The Life
and Times of
Joe McCarthy

Also by Thomas C. Reeves:

Freedom and the Foundation: The Fund for the Republic in the Era of McCarthyism (1969)

Foundations Under Fire (editor, 1970)

McCarthyism (editor, 1973)

Gentleman Boss: The Life of Chester Alan Arthur (1975)

The Life and Times of
Joe McCarthy

A Biography

Thomas C. Reeves

Blond & Briggs

First published in Great Britain 1982 by
Blond & Briggs Limited, London SW19 7JU

Copyright © 1982 Thomas C. Reeves

ISBN 0-85634-131-2

Manufactured in the United States of America

To Kirsten

CONTENTS

Preface   xi
Prologue   xiii
  1. Rural Beginnings   1
  2. Marquette   11
  3. Small Town Lawyer   19
  4. Speedy Justice   33
  5. Tail Gunner Joe   45
  6. Working Toward Washington   63
  7. The Remarkable Upstart   109
  8. Housing Problems   133
  9. Malmedy   161
  10. Communists and the *Capital Times*   187
  11. Wheeling   205
  12. The Top Russian Spy   235
  13. The Tydings Report   287
  14. Revenge in Maryland   315
  15. Combat Duty   347
  16. The Hennings Report   377
  17. Liking Ike   417
  18. No Team Player   459
  19. Devices   493
  20. Declarations of War   509
  21. A National Obsession   561
  22. Point of Order   595
  23. A Matter of Morality and Conduct   639
  24. Dies Irae   665
Chapter Notes   677
Bibliography   783
Index   801

The tragedy of Joe McCarthy isn't that he had so little, but that he had so much and did so little with it. . . . He was a sometimes brilliant, frequently likable demagogue who destroyed many a good thing by the intensity of his hatred for the bad things.

—Leroy Gore

He was an opportunist who happened to stumble onto an idea. He climbed on a political horse and rode it to death, his own included.

—Ralph Zwicker

He was one of the great crusaders of his age. His courage and sincerity in battle against all subversive elements were great contributions to the protection of our American way of life. History will record him as one of our outstanding American patriots.

—Styles Bridges

Joe McCarthy became the center of the century's most scandalous fracas because he had the strength and the defects of organic innocence.

—William S. Schlamm

Joe McCarthy—and he was "Joe" to everyone who knew him—was compounded of many elements. He had strength. He had great courage. He had daring. Joe McCarthy had a rare quality which enabled him to touch the hearts and the minds of millions of his fellow men.

—Lyndon Johnson

PREFACE

This study grew out of a long-standing personal suspicion about the two major biographies of Joe McCarthy, written by journalists and published in the 1950s. One, *McCarthy: The Man, the Senator, the "Ism"* by Jack Anderson and Ronald W. May, seemed obviously designed to contribute to McCarthy's defeat at the polls in 1952. The other, Richard Rovere's widely read *Senator Joe McCarthy*, appeared more rhetorical than factual and had been greeted too warmly for my comfort by the senator's bitter enemies. Both books portrayed McCarthy as the most wicked of villains and heaped uncritical accolades upon those who opposed him. Neither biography displayed a serious commitment to historical research.

Conversations in Wisconsin with several people who had known McCarthy personally quickly increased my curiosity and began to reveal the outlines of a personality that had only been suggested by the senator's critics. They also contributed answers to one of the most fascinating questions of recent political history: How could such an allegedly evil man be elected to office repeatedly in one of the nation's most enlightened States? A preliminary examination of documents surrounding McCarthy's career as a judge, Marine officer, and fledgling United States senator persuaded me to reexamine the whole of his life, a task that ultimately took six years. The Joe McCarthy who emerged from this period of labor and appears in these pages is not the fiendish figure so familiar to history students. Nor is he the saintly patriot his most fanatical admirers have depicted. I have carefully tried to portray this extraordinary and tragic man as he was, grounding the story on evidence and avoiding caricatures posited over the years by both the Left and Right.

Historical objectivity is a much-abused and rather oldfashioned goal, to be sure. But this study has reinforced my belief that the historian's tools can often yield more that is instructive and relevant than is commonly thought. The real Joe McCarthy, I think, is more interesting than the ape-like cartoon figure that haunts our imaginations and our textbooks.

I am deeply indebted to the scores of people who shared their memories and wisdom with me and to the many librarians and archivists who were unfailingly courteous and helpful. I am grateful as well to the American Philosophical Society, the National Endowment for the Humanities, and the Committee on Research and Creative Activity at the University of Wisconsin-Parkside for timely research grants. Lorman Ratner, Nicholas Burckel, Lawrence Crumb, and Dorothy Crowell deserve special thanks for their encouragement and assistance.

PROLOGUE

He seemed so confident. Smiling, laughing, grabbing outstretched hands, he greeted almost everyone he saw—somehow—by their first name and swung young girls in the air and loudly asked beaming old ladies if they hadn't been college classmates fewer than twenty years earlier. Joe McCarthy was again in his native Wisconsin, communicating joyfully with the people he called the "real" Americans.

It was mid-November 1954, in Milwaukee's Pfister Hotel. So many people had sought tickets for the testimonial dinner that the crowd was seated in seven private dining rooms and spilled over into the hotel's main restaurant. Huge banners asking "Who Promoted Peress?" could be seen from every angle, and McCarthy buttons and matchbooks and copies of a congressional report distributed at the door seemed everywhere.

When the senator and his wife entered, 1,500 men and women leaped to their feet, and the roar was deafening. Many pushed and shoved to get closer. One breathless matron in a mink coat told a reporter, "I actually touched him." Later in the evening, when Joe left the speaker's table briefly, a crowd followed. And when he returned, he was cheered. A band blared, and the audience broke into spirited singing in honor of Joe's 46th birthday. The bandleader, Steve Swedish, had his vocalist sing a new song written by a friend and dictated, words and music, that afternoon by telephone from New York:

"That terrible man McCarthy," cries Mrs. Van Soame.
"That book-burning demagogue," shrieks Linus Double-
   Dome.
"McCarthyism sweeps the land," the *Daily Worker* screams,
   And through the press, radio, the Party's poison streams:
"Joe must go, Joe must go."

The last strain of the verse was sung to the tune of "The Volga Boatmen"
and brought gales of laughter. The song continued:

Nobody's for McCarthy but the people, and we all love our
   Joe.
Nobody's for McCarthy but the people, and our letters tell
   him so.
Now little Betsy Williams and old Billy Brown, and all us real
   Americans want Joe to go to town.
Nobody's for McCarthy but the people, and we just love our
   Joe.
Nobody's for McCarthy but the people, and our votes will tell
   him so.

Joe and Sen. Barry Goldwater of Arizona, also at the head table, both threw
their arms around Swedish at the conclusion of the song, while the standing
audience applauded wildly.

On the minds of everyone connected with this dinner was the apparent
certainty that Joe McCarthy was to become the fourth man in American
history to be censured by the United States Senate. Five years earlier
virtually no one outside Wisconsin had heard of the state's junior senator.
Now he was an internationally known political figure, hated and feared as
few men have ever been, admired and exalted by more people than most
learned observers of American politics cared to admit.

To Joe's most militant defenders, the Senate seemed about to do the
work of the very Communists and pro-Communists Joe had been attacking
since that day in February 1950 in Wheeling, West Virginia, when he
alerted the nation to the presence of traitors in the State Department.
Senator Goldwater warned the crowd at the Pfister that subversives were
"way down deep" in secret government positions and that if the Senate
censured McCarthy the next target would be Vice-President Richard
Nixon. "What they want is not only Joe McCarthy but any man who dares
to speak out against Communism."

It was soon McCarthy's turn to speak, and the receptive audience repeatedly interrupted his brief remarks with cries of "We want Joe." For years he had scoffed at his detractors, and over the past few tempestuous months he had mocked and taunted the senators who proclaimed him a disgrace to the Senate and a danger to his party and country. He seemed no less bold and self-assured now. "We are in the midst of a movement of massive appeasement," he charged. "It is a movement of people who are not loyal to our country." It made him sick "way down deep inside," he said, to think that the Senate was wasting its time debating the merits of his struggles against subversives. "As far as I am concerned, what is done at this—circus—whether I am chairman of a subcommittee; whether I am censured or not; I intend doing this job until we win this war on Communism or until I die." Wave after wave of applause echoed through the hotel.[1]

Steve Swedish had known Joe McCarthy rather well since the early 1930s when the latter was a student in law school. The handsome, jovial, and boisterous young man with whom he used to enjoy fishing on Shawano Lake during the Depression little resembled the man who sat slumped in a chair before the fireplace in the fall of 1956. Joe had come to Milwaukee to act as a godfather at a christening and while in town dropped by the Swedish home. Censured by the Senate almost two years earlier, snubbed by the President, ignored by Republicans as well as Democrats, and virtually forgotten by the press, Joe stared blankly into the flames. His face was swollen and flushed. When he moved he did so slowly and seemed often in pain. His drink spilled slightly on the floor, and when Swedish asked him what was wrong, tears welled in his eyes. "I can't take it, Steve. I can't take it. They're after me. They're out to destroy me." The large body shook. "I'm trying, I'm trying. I'm doing everything I can to ferret out these rats, these people who want to destroy our country. . . . No matter where I go, they look on me with contempt. I can't take it anymore."

The last time Swedish saw Joe was in the Pfister Hotel in April 1957. They met accidentally in a hallway. Joe looked sick and he staggered slightly when he walked. As he was being seated, he told the bandleader that people were calling his unlisted telephone number at all hours of the day and night with threats and obscenities. Changing the number did no good. Communists were in the communications industry, he said. "Steve, I can't take it anymore. I can't take it anymore. They're murdering me." Swedish sadly wondered how long Joe could live.[2]

RURAL BEGINNINGS

It was a familiar story. Stephen Patrick McCarthy was one of perhaps a million Irishmen who fled the land of their birth in the mid-nineteenth century in search of prosperity. Born in 1820 in Tipperary County, he was not quite 28 when he arrived in New York.

For ten years McCarthy toiled as a farmhand in Livingston County, New York, sending money to his widowed mother and brothers and sisters in Ireland and saving what he could. Eager to own land of his own, in 1855 he purchased for $600 a half section, sight unseen, in Center township, Wisconsin, about 100 miles north of Milwaukee. Three years later, with a wagon and a team of oxen, he set out alone for that wild, wooded land.

McCarthy's property was about seven miles northwest of Appleton, on the north side of the line that separated Center from the township of Grand Chute. Settlers had only recently entered the area. The first house in Appleton was built in 1848; Grand Chute was organized a year later. Wild animals still roamed the wilderness unmolested. The low price of land—three to ten dollars an acre in the mid-1850s—and the thick forests quickly drew hundreds of farmers and lumberjacks. Germans, Dutch, and Irish poured into the area, and by 1861 over 3,000 people lived in Appleton and Grand Chute.

McCarthy built a log cabin, cleared his land, purchased dairy cattle, planted feed crops, and soon was able to send for his mother. In 1862 he married 20-year-old Margaret Stoffel, who had been born in Bavaria and whose parents farmed eighty acres across the road. She learned English from her husband and had a thicker Irish accent than his.[3]

The couple was soon able to afford a brick home, which had to be large because of a growing family. Ten children arrived over the next two decades, an average number for the Catholic farm families of the area. The third child was born in 1866 and named Timothy. Tim was later to be known outside his quiet, rural community as the father of one of the best-known politicians of the next century.

The McCarthy children attended a parochial grade school in Center and then, as was common, devoted their energies to work on the farm. Tim grew to be a small, wiry, hard-working young man. His Irish brogue, charm, and friendliness were widely admired, even by the Germans, who were a majority of the local population. In the mid-1890s Tim started his own dairy farm on 142 acres purchased by his father. The land lay across the township line in Grand Chute, a short distance from his parents' house.

Nearby, to the east, was the farm of Dennis Tierney and his wife, the former Margaret Ellen Canall. Both had been born in Ireland, and they became good friends with the McCarthys soon after arriving in the area. The fourth of their five children, Bridget, was born in 1870.

"Bid" or "Biddie," as Bridget was called, was a tall, rather homely, heavy-set, jovial young woman, thoroughly domestic in her interests, and a skilled cook.[4]

Tim and Bid were married in 1901 and moved into a log cabin on their property. By all accounts, the marriage was a happy one. The couple was seen in Appleton on occasion holding hands, and one neighbor woman decades later described them as "lovey-dovey." On Sunday afternoons they were often seen strolling hand in hand across the farm, admiring all that was theirs.[5]

While the soil on the farm was not particularly good, the McCarthys managed to raise corn, oats, hay, barley, and cabbage. They had a couple of dozen cows, some chickens, and a few horses. The family's income, by local standards, was average. There was never much money on hand, but people ate well and always seemed to make ends meet. Tim owned one of the best teams of horses in the region, and within a few years after his marriage he built a large barn and an eight-room white clapboard house—both still in use today.

The first four of the seven McCarthy children were born in the log cabin. Mary Ellen (Nellie) arrived in 1902, followed by Margaret Olive (Olive or Ollie) in 1904, Stephen Timothy in 1905, and William Patrick in 1907. The fifth child was the first to be brought into the world in the freshly painted surroundings of the new home.[6]

The boy was born in the afternoon of November 15, 1908, and named Joseph, after a deceased brother of Tim's who had been a Milwaukee dentist. A middle name, Raymond, was added shortly afterward at the boy's baptism; according to a brother and sister, the parents had no specific reason for selecting it.[7]

The McCarthys were a close, happy family—hard-working, very religious, proud of their ancestry, distinctive in no readily observable way from other families in the strip of farms called "the Irish settlement." Tim toiled in the fields with the boys and taught them the rudiments of farm life. (Joe would refer in later years to the disagreeable but necessary job of "digging out" skunks.) Bid saw to it that the girls mastered a number of household skills. The family rode to Appleton for mass and catechism at St. Mary's Church no matter how fierce the weather.[8]

Tim and Bid shared authority in the family, a departure from the stern patriarchal pattern common at the time. And they both urged their children to make the most of themselves. "Man was born to do something," Bid often told them. Don't fear for the future, she would say, for "nobody ever goes hungry in America." Joe later quoted his mother as having chided, "Dog bite Indian once, dog's fault; dog bite Indian twice, Indian's fault."[9]

Bid's sense of humor left a strong impression on her son. She once observed a boyish feat of daring with the wry comment, "Joe's not afraid of anything because he's too dumb." Of course, she was keenly aware of his considerable mental ability.[10]

Joe entered Underhill School, less than a mile south of the farm on what is now called McCarthy Road, in the fall of 1916. It was a classic, rural, one-room schoolhouse in which a single teacher taught from 25 to 40 children in grades one through eight. By the third grade Joe began to blossom, scoring 98 out of 100 in arithmetic at year's end. Three years later he was evaluated as "very good" and "very studious." He was one of four children who completed seventh and eighth grades in a single year, earning top marks in the school. Years later, one teacher recalled Joe's highly retentive mind. Another called him "a lovable sort of guy."[11]

Joe was a dark, good-looking, muscular young man of fourteen when he emerged from elementary school. His pale skin, blue eyes, and black hair were typically Irish, as was the slight brogue in his speech. But in other ways he was already distinctive.

In later years political opponents would conjure up an unflattering story of Senator McCarthy's youth to attempt to explain his complex and peculiar personality and lay the groundwork for the false charge that he was a homosexual. A campaign book of 1952, employed to this day by journalists and historians, described Joe as an ugly duckling, hiding in his mother's skirts, afraid of his classmates, his brothers, his father ("a demanding taskmaster"), and the world in general. Bid, whose "entire universe" revolved around the gawky, ape-like boy, allegedly provided him with the necessary courage to confront the human race. This happens to be entirely contrary to the facts.[12]

What we know about Joe McCarthy's childhood and youth does not really explain his subsequent conduct. His brothers and sisters, products of the same environment, were quite unlike him and chose paths in life that were humble and predictable. When interviewed, they can say only that from his earliest years Joe was in some ways unique. But if causation eludes us, description does not.[13]

Joe was an almost totally extroverted boy, loud, fun-loving, constantly in the thick of things, and extremely popular. Wherever he was, a sister later recalled, there was a crowd. He was also hyperactive, needing at most only a few hours of sleep at night and capable of feats of sustained physical energy that often left others dazzled. His older brother Steve remembered him as always on the move, daring, willing to take chances. When Steve brought home a motorcycle, Joe, about thirteen, couldn't wait to get on it, and roared back and forth across the farm until he hit the corncrib and broke an ankle. The accident slowed him down only briefly.[14]

Joe was frequently playful and enjoyed planning and executing a stunt or trick that would leave playmates roaring with laughter. He could also laugh at himself and took delight in the pranks that were at his own expense. He once designed a pair of wings and persuaded his younger brother Howard to put them on and leap from a high haymow. It wasn't so funny when Howard was knocked unconscious by the fall.[15]

Joe was also aggressive. Tim taught his son to box when Joe was about twelve, and neighborhood boys sometimes avoided the McCarthy farm because of Joe's strength and love of a scrap. In his teens he enjoyed wrestling with local boys at church picnics, a common activity at such events, and seemed afraid of no one. Not very well coordinated, he played a rough game of basketball and suffered a broken nose in baseball. Howard later remarked, "Joe was like any other kid, except that he was generally three steps ahead of them. After he was able to walk, Joe always knew how to take care of himself."[16]

More than any other member of his family, Joe was ambitious. His younger sister Anna Mae recalled, "Joe always wanted to do something big. . . . He never kept still. He was always exploding on something." A neighboring farmer, Jim Heenan, remembered him as "always driving, always driving."[17]

Unlike many rural parents at the time, Tim and Bid were both eager for their sons to enter high school and college. But one by one the boys expressed a lack of interest in further education and dropped out of school after the eighth grade. Steve, the oldest, left the farm at fourteen and in a few years was hired by an Appleton paper company where he was to be employed for forty years. Joe did his chores on the farm for a couple of years but became restless and bored and decided to create a business and make some money of his own.[18]

With $65 he earned working for an uncle in his spare time, he purchased some chickens, fenced them into a part of the property nearest the road, built an insulated 60′ x 90′ shed, and started a chicken farm. He worked diligently on the project; friends recalled his trips to the barn on freezing nights, wearing two coats and returning with chicken droppings all over both layers of garments. He was soon able to purchase a battered old truck, and he traveled to area stores selling eggs by the case. Francis Sumnicht and Howard Crabb of Appleton later recalled with fondness Joe's visits to their fathers' grocery stores. He wore old overalls, stuttered slightly, and was husky-voiced, friendly, and smiling. While always busy, he could never resist the temptation to swap a yarn and "kid around."

Joe invested his profits in his business, and by the time he was seventeen owned 2,000 laying hens and 10,000 broilers and was driving to Chicago to market poultry. He once proudly wrote a personal check for $1,328 in payment for a batch of feed and some chicks.

On one trip to Chicago his truck overturned, killing a number of chickens. Joe later laughed about the incident, telling friends that the Jews on Maxwell Street would buy them "dead or alive." One listener thought the remark anti-Semitic, but Joe was not really prejudiced, then or later.

In the winter of 1928, while much of the rest of the nation was glorying in unprecedented prosperity, Joe suffered financial ruin. Frigid nights attending to the chickens brought on a serious case of influenza that kept him in bed for several weeks. Neighborhood boys, charged with looking after things, were careless, and coccidiosis swept through the flock, killing thousands of chickens. At twenty years old, Joe was broke, poorly educated, and experienced only in farm labor. With his health restored, he tried to rebuild his flock, but his enthusiasm was gone.[19]

Joe quickly wangled a job as a clerk in an Appleton Cash-Way store and was so hard-working and popular that he soon became manager. In a short time, he was transferred to the small (population about 700) town of Manawa, thirty miles away, where he became manager of a new Cash-Way market.[20]

Joe took his sister Olive with him to Manawa, and the two rented rooms in the home of Mrs. Frank Osterloth, an elderly widow whom Joe soon called his "second mother." The grocery opened on May 11, 1929, and Joe and Olive, who worked as a clerk, soon had it operating at a profit. Before long, the Manawa outlet, smallest in the chain, led the 24 others in sales.

To achieve this, Joe employed some rather unorthodox techniques. He walked up and down country roads introducing himself to farmers and their families and inviting them to stop by the store, say hello, and shop. He encouraged customers to wait on themselves, which they saw as an unusual privilege and a sign of trust. He purchased commodities in large quantities and stayed open Saturday evenings to help sell them.

But what most strongly attracted people to the Cash-Way was Joe himself. One woman later recalled, "He sparkled!" Honor Testin, a high school girl at the time, remembered Joe as "a bungling, outgoing kid," full of Irish humor and very courteous and kind. He was a hit especially with elderly ladies, who enjoyed his flattery and special attention, and teenagers, who hung around the store in such numbers that it seemed to be a community center.[21]

For all of his charm and bravado, Joe seemed insecure to some of the more sophisticated young people. Honor Testin recalled his social awkwardness and frequent nervous giggle, "as though he were almost apologetic, almost as if he might be ashamed of having said something." (She noticed the giggle again almost a quarter of a century later during the televised Army-McCarthy hearings.) Around young women, with whom he had had virtually no experience, he was bashful and nervous. He couldn't dance and at first made no effort to participate in local social events.[22]

However, he was good looking enough to attract attention from the opposite sex. He stood five-foot ten-and-a-half inches tall, weighed just over 160, was powerfully built—his wrists and hands were those of a much larger man—and had thick black hair. He wore glasses, which in later years he would remove at the approach of a camera. He coughed and sputtered frequently, the result of severe maxillary sinusitis which had been operated on crudely and ineffectively some years earlier.[23]

Joe seemed religious to observers. He regularly attended mass and was often seen with a local priest, who befriended him and was soon to help him learn Latin. Years later, a reporter from *Time* magazine, probing Senator McCarthy's past, learned that Tim McCarthy's parting words, after a visit from his son, were invariably, "Don't forget to say your prayers, Joe." He never would, and in his youth he wore a scapular and holy medals.[24]

Honor Testin also remembered Joe's sense of daring at the time. Some promoters brought an airplane to Manawa, advertising rides for one cent a pound. Joe invited Honor to join him in a four-mile trip to the town of Symco; it was the first flight for each of them. Before boarding, Joe secretly slipped the pilot some extra money and requested him to perform stunts. Honor was horrified to find the plane rolling, looping, and diving with only a single strap holding her to the seat. Joe enjoyed himself immensely.[25]

Joe later told Honor that she was responsible for his return to school. To reporters, he gave the credit to his kindly landlady, Mrs. Osterloth.[26] At any rate, it was apparent that his prospects for the future were severely limited in a small-town grocery and that further education was necessary in order to achieve very much. The Little Wolf High School in town was not obliged to admit anyone over the age of nineteen, so Joe paid a visit to Leo D. Hershberger, the high school principal.

Joe explained that he would like to get through school as quickly as possible; he didn't know how long it would take but was confident that he could complete the program in less than the usual four years. Hershberger immediately took a liking to the earnest young man and decided to ask the school board for guidance. The board returned the responsibility to the principal and, after consulting with the faculty, he admitted Joe as a freshman that fall.

In existence at the time was a new program (Hershberger later called it a "fad") that permitted students to advance at their own pace. Teachers prepared three levels of written assignments for each subject they taught, and students could select a level depending on the amount of work they intended to do. Passing the easiest level earned a "C," the next level a "B," and the most difficult an "A." When a student completed the mimeographed assignments, he or she would appear before a teacher to take a brief oral examination and a written final. When the course was passed, one could move on to another subject.

Joe was one of 44 freshmen in the tiny school. He said later, "The day I first walked into that classroom and sat down with those thirteen- and fourteen-year-old kids I would have sold out for two cents on the dollar, but they all knew me pretty well, so I got along all right."[27]

He requested A- and B-level assignments and threw himself into his schoolwork with a passion, working far into the early hours of the night, then grabbing a couple hours of sleep before opening the grocery. Mrs. Osterloth kept him supplied with plenty of coffee and encouragement.

Within a short time, a Cash-Way official told his young manager that he would have to either go to school or run the store. Joe quit, but Olive stayed on, at twenty-five cents an hour, to help make ends meet.

Joe's good mind and highly retentive, almost photographic, memory impressed everyone who knew him even slightly. In later years, his memory would be one of his strongest political assets, for he could literally call thousands by their first name and recall facts about people he had met only briefly a decade or more earlier. Now able to devote his full attention to his studies, he quickly made up for the years away from books.

He arose at five in the morning, studied before school, and worked on his assignments for the next twelve hours until the high school closed. Soon he was no longer required to attend class but allowed to sit in the front seat of the study hall, working by himself with a textbook and a class outline, and reporting to a teacher when he thought himself ready to be examined. He astounded everyone. Within six weeks he completed first-year algebra, Latin in seven. By Thanksgiving he was a sophomore; by mid-year he caught up with the juniors; and by Easter he was doing senior-level work. The majority of his grades were A's.

The faculty was solidly behind Joe's efforts. He later recalled, "The teachers were swell, and gave me special instruction after school, and at noon, and at night."[28] Students delighted in his successes; Honor Testin recalled, they were "so darn good to him." Hershberger feared for Joe's health, for he lost weight and often appeared haggard. (Olive thought "he looked like a corpse.")[29] But Joe smiled at his principal's concern and said that he was all right as long as he got some exercise every day.

He hiked and played forward on a town basketball team (being too old for the school squad), and Hershberger personally selected boys to learn boxing from him. He devoted an hour a day to this instruction, spending fifteen minutes apiece with the delighted youngsters.

Somehow, Joe also found time to be active in school affairs. He was vice-president of the freshman class; president of the "We're Citizens" society, created in his citizenship class; he was on the entertainment committee for the school Halloween party; he was a candidate for "Most Lovable Man" at a dance in the gym; he served on a Pep Club committee created to decide a crucial issue about seating at basketball games. During National Education Week he gave a speech entitled "Education is Power." But girls were still beyond his reach, and Honor Testin had to supply him with a date for the senior prom. (Years later, to conceal this embarrassment, Joe told reporters a yarn about taking a teacher to the prom, wooing her on the dance floor to such a degree that she agreed to help him graduate.)[30]

But mostly he studied: every weekday morning, afternoon, and evening, all day Saturday, after church on Sunday, all through the holidays. English, biology, geometry, American history, physics . . . he was never off the honor roll. In March the *Milwaukee Journal* published its first story on Joe McCarthy, describing his rapid progress in school.[31]

Principal Hershberger, weighing the young man's success, worried that perhaps teachers were being a bit easy on him. At Easter, an opportunity arose by which other educators could test Joe's ability. He expressed a desire to study engineering at Marquette University and thus would need advanced algebra for admission. The high school lacked the personnel to teach the subject, so he enrolled in a class offered by the University of Wisconsin's extension division.

Joe completed the correspondence course at home; he asked only a single question of the teacher assigned to help him. He took the final examination a week before graduation in Hershberger's front room, the principal nervously eyeing his fledgling scholar. At one point, the Hershbergers' five-year-old son burst into the room, whooping and hollering. As both parents grabbed for the boy, Joe said, "Never mind, I always work better with a little opposition." He scored 93 out of a possible 100, and Hershberger had no more doubts.

Joe McCarthy was one of 39 seniors to receive diplomas in the spring of 1930; it was the largest graduating class in Little Wolf's history. The principal waited until the end of the ceremonies to award Joe's diploma. The entire McCarthy family beamed with pride as Hershberger declared: "We never graduated a student more capable of graduating," and spoke of Joe as "the irresistible force who overcame the immovable object." In twenty-two years of teaching he had never heard of anyone else completing four years of high school work in nine months. Almost a half century later, he still hadn't.[32]

Having reached this goal at such a dizzying pace, it made sound sense to Joe to keep going. Marquette, a Jesuit institution in Milwaukee, was his first and only choice. By now the Great Depression had descended upon the nation, and a more cautious young man might have had second thoughts about raising the necessary fees and living expenses. But Joe still had a little money from his chicken farm put away, and he could work off campus and perhaps borrow if he still ran short. He wanted to be an engineer and did not doubt he could make it.

When the application form from Marquette arrived at the principal's office, Hershberger noted that an admission requirement was four years of high school. After thinking about it awhile, he wrote that Joe had completed "four-years' work." He told Joe what he had done and asked him to keep quiet about his high school feat for at least a quarter, until his initial grades were recorded and it was demonstrated that he could do college-level work. Then, no doubt, university officials would not care about the slight, technical breach of their rules. Joe's initial grades were two As and a B, and Hershberger breathed more easily.[33]

Leo Hershberger and Joe McCarthy were thereafter lifelong friends. The principal invited the college student to return to talk about the value of education and serve as a model of what he called "stick-to-itiveness." In the 1950s Hershberger spoke at several McCarthy rallies, where he proudly— and accurately—retold the story of Joe's high school achievement. In 1953 Joe gave him a desk set on which was engraved: "To L. D. Hershberger, The Father of McCarthyism." The elderly educator beamed as he showed it to guests.[34]

2

MARQUETTE

Joe spent the summer of 1930 working in a Cash-Way store in the town of Shioctin, 20 miles from Manawa. In September he traveled to Milwaukee and took a room in a boardinghouse where his brother Bill was living, five blocks from the Marquette campus. The three-story building was owned by John Kuhn, a short, stocky German who sported a thick accent, boots, and an outspoken love of his native land. The eighteen young men who inhabited the rather noisy domicile called it "the famous house of Kuhn." Joe enjoyed his new surroundings from the start and became fondly attached to his friendly landlords, calling Mrs. Kuhn "mother" the rest of her life. His roommate of a year later, George H. Lubeley, remembered McCarthy as a smiling, generous, popular fellow who enjoyed a joke, a game of cards, and the young ladies.[1]

Marquette was celebrating its "Golden Jubilee Year" when Joe arrived and had almost 5,000 students. On the first day of school, Joe sauntered over to the football field to try out for the team. Having no experience, he was denied the opportunity. Clifford Mullarkey, who had met Joe in Manawa and walked with him to the stadium, admired his boldness and later reflected upon his friend's intense determination to *be* somebody.[2]

The first two years of the engineering program at Marquette were made up of fundamental courses in mathematics, science, English, economics, accounting, and public speaking—"basic subjects for any profession," the

11

catalogue stated. Joe took a course entitled "Argumentation and Debate" from William M. Lamers, who thought him an above-average to excellent student and a very polite and pleasant young man. At first, Joe could barely speak in front of an audience. Classmate Fred Sturm, from Manawa, remembered an early attempt: his feet shifted mechanically; his hands were often extended, almost as if he were afraid of losing his balance; his nervousness was such that he couldn't talk for a time. But with instruction and practice, Joe became a fairly articulate speaker. He soon developed the flat, droning tone in his voice later associated with his political rhetoric.[3]

He did well in his other classes also, particularly in mathematics. At one point he worked briefly in Milwaukee foundries as a course requirement.[4] His schoolwork might have been truly outstanding had he been able and willing to devote more time to it.

To meet his college expenses and the eight dollars a week for room and board, Joe, like so many of his classmates during the Depression, took a number of jobs. His astonishing stamina usually permitted him to hold several at once. He and another friend, Charles Hanratty, once carried the contents of an entire tavern from one location to another for a small fee. (Both young men sold their blood to hospitals half a dozen times.) Joe did odd jobs, yard work, and janitorial drudgery for a generous and slightly notorious tavernowner called "Dirty Helen." He sold flypaper door to door, with a sales technique so effective that at times he brought in up to $100 weekly. He washed dishes and served as a short-order cook in a beanery (developing a life-long fondness for cooking). He worked on a construction gang—with so many Italians that he later told reporters he could speak their language. (He couldn't.) One summer he went into the window-caulking business with three boardinghouse buddies, Hugo Hellman and track stars Jack and Arnold "Pete" Walter. (He failed to pay his share of the cost of ladders, and one observer later thought him "shrewd.") By the end of his second year at Marquette, he was managing two service stations, working ten to twelve hours a day in one of them at East North Avenue and Oakland in Milwaukee, for thirty-five cents an hour plus tips.[5] And beyond his jobs and school work, Joe found time for boxing.

Boxing was an intramural sport at Marquette, introduced the year Joe arrived and available for gym credits. Training started in the fall and led to two boxing shows (soon combined with wrestling) in the spring. By October Joe was one of five freshmen singled out by the coach for special notice. The first reference to him in the *Marquette Tribune* declared, "McCarthy is a husky, hard-hitting middleweight who promises an evening's work for any foe."[6]

Charles Hanratty sparred with him in training often. He later recalled that Joe was more of a slugger than a boxer; he was slow and not a particularly good puncher but strong and absolutely fearless. He would charge an opponent with a flurry of blows, not worrying about a defense. (Several commentators later noted a parallel between his boxing and political methods.) Joe hit extremely hard, once landing a punch over Hanratty's heart that knocked him down and left him stunned.[7]

Tom Korb, a six-foot, Irish football player, and soon one of McCarthy's closest friends, first met him in the gymnasium. Joe sized him up, asked what he weighed, and said, "Let's box." Korb never forgot the punishing encounter.[8]

Joe had four official fights during the two years he boxed at Marquette. They were three-round events, with three-minute rounds. In mid-March 1931, 900 fans saw Joe batter a husky business administration major named Al Razor to the canvas three times in the first round. He coasted to an easy victory. In May he lost a decision to a much more experienced fighter, Frank Didier.

In 1932 "Smiling Joe," as the student newspaper dubbed him, twice fought a heavyweight named Stan Balcerzak. He dropped the first bout by decision, before a cheering crowd of 3,500. In a rematch, requested by the loser, Joe belted his opponent to the canvas for a count of nine, took a smashing right hand to the chin, and hung on for the win.[9]

Seeking more experience, Joe and a few companions on the boxing team dropped by the new Eagles Club gymnasium from time to time. They sparred a bit, gawked at some local professionals, and picked up a few tips from the boxing instructor, Fred Saddy. One day, Joe decided to turn professional, and he asked Saddy to be his manager. The instructor liked Joe immensely and thought that he might be able to turn him into a fairly good fighter, but he urged him to stay in college, saying that he personally would not trade a university diploma for the heavyweight championship. Joe accepted the advice and later paid warm tributes to his friendly counselor. In 1950 Senator McCarthy flew from Washington to Milwaukee to participate in a dinner honoring Saddy, then president of the National Boxing Association.[10]

In the fall of 1932, Marquette's boxing coach, Curtis Brown, left, and Joe volunteered to take his place for a year. He soon found himself supervising the instruction of more than 70 would-be pugilists, five days a week. He proved to be a popular and effective instructor who constantly stressed the importance of self-confidence.[11]

The sheer weight of Joe's daily schedule would have broken most people.

But he was a whirlwind, not certain where he was going but in constant, fervid motion. The uncertainty was beginning to clear, however, for as he started his third year at Marquette, he entered the law school.

Joe had met several law students at his boardinghouse and found their conversation about tough verbal clashes and swashbuckling victories in the courtroom far more appealing than the dry, technical fare that lay ahead in engineering. Moreover, Tom Korb, Charles Hanratty, and Clifford Mullarkey were all aiming toward legal careers, and Joe was undoubtedly influenced by their aspirations.[12] The law school accepted his two-year preparation for engineering as the equivalent of the regular two-year prelegal program. It had been a brief and superficial introduction to the liberal arts, but few Marquette law students could boast of more serious encounters at the time. And Joe's grades were above the C average required for admission.

Marquette University's law school, which opened in 1911, took pride in the fact that it was one of sixty such schools in the nation approved by the American Bar Association. It was housed in a handsome building dedicated less than a decade earlier. Its library housed 50,000 books, and its law review appeared quarterly. There were thirteen faculty members during the Depression years, some of them part-time. The school had adopted the fashionable case system of legal education in 1929.

Still, for years many had thought the school inferior to the University of Wisconsin law school because the state required Marquette's graduates to pass the bar examination while exempting the young men and women who took their diplomas in Madison. The legislature equalized the standards in 1933, and members of Joe's class would be sworn in as attorneys immediately after graduation.[13]

Law school classes met from early morning until noon. For the rest of the day students were expected to be in the library or down the street at the federal courthouse observing trials. In reality, many of them held jobs.

Joe worked up to 80 hours a week at the Standard station. He got off at 11:00 P.M., sometimes went with Tom Korb to a saloon that featured a free lunch, and then headed home to activities that often lasted until the dawn of the next day.

Soon after transferring to the law school, Joe joined a legal fraternity, Delta Theta Phi, comprised of about 35 young men who rented an old house on West Kilbourn Avenue where Joe and about half of the members lived. (They couldn't make the rent in 1934 and were forced to move to other quarters on North Twelfth street.) The fraternity existed almost exclusively for social purposes and was like many similar organizations on campus in the 1930s. There were silly initiation rites (some involving Limburger cheese), a "hell week," during which newcomers were paddled, and a "quest," in which initiates were required to chase around the city looking for a hidden object.

The fun started about midnight. Beer bottles popped open (during and after Prohibition), several card games—poker, bridge, hearts—often went on at once, a Ping-Pong table was in constant use (after each game a volume of *Wisconsin Reports* was placed on the floor next to the winner), parties were frequent.

Joe was extremely popular at the fraternity; Harold V. Shoenecker later recalled, "His face would beam when you met him. . . . I don't think he had an enemy in the class." The hilarity seemed to intensify as soon as he came through the door. He drank beer (a few glasses were his limit), told stories, played tricks, kidded everyone in sight, and gambled recklessly. It was a far cry from life on the farm—with a teetotaler father—and in Manawa. Once he and a couple of others stole huge urns from in front of an apartment house and put them in the Delta Theta Phi quarters as ashtrays. On another occasion he swiped a large container of beer from a truck and shared it with delighted party-goers.

Joe was a daring but not particularly skilled poker player. He would bet on cards face down; he would trade hands without looking at his cards. He played for the sheer love of competition and hated to quit. If a player went broke, he would shove a pile of chips in front of him to keep the game going. When he won, he would buy sandwiches and Cokes for everyone.

Money meant nothing to Joe McCarthy; his irresponsibility with it would plague him for the rest of his life. Tom Korb was persuaded that Joe could never balance a checkbook. He made money to spend it, gamble with it, give it away—his generosity would become legendary among friends. He rarely knew how much he was carrying, how much he owed, or how much he would need to get through the week. He constantly borrowed, and this in particular would haunt him in the future.

Joe's income during his years at Marquette was at times fairly comfortable; he was the only member of the fraternity to own an automobile. But money came and went. Joe simply paid no attention. He borrowed from his father and two brothers to complete his schooling; Howard was an auctioneer and real estate agent in Appleton, and Bill had a good job in a local factory.

More than a little of Joe's money was spent on girls. He surrounded himself with the most attractive coeds on campus and was the envy of the fraternity. Because of his roadster convertible, friends were eager to go on double dates, and several, such as Gerald T. Flynn, remember Joe as a "womanizer" and a "wolf." But he wouldn't become emotionally or romantically attracted to any girl for long. One statuesque redhead, Mildred Byrnes, was a favorite, but the relationship was stormy and broke off.

Robert Stoltz, a fraternity member, recalled a bull session in which friends talked about their marriage plans. Joe said that he didn't intend to marry, at least not until late in life. Marriage would bring responsibilities that could detract from a career. Stoltz's strongest recollection of Joe was his burning desire for achievement.

Joe attended class regularly but was not considered among the better students. He would bluff occasionally when called upon and would sometimes make a wisecrack that would break up a class with laughter. One hot day in May, a professor droned on about a complex case in California involving a dog. Couldn't the principle be equally applied to a cathouse? Joe asked with a grin. In private, he would mimic the speech impediment of an elderly priest, the Rev. Hugh B. MacMahon, S.J., who taught an especially dry course in legal ethics. Joe rarely entered the library and read little.

The law school curriculum was not especially demanding and primarily involved memorization. This, of course, was easy for Joe, and he prepared for examinations swiftly and at the expense of more studious friends.

Delta Theta Phi had a file of old tests (this was legal), and, two or three weeks before the semester examinations, small groups of fraternity members would study them, go over lecture notes, and discuss cases that had been briefed. Joe would join one or more of these groups, sit quietly in a corner, close his eyes, and absorb the conversation fully and in detail. He attended similar sessions at a nearby rooming house in which Charles Curran, one of the top students in the law school, was a participant.

Whatever Joe's exact grades (Marquette refuses to release them), they were high enough to earn a "hunting license," as the students called the law degree. (They joked about using it after graduation to hunt for a job in the Depression years.[14])

During his first two years of law school, Joe was a member of the Franklin Debating Club, coached by his speech professor, William Lamers. He joined to improve his forensic skills and also, no doubt, for the sheer love of competition. The club was one of several extracurricular debating societies on campus. Members met weekly and debated each other, being required to argue both sides of a topic. Dr. Lamers once selected, "Resolved: That Modern Woman Is a Curse." There were graver topics as well.

By this time Joe was a competent public speaker and debater. He might have become sufficiently skilled to make the varsity team had he taken the time to prepare his arguments. Instead, he always talked off of the top of his head. Club members knew he was bluffing, of course, but they respected his ability on the rostrum.[15]

Joe was rarely serious, but from time to time at the Franklin Club and in the fraternity house he revealed a side of himself that would attract much attention in later years. When he got into an argument over a matter that concerned him, he could become extremely angry and would charge an opponent verbally, becoming intense and abusive. Then, very quickly, he would forget the entire encounter and commence buying Cokes, slapping people on the back, and swapping jokes. Nobody could stay angry at Joe McCarthy. He wouldn't let you.[16]

Within his first semester in the Franklin Club, Joe brashly announced that he was a candidate for its presidency. It was his first race for office, and he lost. But he took defeat graciously and congratulated the winner, Charles Curran.

Curran was deeply fond of his law school classmate because he was one of many to whom Joe had shown kindness and generosity. When Curran's father died in the fall of 1933, Joe appeared at his rooming house door asking if he could help arrange the train trip home to Mauston, Wisconsin. That done, he borrowed an old Model-T Ford (not yet having a car of his own) and drove to Mauston himself to attend the funeral. Almost twenty years later, Curran told a reporter, "He cut classes, left his job, and borrowed money to get there. He did that for me, and he'll always be my friend."[17]

Soon after the Franklin Club elections, Joe and Charles Curran were again competitors, this time for the presidency of their law school class. It was largely an honorary position; each school at Marquette elected class officers. Joe represented the fraternities, and Curran was the independent, or nonfraternity, candidate.

At the time both young men were nominated, they agreed to vote for each other. When the campaigning ended, the race ended in a tie. The dean called both candidates into his office and suggested that they cut cards, draw straws, or flip a coin to determine the winner. Curran was willing but Joe sought a new election, and the dean consented. After another two-week campaign, Joe won by two votes. One person had switched his ballot, and Curran soon asked Joe if he had been the party in question. "Sure," came the reply. "You wanted me to vote for the best man, didn't you?" Curran wasn't resentful; the contest was unimportant. But it was another side of Joe McCarthy that had not been apparent in Manawa.[18]

Contrary to later stories (some of which were his own invention), Joe did not have any lofty goals in mind as he neared the end of his formal education. He did not talk about running for political offices or betray a longing for Washington. And he neither discussed—nor comprehended—the "isms" that were stalking the world during the 1930s. His sole aim was to gain a law degree, settle down somewhere in Wisconsin, and try to make a living, a goal he shared with virtually all of his 56 classmates.

He would sometimes talk about politics in fraternity bull sessions. The McCarthys, like almost all of the Irish in the Appleton area, were staunch Democrats, and Joe firmly supported Roosevelt's candidacy in 1932. But his interest in and commitment to political thought ran no deeper than the prejudices of Tim and Bid.[19]

Joe's schooling had failed to provide him with the solid educational foundation that a man of his later responsibilities would find useful. He emerged from Marquette with only hazy and simplistic historical and philosophical perspectives. He had not even been required to learn to write out his thoughts logically and clearly. (Writing would be a sore point with him in later years.)

Joe could have overcome this deficiency, of course, had he developed a taste for reading, study, or contemplation. But he never would. Instead, he put great store in hasty memorization, shortcuts, and the occasional bluff—techniques that brought him from a grocery store counter to a law office in less than six years. His enormous energy would always be spent chasing back and forth from the gas station to the parties in the fraternity house.

Joe's personal magnetism was his strongest asset, and many a man, unfamiliar with the contents of libraries, has parlayed such a gift for great profit.

Right after graduation, Joe was scheduled to drive with Charles Hanratty and his brother to Madison to be sworn in as an attorney. He drove up in a brand new Ford containing six new suits. Astonished, Hanratty asked him how he managed the sudden display of affluence. Joe wasn't talking. Following the ceremony in the state capital, he suggested a drive up to Waupaca, a small town only a few miles southwest of Manawa. On arriving, Joe brought gasps from his friends by pointing to an upstairs office window bearing his name.

To win a bet from a classmate, he had opened a law office within six hours of being sworn in. Not content with that, he had borrowed enough money from someone to give himself the appearance of being a prosperous attorney. How he would repay such a sizable debt from a nonexistent practice in the middle of the Depression was of no concern. Hanratty just shook his head and smiled. That was Joe.[20]

SMALL TOWN LAWYER

Waupaca was a county seat, and Joe's office was on the second floor of a large stone building on Main Street, a block from the courthouse. The Waupaca Abstract and Loan Company occupied the first floor, while upstairs there were apartments, two dental offices, and a beauty parlor, in addition to the city's newest attorney.

There were five other lawyers in town, and with hard times and a population of little more than 3,000, Joe's prospects for immediate prosperity looked dim. He made a down payment on a set of law books and furnished his office with some creaking wooden furniture and a used typewriter. At first, he wisely spent much of his time in the courthouse observing the maneuvers and absorbing the arguments of his competitors.[1]

Joe roomed in the home of a local dentist, W. H. Rummel. The two had become friends in Manawa, and Joe was not charged rent. He was rarely found in his room. He kept his office open evenings to attract clients, and he busily introduced himself to scores of people, joined civic organizations, and became involved in local charitable drives. In January 1936 the *Waupaca County Post* reported him active in the Lions Club and selling tickets for a polio benefit dance.[2]

Shortly after he arrived in town, a civic group sponsored a donkey baseball game, and Joe signed up to play. These games were popular in rural areas at the time and always attracted crowds. Regular baseball rules prevailed except that all players—excluding the pitcher, catcher, and batter—were mounted on donkeys and would have to coax and prod them to the spot where a ball landed. Batters would stand at the plate, hit the ball, and then try to navigate a donkey to first base. The obstinacy of the animals and the frustration of their riders brought rollicking laughter from audiences.

When it was Joe's turn to bat, he made a solid hit and then discovered that he was unable to get his donkey to move an inch. Determined, he picked up the 200-pound animal and carried it to first base. The crowd cheered and applauded. One spectator, Waupaca attorney Ed Hart, couldn't help laughing as he told the story forty years later. "Joe was a very strong farm boy."[3]

In the absence of much legal business, Joe found a lot of time to enjoy himself. He played softball with local businessmen, treated youngsters to a boxing class, and bowled in a local league. He often played poker, which he took very seriously, and would at times win sizable pots—in the twenty-dollar range—with daring bluffs. He was always in the company of a pretty girl and was rarely seen with the same one twice.

One night, at a bar west of town on Highway 10, he got into a poker game that lasted until 4:00 A.M. His date for the evening, who had come all the way from Milwaukee, was ignored. The challenge, the risks, the excitement of the gambling could completely consume Joe's attention. Moreover, Andrew Parnell, a local attorney and a shrewd McCarthy observer, thought Joe relatively uninterested in girls. Their presence, like the new car and suits, enhanced his image and his vanity. Joe's closest friends recall that he rarely talked about sex.[4]

Joe became friends with many of the attorneys in the area and would often drop by their homes unannounced, bearing small gifts for the women and children. He would play with children for hours, and they would squeal with delight as he chased them with a squirt gun or wrestled with them in mock combat. Years later, when Senator McCarthy was alleged to be one of the most fearsome men in the western world, spectators would marvel at his fondness for youngsters.[5]

He occasionally drove home to see "mither" and "fither," as he called his parents (although by now his brogue had almost completely disappeared). Joe would throw his arms around them after vaulting from his car, and he was soon chomping on a piece of his mother's home-made bread. Only Olive was still at home with Tim and Bid; the other girls were married, and the boys had taken jobs in cities. The only McCarthy making much money, however, was Howard, and Joe's friends used to kid him by claiming that his younger brother had all the brains in the family.[6]

In the nine months Joe practiced law in Waupaca, he handled only four civil cases: an auto collision, a mortgage foreclosure, and two small collections. Three of the four were settled out of court. His income for 1935 was $771.81.[7]

At least one of these cases, Ed Hart later recalled, was taken away from another attorney in town, who complained to a local court about Joe's tactics. While Hart liked McCarthy, as did almost everyone in town, he didn't entirely trust him and thought him extremely aggressive.[8]

One afternoon in early 1936, Mike G. Eberlein strode into Joe's office. Eberlein was a brash, aggressive, and highly successful attorney in Shawano, 45 miles away; an outspoken, colorful courtroom performer, he specialized in accident and insurance cases. One of the men in his office had left, and he was looking for a replacement. He had seen McCarthy in court, liked his style, and decided to offer him the job. Though they differed in age, the two men were much alike.

"Why don't you close up this dive and come to work for me?" Eberlein said bluntly.

"Why don't you close up that dump of yours and come down here and work for me?" Joe replied.

When Eberlein mentioned a salary, Joe grinned and accepted the offer. A few weeks later, in mid-February, he was on his way to Shawano.[9]

Eberlein was a leading Republican in Shawano County, and Joe smilingly told a Waupaca reporter, "I'll have to make hasty transition from a Young Democrat to a Young Republican." The *Post* said playfully, "... just to add a dash of zest in the life of Mike Eberlein's new hired man, we carefully padded his brief case with a couple of copies of the *New Masses,* a recent edition of the *Daily Worker,* and a vest-pocket-size *Das Kapital.*"[10]

When Joe drove into Shawano, he was 27 years old and very nearly broke. He sold his typewriter for fifteen dollars and took a room in a boardinghouse run by Mrs. Edith Green, where several young attorneys lived.[11]

Eberlein owned the building on Division and Main and had two law offices on the second floor, above the *Shawano County Journal.* When Joe first entered the offices, he was introduced to Eberlein's secretary, Mrs. Mae Voy. He warmly shook her hand and said in a loud voice, "You watch. In a few years I'm going to be at the top of the heap around Shawano." Unimpressed by such cockiness (to which he himself was prone), Eberlein cracked, "She's been here quite a few years, Joe, and I'll wager for the first six months she will be able to teach you some law."[12]

Joe did not drum up much business. The Shawano newspaper announced his employment with a biographical article containing the story of his swift journey through high school, and some people in town, particularly the attorneys, were jealous, calling him a "boy wonder," and worse. (Joe sweetened the article with the fable that he had once been associated with a Milwaukee law firm.) Others thought him overly aggressive. He would enter a tavern and almost attack people at the bar with handshakes, noisy introductions, jokes, stories, and backslapping. Still others were suspicious of him. He would cheat at cards, and roar with laughter when caught. It wasn't for the money; he merely wanted to see what he could get away with. Some players were not amused.[13]

Eberlein paid Joe a monthly salary of $200, but the money was spent almost as quickly as it was received. Eberlein later recalled, "Joe was always broke. He had a poor business head. He never could save." To assist his young associate, Eberlein gave him half his salary at the first of the month and put the other half in an account that was turned over to him at the end of the year. The techniques failed, for Joe borrowed on the amount placed in reserve.[14]

He dropped by Walter Jolin's house regularly. The two first met when Joe was a teenager, and Jolin, a lumber executive in Shawano, enjoyed the young man's vivacious company. Joe usually appeared about dinner time, and Mrs. Jolin would smile knowingly and invite him to dine. It was often his only meal.[15]

On occasion, Joe traveled to nearby Tigerton, where he accepted free meals from Anthony (Tony) Swanke, a friend since Marquette whose wealthy family virtually ran the town.[16]

For extra money, Joe wrote political editorials, at five dollars apiece, for the *Shawano County Journal*. The newspaper was staunchly Republican, but that didn't matter. Joe knew what editor Harold A. Meyer wanted, and he obliged.[17]

There were very few Democrats in the Shawano area, but Joe joined a local club and was soon elected president of the Young Democratic Clubs of the Seventh District, encompassing ten counties. He attended a state convention of Wisconsin Young Democrats in Clintonville and helped select a state central committee. Probably for the publicity, he entered the race for district attorney on the Democratic ticket. The Republican candidate was another young lawyer who lived at Mrs. Green's, Ed Aschenbrenner. Louis Cattau, the Progressive Party incumbent who had practiced law in the county for a decade, was the heavy favorite.

Joe painted his car with "Elect Joe McCarthy" signs, buttonholed people on street corners, and spoke at at least one Democratic Party rally, exuding friendliness and platitudes. In August he advocated placing the district attorney's office on a part-time basis, thereby reducing costs by 50 percent.[18]

Although Mike Eberlein was a staunch Republican, Joe's candidacy didn't bother him. Mrs. Voy thought her boss amused by the bravado. Eberlein bristled a bit, however, when Joe distributed Roosevelt-for-President buttons in the office to scores of admiring grade-school children.[19]

In the primary, Joe placed last, garnering only 577 votes to Aschenbrenner's 692 and Cattau's 3,014. He promptly changed his strategy and intensified his efforts. He gave numerous speeches—fourteen in one two-day period—and began hammering at Republicans. He called Alf Landon "William Randolph Hearst's puppet from Kansas," and sneered at the G.O.P. candidate's platform with extraordinary language: "Of all the brainless, half-baked, cockeyed pleas which have ever been made to a voting public, that absolutely tops the pinnacle of them all in asininity." Joe much preferred Roosevelt, "every drop of whose blood and every faculty of whose mind and body is devoted to that great noble, unselfish task . . . of serving all the American people."

Joe also published a pamphlet accusing District Attorney Cattau of engaging in private practice, which violated a local ordinance. The charge was accurate but involved only a small amount of time and money. Cattau was furious and accused McCarthy in a newspaper advertisement of being an "unscrupulous" politician who had "grossly" misstated the facts.[20]

In the general election Joe polled almost seven times as many votes as he had in September. The final tally: Cattau, 6,175; McCarthy, 3,422; Aschenbrenner, 2,842. The furious activity and the slashing attacks had appeared to pay off. Joe would not soon forget this lesson in campaigning.

Eberlein made Joe a partner in 1937. It was an act of friendship; the young attorney did not have to buy into the firm, and he remained on his small salary. Joe beamed at the "Eberlein & McCarthy" sign on display in downtown Shawano. Two years earlier he had been a student.[21]

He remained active in local civic affairs. In April he spoke before the Lion's Club on miscarriages of justice in the legal profession. In July he told the Rotary Club of a trip he and Tony Swanke had just made to the Pacific Northwest and Canada. They did not exactly absorb local history and culture, driving 8,700 miles in two weeks. Joe warmly praised Canadian roads.[22]

Mrs. Ruth Meyer, wife of the local newspaper editor, recalled that Joe could address almost everybody in town by their first name—waitresses, street cleaners, the mayor, anyone he met. This won him many admirers.[23]

Mrs. Voy thought he had "a heart as big as a hotel" and remembered several acts of charity, including having old suits cleaned and pressed for personal delivery to the poor. Her son Peter called him "Uncle Joe" and decades later continued to cherish a musical rocking chair McCarthy gave him for Christmas.[24]

Francis Werner, a well-to-do New London attorney, recalled the many practical jokes Joe and his friends exchanged. Joe was a particularly vulnerable target. Once he was talked into holding a glass of water on the ceiling at the end of a broomstick on the pretext that a crony would soon be tricked into assuming the position. On a fishing trip he complained of the quality of his beer, only to learn that a friend had been dipping the bottle into the Wolf River. Werner came home one night to find his front yard covered with "Worms For Sale" signs. It was innocent fun, and many of Joe's friends often later regretted that he had not remained a small-town lawyer.[25]

Ed Hart remembered the many pretty girls who tried to bring Joe to the altar. He was engaged twice during these years: to Mary Louise Juneau, a student at Mt. Mary College, who was dark, fairly tall, and very beautiful; and to Maybelle Counihan, who was a short, attractive nurse who moved from Milwaukee to Appleton after meeting Joe. He also went with one of Tony Swanke's sisters for a time. But there were others, many others. "He would do anything for you," said one. "Women appreciated that." Joe became a good dancer and was often seen at local balls and parties.[26]

No one in the Shawano area can recall seeing Joe McCarthy somber, serious, or in any way intellectual. William Flarity, a young attorney in Tigerton, used to talk with him at length in local taverns. (He drank little; taverns were the region's social centers.) The conversation was largely about sports and current events. They rarely discussed law, both admitting that they knew little of it.[27]

Joe seemed almost totally extroverted, highly aggressive, fun-loving, loud, generous, and constantly in motion. After an appendectomy, a local physician confined him to a hospital bed for an extended period. A nurse soon found the bed empty; Joe was elsewhere.[28]

Almost all of the legal work he handled involved bits and pieces of cases directed by Mike Eberlein. Joe learned about courtroom procedures from his employer and was schooled by example in the clever and sometimes subtle strategies that wring tears and sympathetic verdicts from juries.

He was once assigned the task of introducing a suit involving an automobile accident in which his client had been crippled by another man's negligence. He was nervous and asked a friend to watch him carefully so that he might later evaluate his performance. With his client on the stand, Joe carefully arranged and rearranged a cushion for the witness at the slightest evidence of his discomfort, to maximize the gravity of his injury. He played up to jury members and used toy cars to reenact the accident for them. Eberlein appeared later in the day and overshadowed his partner, but the case was won and Joe could claim some of the credit.[29]

Joe's ambition was such that he could not remain long in anyone's shadow. He observed Roosevelt's "court-packing" plan of 1937 and listened to the President's plea for younger, more vigorous judges. He also noted the defeat of a Shawano County judge named Jaeckel later that year by a young attorney who harped on the judge's advanced age. The idea soon dawned upon Joe that he might run for a judgeship himself. He had enjoyed the race for district attorney and was proud of his vote total. The local Tenth Circuit judge, Edgar V. Werner, was elderly, and there were grumbles about his efficiency. Why not?

He mentioned the idea to Bill Flarity over a beer one evening. The young attorney laughed and told Joe he was talking off the top of his head. He bounced the plan off of some of the lawyers at Mrs. Green's, who thought him crazy to believe he could be elected. Circuit judgeships traditionally went to distinguished, successful attorneys. And Judge Werner had served over twenty years on the bench, six years as district attorney, and six years as Shawano city attorney. Charles Hanratty was scornful when the idea was put to him. How could Joe campaign? He was broke. "Watch me," came the reply. "I'll go door to door."[30]

The campaigning started in the spring of 1938. To present himself as a mature, contemplative man, Joe gave a speech entitled "Americanization" before the Shawano Junior Women's Club. There was no more prattle about sight-seeing or roads. "Tracing the progress of various great civilizations," an awed reported observed, "Mr. McCarthy described their life cycles, showing their rise and fall, and compared their attitude to other people. He discussed particularly those civilizations which flourished along the great rivers of the world." It was an example of what a close friend, Urban P. Van Susteren, often called Joe's "pure Irish bullshit."[31]

Only a few people knew of Joe's intention to enter the nonpartisan race against Judge Werner, and Mike Eberlein was not among them. It was widely known that he had designs on the judgeship himself. When Joe officially announced his candidacy on December 28, 1938, Eberlein read about it in the newspaper. He was irritated and jealous at first, but quickly got over it. The friendship would remain strong for years. Even during the campaign, Joe told an assistant that if funds ran out "Uncle Mike" could be depended upon.[32]

To finance his campaign, Joe borrowed from dozens of people. Ten dollars here, $500 there—he signed some notes, oral promises covered the rest. Defeat at the polls would make repayment extremely difficult, but Joe had great faith in his own charm and energy and in his decision to go "door to door." He bought a new Oldsmobile on credit and equipped it with a dictaphone.[33]

He also opened a small office of his own in Shawano. This was Eberlein's dictum. If Joe somehow won the election, he would be practicing before him, and he wished to avoid any suggestion of conflict of interest. Joe handled some legal business in the new location, but it largely served as campaign headquarters.[34]

At the suggestion of a mutual friend, Joe hired an attractive young Shawano girl, Dottie Druckrey, as his secretary. She was attending a business college in Oshkosh, but after meeting Joe she agreed to drop out for a semester. At noon of the first day, having taken shorthand all morning, she realized that the office lacked a typewriter. Joe laughed loudly. It was a detail he had overlooked.[35]

Joe had worked out a campaign strategy that he thought unbeatable. The Tenth Judicial District encompassed Outagamie, Shawano, and Langlade counties. With the exception of Appleton, the region was largely rural. He intended to visit as many farmers as possible, introduce himself, chat with them about their families and agricultural conditions, and drop them a personal note before the election, scheduled for early April. The approach, he believed, could win hundreds and perhaps thousands of votes, and overcome the handicaps of youth and inexperience that prompted some people to laugh at his candidacy. He told friends that people really weren't interested in politicians or political issues, and that they needed only a single reason to vote for a candidate. That reason could be a handshake, a smile, a note telling them that they were remembered, and implying that they were special.[36]

It was a novel and daring plan; the physical demands alone would be grueling, especially in the dead of winter. But it was exactly the sort of challenge Joe found irresistible.

For the next three months, six and seven days a week, Joe traveled over icy rural roads, knocking on doors, shaking hands, swapping farm stories, complimenting wives on their cooking, patting children on the head; he even milked a few cows. (He was frequently accompanied by John Reed, a young admirer who spelled him at the wheel.) When out of sight of a farm he had just left, Joe dictated details of his visit into the recording device he kept in the car. On returning to Shawano, he gave the cylinders to Dottie, who used the data to write postcards bearing personal references. She signed each with Joe's name. On the opposite side of the postcard was a photograph of the candidate in suit and tie, wearing his glasses and appearing earnest and responsible.

Joe also spent considerable time in the scores of little towns within the district, walking up and down what was invariably called Main Street and darting in and out of stores, barbershops, and restaurants introducing himself. He overwhelmed tiny Bear Creek. He had somehow learned the names of many townspeople, and they were startled and pleased when he strode into their shops beaming and greeting them as old friends. At the end of a frantic day of handshaking Joe pretended not to know anything about sheepshead, a popular card game, and asked if he might sit in for a bit and learn while playing. He won several pots and spent the proceeds buying drinks for his competitors and spectators. One resident later recalled that McCarthy's appearance "was like having the Ringling Brothers Circus come to town."

The name of anyone Joe met on his travels and had a chance to talk with for more than a few seconds was fed into his dictaphone. Dottie worked all day, every day, writing postcards. She later remembered having completed "thousands." Joe went through them to check their accuracy and mailed them himself.[37]

But Joe had more in store for the incumbent than this. In announcing his candidacy, he charged that Judge Werner lacked the "direct experience in ordinary business affairs" that he possessed:

> In a circuit such as this the judge is continually coming into
> contact with workaday problems of the farmer, the laborer,
> and the small businessman. It seems to me that in addition to
> a good legal mind, trial law experience, and a discerning sense
> of fairness, a judge in such a circuit should include among his
> qualifications, personal experience in each of these fields of
> endeavor.[38]

When this drew no discernable response, Joe tried another, more clever, approach.

Edgar Werner was 66 years old. He was stuffy and pedantic but in good mental and physical health. As a candidate for the office in 1916 he had listed the year of his birth as 1866, instead of 1872, in order to impress voters with his maturity. Later, he neglected to correct the fabrication. Joe spotted the date in the Martindale-Hubbell directory of attorneys and decided to hold the judge to it.

In early 1939 he made public a letter to friends contending that Judge Werner was in his 73rd year and if reelected would be approaching 80 by the end of his term. He knew better, of course, but hoped that voters would think the judge senile. Werner strongly objected, gave his true age, and asked that his opponent make a retraction. On February 22, Joe published a letter that gave Werner the benefit of the doubt but unmistakably implied that he was lying. "Even though a sense of loyalty to the office makes him willing to sacrifice himself and his health," Joe wrote, "perhaps as a kindness to him and in fairness to the public he should not be burdened with another six-year term."

The advertisement also asserted that Werner had earned between $170,000 and $200,000 in public office. When divided by Werner's years of service, the annual figure is moderate and equals an average attorney's income. But the lump sum seemed gigantic to people who were barely emerging from the ravages of the Depression.[39]

This was the Joe McCarthy poker players knew. Louis Cattau liked and admired him but warned that he was "tricky, very tricky." Andrew Parnell thought him charming and brilliant—but ruthless if you were in his path.[40]

A few days before the election, Joe ran another advertisement, topped by a photograph, a slogan—"JUSTICE is TRUTH in ACTION"—and a blaring headline: "WHAT ABOUT THIS AGE QUESTION??"

Joe repeated his charges about the birthdate, "much against my will," and added to the confusion by citing a newspaper article of 1900 giving Werner's year of birth as 1870. Who was right, he asked, Martindale-Hubbell, the clipping, or Werner? "Certainly, I cannot know which, if any, of the three claims is correct." Werner's complaints about Joe's campaigning were "ill-timed and unfair," in view of "his own apparent indecision over the last half century as to whether he should pick 1866, 1870, or 1872 . . ."

For good measure, Joe again printed the total income figure he had devised to cover Werner's more than 35 years in public office and suggested that "it might be well for him to retire."[41]

What any of this had to do with Joe's qualifications for the circuit judgeship was at best obscure, as he well knew.

Almost all of the scores of people who labored for the election of Joe McCarthy were primarily attracted to the campaign by his personality. Urban Van Susteren, a young attorney from Little Chute, was first introduced to Joe at a March of Dimes dance in Appleton and was fascinated by the flow of energy, friendliness, and self-confidence that radiated from the youthful campaigner. When Joe asked if he would lend a hand, Van Susteren casually agreed, thinking that he might stuff an envelope or lick a stamp some time. Early the next morning he was rousted from bed by McCarthy, who already had a dozen chores for him to do.[42]

Gus Keller was also at the dance and was asked to help. He was a native of Appleton, an attorney, a member of St. Mary's, and a Democrat. He first met Joe when he was a farm boy of fifteen or sixteen and had long enjoyed his constantly high spirits. Joe told him at the dance about introducing himself to local Menominee Indian leaders as the man running against "that feeble fellow" serving as judge. They both laughed heartily.[43]

Henry J. Van Straten was the Outagamie County superintendent of schools. He heard Joe give a speech before the Kiwanis Club in Appleton and thought him "dynamic, full of life, interesting." They quickly became friends, and Van Straten offered his services for the campaign.

Two years earlier, Van Straten had devised and successfully employed a campaign technique in his bid for public office that he now passed on to Joe. He had sent a printed postcard to every household listed in local telephone and city directories, containing a pitch for his candidacy and bearing a handwritten signature. He and his wife had labored for weeks on the signatures, and friends had helped with the addressing and mailing. Joe eagerly adopted the tactic; it paralleled his method of reaching farm families and brought his candidacy directly to the attention of thousands of people he would be unable to contact in person. It jelled perfectly with his philosophy—somewhat primitive, perhaps, but perceptive—of giving people a reason to vote for him.[44]

Joe modified the concept by having the entire message, as well as the signature, written by hand, and by having all the work done by others. Recipients would think he had taken the time and effort to compose and sign a personal appeal for their ballot. It was a technique based on deception, of course, but neither Joe nor the scores of helpers who filled out the postcards lost any sleep over that.

Joe deposited boxes of blank postcards and piles of telephone books and city directories at the offices of friendly attorneys. (Some legal secretaries groaned at the sight of the candidate with yet another arm load.) High school students from Shawano volunteered their labor. Admirers throughout the judicial district devoted long days and nights to the project.

There were two types of postcards. One included the sentence: "The present judge, Edgar V. Werner, was born in 1866 (according to Martindale's Legal Directory) and if he were reelected he would be in his eightieth year at the end of the term. Certainly, one who has reached his age is entitled to retire." The citation in parenthesis was included at the suggestion of Francis Werner (no relation to the judge), who thought it wise for Joe to document the allegation. Many families would also receive a second postcard. It was addressed to the spouse of the initial recipient (first names came from the city directories), whose name was dropped in the text of the brief message. Joe was hoping, of course, that recipients did not compare the handwriting on the postcards.

A few days before the election, Joe hauled dozens of sacks full of campaign postcards into post offices throughout the three counties. He continued visiting farms until the day the polls opened.[45]

Almost no one outside the McCarthy camp gave Joe's candidacy serious consideration. Judge Werner came from populous Outagamie County and was thought certain to win heavily there, especially in Appleton, where he had served in the courthouse for nearly a quarter century. Another candidate, Judge A. N. Whiting of Antigo, could easily carry his native Langlade County, observers agreed. Whiting and McCarthy were expected to split the vote, allowing the reelection of Judge Werner.

The final tally on April 5 came as a shock; the *Appleton Post-Crescent* called it "one of the most astonishing upsets in the history of the Tenth Judicial Circuit." The youthful attorney from Shawano defeated Werner in all three counties in the circuit and narrowly lost to Whiting in Langlade county. Werner took the city of Appleton by a few hundred votes over McCarthy but was crushed in the rural areas of Outagamie County. The totals read: McCarthy, 15,160; Werner, 11,154; Whiting, 9,071. At 30, Joe was the youngest man ever to be elected a circuit judge in Wisconsin. Only ten years earlier, he had been a bankrupt chicken farmer with a grade-school education.[46]

When interviewed about his victory, Joe said modestly, "The campaign was a big job, but I have a bigger one ahead of me. The only thing that will overcome the handicap of my youth is unremitting hard work." A few years later, looking back on the election that initiated his ascent to political prominence, Joe remarked, "I figured I could win. They told me that was impossible. I didn't like that.[47]

Tony Swanke hosted a lavish victory celebration at his home in Tigerton. He had traveled with the candidate at times during the campaign and had paid a few bills when asked.

By now Joe owed about 100 people a total of $7,000. He had borrowed recklessly to keep the campaign going and for money to live on. (He reported campaign expenditures of $1,221.58, undoubtedly much less than he actually spent.) He would not take office until the first day of 1940, his law practice amounted to almost nothing (his reported income for 1939 was $1,055), and there was no way to begin making payments to creditors. To ease his friend's financial misery, Swanke arranged a secret $7,000 loan through a bank in Tigerton controlled by his family. Since Joe had no collateral, he was required to agree to a note assigning his future paychecks from the state to the bank, which was given the power of attorney to cash them. When the appropriate interest and principal were subtracted from each paycheck, plus a payment on a life insurance policy for $7,000 to protect the loan, Joe would receive the balance. Although he could look forward to an annual income of $8,000 for at least the six years of his term in office, Joe would still be chronically short of funds and would borrow constantly.[48]

To celebrate the election win and the new financial arrangement, Swanke treated Joe to a three-week vacation in Gulfport, Mississippi. While relaxing one evening in the southern resort town, Joe pondered the fact that he didn't know a great deal of law and was ill-prepared to be Judge Werner's successor.[49]

Werner, meanwhile, fumed over his defeat by the young upstart and was the first of a great many over the years to condemn Joe McCarthy's political tactics. Werner's backers demanded an investigation into the campaign, charging that Joe had overspent the statutory allowance, thereby violating Wisconsin's corrupt-practices law, and had deliberately misrepresented the judge's age. As late as 1951 Werner's son told a reporter, "He not only drove my father to his grave but turned longstanding family friends against our whole family. He didn't just add years to my dad's age; he accused him of all sorts of evil. It was amazing how one man could wreck the reputation of a man loved and honored in this community."[50]

McCarthy's conduct was upheld following a lengthy post-election investigation by state officials (who did not know about the loan from Swanke or the dozens of other loans it covered). Still, Joe had revealed in this campaign not only a brazen ambition, a ferocious capacity for sustained effort, and a powerful ability to charm voters, but also a considerable capacity for deviousness.

SPEEDY JUSTICE

While waiting to take office, Joe stayed in Shawano, visiting friends, playing cards several nights a week, and trying, without much success, to drum up a little legal business. Dottie Druckrey left his office in the summer to return to school. Her starting salary had been $10 a week and had risen to $18. Joe often gave her all the money he had. Before she left, Joe told her that his goal in life was to reach the United States Supreme Court.[1]

On Independence Day he spoke at a park in Appleton, urging the United States to remain aloof from the struggles of European nations. He denounced "the damnable flow of war propaganda" and warned against "another futile slaughter."

> We would like to see all the peoples of the world enjoying the liberty and freedom that we have. But it is written in history that when an autocracy is removed by powers other than the people themselves, that autocracy will be replaced by an autocracy even more vicious.
>
> Democracy has never been bestowed upon a people by an outside paternal hand. It is only when their liberty is purchased by their own blood and courage that people are willing to fight to preserve that liberty.[2]

Such isolationist rhetoric was common in Wisconsin at the time, and Joe knew that his remarks would be greeted with enthusiasm. Still, as far as he understood the issues involved, Joe no doubt meant what he said. His closest friends always recognized a genuine sense of idealism in him. Despite his opportunism and capacity for trickery, Joe was in some ways an innocent, an utterly unsophisticated person intellectually who could find it easy to become a true believer. He usually saw things in black and white; Urban Van Susteren knew him to be helpless with abstractions.[3] But when he thought himself on the side of justice and truth, he could be inflexible toward the opposition.

In 1939, however, Joe McCarthy was years away from finding a cause that would claim his total attention. He thought of himself merely as a Young Democrat, and even that allegiance was superficial. His primary concern was the immediate task at hand: becoming a competent judge of the Tenth Circuit.

After being sworn in, Joe attended the annual convention of the Wisconsin State Board of Circuit Judges, absorbing talks on pretrial procedures and personal injury cases. The circuit court was the highest court of original jurisdiction in Wisconsin. It ranked below the state supreme court, to which appeals were directed, and above the scores of county, civil, and municipal courts that dotted the state. He received a formal welcome by the Outagamie County bar association a couple of days later and began his judicial duties by hearing equity cases in Milwaukee.[4]

Back in the courthouse in Appleton, Joe appointed Urban Van Susteren his divorce counsel. The position was part-time and netted the attorney about $1,500 a year. There was minor criticism at the time. Van Susteren was unmarried and only in his twenties. Moreover, he had played an active role during the campaign in the Little Chute area, which went heavily for McCarthy, and at least one rival for the job charged political payoff. But the post was essentially administrative, and it was common and legal to appoint friends to such positions. Joe somehow wangled a down payment on a small house in Appleton and gave Van Susteren a key. The two saw each other almost every day.[5]

Joe's court reporter was Pat Howlett, a bald, middle-aged gentleman who took accurate notes in longhand. He was with Judge McCarthy constantly and could never quite get used to the frantic activity generated by his new thirty-one-year-old boss.

Edgar Werner had believed in slow, deliberate action by the court; some attorneys resented his constant lectures in the courtroom and complained about lengthy delays. Almost 250 cases were in backlog when Joe assumed the banch. To the delight of local lawyers and their clients, he tackled these cases with a vengeance.[6]

Joe often kept his courtroom open for more than twelve hours a day. In one 44-day period it was in session twelve times beyond midnight. He would work Saturdays, and he once tried 40 cases in 40 days. Whenever possible he invited opposing attorneys into his chambers and helped them reach out-of-court settlements. Divorces were often handled swiftly, sometimes in five or ten minutes if nothing was contested. The procedure was legal, if not ceremonious, and no one complained. Litigants got what they came for. Joe proclaimed in a later campaign, "Justice delayed is justice denied."

While Judge Werner used to appear in Shawano a couple of times a year, Joe drove there every Monday morning, and he handled cases in Antigo in the afternoon. He scrapped the court calendar and announced that he would go anywhere in the district to hear cases whenever attorneys were ready.

Within a few months the backlog of cases had disappeared. A weary Pat Howlett later commented, "Joe always drove himself hard. Sometimes I couldn't keep up."[7]

While McCarthy was not a student of the law—Van Susteren thought that he knew nothing of the rules of evidence—local attorneys admired and respected him as a judge. He revealed a shrewd ability to get to the heart of a matter rapidly and a strong concern for justice. Andrew Parnell, later a judge himself and a frequent McCarthy critic, strongly praised Joe's almost instinctive capacity for handling the bench. He was unorthodox at times; he would grill witnesses, bluff, and occasionally bully and abuse people. Parnell later accused him of making sly remarks in the presence of a jury to influence the outcome of a case. But on the whole, he was praised throughout the circuit as a hard-working and fair-minded judge.

The *Milwaukee Journal* editorialized: "Breaking with the 'horse-and-buggy' tradition that has tied up the calendars of most Wisconsin circuit courts, young Judge Joseph R. McCarthy of Appleton has streamlined his tenth district . . . and has made a hit with lawyers and litigants alike." Another Wisconsin newspaper said that Judge McCarthy "administered justice promptly and with a combination of legal knowledge and good sense."[8]

People also enjoyed the informality and humor found in Joe's courtroom, and there was always an adequate supply of jurors. The Judge frequently brightened stodgy proceedings with wisecracks and good-natured kidding. He once told an attorney for the plaintiff in a traffic accident case, "Every time a doctor comes in here, he tells me his patient was seriously injured and his bill was reasonable. I'm still waiting for the day when a doctor comes in and says, 'No, my patient wasn't hurt so bad, and my bill was way too high.' "[9]

At times the humor was at Pat Howlett's expense. "Now gentlemen," Joe would say, "I would like to continue these proceedings further. But Curly down there wants to go home." Howlett, without a hair on his head, would invariably blush.[10]

Joe well knew how to appeal to lawyers. Before making an important ruling in a case, he would say to one, "Now, Andy, what have you got to say on this point?" When Andy was through, he would turn to his adversary and say, "Now, Chuck, how would you answer Andy?" This flattered attorneys, who thought their learned opinions were being weighed carefully by the judge. Sometimes they were, especially when Joe was uncertain of the law.[11]

On more than one occasion insiders saw examples of McCarthy's kindness. He once learned that a woman convicted of murdering her husband (she had aimed at his testicles and missed) was a heavy smoker and without funds. Joe's serious sinus condition made him unable to tolerate smokers; he once barked at an attorney, "Bill, if you want to win a case in this court, put out that cigar!" But he gave the jailer ten dollars to keep the woman in cigarettes. Joe thought her husband a bad man who deserved killing.[12]

With his court docket up to date in May 1940, Joe and his old friend Clifford Mullarkey, now an attorney in Clintonville, went on a vacation to the Deep South, which Joe had seen for the first time a year earlier. On the way, they attended the Kentucky Derby. Joe found horse racing extremely exciting, and he gambled impetuously. Time after time he placed bets on losers. Finally, he asked Mullarkey if he had any money left. About twenty-five dollars, Mullarkey replied. Why? Well, Joe explained, he was going to have an important conversation in a few minutes and wanted to be able to flash at least twenty dollars. Mullarkey emptied his wallet.

During the next race Joe began to cheer and wave his arms. He stood on his chair yelling as the horses crossed the finish line. He then threw his arms around Mullarkey and told him that he had bet their last twenty-five dollars on the winning horse, "Getaway Jack."

In Biloxi, Mississippi, at the Boardwalk Hotel, Joe played roulette recklessly and lost all of the racetrack winnings. Mullarkey watched in silence as Joe plunged their last silver dollar into an unfriendly slot machine. The judge had to wire Pat Howlett the next morning for money to buy coffee.

In New Albany, Mississippi, the next evening, the two went into a nightclub. Joe set his sights on a beautiful young lady who turned out to be the daughter of the local newspaper editor. He so captivated her father that a large article soon appeared on the nation's youngest judge and his friend. The girl later traveled all the way to Appleton to visit Joe.[13]

Urban Van Susteren became deeply attached to McCarthy. He was by no means a blind admirer, and recognized numerous limitations and faults. But Joe continually fascinated him. He had never met or read of anyone quite like him. He was always to think him unique.

Van Susteren was impressed by what he considered a "lightning-quick" mind, though he knew that outside of court, Joe read almost nothing. He bolted through newspapers in a few minutes and could not sit still long enough to grapple with a book. The only volume Van Susteren saw him with was *Mein Kampf.* "He read only half of it, and it was my book." Joe enjoyed shocking attorneys in his chambers by smilingly pointing to it and noting that this was the way to get things done. (Somehow this eluded reporters in the 1950s, who would have concluded immediately that McCarthy had been a Nazi.) Van Susteren thought that Joe's considerable intellectual powers were most obvious in court and with concrete rather than abstract matters. "He knew so little, but what he knew he knew so well."[14]

Joe was in awe of no one, Van Susteren believed, and was absolutely fearless. He detested weakness of any sort, especially self-pity. A favorite expression was, "The son of a bitch sucks eggs," a barnyard allusion to a weasel or skunk. Joe rarely talked about himself and refused to complain about anything personal.

He loved a fight and could be fierce in combat. When attacked he would return the blow twice as hard. "You could watch Joe's eyes light up," said Van Susteren, "as he figured out almost immediately how to screw an opponent."[15]

Yet this same man could be tenderhearted and even sentimental, funny, generous, religious, and conscientious. He regularly recited the rosary while speeding along a highway, and he knelt for evening prayers no matter where he was.

He disdained material things, never owning good luggage, expensive suits, or even bedroom attire. (He often greeted visitors in stocking feet, wrapped in a blanket.) Yet he would gamble daringly all night long and would soon become obsessed with the stock market.[16]

Joe McCarthy was an anomaly. His closest friends accepted the fact and liked him for what he was.

Van Susteren also observed Joe's helplessness with detail and his frequent disorganization. He was always losing or forgetting something. He would prepare for a trip by throwing whatever was in sight into a suitcase. He left rumpled clothing in hotel rooms wherever he traveled.

His speeches were invariably whipped together at the last minute, and they almost always contained exaggerations, fruits of Joe's lack of preparation.

He would never admit a mistake.[17]

Everyone was aware of Joe's ambition. Some people thought he was continuously campaigning. But even Van Susteren was shocked when his friend calmly told him one evening that he was going to run for the United States Senate.

In early 1941 Joe confided to several intimates his desire for the Senate and his plan for getting there. The odds against him were overwhelming, of course. He was virtually without qualifications for such a position. He had no money and was unknown throughout most of the state. He was a Democrat, a serious handicap in Wisconsin. The stature of the two incumbents, Robert La Follette, Jr., and Alexander Wiley, was immense. Moreover, it was illegal under state law for a judge to run for a nonjudicial office. The candidate would be guilty of a felony and forced to relinquish his seat.[18]

But Joe's confidants didn't snigger at his proposal. Not after the 1939 campaign.

Joe planned to become better known by interchanging positions with other circuit court judges. This would give him an expense-free introduction into a large number of communities where he could give speeches and construct a network of friends. He would change his party affiliation by simply proclaiming himself a Republican; he hadn't the slightest scruple about that. He didn't worry about campaign funds and dismissed the question of his own qualifications. People weren't interested in issues anyway. They voted for personalities. And Joe was convinced that his was the best around.

As for the legal prohibition, he had friends in the state legislature and would find a way to get the statute repealed.[19]

It was as simple as that.

He wasn't sure when he would run. Nothing was certain with a war on. Senator Wiley would be up for reelection in three years; perhaps then. At any rate, the time to begin was at hand.

Joe had a potential rival and was keenly aware of it. Carl Zeidler was a tall, blond, handsome "boy wonder" who had upset a heavily favored Socialist candidate a year earlier to become the mayor of Milwaukee. His political future was thought to be extremely promising.

One evening in Wausau, Joe learned that his date had recently met Zeidler at a reception. He asked her to describe the mayor's handshake. Did it seem as warm and friendly as his own?[20]

Joe began rehearsing speeches in front of his cardplaying buddies and their wives, asking for constructive criticisms. The speeches were rather poor and marred by repetitions. The nasal quality so famous later was present slightly. But Joe kept trying to improve, and his friends knew why.[21]

He accepted as many invitations to speak and to fill in for other judges as he was able to find. He raced across the state, impressing people with his cheeriness and well-developed handshake. He read hundreds of names and details into his dictaphone for future reference.[22]

One night in Antigo he told Pat Howlett that they were to be in Racine the next morning to try cases. The exhausted court reporter refused to make the 300-mile trip without any sleep, even if it cost him his job. Joe snapped, "I haven't got time to argue," and drove all night through a blizzard to reach *the Belle City*. At 9:00 A.M. he appeared on the bench ready for a day's work.[23]

Within his own district, Joe would sometimes drive furiously to a nearby town and back to give a speech during a brief trial recess.[24]

Joe began to drink during this period, although his consumption was not extraordinary. To the envy of Van Susteren, he never suffered a hangover.[25]

He enjoyed gambling at the Racine Elks Club, where the card games started at midnight. Once he played until 7:15 A.M., showered, and then went to court. On another evening he feigned ignorance about gin rummy. By the time he was "instructed," he had won close to $2,000.

One night he and the attorneys in a trial were in a game at the Elks Club when word came that the jury had returned a verdict. They stuffed their cards in their pockets and returned to the courtroom. The game resumed later, as though without interruption.[26]

One man who played poker with Joe about this time called the experience "wild." The judge enjoyed raising the ante until people dropped out from fear. No one could tell if he was bluffing.[27]

Joe's record as a jurist was marred in 1941 in a controversial case that still presents historians with unanswered questions arising from conflicting testimony. Critics would often point to the case in later years as an example of McCarthy's irresponsibility.

In 1935 the state legislature had given the Wisconsin Department of Agriculture the power to regulate the dairy industry, a move designed to stop cutthroat competition, low prices, and bankruptcies. The department issued detailed orders for all areas of the state and established relatively high prices for milk. The law was to expire on the last day of 1941.

In 1940 the Quaker Dairy Company of Appleton violated a local market order by selling milk at a low cash-and-carry price. The company president, Ben Cherkasky, was undercutting his competition. While many consumers applauded, other milk distributors in the area turned to the department of agriculture for relief. In November the department filed suit in Judge McCarthy's court to require the company to obey the law. Trial was set for April 19, 1941.

Having no defense, and with an eye on the expiration date of the statute governing the dairy industry, Cherkasky decided to stall. He replaced his Green Bay attorney with Mark Catlin, Jr., a Republican state assemblyman from Appleton. A state law permitted the temporary adjournment of a case involving an attorney who was also a state legislator until the conclusion of a current legislative session. The case was rescheduled for early June. When the legislature adjourned, Catlin was paid and dismissed by the company, which returned the case to its regular lawyer, assisted by Appleton attorney Andrew Parnell.

Meanwhile, the counsel for the agriculture department's Milk Control Division, Gilbert Lappley, hounded McCarthy to issue a temporary injunction preventing the company from violating the law. Joe complied on May 20. A short time later Cherkasky called on the judge in his chambers and apparently convinced him that the 1935 statute was unreasonable, given current economic conditions, and that the injunction would destroy his business. On May 25, without consulting Lappley, Joe reversed himself and suspended the injunction. Cherkasky also told the judge he had been "reliably informed" that the legislature was about to annul or repeal the 1935 statute. A week later, Joe ordered the department of agriculture to appear before him on June 7 to show cause why the temporary injunction should not be stayed "pending the outcome of proposed legislation" in Madison.

The legislature adjourned on June 6, having taken no action on the milk statute. The next day Lappley contended before McCarthy that the Quaker Dairy Company must now obey the law. Andrew Parnell argued that the injunction should not be continued because the statute would expire on

December 31 and that thereafter his client's actions would be legal. He also claimed that the injunction would ruin the company financially. McCarthy ruled in favor of the company and ordered the injunction quashed. What exactly happened then remains uncertain, but Lappley's account of events was more persuasive than McCarthy's.

When Lappley requested an immediate or at least early trial to appeal the order, he later explained, Joe launched into a lengthy discourse about the entire case. He said that a trial would be "a waste of the court's time," as all the facts in the matter had been amply presented. He castigated the Quaker Dairy Company for its devious employment of Catlin and admitted that "as a matter of strict law" the department of agriculture's position was the proper one to follow. He justified his order by agreeing with Parnell's argument that the statute's expiration in a few months would make the matter moot.

Four days later Lappley petitioned the Wisconsin supreme court for a writ of mandamus. The supreme court responded immediately and requested all of the records in the case. When the documents arrived, a page was discovered missing from the trial record, and the court demanded an explanation. Joe claimed that after the June 7 hearing he had read some flattering remarks about Lappley into the record at the attorney's request. He had recently ordered that portion of the record destroyed, he said, because its contents were "deemed improper and immaterial" to the case. (Joe told friends privately that his action was pure revenge, prompted by Lappley's sudden decision to appeal.) Joe no doubt also sought to conceal from the supreme court his informal comments on the case, in particular his assertion that a trial would be a waste of time. He also was loathe to reveal his criticism of Catlin, a prominent Republican, who was soon to be of use to him.

The supreme court issued an opinion shortly, written by Chief Justice Marvin B. Rosenberry, sharply rebuking McCarthy. The judge's personal views of the statute in question, wrote Rosenberry, were irrelevant. "Whether or not there shall be a law under which the production and sale of milk should be regulated is a matter wholly within the province of the legislature. When a court undertakes to say a law shall not be enforced, the court takes over the legislative function and in effect declares that the act of the legislature should be suspended." The court found that the grounds on which McCarthy acted "constituted an abuse of judicial authority."

Rosenberry declared the destruction of the court notes "highly improper." He tended to accept the agriculture department's contention that they contained information pertaining to the judge's ruling. At any rate,

Rosenberry wrote, "In this proceeding, this court is the judge of the materiality of the notes." McCarthy was ordered to reissue restraining orders against the dairy and rehear the case.

In early July Joe defiantly ruled again in favor of the Quaker Dairy Company. He based his decision on a new argument submitted by Parnell that the agriculture department had exceeded its authority in regulating the cash-and-carry distribution of milk. He also lashed out at the department for oppressing the poor by maintaining artificially high milk prices during a period of economic recovery and milk shortages. Technicalities aside, he wrote, "the department's attempt to dictate that those in the lower-income brackets must pay for a delivery service which they don't want, a service which they don't need, and a service which they can ill afford to pay is ridiculous in the extreme."

McCarthy's ruling was greeted favorably by the public and the press. The department of agriculture, at the urging of the local milk industry, did not appeal. It suspended enforcement of price controls in the area, which meant lower milk prices for everyone. Politically, the encounter with the Madison bureaucrats seemed to be a plus for the Judge.[28]

Did the supreme court censure McCarthy in the Quaker Dairy case, as critics later contended? Although the word "censure" did not appear in Rosenberry's remarks, it is possible to interpret the 1941 decision in such a light. Surely the destruction of the court reporter's notes was a serious error. It is clear, however, that Joe remained in good standing with the state's highest court. In a later decision involving McCarthy, Chief Justice Rosenberry wrote, "The defendant practiced law for many years, and in his relations to his clients and the courts has never been derelict in the discharge of his duties and obligations as a lawyer.[29]

No one charged McCarthy with moral turpitude in the Quaker Dairy case or with profiting in any way from his decision. A shrewd (and hostile) reporter who studied these years in 1951 thought Joe's record as a lawyer and judge virtually unassailable: "As a blemish on McCarthy it has about the same standing as his vaccination."[30]

Young men all over the nation were entering the armed forces in early 1942. Carl Zeidler made front-page headlines when he joined the Navy. Urban Van Susteren applied for active duty and was summoned by the Army to report for a physical.

As a judge, Joe was automatically deferred from the draft. But he felt guilty about staying behind and wondered if he should enlist in the Army. If he wanted to be a hero, Van Susteren advised, bigger than Zeidler, he should join the Marines. Joe asked why. His poor education was showing again; he knew nothing of the Marine Corps' history or image. Van Susteren patiently explained the possible political advantages of a Marine background when the war was over and challenged his friend to sign up. "You got shit in your blood?" he asked, meaning was Joe afraid? There was no reply.[31]

On June 2, Joe wrote a letter to a Marine recruiting officer in Milwaukee, applying for a commission. He then made arrangements for a leave of absence, during which other circuit judges would handle the district's trial work. On June 3 he drove to Milwaukee, and he enlisted the next day.

He told reporters that he was entering without any promises of a commission or special favors but that he hoped to be able to get into officer's training school. At the moment, he said, he was "more interested in a gun than a commission." Van Susteren laughed heartily when he read that. Pure Joe.[32]

The *Appleton Post-Crescent,* managed by John Reidl, a longtime friend who considered himself Joe's political mentor, ran a headline declaring that Judge McCarthy had enlisted as a buck private. For the rest of his life, Joe would contend that he first entered the Marine Corps as a "buck private" or "private." He included the assertion in campaign literature and in biographies prepared for the *Congressional Directory* and *Who's Who in America.* He said in 1944 that he had "earned" a second lieutenant's commission.

Actually, Joe received a direct commission as a first lieutenant on July 29 and was sworn in on August 4 at that rank. He at no time served in the Marine Corps as an enlisted man. (This fact would become public knowledge in 1951.) He was ordered to report to the Marine base at Quantico, Virginia for basic training.[33]

Before leaving, Joe sold his house and auctioned off his two-year-old furniture to friends at what Van Susteren thought were ridiculously low prices.[34]

He turned up at Charles Hanratty's house in Milwaukee with a blonde on his arm. Hanratty was ill and in bed. Joe took a roll of bills from his shirt pocket and, without looking at it, tossed it on the bedspread. He was going into the Marines the next day, he said, and wouldn't be needing money.[35]

The following morning, in uniform, he presided briefly in a Milwaukee courtroom. It made quite a splash in the newspapers.[36]

TAIL GUNNER JOE

Judge McCarthy was 33 when he reported for active duty. "I thought I was in good shape," he said later, "but in that first week's training at Quantico I thought I'd die and was afraid I wouldn't. I was in a group of eighteen- and nineteen-year-old kids, most of them good athletes. We either captured or lost every hill in Virginia before we finished our training."[1]

During the remainder of 1942 and into the following year, Joe received additional training at a number of stations. In Harrisburg he attended the Army Intelligence school. In the fall he found himself at Camp Lejeune, in New River, North Carolina.

There he ran into Leo Day, a young friend from Wausau, who was in the Naval Medical Corps. Both men had 72-hour passes and decided to spend the time together. They flew to Washington, Joe saying that he wanted to look over his future place of residence. They exchanged pleasantries with Senator La Follette and that evening toured the city's nightclubs. Day thought his companion one of the most jovial and pleasant people he had ever known.

They then proceeded to Baltimore. That night, following another round of nightclubs, both became dead drunk. They awoke the next afternoon in the Waldorf Astoria Hotel in New York City. Neither knew how they got there.[2]

From January through March 1943, Joe trained at the Marine Corps Air Station, El Centro, California. Now a captain, he was the intelligence officer for a newly formed dive-bomber squadron, VMSB-235. When in combat, his job would involve briefing the 40 pilots prior to their flights, interrogating them on their return about targets, enemy resistance, and the like, and preparing intelligence reports to be sent up the chain of command. His responsibilities were supposed to confine him to a desk.

McCarthy immediately became one of the most popular men in the squadron. Many of his buddies took pictures, and the photographs show him trim and smiling, slightly balding, with a crew cut. (Overseas he would sport a beard.) He was called "Mac" by some and "Joe" by others and was the life of more than one party. Ken Smedley once introduced him to his parents, and his mother was particularly taken with the captain.[3]

On March 31 the squadron arrived in Pearl Harbor aboard the USS *Kitty Hawk* and was assigned to the Marine Corps Air Station at Ewa, Oahu. Following two months of further training, during which flights were made to Midway and outlying islands, it embarked on June 12, with another squadron, for the South Pacific. Joe was on the Navy's seaplane tender *Chandeleur*. He would spend sixteen months overseas (and always say eighteen).

One Marine, who kept a diary, quickly struck up a friendship with Joe. "We weren't long out of Pearl before I decided that McCarthy was the most interesting character aboard." They enjoyed long talks on deck. Joe often spoke of Maybelle Counihan, whose picture he displayed on the desk in his cabin. When politics came up, Joe told his friend that he had voted for Franklin D. Roosevelt three times.

The days at sea were quiet and uneventful, and there was time for more than chatting. The Marine recalled:

> Joe was quite popular with all the officers. Not only was he a fine conversationalist, but he also had found a way around the regulation banning liquor on board. He had three trunks marked "office supplies—squadron 235" and all those supplies were liquid.

Joe's shipmate considered him a "fabulous" poker player.

> He'd sit in a game and suddenly, for no reason at all, bet $101.15, or $97.90. Not only would the bet knock other players off balance, but they'd have the problem of counting

out the exact sum. Most times, they'd let him have the pot just
to get on to the next hand.

Things were so peaceful that Cmdr. Albert K. Morehouse gave the men
permission to stage a "shellback" initiation ceremony on June 22, the day
the *Chandeleur* crossed the equator. The gaiety started with the announcement that the uniform for "polliwog" initiates consisted of pajamas, overseas caps, and bare feet.

> The war was completely forgotten as we appeared before
> Neptunus Rex, the enlisted man enthroned on the boat deck.
> Rank meant nothing, of course, as we were paddled, soaked
> with hoses, speared by the electric trident, and generally
> abused. One marine officer did an elaborate striptease, and
> someone else read a long defense, typed on toilet paper. It
> was comic relief from the war, still hundreds of miles ahead
> of us.[4]

Joe had nearly completed the initiation when he suffered an accident.
Climbing down a ladder with a bucket fastened to his right foot, he slipped.
His left foot caught on a lower rung, and he fell backward, causing a fracture
at the base of the fifth metatarsal.

The squadron medical officer, Dr. George B. Barnes, put a cast on the
foot. Joe had several drinks and told a friend, "Don't tell Maybelle I broke
my foot in this silly way."[5]

Later, when the cast was about to be removed, the corpsman assigned the
task used glacial acetic acid rather than the regular vinegar to soften the
plaster of Paris before cutting it. The acid caused a chemical burn on Joe's
left leg that took several weeks to heal and left what Doctor Barnes later
called a "fairly large" scar.[6]

The accidental fracture and burn were the only injuries Joe would suffer
while in the Marine Corps.[7]

Joe was quick to recognize the political profit in any sort of war-related
wound and was not above transforming his prank-caused mishap into an
act of combat heroism. In July, newspapers carried the story that he had
received a "facial injury and more serious injuries to a leg and a foot" and
would be hospitalized for about eight weeks. In November, a press release
declared that he had been wounded in action.[8]

In the spring of 1944, in time for his initial race for the Senate, Joe
sported a citation signed by Adm. Chester Nimitz, commander-in-chief of

the Pacific Fleet. It commended McCarthy for his very real participation as
a rear gunner and photographer in the Solomon Islands "from September 1
to December 31, 1943" but altered the date and circumstances of Joe's
injury:

> He obtained excellent photographs of enemy gun positions,
> despite intense anti-aircraft fire, thereby gaining valuable
> information which contributed materially to the success of
> subsequent strikes in the area. Although suffering from a
> severe leg injury, he refused to be hospitalized and continued
> to carry out his duties as Intelligence Officer in a highly
> efficient manner. His courageous devotion to duty was in
> keeping with the highest traditions of the naval service.[9]

The citation resulted from a letter of recommendation dated February
19, 1944, and bearing what purported to be the signature of Maj. Glenn A.
Todd, then McCarthy's commanding officer. In fact, Todd neither wrote
nor signed such a letter. It seems certain that Joe himself was the document's author. As Todd explained in 1977, "Intelligence officers had very
little work to do so we gave them all sorts of odd jobs. They wrote citations
for awards." (The Marine Corps stated reluctantly in 1978 that it had
destroyed the original letter five years earlier as part of an effort to obtain
additional storage space. A typed copy was kept.) After apparently forging
Todd's signature to the letter, Joe sent it through the proper channels.
Admiral Nimitz routinely signed thousands of such documents during the
war.[10]

McCarthy would give several different accounts of his wound in the
future. At political gatherings he would occasionally feign a limp and say
that he had ten pounds of shrapnel in his leg. Van Susteren heard him make
the contention once and thought it typical McCarthy hyperbole. At one
point he asked him specifically about the injury. Joe rolled up a pantleg and
showed him the scar. "There, you son of a bitch. Now let's hear no more
about it." He later denied ever having claimed to bear shrapnel and blamed
the story on a reporter who had once been a Communist.[11]

The account he gave most often was that he had suffered a leg injury
when a plane he was in ground-looped on landing and overturned and
burned. He escaped, spurned medical attention, and went to the Intelligence shack to type a report. A plane did ground-loop that fall, breaking the
pilot's arm. There was no fire; Joe was not aboard. It was the only casualty
sustained by the squadron in over 8,000 hours of flying.[12]

When someone would note that he had not received a Purple Heart while in the service, Joe would always point to his citation, which he published in campaign literature. In 1952 he told a reporter, "I had a leg badly smashed up, burned, and broken. In fact, I got a citation from Nimitz based on that."[13]

That same year, in a deposition, he was asked if he had suffered an injury during a shellback ceremony in 1943. Under oath, Joe replied, "Oh, a minor—I forget what it was. I did suffer some minor injury."[14]

The *Chandeleur* docked at the New Hebrides on July 3, and the entire squadron was soon based at Espiritu Santo. On September 1, VMSB-235 arrived at Henderson Field, Guadalcanal, and three days later flew its first combat mission. Before long, pilots hit gun emplacements at Vila and Balale and spotted artillery for Allied troops on Arundel and New Georgia.[15]

The assignments were important and at times dangerous. The Japanese fought back with anti-aircraft weapons. Maj. Everett E. Munn told of the raid on Japanese-held Balale Island in the Solomons, in which Marine, Navy, Army, and New Zealand air units participated:

> My section came in first, diving through intense anti-aircraft fire. Several of the planes were hit by bits of shrapnel but all made it back to our base. I dumped my 1000-pound bomb right in the middle of my target and pulled out at about 2000 feet. The rest of the boys followed us down and did a magnificent job. By the time the last planes had released their bombs, anti-aircraft fire had ceased entirely. We must have knocked out every big gun position on the island. After our dive bombers finished their job, Marine and Navy torpedo bombers swooped in and laid huge bombs down the center of the airfield.[16]

Joe carried out his less exciting duties on the ground efficiently and responsibly. And he always found time for fun. One night, as a volunteer mess officer, he helped supervise the digging of barbecue pits and a feast that featured nine roasted cows, five gallons of "torpedo juice," and 130 cases of beer "borrowed from the Navy." He often wangled access to airplanes and would fly in canned grapefruit juice, medicinal brandy, canned turkeys, and other rare delicacies which he distributed freely. One grateful recipient later recalled, "You'd see Joe McCarthy come up with an airplane full of goodies from the rear area . . . kind of like Santa Claus coming in the Mason's parade."[17]

Joe joined two other squadron members, Jerome Wander and John A. "Jocko" Kidney, in a profitable liquor smuggling enterprise. Captain McCarthy contacted British and Australian ships in the Pacific and purchased the beverages. Kidney loaded them aboard a seaplane and flew them back to the squadron, where Wander handled distribution. All went well until Joe and Kidney quarreled over a division of the profits. This led to a brutal fist fight between the two that Wander later described as "unbelievable." As tough as Joe was, Kidney, an ex-hockey player from Dorchester, Massachusetts, was his equal. The partnership dissolved with both men lying in the dirt covered with blood.[18]

Master Sergeant Wander was the squadron's head gunner. He and Joe were the oldest among the 40 pilots and 40 gunners and were close friends. Before long, Joe persuaded the sergeant to teach him to shoot the "twin 30's" in the two-man SBD bomber's rear seat. The instruction took place on the ground in an old dive-bomber, and Joe was an enthusiastic student. At one point, he swung the machine guns around too far and accidently shot holes in the plane's tail.

Joe told Wander that he was going to be Wisconsin's next senator and made it clear that his campaign would be helped by pictures and stories linking him with combat duty. Moreover, the captain was anxious to participate in some of the adventures pilots described to him daily.[19]

As Joe told the story of his first overseas flight in 1946, he had become dissatisfied with the quality of the high altitude photography taken during dive-bombing because the pictures failed to reveal gun positions accurately. After he had complained several times, Major Munn "invited" him to take the pictures himself, giving him 30 minutes to learn how to operate a camera before the next dive-bombers took off. Joe recalled, "I was the most involuntary volunteer you ever saw."

The pilot was Major Todd, the squadron executive officer. Joe asked himself, "McCarthy, what in heck are you doing here?"

As the plane dove toward the island and dropped its lethal cargo, Todd later recalled, tracer bullets ripped through the air and appeared to hit the gunner's cockpit. Todd anxiously called Joe on the interphone but received no reply. He turned the squadron over to his wing man and headed for the nearest airfield for help. The radio soon squawked, and it was Joe saying he was all right. He had tied down the camera with his microphone cord in order to fire the machine guns.

Joe later admitted that he was "scared stiff" when he saw the tracer bullets coming at him, but his first inclination, of course, was to fight back.[20]

Joe flew with several pilots on squadron missions. He went up two or three times with Ken Smedley and six or eight times with W. H. Montfort. He strafed areas during pull-outs after bombs were released and shot at a number of specific targets such as supply and fuel dumps, barges, and bridges. At Bougainville, he and Montfort badly damaged a Japanese truck convoy crossing a bridge. On several occasions his own plane was under fire. But Wander restricted Joe's participation largely to safer local strikes called "milk runs." On the really dangerous missions, such as at Rabaul, pilots did not want an intelligence officer seated behind them. (Joe would always falsely claim, even in his official biography written for the *Congressional Directory*, that he had participated in the air strikes over Rabaul.)

"The judge loved to shoot guns," one pilot said later. "He was really eager in that rear seat." Joe claimed to have fired 4,700 rounds of ammunition during three missions in a single day, and he made sure that the public relations officer on Guadalcanal got that figure into a press release. As a gag, men in the squadron awarded him a plaque "for destroying more coconut trees than anyone else in the South Pacific." He was also served with a formal "summons and complaint" signed by "Lever Brothers," soap manufacturers who owned many of the trees in the area.[21]

How many strike-flights did Joe make? His figures varied, rising each time he ran for the Senate. In 1944 he said fourteen. Two years later he claimed seventeen. In 1951, applying for medals, the total became 32. The Marine Corps accepted the last figure, and in 1952 it awarded Senator McCarthy the Distinguished Flying Cross, bestowed upon those who completed at least twenty-five combat missions, plus the Air Medal and four stars. Joe said, "I have never received and never expect to receive anything I will value more highly." The extravagant praise in the DFC citation made no mention of his "injury."[22]

Flight officers kept flight logs during the war that were certified monthly and served as the official record of one's participation in combat missions. Joe's was filled out by Major Todd. When the war was over, the flight logs were given to the participants.

In late September 1951, Joe supported his request for Air Medals with "certified copies from his flight logbook," signed, he said, by Major Todd and verifying 32 missions. Reporters, by this time highly suspicious of the senator's war record, thought it curious that the commandant of the Marine Corps consented to certify only eleven strike/flights and recommend two Air Medals (one medal was awarded per five flights). At some point the commandant placed an undated statement in Joe's file: "It is the opinion of the Headquarters that Major McCarthy participated in combat flights in addition to those used as the basis for the recommended awards; however, official records cannot be used to substantiate this opinion." Marine Corps leaders were well known to be sympathetic to Senator McCarthy. Major Todd was in Indonesia and received what he considered a "very strange" order from Marine Corps headquarters forbidding him to comment on McCarthy's missions or citations. Newsmen did not contact him.

Actually, Major Todd certified eleven strike/flights after Joe sent him his flight log in the spring of 1949. He authorized two Air Medals. The figure eleven came from his wartime entries in the log, entries that jibed perfectly with his memory of events. He was unaware that Joe had received the Distinguished Flying Cross until told by the author in 1977. (At first he was unwilling to believe it and requested official documentation.) He strongly denied the possibility of McCarthy's participation in 32 flights, or even twenty. He himself only flew in fourteen combat missions. Major Munn flew in fewer than twenty.[23]

In 1977, following a television program on McCarthy, Jerome Wander checked his wartime records to see how many flights they revealed for the captain. The figure corresponded exactly with Todd's recollection and the Marine Corps' official records.[24]

Todd, Munn, Wander, Montfort, and Smedley unanimously reject the figure of 32 as far too high. Marine Corps records show that Air Medals were awarded in 1952 for flights that occurred a few days before Joe's initial trip with Todd and two months after he left the squadron. (Which is why he later claimed to have been overseas for eighteen months.)[25]

Other circumstances surrounding the issuance of Senator McCarthy's awards raised eyebrows at the time. President Truman's Secretary of the Navy, Dan A. Kimball, granted final approval on the recommendation of Assistant Secretary John F. Floberg. Floberg assured his superior that the matter was "routine." When reporters reached Kimball at home in California, he was said to have understood that the senator was to receive only a single Air Medal. Floberg, it was noted, had been a member of an important law firm in Chicago that represented the vociferously pro-McCarthy *Chicago Tribune*.[26]

Whatever the machinations involved, the Distinguished Flying Cross bestowed upon Senator McCarthy near the height of his national political prominence was clearly unearned and was granted with the collusion of top Marine Corps officials, who were fully aware of his actual service record. The senator was tight-lipped about the subject and in 1952 attributed all queries into his wartime experiences to sinister, subversive forces.

In late 1943 and early 1944, Joe was determined to get as much publicity back home as possible, for three developments had persuaded him to run for the Senate against Alexander Wiley, a campaign that would have to be waged, apparently, from the Solomon Islands.

In the first place, Carl Zeidler had been declared missing in action a year earlier, eliminating a major political rival. In 1975 it was finally established that his ship had gone down near Capetown in November 1942.

Secondly, friends in the Wisconsin state legislature, led by G.O.P. assembly floor leader Mark Catlin, had quietly secured the repeal of the state law making it a felony for a judge to seek election to any other office. There was still a barrier against the same activity in the state constitution; the statute had actually been a criminal provision of the constitutional prohibition. But Joe had worked out a way to circumvent the document and was not troubled by it.[27]

Most importantly, for the first time in his life Joe had some money. By selling almost everything he owned before entering the service, he scraped together about $2,200. On a tip from an Appleton friend, and buying through a 40 percent margin account with Wayne Hummer and Company, a stock brokerage firm with an Appleton office, he purchased bonds of two nearly defunct railroads that soared in value with the resurgence of business brought about by war orders. Through this and other investments, Joe realized a net profit in 1943 of $40,561.67.[28]

This sum would make a healthy campaign fund. There was a state law limiting a candidate's personal expenses to $5,000. But Joe had figured out a way to get around that too.

Joe courted newspapermen and photographers who were in the vicinity of his squadron. He had pictures taken of himself in a dive-bomber, next to the machine guns and wearing a flying helmet. These were for display in campaign literature, in which he would style himself "Tail Gunner Joe." When his name appeared in a press release about a bombing raid to Bougainville, he told his public relations officer on Guadalcanal, Lt. P. T. Kimball, "This is worth 50,000 votes to me. Come, have a drink on it."[29]

Joe especially liked one story that made his home town newspaper, glorifying his role as an intelligence officer:

> Every evening "the judge" holds court in a dilapidated shack just off a jungle airstrip deep in the South Pacific combat zone.
> The folks back in Wisconsin might be a trifle shocked at his lack of dignity now. He stands barechested before his bench, an ancient table reeling on its last legs, and opens court with:
> "All right, what kind of hell did you give the Japs today?"[30]

Friends sent clippings that included his name, and he carried them around, showing them to whoever might be interested. He was pleased by one dispatch about the "flying judge." One fellow officer, Capt. Jack Canaan, later recalled, "At the time, I was young and didn't understand the significance of his knowing wink that this clipping and picture of himself in a helmet would help out in the States."[31]

Joe put signs on two trucks and a jeep: MCCARTHY FOR U.S. SENATOR, and painted HEADQUARTERS, MCCARTHY FOR U.S. SENATOR across his tent.

He sought out troops from Wisconsin, introduced himself, and said that he was running for office. John F. Thompson of Racine thought him extremely ingratiating. Joe seemed interested in the man he was meeting and wanted to know all about his family. (In 1952, Joe spotted Thompson in the audience at a rally in Racine and immediately left the stage to shake his hand. They had not seen each other since 1944 at Bougainville.)[32]

At home, preparations for the campaign began in Appleton in early March. Joe filed by mail and formally threw his hat in the ring in late April. He did not expect to take any part in the campaign, he wrote, and did not expect to be in the United States before the August 15 primary. He acknowledged that military regulations prohibited servicemen from speaking on political issues while in uniform, but said, "I do have a program and this I will submit to the people of Wisconsin as soon as time permits."[33]

Joe's actual plans bore little relationship to his pronouncement. He fully intended to return to Wisconsin as soon as possible and to speak on his own behalf as much as he dared.

In early June VMSB-235 left Efate, New Hebrides, for its fourth combat tour and was soon attacking gun positions at Rabaul. The following month it began flights against targets in New Britain and New Ireland.

But Captain McCarthy was no longer with the squadron. On July 13 Wisconsin newspapers announced that he had arrived on the West Coast and was on his way home.[34]

Joe had no illusions about his brief campaign in 1944. Senator Wiley, who had gone to Washington in 1939, was highly popular throughout the state, and his reelection was considered certain. This initial effort was made to gain a semblance of statewide recognition and to begin construction of a corps of active supporters that would assist him when he launched an all-out campaign after the war.

Some friends, like John Reidl and Tom Korb, advised against the effort. But Joe now had enough money to launch his bid for the Senate, and he saw no reason for delay.[35]

Only a few close friends knew of his sudden financial harvest, and Joe was determined to keep the matter confidential. He even decided not to file a state income tax return for 1943, on the ground that he was not a resident of Wisconsin during the year. He wouldn't get away with it, but by the time newspapers picked up the story it was 1947 and he was in the Senate.

During the primary contest of 1944, it was later shown, Joe withdrew approximately $46,000 in profits from Wayne Hummer and Company. Investigators were never able to determine exactly how much of this was spent on the campaign, but their estimates agree with the recollections of friends, placing the figure at between $20,000 and $30,000. Joe signed an affidavit on August 7, 1944, declaring his personal expenditures at $2,741.33, slightly more than half the legal limit.[36]

It seems certain that for the purpose of concealing the amount of money he had made from investments and spent on the campaign, Joe contrived the story that members of his family contributed $17,600—all but $2,208.95 of the total reported received by his campaign committee. Howard was alleged to have given $10,600; Tim, $4,000; and Roman Kornely, Olive's husband, $3,000. These figures became embarrassing when later studied by investigators. Howard's net taxable income for 1944 was $3,692.43 and had never exceeded $4,000. Tim's income was so low that he had paid only $2.62 in state income taxes in his life (in 1919) and had not filed a return in almost twenty years. Mr. Kornely, an Appleton clothing salesman, listed his income at only $1,914.

Where could Joe's relatives have come up with such large amounts of cash? And why would Joe have thought it necessary to borrow from them with $46,000 at his disposal?

Actually Joe had turned over his stock-market profits to Gerald Jolin, a close friend and an Appleton attorney, who was to supervise their expenditure in the campaign. Jolin's withdrawal of funds corresponded interestingly with the McCarthy family's alleged contributions. The Committee to Elect Joseph R. McCarthy to the U.S. Senate later reported that Howard and Tim contributed a total of $5,100 on May 12. Subsequent investigation showed that McCarthy stock market profits totaling $17,925.55 were withdrawn between March 1 and May 12. Howard and Mr. Kornely were supposed to have given $6,100 on June 14. Profits totaling $7,000 were withdrawn between May 24 and June 7. Howard allegedly contributed $6,400 on August 2 and 4. The records on Wayne Hummer and Company disclosed that between June 28 and July 14 McCarthy withdrew $13,800 in profits.

When questioned in 1947 about his purported contribution, Howard said, "I must have given it since the report is on file, but that is so long ago I don't recall much about it. It is quite a large sum of money, but I wouldn't answer any questions on it." Roman Kornely claimed that he had contributed personal savings. (Olive refuses to discuss this or any other matter with researchers.) Tim was deceased by this time.

Joe would say only that he was being smeared. The campaign of 1944 was something he avoided discussing at all cost, but it would haunt him for the rest of his life.

When he ran a second time for the Senate two years later, Mr. and Mrs. Kornely listed their campaign contribution as $99.50, Tim reported $554.74, and Howard $49.50[37]

McCarthy's first campaign for the Senate began with considerable enthusiasm. Jolin opened an office in Appleton and draped a banner across the city's major downtown street. He hired a pudgy, cigar-smoking *Milwaukee Sentinel* editor, James Colby, to run the campaign headquarters in Milwaukee. A young woman from Oshkosh, Mrs. Margaret F. Hagene, became secretary-treasurer of the McCarthy for Senator Committee. Charles Kersten, a Milwaukee attorney and personal friend of Joe's, handled much of the strategy in the state's largest city. Other friends pushed for the captain's election elsewhere.[38]

A number of different banners, signs, and newspaper advertisements were produced. A pamphlet using Joe's wartime clippings and designed by an advertising man was printed in huge quantities. Supporters mailed 2.5 million pieces of literature to 80,000 families in the state prior to the primary. The photo-filled campaign materials extolled McCarthy's past (one pamphlet falsely claimed that he was 28 when elected circuit judge) and stressed his role in the war as a tail gunner. "He is ably qualified by training and experience—much of which he obtained on the battlefields of the South Pacific."[39]

By and large, however, the campaign effort was hastily conceived and unimpressive. When Joe arrived in Wisconsin, he had angry words with Jolin, claiming that much of the money he had left in his charge had been squandered.[40]

While Joe was still in the South Pacific, Secretary of State Fred R. Zimmerman challenged his right to be on the ballot. This stemmed indirectly from charges made by Fred Felix Wettengel of Appleton. Wettengel, an insurance executive and slightly eccentric crusader for conservation and clean government, was a good friend of Edgar Werner's and was deeply embittered by his defeat at the hands of McCarthy. Wettengel vowed revenge and devoted much time, energy, and money during the 1940s and

50s attempting to thwart Joe's political ambitions. In late 1943 he wrote to the governor requesting that the Tenth Circuit judgeship be declared vacant due to McCarthy's extended absence. He was delighted by the action of his friend and fellow Republican Fred Zimmerman and urged him also to investigate McCarthy's nomination papers.[41]

Zimmerman contended that the state constitution prohibited Joe's candidacy during the judicial term for which he was elected. The state's attorney general, citing a 1922 decision, ruled, however, that the issue of McCarthy's eligibility "must await future determination," and instructed Zimmerman to proceed to certify the candidate's name on the ballot.[42]

McCarthy and his friends were well prepared for this challenge. Arlo J. McKinnon, Charles Kersten's law partner, had earned $1,000 for his firm for briefing the law on the matter. (Half of the fee was rebated to the campaign when no further legal action was taken.) He determined unequivocally that states could not prescribe the qualifications of United States senators. The issue would emerge again when Joe became a more prominent candidate.[43]

Senator Wiley didn't know what to make of Captain McCarthy's opposition. Friends said that Joe was a Democrat who mysteriously had between $30,000 and $50,000 to spend. Wiley came to the conclusion that he was an agent of some nefarious New Dealers. Even McCarthy's war record was confusing. A Wiley supporter from Appleton wrote, "One bit of his publicity was a claim that he had been injured, presumably at the front. Inquiry at the Marine headquarters stated that he had no medical or surgical history."[44]

Joe arrived in Milwaukee on July 20. While overseas he had served with VSMB-235 on two combat tours, from September 1943 through March 1944. He spent April through June at Bougainville. In early July he was routinely transferred to the Marine Air Fleet in San Diego and given an automatic 15-day leave, which he used to speed toward Wisconsin.[45]

He proudly displayed his uniform and ribbons, and showed reporters the Nimitz citation and a commendatory letter from a major general. He limited his conversation with the press to modest pleasantries. When asked about missions as a tail gunner, he replied, "All I can say is that I've ruined a hell of a lot of coconut trees on those islands." When a reporter wanted to know what the troops talked most about overseas, he grinned and said, "What do you think?" "Next to that, what?" the reporter continued. "The same thing," Joe replied.[46]

He appeared at a few meetings and gave brief talks before the Milwaukee and Appleton chapters of the League of Women Voters. His remarks became directly political only when he spoke out for postwar jobs for veterans and some sort of international peace organization:

> There ought to be machinery to back such an international tribunal with force. As a circuit judge, my judgments would not have been worth the paper they consumed without the authoritative presence of the sheriff's department on another floor of the courthouse.[47]

Even if he had been permitted to speak more frankly about the election, his speeches would have been superficial. Joe was not prepared to discuss issues in any greater depth. Moreover, he was convinced that people weren't interested in issues. He had come home to be seen—in his uniform, smiling.

Joe dashed around the state greeting supporters. Colby later observed, "I'd get mad at him sometimes. I'd arrange a meeting in Milwaukee, and he'd turn up in Fond du Lac." But he wasn't campaigning as he had in 1939; there wasn't time, and he had no pretensions about winning the election. He spent a full week entertaining friends at Shawano Lake.[48]

Four newspapers endorsed McCarthy: the *Appleton Post-Crescent,* the *Green Bay Post-Gazette,* the *Shawano Evening Leader,* and Madison's *Wisconsin State Journal* (where Rex Karney, a friend from Shawano, was a political writer). This support was largely local and almost entirely personal. John Reidl wrote in the *Post-Crescent*:

> McCarthy, about 35 years of age, had the wholesome judgment to hang his robe as circuit judge in the closet, ignore the adequate income to which the law entitled him and shove off with the tough young fellows in the Marines. If a combination of the McCarthy qualities cannot make a statesman, then what can?[49]

Joe had no luck with the G.O.P. party organization in the state. He even failed to win the support of a single member of the Outagamie County Republican Committee. But then he had only declared himself a Republican a few months earlier when announcing his candidacy. One Appleton Republican stated firmly before the election, "He is a DEMOCRAT—climbing on the Republican band wagon ..." Fred Felix Wettengel growled, "He is a DEMOCRAT to the core and a *New Dealer* at that."[50]

Senator Wiley won renomination easily and would go on to be reelected. But Joe placed second in the primary and garnered almost 80,000 votes. He solidly won the counties within his judicial district and came close to victory in seven other counties. He was elated at the outcome and grew anxious to run for the Senate full time.[51]

Wiley was grateful that the primary race had been "exceptionally free from mudslinging and personalities" but was piqued by McCarthy's challenge (he would never forgive him) and wondered how he could possibly have won so many votes.[52]

Harold A. Meyer, chairman of the Shawano County Republicans, pointed to the money Joe spent on the region and to the newspaper support he had. He also described Joe's personal popularity.

> He was a favorite-son candidate, lived here for some years, everyone knew him. He is a backslapping politician. He is the circuit judge and folks consider him a hometown boy.... Also the glamor of a uniform with all the stripes seemed to help as it does in many cases.... McCarthy has a magnetic personality, a great backslapper and a good-natured Irishman . . .[53]

Wisconsin had open primaries, and Meyer and Elmer Honkamp, Outagamie County district attorney, noted that many Democrats had voted for McCarthy. "They voted for him personally," Honkamp advised Wiley, "because they felt he is more of a Roosevelt supporter than otherwise."[54]

Joe returned to California the day after the election, leaving behind a letter urging his backers to support Senator Wiley and the entire Republican ticket in November. A few weeks later he contacted Wiley personally and provided him with the names of his campaign leaders. "My spare time is extremely limited but I have managed to write a few of my friends that, even though I haven't always agreed with the positions which you have taken, I do consider you immeasurably better fitted to the Senate than either of the other two candidates." Wiley was not particularly thrilled by Joe's tepid enthusiasm.[55]

Captain McCarthy reported to El Centro in August and was soon at El Toro, another Marine training base in California. Joe knew that he was eligible for more overseas duty early the next year. On October 19 he applied for a four-month leave, pleading pressing duties at home. In fact, he was up for reelection to his judgeship in 1945 and wanted to be on hand to prepare for the contest. The Marine Corps rejected the request but gave Joe the option of resigning. He took that route on December 11, 1944, and was home in late January.[56]

Joe publicly attributed his departure from the Marines to his "war wound." When he arrived in Milwaukee, he told reporters that he had recently been confined to a hospital bed at El Toro, suffering from a leg injury. (In 1951 he would have Sen. Harry Cain declare that he resigned after telling the Marine Corps that "it would either be necessary to place him in a naval hospital or permit him to return home so that his leg could benefit from medical attention.") No one noticed a limp. That would come later.

Rather than mentioning his resignation, he said that he would be on furlough until February 20 and thereafter go on inactive duty. He was back on the bench in Appleton, wearing his uniform, the next morning.[57]

Joe was reelected in April, without opposition, and almost immediately began preparations for the race against Senator La Follette in 1946. When Urban Van Susteren returned home from the Army a few months later, he was astonished to learn that Joe had his campaign strategy completely mapped out.[58]

Critics would often only publicize Joe's exaggerations and distortions of his military record and note that his resignation from the Marines exempted him from some of the most bloody battles in the war: the return to the Philippines, Iwo Jima, Okinawa. But in fairness it must be said that he served the corps and his country ably and with distinction. He risked his life on several occasions and not entirely for the later political dividends. Posing in the gunner's seat and one or two flights would have been adequate for campaign advertising.

Those who served with Joe admired him greatly. Colonel Todd recalled, "He was a sincere, patriotic, excellent Marine Corps officer and as brave as the rest of us." Maj. Gen. Field Harris, air commandant of the Marines, wrote, "Without exception, the commanding officers under whom he served spoke of the performance of his duties in the highest terms..." One of them, Maj. Gen. H. R. Harmon, contributed the following:

> This officer has shown marked qualities of leadership, cooperative spirit, and loyalty. His initiative, good judgment, determination, and diligence have made him an unusually useful member of the section in which he was assigned, and his unfailing good nature and ready wit made him well liked and respected by his associates. This officer should be classified as "excellent."

The *Wisconsin State Journal,* quoting the last two commendations in 1946, felt obliged to add: "He didn't have to go to war, but he did. There's nothing forcing him to run for the United States Senate either. Joe just feels that 'there's a job to be done' in Washington."[59]

WORKING TOWARD WASHINGTON

Wisconsin politics before World War II were dominated by the G.O.P. Anti-Monopolists, Greenbackers, and Populists enjoyed brief successes in rural areas while Democrats and Socialists won support on occasion in the industrial centers along Lake Michigan. But Wisconsin, like several other Midwestern states, was largely in the grasp of Republicans, who at times fought bitterly with each other for the power and spoils that the party regularly commanded.

From the earliest days of the twentieth century, the Wisconsin G.O.P. was divided into two camps that eyed each other with suspicion and frequent hatred. The Progressives were dominated by Robert M. La Follette, a colorful, magnetic, and brilliant figure in the history of American reform, who captured the Republican machinery in 1900. He served as governor from 1902 to 1906 and then went to the United States Senate, where he remained until his death in 1925. Robert M. La Follette, Jr., was elected to his father's unexpired term and won reelection three times. His brother Philip was Wisconsin's governor from 1931 to 1933 and from 1935 to 1939. As a political dynasty, the La Follettes were without peers.

By 1904 the more conservative Stalwart wing of the G.O.P. was at war with the Progressives. The hostility flared fiercely during the Depression when Philip pushed for sweeping government relief programs, Stalwarts charging the governor with promoting a revolution in league with Communists, Jews, socialists, and assorted other traditional scapegoats. The rhetoric was effective briefly, and Stalwarts swept the 1932 primaries. But their candidates were crushed in November by the Roosevelt landslide.

In 1934 the La Follettes pulled out of the G.O.P., forming the Progressive Party of Wisconsin. The new party cooperated closely with the Roosevelt administration and was rewarded with state patronage. The Progressives were actually Wisconsin's New Dealers. State Democrats, conservative and ineffective, were largely ignored by Washington.

The Progressives prospered, and by 1936 they dominated the populous industrial areas of southeast Wisconsin. They backed FDR's reelection and appeared to have a rosy future. Over the next two years, however, the La Follettes soured on the New Deal because of the recession, the slowdown of reform after the Supreme Court battle, and the President's increasing involvement in international affairs. On April 28, 1938, they announced formation of a new national party, the National Progressive Party of America. The movement failed for a complex of reasons, and Philip was defeated in his bid for another term as governor. Senator La Follette tried to regain the favor of the Administration, but his intense isolationism placed him at odds with Roosevelt. In 1940 he was reelected, but with difficulty. Progressives suffered serious defeats in 1942 and 1944.

During the war, Senator La Follette urged Progressives repeatedly to cling to their membership in the third party, but it swiftly disintegrated despite his appeals. It lacked a solid and distinctive platform and was virtually without leadership when Philip La Follette went into the Armed Forces. It disappeared in many parts of the state in 1945 and 1946.

Where Senator La Follette would turn in 1946, facing reelection and with the Progressive Party in ruins, was the subject of much speculation by the time Joe McCarthy began his second drive for the Senate. After the war, in the industrial counties along Lake Michigan, Progressives began moving into the traditionally moribund Democratic Party, and they received the support of the Truman administration. In rural areas, Progressives were again becoming Republicans. The G.O.P., however, was firmly controlled by Stalwarts, in their seventh year of political control and far from eager to share their power with traditional enemies.

The major figure in Wisconsin's Republican Party was Thomas E. Coleman of Madison. Now in his early fifties, Coleman had succeeded his father in 1927 as president of the Madison-Kipp Corporation and had served many years as a bank director and president. He managed a successful gubernatorial campaign in 1928 and from that point on devoted much of his time and energy to the G.O.P. Tall, handsome, gray-haired, genteel, and domineering, he was called "Boss" Coleman by critics, a title he despised. A friendly political commentator observed, "There is no other man in Wisconsin politics who has worked quite as long, or as consistently or as loyally or as shrewdly for his chosen political cause as has Coleman, and who has never betrayed any motive for personal gain in the process." At any rate, in party matters, he almost always got his way.[1]

Coleman's authority was based largely upon his ability to tap wealthy industrialists for campaign contributions. There were other successful Republican fund-raisers: Sam Pickard of Neenah, William Campbell of Oshkosh, Cyrus Philipp, Joseph Heil, and Walter Harnischfager of Milwaukee. But they all deferred to Coleman's zeal and persuasiveness. One close associate contended that he could raise $100,000 over the telephone in a half hour without the slightest difficulty.[2]

Funds were channeled into G.O.P. activities through the Republican Voluntary Committee, an organization created in 1925 to permit Republicans to avoid the financial limitations upon campaign expenditures placed upon the regular party organizations by Wisconsin's corrupt-practices act. By 1945 the Voluntary Committee, headed by Coleman, was in firm control of the party's patronage and purse strings. Anyone who sought to run a serious, well-financed campaign on the Republican ticket would have to acquire Tom Coleman's personal endorsement.

This posed an enormous obstacle for Senator La Follette, should he wish to return to the G.O.P., for Coleman had a fierce dislike for the entire La Follette family. Some thought it could be traced to a childhood squabble. Others believed it started in 1930 when Philip La Follette defeated Gov. Walter Kohler, Coleman's candidate for reelection. In any case, Coleman was bitter about the departure of the Progressives in 1934 and vowed to resist the return of their leaders to the Grand Old Party.

He was outraged in 1944 when moderate Republican Gov. Walter E. Goodland invited Senator La Follette to rejoin Wisconsin Republicans, and he and other Stalwarts pushed a bill through the legislature forcing Progressives to run on their own party ticket. When Goodland unexpectedly vetoed the bill, Coleman added the elderly governor to his list of party enemies.

At about the same time, Coleman took an active interest in the rise of the Young Republicans, defunct since the late 1930s. Loyal Eddy, an affable, heavy-set, 35-year-old bank equipment salesman, started a group in Milwaukee right after the war. Before long, he was invited to lunch with Tom Coleman, who asked him to organize a statewide group and pledged his support. Coleman wanted to bring young veterans into the G.O.P.; some

300,000 men and women from Wisconsin had served in WW II, and many
of them would be voting for the first time in 1946. Eddy was elected
president of the Young Republican Federation of Wisconsin in early
December 1945 and proceeded to assist in the creation of the first national
convention of Young Republicans.

Shortly after the luncheon with Coleman, as plans for the new organization began appearing in newspapers, Eddy answered his doorbell one
evening and was effusively greeted by a man who introduced himself as
Judge Joe McCarthy. He was running for the Senate, he said, and wanted
Eddy's support.[3]

Among the first things Joe did upon resuming civilian life was to begin a
lengthy and complex financial relationship with the Appleton State Bank
and its president, Matt Schuh, that would make headlines in the 1950s,
revealing McCarthy's wild and reckless use of money and his passion for
stock market speculating.

Having tasted and enjoyed the easy profits of 1943, Joe was eager to latch
on to a similar windfall. As a newcomer to Republican circles and a relatively unknown political figure in the state, he knew that fund-raising
would be difficult. Some fortunate investments could make a big difference
in his drive for the G.O.P. nomination, and he determined to secure the
means to make them.

In February 1945 he borrowed $1,800 from the Appleton State Bank and
opened a checking account. In July, the bank loaned him $73,000 to
purchase stocks and bonds on margin through Wayne Hummer and
Company. After several months of buying and selling, in December Joe
borrowed $149,176.06 from the bank for further investment, bringing his
total indebtedness to $169,540.70, $69,540.70 over the bank's statutory loan
limitation. To make things appear proper, the sum of $69,540 was trans-
ferred to a loan ledger in Howard's name. This fictitious loan was quietly
liquidated the following spring.

In 1945, with an annual salary of $8,000, Joe borrowed a total of $226,000
from the bank. The borrowed funds were invested, and the collateral, by
and large, consisted of the securities purchased with the borrowed funds. It
was a risky game that would begin to worry the players within two years
when the value of Joe's collateral plunged. Senator McCarthy would then be
driven to seek funds to cover his investments from sources that would cause
him considerable political damage.[4]

For the present, however, the entire matter was private. Friends noticed
that Joe talked incessantly about the stock market and was frequently on

the telephone with brokers, but almost no one knew the extent of his involvement. He was thought to be a man of very modest means—his clothes were shabby, and he seemed always to be broke. "Gimme fifty," he would say to friends to cover a bet, a dinner check, or a round of drinks. He would repay them but quickly run short of funds and borrow some more.[5]

Joe's principal preoccupation in 1945 seemed to be to meet as many people as possible and to tell them of his candidacy. He shot back and forth across the state, once again seeking and accepting as many invitations to sit for other judges as possible. It was said that when he entered a circuit he would obtain a list of area Republicans, find someone who could give him their nicknames, and begin calling on them.[6]

Miles McMillin, a fellow "black Irishman" who was shortly to become one of McCarthy's harshest critics, went on vacation with Joe that summer and observed his campaigning with admiration and awe. One evening the two of them were with a party that entered a tavern in northern Wisconsin. McMillin spotted former Assemblyman Morris Fitzsimmons of Fond du Lac and mentioned him to a friend, who said he would go over and say hello. "No," Joe said immediately, "let me go. What did you say his name was?" After being told, he strode across the tavern, slapped Fitzsimmons on the back, and in a booming voice greeted him with "Hello, Morrie." Within a few minutes, Joe had given his new friend a full account of his campaign for the Senate.

On another evening, the two were part of a group that had dinner in a night club. The tab was too expensive for one person to pick up, and everyone contributed to a kitty which Joe collected. When paying the bill, he told the owner that he was bearing the costs of the evening himself and introduced himself as Judge McCarthy, the "man who was going to defeat La Follette in the next election."

McMillin observed, "It is doubtful whether Wisconsin has ever seen a politician who is more ambitious politically or more untiring and unremitting in his campaigning. He never ceases to campaign. He seems to have no other interest than political power."[7]

Joe's style was entirely personal. He didn't offer substantive opinions on any subject to those whose support he requested. The only indication that he took a position on anything at this time occurred during a public debate in Appleton sponsored by an American Legion post on the subject of compulsory military training. His opponent was a good friend, attorney James R. Durfee. Durfee defended a proposal backed by the Legion, the V.F.W. and other veterans' organizations to create a system of universal military training in the United States. Joe argued against it, calling for a highly trained volunteer army. At one point, he became angry: "The stand the Legion is taking is viciously, dangerously wrong," he warned. Even though Joe had recently joined the American Legion, surely a few members of the audience must have thought him dangerously liberal.[8]

Loyal Eddy was greatly taken with Joe, and the two became good friends. Eddy found the judge a joy to be around, but he also recognized his intense ambition and thought him at times cagey. Joe repeatedly urged Eddy to endorse his candidacy and bring the Young Republicans into his camp, but Eddy refused, explaining that an endorsement from such a new and relatively insignificant organization wouldn't mean anything.

In the fall of 1945, Eddy began touring the state, recruiting Young Republicans (ages 21-36) and creating local clubs. He usually traveled with Victor Johnston, the suave, handsome, distinguished-looking secretary of the state Republican organization who enjoyed close ties with Tom Coleman. At almost every town in which they held a meeting, Joe would appear, having driven from wherever he was at the time, to shake hands, meet people, and present brief talks on his own behalf. No other candidate for any office was as active. He met thousands of Young Republicans over the next few months in this way and had the ability to recall most of their names later.

After many of these gatherings, Eddy and Johnston would join Joe for drinks. McCarthy was an especially effective campaigner in small taverns and within a few minutes customers would be flocking around him, glowing in the charm and attention he lavished upon them. On subsequent trips through the same towns, Joe would greet scores of people as personal friends, resuming conversations where they had ended sometimes years earlier.[9]

Joe made much of his being a veteran during these first months after the conclusion of the war and let it be known that he was wounded overseas. Eddy noticed that Joe seemed in perfect health, and he once accused him of injuring his leg during a fall from a bar stool.[10]

On December 1, Young Republicans met in Milwaukee to form a statewide organization. Joe was on hand and was nominated for vice-chairman. (He had just turned 37, making him ineligible for YR membership, but he and friends told reporters that he was 35.) In declining the nomination, he let "slip out" the information that he was running for the Senate. It was the first public announcement of his candidacy.[11]

Within a few days, the candidacy was strongly attacked by the *Madison Capital-Times,* soon to become the most implacably anti-McCarthy newspaper in the state. The editorial came from the fiery pen of William T. Evjue.

Evjue was 67, a graduate of the University of Wisconsin who had worked on several newspapers before founding the *Capital-Times* in 1917. He had become an ardent follower of Bob La Follette in the 1920s and served as chairman of the 1934 convention that created the Progressive Party. He was a humorless, aggressive, and untiring champion of liberal causes who used his newspaper as much to air his ironclad opinions on scores of subjects as to report the news. He was miserly and sometimes cruel to his employees; one longtime reporter described the newspaper's staff as "a society of lone wolves, loosely held together by their dislike of Evjue." But when he sensed injustice in the body politic he could rail against an opponent for months, even years, with bludgeoning editorials and, at times, slanted news stories. His eventual successor, reporter and columnist Miles McMillin, was cut from the same cloth.[12]

There were strong rumors throughout the state that Senator La Follette would seek reelection on the Republican ticket. That was reason enough for Evjue to attack McCarthy. But the thrust of the initial volley concerned the right of a circuit judge to run for political office. When Joe responded with a lengthy statement documenting the principle that the federal constitution governs the qualifications of senators, Evjue simply brushed the argument aside.

> Judge McCarthy may talk and talk; he may invoke Blackstone or the U.S. Supreme Court; but he is not going to detract from the firm conviction of Wisconsin voters that he is acting in violation of the Wisconsin constitution and the deeply rooted traditions of the bar and the people of this state by engaging in partisan political activity while holding a powerful position on the bench.[13]

Republicans divided sharply over the rumors of La Follette's return. Moderates were delighted, and several groups called for a La Follette-Goodland ticket that would wrest party control from the Stalwarts. To bolster their revolt, they obtained La Follette endorsements from a variety of national Republican leaders, including Senators Wayne Morse and Robert Taft.

Coleman took to the road, sometimes appearing with Eddy and McCarthy, urging Republicans to unite behind "loyal" party members. He obtained a resolution from the Voluntary Committee vowing to support a single slate of candidates consisting only of those "honestly in favor of the Republican platform and its political principles."[14]

But who was available for Coleman to back in case La Follette resumed

G.O.P. membership? Several possibilities were mentioned in the press, but by late 1945 there was only one active candidate in the field. A number of party notables stayed out of the fray, thinking the La Follette name unbeatable.

Coleman did not favor McCarthy. For one thing, he considered him beneath the social class of the gentlemen who dominated the Republican Party in Wisconsin. His background was rural, his education parochial, and his income minimal. Coleman once invited the judge to meet him at the exclusive Madison Club in the capital city, and Joe turned up in a soiled Marine shirt. Embarrassed, Coleman found the candidate a suitable coat and tie, which permitted him to enter.[15]

Moreover, Joe had been a Democrat; to Coleman that was a badge of dishonor not easily forgotten. And he was youthful. A senatorial nomination would normally be a prize awarded to someone who had served the G.O.P. for decades.

The story was told that Coleman said to McCarthy one evening over drinks, "Joe, you're a nice guy and I like you. But you're a Johnny-come-lately in Republican politics. You just don't have a part in the senatorial picture for next year. If you work as hard as you have been working and gain more support, you may have a chance some time in the future."

Joe took a casual sip of his bourbon and water and replied, "Tom, you're a nice guy and I like you. But I got news for you. When that convention is over next year, Joe McCarthy will be the Republican-endorsed candidate for U.S. senator."

Unlike Mike Eberlein, Coleman didn't appreciate brashness. "What you need is some self-confidence," he said dryly and left the table.[16]

And then there was the question of what McCarthy stood for. He stuck to generalities for the most part in his brief spiels before Young Republicans. Evjue complained, "We do not know how he stands on any of the major issues he would be asked to vote on if he became a member of Congress."[17]

In mid-February 1946, Joe opened campaign headquarters in the law offices of a friend, Max Litow, in downtown Milwaukee. Litow was named counsel for the organization and Arlo McKinnon secretary. McKinnon's law partner, Charles Kersten, was helpful but was busily laying plans of his own to become the district's Republican candidate for Congress.[18]

By this time, the clamor for Senator La Follette to announce his intentions had become shrill. The Democratic state central committee had passed a formal resolution inviting Progressives to join the party, and the state chairman and other party leaders had personally appealed to La Follette to become the Democratic candidate. Secretary of Commerce

Henry A. Wallace sent a letter expressing the wish that all Wisconsin Progressives would link themselves to the party of Roosevelt.

On March 15, Governor Goodland unexpectedly announced his bid for reelection and repeated his earlier invitation to the Progressives to become Republicans. But his was a minority view within the G.O.P. Coleman held the reins, and he had been touring the state condemning La Follette, Evjue, and Progressive Party state chairman Glenn D. Roberts for their financial interest in two Wisconsin radio stations. Of La Follette, he said: "In view of his years of hammering away at special privileges, does he now contend that it is proper and ethical for him, a U.S. senator, to use any influence on a federal agency which permits him to make additional income far greater than his salary as U.S. senator?"[19]

Many reporters thought that despite the Stalwarts, La Follette would return to the G.O.P. It was by far the majority party in the state, and its senatorial nomination seemed easily within the incumbent's grasp. Coleman apparently had no alternative candidate.

The senator said little, remaining in Washington and devoting his energies to Senate business and world affairs. A somewhat frail and withdrawn man, he had considered retirement rather than be forced to wage a tough campaign for reelection. After much fretting and hesitation, La Follette appeared at Portage on March 17 at a convention of the Progressive Party and, as predicted, led his followers back into the G.O.P. But not without several blasts at Coleman. "True, we have had no invitations from the self-appointed boss of the Wisconsin Republican Party or from the Communist party. But Progressives would be insulted if they received engraved invitations to join up with either Colemanism or Communism."[20]

Coleman replied angrily, "Their shift is not to the Republican Party. It is to the Republican primary. Pure expediency is the motive." It appeared that Wisconsin politics would be red-hot until the August 13 primary election, assuming that Coleman could produce an opponent who could give La Follette a genuine tussle. Indeed, Coleman's authority in the party depended upon his discovery of such a candidate.[21]

Joe McCarthy also responded to the political shift at Portage, with words shrewdly calculated to appeal to Coleman and the Stalwarts.

> The party history of the La Follette brothers (Robert and Phil) is one of successive and successful party destruction. Twelve years ago they temporarily wrecked the Republican Party. Then, by playing with the New Dealers in Washing-

ton, they wrecked the Democratic Party in Wisconsin. They
now allow their own child—the Progressive party—to die.
And they are about to attempt their fourth wrecking job.

Joe concluded, "Personally, as a candidate, I am glad to see Bob come over
and fight in my own backyard. I can assure him that the fight will be very
rough, but clean."[22]

The Young Republicans held a state convention in Eau Claire in late
April, and, because of his close association with the group's leaders, Joe
gave the keynote address. The speech was significant, for it contained
McCarthy's first statement of his positions on a number of domestic and
foreign issues and contained seeds of thoughts and expressions that were in
a few years to become famous internationally.

On domestic subjects, he condemned "an entirely new theory of
government" that had developed under Democratic leadership, the "theory
that for every problem that arises a new bureau should be created."
Government bureaucracy, he said, was "sucking the very life blood from the
nation and stifling the type of initiative which had previously made this
nation the greatest on earth." This had been standard G.O.P. rhetoric since
1933, and the Young Republicans loved it.

Veterans especially, he continued, were "presently being plowed under a
smothering mass of red tape" and were demanding "nothing except the
right to live under a sane, sensible form of government rather than a
stifling type of bureaucracy." Joe came out for a volunteer army, featuring
increased salaries, elimination of the caste system, promotion by merit, and
a fair system of justice at courts-martial. Reporters noticed that most
conventioneers wore honorable discharge buttons on their lapels next to
McCarthy-for-Senator buttons.

Joe accused the Truman administration of being "viciously antilabor" for
causing postwar labor strife by announcing that wages could be raised
without advancing prices. He criticized Senator La Follette for opposing an
amendment to the minimum-hourly-wage act that would have permitted
an increase in agricultural prices so that farmers could afford to pay higher
minimum wages. He recommended a four-point program for labor:

1. All unions should be required by law to account to the
   membership for all monies received and spent.
2. Labor unions should be prohibited from making contributions to political campaigns just as corporations are now
   barred.
3. There should be teeth in the law to prevent wildcat and
   jurisdictional strikes.

4. When a contract is approved between management and labor, both sides should be absolutely bound to the contract and the party guilty of a breach held liable for damages.

He soon added to the list a call for compulsory arbitration of public utility strikes and a required cooling-off period in all strikes. Tom Coleman and his wealthy friends were bound to be appreciative.

The 75,000-member state CIO contained numerous Communists, and some had worked their way into positions of authority. Local 248 of the United Automobile Workers had been controlled by Communists since 1938. (A few days after the speech, Local 248 called a strike at the huge Allis-Chalmers plant west of Milwaukee, which led to a bitter struggle between Communists and anti-Communists for leadership of the union.) Joe referred to the fact by declaring that "Republicans do not confuse the Communistic anti-American individuals who act as [a] disrupting influence in labor unions with the huge mass of honest, loyal American workers, who may at times be temporarily misled."

Joe became intense as he spoke of foreign affairs. Administration bungling, he charged, had lost all that the United States had gained from the war.

> We retreated mentally and morally in Austria, in Poland, in the Baltic States, in the Balkans, in Manchuria, and today in Iran, and there is no reason to believe that tomorrow we shall not do the same thing in Norway, Sweden, and Turkey, which apparently are next on the agenda.

The Four Freedoms "are even now more of a hollow mockery than the Fourteen Points were after World War I."

He attributed " a large part of the blame" to "starry-eyed planners" and called for their removal.

> All of the festering, cancerous sores are there, but growing ever larger. It is crystal clear that unless they are removed and the sores washed out—unless that is done and done now, then just as certain as the sun is to rise out of the east in the morning there shall be another war.[23]

Joe did not win an official endorsement from the Young Republicans, but by all accounts his keynote address was a great success. The Republican Voluntary Committee was set to meet in Oshkosh less than two weeks later, and McCarthy and Loyal Eddy were more determined than ever to use that interval to win over Tom Coleman.

Both had encouraged Young Republicans to be delegates at Oshkosh; they would comprise about 20 percent of the voting delegates. Joe threw a beer party for those who were to attend and confirmed their virtually unanimous backing.[24]

Over the signature of Republican district chairman L. R. "Bob" Watson, Joe and Urban Van Susteren sent some 600 or 700 letters to members of the Voluntary Committee urging them to endorse a candidate against La Follette. The committee, unlike the regular party structure, could vote to endorse in a primary, and it had done so in 1942 and 1944 (when it supported Wiley over McCarthy). The letters stressed McCarthy's adherence to Republican principles.[25]

Joe bought a new Oldsmobile and sped furiously—at times up to 80 miles an hour—from one meeting to another, selling people on the importance of an endorsement policy and his own candidacy. As the convention approached, he had appeared in a total of 71 cities and towns while handling his full schedule of judicial duties. He also paid personal visits to potential rivals, assuring them of his commanding lead in the race and suggesting that they avoid humiliation by dropping plans to run against him. One by one they took his advice.[26]

Only two possible competitors remained in the field as the Oshkosh convention neared. One was 42-year-old Walter Kohler, Jr., a wealthy veteran whose father had been Wisconsin's governor from 1929 to 1931. In a Fond du Lac bar one evening, Kohler asked Joe if he would drop out of the race if Kohler won the Voluntary Committee's endorsement. Joe said flatly that he would not, and the matter was dropped. At a later meeting between the two, Kohler's divorce was discussed. Miles McMillin claimed in 1951 that Joe threatened to make the divorce a campaign issue, ruining Kohler's chances with Catholic voters. Kohler later denied this. At the time, Joe simply assured Van Susteren that Kohler was no longer a problem and didn't offer an explanation. At any rate, Kohler decided not to run.[27]

This left only Julius P. Heil, the wealthy, rotund, 69-year-old ex-governor, who arrived in Oshkosh the day before the convention opened hoping for a draft. At a party in the hotel lobby that evening delegate after delegate approached, expressing personal support but gravely reporting that all other members of their delegations were solidly behind McCarthy. When Heil heard the story about ten times, he had had enough, and the next morning he pulled out of the contest. It was soon discovered that all ten delegates were Young Republicans instructed and dispatched by McCarthy. The field had been narrowed to a single contestant.[28]

Loyal Eddy had been prodding Tom Coleman for months to back McCarthy, but without success. In a motel room they shared just prior to the convention, Eddy tried again. Joe was young, energetic, a combat veteran; he could win, Eddy pleaded. And besides, who else was there? Did Coleman want to hand the nomination to La Follette?

The next morning at breakfast, Coleman asked Earl Kidd, a wealthy party leader from Owen, about McCarthy. Joe had been to see him and had won his support. Moreover, Kidd predicted a McCarthy endorsement in Oshkosh. Robert Pierce, Frank Cornelisen, and a number of other leading Stalwarts were in the McCarthy camp by this time. Young Republicans were working in every hallway at the convention hotel for McCarthy. The candidate himself seemed to be in all the rooms at once. He had the northern part of the state locked up and enjoyed surprising support elsewhere, including Milwaukee.

Reluctantly, and with serious reservations, Coleman gave in. He would back the endorsement, the nomination, and the election of Joe McCarthy. He didn't seem to have much choice. And he would do anything to defeat La Follette.[29]

By the time the convention was called to order, Joe's selection was merely a formality. The Voluntary Committee voted to endorse candidates on the first day, and on the second Frank Cornelisen of Green Bay placed McCarthy in nomination. Responding to earlier criticisms, Cornelisen read from a legal brief substantiating the candidate's contention that a state judge could run for a federal office. (When Fred Felix Wettengel tried to get the platform for an attack on this point, he was ruled out of order.) The speaker also replied to charges that Joe had been a New Dealer. "We aren't going to hold that against him," he said. "That happened during his first year out of law school."

Cornelisen won cheers from the crowd by shouting the thought that was on everyone's mind: "As a result of our endorsement of McCarthy, Senator La Follette, by the grace of God and the will of the people of Wisconsin, will be retired forever August 13." Seconding the nomination, Mark Catlin stressed the same theme: "It is time for Wisconsin to have two U.S. senators again. Let's retire La Follette to Virginia." (La Follette had once owned a house in Virginia but now lived in Washington. Joe would often refer to the "gentleman from Virginia" during the campaign. Still, there was truth to the charge that La Follette rarely visited Wisconsin.)

On the first ballot, Joe received 2,328 votes to 298 for J. Perry Stearns, an obscure Milwaukee attorney. Following Coleman's wishes, the convention brushed aside Walter Goodland's candidacy for reelection and endorsed Delbert J. Kenny of West Bend, a colorless Stalwart.

In his acceptance speech, Joe made a single vow: "I don't claim to be more brilliant than the next man, but I have always claimed that I have worked harder. I am going to work harder. That's a promise." After a few references to excerpts from his Eau Claire speech, he admitted that he had looked forward to the nomination "for days and nights, weeks and months—yes, years." The large crowd roared its approval.[30]

Republicans across the country held great hopes for the 1946 elections. Americans seemed weary of the Democratic Party's lengthy domination of Washington and appeared eager to return to normalcy and free enterprise. Truman, besieged with postwar problems, was growing increasingly unpopular, and there was already a scramble within the G.O.P. for the presidential nomination and almost certain victory two years later.

But in Wisconsin, Republicans had less to cheer about. The party was split between Goodland and La Follette on one side and McCarthy and Kenny on the other. Coleman and the Voluntary Committee were backing virtual unknowns against two of the most popular politicians in recent state history. To make things worse, a few days after the Oshkosh convention, Ralph M. Immell entered the governor's race on the G.O.P. ticket. Immell had been adjutant general of Wisconsin since 1923 and had many friends in both Progressive and Republican circles.

Attacks against McCarthy's candidacy began immediately, initiated predictably by William T. Evjue, who was backing La Follette. The *Capital Times* charged that Joe was "Boss" Coleman's "hand-picked favorite," and it condemned him for "seeking public office in violation of the Wisconsin constitution, the code of ethics of his profession, and the long-standing tradition of this state against a political judiciary." The *Milwaukee Journal* soon called for McCarthy's withdrawal from the race on the same ground, adding:

> Judge McCarthy, morally, is barred by the constitution and the statues from holding any office of public trust, other than a judicial office, during the term for which he was elected circuit judge. He was elected for a six-year term and still has five years to serve. What the Wisconsin constitution says is that he is barred for those five years, whether he resigns or not.[31]

Article VII, Section 10 of the state constitution contained the following reference to state circuit and supreme court judges: "They shall hold no office of public trust, except a judicial office, during the term for which they are respectively elected, and all votes for either of them for any office, except a judicial office, given by the legislature or the people, shall be void." Moreover, the canons of ethics of the American Bar Association said: "While holding a judicial position (a judge) should not become an active candidate either at a party primary or at the general election for any office other than judicial office."

But these proscriptions did not ruffle McCarthy backers. The Voluntary Committee published a pamphlet spelling out numerous precedents, as early as 1856, for the election of judges to congressional seats. Sen. Homer Ferguson of Michigan had been elected while a state judge, and the Michigan constitution was similar to Wisconsin's. The brochure went on to deny that Joe should resign his judgeship while Senator La Follette "continues to accept government pay while he runs for reelection." Sources of the senator's private income were then cited. "Is it La Follette's privilege, then, to collect this fortune during his campaign, while his supporters demand that Judge McCarthy, after several years in the Marines, resign his own sources of living income?"[32]

When the Wisconsin state bar association convened in late June, several leaders spoke out against McCarthy's candidacy. But a resolution to condemn the participation of state judges in political campaigns was tabled. The retiring president of the association said, "I can see arguments on both sides of the question." Evjue was furious, charging the association with cowardice and "majestic hypocrisy."[33]

But the La Follette forces did not push the issue much further, for the senator enjoyed a comfortable lead in public opinion polls. Commentators were predicting that McCarthy didn't have "a ghost of a chance" and would suffer "the soundest drubbing any candidate for high office ever received in decades."[34]

However, McCarthy's candidacy appealed strongly to a number of people. Some veteran campaigners were in the ranks, but Joe's most ardent supporters were youthful newcomers to politics. They were conservative, to greater and lesser degrees, and largely uninterested in intellectual and ideological matters; they were at home with campaign slogans on buttons, banners, and bumper stickers. Their activity in the senatorial race was grounded almost exclusively on an intense attraction to Joe McCarthy and a belief in his integrity, ability, and promise. Some of the men and women who labored on his behalf had known him for years. Others became partisans the first time they met him.

Lloyd Tegge was a huge ex-Marine sergeant from Waukesha, a Milwaukee suburb. He had served overseas for 36 months and bore a long vertical scar on his left cheek as evidence of the combat he had seen. The scar, his size, and a crew cut presented a formidable figure. (At an interview in 1975 he wore numerous buttons and sported red-white-and-blue socks.) He sold insurance after the war and got interested in rebuilding the Young Republicans through Loyal Eddy. He first met McCarthy in Eau Claire at the state convention and was greatly taken with him. "It was a personal thing," he said later. Joe seemed warm, enthusiastic, persuasive, and "he looked like a typical Marine."

The two quickly became close friends, and Tegge frequently accompanied the candidate to political meetings and, afterward, to nightclubs and bars. To Tegge, Joe was the "funnest." He enjoyed people and could make friends with anyone. He would walk up and down along a bar, greeting patrons, sipping drinks, even taking an occasional bite from a sandwich. He would always throw his arm around a man while shaking his hand and give his wife a hug. Joe was even-tempered and almost always smiled. He could also be playful: while serving as best man at Tegge's wedding that October, he pretended for a moment to have forgotten the ring.

Joe drank more than a little in 1946 and had put on 30 pounds since his college days. But he exercised regularly and was in excellent physical condition. He could swiftly pin Tegge's arm in Indian wrestling. He enjoyed the outdoors and once quietly took a brief job with some loggers. "He was at home in a Pendleton shirt and a pair of boots," Tegge later recalled.

Tegge especially appreciated Joe's generosity. He was always grabbing checks at meals and bringing gifts. Joe even bought a $60,000 life insurance policy from Tegge as a favor and gave him a personal check for $200 to defray his expenses during the campaign. For years he sent the Tegges anniversary presents.

When you really got to know Joe McCarthy, Tegge recalled, "he became part of your family."[35]

Ray Kiermas was a high school dropout who worked as a milk grader in tiny Nichols, Wisconsin, during the Depression. Before long, he rented a general merchandise and appliance store from his father-in-law in nearby Stephensville for fifteen dollars a month and opened a small locker plant. The business flourished, and a second locker plant was opened in Shioctin. After years of financial hardship, Kiermas suddenly found himself quite prosperous, and he became interested in real estate and the stock market.

He met Joe McCarthy in 1945 outside his father-in-law's tavern. He was soon invited to play in a semiweekly game of sheepshead with Joe, Henry

Van Straten, and several others. Kiermas and McCarthy became good friends and spent long hours discussing investments. Joe was "a wild man with a buck," Kiermas recalled years later.

The judge impressed Kiermas as a total extrovert, utterly self-confident. His persistent sense of humor made him a joy to be around. He was capable of great tenderness—children adored him. But Kiermas recognized in him a capacity for guile. Joe was also a busy man with the ladies. "Like Jesus Christ, he loved them all."

Kiermas had not been interested in politics and was thus surprised in the spring of 1946 to receive a call from Tom Coleman asking him to handle McCarthy's postcard campaign. "You were well recommended," Coleman said. Out of friendship for Joe, Kiermas deferred plans to open a Milwaukee real estate and investment business, and he accepted the campaign job at a salary of $175 a week.

His mission was to send a "personalized" McCarthy postcard to every voter in the state, and so he began collecting telephone books, and city and county directories, and recruiting help. That was the easy part. He offered a half cent for each postcard filled out, and scores of Appleton area retired people, housewives, and college students applied. (One woman somehow managed to complete 1,000 cards a day.) Kiermas opened an office in the Appleton hotel and provided his employees with an instruction sheet. There were three different postcards; each bore a McCarthy photograph, and on the other side the address was filled in along with "Your vote Tuesday will be greatly appreciated by Joe McCarthy." Kiermas was unaware of Joe's postcard blitz of 1939 and was sure that the idea and the wording on the cards came from the candidate.

As the weeks wore on, mountains of completed postcards piled up in his small basement office. About $3,000 had been spent on the effort when Coleman told Kiermas that there was no money for stamps. Kiermas offered to put up the necessary $7,500 if he would be assured of repayment. Coleman chuckled over the telephone; how binding were oral agreements? But Kiermas went ahead and was later repaid. The stamps were purchased in Appleton, but because of suspicions about the Democratic postmaster the postcards were driven to various locations by volunteers for mailing.

Kiermas was not to open a business in Milwaukee. Before long, he was on his way to Washington with McCarthy.[36]

Harold Townsend was a wealthy Milwaukee construction executive in his early forties who had played no active role in politics before 1946. He considered himself an "independent Republican" and had voted for La Follette and Roosevelt as well as Harding and Coolidge. That spring he was asked by Milwaukee industrialist Harold Falk, Sr., to work for the election of Joe McCarthy to the Senate. Falk stressed the importance of defeating La Follette, whose liberalism, in his judgment, bordered on subversion.

Townsend agreed to the request only after meeting McCarthy a short time later. He seemed cheerful, warm, and dynamic. And the two of them talked about protecting "our way of life." Joe was aware of the dangers of socialism and Communism in 1946, Townsend later recalled, even though the issue was not yet dominant.

Townsend decided to devote six months to the campaign, accepting no compensation. He began by inviting about 70 Milwaukee business associates to join him in forming an independent campaign committee, and he was soon elected chairman. Among those who signed up was Walter Harnischfager, the wealthy and ultraconservative Milwaukee industrialist whose general counsel was Tom Korb, Joe's law school pal. Another was Walter Hagerty, an executive at General Electric. He and his wife Katheryn were greatly attracted to Joe, and for years he would stay in their home while in Milwaukee. The Hagertys were seriously concerned about Communism, and Mrs. Hagerty later recalled hearing Joe discuss the issue with campaign workers.[37]

Townsend opened a headquarters in downtown Milwaukee, staffed by volunteers, and set up ward units and clubs. He and Falk won the backing of Edward V. Dostal, who ran an influential Polish-language newspaper in south Milwaukee and was strongly antisocialist and anti-Communist. Townsend raised funds and purchased radio time and newspaper ads. He supervised and paid for a postcard campaign in the Milwaukee area. Traditionally, the G.O.P. was weak in the county, and Townsend was aware of the difficulty and importance of his task.

He also traveled throughout the state with his sales manager, James T. Ryan, lining up speaking dates for the candidate and accompanying him to rallies. Traveling between meetings, Joe would close his eyes for ten or fifteen minutes and wake up completely refreshed. At times he would ask Townsend to stop the car so that he could chat with a farmer he had spied from the window.[38]

Otis Gomillion was about ten years older than Joe. He was tall, light-complexioned, balding, gaunt, hunch-shouldered, and slightly potbellied. He had served in both World Wars and had once been with the Secret Service in Canada. With an Alabama accent, he told of chasing Baby Face Nelson and John Dillinger at one point in his life, and he listed General Chennault and Jimmy Doolittle among his friends.

He first became acquainted with McCarthy in 1932 when Joe serviced his car. "He was a hell of a good gas station man," Gomillion later recalled. The two were much alike and became fast friends. They would swap stories, kid each other, and play pranks for hours.

After the war, Gomillion became a Milwaukee private detective, but he often neglected his business and his family to chauffeur Joe to and from political engagements and run out for sandwiches and drinks when needed. He also helped Joe wade through crowds, and the candidate always introduced him as his bodyguard. People often noticed the bulge in his suit coat. In the 1950s, Gomillion would have the honor of carrying Senator McCarthy's briefcase at meetings. His loyalty was entirely personal.

In 1946 his services were indispensable. By the end of the summer, Gomillion and McCarthy had traveled 33,000 miles together and worn out two automobiles.[39]

Joe's calendar consisted of long, grueling days that left hundreds of voters beaming and his campaign workers wilted and exhausted. The candidate was determined to greet as many people in Wisconsin as possible before August 13, and even his closest friends were in awe at the pace he set for himself.

One summer morning he drove from Milwaukee to Janesville, in the south central part of the state, picked up two local Republican leaders, and sped to Evansville. He walked up and down the main street, into the bank, hotel, barbershop, and newspaper office seeking votes. He visited with local attorneys and got the mayor to promise to hand out campaign literature.

He then drove to Edgerton and was again in and out of stores, shaking hands with shoppers, stopping to greet the elderly men snoozing in front of the small town's tavern. At one point, a farmer stepped out of his car right into the candidate's grasp. "I don't want to lose your vote, sir. My name's McCarthy. I'm running for the United States Senate—against Bob La Follette, you know." The farmer grinned, "Glad to know you."

Joe hurried back to Janesville for a luncheon meeting at the YMCA. He answered questions with generalities from his Eau Claire speech. When asked what was the major issue in the campaign, he replied, "I believe in government by legislators and not by bureaucrats."

He then went to Footville and was soon on his way to Beloit. In this city of more than 30,000 he toured two factories, enjoyed a reception and dinner, and spoke at a park rally. Joe condemned corruption in Washington and echoed Coleman's attack on La Follette's wartime profits from a Milwaukee radio station. "If our nation is going to be destroyed it won't be by outside isms but by things like this and the resultant disgust of the people with public officals."

Joe was eager to stress his war record. In the factories he asked young men if they were veterans, and if they were he would tell of his exploits in the South Pacific. At the park rally he urged veterans of both wars to work for a change in Washington so that "the curtain that is hiding the graft and corruption of war days can be torn away."

> There are too many men in Washington trying to pit class against class, group against group. Our soldiers didn't fight and die as classes—they did it as Americans. The present Progressive senator and the New Dealers are doing this dividing of the people—if they get reelected they will destroy this nation.

(The exaggerated language and the Populist, conspiratorial rhetoric later associated with McCarthy were clearly in evidence during the primary race of 1946.)

After the rally, Joe visited the American Legion clubroom, the Eagles Club, and the Veterans of Foreign Wars. At midnight he concluded fourteen hours of nonstop campaigning. It was a typical day on the hustings.[40]

One morning he was up at 5:00 A.M. for a 250-mile drive across the northern part of the state from Marinette to Superior, where he was scheduled to give a radio speech at 5:00 P.M. and make a public appearance at 8:30 P.M. Along the way, he stopped in numerous towns, meeting people and giving street-corner talks. In the first 100 miles, driving over poor roads, three tires blew out. He left the car in Rhinelander and took passage on a small plane bound for Superior. The airplane developed an oil leak and was forced to land in an oat field near Butternut. Joe hitchhiked to Park Falls, then took a taxi to complete his journey. When its engine conked out at Ashland, he chartered a plane to Superior. He missed the radio speech but was on hand for the public meeting.

In a four-day period he made appearances in Owen, Thorp, Neillsville, Fairchild, Augusta, Eau Claire, Osseo, Alma Center, Black River Falls, Blair, Whitehall, Independence, Arcadia, Mondovi, Durand, Ellsworth, River Falls, Hudson, New Richmond, Menominie, Barron, Cumberland, Rice Lake, Cameron, Chetek, Bloomer, and Chippewa Falls. While maintaining this pace week after week, Joe was able to continue his judicial duties without interruption.[41]

During most of his travels McCarthy shared the driving with seventeen-year-old Patrick Flanagan, the son of a Kaukauna physician. For the first two weeks of his employment Flanagan often suffered from motion sickness brought on by the top speeds at which the men traveled. Joe was a "wild" driver, and he encouraged his young friend to be just as daring. There were thousands of people to meet.

As McCarthy drove into one small town, he reached for his razor on the seat and accidently cut his right hand. He turned pale at the sight of his own blood, stopped the car, and quickly took six swigs of brandy. It was the only time Flanagan saw him drink more than casually. Joe wrapped his right hand and was soon greeting voters with his left. This helped people remember him, Joe soon concluded, and he kept his right hand wrapped for two weeks. He told Flanagan to explain that he had cut himself changing a tire; he didn't want to appear awkward. At one picnic he told an audience that Flanagan had dropped a tire jack on him![42]

Wherever Joe traveled he carried quantities of campaign literature. The mainstay was a 4-x-7-inch booklet entitled *The Newspapers Say,* containing photos of the candidate and brief, commendable quotations from newspapers. The title was Joe's idea; he told his campaign manager Urban Van Susteren that if the cover read *Joe McCarthy for Senator* no one would open it. The booklet, assembled by advertising man Robert Murray, emphasized Joe's youth, his capacity for hard work, and his military and judicial records. It contained virtually nothing about issues beyond a strong endorsement of federal aid to veterans and their families.

Van Susteren employed two people to conduct surveys in three small towns to test the booklet's effectiveness. It was an amateur undertaking; the surveys were limited and unsophisticated (results were placed in shoe boxes). But it proved valuable.

In West De Pere polls showed that a saturation mailing of the booklets brought McCarthy from a more than two-to-one deficit to an even split with La Follette. The same thing happened in Two Rivers. In Nekoosa the booklets reduced a three-to-one La Follette advantage to three-to-two. Tom Coleman was so impressed that he gave Van Susteren $30,000 to enable 700,000 copies of the booklet to reach Wisconsin voters. According to official campaign records, he turned over another $30,000 to various "McCarthy for Senator" clubs in the state to cover additional expenses. Coleman was pulling out all the stops to beat La Follette. Voluntary Committee literature stressed McCarthy's candidacy. And, in a rare move, Coleman himself gave speeches all over the state on Joe's behalf.[43]

As the primary neared, Joe's attacks on La Follette intensified. In late July at Madison he linked the senator with a current investigation of wartime financial dealings by Rep. Andrew J. May of Kentucky. "Representative May, as chairman of the military affairs committee, apparently directed war department contracts to a private business in which he was interested. Senator La Follette's radio station made a 314 percent profit by virtue of a license granted it by a federal agency that depended on the Wisconsin senator's vote for its appropriation." Joe contended, without substantiation, that the senator "fought long and hard to give the FCC a larger appropriation than anyone else thought it should have." He lashed out against "politicians who grew fat on both ends" during the war.[44]

Two days later in Kenosha, Joe challenged La Follette to a public debate. "I am ready to meet my opponent for the Republican nomination for the senatorship at any time, anywhere in Wisconsin." When the only reply was lofty silence, Joe became rougher. He charged in a "guest editorial" for the *Wisconsin State Journal* that La Follette had helped create "a bureaucratic nightmare" that "in most cases hindered the normal functioning of a free and prosperous America, and which in all instances provided jobs for the La Follettes and other New Dealers." He noted a La Follette endorsement by Leo T. Crowley, a leading state Democrat, and, in a sentence worthy of McCarthy in the 1950s, he wrote: "According to a recent newspaper report, he profited by some $370,000 from utilities and other corporations in which he was interested, firms that in some cases were dealing with the federal government or federal agencies." Joe then proceeded to repeat his charges against La Follette's radio station profits. "Not bad—far more than $50-a-day wartime profit at a time when the young men of this state were fighting a war for the magnificent sum of $50 a month." In Washington, he wrote, "The air seems to reek with intrigue."

Joe criticized Senator La Follette's isolationism and called for "fresh thinking" and "some courage in our handling of America's international relations." Foreign affairs at present, he wrote, were being handled by "mental fuzzy-wuzzies."[45]

In a radio speech in Appleton, Joe went further, charging that La Follette's isolationist tendencies were "playing into the hands of the Communists."

> Doesn't the Progressive New Dealer realize what it would mean for the future of human liberty if the Communists move in, or does he care? Doesn't he realize what it would mean for the rank and file of the people of all the nations of Europe?[46]

In a Milwaukee radio address, Joe charged:

If those men who died in WW II could return, they would say, "Forever sweep from power those men of little minds, who, by their failure to see what even the blind could see, obstructed every effort to prepare us for war—those men of little minds who now talk glibly of world cooperation while attempting to scuttle every specific effort toward that cooperation."[47]

A few days before the election, Joe again challenged La Follette to debate publicly. In a telegram released to the press, he charged, among other things:

1. That by your New Deal voting record on domestic issues you have done tremendous damage to the people of Wisconsin.
2. That you and the Truman administration, in adding 300,000 federal employees to the national pay roll since the war, are increasing the already staggering tax burden.
3. That by your failure to do anything to promote industrial peace you are playing into the hands of the Communists.
4. That your shortsighted views on international affairs kept us unprepared for World War II, and are leading us into World War III. . . .
5. That you and Shipstead and Wheeler, by your votes against the Connally Resolution, in effect voted against every small nation and paved the way for what the Communists have since done in Poland and the rest of Eastern Europe.[48]

If there is a point in Joe McCarthy's political career that he first qualifies as a demagogue, it is surely here, three-and-a-half years before the famous speech in Wheeling, West Virginia. La Follette might have responded with a roar and an avalanche of facts. Instead, he replied that "lack of time" would make a public debate with McCarthy impossible. Moreover, he said, "I don't see why I should help him draw a crowd."[49]

During more than two decades in the Senate, Robert M. La Follette, Jr., had proven himself loyal to the spirit of liberal and humane social and economic reform long associated with his family's name. He had fought for unemployment relief, public works, and tax reform during the Depression and had headed a Senate committee that championed the rights of organized labor. His integrity was unexceptionable. He had made a handsome profit during the war from a part ownership in a radio station, but no one produced evidence of corruption or fraud in the arrangement or in the senator's routine vote to approve funds for the Federal Communications Commission. La Follette's isolationism had been tempered only slightly by the war; he was one of five senators to oppose the Connally Resolution of 1943 favoring an international organization to guarantee the peace, and he remained unsympathetic to the United Nations. But he was militantly anti-Communist and was on record warning of the evils of Soviet expansionism.

Unlike his colorful and tempestuous father, he was a moderate, shy man who devoted much time to the art of legislative technique. He preferred to work in closed rooms with colleagues rather than make dramatic appeals on the stump. He was highly respected on Capitol Hill and was often labeled a "senator's senator."

In January 1945 Democrats appointed La Follette chairman of the Joint Committee on the Reorganization of Congress. Over a year later the committee presented its recommendations for a modest congressional overhaul. During June and July 1946, while his opponents in Wisconsin railed against his reputation, La Follette led the fight to get the bill through congress. It was signed by President Truman eleven days before the Wisconsin primary. "To push it through," wrote the editors of *Life* magazine, "required a rare combination of high political seriousness and parliamentary skill. La Follette has both."[50]

The senator had paid little attention to Wisconsin politics since 1930. In 1942 and 1944 he devoted only a week to campaigning for the Progressive ticket. In late 1945 he chose to go to a football game in Madison rather than attend a meeting called to determine the fate of the Progressive Party. La Follette detested the clamor and fatigue of campaigning, and he distinctly lacked the common touch. For all of his efforts on behalf of "the people," he preferred to meet them in person, if at all, in his Washington office. He told supporters in 1946 that he was obligated to remain in the nation's capital during the heat of the primary race to secure passage of the reorganization bill.[51]

Privately, La Follette was strangely ambivalent about the race against McCarthy. He was an ill, moody man, easily given to depression. (He would end his life by suicide in 1953.) Pollsters predicted a landslide victory, but the senator expressed doubts about his success and at times seemed uninterested in the primary. Glenn D. Roberts, a close friend and political associate, said years later, "Bob didn't care if he was reelected or not." He did little on his own behalf. His only direct contact with Wisconsin voters, until eight days before the election, was a weekly radio broadcast from Washington begun in mid-May. On the initial program he declared:

> With twenty years of service spelling out in detail on the
> public record, I think you have an ample basis for making an
> appraisal of my candidacy—without numerous political
> speeches on my part. . . . I am running on my record. All the
> evidence is there for you to read, discuss, debate, and de-
> cide. . . . I merely want to say that I have worked hard at my
> job. I believe I can say, without boasting, that I have mastered
> the techniques of government, which have become extremely
> complicated. . . .[52]

This was bland and stuffy, not nearly as effective with voters as a photograph of a good-looking Marine tail gunner, a handwritten postcard, a warm handshake in a local tavern, or a sweeping generality about the need for youth and vigor in Washington. "Joe McCarthy is a new blood for the anemia which besets us in Washington," said the *La Crosse Tribune and Leader Press*. "He stands as Wisconsin's hopeful contribution to a transfusion sorely needed in the halls of Congress."[53]

When Senator La Follette returned to Wisconsin for a week of campaigning, he was acutely aware that his political future was in jeopardy.

The incumbent also found himself under fire from Democrats, who had failed to woo him into their ranks. After an encouraging showing in 1944, the Democrats hoped to assume the mantle of liberal reform in the state, win over Progressives who would not follow La Follette into the G.O.P., and become a major political force in Wisconsin. They strongly desired La Follette's defeat in the primary because his proven popularity might add to Republican vote totals in November. Moreover, they preferred to face the relatively unknown Stalwart Republican candidate in the general election.

The sole Democratic aspirant for the Senate was 45-year-old Howard J. McMurray, a former New Deal Congressman and defender of organized labor, who had been the party's candidate in 1944. While seeking office in 1946, he was a lecturer in political science at the University of Wisconsin.

McMurray announced his candidacy in May, receiving strong labor support, and soon launched a series of harsh attacks against La Follette, whose record he had praised a few weeks earlier while seeking to persuade him to run as a Democrat.

McMurray most sharply assailed the senator's isolationist record and revealed a penchant for hyperbole that easily rivaled McCarthy's. He repeatedly reminded voters of La Follette's resistance to President Roosevelt's foreign policy prior to Pearl Harbor. He could not understand, he said, "how any of the young men who have returned from fighting this war can consistently support a man who did everything in his power before Pearl Harbor to prevent us from winning that war—nor can the parents of those who fought and died ever forgive that lack of statesmanship of Bob La Follette."

In one speech, McMurray charged that "Nazi and fascist newspapers" were backing the senator. "He promoted ideas all the fascists like, just as they liked the ideas of Burton K. Wheeler."

A full-page ad in the state's major newspapers featured a headline "Goodbye Isolationists," beneath which were the names of Senators Shipstead, Wheeler, Nye, and former Representative Fish. Their names were crossed out, followed by the declaration, "Goodbye La Follette!"

McMurray also pictured the senator as a lapsed liberal, frequently calling attention to an endorsement by Sen. Robert Taft. One advertisement read: "La Follette Poses As a Liberal—yet Senator Taft, Arch-Reactionary, Endorses Him. La Follette Betrayed the Progressives. La Follette Betrayed President Roosevelt. La Follette Will Betray the Republicans." Actually, Taft was a close personal friend who hoped that his support would ease La Follette's return to the G.O.P. The two men differed substantially on numerous issues.

McMurray assured voters that the President was backing him and was angry over La Follette's lack of support in 1944. He allegedly said, "Howard, I've made many mistakes in office and one of my worst ones was in Wisconsin. But we'll correct that in 1946."

Four days before the primary, McMurray took a line from the Coleman-McCarthy campaign book: "Bob La Follette can skip nimbly from party to party whenever he feels the ground slipping beneath him, but in one respect he never shifts. He never changes his lifelong slogan, 'I am for me.' "54

Communist leaders within the state C.I.O. had been blasting La Follette in the *Wisconsin C.I.O. News* for two years over speeches critical of the Soviet Union. Once the senator chose to run as a Republican, C.I.O. leaders opened up an attack against his domestic record and, like McMurray, pointed to the Taft endorsement as conclusive proof that he had abandoned liberalism. (Nine days before the election, the La Follette forces quietly dropped Taft's name from an advertisement listing senatorial endorsements.) An embarrassing and quickly repudiated endorsement by ultraconservative Gerald L. K. Smith prompted headlines such as "La Follette Shields Role of Reactionary" and "Pro-Fascist Group Supports Bob."

The national C.I.O. and its newly formed Political Action Committee worked closely with Democrats in 1946. Moreover, Communists occupied several positions in the C.I.O. executive board and the P.A.C. and were not disposed to favor La Follette. The senator's primary campaign was largely

ignored by national C.I.O. leaders, including officials of the United Automobile Workers, who had received La Follette's support in a recent strike
against General Motors.

While national American Federation of Labor leaders, including Pres.
William Green, endorsed La Follette publicly and blanketed the state with a
four-page issue of *Labor* devoted to the senator's cause, their Wisconsin
counterparts chose to remain silent during the primary contest. They had
long supported the senator under the banner of the Progressive Party, but
in 1946 they were unwilling to back Republicans no matter how friendly
they might be.

Labor papers in the heavily populated blue-collar areas of southeast
Wisconsin refused throughout the campaign to print either speeches or
press releases by La Follette.

Wisconsin laws permitted people to vote in the primary of only one
party, although at each primary election they were free to select what party
that might be. Organized labor's support of Democrats and its indifference
and hostility toward La Follette seriously threatened the senator's reelection, for thousands of working people would vote in the Democratic
primary and thus be rendered unable to back the incumbent.[55]

La Follette toured the Milwaukee area for three days, giving brief talks
and distributing a modest supply of pamphlets. (La Follette's backers were
to spend only $13,000 on the primary, and well over half of the money came
from the senator's family.) Knowing that he was in trouble with many
voters, he pleaded with the editors of the influential *Milwaukee Journal* for
an endorsement. By a narrow vote, the editors chose to remain neutral.
They had opposed the senator for years on the issue of isolationism but
might well have backed him in 1946 had he not been running as a
Republican.[56]

In Racine, five days before the primary, La Follette compounded his
difficulties by unexpectedly endorsing Ralph Immell for governor. Immell
and Governor Goodland had remained neutral in the senatorial contest,
and to this point La Follette had sided with neither of his former associates.
But he had been under pressure from Immell's camp, which assured him
that an endorsement would not be harmful personally and would repay the
adjutant general for many years of political loyalty.

The endorsement shattered the ranks of the former Progressives.
According to La Follette's Milwaukee campaign manager, the Goodland
forces immediately sent over 10,000 telegrams across the state urging
support for McCarthy. Tom Coleman abandoned the limp candidacy of
Delbert J. Kenny and threw the weight of the G.O.P. organization behind

Goodland. An Immell victory would signify a triumph for La Follette, something Coleman was determined to prevent.[57]

La Follette's candidacy was clearly damaged by his impetuous action in Racine, and no doubt thousands of Goodland supporters went to the polls eager to revenge themselves against the senator. While not endorsing McCarthy formally, the governor called him "an able young man," adding, "I'm not sure but what he would make as good a representative in the Senate as La Follette."[58]

The obvious winner in this sudden political skirmish a few days before the election was Joe McCarthy.

Joe continued his breakneck pace across the state, meeting and greeting hundreds of people a day while the more experienced politicians wrangled and plotted. He was well aware of La Follette's difficulties with organized labor and spoke out several times on the senator's labor record, varying his remarks to suit his audience. In conservative La Crosse he told a group of admirers that "people should know how La Follette has catered to labor and how he has damaged . . . other groups—the farmer, industry, business, and the misreferred-to white-collar worker. . . ." At Eau Claire he chastised the senator for failure to support the harsh Case bill, a measure roundly excoriated by organized labor, that McCarthy called "labor legislation which would benefit labor itself." In Oshkosh he accused La Follette of encouraging union violence, in part because of his failure to condemn the "radical Eastern labor bosses."

In a statewide address of August 7, however, Joe blamed the "vast majority" of the strikes then plaguing the country on "a combination of a few hardheaded, shortsighted men in industry who have not yet learned that labor unions are as much a part of the American way of life as industry itself, and by the few shortsighted political labor bosses who use the workingman and the unions for personal power." "The workingman has earned all his rights and should retain all of them," he added. "I do not blame labor for strikes and stoppages." He called for compulsory arbitration of labor disputes in industries affecting public health and safety and contended that a recent Milwaukee gas strike should not have been permitted.

He soon followed this up with a newspaper advertisement that flouted judicial ethics by citing four of his decisions from the bench under the headline "Labor Record of Judge Joe McCarthy, Candidate for U.S. Senator." Three of the decisions favored trade unions, and the fourth granted tax relief for a retired railroad employee. The ad concluded: "As to Judge

McCarthy's personal record, he was a member of local labor union No. 18617 during the years that he attended Marquette University and was employed as a laborer; he has three brothers, one of whom is a farmer and auctioneer, the other two are laborers and both belong to labor unions."[59]

Joe ran many more newspaper advertisements than La Follette. (A large percentage stressed his alleged military heroism.) He also won more editorial endorsements. Evjue's *Madison Capital Times* was the only prominent newspaper in the state to support the senator. McCarthy captured the backing of six and enjoyed the favorable commentary of a number of conservative newspapers, like the *Milwaukee Sentinel,* that chose to remain neutral.

One careful student of the subject has noted that inadequate reporting also assisted McCarthy's campaign. Reporters failed to inquire into Joe's military record or his previous senatorial campaign, and few editors questioned the legality or ethics of a judge running for another office. This was undoubtedly because so few newspapermen took McCarthy's candidacy seriously. On election eve, James Reston of *The New York Times* wrote, "Sen. Robert M. La Follette is expected to prove tomorrow in the Wisconsin primary election that a man can bolt the Republican party and get away with it."[60]

But Reston was among many who misread developments in Wisconsin and especially underestimated the zeal of many McCarthy supporters.

For several months, Young Republican leaders in the state, with the backing of the regular Republican organization, had been busily planning what they described in an internal memorandum as "THE DETERMINING FACTOR IN THIS ELECTION." It was a secret effort to enlist 1,000 Young Republicans in a massive distribution of McCarthy campaign literature that would reach every town in Wisconsin with a population over 500 during the weekend preceding the election. Many veterans were involved, and the project was privately described as "a statewide vote attack." Car drivers were "flight captains," pilots were "bombardiers," and local leaders were "squadron commanders." They were all part of the "flying badgers."

Three airplanes dropped bundles of campaign folders at airports all over the state. More than 200 cars, each carrying a team of four volunteers, picked up the packages and headed for local towns, villages, and county fairs. The four-page folder they passed out urged voters to back all the "regular Republican" candidates and emphasized the importance of McCarthy, who warranted a full-page photograph.

The idea had come from Victor Johnston, a state G.O.P. official who had

seen it bring victory in Minnesota. Loyal Eddy, who supervised the operation in Wisconsin, was persuaded that the effect of the "Flying Badgers" at
the polls was considerable. After the primary he wrote to participants:

> Your last-minute blanketing of the State by one thousand
> spirited volunteers moving as one team through every part of
> Wisconsin, arousing friends and neighbors to their duty of
> actively protecting the type of government they wanted and
> believed in, was a political phenomenon. It was the final
> touch in one of the most important elections of our time.[61]

Only a third of the eligible voters turned out for the primary. There was
no national election to stimulate public attention, and throughout the
campaign observers had warned of voter apathy.

Joe finished his campaigning at a Soldiers' Home in Milwaukee and
drove to Appleton where he and a crowd of friends sat around the radio at
Urban Van Susteren's house listening to returns. Joe predicted victory by a
5 percent margin, but that was generally discounted even by his closest
supporters.

La Follette enjoyed an early lead as returns from the rural areas were
counted. But when the results from Milwaukee County came in at dawn,
McCarthy emerged victorious by the thin margin of 207,935 to 202,557.
The election was decided along the industrial lakeshore, Joe winning all of
the counties from Kenosha to Sheboygan. In 1940 La Follette had carried
Milwaukee County by 55,000 votes; six years later he lost it to McCarthy by
more than 10,000 votes.

By six A.M. reporters were clamoring for a victory statement. Amid the
cheers and tears, Joe issued a terse declaration that began, "This campaign
was a contest not between men but between issues and the theories of
government." La Follette could bring himself only to send a one-word
telegram to McCarthy: "Congratulations."

Appleton exploded in jubilation over the triumph of its native son.
Throngs of well-wishers prevented Joe from getting any sleep at his hotel,
and he went to his office where telephones rang incessantly, telegrams
poured in, and crowds pushed and shoved to greet the judge with "Hi there,
Senator." That afternoon's issue of the *Milwaukee Journal* called Joe's
victory "one of the most startling stories in the political history of Wisconsin, an upset that not only stunned the state but bewildered political
observers all over the nation."[62]

La Follette was deluged with telegrams and letters expressing shock and sorrow. Congressman Estes Kefauver wrote, "In all of my public career I have never felt worse about a defeat than I have about yours. I felt that you were one of the two or three most valuable men in the Congress and the government of the United States . . ." Sen. Edwin C. Johnson of Colorado (who in a few years would be selected to serve on a committee considering the censure of Senator McCarthy) wrote, "You must know how bitter I feel over the mistake the people of Wisconsin have made."[63]

Tom Coleman told friends for years that La Follette's defeat marked the greatest night in his life.[64]

On election eve, La Follette ranked Communists along with Coleman as his chief opponents. After the primary, he bitterly attributed his loss to Communists within the labor movement who were critical of his stand against Stalin.[65]

This explanation of the election was resurrected in 1950 by the *Madison Capital Times* and has become part of the standard account of McCarthy's rise to power in Wisconsin. The story was irresistible by 1950 because of its obvious irony: the arch anti-Communist was elected to the Senate by Communists. Two quotations were fabricated to substantiate the charge: Joe was alleged to have welcomed Red support in 1946 by saying, "Communists have the same right to vote as anyone else, don't they?" During the campaign he was also supposed to have revealed pro-Russian sympathies by a remark crediting Stalin with sincerity about world disarmament.[66]

An objective analysis presents a more complex picture. It is impossible, of course, to offer a simple explanation of the origins of the 5,378 votes that separated McCarthy and La Follette. Many things could have been—and probably were—responsible for the slim margin.

Joe's feverish activity across the state no doubt brought thousands to the polls and must not be overlooked in summarizing the campaign. The considerable sum of money behind his candidacy was also significant: the advertisements, campaign literature, and hundreds of thousands of postcards—mailed just before the election—were bound to be influential. Numerous reports persuaded Ray Kiermas that a great many voters were flattered to think that a candidate would take time to write a personal appeal for their vote.[67]

Joe's friends were highly important to his victory. Harold Townsend's zealous work in Milwaukee obviously paid off. His ties to ethnic groups in the labor wards of the south side were significant; voters from these wards who entered the Republican primary selected McCarthy over La Follette in disproportionate numbers.[68]

"The flying badgers" alone could have made the difference in the election. They would have accounted for the winning margin if each team of Young Republicans turned out only 26 additional votes for McCarthy in the course of the weekend they combed the state.

La Follette's curiously inept performance paved the way for his defeat. Selecting the G.O.P. as a vehicle for reelection cost him the support of organized labor in Wisconsin, which was perhaps crucial. It alienated many liberals. It led to the failure to win the endorsement of the *Milwaukee Journal,* which could have easily cost him 5,000 votes. It also inspired Coleman and the Stalwarts to throw their complete support behind McCarthy. The extremely brief campaign effort, highlighted by the Immell endorsement, compounded by the refusal to respond to any of McCarthy's charges, seriously damaged the senator's cause at the polls.

The myth that McCarthy would not have won the election without the Communist vote is without foundation. Communist attacks on La Follette, coupled with appeals to vote in the Democratic primary, undoubtedly took some votes away from the senator, but the impact of the Communists on the campaign appears to have been rather unimportant. For one thing, the extent of their attacks has been exaggerated; in the three months prior to the election, the *Wisconsin CIO News* made only two references to La Follette. No evidence suggests that Communist labor leaders urged voters to back McCarthy; indeed, they ignored his candidacy. They were primarily concerned with securing the election to Congress of Edmund Bobrowicz, running on the Democratic ticket in Milwaukee's Fourth Congressional District. Bobrowicz was an official of the Red-dominated International Brotherhood of Fur and Leather Workers; he won the primary but lost in November after the *Milwaukee Journal* exposed his Communist ties.

There is even reason to doubt that Communists had much actual influence over Wisconsin CIO members. One scholar who analyzed the issue concluded that the role of Communists in the 1946 primary was "almost insignificant."[69]

McMurray's attacks no doubt also hurt La Follette. The Democratic candidate received 62,361 votes; slightly more than half of the total came from Milwaukee County, and another 8,000 votes were from Racine and Kenosha counties.

Popular governor Walter S. Goodland won a large victory at the polls.[70] Joe sped to Madison for an interview with the 83-year-old governor, and after less than five minutes told reporters that he would be delighted to campaign with him. "I consider the governor living proof of the fact that you can't measure age in the number of years." (People in Shawano who remembered the campaign against Judge Werner must have smiled at that.) For months, prior to Coleman's sudden turn to Goodland when La Follette endorsed Immell, G.O.P. literature had criticized the governor's age. Photographers now snapped pictures of the two victorious Republicans shaking hands. "He is so definitely far younger mentally and as far as ability is concerned as a man of 50 or 60," Joe awkwardly bubbled. Goodland remained silent. (He would avoid all opportunities to appear with McCarthy during the campaign.)[71]

Before long, the Voluntary Committee was distributing over 15,000 placards and posters bearing specially drawn portraits of McCarthy and Goodland. Tom Coleman was still prepared to spend lavishly. Harold Townsend's Milwaukee McCarthy headquarters privately created an estimated budget dated September 30 that totaled close to $58,000. Nearly $10,000 of this sum was allocated for newspaper advertising; over $7,500 was for the printing and mailing of 350,000 pieces of literature; billboard advertising would cost $14,549.[72]

Given the dominance of the G.O.P. in Wisconsin, there was reason to suggest that Joe should start packing his bags for the trip to Washington. Republican senatorial candidates collected seven times more votes in the primary than McMurray. Democratic Party leadership was virtually nonexistent. One official later lamented to Daniel Hoan, "The present state central committee is a joke as far as any real organization is concerned. Outside of writing a few letters they did not function at all, and as a campaign organization must be disregarded."[73]

But Republicans chose not to be complacent. After a brief vacation in northern Wisconsin, Joe resumed his personal appearances across the state. He had seen McMurray's biting speeches and advertisements, and he had no illusions about coasting to victory. Tom Coleman had been in politics long enough to know that the opposition would not play dead. He anticipated a barrage of attacks that would continue until the last vote had been cast, and with a large turnout at the polls on November 5 anything might happen.

The opening volley against McCarthy began a few weeks after the primary. Ironically, it came from within the G.O.P.

Fred Felix Wettengel, in league with Milwaukee attorney Perry Stearns, who had twice trailed Joe in senatorial races, requested that the secretary of state refuse to authorize the printing of McCarthy's name on the ballot on the ground that his candidacy violated the state constitution. When this effort failed, Wettengel petitioned the state supreme court. The case was

argued on September 20—Mike Eberlein was one of Joe's two attorneys—
and a week later the court ruled unanimously in McCarthy's favor, backing
the contention that jurisdiction over his qualifications rested exclusively
with Congress. Joe was elated, telling reporters, "The decision is precisely
what I have maintained the law to be."[74]

Undaunted, Wettengel, Howard McMurray, and the *Madison Capital
Times* interpreted the decision to mean that the state supreme court had
merely refused to accept jurisdiction in the case and had in no way sanctioned McCarthy's candidacy. It was a clever distinction, bound to confuse
voters; the author of the decision, Chief Justice Marvin B. Rosenberry,
refused further comment. In his campaign speeches, McMurray then began
quoting the canon of ethics of the American Bar Association, which
frowned on the practice of judges running for nonjudicial offices.
McCarthy's opponents were by no means ready to abandon the issue of his
presence in the race. In a few years the matter would reappear before the
state supreme court.[75]

In late September, the *Capital Times* declared that in recent weeks Joe
had granted extraordinarily swift divorces to two couples whose Milwaukee
attorneys were close McCarthy friends and political backers. The *Milwaukee Journal* quickly joined the attack against "quickie" divorces, crying out,
"Judge McCarthy, whose burning ambition for political advancement is
accompanied by an astonishing disregard for things ethical and traditional,
is doing serious injury to the judiciary of this state." Howard McMurray
raised the issue in speeches throughout the state. In later years, the litany of
injustices attributed to McCarthy by his opponents invariably included this
charge against his conduct on the bench.

Wisconsin law permitted residents to initiate a divorce proceeding in any
county in the state. Residents of Milwaukee County frequently took their
cases elsewhere to avoid publicity and the congested calendars of the local
courts. In Milwaukee, even in uncontested divorces, hearings might take
several months.

Circuit judges were required by law to grant relief when uncontested
divorces were brought before them. A few years earlier, a judge in Waukesha had received so many cases from Milwaukee that he began delaying
final judgments. He was an exception, however. It was common for
Milwaukee attorneys to satisfy their clients' demands for quiet, prompt
divorces in out-of-town courts.

Joe had handled only four divorces from Milwaukee during a period of
six to eight months preceding the charges made in September. The cases

were uncontested: the parties had already agreed to terms, and a divorce counsel had reported that there were genuine grounds for separation. Not one of the litigants or their attorneys complained about Judge McCarthy's conduct. That was left to others with political motives.

One of the two cases in question involved Chester G. Roberts, chairman of the Milwaukee County Young Republicans. Both the *Capital Times* and the *Journal* charged that he had been granted a divorce a mere two days after the case had been filed in McCarthy's court. Mrs. Roberts' attorney was Max Litow, a friend of the judge's, who, the newspapers reported gleefully, had contributed $46.93 to the Milwaukee County McCarthy for Senator Club.

It was misleading to cite the date papers were "filed" to give the impression that a suit was thus initiated; the filing often occurred on the day a judgment was rendered. In fact, the Roberts case had begun in March. Mrs. Roberts filed for separate maintenance in a Milwaukee court, charging her husband with excessive drinking, physical abuse, and desertion. She was granted temporary alimony pending outcome of the case. After six months passed without the case coming before a judge, Litow sought a final divorce in McCarthy's court. The fact that Litow and Mr. Roberts were friends of McCarthy and Van Susteren (the divorce counsel) was wholly irrelevant, as was the political contribution. The divorce was legal, in no way unusual, and all parties were satisfied. Joe had not, as was charged, transplanted Reno to Appleton.

In the second case, a divorce was sought by Mrs. Verna Kordas against her husband Leopold. Her lawyer was Arlo McKinnon. Newspapers hostile to McCarthy's candidacy published a photograph of the financial statement revealing that the law firm of Kersten and McKinnon had contributed $500 to the 1944 Senate race—described as a mysterious "Rebate on Legal Fee." (Charles Kersten quickly explained the simple transaction.) It was also noted that McKinnon had contributed $50 to Joe's 1946 campaign.

The *Capital Times* claimed that the Kordas divorce was granted in only three days; the *Journal* said two. The suit had actually been started in Milwaukee a year earlier and finally taken to Appleton for action. One of the attorneys in the case neglected to have the initial action dismissed until after the suit was completed in McCarthy's court. It was simply a clerical error, without consequence, and was rectified by an order from a Milwaukee judge two weeks later. But evil collusions were suspected by anti-McCarthy newspapers, and a later polemic termed the matter a "cover-up."

Howard McMurray told a Milwaukee audience in October:

> If you belong to the right political party you can get divorces.
> If you make campaign contributions to the right candidates
> and employ the right attorneys you can remove your divorce
> cases to the right court and get a divorce in from three to 10
> days.[76]

McMurray also charged that McCarthy had the backing of American Action, Inc., an ultraconservative, isolationist organization supported by Col. Robert R. McCormick of the *Chicago Tribune* and a number of other right-wing industrialists. McMurray contended that American Action, Inc., was "subversive" and in the control of people "who make Communists," people "infinitely more powerful than the Communists." He thought the organization should be "driven from America's political life" along with its counterparts on the Far Left. "Two-Job Joe McCarthy," as McMurray labeled his opponent, was thus tarred with the brush of subversion.

Moreover, Joe had been seen by a *New York Times* reporter coming out of Colonel McCormick's Chicago office. McMurray charged that McCormick and his political allies were pouring money into McCarthy's campaign coffers. Hadn't the colonel once boasted that Wisconsin was his territory? McMurray asked. *Racine Labor* trumpeted, "Is McCarthy to be his stooge?"

The facts of the matter bore no such sinister overtones. In 1944 Joe had been friendly with the Milwaukee correspondent for the *Chicago Tribune*, James Maxwell Murphy, describing him to Senator Wiley as "the only man whom I know who can actively deliver votes—and in sizable numbers." In 1946 Murphy urged McCarthy to drop in on his boss and introduce himself. In response to an invitation from McCormick, Joe did meet with him while in Chicago to deliver a speech. Joe said that the meeting lasted five minutes and was purely social, and there is little reason to think otherwise. When he was asked by reporters if he had been won over to McCormick's isolationism, Joe bluntly replied, "Hell, no!" The newsmen had apparently forgotten McCarthy's recent attacks against La Follette's isolationism. In speeches throughout the campaign Joe persistently reminded voters of America's international obligations. At a dinner in Green Bay in early October he declared, "The best insurance which we can have against ever having to fight another war is to be prepared up to the very minute it appears that the United Nations actually will work."

American Action, Inc., supported McCarthy publicly because, in the words of its Milwaukee representative, "He has a good war record, and he's in favor of the American Constitution." He was also a Republican. Joe's name was listed in a few American Action newspaper advertisements promoting the defeat of "radical and Communist" congressional candidates. The organization's financial contributions to McCarthy, if any, were insignificant; Urban Van Susteren could not later recall any involvement by the organization in the campaign. Its influence on Wisconsinites had to be extremely minimal.

Joe disavowed the endorsement and revealed considerable confusion about the organization. "I know nothing about American Activity, Inc., if that's its name," he told a Milwaukee audience. "If it is, as some newspapers have said, the old America First crowd, I want nothing to do with it. I want nothing to do with any group that goes in for racial and religious hatred."[77]

In late October, Miles McMillin published a lengthy story in the *Madison Capital Times* based on his discovery that members of McCarthy's family had insufficient incomes to contribute as handsomely to the 1944 campaign as reported. Joe surely fumed about McMillin's painstaking research because he knew that he was vulnerable to this charge. He chose to say nothing about the attack during the campaign, and McMillin didn't press the issue until after the election, when he was in better command of the data.[78]

McMillin also brought the Quaker Dairy case to public attention, quoting the order by Chief Justice Rosenberry in the hope of casting a shadow over McCarthy's judicial record. He attacked Van Susteren for serving as a campaign manager while holding the nonpartisan office of divorce counsel and for mailing solicitations for funds. (Van Susteren's activities were legal and highly common.) "What a spectacle this is!" Evjue moaned sanctimoniously.[79]

Joe spoke out often on his own behalf and appeared in debates with McMurray on several occasions. From the first, the debates were angry, nasty events, with each man displaying his powers of invective and sarcasm and his disregard for the rules of logic. McMurray rankled McCarthy with charges involving judicial ethics and alleged isolationist ties; at times Joe would spring to his feet in anger. He fired back with a series of irresponsible blasts against McMurray's patriotism that served as previews of the technique known internationally in a few years as McCarthyism.

It was not unusual for a Republican candidate in 1946 to be hurling charges of treason and pro-Communist activity at Democrats. Throughout the New Deal, the G.O.P. often linked Roosevelt's fumbling efforts to preserve capitalism and restore prosperity with the most incendiary dogmas of Marx and Lenin. In 1944, when the C.I.O.'s Political Action Committee began to assist Democrats, Republicans were just that much more willing to use the Communist issue. G.O.P. Vice-Presidential candidate John W. Bricker charged repeatedly that F.D.R. depended upon the support of "Communist and radical elements" and contended in Dallas that "the great Democratic party has become the Hillman-Browder communistic party with Franklin Roosevelt at its front." Representative Clare Boothe Luce, wife of publishing magnate Henry Luce, contended that on orders from Moscow the American Communist party "has gone underground, after the fashion of termites, into the Democratic Party."[80]

Two years later, with the wartime alliance between the United States and the Soviet Union shattered and the Cold War beginning to dominate headlines, these charges became prominent in a large number of political races (outside the South, where Republicans were few and the conservative Democrats were immune to such tactics). Democrats were linked with Communism by such G.O.P. notables as Sen. Robert A. Taft, House Minority Leader Joseph W. Martin, Republican National Chairman B. Carroll Reece, and New York Governor Thomas E. Dewey. Reece charged that "Democratic party policy, as enunciated by its officially chosen spokesmen . . . bears a made-in-Moscow label. That is why I believe I am justified in saying that from a long-range viewpoint the choice which confronts Americans this year is between Communism and Republicanism." publicanism."

In Missouri, Sen. Harry S. Truman's G.O.P. opponent called him "soft on Communism." In California, Richard Nixon's supporters told voters by telephone that the incumbent congressman had strong Communist sympathies. Republican Senator Hugh Butler of Nebraska warned that "if the New Deal is still in control of Congress after the election, it will owe that control to the Communist party in this country."

Many Wisconsin Republicans joined the chorus. Charles Kersten, running for Congress in the Fifth District, declared that there was no difference between "New Dealism, National Socialism, and Communism," and condemned his opponent, Rep. Andrew J. Biemiller (a moderate liberal), for "going down the line with the inner group of the CIO-PAC . . ." Rep. John W. Brynes of Green Bay declared that the G.O.P. wanted no part of "Russia Firsters, the pinkos, the fellow travelers, the Red Peppers and the Two-World Wallaces." Alvin O'Konsky of Rhinelander vowed if elected to rid the federal government of "Communists," "New Dealers," and "Communist New Dealers," and he told voters that Stalin had personally sent "a CIO-PAC fieldman to purge me." In Governor Goodland's single speech of the campaign he referred to his Democratic challenger as "Comrade Dan."[81]

The politicians were not alone in planting the seeds of what would later become the second Red Scare. Leading business organizations such as the United States Chamber of Commerce distributed hundreds of thousands of publications associating postwar labor demands with Kremlin conspiracies. *Nation's Business* stated in September 1946, "Whoever stirs up needless strife in American trade unions advances the cause of Communism." The American Legion and the House Committee on Un-American Activities (HUAC) joined the hue and cry. The Hearst and Scripps-Howard newspaper chains devoted large headlines to labor disturbances and spy cases.[82]

American Roman Catholic leaders, traditionally conservative and militantly anti-Communist since the late 1930s, added their voices to the growing fear of subversion. Francis Cardinal Spellman said in October 1946 that the Communists "are today digging deep inroads into our own nation" and are "tirelessly trying to grind into dust the blessed freedoms for which our sons have fought, sacrificed, and died." Bishop Fulton J. Sheen condemned "the fellow travelers in the United States and those whose hearts bleed for Red fascism," and announced that a congressional committee had discovered a "full-fledged Soviet agent" (whose existence was never authenticated). The 600,000-member Knights of Columbus called for an all-out attack upon "infiltration of atheistic Communism into our American life and economy," and a New York Knights group called for the boycotting of state and screen entertainment in which Communists or their "sympathizers" had a hand.[83]

Many of the most militant anti-Communists based their charges on statements and statistics issued by the Federal Bureau of Investigation. (As is now known, there was an active covert traffic between FBI agents and ultraconservatives lasting several decades.) On September 30, 1946, J. Edgar Hoover warned the American Legion, "During the past five years, American Communists have made their deepest inroads upon our national life. . . . Their propaganda, skillfully designed and adroitly executed, has been projected into practically every phase of our national life." The FBI director presented a picture of hundreds of thousands of Communists and their dupes (including "so-called progressive and phony liberal allies") infiltrating and influencing newspapers, magazines, books, radio, movies, unions, churches, schools, colleges, and fraternal orders. "Let us no longer be misled by their sly propaganda and false preachments on civil liberty," he said.[84]

Given the growing climate of opinion at the time, especially within the G.O.P., it does not seem unusual that Joe McCarthy employed Red Scare rhetoric in his bid for the Senate. Communist infiltration of American institutions was not yet the dominant theme in political campaigns, but its effectiveness as an issue was being eagerly explored throughout the country. Indeed, Joe might well have used it to a greater extent against McMurray had he been less confident of victory.[85]

In mid-October the candidates met in the Milwaukee suburb of Shorewood. McMurray leveled a number of stinging charges against McCarthy concerning his candidacy and "quickie" divorces, as he had in an earlier meeting in Milwaukee, and raised the issue of American Action, Inc. Joe flatly repudiated the organization but then suddenly added that "if American Action Incorporated is organized to help fight Communism as they say, then I welcome their help in defeating Communists and those who are communistically inclined like Howard McMurray."

McMurray fired back, "I have never had a responsible citizen—I say responsible citizen—challenge my loyalty before. I am sure my friends and my students in my political science courses of past years will not challenge my loyalty. This statement is a little below the belt."

Joe then asked if McMurray welcomed "the endorsement of the *Daily Worker,* which referred to him in a recent issue as a 'fellow traveler,' according to quotations in the *Appleton Post-Crescent* and the *Green Bay Press Gazette?*"

McMurray replied, "I have not seen the reported statement in the *Daily Worker,* nor comments of those two reactionary newspapers in Appleton and Green Bay. I certainly repudiate that paper [*Daily Worker*] and their whole tribe."[86]

Several weeks earlier, McMurray had been endorsed by Fred Blau, chairman of the Wisconsin Communist party, in an open letter to the *Daily Worker.* The endorsement had gone virtually unnoticed until Socialist leader Norman Thomas, bitter over the Democrat's attacks on La Follette, mentioned it in Milwaukee. In early September, the pro-McCarthy *Green Bay Press Gazette* and *Appleton Post-Crescent* wondered, in identical editorials, why McMurray had failed to respond to Blau's endorsement. "Does Mr. McMurray repudiate the Communists who have infiltrated into the New Deal political machine in this state? Or does he crave political success so deeply that he would accept any support disregarding its origin and sinister purpose?"[87]

Joe concluded that the endorsement revealed McMurray's penchant for Communism.

McMurray also received support from the C.I.O.'s Political Action Committee, and in mid-October Urban Van Susteren sent out an appeal for funds contending that the Democratic candidate had "all-out aid from the Communist-dominated PAC."[88]

A few days later, the two candidates met in Appleton for what one reporter called "another verbal slugging match." McMurray set the tone of the confrontation by noting Van Susteren's fund-raising letter and observing sarcastically, "They need money to hire girls to address postcards and sign the name 'Joe.'" He then launched into an attack on the ethics of McCarthy's candidacy.

Joe quickly counterattacked with charges demeaning McMurray's loyalty, saying piously that he regretted bringing up the issue but was forced to do so by his opponent's introduction of "petty personalities" into the discussion.

He alleged that the Communist *Daily Worker* had called McMurray a fellow traveler, "meaning a Communist," and that the newspaper had endorsed him. He went on to condemn McMurray for remaining silent during the *Milwaukee Journal*'s "exposé" of Edmund Bobrowicz, Democratic nominee for Congress in the Fifth District, as a Communist. Therefore, Joe implied, McMurray and Bobrowicz were two of a kind. McMurray proceeded to point out that he had helped write a repudiation of Bobrowicz signed by Democratic National Committeeman Robert E. Tehan. Joe may or may not have known this. He certainly didn't care.

The debate returned to the ethics of McCarthy's candidacy—but not for long. Joe affirmed his belief in the policy of "firmness" toward Russia and criticized what he called the Wallace-Pepper policy of "leaving the job in Europe half done and turning eastern Europe over to Soviet domination."[89]

Joe had quickly learned—in the second and third debates of his political career—how useful Red Scare rhetoric could be. It frustrated an opponent, diverted his attacks, and appealed strongly to voters eager for simple, clear-cut explanations about why things seemed to be going wrong in the postwar world. Joe knew that Communism was bad, but his grasp of the subject went little beyond that; he defined the term in a most elementary way during one debate. He was equally uninformed about the distinctions between reformers, radicals, and Reds. At this stage of his career he was impugning his opponent's loyalty strictly for its effect on an audience. He meant no particular harm by the tactic; he was warm and friendly to McMurray off stage.[90]

Joe also employed other clever devices to counter the thrusts of his eloquent opponent. Asked how Republicans would reduce taxes, he said that he would "dismantle a vast number of unnecessary bureaus"—the sort that studied the "care and feeding of goldfish." When McMurray mentioned the Coleman "machine," Joe said that the "vicious" machines, like those of Kelly, Hague, and Pendergast, belonged to Democrats. He then labeled the C.I.O.'s Political Action Committee a "machine." When asked how his background compared with McMurray's, he said, "I'm just a farm boy, not a professor." The audience loved it.

Joe took a new approach to the issue of his candidacy during the Appleton debate. After McMurray read aloud Section 30 of the American Bar Association canon of ethics ("If a judge should decide to become a candidate for any office not judicial he should resign in order that it cannot be said that he is using the prestige of his judicial position to promote his own candidacy or the success of his party"), he said that he did not belong to the A.B.A. and was therefore not subject to its canon. "I am bound only by the laws of Wisconsin." No more than 15 percent of the state's lawyers were A.B.A. members, he asserted. When asked if the Wisconsin bar association supported the A.B.A. principles, he replied, "No, they do not apply."

McMurray contended with considerable authority that the state supreme court had often written the A.B.A. code into its opinions and that it had the force of law. Joe flatly denied it.[91]

In a speech at Madison a couple of days later, carried over twenty radio stations across the state, Joe claimed that he had not resigned his judgeship because he needed the salary.

> I did give up my job and my salary in 1942 for a period of nearly three years, which time I spent in the U.S. Marine Corps.
> Now, ladies and gentlemen, it so happens that I am not a rich man or I could and perhaps would give up that salary again. My job is my means of support.

Almost no one knew of the scale to which this "farm boy" had become a successful stock market investor.

A few minutes later he was lashing out at the "typical Communist-PAC campaign of personal smears and deliberate falsehoods" and charging McMurray—"the Democrat candidate"—with being a "little megaphone" used by the "Communist-controlled PAC."

Referring to McMurray's promise that leftward-leaning Henry Wallace, the former Vice-President, would appear in the state to speak on foreign affairs, Joe shouted, "Now I warn Mr. Wallace that the people of Wisconsin completely understand only one language—the American language, and Mr. Wallace does not speak that language."[92]

As the election neared, red-baiting became one of the McCarthy campaign's most distinctive features. In Eau Claire Joe promised over a statewide radio hook-up to "make every effort toward removing the vast number of Communists from the public payroll." The hotels in many rural areas were packed, he said, because 50 percent of the guests were government agricultural experts. "Luckily the President's 'experts' were unsuccessful, at this time, in their attempts to communize or Sovietize our farms."[93]

In a radio broadcast from Janesville he charged, "We have been victimized by a seditious serpent, which has wrapped us in its cunning constrictions until we stand in a perilous position. That snake is Communism." Persons with foreign ideologies had crept into positions of importance in government, industry, and labor, he said. "This Communist infiltration is a vital issue in America. . . . It is also a vital issue in Wisconsin." The opposition party, he charged, was infected with subversion. "All Democrats are not Communists. . . . But enough Democrats are voting the Communist way to make their presence in Congress a serious threat to the very foundation of our nation." The PAC had named him its number-one candidate for defeat, Joe added.[94]

Pro-McCarthy newspapers were often reckless in their denunciations of McMurray. The *Appleton Post-Crescent* called him, "a noisy, unbearably egoistic gentleman upon whom the American editor of the Moscow *Pravda* slobbered." The *Green Bay Press Gazette* said that he was "in favor of the enemies of our country." It continued, "When Judge McCarthy faced the Japs on Guadalcanal, he became accustomed to men like McMurray, but it would be said that even the wily Japs had some courage."[95]

Many such newspapers printed Joe's charges against the loyalty of his Democratic opponent but would not run McMurray's rebuttals. The *Wisconsin State Journal* printed only two stories on McMurray longer than five inches, while several stories on McCarthy reached forty inches.

(Charges by the *Madison Capital Times* concerning the 1944 campaign and the Quaker Dairy case were ignored by the press throughout the state. The "quickie" divorce issue was mentioned in only four Wisconsin newspapers. As in the primary, no one thought to investigate Joe's war record.)[96]

Some Democrats were afraid that the red-baiting was having an effect on Catholics. One party leader in Green Bay thought that local Catholics were aroused by the issue. A priest at St. Joseph's Catholic church in Appleton urged parishioners to vote against the "Communist candidate." One reporter sensed deep religious divisions in a Madison audience attending a debate between McCarthy and Baptist McMurray.[97]

When not defending his reputation or railing about Reds, Joe stuck to the basic collection of safe generalities that had helped him win the nomination and defeat La Follette. He was against Big Government, Big Labor, and isolationism. The answer to most domestic problems, he said, was less government control over the economy and the individual. This was standard fare for Republican candidates in 1946.

On one occasion he called for the maintenance of rent controls until the postwar housing crisis eased. But he soon blamed the housing shortage on government planning and said simply that the solution lay in the removal of government controls and priorities. "A veteran cannot live in a priority. What he wants is a house."[98]

Before a rural audience in Eau Claire, he called for a program of federal research laboratories to find new uses for farm products. But even that, he said, should be carried out in cooperation with the states and should not be wholly controlled in Washington.[99]

McMurray was even less stimulating. When not condemning McCarthy, he blandly declared his faith in the New Deal and seemed unable to come up with any attention-getting ideas or even slogans. The two candidates were in accord with peacetime conscription and foreign policy. When asked during a debate what he thought about electing United States delegates to the United Nations, McMurray replied, "Don't faint now, but I agree with Mr. McCarthy."[100]

The Democrat's campaign was underfinanced and poorly organized. Even some Progressives, bitter over his attacks on La Follette, failed to support McMurray. The Milwaukee County Progressive Organization came out publicly for McCarthy. Few experts gave McMurray a chance at the polls.

A week before the election, a new wave of handwritten postcards, identical to those sent out before the primary, arrived in thousands of mailboxes across the state. One card was addressed to William T. Evjue. "Are the people of Wisconsin going to fall for this kindergarten stuff?" he asked his readers.[101]

On election eve, Joe predicted victory by 227,000 votes. (He later told a reporter that he arrived at the figure in part by secret straw votes taken in schools!)[102]

It was a remarkably accurate guess. The final tally showed Joe with 630,430 votes to McMurray's 378,772—a margin of 241,658. Two other candidates shared 12,000 votes. He took 70 of the state's 71 counties, winning by a sizable margin in Milwaukee (151,104 to 117,163) and losing in Dane, home of the *Madison Capital Times,* by fewer than 2,000 votes.

Republicans were highly successful in the state and throughout the country in 1946. McCarthy was not the leading G.O.P. vote-getter in

Wisconsin. He collected 61,000 fewer votes than perennially popular Secretary of State Fred Zimmermann, 1,500 fewer than Governor Good-land, and he trailed the G.O.P. congressional candidates by an average of 4.2 percent. But his margin of victory was larger than Goodland's, he was far more impressive in populous Milwaukee, and he took more counties than the veteran campaigner. By anyone's calculations, Joe had won an impressive victory.[105]

After an election night party in Appleton, Joe, Otis Gomillion, and Harold Townsend quietly headed north to the Michigan border resort town of Land O' Lakes for some much-needed rest and relaxation. Joe calculated that since April 1945 he had driven 80,000 miles campaigning. He went to bed at 7:30 P.M. on Wednesday and slept until 3:30 P.M. Thursday. He downed two thick steaks and at 10:00 P.M. was again in bed. When a reporter called at noon the next day, Joe demanded to know why he was being disturbed "in the middle of the night."

Completely rested by Saturday, Joe led his friends on a fourteen-mile hike through the woods. A *Milwaukee Journal* reporter, Laurence Eklund, caught up with the three men as they returned to their hotel. Joe strode merrily ahead of his panting companions, and Eklund described him as "fit and trim at 193 pounds."

Eklund was soon fascinated by the apparent simplicity of the senator-elect, noting that he pressed his pants by putting them under the mattress at night and sharpened his double-edged razor blade on the palm of his hand. (The latter was done for effect. Joe's older brother Steve once pulled a similar stunt with a hunting knife, sending a prying reporter fleeing through his screen door.)

The *Journal* reporter took seriously some rhetoric about "a really forward-looking Republican party" and wrote,

> In talking with McCarthy one gets the impression that he will make a record as a liberal Republican, and that he will be closer to Republicans of the type of former Gov. Harold E. Stassen of Minnesota and Senators Wayne Morse of Oregon and Joseph Ball of Minnesota than he will be to Sen. Robert Taft of Ohio, the apparent conservative choice for president in 1948.

The influential *Milwaukee Journal* had refused to endorse McCarthy before the primary (the candidate was rudely snubbed when he applied) and afterward attacked him with stories from the *Madison Capital Times*. It now put a rosy hue on his election and hoped for the best: "We think that

Joseph McCarthy has it in him to be a good senator and a good representative of his state." If he uses "his talents and his experience in behalf of the people of Wisconsin and the people of the United States, he can have a bright future in the United States Senate."

Joe returned to a familiar theme when Eklund asked him to comment about his future plans. "I don't claim to be any smarter than the next fellow, but I do claim that I work twice as hard and that's what I intend to do in Washington the next six years."[104]

THE REMARKABLE
UPSTART

At 38, Joe McCarthy would be the youngest member of the Senate. (In his official biographical sketches for the *Congressional Directory,* he claimed to be a year younger, and some authors continue to list the year of his birth as 1909.) He was a decade junior to the average incumbent and over a quarter century younger than the average committee chairman. His class origin was lower than most senators, and he lacked the learning, social graces, personal wealth, and political and business experience of the great majority of his new peers. But these were matters Joe ignored. He had come too far too fast to acknowledge any handicaps. His natural brashness had been magnified considerably by his stunning victories at the polls. (Several old friends, such as Loyal Eddy, would soon be uncomfortable around him.) Joe now thought himself able to win any state election; his "system" was unbeatable, he once bragged to Ed Hart. And if he could win over Wisconsin by charm and hard work, why not Washington? He considered himself the equal, if not the superior, of any man in town and eagerly awaited the first opportunity to prove it.[1]

In later years it would be fashionable to contend that McCarthy suffered from a profound sense of inferiority. Two highly biased studies done in the 1950s by psychiatrists who had neither met McCarthy nor conducted original research into his life concluded, as one of them put it, that the key to the man "is a recognition of his basic insecurity, self-doubt and self-contempt." This assertion was widely publicized and made gospel by liberal writers such as Richard Rovere and Eric Goldman—who also failed to attempt virtually any original research on McCarthy. The passing of time has added little to the picture. In 1970 the able scholar Robert Griffith, leaning heavily on Rovere's popular 1959 biography, wrote of "those demons of fear and self-hatred which pursued him on his short race through life."

But those who knew McCarthy best, from siblings to implacable enemies, scoff at such assertions as the exact opposite of the truth: Joe's self-confidence was unparalleled in their experience. It was often graced by charm and a certain innocence that stemmed from his hurried education and continued unwillingness to read or study anything of value. On rare occasions he would privately lament his lack of intellectual preparation. He could be briefly in awe of the rich and powerful upon a first meeting, and he was much more sensitive to criticism than he admitted. But in general, for sheer temerity Joe had few if any peers. To understand McCarthy, Andrew Parnell once observed unsmilingly, you must realize that he thought he regularly talked with God! When Clifford Mullarkey was asked to name someone like McCarthy, he thought for almost a full minute before volunteering "Evel Knievel."[2]

From the very beginning, Joe was determined to be a major political figure in the nation's capital. He set out to tackle Washington the way he did Shawano. He wasn't sure for a time how to reach the top, but he knew that the right avenue would present itself sooner or later. It always had.

McCarthy was relatively unknown on the East Coast, and his arrival in Washington with Victor Johnston on the first day in December went unnoticed by newsmen. As the train pulled into town on a gray, wet afternoon, Johnston asked his friend to say something for posterity on his initial entrance to the nation's capital as senator-elect. Joe looked out of the window and replied, "Oh shit. It's raining."

Joe was determined to shed his obscurity in record time, and the next day he summoned reporters to the President's room at the capitol for his first press conference. Twenty-eight newsmen and a battery of photographers appeared. The questioning began with a testy reporter asking, "You're a new man here. Why did you call a press conference?" Joe avoided the question and proceeded to expound upon his views of the current strike by the United Mine Workers. He rashly recommended legislation drafting all miners and their union officials into the Army, which could proceed to order the production of coal. What would happen if John L. Lewis refused to obey? a reporter asked. "Have you ever been in the Army?" Joe replied.

"Continuing disobedience of any order in war brings punishments up to and including the death penalty. We are still in war. I think this is the only way to get mines back into operation."

Joe added that he would have opposed President Truman's similar proposal in May to draft members of two striking railway unions into the Army and charge the Army with running the trains. That, he said, would have given the Chief Executive "blanket powers to socialize all industry."

It was an unimpressive debut for the fledgling senator-elect. One sympathetic Wisconsin newspaper urged, "Keep your eyes and ears open and your mouth shut. If you don't, you'll be meat for the wily newspaper correspondents in Washington." Joe realized that he would have to be a bit more cautious in the future, and he soon was advising newcomers to Washington to avoid looking like "upstarts." But he was clearly delighted by his discovery of the ease with which United States senators could make headlines nationally. A brief account of his news conference appeared in *The New York Times* and reached newspapers across the country through the wire services. He told one reporter that the next six years would be "twice as exciting as shooting up Lever Brothers' coconut trees in the Solomons."[3]

Joe quickly took steps to make friends with newsmen. Even before he was sworn in, he donated several large, hard-to-obtain Wisconsin cheeses to the National Press Club bar and went out of his way to tell reporters of his accessibility. A few weeks later he invited eight women correspondents from the Senate press gallery to the Georgetown home of a G.O.P. official and cooked a fried chicken dinner for them. This resulted in a number of lengthy articles lauding the chef's rags-to-riches background as well as his culinary expertise. The Associated Press story, appearing throughout Wisconsin, glowed with praise for the good-looking young politician.[4]

Senator Wiley introduced Joe to more than a dozen colleagues on his first day at the Capitol, including powerful Robert A. Taft of Ohio. He lunched with Henry Cabot Lodge of Massachusetts, who outlined a few of the senatorial perquisites. Joe was eager to impress the veteran politicos and made it known that he sought one of thirteen seats on the prestigious Senate Armed Services Committee. A longtime friend, journalist John Wyngaard, reported that McCarthy was continuing "the same grueling, tireless pace" that had brought him to power in his native state.[5]

Two Pullman cars full of McCarthy supporters, including 60 Milwaukeeans, came from Wisconsin to see Joe sworn in on January 3, 1947. A dinner party organized by Harold Townsend followed the inauguration, and the new senator was repeatedly toasted and cheered.[6]

Several weeks later, at a fashionable Washington cocktail party, Joe stood in a corner with a friend surveying the celebrities who glided by in tuxedos and furs. "I wonder what these people would think," he chuckled softly, "if they knew I once raised chickens."[7]

Joe wanted his close friends Henry Van Straten and Ray Kiermas on his staff and brought them to Washington with him. Van Straten quickly realized that he couldn't adjust to the fast pace of the city and returned home. Kiermas, although he lacked any experience for the position, was hired as McCarthy's office manager. He thought he would give it a try for a year. He was to remain in the senator's office throughout the next turbulent decade.[8]

The first administrative assistant in McCarthy's office was Victor A. Johnston, a tall, affable, distinguished-looking gentleman about ten years Joe's senior who had worked for Harold Stassen before being employed by Tom Coleman and the Voluntary Committee. He was thought to be an important asset to the new senator because of his many friendships with Washington politicians and newsmen; one Chicago reporter called him a new Mark Hanna. In fact, Johnston was rather inefficient and lazy and contributed more than his share to the general confusion that prevailed in Joe's office during the first few years. On occasion, while strolling with McCarthy, Johnston's appearance and tailoring were such that he was mistaken for the senator.[9]

Joe was given Senator La Follette's office. Secretaries were hired and a young University of Wisconsin graduate was employed to handle veterans' affairs. (He was later arrested as a homosexual and promptly fired.) More than 1,500 letters a day were soon pouring in upon the new senator.[10]

Joe moved in with Ray Kiermas, his wife, and daughter, and lived with them until his marriage in 1953. Washington was acutely short of housing after the war, and Kiermas was forced to rent an expensive furnished house before locating a small, two-bedroom apartment in Anacosta. Joe was given one bedroom, and the teenage daughter slept on the couch. A few years later Kiermas built a handsome ranch-style home in a new tract called Connecticut Woods, where the neighbors included J. Edgar Hoover and Robert Taft.

Joe's room was simply furnished and barren of photographs or personal knickknacks. One visitor noticed three bottles of eau de cologne on the dresser, a frond of palmleaves hanging from a mirror awaiting Ash Wednesday, and a pile of pulp western magazines on a bedside table—the senator's late evening reading.[11]

Ray Kiermas's wife Delores was hired as a file clerk in the McCarthy office soon after it was established. The senator called her "mother," and she did her best to see that he was properly dressed and fed. Joe was extremely careless about clothing. Stockings and underwear were frequently scattered all over his room; he left a trail of hats wherever he went. When packing a suitcase, he would grab whatever was in sight. He borrowed spare clothes when necessary. His shirts were often rumpled and dirty. "I never get around to buying shirts, ties, and socks—the girls in the office do it for me," he once said. His often garish ties were frequently askew and soiled. "Once when I was riding with him on his way to make a big speech in New Jersey," an associate later recalled, "I saw that his tie was covered with soup spots. Horrified, I loaned him my tie for the speech— and found out later that my tie was the *second* tie forced on him that evening. The soupy tie had replaced the one he'd originally worn. . . . I hate to think what that other necktie looked like!"

Throughout his years in Washington Joe wore inexpensive, ready-made, double-breasted dark blue suits. He purchased them four at a time in twenty-minute excursions into a men's store. He frequently perspired through one of them by midday and would change into another. The suits were worn until they were frayed and shiny, and office secretaries nagged their boss into replacing them.[12]

At first, Joe set out to accept every invitation he received. He hurriedly bought a dinner jacket at a cut-rate store and began attending up to five and six engagements in a single evening. "Still a bachelor," one observer wrote, "he is handsome in a dark, square-jawed way that has kept the Washington society columnists chirping excitedly ever since he alighted on the capital roost. . . . The scratching for the decorative McCarthy's presence at dinners and cocktail parties is particularly furious." Even Joe could not continue at such a pace, and he began to accept only those invitations that might benefit him politically. When his furious party-going reached the press, Joe made it a point to tell an Appleton reporter, on a trip home, that he rarely went out. "I'm getting a great deal of pleasure out of my work, and it's keeping me busy. I haven't felt the need for other recreation."[13]

Attractive women flocked around the senator. Patricia Corry of Menasha, Wisconsin, came to Washington for the swearing-in ceremony, and reporters labeled her Joe's fiancee. But she was only one of dozens of young ladies Joe dated. As had long been the case, their presence fed his ego and enhanced his public image. "McCarthy loved to squire pretty women," John Wyngaard later recalled, "the more numerous the better." When a reporter asked him a few years later why he hadn't married, Joe quipped, "I can't work at politics if I can't stay away from supper when I want to."[14]

McCarthy soon became one of the most popular men on Capitol Hill. He wanted everyone, from the loftiest senator to the lowliest scrubwoman, to call him "Joe," and they did. His senatorial frank, appearing on his mail, listed him simply as "Joe McCarthy." He could greet hundreds of people by their first name, and he went out of his way to be kind to the "little people" of the Capital. Ray Kiermas later recalled that as he and the senator once walked past a construction excavation Joe stopped and chatted with two Negro workmen about their activities. A large black woman in the Senate restaurant's carry-out service thought so much of the senator that she always put extra meat on his sandwiches. Even as Joe was about to be sworn in, he turned a Negro doorman's collar up and smiled. The man beamed in return and never forgot the friendly gesture.[15]

Children swarmed all over Joe in his neighborhood. Kiermas called him a "pied piper." On one Sunday morning he played so hard with local kids that he perspired through his suit and had to change completely before attending church. Van Susteren was once almost thrown through a windshield when Joe suddenly stopped his car to retrieve a baseball that had rolled into the street, tossing it back to the children with a grin.[16]

Joe was once tipped off in advance that Van Susteren's young son Dirk was going to appear in Joe's office with a cap pistol. When the boy entered the office, the senator whipped out two cap guns of his own, ducked behind his desk, and began firing away at his astonished visitor.[17]

Joe worked hard at courting the press and delighted many reporters with free drinks, dinners, and occasional news tips. He once surprised Mrs. Kiermas by suddenly inviting eighteen newsmen to dinner just before moving day. She dutifully unpacked the dishes. Joe joyfully donned an apron and began preparing one of his specialties: very well-done steak. "I cremate it," he said.[18]

One of Joe's best friends on Capitol Hill was Jack Anderson, a reporter who worked for columnist Drew Pearson. Hoping for favorable mention by Pearson, McCarthy "leaked" information to Anderson regularly and would sometimes telephone colleagues with important questions and permit Anderson to listen in and take notes. It wasn't ethical, but neither the senator nor the reporter (later to be bitter enemies) suffered any qualms. Joe attended Anderson's wedding and brought a handsome gift certificate.[19]

In early August the *Saturday Evening Post* ran a lengthy feature article on McCarthy entitled "The Senate's Remarkable Upstart." The piece contained valuable information on Joe's career in addition to a sizable number of the senator's distortions about his past, his military record in particular, but its emphasis was almost exclusively positive. "He is a muscular six-footer, with long arms and square, capable hands, and his physical movements are the quick, purposeful ones of the good athlete."

The article noted that Joe was studying Russian. (He wouldn't concentrate enough to learn more than a few words.) A senator never knew from day to day whether he would be in Moscow next Sunday or not, McCarthy explained, and he wanted to be prepared. Friends remarked that Joe had hopes of getting on the Senate Foreign Relations Committee and of charming Joseph Stalin in his own language, the way he charmed shoppers in Manawa.[20]

The nation's youngest and perhaps most audacious senator was making quite a splash in Washington and seemed by all accounts to have an extremely bright future.

G.O.P. gains in the elections of 1946 were so great that Democratic senator J. William Fulbright of Arkansas suggested that President Truman appoint a Republican Secretary of State and resign, thereby permitting the G.O.P. to take over the White House too. Republicans elected twenty-five governors and controlled both houses of Congress for the first time since 1931. Their margin in the House was 246 to 188, and they had 51 seats in the Senate.

The dominant figure in the Senate during the 80th Congress was Ohio's Robert A. Taft, the brilliant and ambitious son of the 27th President, known widely as "Mr. Republican." Taft had long been an isolationist and a bitter foe of the New Deal, and he publicly committed himself and his party to a return to the principles of pre-Roosevelt America. "We have got to break with the corrupting idea that we can legislate prosperity, legislate equality, legislate opportunity," he said. "All of these good things came in the past from free Americans working out their destiny. . . . That is the only way they can continue to come in any genuine sense." Most Republican congressmen agreed, and they appeared to have a strong mandate from the American people, who had "had enough," as the G.O.P. slogan put it, of high taxes, high prices, shortages, labor disturbances, and weak Democratic leadership. Of the 77 congressmen who were given a rating of at least 80 percent liberal by the *New Republic* magazine, only 36 were reelected in 1946.[21]

Joe did not obtain his first-choice committee assignments but was placed on the fairly prestigious Committee on Banking and Currency, chaired by moderate Republican Charles W. Tobey of New Hampshire, and was also assigned a seat on the Committee on Expenditures in the Executive Departments, which McCarthy was later to make famous.

It was an unwritten rule that freshman senators should be seen and not heard. There were not enough elder statesmen available in the 80th Congress to observe the maxim strictly, however, and newer men were given active roles in creating legislation. Of course, Joe would have been seen and heard had the Senate been composed of patriarchs.

Two weeks after being sworn in he made *The New York Times,* criticizing an anti-closed-shop bill of Minnesota senator Joseph H. Ball. His maiden speech in the Senate was delivered several days later—a terse, emotional appeal to continue the National Defense Program Investigating Committee. Joe had spent three hours at Walter Reed hospital the night before chatting with veterans, he said, and one of them, a Marine with both legs missing, claimed that many of his comrades had died because "of the graft and corruption which the Senate proposes to investigate." Another veteran, he claimed, asked: "What are you gentlemen up there thinking about? You are the body who voted us into war. Now why do you object to investigating the graft and corruption which occurred during the war?" Joe said that he did not speak on behalf of the 15 million men who had fought in the war, "but I speak as one of them." Several Republicans warmly congratulated the junior senator from Wisconsin for his performance. The Senate voted 49 to 43 in favor of continuance, and McCarthy was later placed on the Special Committee to Investigate the National Defense Program.[22]

There was nothing difficult about that. As Joe had thought from the beginning, Washington was not that different from Shawano.

Two days later Senator McCarthy introduced his first bill, one of scores of bills and amendments designed to crack down on trade unions. There was considerable public pressure for such legislation. When a Gallup poll asked people in October 1946, "Should the Congress elected in November pass new laws to control labor unions?" the response was 66 percent affirmative.[23]

Joe's proposal was more moderate than many then under discussion: it would permit the continued existence of the union shop and closed shop if two-thirds of the employees sought it and would leave "preferential hiring" and "maintenance of membership" to be decided by collective bargaining. Ten of the twelve other bills and amendments before Congress concerning the closed shop or union shop either prohibited such contracts or made them unfair labor practices. The McCarthy bill favored employers largely by permitting an employee to continue working at a plant if he was expelled by a union for anything but failure to pay union dues. This angered Wisconsin labor leaders, who thought the bill an effort by Boss Coleman to subvert trade unionism. The *Madison Union Labor News* assailed the proposal as "an entering wedge for conniving employers and scab-hearted workers to break the union," and contended, "Under McCarthy's bill, a man could connive with the boss to work for less than the union scale or to undermine conditions in some way, and the union would be helpless to discipline such a traitor."[24]

Still, McCarthy was not as hostile toward unions as many of his colleagues. When an arbitration pact within the construction industry was signed in early February, Republican senator Homer Capehart of Indiana called it a "step in the right direction" but hoped it would not stop Congress "from enacting constructive labor legislation." Everyone knew what ultra-conservative Capehart meant by "constructive." McCarthy boldly told reporters that if the new pact proved workable "it might well temper some of the labor legislation now being considered, making it unnecessary to take some of the drastic steps that have been proposed." That Joe would publicly clash with a senior colleague and label G.O.P. proposals "drastic" did not escape notice in the press. *The New York Times* ran his quotation on two separate days.[25]

As the debate over labor proceeded into the spring of 1947, however, McCarthy's initial resistance to harsh legislation subsided, and he voted for the Senate version of the Taft-Hartley bill, the Senate-House version, and the override of President Truman's veto. This legislation, called by union leaders the "slave labor act," outlawed the closed shop, secondary boycotts, the automatic "checkoff" of union dues, and strikes by federal employees, permitted states to enact "right-to-work" laws that prohibited compulsory membership in a union shop, required annual financial and organizational statements and non-Communist affidavits by union officials, shut off political contributions, and required sixty- (sometimes eighty) day written notices in advance of strikes. The President called the act a "clear threat to the successful working of our democratic society."

How carefully Joe studied the measure he voted for is uncertain. A few days before the final version of the bill cleared Congress, he told the Brooklyn Chamber of Commerce that the measure being hammered out in committee was not antilabor, and he predicted that the version proposed by Senator Taft would be signed by the President.[26]

McCarthy usually voted with Taft on bills directly affecting industry and labor and became known early in the 80th Congress as a conservative on domestic issues. The CIO-PAC considered his voting record one of the poorest in the Senate; of the 76 senators who served continuously from 1947 through 1949, he was ranked ninth from the bottom, tied with

Senator Taft. A tabulation of the votes of both men on 26 domestic bills and amendments considered important by the CIO-PAC revealed each voting "correctly" only twice.[27]

Within his first month in the Senate, Joe joined other conservatives in attacking O.P.A. rent controls. He was one of five authors of a bill calling for a 15 percent increase in rent ceilings (a figure favored by the real estate industry) and the removal of controls on new housing units. He also worked with Senator Taft on a bill to create a Rent Adjustment and Decontrol Board and affixed a decontrol amendment (subsequently removed) onto a rent extension bill.[28]

Like any perspicacious congressman, McCarthy was responsive to the desires of Wisconsin industries. Among his earliest activities in the Senate was the successful co-sponsorship with Senator Wiley of an amendment exempting inexpensive fur-trimmed coats from excise taxes. This was a boon to the fur industry that cost the Treasury $4,500,000 annually. Of course, it also benefited low- and middle-income consumers.[29]

In early March the Wisconsin state legislature sent a joint resolution to the Committee on Banking and Currency, through McCarthy, urging immediate removal of all wartime controls upon the production and sale of sugar. Housewives and an assortment of industries badly needed sugar, the memorial asserted; Wisconsin fruits and vegetables were going to waste. The legislature contended that the sugar supply was ample and that continued controls were indefensible.[30]

Republicans had campaigned against government interference with the economy and were anxious to decontrol sugar. Joe had heard many complaints from rural housewives during his travels and was determined to do something about them. He was appointed to a subcommittee on sugar headed by Ralph Flanders of Vermont and quickly absorbed the complex data presented in three days of hearings by a number of authorities and interest groups.

The continuation of wartime rationing was favored by a battery of large industrial users and the sugar industry itself. Rationing guaranteed supplies, kept prices high, and discouraged new competition. The Agriculture Department also favored continued rationing, taking a cautious approach to the statistics on world sugar supplies.

In the subcommittee hearings McCarthy clashed repeatedly with representatives from industry and government. He argued that sugar supplies were underestimated by many authorities, and he staunchly defended pleas by housewives and veterans for more sugar to increase domestic canning and enable the creation of new businesses. Two days after inserting the memorial from the Wisconsin legislature into the *Congressional Record* he co-sponsored a bill to end sugar rationing immediately.[31]

Senator Flanders and Banking and Currency Committee chairman Tobey agreed with Agriculture Department estimates of current supplies and urged restraint. (G.O.P. conservatives considered both men rebels.) Tobey introduced an amendment to a committee bill guaranteeing 35 pounds of sugar per housewife—up from 25 pounds in 1946—and giving the Secretary of Agriculture authority to distribute any surplus to housewives, up to the prewar limit of 50 pounds each.

McCarthy strongly disagreed with his committee chairman's position from the start, and the two men exchanged angry words on the Senate floor over a McCarthy move to table the amendment. The motion was defeated 48-26, but Joe vowed to defeat the amendment when it appeared for debate the following day.

McCarthy backed an amendment by Republican senator Kenneth B. Wherry of Nebraska that would increase the householder's allocation to 40 pounds with a possible increase to 50 pounds, any surplus being divided equally between industrial and home users. The difference between the two amendments was insubstantial; well into the debate Sen. John Sherman Cooper of Kentucky confessed that he was unable to discern any distinction. But Joe thought his case unassailable and was willing to slug it out with any and all Senate opponents regardless of their seniority and power. Moreover, he was anxious to get credit for sugar decontrol, to put his name in headlines as the champion of millions of housewives. The junior senator from Wisconsin threw himself into the debate of March 27 with a passion that left colleagues and newsmen aghast.

Joe called Tobey's amendment "completely meaningless," "completely deceptive," "fictitious," "ambiguous," "a mere well-meaning, pious hope and desire." He charged Flanders with placing the demands of industrial users over the needs of housewives. "I know that many women use 100 pounds of sugar during the canning season. My mother, who had seven children, used to get 100 pounds of sugar to put up her fruits and berries."

McCarthy presented a flood of facts and figures to document his assertion that world sugar supplies were plentiful. At one point he claimed to have been told by the Department of Agriculture within the past ten minutes that it had gone over his subcommittee figures and now wished to discuss the possibility of agreeing to allot sugar along the lines of his proposal. When challenged by Tobey, he amended his statement to say that he had received this information from one of Senator Wherry's assistants. Tobey then triumphantly announced that he had just telephoned Agriculture Secretary Clinton P. Anderson, who denied having personally told McCarthy anything of the kind and said that he continued to endorse Tobey's amendment. Joe fired back, "Then, Mr. President, let me say that in view of the unquestioned figures, I do not give a tinker's dam what Secretary Anderson says about the matter. The sugar is here." He proceeded to claim that Flanders had told him earlier he was going "to introduce some type of fictitious amendment which in effect will do nothing more nor less than deceive the housewife." This left both Flanders and Tobey sputtering in rage.

Tobey's amendment passed 49-32. Sen. Scott Lucas of Illinois perhaps expressed the thoughts of many when he said that he did not wish to go on record as opposing 35 pounds of sugar for housewives. McCarthy and most G.O.P. conservatives voted against the measure, holding out for the higher figure. After some further skirmishing, during which Joe rudely interrupted efforts by Tobey and Flanders to state their case, he introduced an amendment to end rationing on October 31, a date already approved by the House. Senators from sugar-growing states had told him, he explained, that the immediate decontrol he sought earlier would overly benefit Cubans.

By this time Tobey was almost hysterical, shouting his opposition to the amendment and claiming that speculators and their minions were responsible for it. "I want the country to know where the blame lies. It lies with a group in my own party, the Republican Party, who have sabotaged this measure at every possible opportunity with their eyes open."

McCarthy's amendment passed 45-35, and in mid-April President Truman signed the final bill "with reluctance," claiming that the October 31 deadline was "too early."[32]

As it soon turned out, McCarthy's view of sugar supplies proved more accurate than the Administration's. A large surplus appeared by late April. In mid-May Joe called rationing "an incredibly fantastic farce," piling up "tremendous surpluses" while "the average farmer's wife, as well as many other housewives, beg for sugar so that the food which they ordinarily preserve does not go to waste." He co-sponsored a bill proposing immediate decontrol, and he and other Republicans forced Agriculture Secretary Anderson to abandon consumer rationing on June 11. On July 28 rationing to industrial users was discontinued, and all rationing and inventory controls were lifted on August 30. By that time supplies were such that plans were being laid to ship surpluses abroad.[33]

Shortly after McCarthy took office, William T. Evjue's *Madison Capital Times* launched a new series of attacks against the senator. Included in the barrage was the charge that he was the tool of the Pepsi-Cola company in the fight to decontrol sugar. Washington reporters, Evjue claimed, were calling him "Pepsi-Cola Joe," an epithet the journalist found irresistible. (Jack Anderson later changed it to "the Pepsi-Cola Kid.") In 1952, when McCarthy sought reelection, the charge was raised again, and it has found its way into virtually every biography of the senator.

As the story goes, Joe was seen at parties with Walter Mack, president of Pepsi-Cola. His own inaugural party was suggested by Milton R. Polland, a lobbyist for the Allied Molasses company, which had illegally helped Pepsi-Cola obtain sugar during the war. John Maragon, a lobbyist for Polland who later went to prison, "promoted" the party, "and over a sumptuous meal in Washington's Old New Orleans restaurant, Maragon and McCarthy sealed their new friendship in wine." Moreover, when McCarthy ran into financial difficulties at the end of 1947, he secured a note for $20,000 from Russell M. Arundel, who owned the Pepsi-Cola bottling plant on Long Island. Approximately the day after the loan was made, Joe appeared before the Senate Appropriations Committee to interrogate the Secretary of the Army about the Army's purchase of Cuban sugar, a purchase previously criticized by Pepsi-Cola.[34]

The story clearly implied bribery. Richard Rovere's biography carries it in full and solemnly declares of the young senator, "He soon fell in with the seediest lot in Washington—men with their sights fixed not on power in the grand, malevolent sense in which he was to come to know it, but on the fast buck."[35]

The allegation is based almost wholly on circumstantial evidence and swiftly crumbles under scrutiny. It is one of many charges against the Wisconsin senator that illustrate a willingness of his opponents to use the smear technique they bitterly condemned as "McCarthyism."

Joe certainly attended parties at which wealthy Republican Walter Mack was present; he went to dozens of parties during his first months in Washington. Russell Arundel recalled seeing McCarthy "innumerable times . . . at parties and here and there." But no evidence suggests any personal or business relationship between the senator and the executive. Both men wanted decontrol of sugar, but for different purposes. Mack sought sugar to boost the production and sale of his company's product, and he contended that the average housewife was unable to use the 35 pounds of sugar allotted her. Joe, on the other hand, spoke out forcefully during the subcommittee hearings and the Senate debate against the soft drink industry's demand for sugar, arguing that housewives had a superior claim and that 35 pounds were insufficient.[36]

The inaugural party in Washington on January 3 was planned by Harold Townsend, not Milton Polland. It was a private affair attended largely by Wisconsinites and was never "promoted." Polland, a Milwaukee insurance executive (and never a lobbyist), was invited to the affair by Townsend, who was a business associate and friend. Polland had not been active in the election campaign, and he met McCarthy for the first time at the party.

Polland had introduced John Maragon to Townsend earlier in Milwaukee. Maragon knew Washington well, and after the election Townsend asked him to find lodging and banquet facilities for the Wisconsin visitors. He refused to accept any compensation for his efforts. Maragon also met McCarthy initially at the party.

Neither Polland nor Maragon was a friend of the senator or thereafter engaged in any dealings with him; their attempts to secure molasses for a company owned by Polland's nephew did not involve McCarthy and largely preceded his Senate term.

In 1949 Joe was harsh toward Maragon during questioning in a "five-percent" probe and called for his indictment for perjury. To embarrass the senator Maragon told newsmen about arranging the party in 1947. But he added, "As for Senator McCarthy, I never asked him for a damn thing. I never even got a cigaret out of it."[37]

Russell M. Arundel was a wealthy Virginia sportsman who first met McCarthy at the Warrenton racetrack in early 1947. They saw each other thereafter many times at social gatherings and became friends. Joe frequently borrowed money from friends, and in early December 1947 he asked Arundel to sign a six-month note for $20,000. The stocks he was using to secure his loan at the Appleton State Bank had dropped in value, he explained, and the note would serve as additional collateral to please bank examiners. Arundel signed the note without hesitation. The amount was reasonably small, and McCarthy showed him a list of his securities, revealing sizable financial resources. He said later, "I'd do that for any friend; it was a banking proposition." Joe did not pay off the note as promptly as promised, but he attended to the matter about six months after it came due. Arundel had no complaint and forgot about the note until a Senate probe of 1952 brought it to public attention and attempts were made to connect it with McCarthy's alleged interest in Pepsi-Cola.

What was often overlooked was the fact that Arundel was a bottler, and that he and many other bottlers were at odds with Walter Mack on the question of sugar. Pepsi bottlers could charge high prices during and after the war because of the scarcity of soft drinks; rationing propped up their profits. "I was opposed to the parent company's viewpoint at that time,"

Arundel explained. "I was very violently opposed to the end of sugar rationing." Had he ever heard McCarthy called "the Pepsi-Cola Kid?" a reporter asked. "Well, he's not my kid," Arundel replied, and he emphatically denied ever discussing sugar rationing with the senator.[38]

McCarthy's appearance before the Senate Appropriations Committee on December 9, 1947, was part of an effort by his friend, Republican Styles Bridges, the committee chairman, to determine whether or not federal employees or officials were secretly speculating in the grain and commodity markets. The Army had asked Congress for a deficiency appropriation of $400,000,000 for relief in occupied areas, and rumors were afloat that speculators had a hand in the request. Joe was summoned because of his knowledge of the sugar issue. He grilled Army Secretary Kenneth C. Royall and his associates about a purchase of 500,000 tons of raw Cuban sugar in September at a cent a pound higher than the existing world price. Joe charged that the purchase was made to support the price of Cuban sugar, and he said of the Army, "I think someone over there is inconceivably incompetent or worse." Years later it would take genuine creativity by McCarthy critics to link this hearing with Russell Arundel and the Pepsi-Cola company.[39]

By 1947 Soviet-American relations had taken a sharp turn for the worse. The nervous wartime alliance that Roosevelt hoped would prosper when the fighting stopped lay in ruins, and both world powers glared at each other with mutual suspicion and fear. Early in his presidency Harry S. Truman became persuaded of Joseph Stalin's perfidy, and he responded warmly to Winston Churchill's famous "iron curtain" speech of March 1946 warning of Soviet ambitions and pressures. Several months later he enraged many liberals by dismissing Secretary of Commerce Henry Wallace for delivering a speech mildly sympathetic to the Russian position. In March 1947 he declared the sweeping principles of the Truman Doctrine, which committed the United States to the containment of Communism, and requested $400 million to assist the beleaguered governments of Greece and Turkey. In June, Secretary of State George C. Marshall called for what would become known as the Marshall Plan, an unprecedented, multi-billion dollar effort to reconstruct Europe economically for the purpose of deterring Communist expansion.

At the same time, there were warnings of dangers posed by Communists to the internal security of the United States. In 1945 a large number of stolen government documents had been found in the possession of the editor of *Amerasia*, a pro-Communist magazine designed to influence

American Far East policy. The following year a report of the Canadian Royal Commission on Soviet espionage labeled the Canadian Communist party a Russian puppet, pointed to the existence of several Soviet spy rings, and declared that twenty-three Canadians "in positions of trust" had been involved in sending atomic secrets to Moscow.

In March, 1947, FBI Director J. Edgar Hoover branded the American Communist party a "fifth column" and warned that while in 1917 there was only one Communist for every 2,777 people in Russia, thirty years later there was one Communist for every 1,814 persons in the United States.

The House Committee on Un-American Activities (HUAC) made headlines regularly in 1947 with often reckless charges of Red infiltration. In May it launched a series of well-publicized hearings on subversive activities in the motion picture industry that resulted in the imprisonment of ten Hollywood witnesses who refused to cooperate with the committee and soon led to the deprivation of employment, "blacklisting," of scores of actors, writers, producers, directors, and technicians. One of the most outspoken members of the committee, deeply concerned, he said, about Communist propaganda in movies, was a young newcomer to Congress from California named Richard Nixon.

Stories of organized labor's successful efforts to purge itself of Communists appeared frequently in the media. "Anti-Communist Momentum" was the title of a gleeful report published by the conservative *U.S. News and World Report* in March, 1947.[40]

Unlike most conservatives, liberals were badly split over the question of Russian intentions and over the hotly disputed issue of whether the American Communist party was a genuine political party or a foreign-controlled conspiracy. Henry Wallace, thought by some to embody the highest principles of the New Deal, attracted those on the left most inclined to be tolerant toward Communists at home and abroad. In January 1947 a number of prominent New Deal liberals formed Americans for Democratic Action to put visible distance between themselves and Wallace and to build a "vital center" that could oppose the extremism of the Far Left and Far Right. Communists were specifically excluded from membership. James Loeb, one of ADA's founders, called the creation of the organization "a declaration of liberal independence from the stifling and paralyzing influence of the Communists and their apologists in America."[41]

In response to public fears, partisan charges, and a genuine personal concern about espionage, President Truman established a Temporary Commission on Loyalty in November 1946 to study the government's loyalty program. Its report was the basis for an Executive order of March

21, 1947, that considerably altered the conditions of federal employment and dramatically reflected a growing anxiety about internal subversion.

Under the new program all persons entering civilian employment in the Executive branch were subject to an extensive investigation of past activities and associations. Agency and department heads were responsible for the investigations, which were to include examinations of school records and the files of local law-enforcement bodies, the FBI, HUAC, the Civil Service Commission, and Military and Naval Intelligence. Questions would be asked of former employers and personal references sought, and testimony by those wishing their names to remain confidential was welcome. FBI checks were to be made on all incumbent employees of the Executive branch as well.

The standard for denying employment or removal from office was that "on all the evidence, reasonable grounds exist for belief that the person involved is disloyal to the government of the United States." Grounds for disloyalty included: sabotage, espionage, or knowingly associating with saboteurs or spies; treason or sedition or advocacy of either; advocacy of revolution by force and violence; intentional, unauthorized disclosure of documents or information of a confidential or nonpublic character in circumstances that indicated disloyalty; performing or attempting to perform duties ("or otherwise acting") so as to serve the interests of a foreign government in preference to American interests; membership in or affiliation or sympathetic association with an organization or group declared by the Attorney General to be totalitarian, fascist, Communist, or subversive. (In November the Attorney General issued a list of 82 organizations the FBI considered disloyal, and more names were added later.)

A loyalty board was created in each department and agency to handle appeals. Further appeals could be made to the department or agency head and then to a new three-man Civil Service Commission loyalty review board. During the appeal process an officer or employee might be suspended at any time, pending a judgment in his case.

Many liberals were appalled by the new program, arguing that it repeatedly violated constitutional rights. They pointed to the vagueness—"sympathetic association with"—of the disloyalty standards. "Here is the doctrine of guilt by association with a vengeance," one critic wrote. They objected to the inability of the accused to subpoena witnesses, to cross-examine informants, and to have access to all of the confidential information used in his case. They lamented the absence of a court review of Loyalty Review Board determinations. And they worried about what organizations an unscrupulous Attorney General might chose in the future to designate subversive. Historian Henry Steele Commager declared the program "an invitation to precisely that kind of witch-hunting which is repugnant to our constitutional system."[42]

Many conservatives, on the other hand, thought the program timid and full of loopholes. Republicans in the House sponsored a bill calling for a full-time, bipartisan, five-man loyalty review board, an independent agency with a statutory base. Several subordinate loyalty boards, beyond the reach of incumbent department and agency heads, were also proposed. During the debate, Democratic congressman Adolph J. Sabath of Illinois called the proposal "the most drastic and far-reaching bill affecting the rights of Federal employees ever to reach the floor in my 41 years of service," and thought it "merely a belated effort of the Republicans to get back in the groove of their Red-baiting campaign." The bill cleared the House on a 319-61 roll call—few congressmen wished to appear soft on security—but was never considered by the Senate.[43]

Very early in his Senate career Joe McCarthy placed himself squarely within the ranks of the Republican right wing on the issue of loyalty. This should not have surprised anyone familiar with his rhetoric in the recent Wisconsin campaign.

In March 1947, he joined a minority of conservative senators in opposing President Truman's choice of David E. Lilienthal as chairman of the new Atomic Energy Commission. Lilienthal, 47, was a moderate, respectable Washington insider who since 1941 had served as chairman of the Tennessee Valley Authority. In 1946 he had chaired a distinguished committee appointed by the Secretary of State to study the international control of atomic energy, and that October he received an interim appointment to the A.E.C. from the President. Scientists praised his nomination, and it was accepted in committee by a vote of eight to one. But opposition appeared on the Senate floor from those who thought TVA "socialistic" and riddled with subversives. Despite treacly testimony by Lilienthal condemning Communism and lauding the American way of life, Robert Taft joined the ranks of his opponents. A bitter struggle ensued, lasting three months and leaving Lilienthal badly shaken.

Working quietly behind the scenes against confirmation was J. Edgar Hoover, who sent FBI reports to the Senate containing charges against a few of Lilienthal's commission appointees and their relatives. One assistant counsel had reportedly added the words "Insofar as my conscience will allow me" when taking an oath supporting the Constitution. The wife of another employee was said to have left-wing connections. Another employee's brother was allegedly a member of the Communist party.

This sort of "evidence" against Lilienthal carried little weight with most senators, and confirmation seemed assured even before the formal Senate debate began. But Joe was deeply impressed by the FBI reports and swallowed their contents whole. He was shocked by the sentence added to the loyalty oath. "That is not the type of reservation that I believe a man should make, especially when he is a man who has been chosen for such a job as this man." He called the employee's wife mentioned by the FBI "actually communistically inclined." He said of Lilienthal, "I'd much rather run the risk of discarding a competent man than run the risk of being stuck with a dangerous man."

McCarthy co-sponsored a bill to replace the Atomic Energy Commission with a five-man board headed by Secretary of State Marshall. (He would later choose to forget the authority he once tried to hand George Marshall.) The plan would not only have defeated Lilienthal's nomination but would have eliminated the concept of civilian control of atomic energy.

Lilienthal was confirmed on April 9 by a vote of 50-31. Thirty-six Republicans were opposed, including Taft, Wiley, and McCarthy, while twenty Republicans joined with 30 Democrats to provide the necessary majority.[44]

A few days before the final vote on Lilienthal, Joe participated in a debate on "America's Town Meeting of the Air," broadcast nationally. He argued in favor of outlawing the Communist party (61 percent of the American public agreed, according to a Gallup poll), and he presented a five-point program he declared necessary "if we are to survive the Communist menace." The Justice Department, he said, should rule the party an agency of a foreign power. The FBI should be empowered and directed to publish the names of all Communist-front organizations. "All Communist aliens should be forced to leave the country." Communists should be barred from representing clients before labor boards and similar bodies. "Communists and members of Communist-front organizations should be required to register with a federal agency and be fingerprinted." This was as stiff a set of proposals as any being circulated on the Far Right. Joe warned, "The Communist threat is becoming more and more great."

In the course of his speech, McCarthy quoted from an oath taken by members of the Communist party, declaring allegiance to the Soviet Union. Another debater, Leo Cherne of the Research Institute of America, correctly pointed out that the oath had not been used since 1936. The audience laughed, and Joe fired back, "You don't think for one minute that the Communists have changed because they have stricken some words from the oath?"

Joe also launched into a lachrymose yarn involving his overseas duty that proved so effective he would use it repeatedly (with modifications) in later years.

> The whole picture of an early morning is painfully clear before my eyes at this instant. Let me paint it for you. It was before one of our first and roughest bombing attacks on the airfields and shipping in the Rabaul area. All of the pilots and gunners of our dive and torpedo bombing squadrons had been crowded into their ready tent.
>
> After the briefing had been finished, after each squadron and each division and each section had been assigned its job in that day's bombing, my skipper, then Major Munn, turned to the chaplain and said, "Chaplain, we know that some of us shall die today. Might you have a few words to say?"
>
> As the chaplain rose, no other sound could be heard. That chaplain's body today lies on the floor of a vast moon-swept, wind-tossed Pacific, but his words I know are burned deep into the hearts and minds of each of those young pilots and gunners who still live, and this is what he said:
>
> "If each of you young men shall remember two fundamental truths, two truths taught by all religious groups since the beginning of time, if you will remember first, that there is a God who is eternal, and second, that each of you has a soul which is immortal, then regardless of whether you die within the next few hours or live another 50 or 60 years, you shall serve yourself, your country, and your God to the last full measure."
>
> That, ladies and gentlemen, is the American concept of life, a concept so foreign to the communistic concept, a concept preserved over the years by the expenditure of blood and flesh and steel. That concept of life we must preserve. That concept of life we shall preserve.

The large studio audience applauded. As Joe knew it would.[45]

At a press conference in Madison a few days later, Senator McCarthy revealed yet another point of view linking him to the G.O.P.'s right wing: he accused the Administration of "blackjacking" the government of China "to take in the Communists." When asked to list the important tasks facing the government, his top priority was "to stop the spread of Communism."[46]

His second item was "to encourage and give aid to democratic governments," and later in the month McCarthy voted in favor of the $400 million

Greek-Turkish aid bill requested by the President. The vote was lopsided, 67-23, and many prominent Republicans, including Taft and Wiley, backed the bill.[47]

During the debate over the Taft-Hartley bill in May, McCarthy introduced an amendment permitting union members to seek from their employers the dismissal of any employee ejected from the union for "being a member of the Communist party or actively and consistently promoting or supporting the policies, teachings, and doctrines of the Communist party, or advocating, or being a member of any organization that advocates, the overthrow of the United States Government by force or other illegal or unconstitutional methods." The amendment was hastily written, poorly thought out, and of very dubious constitutionality. Its appearance was apparently sparked in part by a confrontation that morning between several Communist party leaders and two Wisconsin congressmen, one of whom was Charles Kersten, Joe's ultraconservative friend from Milwaukee. Senator Taft shrugged off the proposal as "unnecessary." Senators Langer and Magnuson patiently reminded McCarthy that the Communist party was still a legal political body in the United States.

Joe would not give an inch; he became emotional, repetitious, and occasionally rude. "Let me finish," he sputtered at Taft. At one point he argued, "It is not a political party; it is a way of life; it is a religion." He vigorously pounded his point home. "I submit that any man who joins the Communist party, knowing that the Communist party is dedicated to the overthrow of our government by force, is guilty of treason the minute he joins the party, regardless of whether or not the State allows the Communist party to be on the ballot."

McCarthy altered the wording of the amendment at the suggestion of Millard Tydings of Maryland, who expressed fear of a "witch-hunt," but it still failed to win any discernible support. Joe requested a vote. None was taken, and the embarrassing proposal went into the official record simply as "rejected."[48]

In July, McCarthy appeared on the nationwide radio program "Meet the Press" and discussed an investigation of alleged frauds in war-surplus disposal. When asked about the need for a standing army, he said, "We are at war. We've been at war with Russia for some time now, and Russia has been winning this war at a faster rate than we were, during the last stages of the last war. Everyone is painfully aware of the fact that we are at war—and that we're losing it."[49]

McCarthy had been in office only five weeks when the *Madison Capital*

Times initiated a blistering series of attacks against the senator's financial dealings that would continue on a regular basis for the next eight years. William T. Evjue had launched the investigation of McCarthy shortly after La Follette's defeat, and he pursued his friend's conqueror with a passionate blend of vengeance and righteousness. At first the charges were reported only in Madison and in Milwaukee by the *Journal,* but as more facts emerged and Joe became increasingly prominent others joined the probe and the results became international news.

The first stories, stemming apparently from an illegal leak of McCarthy's federal income-tax returns, revealed his large wartime investment profits, disclosed an assessment by the federal government over disputed deductions, and pointed to his failure to file a state return in 1943. More importantly, they again raised serious questions about the financing of his candidacy for the Senate in 1944. McCarthy family incomes were published, and relatives made awkward replies to questions about their alleged campaign contributions.

The federal assessment totaled $3,500 and arose over deductions incurred in the handling of stock transactions in 1943. Joe did not contest the finding and agreed to pay. His failure to file a Wisconsin return in the year of his stock market bonanza, however, was a more serious matter, because it appeared obvious that Joe was attempting not only to avoid taxes but to conceal the profits from public scrutiny and sidestep the election laws.

While overseas, Joe wrote a letter to the Wisconsin State Assessor of Incomes for the Appleton district denying residence in his native state.

> During the entire year of 1943 I was serving in the armed forces of the United States, during which I spent no time in Wisconsin. I had no property in the state and received no income from within the state, having waived collection of my salary as circuit judge. Therefore, I assume it unnecessary, under present laws, to file a return. If you do not so understand the law I shall be glad to file a return.

When no response was forthcoming, Joe thought he was safe. And he might have been had not Evjue prompted an investigation into the matter. If McCarthy was not a resident, the editor asked, how could he be a circuit judge on leave or a Senate candidate?

His Madison antagonist had drawn blood, and at first Joe angrily refused comment. A formal statement, issued shortly, was largely designed to confuse the issue. The *Appleton Post-Crescent* referred to the attack on

McCarthy as "character-assassin effrontery," "sloshy tripe," and "a mixture of subtle slander and splash defamation now known as the Fellow Smear[,] full brother of the Fellow Traveler. It belongs to the Kingdom of Blotch."[50]

On advice from Urban Van Susteren, Joe reluctantly filed a state income-tax return and paid $2,677.86 for the delinquent tax and interest. The *Capital Times* and *Journal* filled page-one columns with Joe's financial records and his letters to state officials, and devoted regular editorials to the affair. Evjue gloated, "The people of this state are catching on to the clever McCarthy . . ." He was planning further stories on the junior senator.[51]

In the course of writing a letter to a state tax official defending his position, Joe referred to himself several times as "McCarthy." Interestingly, his first reference to himself in the third person occurred when under fire and in trouble.[52]

The schoolhouse McCarthy attended. *(Photo courtesy Jim Heenan)*

McCarthy in grade school. He is in the middle, without a cap. *(Photo courtesy May Voy)*

The 1930 class of Little Wolf High School. Mc-
Carthy is fourth from the right in the front row.
(Photo courtesy Paul Sturm)

The same class in cap and gown. McCarthy is
the middle of the third row from the botto
(Photo courtesy Honor Testin)

McCarthy's high school graduation photograph.
(Photo courtesy Honor Testin)

McCarthy on active duty in the Marines during World War II. *(Photos courtesy May Voy)*

Ray Kiermas and McCarthy in 1947. *(Photo courtesy Ray Kiermas)*

McCarthy (third from let
at a GOP picnic, lat
1940s, Shawano Count
Park. (Photo courtes
Ruth Meyer)

McCarthy and his clos
friend Tom Korb, circ
1952. (Photo courtes
Tom Korb)

HOUSING PROBLEMS

One of the most urgent and complex problems facing Congress after the war was the housing shortage. Home construction had been hard hit by the Depression, falling from 937,000 new housing starts in 1925 to an average of 273,000 a year in the 1930s. The number of starts increased in 1941 to 706,000, but war priorities prompted a sharp decline in the figure. With almost 15 million veterans returning in 1945, housing demands became acute. Chicago reported 100,000 homeless veterans; 2,000 people answered an advertisement for a vacancy in Atlanta; a classified ad in an Omaha newspaper read, "Big Ice Box, 7 by 17 feet. Could be fixed up to live in."[1]

President Truman, long concerned about housing (and with a keen appreciation of the importance of urban areas to the Democratic Party), warmly endorsed public housing, slum clearance, and a variety of aids to private housing, and he urged Congress to take action. In November 1945, a comprehensive, bipartisan bill was introduced in the Senate containing a national housing policy, expanded lending powers for home-loan banks, relaxed FHA insurance terms, home-improvement loans for farmers, housing research, slum clearance, and construction of 500,000 public housing units over a fourteen-year period.

The bill was sponsored by Democratic senators Robert F. Wagner of New York and Allen J. Ellender of Louisiana, along with Republican Taft. Taft faced serious opposition within his party for his support of public housing, but he remained a staunch proponent of the principle, arguing that good housing meant good citizenship. His enthusiasm was tempered by his demands that public housing be modest, that it be available only to those in genuine need, and that its presence avoid injury to the private housing industry.[2]

The Wagner-Ellender-Taft Bill passed the Senate without modification on April 15, 1946, but was killed in the House Banking and Currency Committee, chaired by Michigan Republican Jesse P. Wolcott, an indefatigable foe of public housing widely thought to be in league with the real estate lobby.[3]

The following year, responsibility for steering what was now called the Taft-Ellender-Wagner Bill through the 80th Congress fell to the Senate Majority Leader. Despite his authority in such areas as labor, Taft was unable to win the support of a substantial number of fellow Republicans on the public housing question. Sen. Homer Capehart of Indiana growled, "I'm against anything that even looks like it might have socialism in it." Congressman Wolcott let it be known that no matter what the Senate did any measure containing public housing would never clear his committee.

The bill passed the Senate Banking and Currency Committee by a slender seven-to-six margin and Taft abandoned the bill temporarily, conceding that further effort would be unproductive. Instead, he put his weight behind a bill co-sponsored by Senator McCarthy calling for a new study of the entire housing situation.[4]

Joe had taken an early and outspoken interest in housing. Along with many other politicians, he knew that it was one of the hottest issues around and could be generously exploited for personal publicity. Moreover, he was genuinely concerned about the shortage and was especially moved by the plight of the very poor, trapped in slums, and by the thousands of homeless veterans and their families.

Joe did not like public housing; it smacked of big government, bureaucrats, and waste. He voted against the Taft-Ellender-Wagner Bill in the Banking and Currency Committee, and after touring a run-down public housing project in Queens in August 1947 he called the complex "a deliberately created slum area" and referred to "breeding grounds for Communism."[5]

Still, he recognized that a limited amount of public housing was necessary. "I'm for public housing," he told reporters, "but it's only a part of the answer." The proper extent of the federal government's role in tackling the housing crisis was uncertain, in Joe's opinion. He agreed with other Republicans who thought it depended upon a lengthy and detailed examination of the reasons private industry had failed to provide adequate low-cost housing. However cynical men like Wolcott were in urging further study of the housing issue—liberal Democrat Robert F. Wagner charged, "Domestic treason is being perpetrated on the American veterans and their fellow citizens by the money-mad real estate lobby and their unholy representatives in Congress"—McCarthy was convinced that the project was necessary. And he was determined to play a prominent role in it.[6]

The proposal introduced by McCarthy and West Virginia Republican Chapman Revercomb sought the creation of a fourteen-member House-Senate committee to study the entire field of housing—"From A to Z," Joe bubbled to reporters. Seven members were to come from the Senate—including at least three from the Banking and Currency Committee—and an equal number from the House. The joint committee was charged with submitting a report and recommendations to Congress no later than March 15, 1948. The bill sailed through the House and Senate without a dissenting vote, and the committee received a $100,000 expense account. It was decided to send four subcommittees across the country, beginning in September, to gather relevant information.[7]

Joe saw to it that he was named to the joint committee. The others from the Senate were Charles Tobey, chairman of the Banking and Currency Committee, Ralph Flanders, Harry P. Cain of Washington, Robert F. Wagner, Glen H. Taylor of Idaho, and John J. Sparkman of Alabama. Except for Cain, an ultraconservative and a leading opponent of all public housing, senators on the joint committee were capable of looking objectively at the housing problem. The Speaker of the House appointed Ralph Gamble of New York, Frank Sundstrom of New Jersey, Rolla C. McMillen of Illinois, Charles K. Fletcher of California, Wright Patman of Texas, Albert Rains of Alabama, and Hale Boggs of Louisiana.

When the joint committee met in a closed-door organizational meeting in August, only nine members appeared. Tobey was holding four proxies and assumed that with them, his own vote, and the votes of three members in attendance his election as chairman was assured. While most Senate committees employed proxies regularly, House rules prohibited their use in committees. In an act of pure spite against Tobey, Joe moved to bar them. With several senators absent, the motion carried. Joe then nominated Congressman Gamble as chairman and accepted the vice-chairmanship himself. Tobey and his supporters lost each vote cast by a margin of one vote.

Pale and enraged, Tobey immediately summoned an impromptu news conference. He contended that a "sinister group" was behind his defeat, he charged McCarthy with bad faith, and he sputtered fulminations against the joint committee: " 'Behold, I was shapen in iniquity, and in sin did my mother conceive me.' "

With the New Hampshire senator sputtering down a nearby hallway, Joe told reporters that he had not wanted Tobey to be chairman. "He thinks the sole answer to the problem is public housing." More to the point, he acknowledged that he and Tobey had been feuding since the struggle over sugar rationing. "All this bitterness is something carried over from that." Now that he had enjoyed his revenge, Joe sought to shrug off the matter. "It doesn't make much difference who the chairman is. We shouldn't be sidetracked by personal animosity between two senators."

Representative Gamble was somewhat embarrassed by the heated proceedings and vowed to carry out his duties responsibly. "We are going to have a full investigation in accordance with the resolution," he told reporters. "I have no preconceived ideas. I didn't have the remotest thought of being chairman. I certainly didn't seek it. It was thrust upon me, you might say."[8]

Shortly after introducing legislation calling for the creation of the joint committee, Joe made an impassioned plea on the Senate floor on behalf of a bill he co-authored to pay half the cost of specially built houses, up to $10,000, for some 1,700 totally disabled veterans confined to wheelchairs. Most of the veterans lived in hospitals and were unable to obtain G.I. housing loans because of their lack of income. Joe had led a subcommittee that studied the issue for three months, and his bill cleared the Banking and Currency Committee by a unanimous vote.

Joe said that he had personally interviewed about 300 of the veterans and knew of their desperate need for homes. A dozen veterans in wheelchairs attended his presentation; "there are some of them in the gallery, and I wish senators would look up and see them," Joe cried. "If we vote down the measure we will be sentencing these men to an indefinite stay in a hospital."

Joe would brook no opposition to his proposal and became abusive toward critics. When Senator Taft questioned Joe's assertion that Gen. Omar Bradley had been consulted, Joe glared angrily at the Majority Leader and said, "Personally, I do not give a tinker's dam whether General Bradley approves legislation which we propose to pass."

On Senator Taft's motion, the Senate recommitted the bill by a vote of 40-37. McCarthy smarted over his defeat but determined to try again.

Throughout the following year of study and debate on the nation's housing needs, Joe would remind colleagues repeatedly of the plight of totally disabled veterans and attempt to tack his bill onto major housing legislation.

There was no appreciable political gain to be had in this persistent effort. Later McCarthy biographers, eager to portray the senator as the consummate cynic, chose to ignore it.[9]

Joe proceeded to work on the complexities of postwar housing with the sort of intensity that had propelled him through Little Wolf High School in record time. Never one to go into anything he was concerned about halfheartedly, he soon told reporters that he was dropping all other committee work to devote himself exclusively to the issue.[10]

That summer McCarthy successfully sponsored an amendment to the Housing Act of 1937 authorizing cities to complete local public housing units by raising funds to make up the difference between statutory cost limitations and the current cost of construction. Critics who were anxious to prove the senator implacably hostile toward public housing would neglect to mention the McCarthy bill.

Joe resisted efforts in the House to amend his bill to prevent the eviction of public housing residents with ample incomes. The proposal struck him as "very, very wrong" given the needs of the poor. As he soon explained, "I took the position I would rather see my bill defeated rather than to have that amendment."[11]

Before starting across the country on committee hearings, Joe consulted with scores of government and housing industry officials and sent letters to all members of Congress seeking suggestions about housing. He told reporters that he was especially interested in grappling with such "roadblocks" as outmoded building codes, archaic designs, outdated materials, high labor costs, restrictions on the labor supply, faulty distribution, financing and insurance costs, and local taxes. Reporters were learning that it was Senator McCarthy rather than the more reserved and detached Congressman Gamble who would provide them with a colorful story on housing. He told one crowded press conference, "We can find the answer to housing, or the whole Congress should resign and go back home."[12]

When the American Legion created a housing committee, Joe took an immediate interest in its members, toured public housing projects with them, and persuaded them to come out against the Taft-Ellender-Wagner Bill in a report to the national convention. While he recognized that the bill contained many good features, the new joint committee had now assumed the responsibility for future legislation. "I frankly felt for the Legion or any other group to go on record for the Taft-Ellender-Wagner Bill in view of the unanimous and bipartisan action of House and Senate was a mistake," he told a *New York Times* reporter. This was to be McCarthy's show.[13]

The joint committee divided into subcommittees and held formal hearings in a total of 33 cities, compiling testimony from 1,286 witnesses covering 7,000 pages. Senator Flanders was asked to study "cost factors and cost reduction in housing," and he filed an extensive report on the subject in early 1948. Senator Tobey worked on taxation, Senator Sparkman examined Joe's pet project, housing aid to physically handicapped veterans, Congressman Patman studied rural housing, and Congressman McMillen became an expert on building codes.

Senator McCarthy assumed more than his share of the labor. He was not assigned a specific topic, and he delved into a broad range of complexities, from the availability of castiron soil pipe to federal mortgage-insurance legislation. He participated in public hearings in Pittsburgh, Cleveland, Detroit, Indianapolis, St. Louis, Cincinnati, Little Rock, Dallas, San Antonio, Columbus, New Orleans, Chicago, and Milwaukee in October and November 1947, and he played a prominent role in a series of nine Washington hearings in early 1948. He also held scores of private sessions with housing experts across the country and soon claimed to have traveled 30,000 miles in the joint committee's service.[14]

Joe dominated almost all of the public hearings he attended. In part, of course, this was a reflection of his personality. But his dominance also resulted from the fact that he worked harder on the housing question than his colleagues and had a better command of details. In Pittsburgh he skillfully questioned the president of a lumber company on local lumber prices, comparing them with data provided by the Bureau of Labor Statistics. In New Orleans he expounded on the nation's supply of nails and plaster lath. While he confessed in Columbus, Ohio, that "the largest building I have ever built was a chicken house on the farm," no one challenged Senator McCarthy's credentials to discuss postwar housing knowledgeably.[15]

The senator often stressed his own and the committee's objectivity. He told two Milwaukee labor leaders, "We do not restrict any witness, and we want to hear everything that goes on and that can be said. We walk on toes, and we do not give a damn, and we are not out for labor, industry, public housing, or the real estate board." He was especially hostile to charges by liberals and labor leaders that he was a tool of business lobbyists. He said in New Orleans, "You have got that lobby on both sides: a public housing lobby and a real estate lobby. They are both doing the nation, I think, an infinite amount of damage. I think one is as bad as the other."[16]

Still, several of Joe's preconceived ideas about housing were observable throughout the hearings. He made little effort to disguise his distaste for public housing. "I don't think there is anyone that thinks less of public housing than I do," he said in Columbus. He referred repeatedly to a study revealing extensive bookkeeping errors in the Federal Public Housing Authority; they pointed to typical bureaucratic bungling and waste if not outright fraud, he charged. In New Orleans he stated that the committee preferred subsidization of private enterprise to further investment in public housing. But he acknowledged that public housing might be an inevitability and was critical of several witnesses who chose to attack public housing without proposing a feasible alternative. "The question is, how can we give . . . help most efficiently? How can we get the most for every dollar?"[20]

Joe revealed a strong desire to persuade municipalities to simplify and modernize the nation's two- to three-thousand building codes in order to clear the way for the mass production of homes. He was interested in the potential of the new prefabricated housing industry but not nearly to the degree that McCarthy critics would later claim. Senator Flanders was the most ardent proponent on the joint committee of the factory production of homes. It was liberal Wilson Wyatt, the Administration's former Housing Expediter, who had sought huge federal loans for the "prefab" industry. Among his favorite companies was the Lustron Corporation, later to be identified with Senator McCarthy.[18]

Joe expressed angry opposition to a group of shady characters called gray marketeers, who hoarded hard-to-get building materials and sold them to contractors at exorbitant prices. While their activity was legal, it slowed housing production and drove up costs. Determined to shut off their sources of supply, Joe subpoenaed and grilled several gray marketeers and gave their names and copies of their testimony to building material companies.[19]

Among the most prosperous gray-market operators was Isidore Ginsberg, a pugnacious, articulate, 310-pound New York attorney. Called before the joint committee, Ginsberg bitterly denounced the probe and denied that legislation could be passed to outlaw his business. "Only in Russia could that be done." McCarthy countered with the charge that Ginsberg was "the most vicious of the gray marketeers" and threatened to cite him for contempt if he failed to name his suppliers.

At one point Ginsberg loudly protested, "We deal in nothing but free enterprise and take a reasonable profit, and nothing more, not any greater profit than the gypsum companies take for their material." Joe replied coldly, "Your enterprise is just too damn free, Ginsberg."

During a committee session in late January, McCarthy revealed that Ginsberg had been arrested three times for grand larceny and was currently involved in a mail-order swindle of a crippled veteran, which made Joe particularly furious. Congressman Patman objected to the introduction of this information almost as strenuously as Ginsberg, but Joe was unmoved, angrily determined to put Ginsberg out of business at all cost.[20]

Reports of these tumultuous clashes were carried in newspapers across the country. The *Washington Times-Herald* thought that McCarthy "seems to aspire to the title of the Republican Huey Long." William Evjue solemnly declared (in unusually awful syntax), "Such as McCarthy would wind America up in the straitjacket of Russia if their meddling were not fought off by such as Ginsberg."[21]

As he promised in the hearings, Joe turned over the results of his investigation of Isidore Ginsberg to the District Attorney of Queens County, New York. Several months later Ginsberg was convicted of grand larceny and faced trial on 39 counts of mail fraud. With considerable self-satisfaction, Joe soon told reporters of a "noticeable drop" in gray-market complaints since the conviction.[22]

On several other occasions during the hearings McCarthy got into nasty quarrels with witnesses, at times exhibiting a hot temper and a flagrant disregard for established committee procedure and even common courtesy. His most fiery outbursts were reserved for those who questioned the joint committee's (and thus McCarthy's) importance and called for blanket approval of the Taft-Ellender-Wagner Bill. He frequently interrupted testimony by such witnesses and threatened to remove anyone from the hearing room who interrupted his own statements. A real estate broker in Cleveland said of Taft-Ellender-Wagner, "We believe in that bill, the broadening of its provisions, to take care of providing temporary housing or permanent housing at the levels where they are needed. That bill should be passed, yes, I do say that."

> The Chairman. Where in that bill do you find that provision?
> Mr. Worley. I said the bill must necessarily be broadened. Would you give me a minute to tell you why I think—
> The Chairman. No; tell us where it should be broadened.
> Mr. Worley. I will tell you where it should be broadened.

We have got to provide housing in a situation of this kind. We have in Columbus, Ohio, at the present time—

The Chairman. Forget about Columbus. Tell me where the bill should be amended and broadened.

Mr. Worley. It should be broadened to provide temporary housing for people who can only afford to pay $20 to $50 a month until such time as private enterprise can provide housing at that level.

In Columbus we are asked to have people buy 260 square feet of property in a little house that is only—a little 260-square-foot-house for $3,500 and $3,950. I say that the Government has got to broaden—

The Chairman. Now, listen to me. I want you to stick to this bill. We will get to Columbus after a while. We are coming to Columbus to hold a hearing on the 1st of November.

Mr. Worley. I was told you wouldn't.

The Chairman. I want you to stick to this bill. Do you understand that? I want you to answer my questions.

The Senator charged several advocates of the Taft-Ellender-Wagner Bill with complete ignorance of its contents. He asked a Racine, Wisconsin, housing official, "Do you favor all parts of that bill? Do you know anything about the bill?"

Mr. Norstrom. I read the bill, and the bill proposes a decent home for every American family, and that is a good goal.

Senator McCarthy. In other words, you favor the preamble, and I think we all do.

Mr. Norstrom. Yes.

Senator McCarthy. Do you know what is in the bill? If you know what is in the bill, that is all right.

Mr. Nordstrom. I am not familiar enough with the bill to go into it in detail.

Senator McCarthy. That seems to be the prime requisite for testifying for the bill, not to know anything about it at all.[23]

On the whole, however, McCarthy's conduct was reasonably dignified throughout the lengthy hearings, and he earned as much applause as criticism from observers. Elements within organized labor were hostile toward the joint committee, suspecting a right-wing plot to kill public housing. McCarthy sparred lightly with two C.I.O. officials in Pittsburgh and became upset over an agreement uncovered in the New York City area under which union steamfitters would install only equipment supplied by the contractors for whom they worked: "a viciously collusive thing." But his approach toward labor was moderate and positive. He worked closely and amicably with the American Federation of Labor's Building and Construction Trades Department, obtaining crackdowns on several worker abuses. In Washington he publicly expressed the judgment that "the committee has been very happy about the type of cooperation we are getting from labor." McCarthy consistently advocated an increase in apprentice programs to provide more skilled journeymen, and in Cleveland he urged the lifting of all racial restrictions by organized labor.[24]

Joe was unruffled when the secretary of the Communist party of Pittsburgh testified, castigating both major political parties and calling for government housing programs and rent controls. But when Congressman Edward H. Rees told the joint committee of testimony by confidential sources linking a regional director of the Federal Housing Administration to the Communist party, the senator showed extreme concern. "If there is a member of the Communist party in charge, if he is regional director of FPHA, he certainly shouldn't stay there any more than about ten seconds, I would say, at the most."[25]

Joint committee members were obligated to submit reports to Chairman Gamble describing the fruits of their labor. In early February 1948, Joe filed an extensive and detailed analysis of the entire housing situation, complete with recommendations for legislation. He called the attention of the press to his report, predicted passage of a housing bill in the current session of Congress, and told reporters that he was personally framing legislation.[26]

Two weeks later Joe introduced a draft of a proposed bill to the joint committee designed to assist the construction of 1.5 million housing units over the next decade. It was not a reactionary proposal, as some critics charged. Indeed, it bore similarities to a presidential message on housing issued a few days earlier.

The proposed bill contained tax exemptions and generous depreciation allowances to encourage low rental housing, assistance to cities for slum clearance, the extension of F.H.A. mortgage insurance, and the creation of a federal housing and home-financing agency to push for municipal standardization of building codes and a standard system of measurements. "If that program has not produced several hundred thousand low-rental houses a year from now," Joe chortled to reporters, "I'll buy you each a steak." He estimated the cost of the package at about $1,000,000,000 for the first five years.

McCarthy's proposal differed most sharply from the President's on public housing. While Truman urged the construction of 100,000 such units over the next five years, Joe and other Republican leaders, including Congressman Wolcott, sought to omit the controversial issue from legislation entirely. Joe was not as militantly opposed to public housing as some of his colleagues, but he sought swift passage of a bill (hopefully bearing his name) and thought this approach to the matter the only way to achieve it.

This calculation collapsed when Senators Taft and Ellender, miffed over the apparent scuttling of the Taft-Ellender-Wagner Bill, announced that they would introduce a public housing amendment if the bill reached the Senate floor. Eagerly joining their ranks, Senator Tobey told a national housing conference of 1,500 veterans that the proposed bill was a product of the real estate lobby. Mayor Francis Wendt of Racine, Wisconsin (a long-time La Follette supporter), earned headlines by calling Joe "the water boy of the real estate lobby." Not to be outdone, William Evjue echoed the contention and added inaccurately, "McCarthy has charged that it is the Communists who are agitating for public housing."[27]

No evidence even indirectly connecting the senator with the real estate lobby was produced by his critics. But that was largely overlooked at the time in the clash of partisan rhetoric. (Historians of the period have less excuse.)

The fourteen-man joint committee endorsed McCarthy's housing proposals, with the exception of an income-tax exemption for producers of cheap rental housing. Joe accepted the modification and assumed that his proposed bill was now ready for introduction.

Senator Flanders wrote most of the committee's final report, however, and the document called for 500,000 units of public housing. Then, in McCarthy's absence, the Senate Banking and Currency Committee voted to introduce new housing legislation as an amendment to Taft-Ellender-Wagner. The "Flanders amendment" contained public housing proposals, and it squeaked through the committee by a 7-6 vote.

Taft had obviously had a hand in this sudden turn of events, and Joe was furious. He alone refused to sign the joint committee report, and when it was presented to the Senate he hurled sarcasm at Flanders for attempting to deprive him of the credit for housing legislation. "I should like to compliment the senator from Vermont for his good judgment and broadmindedness in filing a report which contains every single element of the bill which I have been drafting for the past three months."

He did not oppose public housing entirely, he explained. Even 100,000 units a year were acceptable "provided we could do it with some semblance of assurance that it would be intelligently handled and that one dollar's value would be received for every dollar of taxpayer money spent." But the Public Housing Administration was rife with waste. And public housing might deprive private industry of scarce building materials.

McCarthy was sincere about these objections; he had expressed them before. But more to the point was his well-informed belief that Congressman Wolcott would not permit a bill containing public housing to reach the floor of the House. And that would mean that all of Joe's work on housing had been in vain.[28]

During five days of often heated debate on housing, McCarthy and Taft clashed repeatedly. At first Joe sought to tack sixteen amendments of his own onto the Taft-Ellender-Wagner Bill and prevent introduction of the Flanders amendment. Taft charged that Joe was "rather wasting our time," and at one point exclaimed, "Frankly I do not know exactly what he is trying to do." Joe angrily proclaimed his expertise in the matter: "I have had practically everyone who has driven a nail tell me what he thinks is the solution to the housing problem." Then he questioned Taft's credentials. "I wonder if he is aware of the history of the housing legislation and will understand why we are taking it up."

After much skirmishing, Taft threw up his hands and said that the junior senator from Wisconsin could amend to his heart's desire. He would proceed to introduce the Flanders amendment and thus cancel out the very similar McCarthy amendments. Joe glared at the Majority Leader and growled, "I do not know the reason for this last-minute maneuvering. I do not know why we cannot forget about politics for a day or two and get some housing legislation." Fourteen McCarthy amendments passed, including one calling for aid to paraplegic veterans.

Joe repeatedly sought to separate public housing from a general housing bill. "If that is not done I fear that both public housing and the other much needed housing legislation may be defeated." He made it clear from the start, however, that if the attempt to separate failed, he would back a bill containing public housing. (When Tobey launched into another tirade about the real estate lobby, McCarthy observed that the lobby "has done more to convince me that public housing is needed than those who have been lobbying in favor of public housing.") Joe supported a motion by Senator Cain that would have divided the measures. After its defeat, true to his word, he made up with Taft and assisted him in the creation of a bill that closely resembled Taft-Ellender-Wagner and was passed by acclamation.

Joe was bound to get at least a measure of credit for the legislation. And in the course of the struggle he secured an amendment to make public housing more available to lower-income families and won support for housing assistance to paraplegic veterans.[29]

As McCarthy feared, anti-public housing Republicans in the House, led by Jesse Wolcott, Speaker Joe Martin, and House Whip Charles Halleck, stymied efforts to bring the Senate bill to the floor. Wolcott pushed through a conservative bill of his own that was received by the Senate on the last day of its regular session. Tobey bitterly denounced it as "a phony housing bill," "a hollow sham," and a "monstrosity," and Allen Ellender called Wolcott "a little czar." Since there was no time to take the House bill through a committee, unanimous consent was necessary to bring it before the Senate. A number of senators, including Taft and McCarthy, favored that route, hopeful of a last-minute compromise; Joe noted that he had been meeting with Wolcott privately, attempting to reach an agreement. But Ellender refused, smarting over the continued obstruction by House leaders. McCarthy complained of a "one-man veto" and charged the Louisiana senator with arguing over whose name would appear on the bill. Ellender would not budge, however, and further action was impossible.

This session of Congress was only able to pass a weak housing bill that provided limited assistance to veterans. It was sponsored by Republican ultraconservative William Jenner, and the President soon called it "slipshod" and "teeny weeny."[30]

Truman took delight in the turmoil within the 80th Congress, labeling it "do-nothing" and "the worst." On his whistle-stop tour to the West Coast in June he repeatedly called attention to the Senate's housing bill and blamed all G.O.P. congressmen for its fate. Congressman Wolcott and his allies had given the Chief Executive exactly the ammunition he needed to revive his sagging political prospects. In Jefferson City, Missouri, he declared, "There is just one big issue. It is the special interests against the people.... You now have a special interest Congress because only one-third of you voted in 1946. You are getting just what you deserve."[31]

When McCarthy was not devoting himself to the housing problem, he was campaigning for Harold Stassen. The tall, good-looking former governor of Minnesota was only 40 when he declared his candidacy for the presidential nomination in the winter of 1947. Within twenty-four hours, Joe announced his support, and that May he was elected temporary chairman of a Wisconsin Stassen-for-President club. He headed the statewide campaign for a slate of Stassen delegates to the 1948 G.O.P. national convention and delivered numerous speeches for the candidate across the country. In November 1947, he drew an angry reply from normally sedate

Thomas Dewey for asserting that the New York governor had "slipped tremendously" in his drive for the nomination due to "his refusal to discuss the issues."[32]

McCarthy's ties to Stassen were largely personal; the two were good friends and similarly energetic campaigners. Victor Johnston, in Joe's office, had been a Stassen publicist for years and spent most of early 1948 campaigning in Wisconson and running Stassen headquarters in Washington. Tom Coleman favored Taft, but he knew that the dour, blunt Ohio senator could not win in Wisconsin, and he supported Stassen in preference to Dewey.[33]

A curious coalition of conservative and progressive Republicans, including Fred R. Zimmerman and Philip La Follette, thought that Gen. Douglas MacArthur was the best choice to sweep Truman from office. The Hearst newspapers and the *Chicago Tribune* boosted the general's candidacy, calling him "Wisconsin-born," and hundreds of campaign billboards sprouted throughout the state.

McCarthy countered with a letter to constituents that contained a type of attack reminiscent of the 1939 campaign against Judge Werner.

> Governor Stassen is in the prime of life. He will be the same age as Teddy Roosevelt was when as President he handled the Panama Canal and the Alaskan situation without getting our country into trouble.
>
> General MacArthur has been a great General. But he is now ready for retirement. He would be 72 years old before a term as President ended. Twice before we have had Presidents who became physically weakened during their term of office and both times it had very sad results for our country. . . .
>
> General MacArthur would be much older than either of these two men [Franklin Roosevelt and Woodrow Wilson] were. It has been 50 years since he commenced his Army career, and he has been out of touch with civilian problems of government and has not been in the United States for ten years. That is why I believe that we should give the general his well-deserved hero's acclaim and retirement when his job is done and not try to have him undergo the strain of years as President of our country in this difficult time.

Joe went on to point out accurately that the general had been born in

Housing Problems 147

Little Rock, Arkansas, not Wisconsin. He then proceeded to bludgeon readers with an item that could not fail to affect the state's large Roman Catholic and Lutheran populations.

> Neither his first nor his second marriage, or his divorce, took place in Wisconsin. He was first married in Florida to Mrs. Walter Brooks of Baltimore, who now lives in Washington, D.C. After she divorced him in Reno, Nevada, he was remarried in New York City. Neither wife ever resided or voted in Wisconsin. In a sworn marriage application for his second marriage he did not claim Wisconsin as his residence, but gave Manila as his residence and Baltimore, Maryland, as the domicile of his former marriage.[34]

MacArthur failed to return to the United States or make his views known to the voters, and his candidacy made little headway. In the April 6, 1948, Wisconsin primary, Stassen supporters won nineteen of the 27 delegate seats; MacArthur took eight and Dewey none. Due to his political position, his labors, and his possession of Stassen's personal backing, Senator McCarthy should have been elected chairman of the delegation to the national convention in Philadelphia. Instead, Tom Coleman, with the assistance of aggressive young Melvin Laird and his mother, had Walter Kohler elected. Coleman was grooming Kohler to be the G.O.P. candidate for governor. Joe was irritated by the move, but he shrugged it off and smilingly agreed to become merely one of the delegates.[35]

In May Joe traveled to Oregon with Stassen to serve as the candidate's campaign manager. This was the last of a series of primaries, and many observers considered it crucial. Stassen's proposal to outlaw the Communist party, which contributed to his defeat at the hands of Dewey, was a position McCarthy concurred in. Joe was present during the famous nationwide radio debate between the two presidential aspirants as Stassen accused his opponent of a "soft policy toward Communism."[36]

After the loss in Oregon, preceded by defeats in New Hampshire and Ohio, Stassen's candidacy was dead. McCarthy played no significant role during the Republican convention and, like Coleman, remained relatively unenthusiastic about Dewey's nomination. (Truman would carry Wisconsin by 56,351 votes in November.)

Joe did take a keen interest in the framing of G.O.P. platform language about housing. The Republicans took the position that federal aid to states for slum clearance and low-rental housing should be extended only as a last resort, when private industry and state and local governments were unable to meet housing needs. Who exactly should decide when federal assistance was needed was deliberately left unclear.[37]

The Democratic platform relied much more heavily on the federal government to solve the housing problem and urged large-scale public housing, slum clearance, and increased rent controls.

Truman shocked and delighted the Democratic convention delegates by announcing in his acceptance speech that he was calling a special session of Congress, daring Republicans of the 80th Congress to pass legislation they said they favored.[38]

Two weeks later, in a message to the special session, the President called specifically for passage of the Taft-Ellender-Wagner Bill. "This is the bill we need. We need it now, not a year from now." He knew, of course, that the G.O.P. was sharply divided over the bill and that Jesse Wolcott would continue to block its passage in the House. His strategy was to embarrass the Republicans and publicize the distinction between their rhetoric and their record.[39]

G.O.P. leaders fumed over Truman's clever tactic and claimed that at least six months would be needed to consider the legislative package the President claimed could be passed in fifteen days. They asserted that under their control of Congress a million new dwelling units were under construction in a year, more than twice the number built while the Administration "was fumbling with the situation." For the sake of party unity, Taft agreed not to press for the Taft-Ellender-Wagner Bill during the brief midsummer session, but he vowed to reintroduce the bill in 1949. There remained the belief that some action on housing would be taken in 1948, perhaps in the form of short-range amendments to legislation passed in the recent regular session.[40]

Joe was dissatisfied with the Republican response to Truman's challenge. He saw in the special session another opportunity to pass a housing bill, perhaps bearing his name, and he simply ignored the determinations of the party's elder statesmen. On August 2 he sent a letter to Taft, with copies to each member of the Senate, calling for a new housing bill and making detailed suggestions for its contents. "In addition to being concerned over the vast number of people who are inadequately housed, we should also be deeply concerned over the health of the building industry inasmuch as a serious slump in building, which may well come if we fail to pass adequate housing legislation, might well be the beginning of a serious depression." He urged the immediate calling of a conference of congressional leaders "and those members of the Joint Housing Committee who have spent much time in a detailed study of the housing problem" to draft legislation. "I strongly feel that if this Congress adjourns without first having passed workable housing legislation, it will be an admission that we are incapable of solving our number-one domestic problem."[41]

Senator Tobey appointed Joe to a three-man subcommittee of the Banking and Currency Committee created to work out a compromise bill with counterparts from the House. The subcommittee returned with a proposal that contained several elements from the earlier Senate bill that Wolcott had stymied, but it deleted public housing and slum clearance (as well as aid to paraplegic veterans). Tobey and Flanders objected strongly, and with their support the full committee voted 7-5 to back the Senate's bill instead of the compromise.

In a tense Senate session on August 5 Joe offered an amendment to the Banking and Currency Committee's bill that embodied his subcommittee's proposal. (At one point he confessed, "I do not know the parliamentary rules too well, so I would ask the opinion of the Chair.") He explained the obstinacy of House Republicans and argued that the continued insistence by the Senate on its earlier bill would doom any housing legislation until the following year. "It will mean there will be thousands, perhaps millions of veterans who simply will not have a decent place in which to live. . . ."

Senator Tobey flew into a rage against McCarthy and House Republicans, and launched into an oratorical flight that included references to Lincoln and a discourse on the meaning of democracy.[42]

All of this intraparty warfare was exceedingly embarrassing to Taft. The next day, for the sake of party unity, he backed McCarthy's amendment, pointing to its many positive features and promising to offer legislation containing public housing and slum clearance in January.

Joe was elated and proceeded to warn colleagues that "a vote against the McCarthy amendment is a vote against any and all housing legislation. . . ." Tobey again fired off a blustery tirade against the Wisconsin senator, predicted victory for his cause, and bellowed the words of Admiral Farragut: "Damn the torpedoes. Full speed ahead."

McCarthy's amendment passed the Senate 48-36. Thirty-seven Republicans, all party regulars, were joined by eleven Democrats, nine of them Southerners, in support of the bill. The opposition came from twenty-four Democrats and twelve rebel Republicans. The next day, G.O.P. leaders (under heavy pressure from Taft) helped steer the measure through the House with a whopping vote of 352 to nine.[43]

The McCarthy-Wolcott bill contained many positive provisions designed to improve the housing situation. Down payments were lowered to 5 percent on homes costing less than $6,300, maximum mortgage terms were extended to 30 years, insurance companies were guaranteed a 2.75 percent return for investing in big rental projects, private loans by builders of low-cost apartment houses were guaranteed up to 90 percent (thereby aiding veterans' cooperatives) and loans for the construction of small homes were similarly guaranteed, prefabricated housing received new credit incentives, research was funded to improve building codes and standardize measurement of housing materials, and apartment houses receiving federal assistance were prohibited from discriminating against couples with children. New authorizations of government funds totaled $835,000,000.

Liberal critics charged immediately that private builders were the principal beneficiaries of the legislation, without mentioning the corresponding benefits to lower-income consumers. It should be noted that the bill contained a large number of proposals requested by President Truman in his special message to Congress of February 23, 1948. Federal aid to home builders was a well-established principle, long endorsed by both major parties. Liberal senator Robert F. Wagner was on record as saying, "We want private enterprise to do the largest possible share of the total housing job." It was Truman's Housing and Home Finance Agency administrator, Raymond M. Foley, who told a meeting of the National Association of Home Builders, "The chief activity of government in housing should be to aid and stimulate private enterprise in reduction of housing cost and in attack upon its problem areas."[44]

Truman signed the Housing Act of 1948 on August 10 because, he said, it would be of some help in meeting the housing shortage. But he called it "an emasculated housing bill" and asserted that Republicans had "deliberately neglected" large groups of poor people by failing to include public housing and slum clearance. Throughout the rest of his successful political campaign the President irresponsibly labeled all G.O.P. congressmen callous "messenger boys" for the real estate lobby and called the Housing Act "fake" and "phony." He was particularly abusive toward Taft, "a cold-hearted, cruel aristocrat." Thomas Dewey stuck to platitudes, and the many positive features of the new housing legislation went largely unheralded.[45]

Eight months later Senator Ellender reported to the Senate that the 1948 Act had been successful on a variety of fronts. But by this time all attention was on what became the Housing Act of 1949, which one historian has called "the major Fair Deal legislative triumph."[46]

Overall, Joe McCarthy received little attention for his industriousness in the field of housing. In Wisconsin, where housing was not a major issue, newspapers virtually ignored the junior senator's work. The state American Legion, which might have applauded his efforts on behalf of veterans, limited its commentary to criticism of his opposition to universal military training. What attention was paid to housing came largely from the *Madison Capital Times,* which linked McCarthy to the real estate lobby and branded his record "one of the most reactionary in the Senate." Evjue proudly reported that he had awarded Joe's entire voting record "an even zero."[47]

On January 5, 1949, the day Truman presented his Fair Deal message to the 81st Congress, administration Democrats introduced a bill in the Senate calling for the construction of 1,050,000 public housing units over a seven-year period, a five-year slum clearance and urban redevelopment program costing $1.5 billion, an appropriation of $250 million in loans for repair of rural housing, and an extensive housing research program. Taft, Flanders, Tobey, and other Republicans proposed a more modest public housing figure, and compromise was reached in the Senate Banking and Currency Committee, which reported a bill providing for the construction of 810,000 units over a six-year period. The bill had twenty-three sponsors by the time it reached the floor in mid-April, and it satisfied the leadership of both parties. Opposition stemmed from ultraconservative Republicans, led by Harry Cain and John Bricker.

Joe backed the bill from the start, but not uncritically. He objected to language that he feared would prevent the poor from obtaining access to public housing. And he criticized a farm housing section—"ridiculous to the point of being ludicrous"—that would appoint what he called a "political army" of county commissioners to aid low-income farmers and grant $500 to each submarginal farm for the installation of a toilet. "I lived on a farm for a number of years and that was not the principal need, as I recall." He declared himself in favor of banning racial and ethnic discrimination in public housing units, giving communities the right to vote upon local public housing and slum clearance projects, granting welfare agencies the authority to select public housing tenants, and prohibiting all government employees access to public housing. He moved three minor amendments to the bill and twice became so involved in prolonged squabbles that weary colleagues cried out, "Vote, vote." The bill passed on April 21, 57-13, with McCarthy's support.[48]

Despite frantic efforts by Congressman Wolcott and the real estate lobby, the House passed a similar bill in late June, 227-186, and conferees accepted the Senate figure of 810,000 public housing units. An elated President signed the bill into law on July 15. "I know this satisfaction is shared by the members of Congress of both political parties," he said, "and by the many private groups and individuals who have supported this legislation over the past four years against ill-founded opposition."[49]

In late February 1949, Joe called a press conference and announced the appearance of his first publication. It was a 37-page article entitled "Wanted: A Dollar's Worth of Housing for Every Dollar Spent" that appeared within a paper-bound booklet called *How to Own Your Own Home.* The publisher was the Lustron Corporation of Columbus, Ohio, manufacturer of all-steel prefabricated housing.

The beaming senator explained that the purpose of the 94-page booklet was to describe "in four-letter words" exactly what federal assistance was available to veterans and nonveterans and how to proceed to build or buy a home. Joe expressed pleasure at Lustron's willingness to publish this information, bringing the price down to 35 cents a copy. The first printing was 20,000 copies, he said, and the company hoped to sell half a million. He explained that while he wrote only the one article in the booklet, he "edited" the other material. He declined to reveal what he was paid for this service, saying only, "It's embarrassingly small. Besides, I have to split it with ten people who helped me."[50]

The article and booklet were forgotten for well over a year. In mid-June 1950, when McCarthy was world famous and under intense attack, it was revealed at a bankruptcy proceeding of the Lustron Corporation that the senator had received $10,000 for his article. Federal Receiver Clyde Foraker called the commissioning of the article "unethical," and referring to the sum paid to McCarthy added, "I'll bet he wouldn't have gotten it if he hadn't been a United States senator.[51]

Over the following two years, as McCarthy's star continued to rise and his reelection campaign neared, critics became increasingly desperate to discredit his reputation. Journalists and congressional committees looked into the history of the housing article and widely publicized several serious charges against the senator which historians have accepted as factual. A careful reconstruction of the story, however, based primarily upon congressional hearings, reveals a far different picture.

Shortly after Joe became a member of the Joint Committee on Housing in July 1947, he suggested that the committee create a publication that would explain to veterans, in nontechnical language, how they might take advantage of the laws designed to help them buy or build a home. The committee agreed on the importance of the proposal but failed to imple-ment it. On his own, Joe hired a married couple to write what he thought would be a low-priced paperback book. When this effort proved unsatisfac-tory, the senator decided to prepare something himself.

By early 1948 he had completed an introduction and a single chapter, which he sent to an assortment of publishers, seeking a contract. Editors rejected the proposal largely on the ground that the book would be too specialized and that the senator's suggested one-dollar price offered insuffi-cient profit.

In mid-August, with the Housing Act on the books, Joe proceeded to update and expand his manuscript. He contacted Raymond Foley, chief of the Housing and Home Finance Agency, and sent over a newly employed research assistant, Jean Kerr, to gather information and acquaint herself with the subject of housing. Miss Kerr was referred to Walter Moore Royal, Jr., a special assistant to the director of information, and the two of them soon developed an outline that was submitted to McCarthy. Over the next several weeks, Royal and about a dozen other H.H.F.A. experts reviewed three different drafts of what became a lengthy article instead of a book. Miss Kerr also consulted with officials of the Veteran's Administration and the Federal Housing Administration about particular issues.

Numerous people, including Miss Kerr, an experienced writer, no doubt contributed to the finished product. But Joe wrote or at least dictated much of it: the corny opening paragraphs are clearly his, as no doubt is one 134-word sentence (on page 43 of the Lustron booklet). He was seen making minor revisions in the manuscript until almost the day it was published. When grilled about the question during a 1952 deposition, Joe at first claimed to be the sole author but later softened this to contend that every line "went through my hands."

Foley and Royal were enthusiastic about the project, recognizing the genuine need for such a publication. Both strongly denied later allegations of improper conduct. "It is the firm policy of the Housing and Home Finance Agency to furnish information and data on housing matters in response to a request from any member of Congress," Foley stated in 1951. Royal noted that his office regularly provided similar assistance. "We do it every day for newspapers, trade journals, magazine writers, book writers, and who not." The explanations were persuasive, and formal charges were never brought against the officials.

Both Foley and Royal understood that McCarthy's manuscript would be offered without charge to national magazines. It was, and *Life, Colliers,* and the *Saturday Evening Post,* among others, rejected it.

In October 1948, Joe met Carl G. Strandlund, president of Lustron, at a racetrack. A short time later, the senator sent his manuscript to Strandlund and invited the corporation to publish it. The piece was warmly endorsed by Lorenzo Semple, a vice-president, and R. Harold Denton, the director for market development, and Strandlund accepted the offer.

McCarthy was delighted with the terms of the contract negotiated with Semple. The corporation planned to place his article within a booklet costing only 35 cents. He was to receive $10,000—a guarantee of ten cents a copy for 100,000 copies—and was obligated to keep his contribution up to date until 1952. Joe requested the $10,000 figure, for at the moment he was under pressure to beef up his collateral with the Appleton State Bank for an investment account that required 120 percent of margin.

The corporation proceeded to hire a writer named Maron J. Simon to prepare the rest of what became the Lustron booklet. He was paid $2,000 for his services and also received assistance from the Housing and Home Finance Agency.

Joe fumed over Denton's decision to place some of Simon's material ahead of his own in the booklet's format. He refused to let a word of his piece be altered. And he demanded that his name appear on the cover. (It did, twice.) There were few things in his life Joe was as proud of as the Lustron booklet. In 1952, while under severe attack on its account, he called it "an excellent, excellent booklet, one badly needed."

Lustron widely advertised the publication in 1949. *Architectural Forum* reported:

> The unique feature . . . is its clear, thorough account of home financing through FHA and VA loans. It tells in simplest terms how much one can borrow, how to go about borrowing it and what the terms of repayment will be. There are also several sensible chapters on points to look for in choosing a house and neighborhood and points to look out for in closing a deal. In addition, a chapter by Senator Joe McCarthy, vice chairman of the Joint Congressional Committee on Housing, sizes up the housing problem as a national headache, with hints on how the law may be applied as a remedy.

The corporation received over 10,000 requests for the booklet and distributed 13,662. Future sales were curtailed by Lustron's mounting financial difficulties.

After Lustron's bankruptcy in mid-1950, McCarthy critics claimed that the housing booklet was an advertisement for Lustron homes and that the senator degraded his office by participating, for money, in a commercial venture. There is a grain of truth in the charge, for the booklet promoted Lustron homes. But the sales pitch appeared almost entirely within the last fourteen pages; the thrust of the booklet was educational. More to the point, McCarthy's article was free of commercial overtones. Joe declared accurately in 1950, "There is nothing in my material which in any way could be considered a promotion for any particular prefabricated house or any other type of housing. It deals strictly with general information which I consider of value to young men trying to buy or build a house."

It was also charged that the $10,000 payment was "influence money," that Carl Strandlund was in effect buying a senator to look after his interests in Washington and see to it that the RFC loans Lustron depended on continued to pour forth at a time when the corporation was financially unhealthy.

Strandlund was attracted to McCarthy's article in part, as he freely admitted, because the senator was an acknowledged authority on housing and was vice-chairman of the joint committee. The corporation proudly trumpeted Joe's credentials on the booklet's cover (at the senator's insistence) and throughout the text. And Strandlund, like any other business— many with dealings in Washington, was not averse to having political influence; indeed, he hired ex-Congressman Frank Sundstrom, a former member of the joint committee, as Lustron's sales manager and placed him on the board of directors. But no one was able to prove the McCarthy ever directly lifted a finger on Lustron's behalf. Joe gloated to a congressional committee in 1952, "I understand that even though your investigators have been very painstaking in their attempts, they have been unable to find even a telephone call I made to anyone on behalf of Lustron." Indeed, during debates over the Housing Act of 1949, Joe opposed legislation favored by Democratic Senator Burnet Maybank, chairman of the Banking and Currency Committee, that would have benefited Lustron. And Strandlund could hardly have counted on McCarthy to influence the Administration on his corporation's behalf, for Joe's contract was signed ten days after Truman's smashing victory at the polls.

Strandlund denied accusations that he had boasted publicly of having friends in high places and attributed the rumor to an RFC director who, he contended persuasively, was part of a conspiracy to take over the Lustron Corporation. However that may be, no evidence appeared linking McCarthy with Lustron after publication of the housing booklet.

Some critics argued that the $10,000 figure was exorbitant and in itself indirectly implied bribery. "The payment represented something of a new world's record in the literary field," Jack Anderson wrote in 1952, "$1.43 a word, 43 cents more than the previous record set by Winston Churchill when he sold his war memoirs." In fact, the figure represented about 14 percent of Lustron's advertising budget for the month of November 1948. Moreover, it should be repeated that no one, including Strandlund, denied that the reputation of the author was as important as the article itself. One would expect to pay more for, say, a piece on foreign affairs by Sen. Arthur Vandenberg than by an unknown. How much more is a negotiable question and need not on its face imply anything, within reasonable limits. The Lustron Corporation was completely confident that it could sell at least 100,000 copies of the booklet; it had a mailing list of some 300,000 names of people who had already requested housing information. Justifiably, it can be argued, McCarthy did not think ten cents a copy an exorbitant royalty.

(Joe did not split the $10,000 fee, as journalists discovered and as he admitted in a 1952 deposition. Miss Kerr, he explained, was on his payroll, and the federal housing officials were simply doing their duty. The press conference assertions about splitting the fee and having "edited" the whole of the Lustron booklet were typical McCarthy blarney, born of the exuberance of the moment.)

But there was also a report that Strandlund had cashed checks for McCarthy at racetracks and had torn them up, boasting that he usually did that for the senator. The story was investigated thoroughly; Joe cooperated with one committee and submitted a canceled check that corrected a faulty recollection by Strandlund.

In the spring of 1949, Strandlund bumped into McCarthy briefly during the Preakness, at Pimlico. As usual, Joe was broke from extravagant betting and was borrowing money as fast as he could to place even more bets. When others in his party ran out of funds, Joe asked Strandlund if he would cash a check for $50, and the executive complied. Joe returned a short time later, again broke, and asked if Strandlund would cash a second check for $100. Strandlund agreed and tore up the first check. Joe's second check cleared the bank, and Strandlund forgot the matter until it was brought to the attention of investigators more than a year later by Merl Young, a shady figure Strandlund blamed in large part for the downfall of Lustron. Young also supplied the alleged comment by Strandlund that journalists soon turned into a direct quote: "I do that quite often for McCarthy."

There was nothing illegal or unethical about the small, utterly insignificant racetrack transaction. But anti-McCarthy forces made much of it in the early 1950s, repeatedly portraying the scene of a sleazy businessman slipping money into the pockets of an immoral senator.

Was Lustron dependent upon McCarthy's political influence to continue its federal loans? It is true that the Housing Act of 1948 authorized the RFC to make loans to prefab manufacturers totaling up to $50 million and that Lustron received $12 million after the bill was signed. It is also true that McCarthy urged passage of a housing bill specifically to assist the builders of prefabricated housing. But this was before Joe knew Strandlund and before he had begun serious work on his manuscript. Joe had long favored prefabricated housing, a position he shared with the President and a majority of Congress. Moreover, of the $37.5 million in loans Lustron obtained from the RFC, $25.5 million had already been received before the Housing Act became law.

In summary, convincing bribery charges must be made of much stronger stuff, and it is no wonder that such allegations against McCarthy were ultimately abandoned by investigators.

Joe also came under fire for having signed the booklet contract at a time when Lustron was allegedly losing $550,000 a week. In fact, these "losses" were start-up costs plus interest to the RFC. The plant would begin production in June 1949—ahead of schedule. RFC officials monitored the corporation's books with extreme care. (They were fully aware of the $10,000 payment to McCarthy. "It was right out in the open and part of our company business," Strandlund later testified.) By every indication, the Lustron Corporation was in excellent financial shape in November 1948 and, in McCarthy's words, "It had the possibility of becoming one of the largest and most successful manufacturers of prefabricated housing." During its brief operation the plant produced more than 2,500 houses, 700 in a single week.

But wasn't the corporation under investigation by a committee McCarthy sat on when the contract was signed? William P. Rogers, chief counsel of the Investigation Subcommittee on Expenditures in the Executive Departments did write a letter to an RFC official on November 5, 1948, requesting information and implying that Lustron loans were being based on purchase orders the corporation could not fill. But this was a staff memorandum, as opposed to a formal investigation, and McCarthy was presumably unaware of its existence. The RFC continued to lend money to Lustron until August 1949. No evidence supports the allegation that McCarthy attempted to delay an investigation of Lustron.

It was also charged that since the Banking and Currency Committee had jurisdiction over the RFC, McCarthy should not have profited personally from a recipient of its funds. This is debatable, at best. If all congressmen were that scrupulous, their outside incomes would fall sharply. (Senators earned more than three-quarters of a million dollars in outside income in 1976 just for speeches delivered before lobbying groups, trade unions, charities, and educational organizations. Wisconsin Democrat William Proxmire, McCarthy's successor, received $23,500.) And it isn't that McCarthy "took money" from Lustron, as Sen. William Benton was to contend; he sold the corporation a carefully researched and useful manuscript.

In February 1950 the RFC foreclosed the mortgage on the Lustron plant amid charges of scandal. Whatever the facts of the matter—and they remain highly debatable—it should be emphasized that Senator McCarthy played a very small and poorly understood role in the corporation's existence.

If all the above charges were insufficient to blacken Joe's reputation as a housing expert, hostile newspapers devoted shrill headlines in 1951 and 1952 to a story that McCarthy had once been involved in a wild dice game at a Columbus, Ohio, hotel and "welshed" on a $5,500 gambling debt to a Columbus builder. The source of the story was a Lustron competitor, Robert Byers, Sr., who also claimed, wrongly, that a former employee of his, Clark Wiedman, had co-authorized the Lustron booklet. During the investigation of these charges, Byers was committed to a mental institution— which Joe found a fine joke on his accusers.

The investigation revealed that in March 1949 Joe flew to Columbus to appear at two dinners and deliver a speech on current housing legislation before an audience of real estate dealers, bankers, and government housing officials. Byers paid him $500 and expenses. (Jack Anderson referred to "a business flirtation" that profited McCarthy "at least $1,000" plus "whiskey and entertainment.")

At a party in Joe's hotel room on the evening of March 20, a dice game started. Clark Wiedman later testified that the game was simply a demonstration prompted by an inquiry from his wife. It was "horseplay" with largely "fictitious sums of money" and did not involve the senator, who was in and out of the room. Late in the evening, Wiedman stated, Bob Byers, Jr., had won what represented $2,400. To persuade his guests to go home, Joe urged Byers to roll a last time, double or nothing, saying he would cover the bet. Byers threw the dice, lost, and retired. Wiedman said that in a conversation he had recently had with McCarthy, the senator could barely remember the incident. Joe had also told Wiedman that he did not know much about dice (which was blarney).

Whatever the precise facts were, the story is inconsequential. McCarthy critics made much of it solely to hurt the senator in public opinion polls and at the voting booth. Sen. Thomas Hennings, a prominent Democratic member of the committee investigating this and similar charges against McCarthy, commented, "I say, if a man wants to engage in gambling games and pays a debt or does not pay it, that is not a matter the United States Senate is really concerned with."[52]

MALMEDY

By early 1949 Joe was worried by the fact that his strenuous efforts with sugar and housing legislation had earned him little or no public attention in Wisconsin. State newspapers outside the Appleton area seemed to either ignore him or publicize Evjue's charges. And with Democrats in control of Congress after the recent elections, he was fearful of being shunted to an insignificant committee, denying him a forum in which to enhance his image. He appealed to Republican Senator Hugh Butler of the Committee on Committees, who tried to persuade colleagues to yield a committee seat temporarily to McCarthy. "We are as anxious as you are," Butler wrote, "to get you in a position so you can accomplish what you want to up there in Wisconsin." But the Nebraska legislator was unsuccessful, and this was no doubt a reflection of the reputation McCarthy had earned within the Senate in his first two years.[1]

Joe was still personally popular. Off the Senate floor he never stopped smiling and backslapping, and his personal generosity was widely known and appreciated. But McCarthy had too often violated the genteel mores of the Senate by launching personal attacks on colleagues and showing disrespect for seniority. His aggressiveness and unpredictability disturbed many senators, among them South Carolina's aristocratic Burnet R. Maybank. When Maybank became chairman of the Senate Banking and Currency Committee, he insisted on "bumping" McCarthy, telling Democratic

Majority Leader Scott Lucas that he would not serve as a member of the committee alongside the Wisconsin "troublemaker." Joe's worst fears were realized when he was assigned to the Committee on the District of Columbia, the least prestigious of all Senate committees. With this and a seat on the Expenditures in the Executive Departments Committee, McCarthy's opportunities for attention appeared extremely limited. Joe told Sen. Robert Taft that his assignments "will be extremely embarrassing to me in my state" and complained of an "awfully foul deal."[2]

A year earlier Joe had become interested in the postwar repatriation of German prisoners of war, an issue likely to carry appeal in Wisconsin. By his estimation, some 640,000 Germans remained captive in Russia, despite a 1947 agreement in which the Soviet Union promised prompt repatriation. In early 1948 McCarthy introduced an amendment to the European Recovery Act, approved by powerful Sen. Arthur H. Vandenberg, requiring the return of all war prisoners by the end of the year as a precondition for economic assistance. In a letter written a few months later he went a step farther, calling for the repudiation of the Yalta and Potsdam agreements, which had sanctioned the use of war prisoners as reparations, a principle "which is repulsive to all American ideals."[3]

In early 1949, as a member of the Expenditures in the Executive Departments Committee, McCarthy became intensely involved in another case involving Germans—this time a number of SS men convicted of a mass atrocity against American troops and Belgian citizens in the vicinity of Malmedy, Belgium.

When Joe's college chum, attorney Tom Korb, came to Washington in May, on loan at McCarthy's request from the Harnischfager Corporation of Milwaukee to help organize and streamline the senator's office, he found Joe completely committed to the truth of reports that the United States Army was responsible for torturing Malmedy confessions out of SS men after the war and of giving them a sham trial. Korb strongly urged his old friend to drop the matter. It was politically unwise; no one in Wisconsin—or anywhere else—sympathized with Nazis. And it made no sense for a freshman senator to take on the Army. But Joe dismissed the objections out of hand. The issue, he argued passionately, had to do with simple justice and the integrity of America's image overseas. After a heated argument, Korb shook his head and went about his business. There was no moving McCarthy when he thought he was right.[4]

On December 16, 1944, German troops began a last-ditch effort to crush the advancing Allied armies, a desperate drive known as the Battle of the Bulge. One of the German units leading the penetration of Allied lines was the First SS Panzer Regiment Leibstandarte Adolph Hitler. It was fresh from Russian combat and was led by brilliant and ruthless 29-year-old Lt. Col. Joachim Peiper. On December 17 Peiper's men swiftly overpowered a convoy of American troops about two miles south of Malmedy and herded scores of disarmed survivors into an open field. A few minutes later eight machine guns fired into the group, and before the Nazis were through, 83 Americans lay dead. The "Malmedy massacre" was quickly recognized as among the most heinous offenses committed by the German Army.

Survivors attributed the massacre to the First Panzer Regiment, and after Germany's defeat about a thousand members of the regiment were collected from across Europe and sent to a war-crime unit near Zuffenhausen for interrogation. In late December 1945, over 400 of the prisoners were taken to a German prison in the small town of Schwabisch Hall, near Stuttgart, for more intensive questioning.

At Schwabisch Hall American personnel learned of further atrocities in the Malmedy area: within approximately three weeks German troops had murdered more than 500 soldiers and civilians at thirteen different locations. Seventy-four SS men were charged with the crimes and sent to Dachau in mid-May 1946 for trial. Eight weeks later the court unanimously found all but one of the accused guilty (a French national was turned over to French authorities) and sentenced 43 to death.

The matter largely dropped from public view until mid-December 1948, when the National Council for Prevention of War issued a press release that reverberated throughout the Western world. The council had been founded in 1921 by Frederick J. Libby, a determined pacifist, tireless crusader for peace, and a longtime advocate of American isolationism. Libby and his small, Quaker-run organization strongly opposed American involvement in the Second World War (even after Pearl Harbor), and when the fighting ceased they devoted their energies toward international reconciliation. Neither pro-Nazi nor pro-Communist, the council took a special interest in providing Germany with food and hope.[5]

The press release contained charges ascribed to Judge Edward L. Van Roden of the Orphan's Court of Delaware County, Pennsylvania, who had recently returned from Germany where he served as a member of a three-man commission, headed by Justice Gordon Simpson of the Texas supreme court, created by Army Secretary Kenneth Royall to investigate allegations of American brutality against the Malmedy prisoners at Schwabisch Hall. Van Roden told of a variety of grisly tortures and threats employed to extract false confessions. The council sent hundreds of copies of the press release to newspapers, magazines, bar associations, and members of Congress, and called for an investigation. Soon the Federal Council of Churches, the *Christian Century* magazine, and the American Civil Liberties Union echoed the appeal for a full-scale probe.[6]

On January 6, 1949, Army Secretary Royall responded by making public portions of the report of the Simpson Commission, which had studied 139 capital cases, including the remaining twelve Malmedy death sentences. (Gen. Lucius D. Clay, American military governor for Germany, it was revealed, had earlier commuted 31 of the original 43 death sentences.) The commission recommended commutation of all twelve remaining Malmedy death sentences to life imprisonment on the grounds that the massacre had occurred "in the heat of one of the most ferocious battles of the war" and that some confessions by SS men were obtained by "mock trials," casting doubt upon the entire legal proceedings. The public also learned that the Simpson Commission was created in July 1948 in response to a petition before the United States Supreme Court submitted in May by Lt. Col. Willis M. Everett, Jr., of Atlanta, who was chief defense counsel for the Malmedy prisoners.[7]

Time magazine devoted an article to Everett, revealing that he had been quietly pleading his case for two years and describing his Supreme Court petition as "an incredible report . . . which read like a record of Nazi atrocities." Everett charged that United States interrogators at Schwabisch Hall kept German prisoners in dark, solitary confinement at near starvation rations for up to six months, applied such tortures as the driving of burning matches under prisoners' fingernails and administered beatings resulting in broken jaws and arms and permanently damaged testicles. He also contended that false confessions were obtained through "mock trials," at which "the . . . plaintiff would see before him a long table . . . with candles burning at both ends . . . and a crucifix in the center. . . . The Germans were informed or led to believe that they were being tried by Americans for violations of international law. At the end of the table would be the prosecutor, who would read the charges, yell and scream at these eighteen- and twenty-year-old plaintiffs and attempt to force confessions from them . . ." *Time* concluded that Everett's findings "would remain as a terrible warning that, at times, the judges can be conquered by the forces of evil they are supposed to try."[8]

By now a storm was brewing over the unanswered charges. Two resolutions were introduced in the Senate calling for an investigation; one of the authors, Republican William Langer of North Dakota (an isolationist, pacifist, and good friend of the National Council for Prevention of War) reviewed the record of the American military government court at Dachau and contended that it "may well turn out to be, upon investigation, one of the most deplorable miscarriages of justice in history." Two officials of the Federal Council of Churches visited the Attorney General seeking a review of the charges. A Democratic senator and two House members called upon Secretary Royall and obtained a 60-day reprieve for the twelve prisoners sentenced to death. Newspapers in Germany carried blazing headlines about American atrocities. Langer gave another speech on the Senate floor, this time warning, "It must be clear now to the American people that there can be no hope of peace whatever, until this government abandons the role of hate-happy hangman and restores some semblance of sanity to our relation with the vanquished peoples in central Europe."[9]

An article by Judge Van Roden then appeared in *The Progressive,* a fervidly liberal magazine published in Madison, Wisconsin, including some of the most shocking charges yet revealed. All but two of the 139 Germans investigated by the Simpson Commission, he wrote, "had been kicked in the testicles beyond repair." "Our investigators would put a black hood over the accused's head and then punch him in the face with brass knuckles, kick him, and beat him with a rubber hose." One eighteen-year-old Malmedy defendant had hanged himself after reaching the sixteenth page of a forced confession; Germans in nearby cells heard him mutter, "I will not utter another lie." In another instance an interrogator dressed as a Catholic priest, heard the confession of a prisoner in his cell, declared absolution, and then urged, "Sign whatever the investigators ask you to sign. It will get you your freedom. Even though it's false, I can give you absolution now in advance for the lie you'd tell." Van Roden angrily called for an investigation, declaring, "The American investigators who committed the atrocities in the name of American justice and under the American flag are going scot free."[10]

On March 2 *The New York Times* ran a lengthy piece on the Malmedy cases, noting that Everett was drafting a petition to the International Court of Justice to save the lives of the twelve condemned prisoners. The article contained lengthy interviews with Van Roden and Herbert Strong, an associate defense counsel at the Malmedy trial, who complained of a lack of time to prepare a case and confirmed several reports of abuse to prisoners.[11]

Three days later the *Times* carried news of another study of the Malmedy affair, this time by the Army's Administration of Justice Review Board. The three-man board, consisting of Col. J. I. Harbaugh, Jr., Col. John M. Raymond, and a Harvard political scientist, Carl J. Friedrich, was asked by

General Clay in May 1948 to investigate Colonel Everett's charges. It concluded, among other things, that American interrogators held "mock trials" in eight or ten instances and occasionally employed threats, inducements, and stratagems to obtain confessions, and it determined that some physical force was used on recalcitrant suspects. The board told of an affidavit from a prison dentist saying that he treated fifteen or twenty Malmedy prisoners at Schwabisch Hall for injuries to the mouth and jaw, apparently inflicted by blows.

On the other hand, the board found that the defense attorneys had been given ample time before the trial to prepare their case. It also dismissed most of the specific charges of physical brutality, noting that almost all of them had first appeared in affidavits written a year and a half after the trial. Why had the defense failed to bring the crimes to the attention of the court? the board wondered. One prisoner who testified at the trial and made no mention of mistreatment later claimed to have been kicked and beaten in the face and abdomen.[12]

Reporters were soon summoned to a press conference by the Society for the Prevention of World War III, headed by writer Mark Van Doren. Maj. Dwight Fanton and Morris Elowitz, two major figures in the prosecution of the Malmedy prisoners, denied that force, brutality, or improper methods of any sort were used at Schwabisch Hall, and the society sent a cable to General Clay calling for immediate execution of the twelve death sentences.[13]

General Clay had promised to reconsider the sentences in light of reports by the Simpson Commission and the Administration of Justice Review Board, and in late March he reaffirmed the death sentences of six of the twelve prisoners and commuted the remainder to life imprisonment. The general clearly accepted at least some of the brutality charges. He commuted the sentence of a first lieutenant who signed a confession that he had ordered American prisoners shot. Corroborating testimony consisted of eight other confessions, seven from coaccused SS men. Clay believed the lieutenant guilty but feared that all of the confessions, now repudiated, were obtained by "improper methods." Army Secretary Royall ordered a stay of execution of the six until more of the facts of the case were made known by Congressional inquiry.[14]

The uproar over Malmedy earned the attention of members of the Senate Armed Services Committee, the Senate Judiciary Committee, and Joe McCarthy. Joe's initial interest may have been political; Appleton newspaperman John Riedl later told friends that he had advised the senator to enter the case as a way of bolstering his sagging political fortunes. If true, it was a miscalculation for Malmedy was almost completely ignored by the Wisconsin press. At any rate, McCarthy's concern quickly rose above his own political considerations and assumed characteristics of a personal crusade against the forces of evil.[15]

The Special Investigation Subcommittee of the Expenditures Committee had recently investigated the case of Ilse Koch of Buchenwald infamy, and Joe argued that it should assume authority in the Malmedy case. The Armed Services Committee was asked if it was planning an investigation, and when the reply was negative McCarthy and other subcommittee members voted unanimously to conduct hearings. The Judiciary Committee appeared satisfied with the arrangement. But suddenly Democratic Senator Millard E. Tydings of Maryland, chairman of the Armed Services Committee, objected and claimed jurisdiction. Without even notifying McCarthy's subcommittee, Tydings swiftly appointed a subcommittee of his own, chaired by Republican Raymond E. Baldwin of Connecticut, and publicly announced a formal investigation.[16]

Tydings was responding to pressure from the Pentagon (or so McCarthy said later) and from Senator Baldwin himself. On the Senate floor in late January Baldwin had revealed that one of the prosecutors in the Malmedy case was a longtime acquaintance. This "young man in the state of Connecticut" had strongly denied allegations of brutality and impropriety and argued that previous investigatory bodies had ignored the prosecution staff. He sent Baldwin a request for a probe that would permit the other side of the story to be heard. Baldwin expressed warm support for his constituent and his colleagues and dismissed charges against them as "groundless." "Mr. President, these men were in the performance of their duty, they were dealing with one war crime which is the one in which our nationals were involved, our own soldiers, our own boys in uniform, men who now lie beneath the sod in France and Belgium, and have no one to speak in their behalf."[17]

Frederick J. Libby learned that Baldwin's "young man" was actually Maj. Dwight F. Fanton of the war-crimes branch of the Office of the Judge Advocate General, the officer who had direct supervision over the interrogators at Schwabisch Hall when the Malmedy prisoners were questioned. Moreover, Fanton was a member of Baldwin's law firm, a fact the National Council for Prevention of War presented to the Armed Services Committee and the press.

McCarthy was outraged by Tydings' tactics and Libby's disclosure and told reporters that the Armed Services Committee was planning a "whitewash." Baldwin offered to withdraw but decided to remain following a vote of confidence by the full committee. As a peace offering to McCarthy, both the Judiciary and Expenditures Committees were invited to send an observer to the hearings. Joe accepted immediately, fully intending not to be a silent observer.[18]

On the face of things, McCarthy had good reason to be suspicious of the new three-man subcommittee. A Democrat had appointed a Republican chairman. All three senators, curiously, were freshmen. Even more to the point was the fact that an officer named Ralph Shumacker, who replaced Fanton at Schwabisch Hall and later served with the prosecution staff at the Dachau trial, was a close personal friend of subcommittee member Estes Kefauver and a former member of the senator's law firm. Thus the subcommittee appeared deliberately stacked in favor of the Army, and an impartial, objective investigation seemed improbable if not impossible.[19]

But the subcommittee's initial appearance was deceiving. Baldwin had twice been governor of Connecticut and had recently announced his intention to resign from the Senate to accept appointment to the Connecticut supreme court. He was a moderate Republican who had strongly urged support for the Marshall Plan. Sen. Scott Lucas accurately described him as "a gentleman, of the old school . . . courteous, kind, tolerant, and fair, one whose integrity could not be questioned." It was clear from the start that Baldwin was extremely skeptical of the charges by SS men against American personnel, but he was to make good his repeatedly declared intention to pursue the facts of the highly complex Malmedy case with objectivity and thoroughness.[20]

Democrat Estes Kefauver of Tennessee, 45, had served in the House for ten years before being elected to the Senate in 1948 and was widely admired for his soft-spoken liberalism. He chose to play virtually no role in the Malmedy hearings, rarely being in attendance. At one point he confessed that he had read only portions of the transcripts of earlier sessions.[21]

The third member, Wyoming Democrat Lester C. Hunt, 56, was a onetime governor of his state who had recently entered the Senate. He was often preoccupied with other committee assignments and was to be of marginal importance in the work of the Baldwin subcommittee.[22]

The counsel was retired Marine Colonel Joseph M. Chambers, a Congressional Medal of Honor winner who would share the bulk of the subcommittee's labors with Baldwin and prove himself perceptive and intelligent.

McCarthy was assisted in his study of the Malmedy case by attorneys Francis Flanagan and Howell J. Hatcher of the Expenditures Committee staff. Joe read the reports of the Simpson Commission and the Administration of Justice Review Board, Van Roden's article in *The Progressive,* and

Everett's petition to the Supreme Court, which contained many affidavits from German prisoners alleging brutality and deception. The National Council for Prevention of War soon sent him statements from two German bishops and other materials confirming the alleged abuse of German prisoners. Colonel Everett telephoned, deeply impressing Joe with his sincerity. And a few letters arrived from witnesses to events at Schwabisch Hall. The evidence the senator saw was almost entirely one-sided, and Joe quickly absorbed it, accepting every assertion as fact, steeling his early conviction that the Army had committed crimes that were a national disgrace. He did not read trial transcripts or interview any American military personnel connected with the Malmedy case. And he entered the hearings firmly convinced that the subcommittee conducting them was part of a conspiracy to whitewash the entire matter.[23]

On April 18, 1949, the first of twenty-nine hearings began in Washington with the swearing-in of Army Secretary Kenneth Royall. McCarthy dominated the session almost immediately, explaining profusely the origins of his interest in the Malmedy case. He did not want guilty Nazis to go unpunished, he assured his audience. "As to the gruesomeness, there is nothing that any of us can recall in recorded history that approaches the unwarranted type of mass slaughter that occurred in Malmedy, and we always like to see the men responsible brought to justice." Indeed, "it is entirely possible that some incompetent prosecutor, by using illegal methods, may be responsible for some of these guilty men going free." His concern focused, he said, on the ways convictions were obtained. "We have been accusing the Russians of using force, physical violence, and have accused them of using mock trials in cells in the dark of night, and now we have an Army report that comes out and says we have done all the things that the Russians were ever accused of doing, but they are all right because it created the right psychological effect to get the necessary confessions." Joe returned to this theme repeatedly during the hearings: the United States had used Russian methods to have its way, which shamed us before the world, damaged such efforts as the Marshall Plan, and aided the expansion of international Communism. At one point, in a letter to Baldwin, he declared, "I think this is one of the most important investigations which the Senate has conducted for some years. I think it doubly important in view of the billions of dollars we are spending in Europe to create goodwill toward this Nation and the amount of money and effort we are expending to sell to the peoples of the world democracy and American concepts of justice." He often expressed his desire to court-martial guilty American interrogators and prosecutors.[24]

When Lt. Col. Burton F. Ellis of the Judge Advocate General's Department took the stand, Joe bristled. Ellis had been the chief prosecutor at the Malmedy trials, and he defended his conduct and that of his subordinates forcefully and persuasively. There had been no physical violence at Schwabisch Hall, he declared; the German affidavits were products of desperate men. He contended that the mock trials, actually called the "Schnell procedure" by interrogators, were rarely held (six or seven times during the questioning of over 400 prisoners), produced little evidence, and made no difference at the trial.

Joe quickly sailed into the witness, rudely interrupting Senators Hunt and Kefauver when they got in his way. He showed that Ellis had been without experience in criminal law before entering the Army and proceeded to assault his reputation as an attorney. At one point he said, "I have been a judge so long, and have tried enough criminal cases that it makes me rather sick down inside to hear you testify what you think is proper or improper." At times Ellis was not even permitted to reply to a loaded question or a barb. "When I am talking," Joe growled, "if you won't talk, then I won't talk when you are talking." When Senator Hunt suggested that McCarthy ease off a bit in his attack, Joe threatened to return to the Expenditures Committee and commence an immediate investigation of his own.[25]

This encounter was a forecast of what was to come, for McCarthy would dominate each of the sessions he attended and verbally bludgeon anyone who disagreed with either his methods or his conclusions. At times his questioning was extremely impressive; these hearings reveal the flash and thunder of Joe's legal mind as no other source. But his emotions frequently overcame him, and the proceedings degenerated sometimes into shouting matches.

The extremely friendly senator who met you in the cafeteria or hallway with a grin and a joke became a rough, insensitive, almost brutal figure in the hearing room. Lawyers, of course, were used to playing one role in the courtroom and another behind the scenes, out of the sight of clients. But Baldwin and his colleagues and staff were shocked by the intensity of McCarthy's transformation once a hearing was called to order. And what did the senator have to gain personally in this case? Who could explain his passion? Certainly no one at the time suggested he was cynical. That would come later.

Joe's sinus difficulties became acute during the hearings, and he was forced to report to a local hospital several times for painful minor surgery. This did little to improve his temperament, of course. But McCarthy's

closest friends knew that the source of his often extreme behavior lay
deeper, involving his susceptibility to belief, in his essentially naive and
romantic approach to life, as Tom Korb was to put it.

Joe's mind was made up about the Malmedy case. He thought he
understood perfectly the nature of the Russian-like crimes committed in
the guise of American justice and knew essentially who was guilty—even
before all the evidence was in. And he was determined to step on anybody
who thought otherwise.

Col. John M. Raymond, who headed the Administration of Justice
Review Board, did not turn out to be friendly to McCarthy's position. He
defended the use of mock trials and observed, "I think that many of the
statements in all the affidavits submitted by these Germans are grossly
exaggerated." Joe tore into his credentials as an attorney, pointed to glaring
omissions in the board's lineup of witnesses, and concluded by labeling the
board's report "completely incomplete."[26]

When the subcommittee invited an American survivor of the Malmedy
massacre to appear, McCarthy became incensed. "On the face of it, this
would appear to be an attempt to put those of us who feel this thing should
be investigated into the position of appearing to defend the actions of these
German storm troopers—which we don't." The move was "completely
inexcusable," "entirely improper," "part of a Roman holiday."[27]

On April 29 Joe brought a witness of his own to testify, a court reporter
who worked with the interrogators at Schwabisch Hall. He told of seeing
an interrogator slap and knee a prisoner once or twice, reported seeing
nooses placed around prisoners' necks, and said that he was told of a mock
hanging. Only two other witnesses out of the 108 who testified (excluding
prisoners themselves) mentioned similar incidents, and they were far less
dramatic. The court reporter's testimony, while never fully rebutted, was
depreciated considerably by many other witnesses.[28]

Judge Gordon Simpson, chairman of the Simpson Commission, dealt
unexpected damage to McCarthy's claims. The judge was eager to defend
the prosecution team at Schwabisch Hall. "I found an honorable and
devoted group of officers when I went over there to investigate these
things, people who wanted to do what was right." He and his colleagues
had verified the existence of mock trials, Simpson said, but he called
attention to the fact that the prosecution had openly admitted at the trial
that this technique was employed. The commission had found no evidence
of inhumane or brutal methods used at Schwabisch Hall or that anyone had
masqueraded as a priest. Simpson scoffed at the charge that prisoners'

testicles had been irreparably damaged, labeling it "absurd." "The affidavits made by the accused after convictions," he warned, " . . . must obviously be received with a great deal of caution. . . ."

Joe flew into Simpson, on occasion exaggerating evidence and loading questions with presumptions that bolstered his own views. He was particularly furious about the legal standards used at the Dachau trial. Simpson pointed out that the rules of evidence included hearsay, a departure from American standards that was employed in the Nuremberg trials. Joe shouted, "Should we adopt Hitler's rules of evidence or follow our own? . . . These are American courts, American prestige to a great extent depends on the way we mete out justice," and he launched into an exhausting grilling of the judge on the point. Before long, he had Simpson saying sheepishly, "I generally thought the proceedings were fair, but I might be mistaken about it. It is a matter I am glad you gentlemen are looking into."[29]

When Simpson's colleague on the commission, Judge Edward L. Van Roden, took the stand, Joe quickly resumed his questioning about the rules governing the trial at Dachau. Senator Baldwin patiently explained after a time that the Allied Powers had agreed on the standards and produced a booklet of rules and regulations that was followed by the Army court. Joe angrily replied, "It was not any Russian standard, any German standard, any other standard that would justify or authorize them to beat these men up, have mock hangings, mock trials."

Van Roden revealed that the Simpson Commission had been given only six weeks in Munich to study about twelve-and-a-half tons of trial records and evaluate the death sentences of 139 prisoners, including the twelve convicted of Malmedy atrocities. The commission heard testimony from a battery of Germans claiming brutality against prisoners but had failed to interview prosecution, administration, or medical personnel at Schwabisch Hall. Moreover, it had access to only a limited quantity of the prosecution staff's affidavits requested earlier by the Administration of Justice Review Board.

Van Roden readily accepted some of the charges McCarthy believed in, but he hedged on others and revealed a general confusion about the Malmedy cases that Joe clearly found embarrassing. He frankly acknowledged that some of his testimony clashed with Judge Simpson's.

The witness's admission that he had not written the article bearing his name in *The Progressive* was a bombshell. In fact, the author was James Finucane of the staff of the National Council for Prevention of War. Van Roden testified that Finucane wrote an elaboration of the council's press release and went over the piece with him on the telephone. While Finucane explained, "This is going to be under your byline," Van Roden claimed that he had not known the meaning of the word "byline" and was shocked to be represented as the author.

The judge was eager to disassociate himself from the article, claiming that most of it came from Finucane's imagination and had not been personally approved over the telephone. (This claim was unconvincing. Subsequent testimony by Finucane revealed that Van Roden was under pressure from the Army to recant. Moreover, the contents of the council's press release—including a revised version requested by the judge, and *The New York Times* interview published on March 2 showed the judge's commitment to some of the most bizarre assertions. For several weeks prior to his discovery by Frederick Libby, Van Roden had been giving speeches before Rotary Clubs and the like featuring lurid charges from the affidavits of Malmedy prisoners.) Even when he took responsibility for a contention, Van Roden was unable to substantiate it with anything other than vague generalities. "It may have come from the defendant's side of the case. I do not know." "I got that from some of the records over there. Where I cannot tell."

McCarthy had several times cited the article's assertion of appalling damage to prisoners' genitals. Van Roden said in answer to detailed questioning by subcommittee counsel Chambers:

> Now, in the next paragraph where it says, "All but two of the Germans, in the 139 cases we investigated, had been kicked in the testicles beyond repair," I did not say that. What I said was that all but two were recommended for commutation to life imprisonment, and the other two for other sentences. I do not know how many we heard or how many may or may not have been kicked or kneed in the testicles. We learned some had been but that figure is absolutely wrong. I do not know how many were kicked or abused in the testicles.

A few minutes later Joe asked to be excused and left the hearing room.

When Maj. Dwight Fanton appeared as a witness, Baldwin offered to withdraw temporarily, in deference to further charges of conflict of interest. He consented to remain as an "unofficial observer" only at the urging of Senators Hunt and McCarthy. Joe expressed profound confidence in Baldwin. "I might say I think the chairman is absolutely fair. . . . I am sure he will not in any way try to protect Mr. Fanton more than any other witness that has appeared."[30]

Joe had made similar statements during the hearings. On April 22 he made public a letter he had written to Baldwin containing, "I want you to know that I have no criticism whatsoever of your handling of this investigation. I think you have been eminently fair and certainly have accorded every opportunity to the Expenditures Committee and the Judiciary Committee to participate in this investigation." On other occasions, however, Joe bitterly attacked the subcommittee chairman, questioning his judgment and motives, and at one point threatening to appeal a decision to the full Senate.

McCarthy was obviously rattled by the realization that Baldwin was almost totally impervious to his emotional outbursts. While other men shook and stuttered at Joe's badgering, his glare, his monotone delivery, Baldwin was as often as not patronizing, urging Joe—sometimes indirectly—"to keep a cool head" and remain fair, courteous, and rational. He once urged McCarthy publicly to apologize for calling members of the military court at Dachau "morons." Baldwin would not be pushed around; McCarthy wasn't used to this, and he responded with both admiration and loathing. Sometimes his extravagant praise and harsh criticism would appear during the same hearing, leaving observers puzzled and flabbergasted.[31]

During his interrogation of the court reporter, McCarthy had charged Baldwin with discourtesy for attempting to interject a few questions. When Baldwin calmly reminded the junior senator from Wisconsin that he was, after all, the subcommittee's chairman and had some responsibility to "get the record in such shape so that it is best readable and understandable," Joe fired back, "I am sure the chair can complete his record without insisting upon interrupting me when I am conducting an examination." When Fanton's name was mentioned a minute later, Joe leered at Baldwin. "I might say, if there is some doubt in the chairman's mind, I have not accused Fanton of any misconduct. . . . I know he is the chairman's law partner, and I am not attempting to go into that and prove there is anything wrong with what Fanton did unless—" It was a low blow that escaped no one's attention.[32]

Fanton began his testimony with a lengthy and articulate statement defending the conduct of American Army personnel at Schwabisch Hall. He called all charges of physical abuse "pure fabrication," stating flatly that "those detained at this interrogation center were given the best treatment possible under the circumstances and were at no time subject to acts of violence, coercion, or threats in the course of their interrogation." Prisoners were not starved; their diet was superior to that of the German civilian population. They were once put on bread and water briefly for attempting to send messages to each other, but such punishment was standard in the military. The "Schnell procedures," or mock trials, Fanton said, were brief, ineffective attempts (later shown to be based on European pretrial procedures) to get confessions from a few of the more simple-minded prisoners. The crucifix, black cloth, and candles were designed to impress the accused with the solemnity of the interrogation. Confessions were neither forced nor dictated, he stated, and every precaution was taken to assure their accuracy.

Fanton had been present in the cell when a prisoner named Christ signed his confession. "I know, I am absolutely certain, that there certainly was no physical force used." Recently, the prisoner's sentence was commuted after he claimed that the confession was produced by torture.

Fanton concluded with a fiery blast at his critics:

> We who are testifying for the prosecution do not feel on the defensive. On the contrary we feel that defense counsel Everett, Judge Van Roden, and all the others who have been hawking this sensationalism at the expense of their country and the cause of international law and order should be publicly exposed and made to stand before the peoples of this country and other like-minded nations for proper judgment.

The case against the Army was becoming increasingly untenable as the hearings wore on. But Joe refused to concede a single point and clung tenaciously to his position, contending that every witness who denied the existence of barbarism at Schwabisch Hall was lying and was part of a conspiracy to suppress the truth. He ripped into Fanton when the major made a second appearance before the subcommittee, jeering at his legal credentials ("Let's assume you know some law") and bullying him mercilessly ("I am going to get this from you if I keep you here a week, and I will make you answer all the questions"). He threatened to bolt the hearings if Baldwin interrupted his interrogation.[33]

One of Joe's persistent attacks concerned the charge that SS men had murdered twenty to thirty unarmed American prisoners in a churchyard at La Gleize. Colonel Everett claimed in his Supreme Court petition that an affidavit by a local priest proved that nothing of the sort occurred. McCarthy championed the contention and sarcastically asked numerous witnesses how prisoners could freely confess to a crime that didn't happen. During testimony by an Army investigator it was revealed that Everett's description of the affidavit was at wide variance with the document itself—

part of the trial record that Joe had not read. This failed to phase the senator in the slightest, and he soon resumed his questions about La Gleize, fully assuming the accuracy of Everett's petition.[34]

One of the American defense attorneys then revealed that the first allegations of physical abuse appeared at Dachau in questionnaires (now lost) filled out by the prisoners shortly after arriving from Schwabisch Hall. Only a small number claimed mistreatment, the complaints were of a very minor nature, no physical damage of any kind was evident, and defense attorneys made no effort to have the prisoners examined by physicians. The witness also noted that the defense put only nine of the accused on the stand during the trial because several of those who appeared lied extravagantly to save themselves.[35]

By this time McCarthy knew that his case was in shambles. But it was not in his nature to admit that he had been wrong, or even to recognize his error. His reaction, as it had so often been in poker, was to bluff. He claimed that he was suddenly privy to information containing "charges of a very serious nature that go beyond the Malmedy case," charges that "can do irreparable damage to the Army . . . and make it difficult for our State Department to operate." He sought an immediate executive session and was clearly attempting to curtail all subsequent public hearings. Baldwin didn't fall for the tactic, however, and the hearings continued. McCarthy's burning information was quickly forgotten by everyone, including Joe himself.[36]

On May 13, the twelfth day of the hearings, the witness was William R. Perl, the Schwabisch Hall interrogator most often linked with reports of violence and coercion. Perl was a 42-year-old Jewish refugee from Austria who had become an American citizen in 1943 after joining the United States Army. An experienced interrogator, he had been responsible for the decision to place the Malmedy prisoners in Schwabisch Hall and had personally devised the "Schnell procedure." Having a Ph.D. in law and years of criminal law practice, he proved to be a formidable witness.

Not long after Perl began a careful and persuasive description of his interrogation methods and the theories behind them, McCarthy interrupted the hearing with a demand that the witness and two other interrogators be given a lie-detector test. Turning to Perl, he said:

> I think you are lying. I do not think you can fool the lie-
> detector. You may be able to fool us. I have been told you are
> very, very smart. I know you are a psychologist and psychia-
> trist and work at it. I have been told I can get nothing from

you in cross-examination, and I think that is true. I am convinced you cannot fool the lie-detector.

Perl unenthusiastically agreed to the proposal, but Baldwin expressed initial reluctance. At this, Joe exploded. "The Chair seems to be afraid of the results of that test."

> ... this confirms what I have suspected all along and that is: This committee is not concerned with getting the facts. Further, this committee is afraid of the facts, and is sitting here solely for the purpose of a whitewash of the Army and that phase of the military government in charge of those trials.
>
> And I think it is so ridiculous, so unheard of, so inexcusable, for the chairman to say that we will not allow these three key witnesses, whom many of us think are deliberately lying—

Baldwin interrupted, attempting to calm him down, noting that while McCarthy was only an observer at the hearings he had been given every courtesy by the subcommittee and access to all of its documents. Baldwin proposed that the matter be taken to the full Armed Services Committee. Joe angrily brushed aside these soothing words and repeated his charges of whitewash.

Not more than a minute later, he calmly asked Baldwin if the subcommittee would alter its hearing schedule "as a favor" since he had an important engagement. The chairman wearily agreed. "May I state for the benefit of the record: Not only on this occasion, but on many occasions I have tried and have, I think, acceded to the requests of the senator from Wisconsin in every single way I could meet his convenience, even at great inconvenience to myself and Senator Hunt, the other member of the committee, and the staff, and the witnesses."

When Perl returned for a second day of testimony, McCarthy assailed him to the point that Baldwin was forced to say, "There has to be some order to this thing." For a third and fourth day Joe harrassed and badgered the witness. Perl once protested to the chairman, "I was asked a question before, and I had no chance to answer it. I am shouted at one question after another, and I never get the chance to answer it." In the course of one harangue, McCarthy said that in his court someone in Colonel Ellis's shoes would be "immediately disbarred" and that Joe would "perhaps first commit him to an institution for observation."

Time after time Baldwin tried to restore the proper decorum to the proceedings. "Senator, I have tried to conduct this matter in a manner not to interfere with you, and I think it is only fair that you reciprocate with the same kind of treatment." But McCarthy paid not the slightest attention.

On May 19 Baldwin reported that members of the subcommittee and a quorum of the Armed Services Committee had voted unanimously against the use of a lie-detector; the senators did not wish to set a precedent that could make a travesty of subsequent congressional investigations, he soon explained. The following day McCarthy publicly condemned the subcommittee and announced his departure. A press release (toned down by Tom Korb) stated:

> I accuse the subcommittee of being afraid of the facts. I accuse it of attempting to whitewash a shameful episode in the history of our glorious armed forces. I accuse it of compounding a wrong, perpetrated by a few members, and impugning the fair name of the millions of men and women who served with valor and distinction in the armed services. I accuse it of sabotaging our efforts under the European Recovery Act, setting at naught that which we spent and are spending billions to prove.

Baldwin replied, quietly and with a smile, "The chairman regrets that the junior senator from Wisconsin, Mr. McCarthy, has lost his temper and with it the sound impartial judgment which should be expressed in this matter." A bit later he stated, "The committee does not intend to be swayed by any emotional threats or charges" and announced that he would ask the Expenditures Committee if it would like to send another representative to attend the hearings.

Baldwin's lofty and dispassionate air threw Joe into a rage. "I might say I think the chairman is inherently so fair and honest that the day is going to come when he is going to bitterly regret this deliberate and very clever attempt to whitewash. I think it is a shameful farce, Mr. Chairman, and inexcusable. Goodbye, sir." And he stormed from the hearing room.[37]

With McCarthy's exit the hearings became considerably more productive, and the unreliability of the Nazi charges appeared increasingly obvious. Both physicians who had served at Schwabisch Hall while the Malmedy prisoners were being questioned were among a parade of witnesses who neither saw injuries nor heard rumors of mistreatment. A lieutenant colonel who conducted an early investigation of prisoner charges reported that the initial complaints to defense attorneys on the questionnaires focused upon the mock trials; only four prisoners claimed to have been punched while being moved between cells, and no one attempted to relate violence to his confession.[38]

Another officer produced notes of a conversation he had with one condemned Malmedy prisoner who admitted that the defendants were attempting to save themselves with trumped-up charges. Several witnesses reported that Colonel Peiper had denounced the brutality allegations by his men and expressed satisfaction with their treatment.[39]

Following the conclusion of the Washington hearings on June 6, the subcommittee made plans to travel to Germany to interview additional witnesses. Before its departure, McCarthy read an angry speech on the Senate floor condemning the Malmedy hearings, followed by a bitter personal attack upon Baldwin that drew heated replies from Baldwin, Hunt, Kefauver, and Joe's arch-enemy Senator Tobey.

The speech, published in full in the *Green Bay Press Gazette,* repeated all of Joe's earlier "whitewash" charges and condemned the Army for "brutalitarianism":

> Regardless of the fact that the Nazis committed horrible acts of cruelty before and during the war and regardless of the fact that those guilty of war crimes are entitled to no sympathy, the fact is that representatives of the American people and of the United States Army are guilty of sacrificing the basic principles of American justice, guilty of failing completely to protect the rights of the innocent and convict only the guilty, and guilty of adopting many of the very same tactics of which we accuse Hitler and Stalin. The cost of their ignorance, bungling, and incompetence has been to almost completely nullify any moral value which the war crimes trials might have had.

The speech was heavily slanted to strengthen McCarthy's case, and it contained numerous factual errors. Joe treated allegations in the prisoners' affidavits and in testimony by the court reporter as self-evident truths. He took the Simpson Commission report at face value, without reference to testimony by Simpson or Van Roden. He distorted findings of the Administration of Justice Review Board. And he simply ignored the abundance of testimony supporting the Army's position.[40]

Two weeks later the full Armed Services Committee passed and made public another resolution of confidence in Baldwin. "We, his colleagues on the committee, take this unusual step in issuing this statement because of the most unusual, unfair, and utterly undeserved comments" made about the Connecticut senator. This was a direct slap at McCarthy, signed by some of the Senate's most powerful figures: Democrats Richard Russell, Millard Tydings, Harry F. Byrd, and Lyndon Johnson, and Republicans Styles Bridges, Leverett Saltonstall, and William Knowland. There could no longer be any doubt about McCarthy's relationship to the "Senate Establishment." Joe was an outsider, a renegade, a man who could not be trusted.[41]

The Baldwin subcommittee's hearings in Germany were held throughout the month of September and included testimony by five Americans formerly involved in the Malmedy case, two German attorneys representing prisoners, a former dental assistant at Schwabisch Hall, and a three-man medical team sent from the United States to examine all of the Malmedy prisoners.

The ex-interrogators and translators described their activities at Schwabisch Hall in detail and persuasively denied allegations of brutality and torture. One interpreter, against whom serious charges had been made, produced a letter of commendation signed by Colonel Everett after the war crimes trial.[42]

Col. A. H. Rosenfeld, a highly experienced trial lawyer who had served as the legal adviser to the court at Dachau, carefully explained a technical ruling about cross-examination that had inflamed McCarthy. If the senator had read the full account of the ruling in the trial record instead of merely that portion of the record contained in Colonel Everett's petition, Rosenfeld pointed out, there would have been no ground for controversy. He noted, too, that a lawyer who had misquoted him, described by McCarthy as "one of the prosecuting attorneys," was not connected in any way with the Malmedy trial. Rosenfeld also described the blend of Anglo-American and European rules of procedure that governed the trial, rules that McCarthy loudly condemned but never fully understood.[43]

The German prisoners proved almost comical on the stand. One said he was questioned day and night for eight days, stabbed repeatedly in an arm by interrogators, severely burned by matches placed under his fingernails, beaten savagely with fists, rubber sticks and baseball bats, and subjected to a mock hanging. The witness was caught lying numerous times during his testimony and admitted falsifying his identity on the 1947 affidavit that contained his charges. He turned out to be an ex-convict whom the American physicians labeled "a psychopathic personality and a pathological liar." Further investigation failed to produce positive proof that he had ever been imprisoned at Schwabisch Hall; the three major interrogators had never heard of him.[44]

When the Public Health Service medical team completed its examination of sixty men, only ten showed traces of physical damage possibly resulting from trauma. Dr. Luther Terry testified, "When these findings are compared with the allegations of physical mistreatment in the prisoners' histories, there is a striking conflict of evidence." The report of massive dental damage, contained in the affidavit of a German dentist (recently deceased) and reaffirmed at the hearings by his assistant, proved groundless.[45]

Colonel Everett was ill and unable to attend subcommittee hearings. (He had spent "over $30,000 from the principal of my estate in fighting this case . . . and ended up with a heart attack.") In a deposition he said that he and his colleagues did not request physical examinations for the defendants because their complaints on the questionnaires filled out at Dachau did not involve serious injuries. He sought to make clear, however, that his long battle on behalf of the Malmedy defendants was based upon the original charges rather than the affidavits that surfaced a year and a half after the trial. He had received several of the latter from a German attorney and attached them to his Supreme Court petition without understanding their contents; he couldn't read German. When asked if the affidavits might have been written to secure commutations, Everett replied, "That is entirely possible."[46]

There is compelling evidence to dismiss virtually all of the charges made by Colonel Peiper's men before and after their conviction for the Malmedy massacres, and such was the conclusion reached by the subcommittee in a carefully reasoned final report delivered by Baldwin to the Senate in mid-October. Joe broke into the address repeatedly, and at one point brushed Baldwin aside with, "If the senator will refrain from interrupting until I get through, I will appreciate it." Baldwin remained dignified but was obviously boiling. "Let me say to my distinguished friend that I am not going to let him incorporate misstatements of fact in this case, because sometimes, in his exuberance, he is a little reckless in statements which do not normally appear in the testimony." Joe soon stormed back with some sentiments that pointed again to the primary reason for his fierce commitment in this case:

> I would say that if the system of justice in Europe was not
> resulting in the conviction of the guilty and the protection of
> the innocent, then it was fundamentally wrong, and, sec-
> ondly, I say that each and every case must be examined on its
> merits. The life or death of one person may not seem to be
> important to the senator from Connecticut, the freedom or

> liberty of one person may not seem so important to him, but
> it is to me. I very strongly feel that a conquering nation which
> has the power of life and death over a people must be very
> meticulous in protecting these liberties.[47]

Despite the subcommittee's almost clean bill of health for the Army (Baldwin told the Senate, "I am convinced the Army did the best it could"), the hearings revealed a number of egregious blunders by Army personnel, several of which escaped mention or emphasis in the subcommittee's final report.

Officials should have selected defense attorneys of a higher professional caliber. Colonel Everett had participated in only three criminal cases when appointed chief defense counsel and was unfamiliar with criminal trial procedure. He made costly errors during the trial and in his affidavit revealed continued confusion about the rules governing the events at Dachau. His colleagues were equally inexperienced. One, Lt. Col. John S. Dwinell, confessed to grave weaknesses in defense tactics. He was later appointed as a consultant to a military board of review and became a persistent advocate for the convicted Germans! He also assisted Everett with his Supreme Court petition. It is hard to escape the conclusion that efforts by Everett and Dwinell to win new trials for the Malmedy prisoners were motivated in great part by guilt.[48]

Moreover, as both McCarthy and the subcommittee noted, the Army should have employed civilian interrogators and interpreters who were more objective toward captured Germans. Almost all of those who figured most prominently in prisoner accusations were refugees from Hitler. One was convinced that Nazis had killed his mother; another's wife had been in a Nazi concentratin camp. Despite a plethora of denials to the contrary, there is little doubt that some of these men shoved, slapped, and threatened prisoners occasionally. While these minor incidents, like Perl's "Schnell procedure," had little or no effect on the overall justice of the situation or the trial verdict, they were wholly unnecessary and served as grounds for future complaints.[49]

(Before the trial had concluded, one intoxicated interrogator escorted several of the German prisoners' wives to a local officers' club. This was later made public by the Administration of Justice Review Board and drew widespread criticism. McCarthy inaccurately implied that the incident contained sexual demands.)[50]

Several Army review boards examined the Malmedy verdicts, and all failed to conduct anything resembling a thorough investigation. The Administration of Justice Review Board met only five times on the matter, heard testimony from seven witnesses, and did not study the trial record. The board gave credence to the German dentist's affidavit without interviewing the author. It accepted a number of prisoner allegations for subjective reasons; one member said later, "From the testimony, why, it was a ladies' seminary, and that didn't strike us as being true to life, and we just used our judgment of what we had." The board's conclusions in its final report inadequately reflected its detailed findings and were obscure and misleading in places. General Clay clearly erred in relying upon the board's hasty activity, and he should have been even more skeptical of the Simpson Commission. All of the death sentences were eventually commuted, and by the late 1950s all the prisoners had been released.[51]

The Baldwin subcommittee might have been content to dismiss most of the charges against the Army, but it went further to allege that Communists were behind the effort to collect sensationalistic affidavits from Malmedy prisoners for the purpose of reviving German nationalism and pushing the German people closer to the Soviet Union.

The subcommittee chose not to spell out details of the plot, but evidence later emerged of a secret subcommittee report charging that Rudolf Aschenauer, a German attorney who had been interviewed in Munich, was a Communist. He had sent affidavits to James Finucane of the National Council for Prevention of War, the report continued, who in turn passed them on to McCarthy. With this information at hand in 1951, McCarthy critics claimed gleefully that the senator had been a Red "dupe" while defending the Malmedy prisoners two years earlier. Richard Rovere later declared, "McCarthy had been had by a Communist agent."[52]

The accuracy of the secret report cannot be confirmed due to a lack of conclusive evidence, but on the basis of the hearings the charge seems improbable. Aschenauer, 35, had not participated in the trial of the Malmedy prisoners. He was the legal adviser on war crimes to Bishop Johann Neuhausler, Roman Catholic bishop of Munich, and the Protestant Church Council in Bavaria, and he represented several of the Malmedy prisoners. In his testimony before the subcommittee he stated that his role in the cases to date had been principally to check the accuracy of affidavits submitted to churchmen. He said that he had had no direct contact with McCarthy. (Joe later affirmed this in sworn testimony.) He corresponded with the National Council for Prevention of War one to three times a month, but largely because the council was in constant touch with his church clients about the work of the Baldwin subcommittee.

In 1951 Bishop Neuhausler swore to James Finucane, "as God is my witness," that Aschenauer had not been a Communist.

The man apparently most responsible for collecting the affidavits from prisoners was another German attorney, Eugen Leer, who served as a spokesman during the subcommittee's hearings in Munich for the German lawyers who had been present at Dachau. No one claimed that he was a Communist.

The Baldwin subcommittee suggested that the National Council for Prevention of War was part of the alleged Red plot and should be investigated. However, all available information indicates that although council leaders Libby and Finucane were intensely idealistic and eager to believe virtually any charges against the American military their loyalty to the United States was unimpeachable.

After the council's press release of mid-December 1948, it received numerous affidavits from German churchmen and attorneys—including Aschenauer—which it distributed to McCarthy and others. These affidavits had been sent earlier to Colonel Everett, the review commissions, and General Clay. The documents were clearly responsible for most of the uproar over the Malmedy verdicts, but whether or not they were products of a Communist plan to humiliate the United States cannot be known with certainty. If McCarthy was a "dupe" in the matter, so were scores of others, including some of Germany's most prominent clergymen.[53]

The hearings indicate that the Baldwin subcommittee learned of the charge against Aschenauer fairly early in its deliberations and that it readily accepted the conspiracy thesis. McCarthy must have been privy to the allegation, since the subcommittee provided him with all of its evidence, and rejected it out of hand. At any rate, he continued to shout "whitewash" even after the final report was published.

In 1952 McCarthy critics not only portrayed the senator as an unwitting tool of the Soviets, but charged that he had entered the fray over Malmedy to placate the Milwaukee industrialist Walter Harnischfager, a conservative of German descent. Tom Korb's presence in Joe's office fueled the story, and for good measure critics contended that Harnischfager's attorney had helped write a Senate speech of McCarthy's on Malmedy.

This wholly inaccurate tale, accepted by some to this day without a shred of supporting evidence, can be traced to Miles McMillin of the *Madison Capital Times*. The alleged association with Harnischfager was used by Jack Anderson to imply that McCarthy was anti-Semitic and pro-Nazi; he was "the fellow traveler of the Axis." (I.F. Stone had made identical charges earlier without knowledge of Harnischfager.)

Senator Flanders would mention the Malmedy hearings in 1954 while attempting to drive McCarthy from the Senate. Joe's involvement, he was to contend, fitted in "neatly with other parallels between the amateurish senator from Wisconsin and the accomplished and successful dictator of Germany."[54]

Joe's brief but explosive encounter with the Malmedy case was a portent of his rendezvous with anti-Communism. He entered the picture perhaps thinking about his political future, quickly became swept away by a Cause, and was vicious and reckless toward all who challenged him. The seeds of this conduct can be seen earlier in his life, especially in his Washington career. But Joe exhibited a passion and a frenzy in the spring of 1949 that was extraordinary and at times shocking. Tom Korb was aware of the change in his old friend but later could not account for it.

Surely a large part of the explanation involves the frustrations of the previous two years. For not only had he failed to gain the recognition he had toiled so hard to achieve, in Wisconsin he was under severe, almost daily attack by forces trying to wreck his political career and drive him from the legal profession.

10

COMMUNISTS AND THE
CAPITAL TIMES

In the summer of 1948 Joe had escaped the tensions of the nation's capital by traveling to southwestern North Dakota and working on a wheat farm for two weeks. (A friend came along: a United Press reporter who gave the "vacation" national publicity.) He zealously plunged into the manual labor of his youth and was later termed a "darn good" farmhand by his elderly host—who at first had not known who Joe McCarthy was. "Why, when it rained and the men couldn't work in the fields, he had them cleaning granaries and any number of other jobs." The farmer's grandchildren delighted in their visitor and called him "uncle Joe." (For years he sent them gifts under that name.) One night he and the reporter drove a small farm tractor with a scoop-shovel attachment into the town of Lefor and bought a case of beer. McCarthy placed the refreshment in the scoop, raised high and out of the sight of passing townsfolk. "Joe got a big kick out of that," the reporter recalled. When the time came for the senator to return to Washington, the farmer insisted that he be paid for his labor. Joe acquiesced reluctantly. The farmer's wife later observed, "He said he would frame the check, and he must have because it never came back."[1]

A year later, Joe decided against taking a vacation. His physical condition was not as strong as it had been the previous summer; he was increasingly bothered by painful sinus flare-ups, and in July he was hospitalized for viral pneumonia. Moreover, he was deeply troubled by an effort in his home

187

state to disbar him. He nervously scanned the newspapers and mail daily for word of a decision by the Wisconsin supreme court that could have a profound effect upon his political future.[2]

In early 1948 Miles McMillin was urging William Evjue to initiate disbarment proceedings against Joe McCarthy, using a charge made by Howard McMurray during the 1946 campaign. There was little to lose, for the *Capital Times*'s expose of the senator's financial affairs and its continuously critical editorials had failed to produce a strong anti-McCarthy movement in the state and had not received attention outside Wisconsin. (McMillin would almost come to blows with syndicated columnist Drew Pearson while attempting unsuccessfully to persuade him of McCarthy's rascality. Pearson and McCarthy were still friends. Indeed, the senator would feed information to the newsman about the 1949 "five-percenter" investigations through Jack Anderson.) Evjue was reluctant to accept the suggestion because his newspaper's attorney, W. Wade Boardman, was a member of the five-man State Board of Bar Commissioners that would hear the complaint, and Boardman advised against the move, fearing conflict of interest charges. By July, however, Evjue was persuaded to intensify his attack against McCarthy. He approved McMillin's proposal, got Boardman to disqualify himself from the case, and prepared his newspaper to launch another no-holds-barred campaign against the junior senator.[3]

McMillin, an attorney, filed the complaint on July 7, printed in full with appropriate headlines and editorials in the *Capital Times*. McMillin contended that McCarthy should be disbarred for violating Canon 30 of the canons of judicial ethics of the American Bar Association by running for the Senate while continuing to serve as a circuit judge. The canon read: "While holding a judicial position he [a judge] shall not become an active candidate either at a party primary or at a general election for any office other than a judicial one."[4]

Joe misunderstood the charge at first, thinking it identical to the issue settled in his favor by the state supreme court during the campaign. He was soon apprised of his error by the board and informed that he must attend a closed hearing on the complaint. Pleading business elsewhere, he hired two Janesville attorneys to represent him.[5]

The board mulled over the case for several months. In the meantime, Evjue lashed out at the board on his radio program and in editorials for procrastination and predicted a whitewash. On December 10 board members voted unanimously to present the state supreme court with a complaint against the senator, and the action became public a few days later. The complaint charged that the state bar association had approved the American Bar Association's canons of ethics and that McCarthy had violated Canon 30 as well as his oath as a member of the bar by running for the Senate in 1946 without resigning or surrendering his office as circuit judge.[6]

The story of McCarthy's serious difficulty in his home state was carried in newspapers all across the country. Joe affected nonchalance when reporters requested a comment. "I discussed the matter freely with the voters during the campaign. The voters of my state passed on this issue and elected me by a majority of a quarter of a million votes. I certainly have no objection to the supreme court going into this matter now."[7]

The senator's official reply to the complaint was contained in an affidavit delivered to the state supreme court in early January, 1949. In it McCarthy stated that he was not a member of the American Bar Association or the Wisconsin state bar association, and he denied that he had violated his oath as attorney or judge. Evjue labeled the affidavit "fantastic." A member of the State Board of Bar Commissioners observed privately to his colleagues, "I just ran across a copy of the proceedings of the state bar association for 1946, and I see that there is a fellow named Joseph McCarthy, Appleton, Wisconsin, listed as a member. That must be 'Slippery Joe.'"[8]

The case was argued before the state supreme court in June, two weeks after McCarthy angrily quit the Baldwin subcommittee hearings. The counsel for the State Board of Bar Commissioners, Portage attorney Harlan B. Rogers, did not have a strong case and had privately expressed qualms about it several months earlier. While McCarthy had undoubtedly violated the A.B.A. canon, the state supreme court had declared that his candidacy was in accordance with the provisions of both state and federal constitutions. Was sufficient "moral turpitude" involved to demand disbarment? Rogers boldly argued the affirmative before the state supreme court. "It is difficult to conceive of any conduct upon the part of a presiding judge which would bring judges and courts into greater disrepute and contempt than the conduct of the defendant challenged in this proceeding."

McCarthy's attorneys pointed to the clear legality of the judge's candidacy in 1946 and argued cleverly that the State Board of Bar Commissioners itself failed to make notice for two years of any alleged legal or moral impropriety.[9]

On July 12 the state supreme court issued a twenty-page decision declaring that McCarthy had violated the state constitution, Canon 30, and "the moral code" and was thus deserving of "just censure." The court dismissed the disbarment action, however, on the ground that the offense was of insufficient gravity to warrant such a drastic action; it was "one in a class by itself that is not likely to be repeated," and it "did not meet the condemnation of a majority of voters in the 1946 election." The justices moreover thought it important to note that "the defendant practiced law for many years, and in his relations to the court, so far as the record shows, he has never been derelict in the discharge of his duties and obligations as a lawyer."[10]

The *Capital Times* called the decision "shocking" and "astonishing," and one of its columnists gasped, "I have read and reread the court's decision seeking some ray of understanding, some logic, and even some common sense in it. I have found it barren of all three." On the other hand, McCarthy's friends at the *Green Bay Press-Gazette* hailed the opinion and dismissed the senator's attackers as "fishy-eyed marplots who supported Mr. McMurray [,] who had been knighted by the *Daily Worker...*" John Wyngaard was more reflective, pondering the effect of the censure on McCarthy's reputation. "The language was tough. It is not the kind that will be calculated to help in his future political career." The columnist predicted that the decision would be the opposition's chief document in the 1952 campaign.[11]

Joe responded angrily to the opinion, handing reporters a statement that branded the complaint against him "a disgrace to every honest, decent lawyer in the state" and calling upon members of the State Board of Bar Commissioners to resign.

> In view of the unanimous decision of the supreme court in dismissing this action, it must be assumed that either the bar commissioners knew that their case had no merit and were playing politics or that they are completely incompetent as lawyers.

For good measure, he charged that one board member was on the payroll of the *Madison Capital Times,* "my most radical opposition." Joe undoubtedly knew that Boardman had disqualified himself from the case; his signature was notably absent from the complaint, and as the president of the board soon observed, "It's a matter of common knowledge that Wade Boardman took no part whatever in the proceedings."[12]

A short time later, Joe was informed by state tax officials that a five-year audit of his returns, for which the *Capital Times* took credit, resulted in a refund of $1,100. McCarthy's financial records were chaotic; and auditors disallowed some of his deductions. Nevertheless, the senator had been given, as he put it, "a clean bill of health." (A federal audit for the years 1946-52 would result in a refund of $1,056.) When the *Capital Times* refused to publish the story, mocking even the appearance of journalistic objectivity, Joe flew into a rage, vowing revenge on his tormentors. The form this expression took is of special interest, for it revealed McCarthy's rather sudden and dramatic willingness to employ the tactics and rhetoric of right-wing extremists who had been making colorful headlines for many months with loose and often irresponsible charges of the presence of Communists in American life.[13]

On November 9, 1949, two days before he was scheduled to give a speech in Madison, Joe mailed an eleven-page, 3,000-word statement to 400 daily and weekly newspapers in Wisconsin, and to all state radio stations, and to the school clerks of Dane County (which includes Madison). The mimeographed documents were mailed at government expense by way of the senator's franking privilege, and attached to each was a personal note: "Enclosed is a document which I thought you might be interested in. I intend to discuss this matter in some detail while back in Wisconsin."

The statement began with a rhetorical question: "Has the Communist party with the cooperation of the Capital Times Corp. won a major victory in Wisconsin?" J. Edgar Hoover, McCarthy stated, had termed it a major aim of the Communists to plant its members in important positions in newspapers—especially in college towns "so that the young people who will take over control of the nation someday will be getting daily doses of the Communist party-line propaganda under the mistaken impression that they are absorbing 'liberal' and 'progressive' ideas from an American newspaper." McCarthy then proceeded to charge that Cedric Parker, city editor of the *Capital Times,* had once been a Communist. As proof, he contended that on March 14, 1941, William Evjue had called Parker "the Communist leader in Madison." Moreover, Parker had been named a Communist during the mid- and late 1930s in sworn testimony by two former members of the Communist party in Wisconsin. He had been a sponsor of a 1938 meeting of the American League for Peace and Democracy, since condemned by the Attorney General and HUAC as a subversive organization. In 1934 he and Eugene Dennis, recently convicted leader of the Communist party in the United States, organized and sponsored the State-Wide Conference on Farm and Labor Legislation, since labeled by HUAC as Communist controlled. In 1940 Parker attended a meeting of the Wisconsin Conference on Social Legislation, listed by the Attorney General as a Communist organization. And the city editor had also been affiliated with the Citizen's Committee to Free Earl Browder. The Attorney General and HUAC had branded the committee subversive.

The public record, McCarthy asserted, "would indicate that Parker was at one time a member of the party and was closely affiliated with a number of Communist-front organizations, and there is nothing in his writings which has been brought to our attention which would indicate he has in any way changed his attitude toward the Communist party." Left unsaid, of course, was the fact that before being named city editor in 1948, Parker, as a reporter, had made the "quickie divorce" charges and had done almost all of the research into McCarthy's tax records, uncovering the attempt to side-step state taxes on his 1943 investment profits.

Then McCarthy asked, "Is the Capital Times Corp. the Red mouthpiece for the Communist party in Wisconsin?" His reply was revealing:

> The simplest and most infallible way to answer this question is to examine the method of handling news by the Capital Times Corp. to see whether it follows the Communist party-line . . . for as someone has said, if a fowl looks like a duck, walks like a duck, swims like a duck and quacks like a duck, then we can safely assume that it is a duck.

The senator proceeded to give examples of "similar" positions taken by the *Capital Times* and the *Daily Worker*. On April 11 the Madison newspaper had criticized "our entrenched economic order" for "implanting in the people a fear of Communism." The *Daily Worker,* Joe advised, "likewise rails at those who 'implant in the people a fear of Communism.'" The *Capital Times* applauded the speech by Henry Wallace in 1946 that led to his resignation as Secretary of Commerce. In doing so, it "withheld comment until the day after Radio Moscow praised Wallace." In May the *Daily Worker* came out in favor of the Wallace-Stalin proposal, and the next day the *Capital Times* followed suit.

Moreover, McCarthy continued, the *Capital Times* "viciously" attacked the American Legion, which is "the typical Communist party-line attack upon the successful middle class . . ." In June 1948 Evjue complained of a double standard of justice in the United States—one for the rich and another for the poor. "This is the type of charge repeatedly made by the *Daily Worker*," McCarthy commented. And in August 1948 Evjue had condemned Congress for investigating Communists and ridiculed anti-Communist newspapers and radio commentators.

Joe also cited the *Capital Times*'s attack on his efforts in housing legislation, and he quoted Lenin, who said, "Take advantage of the difficulties of the government . . . with the aim of overthrowing it." While McCarthy was exposing gray marketeer Isidore Ginsberg—now a "New York pinko—" the *Capital Times* had defended him, and "in the typically 'honest' fashion of the Communist *Daily Worker,* it repeatedly referred to me as Public Housing Enemy No. 1."

The statement continued with a blast against the investigation of McCarthy's taxes. Joe defended his 1943 failure to file, noted his recent refund and the newspaper's failure to publicize it, and then claimed that the *Capital Times* had left out words and sentences from reprints of his financial correspondence. "This is the type of 'honesty' advocated by Lenin when he urged Communists to 'overlook or conceal the truth' to accomplish their ends."

McCarthy concluded this attack with an appeal for an economic boycott.

> There is no law which prevents the *Capital Times* from hiring Communists as it sees fit. There is no law which prevents the *Capital Times* from following the Communist line right down to the last period, if it so desires. It is for the people of Madison and vicinity to decide whether they will continue by advertisements and subscriptions to support this paper in view of the above facts—especially in view of the fact that the man who is editor publicly proclaimed that the man hired as city editor was an active and leading member of the Communist party.[14]

This last jab made Evjue particularly uneasy, for no matter how quickly he could dismiss the bulk of McCarthy's charges—the silliness about the American Legion, the balderdash about taking orders from the *Daily Worker,* the assertion that because Communists adopted liberal positions (which they often did after the inception of the "Popular Front" in 1935) liberals were therefore Communists—he could not comfortably sidestep the fact that he had printed the charge against Parker in 1941. The allegation stemmed from a battle between Evjue and local CIO officials, prompted by the editor's demand that the union leaders repudiate Communism. Parker, a leader in the Dane County CIO, was at least a fellow traveler in those days and perhaps a Party member, and Evjue's attack had been well aimed. That was all in the past, of course, and Parker was now as willing to condemn Communism as Evjue had always been. The problem remained, however, of finding a way to blunt McCarthy's attack without resurrecting embarrassing details of Parker's past. Evjue had great respect for the equally flamboyant Parker—he once called him a "great newspaperman" immediately after a heated argument between the two—and had been his employer since 1927.[15]

At first Evjue claimed that McCarthy had taken the statement attributed to him from a news story written by a staff reporter, and he threatened to sue. McCarthy immediately fired off a telegram to the editor inviting him to check the editorial page for March 14, 1941. Evjue also told his readers that Parker had "repeatedly assured the management of the *Capital Times* that he is not a member of the Communist party." Why was he obliged to make such assurances repeatedly?, one might ask. Then the editor asserted that Parker had signed a non-Communist affidavit in 1948 when elected president of the Madison Newspaper Guild. McCarthy quickly discovered that such an affidavit had never been filed with the National Labor Relations Board and broke the story in his Madison speech. Evjue had met Joe's attack badly.[16]

Addressing an Armistice Day audience of about 250 at a Madison Shriners Club luncheon, McCarthy dared Evjue to sue him, adding cautiously, however, "I'm not going to tell you that Evjue or Parker or anyone else is a Communist." Joe ran through the charges contained in his 3,000 word statement and held up a photostat of the *Capital Times* editorial of March 14, 1941. It was his duty to expose Communism, the senator explained, and he would resign rather than fail to exercise that responsibility. He exhorted, "I believe . . . that when you can expose a paper as communistic, then I believe businessmen should never send in a check for advertising. When any man pays a nickel for a newspaper, he is contributing to the communistic cause."

The senator said he would be happy to accept an invitation from the *Capital Times* editor to a public forum. "Mr. Evjue can select the time, the place, and the forum and I'll be happy to debate the number of times the *Capital Times* has followed the party line." Joe then claimed that the *Daily Worker* had praised Evjue for an editorial attacking a Hearst piece entitled "I am an American." "I don't know whether Mr. Evjue wrote the editorial, or whether Mr. Parker wrote it, or whether it was assigned to someone else," he said with a grin.

Joe then burst forth into patriotic paroxysm: "We cannot blind our eyes to the fact that we are engaged in a showdown fight . . . a final, all-out battle between Communist atheism and Christian democracy. The chips are almost down today." He warned, "You can hear and feel the rumblings of another war."[17]

The charges against Cedric Parker and the *Capital Times* faded from the public spotlight almost as quickly as they arose. Evjue was delighted to drop the matter, and McCarthy was soon after larger targets. A debate between the two was never scheduled; Evjue offered to send Miles McMillin in his place, and Joe refused to confront "a minor employee." In a public letter to Evjue, Joe chided, "Can it be that the self-styled roaring lion becomes a lamb when his bluff is called?"[18]

The Madison newspaper continued its relentless attacks on the senator, however, and McCarthy repeated his charges against it on numerous occasions, at one point calling it "the closest counterpart of the *Daily Worker* in the United States" and "a disguised poisoned waterhole . . . of dangerous communistic propaganda." After one such blast, Evjue tried to explain his 1941 outburst against Parker by contending lamely, "the word Communist had different connotations than it has today. . . . Ten years ago that label Communist was used broadly in the same sense that the words reactionary, tory, radical or Red were used, and the average citizen dismissed these charges as politics . . ."[19]

Joe's attack on the *Capital Times* in November 1949, won him more publicity throughout Wisconsin than any activity he had undertaken since entering the Senate. The principle was not lost upon him: he could labor for months on housing legislation with barely a ripple of attention in the press, but by calling someone's loyalty into question he became an instant celebrity. The *Wisconsin State Journal* devoted 4,000 words to the controversy, the *Milwaukee Journal* ran about 7,500, and the *Capital Times* printed 8,000. Smaller newspapers all over the state covered the story. *Time* magazine gave the incident national attention. Moreover, the publicity was largely favorable to McCarthy. *Time* described Joe's statement as "blistering," and other articles called his charges "documented" and "from the record."[20]

Fortunately for McCarthy, no one outside the *Capital Times* subjected his undocumented 3,000 word statement to careful scrutiny. Joe quickly learned that newspapermen were more interested in his charges than his sources. The statement actually contained questionable quotations (no one has yet verified the sworn testimony allegedly naming Parker a onetime Communist) as well as misleading innuendoes, non sequiturs, and the technique of guilt by association.

Among its larger flaws was the fact that McCarthy accepted at face value the highly controversial Attorney General's list and information published by the notoriously partisan House Committee on Un-American Activities. This practice, increasingly common at the time, frequently led to errors and gross abuses against personal reputations.

Of what objective value, for example, was McCarthy's contention that, according to HUAC, Parker had been "affiliated with" the Citizen's Committee to Free Earl Browder? Parker flatly denied any connection with the committee. Was it illegal or immoral to "attend" the Wisconsin Conference on Social Legislation? If he had, Parker stated, it was as a reporter. One of the conference's listed sponsors was Perry Hill, in 1949 chief of the Madison bureau of the right-wing *Milwaukee Sentinel.* The State-Wide Conference on Farm and Labor Legislation, which Parker "doubted" he sponsored, was chaired by Paul Alfonsi, who later became a conservative G.O.P. state legislator.

Thousands of loyal Americans attended and sponsored meetings and signed petitions during the Depression that would later be deemed "un-American" by ultraconservative congressmen, newspapermen, and patriotic organizations. The impression given by McCarthy and others that these prewar affiliations and signatures necessarily implied (or worse, proved) current subversive intent was unreasonable and malicious in the extreme.

Of course, Joe's broader charge that the *Capital Times* was a "Red mouthpiece" should have been dismissed immediately by anyone with the slightest knowledge of the newspaper's vigorously anti-Communist history. But editors and reporters for the most part simply placed McCarthy's charges in large headlines and refrained from comment.[21]

Joe knew what he was doing. He was out to "get" the *Capital Times.* And if that meant smearing its leaders—well they had started it. As Urban Van Susteren later recalled, McCarthy delighted in revenge and when attacked would return a blow twice as hard.

Joe also hoped to promote his sagging political career by his assault against the Madison newspaper. He not only ripped into Evjue and Parker in his statement but boasted blatantly of personal achievements in housing legislation. He quickly realized, however, that a reckless brand of anti-Communism, not housing, was the key to future fame and fortune. The Madison audience (as others elsewhere) responded enthusiastically and uncritically to his charges. The eyes of any astute politician would have lit up at the torrent of positive publicity that resulted.

Granted Joe's motives and the important lesson he soon learned, what accounts for the somewhat peculiar content of his statement and speech in the first place? In the past he had occasionally revealed a deep and sincere hatred of Communism and the Communist party and a fear of Russian imperialism. He had employed exaggerated and insulting language, resorted to guilt by association, and had deliberately misquoted people. But

Joe had not hitherto revealed such a strident eagerness to condemn opponents as Communists and to rely upon rightwing sources and rhetoric. Moreover, he displayed for the first time two techniques for which he would soon become famous: the public display of photostatic copies of documents and the call for economic boycott.

In retrospect, the content of the attack upon the *Capital Times* in early November 1949 marks it as a departure, if not a sharp departure, from earlier McCarthy tactics against political opponents, and it is not much of an exaggeration to contend that it signals the beginning of the particular form of irresponsibility that was to characterize his style of public debate. But how is one to account for the timing of the senator's plunge into extremism? Was there more to his method than a sense of revenge and frustration over his sinking political career?

Joe later told different stories about the origins of what he called his "Fight for America." In a book published in 1952 he contended that Navy Secretary James Forrestal subtly alerted him to the existence of traitors in high government positions at a private luncheon held three days after McCarthy's arrival in Washington. Gradually the truth dawned: "Day after day I came in contact with convincing evidence of treason." At some point—the account is vague—Joe decided to retire to rural Arizona where he "carefully laid the plans for the one great fight which, as a senator, I had to make." He observed, "The planning was made infinitely easier by my contact with real Americans without any synthetic sheen—real Americans who are part of the Arizona hills . . ." The first part of the story could not be checked, for Forrestal, racked with emotional depression, had fallen to his death from a hospital window in May 1949. (Joe also claimed in 1952 that he was "hounded to death by the Communists," meaning Drew Pearson.) The rest of the tale, clearly is McCarthy moonshine.[22]

In a campaign polemic of 1952, purporting to be an interview between McCarthy and the editors of *Cosmopolitan* magazine, Joe stated that he first became aware of the existence of traitors and dupes in government shortly after he returned from overseas. He launched the "public phase" of his fight, he said, at Wheeling, West Virginia, on February 9, 1950, "after an unlimited amount of research covering the background of the architects of disaster for America and success for Russia." No mention was made of Forrestal.[23]

Joe told Don Surine, a close associate, that he first became attracted to anti-Communism while looking into the issue of fur imports. In September 1949, the senator unsuccessfully tried to amend the Administration's Reciprocal Trade Agreements bill by imposing import quotas on furs. This was an attempt to protect Wisconsin's fur industry, of course. But in defense of his proposal, McCarthy asserted that Russia was exporting all of its furs to America in order to "implement carrying out her communistic program in our country, first by providing a source of dollars necessary to finance her program, and, second, by being able to maintain a large fur business in the United States, which she's using as a base of operation to legally funnel into and out of our country key communistic supporters." His evidence was a two-month-old clipping from a local newspaper reporting testimony by an FBI agent. (The agent told of the smuggling of atomic research instruments, not "key communistic supporters.")

It seems very doubtful that this matter made much of an impression on McCarthy. He was primarily attempting to bolster the incomes of Wisconsin businessmen, and the reference to the Soviet Union was no doubt merely an effort to persuade colleagues that a vote for his amendment was a vote against the Reds. It was a very common tactic at the time. On this issue, it didn't work.[24]

According to Roy Cohn, McCarthy confided to him that prior to the fall of 1949 he had had no special interest in Communism and was without much knowledge of the subject. Then, shortly before Thanksgiving 1949, he was approached by three men bearing an FBI report, and literally overnight he was persuaded to take up the anti-Communist cudgel.

As Joe told the story, Cohn contended in a ghost-written book of 1968, an Intelligence officer in the Pentagon ("a career man in his late thirties") became disturbed sometime in 1949 by the official neglect of a two-year-old, 100-page report prepared by the FBI, a document that summarized information the Bureau had on Communist subversion in the United States. The G-2 officer and some friends met secretly on the matter and decided to approach four Republican senators with the document in the hope that one of them would take the facts to the American people. The first three senators refused, and that left McCarthy, who "had been placed on the list because he was young and vigorous and had already acquired a reputation for courage in tackling formidable foes." The G-2 officer and two other men talked with the Wisconsin senator for several hours in his office and left the document with him. Joe read it straight through after dinner. He later told Cohn, "After a couple of hours' sleep, I got dressed and went to the office. I had made up my mind—I was going to take it on. It was fantastic, unbelievable. Take any spy story you ever read, any movie about international intrigue, and this was more startling." First thing in the morning, Joe called one of his visitors "and told him I was buying the package."[25]

The story has a certain surface appeal. The timing of the alleged visit by the three wise men roughly corresponded to the date the attack on the *Capital Times* was distributed. Joe certainly was capable of responding to an FBI document in the manner Cohn described. Moreover, McCarthy titled his Madison speech "Communism as a Threat to World Peace" and told newsmen that his appearances in the state comprised a "personal campaign against Communism."

Throughout November and December and into January McCarthy expanded his subversion charges. On November 15, before a meeting of Young Republicans in Kenosha, Joe attacked John Stewart Service and castigated the State Department for having a "red tint" and being "honeycombed and run by Communists." He made similar remarks on December 3 before a group of Philadelphia realtors, two days later at Marquette University, and on the floor of the Senate on January 5, 1950. He told a Madison audience that he had voted against the reappointment of Leland Olds to the Federal Power Commission "because he is a Communist." He urged support of Robert La Follette, Jr., as chairman of the Atomic Energy Commission because "we could trust him and he has no leanings toward Communism." On January 21, and again four days later, McCarthy blasted Secretary of State Dean Acheson for supporting Alger Hiss and a "defeatist policy" in the Far East. On February 8 he called the attention of the Senate to a newspaper article asserting that a top Communist spy was using a Supreme Court justice as a "front."[26]

All of this was before McCarthy's famous Wheeling speech of February 9, the traditional date of the birth of "McCarthyism."

Still, the story in Cohn's book is unconvincing. In the first place, no one else close to McCarthy was privy to it. Joe was not one to keep such a dramatic tale to himself and would surely have shared it at some point, at least with Jean Kerr, the research assistant he married in 1953. He did not reveal any information or sources—before, during, or immediately after Wheeling—that would have been contained in a 100-page FBI summary of Red subversion in America. Then too, of course, why did he tell different stories to others? When McCarthy confidant Ed Nellor asked the senator about his initial involvement with anti-Communism, Joe said that there had been no specific incident that turned his attention in that direction; his interest had grown gradually in the course of historical events. This was also the impression Jean Kerr had, and it clearly seems accurate.[27]

Joe's concerted interest in the subject actually began in mid-October 1949, three weeks before the attack on Evjue and Parker and a month before he was allegedly visited by the G-2 officer and his friends. On October 19 he inserted an article into the *Congressional Record* strongly

attacking the State Department, its Far Eastern policies, and Foreign
Service officer John Stewart Service, and he suggested that "some of the
personnel of the State Department are more sympathetic to certain foreign
ideologies than to our own." A few days later, on October 24, Charles H.
Kraus came to work for the senator as a speech writer. Kraus was a political
science instructor at Georgetown University's School of Foreign Service
whose specialty was anti-Communism. His presence was a sign of McCarthy's interest in the field. There is little doubt that Kraus was a major
contributor to the 3,000 word statement and the speech that followed
attacking the *Capital Times,* thus accounting for the distinctive qualities of
the documents. (In a short time, McCarthy was consulting regularly with
Georgetown priests who were leaders in the surge of anti-Communist
sentiment sweeping the country by this time.)[28]

Joe turned toward anti-Communism in mid-October in large part
because he had run out of other issues that could be used to vault his name
into headlines and help insure his reelection. Soon after the housing
struggle became history, he failed in an effort to secure passage of an
amendment requiring states receiving federal aid to pay teachers a minimum salary of $2,850 a year. He earned some minor newspaper attention
for championing the Hoover Commission plan for reorganizing the executive branch, but others got the credit for later reforms. He scored better as a
member of a subcommittee conducting the "five-percenter" investigation,
which began public hearings on August 8. He ripped into Maj. Gen. Harry
H. Vaughan, President Truman's personal friend and aide, during testimony about alleged influence peddling in the White House. But Joe was
forced to publicly withdraw remarks implying that Vaughan had profited
personally in the matter. And by mid-October Democrats had quashed the
probe.[29]

Right-wing anti-Communism was widely embraced by Republicans (and
a sprinkling of conservative Democrats) at the time, and it is entirely
understandable that McCarthy should have joined the parade. His attacks
on the State Department were very familiar by the fall of 1949. The G.O.P.
had been bitterly assailing the Administration's China policy all year, and
when the Chinese Communists assumed authority in the world's most
populous nation, many Republicans became hysterical. Their anxieties
were in no way diminished by the President's announcement in September
that the Soviet Union had exploded an atomic bomb.

All but two Republicans voted against the renomination of Leland Olds
as chairman of the Federal Power Commission, to which he had first been
appointed in 1939. Oil and gas lobby senators from the Southwest, angered

by Olds's belief in public utility regulation and consumer protection, attacked him ostensibly for some socialistic writing he had done a quarter century earlier. McCarthy was among several who were aghast at Olds's youthful sentiments and concluded that the chairman was currently a Communist.

Joe was clearly influenced by the October 14 convictions of the eleven top leaders of the American Communist party for violating the Smith Act, the first peacetime sedition law since 1798. He mentioned the convictions twice in his statement against the *Capital Times* and quoted from Judge Harold Medina, who presided at the trial and was currently a national hero. Other politicians cited the convictions in their rhetoric for years.

McCarthy's comment on the Atomic Energy Commission chairmanship was a swipe at his old foe David Lilienthal, who resigned on November 23 under heavy Republican attack. Charges against Lilienthal by ultraconservative Senator Bourke Hickenlooper of Iowa resulted in 45 separate hearings by the Joint Committee on Atomic Energy.

McCarthy's attacks on Acheson regarding Alger Hiss were among a chorus of similar volleys and were in direct response to Hiss's conviction for perjury on January 21 and the Secretary of State's controversial defense of his longtime friend four days after the conviction.

The spy clipping introduced in early February was no doubt influenced by the fact that five days earlier the British government had shocked the western world with the announcement that Dr. Klaus Fuchs, a high-level atomic scientist, had confessed to being a Soviet spy from 1943 through 1947. This occurred just three days after President Truman announced work on the hydrogen bomb. Hardshell G.O.P. conservative Homer Capehart of Indiana stormed in the Senate, "How much more are we going to have to take? Fuchs and Acheson and Hiss and hydrogen bombs threatening outside and New Dealism eating away at the vitals of the nation. In the name of Heaven, is this the best America can do?"[30]

In late 1949 and very early 1950, then, McCarthy was merely responding to the flow of events with his charges of internal subversion and was following well-worn paths blazed months and even years earlier by others. He was by no means a leading G.O.P. spokesman on anti-Communism and was in fact almost completely ignorant of the subject.

To conceal the truth that there was no initial encounter, Joe later told and wrote different stories about such an encounter with the need for a "Fight for America." With little to lose, he had adopted a standard political weapon and discovered its effectiveness in his spiteful effort to damage the *Madison Capital Times*.

Joe McCarthy went into anti-Communism, as he once frankly admitted to his old friend Mark Catlin, almost strictly for political profit. And yet not all of his actions in this regard are so easily explained. In fairness, we must not overlook McCarthy's genuine concern about domestic and foreign Communism, displayed throughout his public statements. The time would soon come when Joe would think and talk about almost nothing other than anti-Communism. He was to become a True Believer.[31]

There remains the well-known "dinner at the Colony" story accounting for McCarthy's first realization that the subversion in government charge could bolster his campaign for reelection. It was first reported in March 1950 by Drew Pearson. Two years later it was incorporated into Anderson and May's anti-McCarthy polemic and has been accepted by virtually every historian since.[32]

On January 7, 1950, Joe had dinner at the Colony restaurant in Washington with Charles Kraus, William A. Roberts (Drew Pearson's attorney), and Father Edmund A. Walsh, 63, founder and dean of Georgetown University's prestigious School of Foreign Service. After dinner, Joe allegedly confided that he was desperately in need of a 1952 campaign issue. Roberts proposed that he consider the St. Lawrence seaway. Joe was uninterested. "That hasn't enough sex," he said. "No one gets excited about it." The senator then outlined a comprehensive pension plan for the nation's elderly: everyone over 65 would get $100 a month. All three of his friends vetoed that suggestion as economically unsound. Finally, Father Walsh asked, "How about Communism as an issue?" Joe immediately liked the idea. "The government is full of Communists," he observed. "The thing to do is hammer at them." Roberts warned that such a drive would have to be based on evidence, not unfounded charges. McCarthy assured him that he would get the facts. Anderson and May conclude, "His three fellow Catholics went away with the feeling that the sincere McCarthy would do his country a service by speaking out against the Communist fifth column."[33]

Walsh, a conservative anti-Communist who soon broke with McCarthy over the senator's extremism, was angered by the appearance of Pearson's story. He often denied privately that he made any suggestion to McCarthy, and in 1951 he charged that the columnist had "manufactured" the entire incident.[34]

In fact, enough evidence exists to conclude that the dinner did occur and that the discussion was substantially that described in the book by Anderson and May. Moreover, Father Walsh's suggestion may have influenced

McCarthy (although he never mentioned it). The significance of the event, however, has been magnified greatly. By January 7 Joe had been talking loudly about internal Communist subversion for nearly three months, and his attack on the *Capital Times* occurred almost two months earlier. He was not yet certain in early January that anti-Communism was his ticket to reelection and he was obviously still testing the waters, but the pattern of his conduct was well established by the time Father Walsh made his suggestion.[35]

Three others may have played a subtle role in moving McCarthy in the direction of anti-Communism at this time. Joseph P. Kennedy was a conservative Irish Catholic and an isolationist with strong right-wing views on Reds and "pinks." McCarthy may have met his son John in the South Pacific during the war; at any rate, in the late 1940s the senator was often invited to the Kennedy estate in Hyannis Port and flown there in the family's private airplane. He was a favorite with all of the Kennedy young people. Joe was especially fond of Eunice, and he dated Patricia. He once told Ray Kiermas with a smile that if worse came to worst he could marry a Kennedy girl. (In 1953 his wedding present to Eunice and R. Sargent Shriver was a silver cigarette box on which was inscribed: "To Eunice and Bob, from one who lost. Joe McCarthy.") Joe participated several times in the Kennedy clan's grueling weekend sports schedule. He once cracked a rib playing "touch" football and was yanked from a softball game for making four errors at shortstop. Someone was always pushing him into the water. "Christ, I came up there to rest!" Joe once complained to a friend. Several companions later recalled lengthy conversations between the senator and his host, the former ambassador to Great Britain, and it is unlikely that the subject of Communism went unmentioned. After Wheeling, Joseph P. Kennedy was to become one of McCarthy's most loyal defenders and financial supporters, and the senator would give young Bobby his first job.[36]

J. Edgar Hoover and McCarthy became warm friends soon after Joe took office. They were often seen at a local racetrack together, and Joe was the only elected official who used Hoover's private box in the director's absence. They ate dinner together regularly at Harvey's restaurant in Washington—where the FBI chief privately held court almost nightly for two decades without receiving a check. Hoover had quietly leaked tips to right-wing anti-Communists for years, but his chats with Joe in the late 1940s were largely lighthearted and frivolous, according to witnesses. Hoover was attracted by Joe's personality and no doubt failed to take him seriously. Still, McCarthy was a senator, and it seems highly improbable that Hoover failed to talk about the Red menace with him at some point in their many discussions.

When Joe's bluff was called after his Wheeling speech, one of the first people he turned to for help was Hoover. The director swiftly obliged.[37]

Jean Fraser Kerr (pronounced care) had been hired by McCarthy as an assistant clerk in the summer of 1948. Highly intelligent, shrewd, and ambitious, as well as beautiful, she soon became the senator's research assistant and, still in her twenties, the major figure on his staff.

"Jeannie," as friends called her, was of Scotch ancestry. Her father had come to Washington from Glasgow in the early twentieth century and built houses for a living. The Kerr home, which he constructed, was a large white clapboard duplex in the northwest section of the city. Jean, an only child, was born and raised there, and she continued to share the home with her widowed mother until she married McCarthy in 1953. She entered George Washington University in the fall of 1944, following three years in an advertising agency, and earned a journalism degree, with honors, at Northwestern University in 1948. A tall (5 foot, 8 inches), blue-eyed, well-proportioned brunette of striking appearance, she was voted Cherry Blossom Queen in 1946 and at Northwestern was elected to Kappa Kappa Gamma, a glamour-girl sorority, and named the prettiest girl in her journalism class. She also won the university's Alexander Wilbourne Weddell Award for writing the best essay on the subject, "The Promotion of Peace Among the Nations of the World."

Joe first met Jean in 1947, when she was still a college student. She dropped by the senator's office one day during summer vacation to visit his secretary, an old friend. When Joe took one look at her he buzzed his secretary and said, "Whoever that girl is, hire her." Jean declined the offer and went to work for a Senate special investigating committee. McCarthy persisted, however, and persuaded the strong-willed young woman to join his staff after her graduation.

Jean's first love, she often said, was politics, and she took pride in her minor in political science. Her political views were extremely conservative and militantly anti-Communist. While insiders doubt that she played a major role in turning McCarthy toward the Far Right, they agree that she was very close to the senator by late 1949 and welcomed and reinforced his initial probes in that direction as well as his conversion. After Wheeling she was an integral part of all of McCarthy's anti-Communist activities. At times she attempted (usually without success) to restrain Joe, but in public she would always staunchly defend his every move.[38]

WHEELING

A noted scholar once made the distinction between the Communist *problem* in the United States and the Communist *issue*. The differentiation is highly significant, for while the much-publicized rhetoric about subversives at times pointed to reality, far more often than not it was designed for political—and in some cases economic and even psychological—profit.[1]

In 1928, when Stalin consolidated his authority over the Communist party in Russia, the Sixth World Congress, held in Moscow, stated unequivocally that Communists were to refuse to collaborate with all social-democratic forces, especially liberals, Socialists, and trade unionists. Soon the American Communist party—at all times subservient to the Soviet line—harshly attacked the New Deal as a crypto-fascist tool of the capitalists created to forestall a genuine revolution of the proletariat. The party's effectiveness at the time, despite the worst depression in American history, was sharply limited. One congressional committee was able to uncover the presence of only two Communists in the Army and perhaps a dozen in the Navy; less than one percent of the American Federation of Labor was Communist; out of 810 schools in New York, only three contained discernible Communist activity. The vote received by the Communist presidential candidate in 1932 was 103,000.

Threatened by German fascism in 1935, the Seventh World Congress of the Communist International reversed its tactics and ordered a "united front" that would ally Communists with all "organizations of the toilers." Henceforth the American Communist party did its best to infiltrate, invade, and take control of labor unions and socialist and liberal organizations. Communists entered the newly created C.I.O. in large numbers and were soon in positions of considerable authority. They split the socialists badly and made strong inroads into a number of liberal organizations. Party leaders now posed as liberal reformers, uninterested in revolutionary violence, keenly concerned with the rights of minorities, veterans, farmers, and oppressed laborers. Hundreds of Communist fronts bearing reformist titles were created. Roosevelt's reelection in 1936 was quietly supported.

Party membership grew four to five times in the late 1930s because of its guise as the font of humanism and democracy. But it never enjoyed more than 100,000 members (more likely half that number) and was limited to less than one tenth of one percent of the nation's population. A large number of the more intellectual members resigned in 1939 when Moscow suddenly became Hitler's comrade and the American Communist party immediately shifted from interventionism to isolationism.

With the German invasion of the Soviet Union two years later, the party again supported Roosevelt and zealously backed the American military effort. At the same time, the party continued its espionage efforts in the United States and Great Britain, under no delusions about a genuine unity of interest with its wartime allies.

It is clear that Communists entered the federal government throughout the New Deal. That they were involved in procuring secret documents is undeniable. Still, out of a half million Federal workers in Washington, there were probably (according to Whittaker Chambers) only some 75 Communists. A study by Earl Latham of available evidence concludes that the Communists were scattered in small groups, they were not primarily interested in espionage or organized for spying, and they made virtually no impact on the policies of the agencies that employed them.[2]

Moreover, those who were tried and convicted of espionage or treason, well through the McCarthy era, were uncovered by regular law-enforcement agencies, notably the FBI. For all of the thunder in Congress and the White House about disloyalty, all the hearings and the loyalty-security programs were unsuccessful in obtaining a single conviction for substantial acts against the United States.[3]

The same year the American Communist party was organized, 1919, Attorney General A. Mitchell Palmer, with an eye toward his own political advancement, initiated a ruthless assault upon thousands of individuals suspected of radicalism. In December, 249 aliens were deported to Russia. A year later Communist party offices across the nation were raided, and 6,000 Communists were arrested. State governments passed criminal syndicalism laws declaring Communist organizations illegal. Radical meetings of all sorts were frequently broken up. Socialists, Communists, and I.W.W. leaders were beaten, jailed, and occasionally lynched. Five elected Socialist assemblymen were denied their seats in the New York state legislature. This first Red Scare was an ugly, if brief, episode in our history, fueled by labor militancy, runaway inflation, xenophobia and the postwar exhaustion of idealism, as well as by the activities of cynical politicians, businessmen, and fanatics. Little attention was paid to the Bill of Rights, and few took the time to make important distinctions between Communists and others on the Left.[4]

In 1930 a congressional committee headed by Congressman Hamilton Fish of New York investigated Communist activities in the United States and recommended that the party be outlawed. Four years later a probe headed by Congressmen John McCormack and Samuel Dickstein looked into the party and concluded that its growth presented a danger to the country. In 1938, by a vote of 191 to 41, the House created the Special Committee on Un-American Activities, headed by conservative Texas Democrat Martin Dies.

The Dies Committee pioneered virtually all of the techniques later ascribed to "McCarthyism." With strong public support and the backing of the ultraconservative Hearst and McCormick newspapers, as well as the American Legion, the committee recklessly denigrated the loyalty of New Dealers, liberals, socialists, fellow travelers, and Communists, viewing them all as essentially the same. It charged that 1,121 government workers were "sympathetic with totalitarian ideology" and condemned the Roosevelt administration for "coddling" Reds and being "soft" toward Russia. Dies encouraged extremist witnesses, ignored sound rules of evidence, smeared political opponents, and made clever use of the press.

Right-wing newspapers reveled in the committee's every action and often published "leaked" information. The front pages of even the most responsible newspapers were frequently filled with the committee's sensational charges, while denials by the accused—being unsensational—were relegated to the end of articles and back pages. As Alan Barth later observed, "It is the press which executes, so to speak, the sentences passed by congressional committees or by mere individuals speaking under the immunity from suits for slander or libel afforded by Congress."[5]

The committee began to compile huge files on "Un-Americans," based on clippings from right-wing publications and the *Daily Worker,* letterheads of "front" organizations, and other materials from the 1930s. It soon had 600 file cabinets containing more than a million cards, used by thousands of federal officials and others to check up on the "loyalty" of others. In 1944 it published a six-volume report containing the names of 22,000 alleged fellow travelers. A co-author of this formidable blacklist was J. B. Matthews, an ex-radical and Popular Front activist who became the committee's chief research director. A few weeks before being hired, Matthews had appeared as a star witness and cast doubt upon the patriotism of scores of people, including child movie star Shirley Temple.

In 1939 the committee's annual appropriation was increased fourfold to $100,000 (an amount that would soon triple), and throughout the war the House voted overwhelmingly to continue its probes. In 1945 a coalition of Republicans and Southern Democrats made the House Committee on Un-American Activities Congress's first permanent standing committee. This coalition, forged in opposition to the New Deal, would be the primary source of support in Congress for the later excesses of McCarthyites.[6]

In the jittery days before Pearl Harbor congressmen introduced dozens of bills to protect the government from disloyal employees. The McCormack Act of 1938 required agents of foreign powers to register with the government. The Hatch Act of 1939 excluded from federal employment anyone holding membership in a political party or organization advocating the forcible overthrow of the government. This was aimed specifically at the Communist party and the German-American Bund. The Smith Act of 1940 forbade all Americans knowingly or willfully to advocate, advise, abet, or teach the duty, necessity, desirability, or propriety of overthrowing any level of government within the United States. This extremely severe measure enjoyed the support of the President, the Justice, State, Navy, and War Departments, and a long list of patriotic and anti-Communist organizations. One congressman, arguing for passage of the legislation, contended that it went as far as the Constitution permitted to outlaw Communist and fascist organizations. It sailed through the Senate on a voice vote and cleared the House by the overwhelming margin of 392-4.

Several state legislatures passed statutes barring the Communist party from the ballot. In 1940 officials in thirteen states arrested more than 350 party members on a variety of charges. The national mood at the time was such that the House came within three votes of deleting the salary of the American ambassador to Russia from the budget.[7]

After the war, with the advent of hostility between the United States and the Soviet Union, popular opinion about domestic Communists stiffened further. By April 1947, according to a Gallup Poll, 61 percent of the American people supported outlawing the party; by November 1949 the figure had risen to 68 percent. A *Fortune* magazine poll revealed that by February 1948 ten percent of the public thought that the Communist party was reaching the point where it could dominate the nation; another 35 percent believed it was getting stronger and was already in control of important elements in the economy.[8]

Six "little" un-American activities committees were created on the state level, and in 1949 alone fifteen states passed antisubversive laws. The United States Chamber of Commerce began urging Americans to form subcommittees on the local level to identify and expose Communists and those "sympathetic" to their aims, and to build files on "un-American" activities. "In a nutshell, this subcommittee is the eyes of the community."[9]

This growing apprehension was founded in part upon the very real facts of Communist aggression overseas. The coup d'etat in Czechoslovakia in early 1948, the eleven-month Berlin blockade crisis, and the takeover in China, in particular, severely jolted many Americans. The Truman administration's uncompromising portrayals of the Cold War as a struggle between freedom and tyranny, its zealous anti-Communist rhetoric, its prosecution of Communist party leaders under the Smith Act, and its willingness to employ harsh loyalty-security measures, also contributed to public fears. This factor has been greatly exaggerated by the New Left (as it was by the Old Left) but should not be overlooked. Even former Secretary of State Dean Acheson later regretted Truman's loyalty-security program. "I was an officer of that administration and share with it the responsibility for what I am now convinced was a grave mistake and a failure to foresee consequences which were inevitable. That responsibility cannot be escaped or obscured."[10]

More important were the activities of cynical and fanatical politicians and interest groups like the American Legion, eager for votes, power, and influence. HUAC was the leading instrument along these lines during the early years of the Cold War.[11]

In 1945 and 1946 HUAC was dominated by Congressman John Rankin of Mississippi, who had moved to make the body a standing committee. Rankin was a hater: he despised Communists, socialists, liberals, New Dealers, civil libertarians, intellectuals, blacks, aliens, and Jews with fervor. On the floor of the House he once called commentator Walter Winchell "a little slime-mongering kike." "In Rankin's mind," wrote Walter Goodman, "to call a Jew a Communist was a tautology."[12]

J. Parnell Thomas, an ultraconservative New Jersey Republican, served as committee chairman in 1947 and 1948. He was a bitter foe of the New Deal who specialized in bullying witnesses. Robert K. Carr said of him, "Seldom has an important congressional agency been so handicapped by the vulgarity of its leader. . . . Again and again Thomas conducted committee hearings as though he were a cheap comedian or a participant in a street-corner political harangue."[13]

Thomas went to prison in 1949 for payroll padding (having taken the Fifth Amendment before a grand jury), and his successor was John S. Wood, an antilabor white supremacist from Georgia, who had previously been chairman while Rankin captained the ship. With Wood presiding, HUAC was a bit more subdued, but committee members continued to play politics and make extravagant charges of Soviet subversion in all walks of American life.[14]

During the late 1940s HUAC conducted often blatantly publicized investigations of Communists in government, unions, industry, schools, the movies, radio, and the scientific community. It also wrestled with bills to outlaw and circumscribe the Communist party. In the spring of 1948 two members produced the Mundt-Nixon Bill, which would require the federal registration of the party and its front organizations. There was confusion about whether or not the bill would have the effect, forbidden by the Constitution, of outlawing the party. If a Communist failed to register he would be subject to prosecution for defying the law; if he registered he might be jailed for being party to an illegal foreign conspiracy. Nevertheless, the bill whizzed through the House by a vote of 319 to 58. Elections approached, and this was no time to be "soft on the Reds."[15]

HUAC would never obtain more publicity than it did in 1948. In March it clashed with the President over its demand for access to the loyalty file of Dr. Edward U. Condon, a noted physicist and director of the National Bureau of Standards, whom Thomas labeled "one of the weakest links in our atomic security." Determined to protect federal employees from periodic witch-hunts, Truman issued a directive on March 13 that sealed all of the files, basing the order on the principle of executive privilege. Republicans fumed, and the G.O.P. national chairman grumbled about impeachment. The House passed two bills by overwhelming majorities backing its committee. But the President held his ground, and the files remained confidential. To men like Thomas and Nixon, Walter Goodman later mused, "A loyalty file, rich in allegations, hints, rumors, conjectures, was as tempting . . . as a key to the local arsenal would be to delinquent teenagers, and as risky for anybody in the neighborhood." Soon, during a whistle-stop in Oakland, Truman labeled HUAC "more un-American than the activities it is investigating."[16]

In July the committee displayed Elizabeth Bentley, dubbed the "blonde spy queen" by a New York newspaper. She now stated publicly what she had revealed to the FBI three years earlier and had recently told the federal grand jury that indicted eleven Communist party leaders for violating the Smith Act. She had joined the Communist party in 1935, she said, for idealistic reasons. Three years later she met and fell in love with a Soviet agent named Jacob Golos. From 1941 until 1944, shortly after Golos died, Miss Bentley served as a courier in the Communist underground, collecting information in Washington of value to the Russians from over forty government employees and transmitting it to superiors. She worked for a second spy ring briefly before quitting the party and going to the FBI. Among a score of those she named before HUAC and a Senate subcommittee as espionage contacts were Nathan Gregory Silvermaster, an economist with New Deal agencies from 1935 to 1947; William Remington, formerly with the TVA and the War Production Board and currently in the Commerce Department; Lauchlin Currie, who had been an assistant to President Roosevelt for six years; and Harry Dexter White, one of the chief architects of the International Monetary Fund and a former Assistant Secretary of the Treasury.

In due time, Miss Bentley would testify on eight occasions before Congressional committees and in four trials, and she would identify forty-three people as members of the Communist underground. Her story helped convict four persons and resulted in the dismissal of many others. In 1948 HUAC was interested in her primarily as a weapon against the Administration. Her testimony was presented during the special session of the 80th Congress called by the President to challenge the G.O.P. platform. Rather than pass legislation they claimed to support, Republicans began investigating Communism in Democratic administrations.[17]

On August 3 HUAC summoned Whittaker Chambers to the stand to substantiate Miss Bentley's recollections. Chambers, 47, a short, pudgy, unattractive, intelligent, and intensely self-conscious man, was a senior editor of *Time* magazine. He had joined the Communist party in 1924, had been part of the Communist underground apparatus in the mid-1930s, and had been quietly telling his story to various federal officials since 1939. He now made headlines across the world by charging that Alger Hiss had been a Communist from at least 1934, when he first met him, to 1938. This was a name Miss Bentley did not know and had not mentioned. It was a name that was to capture the public's attention for decades. "In the perspective of twenty-five years," Cabell Phillips later wrote, "it can safely be said that no conflict in this century over one man's veracity, no probing into the dark labyrinths of treason and espionage has so roiled the emotions of the populace as this."[18]

Alger Hiss was the embodiment of the liberal elite—the "bright young men" who had flocked to Washington during the New Deal to save the republic, and he was thus the symbol of almost everything most Republicans, particularly in the Midwest, despised. Tall, handsome, urbane, a Phi Beta Kappa graduate of Johns Hopkins and Harvard Law School, Hiss had served as a law clerk to Supreme Court Justice Oliver Wendell Holmes before entering the Agricultural Adjustment Administration in the earliest days of the New Deal. In 1936 he began a career in the State Department. He rose swiftly through the ranks and served as an adviser to President Roosevelt at the Yalta conference, was executive secretary for the Dumbarton Oaks conference, and was a principal adviser to the American delegation at the United Nations Charter Conference in San Francisco. In 1947, at 42, he became president of the highly prestigious Carnegie Endowment for International Peace.

Republicans realized that if Chambers's charge against Hiss could be substantiated the political harvest might be enormous. If Hiss, with his credentials, had been a Communist, then any New Dealer might have been, and the integrity of all recent liberal legislation and Democratic foreign policy could be questioned.

On August 5 Hiss so impressively denied Chambers's allegation that most HUAC members sought to drop the matter. President Truman denounced the investigation as a "red herring" and charged that all of the revelations now on the front pages were known to the FBI and had been presented to a grand jury, which chose not to take action. But Richard Nixon, shrewdly noting the studied evasiveness of many of Hiss's denials, urged his colleagues to persevere. After several private visits with Chambers and an executive session with Hiss, and after quietly receiving direct and indirect leaks of information from FBI officials, Nixon was convinced that his earlier suspicions had been correct. From this point on he staked his political future on Hiss's guilt.

At a committee executive session on August 17 Hiss confronted Chambers, admitting finally that he had known him in the thirties as George Crosley, an impoverished free-lance writer he had helped out for a short time. Fists clenched, Hiss angrily dared his accuser to make his charges in public, thus exposing himself to a law suit.

A nine-hour public hearing followed on August 25, which captured the attention of the nation. Hiss was again evasive and cautious, while Chambers appeared to have nothing to hide. When asked about what motive he might have for destroying Hiss after all these years, Chambers replied, "We were close friends. But we got caught in the tragedy of history. Mr. Hiss represents the concealed enemy we are all fighting. I am testifying against him with remorse and pity. But in this moment of historic jeopardy at which this nation now stands, so help me God, I could not do otherwise."

A few days later, on the radio program "Meet the Press," Chambers stated that Hiss had been a Communist and "may be one now." A month passed before Hiss sued for libel.

Hiss could boast a formidable array of personal references: many of the nation's foremost political leaders, top State Department officials, and two Supreme Court Justices. It became an indispensable part of the liberal-radical credo to believe in Hiss's innocence. (And so it remained in 1978 when an explosion of criticism greeted a study by historian Allen Weinstein concluding that Hiss was guilty.) Hiss correctly pointed out that political opportunists like Nixon and Thomas were actually seeking grounds to taint the entire New Deal, the peace agreements, and the United Nations with subversion. But his name-dropping and his protests, however persuasive to the Left, were inadequate responses to Chambers's charge.

The Communists-in-government issue, as we have seen, was not of major importance in the 1948 elections. Republicans were too confident of victory over the fumbling little man in the White House to do more than smile condescendingly and rent ballrooms for election night celebrations. When Truman upset all predictions with his narrow victory, he ruptured a pattern in the political process that should have turned the Democrats out of office. Republicans, reeling from their fifth consecutive defeat in a presidential election and led by frustrated conservatives who had long cried in vain for the party's top nomination, flew into a boiling rage that quickly erupted into the second Red Scare. Political scientist Earl Latham, a careful and wise student of these matters, wrote, "McCarthyism may have been more than a political phenomenon—but it was at least a political phenomenon. McCarthy acquired his vogue and most of his meaning from the immediate political circumstances which begot him, and for which he was the temporary instrument." With the aid of some conservative Democrats, G.O.P. leaders were determined to damage and defeat at all cost the liberals who chortled and sniggered at the *Chicago Tribune*'s headline declaring Dewey the winner. The main thrust of their bombardment in the next several years was to be the Reds-in-high-places pitch that had proven newsworthy before the fateful election. The Hiss case was the cutting edge for the attack.[19]

At a pretrial examination in mid-November Chambers accused Hiss for the first time of espionage and produced copies of State Department documents he said Hiss had transmitted to him. Hiss had sworn that he had not seen George Crosley after January 1, 1937. Chambers's documents were from 1937 and 1938. If it could be proved that the documents had been copied by Hiss and given to Chambers after the first day of 1937 the accused would be discredited. A few days later, with a burst of publicity, HUAC investigators revealed the existence of microfilms of further State Department documents Chambers said he had received from Hiss and recently hidden in a hollowed-out pumpkin on his Maryland farm. Republican Karl Mundt boasted to reporters that the new evidence contained "definite proof of one of the most extensive espionage rings in the history of the United States."

On December 15 a federal grand jury indicted Hiss on two counts of perjury. The statute of limitations on espionage had run out long before, so Hiss was charged with lying about not having seen Chambers after January 1, 1937, and about not having turned over copies of State Department documents to him. The indictment might only involve perjury, but everyone understood that the real issue in question was whether or not the genteel, sophisticated, self-assured, influential, Ivy League New Dealer had once been a Communist spy.[20]

As the Hiss case traveled through the courts in 1949 other events, domestic and foreign, heated up the political atmosphere and provided Republicans with ample grounds for anguished oratory. "The shocks of 1949," wrote Eric Goldman, "loosed within American life a vast impatience, a turbulent bitterness, a rancor akin to revolt. It was a strange rebelliousness, quite without parallel in the history of the United States."[21]

In March, Judith Coplon, a Department of Justice employee, was arrested as a Soviet spy. Richard Nixon demanded a congressional investigation: "This case shows why the department may be unfit and unqualified to carry out the responsibility of protecting the national security against Communist infiltration."[22]

HUAC published a booklet entitled *Spotlight on Spies,* adding it to its popular *100 Things You Should Know About Communism* series. According to *The New York Times,* "spy stories" of one kind or another occupied 32 percent of the combined front pages of the New York daily newspapers during one week in June.[23]

The Educational Policies Commission of the National Education Association reported in June that twenty-two states required oaths of allegiance for teachers; that thirty-eight states had general sedition laws; that twenty-one states forbade seditious teaching; that thirty-one states prohibited teachers from belonging to groups that advocated sedition; that twelve states had authorized the dismissal of teachers for undefined "disloyalty."[24]

The American Civil Liberties Union entitled its 29th annual report, which told of an anti-Communist wave sweeping the country, "In the Shadow of Fear." President Truman said the nation was on the verge of a Red hysteria and likened the era to that which produced the Alien and Sedition Acts.[25]

On August 5 Secretary of State Dean Acheson Released a White Paper of more than a thousand pages explaining why the Nationalist government of China was on the verge of collapse and portraying Chiang Kai-shek's administration as corrupt, reactionary, and incompetent. Republicans cried whitewash and renewed their charges of an anti-Chiang plot in the State Department. Alfred Kohlberg, spearhead of the China Lobby and a close associate of many right-wing Republicans, declared, "The real purpose of the White Paper seems . . . to be to reveal to the chancellories of the world the story of the American betrayal of the Republic of China. What could be of greater aid to the Soviet Union than this?"[26]

September brought the stunning announcement of Russia's atomic explosion. A few weeks later the eleven top American Communist party leaders were convicted. In December Chiang and his Nationalist government fled mainland China for the island of Formosa, and all of Asia seemed threatened with absorption by the Communists.

In its annual report for 1949 HUAC warned, "We feel more than ever impressed with the insidiousness and vastness of the ramifications of the Communist movement and the urgent necessity for unflagging efforts to expose and curb its machinations."[27]

The United States had long had a somewhat romantic attachment to China. Missionaries had been active there for more than a century, and Americans continued to believe that the Open Door policy had been a diplomatic triumph that had saved the vast country from European exploitation. We had a sense of responsibility toward China, a feeling that we were somehow morally responsible for her fate. In 1951 George Kennan spoke of "a certain sentimentality toward the Chinese," which, he warned, was both patronizing and dangerously naive.[28]

China had been engaged in a fierce civil war since the 1920s. The Chinese Communist party, founded in 1921 and led by Mao Tse-tung, had collaborated with Sun Yat-sen and the Kuomintang, or National People's Party, in the early 1920s. With Sun Yat-sen's death and the rise of anti-Communist Chiang Kai-shek, however, the veil of friendship vanished, and the Communists and Kuomintang were soon locked in deadly combat for control of the country. By 1931 there were actually two Chinas. An alliance was worked out between them in 1937 in response to attacks by the Japanese, and during the Second World War Chiang was acknowledged to be the nation's leader. But throughout the years of fighting neither side lost sight of its ultimate aim, which was the destruction of the other. By Pearl Harbor the Communists were in control of an area of 150,000 square miles, containing over 50 million people. At every opportunity during the war they sought to expand their authority.

Chiang had strong support in the United States. Henry R. Luce, for example, born in China to Presbyterian missionaries, intensely admired the Chinese leader, especially after Chiang's baptism as a Methodist in 1931. Luce's supreme goal in life was the Christianization of China, and in Chiang he believed he had found an unblemished savior. His influential *Time* magazine lavished praise upon Chiang and his attractive wife for years. (By 1944 Luce's holdings in the media were such that an opinion of his could reach at least a third, and perhaps considerably more, of the nation's literate adult population.) Luce was also the spearhead of United China Relief, which had a prestigious board that raised millions of dollars for Chiang during the war.[29]

With the outbreak of World War II, President Roosevelt treated Chiang as the leader of a great power and saw to it that he received a half billion dollars from the United States. It was the President's hope that the Generalissimo (who had sought twice that amount) would bolster his military forces and engage as many Japanese as possible in combat while the Allies concentrated their initial wartime efforts in North Africa and Europe.

In January 1942, Secretary of War Henry L. Stimson selected Gen. Joseph W. (Vinegar Joe) Stilwell to be Chiang's chief of staff and head of operations in the China-Burma-India theater. Stilwell, 58, was a hard-driving, outspoken West Point graduate who had served two tours of duty in China. Placed in command of two Chinese armies, he was soon given the task of preparing for the reconquest of Burma. Almost immediately Stilwell became a bitter critic of Chiang Kai-shek, charging that he sabotaged Stilwell's authority and was more interested in stopping the Chinese Communists than the Japanese. Before long he referred to the Generalissimo as the "Peanut" and described him to Theodore H. White as "an ignorant, illiterate, peasant son of a bitch." Stilwell also clashed with Maj.-

Gen. Claire Chennault, an arch-conservative who served as Chiang's chief aviation adviser and enjoyed direct access to President Roosevelt.

At Stilwell's request, the State Department assigned John Paton Davies, Jr., to his staff. Davies had been born in 1908 in China, where his parents served as Baptist missionaries. He was widely respected as an expert in Chinese affairs and had long been critical of Chiang and the Nationalist government. Along with other State Department "Old China Hands," John Stewart Service (also born in China to missionaries) and John Carter Vincent, with the American embassy in China in 1942, Davies had confidence in the Chinese Communists' willingness to fight the Japanese and saw them as a positive, popular contrast to what Service contemptuously referred to as the "Kuomintang dictatorship." These experienced, well-trained, Chinese-speaking Foreign Service officers were not Communists or part of a conspiracy to turn China over to the Communists. (More than a dozen of the China Hands would later be charged with the "loss" of China.) They were, however, extremely displeased with the military foot-dragging, reactionary policies, and sordid corruption of Chiang's regime and, like many journalists on the scene, were impressed by the Communists' personal austerity and charm and by their espousal of liberal economic policies and orderly democratic growth. Most of the China Hands believed that the Communists were destined to rule China and hoped that the United States would encourage their independence from Russia and win their friendship. Several of them advocated direct American aid to the Communist armies in order to battle the Japanese more effectively and force reforms upon the Kuomintang, which would be compelled to compete for the favor of the Chinese people. Stilwell agreed, but the proposal was ultimately rejected.

At a time when Americans and Russians were allies, it was United States policy to promote collaboration between the two Chinese rivals. Roosevelt sent Vice-President Henry Wallace to confer with Chiang in June 1944 to persuade him to create a united front with the Communists against the Japanese. Wallace was accompanied by John Carter Vincent, then chief of the Division of Chinese Affairs in the State Department, and Owen Lattimore, an official of the Office of War Information and an authority on Asian affairs. Chiang rejected the Vice-President's naive suggestion, demanded impossible concessions from the Communists, and stated flatly that he lacked confidence in Stilwell. A few months later Stilwell, who had fought heroically alongside Chinese troops in North Burma, was replaced by Lt. Gen. Albert C. Wedemeyer. Wedemeyer was an admirer of the Generalissimo and was soon critical of Davies, Service, and several other Foreign Service professionals he inherited.

In August the President sent Maj. Gen. Patrick J. Hurley to China as his personal representative, instructing him to attempt to unify military forces in China. Hurley was a combative, fast-talking, ultraconservative, 61-year-old Oklahoma oil and gas attorney who lacked virtually any knowledge of China. He was convinced that the State Department was full of pro-Communists and pro-Zionists.

On his way to China, Hurley was persuaded by Foreign Minister Molotov in Moscow that the Chinese Communists were not genuine Communists. He later told a news conference:

> All the demands that the Communist party have been making have been on a democratic basis. That has led to the statement that the Communist party in China are not, in fact, real Communists. The Communist party of China is supporting exactly the same principles as those promulgated by the National Government of China and conceded to be objectives also of the National Government. . . .

Hurley was able to obtain a draft agreement, signed by Mao Tse-tung, calling for a "coalition National Government." His buoyancy was short-lived, however, for Chiang turned up his nose at the idea of sharing his absolute power with another absolutist, ever mindful of the total authority he wished to possess in postwar China.

When Hurley resigned in November 1945 he cast the full blame for the failure of his mission upon State Department officials and Foreign Service experts. In a bitter letter to President Truman, he wrote:

> The professional foreign service men sided with the Chinese Communist armed party and the imperialist bloc of nations whose policy it was to keep China divided against herself. Our professional diplomats continuously advised the Communists that my efforts in preventing the collapse of the National Government did not represent the policy of the United States. These same professionals openly advised the Communist armed party to decline unification of the Chinese Communist Army with the National Army unless the Chinese Communists were given control.

In an appearance before the Senate Foreign Relations Committee he named Service, Davies, Vincent, and several other China Hands as the culprits. Earlier in the year he had had Service recalled to Washington after Service had drafted a policy statement, signed by every political officer in the American embassy in Chungking, that the general considered insubordinate.

The day after Hurley submitted his resignation, President Truman named General of the Army George C. Marshall as his personal representative in China and authorized him to offer China a loan of a half billion dollars if a coalition government could be formed to administer it. The wartime goal of unification was now extended to peacetime in the hope of creating political stability. The retired Chief of Staff struggled in vain for more than a year; neither the Kuomintang nor the Communist leadership was willing to abandon its desire to eliminate the other. The President recalled Marshall on January 6, 1947, appointing him Secretary of State within the month.

No further missions were sent to China, and a feeling of helpless resignation prevailed in Washington. The United States continued to give economic and military aid to Chiang: from 1940 to war's end $645 million in loans and $825.7 million in Lend-Lease aid went to China; from V-J day to mid-1949 the National Government received more than two billion dollars in grants and credits plus great quantities of weapons. We would not, however, become more directly involved in a civil war.

Nationalist weapons often wound up in Communist hands, being abandoned in the field or sold. In the last three months of 1948 about 60 percent of all American military supplies were captured intact by the Communists. Whole divisions of Chiang's troops deserted to the Red revolution sweeping the country. When Secretary of State Dean Acheson issued the White Paper in August 1949, he declared:

> The unfortunate but inescapable fact is that the ominous result of the civil war in China was beyond the control of the government of the United States. Nothing that this country did or could have done within the reasonable limits of its capabilities could have changed that result; nothing that was left undone by this country has contributed to it. It was the product of internal Chinese forces, forces which this country tried to influence but could not. A decision was arrived at within China, if only a decision by default.[30]

At this same time increasing publicity was being given to what was called the "China Lobby," and Democratic Representative Mike Mansfield of Montana unsuccessfully requested a congressional investigation of it. The China Lobby was a loose association of Chiang Kai-shek supporters that spent large sums of money promoting the interests of Nationalist China.

Its roots could be traced at least to 1940, and it became a prominent force in Washington, especially after the war when the internal power struggle in China intensified. In 1948 the lobby became closely associated with the G.O.P., convinced that Chiang would be treated more generously by a Dewey administration. After Dewey's defeat and the advent of the second Red Scare, large numbers of Republicans embraced the China Lobby's view that the ascent of Communism in China was the responsibility of traitors employed by Roosevelt and Truman. The right wing of the G.O.P., especially Senators Styles Bridges of New Hampshire, William Knowland of California, Kenneth Wherry of Nebraska, and Congressman Walter Judd of Minnesota (a former medical missionary in China), was extremely vocal on Chiang's behalf, and Senators Vandenberg and Taft lent their considerable prestige to the outcry. Senator Pat McCarran, a maverick Democrat rumored to have close ties to the gambling interests in his home state of Nevada, was also in the thick of things. HUAC's hearings into alleged internal subversion provided pro-Chiang writers with excellent targets, and for years they would argue that Lauchlin Currie, Harry Dexter White, and Alger Hiss were part of the plot to give China to the Reds. The Old China Hands were condemned persistently as handmaidens of the Communists.

China Lobby authors included such ultraconservatives as Joseph P. Kamp, John T. Flynn, and Freda Utley; Henry Luce gave the support of his huge publishing empire and put Chiang on the cover of *Time* magazine for a record seventh time. There were also newspaper editors like the fiery New Hampshire extremist William Loeb, businessmen, religious leaders, military men, and others who backed Chiang and contributed to the flow of propaganda and influence-peddling on his behalf. Some of them were concerned citizens, some were fanatics, others were deeply cynical and looking for political or economic advantages.[31]

Critics often stressed the economic motivation, charging for example that China Lobby figures T.V. Soong and H.H. Kung, both relatives of Chiang, had grown extremely wealthy on American aid to China and were after more money. Gen. Claire Chennault, it was said, was set up in a lucrative airline business with American dollars. Some politicians, including Styles Bridges in 1948, received campaign donations from China Lobby sources. A New York public relations expert, on the payroll of the Bank of China, flew to California in 1950 to organize an "independent citizens committee for Nixon."[32]

The central figure in the China Lobby was Alfred Kohlberg, a short, rotund, bald, New York textile manufacturer and importer in his early sixties. Kohlberg first visited China in 1916 and soon created a business that eventually brought him $1.5 million a year. He shipped linens from Ireland to southeastern China, had them embroidered by thousands of young people working for the barest of salaries, and sent the finished products to the United States. (In 1943 the Federal Trade Commission ordered him to stop selling Chinese-made lace under fancy European names.) Kohlberg's profits depended upon Chiang's control of China, and this undoubtedly played a role in his militant defense of the Generalissimo. But there was surely more to the story, for Kohlberg was a tireless zealot, ever eager to persuade the world that the popular ruler of China had been stabbed in the back by Communists and pro-Communists in the United States.

Self-educated about Communism and unable to speak Chinese, Kohlberg said that he first became aware of a conspiracy against Chiang among American embassy officials in 1943. In 1944 he began a three-year attack upon the Institute of Pacific Relations, to which he belonged, for following the Communist "party line" on China. A year later he encouraged Patrick Hurley to resign and was soon working to defeat the Senate confirmation of John Carter Vincent for the Foreign Service rank of career minister. As Chiang's fortunes continued to decline, Kohlberg sent thousands of letters to newspaper editors, government officials, and prominent citizens; he wrote articles, subsidized at least two right-wing magazines, and in 1946 was the driving force in the newly formed American China Policy Association, led at different times by Clare Boothe Luce and William Loeb. Kohlberg also served as president of the American Jewish League against Communism and as an adviser to the Committee for Constitutional Government. The latter organization had a mailing list of 350,000 names by 1950 and distributed tons of pro-Nationalist propaganda written by Freda Utley and John T. Flynn, among others.[33]

By early 1950 literature and rhetoric about spies, traitors, and betrayals were commonplace across the United States. When Alger Hiss was convicted of perjury on January 21 (his first trial had resulted in a hung jury), the political atmosphere crackled with even greater suspicion and frustration. The conviction was a stunning vindication for Richard Nixon and HUAC and a severe jolt to all of the "respectable" people who had testified on behalf of Hiss's integrity and patriotism. Congressman Mundt urged the President now to begin to weed out the government employees "whose Soviet leanings have contributed so greatly to the deplorable mess of our foreign policy." Nixon called the Hiss case only "a small part of the whole shocking story of Communist espionage in the United States."[34]

When President Truman informed the world on January 31 of the nation's intention to develop the hydrogen bomb, Dr. Albert Einstein warned that all life could be obliterated by the weapon, and Dr. Vannevar Bush declared that no defense could be constructed against it. Americans were soon speculating about bomb shelters, and there was talk about the possibility of digging mass graves in Central Park in case of a nuclear attack on Manhattan.[35]

On February 3 came the news that Dr. Klaus Fuchs, a British physicist who had worked at the Los Alamos project during the war, had been arrested as a Soviet spy. The *Chicago Tribune* headline screamed "REDS GET OUR BOMB PLANS!" Republican Senator Styles Bridges called J. Edgar Hoover's report of the arrest "one of the most shocking things I have ever listened to." G.O.P. Senator George W. Malone of Nevada (soon to join McCarthy at two of his Lincoln Day appearances) warned against anyone who criticized the FBI, which had spearheaded the investigation of Fuchs. He also observed, "Every move the State Department has made since 1934 when we recognized Russia has been toward strengthening the Communists."[36]

On February 6 Republicans adopted a supplement to their 1948 platform condemning "the dangerous degree" to which Reds and fellow travelers had worked their way to high government posts and deploring the "soft attitude" of the Truman administration toward government employees who held or supported Communist positions. The next day J. Edgar Hoover (eager to secure funds to hire 700 more FBI employees) talked further to senators about Fuchs and contended that the United States contained about 540,000 Communists and fellow travelers. Republican Senator Homer Capehart of Indiana gasped, "I am flabbergasted. It is the most alarming thing I have heard in a long time. Think what a powerful 'fifth column' that would make if we ever got into a war." All across the nation Republicans filled Lincoln Day speeches with references to the Reds and pro-Reds who were running loose and formulating American policies.[37]

Joe McCarthy agreed to make five Lincoln Day appearances on the rubber-chicken circuit to fulfill his responsibility to the party. The scheduling was drab, fit for only the least conspicuous of senators: the tour was to begin in Wheeling, West Virginia, and end in Huron, South Dakota. The only bright spots were stopovers in Reno and Las Vegas, where Joe could exercise his passion for gambling.

McCarthy didn't give much thought to the content of the speeches he was obliged to deliver; it mattered little, for news coverage was likely to be minimal at best. He decided to have his office whip up a talk on housing and find somebody else to write a piece on Communists in government, a proven crowd pleaser. Two reporters for the ultraconservative *Washington Times-Herald,* Ed Nellor and Jim Walters, were suggested as possible authors of the second speech. Someone in McCarthy's office called the *Times-Herald* and mistakenly contacted George Waters (instead of Jim Walters), a city desk man, offering him the paid assignment. Waters accepted enthusiastically. Soon, however, he found that he needed help and turned to Nellor, who had covered the Hiss case and similar probes for the *New York Sun* as well as the *Times-Herald.* Waters also asked assistance of *Chicago Tribune* reporter Willard Edwards, a friend who furnished some of his recent clippings. The final product, pieced together by Waters, came largely from the pen of Ed Nellor. Joe took a strong liking to both men, hiring Waters as his press secretary and inviting Nellor to become his speech writer. (Joe would later state under oath that he was the sole author of the Wheeling address. "No one else had anything to do with writing the speech.")[38]

There was nothing very original about the brief address McCarthy took with him to Wheeling on February 9. It bristled with standard right-wing rhetoric about traitors in high places and bore down heavily upon the State Department and Alger Hiss. Portions of the introduction were taken word for word from the speech McCarthy gave in Madison attacking the *Capital Times.* Data cited concerning the alleged growth of Communism since the end of the war could be found in numerous speeches given by Republicans at the time. (McCarthy's speech badly distorted the figures, however. While Richard Nixon had said two weeks earlier that there were currently 540,000,000 people "on our side," 600,000,000 neutrals, and 800,000,000 on the Russian side, Joe's address declared that there were 80,000,000,000 "under the absolute domination of Soviet Russia," while "on our side, the figure has shrunk to about 500,000.") Three paragraphs on the State Department came from a Willard Edwards piece published a week earlier in the *Chicago Tribune.* A blast against John Stewart Service had appeared originally in the *Washington Times-Herald* and had been read into the *Congressional Record* by McCarthy on January 5. Language used to condemn Hiss was almost identical to that employed by Richard Nixon in a speech before the House on January 26. An excerpt from the testimony of an FBI man alleging to show that the State Department had quashed the exposure of spies in its midst was taken from hearings before the Senate Judiciary Committee in 1949.[39]

The speech singled out for attack not only Hiss and Service but also Gustavo Duran ("He was taken into the State Department from his job as a lieutenant colonel in the Communist International Brigade"), Mrs. Mary Jane Kenney ("from the Board of Economic Warfare in the State Department, who was named in an FBI report and in a House committee report as a courier for the Communist party while working for the government"), and H. Julian Wadleigh, incorrectly cited as Julian H. Wadleigh ("After the statute of limitations had run so he could not be prosecuted for treason, he openly and brazenly not only admitted but proclaimed that he had been a member of the Communist party—that while working for the State Department he stole a vast number of secret documents—and furnished documents to the Russian spy ring of which he was a part"). All of these names, products of HUAC probes and the *Amerasia* case, were familiar in right-wing circles.[40]

The most explosive sentence in the speech contended that McCarthy was privy to information that would in effect prove Secretary of State Acheson guilty of treason:

> And ladies and gentlemen, while I cannot take the time to name all the men in the State Department who have been named as active members of the Communist Party and members of a spy ring, I have here in my hand a list of 205—a list of names that were made known to the Secretary of State as being members of the Communist Party and who nevertheless are still working and shaping policy in the State Department.

The unmentioned source of the figure 205 was a letter written on July 26, 1946, by then Secretary of State James F. Byrnes to Democratic Congressman Adolph Sabath of Illinois, a document promptly inserted into the *Congressional Record*. The letter was a reply to an inquiry about the screening of approximately 4,000 federal employees who were transferred to the State Department from wartime agencies. Some 3,000 case histories had been examined, Byrnes stated, resulting in a recommendation against permanent employment in 285 cases. To date, 79 had been "separated from the service," 26 because they were aliens and therefore ineligible for peacetime government employment. Seventy-nine subtracted from 285 is 206; a slip in arithmetic made it 205.

As would soon be noted, the Byrnes letter contained no reference to Communist party membership, a list of names, or Dean Acheson. And, of course, it was three-and-a-half years old. How many of the 205 were still on the department's payroll, let alone in policy-making positions, was in fact unknown.

Joe arrived in Wheeling on Thursday afternoon, February 9. He was met at the airport by Thomas B. Sweeney, a former Republican senatorial candidate and McCarthy's host for the evening; Frank Desmond, a reporter from the *Wheeling Intelligencer;* and Francis J. Love, a local attorney and former G.O.P. congressman. During the drive to Wheeling, Love informed the senator that his speech that evening would be broadcast over a local 50,000-watt radio station, WWVA, and that the station management had requested an advance copy. Joe replied that he had a rough draft of two speeches, one on federal housing and the other on Communists in government. Love suggested that he talk on the latter topic, and Joe agreed. He gave one copy of his thirteen-page speech to Sweeney, who was to take it to the radio station, and another to Desmond. He kept a third copy, explaining that he intended to work on it further in his hotel.[41]

That evening more than 275 people were present in the Colonnade room of the McClure Hotel for the Lincoln Day festivities sponsored by the Ohio County Republican Women's Club. After the invocation by a Presbyterian minister and a "group sing" led by a state senator, the introductions were made and Senator McCarthy strode smiling to the podium.[42]

How closely did Joe stick to his prepared speech? Did he read the sentence about having a list of 205 Communists in the State Department? Politicians, congressional investigators, journalists, and historians would argue about that for years.

Although we cannot be certain, it seems very likely that Joe closely followed the speech he distributed earlier and that he did read the controversial "205" sentence. James K. Whitaker, WWVA's news editor, supervised the taping of McCarthy's speech and followed the manuscript as Joe spoke. He later swore to Tydings Committee investigators that the senator had read the address as written, with the exception of a few connective phrases that did not materially alter the meaning of the text. Although the radio station's program director, Paul A. Myers, virtually repudiated a similar statement under careful interrogation, he distinctly remembered hearing the figure 205 while listening to the tape recording of the speech.[43]

On the other hand, several who attended the Wheeling speech reported to Tydings Committee investigators that McCarthy seemed to speak extemporaneously, that he walked around the platform and only occasionally referred to his manuscript (also described as a sheaf of papers and notes). William Callahan, who introduced McCarthy, questioned Whitaker's ability to follow McCarthy's manuscript carefully while handling recording details. He thought that the senator had used two different figures in his speech. Francis Love also recalled two figures but could not remember if 205 was one of them. Herman E. Gieske, editor of the *Intelligencer,* attended the speech and did not recall a mention of the figure 205.[44]

McCarthy himself later told several different stories about what had happened, but at times he admitted saying 205 and using the Sabath letter in Wheeling. He made five references to the letter and the figure (twice cited as 207) during and immediately after the remainder of his tour: in Denver, Salt Lake City, Reno, Los Angeles, and Milwaukee. On the Senate floor, on February 20, he reluctantly conceded that he had said 205 in Wheeling. In a 1951 interview with *U.S. News and World Report* he stated:

> Up in West Virginia we read to the audience a letter written by Jimmy Byrnes, the then Secretary of State, to Congressman Sabath, in which he said that out of 3,000 employes screened—employes who were being transferred from other departments into the State Department—they found 284 unfit for Government service. He said of the 284 we discharged 79, leaving a total of 205. That night I called upon Acheson and the President to tell us where those 205 were, why they kept them in if the President's own board says they were unfit for service.[45]

In his 1952 *McCarthyism, The Fight For America,* Joe made the same contention but added, "At Wheeling, I said that while I did not have the names of the 205 referred to in the Byrnes letter, I did have the names of 57 who were either members of or loyal to the Communist Party."[46]

Unfortunately, the tape recording was routinely erased after the speech was broadcast. The *Intelligencer* account, written by Frank Desmond, contained the full "205" sentence. But under questioning by Tydings Committee investigators, Desmond later admitted that he had taken the figure from the manuscript McCarthy had given him and that he had listened to the speech the night before only "in a general way."

When a part-time Associated Press correspondent, Norman L. Yost, called in a paragraph or two from the story, Charles R. Lewis, night editor in the Associated Press bureau at Charlestown, West Virginia, was astonished by the claim of 205 Communists in the State Department and asked Yost to verify it. Yost told Lewis to hold on while he had his reporter check with McCarthy. A moment later Yost returned to the telephone and said that the figure was accurate. Just before 2:00 A.M. on February 10 the 110-word story sped to newspapers across the country.[47]

At first it barely stirred a ripple. One study of 129 newspapers, including samples from every part of the nation, revealed that only eighteen carried the Associated Press account on Friday, February 10. Ten others, employing the United Press, ran a similar story on February 11, along with a denial by the State Department that it was harboring 205 Communists. Only three of the original eighteen gave the story page-one coverage, and two of them were fairly small newspapers. Perhaps many news editors failed at first to grasp the significance of the charge; after all, Republicans had been ranting about the State Department almost daily. Others may have been suspicious, wondering why the Associated Press assigned so little space to such a powerful allegation.[48]

When Francis Love drove McCarthy to the airport on the morning of the 10th he proudly showed the senator the *Wheeling Intelligencer,* containing excerpts from the speech. Joe thus realized as he left Wheeling for Salt Lake City that the charge in his prepared speech would reach a wide audience. He did not yet know how wide, but it was certain that sooner or later someone would demand to see his list of 205 Communists.[49]

It didn't take long. During a half-hour stopover in Denver reporters asked the senator to comment on the State Department denial of his charges. As he had done so many times in his life, Joe decided to bluff. He possessed a list of 207 "bad risks" still working in the State Department, he said, and would be glad to display it. Unfortunately, it was in a suit he had left on the plane. ("Left Commie list in other bag" was the line the *Denver Post* ran under a photograph of the senator pawing through his briefcase.) If Dean Acheson would call him in Salt Lake City, he said, he would be pleased to read the list to him.[50]

Of course, McCarthy did not have a list; the Sabath letter did not contain names. Joe elected to switch his evidence, and this required him to alter the figure on Reds in the State Department.

Ed Nellor had passed on to McCarthy a report he had received from Robert E. Lee, an ex-FBI man who became chief of staff of the House Committee on Appropriations in 1947. A subcommittee of this body, during the 80th Congress, had conducted an investigation into the State Department's personnel security program and (prior to Truman's order to the contrary) had enjoyed access to the department's loyalty files. Lee and other investigators sifted through hundreds of files for six weeks and wrote a report containing summaries of 108 individual cases Lee called "incidents of inefficiencies." No Communists had been discovered, but of the 108 Lee personally questioned the loyalty of 45 or 50. Hearings were held in early 1948, and the State Department defended itself sufficiently to satisfy House Republicans, who declared it free of subversives. (Lee angrily sent a copy of the report to HUAC.) In March the department presented statistics showing that as of that time 57 of the 108 persons on the list were employed in the department and 51 were not. Of the 57, more than half had been investigated and cleared for employment by the FBI; twenty-two cases were still being probed.[51]

McCarthy twisted this information for his own purposes. The 57 who were still employed in March 1948 became 57 "card-carrying Communists" in the State Department as of February 1950. In a radio interview in Salt Lake City, picked up by the Associated Press, McCarthy declared that the night before in Wheeling he had said that he possessed the names of "57 card-carrying members of the Communist party" at work in the State Department. "Now I want to tell the Secretary of State this, if he wants to call me tonight at the Utah Hotel I will be glad to give him the names of those 57 card-carrying Communists." Joe protected himself, however, by declaring that he would turn over the names only if Acheson would provide "all information as to their communistic activities" to a congressional investigating committee. This would mean violating the President's order closing the department's loyalty files. Joe knew perfectly well that the Secretary of State could not and would not take such action; again, he was bluffing. McCarthy did not have a single name. The "Lee list" of 108 case summaries used numbers rather than names to identify individuals, and only two congressmen on the subcommittee had been given names to match the numbers.[52]

Why did Joe switch from the Sabath letter to the Lee list, given the fact that neither provided him with names? Perhaps because the Lee document at least contained a lot of information. It also was of more recent origin and had come from a Republican-dominated subcommittee.

More importantly, McCarthy at this point did not always understand what he was saying. He switched from 205 to 57 without batting an eye, but he then continued at times to mention 205 and kindred figures, giving headaches to reporters who were trying to keep things straight. In Salt Lake City he said that the 57 were "not necessarily" all among the 205! When Sen. Clinton P. Anderson asked privately about the numbers a short time later, Joe was confused, admitting to his friend, "I guess I made a mistake in not reading very carefully and I threw them all in together." The terminology of loyalty-security matters escaped him completely. "Bad risks" and "Communists" appeared at times to be synonyms. And he spoke of "card-carrying" Communists at a time when no Communist carried a card. (The party had recalled them several years earlier.)[53]

Then too, he was deliberately distorting the information he possessed. This was still merely a political game to Joe, and he chose not to be cautious or scrupulous about his charges. Why not summon a few headlines by baiting the Secretary of State? Other Republicans had done the same. So he couldn't produce 57 names. Who would ever know? Who could force him to reveal his sources? If he riled a few Democrats and diplomats, so much the better. The G.O.P. would know he was doing a good job on Lincoln Day.

Moreover, McCarthy failed to comprehend at first the distinctiveness of his claim to be able to identify specific Communists in the State Department. Richard Nixon and Karl Mundt might vilify bureaucrats and talk about subversion in high places, but they never used precise figures or pretended to know exactly who the large numbers of subversives were. McCarthy had recklessly exaggerated fairly standard and usually carefully calculated right-wing political rhetoric and was unaware of the potential consequences.

On Saturday morning, February 11, he flew to Reno where he received a telegram from Deputy Undersecretary of State John E. Puerifoy requesting the names of the 205 Communists allegedly in the State Department. Never one to shrink from a challenge and sensing the possibility of some sizable publicity, Joe shot off a letter to President Truman, released to the press by his Washington office. Despite the "blackout," McCarthy wrote, he had compiled a list of 57 Communists in the State Department. "This list is available to you, but you can get a much longer list by ordering Secretary Acheson to give you a list of those whom your board listed as being disloyal and who are still working in the State Department." He then muddled the figures in the Sabath document by claiming that only 80 of 300 State Department employees certified for discharge had actually been dismissed. And those dismissals, he charged, had been achieved only "after a lengthy consultation with Alger Hiss." (Joe had no such evidence; he was compounding his bluff.) He concluded by warning the President that if he refused to require Acheson to reveal all information on State Department suspects, including "those who were placed in the department by Alger Hiss," and if he failed to revoke his order sealing the loyalty files, he would be labeling the Democratic Party "the bed-fellow of international communism."[54]

Later that day two local reporters tracked McCarthy to Sen. George Malone's office. The door was unlocked and they walked in. Joe was alone, talking on the telephone, and it soon became apparent that someone on his staff in Washington was on the other end of the line. Joe was asking how things were going. Had his charges yet generated any publicity? He tapped the telephone mouthpiece with his fountain pen from time to time, explaining to his startled visitors that he was breaking up a wiretap. (The FBI would later discover illegal wiretaps on the telephones of two McCarthy employees, Don Surine and Ed Nellor.) "That's great, great," he said at one point, writing furiously. "Give me some more names." One reporter looked over the senator's shoulder and saw him write "Howard Shipley" on a pad.

After Joe had hung up, the reporters interviewed him about his allegations and requested some names of Communists. When Joe mentioned three or four names, one of the reporters asked if he intended to repeat them in his speech that evening; he didn't want to print them unless the senator was willing to be quoted. Joe curtly reminded the young man that he was an attorney and asserted that he knew more about libel than the reporter did.

Before delivering his address, according to *Nevada State Journal* reporter Edward Conners, Joe scratched out the 205 figure and wrote in "57 card-carrying members."[55]

That evening, before a crowd of over 400 Republicans in the Mapes Hotel, Joe again presented the speech he had given in Wheeling. According to press reports, he followed his manuscript fairly closely. Besides the statistical alteration, however, he also made a change in his four specific examples. He mentioned Service, Duran, and Kenney but substituted Harlow Shapley for H. Julian Wadleigh. It was apparent to the two reporters who had met him earlier in the day that the senator had been given the name over the telephone, copying it incorrectly at first, and probably knew nothing about the man. Joe again used the erroneous figures 300 and 80 when referring to the (still unidentified) Sabath letter. And he muffed Service's name, referring to him as "John W. Service."[56]

After the speech, a reporter asked the senator if he had actually called the four people he named traitors. "I did not," Joe replied, "and you will notice I didn't call them Communists, either." "I don't care if these people sue me," he added. "It might give me a platform from which to expose them." Of course, this disavowal was made specifically to avoid law suits; McCarthy did not enjoy congressional immunity on this junket. Reminded that the four names were described as "specific cases," Joe was asked "specific cases of what?" "Well, I should have had a line in there saying they were specific cases of people with Communist connections," Joe answered.[57]

Later that evening Joe and the two reporters he had met in Senator

Malone's office got roaring drunk in the Mapes Hotel bar. By three o'clock in the morning they were loudly exchanging insults, the reporters calling McCarthy a phony and the senator replying in kind. At one point Joe began screaming that the two newsmen had stolen his list of Communists. "He lost his list," one of the reporters later recalled, "between his eighth and ninth bourbons."[58]

On Monday, February 13th, Deputy Undersecretary of State Puerifoy held a news conference in Washington. He said that only one of the four persons attacked by McCarthy in Reno, John Service, was currently a State Department employee, and that Service had been cleared of all charges made against him. Puerifoy flatly rejected the assertion that 300 employees had been certified as disloyal by the President's loyalty board and that only 80 had been dismissed. He also denied that there were 57 card-carrying Communists in the department. In fact, the FBI had checked the records of 16,075 employees and had failed to find a single person who was disloyal. Two had been labeled "security risks" and were promptly fired. Another 202, about whom security questions had been raised, had left the department since January 1, 1947, either through resignation or reduction in force. Should he learn of a single Red currently in the State Department, Puerifoy assured reporters, the man would be "fired before sundown." This was the third departmental response to McCarthy in four days.[59]

By this time his charges were beginning to generate the headlines Joe eagerly anticipated. Many editors were cautious about the senator's assertions and acknowledged his hedging. The *Chicago Sun-Times* wrote, "Senator McCarthy Names 4 'Reds,' Then Backs Down." The *Baltimore Sun* declared, "McCarthy Names Names in Four 'Cases;' Senator, However, Calls None 'Communist' or 'Traitor.'" But other newspapers were less wary. The *Boston Herald* trumpeted, "Senator Lists Shapley as Among Four Pro-Reds Tied to State Dept." The *San Francisco Examiner's* front page headline read, "4 in State Department Named as Reds."[60]

Many of the initial editorials were hostile. Under the heading "Utterly Irresponsible," the *Raleigh, North Carolina News and Observer* wondered why the Wisconsin senator did not turn over his list to the President or the State Department. The liberal *Washington Post* ran a stinging editorial entitled "Sewer Politics," excoriating McCarthy for evasion and "political foul play of a characteristically Communist kind." "Rarely," said the *Post*, "has a man in public life crawled and squirmed so abjectly."[61]

Joe next appeared in Las Vegas on the 13th for another Lincoln Day dinner. "John W. Service" was one of the 57 "who have not been cleared by loyalty boards," he was reported saying. The following day he held a press conference in Los Angeles and condemned the President for closing the loyalty files. "Never before in the history of the country have employee records been made secret," he claimed. Upon his return to Washington, Joe said, he would request an appearance before a Senate subcommittee and disclose the names of the 57 Reds in the State Department. He also declared that the President's Loyalty Board had found "207 or 209" employees unfit because of disloyalty and that of these "79 to 81" were fired. "I do not know if the 57 are on the list of those recommended for dismissal," he said. [62]

On the 15th he gave his speech before 300 people in the First Presbyterian Church, Huron, South Dakota. He again said "John W. Service" and stated that the names he was revealing were not on his list of 57 Reds. Joe clearly was a hit in Huron. The local newspaper gave a rave review, and one member of the audience wrote to the editor, "He left us feeling proud we were Republicans, and that feeling will last longer than the trite worn-out phrases and pointless flattery of others will be remembered. McCarthy is a thinking, acting leader, not just a politician. There is a tremendous difference."[63]

His speaking engagements completed, Joe flew to Milwaukee on Thursday, February 16, on his way to Appleton for a brief visit with friends and relatives. At the Milwaukee airport he was greeted with the news that President Truman had told a press conference that there was not a word of truth in any of the senator's charges. As reporters thronged around him, shouting questions and pleading for comments, Joe again realized that anti-Communism was his ticket to the front pages. First it was the State Department issuing repeated denials, and now he had gotten the attention of the President. The bravado and the bluffing were paying off handsomely.

"President Truman should refresh his memory about certain things," Joe told reporters. He then revealed the source of his "205" charge: the 1946 letter from Byrnes to Sabath. He repeated his claim to have the names of 57 active Communists in the State Department and said that he would give the list to the President as soon as he opened the department loyalty files. "I want to be sure they aren't hiding these Communists any more," Joe said solemnly.[64]

Two days later he was back in Milwaukee awaiting a plane that would take him to the nation's capital. He called Paul Ringler, the *Milwaukee Journal*'s editorial writer, and suggested lunch. Joe could not believe that anyone could resist his charm forever. Wanting to probe McCarthy about his recent charges, Ringler accepted the invitation and brought along two *Journal* reporters, Robert Fleming and John Hoving, as witnesses. The quartet met at Moy Toy's, a small Chinese restaurant near the *Journal* offices.

The three newspapermen cajoled, badgered, and even insulted McCarthy throughout the luncheon, seeking some hard evidence to support the much-heralded charges. When Joe continued to be evasive, Ringler said in disgust that he didn't believe Joe had anything concrete at all and that his assertions were mere political hogwash. Flushed with anger, Joe pounded the table and shouted, "Listen, you bastards. I'm not going to tell you anything. I just want you to know I've got a pailful of shit, and I'm going to use it where it does me the most good."[65]

Later that day he told a news conference that on Monday he would give the Senate "detailed information" about the Communists in the State Department.[66]

Only a week earlier, in Wheeling, Joe McCarthy had been one of the least known senators in Washington. He was now in the nation's headlines. And he intended to stay there.

THE TOP RUSSIAN SPY

On Monday morning, in Washington, McCarthy's office was crowded and the telephone rang incessantly. Two newsmen, William S. Fairfield, who wrote a weekly column for six Wisconsin newspapers, and John Dear, a Washington correspondent and co-owner of a chain of small daily newspapers, managed to elbow their way into the senator's inner office for an interview. Dear requested the names of the 205 State Department Reds (that being the only figure he had read).

"Look, you guys," Joe said. "That was just a political speech to a bunch of Republicans. Don't take it seriously."

"Don't you have any names?" Dear asked.

"Oh, one was a college professor," Joe replied.

"Where?" Dear asked.

"A professor of astronomy," Joe said. "Another was a professor of anthropology, a woman. But it was just a political talk."

Fairfield's subsequent article consisted largely of a summary of the numbers McCarthy had used in his speeches. Like the reporters in Reno, Fairfield failed to reveal his own misgivings or note the senator's attitude toward his charges. Newsmen at the time were trained to report only what happened in public.[1]

A daring and incredibly irresponsible plan lay behind Joe's announcement of his speech that evening. He intended to go before the Senate and present a majority of the cases on the Lee list, changing their numbers and extemporaneously altering the text to conceal his source. He would then claim that his information came directly from the State Department files through loyal informants. Since the President's 1948 executive order closed the files, there was no way to check. And if Truman buckled under at some later date, Joe perhaps reasoned (if he thought that far ahead), the McCarthy charges would quickly be lost in a barrage of similar assaults by the G.O.P. Joe requested four or five hours of Senate time for his performance. It was bound to make headlines everywhere.

McCarthy's temerity was intensified by rage when he read that Democratic Majority Leader Scott M. Lucas stated in a Chicago speech, "If I had said the nasty things that McCarthy has about the State Department, I would be ashamed all my life." Moreover, Lucas had let it be known that no votes would be taken on the evening of February 20th, and when Joe entered the Senate only two or three Democrats and a half dozen Republicans were present.

Joe strode to the podium very confidently, carrying a bulging briefcase. "Mr. President," he began, "I wish to discuss tonight a subject which concerns me more than does any other subject I have ever discussed before this body, and perhaps more than any other subject I shall ever have the good fortune to discuss in the future." Joe was spoiling for a fight, and a few seconds later he attacked Lucas, "the Democratic leader of the Senate—at least, the alleged leader," for his speech in Chicago. This quickly led to a broader assault. "I do not feel that the Democratic Party has control of the executive branch of the government any more." Then the attack became bipartisan. "I think a group of twisted-thinking intellectuals have taken over both the Democratic and Republican Parties to try to wrest control from them."

Scott Lucas, 58, had entered the Senate in 1939 from Illinois. He was a tall, impressive-looking, affable, and decent man who enjoyed membership in the Senate Establishment. But he was also moody, insecure, and of mediocre intelligence; he did not have a solid command of his duties as Majority Leader and was known to lean heavily upon Sen. Richard Russell of Georgia, who had tapped him for the post. Lucas had little or no respect for McCarthy before the latter's recent wave of charges and greeted newspaper accounts of Joe's Lincoln Day speeches with contempt. This was simply cheap politics, he thought, that could easily be exposed and dismissed. In short, Lucas badly underestimated McCarthy and the fears and tensions on which he fed.[2]

Almost immediately, Lucas chose to interrupt Joe's speech with repeated challenges, loaded questions, and snide barbs. This tactic was to backfire, for McCarthy, as was his style in the ring at Marquette, thrived upon direct attack and counterpunched with reckless abandon. The exchange generated the headlines both McCarthy and the conservative Republicans relished. Moreover, the Majority Leader's often emotional and highly partisan language drove even moderate Republicans into McCarthy's corner.

Soon after Joe began to speak, Lucas demanded that he provide the names of the card-carrying Communists in the State Department. Now that McCarthy enjoyed congressional immunity, Lucas sneered, he no longer had to talk merely about numbers. Joe fired back, "I will not say anything on the Senate floor which I will not say off the floor. On the day when I take advantage of the security we have on the Senate floor, on that day I will resign from the Senate. Anything I say on the floor of the Senate at any time will be repeated off the floor." That was a statement his critics would never let him forget.

When Lucas asked what number McCarthy had used in Wheeling, Joe replied that the speeches in Wheeling and Reno were recorded and that there could be no doubt about what he had said. "I do not believe I mentioned the figure 205. I believe I said 'over 200.'" He then proceeded to read what he falsely contended was a transcript of the recording made at Wheeling. "I did not use a written speech that night." (Later in his talk he said Reno. In fact, there was no extant recording or transcript.) The Lincoln Day speech now contained several modifications. The statistics about the increase of Soviet influence were corrected. Dr. Harlow Shapley's name replaced H. Julian Wadleigh's. And the critical sentence about Reds in the State Department read, "I have in my hand 57 cases of individuals who would appear to be either card-carrying members or certainly loyal to the Communist party, but who nevertheless are still helping to shape our foreign policy." This was far more cautious than anything Joe had actually said on his tour.[3]

When Lucas continued to ask if McCarthy had said 205 in Wheeling, as reported in the press, or 57, Joe floundered badly, grew angrier, and labeled the question "silly." He finally said that he had used both figures in Wheeling; the 57 were Communists, the 205 were "unsafe risks." (A short time earlier he had denied saying 205 at all.) Then he charged that some of the 57 were from "this group of 205." Here he separated the categories. And shortly afterward he proceeded to mention the figure 206. The absurdity of it all was apparent to Lucas, who was completely confident that no one could take McCarthy seriously.

Joe claimed that his briefcase was full of photostatic copies of information about the Communist character of 81 State Department employees. He soon conceded, however, that some of the 81 were no longer in the State Department but had worked there "at one time or another." His information, he said, came straight from the State Department files, provided by "some good loyal Americans" whose identities would forever remain confidential.

> The files which I have here show the source of the information. I contacted one of the Federal intelligence agencies, one of the investigative units. I asked them if they would care to go over what I have to say before I say it, and red-pencil anything which they thought might in any way divulge the source of information, that would in any way inform the Communist spy ring of the information they have. The answer was, "Well, you have gotten all of it from the State Department files, and the Communists within the Department can see those files, and I will show you which Commies have the top-secret clearance, so if they have seen it, it does not do much damage for the Senate to see them."

When Brien McMahon asked if he actually possessed complete State Department files, Joe said that he had only a "resumé" and was eager to open the actual files. In response to a question from veteran legislator George Aiken, he said, "This information is nothing new. It has been there a long time. If the senator or anyone else who is interested had expended sufficient effort, he could have brought this to the attention of the Senate."

Joe announced that he had the names of all 81 suspects. "The senators may have them if they care for them," he said, and he invited Lucas and hostile Garrett Withers to come to his office later to see them. Of course, Joe was bluffing. So he took the position that he thought it improper to make them public until an appropriate Senate committee could study them in executive session. After all, he said, "If we should label one man a Communist when he is not a Communist, I think it would be too bad." Surely the Senate would honor his desire to protect the innocent. He withdrew the offer to Withers and reneged on a promise to give reporters copies of the materials in his briefcase.

Joe did not claim to have enough evidence on the 81 to convince a jury. "All I am doing is to develop sufficient evidence so that anyone who reads the RECORD will have a good idea of the number of Communists in the State Department." Of critical importance, he said, were cases numbered one, two, and 81; they were "the big three" Reds, and their dismissal would "break the back of the espionage ring within the State Department." This was a crude and transparent effort by McCarthy to retain his audience until the completion of his histrionics.

Joe then began to fish papers out of his overstuffed briefcase and present his "evidence." The Associated Press reported that he had "photographs of records," which falsely conveyed a sense of authority. In fact, Joe had only the Lee list, a document that when later published by the Tydings Committee encompassed 42 pages. For the next several hours Joe went through the list, interrupted repeatedly by Democrats Lucas, McMahon, Withers, and Herbert Lehman, who expressed frustration, anger, and even disbelief at what they were hearing on the floor of the United States Senate.

McCarthy had renumbered the cases on the Lee list at random, so that the list's number 51 became his number one, number 52 became number two, 99 became nine, 107 became twelve, and so on. (The Tydings Committee later published a complete cross-listing.) Joe altered, twisted, and improvised upon the cases he used to make them appear sinister and sensational. He recklessly omitted lines, eliminated modifiers, added phrases, and exaggerated freely. A person reportedly "inclined toward Communism" became "a Communist." An "active fellow traveler" became an "active Communist." An unsuccessful job applicant was said by McCarthy to have been given "top-secret clearance." Where the Lee investigators had reported the absence of memoranda from a file, Joe said, "Upon contact with the keeper of the records, he stated that, to the best of his knowledge, the major portion of the file had been removed. He did not mention any name, but he said, 'He was put in some high-brass job about two years ago.'" The list's "He was recommended by E-21, who is a suspect in a Soviet espionage case" became "He was recommended for the position by an individual who is listed by the FBI as a principal in a Soviet espionage case."

From the Lee list:

> The subject was described in reports by various witnesses as interested in communism as an experiment but his political philosophy is in keeping with liberal New Deal social reform under democratic processes of government; "he is a very ardent New Dealer; he is a live liberal;" but an informant who also lived in the International House at one time said, "He was one of those accused of being a Red here but the people who do get up and talk communism are refuted."

McCarthy:

> He was described in reports by various witnesses as inter-
> ested in communism and by his roommate at the Interna-
> tional House as a Communist.

From the Lee list:

> This employee is with the Office of Information and Edu-
> cational Exchange in New York City.
> His application is very sketchy. There has been no investi-
> gation. (C-8) is a reference. Though he is 43 years of age, his
> file reflects no history prior to June 1941.
> Case is awaiting a report from the New York Office.

McCarthy:

> This individual is 43 years of age. He is with the Office of
> Information and Education. According to the file, he is a
> known Communist. I am not evaluating the information
> myself. I am merely giving what is in the file. This individual
> also found his way into the Voice of America broadcast.
> Apparently the easiest way to get in is to be a known
> Communist.

A few of his cases, Joe made clear, involved homosexuality. The file on number 62 (the Lee list's 73), he said, revealed "unusual mental aberrations of certain individuals in the department." He quoted "one of our top intelligence men in Washington" as saying, "You will find that practically every active Communist is twisted mentally or physically in some way."

The extemporaneous nature of the performance and the interruptions by Democrats caused McCarthy to stumble several times. He skipped his own number 15, 27, and 59; nine and 77 were identical, he said; numbers 21 through 26 were "substantially the same," and he didn't go into them. Of case 40 he said, "I do not have too much information on this, except the general statement by the agency that there is nothing in the files to disprove his communistic connections." (The Lee list's number 45, on which this was based, actually concerned a woman.) Case 72, Joe explained, described a man who was in fact anti-Communist.

Lucas forced McCarthy to admit that he was uncertain if any of the 81 had been checked by the State Department's Loyalty Board. Joe was unfamiliar with the personnel of the board. Indeed, he was unsure about loyalty-security procedures in general in the department and even had no idea who screened the 3,000 employees mentioned in the Byrnes letter.

What made headlines, however, was McCarthy's charge that his case number nine was a White House speech writer. From Jack Anderson, Joe had discovered that number 99 on the Lee list was David Lloyd, a founder of the anti-Communist Americans for Democratic Action, an important figure in Truman's election campaign, and currently a presidential assistant. Joe claimed that this case number nine had failed to obtain a State Department security clearance, that he and his wife "are members of Communist-front organizations," and that he "has a relative who has a financial interest in the *Daily Worker.*" Joe gloated, "So that there may be no question about this, we will refer directly to the investigative file. I think I am doing Mr. Truman a favor by telling him this. I do not think he knows it."

Actually, the Lee list's number 99 noted that the subject "was not employed inasmuch as security clearance was not given soon enough and he accepted another position." The case was still pending in October 1947. A week after McCarthy's speech, Lloyd revealed that he and his wife had belonged to several left-wing organizations "a long time ago" and that the relative with financial ties to the *Daily Worker* was his great aunt, who had died in 1941.[4]

Joe's Republican colleagues came to his support early in the presentation. Victory in the 1950 elections was thought vital to the future of the G.O.P., and the Reds-in-government issue was an integral part of the party's strategy. Even before McCarthy began to go through his 81 cases, moderate Henry Cabot Lodge of Massachusetts suggested that the Senate Foreign Relations Committee examine the charges. Joe greeted the idea enthusiastically; such an investigation could guarantee headlines for months.

At 7:30 P.M., after fourteen cases were read, Democrats and Republicans wrangled bitterly over the absence of a quorum. A move by Lucas to adjourn was defeated by a straight party vote, and this led to an agreement to direct the sergeant-at-arms to "compel" the attendance of 72 absent senators, the first time in nearly five years that such a procedure had been employed. One by one they appeared, responding to frantic telephone calls, wondering what urgent matter necessitated their presence at this hour. Within forty minutes a quorum was present, and McCarthy resumed his presentation, with the support of right-wing Republicans Wherry, Dworshak, Mundt, Capehart, and Brewster. This sort of attack was how we caught Hiss, Mundt chortled. Democrat Brien McMahon, summoned from a Georgetown

party, turned up in white tie and tails. After trying repeatedly and unsuccessfully to argue rationally with McCarthy, he announced that by the time
the senator had completed his 81 cases he hoped to be at home and in bed.

Joe urged a bipartisan investigation of his charges. "All I am doing is
presenting enough of the picture so that I hope both the Democratic and
the Republican side will forget politics and clean house." But the political
overtones of his attack escaped no one present. During one heated
exchange between McCarthy and Lucas, Joe snarled, "Nothing the senator
from Illinois has done here tonight indicates that he even remotely realizes
the seriousness of this problem." Lucas angrily replied, "Let me say that
when he makes that statement, he simply does not know what he is talking
about." The Majority Leader promised a complete investigation of McCarthy's charges, "from top to bottom."

One G.O.P. conservative, Homer Ferguson of Michigan, apparently had
a copy of the Lee list and followed it as McCarthy went through his 81 cases.
At one point Ferguson asked, "I wondered why the senator took them out
of order. Is there any reason why he did not take them in order, beginning
with number one and going down through them?" The Lee list was a
House document and thus virtually unknown to senators. Then and there
Ferguson could easily have exposed the origin of McCarthy's charges and
destroyed their credibility. But Ferguson was apparently disinclined to
discourage or discredit a political attack that might eventually reap votes.

In all, Joe's speech lasted five hours (he said eight), and the exhausted
senators voted to adjourn at 11:42 P.M. It had been one of the most fantastic
and supremely dishonest performances ever witnessed on Capitol Hill.
Even McCarthy apologists William F. Buckley, Jr., and L. Brent Bozell later
said that Joe deserved Senate censure for lying about the source of his
information.[5]

The true nature of McCarthy's charges could not be readily understood by
those reading newspaper accounts of the events of February 20, however,
and not many editors were yet prepared to join *The New York Times* in
denouncing "the campaign of indiscriminate character assassination on
which the senator has embarked." Many Americans quickly concluded that
the young Wisconsin lawmaker had actually discovered scores of spies and
was acting upon the most patriotic motives. More sophisticated observers
had a clearer perception of McCarthy and rapidly began to gird themselves
for the fierce political battle that seemed imminent.[6]

Democratic Party leaders met on the morning of February 21 with Tom
Connally of Texas, chairman of the Senate Foreign Relations Committee.
They voted to press for an immediate investigation of McCarthy's charges

by Connally's committee. To get things speedily underway, however, Lucas was forced to accept Republican demands to broaden the scope of the inquiry, permit open hearings, seat five members, and authorize the investigating committee to subpoena the State Department's loyalty and employment files. McCarthy favored all of these amendments and was especially intent on gaining access to the files. Without the power to subpoena them, he cried, "the investigation will be completely useless, it will be a complete farce, and nothing but a whitewash."

At one point in the proceedings Joe asked warily if he would be required to give an investigating committee the names of his 81 State Department figures. "Of course, it is of no personal concern to me. I do not care, personally, whether the Senate says 'yes' or 'no.'" Lucas declared that it was McCarthy's duty as an American citizen to both cite his sources and name names. "A heavy responsibility lies on his shoulders." Joe replied that Lucas "knew perfectly well" that he always stood ready to assist any investigating committee.

Senate Resolution 231, adopted on February 22, authorized and directed "a full and complete study and investigation as to whether persons who are disloyal to the United States are or have been employed by the Department of State."[7]

At a presidential news conference the next day Truman branded McCarthy's charges false and refused to open the files. Senator Wherry proposed that Secretary of State Acheson be prosecuted for contempt if a subpoena was rejected. Joe told reporters, "I do not think the Senate will allow the President to get away with his boyish thumbing of his nose at all the senators who represent the forty-eight states."[8]

It took State Department security officers only a few days to discover the link between the Lee list and McCarthy's Senate speech. Acheson, who had loftily declared that he refused to be part of any quarrel with McCarthy, told a news conference that "similar—perhaps identical—charges have been aired and thoroughly investigated before." Columnist Drew Pearson, no longer friendly, soon carried the story in further detail, and the fraudulence of Joe's presentation before the Senate was public. Democrats were now more confident than ever that they could swiftly crush McCarthy's allegations and taunt the G.O.P. with their success until the polls opened. Senator Connally turned the McCarthy probe over to a subcommittee. When asked why, he reportedly said, "I have more important things to do than go to a skunk hunt."[9]

Connally named Maryland Democrat Millard E. Tydings chairman of the subcommittee. Tydings, 59, had served two terms in the House before moving to the Senate in 1927. A shrewd and articulate conservative, he had survived Franklin Roosevelt's "purge" of 1938 and was currently chairman of the powerful Armed Services Committee. Tydings had crossed swords with McCarthy earlier in the year over naval matters and disliked him personally, but he promised "a full, fair and complete investigation" and told reporters, "We shall let the chips fall where they may. This is neither a witch-hunt on the one hand nor a whitewash on the other."[10]

Democrat Brien McMahon of Connecticut, 46, was also appointed to what was soon called the Tydings Committee. A skilled attorney and former head of the Criminal Division of the Department of Justice, he was elected to the Senate in 1944 and five years later became chairman of the Joint Committee on Atomic Energy. He had made his hostility toward McCarthy's charges of February 20 a matter of public record.

Eighty-two-year-old Theodore Francis Green of Rhode Island was the third Democrat on the committee. He had been a New Deal governor of his state before joining the Senate in 1937 and was now widely acknowledged to be a pillar of the Senate Establishment. Well-educated, bright, and perceptive, he would prove to be the committee's most astute interrogator.

Republican Henry Cabot Lodge of Massachusetts was tall, handsome, and sophisticated. His family was one of the oldest and most aristocratic in New England, and he was the grandson of the more famous politician of the same name. While only 47, he had been in the Senate for eleven years. Lodge was a G.O.P. moderate or liberal; he backed modest domestic reforms and supported a bipartisan foreign policy. Unfortunately, he was not a particularly industrious individual and despite his education at "proper" schools was not among the more intelligent members of the Senate. He would consistently be the least-prepared member of the Tydings Committee and often appear uneducable.

The other Republican assigned to the committee was Bourke Hickenlooper of Iowa, 53, a rock-ribbed right-winger who had entered the Senate in 1945 after a term as governor. Hickenlooper ("Hicks" to his friends) had given strong support to every effort by the Far Right to point to conspiracy and treason in high places, and his appointment to the Tydings Committee was widely recognized as a sop to McCarthy. Wily, zealous, totally partisan, and up for reelection in the fall, Hickenlooper was to have more of an impact on the investigation than Democrats anticipated.

The committee's chief counsel was Edward P. Morgan, 36, a former chief inspector of the FBI, a widely respected lecturer on Communism (he had warned audiences all over the nation against Henry Wallace and his Progressive Party), and a onetime associate counsel to the Joint Committee of Congress on the Pearl Harbor disaster and author of the committee's final report. Recommended by Senator Green, Morgan was to prove to be highly competent and fair-minded.

One of the four assistant counsels, hired at the insistence of committee Republicans, was New York lawyer Robert Morris, a militant conservative with close connections throughout the Far Right. Morris would work diligently on McCarthy's behalf throughout the hearings and later join the senator's staff.

It was no secret in Washington that McCarthy was in deep trouble, and few were more keenly aware of this than those on the Right with years of experience in the anti-Communist field. Joe's innocence of domestic subversion was obvious to experts; his unsophisticated terminology, the jumbling of the numbers 57, 81, 205, and the rest, the incredible February 20 speech, and his willingness to stand before an investigating committee with nothing but the outdated Lee list were the trademarks of a reckless novice. This worried conservatives and ultraconservatives, for if Democrats were permitted to expose McCarthy's charges for what they really were, the political impact could be explosive, and the Red Scare that had been building since the 1948 elections might be severely crippled or destroyed. Decisions were made by some people to come to the aid of the floundering senator. There was also the thought that with some education McCarthy might become a useful ally. Ultraconservatives found him personally likable and capable, and he was obviously intrepid. He had hitherto been thought of—if at all—as a sort of moderate liberal, and many on the Right were delighted by his apparently sudden transformation.

Joe, too, was cognizant of his hazardous situation and turned to others for information to bolster his charges. According to William C. Sullivan, the FBI's number-four man, McCarthy telephoned J. Edgar Hoover soon after the Wheeling speech and said, "This caused headlines all over the country and I never expected it, and now I need some evidence to back up my statement that there are Communists in the State Department." Hoover gave orders immediately to review the files and obtain anything that might help the senator.[11]

Still, Hoover was furious with McCarthy over the Wheeling speech. A close Hoover aide, Louis B. Nichols, later stated that the director gave Joe "unshirted hell" for his bluffing. Hoover was an extremely shrewd and cautious manipulator, and a true believer who took his anti-Communism very seriously. Since the war he and his top aides had repeatedly leaked information to "friendly" sources in Congress, the media, and ultraconservative patriotic organizations. (Hoover was very close to Hearst columnist

George Sokolsky and checked matters with him, through Nichols, almost daily for twenty years. Nichols later called Sokolsky "a great American. A great Jew, too.") The FBI had a strong vested interest in the Red Scare; it was ideologically exhilarating, and at the same time it reinforced the director's authority and insured hefty annual congressional appropriations. McCarthy's crudity had handed important advantages to the Tydings Committee and placed the entire battle against subversives and their sympathizers in jeopardy.[12]

Hoover not only ordered information passed to McCarthy, he supplied him with an investigator. Donald A. Surine, 34, had served for more than ten years with the FBI before being dismissed on February 9 for becoming entangled with a prostitute during a white-slavery investigation. Hoover regretted having to take the action, for Surine was the kind of man he sought for the bureau: a true believer, an indefatigable worker, and a man with a fierce loyalty to the director. Soon after Joe returned to Washington, he hired Surine at Hoover's recommendation and told him to begin gathering information on State Department suspects. For the next several years he was to be among the most active and important people on the senator's staff. Surine told the author that almost every week during his employment with McCarthy he and Joe met secretly with Hoover and Clyde A. Tolson, the bureau's number-two man, to share information over lunch. FBI documents obtained by Owen Lattimore through the Freedom of Information Act reveal Surine and others on McCarthy's staff in constant contact with bureau officials and agents. (They also paint a somewhat darker picture of Surine's early relationship with his former employers. Bitter over his termination from government service, Surine occasionally attempted to "scoop" the FBI on stories. In April 1950 he tried to drive agents away from the scene of one probe, displaying his ten-year pin and claiming falsely that he was working in complete cooperation with the bureau and was about to report to Hoover. At least some bureau leaders considered him an unreliable source of information, and Hoover told agents to keep him at a distance and maintain a strictly formal relationship.)[13]

According to Richard Nixon, McCarthy first asked him for assistance during the Wheeling trip, shortly before the Los Angeles news conference of February 14. Back in Washington, McCarthy called again and requested HUAC materials. Nixon said later that he lent him portions of his files, which no doubt contained HUAC data. During the next several months, Nixon met privately with McCarthy on numerous occasions, attempting to educate the Wisconsinite in the politics of anti-Communism. Nixon constantly urged restraint, he later recalled, but Joe did not listen.[14]

Joe had also gone to Jack Anderson for help. He was completely candid with his reporter friend: he had a terrific political issue but no evidence. Anderson dug out some information from Drew Pearson's files, including the tip on David Lloyd, which Joe proceeded to use publicly in its raw state, without checking a single fact. Pearson then swiftly severed relations with McCarthy and became the first syndicated columnist to attack him.[15]

McCarthy asked *Washington Times-Herald* reporter Ed Nellor to join his staff as a speech writer, hoping to lean upon his experience with anti-Communist probes. Nellor was about to join *Look* magazine and declined the offer. A few weeks later *Look* loaned Nellor to McCarthy on a full-time basis free of charge; the deal was urged by G.O.P. National Committeeman Arthur Summerfield, who placed expensive Chevrolet advertisements in the magazine. Nellor was given a hideaway office in a Washington home owned by the mother of McCarthy staff member Jean Kerr, and he was soon churning out scores of speeches and snappy remarks for the senator.[16]

Telephone calls to Wisconsin yielded important dividends. Milwaukee attorney Charles Kersten was glad to hear from McCarthy; he had lost his bid for reelection to Congress and readily accepted his old friend's offer to return to Washington during the Tydings Committee hearings. Kersten had many ties to the Far Right that McCarthy knew would be useful. At first Joe tried to have him appointed assistant counsel to the Tydings Committee. When this was blocked by Senator Lodge, Joe put Kersten on his own payroll and quietly installed him in a suite in the new Congressional Hotel near the House Office Building. The ex-congressman quickly went to work contacting sources and collecting evidence about State Department personnel. He was to continue on the job until May.[17]

Tom Coleman flew to Washington soon after Joe contacted him and spent the first week in March drumming up support for McCarthy among right-wing newsmen and key Republicans (including Senators Lodge, Hickenlooper, and Taft) and collecting what information he could to help McCarthy defend himself before the Tydings Committee. He then proceeded to raise funds for the senator, sending pleas to friends all across the country and gathering additional leads from ultraconservative Emerson P. Schmidt of the United States Chamber of Commerce. Albert B. Hermann, executive director of the Republican National Committee, and Arthur E. Summerfield were among early contributors. Sewell Avery of the Montgomery Ward company donated $1,000. By late June Coleman had raised $5,475, and he continued to solicit funds for several weeks, by which time money was pouring into McCarthy's office from other sources. In August Arthur Summerfield sent checks from two friends to McCarthy through Coleman totaling $6,000.[18]

Milwaukee industrialist Walter Harnischfager volunteered assistance when he read of McCarthy's attacks on the State Department. Through his attorney Tom Korb, Joe's law school friend, he suggested numerous sources of information, including a former Undersecretary of State, the head of the Passport Division, and the former head of the New York Police Department's detective bureau. Harnischfager also urged McCarthy to go through Kersten to reach Louis Budenz, one of the best-known ex-Communist witnesses, who had expressed interest in helping the Wisconsin senator. Korb added several tips of his own and passed along a recommendation from a former J. Edgar Hoover associate to contact the editors of *Counterattack,* one of the Far Right's favorite periodicals.[19]

Numerous right-wing leaders rushed to McCarthy's aid once the Tydings Committee was formed. Senator Styles Bridges of New Hampshire invited several veteran anti-Communists to his apartment to talk things over with Joe and map future strategy. In attendance were Congressman Nixon and Senator Knowland of California, Congressman John Taber of New York, Robert E. Lee, and R. W. Scott McLeod, Bridges's administrative assistant. Senator Wherry of Nebraska soon confided to a visitor, "Oh, Mac has gone out on a limb and kind of made a fool of himself, and we have to back him up now."[20]

Alfred Kohlberg quickly ingratiated himself and was a frequent visitor to McCarthy's office and Mrs. Kerr's home. He soon boasted of providing McCarthy with "documentary material" and declared his admiration for the senator. William J. Goodwin, a Kohlberg associate and registered lobbyist and agent for the Chinese Nationalists, said in mid-April that he had "laid the groundwork" for some of McCarthy's charges and had recently entertained the senator at dinner. (Joe later denied even knowing what Goodwin looked like.) China Lobby Congressman Walter Judd also said that he had given information to McCarthy, at the senator's request. ("It was not enough to convict anybody as a Communist," Judd added.)[21]

J. B. Matthews, a highly paid anti-Communist "expert" for the Hearst organization, also provided information for McCarthy. Reporters, columnists, and radio commentators paid by the conservative Hearst, Scripps-Howard, and McCormick chains flocked around Joe, feeding him data and championing his every move. Hearst's Larry E. Kerley, George Sokolsky, and Ken Hunter were soon revealed to be involved with witnesses appearing before the Tydings Committee. According to Ed Nellor, Tony Smith of the Scripps-Howard newspapers helped write a McCarthy speech delivered during the hearings. Before long, Joe and Jean Kerr were paying visits to Whittaker Chambers at his farm in Maryland, receiving instruction in how Red agents worked and listening in awe as the former *Time* editor pondered aloud about who the person he called the "master spy" might be.[22]

Those experienced with the struggles of the Far Right were astonished and sometimes amused to learn of McCarthy's ignorance of Communism. At the meeting called by Styles Bridges, Joe revealed that he had never heard of former American Communist party leader Earl Browder. Ed Nellor and Don Surine discovered that the senator was completely unprepared on the subject of domestic subversion. Frank Waldrop of the *Washington Times-Herald* thought Joe a simple man, "an innocent." When the *Chicago Tribune*'s Willard Edwards first met McCarthy that summer he quickly realized that Joe knew virtually nothing about Communist theory, history, or strategy.[23]

(Edwards later described his first impression of the senator as "very revealing." At a social gathering in Ray Kiermas's home Joe was involved in a game in which he would ask a guest to balance a marble on his forehead and drop it into a funnel McCarthy inserted in the front of the guest's trousers. As the victim looked to the ceiling, concentrating on the marble, Joe would pour water into the funnel and roar with laughter.)[24]

The Tydings Committee opened its hearings on Wednesday morning, March 8, in the Senate caucus room. Scores of newspaper, newsreel, and television photographers were on hand, along with dozens of reporters and a capacity crowd of spectators. After Senator Tydings read Senate Resolution 231, authorizing the committee's creation and defining its duties, he called upon Senator McCarthy, who swore to tell the truth, the whole truth, and nothing but the truth. Beaming and apparently very self-confident, he had already distributed press releases concerning his impending testimony.

Chairman Tydings was fully aware of the origin of McCarthy's 81 cases and chose to treat him with contempt and scorn. He interrupted and challenged Joe repeatedly and promised, "You are going to get one of the most complete investigations ever given in the history of this republic, so far as my abilities will permit." The tactic backfired, for it angered Lodge and Hickenlooper and led to intense partisan wrangling. Lodge complained bitterly of "this Roman holiday" and "some sort of a kangaroo court."

In response to Tydings's taunts, Joe asserted that his evidence on the 81 suspects had been gathered "over painstaking months of work," and that he had the names of all 81 and would gladly submit them shortly. (In fact, he was still in the process of obtaining the names. He had asked George Waters to get the key to the Lee list that would translate the numbers into names. Waters would go to Nellor, Nellor would consult Lee, and Lee would acquire the relevant document from Congressman Taber. All of this was to take ten days, and Joe would continue to bluff during the interim.) But he did display some reluctance. "Let me make my position clear," he told the committee on the first day. "I personally do not favor presenting names, no matter how conclusive the evidence is."[25]

Tydings sought to embarrass McCarthy by asking him to identify a high State Department official, in his case number fourteen, who had allegedly blocked the dismissal of a homosexual employee. This was a clever ploy, for the chairman had discovered that McCarthy's number fourteen corresponded to the Lee list's number ten, and that the official in question was J. Anthony Panuch, now a contributor to Alfred Kohlberg's right-wing magazine *Plain Talk* and a man McCarthy had praised in his Salt Lake City speech and in the Senate on February 20. Joe avoided the trap by acting as though Tydings had said "57" instead of "fourteen" and asserting that he did not choose to discuss his cases out of numerical order. In due time, he assured the chairman, he would get to number 57. "Let me add this, too. If you are eager to get to that case today, when the testimony ends this morning if you will come to my office I will dig that case out and give you all the names in the file, all the information you want." Moreover, he said, he had prepared more important cases for the committee's immediate attention.

Joe knew that he would have to come up with something specific in order to keep the press interested and prevent the committee from humiliating him. While awaiting the names from the Lee list, he began to present a few cases based upon the information he and his staff had hurriedly scraped together over the past several days. The first name he announced was that of Dorothy Kenyon, a 62-year-old New York attorney.

Armed with photostatic copies of documents and newspaper clippings, Joe claimed that Miss Kenyon was "in a high State Department position" and "belongs" (at times he said "belonged") to 28 organizations cited by the Attorney General and House and Senate committees as "subversive or disloyal." (He later said "declared subversive by an official government agency.") His first exhibit was a copy of a 1940 advertisement in the *Daily Worker* showing Miss Kenyon's name on a lengthy petition to the President and Attorney General protesting attacks upon the Veterans of the Abraham Lincoln Brigade. The brigade was later cited as subversive by

HUAC, the California Un-American Activities Committee, and the Attorney General. Following the Far Right's customary reasoning, Joe asserted that Miss Kenyon was thus currently a danger to the State Department and to the United States. Senator Tydings noted that the petition also contained the signatures of many prominent Americans of unimpeachable reputation, and he proceeded to read all of the names into the record. This did not set well at all with Lodge and led to further quarreling. At one point Joe glared at Tydings and snapped, "Let's have an agreement. When you ask a question, let me finish my answer, will you?" The pattern of events was soon repeated.

The weakness of McCarthy's case was obvious. He did not know, for example, the dates on which several organizations linked with Miss Kenyon had been labeled subversive. "I think much of the material the Chair wants will have to be developed by the committee," he said. "I just cannot afford to hire the investigators to present a court case to the committee." Joe treated declarations by the Attorney General, HUAC, and its California counterpart as truth, even those that were highly dubious. He avowed faith in the doctrine of guilt by association. He revealed ignorance of the historical circumstances that drove liberals and Communists together at times in the 1930s and 1940s and expressed amazement that Miss Kenyon could have ever been involved with 28 "Communist-front organizations." "I might say that I personally would not be caught dead belonging to any one of the 28." It was his judgment, he said, that Miss Kenyon was "an extremely bad security risk" and should be driven from the State Department within the hour.[26]

Joe also briefly mentioned Dr. Philip C. Jessup, the State Department's ambassador-at-large, as having an "unusual affinity . . . for Communist causes" and promised to develop the case later in the hearings. He was not to mention Jessup again during his three remaining days of testimony. Jessup had already been attacked in January by Nixon, Karl Mundt, and Styles Bridges. Nixon had called him "the architect of our Far Eastern policy" and was perhaps responsible for McCarthy's sudden interest in the diplomat.[27]

That afternoon Dorothy Kenyon told reporters, "Senator McCarthy is a liar," and quickly requested an appearance before the Tydings Committee. The State Department issued a statement pointing to the fact that Miss Kenyon was not an employee; a three-year term as an American representative on a United Nations commission had expired in December. That had been her only connection with the department.[28]

Still, the true nature of McCarthy's performance was not easily perceived from newspaper accounts. (This was ever to be the case.) Wire service reporters, for the most part, attempted merely to describe the flow of events. Stories were often brief and void of all but the most inflammatory charges. Headlines invariably featured McCarthy's most sensational allegations, while denials often appeared toward the end of articles, escaping attention. Right-wing newspapers, of course, portrayed McCarthy's testimony as revelation; an eight-column headline in the *Washington Times-Herald* read "JESSUP PAL OF REDS—MCCARTHY."[29]

Joe was delighted by events of the first day's hearings. He wired Tom Coleman, "THINGS WENT VERY SATISFACTORILY SENATOR FROM MASSACHUSETTS WAS VERY HELPFUL MANY OF YOUR EXCELLENT SUGGESTIONS COULD NOT BE USED TODAY BUT WILL BE USED LATER." The headlines had just begun.[30]

The next day, March 9, Joe opened the proceedings with another daring bluff. He submitted to the committee what he said was the name of the State Department employee who was case number fourteen. What had been asked for earlier, of course, was the name of the department official who had shielded number fourteen. When that request was renewed, Joe said that he had not had access to it. "The name of the individual is not in my file number fourteen, period; at least, not that I know of." The Chair could obtain the name from the State Department files, Joe added; "I have no objection whatsoever to recessing the hearings until the committee obtains the files."

Committee Democrats were not about to let the witness escape that easily, however. They hammered at him with questions about his sources, and Tydings threatened to subpoena his files. Joe became angry and abusive, shouting at Green, "You be quiet until I finish"; bellowing at Tydings, "You are not fooling me, Senator"; and calling the committee "the tool of the State Department." The committee was simply fishing for the names of his loyal informants, he charged, "so their heads will fall." He also reported rumors that the department was rifling its files. Hickenlooper soon claimed that department officials had been burning documents for three months.

Joe was a little better prepared for this session of the hearings. The Civil Service Commission had provided him with a list of loyalty boards, and his lengthy conversations with Surine enabled him to discuss the FBI with some authority. Still, he did not know the full name of the man who headed the State Department Loyalty Board and was badly confused about the current board's relationship to his 81 cases and Dorothy Kenyon. When Brien McMahon suggested that board members be subpoenaed and questioned by the committee, Joe labeled the tactic "completely ridiculous" but asked to sit in should the board appear. No doubt mindful of McCarthy's contributions to the Malmedy hearings, McMahon dropped the idea.

Joe continued to present his case against Dorothy Kenyon, providing photostatic copies of clippings and letterheads that showed her support of various organizations during the two previous decades. When he came to the League of Women Shoppers, he leered:

> As an indication of the far-reaching power and influence of this Communist-front organization, the committee might be concerned to know that Mrs. Dean Acheson, the wife of the Secretary of State, is listed on page 1023 of appendix 9 of the records of the House Committee on Un-American Activities as a sponsor of its Washington branch. There is no length to which these purveyors of treason will not go to bring into their fold the names of unsuspecting and misguided men and women who are influenced by a glib story of social or economic improvement and thus lend prestige to a sordid and dissolute cause.

Secretary Acheson later told a news conference that his wife recalled paying two dollars, possibly twice, a decade earlier for data on local stores supplied by the league.[31]

The New York Times observed that McCarthy was off to a "feeble start" if he intended to prove that there were 57 card-carrying Communists in the State Department. To date he had submitted only a single name, and Dorothy Kenyon was accused merely of membership (along with many other respectable citizens) in organizations that hoped to nurture friendly relations between the United States and the Soviet Union during the war. Eleanor Roosevelt, a friend of Miss Kenyon's (and a nemesis of the Far Right), said in her syndicated column that McCarthy's charges were "very ill-informed" and humorous. "If all of the honorable senator's 'subversives' are as subversive as Miss Kenyon, I think the State Department is entirely safe and the nation will continue on an even keel."[32]

Impervious to such criticism, Joe announced that he was at work on further cases, and that the next one to be placed before the committee would reveal a situation "infinitely worse" than what he had dealt with earlier.[33]

When the Tydings Committee assembled on March 13 for its third session, members had voted to refrain from further interruptions of the witness in order to hasten the proceedings. Chairman Tydings seemed especially eager that subsequent hearings appear more dignified and less partisan. Joe no doubt welcomed this new approach for it permitted him to introduce his charges virtually without challenge, which meant that the headlines, for as long as he could hold the stage, belonged to him.

The first name he presented was Haldore Hanson, executive director of the Secretariat of the Inter-Departmental Committee on Scientific and Cultural Cooperation. Hanson had been called to Joe's attention on March 7 by Emerson P. Schmidt, who had been contacted by Tom Coleman. Schmidt urged McCarthy to check *Congressional Record* entries of 1947 and a recent story in the *New York Daily News* noting that Hanson was to be named to a post in the Point-Four Program.[34]

Drawing upon a 1947 attack by Republican Congressman Fred Buseby of Illinois, plus additional materials probably supplied by Kohlberg, McCarthy charged that Hanson was a "pro-Communist" whose record of sympathy toward the Chinese Communists could be traced to 1938, four years before he joined the State Department. He had run a Communist magazine in Peiping when the Japanese-Chinese war broke out, Joe claimed. He had published articles in *Pacific Affairs,* the official publication of the Institute of Pacific Relations, headed, Joe said, by an admitted Communist. He had also published in *Amerasia,* whose managing editor, Philip Jaffe, was involved in the illegal possession of government documents. Hanson had spent several years with the Communist armies in China, Joe stated, and had written a book extolling them. McCarthy then read several excerpts from Hanson's 1939 volume *Humane Endeavor,* changing a description of the Communist Chinese leaders as "hard-shooting realists" to "straight-shooting realists." He had clearly not read the book and could not even think of its title when asked. Nevertheless, he compared it to *Mein Kampf.* Hanson, he cried, was a man with "a mission to communize the world" and was "one of the architects of our foreign policy in the State Department today." Joe warned, "Gentlemen, if Secretary Acheson gets away with his plan to put this man, to great extent, in charge of the proposed Point-4 program, it will, in my opinion, lend tremendous impetus to the tempo at which Communism is engulfing the world."[35]

McCarthy's second case of the day focused upon Esther Caukin Brunauer, a member of the State Department's United Nations relations staff. This was another well-worn case, handled in 1947 by HUAC. Joe discovered and announced that it was number 47 on his list of 81 (his distorted version of the Lee list's number 55).

The senator charged that Mrs. Brunauer had been associated in the 1930s and 40s with a few groups later cited as Communist fronts and that she had served as Alger Hiss's first assistant at the San Francisco conference. From this he implied that she was a Communist, not just a dupe or a sympathizer, and exclaimed, "This is, in my opinion, one of the most fantastic cases I know of." He was also concerned, he said, about Mrs. Brunauer's husband, Stephen, a Navy Department employee who allegedly had admitted to associates that he was a Communist and who was a "close friend and collaborator" of Communist Noel Field. Joe claimed that Stephen Brunauer was a scientist whose work "has involved some of the topmost defense secrets which the armed forces of this country possess." He advised committee members to seek corroborating evidence on the Brunauers in the files of the State Department, Naval Intelligence, and the FBI, implying that he had already consulted these sources.[36]

McCarthy then raised the name of Owen J. Lattimore, director of the Walter Hines Page School of International Relations at Johns Hopkins University. Lattimore had been attacked for several years by Alfred Kohlberg and the China Lobby, and his name was well known on the Far Right.[37]

Dr. Lattimore was the author of eleven books and hundreds of newspaper and magazine articles and was an internationally recognized authority on the Far East. Fluent in several Asian languages, his specialty was Mongolia, an area little known to other Western scholars. From 1937 to 1941 Lattimore had served on the editorial board of *Amerasia,* and from 1933 to 1941 he had edited *Pacific Affairs,* a scholarly journal produced by the Institute of Pacific Affairs. The institute was an association of national councils in ten countries, founded in 1925 to study the Far East. It had many distinguished supporters and received funds from several major foundations. During the Depression the institute had been infiltrated by Communists and fellow travelers. Lattimore himself was no doubt a fellow traveler, and *Pacific Affairs* featured many articles by left-wing authors and often revealed a pro-Soviet bias. (His quickie book *Ordeal by Slander,* justifying his past and describing his experiences with McCarthy and the Tydings Committee, was as cynical a piece of writing as almost anything published at the time by ultraconservatives.) The I.P.R. and its publications had no demonstrable effect on the White House or the State Department, however, and efforts such as Kohlberg's to prove a gigantic conspiracy to aid the Chinese Communists would never be successful. Secretary of State Acheson had not heard of Owen Lattimore until McCarthy put his name in headlines on March 13.[38]

Joe called Lattimore "one of the principal architects of our Far Eastern policy," a "pro-Communist," "an extremely bad security risk" who had been one of the State Department's "outstanding experts" for several years. He pointed to Lattimore's brief service in 1941 as a political adviser to Chiang Kai-shek, his wartime duty with the Office of War Information, his assignment to accompany Henry Wallace on a diplomatic tour of Siberia and China, and a recent State Department mission to India as examples of his influence. He was still a department consultant, Joe claimed. "I think the Chair will find upon investigation that he has a desk which is kept there for him constantly, kept for his sole benefit, and he comes in at will."

Joe introduced I.P.R. materials and excerpts from Lattimore's writings into the record and read from a lengthy article written by the Rev. James F. Kearney, S.J. (whose information had come from Kohlberg). The senator stated that he and his staff were working night and day to provide the committee with further information. "There is a great wealth of material to be done over. . . . In fact, much of the material that I am presenting tomorrow morning frankly was not in my hands the day I spoke on the Senate floor."[39]

On March 14 Joe appeared for three hours, presenting five more cases to the committee. The first involved Gustavo Duran, whom McCarthy had first mentioned in his Wheeling speech. Charges of disloyalty against Duran, a State Department employee from 1943-46, had been studied and dismissed by the State Department Security Committee and HUAC in 1946. Joe now dusted them off and claimed that Duran was "well known" for Communist beliefs and had once been active in secret Soviet operations in the Spanish Republican Army (he produced a photograph of Duran in uniform). He read from one document that asserted that Duran was a homosexual. He added that Duran's brother-in-law, Michael Straight, was "the owner and publisher of a pro-Communist magazine called the *New Republic*." Duran had been recommended for his current position with the United Nations, McCarthy claimed, by a current member of the President's cabinet. He worked for the International Refugee Organization and was screening refugees being admitted to the United States. Along the way, Joe cast doubt upon the loyalty of Spruille Braden, a top State Department official.

The second case was that of Dr. Harlow Shapley, the Harvard astronomy professor whose name McCarthy added to his Lincoln Day speech in Reno. Shapley belonged to 36 Communist fronts in the 1930s and 40s, the senator said, and he read a list (that perhaps came from J. B. Matthews). To counter the State Department's denial that Shapley had ever been an employee, Joe noted his two appointments in 1947 by the Secretary of State to the National Commission for UNESCO. By law these involved transportation expenses and $10 a day!

Joe then raised the alleged case of a convicted homosexual who had resigned from the State Department in 1948 and was currently enjoying a "top-salaried, important position" with the Central Intelligence Agency. The senator would divulge the man's name only in executive session, he said, but in public he demanded his immediate dismissal. "I might say, in connection with that, it seems unusual to me, in that we have so many normal people, so many competent Americans, that we must employ so many very, very unusual men in Washington. It certainly gives the country an odd idea of the type of individuals who are running things down here."

The next case involved John Stewart Service, a longtime target of the China Lobby and right-wing Republicans. Despite having been cleared three times in the last five years, he was again under scrutiny by the State Department Loyalty Board. McCarthy called him "one of the dozen top policymakers in the entire Department of State on Far Eastern policy," and "a known associate and collaborator with Communists and pro-Communists." Joe read many allegations into the record and focused upon the Foreign Service officer's role in the *Amerasia* case, citing in particular an article in Kohlberg's magazine *Plain Talk* by Emmanuel Larsen, a defendant in the case.

The last name to be brought before the committee by McCarthy was that of Dr. Frederick L. Schuman, a professor at Williams College. Joe claimed that he was a "highly placed" lecturer in the State Department, "a consultant" who was "one of the closest collaborators in and sponsors of Communist-front organizations in America." Like Service, Schuman was among a small group of untouchables "who determine, force through, and carry out the foreign policy of this country." If the professor was not actually a card-carrying Communist, Joe remarked, "the difference is so slight that it is unimportant."

Before concluding his testimony before the Tydings Committee, Joe submitted a list of twenty-five names "which requires further investigation." "All of these individuals to the best of my knowledge are either in the State Department or in closely related agencies," he said. "At least they were very recently." Evidence against all twenty-five could be found in the files of the FBI, he asserted. Joe was frank to admit that the twenty-five names were not among his earlier 81. He and his staff were still at work on that list, he said. (In an executive session a week later, he amended this statement. "In the twenty-five there is actually a duplication of two. Two of the twenty-five I understand are in the 81." After committee members revealed considerable confusion, Joe warned, "I want the record to show that there is in that list of twenty-five one man who is utterly dangerous.")[40]

To well-informed, objective observers, McCarthy's four-day public testimony was appalling. He had failed to straighten out the discrepancies in the numbers he had used since Wheeling to point to the presence of Reds in the State Department. He had failed to turn over the names linked to the 81 cases described on the Senate floor. (The committee would receive the names from the Lee list on March 20, exactly one month after McCarthy's speech.) He had failed to reveal an "espionage ring" or anything like it; indeed, he had yet to charge a single current State Department employee with being a Communist. All of the names Joe presented were familiar, as was his evidence. The documentation could appeal only to those who found guilt by association persuasive and enjoyed wrenching facts out of their historical contexts. Shameless bluffing was evident throughout the testimony.[41]

Several of the nine public cases presented could be dismissed out of hand (and later were by the committee). Gustavo Duran had resigned from the State Department on October 3, 1946, before the institution of the current loyalty program, and could hardly have been one of Joe's 205, 57, or 81. The allegations McCarthy cited were false and were taken from a 1946 article published by the Falange party of Franco Spain, angry over Duran's service with the army of the Spanish Republic. Duran had never been employed by the International Refugee Organization and at no time had anything to do with screening refugees for entry into the United States. He swore that he was not and had never been a Communist.[42]

Harlow Shapley had never been on the payroll of the State Department and could not be considered a department employee. His appointment to the United States National Commission for UNESCO was a pro forma action by the Secretary of State, in the spirit of relevant legislation, following Shapley's designation by the executive committee of the American Association for the Advancement of Science.[43]

Frederick Schuman had never been a State Department employee, and his only connection with the department consisted of giving a one-hour lecture, free of charge, at the Foreign Service Institute in 1946.[44]

McCarthy claimed that he had additional materials to present to the committee, and Tydings invited him to return to the stand at any time to testify further. (Before leaving, McCarthy quarreled bitterly with the chairman, offering to repeat his February 20th Senate speech under oath "this afternoon.") The committee then chose to honor requests by the accused to respond publicly to McCarthy's charges.[45]

Dorothy Kenyon appeared on the afternoon of March 14th. (McCarthy was absent, leaving his charges and evidence with Hickenlooper.) The

New York attorney and former municipal judge was an impressive and thoroughly persuasive witness. "I am, and always have been, an independent, liberal Rooseveltian Democrat," she said firmly, "devoted to and actively working for such causes as the improvement of the living and working conditions of labor and the preservation of civil liberties." Miss Kenyon was admittedly—and proudly—an outspoken political activist who had joined dozens of organizations over a busy lifetime. She was currently engaged in the work of Americans for Democratic Action, the American Civil Liberties Union, the League of Women Voters, the American Association of University Women, the Association for the Aid of Crippled Children, and a number of similar groups. She flatly denied having ever been a Communist or fellow traveler and stated that she had never joined or assisted any organization known to her to be "even slightly subversive." She could not recall several of the 28 Communist-front groups McCarthy cited (two of the 28 had not in fact been labeled subversive by anyone other than McCarthy), and in some cases her name had apparently been used without her knowledge. She had never belonged to some of them. She had associated with others only briefly, on the recommendation of prominent friends or to support a worthy-sounding cause.

Miss Kenyon presented documents revealing that as early as 1940 she had resisted efforts by Communists to take over the American Labor Party and that since that time she had often taken positions hostile to the Russians. As a delegate to the United Nations Commission on the Status of Women from 1947 to 1949 (her only slight connection with the State Department), she had sparred repeatedly with Soviet representatives and had been severely criticized by Moscow.

Democrats on the committee, particularly Senator Green, were obviously sympathetic to Miss Kenyon. They shared many of her basic assumptions, personal friends, and political associates, and they realized that only extremists could adhere to the fantasy that she was a loyalty or security risk. Even Republican Hickenlooper, who resorted to probing Miss Kenyon's 1928 college-reunion class book for hints of treason, acknowledged frankly that he did not consider the witness disloyal or "subversive in any way."

At Senator Green's invitation, she spoke out forcefully against guilt by association, which she declared a violation of due process. The organizations McCarthy had cited,

> ... have never been found subversive by a court of law or by
> any process other than an administrative edict; and adminis-

> trative edicts or fiats or whatever you call them sound to me
> like Mr. Hitler and Mr. Stalin; therefore, I think that the
> terming of an organization subversive is in itself a violation
> of civil liberty.
>
> And then from that to jump to the fact that a person who is
> a sponsor or a member or participates in one tiny little
> project for a short period of time is therefore tarred with the
> same brush and is therefore himself or herself subversive
> seems to me a non sequitur. Very frequently it just is not true.

At one point in her presentation the audience burst into applause, prompting a mild rebuke from Senator Tydings. The *Washington Post* commented, "In truth Case No. 1 turned out to be not only an outraged and innocent American, but also a woman of spirit."[46]

By this time the liberal *Post* was only one of many sources of increasingly hostile reaction toward the exploits of Wisconsin's junior senator. The *New Republic,* for example, published a solid analysis of McCarthy's charges against the State Department. Columnist Marquis Childs condemned "this 10-cent Robespierre" for his technique of "indictment by association and smear." Columnist Dorothy Thompson pointed out some of the absurdities in the Kenyon case. And at the State Department Deputy Undersecretary John E. Puerifoy expressed the "sympathy and good wishes of the entire department" to John Stewart Service and his family, and condemned McCarthy for reviving "dead, discredited, disproven" charges against the Foreign Service officer.[47]

Another style of attack was also underway by mid-March. Drew Pearson, in contact with the *Madison Capital Times,* attributed Joe's interest in Communism to the dinner with Father Walsh and filled his syndicated column with half-true stories of McCarthy's tax problems, "quickie" divorces, and the effort toward disbarment in 1946. I. F. Stone published a distorted account of the Malmedy hearings which bore the headline "When McCarthy Stood Up For Malmedy Murderers."[48]

Joe counterattacked with almost daily press releases and interviews. Having two veteran Washington reporters on his staff, he learned about newspaper deadlines and timed his handouts and comments to obtain maximum newspaper coverage in morning and evening editions. In the future he would often top an unfriendly headline by knowing exactly when to make a new, sensational charge. Careful timing also denied opponents an opportunity to reply effectively.[49]

On March 16 he said that he had written to the chairman of the Civil Service Loyalty Review Board asking him to explain allegedly delayed action on the Service case. The next day he claimed that the State Department had issued a mandate for a "complete and thorough whitewash" of Service. On a television program two days later he called for the ouster of Acheson and said, "We still have most of the Hiss ring" in the State Department, including "the top man" and several other "extremely dangerous men."[50]

The next morning Ambassador-at-Large Philip C. Jessup took the stand to answer McCarthy's brief slur about his "unusual affinity" for Communist causes. Jessup had been in Pakistan on an official mission when word was received of the charge against him and had flown home for the purpose of addressing the committee publicly. Bristling with anger and contempt for McCarthy, who observed the proceeding quietly, Jessup questioned whether the senator was doing the work of the Communists by attacking him. (He reluctantly concluded in the negative.) He displayed his impressive Establishment credentials, brandished a lengthy record of hostility to Communism, defended his relationship with the Institute of Pacific Relations, and submitted strong letters of support from Generals Marshall and Eisenhower. The former wrote, "I am shocked and distressed by the attack on your integrity as a public servant."

Committee Democrats were openly sympathetic, and Tydings brushed aside Joe's request to interrogate the witness. Hickenlooper stumbled at times during his lengthy exchange with the articulate ambassador and was clearly in awe of him. The audience applauded when Jessup contended that "Senator McCarthy's charges and insinuations are not only false but utterly irresponsible and under the circumstances reveal a shocking disregard for the interests of the country."[51]

Joe had little to say after the hearing; even he must have been sobered slightly by the public collapse of his credibility. But he quickly shook off whatever humiliation he may have experienced and resumed the attack, calling Jessup "sincere and well-intentioned but completely fooled . . . the voice of Lattimore."[52]

After Jessup's appearance before the committee, Tydings told a news conference that to date McCarthy had not yet provided committee members with the name of a single person accused of being a Communist. Over a hundred names had been submitted, Tydings acknowledged, but McCarthy had not lodged definite charges against any one on the list. When reporters confronted Joe with this statement he once again chose to bluff. He had just given Senate investigators, he said, "the name of the man—connected with the state department—whom I consider the top Russian espionage agent in this country," describing him as Alger Hiss's onetime boss "in the espionage ring in the department." (This took headlines away from Tydings in newspapers all over the nation.) He then contacted Tydings and asked to appear before an executive session of the committee.[53]

That afternoon, March 21, Joe told the senators that the man in question was Owen Lattimore. Speaking impromptu and obviously trying hard to regain his credibility with committee members, Joe promised his colleagues, "If you crack this case it will be the biggest espionage case in the history of this country." Lattimore was definitely an espionage agent, "the top of the whole ring of which Hiss was a part." "I think he is the top Russian spy," he exclaimed. He admitted, however, that he had no additional information to provide the committee. The government files would prove his case, Joe claimed repeatedly. Lattimore's FBI file would "prove that I am completely wrong or it will prove that I am 100-percent right." Had McCarthy actually seen the FBI files? McMahon asked. "I think I know what is in them," Joe blurted out. He then quickly stated that he had not personally seen the original files and denied having spoken with J. Edgar Hoover about the case.[54]

Having recklessly staked his political future on this charge—"I am willing to stand or fall on this one," he soon told reporters—Joe labored furiously over the next several days to secure more data on Lattimore. Don Surine, Jean Kerr, and Charles Kersten worked around the clock on the project. Joe and Alfred Kohlberg spent eighteen uninterrupted hours together discussing Lattimore.[55]

As he frantically gathered information, Joe made a lot of noise in public about the unavailability of the government's loyalty and security files. The issue diverted attention from his own failures, placed blame on the Administration, and rallied support among numerous Republicans. The obvious flimsiness and irresponsibility of McCarthy's charges irritated many thoughtful G.O.P. leaders. Henry L. Stimson, one of the party's most distinguished elder statesmen, wrote a letter to *The New York Times* praising Acheson and warning, "The man who seeks to gain political advantage from personal attack on a secretary of state is a man who seeks political advantage from damage to his country." No name was mentioned, but the allusion to McCarthy was unmistakable. (Truman sent Stimson his congratulations.) The letter was inserted in the *Congressional Record* by Sen. Irving Ives of New York, a party moderate. John Foster Dulles and Senators Ralph Flanders and Leverett Saltonstall also backed Acheson. Sen. H. Alexander Smith of New Jersey defended Philip Jessup on the floor of the Senate and urged that the Tydings probe be continued behind closed doors. The G.O.P. Senate leadership made it known that McCarthy's charges were "not a matter of party policy." On the other hand, Senator Taft, worried about his reelection in 1950 and eager for the presidential nomination two years later, was not above courting support from the extreme right-wing. He publicly encouraged McCarthy and allegedly advised him to "keep talking and if one case doesn't work out he should proceed with another."[56]

On March 22 McCarthy told a news conference that he had given the Tydings Committee the name of the nation's "top Russian espionage agent" and that it was now Truman's responsibility to open the files. "It is up to the President to put up or shut up. Unless the President is afraid of what the files would disclose he should hand them over." The next day McCarthy displayed a lengthy telegram he had sent to the President in which he stated, "I feel that your delay of this investigation by your arrogant refusal to release all necessary files is inexcusable and is endangering the security of this nation."[57]

Tydings had written to Truman on the 22nd, on behalf of his committee, requesting access to the files of the nine individuals publicly accused by McCarthy and the files of the 80 other names on the Lee list. Wishing to avoid a confrontation, Tydings had chosen not to send a subpoena, as he was authorized and as some Republicans urged. The President had said, in any case, that he would ignore such a subpoena.

Truman, on vacation in Key West, was known to be considering a grant of at least limited access to the files. He was concerned about setting a dangerous precedent for later G.O.P. "fishing expeditions," however, and knew that Attorney General McGrath, FBI director Hoover, and Loyalty Review Board chairman Richardson were strongly opposed to letting congressmen peer into the raw data contained within the FBI files. To placate Tydings—and deflate McCarthy—the President ordered Hoover to present an analysis of Owen Lattimore's FBI file for committee members. The Justice Department announced the move the following day, without mentioning Lattimore's name. After studying Hoover's report, the committee members (with the exception of Hickenlooper, who was out of town) joined Hoover and Attorney General McGrath in concluding privately that there was nothing in the file to show that Lattimore was or ever had been a Communist or had in any way been connected with an espionage ring.[58]

Tydings told a news conference that McCarthy's unnamed "top agent" had been employed or connected with the State Department only once, five years earlier, and had thereafter given only a single speech to a group of

State Department employees. Joe called the announcement "a deliberate misstatement of the facts" and "another one of those obvious attempts to twist and distort the truth." The accused, he said, has a desk in the State Department, "or at least he did until three or four months ago." He added, "He is one of their top advisers on Far Eastern affairs, or at least he was until three or four weeks ago."[59]

Off the record, McCarthy leaked the identify of his "top agent" at a news conference. Newspapermen would not print the story for fear of libel, but soon all Washington was buzzing about Lattimore. A few days later Joe gave Jack Anderson, with whom he was still friendly in spite of his fight with Drew Pearson, permission to publish the professor's name. "In deadpan seriousness," Anderson later recalled, "Joe told me a gothic tale about Communist spies who had been landed on the Atlantic coast by an enemy submarine and who had hastened to Lattimore for their orders." Anderson's employer, Drew Pearson, identified Lattimore on his weekly radio broadcast of March 26, adding, "I happen to know Owen Lattimore personally—and I only wish this country had more patriots like him." Lattimore, in Afghanistan on a United Nations mission, called McCarthy's charges "pure moonshine" and soon prepared to return home.[60]

Four Democratic senators, including Theodore Green of the Tydings Committee, excoriated McCarthy on a radio network program hosted by Mrs. Eleanor Roosevelt. Green declared that the Wisconsin senator's attacks were reckless and unfair and charged that they had done irreparable damage abroad. In a Maryland radio broadcast Tydings chortled that no one in the State Department could locate Lattimore's desk.[61]

The next morning Esther Caukin Brunauer testified before the Tydings Committee. One of the nine publicly named by McCarthy two weeks earlier (the only one of the nine also on the Lee list), Mrs. Brunauer was a $9,706-a-year assistant director for policy liaison with UNESCO. She had been with the State Department since 1944 and had been cleared of all loyalty-security charges in 1948, following a full field investigation by the FBI. The witness declared that she had never been a Communist or a Communist sympathizer, she denied having had any official or personal contact with Alger Hiss at the San Francisco conference (she assisted the late Congressman Sol Bloom), and she demolished allegations that she had knowingly associated with Communist fronts. She introduced numerous letters from distinguished Americans, including Milton Eisenhower, Republican Senator Joseph Ball of Minnesota, and Democratic Senator William Benton of Connecticut, attesting to her loyalty and competence. And she stoutly defended the patriotism of her husband, who had discontinued associations with Communists in the late 1920s (he had never joined the party) and was described by Senator Ball as "perhaps the most violently anti-Communist person I know."[62]

Mrs. Brunauer's testimony left McCarthy's charges against her in shambles. Hickenlooper was reduced to sputtering halfheartedly that all of the facts in the case were not available. After the appearance of three defense witnesses it was becoming increasingly apparent that Senator Benton was correct when he labeled McCarthy's charges "indeed irresponsible."

Attorney General J. Howard McGrath then took the stand and argued against opening the files. He discussed the separation of powers and contended that congressional access to the files would abridge the rights of government employees and hinder the effectiveness of the FBI. (He spoke in awe of the FBI files: "We never go near the raw files because we hold them in such sacred trust." Almost trembling, he denied that he actually gave orders to J. Edgar Hoover.) He also read Henry L. Stimson's letter to *The New York Times* into the record, making it plain where he stood on McCarthy.

Hoover appeared briefly, explaining that the bureau's files contained the identities of confidential informants, full details of investigative techniques, and information about the private lives of those under investigation. He declared that the files should always remain confidential and even opposed providing summaries for the committee. He brusquely denied that anyone in the FBI had ever made confidential bureau reports available to a congressman.[63]

Never quiet long, Joe sent a public apology to Hoover for his absence. He was preparing a Senate address on Lattimore, he said through Hickenlooper, and asked the director to have an agent on hand for the speech to receive important documents. A weary Justice Department official told reporters privately, "It would be a little more helpful if Senator McCarthy would give us that information before he makes a Senate speech about it."[64]

That evening Styles Bridges, one of six senators who voted against Acheson's confirmation, initiated what he predicted would be an outburst of G.O.P. outrage against the Secretary of State. "We must find the master spy," he told his colleagues, "the servant of Russia who moves the puppets Hiss and Wadleigh and the others in and out of office in this capital of the United States, using them, and using our State Department as he wills." Bridges demanded to know who hired the 91 sex perverts the department said it had discharged over the past two years.[65]

The next day, March 28, Haldore Hanson came before the Tydings Committee. He had requested a hearing in a bitter letter to the chairman, complaining that since McCarthy's charges some of his Virginia farm neighbors had begun to refer to him as "that Communist" and "that Russian spy" and had circulated a petition urging him to leave the community. (The Brunauers had received anonymous telephone calls and threats from neighbors.)[66]

The 37-year-old State Department official dared McCarthy to repeat his allegations without benefit of senatorial immunity. If he would, "I assure him that he will be called upon to answer me in a court of justice at the earliest possible moment."

Hanson convincingly refuted each of McCarthy's charges. He had never held a position bearing responsibility for Far Eastern policy, he stated, or in which his advice on such policy was requested. His only association with the Communist Chinese army occurred in 1938 when the troops were under the supreme command of Chiang Kai-shek. He had spent four months with the army on assignment by the Associated Press as a war correspondent.

The witness read excerpts from his 1939 book *Humane Endeavor* containing favorable references to Nationalist leaders and cited reviews praising the book's objectivity. He pointed to errors by McCarthy in quoting and interpreting the study. Chapters from the volume were sold to *Pacific Affairs* and *Amerasia,* he explained, because they were then the most eminent and scholarly journals in the field. Hanson commented, "If we have got to the point in America where writers must assume responsibility for the political opinions, the morals, and the public activities which all of the editors or owners, or stockholders or writers that magazine may hold or later develop, then we have traveled far indeed from these basic principles upon which this country was founded."

As for the contention that he ran a Communist magazine in Peiping in the late 1930s, Hanson noted that the magazine in question existed for only three months and that he was on its board of editors for two issues and attended only one board meeting. The magazine was created to promote a united front against the Japanese, and the only people Hanson knew connected with it were not Communists. Indeed, one board member belonged to Chiang Kai-shek's executive committee.

Hanson added that the FBI had given him a full field examination and that the State Department had cleared him for top secret information. Congressional immunity might save McCarthy from a lawsuit, he said solemnly, "but it will not save him from moral accountability."[67]

The next morning the *Washington Post* carried an instantly famous cartoon drawn by the brilliant political satirist Herbert Block (Herblock). It featured the G.O.P. elephant being dragged and pushed by right-wingers toward a stack of dripping tar buckets topped by a barrel bearing the word "McCarthyism." "You mean I'm supposed to stand on that?" asks the struggling elephant. The new term Herblock coined caught on immediately and was soon in dictionaries. One defined McCarthyism as a political attitude "characterized chiefly by opposition to elements held to be subversive and by the use of tactics involving personal attacks on individuals by means of widely publicized indiscriminate allegations esp. on the basis of unsubstantiated charges." Privately, Joe was stung by the term and despised it. To conceal this reaction, with Ed Nellor's assistance he took the public position that "McCarthyism" was a synonym for "Americanism" and that he welcomed the new word. "In my state," he would tell an audience in 1952, "McCarthyism means fighting Communism. People write in all the time saying they wish there was more McCarthyism." He and his allies often revealed their sensitivity to the formally negative nature of the term, however, and would usually attribute its authorship to Owen Lattimore. In fact, the professor was in Karachi, Pakistan, when the Herblock cartoon appeared.[68]

The search by Joe's staff for information about Lattimore yielded an abundance of material. Ultraconservatives were eager to help McCarthy. Kersten and Surine labored furiously, at one point rousting the president of Johns Hopkins University and his wife out of bed at 11:00 P.M. to check a rumor they had heard from an Irish professor at the university.[69]

Kersten had known Louis Budenz during the 80th Congress when the former managing editor of the *Daily Worker* helped him, John F. Kennedy, and other members of a House committee bring about the perjury indictment of Milwaukee labor leader Harold R. Christoffel, who had denied membership in the Communist party. Kersten contacted Budenz and asked about Lattimore, recording the telephone call in McCarthy's office. Budenz stated that Lattimore had indeed been a member of the party and was the individual in charge of Asian affairs. He had a code name that was used on documents, Budenz said, and whenever a story would come into the *Daily Worker* bearing the name, staff members would know what the new Moscow line was. When Kersten played the recording to the senator, he later recalled, Joe "danced with glee."[70]

McCarthy's Senate speech on Lattimore was written in a single evening at Ed Nellor's hideaway office in Mrs. Kerr's home. Joe was present, along with Nellor, Jean Kerr, Don Surine, Scripps-Howard reporter Tony Smith, and a man from the staff of Sen. Pat McCarran. Nellor actually composed the lengthy address at his typewriter, pausing frequently for input from the others in the room. The entire office staff worked until two in the morning of the day the speech was to be delivered, preparing copies for distribution. After a few hours' sleep, they were back on the job.[71]

Joe advertised the speech among friends and associates. He sent telegrams on March 30 to members of the Republican House delegation: "Would like to have you share some pumpkin pie with me this afternoon on the Senate floor." He wired Tom Coleman, "The seeds you sowed will bear pumpkin this afternoon." (These were allusions to the 1948 incident in which Whittaker Chambers revealed microfilmed documents that had been hidden in a hollowed-out pumpkin.) When he strode onto the floor that Thursday afternoon, the galleries were packed with noisy partisans. Only 36 Senators, including eight Democrats, were on hand.[72]

Joe attacked the Tydings Committee early in the speech for forcing him to disclose publicly the names of the accused. He would have preferred to handle all such matters behind closed doors, he said. Tydings was guilty of "clever maneuvering." For those who had carefully followed events of the past several weeks, McCarthy's current posture as a civil libertarian shrinking from publicity seemed bizarre.

He repeated his contention that Lattimore was "a Soviet agent," adding that "he either is, or at least has been, a member of the Communist party." He charged that the professor had "a dominant influence over the formation and implementation of the policy which has delivered China to the Communists" and claimed that two branches of the State Department, the Far Eastern division and the Voice of America, were "almost completely controlled and dominated by individuals who are more loyal to the ideals and designs of Communism than to those of the free, God-fearing half of the world." Secretary of State Acheson, he said, was simply "the voice for the mind of Lattimore." Philip Jessup was "a very willing stooge" for Lattimore.

Joe claimed that he could produce a mystery witness who would testify that Lattimore was a member of the Communist party for several years. (Reporters quickly and correctly guessed that the reference was to Louis Budenz.) He read from an affidavit of another unnamed potential witness (Freda Utley) who claimed that "he" had met Lattimore in Moscow in 1936 when the professor "was receiving instructions from the Soviet government." McCarthy also read excerpts from a letter Lattimore had written in 1943, allegedly revealing his treachery toward the Chinese Nationalists. Another affidavit, he said, tied Lattimore to John Stewart Service. The night before Service was arrested, in 1945, for unlawful possession of secret documents, he was seen with Lattimore at a private home. A guest saw the latter going over some papers, and Lattimore explained that he was "declassifying secret documents in favor of some friends."

Throughout Joe's speech he was interrupted repeatedly by angry Democrats. Senators Herbert H. Lehman, Charles Tobey, Dennis Chavez, Hubert Humphrey, Clinton Anderson, and Brien McMahon stood at one time or another to raise objections. Lehman was especially incensed when McCarthy made it clear that he would turn his information over to the FBI and not the Tydings Committee. "You are making a spectacle to the galleries here and to the public where a man accused has no chance to answer," he charged. Joe shot back, "Crocodile tears are being shed for traitorous individuals, but forgotten are the 400,000,000 people who have been sold into slavery by these people." At another point Lehman sought to have the entire letter written by Lattimore in 1943 read to the Senate, fearing that McCarthy's quotation was taken out of context. Joe invited the New Yorker to step across the chamber "so that I can show him why a fuller disclosure would be completely unfair." Lehman walked over, saying "I want to see the letter." Joe would not hand it over, and announced, "I don't yield any further." Applause thundered from the galleries.

The speech lasted more than four hours. Midway through it, Joe pulled a small brown bottle from his pocket and took a swig of its contents. Smiling, he said it was cough medicine. It was. He entered the hospital the next day for further treatment of his painful sinus condition and a cough. When Senator Wherry announced that fact to the Senate, Sen. Tom Connally, who had sat in on some of the Tydings Committee hearings, asked how long McCarthy would be absent. Wherry said, "Just today." "Is that all?" Connally exclaimed.[73]

Wherry, a mortician from Pawnee City, Nebraska, was ecstatic over McCarthy's speech. In his view it contained "a case that is clear cut." "The Administration will have to take cognizance of it," he said. "It's up to the State Department to refute these charges if it can."[74]

Even before McCarthy had concluded his speech, President Truman called a rare vacation news conference in Key West and unleashed his fury on Senators McCarthy, Wherry, and Bridges. They were playing politics with American foreign policy, he said, and were undermining constructive bipartisanship. He told reporters that McCarthy was the greatest asset the Kremlin had—but then refused to be quoted directly. (He was anyway.) He had ample praise for Acheson, Jessup, and Lattimore, as well as for moderate Republicans Vandenberg, Saltonstall, and Stimson. Truman flatly dismissed the charge that Lattimore was the top Russian agent as silly.[75]

Senator Taft quickly responded to what he called a "bitter and prejudiced attack on Republicans." "The greatest Kremlin asset in our history," he charged, "has been the pro-Communist group in the State Department," and such people could not be rooted out by men who think Communists are only "red herrings." McCarthy, he said, was "a fighting Marine who risked his life to preserve the liberties of the United States."[76]

Even Senator Wiley, who had long remained silent about his colleague and had opposed McCarthy's votes for the Kerr natural gas bill and the central Arizona projects—widely considered favors to private interests— joined the chorus of Republicans who lashed out against the President's rebuke. "The nation wants to get the facts and it does not want to see Senator McCarthy or any member of the Senate smeared merely because he has the guts to seek those facts on behalf of the American public."[77]

It was becoming obvious that McCarthyism was to be among the central issues of the 1950 congressional campaigns. Senators were already reporting the arrival of thousands of right-wing postcards daily at their offices. A typical card read "Why don't you get the Red rats out of the State Department," the words heavily underlined in red ink. Those experienced in evaluating postcard and letter campaigns, William S. White wrote in *The New York Times*, were alarmed at the tone of the current messages. At the same time, McCarthy's office was being flooded with favorable letters. Some were beginning to contain financial contributions.[78]

Whatever slim chance the Tydings Committee had of producing a statement on McCarthy and the State Department that would lift foreign policy above the political fray and quell public rancor was already long lost. Senators Green and Hickenlooper were arguing publicly about the wisdom of sending a subpoena to McCarthy in order to obtain the Lattimore materials for the committee. Senator Lodge, echoing an earlier proposal by Congressman Nixon, called for a new twelve-member nonpartisan commission. "All we can learn so far," he told the Senate, "shows clearly that none of the current charges has been proved." From his hospital bed, Joe backed the proposal. "Anything would be better than the committee we now have." Administration leaders vetoed the idea, however, on the ground that the current Senate probe had progressed too far to be stopped.[79]

The committee served subpoenas on Acheson, McGrath, and Chairman Harry B. Mitchell of the Civil Service Commission, seeking access to the files of the accused that Tydings had earlier requested from the President without success. Truman ordered the three to ignore the subpoenas. "No president has ever complied with an order of the legislative branch directing the executive branch to produce confidential documents, the disclosure of which was contrary to the public interest," Truman wrote Tydings. Senator Connally predicted that the Senate would not vote contempt citations against the three officials. (Wherry wanted Truman cited for contempt.) Faced with the unlikelihood of obtaining evidence from the files of the State Department, the Civil Service Loyalty Board, or the FBI, and unable to gain access to McCarthy's Lattimore documents, Tydings wondered aloud how his committee might achieve its goals.[80]

Committee hearings resumed on April 5th. Donald Nicholson, a former FBI agent and since 1948 chief of the Division of Security for the State Department, explained the stringent loyalty-security program in detail for the senators. "As far as we know," he said, "there is no card-carrying Communist in the State Department. If there were, they would be terminated by noon."

Gen. Conrad E. Snow, chairman of the State Department's Loyalty and Security Board, appeared next, accompanied by seven of the eight distinguished citizens who comprised the board. Snow, a 60-year-old Republican, had been chairman of the body since 1947 when the President's loyalty program was initiated. He thoughtfully explained board procedure, expounded upon the care with which an individual's membership in Communist fronts in the 1930s and 1940s had to be weighed, and discussed the uses and misuses of guilt by association. The board's record was sound, he pointed out. During the past three years the board had determined 246 cases, 199 of which were postaudited by the Loyalty Review Board. Only three were remanded for a hearing and not a single case was reversed. Of the 246 cases, the board judged two employees to be security risks; five others resigned with charges pending. Any reasonable doubt about an employee's loyalty, if based on solid evidence, was resolved in favor of the government, Snow observed. Not only was the loyalty-security program effective but the McCarran rider, approved by Congress in 1946 and renewed repeatedly in subsequent appropriation acts, gave the Secretary of State absolute discretion to fire any department employee whenever he thought the action necessary or desirable. "If there are any Communists in the State Department," he said, "the Loyalty-Security Board is uninformed of their existence."

Seth W. Richardson, chairman of the Civil Service Loyalty Review Board, followed Snow to the stand. The 70-year-old former Assistant Attorney General in the Hoover administration added further details about procedures followed under the loyalty-security program and presented a highly positive picture of the men and women employed by the federal government. The FBI, which was responsible for examining files of applicants and employees, had considered 3,000,000 cases, he noted, giving more than 10,000 files a more thorough (field) investigation. Not a single case of espionage was disclosed. "We have not received any evidence," he stated, "of any card-carrying Communists in the State Department, up to the present time."[81]

The stage was now set for the appearance of Owen Lattimore. He had returned to the United States from Afghanistan less than a week earlier, telling reporters at the airport that he was not a Communist or a fellow traveler and calling McCarthy a "base and miserable creature." In his absence, Mrs. Lattimore had requested an appearance before the Tydings Committee and had employed attorney Abe Fortas, a prominent Democrat, a former Undersecretary of the Interior, and a future Supreme Court Justice. (Reacting against McCarthy, Fortas took the case after asking only a single question of Mrs. Lattimore, whom he had met once socially. "Will he fight?") Aided by many of Lattimore's friends, colleagues, and students, Fortas swiftly prepared an elaborately detailed defense, pointing to almost 100 factual errors in Joe's March 30th speech alone.[82]

McCarthy countered Lattimore's airport remarks with a demand from his hospital bed that the State Department make public a confidential memorandum submitted by Lattimore the previous August to a departmental advisory group. When the State Department declined, Lattimore released the document himself. The professor had advised the United States to abandon further support of Chiang Kai-shek, avoid bringing trade pressure on Communist China, and withdraw as quickly as possible from "entanglements" in South Korea.[83]

The day before Lattimore's scheduled appearance before the Tydings Committee, McCarthy asked for the right to cross-examine the witness. The committee denied the request but gave Joe permission to submit questions through committee members. He flatly rejected the offer.[84]

The Senate caucus room was packed on April 6 when Lattimore was sworn in. The 49-year-old, bespectacled professor was startled at first by the hot and almost blinding klieg lights for the newsreel and television cameras and by a knot of cameramen jockeying for position in front of him and igniting flashbulbs in his face. His parents were present, along with a large number of friends, but most of those on hand were strangers, and Lattimore knew that they were eager for sensation. Abe Fortas was seated next to him at a small table in front of the committee; Mrs. Lattimore and Fortas's partner Paul Porter sat slightly behind them. The witness recognized the senators in the room from photographs. Tom Connally was seated with the committee members, and behind them were Senators Lucas, Tobey, Mundt, Knowland, and McCarthy. Joe sat behind and slightly to one side of Senator Tydings, so that whenever Lattimore addressed the chairman, he also saw his accuser. "I soon found out something interesting," he later wrote. "Joe McCarthy cannot look you straight in the eye."[85]

Lattimore began by reading a 10,000-word prepared statement that took an hour and forty-five minutes to deliver and won prolonged applause from the spectators. It opened with fiery and often sarcastic denunciations of McCarthy, labeling his conduct "unworthy of a senator or an American" and his charges "base and contemptible lies." McCarthy had become a "willing tool" of the China Lobby, he charged, "the simple dupe of a group of fanatical persons who have been thoroughly discredited." He presented an analysis of McCarthy's charges, showing their similarity to Alfred Kohlberg's. "It is easy to understand," he said, "the joy of Kohlberg and his associates when they found the willing hands and innocent mind of Joseph McCarthy." (Kohlberg soon admitted that he had given "documentary material" to McCarthy but denied telling the senator that Lattimore was an actual Communist.) Lattimore recalled McCarthy's pledge to resign from the Senate if he failed to repeat any charge in public made under the cloak of immunity. "He has failed to do so," the witness said, "and he has not resigned." He accused McCarthy of using secret government documents without authorization, of refusing to submit evidence to a duly constituted committee of the Senate, of vilifying American citizens without giving them an opportunity to defend themselves, of instituting a "reign of terror" among federal employees, and of making the government "an object of suspicion in the eyes of the anti-Communist world, and undoubtedly the laughingstock of the Communist governments."[86]

Lattimore cited three brief associations with the State Department: he had served for three or four months on a reparations mission to Japan in 1945, he had participated in a two-day panel discussion on China the previous October and had submitted a memorandum of his views at the request of the State Department, and he had delivered a single speech at the Department, one in a series of lectures designed to present various points of view. Beyond that, he said, he had had no connection with the State Department. He did not have a desk or a telephone at the Department and did not enjoy access to its files. "I think I can fairly claim," he said, "with great regret, that I am the least consulted man of all those who have a public reputation in this country as specialists on the Far East.... I wish that I had in fact had more influence," he added. "If I had, I think that the Communists

would not now control China." He inserted flattering wartime letters from
Chiang Kai-shek and his wife into the record, along with recent letters of
recommendation from relevant observers and authorities.

Lattimore vigorously denied McCarthy's espionage charge. "I cannot
even imagine anything that I ever did or said which might conceivably have
suggested this even to a perverted mind." He effectively challenged the
several assertions McCarthy had read in his lengthy Senate speech alluding
to spying, including the charge that he had declassified government documents in 1945 in the company of John Stewart Service. He also presented a
sampling of McCarthy's quotations from his publications to demonstrate
that they were distorted and inaccurate.

Bourke Hickenlooper dominated the remainder of the session, pressing
the witness hard with a battery of questions focusing upon the fall of China
that were at first ascribed in part to McCarthy. Lattimore responded
eloquently and persuasively, revealing a wealth of information that left
Hickenlooper sputtering and Lodge pleading for closed sessions. Lattimore's position on China was virtually identical to the Administration's.
He blamed the Nationalists for losing the support of the Chinese people,
he backed the Foreign Service officials who were on the scene, and he
supported the Marshall mission. Lattimore also expressed his highly un-
fashionable belief that the Chinese Communists should receive diplomatic
recognition from the United States. In addition, he warned against further
American involvement in Korea on the ground that the nation was backing
another Chiang, a position "untenable for a democracy."

At one point Hickenlooper pulled from his papers a copy of a classified
letter Lattimore had written in 1943 while in the Office of War Information, and asked the witness to identify it. Realizing that McCarthy had cited
the letter in his Senate speech, Lattimore had it declassified by Tydings and
read into the record. The full text cleared Lattimore of Joe's contention that
the letter revealed pro-Communist treachery and proved once again that
McCarthy had twisted a quotation for his own purpose.[87]

It was clear from their earliest questions that committee Democrats were
sympathetic to Lattimore. (Tom Connally shook hands with the witness
during the noon recess and said a few harsh words about McCarthy.)
Tydings intensified the atmosphere of partisanship by announcing the
committee's earlier study of a summary of the professor's FBI file and the
unanimous judgment that he was innocent of all charges. This revelation
deeply upset Hickenlooper, who had been out of town when J. Edgar
Hoover and Attorney General McGrath presented the summary of the file

to committee members. (Two days later, having seen the summary, he strongly dissented from the findings of the others who had consulted it.) To make things worse, the chairman also condemned Republicans for defeating aid to Korea and for failure to support the Marshall Plan. The G.O.P., in short, was soft on the Reds.[88]

Joe remained impassive throughout the hearing. At its conclusion, however, he angrily told reporters, "I am not retracting anything. I intend to prove everything I have said." When asked about the FBI summary, he stated, "Either Tydings hasn't seen the files, or he is lying. There is no alternative." He did not know what Hoover had shown the committee members, he admitted, "but I know what is in the files." He also said that he would not repeat his charges against Lattimore without congressional immunity until the government surrendered its files for inspection.[89]

On April 8 Joe delivered a speech in Passaic, New Jersey, where he received the 1950 Americanism award from the local Marine Corps league. He accused Jessup, Service, and Lattimore of following and advocating policies identical with those of the Communist party, and he invited the three to sue him. At no point, however, did he call them Communists. In Washington, Lattimore told reporters that McCarthy was "weaseling." John E. Puerifoy of the State Department taunted the senator for using "carefully phrased innuendo." A formal statement said, "Senator McCarthy roared like a lion when he wore the cloak of congressional immunity. Now he discards his immunity, strikes the pose of a hero, and bleats like a lamb." Drew Pearson soon offered to pay McCarthy's legal expenses for a libel suit if the senator would repeat his charges against Lattimore off the Senate floor.[90]

In a telegram to Acheson, released to the press, McCarthy expressed shock at the State Department's attack and hinted that conclusive proof of Lattimore's treason was forthcoming. The next day he told reporters that he had given Senate investigators the name of a mystery witness who would swear that Lattimore was currently or at one time a Communist. Tydings dispelled the air of suspense by announcing that Louis Budenz was McCarthy's witness and that he had been ordered to appear before the committee in public session. Privately, Tydings again appealed to the President to release the files so that "the present Communist inquiry be not allowed to worsen."[91]

Truman's position on the issue remained unchanged for the time being, but he soon fired a new blast at McCarthy during a news conference, questioning whether it was possible to libel the Wisconsin Republican. He

infuriated Joe a couple of weeks later by inviting William T. Evjue to the
White House and providing the *Capital Times* editor a national forum for
his bitter and often inaccurate attacks on McCarthy's past.[92]

On the 20th of April, 700 people waited outside the Senate caucus room
twenty minutes before Louis Budenz was scheduled to testify. Five hundred
were seated, and spectators lined the walls and filled the aisles. Senators
Connally, Wiley, Ferguson, Wherry, Knowland, Mundt, and McCarthy
were in evidence, along with the committee members. Joe's ever-present
leather briefcase bulged so large that one reporter compared it to an
overnight bag. He again seated himself slightly behind the chairman.

Budenz, 58, was an assistant professor of economics at Fordham University. After more than two decades of participation in radical politics, he had
joined the Communist party in 1935, becoming managing editor of the
Daily Worker in 1941. He held the post until he resigned from the party in
October 1945, claiming disillusionment with Communism and the Soviet
dictatorship. With the assistance of Msgr. Fulton J. Sheen, Budenz returned
to the Roman Catholic Church, in which he had been born and raised, and
was given a job at Notre Dame University. In early 1946 Budenz went to
the FBI to confess all, and he soon became a star witness at congressional
hearings, trials, and administrative proceedings. In 1950 he continued to
provide evidence for the FBI, sometimes devoting up to eighteen hours a
week to the task. When he appeared before the Tydings Committee he said
he was working on a list of 400 concealed Communists in the United States.
Budenz was also an author and lecturer, and in 1953 he would claim gross
earnings of $70,000 from his anti-Communist activities.[93]

With Lattimore seated behind him, grimly taking notes with a gold
pencil on a stenographer's pad, Budenz testified that he had been told by
Communist leaders in 1937 that Lattimore was part of a party cell centered
at the Institute of Pacific Relations. Lattimore, Philip Jaffe, Frederick
Vanderbilt Field, and other cell members were ordered to portray the
Chinese Reds as agrarian reformers. Budenz testified that Field com-
mended Lattimore's zeal in placing Communist writers on the magazine
Pacific Affairs.

In 1943, Budenz said, he heard that Lattimore, through Field, had
received word that the new line was to attack Chiang. (He soon contradicted himself, saying that Lattimore had told Field about the new line.) A
year later, he reported, Communist leader Jack Stachel advised him "to
consider Owen Lattimore as a Communist." The advice came, he said, at the
time Communists were discussing Lattimore's trip to China as an adviser to
Vice-President Henry Wallace.

Budenz also testified that he had seen secret politburo reports, written on onionskin paper, which contained information so confidential that recipients were not permitted to burn them for fear of leaving embers. "We had to tear them up in small pieces and destroy them through the toilet." Whenever "L" or "XL" appeared on one of these documents, party leaders told him, it came from Owen Lattimore.

In response to shrewd questioning by committee Democrats and chief counsel Morgan, Budenz admitted, however, that he had not told the FBI about Lattimore's alleged Communist membership until a couple of weeks earlier when he learned that the Tydings Committee had seen a summary of the professor's bureau file. His explanation was simply that he had lacked sufficient time over the past four years. Calling himself a reluctant witness, he acknowledged discussing Lattimore recently with Alfred Kohlberg, Charles Kersten, Robert Morris, and J. B. Matthews, and he admitted furnishing information to McCarthy. He stated flatly that he had no personal knowledge of Lattimore's party membership. And when asked if he considered Lattimore the top Russian spy in the United States, he replied, "Well, to my knowledge, that statement is technically not accurate. I do not know, of course, the whole story, what other evidence there is, but from my own knowledge I would not say he was a top Soviet agent."

Budenz was often shifty and ill-prepared, and at times he gave the (probably correct) impression that he had agreed to appear before the committee only under extreme pressure from right-wing friends in order to save McCarthy. He admitted knowing virtually nothing about Lattimore's writings and noted that he had never seen or met the accused. He resorted to evasion when asked to explain a transcript of a 1949 conversation he had had with the editor of *Collier's* magazine in which he specifically denied that Lattimore was a Communist agent. He was forced to acknowledge that his new book, designed to expose the Soviet fifth column in the United States, contained no reference to Lattimore. "However," he promised, "in another book which I am writing Mr. Lattimore is very prominent."[94]

Budenz was followed to the stand by retired Brig. Gen. Elliott R. Thorpe, an Army Intelligence expert who had served on Gen. Douglas MacArthur's staff during the war. On three different occasions, Thorpe testified, from the early 1930s through 1947, he had carefully examined Lattimore's loyalty. He assured the committee of his total confidence in the professor's patriotism and attributed the charges against him to "the protagonists of Nationalist China." In all his years of Intelligence work, he said, he had never "heard a man so frequently referred to as a Communist with so little basis in fact."[95]

That evening, his case against Lattimore in ruins, Joe broadened his attack against the State Department. In a formal speech before the American Society of Newspaper Editors, he donned the mantle of martyrdom, claiming that his critics were attacking him solely because he had challenged Communists and their agents in the United States. "I knew it would be thus—that vilification, smear, and falsehoods would follow, peddled by the Reds, their minions, and their egg-sucking phony liberals who litter Washington with their persons and clutter up American thinking with their simple-minded arguments."

It was clear that McCarthy included journalists among his targets (Drew Pearson had just begun devoting articles to the Lustron story.) "Some write columns for your newspapers. It is your privilege to buy them; mine to ignore them." He had nothing but scorn, Joe sneered, for "the pitiful squealing of those who would hold sacrosanct those Communists and queers who have sold 400 million Asiatic people into atheistic slavery and have the American people in a hypnotic trance, headed blindly toward the same precipice."

In a question-and-answer period that followed, Joe called Acheson "completely incompetent" and implied that he was a tool of Stalin. Not content to stop there, he labeled former Secretary of State George Marshall "completely unfit" for the cabinet post and said "it was a crime ... a pathetic thing" to put him in charge of John Stewart Service. Marshall, he claimed, "boned up" on China by reading the works of Owen Lattimore.[96]

Reporters were surprised by McCarthy's attack on Marshall, for however much Republicans had grumbled about his unsuccessful mission to China they had almost always avoided direct criticism of the revered wartime Chief of Staff. Acheson called Joe's charges "mad and vicious." Marshall declared that the senator's activities "undermine and weaken our position before the world and actually lend assistance to powers that would destroy us."[97]

In response to letters from Senator Tydings, four Secretaries of State—Cordell Hull, James F. Byrnes, Marshall, and Acheson—denied in writing that Lattimore had had anything to do with American foreign policy in the Far East. Marshall, like Acheson, had never met the accused. Hull could not remember having consulted with him at any time on any subject. Senator Tydings released these declarations to the press, and some top Republicans began to talk of a committee boycott by Hickenlooper and Lodge.[98]

On April 24 the Tydings Committee met in executive session with McCarthy. Green and Hickenlooper could not attend, and no transcript was made of the proceeding. From minutes subsequently submitted by committee counsel Morgan, it is known that Joe was questioned about the wording of his Wheeling speech. Committee investigators were in Wheeling at the time taking testimony about the charges of February 9. According to Morgan's minutes, Joe denied having said that there were 205 Communists in the State Department, and he stated that he could not specifically recall using the expression "card-carrying." The only figure he had employed in West Virginia, he told committee members, was 57.

Joe was not sworn in at this session, but because he had taken the oath earlier it was binding throughout the balance of the investigation. Critics were to contend that McCarthy was guilty of perjury for his statements at this executive session. If Morgan's minutes were accurate, the critics were no doubt correct, but the charge was never to stick because of the general confusion surrounding the contents of the Wheeling speech.[99]

The next day the full committee met in executive session with Louis Budenz. McCarthy asked for permission to attend and interrogate the witness. The committee denied the request and also barred Robert Morris from the session, no doubt because of his complicity in Budenz's earlier appearance. Joe fumed to reporters, "I was not allowed to be present when my witness was testifying."[100]

Budenz introduced what he said was a list of Communists who had published in *Pacific Affairs* while Lattimore was editor. But under questioning he admitted that he had no proof that Lattimore had solicited the articles or given their authors instructions, and he did not know when the contributors first began to publish in the journal. He expressed considerable ignorance of the articles themselves: "A long time ago I glanced through them." He even acknowledged that some of the pieces might not have been pro-Communist. "You see, Communists do not always write Communist articles."

The witness also revealed that he did not possess records that could document any of his statements about Lattimore. He would not deny having told a special agent of the State Department in 1947 that he was unable to recall any incident that would definitely show Lattimore to be a member of the Communist party. And he further acknowledged his recent contacts with Kohlberg, Kersten, Matthews, and Morris.

Budenz startled Senator McMahon by claiming that he knew "from official reports" that Haldore Hanson was currently a Communist. When pressed, however, the witness acknowledged that his statement about Hanson was based solely on oral evidence, and he was uncertain of its source. He also admitted that he first told the FBI about Hanson's alleged party membership during the past week.[101]

McCarthy reported to the Senate later that day that Budenz, during his testimony before the Tydings Committee, had identified a man in a "very, very important" State Department position as a Communist. (Two days later he named Hanson, who had never held a policymaking post in the Department.) He also told his colleagues that he had given the committee the name of a man who had a police record as a homosexual and still held "an extremely sensitive position" in the Central Intelligence Agency. Senator Wherry informed McCarthy that the person in question had already resigned, and he shouted encouragingly, "You're going to get some more resignations. This is not the only man."[102]

That evening, in the presence of another overflow crowd (including McCarthy), the Tydings Committee heard testimony from New York attorney Bella V. Dodd. Dodd had been active in left-wing politics since the early 1930s and in 1943 had joined the Communist party. She rose quickly in party circles and soon held a seat on the national committee. In 1949 she was expelled from the party following what she described as a four-year struggle against "certain policies."

Dodd stated that in her fourteen years of association with the party, as a fellow traveler and member, she had never heard of Owen Lattimore. Moreover, she had recently read his two latest books and found them unrepresentative of the Communist position on China. She sharply ridiculed Budenz, disputing many of his assertions about party discipline and secrecy and likening his "onionskin document" recollection to "dime detective stories." She was also critical of McCarthy. "Smearing of public citizens has become a greater racket in the United States than horse racing or gambling and almost equally profitable for the individuals engaged therein."

Responding to questions from Hickenlooper, however, Dodd appeared to be something less than the heroine of civil liberties liberals saw on the stand. She revealed considerable sympathy for the Communist party, Stalin, and the Soviet Union, and even denied at one point that the American Communist party took orders from Moscow. "The Communist party of the United States is looking to take over the United States government just as the Republican Party is looking to take it over in this next coming election."[103]

The next witness was Larry E. Kerley, 35, an ex-FBI man, a member of the editorial staff of Hearst's *New York Journal-American,* and a friend of McCarthy's. A week earlier, Joe had requested that the committee subpoena Kerley and one John Huber, whom Kerley had set up as an FBI undercover agent in the Communist party in 1939. Kerley testified that Huber had come to his office after reading McCarthy's charges against Lattimore and told him that the professor had been a Red agent. McCarthy was contacted; both men were subpoenaed, and they came together to Washington. Kerley was to substantiate Huber's credentials, and Huber was to condemn Lattimore. Things did not work out, however, for Huber apparently got cold feet and disappeared from the Carlton Hotel. Kerley testified that he knew little about Huber's undercover work and nothing about Lattimore.

Huber turned up in Manhattan the next day, saying that he had "blacked out" in Washington and did not know how he got to New York. Liberals chuckled for weeks over McCarthy's embarrassment. Subsequent testimony in executive session revealed that Huber had met with Kerley, Robert Morris, George Sokolsky, and J. B. Matthews before he was scheduled to appear before the Tydings Committee. It was merely a social gathering, staff member Morris sheepishly told the senators. "Naturally," however, "the Lattimore subject was in all the papers and everyone was talking about it." In January 1951 McCarthy would put Huber on his personal payroll.[104]

On April 27 the committee heard former Communist party leader Earl Browder. Browder denounced Budenz as a "professional perjurer" and challenged his testimony in detail. He had never met Lattimore or heard his name mentioned in party circles, he said. "He was definitely known to me as a person of anti-Communist views, of a very decided and profound character." Browder also defended the Communist party vigorously and on several occasions refused to answer questions. The committee later voted to cite him for contempt.[105]

The next day Frederick Vanderbilt Field appeared before the committee. A wealthy man who had long been associated with the Institute of Pacific Relations and *Amerasia* magazine, Field was commonly thought to be a Communist or a hard-line fellow traveler. Budenz had called him a Red spy. He took the Fifth Amendment when asked about party membership and was also cited for contempt at a later date. Field defended Lattimore's scholarly objectivity and condemned Budenz's assertions about himself and the professor. He and Lattimore were "pretty much in disagreement on political questions," he said.[106]

The testimony by Dodd, Browder, and Field did nothing to strengthen the committee's reputation. More than one observer wondered why objective men in the exercise of good judgment would pay any attention to what such witnesses said of Owen Lattimore. Asking Browder about the accused, said Senator Jenner, was like "sending Baby Face Nelson to investigate John Dillinger." Joe called the action "ridiculous to the point of being ludicrous."[107]

Equally partisan and predictable was the testimony of Freda Utley, who appeared before the committee on May 1. A former member of the British Communist party, Utley had flirted with the Nazis in 1940 and later became closely associated with Alfred Kohlberg and the China Lobby. A fiery, emotional witness, she condemned Lattimore, a onetime personal friend, as a "Judas cow," an "out-and-out defender of the Soviet government," a man who "can be said to have done more than anyone else to poison the wells of opinion with regard to China." "His function has been to lead us unknowingly to destruction," she cried. She was unable to prove, however, that Lattimore had influenced American foreign policy. She admitted ignorance on the question of his membership in the Communist party. And she declined to support McCarthy's charge that the professor was the top Russian spy in the country.[108]

Lattimore was granted a further appearance on May 2 that spilled over into the next day. In a lengthy statement, interrupted by applause from the crowd that packed the caucus room, he castigated McCarthy for his unsupported contentions, countered with a number of charges against his accuser currently popular in the press (involving the 1944 campaign, the Quaker Dairy case, and Malmedy), and systematically rebutted statements made by Louis Budenz, even implying that the ex-Communist was a homosexual. "We cannot allow this man to run wild any longer," he demanded. He also presented evidence showing that he had not filled the pages of *Pacific Affairs* with the writings of subversives during his editorship. And he presented about 170 letters from scholars and writers on the Far East deploring McCarthy's charges against himself. He asked, "Will you, gentlemen, seriously consider the uninformed, reckless, mad denunciations of McCarthy and Budenz against the informed conclusions of citizens like these?"

Lattimore was not so cocky, however, when carefully questioned by committee counsel Morgan about certain statements from his publications. What had he meant by Russian "democracy"? How did he explain his judgment that in China "the political structure under the Communists is more nearly democratic than it is under the Kuomintang"? What did he mean by writing in 1945, "When Japan begins to show an ability to make progress politically, we must expect the leadership to be left of center and at least liberal enough to be friendly with Russia"? Hadn't he written in 1940 that the Chinese Communists were "agrarian radicals rather than true Communists . . . "? Lattimore's answers were all too often prolix and evasive.[109]

However unconvincing Lattimore was at portraying himself as an intellectual independent and a devout anti-Communist, it should have been clear to any fair-minded observer that McCarthy's sensational charges against the professor remained without substantiation. Louis Budenz was the best witness McCarthy and his allies had come up with, and his testimony had fallen far short of their expectations.

Indeed, almost 90 days after the Wheeling speech, not one of Joe's allegations of treason in the State Department could be judged by reasonable men as documented or even persuasive, and the fraudulence of most of them was already obvious. Democratic Congressman Frank M. Karsten of Missouri, examining the source of Joe's February 20 speech to the Senate, asked for an investigation to determine whether McCarthy's charges constituted "a hoax, a deceit, or a fraud ... upon the American people."[110]

But the political atmosphere in the spring of 1950 was such that evidence and logic were often avoided. Growing numbers of Republicans were convinced that McCarthyism was their ticket to political power and were determined to back Joe's Red hunt as long as the headlines continued to bombard the Administration. *New York Times* columnist James Reston quoted Tom Coleman as saying, "The issue is fairly simple, and it was made by the newspapers. It is now a political issue, and somebody is going to gain or lose politically before it's over. It all comes down to this: are we going to try to win an election or aren't we?"[111]

G.O.P. leaders were encouraged by polls showing sizable public support for McCarthy's efforts. A Minnesota poll found that 41 percent believed the charges of Communist infiltration in the State Department, while 29 percent did not. A Gallup poll discovered that 39 percent of those interviewed thought McCarthy's charges were "a good thing," while 29 percent considered them "doing harm."[112]

On May 3 Republicans and Democrats clashed in what a *New York Times* reporter called "one of the harshest Senate scenes in many years." It began with Senator Lucas reading a statement by Deputy Undersecretary of State Puerifoy that accused McCarthy of reviving "shop-worn" charges that had been examined and dropped in the 80th Congress. Wherry rose to object, contending that Lucas was defaming a colleague. A short time later Lucas resumed reading the statement and noted that the press had reported the number 205 after Joe's Wheeling speech. "The time has now come to call a spade a spade," Lucas shouted. Facing McCarthy, he said angrily, "I am willing to take what the press of the country said, and not what McCarthy says he said on that occasion." Democrats Matthew Neely and Harley M. Kilgore of West Virginia then offered the *Wheeling Intelligencer* account of McCarthy's speech and affidavits taken by the Tydings Committee staff affirming the number 205. Neely said sternly, "If there is no foundation for this charge of 205 Communists in the State Department I think the senator will have destroyed himself in the Senate and will have destroyed his usefulness to the country."

Boiling with rage at this obviously planned attack by Senate Democrats, Joe managed to sputter through an explanation of what he had said in Wheeling that no doubt merely confused colleagues on both sides of the aisle. He also tried to be evasive. "Let's be done with this silly numbers game. If a word I have said is not true, the President has only to open the loyalty files to show it." Neely continued to bear down, however, and Tydings soon joined in, contending that the question of whether or not Joe had said there were 205 card-carrying Reds in the State Department could be answered yes or no "by an honest man." Neely declared at one point, "Somebody is lying at the rate Ananias never lied." Wherry bellowed, "The American people want an investigation not of Mr. McCarthy but of subversives in the State Department."[113]

Late the next day President Truman agreed to let the Tydings Committee study the loyalty files of the 71 identifiable cases McCarthy had referred to in his February 20 Senate speech. Committee members would not have access to the "raw" FBI files, Tydings announced, but added that "there will be FBI material" in some of the State Department files made available. The senators were to examine the files at the White House and would not be allowed to take notes. Committee staff members were not to be permitted to participate.

The President had obviously given in only after intense pressure from Senate Democrats, eager to deflate McCarthy and his G.O.P. allies. After the heated Senate session of May 3 Lucas had told reporters, "We have just started to fight." The next day he said that Democrats in the Senate "are tired of being kicked around and of listening to that claptrap on the other side [of the aisle]." Truman, moreover, was about to embark upon a "nonpolitical" junket across the country and was undoubtedly glad to be rid of Republican "cover-up" charges. He had also been persuaded that since the files of those on the Lee list had already been inspected by four committees of the 80th Congress prior to his executive order, his permission did not involve a harmful precedent.[114]

The files would reveal, of course, what Tydings and Truman already knew: that on February 20 McCarthy had merely shuffled sentences and numbers from the Lee list and that there was no additional evidence to support his assertions. To ward off the impact of this inevitable finding, Joe had no other recourse than to contend that the files committee members were to examine had somehow been tampered with after he had studied them. In a perfervid speech before the Midwest Council of Young Republicans he called the files "phony" and charged that they had been "raped." He referred to the Tydings Committee as "the famous Lucas-Tydings-McMahon OPERATION WHITEWASH." He demanded that the President call in J. Edgar Hoover and other top security officials and authorize them to compile a list of the federal employees who were dangerous to the Republic. "Tell them to study the list, use tough standards, cut them to fit the cloth of Communist treachery, and tell you who to fire. Take their word for it, Mr. President, not McMahon's, not Tydings,' not Earl Browder's."[115]

THE TYDINGS REPORT

At some point in his post-Wheeling struggles Joe became persuaded of the overall truth of the Communist conspiracy charges that dominated his political career for the rest of his life. The frank cynicism revealed to the *Milwaukee Journal* reporters at the conclusion of his Lincoln Day speeches was soon replaced by an intense, almost fanatical interest in the Reds who lurked in high places. This obsession often wearied his staff, bored old friends, and astonished several Senate colleagues. It was ironic that while ' critics railed at McCarthy for being wholly cynical, immoral, and even amoral, those closest to him knew that he had become a zealot.

The transformation occurred very soon after his return to Washington in mid-February. Ray Kiermas, with whom Joe lived and worked daily, watched with fascination as his longtime friend became completely absorbed by anti-Communism. Don Surine later said that he never doubted his employer's sincerity, although he acknowledged Joe's early lack of information. Ed Nellor, the principal author of the Wheeling speech, knew that McCarthy was merely playing politics on his Lincoln Day tour. But when Joe was "educated" by veteran anti-Communists after returning to Washington, Nellor later recalled, he was "like a kid opening a Christmas present." He immediately became enthusiastic, eager to kick the Reds out of Washington. "Joe got an eyeful, quick."[1]

Joe's basic innocence of history made him a natural prey for the hard-line right-wingers who flocked around him after his Lincoln Day charges. Hoover, Nixon, Bridges, Kohlberg, Sokolsky, Matthews, and the others flattered him, defended him, and filled his office with more documents than Joe would ever find time to read. Staff members Surine, Nellor, Kersten, and Jean Kerr, true believers all, backed his every move and sometimes worked seven days a week until all hours of the morning to strengthen his charges and lay the groundwork for new allegations. Of course, as a former judge with a good mind and a capacity for sustained labor, McCarthy should still have been able to weigh the evidence with greater care and fairness. Joe, however, had long since revealed his capacity for uncritical belief and an ability to ignore the promptings of his intellect.[2]

McCarthy's new mentors also told him what he wanted to hear, which undoubtedly accelerated his commitment to right-wing extremism. He had been desperate for a political issue that would bring him the attention his ego had demanded since he first ran for district attorney in 1936. Joe was now in the headlines, the editorial pages, even in the political cartoons, almost daily. He clearly became addicted to the publicity, as many public figures do, and was unwilling to surrender the spotlight.

Joe would glow as reporters surrounded him, pleading for a statement or a comment. He knew most of the Washington newsmen by their first names and delighted in furnishing them with stories, remarks, and tips that would please editors and land himself on the front page. There were three wire services in the nation's capital—the Associated Press, United Press, and Hearst's I.N.S.—and reporters from each competed for sensational stories and the raises and bonuses that went with them. Washington correspondents from the larger newspapers were equally eager to scoop colleagues. Joe understood this struggle and frequently exploited it. Almost anything he said, no matter how extreme, was considered highly news-worthy and was soon read by tens of millions. Bill Theis, a veteran I.N.S. reporter, became physically ill nightly at the thought of printing another McCarthy charge that he personally considered irresponsible.[3]

Reporters usually confused McCarthy's eagerness for publicity with political cynicism. Joe was fully aware, of course, of the political uses of his brand of anti-Communism and was determined to exploit them to the fullest. This recognition only proved, however, that McCarthy was a skillful politician and did not necessarily indicate hypocrisy on his part. Jack Anderson was shocked to learn that McCarthy was sincere. One day he and the senator were alone in the latter's office when Joe began to lecture about the Communist conspiracy in Washington. Anderson asked his friend to stop the performance; he knew it was an act and was unimpressed. "No, no, no," Joe said earnestly, "this is the real thing, Jack. This is the real thing."[4]

Requests for personal appearances began to pour into McCarthy's office during the Tydings Committee hearings. Basking in his sudden fame, in May the senator gave speeches in Chicago (over a national radio hookup); Janesville, Wisconsin; Atlantic City; Rochester, New York; and West Allis, Wisconsin. Audiences were enthusiastic and demonstrative. "My topic wasn't hard to pick," he said in Janesville, "since there is one subject you would all like to hear about—the Communist investigations." He reported in the same speech that a heavy volume of mail arriving daily at his office indicated strong national approval of his efforts.[5]

Joe's mail continued to bring numerous financial contributions for his anti-Communist crusade. On May 5 he quietly opened a special account at the Riggs National Bank in Washington as a depository for the funds. Checks, money orders, and cash were deposited regularly, and by the end of the year funds in the account totaled $15,428.52. The 392 checks and money orders received averaged under $40 apiece, indicating that they were sent in by people of average incomes. The funds being gifts, Joe was not required to pay taxes on them or account for them in any way. He no doubt paid Kersten from this account, and he hired as many as five investigators at one point later in the year to accelerate his probes. Later investigations were to show that Joe also used a portion of the funds for personal investments and expenses.[6]

Joe was no doubt also attracted to anti-Communism as a weapon against his critics. Since Wheeling he had been under relentless attack for his State Department charges. And within a short time Evjue, Drew Pearson, and others were condemning his 1944 campaign and his record as a judge and as a senator. The charge concerning the financing of the wartime campaign, as we have seen, was painfully accurate, as other allegations would be. Joe took obvious delight in lashing out at his detractors, especially in his speeches, tying their attacks to similar blasts from the Communist press and concluding, inevitably, that all of his critics were cut from the same Red cloth. McCarthyism became a form of self-protection and a device for revenge.

McCarthy devoted almost all of his energy to anti-Communism after Wheeling, badly slighting his other senatorial duties. He drove his staff, especially Surine, very hard; Robert E. Lee thought that Joe virtually set quotas for the discovery of Reds. He loaded his personal letters and speeches with self-serving references to sacrifice, persecution, and martyrdom. He was also privately convinced that State Department agents were tailing him, and he told friends that he feared for his life. He would not go near an open window for fear of being an assassin's target. He kept a loaded pistol in his office desk and often surrounded himself in public with armed bodyguards. A former FBI undercover agent later testified that a "goon squad" organizer had been selected by the Communist party to murder McCarthy. Don Surine claimed that the senator occasionally found the nuts on his car wheels loosened. (Surine also claimed that his own telephone was tapped by five government agencies and that the Truman administration once put him under twenty-four-hour-a-day surveillance.)[7]

Democratic Senator Clinton Anderson of New Mexico was a friend of McCarthy's during the late 1940s and later wrote about the change he saw in his colleague after the Wheeling speech. During Joe's first two years in Washington Anderson thought of him principally as a rather wild and unsuccessful card player. When he failed to beat Robert Kerr of Oklahoma at gin rummy, he hired an expert to give him lessons. With his game improved, he would periodically brag, "I really got him bloodied last night, Clint." Anderson did not take the Wisconsin Republican very seriously.

After his Lincoln Day charges, however, McCarthy appeared noticeably different to Anderson. "His accusations, naturally, attracted widespread publicity, and when he returned from his speaking tour he seemed to be a changed man." Anderson was shocked by the February 20 speech and soon discovered that McCarthy did not respond to his gentle pleadings and reasoned arguments. He was revolted by Joe's "blustering and raging" and watched sadly as his former friend "lost perspective and chose to take on bigger and bigger game."[8]

On May 4 the Tydings Committee launched a probe of the *Amerasia* case, an inquiry that was to dominate the remainder of the committee's hearings. The case first came to light in June 1945 when the FBI arrested six persons on charges of conspiracy to violate the Espionage Act. Some 1,700 government documents, copies of documents, many of them classified, and newspaper clippings were recovered in the office of the fortnightly *Amerasia* and elsewhere. One of the suspects was John Stewart Service, the China Hand who had clashed with Gen. Patrick Hurley. Emmanuel Larsen, another State Department employee, was also arrested, as were Philip Jaffe and Kate Mitchell, co-editors of *Amerasia*; Andrew Roth, a Navy officer formerly assigned to the Office of Naval Intelligence; and Mark Gayn, a writer for *Collier's* magazine.

Three of the six arrested—Service, Gayn, and Mitchell, were not indicted by the grand jury that heard the case. Larsen pled nolo contendere and was fined $500. Jaffe pled guilty to a lesser charge and paid a fine of $2,500. A House subcommittee chaired by Alabama Democrat Samuel F. Hobbs investigated the matter behind closed doors in 1946 and concluded that justice had been done.

Republicans had cried "whitewash" ever since. The right-wing press, especially the Scripps-Howard and Hearst newspapers, had kept the Administration under steady fire, bearing down especially on Service. McCarthy was attacking Service by November 1949 and had taken aim at the Foreign Service officer in his Wheeling speech. In the speech of March 30 he stated that "a number" of members of the grand jury had voted to indict Service (the vote was actually 20-0 to no-bill) and that J. Edgar Hoover had declared the *Amerasia* case "100-percent airtight" (which the director later denied saying, according to the Justice Department).[9]

Whether Joe correctly quoted Hoover or not, it seems clear that the FBI was behind much of the fury from the Far Right about the *Amerasia* affair. As testimony would reveal, blunders by bureau agents had badly damaged the case against the two key suspects. FBI leaders, unwilling to admit the blot on the bureau's record, angrily cast the blame for the outcome of all the cases on government attorneys and the Administration.

The hand of Alfred Kohlberg would also be seen in the sustained uproar. The China Lobby had pictured *Amerasia,* Owen Lattimore (a member of the journal's editorial board from 1939 to 1941), and Service as major factors in the Communist takeover in China. What could be more natural than that the Democratic administration would come to the aid of its co-conspirators?

The Tydings Committee elected to hold its hearings on the case in executive session, hoping to decrease the publicity surrounding the investigation. McCarthy disliked the decision and wrote a protest letter to Tydings which he defiantly made public at a news conference. He told reporters that the committee's first witness, who was then on the stand, was 60-year-old private detective Frank Bielaski and that he would testify: (1) that six months before the atomic explosion at Hiroshima persons connected with *Amerasia* were "collecting and transmitting to Soviet Russia the secrets of the atomic bomb," (2) that top secret government documents were discovered in the *Amerasia* office, and (3) that the immensity of the espionage operation was such that the witness took fifteen copies of documents from the office "which were never even missed." Reporters eagerly rushed the story into print without asking for the source of McCarthy's information.[10]

In fact, Bielaski did not quite live up to Joe's advance billing. In 1945 the witness had been director of investigations for the Office of Strategic Services. When, in late February, one of his men pointed out that *Amerasia* carried a verbatim record of a secret O.S.S. document, he and several associates broke into the journal's office and discovered hundreds of documents and copies of documents, some labeled "Top Secret." They appeared to have come from every department of the government except the FBI.

One document was simply marked "A" and had to do with a bomb, Bielaski said. "I have racked my memory time and again to produce more, and I don't know whether it was a progress report or a plan report or what; but it had to do with a new piece of, as I thought, ordnance." He had not mentioned an "A" bomb document in earlier testimony before the Hobbs Committee. Bielaski said that he took twelve to fourteen other documents with him from the *Amerasia* office as evidence of what he had seen, and in a short time the FBI was alerted. FBI agents reentered the office ten days later and found many documents, but they were apparently not those described by Bielaski. Six suspects were placed under surveillance, and the arrests were made on June 6. One FBI agent admitted to Bielaski that he had entered the apartment of one of the suspects, Emmanuel Larsen, and Bielaski thought the entry was "a black-bag job," without a warrant.

Bielaski repeatedly mentioned the FBI's bitterness over the results of the case. "I know that the Federal Bureau of Investigation men who worked on this felt that they had gotten the most severe kick in the face the department had ever gotten. They feel that way today." He hinted at dark plots in high places. Three weeks later, over N.B.C.'s "Meet the Press," he declared "very definitely" that there was "a concerted effort on the part of someone to whitewash the *Amerasia* case."[11]

After a brief interrogation of Assistant Counsel Robert Morris, who shared Bielaski's suspicions about the handling of the case, Assistant Attorney General James M. McInerney was sworn in. McInerney was the Justice Department official who supervised the prosecution of the case in 1945. Carefully and convincingly he explained the facts of the complex case that dictated its outcome. The documents involved, he said, "were of innocuous, very innocuous character . . . a little above the level of teacup gossip in the Far East . . ." The classifications were "nothing short of silly." McInerney doubted that more than one percent of the documents related to the national defense. Secondly, surveillance of the suspects had failed to reveal the transmission of any documents outside the circle of the suspects themselves. Senator Lodge was shocked to hear the witness state categorically, "No document was ever traced out of *Amerasia*'s office to anyone else—not one . . . and, there was no instance of anybody ever using one of these documents for anything except the purpose of publication in *Amerasia,* or elsewhere." Thus the grand jury was unsympathetic to the espionage charge. Thirdly, the FBI had made illegal entries into the *Amerasia* office and into the homes of several defendants, and had employed unauthorized wiretapping. (The O.S.S. and FBI committed a total of thirteen illegal entries in the case.) Emmanuel Larsen got wind of entries into his apartment through the slip of an agent's tongue at his arrest and then learned that his telephone had been tapped for months. His attorney quickly filed a motion to quash the indictment against him. McInerney kept the news of the filing from Jaffe's attorney, who could have made a similar motion, and offered him a reduced charge in return for a guilty plea. A judge was hastily summoned on a Saturday morning, and the deal was consummated. Through this ruse the government was able to salvage at least some satisfaction in the case. Larsen's attorney settled for a nolo contendere plea and a small fine. The case against Roth, the third man indicted, was dropped for lack of evidence.

McInerney stated that he had never heard of Bielaski's "A" bomb document at any stage of the case's development, from the FBI or anyone else. When asked if he had received any pressure from the State Department, he replied that department officials had taken a strong interest in the case, had followed it closely, and were eager for the prosecution of the suspects. (Later testimony would show that when President Truman heard a rumor that the White House was urging delay in the case, he personally ordered the FBI to pursue it vigorously.)[12]

Two FBI officials appeared before the committee on May 31 in response to written questions submitted by Tydings. D. Milton Ladd, assistant to the director, and Louis B. Nichols, assistant director, were extremely defensive about the FBI's role in the case. Ladd even denied that bureau agents had entered the apartment Larsen was arrested in and glossed over the charge that an agent tipped off the suspect. (The bureau had submitted a memorandum to the Justice Department setting forth eighteen points to be used in refuting Larsen's attorney's motion to suppress.) Still, virtually all of McInerney's statements about the case were substantiated. Ladd also noted that the bureau knew nothing of Bielanski's "A-bomb" document. Senator McMahon observed that journalists had coined the term "A-bomb" many months after Bielaski's break-in.

At one point during his interrogation Ladd inadvertently quoted from a recorded conversation between Service and Jaffe. No one outside the bureau had been privy to this source of information before, and in a short time Ladd's blunder was to interest Senator McCarthy as well as the Tydings Committee.[13]

Emmanuel Larsen told his story to the committee on June 5 and 6. An articulate but somewhat unstable man of 52, Larsen had grown up in China and possessed considerable linguistic talent. He was hired by the Office of Naval Intelligence in 1935 and transferred to the State Department in 1944. He served on the Postwar Policy Committee and the research and planning unit of the Far East Division and was given a gold badge that entitled him to remove documents from his building for official purposes. The federal government's record-keeping during the war was often extremely sloppy, and Larsen and many other colleagues took documents and copies of documents home and elsewhere as they saw fit. Larsen often filled his briefcase at the end of the day, for he enjoyed working at home and had long been building a biographical file on Chinese personalities.

In mid-1944, while Larsen was still with Naval Intelligence, Lt. Andrew Roth suggested that he meet a friend named Philip Jaffe and exchange information about China. The two quickly became friends, and about once a month, until their arrest, Jaffe supplied Larsen with data about Chinese personalities and Larsen loaned the editor of *Amerasia* copies of documents and biographical cards kept at his home. Larsen assumed that Jaffe's interests were journalistic, although at times the editor revealed a leftist bent that Larsen did not care for. (The FBI considered Jaffe a Communist, according to McInerney.) Larsen never had access to top-secret reports and, in his judgment, the information he shared with Jaffe did not involve national security. He noted that a great many government documents were marked "confidential" by youthful officers eager to impress others with their importance. "There isn't much humor in Naval Intelligence, but we had our daily constitutional laughing at the very, very ridiculous things that were said and done." More than 700 documents, copies of documents, and newspaper clippings were found in Larsen's home at his arrest. He had loaned Jaffe no more than twenty copies of documents, he said, and did not know the source of the scores of other documents found in the *Amerasia* office. (It was to remain a mystery.) He had not conspired with Jaffe or any of the others arrested, he stated, and had not even heard of Mark Gayn.

Larsen described in detail how an FBI agent accidentally alerted him to the fact that his apartment had been entered clandestinely. He checked his suspicion with the landlord and also learned that his telephone was tapped.

Larsen's testimony revealed that he had been unemployed since his resignation from the State Department in 1945. He tried to land a job with the War Department in March 1946 but was rebuffed when a Hearst reporter, friendly with Congressman Dondero, published an article calling him a Communist. The reporter and the congressman made it clear that their favor could be won only by a public statement accusing the State Department of harboring Communists and pro-Communists. Desperate for employment, and having been told falsely that Service had made him a scapegoat before the *Amerasia* grand jury, Larsen went before the Hobbs Committee and blasted Dean Acheson and the China Hands as part of a pro-Communist "gang." Obviously embarrassed, Larsen told the Tydings Committee that he had been misquoted in 1946, and he vouched for the loyalty of each of those he had earlier condemned.

In August 1946 two ex-FBI men had visited Larsen, still unemployed, and invited him to come to New York and write an article for Alfred Kohlberg's *Plain Talk* magazine. At first he refused, but when his visitors promised money, publicity, and an opportunity to clear his name, Larsen gave in. Kohlberg and Don Levine, the magazine's editor, were disappointed with the piece Larsen produced, and when cajolery failed to yield an acceptable revision they rewrote the article to suit their needs and published it under Larsen's name. "The State Department's Espionage Case" contained scathing attacks against the loyalty and integrity of George Marshall, John Service, and others, and was quoted by McCarthy before the Tydings Committee on March 14, 1950, and before the Senate on March 30.[14]

Larsen also revealed that in mid-March McCarthy had called him into his office to learn what he knew about the *Amerasia* case. Joe was pestered so frequently by telephone calls during the interview ("Tell them I have to go to China, or I'm having a baby," he shouted to his secretary) that he turned Larsen over to Don Surine. In his small basement room in the Senate office building, loaded with office and electronic equipment, Surine pointed squarely at his visitor and threatened, "You are equally guilty with the others, but if you will testify correctly you can be of great help to us and everything will be much easier for you." However, when Surine learned that Larsen would not stand behind the *Plain Talk* article, he quickly dismissed him.

Also in recent months, Senators Wherry and Ferguson, who were both aware that Larsen had seen McCarthy, Congressman Dondero, and Hearst reporter Ken Hunter had been pressuring Larsen to testify against Owen Lattimore. Larsen had no knowledge of the professor, and said so flatly. Wherry implied that Lattimore was a homosexual. (Shortly after hearing this, Brien McMahon asked dryly, "When Senator Wherry said he was the expert on homosexuality in the State Department, did he state his qualifications?")[15]

While the Tydings Committee grappled with the complexities of the *Amerasia* case behind closed doors and quietly studied loyalty files in the White House, Joe remained in the headlines on a regular basis. In Janesville he charged that an unnamed U.S. envoy to an unidentified foreign country was a "foreign agent." It was his "case number two" among those handed over to the Tydings Committee, he said. (McCarthy's number two was the

Lee list's number 52. It concerned hearsay about a man who occupied "a high diplomatic post" in 1948.) A week later he accused Dean Acheson of betraying the United States in Asia and demanded that the President dismiss his Secretary of State, Philip Jessup, and Owen Lattimore. "Come home, Mr. Truman, and fire the pied pipers of the politburo." This was followed by a new blast at the Tydings Committee, which was engaged, he said, in doing a "foul job, and deliberately." He raised more charges against Lattimore. He then labeled the *Washington Post* the "Washington Daily Worker" and added it, the *New York Post,* and the *St. Louis Post-Dispatch* to his list of pro-Communist newspapers, along with the *Madison Capital Times.* The new entries were liberal and staunchly anti-McCarthy. They were part of a swelling tide within the fourth estate increasingly critical of the senator editorially. Even the Scripps-Howard newspapers declared, "We wish Sen. McCarthy would keep his big mouth out of the *Amerasia* case. This case is too important to be bungled and it surely will be bungled if the senator from Wisconsin keeps gallumphing in with his wild exaggerations."[16]

Democrats were far from silent during the turmoil. On May 8 Millard Tydings, in the presence of Brien McMahon, privately asked freshman Senator William Benton of Connecticut and veteran Dennis Chavez of New Mexico to attack McCarthy. Benton took the Senate floor the next day, denouncing McCarthy as a "hit-and-run propagandist of the Kremlin model." Chavez followed suit two days later with a stinging condemnation of Louis Budenz. (Joe was persuaded that Chavez's speech had been written by Abe Fortas, Lattimore's attorney. He told reporters that the author was an unnamed Communist lawyer.) Tydings himself claimed that his committee's investigation had delayed legislation "vital to national security," i.e., Joe was helping the Reds. He also released a statement revealing portions of testimony given in executive session by a government prosecutor in the *Amerasia* case, Robert M. Hitchcock. This called public attention to the fact that the major evidence in the case had been illegally obtained and that government efforts to prosecute the suspects had thus been hindered.[17]

The State Department issued several blasts at McCarthy, accusing him at one point of "a further rape of the facts" and declaring at another that "the facts do not deter him from his reckless course." Press officer Lincoln White even told reporters about the Quaker Dairy case and contended that Chief Justice Rosenberry's opinion revealed McCarthy's "abuse of judicial power."[18]

The President also joined the attack. When William Evjue published an editorial entitled "We Apologize, Mr. President," rehashing many of the earlier charges against McCarthy and apologizing on behalf of the people of Wisconsin for electing Joe, Truman aide Harry Vaughan told reporters, "He appeared very excited about it, and was highly pleased."[19]

On June 1 the Senate's only woman member, freshman Republican Margaret Chase Smith of Maine, shocked colleagues by reading on the Senate floor a "Declaration of Conscience," which she and six other liberal Republicans had signed. The declaration was a terse, stern attack on McCarthyism and on the right wing of the G.O.P. that nurtured it. "Certain elements of the Republican party have materially added to this confusion in the hopes of riding the Republican party to victory through the selfish political exploitation of fear, bigotry, ignorance, and intolerance." It appealed for an end to "totalitarian techniques" and called for a bipartisan reconsideration of the meaning of American civil liberties, "national security based on individual freedom." At the same time, the statement took some solid shots at Democrats, including the charge that the Administration had shown "complacency to the threat of communism here at home."

Mrs. Smith, who had served in the House for eight years, had been the target of right-wing Republicans in Maine during the 1948 senatorial primary. Anonymous smear sheets appeared throughout the state claiming that she was a pro-Communist, a tool of the C.I.O., and a political ally of radical left-wing Rep. Vito Marcantonio of New York. Her somewhat timid and defensive reply noted that she had voted with her party almost all of the time and had backed HUAC sixteen times.

Mrs. Smith's attack on McCarthy may have had roots deeper and more personal than her devotion to civil liberties. She had served with Joe on the Executive Expenditures Committee during her first two years in the Senate, and they became close friends. Joe appointed her to his Permanent Investigations Subcommittee, invited her to address a Marquette University journalism sorority, and told her that she was his personal choice for Vice-President. Mrs. Smith, 53 and a widow, may have taken Joe's flattery too seriously. Ray Kiermas later recalled seeing personal letters from the Maine senator containing curiously vague references. Joe would shrug them off and assign Kiermas to write bland, official replies. Kiermas was convinced that the "Declaration of Conscience" was an act of personal revenge.

However that may be, Mrs. Smith later claimed that she turned against McCarthy when she realized that the copies of documents he often distributed during his speeches did not prove his charges. After consulting several friends, she worked on a draft of an anti-McCarthy statement and showed it to veteran Sen. George Aiken of Vermont. They decided to invite five other

Republicans to join them in a formal declaration: Charles Tobey of New Hampshire, Wayne Morse of Oregon, Irving Ives of New York, Edward Thye of Minnesota, and Robert Hendrickson of New Jersey. When the declaration was presented on June 1, accompanied by a speech by Mrs. Smith, H. Alexander Smith of New Jersey publicly expressed his agreement as well. Almost everyone else was silent, Mrs. Smith later recalled, for "Joe had the Senate paralyzed with fear. The political risk of taking issue with him was too great a hazard to the political security of senators."[20]

Of those Republicans who signed and supported the declaration, only Wayne Morse was to hold his ground against McCarthy in the long run—and he would leave the G.O.P. It took Senator Ives less than a week to observe publicly that the Tydings Committee appeared to be "trying to whitewash the state department."[21]

Tydings called Mrs. Smith's presentation "temperate" and "fair" and an act of "stateswomanship." At his afternoon press conference, President Truman replied to a question about one of Mrs. Smith's assertions with a broad smile, noting that he would not want to say anything that bad about the Republican party.[22]

Joe sneeringly labeled Mrs. Smith, her co-signers, and Senator Smith of New Jersey "Snow White and the Seven Dwarfs" and resumed the offensive a few days later. On June 6 he told the Senate that a 1946 report prepared by a State Department investigator referred to an FBI chart listing the presence of 124 Communist agents, Communists, sympathizers, and suspects in the State Department. After distributing copies of the document, he claimed that at least three of those listed as Communists were still holding high positions in the State Department. The three were among the names he gave to the Tydings Committee, he said.[23]

State Department officials quickly termed the assertion "absolutely false" and stated that the Justice Department had informed them that the FBI had never prepared such a chart. A further State Department analysis released a short time later revealed that the chart was a work sheet prepared by subordinates in the department's own security office and was based on allegations received as of May 15, 1946, appearing to warrant further investigations.[24]

Joe could easily have discovered through Surine or Hoover that the FBI did not create the chart. Perhaps he actually knew the origin of the document and simply could not resist the lure of the inevitable headlines that would result from his charges. The assertion that at least three of the Reds named in 1946 were still in the State Department was undoubtedly another McCarthy bluff. The page-and-a-half document distributed to the Senate did not contain names.[25]

In a keynote speech before 2,500 cheering delegates to the Republican state convention in Milwaukee on June 9, Joe passionately lashed out at his critics, who resorted, he said, to "screaming, squealing, and whining smear." He stated that he had a list of 106 (a new number) names of State Department employees who were either Communists or loyal to the party. "The time has come," he cried, "to pinpoint individually the most dangerous Communists, and if lumberjack tactics are the only kind they understand then we shall use those tactics." He charged that Dean Acheson had admitted in sworn testimony that he received a fee of over $50,000, while serving as Assistant Secretary of State, when his law firm was retained by the government of Poland after the war to obtain a 90-million-dollar loan from the United States. "It was Mr. Acheson who placed the guns, the whips, the blacksnakes, and clubs in the hands of those Communists," he declared. "It was Mr. Acheson who furnished them with bullets to keep a Christian population under Soviet discipline." The Secretary of State had condemned Communism only in general terms, Joe said, "with a lace handkerchief, a silk glove, and with a Harvard accent."

McCarthy received a standing ovation before and after he spoke, and his speech was interrupted nineteen times by applause. Delegates scrambled over each other to obtain some 2,000 manila envelopes containing photographic copies of what Joe claimed was his evidence. It included the 1946 document he had distributed to the Senate a few days earlier. The chart, Joe said once again, was created by the FBI.[26]

It took more than a week for the State Department to point out eleven "misstatements" in McCarthy's speech. Among other things, it noted that Dean Acheson had completely severed all connections with his law firm before the Polish loan was approved by the United States. But the State Department press release did not nearly draw the attention that McCarthy's speech had. It was drab and colorless, however accurate.[27]

Deputy Under Secretary of State John E. Peurifoy appeared before the Tydings Committee on June 21 at his own request to answer charges made by McCarthy in a speech that he had attempted to influence Emmanuel Larsen's testimony and had granted him a loyalty clearance "for any job in the government." After describing a brief interview with Larsen and explaining that he had no personal authority to give anyone a loyalty or security clearance, Peurifoy, with the assistance of Chief Counsel Morgan, launched an attack against McCarthy. He noted that a State Department analysis had confirmed the relationship between Joe's February 20 speech and the Lee list. He stated that an FBI investigation had dismissed McCarthy's assertion that the government files being studied by the committee had been "raped." He also read into the record a letter from J. Edgar

Hoover flatly denying that the FBI had made the chart McCarthy was flaunting in public appearances.

Stung by the effectiveness of Peurifoy's testimony, Senator Hicken-looper responded with a tirade against the State Department and "this pseudo-liberal philosophy in this country." The witness was quickly intimidated by the right-wing rhetoric and sputtered in his own defense, "My people came to this country in 1619 [sic] on the *Mayflower*.... I went to the United States Military Academy, where I do not believe they teach Communist beliefs; and my whole background is against this philosophy. I myself believe anyone who believes in Communism does not believe in God."[28]

After the executive session Tydings told a news conference that McCarthy's charge about State Department files he had been examining had been denied by the Justice Department and the FBI. Tydings no doubt thought it justifiable to set the record straight periodically in light of repeated leaks from the committee to McCarthy and the press. (Emmanuel Larsen's entire testimony had found its way to newsmen.) Still, the statement was another example of the political warfare that had characterized each step of the committee's probe and would inevitably tarnish its final report.[29]

John Stewart Service, a slim, good-looking man of 40, appeared before the committee the next day, and at his request the hearing was open. Service had discussed his State Department career and his involvement in the *Amerasia* case several times, and since May 26 his case had been under consideration by the State Department Loyalty-Security Board. Calmly and persuasively he delivered a lengthy autobiographical statement containing a stout defense of his dozen years in China. He observed proudly that his wartime dispatches had recently been studied and defended by George F. Kennan, the renowned diplomat, scholar, and Soviet affairs specialist.

Service explained that his association with the *Amerasia* case was innocent and incidental. He began by pointing out that when Frank Bielaski raided the *Amerasia* office in early March, he was in Yenan, China. This meant that the channels Philip Jaffe had developed for securing government documents were already well established before he returned to the United States on April 12. Moreover, the FBI was prepared to arrest the suspects in the case within a week after Service's arrival. The list could not have included Service, for at that point he was unacquainted with any of the suspects and had only been casually introduced to Lieutenant Roth.

State Department policy, Service observed, encouraged Foreign Service officers who returned from active field posts to supply representatives of the press with background information so that the American people might be better informed of world affairs. Service's rich experiences in China earned him considerable attention after his arrival in Washington, and he discussed Chinese matters with numerous journalists and writers. Mark Gayn had lunch with Service on April 18. The next day, Lieutenant Roth arranged a meeting with Philip Jaffe, whom Service thought to be simply another well-established journalist. Service brought along a personal copy of a document containing a report of an interview with Mao Tse-tung, which he let Jaffe read. A day later Service agreed to lend the journal editor eight or ten personal copies of memoranda on China that were factual in content and did not contain discussions of United States political or military policy. Several of the documents had been written by Service himself, and he had classified them. He explained to the Tydings Committee, "The original need for classification on this descriptive material was by April 1945 no longer necessary. It was material which had become known to the press through writings, through press conference, and so on." None of the documents had ever been in an official file, Service said. Jaffe returned the materials he borrowed a few days later in New York.

During the next few weeks, Service and Jaffe saw each other socially three times (in the company of others soon arrested in the case), they had one conversation in a hotel room, and they exchanged several telephone calls. On May 8 Service delivered to Jaffe an unclassified transcript of a Yenan radio broadcast, a document legally provided by a State Department official. Of course, neither man knew that his movements were being monitored closely by the FBI.

Service was convinced until the day of his arrest, he said, that Jaffe was a reputable journalist. The editor had also told him that he was helping Kate Mitchell gather materials for a book on China, and Service had no reason to doubt him. One of Jaffe's main interests was the trend toward Confucianism within the Kuomintang, Service said, which was a matter of scholarly concern.

Service was "mystified" by his arrest on June 6, he told the Tydings Committee. He was even further confused when he found himself handcuffed next to Emmanuel Larsen, a man he had met only on a couple of occasions. Service gave a full statement to the FBI, waived immunity, and appeared at his own request before the grand jury that voted unanimously not to indict him. While he admitted to the committee that he was guilty of "indiscretion," Service swore that he was innocent of all allegations of treason and repeatedly denied that he was a Communist or a Communist sympathizer.

In the course of his testimony, Service effectively answered McCarthy's charges against him, which were almost exclusively based on the *Plain Talk* article engineered by Alfred Kohlberg. He denounced the undocumented assertion that he had contacted Jaffe from China, as well as the charge (later debunked by the Tydings Committee) that some of his confidential messages to the State Department had reached the *Amerasia* office in New York before they arrived in Washington. He introduced a letter from former Under Secretary of State Joseph C. Grew that quashed the myth that Grew had insisted on Service's prosecution in 1945 and had been forced to resign as a result. He also explained the details of an evening he had spent with the Owen Lattimores at their home and denied McCarthy's charge that government documents were involved. (Joe claimed in his March 30 speech that he had two affidavits proving that Lattimore had declassified secret documents on the evening Service was his guest. The affidavits were never submitted to the Tydings Committee. Moreover, the FBI found no evidence of the presence of government documents during the incident.)[30]

Little of Service's many hours of involved testimony appeared in newspaper accounts of the hearing. The Associated Press story slighted the witness's explanation of his *Amerasia* involvement and featured his less convincing assertions that he had never opposed Chiang Kai-shek and had attempted to prevent the domination of China by the Communists.[31]

Unwilling to concede Service anything in the press, McCarthy attempted to upstage accounts of the hearing by telling reporters that a recording existed of a secretly monitored conversation between Service and Philip Jaffe. This was the recording that FBI official D. Milton Ladd had quoted during his testimony in executive session three weeks earlier. Joe had obviously learned of it from his contacts within the Tydings Committee. The sentence Ladd had read appeared to incriminate Service and was leaked to the press. The Foreign Service officer allegedly told Jaffe, "Well, what I said about the military plans is, of course, very secret." Since the sentence had become public knowledge, the Justice Department agreed to submit a transcript of the full conversation to the Tydings Committee. It did so with great reluctance, not only because of the traditional constitutional barriers but because the conversation had been illegally recorded by the FBI through a microphone hidden in Jaffe's hotel room.

The transcript turned out to be only a partial, barely intelligible record of the conversation. The FBI had apparently botched the recording process, adding to its long list of blunders in the case. Service said that he had no recollection of such a conversation. He noted also that he had had no access to military plans, and he denied ever having discussed secret military information with the *Amerasia* editor. Ex-prosecutor McInerney testified that he had seen a summary of the transcript in 1945 but had been warned that its contents could not be used as evidence. The FBI reported that the disc from which the transcript was taken had been destroyed. Thus the brief flurry over the recorded conversation concluded in confusion. What exactly Service said to Jaffe during a hotel room chat in May 1945, and in what context, remained in doubt.[32]

Joe, of course, was never one to respect ambiguity. Nor did he feel bound to abide by a careful reading of the Tydings Committee testimony. He was soon telling a Wisconsin audience:

> Service was arrested by the FBI in connection with the theft of hundreds of secret government documents. The FBI testified they had microphones in the hotel room of Jaffe, whom they labelled as a Communist, when Service visited him. The microphone recording showed that Service discussed military secrets with this Communist while the war was still on. Service admitted having turned over to him classified State Department documents. At the time Service and his five co-defendants were arrested, J. Edgar Hoover, according to a Washington paper said, 'This is a 100 percent air-tight case of espionage.' But Service did not go to jail. However, Under Secretary of State Joseph Grew, who insisted he be prosecuted, left the Department. Acheson took over and Service was re-hired, promoted and put in charge of placing personnel in the Far East area.
>
> Do you want on your payroll a man who admits turning government secrets over to a Communist and who was caught by the FBI giving secret military information to a convicted Communist thief of government top secrets?[33]

It was virtually impossible for the average citizens of Wisconsin to test the accuracy of their senator's apparently learned, detailed, and sincere assertions. Many, in particular those who had admired Joe as a young man, quickly and proudly concluded that he was cleaning the Commies out of Washington and that it was a patriotic duty to support him. They refused to pay attention to his critics.

Evidence was available to indicate that McCarthy was making a favorable impression upon the general public all across the nation. A Gallup Poll of May 21 discovered that 84 percent of those interviewed had read or heard of the senator's State Department charges and that 39 percent thought that they had done more good than harm (as opposed to 29 percent who thought the reverse). Fifty percent of the Republicans polled backed McCarthy's allegations, while only 35 percent of the Democrats gave their support. Minnesota poll findings published in July showed 45 percent backing McCarthy (with 30 percent taking the opposite position). "If it wasn't for courage like McCarthy's, we'd be run like Stalin runs Russia," a St. Paul woman said. An Ortonville man declared, "He has shown up some of the crooks in the department."[34]

On July 17 the Tydings Committee released a 350,000 word, 313-page final report on its almost five-month investigation. It was signed by the three committee Democrats; Lodge filed a brief minority report, and Hickenlooper chose not to write or sign anything. The majority report drew extensive newspaper coverage, for it denounced McCarthy in scorching language that ignored traditional senatorial courtesy. Joe's charges and methods, it said, were "A fraud and a hoax perpetrated on the Senate of the United States and the American people. They represent perhaps the most nefarious campaign of half-truths and untruth in the history of this Republic." Not content to rest with this unprecedented excoriation, the report continued, "For the first time in our history, we have seen the totalitarian technique of the 'big lie' employed on a sustained basis. The result has been to confuse and divide the American people, at a time when they should be strong in their unity, to a degree far beyond the hopes of the Communists themselves whose stock in trade is confusion and division." Richard Strout of the *Christian Science Monitor* wrote, "Not before in this century have fellow senators denounced a colleague in such searing terms, and the question is raised whether expulsion action will be attempted."[35]

Some reporters became so fascinated with the majority report's fiery language that they overlooked its often painstaking and impressive compilation and analysis of evidence. McCarthy's sweeping claims about Reds in the State Department were carefully examined and dismissed. The report revealed the origins of the figures 205, 57, and 81; it exposed Joe's use of the Lee list; and it observed that of the 81 alleged State Department employees whose names were submitted by McCarthy only 40 were found to be currently employed by the department. (Seven had never been so employed and 33 had been separated either through resignation, termination, or reduction in force—two as early as 1946.) Moreover, committee Democrats wrote, a lengthy review of the loyalty files Truman had reluctantly made available failed to reveal a single Communist or a single instance in which a clearance should have been reversed. The report sharply criticized committee Republicans on this score, for Lodge had read only a dozen of the files and Hickenlooper only nine. "Despite, therefore, the clamor and demand that was raised by Senator McCarthy, along with his associates, that the files be opened by the President, and the assertion that the loyalty files would 'prove his case,' we find the almost unbelievable situation of the members of Senator McCarthy's own party on our subcommittee taking the trouble to read only a very small percentage of the files made available for their examination by the President."

The report went into McCarthy's charges against specific individuals in depth. All of those targeted by name—Brunauer, Duran, Hanson, Jessup, Kenyon, Lattimore, Schuman, Service, Shapley, and Vincent—were convincingly cleared of the senator's allegations. John Service (who was to be cleared by the State Department Loyalty-Security Board a total of six times) was rapped on the knuckles for being "extremely indiscreet"—a verdict Service freely accepted.

Joe's reckless rhetoric and his consistent misuse of evidence were documented fully in the report. When the committee majority examined the file of John Carter Vincent, whose name was number two on the list of 81, it concluded that McCarthy's charges against the China Hand were "absurd." They wrote of the attack on Owen Lattimore, "We have seen a distortion of the facts on such a magnitude as to be truly alarming."

Committee Democrats were also unsparing in their criticism of McCarthy's allies. Testimony by Budenz and Utley was weighed against testimony by Browder, Field, and Dodd and found wanting. Of those behind the *Plain Talk* article that was allegedly written by Emmanuel Larsen, the report said, "The fact that these persons have been reported to us as professional 'anti-Communists,' whose incomes and reputation depend on the developing and maintaining of new Communist fears, while not deemed necessarily significant, has not been altogether overlooked by the subcommittee."

The report's treatment of the *Amerasia* case was remarkably thorough, given the short length of time the committee and its staff devoted to the thorny affair. Staff members reviewed all of the documents seized in the case and concluded, as had the Hobbs Committee earlier, that they were of little or no importance to the national defense. The government's prosecution of the case was found to be wholehearted and judicious. (A New York grand jury had arrived at the same conclusion a month earlier.) McCarthy's contention that the case was the key to an espionage ring in the State Department was effectively demolished.

There were several legitimate grounds on which to criticize the majority report, however. Some found it too political and argued that it would have been more appealing to independents and moderates had it contained less vituperation. The standard reply was that McCarthy's charges were wholly political in nature and that any genuine bipartisanship was impossible from the start. Moreover, McCarthy's abusive behavior toward the committee virtually guaranteed a harsh response. Still, the attacks against Republicans, if not McCarthy, might have been muted somewhat in the interest of harmony. It was unnecessary, for example, to excoriate Hickenlooper and Lodge three times for failing to study the loyalty files.

Some conservatives argued that the committee had done its work too hastily and had not conducted the "full and complete study" of the State Department that Senate Resolution 231 envisioned. Chief Counsel Morgan later conceded privately that the criticism had merit. He explained that Senator Tydings chose to conclude the probe because he was personally weary of the pressures generated by the investigation and because Republicans were threatening to continue the hearings into November, depriving him of the opportunity to campaign for reelection. The majority report acknowledged the need for further study and called for a presidential commission to examine the entire federal loyalty program. (Tydings, McMahon, and Green met with the President and other Administration leaders on June 22 and urged the creation of such a body to thwart McCarthy's impact on the fall elections. Opponents of the plan argued that the Tydings Committee report would be sufficient to expose the Wisconsin senator. Truman deferred action for the time being.)[36]

The report could also have been faulted—but was not—for neglecting to mention the FBI's bumbling throughout the *Amerasia* case and for failing to point to the probability that the bureau was in part responsible for the continued attention paid to the case. (The Judith Coplon spy case would be dismissed in December 1950 because of the prosecution's dependence upon another illegal FBI wiretap. Truman internal security expert Stephen Spingarn also blamed the bureau for the government's inability to convict those implicated by Elizabeth Bentley. "It was pure inefficiency, a rotten, bumbling operation by the FBI.") Instead, the Tydings report slathered praise upon the bureau. This was largely a reflection of the awe and fear in which Hoover and his minions were held. Senator Tydings would reveal shortly that he had daily turned over his own reports of committee proceedings to the FBI director.[37]

Committee Democrats had known all along that Senator Hickenlooper would refuse to sign a majority report, but they held high hopes that moderate Lodge would join them. Tydings showed extreme courtesy to the Massachusetts Republican and granted his request to travel to Europe with Senator Green to conduct a brief side investigation. The first draft of the final report was worded especially to attract his support. Lodge refused to sign, however. His understanding of the issues and evidence was poor, and he was unwilling to set partisan politics aside. In his 34-page minority report he conceded that the charges against Lattimore and Service had not been proved, but he expressed a naive trust in Louis Budenz ("Mr. Budenz's credibility is also completely vouched for by the great university [Fordham] where he is now a teacher") and revealed only a dim awareness of the facts in the *Amerasia* case. He condemned committee Democrats for being anti-McCarthy (although he did not mention the senator by name) and for conducting a "superficial and inconclusive" study. "The fact that many charges have been made which have not been proven," Lodge wrote, "does not in the slightest degree relieve the subcommittee of the responsibility for undertaking a relentlessly thorough investigation of its own." He explained that he had studied only a few of the available loyalty files himself because they were "in such an unfinished state as to indicate that an examination of each file would be a waste of time." (It was uncertain what Lodge meant by "unfinished," but Joe later used the evaluation to buttress his claim that the files had been "raped.") The report concluded with a renewal of Lodge's appeal (opposed by many Republicans) for a bipartisan, independent commission not unlike that requested by committee Democrats.[38]

Joe's reaction to the majority report was immediate. His statement said in part:

> The Tydings-McMahon report is a green light to the Red Fifth column in the United States.
>
> It is a signal to the traitors, Communists, and fellow travelers in our Government that they need have no fear of exposure from this Administration. It is public notification that we will officially "turn our back" on traitors, Communists, and fellow travelers in our Government.
>
> The most loyal stooges of the Kremlin could not have done a better job of giving a clean bill of health to Stalin's fifth column in this country.

The majority on the Tydings Committee, he said, "has degenerated to new lows of planned deception." The fruit of its labors was "a clever, evil thing to behold. It is gigantic in its fraud and deep in its deceit."[39]

(The impact of the majority report was decreased considerably by J. Edgar Hoover's perhaps coincidental announcement of the arrest of Julius Rosenberg on the same day the report was released. *The New York Times* ran the two stories in parallel columns. Rosenberg, charged with conspiracy to commit atomic espionage, had first been arrested on June 16 and released. While his crime was committed during the war, and he had nothing to do with the State Department, McCarthy apologists used spy cases to bolster their cries of "whitewash" against the Tydings Committee.)

The Senate Foreign Relations Committee voted eleven to nothing to end the investigation conducted by Tydings and his colleagues. Tempers flared, however, when a motion was made to send the majority report to the Senate. Following what the Associated Press called "one of the stormiest sessions the group ever held," the vote was nine to two in favor, with Hickenlooper and Lodge dissenting. Chairman Connally told a news conference that the question of approving the majority report was not even raised. "We want to go home by Christmas," he said with a grin. Later that day, Senator Taft spoke for the Republican Senate Policy Committee when he called the majority report "political" and "insulting."[40]

One Administration leader in the Senate told reporters later that the Democratic policy committee might consider calling for a formal Senate censure of McCarthy on the basis of the majority report. The *Washington Post* declared editorially, "A motion of censure against Senator McCarthy is clearly in order."[41]

The political situation, exacerbated by the first frustrations of the Korean War, which broke out on June 25, plus the heavily political overtones of the reports emanating from the Tydings Committee, now made McCarthyism a more bitterly partisan issue than ever. Republicans rallied behind McCarthy even though most understood that his allegations were fraudulent. Joseph C. Harsh reported, "There may conceivably be as many as three Republicans in the Senate who sincerely believe that there is substance behind the McCarthy charges, but I doubt it. I would not know where to find one, other than McCarthy himself, who would seriously contend in private and between friends that he believed the charges." The defense of McCarthy became G.O.P. doctrine, and even Margaret Chase Smith and the others who signed the "Declaration of Conscience" found themselves casting votes on the Senate floor on behalf of the Wisconsin Senator.[42]

Tydings pleaded with Democrats to support the majority on his committee, noting the months of harassment and slander he and his colleagues had suffered. Some Southern Democrats, like Lyndon Johnson, were less than enthusiastic about the request; McCarthy was a Republican problem in their judgment, and should be disregarded. Nevertheless, party leaders recognized the political realities involved and agreed in caucus to support the committee majority down the line.[43]

The two sides clashed bitterly on July 20 in one of the wildest Senate sessions since Reconstruction. It began with Tydings submitting his majority report to the Senate, as he had been instructed to do by the Foreign Relations Committee. Vice-President Barkley ordered it filed. Minority Leader Wherry, agitated and highly emotional, challenged the ruling on the ground that the report was not a product of the full Foreign Relations Committee (which Tydings did not claim). The Vice-President's ruling was upheld by an extremely rare straight-party vote of 45-37. Republicans then tried twice to recommit the majority report to the Foreign Relations Committee, a type of repudiation rarely requested in Congress. They were defeated again, each side voting without a single defection.

During the heated oratory surrounding these moves, Barkley repeatedly fought to restore order on the floor and in the galleries, but he met with little success. Hickenlooper angrily blasted "this so-called report" as simply an attack on McCarthy and claimed that he could not remember being invited to a Tydings Committee meeting to vote on the majority report. (Tydings soon produced a copy of the invitation.) Wherry spied Chief Counsel Edward P. Morgan on the floor and started an argument. The two men left the chamber and became engaged in a noisy exchange that some witnesses said involved blows. When Wherry returned to the floor he demanded that Morgan be expelled. Barkley denied the request, and his decision was sustained by yet another straight-party vote. Amid all of the turmoil and shouting, William Jenner managed to capture the floor long enough to ask, "Considering the fact that we are now at war, and considering what has transpired here this afternoon, how can we get the Reds out of Korea if we cannot get them out of Washington?" Many spectators applauded.

Tydings had anticipated the struggle and brought with him that morning some teaching aids: a photograph, eight large charts, an easel, and a five-foot pointer. After some initial sparring with Wherry, he launched into an impassioned two-hour speech condemning McCarthy and summarizing and defending his majority report. His initial offensive was to present the story of how McCarthy changed the number 205 to 57 during his Lincoln Day tour. Looking at Wherry, he observed, "I would not be surprised—and I say this with a smile—if it did not happen in a plane over Nebraska." One of his charts, placed in plain view of all the senators, featured blowups of headlines reporting McCarthy's Wheeling speech. Before long, Tydings displayed other charts showing the parallels between McCarthy's list of 81 and the Lee list. Joe looked on in silence. At one point the veteran statesman glared at him and said, "I have taken in the past three months much punishment in the newspapers by a colleague of mine who has used every epithet and every term of opprobrium and calumny to blackguard me, the senator from Connecticut, and others." Tydings had not returned the fire, he said, "because I do not want to sink to that sort of level, even off the Senate floor; and anything I say on the Senate floor, I shall say outside the Senate floor, and I shall not retract it afterward." Applause showered down from the galleries.

Tydings was not always to exhibit such high-mindedness, however. During his discussion of McCarthy's Lincoln Day tour, Tydings suddenly startled colleagues by asking, "Mr. President, I wonder if I could get unanimous consent to play a radio recording of the senator's own voice on one of these occasions." In the context of the request, it appeared that Tydings possessed a recording of the Wheeling speech that would prove that McCarthy had lied when he denied saying that he had a list of 205 card-carrying Communists. That was exactly the impression Tydings wanted to give. Actually, he was bluffing. Committee investigators had discovered weeks earlier that the recording taken at Wheeling had been erased shortly after McCarthy's speech. As Edward P. Morgan later explained, Tydings was sure that he would not be permitted to play the record, for that would violate Senate rules. When Wherry objected, Tydings quickly withdrew his request, adding, "I will play the record off the Senate floor in due time, but admission will be by card only," a sarcastic reference to Joe's "card-carrying Communists" that drew laughter. If Tydings had been permitted to use the phonograph sitting next to his desk, he no doubt would have reminded colleagues that he said he possessed a recording taken "on one of these occasions," which did not necessarily mean Wheeling. In fact, he had only a recording of the Salt Lake City radio interview in which Joe spoke of 57 card-carrying Communists. Once his bluff could no longer be called, Tydings noted his possession of the Salt Lake City interview. "I shall be delighted to play it," he said, "but I suppose I shall have to play that outside, too."[44]

McCarthy had written to the editor of the *Wheeling Intelligencer* on June 28 offering a reward for a recording of his Wheeling speech. There were no takers, but on July 20 he could not be certain what Tydings had. He told reporters after the Senate melee that he would give anyone odds of 100 to one that Tydings' recording would not disclose him saying 205 card-carrying Communists.)[45]

As Tydings thundered on, his passions got the better of him. He sneeringly imitated McCarthy's voice as he read from the Salt Lake City interview. He saw Scripps-Howard reporter Frederick Woltman in the galleries and charged that he had resurrected the *Amerasia* case because he was being sued for libel "and was using us as a means of trying to secure evidence for his own personal benefit." Then, spotting committee critic William Jenner glaring at him from his seat, Tydings strode across the chamber, pointed a trembling finger at the ultraconservative Indiana senator, and charged that he was soft on the Communists. Jenner had opposed the Marshall Plan, NATO, and the military assistance program. Therefore, Tydings concluded with classic McCarthyite logic, "I find that Joe Stalin and the *Daily Worker* and the senator all vote the same way." He shouted, "I do not start fights quickly, but I do not run away from them when I am attacked." He then began to extol his own military record in World War One.

Twice Homer Capehart requested that Tydings be ordered to take his seat for his abusive language against Jenner. (No one objected to the even nastier bombast used on McCarthy.) Both times the Senate permitted him to continue. Tydings's fulminations, when finally completed, left spectators astonished and shaken. Veteran lawmakers thought that the attack had exceeded anything ever heard on the Senate floor. More than thirty Democrats flocked around Tydings to shake his hand and extend their congratulations.

Joe told reporters afterward, "Today, Tydings tried to notify all Communists in government that they are safe in their positions." His number nineteen, he said, was William Remington, who had just been indicted for perjury in connection with his denial of Communist party membership. He further claimed that another (unnamed) man on the list had recently been forced to resign. "That means two down and seventy-nine to go."[46]

The next day Republicans counterattacked, moderates Ives, Lodge, and Flanders leading the charge. At one point Lodge and McMahon fell into a quarrel of such intensity that the Connecticut Democrat charged his colleague with attacking the FBI—an indictment Lodge greeted with horror and effusive denials. The Far Right took angry blasts at Tydings, and William Jenner, in an unrestrained 1,000-word tirade, contended that Tydings had "conducted the most scandalous and brazen whitewash of treasonable conspiracy in our history." Still boiling over Tydings's speech, he growled, "It is certainly not difficult to call the hand of the senator from Maryland, for the cards he is hiding are so red with the blood of treachery." The attack even included a swipe at Tydings's father-in-law, former Ambassador to Russia Joseph E. Davies, for having written "as foul a piece of pro-Soviet propaganda as was ever designed to corrupt the minds of the American people." Jenner's concluding words alluded to Stalin.

> Mr. President, I desire to say that I have no medals, such as the distinguished Senator from Maryland told us yesterday he has. I did not know the distinguished Senator from Maryland was such a brave and heroic man until he told us from his own itsy-bitsy lips yesterday, but I do know that there is another medal which will probably come to him. It will be very large, and emblazoned with a single name: "Thanks, from good old Joe, for a job well done."[47]

During the uproar Democrats forced Lodge to concede that he had not found any Communists in the State Department, and they managed to make the point that McCarthy had been given every opportunity to provide the Tydings Committee with his evidence. But somehow these brief appeals to reason were lost in the crashing billows of partisan rhetoric. Joseph and Stewart Alsop soon observed, "Everyone must know by now that something has gone wrong, very wrong, in the capital of the United States." It seemed to them that "a miasma of neurotic fear and internal suspicion is seeping in over the nation's capital, like some noxious effluvium from the marshy Potomac."[48]

A few days later Republicans attacked again, this time with McCarthy taking the lead. Joe had obviously been comparing notes with Senators Jenner, Langer, Wherry, and Malone, for the presentation appeared well rehearsed. He had also probably been quietly consulting again with J. Edgar Hoover.

Joe held in his hand, he said, "this FBI secret report . . . a complete FBI case" which was from his list of 81. It was a typical case, he claimed; probably the senators on the Tydings Committee had not seen it, for there was much in "the raped and denuded State Department loyalty files" that had escaped them. Despite the fact that an FBI undercover agent had named "Mr. X" a member of the Communist party, Joe said, and that his wife had also been cited as a Red, the man in question currently held a "very important job" in the State Department. "The FBI did an outstanding job," Joe stated. "But what happens? Material is thrown into a file and allowed to lie there." Moreover, McCarthy charged, "Mr. X" had lied before a loyalty board, Dean Acheson's law firm had represented him, and the charge in the case was reduced before any evidence was taken. The "Red Dean" could add "Mr. X" to his list of crimes, Joe said, for "as a result of the activities of Acheson's law firm that man is today, at this very moment, in the State Department in an important position." The man's file, Joe concluded, contained "a complete and airtight case proving that one of the important officials in the State Department is a Communist."

McCarthy also introduced what he said were four affidavits showing conclusively that the State Department loyalty files had been rifled in 1946. One of the documents was signed by a man who was currently an FBI agent. Joe also produced a letter from Hoover denying that the FBI had ever examined the files and certified that they were intact. The director's statement was a flat contradiction to the claim Tydings had made publicly and included in the majority report. McCarthy later wrote, "Had it not been for J. Edgar Hoover's frank and honest report the truth never would have been known."[49]

Shortly after Joe took his seat, Wayne Morse revealed that "Mr. X" was Edward G. Posniak, a State Department economist who had been numbers nine and 77 on McCarthy's list of 81. Brien McMahon sought to introduce twenty-one affidavits affirming Posniak's loyalty and integrity, and Morse recalled that when he knew Posniak in the Department of Justice in 1938 he appeared to be entirely trustworthy.

In fact, the evidence in this case, available to the Tydings Committee and atypical of the documentation associated with the Lee list, did not substantiate McCarthy's claim to have discovered a Communist loose in the State Department. The anonymous FBI undercover agent had reported that Posniak was a member of the Communist party from 1938 until sometime in 1942. Another unnamed informant had linked him with the party in the late 1930s. For more recent years, the file contained an affidavit from an anonymous "scholar" who had worked with Posniak for two months in 1946 and thought him pro-Soviet. An FBI report stated that the suspect continued to associate with at least three Communists and fellow travelers as late as 1948. At best, these charges raised doubts about Posniak. They fell far short of providing an "airtight case" of Communist party membership in 1950. Moreover, the file also contained ample testimony from Posniak's former employers and associates affirming his absolute loyalty and militant anti-Communism at all times.

In 1948 Posniak was investigated by the State Department Loyalty-Security Board and cleared by a vote of two to one. Posniak's attorney was a member of Acheson's law firm. At the time, of course, no one envisioned the "Red Dean" charges that were to follow. FBI leaders, however, clearly remained as angry about Posniak's clearance as they were about the outcome of the *Amerasia* case.

Posniak's case was soon reopened after McCarthy's Senate attack, and the economist resigned rather than accept a suspension and face another investigation. Joe would therefore imply that he had purged the State Department of a proven subversive. For the vast majority of people, who depended upon the often brief and usually shallow accounts in newspapers for their knowledge of McCarthy's activities, it was virtually impossible to challenge the claim.[50]

The four affidavits Joe submitted to the Senate were first released on July 12. They had been collected by Don Surine after the Tydings Committee had concluded its hearings, no doubt as rebuttal material. The documents were alleged by McCarthy to prove his charge that the loyalty files had been "raped" in 1946. Actually, as the State Department quickly pointed out, the affidavits merely described a postwar reorganization of personnel files— not loyalty and security files, which were housed separately. Undaunted, Joe later published one of the affidavits and claimed that all four affiants "did the actual job of removing from the State Department files all evidence of Communist activities."[51]

The Hoover letter Joe waved before his colleagues was dated July 10. Hoover's contention that the FBI had not actually examined the loyalty files (first made public by Fulton Lewis, Jr.) was apparently correct, despite statements to the contrary by Deputy Under Secretary of State Puerifoy and Senator Tydings. In any case, the Justice Department promptly had the FBI examine the files turned over to the committee. On July 17 Attorney General McGrath reported that the FBI reports in the files—on which Joe based his charges—were intact. This was confirmed by J. Edgar Hoover on September 8 in a letter to Tydings. (The letter may have been drafted reluctantly. Joe claimed that the Justice Department "ordered" the director to write it.)[52]

McCarthy, nevertheless, published only Hoover's July 10 letter in later campaign literature and propounded the fantastic theory that FBI materials were reinserted into the loyalty files after the Tydings Committee no longer had access to them. It was all "rather involved," Joe concluded, but could be summarized as a "typical example" of the Tydings Committee's attempt "to hide behind the excellent reputation of the FBI."[53]

Back in Wisconsin in late July, McCarthy labeled the Tydings Committee majority report "dishonest" and called its authors "well-meaning little men—men without the mental or moral capacity to rise above politics in this hour of the nation's gravest danger." The audience of 4,500 at the Izaak Walton League picnic in Fond du Lac roared its approval.[54]

14

REVENGE IN
MARYLAND

In less than six months after his speech in Wheeling, Senator McCarthy had become one of the best known and most controversial political figures in the world. His face was frequently in newsreels and on television; his distinctive voice could often be heard on radio; flocks of newsmen dogged his every step, eager to rush anything he had to say onto the front pages; he was the G.O.P.'s most sought-after public speaker. No senator in American history had ever generated so much publicity in such a short time.

To his admirers, McCarthy could do no wrong. He was described in the right-wing press, by veterans' and patriotic organizations, and by friendly news commentators as a tough Marine, fighting to keep America free from the enemy within. His unparalleled bravado had made him the symbol of the postwar effort by conservatives and ultraconservatives to vilify and drive from power the liberals and internationalists who had begun to pour into Washington in 1933. The fact that he initially focused his assault upon the State Department and what he called its "bright young men who are born with silver spoons in their mouths" broadened his base of support to include many outside the Right who were disturbed and confused about foreign affairs and resented privilege.

Joe's opponents, conversely, saw him as the embodiment of evil. He was portrayed in the liberal, left-wing and Communist media as a ruthless, reckless, heartless, mindless fiend who had yet to utter his first honest sentence. The unceasing barrage of vituperation against the senator was such that it even extended to descriptions of his physical appearance. While Joe had often been depicted before Wheeling as a rather good-looking and robust young man who attracted scores of Washington's prettiest ladies, the influential cartoonist Herblock, among others, now pictured him as a sort of fearsome ape-man—thickset, ugly, always in need of a shave, frequently scowling malevolently, often sporting a menacing leer. (Herblock's frequent cartoons stung McCarthy; Jean Kerr was sometimes driven to tears. Richard Nixon, another favorite target of Herblock's acid wit, did not permit the *Washington Post* in his home for fear his daughters would see the cartoons.) Jack Anderson, in a 1952 book, described McCarthy in childhood as "an ugly duckling" whose "shaggy eyebrows, blue eyes, and lips that turned downward at the corners" gave him "a serious, brooding look. Big-chested and short-armed, he reminded his older brothers of a cub bear, and they took pleasure in telling him so." This was inaccurate, to say the least. Joseph and Stewart Alsop imagined in mid-1950 that he had "a continual tremor which makes his head shake in a disconcerting fashion." Expanding upon this fiction, Miles McMillin wrote a year later, "I watched him intently when he spoke at Platteville recently. The palsy in his hands was most noticeable and his efforts to hide it, probably from himself, by continuously thumping his fists was obvious. And when he would step back to search his big brief case for some more 'documentation' the nervous twitching of his head was also noticeable."[1]

This perfervid loathing of McCarthy was responsible for numerous charges that were false and defamatory about the Lustron booklet, first investigated in mid-1950, and the Malmedy hearings. On September 12, 1950, William Evjue published a lengthy editorial that attempted to blacken McCarthy's history by focusing upon the Quaker Dairy case, Joe's tax problems, and his eligibility to campaign in 1946. Thousands of copies of the editorial were reproduced and distributed across the country wherever Joe delivered a speech. (Joe countered by charging that Cedric Parker had written the editorial and that copies were distributed "normally by members of the young Communist party [sic].") It was even becoming common for anti-McCarthy speakers and writers to echo Truman's assertion that the senator was assisting the Soviet Union. Esther Van Wagoner Tufty, a Washington correspondent for the *Capital Times,* declared that McCarthy had become "the Kremlin's favorite American." Norman Cousins, editor of the *Saturday Review of Literature,* contended that Joe was employing Red techniques. "I can't think of anyone who has helped Communism more than Joe McCarthy," he said.[2]

Shortly before publication of the Tydings Committee report, the *Capital*

Times and the *Milwaukee Journal* launched another probe into McCarthy's tax returns. Several stories in the lengthy series received national attention. Headlines pointed out that while the senator's total gross income for 1946-49 was $66,938.59, he had paid no state income taxes. McCarthy's official explanation for this fact was that his stock losses for the period totaled $51,298.78 and that his interest payments for the same four years added up to $18,575.96.

Reporters did their best to cast doubt upon Joe's deductions. His interest payments for 1949, based on a 4-percent interest rate, they said, indicated that the senator "might have borrowed some $375,000." Seeing that Howard McCarthy received an interest payment of $2,857.70, they concluded that at a 4-percent interest rate Joe must have borrowed approximately $60,000 from his brother. Howard's tax returns, however, showed net taxable incomes ranging from $3,581 in 1945 to $18,855 in 1948. (In 1950 Joe paid Howard only $877.24.) Howard's refusal to discuss his personal finances fed the newsmen's suspicions.

The largest interest payment for 1949 totaled $9,105.22 and was paid to the Appleton State Bank. Reporters were frustrated that details of this financial arrangement were unavailable and speculated that the loan must have been in excess of $200,000. (It was actually less than a fourth of that sum at the time.) Their spirits brightened considerably when the state tax commissioner announced that a full-scale audit of McCarthy's 1949 tax return was underway. William Evjue chortled, "This man McCarthy has gone far enough in his disregard for the moral, ethical, and legal considerations that govern the rest of us." With a classic use of guilt by association, the editor noted that two of McCarthy's friends, Milwaukee attorneys Charles Kersten and Arlo McKinnon, had once had difficulties with state tax officials. The *Milwaukee Journal* added that Howard and his father Tim (posthumously) had each been found to owe additional taxes at one time.[3]

After an investigation that lasted more than six months, the state tax department cleared McCarthy of his enemies' innuendoes. Joe's financial records were found to be chaotic or nonexistent, and he was ordered to keep detailed accounts for future use by tax officials. A disagreement over a rule resulted in McCarthy having to pay $134.23 plus $4.74 interest. (Joe considered appealing the small assessment but concluded that he lacked the time.) There was, however, no suggestion of illegal activity in the audit report.[4]

Joe's fame was such that mail poured into his office from all over the world, at times amounting to as much as 25,000 letters a day in 1950. Many of the letters contained charges of subversion against people in all walks of life. Joe soon spoke of being "swamped with tips," and bragged, "Since the Communist fight has started any loyal American who knows of Communist activity normally would drop me a letter and tell me about it." Tips came not only in the mail but also by courier and telephone. Don Surine and Ed Nellor later estimated the number of letters received in McCarthy's office from 1950 through 1954 at between ten and twenty thousand. Nellor was sometimes stopped on the street by a person eager to hand him a note, letter, or document; once he collected items left in a telephone booth by an anonymous caller. Generals and admirals, as well as scrubwomen and clerks, were among the donors; Surine later boasted of secret dealings with Generals Charles A. Willoughby, Courtney Whitney, and Douglas MacArthur. Surine sent everything he thought valuable to the FBI, with which he continued to work closely. The sorting, studying, and evaluating of this information often required twenty-hour days and seven-day weeks, not only for Surine but for other office staff members, friends, and the senator himself. Nellor later recalled that his own health was almost ruined by this labor. McCarthy appeared to be indefatigable.[5]

Surine also sought and received a large number of classified government documents, more often than not from friends within investigative agencies of the federal government, especially the FBI, the C.I.A., and Army Intelligence. He later boasted of a network of informants and said that he had been operating on a worldwide basis. During the Korean war, Nellor saw Surine with a document so highly classified that the speech writer refused to read beyond its title for fear of placing himself in legal jeopardy. The senator, of course, worked closely with his investigator in this clandestine and dangerous activity. Many of the purloined documents were kept in McCarthy's office safe.[6]

Joe's prominence also resulted in an acceleration of the financial donations that had begun to arrive in the mail after the Wheeling speech. A spy planted by Drew Pearson in the senator's office for four months in early 1951 quoted Surine as saying that contributions sometimes reached more than $1,000 a day. Probably several bank accounts were opened to contain the tax-free gifts by that time. Ray Kiermas later recalled that one depository contained approximately $125,000 at one point. McCarthy used the funds, in part, to cover investigative costs, including the purchase of information. Pearson's informant said that Surine had boasted of a personal expense account of $700 a week in cash.

As already mentioned, Joe also pocketed some of this money legally; the exact or even approximate amount will probably never be known. He used some of it for personal expenses. *Chicago Tribune* reporter Willard Edwards once watched him open a letter, take out some cash and, with a grin, stuff it into his pocket. Some of these funds no doubt wound up at the racetrack. Ed Nellor cashed as many as $4,000 worth of racing tickets for the senator at one time; Ray Kiermas and Otis Gomillion were constantly driving to the track for the same purpose. Joe also invested some of the money in stocks. Investigators would later document his temporary employment of two donations totaling $10,000 to make a quick profit in soybean commodities.[7]

McCarthy no doubt also used this money to profit from stock market tips emanating from several wealthy Texans who had begun to take an interest in him. Clint W. Murchison, H. R. Cullen, and H. L. Hunt, among others, had long been eager to make friends on Capitol Hill, to protect their oil properties and to promote right-wing legislation. Among their methods for winning allies was the quiet dissemination of stock market "sure things," often involving their own corporations. According to Ed Nellor, Everett Dirksen, Karl Mundt, and Richard Nixon were among many political figures who made money this way. It was legal, whatever the ethics involved; taxes were paid on the profits. By early 1950 Murchison had contacted McCarthy, perhaps through Robert Taft, and Joe was soon receiving highly lucrative market tips. As the senator's fame loomed larger, the relationship grew closer. H. R. Cullen introduced McCarthy at a much-publicized "Americanism" rally in Houston in September 1950. By mid 1954 Murchison would admit to contributing "something under $40,000" toward various McCarthy enterprises.[8]

The senator's celebrity status prompted an avalanche of requests for speeches and public appearances in 1950. Many invitations, of course, were from G.O.P. candidates, eager to persuade McCarthy to tar their opponents with a Red brush. Others were from people who simply wanted to hear more about what the senator would call his "fight for America." Joe accepted an unusually large number of requests. From August 6 through November 6, 1950, he traveled to at least fifteen states, from California to Louisiana to Maryland, delivering scores of speeches and often speaking several times a day. In 1951 he made many dozens of addresses and appearances in at least sixteen states throughout the nation. The Republican National Committee reported that no other person in the party was in such demand.[9]

The strain on McCarthy was enormous. Moreover, he was not in good health much of the time. His sinus condition worsened and gave him considerable pain and irritation. Friends drove him to a hospital as often as once a month, and in March 1951 an operation hospitalized him for two weeks. He also began to suffer from severe indigestion in 1951. At Urban Van Susteren's suggestion, he ate handfuls of baking soda throughout each day to alleviate the discomfort. The problem was discovered to be a herniated diaphragm, and it was repaired after another sinus operation in July 1952. Joe also started drinking more heavily once he became famous. In 1950 one of his sisters confided to Van Susteren that she had seen him drunk during a debate in Green Bay. While still under control, McCarthy's drinking was to increase dramatically as events elevated his career to even greater heights.[10]

Joe might have slowed down, taken more vacations, accepted fewer speaking engagements. Instead, he pushed himself harder with each passing month. Some critics thought that handsome royalties were responsible for his many public appearances. Most of his speeches were free, however, and in 1950 he reported receiving only $2,850 in fees. Some thought him eager for the Presidency or Vice-Presidency in 1952. But in fact he had no such ambitions. Others considered McCarthy driven by the sheer love of publicity and applause, and of course there was truth to that charge. Old friends knew also that Joe had always been hyperactive. Those closest to the senator, however, went a step farther and correctly concluded that the frantic pace was largely the result of a burning desire to preach the internal Communist conspiracy to the American people and to punish those who opposed him. McCarthy's speeches, news conferences, and impromptu remarks revealed a man taken by genuine missionary zeal. He was passionate, inflexible, intolerant, angry.

There was more to a public appearance by McCarthy than the message, however. Like many successful figures in politics, show business, academia, and elsewhere, Joe used a number of techniques for intensifying audience response. He invariably arrived late for meetings and rallies, and when crowd anticipation reached an appropriate level he would suddenly rush in, surrounded by bodyguards, clutching his bulging black briefcase. The bodyguards, who sometimes carried weapons, often intimidated reporters; their presence made McCarthy seem all that more important to his audiences, as did the abundance of "evidence" Joe packed around and inevitably dug into. The senator often made dramatic entrances, preceded by bands, marching units, standardbearers, veterans, priests, and others. At Platteville, Wisconsin, in September 1951, crowds could hear the screaming sirens of his motorcade long before he stepped out of a shiny state patrol car. Soldiers stood shoulder to shoulder to keep a passage open for him to the speakers' platform, while flags waved and thousands cheered. Once Joe reached the platform, the soldiers took up positions around it.[11]

On a stage, platform, or at a head table McCarthy would usually give an effusive bear hug to everyone in the near vicinity. At a Milwaukee Press Club dinner for community leaders in 1952, he grabbed and embraced J. Donald Ferguson, editor of the *Milwaukee Journal,* who was furious. Before his address, Joe would often wade into an audience to greet old friends, slap backs, shake hands, and hug old ladies and pretty girls.[12]

Joe usually opened his speeches in the midwest—and often elsewhere— with a line that varied only slightly from place to place and immediately warmed the hearts of his listeners. In Cudahy, Wisconsin, in April 1951, it went: "I think it is unnecessary for me to tell you that I thoroughly enjoy getting away from Washington for hours and back here in the United States again. It's a good feeling." In Janesville, Wisconsin, that same month the enthusiasm of the crowd was such that before Joe could get to his stock sentence, a local veteran cried out, "Give 'em hell, Joe," and the 700 people at the Chamber of Commerce annual dinner cheered.[13]

Sometimes, when a suitable occasion arose, Joe would also preface his speech with an anecdote about local affairs. In Manawa, in June 1951, he recalled his job years earlier at the Cash-Way store and remarked, "If you folks had only bought a few more groceries from me I'd still be here."[14]

Associated Press reporter Dion Henderson, who covered scores of McCarthy's speeches from 1946 until the senator's death, thought that Joe took a childish joy in being loved by audiences. He gauged crowd reactions shrewdly, Henderson observed, and responded accordingly. During one appearance in Wisconsin the master of ceremonies shouted, "Our senator is a regular fella. A fella in flesh and blood and thinking the way we think. Is that right folks?" Applause thundered from the 10,000 townspeople and farmers in attendance. Henderson and others often heard Joe's "nervous giggle" as he stood at a microphone, smiling and laughing, while audiences cheered.[15]

Once the preliminaries had ended, Joe would become extremely serious, launching into an earnest, often bitter, and frequently sarcastic attack against those who were undermining the country and attempting to discredit his work. He often displayed what he said were documents substantiating his charges. In Wausau, Wisconsin, in October 1950, he held up a reproduction of a set of "secret files" on two Communist Chinese whom he claimed Owen Lattimore had insisted on retaining on his war information staff. (In fact, the four documents involved conflicting reports and opinions about the loyalties of two Chinese in 1942-43. They proved nothing conclusive against Lattimore.) Then he waved a photograph of Lattimore taken at Communist headquarters in Yenan. (At best, this undated photo placed Lattimore in China.) "The Tydings whitewash committee, however, found that Lattimore never knowingly associated with Communists," he said, and the audience burst into laughter. Without a solid grounding in the history of the Chinese Communists in the 1930s, and lacking firsthand knowledge of the Tydings hearings and the committee's final reports, it could do little else. Joe, of course, understood this perfectly. He next produced what he described as a confidential document sent to George Marshall, when the general was Secretary of State. It contained, Joe charged, warning of a "condition that still flourishes in the State Department under the administration of Dean Acheson." "Unfortunately," he added, "Marshall thumbed his nose at this report, as did the Tydings Committee." (The memorandum, dated June 10, 1947, came from a right-wing subcommittee of the Senate Appropriations Committee. Typically, it contained hysterical and apparently partisan charges about subversion under the Democrats.) This was evidence of a plot, he cried, "a deliberate, calculated program being carried out, not only to protect Communist personnel in high places, but to reduce security and intelligence protection to a nullity."[16]

McCarthy soon distributed to his audiences a 45-page magazine-size booklet called *The Party of Betrayal*. Under the title, the cover read:

> A small part of the Administration Commicrat Record is printed in this booklet. It is the record of the Administration Democrat Party. It does not speak for millions of loyal American Democrats.
>
> This record shows that the Administration Democrat Party has betrayed loyal Americans—Democrats and Republicans alike who want no part of protecting Communists and hiding corruption.
>
> The record points unmistakably to one fact—no one can be for the Administration Democrat Party and at the same time against Communism.

The contents of the booklet appeared to be authentic and authoritative. Documents were reprinted, some underlined, some censured, one hand-written, several stamped "Secret." There were photographs of canceled checks signed by Frederick Field. Hoover's letter of July 10, 1950, was reproduced, contradicting a clipping on the opposite page that quoted Tydings as saying that the FBI had investigated the 81 State Department files and found them "intact." The first page of the booklet declared,

> The following material was developed without the right to subpoena any witnesses or cross-examine those few called by

the Committee. The ranking Republican member of the Committee asked that some thirty witnesses be sub- poenaed—witnesses who had been previously interviewed and whose backgrounds had been thoroughly checked by either the Republican counsel or McCarthy's investigators and who had valuable information on Communists in key positions in the State Department. This request was flatly refused by the Democratic members of the Committee.

Few Democrats in the country were prepared to refute the widely read contents of the booklet. (Democratic leaders should have quickly cleared up the misleading assertions about the thirty witnesses.) The nation's most prestigious newspapers and magazines seemed more interested in blacken- ing McCarthy's past and running derogatory cartoons than documenting a detailed defense of the Tydings Committee.[17]

Joe's speeches were often less accurate and responsible than his litera- ture. This was due in part to the fact that he would stray from his prepared text and extemporize, at times making reckless statements that worried his key staff members. Nellor, Kerr, and others would gently urge him to be more cautious in the future. Joe would always agree, and promptly ignore the advice. The prepared addresses themselves, however, largely the pro- ducts of McCarthy's staff, invariably contained distorted, misleading, and inaccurate information.[18]

From a tape recording of an April 23, 1951, speech given in Cudahy, Wisconsin, this is what McCarthy said about John Stewart Service:

> Let's take the case of John Service. You will hear more about poor, innocent John before we are through. He is one of the "innocent people who were smeared," you understand, by "wild and irresponsible" charges. He was the subject of many bleeding-heart editorials. Let's look at the record of Service. Nothing new about this story.
>
> When Pat Hurley was the ambassador to China, he sent back repeated dispatches to the President saying, "Mr. Presi- dent, I can't work with the motley crowd you have over in my office. These men, Mr. President, are not good for America; they are good for Communist Russia. When top-secret mate- rial comes to me, and is seen by these individuals, within a matter of hours or days it shows up at the Communist headquarters at Yenan." Hurley pleaded, "Call them home, Mr. President. One of them, Mr. President, is John Stewart Service." Well, the President called Service back. Keep in mind this is all a matter of record—nothing from secret files.

The President called him back; he was promoted and given a better job in the State Department.

But the picture doesn't end there. Far from it. While he was back in this country he was picked up—he was arrested by the FBI with five other co-defendants. Keep in mind we are talking about one of our planners now, one of the men making the plans which led to MacArthur's dismissal. He and five others were arrested in a case which J. Edgar Hoover was quoted as having referred to as a 100-percent air-tight case of espionage—and J. Edgar Hoover does not make careless statements; he is one of the greatest men we have in Washington. What do you think happened to this case? (1) Service was not convicted; (2) he was not tried; (3) he was not indicted. What did happen? Under Secretary Joseph Grew, who was then Under Secretary of State, insisted that the defendants in this case be tried. He was told, however, that if we tried those people and they were found guilty, then we might make Communist Russia mad. Joe Grew said, "I don't give a tinker's damn whether you make them mad or not; they must go to trial." But they never went to trial. Service was let off. So what happened? Joe Grew resigned, and then Dean Gooderham Acheson took over Joe Grew's job. John Service was not only promptly rehired; he was also put on the board which had complete charge of the promotions and placement of all State Department personnel in the entire Asiatic theater! This was Dean Acheson's first act.

When I named Service as one of those dangerous to this nation, he was holding a top job over in India, one of the trouble spots of the world. He was called back before the unlamented Tydings Committee—after much protest; much editorializing—and the FBI was called before the committee. And under oath the FBI said when Service was back in this country we trailed him from the State Department with large brown envelopes under his arm; we trailed him to the hotel room of Phillip [sic] Jaffe. Phillip Jaffe was known to us as a Communist. Phillip Jaffe had been named under oath as a Russian spy. He was later tried and found guilty in connection with the theft of some seventeen secret and other classified government documents. They said, we trailed this State Department expert to the hotel room of Jaffe. We trailed him away without those brown envelopes. Then we put microphones in the hotel room of this known Communist. We listened to the conversation between this State Department expert and Phillip Jaffe. We heard Service discussing with Jaffe the top secret military information that he had turned over to him.

But the story does not end there. Now the tragic part: the Loyalty Board met, had a hearing, and said, "Now this is an example of McCarthyism at its worst." They said, "By smearing a poor, innocent man like Service who might have been a bit naive (didn't know what he was carrying under his arm, of course) it makes it impossible for us to hire other good, loyal Americans like Service." And they said, "He must be put back on his job in the State Department." That is where he is tonight.[19]

Such travesties of responsible historical narrative were to be found repeatedly in McCarthy's speeches. Philip Jessup, Stephen Brunauer, Gustavo Duran (whose photograph was often displayed), and others were smeared similarly on a regular basis. Joe often took credit for securing the perjury conviction of William Remington, whose name happened to be on the Lee list. (The conviction, concerning Remington's denial of Communist party membership, actually stemmed from testimony in early 1949 by Elizabeth Bentley.) He claimed that the State Department had ordered the destruction of 120,000 tons of ammunition stored in India that would have gone to Chiang Kai-shek. "Finally we got a letter from Major General Witsell," Joe said. "General Witsell admits that this ammunition actually was dumped in the Pacific Ocean." In fact, the Witsell letter was written in 1947, and the correct figure was 120 tons. The ammunition was destroyed because of extreme deterioration and corrosion.[20]

Still, audiences all over the country found it hard to believe that this obviously sincere, personable, self-confident, well-prepared young United States senator was anything other than what he said he was: the savior of his country. The positive impression multitudes came away with after listening to McCarthy at this stage of his career was in large part a product not only of his theatrics and communication skills (not to mention his often breathtaking mishandling of facts) but also of the self-image contained in his speeches and interviews.

In virtually every address Joe spoke of his own courage and manliness. "I will have to blame some of the roughness in fighting the enemy to my training in the Marine Corps," he told audiences on several occasions. "We weren't taught to wear lace panties and fight with lace hankies in the

Marine Corps." "McCarthyism," he often said, "is Americanism with its sleeves rolled up." At times he declared, "If lumberjack tactics are the only thing the Communists understand, then lumberjack tactics are the ones to use." Supporters described him as a "fighter," a "slugger," a "battler." "I might say," Joe told the state Republican convention in 1950, "that I know of not one single reason why Communists should be handled with kid gloves. They don't use kid gloves or powder puffs on us."

McCarthy also spoke of himself as a martyr, a man forced to bear the most outrageous calumny as the price of waging a one-man war against a vicious worldwide conspiracy. Just before the 1950 elections, he said he would "continue to fight Communism as long as I am in the Senate, and I will get nearer and nearer to the crimson clique, which will begin to start screaming louder and louder." A 1952 campaign slogan would read, "America loves him for the enemies he has made," meaning "Joseph Stalin, the pinks, and the Reds."

McCarthy also stressed his personal commitment to principle. He was unashamedly devoted to the Christian religion and the American flag, he told audiences. One admiring editor, John Chapple of the Ashland, Wisconsin *Daily Press,* believed that historians would remember the senator as "the most courageous American" battling against the "pro-Soviet forces of hell." At the Republican state convention of 1951 some Young Republicans broke into song:

> Fighting Joe McCarthy
> We're one and all for you
> Our land you'll save
> The flag will wave
> The true red, white and blue.[21]

The self-image McCarthy presented to the public, which had its parallels, of course, in America's frontier experience, was strikingly similar to the stereotype portrayed in dozens of highly popular films starring John Wayne. (The senator and the actor were to become good friends.) In part Joe was simply reflecting what he actually was. But he also had a shrewd, instinctive understanding of what people liked to hear.

Many people in McCarthy's audiences at this time were undoubtedly unaware that he was even controversial. Conservative newspapers in cities and towns across the country, but especially in Wisconsin, had refused to publish stories critical of the senator. The Catholic press was predominantly pro-McCarthy. Radio and television newscasters were neutral by and large, aside from the stridently pro-McCarthy commentators such as Fulton Lewis, Jr., Walter Winchell, and Paul Harvey. Joe, on the other hand, complained repeatedly of a conspiracy within the media, the press in particular, to ignore and berate him. In August 1950 he mailed a letter to many of the nation's newspaper editors complaining that his charges against Lattimore were receiving too little attention and blaming those elements in the media that "sprang to the defense of Alger Hiss." By mid-1951 he was quoting Louis Budenz, who charged that some 400 active Communist party members were at work in the American press, radio, and motion picture industries. "That amounts to about ten per state," he told a crowd in Spring Valley, Wisconsin. "I sometimes think Wisconsin has far more than its share."[22]

McCarthy seemed to enjoy berating certain reporters who covered his public appearances. At a gathering in Platteville he repeated a standard line: "I sometimes think that Wisconsin has more than her share of Communists." Then he paused, looked down at the press row, spied Miles McMillin, and said in a loud voice, "Hello, Miles." At another meeting in Racine Joe told his audience that Miles McMillin of the "Madison Daily Worker" was present. "Stand up, Miles," he said. "Let the people get a good look at you." There were hisses, boos, and ripples of applause. McCarthy was always asking reporters to stand up and be identified—they never did—as representatives of the "New York Daily Worker," the "Milwaukee Daily Worker," the "Milwaukee Urinal," and the like. In part this revealed Joe's sensitivity to criticism (which he always denied) and his penchant for revenge. But the attacks were also effective platform techniques; crowds invariably responded sympathetically. (Public suspicion of the press did not begin with Spiro Agnew.) Afterward, in the bar, Joe would often slap a flabbergasted reporter on the back and tell him not to take such things seriously. Many journalists were unable to separate this jocular assurance from McCarthy's address. Thus they erroneously concluded that the senator was a consummate cynic.[23]

The Korean War provided McCarthy, and almost all other Republicans, the ideal topic for campaign oratory in 1950. Joe incorporated facts and fantasies about the conflict in virtually every speech once it made the headlines. The fearsome and frustrating war broke out while the Tydings Committee hearings were grinding to a close. Combat stories no doubt blunted some of the effects of the committee's majority report condemning McCarthy. Senator Green received several letters reflecting the strain and anxiety felt by many. "There is something wrong in the government. How else do you account for the tragedy in Korea? We are sick of red herring whitewash etc." "Senator, now after this whitewash proceeding, just how do you feel when you read of the Reds torturing our boys? You must sleep fine." "Kiss the blood off your hands, you lousy New Dealers!"[24]

As the first American combat reports began to be published in July, accompanied by complaints from GIs of a lack of military equipment, tensions soared throughout the country. Senator Taft declared that the Administration's "weak" Far Eastern policy had invited Communist aggression, and he charged that the Administration had spent only $200 (!) to defend the South Koreans. (The Defense Department contended that the replacement value of arms left in South Korea a year earlier was about $110,000,000.) The national commander of the Veterans of Foreign Wars called for the resignation of Dean Acheson and Defense Secretary Louis Johnson. Henry Cabot Lodge declared that he would request an investigation of Johnson's "fitness for office," and he called for an increase of two billion dollars for military assistance in 1950 beyond the $1,222,500,000 already allocated. Maj. Gen. Lewis B. Hershey, head of the Selective Service, warned that it might be necessary to register women for the draft. Henry Wallace astounded his friends on the Left by announcing his support of American fighting men in Korea. President Truman asked Congress for $260,000,000 to expedite development of the hydrogen bomb. Winston Churchill disturbed Americans further by warning of World War III; "I must ask you not to suppose that time is on our side." In September, New York governor Thomas E. Dewey announced that he had been told that war with Russia would come "this month."[25]

It took McCarthy only a week after the war began to charge, predictably, that the crisis was further evidence of Communist infiltration into the highest levels of the Administration. The President's stern and prompt reaction to North Korean aggression and the swift dispatch of American ground troops made no impression on Joe. In a television interview of July 2 he said that "American boys are dying in Korea" because "a group of untouchables in the State Department sabotaged" the aid program Congress had voted for South Korea. In truth, the United States had deliberately withheld tanks, heavy artillery, and planes from the South Koreans, fearing that the government of Syngman Rhee would use them to carry out its threat to unify the country by force. Joe also fired bitter criticism at Acheson, contending that the Secretary of State had been "telling the world" that the United States would not interfere in Korea. In fact, Acheson had stated publicly in January that South Korea did not fall within the defensive perimeter of the United States. The statement was consistent with the wishes of the Joint Chiefs of Staff and Gen. Douglas MacArthur, and with a pronouncement by the President declaring that America would not "pursue a course which will lead to involvement in the civil conflict in China" or "provide military aid or advice to Chinese forces on Formosa." Acheson told the Soviet Union nothing that it did not already know. The North Korean invasion, which caught the American government completely by surprise, resulted in an immediate reversal of the Administration's Far Eastern policy. Republican senators Vandenberg and Taft initially applauded Truman's decision to resist "lawless aggression" by a puppet of the Soviet Union, the former calling it "courageous and indispensable."[26]

But McCarthy credited the Administration with nothing but bungling and treason. In a Senate speech of July 6 he accused Acheson of having "sabotaged and vetoed" a congressional attempt to fortify South Korea and spoke of "highly placed Red counselors" who were "far more deadly than Red machine gunners in Korea." In a public letter to the President of July 12 he repeated his charges, again condemning Acheson, Jessup, and the latter's "super adviser Lattimore" and contending that State Department loyalty files had been rifled in 1946. "Today Korea is the crisis area," he wrote. "Where will it be tomorrow if the same men act as your advisers and mold your thinking, Mr. President?"[27]

Out on the hustings Joe placed great emphasis on Korea, and his simplistic and irresponsible explanation of events that were increasingly disturbing the American people was greeted enthusiastically by audiences from coast to coast. In one speech he cried, "The State Department is again playing politics with the lives of other people's sons," and he warned, "If you want more of that, keep them in office. But if you vote for them, remember this. When the Communist trap to conquer this nation is sprung, it will be your vote that pulled the trigger." At another rally he joined a large crowd in a silent observance of the death of a local young man who was posthumously awarded the Congressional Medal of Honor. "Someone should hang for high treason," he said during the speech that followed, "for the needless loss of life in this war—where our only object is killing more of them than they do of us."[28]

The McCarran Act, passed on September 23 over President Truman's veto, symbolized the increasingly ugly mood on Capitol Hill and throughout the nation during the summer and fall of 1950. The act had its origin in legislation proposed in the House in 1947 by Republicans Karl Mundt and Richard Nixon, both members of HUAC, and both eager to make names for themselves politically. The Mundt-Nixon bill, in part, required "Communist-action" and "Communist-front" organizations to register with the Attorney General and divulge the names of their officers and members. If organization leaders refused to cooperate, individual members were required to register. The bill called for the creation of a five-man Subversive Activities Control Board, appointed by the President and confirmed by the Senate, to determine what organizations must comply. The measure also made it a crime to participate "in any manner" in a movement conspiring to "do anything" leading to the establishment of a foreign-controlled dictatorship in the United States.

Despite the fact that the bill appeared clearly to violate the First and Fifth Amendments, it swept through the House in 1948 by a vote of 319 to 58. The vote was bipartisan; the Democratic Party leadership, fearful of being branded "soft" on the Reds during a presidential election year, offered no official opposition. While the Senate failed to take action on the measure, the Republican platform of 1948 endorsed similar legislation, and Sen. Alexander Wiley, chairman of the Senate Judiciary Committee, called for a G.O.P. victory at the polls in order to pass the Mundt-Nixon bill. Proponents were undeterred by Truman's upset victory. Mundt (now in the Senate) and two colleagues reintroduced what was essentially the 1947 bill, and Nixon presented a companion measure in the House. Senate debate was delayed until the summer of 1950 when American troops were dying in Korea.

President Truman had opposed the registration bill from the start. He promised to "veto any legislation such as the Mundt-Nixon bill which adopted police-state tactics and unduly encroached on individual rights," and he assured lawmakers that he "would do so regardless of how politically unpopular it was—election year or no election year." But the warning was to no avail. A 32-page omnibus bill containing the registration proposal was reported out of the Senate Judiciary Committee, now chaired by the crafty, ultraconservative Nevada Democrat Pat McCarran, and the Republican Policy Committee of the Senate put it on its "must list." A companion measure sailed through the House, with HUAC's endorsement, 354 to 20.

As a hypothetically less drastic alternative to this legislation, Senate liberal Democrats Paul Douglas of Illinois, Harley Kilgore of West Virginia, Herbert Lehman of New York, Estes Kefauver of Tennessee, William Benton of Connecticut, Frank Graham of North Carolina, and Hubert Humphrey of Minnesota co-sponsored a bill authorizing the Attorney General to round up and detain anyone he had "reason to believe" might engage in subversive activities during a presidentially declared "internal security emergency." Such were the tensions of the time that this proposal, dubbed "a concentration-camp bill" by a White House aide, could be championed by those normally eager to defend civil liberties. An aide to Senator Lehman pointed out that the "very bad bill" had "profound constitutional weaknesses in seeking to set aside the right of habeas corpus." Karl Mundt chided, "While I sincerely welcome the support of the Kilgore group in trying to do something about Communism . . . let us not tear the Constitution to shreds; let us not out-Hitler Hitler; let us not out-Stalin Stalin; let us not establish concentration camps in America. . . ." Hubert Humphrey assured colleagues that the bill was "tough," and he labeled the McCarran Bill the "cream-puff special."

Through a complex of maneuvers, the emergency detention proposal ironically wound up becoming part of the McCarran Bill, and the measure rushed through the upper house with only seven negative votes. Douglas, Kilgore, Humphrey, Benton, and other liberals voted in favor of passage. Humphrey later confided to Kefauver that he was "very proud" of the Tennessee lawmaker's negative vote. "I wish I could say the same for myself." The bill passed easily in the House, 312 to twenty. With the war going badly and elections nearing, few members of Congress were willing to risk being labeled "pro-Communist," "anti-anti-Communist" or any of the other epithets in right-wing arsenals. Herbert Lehman later recalled that "the fever of fear was on my colleagues."

Despite urging by the Vice-President, the Speaker, and the Democratic floor leaders of both houses to sign the bill, Truman vetoed it, including in his message some stirring statements on American freedoms. "No considerations of expediency," he wrote, "can justify the enactment of such a bill as this, a bill which would greatly weaken our liberties and give aid and comfort to those who would destroy us." The veto was swiftly overriden in the House 286 to 48. In the Senate, despite a filibuster by liberals (and Republican maverick William Langer of North Dakota) and some arm-twisting by the President, the vote was 57 to ten to override. McCarthy, of course, voted for the Internal Security Act of 1950, as the legislation was officially known, and the override. He did not, however, contribute in any other way to the passage of the act.[29]

The many deeply disturbing and at times unprecedented domestic and international shocks of the years 1949-50, coupled with the popularity of McCarthy's black-and-white explanation of current events, accelerated the trend within the G.O.P. to use extremist rhetoric for political advantage. The campaign theme of Republicans all across the country in the elections of 1950 was the Communist conspiracy within the Democratic administration. The G.O.P. National Committee issued a handbook to party candidates describing contents of the theme and featuring such McCarthy targets as Owen Lattimore and Julian Wadleigh. Even the most distinguished Republicans embraced the views and tactics of McCarthyism. James Reston observed in late October, "If this term means the use of lies or partial truth to score a political point, regardless of the consequences to personal reputation or public trust; if it means public charges before proof, guilt by association, and the elevation of means above ends, as its critics assert, then 'McCarthyism' has been carefully planned, widely used, and even institutionalized in this campaign."[30]

In California, Congressman Richard Nixon ran against liberal Congresswoman Helen Gahagan Douglas for a Senate seat. Boasting of his own record with HUAC, Nixon referred to his opponent as the "Pink Lady" and falsely claimed that she was "a member of a small clique which joins the notorious Communist party-liner Vito Marcantonio of New York in voting time after time against measures that are for the security of this country." Douglas fired back, "On every key vote Nixon stood with party-liner Marcantonio against America in its fight to defeat Communism," and she called Nixon and his followers "a backwash of young men in dark shirts." She spoke of "smears" and warned that "McCarthyism has come to California." But the fiery wife of actor Melvin Douglas was no match for Nixon. He distributed more than a half million leaflets (printed on bright pink paper and thus dubbed "pink sheets") titled "Douglas-Marcantonio Voting Record," alleging that the two had voted the same way 354 times. If Mrs. Douglas had had her way, he told audiences, "the Communist conspiracy in the United States would never have been exposed."[31]

In Illinois, Senate Majority Leader Scott Lucas's bid for a third term was challenged by former Congressman Everett Dirksen, a smooth-talking, exceedingly shrewed politician of ultraconservative proclivity. Dirksen made much of the Communist conspiracy in Washington theme, and claimed that a Republican victory would let Stalin "know that there will be a housecleaning of his sympathizers and party-liners such as this country has never seen before."

Robert Taft, for all of his authority and seniority in Washington (and a campaign war chest containing at least $500,000), was not above using a similar approach to protect his Senate seat in Ohio. "Because of the Administration's strong Communist sympathies," he said in Dayton, "which apparently existed before and about the time of the Yalta conference, we have placed Russia in a commanding presence in Europe...and in

China." He blamed the conflict in Korea (increasingly labeled "Truman's War" by Republicans) on the State Department. He called his opponent, Joseph T. Ferguson, a tool of the C.I.O. Political Action Committee, which he said used "Communist techniques" and was "the Socialist party in this country."

Ferguson showed that Democrats could also sling mud. He condemned Taft's "communistic tactics in branding labor-union leaders and union members as Communists," and wanted to know how "any red-blooded loyal American" could back the incumbent. He asked the senator to explain "his own association with Communist leaders" and distributed a photograph showing him with Earl Browder—conveniently neglecting to note that it was taken in 1936 during a debate. Ferguson also claimed to see a congruence between the voting records of Senator Taft and Manhattan radical Marcantonio.

In Wisconson, Alexander Wiley swallowed much of his personal distaste for McCarthy and his methods. Seeking reelection, he praised the junior senator for alerting the nation to "the danger of Communist penetration" and condemned Democrats for "seventeen years of coddling Communists." Walter Kohler, Jr., the G.O.P. gubernatorial candidate, declared that he had not "the slightest doubt that there are thousands of Communists in key places of the government." A Republican newspaper advertisement, containing the photographs of Wiley and Kohler, bore the headline: "BLUNDERS COST BLOOD! STOP THEM!" The ad continued, "Citizens . . . a vote for a Republican candidate means much to America. The Democrats have stumbled through Asia into their third World War in a generation. They have coddled Communists and fumbled preparedness. Now . . . every day we must pay for their blunders. LET'S STOP THAT! Democrats have fought every effort to rid the government of bad security risks."

In Pennsylvania, G.O.P. gubernatorial candidate John Fine charged that the Truman administration had "flirted with Communism" and said that his opponent, Richardson Dilworth, was courting the votes of "pinks" and subversives. Republican governor James Duff, running for the Senate, condemned the Administration's "socialistic experiments" and waged a blistering attack upon the nation's foreign policy.

In Indiana, Sen. Homer Capehart declared, "We are still appeasing Russia," termed Dean Acheson "Quisling-like," and called his Democratic opponent a "Truman stooge" and a member of the Chief Executive's "red-herring brigade." Alex Campbell, the opponent, had in fact assisted the Justice Department during its prosecution of Alger Hiss. He counterattacked with the charge that both of Indiana's senators had "voted consistently" with Congressman Marcantonio.

Colorado Republican senator Eugene Millikin accused his challenger of "coddling Communists" and blasted the Administration's "appeasement and encouragement of Communism at home" and its tolerance of Reds in the State Department.

In Utah, G.O.P. candidate Wallace Bennett promised to show that Sen. Elbert D. Thomas was the "darlin' of several un-American organizations." A tabloid entitled *Thomas Philosophy Wins Red Approval* blanketed the state containing, among other things, the false charge that Thomas once presided at a pro-Communist fund-raising dinner with singer Paul Robeson.

In Washington State, Sen. Warren Magnuson was linked with a rally of Communists and fellow travelers and was said to have a voting record similar to those of left-leaning Senators Glen Taylor and Claude Pepper.

Similar charges were common in other states, as well. Conservative Democrats employed them in Florida, North Carolina, Idaho, California, Oklahoma, and elsewhere. A character in a Herblock cartoon asked wearily, "Is Joe Stalin running in all these elections?"[32]

President Truman spoke publicly about the elections only twice during the fall contests, once in defense of Helen Gahagan Douglas during a news conference. In a St. Louis speech a few days before the balloting he charged that those who employed the Communists-in-government issue had "lost all proportion, all sense of restraint, all sense of patriotic decency." Republicans, he said in disgust, were "willing . . . to undermine their own government at a time of great international peril.[33]

McCarthy drove himself hard in more than a dozen states during the weeks preceding the elections, not only for the applause and the publicity and the opportunities to tell the public about the Great Conspiracy. He was also interested in revenge. In a speech in Hyattsville, Maryland, he singled out Scott Lucas, Brien McMahon, and Millard Tydings for special attention and accused the Democratic incumbents of shielding the State Department. "Lucas provided the whitewash when I charged there were Communists in high places in government," he said. "McMahon brought the bucket, Tydings the brush." He also determined to campaign extensively in his home state, not only to lay the groundwork for his own reelection bid two years later, but also to clash swords again with the newspaper editors and politicians who had been bombarding him with investigations and hostile commentary virtually every day since Wheeling.[34]

In Illinois, Joe made a half dozen speeches in the Chicago area. He lashed out at Scott Lucas as one of those most responsible for the State Department whitewash. A vote for Everett Dirksen, he exclaimed, would be a "prayer for America" and a "vote against Dean Acheson" and the "Commicrat party." (This vulgar new term was invented by speech writer Ed Nellor.)[35]

McCarthy spoke three times in Connecticut. The state Republican organization chose not to sponsor his appearances, however, and audiences were relatively small.[36]

In Wisconsin, Joe traveled to more than a dozen cities, drawing large crowds wherever he went. In Beaver Dam the Dodge County Republican chairman introduced him by saying, "Some people in Wisconsin have been against Senator McCarthy, but those people are against the American flag." For the most part Joe repeated his familiar charges, employing Nellor's flair for alliteration: Acheson was a "procurer of pinks and punks"; the Democrats were the "party of the puppets of the politburo," and so on. He angrily sparred with *Capital Times* reporters on several occasions and came up with new evidence against the loyalty of the *Milwaukee Journal*: the chairman of the newspaper's editorial board was married to a lady whose sister was married to a New York attorney who was once the lawyer for a now-defunct left-wing periodical!

Joe also flattered Walter Kohler, praised Senator Wiley, and urged the election of all Republicans. He told crowds that a vote for Wiley's challenger, Attorney General Thomas R. Fairchild, was a vote to approve Communist coddling. He referred to the Democratic candidate as "this man who sat out World War II as an OPA attorney."

Some Democrats were eager to return McCarthy's fire. During an appearance in La Crosse, the senator was harassed by two young Democrats named Gaylord Nelson and William Proxmire (later United States senators themselves). They set up loudspeakers across from Joe's hotel and shouted charges and challenges into a microphone.[37]

McCarthy's most famous involvement in a 1950 campaign, the subject of a full-scale Congressional investigation the following year, occurred in Maryland. Joe determined, even before he read the final report of the Tydings Committee, to do everything in his power to drive the haughty committee chairman from office. Ray Kiermas argued against it, pleading that Tydings was a good senator. Joe brushed him aside. "The Irish get even," Ed Nellor said later.[38]

A wealthy Maryland Republican named Louise Gore brought to Joe's attention the name of a candidate to pit against Tydings. John Marshall

Butler was a tall, good-looking, slightly graying Baltimore attorney in his early fifties. (In physical appearance, intellectual capacity, and political philosophy he reminded some of Warren G. Harding.) He had never run for political office and was virtually unknown in the state. But he was eager to be a senator and was willing to wage a strenuous campaign. In early July, Butler met for several hours with McCarthy, Jean Kerr, Robert Morris, and Ruth (Bazy) McCormick Miller, editor of the *Washington Times-Herald* and a close friend of Miss Kerr's. He won Joe's enthusiastic support.

Within two weeks several state Republican leaders huddled with the candidate and Mrs. Miller, in Mrs. Miller's Washington office, to map campaign strategy. At Mrs. Miller's suggestion, Butler hired a personal friend, Chicago advertising man Jon M. Jonkel, as a public relations adviser. Since Butler neglected to employ a campaign manager, those duties soon fell to Jonkel as well. He had had no political experience, and he knew almost no one in Maryland.[39]

Jonkel and Butler, even with McCarthy's backing, had their work cut out for them. Another G.O.P. senatorial aspirant, Gen. D. John Mackey, had almost defeated Sen. Herbert O'Conor in 1946 and was the favorite to capture the Republican nomination. Moreover, Maryland had long been dominated by the Democratic Party, and it seemed improbable that any Republican could defeat Tydings, who had been in Congress since 1923 and had always been a vigorous and popular campaigner.

On the other hand, state Democrats were badly split. In the primary race for the gubernatorial nomination, incumbent W. Preston Lane and George Mahoney fought each other bitterly. Lane, unpopular with many as a consequence of signing into law Maryland's first sales tax, collected fewer votes than Mahoney but won the contest, due to the state's unit rule. The scars were not to heal before the general election. Tydings' primary opponent, Hugh M. Monaghan II, waged a McCarthyite campaign, charging that the Tydings Committee's majority report had "given the green light to Stalin's agents in this country to continue to gnaw at the foundation of our national security." Tydings captured the victory, but 125,849 Democrats who voted for their gubernatorial preference chose not to vote in the Senate race. Nothing like this had ever happened in a Maryland primary.[40]

McCarthy suggested that the Butler camp use his postcard tactic in the G.O.P. primary race. Jonkel agreed, and in the weeks preceding the September 17 primary some 200,000 postcards were filled in by hand, in accord with the formula Joe had developed in 1939, and mailed throughout the state. Jean Kerr provided Jonkel with anti-Tydings information, which he used in writing all of his candidate's speeches. The primary election was extremely close; the result was uncertain for a week. Markey wound up with a larger popular vote than Butler, but Butler picked up enough unit votes to take the nomination.[41]

With Butler now facing Tydings in the general election, McCarthy and his staff and friends stepped up their activities. Joe assigned Jean Kerr full time to the campaign. He enlisted Robert E. Lee and his wife to supervise a more extensive postcard project. He suggested the creation of an anti-Tydings tabloid that could be distributed across the state; he also provided most of its contents, consulted with its author, and arranged for its publication by the *Washington Times-Herald*. He telephoned Clint Murchison and persuaded the wealthy Texan to donate $10,000 to the Butler cause. He was undoubtedly the force behind $5,000 contributions from H. L. Hunt (who gave through another to conceal his identity) and former State Department employee Alvin Bentley. (Jonkel did not report receiving these and other contributions until a congressional committee probed the campaign.) A $500 contribution from Alfred Kohlberg was surely also solicited by the senator. Joe gave two speeches in Maryland on behalf of Butler, one in Baltimore and another in Hyattsville. A third speech, blasting the "whitewash committee" and the "Tydings-McMahon combine" was delivered to the Young Republican Club of the District of Columbia and broadcast by several Maryland radio stations. He was in Jonkel's office at least three times during the campaign. And he placed his entire staff at Jonkel's disposal. Never before had this sort of vindictiveness been displayed by a United States senator against a colleague.[42]

Jean Kerr was extremely busy on Butler's behalf, especially during the three weeks preceding the election. She selected and transmitted McCarthy materials for Butler's speeches and the tabloid, guiding the latter through its prepublication stages and distribution. She contacted printers of campaign literature and postcards, placed orders, and arranged to have hundreds of thousands of items picked up and distributed. She provided the Lees with the name of an addressing firm to assist the postcard project designed for the general election, and she guided the entire effort through to its completion. She also delivered several campaign contributions to Jonkel and others.[43]

Bazy Miller also played an important role in the campaign. Besides recommending Jonkel, she sent longtime family retainer Col. Roscoe Simmons from Chicago into Maryland in early October to win votes among blacks. Simmons, a nephew of Booker T. Washington, gave 56 speeches for Butler in the course of six weeks. Mrs. Miller gave funds to Simmons, contributed $2,000 to the primary race and $5,000 to the general election contest, loaned Jonkel $1,500, and raised additional sums from friends. She assigned her chief editorial writer Frank Smith to write the tabloid, and had the *Times-Herald* publish a half million copies of it at minimum cost.[44]

Don Surine contributed some research work to the campaign and drove 1,700 miles back and forth between Washington and Baltimore during the week before the election, delivering contributions, running errands, and distributing and mailing postcards. Ray Kiermas assisted the new postcard project. The entire McCarthy office staff joined scores of volunteers and others hired by the Hearst corporation and an addressing firm in filling out postcards, at times laboring all through the night and on weekends. The goal was 300,000 postcards bearing a brief handwritten message and signed "John M. Butler."[45]

From mid-October until election day, McCarthy confrere Fulton Lewis, Jr., repeatedly blasted Tydings on his network radio programs, carried over 535 stations, including five in Maryland. Eight broadcasts were devoted exclusively to partisan attacks upon the Maryland senator. The strong resemblance between Lewis's charges and McCarthy's was not coincidental: Ed Nellor was writing for both men.[46]

Lewis, Butler, and Jonkel were privy, before its publication, to a full-page advertisement in the *Baltimore American* that appeared two days before the election. The ad, published under the authority of "Democrats for Butler," echoed charges made against the Tydings Committee by McCarthy and Lewis and contained numerous factual errors. The actual creator of the advertisement was a rather unsophisticated lady, Margaret T. Berndt, whose husband loaned the largely phantom "Democrats for Butler" the necessary funds to ensure the ad's publication. During the congressional investigation she admitted having little knowledge of the Tydings Committee hearings or reports. When asked if she had even read Senator Lodge's minority report, on which she based one of the ad's charges, she replied, "I believe I skipped through it, Mr. Hendrickson. I don't have a copy, and I certainly hope to get one." She also observed about her ad, "I would not have published it without the approval of Mr. Butler's campaign manager, Mr. Jonkel."[47]

Equally in the McCarthy spirit were Jonkel's radio advertisements. (In the last three-and-a-half days of the campaign alone, Butler headquarters purchased 465 spot announcements. They were used before and after every Tydings speech.) One featured the sounds of machine-gun fire and mortar shells. "That is the way the war in Korea sounds," an announcer declared. "Do you, in your heart, believe that we were ready for what happened in Korea, or could have happened some place else? Vote for John Marshall

Butler, Republican candidate for United States senator." In the speeches Jonkel wrote for Butler, the candidate constantly misquoted Truman on Stalin, "I like old Joe. Joe is a pretty good fellow." He also raised the issue of traitors in the State Department and asked audiences, "You are a father, you are a mother, do you believe that we are well organized here? Do you feel that you know for sure that there are no Communists or Communist influence in the top levels of our Government?"[48]

The campaign item that drew the most attention both during and after the election was the tabloid. The four-page, eleven-by-sixteen-inch paper bore the title *From the Record.* It charged, among other things, that Tydings had "sponsored Owen Lattimore in a series of lectures on Communist Russia," that his Armed Services Committee had hamstrung appropriations to arm the South Koreans, and that the Tydings Committee had refused to carry out Senate instructions to investigate disloyalty in the State Department and had ordered William Remington kept on the Commerce Department's payroll. The tabloid also contained excerpts from newspaper editorials hostile to the Tydings Committee, Hoover's July 10 letter to McCarthy about the FBI files, photographs of "State Department pro-Communists" Acheson, Jessup, Service, Lattimore, Hanson, Remington, and Duran, and a number of tidbits and wise sayings, such as "Administration red herrings and whitewashes are making the voters blue."[49]

One photograph, labeled a "composite picture," appeared to show Tydings listening attentively to Earl Browder. The caption implied that the two were allies. This was the work of *Washington Times-Herald* executive Garvin Tankersley (soon to wed Bazy Miller). To get the effect he sought, he had a staff artist reverse a 1938 picture of Tydings and place it next to a recent photograph of Browder. He later said proudly, "We wanted to show that Mr. Tydings did treat Mr. Browder with kid gloves, and conveyed that in the caption."[50]

Tydings was enraged by Tankersley's sleight of hand. "That picture brings into clear focus the intent of the conspirators in their moral squalor to deceive the people of the State of Maryland in the selection of a candidate for one of the highest offices in the world." The "composite" label in the caption was inadequate, he argued, for most people were unfamiliar with the word. When later questioned by a congressional committee, Baltimore attorney Cornelius P. Mundy, Butler's campaign treasurer, called the picture "stupid," "puerile," and "in bad taste." The treasurer of the Young Democrats for Butler, the five-member "organization" listed as the tabloid's sponsor (Mundy actually provided the funds), also disapproved of Tankersley's handiwork.[51]

Jean Kerr first saw the composite picture when the tabloid was in page proofs. She endorsed the idea and thereafter defended it vigorously. "I think his picture certainly did not do Mr. Tydings an injustice," she later testified. "I think it did him a favor." Tydings' pro-Communist treatment of Browder during committee hearings was "a hundred times more damaging" than the imagery conveyed in the composite picture, she charged. (She championed the entire tabloid: "There are no lies about Mr. Tydings in this tabloid. I think it is the kind of campaign literature that we should almost look for because I think the truth should be taken to the voters.")[52]

McCarthy had nothing to do with the creation of the composite photograph. He soon made this clear to Tom Coleman, who called the picture "inexcusable and needless," and he publicly disassociated himself and his staff from it. Moreover, he had greater personal qualms about the tactic than Miss Kerr did. In a later deposition he said that when he first saw Tankersley's picture he advised against it. On the whole, "composite pictures are wrong. They should not be used. . . . Whether the picture is labeled composite or not, I don't think they should be used any more than unfair caricatures should be used. A man in a campaign is entitled to have his picture as is, and not caricatured and not a part of a composite." Still, he did not wish to give the impression that he and his cohorts in the Maryland campaign were at war over the matter. "Luckily, it didn't do any injustice to Tydings because if they had taken the testimony, the statements made between Tydings and Browder, it would have shown the relationship much closer and much more cooperative." In a magazine interview published in September 1951, Joe said of the contest, "I think it was one of the cleanest campaigns in the country."[53]

The most notorious event of the campaign came to light after the election. It involved a small, Jewish (Joe privately called him "a little sheeny"), 40-year-old Baltimore printer named William Fedder, who claimed that throughout the early morning hours of November 6 Don Surine and two other McCarthy men held him captive and threatened him. Millard Tydings passionately condemned "the midnight ride of Mr. Fedder, Chicago gangland style, imported into Maryland for the first time." The congressional investigating committee studied the story at length, and the anti-McCarthy press displayed it prominently for many months. When Ray Kiermas was asked about Fedder more than twenty-five years later, he began: "THAT bastard!"[54]

Fedder had owned and operated a direct-mail advertising and printing plant in Baltimore since the early 1930s. A friend recommended him to Jonkel and, starting in mid-October, Jonkel ordered some half million campaign flyers printed. Fedder was also asked to distribute throughout the state about 70,000 letters and the 500,000 tabloids published by the *Times-Herald.* Jonkel told him not to worry about payment, for Senator McCarthy was going to provide the campaign with ample funds. By the end of the month, however, Butler headquarters owed Fedder more than $10,000, and the printer refused to release or mail much of what he had printed and received for distribution. To expedite matters, Butler signed a personal guarantee of payment "for any of your services that have not been paid for at the time the campaign is completed," thereby unknowingly violating an election law limiting personal expenditures by candidates. With this assurance, and cash provided by Bazy Miller (at Jean Kerr's request) and Jonkel, Fedder released the campaign literature on Saturday, November 4.

That evening, Ray Kiermas telephoned Fedder, at Miss Kerr's recommendation, and asked him if he could arrange to have 50,000 postcards handwritten and stamped within twenty-four hours. The others at work on cards had said they were unable to complete this amount before the election. Fedder accepted the task, drove to Washington and picked up the postcards and 50,000 one-cent stamps.

Accounts of what occurred thereafter vary greatly. It is certain that Fedder distributed cards and stamps to a number of Negro households in Maryland; workers were to be paid one cent per completed postcard. To cover this expense, Kiermas gave Fedder a check for $500 on Sunday, in the presence of Don Surine, and offered him a bonus for completing the project on time. It is also clear that both Kiermas and Surine quickly began to suspect Fedder of fraud.

Kiermas said later that he distrusted Fedder on sight. His suspicion deepened, he said, when the printer sought to mail the postcards as well as stamp them, which would eliminate any check on the number of cards actually completed. Word was also received shortly in McCarthy's office that tens of thousands of copies of the tabloid were discovered at the Baltimore dump. Fedder had to be responsible, and that meant that he was pocketing funds given to him for distribution. Surine soon discovered, moreover, that Fedder had not metered and mailed thousands of letters for which he had received advance payment. He also learned of Butler's guarantee to Fedder and realized that the document broke the law as well as provided Fedder with a blank check.

It seems probable that on Sunday evening, Surine, a physically aggressive and short-tempered man, decided to crack down on Fedder and terminate his relationship with the Butler campaign. With Kiermas scheduled to fly to Milwaukee, Surine asked Ewell Moore, Jr., a strapping young part-time

McCarthy employee, to assist him. Moore invited a friend to come along, Arlington real estate salesman George Nilles, who had been filling out postcards in McCarthy's office for a couple of days. The three men determined to collect and mail the completed postcards, gather the unused stamps (which Kiermas and Surine now suspected Fedder of coveting), retrieve Butler's letter and the $500 check, and turn off the printer's pipeline to further campaign funds.

Shortly before midnight, Moore and Nilles telephoned Fedder's home and learned from his wife that he was out. According to Fedder, the two callers, who remained anonymous, became angry, made threats, and demanded that the printer contact them upon his return. Fedder soon returned the call and was asked how many postcards were completed. When he said that only about 5,000 were ready, the person on the other end of the line became extremely abusive. Probably at this point, as Fedder later claimed, the printer tried to calm his agitated respondent by claiming falsely that he had already mailed another large batch of completed cards. This news made either Moore or Nilles even angrier, and Fedder was ordered to report to the lobby of a local hotel.

About 1 A.M. Fedder met Moore and Nilles, who counted the finished postcards and mailed them. Surine arrived a short time later, and Fedder admitted that he had not mailed any postcards himself. Surine became enraged, according to Fedder. "His eyes looked like they were going to pop out of his head." Jerking the much smaller man by the coat, Surine demanded the Butler letter, threatened to put Fedder through "a McCarthy investigation," and said that his friend Captain Kriss of the local police department would "make it tough" for the printer if he failed to cooperate. When Fedder balked at the demand for the Butler document, he was hustled into Surine's car.

Throughout the next five hours, Surine, Moore, and Nilles drove Fedder around Maryland, at times stopping at private homes to pick up postcards and stamps. Fedder was frightened and shaken, he said later, and was frequently interrogated, badgered, and intimidated. At about 4 A.M. Surine demanded the return of the $500 check. When the four men arrived at Fedder's home to collect it, the printer said later, Surine and his cohorts "insisted on coming in, but I begged them not to do this to my wife and family—that my wife was extremely nervous because of what happened earlier in the evening. They waited on the sidewalk." During the several minutes he was in his house, Fedder might easily have called the police. He said later that he did not for fear of his life. However that may be, Fedder's silence was also prompted by his guilt. Surine, Moore, and Nilles knew about the dumping of the tabloids and the overcharge for the metered letters. Moreover, they were probably correct in concluding that Fedder was attempting to abscond with several hundred dollars' worth of stamps and much of the $500 advance. Fedder's fake claim to have mailed a large quantity of postcards himself was no doubt solid ground for suspicion.

After Fedder reappeared with the check, Surine ordered him back into the car. Over the next two hours, the ex-FBI agent fired questions at Fedder and wrote out a statement of accounts for Fedder's signature. The document noted the contracted duties with the tabloids, the metered letters, and the postcards, and it called for a refund from Fedder, of an unspecified amount, to Butler headquarters. It also concluded the postcard activity with the return of the Kiermas check and 39,000 stamps in Fedder's possession. Fedder made several revisions in the statement and signed it. He was then permitted to get some sleep.

Back in Washington, Surine deposited the check and the stamps in McCarthy's safe and turned the statement over to Cornelius Mundy. When Fedder submitted a final bill after the election to campaign headquarters, treasurer Mundy refused payment.[55]

Fedder brooded for about three weeks, angered by Mundy's neglect and Butler's refusal to return his telephone calls. In mid-December he told the story of "the midnight ride" to a friend, garage owner and former investigator Louis Fried. Fried contacted a businessman named S. Charles Friedenberg, who was a longtime friend of Millard Tydings. An appointment was made with the senator, and Fedder delivered a lengthy—and one-sided—account of his "kidnapping." Fried leaked the story to Drew Pearson, who gave it national exposure over his network radio program. Tydings filed more general complaints with the Subcommittee on Privileges and Elections, chaired by Iowa Democrat Guy Gillette, and denounced the Butler campaign as "scandalous, scurrilous, libelous, and unlawful."[56]

The publicity and complaints, of course, drew public attention after the November elections. The election results themselves, in Maryland and elsewhere, were considered at the time tributes to the awesome—and to some frightening—power of Sen. Joe McCarthy. "In every contest where it was a major factor," Marquis Childs observed, "McCarthyism won."[57]

Richard Nixon won in California by almost 700,000 votes. Everett Dirksen defeated Majority Leader Scott Lucas in Illinois with 294,354 votes to spare. Taft crushed his Ohio challenger, taking 57.5 percent of the vote. In Wisconsin, Wiley and Kohler won easily, as did Charles Kersten, who boasted of his friendship with McCarthy while seeking reelection to the House of Representatives. In Pennsylvania, James Duff ousted Majority

Whip Francis Myers. Wallace Bennett defeated highly respected Elbert D. Thomas of Utah. Homer Capehart won reelection in Indiana, as did Eugene Millikin in Colorado. Results of the Maryland senatorial race astonished many observers: Butler beat Tydings by a majority of 43,100 votes, "the largest majority that has ever been given a Republican senatorial candidate in the history of my state," the winner later boasted. Altogether, Democrats dropped 28 seats in the House and five in the Senate.

G.O.P. gains on Capitol Hill were not overly impressive when taken in perspective, however. They were smaller than Republicans had achieved in 1938, 1942, or 1946, and gave the party control of neither chamber. Democratic losses were only slightly more than half the average suffered in the last three mid-term elections. Moreover, careful analysis of the elections suggests that the impact of McCarthy and McCarthyism was greatly exaggerated at the time.

Lucas's defeat was largely attributable to scandals within the powerful Cook County Democratic machine, brought to light that fall by Sen. Estes Kefauver and his special investigating committee. Taft's victory was in large part the product of the senator's attitude toward organized labor. A statistical study by Robert Fleming of the *Milwaukee Journal* showed that while McCarthy drew crowds in his home state, he did not win votes for the G.O.P. In Kenosha, where his largest audience appeared, Republicans faded from 48 percent of the major party vote in 1948 to 39 percent in 1950. Democrats, on the whole, increased their strength in Wisconsin; their candidates for senator and governor polled an impressive 47 percent of the vote. James Duff's win in Pennsylvania centered around his popularity as governor; he was publicly critical of McCarthy and spoke infrequently about internal subversion. Brien McMahon and William Benton were both reelected in Connecticut. Warren Magnuson easily defeated his McCarthyite opponent in Washington State. Thomas Hennings, Jr., was elected to the Senate in Missouri, despite a speech by McCarthy in Jefferson City in which he tried to link Hennings's father with the "Young Communists" and anti-McCarthy (therefore pro-Red) advertisements in local newspapers.[58]

Even in Maryland there were grounds for questioning McCarthy's effect on Tydings' defeat. Democratic vote totals had been declining in the state for years, and, as noted earlier, Democrats were bitterly divided. When questioned shortly after the election, Tydings attributed the outcome of the race basically to his party's internal dissension, and many Republicans agreed. The recently adopted sales tax undoubtedly hurt Tydings as well; its author, Governor Lane, was defeated by an even larger margin than the senator. Moreover, many Maryland blacks were hostile toward Tydings because of his conservative stance on civil rights. (A Jonkel flyer called "Back to Good Old Dixie," purportedly sponsored by blacks, attempted to exploit this hostility.) Butler carried the vote in Baltimore's black precincts; by 85 percent in one. A prominent black Maryland Republican said after the election, "Of course, Mr. Tydings was not popular with the colored people anyway, because he never did anything for us ... every measure that was passed in Congress, he voted against it." The *Baltimore Afro-American* contended that Tydings' defeat "was not interpreted so much as support of McCarthy's Reds in the government charges but as a protest at the denial of civil rights on the part of the Lane 'machine.'" Others complained that Tydings had lost the common touch during his lengthy career in Washington and had long failed to inspire the average voter. Organized labor supported him only halfheartedly, due to his conservative record on economic legislation. The deteriorating situation in Korea just before the balloting—the Chinese Communists moved south across the Yalu River on October 26—no doubt also damaged Tydings.

The impact of the McCarthy tabloids on the campaign was also questionable. Thanks to Fedder and an eccentric G.O.P. volunteer who destroyed a quantity of them because "they were an insult to the intelligence of the people of Maryland," only some 300,000 (perhaps far fewer) tabloids were ever distributed. Then too, Tydings had gone on radio and television prior to the election and denounced the publication in detail, including the composite picture. Several Maryland newspapers also condemned it before the polls opened.[59]

The political fate of those who voted against the McCarran Act is another indicator of the actual effect of the anti-Communist issue on the campaigns of 1950. Of twenty-one Democratic congressmen who voted no, only five were defeated—two in bids for Senate seats. Twenty-three of the 28 Democratic representatives beaten in the elections had supported the bill. The lone senatorial opponent, New York's Herbert H. Lehman, won reelection handily.[60]

Of course, perceptions of reality are often more important than reality itself. Virtually everyone, across the entire political spectrum, interpreted the elections of 1950 as, to use Sen. Owen Brewster's term, a "triumph" for McCarthy and his "ism." Senate colleagues, according to two influential columnists, credited Joe with Tydings' downfall and believed that he had contributed to the victories of Everett Dirksen, Wallace Bennett, and Herman Welker of Idaho, as well as to the defeats of Frank Graham of North Carolina and Claude Pepper of Florida. (In fact, Welker employed right-wing charges in his campaign, but they may not have been decisive in his victory. Graham and Pepper lost their primary contests largely on the race issue.) Welker later said that except for Joe McCarthy some seven senators might not then be sitting in the upper house. A reporter observed in 1951, "The ghost of Senator Tydings hangs over the Senate."[61]

McCarthy readily accepted all of the plaudits. His ego soared, and he saw himself more than ever as a power to be reckoned with. In his view he had almost single-handedly brought some of the nation's leading Democrats to their knees; he had wiped that mocking smile from Millard Tydings' face. The last election Joe had lost was the halfhearted effort in 1944, when he spent most of the campaign in the South Pacific. He knew how to win at the polls, and he had now proven that he could carry that knowledge effectively into any state in the Union. In the future he would often threaten opponents with references to the defeat of Lucas and Tydings. In August 1951, he scoffed at charges raised by William Benton with the sneer, "Benton will learn that the people of Connecticut do not like Communists and crooks in government any more than the people of Maryland like them." He was supremely confident that he would have a commanding voice in the 1952 contests. In a private letter to Tom Korb, Joe observed, "In my opinion, the result of the elections is the healthiest sign we have seen in this country for a long time. I sincerely hope we can continue on now, and elect a real *American* President in 1952."[62]

Jubilation had swept through the McCarthy office on election night. As the vote totals poured in, everything seemed to be going the senator's way. The results in Maryland, of course, were especially pleasing to McCarthy's staff and friends. All of the long days and nights of speech writing, researching, planning, fund-raising, errand-running, wrestling with mountains of postcards, telephone calling, and the like had paid off handsomely.

Ed Nellor hosted a "victory celebration" late that evening at his handsome home in a northern Virginia suburb. McCarthy and his aides were joined by a large number of Republican congressmen, including Richard Nixon and Karl Mundt. People whooped and cheered, and almost everyone got drunk. At one point in the festivities, the septic tank backed up into the house, and Nellor laughed heartily as he saw Joe and the others wading through the overflow in their bare feet. The symbolism somehow escaped him.[63]

COMBAT DUTY

Emboldened by their victories at the polls, and angered and worried by worsening conditions in Korea, Republicans stepped up their attack on the Administration in late 1950 and early 1951, demanding Dean Acheson's resignation or impeachment, sniping at Gen. George Marshall, the new Secretary of Defense, and dropping hints of plots in high places to fire General MacArthur and undermine the war effort. Several conservative Democrats joined the hue and cry. Pat McCarran and James Eastland echoed the call for Acheson's resignation. Joseph P. Kennedy, whom his son John once described as a "Taft Democrat," termed American foreign policy "suicidal" and "politically and morally bankrupt." He sought withdrawal from Korea and Western Europe, and his plea for neo-isolationism was applauded by Herbert Hoover, Robert Taft, and the Hearst newspapers, among others. Bipartisanship was virtually dead.

The Administration fought back by soliciting supportive statements from foreign policy experts and congressmen. (Crotchety Kenneth McKeller of Tennessee accused Republicans of "helping the Russians.") The President remained firm. At a news conference he snapped, "Dean Acheson would be one of the first, if not the first, to be shot by the enemies of liberty and Christianity." But it was clear that the Truman administration was in deep trouble, at home and overseas. A Gallup poll revealed that of those who could identify the Secretary of State, only 20 percent responded favorably, while 30 percent thought he should be replaced. In early January 1951, after the fall of Seoul, a similar poll reported that 49 percent of the American people thought it a mistake to defend South Korea; 66 percent wanted to pull out.[1]

McCarthy, of course, took a major role in the assault upon the Administration. If the President refused to end the "treasonable farce" of leashing the forces of Chiang Kai-shek in Asia, he exclaimed in one speech, then Congress should impeach him. On the floor of the Senate he demanded the ouster of Defense Secretary Marshall. He repeated many of his charges about treason in the State Department and continued to portray Acheson as the pinkish bureaucrat most responsible for the American casualties in Korea.[2]

During this post-election period McCarthy's arrogance soared. Now that he had tasted the delights of revenge at the polls, he determined to punish Drew Pearson, who had been attacking him regularly for months. Drawing upon materials from J. B. Matthews' files, including a number of Westbrook Pegler's columns, Joe and his staff went to work preparing a Senate speech linking Pearson with the international Communist conspiracy. McCarthy publicly announced the forthcoming delivery of the address.

Shortly before completing the speech, Joe accepted an invitation to a dinner dance to be given on December 12 by Louise Tinsley Steinman, the wealthy daughter of an Ohio newspaper publisher. Apparently for her own amusement, the young hostess also invited Drew Pearson, choosing not to inform either the senator or the columnist about the other's invitation. Senators Richard Nixon and Russell Long were also to be on hand, along with several others. The scene was set for the upstairs ballroom area in Washington's swank Sulgrave Club.

The first person to greet the astonished Drew Pearson upon his arrival at the Club was Senator McCarthy, who approached with a big grin and extended hand. "Hello, Drew." He then informed the columnist that he was going to take him apart on the Senate floor the next day, and proceeded to get him a cocktail. The details of what followed are unclear, due to conflicting testimony, but it seems fairly certain that McCarthy began to heckle Pearson and that the two fell into a nasty quarrel. At one point, according to Pearson, Joe challenged him to step outside and fight. When this offer was declined, Joe ordered him out of the building. At the mention of his income tax problems, some time later, McCarthy grabbed the back of the older man's neck and again invited him outside to settle matters. In the downstairs cloakroom, as guests were leaving, Joe pinned back Pearson's arms, kneed him twice in the groin, and took a swing at him. (Under oath,

McCarthy later claimed that he had only slapped him on the cheek.)
Senator Nixon broke up the brief tussle. Pearson thought that McCarthy
was drunk, but on the basis of recollections by others who spoke with the
senator later that night Pearson was undoubtedly incorrect.

Joe telephoned *Times-Herald* editor Frank Waldrop right after the
incident and bragged that he had just kicked Pearson "in the nuts." He
made a similar call to Urban Van Susteren in Appleton. He told Ray
Kiermas that Pearson had jumped three feet in the air. Through Ed Nellor,
Joe gave his side of the story to Fulton Lewis, Jr., who broadcast it nationally
the following evening, including the reference to the three-foot leap. Joe
took delight in telling others of his assault upon the fifty-four-year-old
Quaker pacifist. By his own admission, he described the incident to "a vast
number of people" during the next few weeks. One reporter heard him say
that he had enjoyed the fracas thoroughly. When he detailed it to his friend
George Reedy, his voice became high-pitched, and he giggled like a teenager. Many on the Far Right shared Joe's glee over his senseless act of
violence. Sen. Arthur Watkins said that he had heard two differing reports
about where Pearson was hit and hoped that both were accurate. Tom Korb
gloated in a private letter, "If, as Drew Pearson is quoted, you 'kicked him in
the groin,' I don't know how you could be so stupid, because I think it is well
known that Drew Pearson has nothing there." Someone from Missouri
sent McCarthy an Elgin watch inscribed, "For combat duty on the 12th of
December above and beyond the call of duty."[3]

On December 15 McCarthy delivered a passionate anti-Pearson speech
to the Senate. The columnist, he claimed, was "the voice of international
Communism," a "Moscow-directed character assassin," an "unprincipled
liar and a fake," a man of "twisted, perverted mentality." Pearson had
hounded James Forrestal to his death, Joe cried, he had taken orders from a
Communist named David Karr, and his latest assignment was the destruction of Gen. Douglas MacArthur. McCarthy read quotations from more
than forty prominent citizens, including Presidents Roosevelt and Truman,
condemning the flamboyant columnist and questioning his integrity. He
then called upon the public to urge newspapers and radio stations to halt
the dissemination of Pearson's views. He specifically named the Adam Hat
Company, Pearson's $5,000-a-week radio sponsor, as a target and sug-
gested a boycott. "It should be remembered that anyone who buys an Adam
hat—any store that stocks an Adam hat—anyone who buys from a store
that stocks an Adam hat—is unknowingly contributing at least something
to the cause of international Communism by keeping that Communist
spokesman on the air." A privately financed pamphlet containing this and

two subsequent anti-Pearson speeches was soon mailed to every newspaper in the country, courtesy of Joe's senatorial frank.[4]

Pearson vehemently denied the charges and threatened to sue. Karr, a former Pearson employee who had once been investigated by HUAC and a House Appropriations subcommittee (being cleared by the latter), replied that "within his lying heart, McCarthy knows that I am not and never have been" a Communist or fellow traveler.[5]

McCarthy's Senate speech was followed up by almost nightly appeals from Fulton Lewis, Jr., (reading Ed Nellor scripts) for letters to the Adam Hat Company. It took only ten days for the pressure to pay off and the Pearson sponsorship to be dropped. There were official denials that McCarthy and Lewis had anything to do with the decision, but no one believed them, least of all the jubilant senator. Surely this response by the nervous hatmakers proved that he had enormous potential power in the marketplace. Perhaps this was just the beginning; from now on many more "truly American" corporations might be persuaded to silence those who opposed him. At the very least, the triumph over Pearson was a reaffirmation of the increasing effectiveness of coloring one's opponents Red. Joe was beginning to think himself invincible. "What he is trying to do is not new," the *Washington Post* editorialized. "It worked well in Germany and in Russia; all voices except those officially approved were silenced in those lands by intimidation."[6]

In January, McCarthy renewed his appeal to drive Pearson from the nation's newspapers. The best way for editors and publishers to endanger freedom of the press, he charged, "is to carry in their columns the work of an exposed, known, deliberate liar."[7]

On March 5, 1951, Pearson filed a $5,100,000, multi-count law suit against McCarthy, Lewis, Nellor, Surine, J. B. Matthews, the *Washington Times-Herald,* and a number of others. It was largely a somewhat bizarre antitrust suit designed by Pearson attorney Warren Woods to circumvent McCarthy's congressional immunity. Pearson was personally persuaded (Woods wasn't) that a demonstrable conspiracy existed within the Far Right to destroy him and thought that this action would expose it. The suit survived several motions to dismiss and earned a battery of lawyers some substantial fees, but it never went to court and was dropped in 1956.[8]

In late January 1951 McCarthy avenged himself on Margaret Chase Smith. On the eve of a meeting of the Executive Expenditures Committee, he informed her, by messenger, that she had been "bumped" from the powerful Permanent Investigations Subcommittee in favor of Richard Nixon. Joe had the authority to make the switch as ranking member of the parent committee. Publicly and privately he denied seeking revenge for the "Declaration of Conscience," and contended that he was merely acknowledging Nixon's superior investigative record. But this avowal persuaded no one, especially after Senator Smith angrily pointed out to colleagues that she had served on congressional investigating committees longer than either Nixon or McCarthy.[9]

A few days later the Republican Committee on Committees named Joe to the powerful Senate Subcommittee on Appropriations, which had jurisdiction over State Department funds. This move enraged William Benton, a former Assistant Secretary of State, and in a blistering Senate speech, during which he was twice forced to take his seat by Republicans, he denounced the appointment and the appointee. "The senator from Wisconsin is to be the judge, jury, and prosecutor of the State Department," he declared. "He becomes his own kangaroo court." Senator Jenner replied curtly, "The committee will take no advice from Benton." All in a dither over the attack, Kenneth Wherry felt obliged to assure the Senate that McCarthy had "done more to establish confidence in the hearts of Americans than any other man I know." Joe later issued a statement describing Benton as "this defender of the State Department's Yalta crowd" who "squeals and beats his breast in agony because the day of judgment is at hand for the crimson clique in the State Department."[10]

McCarthy had another excellent reason for believing that he was soon to have the upper hand with Acheson and his friends. In late December the Senate authorized another congressional investigation into internal security matters, and the Senate Judiciary Committee named its chairman, Pat McCarran, to head the new Internal Security Subcommittee. While its membership was balanced by party, its political philosophy was virtually uniform. McCarran, James Eastland of Mississippi, William Jenner of Indiana, and Homer Ferguson of Michigan were militant ultraconservatives; Herbert O'Conor of Maryland, Willis Smith of North Carolina, and Arthur Watkins of Utah were conservatives. All were critical, in varying degrees, of American foreign policy; several, like McCarran, were open partisans of Chiang Kai-shek; and most, again like the chairman, had declared the existence of traitors in the State Department.

McCarran was determined from the outset to reopen McCarthy's State Department charges, and Washington insiders predicted that he and his colleagues would make every effort to vindicate Wisconsin's junior senator. Joe had complete confidence that the prediction was accurate. Publicly, he expressed joy at the McCarran Committee's formation, pledged his total support ("1,000 percent"), and soon admitted that he was providing the committee with evidence. Privately, he had McCarran name his friend and employee Robert Morris chief counsel, with the sole right to pick his assistants. Morris was soon joined by Benjamin Mandel as director of research, a post he had held with HUAC. Joe also assigned Don Surine to the work of the committee. Surine was to be especially active, attending hearings, conducting research, and assisting in the writing of final reports. Years later he would claim responsibility for 80 percent of the McCarran Committee's findings.[11]

The committee made headlines on February 10 with the announcement that it had seized "several thousand" documents from the files of the Institute of Pacific Relations on a farm near Lee, Massachusetts. A week later Karl Mundt boasted to reporters that he and McCarthy had seen some of the documents prior to their seizure, explaining that Don Surine had discovered about fifty "sample" documents at an earlier date and had turned them over to the two senators. When the full story of the I.P.R. emerged later, the close relationship between McCarthy and McCarran became even more apparent.[12]

In the summer of 1949 officials of the institute had transferred several steel cabinets, containing some 20,000 documents, from their overcrowded New York office to a barn at Lee, owned by Edward C. Carter, the institute's former secretary-general. The documents largely pertained to the years 1925 to 1945, and the cabinets were removed to provide additional filing space. Shortly after McCarthy made his initial charges against the State Department in early 1950, institute officials invited the FBI to study their files, both in New York and Massachusetts. A team of about a dozen agents quietly spent six or seven weeks with the records. This probe remained confidential and was not leaked to either McCarthy or Surine.

In late December 1950 a young Maine schoolteacher named Thomas Stotler paid a visit to his aunt, who was the caretaker of Carter's summer place in Lee. In the barn across from the Carter home he stumbled upon the institute's dead files. Thinking them of extreme value, he made a collect call to Senator McCarthy's office in Washington. He breathlessly shared the news of his discovery with Surine and offered assistance in smuggling the documents off of the property. On January 4, 1951, Surine telephoned Stotler in Portland, Maine, and discussed plans for the clandestine operation. He then traveled to New York to make arrangements with J. B. Matthews for photostating the documents. In late January and early February, Surine made two secret trips to Carter's farm. On the second visit he bribed a custodian and removed the locked cabinets to Matthews' office in the Hearst magazine building in New York. By February 3 over 1,800 documents had been filmed. Surine did not know that his moves had been observed carefully by HUAC investigators, who were also aware of the I.P.R. files. The congressmen and staff members of HUAC were by this time increasingly jealous of McCarthy's publicity and decided to put a stop to this new bid for headlines.

When McCarthy and Mundt saw a selection of the documents they were quickly convinced that the I.P.R. dead files contained proof of the State Department's "sell-out" in Asia. Word of Surine's daring deeds spread to a number of Joe's friends, and one of them, the eccentric George Sokolsky, telephoned Edward Carter and told him what had gone on. He also informed Robert Morris that news of the documents was all over Washington. Then a HUAC investigator arrived at Matthews' door with a subpoena for all of the I.P.R. materials.

Surine and Matthews panicked; Surine's actions alone possibly involved, among other things, bribery, breaking and entering, and interstate transportation of stolen property. While McCarthy attempted to cajole HUAC leaders, Surine spirited the documents back to the Carter barn, thus avoiding the subpoena. He and his allies then got the McCarran Committee to issue a subpoena for the papers. On February 7 Surine, Stotler, and McCarran committee investigator Frank Schroeder seized the files legally and drove them through a blinding snowstorm to New York, where they were met by a convoy provided by the Treasury Department.

The headlines were sensational: RED PROBERS SEIZE "LATTIMORE" FILES IN FARM RAID. PROBERS PROMISE FULL STUDY OF SEIZED FILES. DARING RAID NETS I.P.R. FILES. "The files were under guard over the weekend in the Judiciary Committee's rooms here in the Senate Office Building," said one story in *The New York Times*. "Locks on doors were changed as a safeguard that they would not be disturbed." McCarran chortled that his committee had issued the subpoena because the documents were "relevant" to its inquiry. William Holland, the institute's secretary-general, indignantly declared that the organization did not object to "any properly accredited agency" using its files "provided they are used properly." He also noted that the FBI had already studied them.

Karl Mundt soon earned more headlines by leaking the story that he and McCarthy had previously seen the papers and contending that the documents indicated that Moscow had contributed $2,500 to the I.P.R. (Holland explained that the sum had been part of a $12,000 contribution made by the Russian Council of the institute while it was a member from 1935 through 1939. Other councils made similar payments during these years; the United States Council contributed $18,000 in 1935 alone.) Newspapers also carried the story that Senator McCarthy had supplied the tip to McCarran investigators for their "surprise raid." Beaming, Joe later told reporters that the Carter barn had been "crammed with documents," and added, "I succeeded in—I don't like to use the word 'stealing'—let's say I 'borrowed' the documents." For the next few years he would shock audiences around the country by showing them photographs of the remodeled interior of the barn and contending that instead of being a home for harmless bovines it was in reality a center for Russian espionage.[13]

The McCarran Committee was to make much of the seized documents. Hearings on the I.P.R. ran from July 25, 1951, to June 20, 1952, and throughout the proceedings, news releases, tips, and leaks to the press tended to support McCarthy's tales of espionage and treason. On the eve of the G.O.P. national convention, the committee issued a highly partisan final report that concluded that the net result of I.P.R. activities had been "to serve international Communist interests and to affect adversely the interests of the United States." While scrutinizing the I.P.R., the McCarran Committee also held hearings on: subversive aliens in the United States; Communist tactics in controlling youth organizations; subversive infiltration of radio, television, and the entertainment industry; subversive control of the Distributive, Processing and Office Workers of America; subversive infiltration in the telegraph industry; subversive influence in the Dining Car and Railroad Food Workers Union; unauthorized travel of subversives behind the Iron Curtain on United States passports; Communist propaganda activities in the United States; subversive control of the United Public Workers of America; and espionage activities of personnel attached to embassies and consulates under Soviet domination in the United States. The barrage of headlines generated by the committee throughout 1951 and 1952 contributed significantly to the perpetuation of the second Red Scare and to the popularity of Joe McCarthy.

During these prosperous months Joe enjoyed telling a private joke to friends about Dean Acheson. It seemed that the Secretary of State died and entered hell, where he was placed up to his armpits in fecal matter. Resigned to his fate, Acheson sighed, "Well, I guess I'm safe, so long as I can keep my head and shoulders above all this stuff." Suddenly a voice from heaven declared, "Wait until Joe McCarthy comes by in his speedboat."[14]

After the elections of 1950, the Administration sought to counteract the prosperity enjoyed by McCarthy and his allies by supporting a proposal discussed by the President, White House officials, and Democratic congressional leaders in late June and delayed by political considerations and the outbreak of the Korean War. The President's Commission on Internal Security and Individual Rights was to be composed of distinguished citizens who would investigate and report on the government's loyalty program. Members of the President's staff and others were confident that the results of the bipartisan probe would restore public trust in the program and expose the fraudulence of much right-wing rhetoric.

Truman offered the chairmanship of the presidentially appointed commission to Herbert Hoover in late November. (Earlier he had named Republican Seth Richardson as chairman of the Subversive Activities Control Board and appointed Hoover's conservative friend Hiram Bingham as Richardson's successor on the Loyalty Review Board.) The former Chief Executive swiftly declined, no doubt because of his adherence to the G.O.P. "party line" on the Reds-in-government issue. On January 4, 1951, the President made the offer to Admiral of the Fleet Chester W. Nimitz, a war hero and a political neutral. The retired admiral accepted a few days later. On January 23 Truman established the Nimitz Commission by executive order and named eight prominent men and women to the body. At the commission's first meeting in February the President said, "I have the utmost confidence in the manner in which the commission is set up. I have very great confidence in your chairman, and always have had. I am anxious that this job be done in the manner that will stop witch-hunting and give us the facts."

Several right-wing leaders, of course, were less than eager to sanction an objective appraisal of the loyalty programs. George Sokolsky contended that the idea for the commission was conceived by Communists and fellow travelers. Senator Ferguson was convinced that the new panel was an effort to undercut the McCarran Committee. McCarran, despite a personal plea from the President, refused to move through his Judiciary Committee a normally routine request for special legislation to exempt commission members and employees from conflict-of-interest laws. These laws severely restricted the employment of commission staff members. Attorneys, for example, would be barred from having business dealings with the federal government for two years after completing their official duties, a ban that could prove very costly to successful lawyers. McCarran's tactic proved effective, and after several months of effort the Administration conceded defeat. The Nimitz Commission was revoked by executive order in November.

Ironically, the commission's sole contribution as a body won the applause of McCarran, McCarthy, and others of similar bent. All but one of the commission members informally sanctioned a request by the Loyalty

Review Board to change the basic loyalty standard from "on all the evidence, reasonable grounds exist for belief that the person involved is disloyal" to "a reasonable doubt as to the loyalty of the person involved." Truman approved the alteration in late April by executive order, despite serious misgivings by some White House staff members. Executive Order 10241, a further attempt to strengthen the loyalty program's credibility and placate congressional critics, greatly disturbed civil libertarians. The new standard was extremely broad and ambiguous, it placed a greater burden of proof on the suspect, and it freed the loyalty board of having to show present disloyalty. The Loyalty Review Board, under the aggressive leadership of Hiram Bingham, a self-proclaimed "old-fashioned conservative Republican," swiftly applied its new weapon to the 565 cases then under consideration, reopened cases, and expanded its "post-audits" of decisions by departmental boards. By March 1952, 2,756 of the 9,300 employees who had been cleared under the old standard were again under scrutiny.[15]

Several targets of McCarthy's wrath were soon under fire. Stephen Brunauer was suspended by the Navy Department, pending a security investigation. Convinced of his impending dismissal, he resigned in June. The State Department suspended his wife and ultimately fired her as a security risk. China Hand John Paton Davies was suspended by the department in June 1951, pending hearings on security charges. Foreign correspondent Harold R. Isaacs moaned, "Dean Acheson has not broken under fire but he has bent considerably." Davies was cleared, reinvestigated, and cleared again, only to be grilled by the McCarran Committee and threatened with a perjury indictment. O. Edmund Clubb, Jr., director of the State Department's Office of China Affairs, was suspended with Davies, following an appearance before HUAC. He was recommended for dismissal on security grounds, cleared by Secretary of State Acheson, and reassigned to the Division of Historical Research. He chose to retire rather than accept the demotion. In December the department fired John Stewart Service, in response to the Loyalty Review Board's finding that there was a "reasonable doubt" as to his loyalty. The decision was based on the *Amerasia* case of 1945.[16]

The suspensions of Davies and Clubb had prompted McCarthy to ask publicly why similar action had not been taken against Ambassador-at-Large Philip Jessup and John Carter Vincent, now consul general at Tangiers. He claimed to have received from Hiram Bingham a list of twenty-nine employees, including Jessup and Vincent, whose cases had been reopened on security grounds, and he threatened to make the names public unless all twenty-nine were immediately barred from "secret materials." Challenged by the State Department, he read a list on the Senate floor. The twenty-six names he presented on August 9 came from the Lee list and, by his own admission, had been given to the Tydings Committee a year earlier. According to the State Department, the McCarthy list included two persons who no longer worked for the department, fourteen who had been cleared by the department loyalty board, and thirteen cases still under review. It was clear that Joe was principally interested in smearing those on his list and condemning the State Department Loyalty Board, which, he predicted sarcastically, would clear all concerned. *The New York Times* commented in an editorial, "In defiance of every American tradition of decency and fair play he is willing to destroy reputations by publicly denouncing individuals even while their investigations, perhaps founded on nothing more than idle gossip, are actually under way."[17]

When Service was fired, Joe shrugged and said that the China Hand was "only one of many rotten apples in the barrel," and he renewed his demand for the removal of Acheson. It should have been clear to the Administration that Senator McCarthy could not be placated.[18]

Not everything went Joe's way during these months of triumph, however. In December 1950 he was linked with several right-wing crackpots and anti-Semites in a shameful effort to destroy the reputation of Anna M. Rosenberg, forty-nine, a prominent New York manpower and public relations expert long associated with New Deal liberalism.

On November 9 the Defense Department announced that Secretary of Defense Marshall had recommended Mrs. Rosenberg as Assistant Secretary of Defense. Marshall needed assistance with pressing manpower problems caused by the Korean War and was delighted by Mrs. Rosenberg's reluctant willingness to make a considerable financial sacrifice to assume the duties.

The next day, Fulton Lewis, Jr., told his radio audience that Mrs. Rosenberg had once been a member of the Communist-run John Reed Club. His charge was based on data from the Dies Committee, provided by J. B. Matthews, referring to an "Anna Rosenberg." Shortly, Matthews prepared and apparently distributed all over Washington a nine-page sheet linking Mrs. Rosenberg with four Communist-controlled organizations. It was later revealed that he firmly believed that the Anna Rosenberg mentioned by the Dies Committee was George Marshall's choice for Assistant Secretary of Defense. Matthews' charges were soon included in an anti-Semitic tabloid called *Common Sense*. A wealthy New Yorker and self-styled "excommunicated Jew" named Benjamin H. Freedman later admitted distributing 25,000 copies of the sheet, including one to each name in the

Congressional Directory. Also contributing to the ruckus, among others, was Dr. Marjorie Shearon, an ultraconservative polemicist and former Republican National Committee employee who had a long history of emotional disorders and would be described by Sen. James E. Murray as "an hysterical, psychopathic, and completely untrustworthy individual whose testimony is deserving of absolutely no credence whatsoever."

When the thirteen-man Armed Services Committee met on November 29 to consider the nomination, Mrs. Rosenberg displayed her impressive credentials and explained that she was not the Anna Rosenberg cited by the Dies Committee. "I asked the postmaster, Mr. Goldman, of New York, to let me know how many Anna Rosenbergs there were in New York, and at that time there were forty-six of them. My name is Anna M. Rosenberg, and I have very carefully always used that name." She denied all associations noted by Lewis and Matthews, denounced her reputed support of "socialized medicine," and stoutly proclaimed her patriotism. The session lasted only an hour and ten minutes, and the senators voted unanimously to confirm the nomination.

The swift confirmation exacerbated the hostilities of those opposed to Mrs. Rosenberg. Benjamin Freedman flew from New York to Washington and consulted with Mississippi Democratic congressman John E. Rankin, an outspoken racist and anti-Semite who would soon condemn Mrs. Rosenberg on the floor of the House. Rankin telephoned Gerald L. K. Smith, a notorious hater of Jews and a leader of the lunatic Right, who was in town organizing a campaign of his own against the Rosenberg nomination. Freedman and Smith discussed the matter over lunch and decided to join forces.

Freedman returned to New York and, through his attorney, met Ralph De Sola, a forty-two-year-old unemployed "microfilm technician" and former circulation manager for Alfred Kohlberg's *Freeman* magazine. De Sola had been a Communist from 1934 to 1937 and a member of the John Reed Club. He told Freedman that he had seen Anna Rosenberg—the same woman whose photograph was currently in the newspapers—at several meetings of the club and had been introduced to her. His Communist party sponsor, he said, had described Mrs. Rosenberg as a Communist and claimed that she had passed on the appointments of Harry Hopkins and other New Deal figures "who were notoriously liberal in their hiring of known Communists . . ." Freedman obtained a signed statement from De Sola and then called on J. B. Matthews at his New York penthouse. The veteran researcher was aghast to learn of the vote by the Armed Services Committee and urged Freedman to consult the FBI's file on Mrs. Rosenberg, which, he said confidently, would support all of the allegations made against her.

Armed with this new evidence, Freedman hastened back to Washington on December 4 and began calling on congressmen, including Senators Richard Russell and Lyndon B. Johnson of the Armed Services Committee, to demand that the confirmation hearings be reopened. In Congressman Rankin's office he dictated a memorandum of the charges made by De Sola and Matthews and distributed copies all over Capitol Hill.

McCarthy was undoubtedly aware of the charges made against Mrs. Rosenberg from the start, being very close to both Fulton Lewis, Jr., and J. B. Matthews. He was quick to believe the worst about the nominee, if only because she had been hand-picked by George Marshall, and asked G.O.P. floor leader Wherry to block a unanimous consent agreement. He may also have been aware of Don Surine's decision to visit New York and check out Ralph De Sola's testimony. If true, the Rosenberg nomination might have the makings of another Hiss case.

Surine telephoned Ed Nellor and asked him to come along. "I've got a hot one this time," he said exuberantly. On the way to the airport, Surine told Nellor that he had to stop at the Congressional Hotel for a minute to pick up an address. He did not say from whom. A short time later, in the airplane, Surine confided to his friend that he had just called on Gerald L. K. Smith, who had given him De Sola's address and a letter of introduction. Surine had called Freedman earlier, and he had required a letter from Smith before either he or De Sola would grant an interview. Smith's letter read:

> Dear Mr. Freedman:
> Congratulations on the terrific job you are doing in helping to keep the Zionist Jew Anna M. Rosenberg from becoming the dictator of the Pentagon. This is to introduce two gentlemen who are helping us in this fight. One is the bearer of this note. I understand he is Mr. Neller [sic], the chief aide to Mr. Fulton Lewis. Mr. Lewis and Mr. Nellor should be treated very kindly. You should give them any information that will help them, because Mr. Lewis is doing a magnificent job in the Rosenberg matter.
> Please destroy this upon reading it.
> P.S. The bearer and Mr. Neller [sic] are flying up.

Nellor was appalled to learn of Surine's contact with the infamous demagogue, however brief. If word of the visit got out, it could be extremely damaging to McCarthy. Nellor's fears were quickly realized, for a hotel employee leaked the story to Drew Pearson, who transformed it into headlines charging that Senator McCarthy was anti-Semitic. Before long he would obtain and publish a copy of Smith's letter to buttress the allegation. (Joe, accompanied by George Sokolsky, later met with officials of the Anti-Defamation League of B'nai, B'rith, denying any personal anti-Semitism.) Other liberals would tie the Smith incident to the Malmedy hearings, confident that the evidence of Joe's fascism was now certain.

Surine and Nellor interviewed Freedman on the evening of December 5. "We got a good hour's lecture on anti-Semitism," Nellor later testified before the Senate Armed Services Committee. Supplied with a card from Freedman, the two then called on De Sola, some time after midnight. De Sola identified a 1936 photograph of Mrs. Rosenberg as the woman he had met two years earlier and discussed his charges against her. Nellor didn't trust De Sola, but he listened to his story and passed it along to Fulton Lewis, Jr., who broadcast its details and boasted of Nellor's interview.

The pressure was such by this time that the Senate Armed Services Committee decided to reopen the hearings. De Sola and Freedman were summoned as witnesses and traveled together to Washington. Responding to an invitation by Surine, they went directly to McCarthy's office to leave their coats. When this fact became known, the senator's opponents interpreted it as further evidence of his direct involvement in the Rosenberg case. In truth, McCarthy was not in when De Sola and Freedman called, and he was never to meet or speak to either man.

The committee held seven hearings, from December 5 through 14. The case against Mrs. Rosenberg swiftly crumbled. Ralph De Sola turned out to be an unstable person and an unreliable witness. "The danger to the Government of the United States in having a Mrs. Anna Rosenberg near the helm," he cried, "is not merely in her pro-Soviet sympathies and affiliations and her ability to pack the Pentagon with her Moscow-indoctrinated mob, but in the entire set of ideas that she holds with respect to the so-called welfare state . . ." Numerous witnesses refuted De Sola's testimony, including the man who had supposedly introduced him to Anna Rosenberg. The FBI tracked down thirty-five others who De Sola claimed would corroborate his testimony. They discovered that none did. On December 8 De Sola and Mrs. Rosenberg faced each other in the hearing room, and the accuser again identified the woman as the Anna Rosenberg he had known in the thirties. That evening, Fulton Lewis, Jr., said that the dramatic incident reminded him of the occasion "when Alger Hiss was confronted across the table with Whittaker Chambers." But before long even Lewis realized the truth of Mrs. Rosenberg's innocence and condemned those responsible for the charges.

Benjamin Freedman was an equally unpersuasive witness. He shifted the details of his story from time to time and in the end claimed (falsely) that he had torn up and flushed down the toilet his complete files on the Rosenberg case. Marjorie Shearon rambled on to the point of incoherence and had to be restrained by the committee. J. B. Matthews attempted lamely to exonerate himself and blame Freedman, whom he now denounced as "rabidly anti-Semitic." He claimed that two former FBI men had told him that an undercover agent for the FBI reported to the bureau that he had been in a Communist cell with Mrs. Rosenberg. All three men denied any knowledge of the lady. The undercover agent had never even worked for the FBI. Arnold Forster and Benjamin Epstein of the Anti-Defamation League would later observe, "Never before had those seeking to damn an individual through irresponsible charges, innuendo, and guilt by association been able to win so respectful a hearing."

A subcommittee of the Armed Services Committee, which included ultraconservative Harry P. Cain, examined Mrs. Rosenberg's FBI file and found nothing incriminating. The committee voted unanimously once again to confirm the nomination, and the full Senate soon concurred. (McCarthy voted for confirmation.) During its final session the Armed Services Committee inserted into the record samples of the correspondence that had poured in upon them in recent days. The letters and telegrams were overwhelmingly favorable to Mrs. Rosenberg and came from such notables as Senators William Benton and Stuart Symington, Bernard Baruch, James Byrnes, Dwight D. Eisenhower, and Robert M. Hutchins.

A short time later, the FBI located the Anna Rosenberg who had actually belonged to the John Reed Club in the thirties. It turned out that she had left the club to move to California before Ralph De Sola had joined, thus ruling out any chance that De Sola had made an honest mistake. Nevertheless, De Sola continued to contend that the new Assistant Secretary of Defense was the woman he knew to be a Communist. Benjamin Freedman published a newspaper of his own called *Know the Truth* to tell his side of the "Smear Bund" that had "rescued" Mrs. Rosenberg. Gerald L. K. Smith sent out a form letter denouncing Fulton Lewis, Jr., for criticizing him. "When the Jew campaign to whitewash the Rosenberg woman was fully organized," he wrote, "it was discovered that Fulton Lewis was in the thing with me up to his neck. The Jews put on the pressure and the price was 'Repudiate Smith or get off the air.' This is the Jew formula." Lewis, he contended, "has demonstrated one thing: he fears the Jews more than he hates Communism . . ."[19]

This grotesque, anti-Semitic attack upon a respected citizen was roundly condemned in the press throughout the country. McCarthy's name was often included in the cast of villains. William Evjue asked indignantly, "What is the responsibility of the Senate of the United States to investigate the part played by McCarthy, Fulton Lewis, Representative Rankin, and Gerald L. K. Smith?" But the affair was brief, and others rightfully took most of the blame. Joe quickly covered his tracks, telling reporters that his only interest in the case was in assisting the FBI. He abandoned Ralph De Sola as a witness, he said, when De Sola refused Don Surine's invitation to take a lie-detector test.[20]

Public hearings into the Maryland campaign began on February 20, 1951, and ran until April 11. The hearings generated much unfavorable publicity for McCarthy and his associates as the full story of their involvement in the successful drive against Millard Tydings came to light.

The probe was conducted by a special hearings subcommittee created by Guy Gillette, chairman of the Subcommittee on Privileges and Elections. A somewhat conservative and timid man, he named all members of his subcommittee to the new body except himself and gave the chair to freshman Democrat A. S. "Mike" Monroney of Oklahoma. Sharing the duties were newly elected Thomas C. Hennings, Democrat of Missouri, and Republicans Margaret Chase Smith of Maine and Robert C. Hendrickson of New Jersey. Ultraconservatives had a right to complain, for three of the four Monroney Committee members had been publicly critical of McCarthy in the past. Hennings had crossed swords with the Wisconsin senator during the recent elections. Mrs. Smith had authored the "Declaration of Conscience" the previous June and had called for an investigation into the Anna Rosenberg matter in her syndicated newspaper column. Hendrickson had signed the "declaration," although he had defended McCarthy on several occasions thereafter. Kenneth Wherry made a move to oust Mrs. Smith from the subcommittee, but nothing came of it.[21]

At his own request, John Marshall Butler was the first witness to appear at the subcommittee's hearings. Earlier, he had been sworn into office "without prejudice," meaning that the Senate might refuse to seat him at a later date by a simple majority vote. Clearly worried about that possibility, Butler angrily leveled charges against the subcommittee and Millard Tydings, and contended that his election campaign had been conducted honestly and effectively. "First, the question before the committee should not be the Maryland campaign alone, but the campaigns in all forty-eight States. There is no reason for singling out the State of Maryland."[22]

That afternoon, Millard Tydings took the stand and read a lengthy statement condemning the Butler campaign in detail, including the tabloid

From the Record, the misleading newspaper advertisement, the assorted financial irregularities, the importation of black orator Roscoe Simmons from Chicago, William Fedder's "midnight ride," and the attacks by Fulton Lewis, Jr. It was a convincing performance, and throughout the next several weeks Tydings' objections would be documented fully. During the fourth day of hearings, for example, Butler campaign manager Jon Jonkel revealed unreported campaign contributions totaling $27,100—probably a modest estimate. (He soon pleaded guilty to violating Maryland election laws on six counts.)[23]

McCarthy's name, of course, was mentioned frequently during the hearings. Friendly witnesses Jonkel, Robert E. Lee, Ray Kiermas, Don Surine, and Jean Kerr tried to mask the extent of his involvement in the campaign. Kiermas had obviously been coached thoroughly in advance, and his evasiveness on the stand was so blatant that Senator Smith warned him of the penalty for perjury.[24]

McCarthy was in the audience when Miss Kerr appeared before the subcommittee on April 10. Her testimony had been delayed by a broken hip suffered on December 7 while on vacation in Honolulu. (The accident occurred at the home of the head of the FBI in Honolulu. J. Edgar Hoover blamed the mishap on two agents present and angrily transferred them to less desirable climes.) Joe and Jean had unquestionably discussed her testimony in advance, and when Joe was later questioned about the Maryland campaign in a deposition he was fully supportive of his research assistant, despite her lapses into wholly unconvincing forgetfulness.[25]

Ironically, McCarthy did not testify before the subcommittee himself, despite receiving three invitations. He did not refuse to appear, but he made it clear that he was less than anxious to do so, and he did not specifically accept any of the invitations. Subcommittee members, obviously wishing to avoid entanglement with the Wisconsin brawler, were not inclined to press the matter, and the hearings closed without Joe's testimony on the Maryland campaign. The omission damaged the credibility of the case against McCarthy, who soon claimed, "I was available to the committee at any and all times and so notified the committee."[26]

Several months of delay followed the conclusion of the public hearings on April 11. During this interim the Republican Committee on Committees placed McCarthy on the parent Rules Committee, a not overly subtle warning to the nervous senators on the subcommittee against a harsh report. In July Gillette threatened to resign as chairman of the Privileges and Elections Subcommittee, complaining about the inability of Monroney and his colleagues to conclude the Maryland investigation. Hendrickson too threatened to walk out or write his own report. At a meeting of the parent Rules Committee, Hennings placed the blame for the delay on Gillette's failure to provide him with legal counsel. Gillette calmed down, rectified the oversight, and on August 2 joined all of the subcommittee members in signing a final report.[27]

The report condemned the Butler campaign in no uncertain terms. It contrasted the "front-street" campaign waged by the candidate himself with the "back-street" effort "conducted by non-Maryland outsiders," which it labeled "of a form and pattern designed to undermine and destroy the public faith and confidence in the basic American loyalty of a well-known figure." The Maryland campaign, the report declared, "brought into sharp focus certain campaign tactics and practices that can best be characterized as one destructive of fundamental American principles. The subcommittee unreservedly denounces, condemns, and censures these tactics."

The tabloid, the senators said, disregarded "simple decency and common honesty." Its composite photo was a "shocking abuse of the spirit and intent of the First Amendment." The misrepresentation of its sponsorship was a violation of federal and state laws. Butler's campaign financing was also strongly criticized, and the subcommittee announced that it was turning over its evidence to the Department of Justice for possible action. The report largely accepted William Fedder's account of his "midnight ride," and sharply censured the testimony and activities of Don Surine. The subcommittee especially questioned Surine's inaccurate account of his departure from the FBI and suggested that the issue (first raised by Tydings) be examined by the Justice Department.

In order to achieve a unanimous endorsement of the report, however, several compromises had to be made. John Marshall Butler was only mildly chided for his supposedly slight knowledge of elements within the "back-street" campaign, and the subcommittee did not recommend his unseating. The report took no position on the activities of Fulton Lewis, Jr. It praised recently deceased Roscoe Conklin Simmons and slightly understated Jean Kerr's involvement in the campaign. Above all, it soft-pedaled Senator McCarthy's personal contributions to the Butler election drive. Joe was scolded for making his staff available to Butler and for originally suggesting the tabloid; at one point the report declared, "From the testimony it appears Senator McCarthy was a leading and potent force in the campaign against Senator Tydings." But many references and inferences from the hearings to Joe's direct activities went unmentioned, and the report even failed to acknowledge the origin of the postcard campaign concept. The subcommittee's bland list of recommendations made no specific reference to either McCarthy or Butler.[28]

Predictably, Joe lashed out at "puny politicians" and labeled the report "an attempt to whitewash Tydings." "I am not surprised at the action of the two 'Republicans' on the committee," he said. "After all, they went on record last year approving the Tydings whitewash and condemning me for getting rough with the Communists." Pat McCarran leaped to his colleague's assistance the same day by telling reporters that his Internal Security Subcommittee had discovered a Communist conspiracy "to take all of Asia" and that hearings would soon show "how this conspiracy is operating today."[29]

The Maryland election report was accepted shortly by the full Rules Committee on a nine-to-three vote. Smith and Hendrickson joined the Democrats, while McCarthy, Jenner, and Wherry voted no. Word leaked out that during one closed-door committee session McCarthy gave Wherry a tongue-lashing for suggesting that the senators present should protect one of their own. "I don't need your protection and I don't want it," Joe allegedly snapped. "What I resent most in this report is the reference to a little girl who works in my office," meaning, of course, Jean Kerr, whose various campaign activities were described by the subcommittee. "There are a lot of small, evil-minded people in this town," he continued, "who are trying to smear this girl just because she works for me. I'm not going to stand for that. And I don't need anyone on this committee to protect me. I can take care of myself." It was getting dangerous even to be Joe's friend.[30]

Further headlines hostile to McCarthy appeared on February 12, 1951, involving the arrest in Switzerland of a twenty-three-year-old American black named Charles Davis. Davis had been arrested in November on espionage charges and was now telling authorities that he was hired by an American detective in Paris, employed by Senator McCarthy, to spy on State Department personnel. Joe denied employing Davis but acknowledged that he had received information from him, which was turned over to the FBI and made available to the C.I.A. He also admitted that he had an agent in Paris. Several anti-McCarthy newspaper editors made the most of Davis's charge; William Evjue contended that the senator had "a private gestapo."[31]

At his trial in October, Davis told a five-man Swiss tribunal that he had been hired by John E. Farrand, "one of McCarthy's emissaries," to report on social and official relations of American diplomats in Switzerland, in particularly John Carter Vincent, former U.S. minister in Bern. On November 4, Davis said, he sent a telegram to Vincent stating, "Send information on Alex Jordan," and signed it "Emile Stampfi." Jordan was an American black student of left-wing proclivities, and Stampfi was a Swiss

Communist leader. It was clear that Davis had tried to frame Vincent by implying that he was a Red. The defendant also testified that he had been in direct contact with McCarthy and received money from him. Davis was convicted in part for spying on U.S. diplomatic personnel in Switzerland on behalf of Senator McCarthy and was sentenced to eight months in jail and expelled from the country.[32]

The next day William Benton, on the warpath against McCarthy, quoted a letter to reporters from Deputy Undersecretary of State Carlisle H. Humelsine describing Davis as a homosexual and onetime Communist. "Here we have an admitted homosexual ex-Communist convicted as a personal spy on Senator McCarthy's payroll," Benton crowed, "trying to frame an American diplomat—John Carter Vincent—with a fake telegram linking him to Communists." The story was "shocking," Benton said, "indicating that Senator McCarthy's pattern of conduct extends to his employees and that their unethical acts are countenanced by him." Although the Davis matter was later dropped by Senate investigators pursuing Benton's allegations and was forgotten by historians, a careful examination of the facts reveals that the Connecticut senator actually had something of a case against McCarthy.[33]

Charles Davis was born in Dallas in 1927, grew up in Los Angeles, and became a Communist before he was twenty years old. A deeply disturbed young man, he enlisted in the Navy "for the purpose of propagandizing service personnel," he said later, and was dishonorably discharged within a year as an admitted homosexual. He returned to California and became a correspondent for a Communist newspaper.

In September 1949 the left-wing California Labor School sent Davis to Europe to participate in some Communist youth activities. Within a few days of his arrival at Le Havre, France, he called upon the American embassy in Paris asking for money. While in France he attended several Communist meetings and gave a few speeches. He was soon arrested in Lausanne for stealing an overcoat. In November 1949 he turned up at the American consulate in Geneva, offering to switch sides and provide information on local Reds. Vice-Consul S. R. Tyler became interested in Davis and suggested that he maintain his left-wing connections and report regularly to the consulate. For the next several months Davis dutifully informed on his friends, hoping in vain that Tyler would assist him financially.

In late May or early June, Davis told Tyler that he badly needed money. According to Davis, Tyler suggested that he contact Senator McCarthy, who might be happy to pay for information. On June 5 Davis wrote to the senator, congratulating him on his anti-Communist activities, telling of his left-wing associations and personal repudiation of Communist dogma, and offering his services. The letter apparently came to Don Surine, and he brought it to McCarthy's attention. Both men were clearly interested in Davis's proposal. Joe told Tom Coleman later that month that he was going to send Robert Morris to Paris, where Davis was then living, "and perhaps bring back with him what I consider potentially one of the most valuable witnesses we have had."[34] Instead, Morris suggested a friend of his living in Paris, thirty-two-year-old attorney John E. Farrand, to serve as Davis's contact. Joe replied to Davis on August 15:

> I received your letter and thank you very much for your interest in my efforts to expose Communists and subversives in our government. You mention in your letter documents and facts concerning the activities of certain American citizens in Europe. I would be very much interested in receiving from you any or all of the documents you may care to furnish to me, and also, I would appreciate receiving some background facts as to your identity. In the event you do not desire to send the documents to me, I would appreciate your describing the nature of such documents and facts which you have in your possession. In the event you do desire to turn the documents over to a personal representative of mine, I am sure this can be arranged.

While awaiting the senator's response to his proposal, Davis struck up a relationship with members of the American embassy staff in Paris, who provided him with a little money in exchange for reports on his Leftist associates. From July 25 until early November he received a small amount of additional cash for written and oral information about Communists from a legal attaché of the embassy named Jack West, later revealed to be an FBI agent.

On September 9 Davis replied to McCarthy, saying that he was "overjoyed" to receive his letter ("I now hope to be with you exclusively...") and asking for money. The frantic tone of the letter, plus its obvious exaggerations, should have alerted McCarthy and Surine to the instability of the author.

> At the moment I have been in Paris contacting all delegates to Prague from America and Americans in Paris who are Communists and in the French party. The documents are

> copies sent to the top CP man in Switzerland, also some
> papers on atomic theory and American troop movements in
> Germany. . . . Will you telegraph me immediately for these
> papers are top-rank material and can sink all persons under-
> ground in the CP of the USA.

Instead, perhaps encouraged by FBI man West, the senator continued to
show strong interest, and he told Davis (in a letter Joe later tried to conceal)
that he would be contacted by Farrand.

Davis and Farrand met in Paris in late September. The attorney told
Davis that McCarthy was interested primarily in information about Communists in high places, and in particular evidence about John Carter
Vincent and John Stewart Service. Farrand gave Davis between $200 and
$250 which he had received by cable from McCarthy, money used to pay
Davis's hotel bills and travel expenses. The attorney said later that he met
with Davis three times, from late September into early November, finally
realizing that the young man could not come up with anything on Vincent
or Service. Probably on his own, Davis then devised the scheme for the fake
telegram, hoping to impress Farrand and McCarthy. (It was addressed to
"John Vincent Carter," and Stampfi's name was omitted from the telegram
itself.)

Eager for closer ties to McCarthy, Davis called the senator by trans-
Atlantic telephone on November 9, reaching him, after some difficulty, at
home. Joe recognized his caller's name and quickly referred to him as
"Charlie." The two had a pleasant chat, and Joe said that another represent-
ative would be contacting Davis, since Farrand was soon to leave for the
United States. Davis did not mention the fake telegram.

A few days later Davis wrote to McCarthy again, enclosing a copy of the
telegram and appealing for funds. "Wish to act as your investigator until
you send new man here in Europe." He claimed that Vincent would be
staying with him in Geneva soon and asked for money to "have the flat
wired and all talk on tape for you." "I think we have Vincent for good if he
lives at my place," Davis boasted.

When there was no immediate reply, Davis went to the Geneva
consulate and requested travel funds. "He said he was . . . caught between
the Swiss political police on one hand and members of the local Communist
party on the other," Consul Randolph Dickens, Jr., later recalled. Davis
asserted that he had been paid by Senator McCarthy to spy on Vincent, but
he "now thought that . . . McCarthy had gone too far and he wished to get
away from his control." Dickens thought Davis "not mentally normal" and

a "pathological liar." Swiss police arrested the young American three days later.

By this time, Surine had forwarded the Davis telegram to the FBI, and McCarthy had called it to the attention of a top C.I.A. official. When news of the Davis arrest reached Joe's office, McCarthy and Surine suddenly realized their serious error and sought immediately to cut and cover up all ties with the suspect. Surine fired off a letter to Davis curtly informing him that the senator was not interested in hiring any additional investigators, thus asserting for the record that Davis had never been more than an unsuccessful job applicant. (Surine, with his FBI experience, was good at this sort of thing. When the "midnight ride" of William Fedder was investigated, he came up with a backdated memorandum to McCarthy that justified his every action. The Monroney subcommittee chose wisely to dismiss it.)[35] In later depositions, taken under oath, both McCarthy and Surine would admit to only the barest knowledge of Charles Davis and contend that they never at any time took him seriously.

Davis's mental instability was such that he told several different versions of his spy story to reporters and Senate investigators, and few took him seriously very long. He tried unsuccessfully to sell "all his files and information" to William Evjue. He further discredited himself in early 1952 by filing a fantastic $100,000 slander and breach of contract suit against McCarthy, claiming to have made an oral contract with the senator on September 25, 1949, to spy on State Department employees in Europe, and contending that he received a minimum monthly salary of $200, with bonuses ranging up to $600. He also asserted that McCarthy had sent him to Europe in the first place, giving him $400 in traveling expenses. After Joe threatened to press for a perjury investigation into conflicts in Davis's sworn statements, the law suit evaporated, and the young man dropped from sight.[36]

When the *Syracuse Post-Standard* published an editorial in October 1951 contending that Davis was "acting under orders" of McCarthy when he sent the fake telegram to Vincent, Joe filed a $500,000 suit for libel. "I decided sooner or later one of these left-wing smear articles would go so far we would have to teach them a lesson," he told a hostile attorney at his deposition, "and your paper went as far as it can, even farther than the *Daily Worker*." McCarthy won an out-of-court settlement of $12,000 in 1953 and a public apology. The editorial had no doubt been incorrect. But journalists and historians would have done well to probe the Charles Davis case a bit deeper. John Farrand, for example, fully admitted to Senate investigators his dealings with Davis as McCarthy's representative and acknowledged turning over funds to Davis sent for that purpose by McCarthy. This made Davis McCarthy's agent and employee. While no evidence links the senator to the fake telegram, he nevertheless was associated with Davis to a degree that he sought mightily to conceal and could at least be faulted for extreme gullibility and public deceit—not to mention perjury.[37]

McCarthy was in the news again as the clash between Gen. Douglas MacArthur and President Truman boiled to a head in April 1951. When G.O.P. House minority leader Joseph W. Martin, Jr., of Massachusetts read the general's famous letter challenging the authority of the Chief Executive in the Korean War, Joe leaped into the fray with extravagant praise for MacArthur and a warning against the "efforts to aid the Communists that are behind our activities in Asia." "There is no reason to doubt Mr. Truman's loyalty as an American citizen," McCarthy told an enthusiastic audience in Fort Atkinson, Wisconsin, "but it is unfortunate that he is a man of infinitely small mind and tremendous stubbornness."[38]

When the President relieved MacArthur of his command a few days later, Joe was enraged and told the Senate that he would return to Milwaukee "to discuss the fact that the midnight potency of bourbon and Benedictine may well have condemned thousands of American boys to death and may well have condemned western civilization." MacArthur, he said, was "the greatest American I know." In Milwaukee, Robert Fleming of the *Journal* managed to get into the senator's crowded hotel room prior to the speech before the Wisconsin Retail Furniture Association. While Joe was shaving, Fleming casually tossed off a few questions, hoping to obtain one of McCarthy's often extreme off-the-cuff remarks. Did the senator agree with Republicans who were calling for the President's impeachment? the reporter asked. "The son of a bitch should be impeached," Joe shot back, "but on the other hand he's not important. It's the crowd around him that causes the trouble." Fleming rushed the careless sentences to his editors, and they were included (with four revealing dashes substituted for the expletive) in the story about the speech and fired across the nation by the wire services.[39]

In the speech itself McCarthy lashed out at Truman for incompetence and drunkenness. "He is surrounded by the Jessups, the Achesons, the old Hiss crowd. These men have no hypnotic influence; most of the tragic things are done at 1:30 and 2 o'clock in the morning when they've had time to get the president cheerful." MacArthur's dismissal was a victory for the Communists, "homemade and foreign made," he cried, "a victory achieved with the aid of bourbon and Benedictine."[40]

The White House refused comment, but more than a few figures on Capitol Hill were openly angered by the wholly irresponsible indictment of the President. Democratic congressmen Pat Sutton of Tennessee and Franklin D. Roosevelt, Jr., of New York shot a telegram to McCarthy asking him to confirm or deny the hotel room quotation. "If you are quoted correctly we believe your remarks to be contemptible and beneath the dignity of a United States senator." Joe soon told the Senate somewhat sheepishly, "I was not intimating that the President was intoxicated. I do not think he is a heavy drinker. I honestly do not think he is." He did not deny Fleming's hotel room quotation, however. "I may say that, in referring to the President, I was also quoted as using one of the President's pet terms."[41]

Actually, McCarthy's attack on the President had been only slightly more extreme than the highly partisan statements made by other Republicans at the time. Senator Taft and Congressman Martin were among those reported to be discussing the impeachment of Truman, Acheson, and "possibly others"; Taft spoke of the new "appeasement." William Jenner said on the Senate floor, "We must cut this whole cancerous conspiracy out of our government at once. Our only choice is to impeach President Truman and find out who is the secret invisible government which has so cleverly led our country down the road to destruction." Senator Nixon proposed that the Senate censure the President, likening MacArthur's dismissal to appeasement of the Reds. The Republican Policy Committee unanimously approved a declaration asking whether "the Truman-Acheson-Marshall triumverate" was preparing for a "super-Munich" in Asia. The committee's consultant on national defense, Brigadier General Julius Klein, asserted that the United States had not been so humiliated since Bataan and suggested that the Kremlin fire a 21-gun salute in celebration.[42]

If McCarthy suffered any political damage by his outbursts in Milwaukee, it was quickly forgotten as the nation cheered MacArthur's triumphant return to the United States, arranged by the G.O.P. Two-thirds of those polled by the Gallup organization said that they disapproved of MacArthur's dismissal. Some 60,000,000 Americans watched on television as the old soldier delivered his emotional self-defense before a joint session of Congress on April 19. Joe soon told an audience that it was "actually the greatest speech which I have ever heard or hope to hear," delivered by "the greatest military leader and strategist since even before the days of Genghis Khan." Truman's popularity plummeted in the polls to a record low for a president.[43]

Joe made headlines again in mid-June by delivering on the floor of the

United States Senate for two hours and forty-five minutes a harangue that was part of a 169-page, 60,000 word attack against Gen. George C. Marshall. The Secretary of Defense was bitterly assailed as a "mysterious, powerful" figure who, along with Dean Acheson, was part of "a conspiracy on a scale so immense as to dwarf any previous such venture in the history of man. A conspiracy of infamy so black that, when it is finally exposed, its principals shall be forever deserving of the maledictions of all honest men."[44]

Liberal newspapers howled their derision, and Herblock had a field day. Adlai Stevenson, the Democratic governor of Illinois, referred to McCarthyism as a "hysterical form of putrid slander" and thought it "one of the most unwholesome manifestations of our current disorders." *Collier's* magazine, in a full-page editorial, told its 3,000,000 readers that the McCarthy speech set "a new high for irresponsibility," and it urged Republican leaders to disassociate themselves from the "senseless and vicious charges." William Benton thought the speech evidence of either outright lying or of an "unsound mind." Predictably, the Far Right was ecstatic. Columnist John O'Donnell of the *New York Daily News* thought the speech "a coldly documented, carefully edited and restrained indictment in which damning evidence marched steadily on the heels of accusation, where lie and reputation came face to face." The *Washington Times Herald* dismissed McCarthy's critics as the "kept columnists and newspaper errand boys of the Pendergast mobsters."[45]

Marshall, of course, had long been a favorite target of the China Lobby and the Right wing of the G.O.P. In 1950 he had been called an "appeaser" by minority leader Martin and "a living lie" and a "front man for traitors" by William Jenner. Twenty Republican senators tried to thwart his appointment as Secretary of Defense, and eleven voted against his confirmation. McCarthy too had been an outspoken opponent, being particularly aggravated by the general's defense of Acheson, Lattimore, Jessup, and Anna Rosenberg. In April 1950 he had called him "completely unfit" and "completely incompetent" and charged that as Secretary of State Marshall had "boned up" on China by reading the works of Owen Lattimore. That December he had demanded the General's dismissal from the Truman cabinet. McCarthy's wrath was greatly intensified by Marshall's support of the decision to remove MacArthur.[46]

Two days before delivering his Senate speech, Joe had written a letter to each member of Congress announcing his intention to attack Marshall, and he had likewise alerted the press. The galleries were packed when Joe took the rostrum on June 14. (Only a few senators, three at one point, bothered to attend.) Don Surine and Jean Kerr sat on a couch at the rear of the chamber, Miss Kerr's crutches lying between them. As the senator droned on, for an hour, then two, the audience began to thin, and finally even Surine and Kerr left. Before the two made their exit, however, Joe interrupted his speech to give credit to his staff. "I believe most of them are in the gallery today. I salute them; they worked 18, 19, and 20 hours a day in getting the document together."

Later, McCarthy consistently took personal credit for the speech. In an address before an American Legion post in Oconto, Wisconsin, on July 1 he referred to "the history of Marshall as compiled by myself . . ." When the speech was published late in the year in revised form as a book entitled *America's Retreat from Victory, The Story of George Catlett Marshall,* McCarthy was represented to be the author. In an introduction he described at length how he was led to undertake the study of Marshall's life and career, portraying himself as the sole researcher and writer. During a September deposition for the Drew Pearson lawsuit, however, Joe refused to answer when asked directly who had assisted with the research for the speech. Before his attorney, Edward Bennett Williams, could caution him, Joe blurted out, "I can hardly say that I am the author of it."[47]

Anyone who was at all acquainted with McCarthy knew that he could not possibly have written the speech. It was sophisticated, detailed, and scholarly. Its sources included works by Winston Churchill, Cordell Hull, Henry L. Stimson, Robert Sherwood, Sumner Welles, and Hanson Baldwin—books Joe had probably never even seen, let alone read. Privately, Joe would have roared at the very thought of writing: "I am reminded of a wise and axiomatic utterance in this connection by the great Swedish chancellor Oxenstiern, to his son departing on the tour of Europe. He said: 'Go forth my son and see with what folly the affairs of mankind are governed.'" One observer, Douglass Cater, thought that McCarthy's slightly stumbling, emotionless presentation on the Senate floor bore evidence that Joe was reading the speech for the first time. Richard Rovere later surmised that the piece had been written by revisionist historians of the "Georgetown school" such as Charles Callin Tansill and Stefan Possony.[48]

The principal author was actually Forrest Davis, a Washington columnist and editorial writer for the *Cincinnati Enquirer* and a former staff writer for the *Saturday Evening Post.* By the time of his death in 1962 Davis had published more than a dozen books, including *The Atlantic System,* an analysis of Anglo-American relations from 1890 to World War II; and a history of President Franklin D. Roosevelt's wartime policy. Davis was deeply conservative, and he counted Senator Taft, William F. Buckley,

Jr., and John Chamberlain among his close friends. In the early 1950s he was associated with Alfred Kohlberg's magazine *The Freeman*. (Kohlberg distributed a copy of *America's Retreat from Victory* to every daily newspaper in the United States.)[49]

As Davis told the story to Buckley, he and McCarthy were at a party together one evening at the home of Freda Utley and got into a conversation about Communist infiltration. Davis had had too much to drink, and at one point he produced part of a history he was writing under contract to a publisher and handed it to the senator, telling him that if he really wanted to know about the Reds this was what he needed. Joe was flabbergasted and delighted by the manuscript and turned it over to Don Surine and Jean Kerr, who made additions and alterations, giving the impression that their employer was the author of the entire piece. John Chamberlain later noted, "The diplomatic scholar in Forrest moaned to himself—but the Davis who always remained loyal to his friends never complained publicly about what had been done to his original document."[50]

McCarthy did not deliver the full speech to the Senate. He grew weary after almost three hours of speaking and found himself almost alone in the cavernous chamber. As the dinner hour approached he began to skip pages, and finally he relinquished the floor, inserting the remainder of the address in the *Congressional Record*. Some reporters, who possessed copies of the document, had already filed their stories.

Marshall refused to comment on McCarthy's performance. He had learned years earlier to ignore such partisan twaddle and knew that responsible observers of America's postwar foreign policy would assess the senator's speech for what it was and quickly dismiss it. (Which they did.) The leadership of the Democratic Party also remained silent; when one top Democrat was asked if the Administration planned a reply to the speech he asked, "Do you think it requires one?" The State Department, however, responded by releasing extracts from the same books cited in the Davis-McCarthy manuscript that warmly praised General Marshall.[51]

Stewart Alsop thought it a mistake to dismiss Joe McCarthy too lightly: "His charge that Marshall is implicated in 'infamy so black as to dwarf any previous such venture in the history of man' is so ridiculous that it may seem silly to discuss it seriously. Yet a man who has proved that he can use demonstrable falsehoods to devastating political effect cannot be entirely laughed off." One of Joe's colleagues, William Benton, was now of the opinion that the junior senator from Wisconsin had become a national menace, and he soon determined to take steps against him.[52]

On August 6, three days after the Monroney subcommittee released its report on the "back street" campaign in Maryland, Benton told the Senate that McCarthy should resign. "By resigning in the face of such an indictment, he can take the only step now open to him to make amends to the people of Wisconsin, to his predecessors in the seat he now occupies, and to his colleagues in the Senate." As an alternative, Benton introduced an unprecedented and unexpected resolution requesting an investigation by the Rules Committee into McCarthy's activities to determine whether or not the Wisconsinite should be expelled from the Senate. Joe released an angry statement denouncing Benton as "Connecticut's mental midget" and charging him with having "established himself as the hero of every Communist and crook in and out of government."[53]

Reporters noticed that not a single senator entered the fray on Benton's behalf. McCarthy was immune to serious attack, said *Newsweek* magazine, because of the fear he instilled in members of the Senate, who well remembered the election results of 1950. Moreover, many congressmen were afraid that McCarthy's charges against the State Department would eventually be upheld by the McCarran Committee. Benton's resolution was expected to die "a lingering death" in committee. Joseph Harsch of the *Christian Science Monitor* reported, "Benton did what many other senators would like but never would dare to do. The fact is that the Senate is afraid of Joseph McCarthy. He is something its members don't understand." Harsch observed that many Washington insiders thought Benton "went into this thing as an innocent, walking blithely to his doom . . ." Benton confided to a friendly magazine editor that many of the professional politicians "think I am making a mistake in terms of my own political future; but I can only reply that I would rather be right than be senator."[54]

THE HENNINGS REPORT

William Burnett Benton, 51, was far from being a "mental midget." The son, grandson, and nephew of Phi Beta Kappa preachers, teachers, and scholars, he had been a top student at Yale and a recipient of a Rhodes scholarship. He became a millionaire in the advertising business during the early Depression years and in 1936 determined to devote his frenetic energy and intellectual prowess to more challenging fields. His Yale classmate Robert Maynard Hutchins hired him as a vice-president of the University of Chicago in 1937, and this led a few years later to the chairmanship of the board of Encyclopedia Britannica, Inc. "Don't try to understand Bill Benton in human terms," Hutchins was quoted as saying. "He is not a man. He is a phenomenon." In 1945 Benton became Assistant Secretary of State for Public Affairs and for two years made numerous contributions to national and international developments. In 1949 Connecticut Governor Chester Bowles, his former business partner, appointed him to the Senate seat vacated by Raymond Baldwin. (The frustrations stemming from the Malmedy hearings were in part responsible for Baldwin's resignation. Truman later called Baldwin McCarthy's first victim.) The following year, by a razor-thin majority of 1,102 votes, Benton was elected to serve the two remaining years of the term.[1]

Benton was not a member of the Senate Establishment, that coterie of powerbrokers dominated by the likes of Richard Russell of Georgia and

Carl Hayden of Arizona; he not only lacked seniority but was far too independent, outspoken, and liberal. His closest friends in the Senate, Herbert Lehman, Hubert Humphrey, and Paul Douglas, were of similar temperament. On the Senate floor Benton fervently defended the State Department and was consistently one of McCarthy's most fearless opponents. He backed the Administration's decision to dismiss MacArthur in a speech that lasted three-and-a-half hours. "I not only support President Truman's recall of General MacArthur," he said bluntly, "but I telephoned him the day before the announcement, not knowing what was coming, and urged him to make the move." On September 14, 1951, a month after he presented his resolution to investigate McCarthy, he boldly championed Dean Acheson, defying G.O.P. colleagues and needling fellow Democrats for their silence. "I naturally regret that members of my own political party have not stood up more strongly in their defense of Mr. Acheson. This disinclination on their part has in turn generated more and more irresponsible critics."[2]

Benton did not expect his resolution to produce the two-thirds vote necessary to drive McCarthy from the Senate. Senators had long been known to disapprove of motions of expulsion; from 1871 to 1947 the Subcommittee on Privileges and Elections had handled only eight expulsion and exclusion cases based on nonelectoral matters, and in no proceeding did the Senate expel or exclude one of its own. Benton thought it possible, however, to win a vote of censure, which could bear a rich dividend in 1952 when McCarthy stood for reelection. To this end he was eager to call public attention to the Maryland report, to various outrages he had witnessed on the Senate floor, and to other charges he had read about in newspapers.[3]

It was widely assumed that the Benton resolution would be filed and forgotten. Senator Gillette told reporters that he had no plans for hearings, and several other members of the subcommittee said privately that they did not favor an investigation. One encounter with McCarthy per congressional session was surely sufficient. Douglass Cater reported that while several leading Democrats conceded the merits of Benton's case, they objected to the timing of his resolution: it should have been presented in 1950, and it was now too near the upcoming election campaigns. Moreover, they stressed the importance of handling motions to expel with extreme caution.[4]

All might have gone well for Joe had he simply chosen to be silent or at least restrained for a time. But that was not in his nature. "McCarthy seems to thrive on smear warfare," Cater wrote. On August 9, undoubtedly to upstage the Rules Committee's acceptance of the Maryland election report, Joe read his list of 26 names identified as State Department employees "charged with Communist activities." This enraged Senate Majority Leader Ernest W. McFarland of Arizona, who bitterly condemned McCarthy as "a character assassin." When Joe told McFarland that he and other administration Democrats were making the Democratic Party known as "a party of Communists and crooks," the Majority Leader left the ranks of the uncommitted and fearful and turned against McCarthy, despite the fact that he was up for reelection in 1952. William Benton's longtime personal assistant, John Howe, was soon conferring with McFarland staff members.[5]

President Truman, who had been boiling about McCarthy since the Marshall speech, decided to step up his attacks on the senator at the same time. He had recently called attention to a stunt publicized throughout Wisconsin by William Evjue and nationally by Drew Pearson. On Independence Day, 1951, a young *Madison Capital Times* reporter named John Patrick Hunter went out on the streets of Madison to see if people would sign a petition containing the preamble to the Declaration of Independence and portions of the Bill of Rights. Of 112 people asked to sign, 111 refused. This was a result, the President said in a Detroit address, of "lies and slander" being spread throughout the country. Pearson was more blunt: "That is McCarthyism, a disease of fear—unreasoning fear, mortal fear, fear of ideas, fear of books, fear of the good old American right to sign a petition. And that disease is marching like a monster through the minds of its victims." Joe countered by claiming (falsely) that Cedric Parker was behind the petition and contending on the Senate floor that Parker was a Communist. "The next time President Truman wants to slander the people of my state, I want to be sure that he will not use a Communist sheet edited by a Communist city editor in order to do so."[6]

Truman chose to wage his new attack in enemy territory. In a speech dedicating the new Washington headquarters of the American Legion he lashed out at "scaremongers and hatemongers."

> Character assassination is their stock in trade. Guilt by association is their motto. They have created such a wave of fear and uncertainty that their attacks upon our liberties go almost unchallenged. Many people are growing frightened—and frightened people don't protest.

Truman called on "every American who loves his country and his freedom" to "rise up and put a stop to this terrible business." The Legionnaires, for the most part, remained silent during the speech. Robert Taft soon told reporters that he thought the President "hysterical." Sen. Homer Capehart snarled, "All he has to do to stop the honest criticism of 100 percent Americans is to clean house—sweep out the Communists and the pinks in his administration." Capehart added, "Certainly he doesn't mean that we who condemned Alger Hiss were hatemongers."

McCarthy's name was not mentioned in the speech, but Benton, in a comment to reporters, accurately nominated the Wisconsin senator as the object of Truman's attack. Joe accepted the designation and hurled a challenge at the President. "If Truman wants to make the fight against Communism—which he calls McCarthyism—an issue in the campaign, I will welcome it. It will give the people a chance to choose between Americanism or a combination of Trumanism and Communism." He then demanded and received free broadcast time from the radio networks to present a formal "reply."[7]

Two weeks after Truman's blast, Secretary of Labor Maurice J. Tobin excoriated "slanderers" during remarks delivered before the annual convention of the Veterans of Foreign Wars. Columnist William S. White contended that the Administration was planning an all-out counteroffensive against McCarthy. The speech by Tobin, a Roman Catholic, was part of the strategy, he wrote, and was aimed at the large body of McCarthy sympathizers within the Church. The message was lost on the V.F.W. delegates. They went on record demanding Dean Acheson's removal from office and cheered wildly as McCarthy told them that he would resign if a jury trial failed to sustain his charges against Acheson and Jessup. Joe brought a chorus of "oohs" and some low whistles from the audience as he repeated his well-worn charges against Gustavo Duran. "We need a change in '52, if we are to have a housecleaning," he shouted.[8]

On August 20 McCarthy read a lengthy reply to the Maryland election report on the Senate floor. Splenetic and uncompromising, the speech defended every move of the Butler campaign, condemned Senators Smith and Hendrickson for failing to resign from the Monroney subcommittee ("The issue in this investigation was practically identical to the issue involved in the Declaration of Conscience"), and repeated charges against the loyalty of Tydings, Pearson, and Acheson. So extreme was the blast that Tydings was presented as "the symbol of the whitewash and cover-up of Communists in government" and portrayed as William Fedder's employer. Joe's only criticism of the tabloid (perhaps betraying the pen of Jean Kerr) was that it was insufficiently forceful.

Both Senators Hendrickson and Smith were quickly on their feet objecting to this gratuitous attack. Smith was so angry that she again placed the Declaration of Conscience in the *Congressional Record*[9]

In an interview in the September 7 issue of *U.S. News and World Report* McCarthy boasted of taking an active part in the Maryland campaign "because I felt we had to prove to both parties that the American people were sick and tired of the dupes and stooges of the Kremlin determining our policy . . ." He accused the President of using Communist vocabulary against him and said he doubted that Truman knew what Communism was. "He perhaps thinks it's a third party." When asked about Benton's resolution, he said, "I don't think the Senate is ready to expel a senator because he tries to expose Communists."[10]

Joe's confidence in the Gillette subcommittee's quiescence was short-lived, however. His clashes with McFarland, Hendrickson, Smith, and Truman apparently riled subcommittee members to the point that they agreed shortly to set a date for a vote on whether or not to hold hearings on Benton's resolution. When word of the impending meeting reached McCarthy, he proceeded to attempt to intimidate the senators on the subcommittee.

On September 17 he wrote a public letter to Gillette saying that the proposed hearings were designed to expel him "for having exposed Communists in government." He demanded the right to cross-examine witnesses and threatened to take the issue to the full Rules Committee if he didn't get his way. The following day he proposed in another letter given to the press that Thomas Hennings disqualify himself from the subcommittee. Hennings's St. Louis law firm, Joe pointed out, represented the liberal *St. Louis Post-Dispatch.* The newspaper was soft on the Reds, he charged, because it had condemned conviction of Communist leaders under the Smith Act and had "editorialized against my anti-Communist fight along the same lines followed by the *Daily Worker.*" Moreover, one of Hennings's law partners, John Raeburn Green, had recently represented John Gates, editor of the *Daily Worker,* in a Smith Act suit before the Supreme Court. The implication was, of course, that this very action tainted Green's loyalty—and, therefore, Hennings's loyalty as well. Joe's letter concluded with the patronizing advice, "I understand, Tom, that your father has a record as a fine lawyer and jurist. May I urge that you phone him and follow his advice on whether you should insist upon taking part in this Administration-conceived version of a loyalty board for senators." This was no doubt a warning of future attacks, for Joe had harshly assailed Hennings's father less than a year earlier during the Missouri senatorial race. The condescending language may also have included a veiled and sarcastic reference to Hennings's severe alcoholism, which at times incapacitated him and resulted in his absence from Capitol Hill.[11]

Hennings's office quickly defended Green's patriotism and noted that the Gates case was being handled without fee because it involved the issue of free speech. William Benton observed wryly that Joe appeared "worried." Hennings, having tasted a pure sample of McCarthyism, was irate. He wired Joe: "I propose to discuss you in the Senate on Friday. I hope that you will have time to be there even if it requires your temporary absence from inventing smears and lies about others."[12]

On September 19, at a news conference in Savannah, Georgia, Joe charged that "several U.S. representatives and senators have known Communists on their staffs." He refused to name names. Upon returning to Washington he denied having said "known." "I said they have Communists on their staffs." On learning that Benton had asked for evidence to substantiate the contention, Joe snapped, "I am all through paying any attention to what that odd little mental midget, Benton, has to say. His complete lack of intelligence makes him too unimportant to waste time on."[13]

The next day in the Senate, Thomas Hennings delivered a fiery blast against the absent McCarthy, declaring that his letter of September 18 was "an affront to the honor of the Senate and impugns the integrity of one of the Senate committees." It was "a thinly veiled attempt—and not the first one—to discredit the work of the subcommittee and invalidate its findings by devious means and irrelevant attacks on its members." At the conclusion of the speech, Margaret Chase Smith crossed the chamber and shook Hennings's hand. Senators Douglas and McMahon also expressed their congratulations. McCarthy later accused Hennings of making "a personal attack on me" and of being "completely prejudiced."[14]

The letter to Hennings was undoubtedly a serious mistake by McCarthy. The freshman Missouri senator was popular with powerful Southern Democrats, who were reportedly "deeply angry" with Joe for the first time. Moreover, John Raeburn Green was an eminent attorney, a man who, by coincidence, had recently been saluted by the *Journal of the American Bar Association* as exemplifying "what is pure and noble in our profession." It was obviously one thing to malign bureaucrats and liberal Democrats but quite another to attack those favored by the Senate "club." Columnist William S. White reported on September 23 that there was currently a "fairly firm prospect" that hearings would be held on Benton's resolution. The mere calling of such hearings against a senator, he wrote, would be "a heavy blow" to the accused.[15]

The following day the Gillette subcommittee met behind closed doors for more than four hours, voting 5-0 to hear Benton and then determine if further hearings were appropriate. Senator Smith made public a letter she had written to Carl Hayden asking the full Rules Committee to decide if she was qualified to sit with the subcommittee when it heard Benton. This was a direct challenge to McCarthy, of course; knowing the rules of senatorial courtesy, moreover, she was confident of complete support. As expected, she soon received the unanimous backing of the committee. Joe was absent when the vote was taken but sent a proxy ballot favoring Mrs. Smith's right to sit. This was only a recognition of the inevitable, and McCarthy did not abandon his argument that Senator Smith was prejudiced against him. For good measure, he also submitted a proxy supporting Hennings's membership, although the Missouri senator had not requested a vote.[16]

Joe was aware of the fact that the decision by the Gillette subcommittee to air Benton's charges was part of a larger attack now underway by enemies within the press. The liberal *New York Post,* for example, was publishing a highly influential seventeen-part series entitled "Smear, Inc., The One-Man Mob of Joe McCarthy." The authors, Oliver Pilat and William V. Shannon, were principally concerned with mustering evidence to portray McCarthy as a lifelong, cynical huckster, and they did some rather gross smearing of their own while describing the Quaker Dairy case, "quickie" divorces, the campaign of 1946, the Lustron booklet, the sugar issue, and the Malmedy hearings. They even called attention to the brief and wholly accidental presence of a homosexual in Joe's office in 1947: "The man who flamboyantly crusades against homosexuals as though they menace the nation employed one on his office staff for many months." Still, Pilat and Shannon revealed considerable research into McCarthy's personal history and political career, and they raised some solid questions about his military record, his stock market speculations, his jumbled figures on State Department Communists, and his direct involvement in the Maryland campaign. The reporters' grasp of detail had to make Joe extremely nervous.[17]

At the same time a young Madison writer named Ronald May was traveling throughout Wisconsin conducting interviews and gathering information about every aspect of McCarthy's life. He was researching a campaign biography with collaborator Jack Anderson, who soon joined May in Wisconsin. Joe well understood the intentions of Anderson and May. In the depositions required by Drew Pearson's lawsuit, he was asked a wide range of questions about his past, undoubtedly to assist the Anderson-May book. Over the protests of McCarthy attorney Edward Bennett Williams, a district court judge opened the depositions to the press, and

McCarthy's testimony, taken under oath, was displayed throughout the nation's newspapers.[18]

Pearson attorney Warren Woods was also in Wisconsin consulting with editors and reporters of the *Milwaukee Journal* and *Madison Capital Times*. At one point he confided to *Journal* reporter Robert Fleming:

> . . . so far we have only scratched the surface and there are many more sessions of McCarthy's depositions to be had before we are through with him. I do plan to file a motion with the Court to compel McCarthy to answer questions about his borrowings. Of course, since the Court has denied all of the motions filed by the defendants, it is apparent that we are going to come to trial, although perhaps too late to do any good in the Wisconsin primary.[19]

Fleming himself was at work almost full time on McCarthy. He conducted interviews in Wisconsin and Washington (Millard Tydings slipped him relevant materials), checked tax records, legal cases, and government hearings, reported on the senator's appearances in his home state, and consulted with others constructing cases against McCarthy, including Oliver Pilat, Drew Pearson, Jack Anderson, William Benton, and Kenneth Birkhead, an official of the Democratic National Committee and former Thomas Hennings campaign manager. (Birkhead would assist Benton in preparing detailed charges against McCarthy.)[20]

The October 22 issue of *Time* featured Joe's face on its cover over the caption "Demagogue McCarthy." The story, to which Fleming and other Wisconsin reporters made contributions, surveyed Joe's rise from farm boy to senator with tolerable accuracy, described his personality with rare perception, and strongly attacked his credentials as a spy-catcher. The case against Gustavo Duran was singled out for special attention and ridicule. While Henry Luce's magazine was willing to perpetuate the Red Scare and push for G.O.P. victories in 1952, it would be consistently unsympathetic toward McCarthy's excesses. "Experience proves . . . that what the anti-Communist fight needs is truth, carefully arrived at and presented with all the scrupulous regard for decency and the rights of man of which the democratic world is capable. This is the Western world's greatest asset in the struggle against Communism, and those who condone McCarthy are throwing that asset away."[21]

Joe lashed out bitterly against these attacks. He began to quote Louis Budenz's incredible charge that there were some 400 active members of the Communist party holding positions in the American press, radio, and motion picture industries. He dismissed the Pilat-Shannon series as "party line." In a Milwaukee speech he denounced Ronald May as a Drew Pearson "spy," gathering information for a "smear attack." He intensified his penchant for embarrassing reporters at speeches and political gatherings of all sorts. He sued the *Syracuse Post-Standard* for libel. He condemned what he called *Time*'s "degenerate lying," and in a public letter to Henry Luce claimed that a memorandum in *Time*'s own confidential files contradicted the magazine's account of Gustavo Duran's career "in every detail." He soon circulated letters to *Time* advertisers urging them to withdraw their financial support of the magazine. Joe also began filling the *Congressional Record* with items favorable to his anti-Communist efforts. The headlines he placed over the insertions were revealing: "Smear Tactics Cannot Beat Senator McCarthy's Record," "McCarthy Will Beat Down Commies," "Vultures Are After McCarthy."[22]

Equating the hostility of elements within the press with the move by the Gillette subcommittee to hear Benton, and still angry over the Maryland report, Joe predictably determined to defy the Iowa senator and his colleagues. A few days before Benton was to appear, McCarthy released a letter to the subcommittee that stated in part: "I am not in the slightest concerned with what this subcommittee does insofar as my fight to expose communism and corruption in Washington is concerned. This subcommittee can not in the slightest influence my activities." He had heard, he wrote, that Benton would not be testifying under oath. "I think the full committee should reverse this decision and require Mr. Benton be placed under oath if he is to act as the megaphone for the Communist party-line type of smear attack on me."[23]

Gillette invited McCarthy to attend the Benton hearing and even to make a statement if time permitted. But he also advised him that the subcommittee would be meeting in executive session and that only members would be permitted to cross-examine. Joe snubbed the invitation and departed for Santa Fe, New Mexico, to give a speech. With Hendrickson and Hennings dissenting, the subcommittee then reversed its position and opened the hearing to the public. It was clear that the majority of the senators about to hear Benton were far from neutral about McCarthy.[24]

Benton took the oath on September 28 and proceeded to read a 25,000 word statement charging McCarthy with practicing "deceit and falsehood on both the U.S. Senate and the American people." Joe's ouster, Benton said, was "essential to the well-being and security of the American people." The statement presented ten "case studies" that Benton, John Howe, and Kenneth Birkhead had collected from Drew Pearson and others hostile to

McCarthy. The first charged that Joe had lied to the Tydings Committee by denying he had said in Wheeling that there were 205 Communists in the State Department known to the Secretary of State. Secondly, Benton condemned McCarthy for accepting a $10,000 fee from the Lustron Corporation. Case number three blasted McCarthy for his speech on George Marshall. Number four contended that Joe was guilty of fraud and deceit for stating on the Senate floor that Millard Tydings had forced him to make public the names of government officials with Communist membership and affiliation. Case number five focused on Joe's activities in the Maryland campaign. Number six rebuked McCarthy for offering to repeat his charges off the Senate floor and for failing to do so. Seven involved the alleged "FBI chart" Joe once claimed to possess. Case number eight noted McCarthy's promise to give the names of 81 Reds in the State Department and pointed to his reliance upon the Lee list. Nine dealt with the senator's role in the Malmedy hearings. And number ten focused upon the character of people hired by McCarthy; Don Surine and Charles Davis were later named. To highlight this bill of particulars, Benton played a tape recording of Joe's Salt Lake City speech—the same recording that Tydings had once implied was made at Wheeling.[25]

The subcommittee responded by voting unanimously to order its staff to conduct an investigation into the legal and factual phases of Benton's resolution. No one questioned the fact that McCarthy had been dealt a blow.

A week later Benton asked the subcommittee to include in its probe acts committed prior to McCarthy's election to the Senate: the Quaker Dairy case, alleged violations of the Wisconsin state constitution, "quickie" divorces, and the 1943 income tax report. William Evjue cheered, and Drew Pearson stepped up his attacks. Senator Hennings soon revealed that five investigators were at work checking into Benton's charges. Millard Tydings publicly offered a $10,000 reward to McCarthy if he would offer evidence to a grand jury to convict Communists in the State Department. (The reward figure reminded him of the Lustron fee, Tydings said.) The ex-senator attached a photograph to his press release showing frozen bodies of American soldiers killed at Malmedy. "I am sending it to the 400 Wisconsin newspapers," he announced, "for I am certain they will want the 'facts' about a man up for reelection, who has performed such patriotic services in defending the murderers of surrendered American soldiers."[26]

Some Republicans were reportedly becoming uneasy about McCarthy. Robert Taft, having announced his candidacy for the presidential nomination, told reporters that Joe had "overstated his charges" in some cases, and he singled out the Marshall speech for specific criticism. The Ohio senator predicted that McCarthyism would not be a major issue in the 1952 campaign.[27]

Joe blanketed some of the hostile stories with headlines produced by two personal appearances before a subcommittee of the Foreign Relations Committee, in late September and early October, weighing the nomination of Philip C. Jessup to be a delegate to the United Nations General Assembly. In normal times the nomination would have sailed easily through the Senate. Jessup, 54, possessed credentials that were solidly within the perimeters of Establishment respectability. He had come from a distinguished East Coast family with deep roots in politics and the Presbyterian Church. He was a graduate of Hamilton College and Yale Law School; he had served overseas during World War I and back home had commanded the Utica, New York, post of the American Legion; he had married the niece of a Connecticut senator; and he had become a prosperous attorney, respected author, and Hamilton Fish professor of international law and diplomacy at Columbia University Law School. Jessup could also boast of a record of public service that went back to 1924. He had enjoyed the confidence of such eminent public figures as William Howard Taft, Harlan F. Stone, Elihu Root, Harry Guggenheim, and Herbert H. Lehman, and had been confirmed by the Senate five times since 1948 as a United Nations representative and as ambassador-at-large.[28]

But this, of course, was a highly abnormal period in American politics, and superior credentials of themselves meant nothing to leaders of the second Red Scare; Hiss and Acheson had been "respectable" too. Since early 1950 Jessup had been under attack by Styles Bridges, Karl Mundt, Richard Nixon, and McCarthy, among others. He was a symbol to them of "the conspiracy" in the State Department, for he had worked closely with Acheson, edited the department's "White Paper" on China, served as a character witness for Hiss, and played a role in events leading to General MacArthur's dismissal. McCarthy told the Tydings Committee that Jessup had an "unusual affinity" for "Communist causes" and had Bourke Hickenlooper quiz the ambassador about a number of charges then in circulation on the Far Right. Joe contended that Jessup had been affiliated with five Communist front organizations and that his name had appeared as a member of the executive committee of a sixth such organization. The State Department, in a lengthy statement of May 27, 1950, demolished the charge in detail by pointing out that two of the six organizations cited were not Communist fronts, that Jessup had had no connection with two others, that he had only sponsored two dinners (which he did not attend) for a fifth organization, and that he had merely signed a "call" that resulted in the formation of a sixth organization. The department traced another McCarthy charge against Jessup to discredited contentions made by Alfred Kohlberg, and it properly dismissed a further allegation as entirely misleading, being in part a product of Joe's apparent confusion about two unrelated organizations.[29]

Nevertheless, McCarthy continued to repeat his assertions about Jessup in speeches all across the country, drawing rousing responses from huge audiences. By the fall of 1951 he was distributing a 27-page brochure entitled "The Case of Ambassador-at-Large Philip C. Jessup: 'Let Them Fall, But Do Not Let It Appear That WE Pushed Them.'" Among the examples of "documentary evidence" presented were large photostatic copies of letterheads, either undated or from the early 1940s, bearing Jessup's name. They were accompanied by "official citations" from the Attorney General's list, HUAC, and the equally infamous un-American activities committees of California and Massachusetts, labeling the organizations Red fronts. Many of the other names on the letterheads, often those of highly distinguished citizens, were preceded by inserted check marks, cleverly giving the impression that they too were tainted with subversion. Some of the material in the brochure came from the hearings of the McCarran Committee, which was generating extensive publicity through its peregrinations in the I.P.R. files and by a parade of veteran ex-Communist witnesses such as Louis Budenz and Elizabeth Bentley. Budenz alone, enjoying congressional immunity, labeled 46 people Communists who had been "associated"—often very indirectly—with the Institute of Pacific Relations.[30]

Truman's confidence in Jessup was undisturbed by the partisan howls of ultraconservatives and by warnings from within his own party about the political wisdom of further association with the ambassador. On September 3, 1951, the President submitted Jessup's name to the Senate as a member of a new slate of delegates to the United Nations. The matter was turned over to a subcommittee of the Foreign Relations Committee headed by John J. Sparkman of Alabama, a highly respected Senate "insider." Also named to the subcommittee were J. William Fulbright of Arkansas, Guy Gillette, moderate Republican H. Alexander Smith of New Jersey, and McCarthyite Owen Brewster of Maine. McCarthy was the first person to volunteer to testify at the hearings, a move undoubtedly part of a counteroffensive against William Benton.[31]

Joe appeared before the Sparkman subcommittee on September 27, the day before Benton's scheduled testimony before Gillette and his colleagues.

He began by presenting the familiar charge concerning Jessup's alleged affiliation with six Communist fronts. When his documentation was challenged by Fulbright and Sparkman, who were well-versed in the State Department's rebuttal, Joe stumbled badly, sputtered about "the commie-crat party," and took refuge in oratory: "I intend to bring this story to the American people, from the Atlantic to the Pacific, from New Orleans to St. Paul, because it appears now . . . the only way we can get a housecleaning. . . . " In the case of front number one, the National Emergency Conference for Democratic Rights, Joe was unable to say if Jessup had been a sponsor at the time HUAC cited it. Concerning the American Russian Institute, Joe did not know the extent of Jessup's affiliation and could not even cite the year of the dinner invitation he was using as evidence. Sparkman pointed out that another front, the Coordinating Committee to Lift the Embargo, had merely reprinted a portion of a 1939 letter to *The New York Times,* co-authored by Jessup, on the need for isolationism. Joe then tried to link Jessup, who had been an America Firster, with the Communist party line on Spain; he was unable to associate him more closely with the coordinating committee. When the testimony turned to the American Law Student's Association, for which Jessup had been one of fifteen faculty advisers, Joe could not date the letterhead in question, did not know when Jessup had been an adviser, and was unaware of the year HUAC had cited the association as a front. Joe argued that even though individual cases might appear weak, they were each part of a larger pattern pointing to Jessup's loyalty to the Communist cause. Fulbright shot back, "There has to be something in each one of these cases, it seems to me—active participation in the organizations that were subversive. The fact that there were a number of zeros doesn't make it amount to one if you put them all together."[32]

McCarthy made a second appearance before the subcommittee on October 2, following a whirlwind speaking tour that took him to New Mexico, Pennsylvania, and Wisconsin. The session lasted more than seven hours and was marked by a spirit of rancor rarely seen on Capitol Hill. Joe had returned to Washington obviously anxious to wreak revenge upon Fulbright for humiliating him a few days earlier. The scholarly senator from Arkansas was equally determined to expose the irresponsibility of the charges against Jessup. Enjoying a secure Senate seat, his contempt for McCarthy was not muted by fear.

Sparkman opened the hearing by pointing to the fact that, contrary to McCarthy's brochure and testimony, the American Law Student's Association had never been cited as a Communist front. He also noted the names of many distinguished legal scholars who had appeared supportive of the organization in 1939, the period of Jessup's association as a faculty adviser. Joe fumed and stormed and contended that Jessup had known that the organization used a Communist print shop at the time and that alone was evidence of the gentleman's pro-Communist sympathies.

Joe then changed the subject by referring to testimony given a day earlier before the McCarran Committee by G.O.P. presidential hopeful Harold Stassen. His testimony included a reference to a chat with Philip Jessup that had allegedly taken place in October 1949, during an intermission at a State Department meeting on Asian affairs. Jessup, Stassen claimed, had made a remark expressing general sympathy with positions espoused by Owen Lattimore and others at the meeting; among those proposals, he said, was the diplomatic recognition of Communist China. This allegation was sufficient for Joe to proclaim Jessup guilty of hewing to the Soviet line.

When Sparkman subcommittee members pressed for further details of the Stassen testimony, Joe hastily retreated: "I got to town late last night. I read over this testimony. I picked out the points which I thought were the highlights. As to whether there are any other points in here that might be covered, I do not know, Senator. I went over this hurriedly ..." (Jessup soon emphatically denied making the remark to Stassen. The State Department released a transcript of the 1949 meeting, badly damaging Stassen's recollections of the event. Stassen himself proved unconvincing when summoned before the subcommittee. A second charge of his, that Jessup had proposed in early 1949 to end all aid to Nationalist China, turned out to be without substance.)[33]

Fulbright proceeded to bear down hard on McCarthy's evidence. The Arkansas senator's boldness and penchant for inserting sarcasm into his interrogation frequently angered McCarthy, no doubt in part because he was unaccustomed to being the target of his own political weaponry. Fulbright called attention to the fact that Jessup's only association with the China Aid Council, "Communist Front No. 4," was his wife's wartime membership in the affiliated American Committee for Chinese War Orphans, sponsored by Madam Chiang Kai-shek. In reply, Joe resorted to asserting that Mrs. Jessup had been a friend of Mrs. Hiss. At another point Joe quoted from McCarran Committee testimony by Raymond Dennett, a former Secretary of the Institute for Pacific Relations, to prove that the I.P.R. was Communist controlled. Fulbright then read an Associated Press dispatch that quoted further from Dennett's testimony: "Of all the people I was associated with in the I.P.R., the person I never questioned as having any Communist association was Philip C. Jessup." Joe could only sputter, "I am giving what I consider the pertinent parts of the testimony."

Fulbright repeatedly exposed McCarthy's documentation as inaccurate and distorted, and he ridiculed him for his lack of preparation. Joe fought back with loud diversions, personal challenges, and a variety of bluffs. At the conclusion of the grueling hearing, Fulbright declared sternly, "I just want to say for the record that in all my experience in the Senate, I have never seen a more arrogant or rude witness before any committee." Joe made no reply; he had met his match. Soon, however, he was sneering privately about "Senator Halfbright."[34]

Newspaper accounts of the two hearings did not reveal the extent of the damage done to the case against Jessup, and the frequent clashes between Fulbright and McCarthy over facts and evidence appeared to be little more than partisan squabbles. Jessup's point-by-point refutation of McCarthy's charges, presented during several appearances before the subcommittee, were also slighted in deference to the ambassador's often politically colored rhetorical flourishes. "I will introduce evidence that the Communists have attacked me with a violence equal to that displayed by the senator from Wisconsin," he said during his first day on the stand, "and with far greater justification." He made news by labeling as "absolutely dishonest" McCarthy's use of his 1939 letter to *The New York Times* to tie him to the Coordinating Committee to Lift the Embargo. Unwilling to leave it at that, he compared the action to "another trick photograph" used in the Maryland campaign against Senator Tydings.[35]

Newspaper readers may also have dismissed as politically partisan a finding by the Civil Service Loyalty Review Board, released by the Sparkman subcommittee, that there was "no reasonable doubt" about Jessup's loyalty. Joe counteracted the headline by telling reporters that Chairman Hiram Bingham had confided to him that the board would have turned Jessup down "as a bad security risk" if it had possessed the authority. When Bingham flatly denied saying "any such thing," Joe replied, "I wouldn't want to get into a fight with Hiram. He's too good a fellow—too good an American. If he makes a few mistakes, he's entitled to make them."[36]

McCarthy was jubilant when the Sparkman subcommittee surprised some observers by voting 3-2 to reject Jessup's nomination, telling reporters that it was "a great day for America and a bad day for the Communists." Predictably, Sparkman and Fulbright supported the nomination and Owen Brewster opposed it. Insiders had known privately for weeks that Guy Gillette would also vote in the negative. The Iowa senator explained lamely that while he continued to have complete confidence in Jessup's loyalty, he thought that the ambassador lacked the confidence of the public. He acknowledged at the same time that Jessup's reputation may have been damaged principally by "the concerted campaign of unfair and unprincipled attacks made on him." H. Alexander Smith held the swing vote on the subcommittee, and Democrats had thought that he could be won over. He and Jessup were old friends, and on several occasions during the hearings Smith had expressed his faith in the ambassador's integrity and patriotism. After casting his ballot, Smith again expressed his personal belief in Jessup's honor but declared him to be "a controversial figure" and "the symbol of a group attitude toward Asia which seems to have been proven completely unsound." The power of the fears and ambitions that propelled political life in the era of McCarthyism clouded the minds and dulled the consciences of many otherwise decent men and women. "Throughout this whole period," Sen. Henry M. Jackson would later recall, "the major thread was fear."[37]

The day after the subcommittee's action, the Senate unanimously confirmed nine of the ten nominees to the United Nations. Sparkman, fearing defeat in a Senate vote, asked that Jessup's name be withheld until Congress adjourned a few days later. With senators returning home, Truman gave Jessup a recess appointment, declaring accurately, "The record of the hearings shows that charges to the effect that he was sympathetic to Communist causes were utterly without foundation." Senator Taft said angrily that the President's action showed "complete contempt for Constitutional processes and the law of the land." McCarthy boiled over the Democrats' slightly irregular but legal strategem and continued his tirades against Jessup, hereafter adding the charge that a Senate subcommittee had declared the ambassador "unfit to represent this country." He told a group of women Republicans in Michigan that he hadn't thought Jessup "so morally degenerate" as to accept a recess appointment.[38]

On October 1, Guy Gillette again invited McCarthy to appear before the Subcommittee on Privileges and Elections, this time to reply to William Benton's lengthy statement. Joe responded a few days later, "Frankly, Guy, I have not and do not intend to even read, much less answer, Benton's smear attack. I am sure you realize that the Benton type of material can be found in the *Daily Worker* almost any day of the week and will continue to flow from the mouths and pens of the camp followers as long as I continue my fight against Communists in government."[39]

Throughout the next several weeks newspapers were filled with anti-McCarthy charges and information involving the senator's personal income, his tax returns, the 1944 campaign, the "war wounds," Charles Davis, and the like. Investigators from the Gillette subcommittee were

conducting interviews in Washington, Wisconsin, Wheeling, and elsewhere on the full range of Benton's allegations, at times bumping into
reporters asking the same questions. The Administration joined the attack.
Brig. Gen. Conrad E. Snow, head of the State Department's Loyalty Board,
gave a speech harshly critical of McCarthy, contending that over the past
four years "not one case has been found of a present Communist working"
in the department. "This is McCarthyism," Snow said:

> the making of baseless accusations regarding the loyalty and
> integrity of public officials and employees by a person who is
> himself in high public office and who uses his office at one
> and the same time as a platform from which to shout his
> accusations and as a screen to protect himself from action for
> defamation. The purpose of it all is, of course, not the public
> interest but political advancement in a period of public ten-
> sion and excitement.

Attorney General Howard McGrath told reporters that the criminal division was checking testimony by Don Surine in the Maryland election
hearings about his "voluntary resignation" from the FBI.[40]
    During this period there were further indications of unrest within the
G.O.P. Gov. Earl Warren of California, the party's recent vice-presidential
candidate, specifically disassociated himself from Joe's "blanket accusations." Sen. James H. Duff of Pennsylvania, spearheading the Eisenhower-
for-President drive, lashed out at McCarthy's use of "random blanket
charges without specific data to back them up." Even Senator Nixon
cautioned Republicans that "indiscriminate name-calling and professional
Red-baiting can hurt our cause more than it can help it."[41]
    Joe was both aware of these developments and deeply concerned about
them, choosing to counterattack in a fashion that by now had become
familiar. A campaign fund-raising letter, distributed by the thousands in
Wisconsin, claimed that "well-financed agents of the Administration and
the Communist party are traveling throughout Wisconsin attempting to
stir up opposition to McCarthy." On December 6, in a letter given to
reporters, Joe told Gillette that the subcommittee was guilty of "stealing
from the pockets of the American taxpayer tens of thousands of dollars and
then using this money to protect the Democrat party from the political
effect of the exposure of Communists in government." He also challenged
the subcommittee's right to conduct a probe of all of Benton's charges. A
"horde of investigators" had been hired, he said, "to dig up on McCarthy
material covering periods of time long before he was even old enough to be

a candidate for the Senate—material which can have no conceivable connection with his election or any other election." The next day, in another
public letter to Gillette, Joe requested complete information about all
subcommittee staff members.[42]

Gillette dismissed McCarthy's charges concerning appropriations and
staff as "of course, erroneous" and promised an investigation conducted "in
a spirit of utmost fairness to all concerned and to the Senate." He noted that
a study of the legal phases and precedents concerning the probe was
underway. When Senator Monroney offered publicly to put the question of
jurisdiction before the full Senate, assuring reporters that the subcommittee had already consulted the Senate parliamentarian on the matter, Joe
promptly rejected the proposal as "dishonest."[43]

Joe then attacked the subcommittee through one of its former staff
members. Daniel G. Buckley, a New York attorney, had served as assistant
counsel to the subcommittee from October 16 to December 8. He had been
a temporary employee and was one of three workers dismissed in early
December because, in Gillette's words, their services "were no longer
needed." Buckley asked Gillette to be rehired when an opening appeared
and left the senator's office in an amicable spirit. Suddenly, on December
27, Buckley appeared in the Senate press gallery, handed out a mimeographed statement, and disappeared before reporters could ask any questions. The press release claimed that Buckley had been dropped by the
Gillette subcommittee for failing to be anti-McCarthy. He had twice conducted investigations in Wheeling, he said, and had come away convinced
that McCarthy had referred to 57, rather than 205, State Department Reds.
When the chief investigator and Millard Tydings learned of this, Buckley
claimed, his employment was terminated. Buckley also charged that Drew
Pearson was supplying the subcommittee with information and had been
given access to a confidential report. When he suggested to Margaret Chase
Smith that the staff learn from what source Pearson acquired the report, he
claimed, the senator said that the matter should be forgotten. Buckley
concluded that "the Benton investigation is part and parcel of an insidious
campaign which had two major aims: (1) to discredit and destroy any man
who fights Communist subversion—in this case, Senator McCarthy; and
(2) to instill fear in the minds of men—a fear which our enemies hope will
effectively scare loyal Americans, in private life and in Congress, into
silence and prevent them from speaking out against the Communist threat
to this country."[44]

It was all too pat. The jabs at Tydings, Pearson, and Smith, and the very
wording of the press release itself, sounded like McCarthy. Gillette chal-

lenged Buckley to repeat his story under oath, and the subcommittee's chief counsel dismissed the charges as "unfounded and unwarranted." The subcommittee soon learned from telephone company records that Buckley had been in close contact with Jean Kerr and Fulton Lewis, Jr. The press release was reportedly prepared in McCarthy's office. (When soon asked during a television debate if he had said "205" at Wheeling, Joe replied, "You read the other day that one of the investigators who has left the committee went down and completely exploded that story.") Buckley was later hired by the Republican National Committee and subsequently became a member of McCarthy's staff.[45]

Despite Joe's fusillade, the Gillette subcommittee's staff continued its investigation into the full range of Benton's charges and submitted a 300-page, confidential preliminary report on January 18, 1952. While staff members conducted much of the research for the report, they also relied upon information published by Drew Pearson, William Evjue, and others hostile to McCarthy; Democratic State Senator Gaylord Nelson of Madison soon boasted in the *Capital Times* that he had forwarded considerable information and "confidential affidavits" to the subcommittee. Five of Benton's ten "case studies" were considered worthy of hearings: the Wheeling speech, the Lustron fee, the allegation that Tydings forced McCarthy to make public the names of accused government officials, the Lee list speech of February 20, 1950, and the employment of Farrand and Davis. Charges involving the Maryland election, Malmedy, and Don Surine were termed persuasive and already sufficiently documented. In addition, the staff considered censurable several of McCarthy's attacks on the subcommittee, the blast at John Raeburn Green, and one piece of evidence used against Philip Jessup.[46]

A month later, as liberals demanded action from the subcommittee and its members prepared to vote on whether to proceed with the recommended hearings, the preliminary report was leaked to the press, producing anti-McCarthy headlines, editorials, and cartoons in newspapers all over the country. This could only serve to substantiate McCarthy's contention that the subcommittee was politically motivated.[47]

Republican leaders saw the Gillette subcommittee as a source of considerable embarrassment in a crucial election year, and in early 1952 they attempted to stymie the McCarthy investigation. Kenneth Wherry had died in November 1951, and McCarthy was transferred from the Rules Committee to the Appropriations Committee. His replacement was ultraconservative Herman Welker of Idaho. Everett Dirksen of Illinois, another McCarthyite, was soon added to the committee. Henry Cabot Lodge, the

ranking Republican on the Rules Committee, then proposed to replace
Margaret Chase Smith and Robert C. Hendrickson on the Gillette subcommittee with Welker and Dirksen. Mrs. Smith, privately eager to avoid
further clashes with McCarthy, greeted the decision enthusiastically, telling
reporters that she preferred appointment to the allegedly more important
subcommittee on rules. (In fact, this subcommittee rarely met and was
referred to as "the pidgeon-holed committee" by Carl Hayden.) Hendrickson weighed the move briefly, deciding against it after Joe sidled up to him
in the Senate cloakroom, threw an arm over his shoulder and said in a
patronizing voice, "You are doing the right thing by resigning, Bob. It's the
only thing to do with your prejudice." Hendrickson explained to his
brother, "I did not feel that I could run out in the 'midst of a trial,' so to
speak, despite Joe McCarthy's wishes to the contrary."

Democrats complained bitterly about the ploy. Blair Moody of Michigan
called it "one of the slickest tricks of the year by the Senate G.O.P. high
command," adding that it "scarcely indicates a sincere interest in clean
politics or clean government." Benton expressed disbelief and shock.
Gillette said that he would vigorously oppose the move. When the dust
settled, Hendrickson remained on the subcommittee and Welker replaced
Smith.[48]

Mike Monroney thought Welker's appointment "catastrophic." The
subcommittee had been criticized for indecision and delay, and now its
prospects for moving boldly against McCarthy had declined sharply.
Welker soon obtained a pledge from Gillette that the subcommittee would
take no action during the month of February while he was on an extended
speaking tour. Many observers thought that McCarthy and his allies had
hamstrung the entire investigation. William Evjue called for Gillette's
resignation, growling, "What the Senate needs is some guts."[49]

Joe was undoubtedly pleased by these recent developments. Wearing an
overcoat and a confident expression, he posed for a dramatic photograph in
front of the Capitol holding a huge broom sent by constituents from Little
Chute and Appleton. The senator was an "advocate of cleaning Communist
influence from government," said the Associated Press, which distributed a
copy of the picture to every newspaper in Wisconsin. "This broom gag is as
old as politics," Evjue moaned.[50]

President Truman was far less willing than congressional Democrats to
surrender the McCarthy issue. In late January he signed an executive order
authorizing the Gillette subcommittee to check income and other tax
returns in the course of its investigations. This authority had been sought
by the subcommittee staff in its preliminary report and was expected to

shed light on McCarthy's financial activities as far back as 1943. William Benton soon announced that Truman had accepted "with alacrity" an invitation to speak on his behalf during his reelection campaign.[51]

Joe retaliated with a Senate speech claiming that FBI reports closely linked Phileo Nash, a black White House special assistant on minority problems, with Communists in the 1940s. Nash branded the accusation "a contemptible lie" (a special loyalty board soon gave him a complete clearance), and Truman described McCarthy as "pathological" and "a character assassin." In a speech before the Wisconsin Seed Dealers' Association, McCarthy repeated his original statement from the *Congressional Record* "in answer," he said, "to the crocodile tears of the bleeding-heart elements of the press and radio." "There is no immunity here," he assured his audience. "I'm making a tape-recording of everything I say here for their benefit, and they can start their lawsuits this afternoon." Actually, as Joe well knew, his congressional immunity remained in force as long as he quoted his remarks delivered on the Senate floor. "He has made this technique a standard political stock in trade," sighed Miles McMillin. Nash tried unsuccessfully for months to obtain a copy of the tape, which the senator took with him on his return to Washington.[52]

McCarthy then turned his attention to Leon Keyserling, the President's chief economic adviser. In a speech entitled "The Treason of 1952," delivered in Wheeling, West Virginia, on the second anniversary of the "205" charge, Joe contended that an unnamed witness, in secret testimony before the McCarran Committee, had quoted a Communist party organizer as saying that Keyserling was sympathetic to Red aims. He also claimed to possess photostats showing that Mrs. Keyserling had been a member of ten Communist front organizations.[53]

A few days later Joe told an audience in Fond du Lac, Wisconsin, that the nation's leadership was "almost completely morally degenerate." The President, he said, was "a puppet on the strings being pulled by the Achesons, Lattimores, and Jessups."[54]

Brigadier General Snow, on behalf of the State Department, returned some of this fire, stating in a Washington speech that he was confident that the department was free of "known Communists." "Some will say that where there is so much smoke there is some fire," he declared. "There is, however, no excuse for mistaking dust for smoke." Snow continued sternly, "The dust in the present case is created by one man, tramping about the nation and making over and over again the same baseless and disproved accusations." When this blast caught up with McCarthy in Omaha, he sneered, "Snow's speeches are always written for him, and he makes a good delivery. There's nothing vicious or evil about General Snow. He's a poor befuddled old gent who doesn't know enough to come in out of the rain."[55]

By late February Democrats on the Gillette subcommittee had regained their resolve and agreed upon a tactic to revitalize the McCarthy probe. At a March 5 executive meeting of the subcommittee, Mike Monroney reviewed McCarthy's abusive statements concerning the body's motives and methods, appealing to the pride and dignity of his colleagues. On his motion the Senators voted four to one (the one was Welker) to challenge McCarthy to ask the Senate to discharge the subcommittee from further consideration of the resolution to expel; should he fail to take such action, the Rules Committee would bring the issue to the floor itself "for the purpose of affirming the jurisdiction of the subcommittee and the integrity of its members in its consideration of the aforesaid resolution." Subcommittee Democrats knew that they could not lose a vote of confidence. They hoped too to arouse Southerners and other conservatives against McCarthy by revealing his disrespect for Senate traditions.

The next day Gillette sent a lengthy letter to Rules Chairman Hayden containing excerpts of McCarthy's attacks on the subcommittee and condemning his charges as "scandalous," "extravagant and irresponsible," "unwarranted, undignified, and wholly unjustifiable." On March 7 the Rules Committee voted eight to three (Dirksen, Welker, and Jenner dissenting) in favor of the showdown with McCarthy. Gillette's letter was given to the press, and Hayden assured reporters that he would soon be in touch with the Wisconsin senator.[56]

On March 16 Joe appeared on Edward R. Murrow's popular network television program and attacked William Benton for "shouting and screaming to high heaven" about his use of congressional immunity. Joe pretended to read from the first page of Benton's lengthy Senate speech of September 28 to show that the Connecticut senator's charges against McCarthy were also immune: "No part of this must be used by the press until it becomes immune as I testified." Reporters knew instantly that McCarthy had twisted a standard press release statement for his own purpose. The phrase from the Benton document actually read: "The attached . . . must be held in strict confidence for release as it becomes a part of the record of the subcommittee." The nation's viewers, of course, were unaware of Joe's deception, and only a few major newspapers later called it to public attention.[57]

Benton was enraged by McCarthy's tactic. On the Senate floor he challenged the Wisconsin senator's honesty, likened his methods to those of Hitler, and offered to waive his own immunity on any of the charges contained in the September 28 speech. In a strongly worded letter given to the press, Joe dared him to take such a step, threatening legal action. When Benton promptly complied, "to compel him to sue or cease his reckless accusations," McCarthy filed a $2,000,000 libel and slander suit, telling a news conference that he intended to serve as his own attorney so that he could cross-examine Benton under oath. In a later public letter, Joe wrote, "I consider this lawsuit as a means of pinpointing the contest between America and the Communist party."[58]

Joe was now the plaintiff in two libel suits, involving the *Syracuse Post-Standard* and Benton, and the defendant in the Drew Pearson suit. The legal action against Benton was a vehicle for further publicity, part of his arsenal in the struggle against the Gillette subcommittee. Of course, there was also the element of revenge. When Urban Van Susteren chided Joe privately for going to court, saying that he couldn't win two dollars in the case, Joe acknowledged the truth of the assessment. But every morning when Benton was shaving, Joe said, he would look into the mirror and think to himself that Joe McCarthy might take two million dollars out of his pocket. "He'll sweat."[59]

Predictably, McCarthy refused to call for a vote of confidence on the Gillette subcommittee. In a letter to Hayden rejecting the opportunity, he repeated his charge that the subcommittee was guilty of "a completely dishonest handling of taxpayer's money," and he referred to the preliminary report as "scurrilous" and consisting of "cleverly twisted and distorted facts ... 'leaked' to the Left-wing elements of the press and blazoned across the nation in an attempt to further smear McCarthy." With a nod to the inevitable, however, he said that he favored continuation of the subcommittee's investigation.[60]

On April 8 Hayden introduced the resolution to relieve the subcommittee of its McCarthy probe, describing McCarthy's attacks and requesting that certain Senate precedents relating to expulsion, exclusion, and censure cases be published in the *Congressional Record*. Two days later the resolution failed zero to 60. Joe left the floor before the vote was taken but made his intentions clear in order to avoid embarrassment. Minority Leader Styles Bridges dismissed the vote as merely an expression of confidence in individual members of the group and not an indicator of approval or disapproval of their actions. Margaret Chase Smith emotionally labeled Bridges' statement a "face-saving" gesture and argued that the vote meant that Joe's attacks were "false and without foundation."

As was now common, Joe stole most of the day's headlines from his opponents. Before the Senate vote, he offered a resolution calling for a subcommittee investigation of William Benton. The resolution cited six specific cases in need of inquiry: (1) campaign fund violations in the 1950 election race involving Salt Lake City banker Walter Cosgriff, (2) the use of "fake television portrayals of Benton" in his 1950 campaign, (3) the expenditure of State Department funds for Benton's Britannica Films and Encyclopedia Brittanica, (4) "the facts surrounding Benton's printing of Encyclopedia Britannica by cheap labor in England in order to avoid paying the printer's union scale charged in America," (5) Benton's income taxes for the years 1947 through 1950, (6) and "such further investigations with respect to the activities and associations of William Benton" as deemed necessary by the subcommittee. The resolution also condemned Benton's activities in the State Department. Among other things, Joe charged Benton with employing "a number of individuals named by Senator McCarthy as either Communists, fellow travelers, or dupes of the Kremlin" and with purchasing and distributing "lewd and licentious literature which has also followed the Communist party line" and "lewd art works and Communist-produced art works."

In the course of his bitter Senate remarks, Joe also attacked Darrell St. Claire, chief clerk of the Rules Committee, as the source of the preliminary report leak and called him "a shining example of incompetence" when he was connected with the State Department's loyalty program. (Joe had blasted St. Claire in a speech at Rhinelander, Wisconsin, on February 23. This was reported to Carl Hayden, St. Claire's political sponsor and friend, and helped stir the quiet and powerful Senator into action against McCarthy.) In addition, Joe said bluntly that he had "absolutely no confidence" in Democratic members of the subcommittee. Majority Leader Ernest W. McFarland of Arizona gasped at the use of such language. "I've never heard so serious a charge made against the membership of any committee in my time here." McFarland had entered the Senate in 1941.[61]

By now it was clear that McCarthy's unwillingness to control his temper, his tongue, and his pen was producing serious hostility in the Senate. Had he answered his critics in a temperate and reasonable manner, had he exercised the smallest measure of tact and gentility in his dealings with colleagues, the Gillette subcommittee would undoubtedly have shelved Benton's resolution, and the Connecticut senator's charges would have been discounted as campaign rhetoric and eventually forgotten. But Joe preferred combat without civility, the knee in the groin; however, Joe continued to be affable on a personal level. While leaving the Senate floor on April 10, having excoriated the subcommittee and its staff, he stopped to give Gillette an effusive, bone-jarring handshake. Encountering Secretary of State Acheson in a Senate elevator one day, he stuck out his hand and bellowed "Hi, Dean." (Acheson snubbed him coldly.) But before the public and the press, and in his formal dealings in the Senate, Joe was shocking and reckless to a degree unknown by most observers. His own conduct was largely responsible for keeping the McCarthy investigation alive.[62]

Joe's behavior was a product of many complex forces. His temperament, of course, played a vital role; he had never been able to restrain his reactions to harsh criticism, especially when it contained an element of truth. He particularly resented the meticulous probes by enemies into his personal history and financial affairs. He would "blanket" their headlines, challenge their integrity, link them to the Reds, defeat them at the polls—hit them harder than he had been hit.

Joe's ignorance was also a factor. Richard Nixon, for example, studied issues, institutions, and personalities; his manipulations were based upon a shrewd understanding of how things worked and what it took to achieve carefully planned goals. McCarthy, on the other hand, studied little, had no goals (beyond his own reelection), and thought nothing out in advance. As had long been his style, he shot from the hip, bluffed, lied, rushed to get to the plane to take him to a rally in Peoria or a parade in Cheyenne. This approach had yielded positive results in the past but was becoming increasingly dangerous.[63]

Equally important was Joe's very real belief in the internal Communist conspiracy, a passion that prompted him to stump the country as he had once covered his judicial district and then his state. The often wild enthusiasm that greeted him at these public gatherings, reinforced by tons of mail, his staff, G.O.P. colleagues, the right-wing press, and the election returns of 1950 persuaded McCarthy that he was above the petty amenities that guided the conduct of his Senate colleagues. He had the truth and was giving it to the "real Americans." The puny politicians and scribblers who attacked him were hindering his effectiveness and hurting the country; they were unworthy of polite treatment. No one could persuade him otherwise. All suggestions by staff members and friends that he be more courteous, relaxed, and cautious were sharply rebuffed.[64]

Moreover, McCarthy was now beginning to break down physically and mentally, and this deterioration unquestionably contributed to his often choleric behavior. By the spring of 1952 he was drinking so heavily that close friends and a few journalists recognized the signs of alcoholism. He got drunk regularly while staying with the Urban Van Susterens in Appleton. A *Milwaukee Journal* reporter called on Joe at seven one morning, finding him lying nude on his hotel room bed swilling a pitcher of martinis. Associated Press reporter Dion Henderson saw him drink a glass of whiskey for breakfast, flavored with a tablespoon of orange juice. Ex-Communist Harvey Matusow watched Joe drink "a sea of bourbon" during an all-night party in Appleton. Before addressing the Republican State convention in Milwaukee, he stepped into a men's room, took a bottle of whiskey from his briefcase, and downed a large glassful in a gulp.[65]

In July, Joe underwent another operation for maxillary sinusitis. Shortly afterward, having complained of severe stomach problems, he was operated on for a herniated diaphragm. The latter was a serious surgical procedure at the time, requiring a twenty-four-inch incision and the removal of a rib. The operation cost Joe eighteen pounds and left him with a long, painful scar that ran from his stomach, under his arm, to the top of his shoulder. (He would often show it to children and enjoy their astonished expressions.) For a time he was slightly stooped. For the rest of his life he would suffer a dull pain in the area and have a slight twitch of his neck and head in the direction of his right shoulder. At times he took aspirin for the pain. He also took to the bottle.[66]

Still, Joe did not alter his rigorous schedule. Matusow noted that he slept only three hours after his drinking binge in Appleton and awoke ready for another day's activities. He was supposed to take two months to recover from the surgery. He granted his first interview to reporters in less than three weeks, and three weeks after that he was out on the hustings. By early November he was so exhausted and ill that an Appleton physician ordered him to bed and asked that visitors be kept out of his room. An hour later Joe was milling with a boisterous election-night crowd, shaking hands, signing autographs, and quietly enduring the pain as people slapped him on the back.[67]

Pursuing charges originally raised by McCarthy's newspaper critics, the Gillette subcommittee sent investigators to study the senator's federal income tax returns and his brokerage account with the Appleton State Bank. Emboldened by the Senate's unanimous vote of confidence, it voted on May 7 to hold public hearings on Benton's resolution, starting with the Lustron case, and it sent an invitation to McCarthy to appear and present testimony. Joe's reply contained a solid and convincing refutation of the Lustron charges. But he also felt obliged to repeat his contention that the subcommittee was doing the work of the Communist party by attempting to discredit him. "It is an evil and dishonest thing for the subcommittee to allow itself to be used for an evil purpose." He angrily repeated and expanded his charge in a letter of May 11 and ignored the invitation to testify.

> I ask you gentlemen not to be disturbed by those who point out that your committee is trying to do what the Communist party has officially proclaimed as its No. 1 task. You just keep right on in the same honest, painstaking way of developing the truth. The thinking people of this nation will not be deceived by those who claim that what you are doing is dishonest. After all, you must serve the interests of the Democrat Party—there is always the chance that the country may be able to survive. What better way could you find to spend the taxpayers' money? After all, isn't McCarthy doing the terribly unpatriotic and unethical thing of proving the extent to which the Democrat administration is Communist-ridden? Unless he can be discredited, the Democrat Party may be removed from power.[68]

(The increase in Joe's resort to abusive language in official communications was accompanied by a rise in his use of obscenities in conversation. A *Washington Star* reporter noted, "It is difficult for him to talk privately for many minutes without barnyard language getting into the conversation. One listener clocked him at four unprintables in just three minutes." An Appleton reporter heard him at a party refer to Millard Tydings as "a sheep-fucker.")[69]

The public hearings in mid-May produced a spate of anti-McCarthy headlines. Many of Joe's stock market ventures and loans of the late 1940s came to light. Copies of his personal correspondence with Appleton State Bank president Matt Schuh were given to reporters, and many newspapers published the letters in full, revealing Joe's bluffing and stalling to keep from selling collateral to settle his 1945 loan (paid in full in 1951). Editorial writers whooped about Russell Arundel, the allegedly mysterious "Prince of Baldonia," pointing to his $20,000 note to McCarthy and reviving the "Pepsi-Cola Kid" sobriquet. Commentators from coast to coast discussed data from Joe's federal income tax returns. Much was also made of the fact that McCarthy had not done all of the research and writing for the Lustron booklet and that he had once rolled dice with the son of home builder Robert Byers.

But for all of the publicity, with its overtones of bribery and fraud, the hearings failed to produce solid evidence linking McCarthy with a single illegal activity. Many observers, including, no doubt, most Republicans, dismissed the proceedings as election-year prattle. This conclusion was reinforced by the highly partisan nature of the applause sounded for the subcommittee. At its annual convention in Washington, Americans for Democratic Action urged "a full disclosure of the senator's public record in the hearings now being conducted so that the people of Wisconsin may be fully informed as to his performance against the public interest and retire him from the Senate." A Wisconsin group calling itself "Citizens vs. McCarthy, Inc." cited the Lustron fee in an appeal to Republican state convention delegates to drive the senator from the ticket. State Democrats invited William Benton to their convention and roared approval as he dismissed McCarthy as a "slight-of-mouth artist," and a "Joseph-come-lately" in the fight against Communism. Benton also praised the *Madison Capital Times* and the *Milwaukee Journal* as "two great papers."[70]

Democrats on the subcommittee were sensitive to the charge that they were merely playing politics. They were also dissatisfied with the staff's choice of the very weak Lustron case as the focus for public hearings. (As a result, Carl Hayden would soon transfer Chief Counsel John Moore to the parent Rules Committee.) Throughout the month of June Gillette made repeated efforts to bring McCarthy before the subcommittee to testify on behalf of his anti-Benton resolution. Gillette found it puzzling that Joe continued to stall and seek delays, although expressing the desire to appear. On July 1 McCarthy finally agreed to testify two days later. On the morning of July 3 newspapers trumpeted the proclamation by the McCarran Committee that after eighteen months of study it had concluded that Owen Lattimore had been "a conscious articulate instrument of the Soviet conspiracy."[71]

Joe wheeled a cart loaded with documents and reference books into the hearing room and railed against Benton for five hours. Among his charges was the assertion that Benton, as Assistant Secretary of State, had given haven to seven "fellow travelers, Communists, and complete dupes" (including the distinguished Harvard law professor Zechariah Chaffee, Jr.), and that he had moved among "a motley pink-tainted crowd" in the State Department. Benton replied in the public hearing with a four-hour emotion-packed harangue, responding to the charges and angrily denouncing McCarthy as "a hit-and-run propagandist of the Soviet type." Herman Welker, McCarthy's ambassador on the subcommittee, bore down hard on Benton's alleged violations of election and tax laws, calling for a jury decision.[72]

Two days later McCarthy and Benton got into a nasty exchange on the Senate floor. Joe introduced a bill that would bar interstate shipment of educational films on which script writers with records of Communist front activities were employed. This was a direct attack upon Benton's Encyclopedia Britannica Films, Inc. Joe claimed that a random check of seventeen writers at the corporation had turned up eight with a "fantastic record of Communist activities." Prof. Robert S. Lynd of Columbia University, for example, had twenty-three citations in his HUAC file. At one point Joe asked whether "the Senator is either so stupid he doesn't know how Communism works" or whether his stand was "worse."

Benton hotly denied McCarthy's allegations and explained that the films on which Lynd and his colleagues had worked were made before he purchased the film company from the Western Electric Corporation. Did the Wisconsin senator, he asked sarcastically, wish to claim that Western Electric and its parent, the American Telegraph and Telephone Company, were nests of Communists? He supported Lynd's patriotism by observing that as a member of Columbia's faculty the professor had been employed by General Eisenhower, at one time the university's president. Benton accused McCarthy of "blackmail" tactics and said that he represented "the spirit of fascism."[73]

The Gillette subcommittee sank into moribundity while the nation's attention was riveted upon the national party conventions and the primary contests. Hendrickson went to Europe, and Welker retreated to the Idaho hills, making it clear that he wanted little more to do with a McCarthy probe. Gillette did not favor further subcommittee action in the absence of the Republicans. Moreover, he was very jittery about his position on the subcommittee; McCarthy had warned him privately that he would defeat him in Iowa during the next election if he pressed the investigation. Monroney and Hennings also opposed the resumption of subcommittee activity on the ground that it might appear at this time of year to be politically inspired. Rules Committee Chairman Hayden was the only figure connected with the subcommittee who was eager to resume public hearings, and his pleadings were in vain. Drew Pearson reported that Hayden was giving serious consideration to Gillette's removal as subcommittee chairman.[74]

On September 8, one day before the Wisconsin primary, subcommittee investigator Jack Poorbaugh resigned. In a telegram released to the press, Poorbaugh claimed that "restrictions" had been placed on the Benton investigation and that information had been supplied to columnists for the "apparent political purpose of smearing Senator McCarthy." The next day Herman Welker submitted his resignation, charging that the subcommittee was being used as a "political vehicle by the Democratic Party." The orchestration of these actions was obvious. The subcommittee later revealed that Poorbaugh had been in touch with McCarthy associates, including Fulton Lewis, Jr., just prior to his departure. Welker's sympathies had long been known; his resignation was timed perfectly to reach the headlines on election morning in Wisconsin.[75]

The two resignations, followed immediately by McCarthy's overwhelming victory in the G.O.P. primary, were too much for Guy Gillette, and he submitted his resignation to Hayden on September 10. He suggested that since his exit balanced Welker's, the subcommittee should continue to consist of only Hennings, Monroney, and Hendrickson. "As you know, there are no three members of the Senate who are more capable or more high-minded than these men."[76]

Thus by mid-September the McCarthy investigation appeared to be dead. The subcommittee lacked a chairman, a full complement of members, and a chief counsel. All of the information collected so far lay locked in Hayden's private office and could not possibly be published in time to have an impact on the November election. Indeed, it seemed unlikely to many insiders that a final report would ever appear.[77]

Carl Hayden, however, refused to abandon the investigation. Described by George Reedy as "the toughest man in the Senate," the 76-year-old Arizona lawmaker was still boiling at McCarthy's attack on Darrell St. Claire and his contemptuous disregard for Senate traditions. He agreed to proceed with a three-man subcommittee and named Hennings the new chairman and Hendrickson vice-chairman. No sooner had Hennings taken the reins than the third member, Mike Monroney, decided to take an extended European vacation. Monroney had been trembling with fear for some time about the McCarthy probe, confiding to Benton that he thought his mail was being read, his files searched and photographed, and his telephone tapped. (In response, Benton ran private telephones into his own hotel suites, bypassing switchboards, and put his chauffeur-bodyguard on alert. He was certain that some of his mail was opened before delivery.) Hennings angrily asked Hayden to tell Monroney to reassume his subcommittee duties or resign. When Hayden complied, Monroney promptly quit. At Benton's urging, Hayden placed himself on the subcommittee, keeping it legally viable. The body was henceforth called by some the "H-H-H" committee, after its members, Hennings, Hendrickson, and Hayden.[78]

Paul J. Cotter, from the Rules Committee staff, was named chief counsel of the subcommittee, and he was joined by a new group of experienced investigators. Apparently without the knowledge of either Hayden or

Hennings, Cotter quietly placed a "mail cover" on the private residences of McCarthy, Jean Kerr, and Don Surine in late October. This directed the Washington postmaster to provide Cotter with a daily listing of the names and return addresses of everyone from whom McCarthy and his two top aides received mail. Joe was not the only one who could play rough.[79]

Still, there was reason to believe that these efforts to revive the investigation would fail. Hendrickson, the lone Republican on the subcommittee, was under pressure from G.O.P. leaders to let the probe expire, and he seemed to be wavering. When Benton urged him to carry on, he replied, "As you well know, there is little I can promise from our present committee because we are, in the fullest sense, a 'lame-duck' corporation."[80]

Even worse, Thomas Hennings soon dropped from sight. Many close to the brilliant lawmaker realized that his disappearance could mean only one thing: another of his periodic collapses into alcoholism. When the 1952 elections became history, no one knew where Hennings was. The trail petered out in Lincoln, Nebraska.[81]

Three days after the G.O.P. White House and congressional victories, McCarthy's reelection, and Benton's defeat, Cotter sent invitations to McCarthy and Benton to appear before the subcommittee in executive session regarding the resolution each man had sponsored. Joe, on vacation and reveling in the joy of yet further triumphs, had Ray Kiermas send a polite notice of his unavailability. He could not appear, of course, and be faced with the questions contained in Benton's resolution. The subcommittee was especially interested in his finances, and Joe was not about to discuss the campaign of 1944 or his more recent personal uses of campaign contributions. Moreover, there was no reason why he should subject himself to interrogation by the Hennings subcommittee. Time was running out on the eighty-second Congress, and in a short while the Republican majority would cast Benton's charges into the oblivion of history.[82]

Subcommittee members considered issuing a subpoena to McCarthy but abandoned the idea, fearing that Joe would not respond and that they would lack the power or authority to enforce it.[83]

William Benton was more anxious than ever to have the subcommittee complete its work. His defeat at the polls had intensified his loathing of McCarthy and strengthened his desire to see a final report published. Then too, subcommittee data and conclusions would be useful in his defense against McCarthy's law suit. Benton located Senator Hennings in New York, after an extensive canvas of Manhattan bars, and pled with the woozy solon to return to Washington and resume his duties while Democrats retained their control of Congress. When Hennings proved unresponsive, Benton sent for Drew Pearson, a close friend of Hennings and the recipient of many subcommittee leaks.

Pearson and Jack Anderson had been actively lobbying senators to keep the subcommittee investigation alive and had extracted promises from New York Republican Irving Ives, Charles Tobey, and William Fulbright to ride herd on Hendrickson. When Pearson learned of Hennings's whereabouts, he called the senator's wife and rearranged his schedule to fly to New York. Before he could get to the airport, Mrs. Hennings telephoned to say that her husband had arrived at their Washington home in a sorry state and was bedridden. For the next six weeks Hennings stayed at home, departing only to spend numerous evenings in his favorite night spots.[84]

On November 21 Cotter, over Hennings's signature, sent another invitation to McCarthy to appear, specifying six matters the subcommittee would like to take up. When the chief counsel delivered the letter to McCarthy's office, he was informed that the senator was hunting in the Wisconsin woods and could not be reached. Cotter then sent a telegram, in Hennings's name, to McCarthy's Appleton address, with a copy to the Senate office, advising of the letter and inviting Joe's appearance. When the wire reached McCarthy, relaxing in a Wisconsin lodge with friends, he tossed it aside contemputously, cursing his pursuers for playing politics.[85]

On December 1 two letters from McCarthy arrived at Hennings's Senate office. In one, dated November 28, Joe claimed falsely to have just received Hennings's telegram on his return to Washington the day before. In this way he was technically relieved of the charge that he had defied the subcommittee. The second letter, obviously written in a rage, contained a harsh condemnation of the subcommittee's integrity and a one-word answer to the "six insulting questions" contained in the Hennings letter of November 21: "No." Joe added, "I thought perhaps the election might have taught you that your boss and mine—the American people—do not approve of treason and incompetence and feel that it [sic] must be exposed." He made no mention of a willingness to testify.[86]

This intemperate missive of December 1 was another serious blunder by McCarthy. It could only serve to stimulate those who were attempting to embarrass him and anger those who might otherwise have remained neutral. Even more important, the one-word denial served as an official answer to the six questions raised in Hennings' letter of November 21. These included:

> (1) Whether any funds collected or received by you and by others on your behalf to conduct certain of your activities, including those relating to "communism" were ever diverted

and used for other purposes inuring to your personal advantage.

and

> (6) Whether you used close associates and members of your family to secrete receipts, income, commodity and stock speculation, and other financial transactions for ulterior motives.

The subcommittee now had evidence to show that in both cases the proper answer should have been "Yes."

With Hayden's encouragement, the subcommittee staff labored actively to produce a final report. A lengthy document emerged shortly before Christmas, and Hayden, Pearson, and Benton were faced with the challenge of obtaining the signatures of Hennings and Hendrickson.

Pearson, weary of cajolery, warned Hennings that he would publicize his alcoholism unless the senator agreed to resume his duties. He then stationed himself around the clock inside Hennings's home to make sure that the senator did not sneak outside for a drink; Jack Anderson later termed the tactic a "species of house arrest." It took only a couple of days for Hennings to rally, and Pearson got him to a meeting with Hayden and Hendrickson.

Public acceptance of the subcommittee report hinged, of course, upon its bipartisanship, and that made Hendrickson's approval critical. The New Jersey Republican did not like some of the report's wording and may have demanded alterations and deletions. He later told Benton, "I only did for McCarthy what I would do for any other American citizen." At any rate, he agreed to sign only if the report included criticism of Benton's failure to report a $600 gift from banker Walter Cosgriff as a campaign contribution. The case against Benton was, in fact, highly persuasive. Moreover, Cosgriff's nomination as a director of the Reconstruction Finance Corporation appeared directly related to the banker's donation, the first half of which was accepted in cash. When Carl Hayden described Hendrickson's offer to Benton, the outgoing senator accepted eagerly. "Pick anything concerning me that came out of any hearings and make use of it. The important thing is to get a unanimous report signed, published, and submitted to the Senate before the new Congress convenes." What were a few paragraphs spotlighting a peccadillo involving $600 compared to the hundreds of pages of evidence, questions, and conclusions in store for McCarthy?[87]

By this time Joe was aware of the hurried attempt to produce a subcommittee report, and he determined to thwart it by applying pressure on Hendrickson. In late December he telephoned Hendrickson's New Jersey home and gave his twenty-one-year-old daughter "a mean time" when told that the senator was out. Greatly disturbed, the girl called her father in Washington, and Hendrickson telephoned McCarthy. Joe's first question was, "Did you sign that report?" Hendrickson said later that he told McCarthy he had not, but that his name would appear on it—a quibble designed to appease some of Joe's wrath. Hendrickson also assured McCarthy that the report contained a recital of the facts. (Joe was to claim that Hendrickson said he had not even read the report.)[88]

On December 31 Joe flew to Hendrickson's home and spent a half day badgering the nervous Republican. Hayden and Hennings stayed in hourly contact with Hendrickson by telephone and could discern that his resolve was beginning to weaken. Hennings could tell that Hendrickson was drinking. When the senator agreed to return to Washington the next morning, Hayden ordered the Government Printing Office to publish the report. His authority as Rules Committee chairman would expire in 48 hours.

The next day, Hennings took Hendrickson to a quiet spot for lunch, and over several drinks he applied all of his personal charm. After a few hours, Hendrickson summoned the courage to sign the report. At some point, perhaps a few hours later, Hendrickson demanded an addendum to the report stressing the subcommittee's "lack of adequate time and lack of continuity in the committee membership" and contending that a number of the report's points "have become moot by reason of the 1952 election." Hayden and Hennings wearily agreed to include this last-minute effort by Hendrickson to save face with his G.O.P. colleagues.[89]

Hayden had no hope of seeing action against McCarthy taken by the newly constituted Rules Committee; its chairman was to be William Jenner of Indiana, an ardent McCarthyite. Instead, the dour Arizona senator planned to call public attention to the subcommittee report in a news conference held the day before Republicans took over. He intended to challenge McCarthy on the Senate floor when the Wisconsinite was about to be sworn in; he telephoned colleagues all over the country for days in preparation for this move. Hayden was also determined to persuade Internal Revenue officials that McCarthy had violated criminal statutes and should be prosecuted. To the veteran senator's consternation, his three-fold plan to humiliate McCarthy, encouraged and supplemented by Benton, Pearson, Evjue, and other allies, was to yield no immediate results.[90]

Senator Hendrickson did not attend the January 2 news conference, leaving Hayden and Hennings the awkward task of assuring the press that the report was truly bipartisan. Hendrickson stayed at home, claimed to be ill, and refused comment. The next day he collapsed completely from the political heat, telling reporters that the subcommittee no doubt lacked legal authority after the previous Congress adjourned, that the report was "without the force of law," and that he doubted further action would be taken. "McCarthy's secret weapon is the cowardice of his critics," the *New York Post* editorialized. Hendrickson announced his intention to resign from the subcommittee immediately. Benton later called him a "pitiful jellyfish."[91]

Hayden and Hennings distributed the report to reporters, having delivered a copy to each senator. It consisted of 52 pages of text and 348 pages of exhibits, largely McCarthy's financial records. The document began with a lengthy account of the senator's efforts to obstruct the investigation, including his failure to comply with six invitations to testify. It then revealed that the subcommittee had decided to report on only those questions to which McCarthy had responded with "No" in his letter of December 1. These had dealt almost exclusively with financial matters, and this meant that the subcommittee was sidestepping the Communists-in-government claims, the heart of Benton's ten charges and the key to McCarthy's political power. This gingerly approach had been recommended earlier by Senator Monroney. "Mike insisted," Benton later recalled, "that on every other count he [McCarthy] was too clever, too smart, too dextrous—that he could evade us." Furthermore, the report employed innuendos and loaded questions in lieu of conclusions; it implied McCarthy's guilt on almost every page but stopped short of declaring him guilty. "Are there other instances where Senator McCarthy received some consideration from persons or agencies that he was in a position to assist or hurt in his official position as a United States senator?" It also failed to make any recommendations; subcommittee members were content to assert lamely, "The record should speak for itself. The issue raised is one for the entire Senate."[92]

The first case involved the $10,000 fee from the Lustron Corporation, a Drew Pearson favorite. Evidence in the matter was carefully and deliberately skewed to make McCarthy appear guilty of influence peddling and bribery. Joe's protestations and explanations were largely ignored. The report also described how the senator invested the fee in Seaboard Airlines Railroad stock, which later yielded a large profit and enabled him to liquidate his long-standing debt to the Appleton State Bank. "It may or may not be significant," the report stated, "that the Seaboard Airlines Railroad was also financed by the RFC and at the time indebted to RFC in excess of $15,000,000." McCarthyites were correct in labeling this part of the Hennings Report an unadulterated smear.[93]

The subcommittee had a much stronger case when it turned to the matter of McCarthy's expenditure of funds donated to assist his anti-Communist activities. Investigators uncovered a special checking account opened on May 5, 1950, into which checks, cash, and money orders totaling almost $21,000 were placed. The deposits were clearly gifts to McCarthy for his "war against the Reds." Several checks drawn on the account, however, seemed to be intended for McCarthy's personal use, including a $73.80 check to the Collector of Internal Revenue.

A savings account, opened on September 7, 1950, was also discovered. It contained $10,500, and investigators traced all but $500 of this to Mr. and Mrs. Alvin M. Bentley, divorced right-wing admirers of the Wisconsin senator. (Joe stayed a step ahead of the sleuths. Mr. Bentley suddenly produced a curious five-year, non-interest-bearing, $3,000 note from McCarthy. Mrs. Bentley, with Joe's knowledge, fled to Nassau to avoid questioning, escorted by McCarthy aide Harvey Matusow. Matusow soon married Mrs. Bentley, and later, disenchanted with McCarthy, sold the story of the courtship to Drew Pearson for $250.) The report showed that Joe transferred the $10,000 to an old friend, Henry J. Van Straten, to invest in January soy beans. From October 3, 1950, to January 2, 1951, a profit of $17,354.30 was realized. Van Straten returned the $10,000 to McCarthy, who deposited the sum in his general personal checking account. The Hennings Report noted that Mr. Bentley told a subcommittee investigator that his $3,000 "loan" to McCarthy had been earmarked for the senator's anti-Communist fight. Mrs. Bentley, on the other hand, who had contributed a $7,000 check, would only say before her flight that she had never given McCarthy money for political purposes. (According to Matusow, she had actually given Joe more than $75,000 since 1950, money that was used in the campaigns against Tydings and Benton and for a national radio broadcast by McCarthy.)

For all of its research on this point, the report was unable to prove McCarthy conclusively guilty of illegal conduct. The donations were tax-free gifts, and the senator was free to use them as he saw fit. The subcommittee, moreover, could not prove that each donation was designated for a single purpose, and its evidence about specific disbursements by McCarthy was weak and largely speculative. The Van Straten transaction might have produced considerable negative publicity; according to later interviews with Urban Van Susteren, Joe was operating a dummy account in Van Straten's name, reaping the profit himself. But Van Straten was tight-lipped about the issue, and the available evidence was inconclusive. Still, it was hereafter exceedingly difficult to defend McCarthy's answer of "No" to the question about his personal use of these donations.[94]

The third case in the Hennings Report exposed Joe's personal contributions to his 1944 campaign. It also revealed secret and profitable stock market speculations apparently by McCarthy in the names of his brother William and his wife Julia, from 1948 through 1952. William, a Chicago truck driver, declined to be interviewed and was not subpoenaed. In addition, the report went through the tedious details of Joe's dealings with the Appleton State Bank, most of which had long ago appeared in the press, showing his often heavy indebtedness from 1945 through 1951 and his frequent financial transactions with Ray Kiermas. The purpose behind all of this was no doubt lost on many readers. The report's failure to present conclusions based upon its findings strengthened McCarthy's contention that the subcommittee was simply trying to smear him.[95]

Case number four consisted of a rehash of journalistic charges concerning Lustron, Pepsi-Cola, and the China Lobby. Number five returned to the Appleton State Bank transactions, questioning whether tax or banking laws had been violated. (No charges would ever be filed.) The last case again reviewed the campaign of 1944 and then lamely implied that Joe appointed Ray Kiermas to his office staff because Kiermas had been involved with the senator financially. "Of course," the report hedged, "there is no law against friendship and the subcommittee feels sure that Mr. Kiermas' acts were inspired by friendship and loyalty." Then why raise the charge at all? an objective reader might well have asked. Kiermas was not subpoenaed or even requested to appear before the subcommittee. (McCarthy had Kiermas submit to an I.R.S. audit immediately. Nothing illegal was found.)[96]

This hurried and unfair report should have been quickly dismissed by the nation's liberal and intellectual community, for it contained features often associated with extremist literature and condemned as McCarthyism. But the hostility toward McCarthy and the bitterness over the recent election defeats were such that many otherwise reasonable people welcomed the Hennings Report with fanfare and applause.[97]

As expected, Benton, Pearson, Herblock, and a number of Wisconsin Democrats were ecstatic. Benton termed the report's findings "shocking" and said solemnly, "It is manifest that the Senate will be compelled to unseat Senator McCarthy." The *Madison Capital Times* and *Milwaukee Journal* would quote extensively and approvingly from the report for years.

The *New York Post* boasted, "We believe this document will haunt McCarthy for a long time," and published a major portion of it in installments under garish headlines. The *New Republic* issued a condensed, well-advertised version of the report and racked up sales in excess of 150,000 by July. Americans for Democratic Action, deliberately attempting to draw McCarthy into a libel suit, reproduced the full report and quickly distributed almost 7,000 copies. Princeton University political scientist H. H. Wilson declared, "It is probable that no more damning document involving the integrity of a member of the United States Senate has ever been drawn up." Washington correspondent Willard Shelton, writing in *The Progressive,* was critical of "the piled-up agglomeration the Senate subcommittee issued after nearly seventeen months of frittering and twittering" but at the same time labeled the report "a powerful indictment." The April 1954 issue of *The Progressive,* devoted entirely to McCarthy, would cite it frequently and uncritically. Senators Flanders, Fulbright, and Morse, clamoring for sanctions against McCarthy that same year, would all speak glowingly of the Hennings Report.[98]

For the most part, Republicans greeted the report with contempt. Charles Potter of Michigan, assigned to the Rules Committee, said scornfully, "There's nothing new in it—just the same stuff that Drew Pearson has been hashing over." Right-wing newspapers downplayed and buried the story.[99]

After being handed a copy of the report Joe exploded with rage a few minutes before it was released to the press. The subcommittee, he said, had hit "a new low in dishonesty and smear," and he castigated Hayden and Hennings as "lackeys" of "this corrupt administration." "Hendrickson," he added, "is a living miracle in that he is without question the only man in the world who has lived so long with neither brains nor guts." Joe blustered, "They should know by this time that they cannot scare or turn me aside." A short time later, still burning with anger, he telephoned reporters and challenged subcommittee members to bar him from taking his Senate seat. "If they do not, they will have proven their complete dishonesty."[100]

Joe no doubt knew that Hayden, with Hennings's support, had been working on such a scheme for days. When McCarthy presented himself to be sworn in on the first day of the new Congress, Hayden planned to rise and ask him either to "stand aside" or take the oath "without prejudice." The first option meant that Joe would not take his oath of office and could not assume his seat. If the latter course of action was followed, Hayden believed, McCarthy could be removed from office by a majority vote rather than the two-thirds required for expulsion.

The Arizona senator discovered, however, that his plan lacked sufficient bipartisan support. The G.O.P. was to control the Senate in the 83rd Congress by a one-vote margin, 48 to 47 (Independent Wayne Morse of Oregon was the 96th member), and this compelled Republicans to rally behind McCarthy. Moreover, on January 2 McCarthy quietly warned the Democratic Policy Committee that if Democrats challenged him, Republicans would take the same approach toward Dennis Chavez, narrow winner of a disputed election in New Mexico. This threat disturbed several Democratic leaders, and Hayden was forced to drop the McCarthy matter entirely. Hennings later lamented, "The truth simply [was] that we did not have the votes to sustain such a move, and any motion to that effect would have resulted in a vote of confidence in Senator McCarthy and a repudiation of the subcommittee. In our opinion, such a result would have been bad for the country and for the Senate."[101]

When McCarthy's name was called on January 3 there was a hush in the Senate galleries. Joe strode into the chamber, accompanied by Alexander Wiley. He clapped Carl Hayden on the back, grinned maliciously, and walked on amid a spattering of applause. Not a single voice was raised from the floor to contest his right to be seated for a second term. As McCarthy signed the register, a sudden roar arose; Margaret Chase Smith had come up with her new colleague, former Gov. Frederick G. Payne, and Vice-President Barkley, a gallant Kentuckian, kissed her hand. Joe turned around to see what was happening and joined in the laughter.[102]

Jack Anderson later recalled, "By the advent of 1953 we had used up almost our entire bag of tricks against McCarthy, without marked effect.... Lord, three years had passed since Wheeling and he was still coming on stronger."[103]

The two subcommittee Democrats had not completely conceded defeat, however. Hayden persuaded his friend T. Coleman Andrews, the new Commissioner of Internal Revenue, to hire Harvey Fosner, associate counsel of the Hennings subcommittee, for the purpose of further investigating McCarthy's tax returns, but Treasury Secretary George M. Humphrey scotched that arrangement upon learning of it.

Hennings sent his report directly to the Justice Department and the Bureau of Internal Revenue, bypassing Rules Committee chairman Jenner, who was busily firing all but one of the incumbent subcommittee staff members. But the effort proved futile. Several months later the Justice Department announced that a study of the Hennings Report found no basis for a fraud or election-law indictment against McCarthy. The 1944 election question was a matter for state authorities. (And the statute of limitations had expired long ago.) One report declared that these findings were identical to those made by attorneys during the Truman administration. When Joe was asked to comment on the Justice Department study, he told a reporter, "I didn't even know they were working on it."[104]

17

LIKING IKE

Planning for McCarthy's reelection campaign began in the fall of 1951. In late October, Jean Kerr was supervising the creation of a book of questions and answers concerning the senator's anti-Communist charges for use on the hustings. She consulted such friends as Tom Korb, Tom Coleman, and Wisconsin G.O.P. chairman Wayne Hood, soliciting suggestions and evaluations of initial outlines. What emerged a few months later was a 104-page oversized paperback entitled *McCarthyism, The Fight for America*. Skillfully written, heavily footnoted, indexed, and containing photographs of documents and clippings, the book appeared to many average Americans to document thoroughly McCarthy's case against the conspirators in high places and his own detractors. In fact, it contained little other than Joe's well-worn attacks against Acheson, Jessup, Lattimore, the I.P.R., the China Hands, George Marshall, the Tydings Committee, and the like, which were easily vulnerable to the careful scholar. The publication sold for fifty cents, and business was brisk wherever Joe appeared. He signed thousands of copies eagerly thrust at him by cheering crowds. For many years after McCarthy's downfall his admirers would continue to point to this campaign book as the depository of the unchallenged truth of the senator's charges.[1]

In Wisconsin, in late September, Tom Korb, Otis Gomillion, Harold Townsend, Marshfield businessman Steve Miller, and a number of others close to McCarthy, created a statewide McCarthy Club and began laying plans for a gala fund-raising testimonial dinner. As Democratic State Senator Gaylord Nelson soon pointed out, this "voluntary organization" was actually a front for McCarthy's personal campaign, a familiar device for avoiding the state law that set a $10,000 limit on campaign spending by a candidate or his committee. In early December, the club mailed thousands of mimeographed letters, printed in three colors, inviting Wisconsinites to purchase twenty-five-dollar-per-plate tickets and urging them to sell tickets to others. "We need your help. The money raised will be used to spread the truth about Joe's fight against the Communists and fellow travelers." Subversives were already at work to defeat the senator, the letter warned. "Well-financed agents of the Administration and the Communist party are traveling throughout Wisconsin attempting to stir up opposition to McCarthy." This was undoubtedly a reference to investigators for Drew Pearson and the Gillette subcommittee.[2]

About 2,200 people attended the dinner on December 11, 1951, at the Milwaukee Auditorium, including many state G.O.P. leaders. (Only a single major Wisconsin Republican, Secretary of State Fred Zimmerman, had spoken out against McCarthy.) Leo Hershberger, Joe's high school principal, lavished praise upon Joe, as did Republican Senators Herman Welker and John Marshall Butler and Dr. William McGovern, a right-wing political scientist from Northwestern University who had testified before the McCarran Committee. McGovern, who gave the principle address, described the rise of Communism in Asia and said that Americans had failed to heed "those voices of warning from musty classrooms until the clear, small, strident voice of a little boy from Wisconsin, Joe McCarthy, concentrated American attention on disloyalty in our State Department." Congratulatory telegrams were read from Republican Senators Everett Dirksen, William Jenner, Homer Capehart, Andrew Schoepple, Owen Brewster, and Harry Cain.

Many in the audience expected a fiery address from McCarthy, and the crowd roared when the time came for his remarks. Korb had advised Joe to scrap a prepared speech in favor of a brief statement of gratitude. Joe was so shaken by the tributes and constant ovations that he could barely do that. "I used to pride myself on being tough," he stammered, "especially in the last eighteen months when we've been kicked around and damned. I didn't think I could be touched very deeply. But tonight, frankly, my cup and my heart are so full I can't talk to you." Wiping his eyes, he sat down. Not even Miles McMillin or Robert Fleming, covering the dinner for their hostile newspapers, challenged the sincerity of this rare public display of emotion.[3]

The *Capital Times* would later claim that the dinner raised "more than $100,000." Far more realistically, the McCarthy Club reported proceeds of $15,536. (Only 1,777 actually had dinner, and some 400 tickets were complimentary.) The club continued to raise funds through advertisements and mailings, and by February 1952 listed total receipts of $39,635. That August it reported receipts of $30,819, including a $5,000 donation from Texas oilman H. R. Cullen. One of the club's projects was the creation of "Physicians for McCarthy," another fund-raising body, and the delivery of a free copy of *McCarthyism, The Fight For America* to every physician's office in the state.[4]

Gov. Walter J. Kohler was noticeably absent from the McCarthy dinner. A popular and moderate Republican, Kohler was seriously considering a challenge to McCarthy in the G.O.P. primary. He disliked the senator personally and had strong reservations about his anti-Communist campaign, especially the attacks on Gen. George Marshall. Mrs. Ogden Reid, of the *New York Herald Tribune,* quietly traveled to Madison to encourage Kohler to run. Officials of the Wisconsin Federation of Labor promised funds and support. An assortment of "citizens committees" sprang up. But in late January, bowing to pressure from lower-echelon party leaders, Kohler announced that he would seek reelection as governor. This meant that McCarthy would enter the primary without significant opposition. Henry S. Reuss, a Milwaukee Democrat who declared his candidacy for the Democratic senatorial nomination in October 1951, told reporters, "I had hoped that Governor Kohler would carry out the promptings of his conscience and give the decent Wisconsin Republicans a chance to clean up a national disgrace within their party primary."[5]

Wisconsin Democrats were optimistic about their political future. In 1950, party candidates for governor and U.S. senator polled 47 percent of the vote, a far cry from the bleak year of 1938 when Democrats won only 8 percent of the state vote. Numerous young, attractive, and able party leaders were eager to run against Joe McCarthy, among them James Doyle, chairman of the Democratic Organizing Committee; former Attorney General Thomas Fairchild, the party's Senatorial nominee in 1950; State Senator Gaylord Nelson, and Reuss. Private efforts to reach agreement on a single candidate and avoid a primary fight were disrupted by Reuss, who was determined to run no matter what the party hierarchy decided. Reuss was wealthy, well educated, and a tireless campaigner. But he was virtually unknown outside Milwaukee and did not enjoy the confidence of many top Democrats. After much jockeying back and forth, Fairchild, the favorite of party liberals, declared his candidacy on July 8, one day before the deadline, and prepared to face Reuss in the primary. There were no issues between the two, and the struggle became largely personal.

Fairchild's candidacy not only split Democrats but wrecked the senatorial bid of Merrill attorney Len Schmitt, a former Progressive and a G.O.P. maverick who had rolled up 150,000 votes in the race for the gubernatorial nomination in 1950. William T. Evjue hoped that Schmitt, an old friend, would draw a large Democratic crossover vote in the primary. Now, however, the Democrats who might have voted for Schmitt in the Republican primary were sure to support Fairchild instead. Some G.O.P. leaders thought that Fairchild's candidacy would cost Schmitt at least 50,000 votes.[6]

Democrats had begun a concerted effort against McCarthy in June 1951 with the creation of "Operation Truth," a statewide series of public meetings featuring street-corner oratory by party leaders. The intellectual content of the speeches, apparently, left something to be desired. Henry Reuss, for example, charged, "Senator McCarthy is a tax-dodging, character-assassinating, racetrack gambling, complete and contemptible liar." The impact on the electorate soon appeared minimal, even to partisans.[7]

At about the same time, liberals were forming the Wisconsin Citizens' Committee on McCarthy's Record, a bipartisan, 75-member body drawn from across the state to support the production of an anti-McCarthy campaign book. The driving force behind the project was Morris H. Rubin, editor of the Madison monthly *The Progressive*. A year later, in mid-1952, the committee published a 136-page paperback entitled *The McCarthy Record,* edited by Rubin but actually written by Miles McMillin and *Milwaukee Journal* reporter Ed Bayley.[8]

The publication, sold at $1.00 a copy, had several strengths. It was well written and attractively designed; photographs of documents and newspaper clippings were included, imitating McCarthy's method. Quotations from congressional hearings and reports were used extensively to document accounts of the Wheeling charges, the John Stewart Service case, the Philip Jessup nomination, the Maryland campaign, and other relevant issues. Attention was called to polls taken of 128 Washington correspondents and 50 political scientists ranking McCarthy the worst senator on Capitol Hill. A two-page illustration depicted the State Department's elaborate loyalty and security procedures, enacted three years before the Wheeling speech.

On the other hand, the authors painted McCarthy's pre-Senatorial career as black as they could, and their accounts of the Lustron case and the senator's income tax returns were misleading. (The Malmedy case was omitted from the litany of Joe's sins; the charge that Wisconsin Germans were pro-Nazi in 1949 was not likely to be welcomed by state voters.) Some readers were probably repelled by the unrelieved portrayal of the senator as an evil figure. Others no doubt found it hard to believe the claim that McCarthy's anti-Communist activities had actually helped the Reds. "Playing into Communist Hands" was the title of a chapter that might serve as a model of "reverse McCarthyism." A headline over a quotation from a North Carolina newspaper read "Stalin's Man-of-the-Year." Next to a drawing of the FBI director was the heading, "J. Edgar Hoover versus Joseph McCarthy."

On the whole, however, *The McCarthy Record* was more informative and far more accurate than the book produced under the direction of Jean Kerr, but its blatant partisanship may have limited its circulation and reduced its effectiveness. The book became associated from the start with the Democrats, despite the presence of Republicans on the Citizens' Committee, and many Republicans, Independents, and conservative Democrats no doubt dismissed it the way they would a speech by William T. Evjue or an editorial in the *Milwaukee Journal*.[9]

McCarthy officially opened his reelection campaign on May 3 with a keynote speech at the convention of the State Federation of Young Republican Clubs in Racine. He promised to attack the "starry-eyed planners" in the State Department as never before; "now we'll name them for the traitors they are." The brief address, as well as the *McCarthyism* book, clearly defined the perimeters of the campaign. Joe was to wrap himself in the mantle of anti-Communism and rarely discuss anything else, including his overall legislative record. It was sound strategy. *Capital Times* columnist Aldric Revell lamented, "rank-and-file Republicans, especially those in the rural areas, consider McCarthyism to mean anti-Communism, two-fisted fighting against odds, and battling to save America from Communism in the State Department." Revell did not know how to overcome this popular impression. "Inevitably, if the discussion gets down to particulars, the average person will refer to Alger Hiss as the clincher to prove that McCarthy knows what he is doing and is doing a good job. Anyone who wastes his breath pointing out that McCarthy had nothing to do with Alger Hiss is just politically and psychologically naive." When a *New York Times* writer asked a rural Wisconsin newspaper editor for his opinion of the senator, the man replied, "Sure, I'm for McCarthy. I'm against Communism. McCarthy's a real American and he's the only one in Washington doing anything about the Communists." A farmer commented, "Yes, I guess almost everybody in this part of the country is for McCarthy. He's against Communism—and we're against Communism. Besides, if he wasn't telling the truth they'd a hung him long ago. He's one of the greatest Americans we've ever had."[10]

McCarthy and his supporters were supremely confident of his reelection. Wayne Hood toured the state and reported that there was "no question but what Senator McCarthy would be reelected by the largest majority in the history of the State of Wisconsin." Cyrus Philipp told a national G.O.P. official, "I think the general consensus among observers is that Joe McCarthy will win the nomination and election very handily." Enthusiasm was high on all levels of party activity, and Joe was in heavy demand as a speaker. A civic official from Hartland wrote to Hood, "It has been said in our local group that we are going to arrange this meeting when Joe McCarthy can speak to us even if it must be at midnight." Twelve thousand people signed the senator's nomination papers, required by law in Wisconsin.[11]

Republicans of national stature were also flocking behind McCarthy. Robert Taft, eager for victory in Wisconsin's Presidential primary, swallowed his personal misgivings and came out for the senator in early 1952. A form letter written in mid-February explained, "I have disagreed with some of Senator McCarthy's statements and charges just as I often disagree with other Republican senators, but no one can escape the fact that Communists did infiltrate the State Department and that their existence was just as strenuously denied before Hiss was convicted. Many convictions and dismissals since that time, including the recent dismissal of Service, certainly justify the movement started by Senator McCarthy." Those close to McCarthy in Wisconsin returned the admiration. Tom Coleman directed the Taft campaign in the state and was chosen to be Taft's national convention floor manager. Tom Korb became chairman of the Ohio senator's Milwaukee County campaign. Lloyd Tegge resigned as state chairman of the Young Republicans to work with the Young Republicans for Taft. On a swing through Wisconsin, Taft assured Republicans of his complete support for Joe; he told Harold Townsend that he "thought the world" of McCarthy. In the April 1 presidential primary, Taft won 315,541 votes to Earl Warren's 262,271 and Harold Stassen's 169,679.[12]

On his return to the United States in early June, Gen. Dwight D. Eisenhower, the extremely popular candidate of the G.O.P. moderates, refused to comment on McCarthy, saying that he would not "discuss personalities." He added, however, that he stood second to none in his own desire to root out "Communistic, subversive, or pinkish influence" in the government. It was common knowledge among insiders that "Ike" intensely disliked McCarthy because of the attack on Gen. George C. Marshall. Moreover, in late 1951 Joe had added Paul G. Hoffman, head of the Ford Foundation and chairman of the advisory committee of Citizens for Eisenhower, to his public list of those "soft" on Communism. But by failing, for pragmatic reasons, to repudiate McCarthy, and by using right-wing rhetoric in campaign speeches (in Denver he blamed Democrats for the fall of China and the Korean War), Eisenhower was indirectly assisting the Wisconsin senator's reelection.[13]

Richard Nixon came to Milwaukee in mid-June and gave the keynote address to the 3,000 delegates to the Republican state convention. He made it clear that he endorsed his good friend from Wisconsin. The freshman California senator condemned the Administration for its failure to grapple effectively with the "Communist fifth column in the United States" and said that no one should contend that McCarthy's charges were wrong until they received a "fair" investigation by a Republican administration.

Convention delegates gave McCarthy a unanimous endorsement. At the same time, there were strong objections voiced against Fred R. Zimmerman, who had criticized McCarthy publicly. Despite the fact that he had regularly received more votes than any other statewide candidate, Zimmerman was denied endorsement for a tenth term as Wisconsin secretary of state.[14]

As delegates began to gather in Chicago in early July for the 25th Republican National Convention, Eisenhower supporters were stunned to learn that McCarthy was scheduled to give a major address. There were reports that Joe had "bulled" his way onto the convention program, but these were denied by A. G. Hermann, executive director of the Republican National Committee. McCarthy and Senators Cain of Washington and Kem of Missouri were selected to give speeches, Hermann explained, to assist their bids for reelection. Asked why Declaration of Conscience signers Ives of New York, Thye of Minnesota, and Smith of New Jersey, also up for reelection, were not included, Hermann snapped, "They can't get on the program." One senator told a reporter, "Senator Taft controls the national arrangements committee that selected the speakers. It's as simple as that."[15]

The Republican Party at this point in its history was extremely conservative and thoroughly devoted to exploiting the second Red Scare. It was fitting that McCarthy be placed in the limelight. Gen. Douglas MacArthur was to be the keynote speaker at the convention, and Senator Styles

Bridges, Herbert Hoover, and Patrick Hurley would also be giving speeches. The Communists-in government issue was used during the first hour of the first day of the convention, as was the term "Democrat Party." Even before the proceedings got underway, the *Chicago Daily News* reported that Richard Nixon had been selected as Eisenhower's running mate. Insiders understood that Nixon's appeal involved not only geography and youth but above all the senator's close ties to Joe McCarthy and his allies. If the G.O.P. had to swallow Ike, who, like Thomas E. Dewey, was linked in many minds with the Eastern Establishment and New York financial circles, the presence of Nixon on the ticket would do much to appease the Far Right.[16]

Curiously, Joe did not commit himself publicly for a candidate until shortly after the convention was underway. General MacArthur, he told reporters, was "the man who combines the best qualifications of the other leading candidates." Joe was clearly moved by the keynote address attacking "Those reckless men who, yielding to international intrigue, set the stage for Soviet ascendancy as a world power and our own relative decline." He added, however, that he would not campaign for MacArthur during the convention because "both Senator Taft and General Eisenhower are outstanding men."[17]

On the afternoon of July 9, before a nationwide television audience, temporary convention chairman Walter S. Hallanan of West Virginia, a close friend of McCarthy's, took the rostrum to introduce the Wisconsin Senator.

> Ladies and gentlemen of the Convention, the Truman-Acheson Administration, the Communist press and the Fellow Travelers have all joined hands in a gigantic propaganda campaign to discredit and destroy an able and patriotic United States Senator, because he had the courage to expose the traitors in our Government. (Applause.) They have not succeeded and they will not succeed. The fact that Senator Joe McCarthy is the object of such violent hatred by Dean Acheson, the Alger Hiss gang and the Owen Lattimore crowd is a badge of honor in the eyes of every patriotic American. (Applause.)
>
> When anyone tells you that Joe McCarthy has recklessly slandered honorable American citizens ask that person to name one whose name has been unfairly besmirched. (Applause.) One by one those named by him as bad security risks are being publicly exposed or quietly dropped from the rolls of the Federal Government. (Applause.)

> Let us make it clear to the country here today and now that
> we turn our backs on Alger Hiss but that we will not turn our
> backs on any man such as that fighting Marine from Wiscon-
> sin whom I now present to this Convention, the Honorable
> Joseph McCarthy. (Prolonged applause.)[18]

As Joe entered the convention hall, grinning, shaking hands, waving to
the cheering crowd, the band played "On Wisconsin" and the "Marine
Hymn." Miles McMillin observed maliciously that the senator was the only
convention speaker to wear makeup.[19]

Joe's speech was little more than a rehash of the emotional vituperations
against the "Acheson-Truman-Lattimore party" that he had delivered
hundreds of times since Wheeling. The free world was losing 100 million
people a year to international Communism, he cried, and those responsible
"are still in control in Washington and in Moscow." In Korea alone
Democrats "have squandered the blood of 110,631 sons of American
mothers." Unfortunately, he said, "the loyal Democrats of this nation no
longer have a party."

At one point in the speech, Joe's pal Lloyd Tegge and some others
jumped up and began to parade around the hall holding up large red
herrings bearing the names Alger Hiss, Owen Lattimore, and Dean Acheson. A few minutes later Joe called the convention's attention to the
presence of Mr. and Mrs. Robert Vogeler, and he asked the couple to stand.
Vogeler had been the president of the International Telephone and Telephone Company when arrested in Hungary on bogus charges of spying and
imprisoned for seventeen months. He was released on April 28, 1951, after
extensive State Department negotiations. Joe took the position that Mrs.
Vogeler, an ex-Belgian beauty queen, was solely responsible for her husband's freedom because of her efforts to publicize the case. By prearrange-
ment, the television cameras immediately switched to the Vogelers and Joe
shouted, "He is here and not being tortured in a Communist prison cell,
thanks to a courageous wife who has refused to let the State Department
forget him." (The Vogelers were soon to campaign in Wisconsin for
McCarthy.) Joe then repaired to a favorite oratorical device:

> But Mr. Truman says there is nothing wrong in the State
> Department, he says everything is just fine, he has actually
> said that if anyone hears of anything wrong, just call him
> collect and he personally will take care of things.
> Mr. Truman, your telephone is ringing tonight. Five thou-
> sand Americans are calling, calling from prison cells deep

> inside Russia and her satellite nations. They are homesick,
> Mr. Truman. They are lonely and maybe a little afraid.
> Answer your telephone, Mr. Truman. It will be interesting to
> hear what you have to say. Some of them haven't heard an
> American speak for years. But, Mr. Truman, they are getting
> a busy signal on your line. They will call Washington again;
> they will call again when the American people are through
> with you, Mr. Truman, and through with the Achesons, the
> Jessups, and the Lattimores. (Applause.)

Joe made effective use of ultraconservative testimony given before the McCarran Committee, which had conveniently released its final report just before the convention opened. "Listen to what General Willoughby said when asked to give a Senate committee the record of some of the State Department's architects for disaster—records which were carefully documented in Army Intelligence files. Let me read it to you. On pages 387 and 388 of the hearings of August 9, 1951." It all sounded so official and scholarly.

McCarthy stirred the crowd with four thundering sentences delivered with the full power of his rhetorical skill:

> My good friends, I say one Communist in a defense plant is
> one Communist too many. (Applause.)
> One Communist on the faculty of one university is one
> Communist too many. (Applause.)
> One Communist among the American advisers at Yalta
> was one Communist too many.
> And even if there were only one Communist in the State
> Department, that would still be one Communist too many.
> (Applause.)

Toward the end of his speech, Joe trotted out his treacly yarn about the chaplain at Bougainville. "In the South Pacific there had been a dive-bombing attack on our boys," he began. "I guess Truman would call it a police action."[20]

The speech was a solid hit with the delegates, who cheered and hollered boisterously as McCarthy concluded. Of course, almost every word he had uttered, with considerable skill to be sure, was historical and factual balderdash. Taft knew it, and so did Nixon, Dirksen, Bridges, and many others who were willing to use the malevolent innocence of McCarthy for their own political gain.

Those closest to Joe knew that, oratorical flourishes aside, he was entirely sincere. When Lloyd Tegge would ask him privately to soften his charges a bit for fear they were hurting him politically, Joe would launch into a frenetic tirade about Reds in Washington. "He'd tear me apart," Tegge later recalled.[21]

William Randolph Hearst warmly applauded the McCarthy speech in his newspaper chain. *The New York Times,* on the other hand, stated editorially that with McCarthy's appearance the G.O.P. convention "reached rock bottom." Miles McMillin quoted a reporter (probably himself) who referred to a "middle of the gutter speech." President Truman missed the performance but did not think himself deprived of an enriching experience. When reporters asked if he had any comment on "the mistakes of the Acheson-Truman-Lattimore party" as described in Chicago, he said that he didn't know anything about that, "but if McCarthy said it, it's a damned lie, you can be sure of that."[22]

The G.O.P. party platform contained numerous examples of McCarthyism, forecasting the tone of Republican campaigns all over the country. The preamble contended that Administration Democrats had "shielded traitors to the Nation in high places" and were responsible for the Korean War. The foreign policy plank, drafted by John Foster Dulles, condemned Democrâts for the "tragic blunders" of Tehran, Yalta, and Potsdam, the abandonment of Eastern Europe to Communism, the surrender of Manchuria, the fall of China, and the Korean War. It promised an end to "the negative, futile and immoral policy of 'containment' " and anticipated "the contagious, liberating influences which are inherent in freedom." A plank entitled "Communism" accused the Administration of appeasement at home and abroad plus the deliberate obstruction of Communist investigations. "There are no Communists in the Republican Party," voters were assured. "A Republican President will appoint only persons of unquestioned loyalty. We will overhaul loyalty and security programs."[23]

Eisenhower's popularity with the American people was such that his selection by the delegates on the first ballot was anticlimactic. Those on the Far Right, although naturally disappointed by Taft's defeat, had good reason to approve the convention's choice. The nominee violated precedent by telephoning Taft almost immediately, and the two men, smiling and friendly, soon faced reporters together. Nixon's selection, of course, was also highly pleasing. (Dr. Milton Eisenhower later conceded that his brother "was pretty much guided by the advice of the people who had been in politics for a great many years.") There was also the certainty that John Foster Dulles would be named Secretary of State in an Eisenhower Administration. Dulles, a veteran diplomat and descendant of two Secretaries of State, had been the choice of many close to Taft. He had won the hearts of ultraconservatives not only for his experience and militant anti-Communism but also by his right-wing senatorial campaign in New York three years earlier against Herbert Lehman. To the delight of McCarthy and his friends, Dulles and Eisenhower soon conferred with Charles Kersten, an outspoken advocate of liberating all "captive peoples" from the control of the Soviet Union. Shortly, the Republican nominee endorsed this highly controversial policy in a speech before an American Legion convention.[24]

Still, Taft was clearly unenthusiastic about Eisenhower, and many of his partisans dragged their feet. It took another meeting with Eisenhower in mid-September to persuade Taft that his differences with the candidate were only "differences of degree." This cordiality disturbed many G.O.P. moderates but served the purpose of bringing virtually all of the Far Right actively into the campaign. One influential Taftite, Indiana Republican Chairman Cale J. Holder, declared, "It is in the interests of America that Eisenhower . . . be elected."[25]

Joe publicly praised Ike's selection from the start. "I think that Eisenhower will make a great President," he told reporters on the evening of the nomination. "One of the finest things I've seen is Eisenhower going to Taft's headquarters and accepting Taft's offer of cooperation." Governor Kohler, Senator Wiley, and Wisconsin Secretary of State Zimmerman were also early supporters. Democrat Henry Reuss, a former junior officer on Eisenhower's staff, added his admiration for the nominee but predicted that he would be incompatible with McCarthy. "General Eisenhower and Senator McCarthy are at opposite poles of the G.O.P. scale. Where one is honest, the other is devious. Where one is well advised in foreign affairs the other is ignorant. The two are utterly opposed on issues and principles. Therefore, it is obvious that Eisenhower will find it impossible to campaign in Wisconsin. For if he does, he will have to either ignore our junior senator or repudiate him."[26]

The Democrats met in Chicago in late July, and William Benton was a principal convention speaker. Predictably, he attacked Senators McCarthy, Bricker, Cain, and Kem, men who "were members of the freshman class of 1946 and will become the seniors and take over the class of '52." Of course, he reserved his harshest words for Joe, contending that any similarity between the party of Lincoln and Republican orators like McCarthy "is a semantic accident." "Do the American people really want Joe McCarthy as chairman of the powerful Senate Committee on Government Operations?"

he shouted. The delegates roared back "No." Presidential candidates Estes Kefauver and W. Averell Harriman were among several Democrats who strongly condemned McCarthy.[27]

The Democratic Presidential nominee, Gov. Adlai E. Stevenson of Illinois, was a man of splendid intellect, sound education and high principles, and he was one of the party's most articulate spokesmen for Roosevelt-Truman liberalism. "Let's talk sense to the American people," he would urge. The fact that he had once vouched for Alger Hiss's personal integrity made him a certain target for the full force of right-wing bombast, but he did not flinch at this prospect. At the same American Legion convention during which Eisenhower pandered to his hawkish audience by advocating the "liberation" of whole segments of the Communist world, the Democratic nominee attacked McCarthy and McCarthyism. There are among us, he said, those "who use 'patriotism' as a club for attacking other Americans." As a "shocking example" he pointed to "the attacks which have been made on the loyalty and the motives of our great wartime Chief of Staff, General Marshall. To me this is the type of 'patriotism' which is, in Dr. Johnson's phrase, 'the last refuge of scoundrels.'" In this very citadel of the second Red Scare, Stevenson declared to his largely unreceptive audience, "The tragedy of our day is the climate of fear in which we live, and fear breeds repression. Too often sinister threats to the Bill of Rights, to freedom of the mind . . . are concealed under the patriotic cloak of anti-Communism."[28]

One of McCarthy's earliest public comments about Stevenson, made as Joe recovered from his stomach surgery, set the stage for future attacks. Told that the Democratic nominee had asked Eisenhower to repudiate him, Joe said, "Horsemeat Adlai should brush the odor of Alger Hiss off his toga before he advises Eisenhower."[29]

Even in his absence, McCarthy's campaign was well underway and running smoothly. Copies of *America's Retreat from Victory*, the anti-George Marshall book, and *McCarthyism, The Fight for America* were reaching thousands. Walter Kohler, who abandoned his personal reservations about Joe before the national convention assembled, took the stump for the senator in early August, pledging his full support. "You can't write McCarthy off," the governor said. "You can like him or dislike him but the fact remains that all of the things he has said about the Communists in government stack up to the point where there is too much smoke to repudiate McCarthy." The Republican Voluntary Committee ran a full-page "Open Letter from Senator Joe McCarthy" in both Madison newspapers in mid-August. "The Communists and their fellow travelers would have you think this is a personal fight on the part of McCarthy. They want you to think this," Joe wrote. "This is your fight. It is the fight of every American—every loyal Democrat and every loyal Republican—who wants this nation to remain free." In South Milwaukee former Ambassador to Poland Arthur Bliss Lane told an enthusiastic crowd of 1,000, "Senator McCarthy is a symbol of the patriotism that should rule the United States. I am not ashamed to be called a McCarthyite; I am proud. I would rather be accused of being a McCarthyite than be accused of treason." Ex-Communist Harvey Matusow, sponsored by the McCarthy Club, gave five speeches in the state, contending that a "smear campaign" against McCarthy had been launched in 1950 by 40 Reds who were on the staffs of leading New York newspapers; the term "McCarthyism" was a product. The senator, he said, "makes no accusations or says anything about anybody unless there is documentation to back it up." In California a "Hollywood Committee for McCarthy" was at work raising funds. Actors John Wayne and Ward Bond were Vice-Chairmen, and the list of members included Cecil B. De Mille, Harold Lloyd, Louis B. Mayer, Adolphe Menjou, Ray Milland, Dennis Morgan, George Murphy, Leo McCarey, Pat O'Brien, Dick Powell, and Randolph Scott. Hearst columnist Westbrook Pegler, as well, had asked his readers to contribute to the McCarthy campaign, describing Joe as sick and broke. Fulton Lewis, Jr., made a similar plea. Harvey Matusow later recalled seeing money pour into McCarthy Club headquarters.[30]

Joe's opponents were also hard at work before the primary. The *Madison Capital Times* and *Milwaukee Journal* ran anti-McCarthy stories and editorials almost daily, focusing on the latest revelations about the senator's wartime record and the assortment of charges being investigated by the Gillette-Hennings Subcommittee. Evjue displayed the fact that McCarthy had failed to introduce a single successful bill in the 82d Congress. (Senator Wiley had the same distinction.) *The McCarthy Record* became the best-selling non-fiction book in Milwaukee, and sales went over the 15,000 mark by early September.[31]

Len Schmitt, McCarthy's G.O.P. primary opponent, consulted with Millard Tydings and began a series of blistering attacks on the senator. He said repeatedly that he was in the race not because he wanted to go to Washington but because he sought to defeat McCarthy, who had become a disgrace to the Senate. Schmitt hit especially hard at Joe's Reds-in-government charges. If he lost in the primary, he said, he would vote for McCarthy's Democratic opponent.

The device that earned Schmitt the most publicity was the "Talkathon," a marathon radio show, featuring questions and answers, that once lasted twenty-five consecutive hours. Advertising for donations in a Long Beach, California, newspaper, the McCarthy Club referred to a "twenty-five hour radio smear program" and pled, "Although we do not hope to match the enormous amount of money which the opposition is pouring into Wisconsin, we do very badly need campaign funds to bring the facts before the people of Wisconsin to offset this vicious mud-slinging campaign which is being waged against [the Senator]." In fact, Schmitt's coffers were virtually empty. A "Dollars for Decency" drive to raise funds from the "little people" flopped, and an effort by Green Bay Democrat Meyer Cohen to raise $50,000 in New York brought in only about $5,000. The only visible support Schmitt had in the state came from Evjue and a few scattered labor and citizens' groups. Organized labor on the whole ignored his candidacy and backed the Democrats. Conservative newspapers disregarded his press releases and attacked him editorially. G.O.P. officials spoke of Schmitt scornfully if at all.[32]

Democrats Fairchild and Reuss campaigned vigorously across the state, paying far less attention to each other than to the incumbent. Neither candidate enjoyed ample funding. Six state organizations opposed to McCarthy reported spending a total of only $14,923 by early September. Wisconsin trade unions contributed modestly. Efforts by party leader James Doyle and others to raise money outside the state were only partially successful. A.D.A. advocate Joseph Rauh and liberal economist Robert Nathan asked their friends for assistance. Dorothy Schiff, publisher of the *New York Post,* contributed $500, as did Marshall Field, publisher of the *Chicago Sun-Times.* The scale of these donations was not in the same league with the triumphant tally being recorded by the McCarthy apparatus.[33]

Democrats were encouraged by the arrival of President Truman on September 1 for a Labor Day speech in Milwaukee. An estimated 40,000 people jammed a six-block parade route from the railroad station to the new Milwaukee Arena. Fairchild and Reuss were on hand, as was William Proxmire, Democratic candidate for governor. Before a cheering crowd of 11,000 Truman praised the state's "great liberal tradition" and declared, "I am sure that this year Wisconsin will return to that tradition and elect a United States Senator you can be proud of." He was applauded loudly at another point in his address at which he said, "It is time for a change from the Big Lie—from the brazen Republican efforts to falsify history, to smear and ruin innocent individuals, to trample on the basic liberties of American citizens." He did not mention McCarthy by name; but then he didn't have to.[34]

Two days later Joe had recovered from his surgery sufficiently to make his only speech prior to the September 9 primary. A 31-station radio hookup carried the message throughout the state, and a wildly enthusiastic crowd of some 2,000 greeted the Senator in a North Milwaukee suburban high school auditorium. Joe began by expounding for the first time the fiction that the late Navy Secretary James Forrestal had been the instigator of his Communists-in-government charges. He then documented the continued seriousness of the situation in Washington by quoting from a recent Justice Department brief referring to Soviet plans for obtaining blank American passports "from Communists in the State Department." (Attorney General James McGranery quickly explained that the reference was to testimony by an ex-Communist about a plan laid by the Russian Secret Police in 1928! "Nowhere in the entire hearing is there any testimony that the plan was put into effect.")

Before long, Joe turned his attention to the "Democrat candidate" for President.

> Mr. Stevenson, in three of the speeches which you made since you were nominated on the Democrat ticket, you went out of your way to viciously berate me. Why, Mr. Stevenson. Why the bitterness? Could you be disturbed, Mr. Stevenson, because I am checking your record since the day you entered government service at about the same time and in the same department as the Hiss, Abt, Witt, Pressman group? Are you getting worried about what we are finding?

Actually, Stevenson had worked in the Agriculture Department, along with Hiss and the others, for about five months in 1933 and had not perceived the slightest inclination by his colleagues toward subversive activities. He saw Hiss again in 1945-46 in the course of official duties and twice in 1947 at the United Nations. That was the full extent of their relationship. In 1949 Stevenson had declined a request to testify at Hiss's first trial but consented to answer questions submitted under a court order about the reputation of the accused. "I said his reputation was 'good' so far as I had heard from others," Stevenson explained in 1952, "and that was the simple, exact, whole truth, and all I could say on the basis of what I knew." Moreover, he said, "at no time did I testify on the issue of the guilt or innocence of Alger Hiss as a perjuror or traitor. As I have repeatedly said, I have never doubted the verdict of the jury which convicted him." But Joe continued gravely,

You voluntarily submitted to the Hiss judge and jury an affidavit in which you swore to your Almighty God that Alger Hiss (1) has a reputation for truthfulness—you say McCarthy is a liar; (2) you swore under oath that Hiss had an outstanding reputation for integrity; (3) you swore under oath, Mr. Stevenson, that Alger Hiss is a great American—you say McCarthy is un-American. Well, after your entire record is given them, if the American people want you, they can have you. I don't think they do.

Joe made no mention of his primary opponent but concluded his speech with, "So there can be no doubt, let me assure you I need your votes next Tuesday. I need them badly."

There were frequent cries from the audience as McCarthy spoke: "Atta boy, Joe," "Give it to 'em," "Tell it to the *Journal,* Joe." A reference to the "Milwaukee Daily Worker" was met with what Miles McMillin called "shrieks of approval." At the conclusion of the meeting a number of women worked their way through the crowd down to the press section and stood over the newsmen shouting, "Where's the *Journal* reporter? Who writes that dirty stuff?"[35]

During the first week of September every Wisconsin citizen with an address received an eight-page tabloid called *Election News,* paid for by the State Republican Voluntary Committee, and an eight-page, red-white-blue flyer titled "The Truth about Sen. Joe McCarthy," sponsored by the McCarthy Club. Some 700,000 copies of each publication were mailed and delivered by volunteers, part of a week-long Republican blitz that may have cost as much as $50,000.[36]

The skillfully prepared tabloid was reminiscent of its counterpart in the Maryland campaign and was undoubtedly the work of Jean Kerr. Its initial headline blared, "Red's No. 1 Enemy Seeks Reelection," and the claim was made in the opening paragraphs that the McCarran Committee had substantiated the senator's charges. Other headlines read, "Vogeler for Joe," "Homosexuals—125 Found in U.S. Jobs," "Church Men Back McCarthy," "*Daily Worker* Praises the *Capitol* [sic] *Times,*" and "Film Stars Cite Importance of Electing an Anti-Communist." The usual allegations were made against Acheson, Jessup, Lattimore, Service, and others. The Nimitz citation was featured, to answer charges against Joe's war record. A slightly inflated list of legislative achievements appeared which included the senator's work with housing, sugar rationing, price supports for dried milk, disabled veterans, and imported furs. A final item quoted McCarthy's speech before the G.O.P. National Convention: "Our task is merely to give the American people unvarnished truth. Then, don't worry. If the American people have the facts on November 4, it will be a great day for America and for the world."[37]

On the day before the primary, Joe discussed his future with Harvey Matusow during a flight to Appleton. The possibility of a G.O.P. majority in the Senate in 1953 especially interested him, and he thought aloud about his membership on the Government Operations Committee. "I'm just biding my time. I'm the senior Republican, and some day I'll be chairman," he mused. "Some people don't realize it, but it could be the most powerful committee in the Senate." He added, "I can investigate anybody who ever received money from the government, and that covers a lot of ground." The thought made him glow. "There won't be enough trains leaving Washington to hold them if the Republicans control the Senate."[38]

The overwhelming size of McCarthy's victory in the primary stunned political observers throughout the state and nation. *Time* magazine thought that it suggested "a thorough reexamination of the 1952 campaign." Joe trounced Schmitt by a two-and-a-half-to-one margin (515,581 to 213,701), taking all but two of Wisconsin's 71 counties and rolling up 100,000 more votes than all of his Democratic and Republican opponents combined. He won the industrial centers of Milwaukee, Racine, and Kenosha handily, took Dane County, home of the *Capital Times,* and captured the farm vote as well. Many Democrats had obviously supported McCarthy. Fairchild narrowly defeated Reuss (97,321 to 94,379) but the two received only 17 percent of the total vote. McCarthy's victory in November was considered a certainty. Tom Korb confided to a friend that he thought Joe would beat Fairchild "by at least a three to one, and probably a four to one margin."[39]

The McCarthy triumph was attributed by most observers to the Reds-in-government issue. Len Schmitt commented, "I think that Wisconsin people are voting against Stalin." "McCarthy has grown in power," said *Time* magazine, "because millions of Americans think he is 'the only one' really against the internal Communist threat." William Randolph Hearst wrote exultantly, "While Communist apologists and others, including the Democratic Presidential candidate, keep acting as if the Lenin conspiracy never existed, Fighting Joe has appealed to the conscience of a people aroused by the treachery of the Hisses and the other proven associates of the Kremlin." *The New York Times* charged that McCarthy had "profiteered in fear." The *St. Louis Post-Dispatch* echoed, "McCarthy is what he is, not because he opposes Communism but because he exploits the fear of it for his own political gain." *U.S. News and World Report* observed, "McCarthy-ism, as a result, emerges as a political force to be reckoned with, not just in Wisconsin but in other states where others in politics will be tempted to exploit its vote-getting possibilities."[40]

Democratic strategists in Wisconsin, demoralized and pessimistic after the primary, decided to avoid the Communists-in-government issue as much as possible and pin what slim hope they had for victory in November on a continued exposé of McCarthy's unethical conduct and a review of his voting record. Thomas Fairchild, an honest, intelligent, and dignified attorney who lacked much flair as a campaigner, occasionally attacked McCarthy's methods, which he once said were "destroying the rights of free speech and free thought." On the whole, however, he restricted his oratory to the caliber of charges found daily in the *Capital Times* and tried to stir public interest in Joe's pre-Wheeling activities. His newspaper advertise-ments stressed the theme that his election would mean "continued prosperity."[41]

A case could be made for Fairchild's chances against McCarthy. Although Democrats traditionally did not turn out in great numbers for primaries; their presence was felt largely in general elections, and this was especially true during presidential contests. Moreover, Fairchild could count on virtu-ally all of the votes cast for Reuss, a large percentage of those given to Schmitt, and at least a fair share of the support that had gone to minor G.O.P. candidates. In Dane County, William T. Evjue pointed out, Schmitt, Fairchild, and Reuss outpolled the senator by 10,000 votes; in Milwaukee, the anti-McCarthy candidates topped the McCarthy vote by 35,000. "The game hasn't been forfeited to McCarthyism, yet," the editor growled. Patrick Lucey, Fairchild's campaign manager, thought that his candidate would make a better showing in the state than Adlai Stevenson. But such optimism was not widespread among knowledgeable Democrats. The *Milwaukee Journal* examined the primary election results and exclaimed, "This is not only appalling—it is frightening."[42]

Joe's confidence was such that he ignored Fairchild's candidacy alto-gether in favor of attacks on Stevenson and the Truman administration. At Delavan, Wisconsin, in late September, he told a crowd of "Farmers for McCarthy" (another McCarthy Club creation), "This has been a rough fight, and it will be rougher and rougher." He made his point two weeks later, telling a Chippewa Falls audience that he would make a "good American" out of Adlai Stevenson "if someone will give me a good slippery-elm club and put me aboard the Stevenson train and get rid of some of those advisers." He won applause from delegates to the 51st convention of the Wisconsin Buttermakers' and Managers' Association when, in a mock slip of the tongue, he referred to "Alger Stevenson." He assailed Democrats for singing "Happy Days Are Here Again" at their national convention on a day 208 Americans died in Korea.[43]

McCarthy lieutenants canceled numerous in-state speeches and laid plans for a multi-state tour to assist Republican candidates. Both the Republican National Committee and the G.O.P. Senatorial Campaign Committee were eager to exploit McCarthy and his message.[44]

It was hardly a secret within top G.O.P. circles, however, that Eisenhower despised McCarthy and wanted as little to do with him as possible. Ultraconservatives were jolted by a report published by the Alsops that Ike would not campaign in Wisconsin on behalf of McCarthy or in Indiana on behalf of William Jenner. (Ike had, in fact, told his staff to make no plans for visiting Wisconsin.) They noticed too that William Benton's attorney, in connection with McCarthy's libel suit, chose to question Paul Hoffman less than two weeks before the Wisconsin primary, generating harsh anti-McCarthy statements and headlines. When Charles Kersten spoke privately with Eisenhower in Denver, the candidate asked, "What can we do about McCarthy making unproved charges?" *The New York Times* carried a story claiming that even Nixon would shun McCarthy in the fall campaigning.[45]

Sen. Karl Mundt, on the other hand, co-chairman of the Republican campaign speakers' bureau, told reporters that Eisenhower would support McCarthy and all other G.O.P. senators as members of the Republican "team." Nixon agreed publicly that he and Eisenhower would back all Republican Senate and House nominees but without necessarily endorsing their views or methods. When asked specifically about McCarthy, Nixon said that neither he nor the general had had the opportunity to examine the senator's allegations about Communists in government. "I don't intend to comment on his methods or charges until I know the facts," he said.[46]

At a news conference in late August, reporters confronted Eisenhower with Nixon's statement. The general declared that he would back McCarthy "as a member of the Republican organization," but he added forcefully, "I am not going to campaign for or give blanket endorsement to any man who does anything that I believe to be un-American in its methods and procedures." Pressed about the charges against George Marshall, Ike became angry and got up from his desk and began to pace. There was "nothing of disloyalty in General Marshall's soul," he said, and he went on to describe his former chief as a patriot and "a man of real selflessness." "I have no patience with anyone," he stated bluntly, "who can find in his record of service for this country anything to criticize." Associates of the Republican standardbearer told reporters privately that Eisenhower would give only nominal support to McCarthy should he win in the primary.[47]

Joe's triumph on September 9 convinced Eisenhower aides of the absolute necessity of traveling to Wisconsin on the campaign swing through the midwest. Ike fussed and fumed but gave in to the decision. He asked speech writer Emmet John Hughes, however, if his Milwaukee speech scheduled for October 3 might be used as an occasion to pay tribute to George Marshall. Hughes liked the idea of challenging McCarthy directly on his home ground and wrote into the draft:

> Let me be quite specific. I know that charges of disloyalty have, in the past, been leveled against General George C. Marshall. I have been privileged for thirty-five years to know General Marshall personally. I know him, as a man and as a soldier, to be dedicated with singular selflessness and the profoundest patriotism to the service of America. And this episode is a sobering lesson in the way freedom must not defend itself.[48]

Eisenhower's advisers also scheduled him to appear in Indiana, where a confrontation with Marshall foe William Jenner was unavoidable. In a speech delivered in early September before an overflow crowd at Butler University, Eisenhower urged support of the entire statewide G.O.P. slate. He did not mention Jenner's name, although the senator had introduced him and was sharing the same platform. At the conclusion of the address, Jenner leaped to his feet and warmly embraced the startled candidate, a scene captured by photographers and transmitted throughout the nation. "I felt dirty from the touch of the man," Ike later told Emmet John Hughes. Liberals and moderates in both parties groaned at the picture of the apparently chummy duo. The vice-chairman of the National Young Republican Clubs immediately switched to Stevenson, telling reporters, "It is too much for an honest man to swallow."[49]

As the Eisenhower campaign train rolled through Illinois three weeks later, the candidate's advisers argued fiercely among themselves over the wisdom of retaining the strong pro-Marshall statement in the Milwaukee speech. The more pragmatic among them contended that the paragraph was unnecessarily insulting to McCarthy and might damage the success of the entire state ticket. News of the Marshall statement reached G.O.P. leaders in Wisconsin, and on October 2 Joe, Governor Kohler, and national committeeman Henry Ringling flew to Peoria to confront the Republican candidate and his aides before the train traveled northward. For Eisenhower, McCarthy's sudden appearance was another of the campaign's unpleasant surprises.

McCarthy was ushered into the general's suite at the Pere Marquette hotel and spent a half hour with the candidate. Joe made it clear that he did not want a reference to Marshall made in Wisconsin. The conversation quickly became heated, and Eisenhower told the senator exactly what he thought of his anti-Communist crusade. He also defended Marshall and expressed his determination to retain the laudatory paragraph in his speech. One aide later said that it was the only time he had ever heard Ike speak "in red-hot anger." Joe told reporters merely that the meeting had been "very, very pleasant" and announced that he and Kohler would be on the general's train as it entered Wisconsin. Attempts by photographers to get Eisenhower to pose with McCarthy in the rear car were turned down.

The discussion continued the next day as the candidate and his entourage headed for Green Bay, one of six scheduled stops in Wisconsin. When Kohler and McCarthy entered Eisenhower's private car, Ike lectured them briefly about his opposition to "un-American methods in combating Communism." "I'm going to say that I disagree with you," Ike told Joe frankly. "If you say that, you'll be booed," McCarthy replied. Eisenhower shrugged and said, "I've been booed before, and being booed doesn't bother me."

Republican Congressman John W. Byrnes introduced McCarthy and Eisenhower to the crowd of 3,000 at Green Bay. The two did not appear on the rear platform of the train at the same time, however; Joe acknowledged his noisy welcome with a bow and retired. Eisenhower expressed gratitude to the senator for meeting him in Peoria and assured his audience that he and McCarthy differed only about methods not goals. Still, he called for the election of all Republican candidates in the state without mentioning McCarthy specifically. And when discussing the weeding out of Reds in government, he said that the responsibility would fall squarely on the Executive Branch. "We can do it with absolute assurance that American principles of trial by jury, of innocence until proof of guilt, are all observed, and I expect to do it." The crowd cheered rather than booed, and Sherman Adams, Ike's personal campaign manager, later recalled McCarthy "looking very black indeed" as he walked out of the candidate's car.

On the way to Appleton, the next stop of the day, a tense meeting was held between Eisenhower, McCarthy, Kohler, Adams, and several others over McCarthy's request to introduce the presidential candidate in his home town. According to Raymond P. Dohr, a local G.O.P. official who was present, Ike again expressed his dislike of the senator and said that he had no desire to be introduced by him. Dohr, who had known McCarthy since the late 1930s, later recalled that this was the only time he had ever seen Joe appear meek. Ike yielded reluctantly after some strenuous arguing by Dohr and other state politicos.

McCarthy's introduction of the candidate to the crowd of 5,000 was a single sentence: "I wish to present to the people of my home city the next President of the United States—General Dwight Eisenhower." Joe stood on the campaign train platform for the duration of Eisenhower's twelve-minute speech—but next to Kohler, who was on the candidate's immediate left. The general made no reference to the senator.

As the train headed southeast toward Milwaukee, Walter Kohler plead with Sherman Adams to delete the Marshall statement, arguing that it was an unnecessary rebuff to McCarthy and might jeopardize Republican successes locally and nationally. Adams agreed with the governor and brought him to Eisenhower, along with Ike's friend Maj. Gen. Wilton B. "Jerry" Persons, who sympathized with Kohler's position. Ike quickly gave in to the political necessities; "Take it out," he snapped. An adviser later described him as "purple with rage."

McCarthy appeared on the platform at the Milwaukee Arena before Eisenhower arrived, thanking the crowd of 8,500 for his primary victory. Governor Kohler introduced the general, an awkward arrangement that some reporters rightly interpreted as a snub of the state's junior senator. In his prepared remarks Eisenhower made no mention of McCarthy.

The speech undoubtedly pleased Joe, however, for it contained the irresponsible brand of Red Scare rhetoric that had made him famous and that the vice-presidential candidate was freely distributing in his campaign appearances throughout the country. A national tolerance of Communism, Eisenhower said, had "poisoned two whole decades of our national life" and insinuated itself in our schools, public forums, news channels, labor unions, "and—most terrifyingly—into our government itself." This penetration "meant contamination in some degree of virtually every department, every agency, every bureau, every section of our government. It meant a government by men whose very brains were confused by the opiate of this deceit." The candidate attributed the fall of China and the "surrender of whole nations" in Eastern Europe to the Reds in Washington. The effects were felt at home as well, he continued. "This penetration meant a domestic policy whose tone was set by men who sneered and scoffed at warnings of the enemy infiltrating our most secret councils." In short, he said, "It meant—in its most ugly triumph—treason itself."

Reporters had received copies of the full speech and were thus aware of the Marshall statement's deletion. Many Eisenhower supporters were mortified by the decision. Arthur Hays Sulzberger, publisher of *The New York Times,* wired Sherman Adams, "Do I need to tell you that I am sick at heart?" *The Times* reported accurately that McCarthy had successfully sought the deletion. This was denied by all concerned, including Joe; a top Eisenhower aide, who asked not to be identified, told reporters that the senator had not seen the Milwaukee speech until it was in its final form, as delivered. (Eisenhower and Adams continued to deny McCarthy's influence years later in their memoirs.) Joseph Alsop reported that members of Eisenhower's personal staff were privately referring to the Wisconsin visit as the "terrible day."[50]

Adlai Stevenson made much of Eisenhower's capitulation to McCarthy. In a rousing Milwaukee speech, delivered five days after Ike's appearance, he charged that the G.O.P. candidate had deliberately compromised his views on General Marshall and United States European policy in an "opportunistic grasping" for votes. In Waukesha he called the G.O.P. right wing "the most accomplished wrecking crew in this country's history" and said that Eisenhower had given it a first, second and third mortgage "on every principle he once held."[51]

Herblock published a characteristically devastating cartoon in the pro-Eisenhower *Washington Post* showing the leering ape-man McCarthy standing in a pool of filth and holding a sign reading "ANYTHING TO WIN." Next to him, Eisenhower explained to a shocked voter, "Our differences have nothing to do with the end result we are seeking." A *New York Post* headline trumpeted, "He has met the enemy, and he is theirs."[52]

Joe did not complain publicly or in private about his treatment by Eisenhower. When prodded by reporters he stuck to bland generalities expressing his respect and complete support for the candidate. For one thing, Joe was undoubtedly in awe of the storied general. Emmet John Hughes later wrote of Eisenhower's "sheer *presence*" and sense of strength. "The stride and the stance of a man, the timbre of his voice, the command of his eyes, the vigor of his gestures, the authority of his movements—these can affect profoundly the whole world he inhabits." Moreover, Joe knew that the candidate's popularity throughout the country was phenomenal and that his election in November was very likely. Everywhere one saw a sea of "I Like Ike" buttons, and the public opinion polls were encouraging. This was a man whose favor simply had to be courted. At least for the time being.[53]

Despite his weakened physical condition, McCarthy traveled to ten states on behalf of a number of right-wing Congressional candidates. (He would later tell Senate colleagues that he spoke "in practically every state in the Union—sometimes as often as three or four times in one day.") On the western leg of his tour he appeared in Arizona, Nevada, Washington State, Wyoming, and Montana. In Arizona he spoke on behalf of ultraconservative businessman Barry Goldwater, who was challenging Senate Majority Leader Ernest McFarland. In Wyoming he boosted the candidacy of Frank Barrett, Sen. Joseph O'Mahoney's opponent. In Montana he backed Sen. Zales Ecton against his challenger, Rep. Mike Mansfield. In Washington State he defended the record of Sen. Harry P. Cain, under fire by popular Congressman Henry M. Jackson.

The topic of Communist subversion, of course, was the major thrust of every speech. Joe told the United Press in Las Vegas, "I do not plan to take sides" in the Presidential race. "My job is to warn the people about the Communists, our real inner enemies." Sometimes he modified his message to respond to local needs. Mansfield, he said, had once been praised by the *Daily Worker* and must be "either stupid or a dupe." He described Cain as "perhaps more hated by Communists, Communistic and fellow-traveler elements than any man alive, and with good reason." Joe sent Harvey Matusow into Montana, Utah and Washington State to confirm and expand upon his charges of the Communist infiltration of American life.

At times McCarthy stirred intense controversy. In a Las Vegas radio talk on behalf of Sen. George "Molly" Malone, Joe labeled local newspaper editor Hank Greenspun—a foe of Senator McCarran's political machine—an "ex-Communist." (He meant to say ex-convict. The editor later told his attorney that Joe was drunk.) Greenspun, in the audience, interrupted the speech, calling McCarthy "the most vicious type of demagogue." A few minutes later he stormed the stage, took over the microphone, and denounced the senator over the air for 27 minutes, charging, among other things, that in regard to foreign policy he had voted the "straight party line along with the *Daily Worker*."

In Seattle, officials of a local television station refused to permit McCarthy to make a fifteen minute telecast unless he could prove, to the satisfaction of station attorneys, allegations made in his script about two Drew Pearson staff members. Joe could not provide the evidence and would not delete the remarks, so the broadcast was canceled. Joe told reporters that he would ask the Federal Communications Commission to revoke the station's license.

That same day, the senator was greeted with a chorus of boos and cheers at the Washington State Press Club's gridiron dinner. The affair was billed as a lampoon of political parties and candidates, and Joe announced that he wanted to make a serious speech. After the noise died down, he protested indignantly, "I didn't travel 2,300 miles to be funny."[54]

In the midwest McCarthy paid visits to Michigan, Missouri, and Indiana. In Michigan he spoke on behalf of HUAC Congressman Charles Potter, who was running against Senator Blair Moody, and in favor of his friend Alvin Bentley, a candidate for the House. He made two hard-hitting speeches in Missouri to assist Sen. James Kem, struggling to ward off challenger Stuart Symington. In Indiana Joe praised William Jenner for being "a great American" and the target of "Eastern bleeding hearts." Jenner repaid the compliment, saying that he and McCarthy had both been "marked for liquidation by an administration which . . . consorts openly with Reds and pinks."

In addition, Joe traveled to West Virginia on behalf of former Sen. Chapman Revercomb, Sen. Harley M. Kilgore's opponent. He gave three speeches in Connecticut against William Benton; he told an audience in Westbury that his foe was "worth a hundred million dollars to the Kremlin on the floor of the United States Senate." A tape recording of McCarthy's voice was used in North Dakota to defend his friend Sen. William Langer, a member of the McCarran Committee, against charges by local G.O.P. ultraconservatives that the veteran isolationist himself was soft on the Reds![55]

McCarthy chose not to enter Massachusetts, where Henry Cabot Lodge was struggling to ward off the money and glamour of challenger John F. Kennedy. This stirred considerable controversy, for there were 750,000 Irish in the state and their admiration for the Wisconsin senator was well known. It has long been thought that Lodge did not seek Joe's presence, that being a moderate and a leader in the Eisenhower campaign he shunned McCarthy and all that he stood for. (Advocates of this position, such as Kennedy biographer James MacGregor Burns, had obviously failed to read the Tydings Committee hearings.) It has also been reported by Westbrook Pegler, Roy Cohn, and others, that Joseph P. Kennedy successfully urged his Wisconsin friend to stay out of Massachusetts, thereby greatly improving his son's chances for victory. Actually, part of the traditional account is correct and part of it is false.

The elder Kennedy did ask McCarthy not to enter Massachusetts; moreover, he made a sizable contribution to McCarthy's reelection campaign. But these were not the primary reasons for the senator's decision. According to Ray Kiermas, Joe had picked up a rumor in mid-1952 that Lodge and fellow Republicans Herbert Brownell and William Rogers were hatching a political plot of some sort against him. When he confirmed the story two months later in a late night telephone call to Lodge, Joe swore not to lift a finger for his Massachusetts colleague. "I'm going to teach that bastard of a Lodge to suck eggs," he told his office manager.

But, according to Kiermas and Don Surine, Lodge strongly desired McCarthy's assistance; he telephoned the McCarthy office almost daily appealing for the senator's aid. So Joe set an impossible price for his participation: Lodge would have to introduce him personally wherever he appeared and wholly endorse his fight against the Reds. Lodge balked at this, as Joe knew he would, and the requests ended. Lodge never forgave McCarthy for the 1952 campaign and would later play a role in his downfall.

Joseph P. Kennedy did not even want criticism of McCarthy to stain his son's campaign. He prevailed upon Adlai Stevenson to keep silent about the Wisconsin senator during his campaign appearances in Massachusetts. He personally blocked publication of an anti-McCarthy newspaper advertisement concocted by one of his son's liberal advisers. "You're trying to ruin Jack," he shouted. "You and your sheeny friends are trying to ruin my son's career." He may also have been responsible for John Kennedy's failure to give an anti-McCarthy speech aides had been preparing, with the assistance of William Benton, at the request of Democratic Party leaders. (It was later revealed that Joe Kennedy lent the publisher of the *Boston Post* $500,000 shortly after the newspaper switched its support from Lodge to his son.)[56]

In fact, young Congressman Kennedy shared many of the Red Scare views held by his father and McCarthy. He had worked closely with Joe's friend Charles Kersten in a controversial Communist-hunting investigation involving a Milwaukee local of the United Auto Workers, and he boasted of the probe in his senatorial campaign. Adlai Stevenson joined in, asking a Massachusetts audience, "I wonder how many of you know that it was Congressman Kennedy and not Senator Nixon who got the first citation of a Communist for perjury?" In January 1949, more than a year before the Wheeling speech, Kennedy had attacked the policies of "the Lattimores and the [China expert John King] Fairbanks," the Yalta accords, and George Marshall. In November 1950 he told a Harvard University class that he supported the McCarran Internal Security Act, that he lacked great respect for Dean Acheson, and that he was very happy about Richard Nixon's defeat of Helen Gahagan Douglas. He also said that he knew Joe McCarthy "pretty well, and he may have something." In 1952, Kennedy's campaign literature portrayed him as an unyielding opponent of "atheistic Communism," and it chided Lodge for missing his chance to do something about the Reds-in-government by failing to attend most of the

Tydings Committee hearings. The *Chicago Tribune* called J.F.K. "a fighting conservative" and blasted Lodge as a "follower of the Truman-Acheson-Lattimore foreign policy."[57]

When McCarthy wasn't running around the country urging the election of others, he found a little time to campaign on his own behalf. At one point he spent about a week in southeastern Wisconsin traveling with Lowell McNeill of Racine, state chairman of the Young Republicans. McNeill later recalled the senator's "common touch," his striking rapport with the ordinary people of his state. In smallish Burlington, for example, one hot afternoon, Joe asked to stop at a small tavern for a drink. There were only four or five people in the place as they entered. Before long a woman greeted McCarthy with "How are ya, Joe?" Within twenty minutes the tavern was packed, and Joe was the center of attention, laughing, shaking hands, telling slightly risqué stories, genuinely enjoying the company of the people who flocked about him. How could such a man be the immoral monster Democrats were describing? Who could believe that he was the international menace big-city liberals were attacking? To McNeill, McCarthy seemed to be "just another guy," only more brash, colorful and fun to be around. His sincerity and patriotism appeared unquestionable to the Racine banker.[58]

McCarthy's most famous campaign speech of 1952 took place in Chicago and was carried nationally over 55 television stations and 550 radio stations. For weeks Joe had been telling audiences of his research into the life and times of Adlai Stevenson. Without consulting Eisenhower or his advisers, McCarthy suddenly announced his intention to "expose" the Democratic Presidential candidate on October 27. He paid for the network time himself with funds collected by a committee of businessmen headed by Gen. Robert E. Wood, the Sears, Roebuck mogul. This move puzzled and disturbed many top Republicans. Some of them were persuaded that Joe's long-range goal was the G.O.P. Presidential nomination in 1956.[59]

Don Surine had been assigned the task of researching Stevenson, and he arrived in Chicago with what he later described as "ninety pounds" of documents. Joe, exhausted by his travels, saw the material for the first time in his Chicago hotel room and quickly became enthusiastic. On the evening before the address was to be given, a delegation sent by Eisenhower quietly slipped into the hotel. General Persons, Governor Kohler, and General Wood sought to check the authenticity of a rumor started by Stevenson's sister that McCarthy would be labeling the Democratic leader a homosexual and a Communist. Joe sent the visitors to Surine, who passionately argued his case against Stevenson and distributed samples of his documentation. In a short time, according to Surine, the Republicans were won over and Persons telephoned Eisenhower with his approval. The finishing touches were then applied to the prepared text.[60]

In his speech, delivered before a crowd of 1,700, most of whom had paid $50 for dinner, McCarthy claimed to possess "the coldly documented background" of the Democratic presidential candidate. "There is a tremendous quantity of material. That which I present to you tonight is only that portion of it on which I have complete, unchallengeable documentation." Joe charged, among other things, that Stevenson had connived during the war to introduce Communists into the coalition government of Italy; that he had defended Hiss, "the arch-traitor of our time," and lied about introducing him in 1946 at a Northwestern University lecture; that he had been recommended by Hiss and named Communist Frank Coe as a delegate to the 1942 Mont Tremblant conference, sponsored by the Institute of Pacific Relations; and that he had lied about membership in the "left-wing" Americans for Democratic Action. Stevenson, Joe said, was a man who had endorsed "and would continue the suicidal Kremlin-shaped policies of this nation." At another point he contended, "I do not state that Stevenson was a Communist or pro-Communist, but I must believe that something was wrong somewhere." The candidate's liberal, anti-Communist friends and advisers Wilson Wyatt, Arthur Schlesinger, Jr., James Wechsler, Bernard De Voto, and Archibald MacLeish were described in various ways as being soft on the Reds. Joe even claimed that the *Daily Worker* had endorsed Stevenson's candidacy.

McCarthy employed some of his most effective stage techniques before the cameras. He frequently displayed copies of documents in a manner that had by now become a personal trademark; "I hold in my hand . . ." He held up the photographs of the barn at Lee, Massachusetts, and said, "This barn, so crude on the outside, contained a beautifully paneled conference room with maps of the Soviet Union on its walls. In an adjoining room my investigators found over 200,000 astounding documents. They were the hidden files of the Communist controlled Institute of Pacific Relations . . ." He introduced Harvey Matusow in the audience. He delighted his dinner audience, at least four times, with the planned slip of the tongue, "Alger—I mean Adlai."[61]

Democratic Party researchers spent four days tracing McCarthy's sources and then announced, in a 5,000 word analysis, that his speech contained "at least eighteen false statements, distortions or quotations wrenched from context." (Northwestern University law professor Willard H. Pedrick later checked all of the senator's documentation and called the Chicago speech "a most amazing demonstration of studied inaccuracy.") For example, the letter documenting Stevenson's recommendation by Hiss and Coe to the Mont Tremblant Conference was written by I.P.R. official Joseph Lockwood. The only reference to Stevenson was on the second page, where he was referred to incorrectly as "Adlai Stevens." Hiss and Coe also suggested Adolph Berle and Dean Acheson, and Hiss named Harvey Bunde, Assistant Secretary of State under Hoover, and two generals. All of which proved what? Stevenson was not invited to the conference and did not attend.

McCarthy quoted Arthur Schlesinger as having written in 1946: "The present system in the United States makes even freedom-loving Americans look wistfully at Russia." Schlesinger actually wrote in the *Life* magazine article in question:

> The Communists are looking to a next depression as their happy hunting ground. The way to defeat them is not to pass repressive legislation or return Martin Dies to public service, but to prevent that depression and to correct the faults and injustices in our present system which make even freedom loving Americans look wistfully at Russia. If conservatives spent more time doing this and less time smearing other people who are trying to do it as Communists, they would get much further in the job of returning the CPUSA to its proper place beside the Buchmanites and Holy Rollers.

Ironically, Schlesinger had consulted with Whittaker Chambers, among others, while writing the piece. The title of the article was: "The U.S. Communist Party—Small But Tightly Disciplined, It Strives with Fanatic Zeal to Promote the Aims of Russia."

When Joe again trotted out his story of how the Soviet secret police had plans for obtaining American passports from Reds in the State Department, he denied government claims that the testimony behind it referred to conditions in 1928. He shoved a 1952 Justice Department brief in front of the television cameras, read a passage from it, "the passage to which the Democrat candidate took exception," and noted that there was no reference to 1928. In fact, at the end of the sentences quoted one could find two sources cited: Cummings and Crouch. Testimony before the Subversive Activities Control Board by ex-Communist William Garfield Cummings had referred to misused passports in the early 1930s. Paul Crouch had told the S.A.C.B. of a 1928 conversation on the matter. Joe claimed that Harvey Matusow had testified about the passport plot; "His birth is October 3, 1926. So certainly he was not testifying about the Communist party when he was two years of age." Actually, Matusow had not testified about passports; his age had nothing to do with the issue. When Joe mentioned Cummings as another source, he confused the ex-Communist with former Attorney General Homer Cummings. Moreover, Joe claimed that the evidence for the Justice Department brief had "never been made public." This was false, for the Cummings-Crouch testimony had been published and was freely available.[62]

How many McCarthy viewers and listeners studied lengthy newspaper accounts of the Democratic Party analysis cannot be known, of course, but surely their numbers were not great. Most newspapers provided only brief summaries of the document, which were undoubtedly dismissed by many voters as mere partisanship. Then too, stories on the study were often hard to find, as journalists rarely award rebuttals the attention given to sensationalistic charges. Joe's blast against A.D.A. in the speech made page one of *The New York Times*; the liberal organization's responsible reply was buried on page 26. At any rate, by the time the analysis of the Chicago address became public, just before the polls opened, the senator had given similar speeches in Milwaukee and Appleton, held several news conferences, and was again in the headlines with new charges. As had long been the case, Joe excelled at staying ahead of his critics.[63]

The Chicago speech cost about $75,000 to put on the air, and the Appleton talk, broadcast nationally over 530 radio stations, was also expensive. Money was simply not a problem in the McCarthy campaign; it flowed into Joe's Senate office, campaign headquarters, and home town from throughout the country. Urban Van Susteren later exclaimed, "There was money all over the place!" In December the McCarthy Club reported expenditures of $162,832.91, the largest amount spent on a single candidate by one state organization in many years. The Republican Voluntary Committee declared that it spent another half million on McCarthy and other G.O.P. candidates. The exact amount of money at McCarthy's disposal will no doubt always defy detection. There were rumors of unreported funds coming in from Joe's friends in Texas. (The senator appeared at the Inaugural Ball with several Texas oil men. Clint Murchison later admitted contributing funds in Connecticut to defeat Benton.) And it was widely known among insiders that Joe Kennedy's $10,000 contribution was "laundered" to defy detection. The McCarthy Club listed 41 "unknown" contributors in one of its official reports, including two who gave $1,000 each.[64]

Fairchild's forces could not match McCarthy's fund-raising prowess, but they worked exceptionally hard after the primary and succeeded in obtaining more campaign money than local Democrats had ever seen before. The largest contributor was organized labor; the state A.F.L. and C.I.O. organizations spent almost $100,000 on political activities, and most of it was channeled into the effort to defeat McCarthy. Fifteen major union groups outside the state sent at least $21,000 into Wisconsin, and Fairchild received a substantial share. The National Committee for an Effective Congress, a small, liberal, fund-raising organization centered in Washington, D.C., gave between $20,000 and $30,000 to the cause. Americans for Democratic Action contributed over $1,000.[65]

Organized labor's funds were used to publish tens of thousands of brochures, pamphlets, fliers, and tabloids attacking McCarthy's "reactionary" legislative record, his political support, and his personal reputation. Joe's anti-Communist charges were virtually ignored, in part because of Len Schmitt's crushing defeat, and in part, no doubt, because of a fear of clashing with McCarthy on this sensitive and highly controversial issue. One A.F.L. brochure, entitled *Inside McCarthy,* was written by Miles McMillin and contained the slashing attacks that the *Capital Times* continued on an almost daily basis. The C.I.O. brought out a fifteen-page pamphlet called *Smear Incorporated: The Record of Joe McCarthy's One Man Mob Operation.* Radio and television advertising was also purchased. On the last day of the campaign the C.I.O. bought an hour on 31 state stations to present an anti-McCarthy speech by Senator Hubert Humphrey of Minnesota.

State labor journals joined the barrage. The *Milwaukee AFL Labor Press* ran a series entitled "Case of the People Versus Slippery Joe McCarthy." The first article claimed, among other things, that the senator's vote against a federal education bill proved his dislike of children. While commenting on votes against housing and Social Security legislation, the piece asked, "Do you hate the old folks, just as you apparently hate the youngsters, Joe?"

State and regional labor leaders often formed "truth teams" to appear at private and civic gatherings and explain the case against McCarthy. Union wives raised funds for Fairchild through card parties and raffles. State political action committees organized volunteers to telephone union members and distribute literature to them door to door.[66]

The attack on McCarthy, in Wisconsin and elsewhere, was considerably strengthened in early October by the appearance of *McCarthy: The Man, the Senator, the "Ism"* by Jack Anderson and Ronald May. The 431-page book contained virtually every charge ever made against Joe and was cited by Democrats as "proof" of the senator's total malevolence, cynicism, and corruptibility. Largely through oral interviews, the authors had, in fact, collected some interesting details about Joe's life that shed light on his personality and rise to power. But every chapter contained factual errors, slanted interpretations, partisan conclusions, and even occasional fiction. Anderson and May had started the book in the spring of 1950 as a campaign polemic, and they made few pretensions about its lasting value. "The authors acknowledge their limitations; they are not historians; and the scholarly treatment of the baffling postwar phenomenon called McCarthyism must await a detached academician. The authors are journalists; and theirs is a book of journalism..." The fear and loathing of McCarthy within liberal-intellectual circles was such, however, that the volume was greeted with great seriousness in important newspapers and journals. Favorable reviews in the *Saturday Review, New York Herald Tribune,* and *The New York Times,* for example, helped rush the book into the best-seller lists.[67]

Unlike most of McCarthy's Wisconsin opponents, Anderson and May were not reluctant to attack the senator on the issue of his anti-Communist claims. Chapters bore such titles as "205, 81—or 57?," "The Multiple Lie," and "Aiding the Communists." Perhaps thinking they had little to lose, Fairchild and his advisers decided late in the campaign to follow suit, striking directly at the heart of McCarthy's authority. Two days before the election, former Tydings Committee counsel Edward P. Morgan appeared on Milwaukee television with Fairchild and strongly urged McCarthy's defeat. He told of the senator's use of a forged Civil Service Commission report in a Senate speech attacking Reds in government. He also revealed that Joe had come to him privately after the Wheeling speech seeking assistance in identifying a single actual Communist in the State Department.

A Fairchild advertisement in the *Appleton Post-Crescent* erroneously labeled Morgan an FBI man instead of an *ex*-FBI agent, as Morgan had identified himself. Joe caught the error and exploited it in his nationally broadcast Appleton speech. He had just sent a telegram to J. Edgar Hoover, he said, asking whether Morgan was an FBI employee or "a faker." Hoover replied, as Joe knew he would, that Morgan had resigned in 1947 and did not now represent the bureau in any capacity. "So Tydings's chief of staff, Morgan, was brought to Wisconsin at the last minute," Joe gloated, "to falsely pose as a spokesman for the FBI. Don't you wonder just how low they can get in this campaign?"[68]

The second Red Scare, of course, was larger than McCarthy, and in political campaigns all over the country Republicans—and some Democrats—were busily hammering away at their opponents with crimson cudgels. Even before the campaigns were underway, the G.O.P. had determined to stress the theme "Korea, Communism, and Corruption," which party leaders abbreviated in the popular formula K_1C_2. And there was no dearth of candidates eager to endorse Richard Nixon's determination to emphasize the un-American qualities of the opposition.

In West Virginia, for example, foes of Democratic Senator Harley M. Kilgore produced and distributed a vulgar volume entitled *Kilgore's Red Record*. Challenger Chapman Revercomb charged that the incumbent had "aided and appeased Communist causes" and had a record of "continuous sympathy to the Communist thinkers."[69]

In Maryland, G.O.P. Senatorial candidate J. Glenn Beall cried, "We have got to slug it out, toe to toe, with the parlor pinks and so-called liberals, who call themselves Democrats." He decried the nation's headlong plunge "down the paths of precepts dictated by the teachings of Karl Marx" and challenged anyone to identify "one charge that McCarthy ever made that he's been wrong on."[70]

In Ohio, Sen. John Bricker gave McCarthy credit for driving hundreds of dangerous people from the federal government. He called the Korean War "unconstitutional" and demanded an end to "trading the blood of American boys for synthetic propaganda to elect Harry Truman or his satellites."[71]

Senator Jenner, fighting an uphill battle in Indiana against Democratic governor Henry Schricher, warned that if Democrats won in November "the bodies of thousands more American boys will be tossed on Truman's funeral pyre in Asia." If Schricher and Stevenson came to power, he charged, "the Red network will continue to work secretly and safely for the destruction of the United States."[72]

In Montana, Senator Ecton called Congressman Mansfield a "captive candidate of the Truman-Acheson gang" and charged that he had helped give China to the Reds. (Ecton was no doubt relying upon research supplied by McCarthy. Harvey Matusow later recalled, "McCarthy had a violent hatred for Mansfield and told me that if he was elected 'you might just as well have an admitted Communist in the Senate, it's the same difference.'")[73]

Senator Cain, in Washington State, claimed that Henry M. Jackson had "approved each step the Administration took on the road to Korea." He also condemned the congressman for his votes against HUAC, and he claimed to see a parallel between Jackson's congressional record and Vito Marcantonio's. One campaign brochure accused Jackson of "Communist mollycoddling," and a cartoon caption within the publication read, "Unmask Jackson and behind you find the grinning face of Secretary of State Acheson." Republican Governor Arthur Langlie blasted his opponent, Congressman Hugh Mitchell, for his A.D.A. membership and warned against candidates who "play footsie with Communists and their dupes."[74]

William Benton complained bitterly about the attacks waged against him in Connecticut. He was especially angered by the activities of a recent Yale graduate named William F. Buckley, Jr., who chaired a committee to drive Reds from the government and ran what Benton called "scurrilous" newspaper advertisements designed to prove that the senator was Communistic. Benton later wrote to Millard Tydings, "Buckley is a smart, able, aggressive young man. Yes, he is a potentially dangerous young man."[75]

Few campaigners anywhere that year could match the zeal of the G.O.P. vice-presidential candidate. Three days after his nomination, Nixon contended that he had found "as many Democrats as Republicans disgusted with the way the Administration kissed off and pooh-poohed the Communist threat at home." When in mid-September he was nearly driven from the ticket by the famous $18,000 "slush fund" crisis, he cried, "This is another typical smear by the same left-wing elements which have fought me ever since I took part in the investigation which led to the conviction of Alger Hiss." After the "Checkers" speech and the reconciliation with Eisenhower ("You're my boy"), Nixon went all out to paint the opposition pink. He described the President as "spineless" and soft on the Reds. He told an audience in Pittsburgh that the Communists in both Russia and the United States were eager for a Democratic victory. Stevenson became "Adlai the appeaser" who "carries a Ph.D. from Dean Acheson's Cowardly College of Communist Containment." "Somebody had to testify for Alger Hiss," he said at one point, "but you don't have to elect him President of the United States." He would prefer to have a "khaki-clad President," he said, to "one clothed in State Department pinks." He told a Minneapolis audience that if the President and State Department officials had their way, "the traitor spy Alger Hiss would be free today and voting for the Truman candidate November 4." In Superior, Wisconsin, Nixon endorsed the reelection bid of his "good friend, Joe McCarthy."[76]

After a few weeks of this, Adlai Stevenson told a Boston crowd, "This is Sunday, and this is a day of rest for candidates. And, therefore, I am not even going to worry about Senator Nixon's conscience."[77]

Eisenhower himself did not remain above dabbling in the tactics employed by his fellow Republicans. He and his advisers were delighted to leave Wisconsin. (A farewell handshake with Joe was forced and awkward.) "The general's compromises are all behind," said an adviser. "From now on you'll hear more of the old Ike." The candidate soon made numerous references to his distaste for "witch-hunts" and "character assassination," and he told a Salt Lake audience, "We cannot pretend to defend freedom with weapons suited only to the arsenal of tyrants." But in Billings, Montana, he promised, "We will find the men and women who may fail to live up to these standards; we will find the pinks; we will find the Communists; we will find the disloyal." On the same day he called for the repudiation of the Yalta agreements. With pollster Elmo Roper revealing that the Korean War was the leading issue for more than half the public, Eisenhower condemned the Administration for making Korea vulnerable to Communist aggression, repeatedly cited casualty figures, and bemoaned the seeming futility of the conflict. (Ike's promise to visit Korea if elected, an idea conceived by Emmet John Hughes, no doubt assured his victory at the polls.)[78]

More than a few Democrats were willing to sling the same mud. Such mainstream liberals as Stuart Symington, Henry M. Jackson, and Ohio's Michael V. DiSalle, former Office of Price Stabilization director, found an assortment of pretexts, including isolationism and friendship with McCarthy, by which to proclaim their opponents soft on the Reds. Sen. John Sparkman of Alabama, the Vice-Presidential candidate, quoted a 1945 Eisenhower statement that "nothing guides Russian policy so much as a desire for friendship with the United States." He also contended that "there are more Communists and Communist infiltrators" from Columbia University, where Eisenhower had served briefly as president, "than from any other school in the United States." President Truman claimed that Ike's 1945 statement "did a great deal of harm," and he condemned the general for his failure to achieve a firm agreement with Russia over American access to Berlin and for recommending withdrawal of American troops from Korea in 1947.[79]

Stevenson roasted Eisenhower for his concessions to the right-wing of his party. "Joe McCarthy may get him if he doesn't watch out." And he ridiculed ultraconservatives for their failure to back postwar efforts to halt Russian aggression. "By the time it occurred to the Old Guard of the Republican Party that resistance was necessary, we would have been isolated, a beleaguered garrison state in a Soviet-dominated world." "Why is it," he asked, "that these politicians that scream loudest about Communism in America have fought hardest against every Democratic program to fight Communism itself?" In New York he said, "They would rather battle Democrats than Communists any day."

While Stevenson made several eloquent statements on civil liberties, he left no doubt about his firm belief in an internal Red peril. "The Commu-

nist conspiracy within the United States deserves the attention of every
American citizen and the sleepless concern of the responsible government
agencies." He heaped praise upon the FBI "In all this effort, we have had
the faithful and resourceful work in national protection of the Federal
Bureau of Investigation." He "of course" recommended the dismissal of all
Communist teachers. He told a New Mexico audience not to confuse
liberals, socialists, and radicals "in the American sense" with Reds. "But
where true Communists are concerned—men bound to the service and the
defense of Stalinist tyranny—we must root them out and give them the
consequences of treachery to all America holds dearest." In Cleveland,
Stevenson attempted to prove that Eisenhower and Dulles were closer to
Alger Hiss than he was because of their mutual ties to the Carnegie
Endowment for International Peace. (In 1948, Hiss was president, Dulles
was chairman of the board, and Eisenhower was a trustee. Twice in 1949
the board of trustees, including Eisenhower and Dulles, voted to reject
Hiss's resignation.) He declared in the same speech, "For I believe with all
my heart that those who would beguile the voters by lies or half-truths, or
corrupt them by fear and falsehood, are committing spiritual treason
against our institutions. They are doing the work of our enemies."[80]

Some 61.5 million people went to the polls on November 4, giving Ike
nearly 55 percent of the vote and victory in 39 states, including Wisconsin.
Political analysts quickly understood that this was a personal triumph for
the general, as the G.O.P. barely won control of the Congress. The margin
in the Senate was 48-47, and in the House 221 to 213.

All of the major Republican candidates were elected in Wisconsin.
McCarthy won 54 percent of the two-party total, collecting 870,444 votes
to Fairchild's 731,402. The "smashing victory," as Joe's supporters termed
it, resulted in a wild celebration in Appleton. About 1:00 A.M. the weary
and jubilant senator thanked the voters of his state for their confidence in
him. He added, "The election of Eisenhower and most probably a Republican senate and house more than justifies my faith in the intelligence of the
American people. This is a new day for America."[81]

Soon afterward, Tom Korb drove Joe to the airport for a flight to
Washington. Along the way Joe burst into tears, and Korb had to pull off
the road for a while to let him regain his composure. All that loyalty; such
an honor, Joe sobbed. Korb said later that under the surface his old friend
was "a sentimental slob."[82]

Joe's victory was not as impressive as Korb and others had predicted,
however. In fact, of the eleven Republicans on the ticket, he ran last. He
received 12 percent fewer votes than anti-McCarthy Fred Zimmerman, the

party's top vote-getter, 9 percent fewer than Governor Kohler, 7.3 percent fewer than the Republican congressional ticket, and 7 percent fewer than Eisenhower. Joe even failed to equal his 1946 vote total, dropping 112,616 votes.

Election data suggest that McCarthy's relatively weak showing can be explained by considering at least four interrelated factors: union membership, geography, newspaper exposure, and party affiliation.

The full-scale effort by organized labor to convince its members of McCarthy's depravity unquestionably bore fruit. Most union members in the state voted for Fairchild. In the labor wards of Milwaukee and Madison, Joe lost by huge margins and trailed all other G.O.P. candidates. It should be noted that, while no other Republican in Wisconsin had the money and organization enjoyed by McCarthy, no other Republican faced such intense, well-financed opposition. Indeed, Zimmerman and Kohler were confronted by virtually token opponents.

Joe's strength lay in Wisconsin's rural areas; he lost all the major cities in the state. Rural voters were largely non-union and were not exposed to labor's anti-McCarthy literature. Neither did they read the blistering pages of the *Milwaukee Journal, Madison Capital Times,* or *Sheboygan Press.* One study of the election revealed that an overwhelming majority of state newspapers backed the entire G.O.P. ticket, including McCarthy. Pro-McCarthy newspapers awarded far more headlines, front-page attention, and article space to the senator than pro-Fairchild newspapers gave to the Democratic candidate. The *Chicago Sun-Times* observed that "few daily newspapers in Wisconsin have printed in any detail the mounting flow of disclosures detrimental to McCarthy." William Evjue wrote scathing editorials condemning state newspapers for having "suppressed and distorted" the facts about McCarthy's record. In the Appleton-Green Bay area, where Joe received a whopping 69 percent of the vote, the two rabidly pro-McCarthy newspapers had consistently praised the senator.

Joe did well in parts of the state that were traditionally Republican. A University of Wisconsin political scientist wrote in 1960, "The returns demonstrate that the vote was concentrated in areas of Republican strength, and was neither scattered nor distributed in some pattern unique to McCarthy, nor particularly strong." Efforts to prove that he was shown special favor by Roman Catholics, Germans, or Eastern Europeans, and that his support came from an agrarian radical tradition, have not withstood the scrutiny of careful scholars. Michael Paul Rogin, the most impressive of the analysts, concluded that "McCarthy had his most important roots in the conservative Republican Party." He "capitalized on the tradi-

tional party vote." Louis H. Bean concluded in 1954 that McCarthy would
have lost had it not been for the Eisenhower landslide.[83]

Joe's campaigning on behalf of others yielded mixed results. Of the ten
Senatorial incumbents and challengers he supported, four were defeated:
Cain, Ecton, Kem, and Revercomb. The six who won were Malone, Goldwater, Barrett, Jenner, Potter, and Purtell. William A. Purtell's defeat of
Benton, of course, was especially pleasing to McCarthy. On election night at
the Hotel Appleton, where the senator and his well-wishers were celebrating, the election board in the reception room bore the terse announcement,
"Benton went to hell at 8:30.'" The most often repeated remark of the
evening, according to one reporter, was "Joe won in Connecticut." A few
days later, vacationing in Arizona, Joe asked an interviewer, "How do you
like what happened to my friend Benton?" With the destruction of the
political careers of both Tydings and Benton, and the continuation, for at
least six years, of his own, McCarthy's sense of invincibility continued to
soar.[84]

In fact, Joe's power at the polls was as illusory outside Wisconsin as
within. Pollster Louis H. Bean discovered in 1954 that the candidates
McCarthy supported trailed the Republican norm by an average of five
percent. Moreover, in every case the Democratic candidate opposed by
McCarthy ran ahead of the Stevenson-Sparkman ticket. That is to say, Joe
actually hurt the campaigns of those he backed, even those who won.
Eisenhower, not McCarthy, defeated Benton, McFarland, Moody, O'Mahoney, and the others.[85]

In Connecticut, for example, Benton's 1952 tally was roughly equivalent
to his 1950 performance. He collected 41,000 votes more than the national
ticket. Irish Democratic leaders thought that McCarthy had hurt Benton
among Catholics. Statistics do not bear out this impression, however. A
study of Waterbury, where the Catholic population was almost 80 percent,
and where McCarthy made a personal appearance, shows that the traditionally Democratic Catholics of the community went for Benton in 1952 as
they had in 1950. Indeed, Benton made his strongest showing in Windham
County, the most Catholic in Connecticut. Louis Bean concluded that if
there was any religious influence in the election at all, it was "so small as to
be quite undiscernable." Benton was later of the opinion that his war with
McCarthy had actually helped his campaign. He confided to a friend, "there
isn't any doubt that the McCarthy issue pulled in the money and also caused
me to run better in certain of the smaller towns and other Republican
areas."[86]

Moderate Republicans of the Eisenhower type fared better in the 1952
elections than their colleagues on the right. Of thirteen G.O.P. right-

wingers running, only one equaled Eisenhower's share of the two-party vote. Of nine moderates, five bettered Ike's mark. The reason for this, pollsters indicated, was the fact that voters were not perturbed about alleged internal subversion. One study revealed less than 3 percent of the public expressing concern about the issue. Korea and the external Communist threat aroused much voter interest, of course, which undoubtedly benefitted Eisenhower. But no evidence suggests that the rhetoric of Nixon, Jenner, or McCarthy won many votes for the G.O.P. A Gallup poll taken in the spring of 1953 showed that 57 percent of those questioned did not even have an opinion about the Wisconsin senator. Of those who did, 22 percent were unfavorable and 19 percent favorable; 13 percent approved of McCarthy's methods, while 25 percent disapproved. "Support for Eisenhower," wrote Rogin, "indicates more about the mood of the populace in the America of the 1950s than does support for McCarthy."[87]

Almost all of the studies that now guide our understanding of the period, of course, were still in the future. At the time, McCarthy's political significance seemed staggering. *New York Times* columnist Arthur Krock concluded that "the voting majority indicated approval of the objectives of what the Democrats and independents have assailed as McCarthyism." William S. White said that McCarthy reentered Washington "in a position of extraordinary power—in the country as well as in the Senate." His friends were claiming that in the past two years McCarthy had influenced the victories of no less than eight present Senators, White reported. "The simple fact about Senator McCarthy—the profound fact of his well-documented political successes—is not overlooked in a political body." White pointed to the election of Butler, Dirksen, Purtell, Goldwater, Jenner, and Barrett. The Senate currently understood what it suspected in 1950, White wrote. "Senator McCarthy is a very bad man to cross politically."[88]

As if to symbolize Joe's triumph, a panel of the Civil Service Loyalty Review Board, in mid-December, recommended the dismissal of China Hand John Carter Vincent. Using President Truman's "reasonable doubt" standard, the panel concluded, by a 3-2 vote, that the 28-year veteran of the Foreign Service was a loyalty risk, even though he had been given a clean bill of health by the State Department's Loyalty-Security Board four times, once as recently as August 5. Vincent joined John Stewart Service as the second major victim of the Administration's new and highly controversial test of loyalty. McCarthy, Alfred Kohlberg, Louis Budenz, J. Edgar Hoover (who loaded Vincent's FBI file with inflammatory material from people such as neo-fascist Joseph Kamp and constantly pressed for his dismissal), Pat McCarran (whose committee interrogated Vincent for six-and-a-half days and condemned him in its final report), and the rest of the diplomat's detractors could point to yet another victory. Fulton Lewis, Jr., told his radio audience that the Vincent verdict was a "vindication of Senator Joe McCarthy."[89]

Joe soon told an interviewer that the government had merely "scratched the surface" in attempting to rid itself of subversives. When asked what had been the main difficulty up to this point in uncovering disloyalty, Joe said, "The principal hurdle has been the complete, wholehearted opposition from the President on down, the entire Administration, their attempt to protect, to cover up, and their complete refusal to recognize the evidence of subversives when you gave it to them." Asked if he would continue the search for Reds in government with the G.O.P. in power, he replied, "very definitely."[90]

NO TEAM PLAYER

During the campaign Adlai Stevenson warned that the right wing of the G.O.P. would "run the country" in the event of an Eisenhower victory, and he referred specifically to McCarthy. Not long after the ballots were counted, several observers of the rapid developments in Washington thought themselves prepared to confirm Stevenson's disturbing prediction.[1]

According to his seniority in the 83rd Congress, McCarthy could have become chairman of the Senate Appropriations Subcommittee, which supervised the State Department's spending. Joe had larger plans, however. In late November he announced that he would chair the Committee on Government Operations, a relatively minor "watchdog" committee created by the Legislative Reorganization Act of 1946. He would also serve, he said, as chairman of the committee's Permanent Subcommittee on Investigations. This was the true focus of Joe's ambition, for the subcommittee had an investigative staff and enjoyed wide discretionary authority. In the past it had studied "export policy and loyalty" as well as the "employment of homosexuals and other sex perverts in government." No one, including Joe, was yet certain of the scope of the probes to be undertaken by what soon became known as the "McCarthy Subcommittee," but few doubted that the unit would be extremely active. *The New York*

Times listed McCarthy among the six "key men" of the Senate in the new G.O.P. Congress.[2]

From the start it appeared certain that Joe would have a relatively free hand as chairman. On the Republican side the committee included Karl Mundt, Everett Dirksen, Henry Dworshak, John M. Butler, Charles Potter, and Margaret Chase Smith. Only Mrs. Smith was likely to be unsympathetic to McCarthy's tactics. Democratic floor leader Lyndon Johnson appointed three freshmen to the committee: W. Stuart Symington, Henry M. Jackson, and John F. Kennedy. Symington and Jackson were moderate, humane men who might be expected to resist at least some of the antics of the Far Right, and they both had bitter memories of McCarthy's active support of their opponents in the recent election. Still, their opposition to Joe and his allies, in light of Senate rules and traditions, was not expected to be formidable. Kennedy would not make waves. Conservative Democrats John L. McClellan of Arkansas and Clyde Hoey of North Carolina, and liberal Hubert Humphrey of Minnesota rounded out the committee. McCarthy was joined on the subcommittee by Mundt, Dirksen, and Potter, assuring him of a majority. The Democratic members were Symington, Jackson, and McClellan.[3]

Joe seemed unlikely to face serious opposition from the Senate Establishment of either party. G.O.P. leaders such as Robert Taft and William Knowland of California were known to be sympathetic. Leading Democrats, out of a mixture of fear, political acumen, and respect for senatorial courtesy, were unwilling to attack the Wisconsinite. Lyndon Johnson repeatedly referred to McCarthy as a "Republican problem" and once said, "I will not commit my party to some high-school debate on the subject, 'Resolved that Communism is good for the United States,' with my party taking affirmative." J. William Fulbright confided to William Benton, "For a Democrat to take the lead at this juncture would likely cause the Republicans to rally around McCarthy. . . . Unless some leading Republican is willing to take the curse of partisanship off the matter, I doubt that it is wise for a Democrat to make a move."[44]

McCarthy had good reason to believe that the new administration would also be supportive. A short time after the election, he had been invited to the home of William P. Rogers, a Washington acquaintance who was soon to be named Deputy Attorney General. There he spent a friendly evening chatting with Rogers, Richard Nixon, and Jerry Persons. According to Nixon, Joe admitted having been a bit extreme at times, but he expressed his complete sincerity in wishing to drive the Reds out of government. Nixon and the other Eisenhower aides assured the senator that they did not want him to take his eyes off of a single Communist. They urged him, however, to cooperate with his fellow Republicans in the White House in the interest of achieving a truly effective anti-Communist effort. The message seemed clear: as long as Joe remained a "team player" (soon a favorite expression within the new administration), he could expect cooperation from the Executive Branch.[5]

Joe bubbled with optimism at the thought of what might be accomplished during the next four years. Things would be "a lot different" with the G.O.P. in control, he told reporters. "I don't think we'll run into any whitewash or cover-up after Eisenhower takes over." "I like Dulles," he said on another occasion in late November. "I think he's a good American." Joe promised to turn over every particle of evidence he had collected on internal subversion to the new Secretary of State, and he pledged his complete cooperation. "If he does a good job, he will be attacked by left-wingers from one end of the country to the other."[6]

One of the first things Dulles did after taking office was to dissolve a distinguished review panel named by Truman in early January to look into the John Carter Vincent case. The panel, chaired by Learned Hand, former chief judge of the United States Second Circuit Court of Appeals, soon determined informally that Vincent was innocent of the charges contained in the Loyalty Review Board decision. Before it could issue a report, the Secretary of State relieved the panel of its responsibilities. The step was taken a short time after Alfred Kohlberg privately warned Dulles about Vincent and cast doubt on the loyalty of Learned Hand. Vincent's biographer later concluded that Dulles's "first objective was to reassure the McCarthyites that he was not another Acheson, even if it meant destroying State Department and Foreign Service morale." Ironically, Dulles cleared Vincent of all loyalty and security charges, and he permitted the veteran diplomat to resign and retain his pension. The public statement by the Secretary of State spoke vaguely of Vincent's poor judgment. (Three days after the 1954 elections, Dulles would dismiss John Paton Davies, Jr., on the ground of "lack of judgment, discretion, and reliability." Davies had been cleared eight times by loyalty boards.)[7]

Soon after being sworn in, Dulles sent a letter to 16,500 State Department and Foreign Service personnel demanding "positive loyalty" to the Administration and hinting of forthcoming purges. He warned that "the national welfare must be given priority over individual concerns." That same day the first Eisenhower bill to pass the initial legislative stage toward enactment in the 83d Congress emerged from the Senate Foreign Relations Committee. The measure provided for an Under Secretary of State for

Administration and Operations, a new post designed in part to guard against subversive infiltration in the Foreign Service. Senator Wiley said that the position was being created "for the specific obligation of house-cleaning in the State Department."[8]

The new post went to Donald B. Lourie, president of the Quaker Oats Company of Chicago. McCarthy was delighted when Lourie tapped Joe's friend and ally Scott McLeod to be the State Department's chief security officer. McLeod was a former FBI agent and administrative assistant to Sen. Styles Bridges of New Hampshire. The appointment was widely thought to be an act of appeasement by the Administration to the Far Right, and several commentators shuddered at the thought of what the likes of McCarthy and Bridges would do when given full access to the State Department files.[9]

Joe enjoyed speculating about the topics his subcommittee might investigate. At times he talked about concentrating on graft and corruption in government. He also spoke of undertaking extensive anti-Communist probes. "Out of the 81 cases I named in 1950, we have gotten rid of fifteen or sixteen. That's just scratching the surface." In late November he claimed that three senators had requested an inquiry into the Federal Communications Commission. A month later he declared his intention to root out "Communist thinkers" from the nation's colleges. "It will be an awfully unpleasant task," he told an interviewer, adding that he expected "all hell" to break loose and that there would be "screaming of interference with academic freedom." Two days later Don Surine told HUAC officials that McCarthy did not plan to limit his operations to a single field. He was even thinking of subpoenaing Harry S. Truman. "Senator McCarthy isn't afraid of anyone or anything," said Surine. "He means business. You watch and see what he does. It will make history."[10]

In December Joe had asked his friend Robert Morris to leave the McCarran Committee to become chief counsel of his subcommittee. The subcommittee already had a general counsel, former FBI man Francis Flanagan. Matters were complicated further when Joseph P. Kennedy requested that his son Robert be named chief counsel. (McCarthy once passed a note to an associate while the elder Kennedy supplied him with lengthy, unsought advice over the telephone: "Remind me to check the size of his campaign contribution. I'm not sure it's worth it.") After some confusion, Morris decided to remain with the Senate Internal Security Subcommittee, Flanagan was retained, and Kennedy was hired as Flanagan's assistant. The elder Kennedy was placated with the assurance that in due time his son would replace Flanagan.[11]

Twenty-seven-year-old "Bobby" Kennedy had graduated from the University of Virginia Law School the year before. As president of the Student Legal Forum, he had impressed his professors and fellow students by bringing McCarthy and other prestigious family friends on campus to speak. He then worked briefly in the Justice Department's Internal Security and Criminal Divisions, and he helped lead his brother's successful senatorial campaign. More than any of his siblings, Bobby resembled his father. "He's a great kid," Joe Kennedy once said. "He hates the same way I do." Undeniably intelligent and hard-working, Bobby was also extremely ambitious, aggressive, and vindictive. The word "ruthless" was often associated with the young attorney. Politically, Bobby could easily have qualified as a McCarthyite. The University of Virginia still possesses a paper he wrote while at law school attacking Roosevelt's "sellout" at Yalta. Kennedy also had a strong personal fondness for McCarthy that would be exhibited for many years.[12]

Joe remained determined to have a chief counsel, an experienced ultraconservative investigator like Robert Morris who would lead his committee into battle with the Reds and pinks. On January 2, 1953, the same day the Hennings Report was handed to reporters, Joe announced the hiring of twenty-five-year-old Roy M. Cohn as chief counsel. When asked by newsmen about the difference between a general counsel and a chief counsel and about which would have superior authority, Joe grinned, shrugged, and confessed, "I don't know." With the arrival of Cohn, a new chapter in McCarthy's life began, one that would see him elevated to even greater heights of international notoriety and plunged to the lowest depths of political ruin and personal despair.[13]

Roy Cohn was the son of Judge Albert Cohn of the Appellate Division of the New York Supreme Court. Gifted with a brilliant mind and a photographic memory, Cohn graduated from the Columbia University Law School at nineteen and was forced to wait two years until he was eligible to take the bar examination. His father's strong connections within the Democratic Party landed Cohn a clerk-typist job in the office of the United States Attorney for the Southern District of New York. On the day he became a member of the bar, he was sworn in as an assistant United States Attorney. He soon developed an intense interest in the field of subversive activities and became closely associated with the Far Right.

Cohn helped send the "Top Eleven" Communists in the United States to jail for violating the Smith Act, and he worked on the perjury trial of William Remington (who was convicted in January 1953). He assisted in the successful prosecution of Julius and Ethel Rosenberg, a young New

York couple convicted in March 1951 and sentenced to death for participation in a conspiracy to smuggle atomic bomb secrets to the Russians. As a
special assistant to Attorney General James McGranery, he prepared the
indictment of Owen Lattimore on perjury charges stemming from the
McCarran Committee investigation. He also assisted the McCarran Committee during a probe of Red infiltration into the United States personnel
of the United Nations, writing a grand jury presentment that was a
sweeping attack upon the State Department. Cohn could boast of legal
experience in other areas as well, from counterfeiting to narcotics traffic.
Despite his youth, he was considered a veteran investigator. (Some under-
world characters reportedly spent the first few minutes of an interview
with Cohn thinking themselves victims of a practical joke in apparently
being questioned by a schoolboy.)

The young attorney was dark, five-foot-eight-inches tall, weighed 160,
and wore his black hair slicked back in the style then popular. He bore a
rather prominent scar on his nose, the result of a boyhood accident. His
sleepy eyelids often disguised furious mental activity. He spoke rapidly,
seldom smiled, worked tirelessly, and appeared almost perpetually intense.
Not even Bobby Kennedy could match Cohn's arrogance, ambition, and
love of publicity.

When he was hired by the Justice Department in September 1952,
newspapers were tipped off in advance. On his first day on the job he was
sworn in ceremoniously in the Attorney General's private office (the oath
was unnecessary), a departmental press release was altered to mention his
new title, three Justice Department juniors were evicted to make room for
his private office, and he demanded a private cable address and a private
telephone line to his New York law office (from which he continued to
draw a handsome salary). *Time* magazine once said that Cohn showed
"contempt of all but the top boss." While McCarthy was to dote on his
young assistant, everyone who worked in the senator's office and almost all
of Joe's close friends in Wisconsin would despise him.[14]

Cohn's most intimate associates were ultraconservatives, including
Hearst columnists George Sokolsky and Walter Winchell. In 1952 Cohn
struck up a friendship with Sokolsky's confidant J. Edgar Hoover. The FBI
chief attended a private party celebrating the announcement of Cohn's new
position on the McCarthy Committee, as did Vice-President Nixon and
some twenty senators.[15]

Sokolsky later claimed to have introduced Cohn to McCarthy. While
Cohn disputed this in a 1968 book, he acknowledged that the Hearst
columnist, a longtime friend of his father, had played a leading role in the

deliberations that led to his appointment. As Cohn told the story, he first met McCarthy in early December 1952 at a crowded party in the senator's suite at the Hotel Astor in New York. Robert Morris had called a few days earlier to say that McCarthy wanted to talk with him. Cohn would long remember his first look at Joe: "Among the dozens of men and women in formal dress the senator had removed his jacket, shirt, and tie. He wore tuxedo trousers, patent leather shoes—and suspenders over a T-shirt." Joe was fully aware of Cohn's credentials and in a brief conversation made it clear that he wanted the investigator to join his subcommittee staff. He soon telephoned, offering the position of chief counsel. The call was extremely welcome, for Cohn, a Democrat, faced departure from Washington along with the retiring administration. "I couldn't care less about your politics," Cohn remembered Joe saying. "I'm interested only in your ability to do the job."[16]

With Cohn's list of achievements and references, McCarthy had every reason to believe that he would be effective. Joe was soon in awe of Cohn's intellect and breadth of knowledge as well, and became increasingly dependent upon his chief counsel. "Roy is one of the most brilliant young men I have ever met," he would say repeatedly. Joe also told friends that he hired Cohn to escape charges of anti-Semitism. Since the Anna Rosenberg fiasco he had been especially sensitive to this form of attack. In his speeches he avoided mention of the Julius and Ethel Rosenberg spy case, even though it had been in the headlines frequently since the summer of 1950 and helped document the theme of internal subversion. Joe appointed Steve Miller of Marshfield chairman of the McCarthy Club during the campaign specifically because he was Jewish.[17]

Don Surine was named assistant counsel to the subcommittee. He would later be joined by McCarthyites Daniel G. Buckley, the former Tydings Committee staff member, and ex-Communist Howard Rushmore, a Hearst reporter. Cohn was responsible for the hiring of 26-year-old G. David Schine as the subcommittee's unpaid "chief consultant." Schine was tall, slim, and blond; Richard Rovere would describe him as "a good-looking youth in the style that one associates with male orchestra singers." The son of a multimillionaire who owned a string of hotels, theaters and radio stations, Schine had gotten good grades at Fessenden, Andover, and Harvard, and soon after graduation was named president of Schine Hotels, Inc. His interests ran more toward nightclubs, starlets, and fancy cars than business, however, and he distinguished himself largely by owning what was reportedly the world's largest collection of cigars. Schine attracted the attention of right-wingers by writing and publishing an error-filled, six-page pamphlet entitled "Definition of Communism," copies of which were placed in every room in the Schine hotel chain. Cohn and Schine met in late 1952 and quickly became close friends. McCarthy added Schine to his staff in early February to please Cohn, never dreaming of the role this frivolous young man would play in his political and personal destruction.[18]

With his staff fairly complete, Joe initiated a struggle with the Senate Internal Security Subcommittee over "exclusive jurisdiction" in the field of anti-Communist investigations. He proposed creating at least three standing subcommittees of the McCarthy subcommittee which would conduct all probes into subversive activities. He publicly invited Homer Ferguson of Michigan to head one of them, a particularly brazen move given the fact that Ferguson was in line to succeed Pat McCarran as chairman of the Internal Security Subcommittee. A compromise was hammered out within top G.O.P. circles in early January. McCarthy agreed to permit the Internal Security Subcommittee to retain primacy over anti-Communist probes in return for three assurances: William Jenner was to succeed McCarran, McCarran was to remain on the body and continue to be active in its work, and the Jenner and McCarthy subcommittees were to consult on investigations and exchange information. A working agreement was also made with HUAC, chaired by Harold Velde of Illinois, so that forthcoming probes would not compete with each other. On the "Meet the Press" television program, Joe explained that his committee would retain the right to look into any phase of Communism neglected by the other two committees. Asked if he wasn't being pushed out of the fight against the Reds, he replied, "No one can push me out of anything."[19]

In late January, following a McCarthy speech telling of the need to investigate "alarming and disgraceful" practices in the foreign aid program, the McCarthy subcommittee received $200,000 to finance its operation. Jenner's Subcommittee was granted $150,000. Altogether, the Senate appropriated more than $800,000 to its investigating committees. (By mid-April eight investigations would be under way.) Veteran conservative Democrat Allen J. Ellender of Louisiana charged that the Senate was going "somewhat haywire" on probes, and he was especially critical of McCarthy for doubling his subcommittee's budget and staff. "He wants to televise all these hearings," Ellender complained. "He is trying to overdo this."[20]

Once the Senate had granted his budget request, Joe told reporters that he planned a new investigation of the State Department. It would be a study, he said, of alleged "mishandling" of department files rather than a direct probe of Communist infiltration. He also wrote to the President seeking access to all "Federal income tax returns and other related documents" in the Bureau of Internal Revenue. He soon demanded access to the classified files of the Federal Communications Commission. McCarthy was clearly determined to make his subcommittee a substantial power on Capitol Hill. Administration leaders were soon to learn how difficult it was to keep Joe on their "team."[21]

In early February McCarthy took a leading role in opposing the confirmation of Dr. James B. Conant, the President's selection for United States High Commission for West Germany. Conant, retiring president of Harvard University and a member of the Advisory Commission on Atomic Energy, was under fire for opposing a Congressional subversive activities investigation on his campus. This angered anti-Communist militants, for both HUAC and the Jenner subcommittee were planning inquiries into Communism in the schools, and McCarthy had publicly endorsed the idea. The Massachusetts House of Representatives narrowly killed an attempt to invite a Senate committee into the state to search for Reds in universities. Senator Kennedy said that while he intended to vote for Conant's confirmation "it would be a different matter if he were standing for commissioner of education." Conant was also under attack by leading Roman Catholics for a speech allegedly critical of private and parochial schools. Right-wing extremist John T. Flynn contended as well that Conant had supported the Morgenthau Plan for stripping postwar Germany of heavy industry. Flynn told the Foreign Relations Committee that Conant had also called for the formation of a "radical" political party in 1943, had stated that the Harvard faculty was free of Communists (which was unthinkable to the Far Right), and was guilty of holding opinions that "do not represent the prevailing philosophy of the American people."

McCarthy liked Flynn (who had contributed financially to his recent reelection campaign), and he endorsed his objections. Joe asked William F. Buckley to prepare a Senate speech summarizing the case against Conant. When Robert Taft learned of the speech, he persuaded McCarthy not to deliver it, for fear that references to the Morgenthau Plan would hinder Conant's effectiveness in Germany. Instead, Joe wrote a personal letter to the President, later described by Eisenhower as containing "wild charges." Joe let Ike know that he "strongly opposed" the nomination and would vote against it. He would not lead an all-out attack on the Senate floor, however, because such a battle "would furnish the Communists in Europe a vast amount of ammunition for their guns." Implicit in the message was the threat not to be so lenient in the future should the President again fail to exercise good judgment.

The Senate Foreign Relations Committee put Conant through some intensive closed-door questioning. Taft wanted to know specifically about McCarthy target Harlow Shapley, commenting that the Harvard faculty member had "attended every Communist meeting that we had in this country." Conant answered his critics persuasively, proclaimed his own vigorous anti-Communism, and was approved unanimously. Chairman Alexander Wiley told reporters, "Of course, Conant is classified as a great liberal and undoubtedly is not the type some of the committee would have named." The nomination cleared the full Senate two days later.[22]

On February 5, two days after McCarthy wrote his protest to the President about Conant, a White House source announced that Charles E. "Chip" Bohlen, counsellor of the State Department, would be appointed ambassador to the Soviet Union. Bohlen, 48, was an excellent choice to succeed George Kennan: he had worked in the Foreign Service for twenty-four years, spoke Russian and French, and was an authority on Soviet affairs. His nomination had been endorsed by a committee of three former Foreign Service officers, all Republicans and former ambassadors, who had been advising Secretary of State Dulles on appointments. He was also well known and respected by the President.

Still, it was certain that the nomination would raise the hackles of the Far Right, for Bohlen had been an interpreter and adviser at Yalta. Republicans, of course, had made much of the Yalta Conference during the campaign, especially in connection with the presence of Alger Hiss, and several ultraconservatives, including Styles Bridges and Charles Kersten, were clamoring for the formal repudiation of Yalta by the new administration. Bohlen had served in the State Department with Dean Acheson as well, and the appointment violated the determination of many Republicans to "clean house" after the election. Sensing the coming storm, Eisenhower quietly invited Majority Leader Taft to the White House and urged him to support Bohlen's confirmation. The Ohio senator reluctantly agreed to lay aside his natural inclinations and back the President. He warned his host, however, that if the G.O.P. majority failed to accept the nomination, it would be a serious blow to Eisenhower's prestige.[23]

The nomination was sent to the Senate on February 27. Four days earlier the Administration had sponsored a House joint resolution on Yalta that fell considerably short of repudiation. Ultraconservatives were enraged by this move and began speaking of betrayal. Congress, cried the *Chicago Tribune,* should recognize Roosevelt's "high crimes." The Bohlen nomination seemed to be an even more direct affront.[24]

Sen. Homer Ferguson of Michigan questioned Bohlen intensely on the issue of Yalta during the nominee's appearance before the Foreign Relations Committee on March 2. Bohlen placed the midwar conference in its

proper historical framework and answered questions about Hiss, containment, the Truman Doctrine, and similar matters. Committee members
seemed pleased by the witness's frank and learned statements and appeared
to favor confirmation. While the hearing was closed, Chairman Wiley later
gave briefings to the press, and some newspapers ran such headlines as
"Bohlen Defends Yalta Pact." This was a clear signal to McCarthyites to
declare war upon the nomination. As Bohlen later put it, "To the extreme
right-wingers, the gauntlet had been flung down. In their opinion, I was
opposing views that the public had overwhelmingly endorsed in the
election only a few months before."[25]

At the death of Joseph Stalin on March 5, the Foreign Relations Committee summoned Walter Bedell Smith, the former C.I.A. chief, now Under
Secretary of State, to a closed-door briefing. Asked about the vacant ambassadorship to the Soviet Union, Smith urged the committee to act swiftly
upon the Bohlen nomination. "The sooner we get in there, the better;
because there is going to be a very unusual series of developments, one way
or the other, and Mr. Bohlen, of course, is probably the best qualified man
that we have at the present time, and available to go there and make reports
during this critical period." Joe and his allies had other plans, however.[26]

McCarthy's friend Scott McLeod, assistant Secretary of State for Security
Affairs, was enjoying his new job thoroughly: in his first three weeks he
fired twenty-one State Department employees for alleged homosexuality.
He and a team of nearly two dozen ex-FBI agents examined desks, drawers,
file cabinets, and employee reading matter, during and after working hours,
in pursuit of subversives, forcing the State Department to operate in a
police-state atmosphere. Late in the year he would proudly announce that
306 citizen employees and 178 aliens had been removed on numerous
grounds without a single hearing. In early March McLeod learned that an
FBI check on Bohlen, the first ever made on the diplomat, had turned up a
small quantity of derogatory information. One report, Senator Gillette later
revealed, came from a person who claimed to have a "sixth sense" that
detected immorality in Bohlen. Sen. Walter George told reporters that the
information contained an anonymous letter and "hearsay reports" that
Bohlen had associated with "some bad eggs." At any rate, McLeod determined to use the material to stop Bohlen's confirmation. He informed
Dulles of the FBI findings and shared the evidence in detail with McCarthy.
Rumors quickly spread throughout Washington that McLeod considered
the nomination risky. The fears on Capitol Hill were such that the Foreign
Relations Committee delayed action on Bohlen and scheduled another
hearing.[27]

On March 13 Styles Bridges, McLeod's former employer, told reporters that "top" people in the Administration had asked the President to with-draw Bohlen's name. McCarthy announced that he would oppose the nomination, and he was soon joined by Senator McCarran. Taft admitted disliking the choice but said he would support the Chief Executive. "Our Russian ambassador can't do anything," he added. "All he can do is observe and report. He will not influence policy materially."

By this time Dulles was becoming fearful, and he seriously considered abandoning the nomination. He called Bohlen to his office and asked him if there was anything in his past that might be damaging. When assured that there wasn't, Dulles said, "Well, I'm glad of that because I couldn't stand another Alger Hiss." Undoubtedly at Eisenhower's insistence, Dulles decided not to yield to right-wing pressure. When Joe learned of this he told reporters that the secretary was making "a great mistake," although he conceded that Bohlen would be confirmed. Bridges predicted fifteen to twenty votes against the nominee from the full Senate.[29]

Dulles and Bohlen were both scheduled to appear in closed session before the Foreign Relations Committee on the day of the second hearing, March 18. Dulles suggested that they drive separately to Capitol Hill, explaining bluntly that it would be better if they were not photographed together. "His remark made me wonder if he would have the courage to stand up to the McCarthyites," Bohlen later wrote.[30]

The Secretary of State had received the full FBI summary on Bohlen the day before. In an unprecedented action, he personally evaluated the report for the committee and assured its members that it contained nothing of substance against the nominee. "There is not a whisper of a suggestion that I have been able to turn up throwing any doubt at all upon his loyalty or upon his security as a person." Under questioning, Dulles conceded that McLeod had not cleared Bohlen. "In important cases, such as this one," he said, "the task of final evaluation should be passed up to the senior officers." The senators revealed their confidence in the secretary by approving the nomination 15-0. Senator Ferguson said afterward, "Dulles is a good lawyer with the capacity to evaluate the field report. I'm satisfied that he gave us a proper evaluation of it."[31]

McCarthy was furious with Dulles and predicted that the President would withdraw the nomination if he saw "the entire file on Bohlen." This was perhaps a reference to the FBI's "raw files" rather than the bureau summary, and was no doubt a bluff. On the Senate floor he claimed that Dulles had "cleared" Bohlen despite objections by the State Department's top security officer. Pat McCarran agreed, charging that McLeod's judg-ment had been "summarily overriden" by Dulles and recommending that the nomination be delayed until every interested senator had seen "the full and complete FBI file on this nominee." Everett Dirksen told reporters that McLeod should be brought before the McCarthy subcommittee and asked to tell "exactly what he found" in the FBI report.

The Administration struck back quickly. Eisenhower told newsmen that he thoroughly approved of Bohlen's nomination. Dulles called a news conference and, with Senator Wiley at this right, told reporters that he had informed the President of all derogatory material in Bohlen's file. He repeated his support of the nomination and contended that he and McLeod were in accord on the final evaluation of Bohlen. G.O.P. moderate Charles Tobey of New Hampshire angrily told a reporter, "The opposition comes from a little group of willful men. For twenty years," he continued, "we've been trying to get a Republican administration. Instead of upholding the President, they are trying to block him and put daggers in his back. They are attacking the President and trying to undermine his administration. These critics are not worthy to unlace either Acheson's or Bohlen's shoes."

Enraged by this response, Joe demanded that the Secretary of State be "put under oath" and questioned further by the Senate Foreign Relations Committee. He charged that McLeod had been ordered not to appear before the McCarthy Subcommittee until after Senate action on Bohlen's nomination, and he toyed with the idea of issuing a subpoena to Dulles to explain the order. From what he understood, Joe said, Dulles and McLeod were not in agreement over Bohlen. "McLeod is a very truthful man."[32]

McLeod marched over to the White House and spoke for two-and-a-half hours with his friend Gen. Milton "Jerry" Persons, the President's congressional liaison, complaining about the assertion that he and Dulles had agreed on Bohlen. His frustration was such that he threatened to resign, a proposal overruled by presidential assistant Sherman Adams. (Eisenhower later explained to Bohlen that McLeod's appointment was "an error on our part," but added, "My feeling is it would be a worse error to dismiss him.") McLeod secretly reported his White House experience to McCarthy, whose anger at the Administration grew even stronger. According to Persons, Joe soon contacted Richard Nixon and said that he had two speeches prepared on the Bohlen issue: one was "pretty rough" and the other "*real*" dirty." He asked the Vice-President for advice on which to use. No doubt with considerable difficulty, Nixon persuaded his friend to deliver the more temperate address.[33]

McCarthy and McCarran requested delay on the nomination, the latter contending that he had a "chestful" of information for his colleagues about Bohlen. After a private session with Eisenhower, Taft scheduled the debate for March 23 and announced "no change" in the President's position. In defiance of both his party leaders, Styles Bridges quickly renewed his strong opposition to Bohlen before a battery of newsreel and television microphones.[34]

The Senate debate was heated and often bitter. McCarthy, leading the opposition, proposed that Bohlen be given a lie-detector test about allegations turned up by the FBI. "I think Mr. Bohlen would agree with me that if the information in the files—some sixteen pages of it—is correct, Moscow is the last place in the world to which he should be sent." He also suggested that Dulles and McLeod be called before the Foreign Relations Committee for a sort of Hiss-Chambers confrontation. Senators Wiley and Taft staunchly defended the nomination and caustically dismissed McCarthy's objections. Even William Knowland, normally loyal to McCarthy, argued in favor of confirmation. Ralph Flanders angrily told Joe that he should give the new administration an opportunity to succeed. "We have on trial a Republican Secretary of State and, by implication, the Republican President of the United States." Joe fired back, "I do not care whether a President is a Democrat or a Republican; when he has made a bad nomination I intend to oppose it on the floor of the Senate or elsewhere."

It was finally agreed to accept a proposal by Robert Taft to have one senator from each party review the FBI file on Bohlen and report their findings. The Foreign Relations Committee gave the task to Taft and John Sparkman, the 1952 Democratic vice-presidential candidate. They were not permitted to examine the sacrosanct "raw files" of the FBI, but J. Edgar Hoover assured them personally that the bureau summary contained all of the relevant material in the case. Both senators requested and received a statement by McLeod that he had had access only to the summary. In short, Taft and Sparkman would be studying exactly what Dulles and McLeod had seen.[35]

On the second day of the debate, March 25, the two senators reported that they found nothing in the summary to shake their support of Bohlen's nomination. "There was no suggestion anywhere by anyone," Taft said, "reflecting on the loyalty of Mr. Bohlen in any way, or any association by him with Communism or support of Communism or even tolerance of Communism."

Faced with the endorsement of Bohlen by the President, Secretary of State, a unanimous Foreign Relations Committee, the G.O.P. Majority Leader, and a clear majority of senators, the anticonfirmation forces remained unmoved. Styles Bridges leaped to the attack, branding Bohlen an

"exponent of appeasement and containment" and an "experienced failure."
"If we approve the nomination of Mr. Bohlen," he cried, "we put the seal of
approval on the sellout of Poland, and we slap in the face every citizen of
Polish descent in this nation and every free man in this country."

Bridges also challenged Senator Wiley's statement to the Senate that
Bohlen had been recommended by three distinguished ex-Foreign Service
officers, Joseph Grew, Norman Armour, and Hugh Gibson. Gibson was in
the hospital recovering from a heart attack, but his attorney, Bridges said,
denied that he had approved Bohlen. Everett Dirksen telephoned Gibson
and confirmed Bridges' report. Knowland called Dulles, who dispatched a
letter to Capitol Hill signed by Grew, Armour, and Gibson containing a list
of men for numerous diplomatic posts. Attached was a memorandum
listing Bohlen's name opposite the space for the ambassadorship to the
Soviet Union. Since the document contained the names of appointees yet to
be announced, Knowland said that he could not read it into the *Congressional Record*. McCarthy asked that Knowland show the memorandum to
Dirksen "so that there may be no question about it." His integrity challenged, Knowland flew into a rage and exchanged bitter words with Joe. At
one point the California senator shouted, "If we have so destroyed confidence in men who have been selected to hold high places in the government of the United States, God help us; God help us if that is the basis upon
which we have to operate."

With little else to stand on, Joe produced what he said was an affidavit
from one Igor Bogolepov, an ex-official of the Soviet Foreign Ministry. The
highly suspicious document alleged that Bohlen was "evidently" considered
friendly by Soviet authorities as a "possible" source of information. Bohlen
later labeled this tactic "outrageous."[36]

At his weekly news conference on March 26, Eisenhower quashed
suggestions by McCarthy and McCarran that Bohlen was not his personal
choice. He declared the nominee to be the best qualified man he could find
to be ambassador to Moscow and said that he was deeply concerned about
the appointment. He added that he had once been a guest in Bohlen's home
and had played golf with him. The President avoided direct criticism of
McCarthy, saying that he had no intention of trying to interfere with him as
long as the senator thought he was doing the right thing.[37]

Privately, columnist Marquis Childs revealed, Eisenhower was seething
over Joe's conduct. "No incident in his first two months has so stirred the
Eisenhower ire." But the President spurned all pleas to take the offensive
against McCarthy. He soon explained privately to a friend:

This particular individual wants, above all else, publicity. Nothing would probably please him more than to get the publicity that would be generated by public repudiation by the President.

I do not mean that there is no possibility that I shall never change my mind on this point. I merely mean that as of this moment I consider that the wisest course of action is to continue to pursue a steady, positive policy in foreign relations, in legal procedures in cleaning out the insecure and the disloyal, and in all other areas where McCarthy seems to take such a specific and personal interest. My friends on the Hill tell me that of course, among other things, he wants to increase his appeal as an after dinner speaker and so raise the fees that he charges.

It is a sorry mess; at times one feels almost like hanging his head in shame when he reads some of the unreasoned, vicious outbursts of demagoguery that appear in our public prints. But whether a presidential "crack down" would be better, or would actually worsen, the situation, is a moot question.

Eisenhower told Emmet John Hughes and others on numerous occasions, "I just will not—I refuse—to get into the gutter with that guy."[38]

The Senate debate resumed the next day, and McCarthy and his allies again attacked Bohlen, concentrating their fire on his presence at Yalta. "I reject Yalta, so I reject Yalta men," Senator Dirksen growled. But it was clear, as it had been from the start, that the Administration would carry the vote. Too many Republicans wished to remain loyal to the new Chief Executive, however they may have disliked his nominee. Democrats, of course, were more than willing to back a diplomat who had enjoyed the confidence of both Roosevelt and Truman. When the nomination came to a vote Bohlen was confirmed by a rousing margin of 74-13. The eleven right-wing Republicans who cast negative votes were: McCarthy, Bridges, Bricker, Dirksen, Dworshak, Welker, Goldwater, Hickenlooper, Malone, Mundt, and Schoeppel. They were joined by Democrats McCarran and Edwin Johnson of Colorado.[39]

Several insights into the future could be gleaned by the Administration from this initial confrontation with Senate McCarthyites. For one thing, it was clear that Joe and those who backed him were going to operate outside party discipline when it suited them. Appeals to unity and self-interest were of no avail, even when it was certain that the Bohlen nomination would be confirmed. Karl Mundt declared, "Rubber-stamp government in

America died when President Eisenhower took office," and he expressed his confidence that the Majority Leader would not request "blind partisanship" in the future. Taft had shown himself incapable of restraining all of his colleagues on the Far Right. At one point in the debates he harshly informed McCarthy that J. Edgar Hoover was "absolutely opposed" to lie-detectors. Joe abruptly dismissed the Majority Leader with the assertion that he was "incorrect" and continued the attack.

Taft, of course, had been influential in the lopsided vote on Bohlen; numerous Republicans, including the likes of Homer Capehart of Indiana and John Marshall Butler of Maryland, rallied behind the President at his request. But it was certain that the Ohio senator would not always be so loyal. After the vote he sent a pointed message to the White House: "No more Bohlens." Administration leaders had good reason to fear the fate of measures, such as foreign aid, that would unite the Majority Leader with McCarthyites. In the future Eisenhower might be forced to rely heavily upon Democrats to push his programs through Congress, which would divide Republicans even more than the Bohlen nomination.[40]

Many were persuaded by the Bohlen fight that McCarthy was implacably ambitious. Marquis Childs wrote, "His drive for personal power is such that he cannot call off the attack and become one of the ninety-six senators." Columnist Clifton Utley declared, "Many of the seemingly inexplicable antics of Senator McCarthy become perfectly rational and understandable once one accepts the basic premise that McCarthy, whose ambition is limitless, is busily engaged in running for President." Some White House advisers thought that the President's lenient, "hands-off" approach to the Wisconsin senator would ultimately lead to political disaster.[41]

Others were less certain about McCarthy's motives. How was one to explain his eagerness to impugn the honesty and integrity of Secretary of State Dulles and William Knowland, chairman of the Policy Committee of the Republican majority in the Senate? Surely this was not the action of a reasonable, knowledgeable politician, especially an ambitious one. And if such passion could be displayed over the appointment of an ambassador, in the face of certain defeat, what havoc might McCarthy wreak when far more serious matters came before the Senate?

Joe's role in the Bohlen episode angered and irritated Republicans throughout the country, including Wisconsin. The right-wing Scripps-Howard newspaper chain condemned McCarthy's "back-alley tactics," charged him with "vilification by innuendo," and concluded, "The amazing thing is that this loud-mouthed rowdy has attracted a Senate following, which has assisted him in dragging that body into the gutter with him."

The ever-loyal *Wisconsin State Journal* complained bitterly about the senator's treatment of Knowland and sighed, "There are times when Joe McCarthy makes it tough to play on his team."[42]

There was no indication that Joe took his defeat on Bohlen to heart or paid heed to the growing number of his critics. With Roy Cohn at his side, he was engaged in furious activity that kept him in the headlines and made the McCarthy subcommittee one of the most dreaded and notorious public bodies in the nation's history. William S. White would later observe that the marble caucus room in the Senate Office Building, where the subcommittee often met, "stank with the odor of fear and the odor of monstrous silliness."[43]

In his State of the Union message on February 2, Eisenhower repeated a controversial statement he had made in Green Bay during the campaign: the primary responsibility for rooting subversion out of the federal government, he said, rested squarely upon the executive branch. Some journalists interpreted this as an effort by the President to seize control of the Communists-in-government issue from the hands of Congress, and perhaps they were right. But from the opening days of the 83d Congress it was clear that ultraconservative congressmen were intent on pursuing the second Red Scare regardless of the desires of the Chief Executive.[44]

Jenner's Internal Security Subcommittee traveled to New York to probe the loyalty of Americans working in the United Nations and then moved on to Washington and Boston in pursuit of Reds in public and private schools. HUAC, under the direction of Harold Velde, searched for Communist infiltration of education in New York City, grappled with alleged Communists in the motion-picture industry, and examined the patriotism of the state government in Albany. Ex-FBI man Velde told a radio audience that he was considering an investigation of the clergy, a suggestion that stirred a storm of protest throughout the country and earned the President's public opposition. Undeterred, HUAC summoned Methodist Bishop G. Bromley Oxnam to a much-publicized hearing a short time later and cruelly grilled him for ten hours under blinding television lights.[45]

In early February the McCarthy subcommittee began hearings on the State Department files. Two unconvincing witnesses who worked with the files told of sloppy security procedures and hinted at subversion. When one of them, a State Department security officer, was suddenly transferred to a job in which he no longer had access to Foreign Service personnel files, Joe angrily summoned the official who ordered the change and put him through a grueling interrogation on the witness stand. After a closed-door meeting between the subcommittee and Donald B. Lourie, the friendly Under Secretary of State for Administration, the transfer was revoked.[46]

On February 12 McCarthy announced an investigation into possible "mismanagement, subversion, and kickbacks" among employees of the Voice of America. The subcommittee hearings were to be closed briefly and then televised nationally. Joe displayed a letter from Alexander Wiley, chairman of the Foreign Relations Committee, bestowing his blessing upon the probe. Once again, the moderate Republicans were guilty of abetting McCarthy's excesses.[47]

The Voice of America had its roots in the wartime effort by the Office of War Information to wage psychological warfare against the Axis powers. In 1945 the O.W.I. conducted an ambitious overseas program that included the publication of magazines, the distribution of newsreels and photographs, the operation of libraries in some 40 outposts, and Voice broadcasting in 41 languages over 39 short-wave transmitters. After the war the broadcasts became anti-Communist, and in 1948 responsibility for the preparation and transmission of programs was given to the State Department. A year later the Soviets began to jam Voice broadcasts within the Iron Curtain.

In 1952 President Truman placed much of the overseas information program within a semi-autonomous agency called the International Information Administration, headed by Dr. Wilson M. Compton, former president of Washington State College. When the G.O.P. came to power, the I.I.A. employed a staff of 10,000 comprising approximately 40 percent of the total personnel of the State Department, and spent some $100,000,000 a year. The Voice of America was transmitting 50 hours of programs daily in approximately 50 different languages. It had twelve stations within the United States, six overseas, and a mobile transmitter aboard a ship. New high-power stations were nearing completion in Munich, the Philippines, and on Okinawa, and two powerful short-wave stations were under construction at Port Angeles, Washington (called Baker West), and Wilmington, North Carolina (Baker East).

Overseas information programs were familiar targets of controversy, however. As early as 1945 Republicans claimed that the New Deal-created O.W.I. had been infiltrated by Communists. Powerful G.O.P. Congressman John Taber of New York attempted annually to slash appropriations in this field. The South Korean government banned Voice broadcasts during the Korean War, and in early February 1953 a Senate Foreign Relations subcommittee called for a drastic overhauling of overseas information programs, including the Voice of America. When one agency official called on Herbert Hoover in early 1953 seeking support, the former President angrily contended that the I.I.A. was "full of O.W.I. hangers-on," "Communists," "left-wingers," and "incompetents." Taber, chairman of the House Appropriations Committee in the new Eighty-Third Congress, called the I.I.A. "decidedly pinko."[48]

Joe undoubtedly became interested in the Voice of America in large part to make headlines. One veteran I.I.A. official commented in early 1953, "It is his plan to get publicity. There is no necessity for televising these hearings." But the investigation was also part of a long-range, right-wing effort to drive "dangerous liberals" and other antagonists out of the State Department. From the start, Joe had the warm support of Donald Lourie, Scott McLeod, and Carl McCardle, Secretary of State Dulles's press secretary.[49]

Joe also enjoyed the assistance of "friends" within the I.I.A. who supplied him with tips, information and testimony. Calling themselves "the Loyal American Underground," they were eager to increase hard-line anti-Communist propaganda over the Voice and silence those who favored a more subtle approach. Several were junior employees, apparently grown desperate by the threat of personnel cuts. Two were disgruntled former employees who claimed to see treason in the selection of the Baker sites. One, a Rumanian-born member of the French desk who trafficked in gossip and threats, was thought by some of his colleagues to be a McCarthy plant. The most prominent was Miss Frances Knight, a veteran I.I.A. employee and zealous ultraconservative who would later be named McLeod's assistant deputy administrator and in 1955 become head of the State Department's passport office.[50]

The McCarthy subcommittee's closed-door hearings began on February 13, and after a single session Joe gravely announced to reporters, "There are some people in the Voice of America who are doing a rather effective job of sabotaging Dulles's and Eisenhower's foreign policy program." One witness, Lewis J. McKesson, a former Voice radio engineer, criticized the selection of sites for Baker East and Baker West, charging mismanagement of funds and implying that the locations had been chosen because signals from these regions could be more easily jammed by Soviet transmitters. (The sites had been selected by scientists from the Radio Corporation of America and checked by M.I.T.'s Research Laboratory of Electronics. No evidence of sabotage was ever discovered.) Dr. Compton immediately suspended work on the two locations, a fact Joe proudly announced after McKesson's public testimony three days later. Construction of the short-wave stations was later canceled, and McCarthy would boast that his subcommittee had saved taxpayers $18,000,000. The figure was fantastic: Joe used it on February 16 as an estimate of the savings involved in shifting the two stations to sites in southern California and southern Florida. During the course of the hearings Joe claimed repeatedly that the study recommending the original sites cost $600,000, when the actual cost was $6,000.[51]

Dr. Compton's perfunctory change-of-administration resignation was brusquely accepted on February 18, a day after he testified before the subcommittee and conceded the existence of waste within the I.I.A. As a replacement, Dulles selected Dr. Robert L. Johnson, 58, a millionaire Republican and president of Temple University. When asked about McCarthy's investigation, Johnson said, "I think he is trying to be helpful, and maybe he'll dig up stuff that will be very important to us." Joe said of Johnson, "I think he is a good American who wants to see that the Voice works properly." As his operations chief, Johnson picked Martin Merson, a conservative Virginia Democrat who was to write a fascinating book about his turbulent five-and-one-half months in Washington.[52]

The hearings then turned to the subject of the material used in Voice of America broadcasts and included in the libraries of 200 State Department Information Centers in 63 countries. Under the Truman administration a "balanced presentation" policy had been in force, and there was virtually no effort made to exclude the writings of Communists. An agency advisory Committee on Books, headed by Dr. Martin R. P. McGuire of Catholic University, declared in 1952, "any book whatsoever of United States origin, which may be of use to the program, should be made available abroad." The State Department distributed a new policy statement on February 3 that retreated only slightly from the earlier position. One portion of the classified directive read:

> The reputation of an author affects the active utility of the material. If he is widely and favorably known abroad as a champion of democratic causes, his creditability and utility may be enhanced.
> Similarly, if—like Howard Fast—he is known as a Soviet-endorsed author, materials favorable to the United States in some of his works may thereby be given a special creditability among selected key audiences.

The new policy order was smuggled to McCarthy, who exploded with anger before the television cameras, charging that the I.I.A. was encouraging subversion. Fast was promptly called before the subcommittee and brutally berated by McCarthy after refusing to answer all questions about Communism. For good measure, Joe charged that Mrs. Franklin D. Roosevelt had "helped" with the circulation of Fast's writings. The allegation was apparently based upon the fact that Fast had attended a luncheon at the White House some nine years earlier.[53]

The next day, February 19, the State Department issued Information Guide 272, banning the books, music, and paintings of "Communists, fellow travelers, et cetera" from the Voice of America and ordering overseas librarians to remove all publications by controversial authors from their shelves. When McCarthy's staff examined the I.I.A.'s catalogues, Joe charged that there were over 30,000 volumes in agency libraries by "Communist" authors. The figure was actually obtained by listing individual copies of books by 418 writers, including Arthur Schlesinger, Jr., John Dewey, Robert M. Hutchins, W. H. Auden, Edna Ferber, and Steven Vincent Benet. Before long, in the madness that followed, nervous librarians discarded and even burned books placed on what appeared to be a State Department blacklist. Among those whose works were removed were such strange bedfellows as: Vera Micheles Dean, editor of Foreign Policy Association Publications; mystery writer Dashiell Hammett; Theodore H. White; Lillian Hellman; Jean Paul Sartre; Bert Andrews, head of the Washington Bureau of the *New York Herald Tribune;* Joseph Davies, former ambassador to Moscow; Walter White, head of the National Association for the Advancement of Colored People; Foster Rhea Dulles, the Secretary of State's scholarly cousin; Alan Barth; and Whittaker Chambers. Hammett and several other authors had refused to tell congressional investigators about alleged Communist affiliations. A number of the banished books, such as Theodore White's best-selling *Thunder out of China,* criticized American policy in the Far East. Walter White's book (restored after a protest by the author) discussed race relations among American troops during World War II. In all, according to *The New York Times,* several hundred books were removed from overseas libraries. Dulles set the number destroyed by fire at eleven, but in Japan "many" books and periodicals were reported "burned or scrapped for pulping."[54]

The number-two Voice official, Alfred H. Morton, chief of the International Broadcasting Service, wired a protest to his Washington headquarters saying that the I.B.S. would continue "to use the works and words of Communists, fellow travelers, et cetera, to expose them or make them eat their own words, or in the furtherance of the American national interest." Through connections inside Voice offices, Francis P. Flanagan of McCarthy's staff learned of the telegram and informed Under Secretary Lourie, interpreting the wire as an act of defiance. On February 24 Morton was suspended. "I.I.A. at this time," Martin Merson later wrote, "was looking directly to McCarthy for policy. It was quicker that way."[55]

Under Secretary of State Walter Bedell Smith restored Morton to office the next day. A formal letter, released to the press, unconvincingly implied that Morton had not actually written the telegram. *The New York Times* reported that "vigorous protests had been made by leading Voice executives to top Department officials" about the February 19 order. The clamor was to have little lasting effect, however. On March 17 Dulles issued a policy directive that dropped the menacingly vague "et cetera" from the prohibited authors category. But the new statement essentially supported the February 19 order, specifically demanding the removal of works by Communist authors and the withdrawal of individual issues of periodicals "containing any material detrimental to United States objectives." Joe praised the directive as "just the kind of thing we hoped for," and complimented Secretary Dulles[56]

The Administration capitulated to McCarthy again in late February by making ineffective a two-day-old State Department directive giving employees the discretion not to talk informally with a member of a committee or subcommittee staff in the absence of a senator. The directive also forbade employees to remove files, records, or internal executive correspondence in department custody without specific permission from superiors. When Joe heard about the order he roared, "This subcommittee is not going to be hamstrung by the State Department or any other department." After a closed-door session with Under Secretary Smith, Joe announced to reporters that the State Department would henceforth cooperate fully with his investigation. Moreover, he said, the department would appoint a liaison officer to work with the subcommittee in lining up witnesses.[57]

Washington buzzed with reports of sinking State Department morale. *New York Times* correspondent William S. White reported, "No greater series of victories by a congressional body over a senior executive department in so short a time is recalled here." One Voice employee confided to a high federal official, "Just imagine yourself having to work in the same room and directing the daily work of a person who has slandered you in public—before the press and television—and has told absurd lies which can only be explained by psychiatrists." He continued, "No one seems interested in the truth. If you quit it looks like some tacit admission of guilt. If you protest, it is insubordination, and you might find yourself suspended." The head of one office was reported to have said that his staff was able to do only about half its normal output of work. Another was quoted as having confided to a colleague, "I am engaged in an intense effort to fade into the wallpaper." The atmosphere at Foggy Bottom was such that Robert Johnson, the new I.I.A. chief, first met with top advisers in his apartment, fearing hidden microphones and wiretaps in his office.[58]

When Joe was asked about State Department morale, he said that the morale of "good Americans" was at an all-time high. Secretary Dulles, he noted, "hasn't shown he's at all unhappy about what we are doing." When reporters asked the President if he thought the McCarthy subcommittee investigation was helping the Voice of America, Eisenhower said that he could not reply without having more information. Joe praised the response as "a good sensible answer."[59]

One American newsman in Europe reported a "nervous chill" in overseas financial and governmental circles over the ease with which McCarthy appeared to be manipulating the new administration. Many newspapers, he wrote, gave their readers the impression that Washington officials were "living under a kind of terror not unlike those experienced in Europe at various periods." Foreign reporters, for example, made much of the plight of Troup Matthews, editor of the Voice of America's French section. One obviously unstable subcommittee witness charged during a public hearing that Matthews had tried to recruit her into a Communist-style community of "free love." Matthews, a one-legged veteran of World War II, told newsmen, "Communism is utterly abhorrent to me. It embodies all the aspects of Nazism against which I fought." He added, "I'm a firm believer in monogamy, and I've got a wife and four kids to prove it." Matthews' appeal to appear publicly before the subcommittee on his own behalf was ignored by McCarthy.[60]

Numerous confrontations between the subcommittee and its witnesses bordered on the grotesque. Roger Lyons, director of the Voice of America's religious programming, was forced to respond to a charge (supported by an ex-girl friend) that he was, or at least once was, an unbeliever. "I am not an atheist," Lyons insisted during his testimony, "I am not an agnostic. I believe in God." While he did not attend religious services regularly, Lyons said, he had been to church within the past month and had contributed ten dollars recently to a Lutheran church in New Jersey. When the witness mentioned that he had once studied psychology in Switzerland with the renowned Carl Jung, Joe asked if Jung attended a church or synagogue.[61]

Edwin M. J. Kretzmann, chief Voice policy director in New York, was assailed for having told a supposedly closed-door conference of Voice officials that an order by Dulles to cooperate with the subcommittee was "rather depressing." He was soon transferred to the U.S. embassy in Belgrade.[62]

In three days of stormy testimony in early March, Reed Harris, a former O.W.I. employee and recent acting chief of the I.I.A., was attacked repeatedly by McCarthy for sentiments expressed in a book written twenty-one years earlier when Harris was a student at Columbia University. Entitled *King Football,* the book dealt largely with the commercialism of intercollegiate football but also contained a defense of academic freedom, including the right of Communists to teach (a position endorsed by Senator Taft). Despite two favorable "full field" investigations by the FBI and clearance from the Civil Service Commission, Harris found himself under suspicion of harboring disloyal thoughts and ordered to produce documentary evidence of a change of heart. An additional charge, supported by two colleagues, that Harris had deliberately subverted Voice objectives by canceling Hebrew language broadcasts, was highly unpersuasive and was later dismissed by virtually everyone familiar with the facts. Scarred badly by the rough treatment he received at the hands of McCarthy, Harris resigned voluntarily on April 14, "pilloried for sins," Martin Merson later wrote, "that were collegiate, to say the worst about them." "I only hope," Joe commented, "that a lot of Mr. Harris's close friends will follow him out."[63]

At times, the gravity of the proceedings lifted. Robert A. Bauer, acting chief of the Voice's Field Program Service division, appeared before the subcommittee on March 6 to rebut an allegation that a great share of the Latin American broadcasts had been devoted to children's programs and lacked anti-Communist impact. To make his point, Bauer read excerpts from individual broadcasts, interpreting the scripts with dramatic flare and noting with gestures that the villains of every piece bore Russian names. The audience howled over the robust melodrama, which prompted Karl Mundt to suggest that the issue be put "on ice."[64]

But such levity was rare under the boiling television lights, as witnesses struggled to combat often absurd charges, display their unwavering patriotism, and grapple with the abuse McCarthy and his colleagues poured upon them. Those who came before the subcommittee quickly sensed the intensity, suspicion, and anger that hung over every executive session and public hearing. One witness would write, "There were moments during the hearings when I caught myself watching McCarthy with a kind of fascination, trying hard to look behind the masks he wears and almost forgetting that it was my life he was playing with."[65]

Sometimes the subcommittee seemed interested primarily in persecuting a witness. On March 13, for example, Dr. Julius H. Hlavaty was called before the body and questioned about a single broadcast he had made to his native Czechoslovakia over Voice facilities in 1952. The script had been prepared by Voice officials, and even Roy Cohn could find nothing controversial within it. The true purpose of summoning the Bronx High School mathematics teacher, it soon appeared, was to grill him about his personal beliefs (Senator Symington asked if he believed in God) and to demand that he admit to having once been a Communist. The witness bravely defended his intellectual integrity and objectivity as a teacher, but he invoked the Fifth Amendment when questioned about previous party membership. This action, as subcommittee members knew, meant Hlavaty's automatic dismissal from the New York school system, in accord with a section of the City Charter. Despite the teacher's superior record during a career that began in 1929, he was soon unemployed.[66]

James A. Wechsler, editor of the liberal *New York Post,* was summoned twice before the subcommittee in the spring and subjected to blistering excoriations by McCarthy. (The hearings were closed, but newsmen were informed of the proceedings, and the stenographic transcript was soon released at Wechsler's insistence.) Joe was ostensibly interested in the presence of books by Wechsler in overseas libraries. In fact, he desired to harass and bully the editor for years of anti-McCarthy editorials, stories, and cartoons. It was as though Joe had William Evjue or Robert Fleming in his grasp. "You have fought every man who has ever tried to fight Communism," he charged. "Your paper, in my opinion, is next to and almost paralleling the *Daily Worker.*" McCarthy made much of the fact that Wechsler had been a member of the Young Communist League from April 1934, when he was an eighteen-year-old student at Columbia University, through December 1937. Actually, as was well known, Wechsler had been a staunch anti-Communist since that time, and his newspaper had attacked domestic subversion and Soviet foreign policy vigorously and regularly. Joe charged him with having made a "phony break" with Communism. "I feel that you have not broken with Communist ideals," he sneered. "I feel that you are serving them very, very actively. Whether you are doing it knowingly or not, that is in your own mind. I have no knowledge as to whether you have a card in the party."

McCarthy's conduct prompted Senators Jackson and Symington to become restive and speak out on Wechsler's behalf. They did not object, however, to the demand by McCarthy that the editor give the subcommittee a list of the names of everyone he could remember from his youth who had been a Communist or a Young Communist League member. Wechsler complied, with reluctance and remorse.[67]

Fear of persecution by the subcommittee caused Raymond Kaplan, a 42-year-old Voice of America engineer, to commit suicide in early March by jumping in front of a truck. Kaplan had served as a "liaison man" between the Voice and M.I.T. during the selection of sites for Baker East and Baker West. In a farewell letter to his wife and son, Kaplan wrote, "You see, once the dogs are set on you everything you have done since the beginning of time is suspect." He assured his family, "I have never done anything that I consider wrong but I can't take the pressure upon my shoulders any more." Joe shrugged off the incident, noting that he and his staff had no evidence of wrongdoing against the deceased. Moreover, he told reporters, coworkers of Kaplan had expressed "grave doubt" that his death was actually a suicide.[68]

Some hearings were devoted exclusively to attracting publicity. In a rowdy session in late March, Earl Browder and two left-wing authors were brought before the subcommittee—and the television cameras—to explain why their books were in State Department informational libraries. As expected, they took the Fifth Amendment when asked about Communist party membership. One witness, William Marx Mandell, accused the subcommittee of attempting a Nazi-like "book-burning," and at one point he shouted at McCarthy, "You murdered Raymond Kaplan." The strong exchanges prompted Joe to call a Capitol policeman to stand ready to eject the witness. The State Department soon revealed the fact that of 2,000,000 books by more than 85,000 authors in the overseas informational libraries, seven written by the witnesses summoned that day had been discovered on the shelves.[69]

Ultraconservatives were highly pleased with the subcommittee's effort to purge the Voice and cleanse overseas libraries. Karl Mundt, considered one of the "fathers" of the agency, declared that he was still proud of his "baby" but asserted that it contained too many "liberal-minded" holdovers from the O.W.I. and too many others who "do not have their roots grounded in the basic concepts" of America. Majority Leader Taft, whose opinions on this matter were not restrained by the White House, told a television audience that the Voice "certainly was full of fellow travelers," and said that he hoped Secretary Dulles would wipe it out. He termed the subcommittee's investigation "very helpful and constructive."[70]

Not long after Taft cast his vote of confidence, the subcommittee assumed a new role that resulted in an open clash with the Administration. In mid-March McCarthy let it be known that the subcommittee intended to investigate commerce between the non-Communist and Communist worlds, commerce that sometimes was carried in vessels sold by the United

States as war surplus. Joe expressed a particular concern about materials being supplied to Red China that were used in Korea against American troops. This issue, in which Bobby Kennedy had a particularly strong interest, had attracted the attention of conservative senators and State Department officials for some time but had not generated many headlines.

On March 28, the day after Joe's defeat in the Bohlen vote, he called a press conference that was opened to the public and televised. With Kennedy at his side, he announced that he had personally made an agreement with the Greek owners of 242 cargo vessels to break off all trade with Red China and Soviet bloc ports. He had negotiated the deal privately, he said, because "I didn't want any interference by anyone." Joe predicted that it would reduce the Peiping regime's sea-going commerce by 10 to 45 percent "and should hasten the day of a victorious and honorable conclusion of the Korean War." Several subcommittee members were surprised at the chairman's sudden announcement, but all of them gave their support. Joe expressed confidence that Eisenhower and Dulles would be proud.

Instead, recently appointed Mutual Security Director Harold Stassen, who administered the nation's foreign aid programs, angrily charged that McCarthy was interfering with the nation's foreign policy and was "undermining" government efforts to halt shipments from the West to Iron Curtain countries. The State Department announced that the Greek government had already agreed to stop such shipments several days earlier. A high Administration official, who chose not to be identified, labeled Joe's announcement as "phony" as his methods had been "irregular." *New York Times* columnist James Reston said that the Administration was upset that a committee of the legislative branch had negotiated with foreign nationals, an obvious violation of the separation of powers.

Coming to McCarthy's defense, Karl Mundt admitted that the Greek shipowners had agreed to halt trade in return for a promise by subcommittee investigators not to "harass them" by "raking up stuff in the past." At the time, Greeks were under fire from the Justice Department for purchasing war surplus ships through deception. Mundt declared that this was the "kind of thing a congressional committee can do better than the State Department because they are in a position to put public pressure on people." McCarthy and counsel Flanagan warned that if the shipowners violated their agreement they would be hauled up for public interrogation and exposed before the world. Columnist Arthur Krock sarcastically labeled McCarthy the country's "roving, unofficial Secretary of State" and called for a stern rebuke from the President.

Richard Nixon, the Administration's liaison man to the Far Right, hastily arranged a meeting between Dulles and McCarthy in hopes of containing the struggle. At a private, 90-minute luncheon on April 1, according to a Dulles biographer, the Secretary quoted a few pertinent passages from George Washington's Farewell Address, reminding the senator of (or perhaps introducing him to) the proper constitutional functions. Dulles also undoubtedly expressed his strong desire to have Joe back "the team." In a joint communiqué issued after the luncheon, Dulles praised McCarthy for acting in "the national interest," a statement that damaged Stassen's credibility. Joe made the remainder of the concessions, however, acknowledging that it was the prerogative of the President to conduct American foreign policy and promising to convey to the Administration any further facts collected on shipping to Communist countries. The official statement even denied that McCarthy had made an agreement with Greek shipowners: "Certain foreign shipping groups voluntarily agreed among themselves to abstain from participation in the Communist China trade and in inter-Soviet-bloc trade." When Joe was asked by reporters if he would follow up an earlier threat to negotiate an agreement with Greek shipowners in London, who were said to possess 150 vessels, he replied, "I wouldn't say 'negotiations' is the right word. If in the future any group of shippers agrees to withdraw from the China trade, we will report it to the Secretary."

At his weekly news conference, the President sought to smooth things over by claiming that Stassen had meant "infringed" rather than "undermined" (Stassen quickly agreed), and that McCarthy could not have actually "negotiated" a treaty-like agreement. The controversy was caused by a poor choice of words, Eisenhower said cheerfully, and he denied being upset. Privately, Arthur Krock reported, Ike was extremely angry with McCarthy. Once again, however, out of a sense of personal dignity, out of respect for the separation of powers, and from a deep appreciation of the value of the right-wing to his administration, he elected to avoid a direct confrontation.

The Dulles-McCarthy accord did not last long. Two weeks later, in mid-April, Joe announced that he had made an agreement with the Greek shipping men in London to withdraw their cargo ships from trade with Communist China. When Administration officials were unable to persuade McCarthy to reverse his efforts, they went directly to the shipowners and blocked the deal. In a televised news conference, Joe accused Harold Stassen of torpedoing his efforts and said that it was unclear if the United States "really wanted" to stop ship traffic to China. "More Americans will die," he declared, "because of the decision of those Greek shipowners in London."

Two days later, Joe announced that Greek owners of 53 more ships had "volunteered" pledges to the subcommittee. This brought the total to 295 Greek-owned vessels that would no longer trade with the Reds, he boasted. Joe assured reporters that he had forwarded a copy of the agreement to the State Department before making it public. The Administration made no comment.

Joe was soon angered by news that European trade with Red China was increasing and by testimony from a State Department official to the effect that the United States was not attempting to discontinue all trade with the Peiping regime. At the suggestion of Senator Symington, Joe had Robert Kennedy draft a letter to the President asking exactly what the Administration policy was. He signed the letter while at the Bethesda Naval Hospital, where he was undergoing a checkup, and had Kennedy take it to the White House. Administration officials quickly searched for a way around the letter, wishing to avoid a clash with allies, such as Great Britain, that continued to trade with China, as well as a ruckus with ultraconservatives. Nixon was again called upon. The Vice-President telephoned McCarthy and told him that he had fallen into a Democratic trap by sending the request. Joe was persuaded, and he asked Nixon to intercept his letter before it reached Eisenhower. It was returned without being "officially" received. When reporters got wind of these maneuvers, Joe denied ever authorizing delivery of the letter. When a newsman asked Kennedy about his White House visit, the young attorney asked nervously, "Did somebody see me go in there?"[71]

A month later Nixon, William P. Rogers, and Gen. Wilton B. Persons hosted a private dinner for McCarthy. The amiable conversation focused upon the many benefits that would follow if the senator joined the team and became a constructive associate of the President. Joe agreed with all that was said. But the harmony was again to prove illusory.[72]

During April McCarthy's young associates Roy Cohn and David Schine were the focus of a media uproar that delighted the senator's enemies, flustered at least one subcommittee member, John McClellan, and undoubtedly embarrassed numerous Administration officials. Starting on April 4 the two investigators, trailed by batteries of hostile European reporters, traveled swiftly throughout Europe probing American informational facilities. In eighteen days they made appearances in Paris, Bonn, Berlin, Munich, Vienna, Belgrade, Athens, Rome, Paris again, and London. The visits were often extremely brief: seventeen hours in Bonn, twenty-three hours in Belgrade, twenty-four hours in Athens, twenty-four hours in Rome, six hours in London. But wherever Cohn and Schine went controversy followed, and newspapers were ablaze with references to "scummy snoopers," "Mr. McCarthy's distempered jackals," and "latter-day fascism." After viewing one of the duo's many press conferences, the Rome correspondent of the *Manchester Guardian* wrote, "Their limited vocabulary, their self-complacency, and their paucity of ideas, coupled with the immense power they wield, had the effect of drawing sympathy for all ranks of the United States diplomatic service who have to submit to this sort of thing."[73]

Cohn and Schine had taken a strong interest in the Voice of America investigation from the start. They moved into the Schine family's private suite at the Waldorf Towers in New York shortly before the hearings opened, and there mapped subcommittee strategy with the "Loyal American Underground" and summoned scores of Voice employees, often by subpoena, for interrogation. The expression "going to the Waldorf" had a dreaded meaning within the I.I.A. bureaucracy. Subcommittee senators were never in attendance at these private sessions, but it was well understood that Cohn and Schine were operating with McCarthy's complete assent. He signed the subpoenas and would often refer to the pair as "my investigators."[74]

The idea for an overseas trip arose from articles and testimony by Freda Utley and Karl Baarslag, an American Legion official (soon to be hired as the subcommittee's director of research). Both had visited European State Department libraries within the past year and reported seeing numerous Communist and pro-Communist publications on the shelves. Baarslag told the subcommittee on April 1 that he sensed a "planned conspiracy" to aid the Soviets. Utley urged an investigation, "because it is the same attitude of mind that operated in China, the softness, or whatever you would call it." In fact, the overseas libraries, for the most part, had already been weeded in response to State Department orders. But three days after the testimony by Utley and Baarslag, Cohn and Schine landed in Paris. Whether the true purpose of the hasty junket was information gathering (as the sojourners contended), publicity, the intimidation of bureaucrats, or simply the enjoyment of Europe in the spring, Cohn and Schine seriously underestimated the hostility that would greet them. Cohn later wrote, "It turned out to be one of the most publicized trips of the decade. We soon realized, although neither of us could admit to the distressing fact, that it was a colossal mistake."[75]

In city after city the two travelers popped into United States Information Service libraries, called on diplomats, conducted interviews, and collected documents. In Bonn they spent half an hour looking at Radio Free Europe, where 1,200 were employed. They visited the American embassy in Belgrade and interviewed members of the staff. In Rome they held a seven-hour meeting with the leading officials of all United States agencies in the city. In Munich they consulted with two ex-Communists and hired one of them. In Berlin they told reporters that they had been in touch with McCarthy by telephone and had received word that a top American official in Germany would be recalled within "a matter of weeks." At a Paris news conference on April 19 they claimed to have talked with at least 200 persons during their journey and to have discovered numerous books and periodicals written by Reds. At one point they called the liberal, widely respected *Commonweal* a "Communist Catholic magazine."[76]

European newsmen viewed Cohn and Schine with a mixture of disbelief and contempt. They seemed unable to understand how a civilized nation could bestow such authority upon two brash and shallow youngsters. Some observers saw the presence of the investigators as a prelude to the expansion of McCarthyism overseas and wrote fright-filled articles about "book-burners." Others worried about the rise of neo-isolationism in America. A few found grim humor in the situation. State Department employees were known to say privately, "See you tomorrow, come Cohn or Schine." The British took to chanting, "Positively, Mr. Cohn! Absolutely, Mr. Schine!" Many Europeans roared at a report by a German newspaper that Schine was seen chasing Cohn around a hotel lobby swatting him on the head with a rolled-up magazine.[77]

The top American official mentioned by Cohn at the Berlin news conference was Theodore Kaghan, acting deputy director of the Office of Public Affairs in the American High Commission in Germany. His patriotism had first been questioned by a subcommittee witness in late February. Kaghan was openly defiant, calling Cohn and Schine "junketeering gumshoes" and requesting an appearance before the subcommittee to defend himself. On returning to the United States he was sternly interrogated by McCarthy on three occasions, twice in public session, about well-worn charges involving youthful associations and writings from the 1930s. He might have retained his job (he had been cleared for loyalty and security) had he complied with demands to provide the names of left-wing friends and acquaintances from the Depression years. But he continued to resist, pleading a bad memory, and was forced to resign in early May. Later that month some 250 of Kaghan's friends, including Dr. James B. Conant, U.S. High Commissioner for Germany, attended a farewell testimonial party in his honor. State Department investigators were soon reported asking guests to provide the names of others who were present.[78]

The British were disturbed not only by the travels of Cohn and Schine, which *The London Times* called "a grotesque voyage," but by the McCarthy subcommittee's attacks on their trade relations with Communist China. In mid-May British Labor Party leader Clement Attlee strongly criticized the Eisenhower administration for its obsequiousness toward McCarthy. From the Senate floor, Joe angrily replied with a tirade against "Comrade Attlee," accusing him of previous Communist ties and of joining Dean Acheson in past compromises "with treason." He also called for the sinking of every ship carrying material to Red China, "regardless of what flag those ships may fly." These intemperate and irresponsible remarks were hastily disavowed by Alexander Wiley, chairman of the Senate Foreign Relations Committee, and H. Alexander Smith, the committee's next senior Republican member. Wiley called for "the steadying force of patience with our allies, even if some individual loses his head." He added, "Let us prove our adequacy mentally, as well as militarily." Administration leaders had no comment.[79]

Throughout the spring, the Administration fired hundreds of I.I.A. employees, eliminated some of the Voice of America's foreign-language programs, and closed several overseas libraries. Eisenhower endorsed a reorganization plan that placed the Voice and other such units in the State Department within a new organization called the United States Information Agency. All that remained in the State Department, at the recommendation of a Senate Foreign Relations subcommittee headed by Bourke Hickenlooper, was the Fulbright international cultural exchange program. McCarthy strongly objected to this part of the plan, attributing it to "a group of the old Acheson braintrusters" and assailing what he termed the "half-bright program."[80]

The McCarthy subcommittee's I.I.A. investigations petered out in July without uncovering evidence of treason or conspiracy. Before turning to other targets, however, Joe clashed with outgoing I.I.A. chief Robert L. Johnson. With the approval of Dulles and Eisenhower (who said he did not favor the removal of Dashiell Hammett stories), Johnson issued an order on July 8 permitting the use in overseas libraries of books written by Communists and Communist sympathizers, providing that their contents might serve the ends of democracy. Joe objected strenuously, publicly questioned Johnson's judgment and loyalty, and threatened economic reprisals against the information program. At the height of the uproar, the White House, at Karl Mundt's request, imposed a "gag" on Johnson, prohibiting him from holding news conferences, issuing press releases, or giving out statements concerning McCarthy. It seemed to many critics of the Red Scare that the Eisenhower administration would never summon the courage to stand up to the powerful Wisconsin senator.[81]

19

DEVICES OF THE TYRANT

By mid-1953 Joe McCarthy had reached the height of his political power. The President and his leading aides and cabinet officers seemed anxious to please him. Scott McLeod was strategically placed in the State Department. The Senate Internal Security subcommittee, the Senate Appropriations Committee, and HUAC were cooperative and supportive. McCarthy's Senate colleagues knew and feared his influence. William S. White observed, "And to come down to simple reckonings of naked power, who in the Senate has more—not in terms of the legislative hierarchy but in the ability to reward and punish? No one."[1]

Before the summer was over, Joe collected public endorsements from no less awesome a pair than Francis Cardinal Spellman of New York and J. Edgar Hoover. Hoover had just published an article in the *Washington Times-Herald* entitled "You Child Could Become a Communist." Since Wheeling, he had enjoyed a close working relationship with the senator, using him to fan the Red Scare and call public attention to several cases that authorities had not handled as he wished. "I've come to know Senator McCarthy well, officially and personally," he told reporters in La Jolla, California, where he and Joe were vacationing at a resort owned by Texas oil men. "I view him as a friend and I believe he so views me. Certainly, he is a controversial man. He is earnest and he is honest. He has enemies. Whenever you attack subversives of any kind, Communists, fascists, even

493

the Ku Klux Klan, you are going to be the victim of the most extremely vicious criticism that can be made." (When reporters asked Attorney General Herbert Brownell about the FBI Director's comment, he sputtered, "I have not read his statement . . . but the important thing here—I have so much full confidence and admiration for J. Edgar Hoover—I would like to stress that whenever possible.")[2]

Some saw President Eisenhower's Executive Order 10450, which went into effect in late May, as a symbol of McCarthy's authority in Washington. The new program subjected all present and future employees of the Executive Branch to a broad character scrutiny and eliminated the previous distinction between loyalty and security. Henceforth many people could be fired for personal traits, such as alcoholism, homosexuality, or "infamous" conduct, that did not involve loyalty, and the public could be led to think that large numbers of subversives had been caught and dismissed. Before announcing the security program, the President invited McCarthy, Jenner, and Congressman Velde to the White House and reviewed the plan for them. The three committee chairmen warmly praised it and had a photograph taken together to accompany the White House press release. Joe bubbled to reporters, "I think it is a tremendous improvement over the old method. Altogether it represents a pretty good program. I like it. It shows that the new administration was sincere in the campaign promises to clean house."[3]

McCarthy's broader goals at this time continued to puzzle and fascinate observers. Joe said repeatedly that he was simply in pursuit of Reds in government, but friend and foe alike suspected that he was after more. The most common hypothesis was by now familiar: he wanted the presidency in 1956. *Newsweek* and *The New York Times Magazine* carried lengthy articles discussing the possibility. But Joe strongly denied such an ambition and attributed the story to liberals and Communists. He told writer James Burnham that he was confident Eisenhower would be renominated in 1956. "He is more popular than ever with the people. There have naturally been some difficulties in getting the Administration going, after twenty years of the other party. But on the whole Eisenhower is doing a good job, and there is no reason why he will not be reelected." Joe said that his highest ambition was to continue to represent the people of Wisconsin in the Senate. "Over the long haul, a senator can sometimes do more than most Presidents. Don't forget that a senator can serve as much as fifty years, but a President no more than eight." He sought only to retain his seat and best serve the public by kicking the Communists and pro-Communists out of Washington. In mid-June he told a cheering crowd in Madison, "I want to again assure the frantic *Daily Worker* elements of press and radio, regardless of whether they are in New York, Madison, or Milwaukee, there is nothing on earth they can do to stop the investigation and exposure which we promised the American people last fall." Many, however, including his most bitter enemies, dismissed Joe's declared intentions as rhetoric. Misreading McCarthy, they remained convinced that he was a wholly cynical man whose lust for higher office knew no bounds.[4]

Had he possessed the intellectual sophistication necessary to be truly cynical, had he been as crafty and manipulating as, say, a Nixon, Joe would have been less potentially dangerous to the Administration. A few favors and some flattery, and he might have quieted down and been cooperative. But Joe could not be handled that easily—or at all. William S. White reported, "In McCarthy, embarrassed Republican leaders know they have got hold of a red-hot bazooka, useful in destroying the enemy but also quite likely to blister the hands of the forces that employ it. Their private fear is that a lethal rocket may at any moment blast out through the wrong end of the pipe."[5]

As White House insiders knew, Eisenhower privately fumed about reports that books in overseas libraries were being destroyed. In impromptu remarks at the Dartmouth College commencement service on June 14 he denounced "book burners" and appealed to his audience of 10,000, "Don't think you are going to conceal faults by concealing evidence that they ever existed. Don't be afraid to go in your library and read every book as long as any document does not offend our own ideas of decency. That should be the only censorship." Many liberals applauded the President, convinced that McCarthy was the target of the unusual remarks. In fact, of course, he was. But presidential aides quickly assured reporters that Eisenhower was not aiming at any specific individuals. Joe commented simply, "He couldn't very well have been referring to me. I have burned no books." Pat McCarran, fully comprehending the thrust of the Dartmouth speech, labeled it a "pitiful thing" and added that the President "showed no knowledge of his subject. It's bad a man in his position doesn't know more about it. Someone must have sold him a bill of goods."[6]

Faced with sharp questioning from reporters at a June 17 news conference, Eisenhower qualified his earlier remarks and evaded the inevitable reference to McCarthy by declaring that he never discussed personalities. He seemed to say now that he favored the retention of merely controversial books in overseas libraries and endorsed the destruction of books advocating the overthrow of the United States Government. He appeared to reject the idea that any volumes written by Communists, including those of Marx and Lenin, should be retained. Joe soon told reporters, "I think he has given

a commendable clarification of the Dartmouth speech, which apparently
has been misunderstood by many newsmen."[7]

No doubt embarrassed by his news conference statements, Eisenhower
sent an open letter (drafted by anti-McCarthyite Emmett John Hughes) to
the president of the American Library Association a week later calling for
complete freedom of expression in the United States and taking an obvious
jab at those who misunderstood how democracy functioned.

> ... we must in these times be intelligently alert not only to the
> fanatic cunning of Communist conspiracy—but also to the
> grave dangers in meeting fanaticism with ignorance. For, in
> order to fight totalitarians who exploit the ways of freedom
> to serve their own ends, there are some zealots who—with
> more wrath than wisdom—would adopt a strangely unintel-
> ligent course. They would try to defend freedom by denying
> freedom's friends the opportunity of studying Communism
> in its entirety—its plausibilities, its falsities, its weaknesses.
> But we know that freedom cannot be served by the devices
> of the tyrant.

Uncharacteristically, Joe preferred not to comment on the letter. Eisenhower's anger was now public. The widely read columnists Joseph and
Stewart Alsop soon observed casually, "As is well known, the President
personally not only detests Joseph R. McCarthy's methods but also abhors
the man himself."[8]

Eisenhower was not alone in his displeasure with McCarthy. In Congress
there were increasing rumbles of discontent. Joe's most outspoken critic in
the Senate was Herbert H. Lehman of New York. Lehman joined several
other liberals in backing resolutions aimed at reforming the conduct of
congressional committees, and he publicly warned of "creeping McCarthyism," which he called "a subtle poison which has already eaten deep into the
muscles and sinews of our body politic." In June he and McCarthy battled
openly over the New Yorker's effort to mail 100,000 copies of an anti-
McCarthy pamphlet via his franking privilege. (Joe at the time was using
his own frank to mail more than 8,000 copies of a ghost-written newspaper
column every week, at an annual cost to taxpayers of about $30,000.)[9]

Later that month Democratic members of the McCarthy subcommittee
observed that Joe had announced the possible subpoenaing of former
President Truman without consulting them. As would soon be seen,
McClellan, Symington, and Jackson were growing increasingly irritated by
Joe's autocratic and irresponsible tactics.[10]

By this time, Joe's liberal critics outside Capitol Hill were becoming frantic in their denunciations. Officers of the New York-based Freedom House, a highly reputable organization founded in memory of the late Wendell L. Willkie, Republican presidential candidate in 1940, charged the senator with being "a man who is ever ready to stoop to false innuendo and commit as dangerous an assault on democracy as any perpetrated in the propaganda of the Communists." It was increasingly popular to equate McCarthy with Hitler. The senator's investigating tactics "look like Mr. Hitler's methods," Mrs. Franklin D. Roosevelt told a news conference. "The time to have stopped Hitler was when he went into the Rhineland," G. Bromley Oxnam wrote to William Benton. "There is a time to stop McCarthy."[11]

Other prominent clergymen added their voices to the attack. Dr. A. Powell Davies, minister of All Souls Church in Washington, D.C., contended that McCarthy was "to a great extent" ruling the United States and that Secretary of State Dulles "might well be called" the senator's "administrative assistant." Officials of the Presbyterian Church in the U.S.A.—the church to which President and Mrs. Eisenhower belonged—blasted McCarthyism several times during the opening day of its 165th General Assembly meeting in late May. The newly elected moderator, Dr. John A. MacKay, warned of a new "cult" of anti-Communist fanaticism. "A new form of idolatry, a religious devotion to something other than God," he said, "is gripping the popular mind in our country."[12]

About this same time the liberal Washington lobbyist Maurice Rosenblatt quietly organized a small group of friends from within the National Committee for an Effective Congress to collect and disseminate information on the McCarthy issue. The nucleus of the body that was dubbed the "Clearing House" consisted of Rosenblatt, William Benton aide John Howe, former Benton attorney Gerhard P. Van Arkel, and Kenneth Birkhead, staff director of the Senate Democratic Campaign Committee. William Benton provided active but indirect assistance to the group and used his contacts with Marshall Field and Paul G. Hoffman to raise funds. Millard Tydings was also cooperative. In June the Clearing House employed a full-time secretary, Lucille Lang, and began constructing comprehensive files on McCarthy and McCarthyism. Jack Anderson and Ronald May donated the notes and clippings they had collected for their campaign biography. Van Arkel contributed material gathered for Benton. Drew Pearson attorney Warren Woods added information developed for the Pearson-McCarthy lawsuit. The Clearing House operated out of the offices of the Democratic Senate Campaign Committee.[13]

Rosenblatt and his associates saw McCarthyism as a radical, extremely dangerous challenge to democracy, and they drew parallels between America in their own time and Germany in the 1920s and early 1930s. Rosenblatt was convinced that Joe was a totalitarian, a cynical hooligan who would bring down the government merely for the sake of doing it. He thought that efforts to blacken McCarthy's reputation by pointing to the alleged foibles contained in the Hennings Report were futile and played into the senator's hands by distracting attention away from the deeper issue. McCarthy was asking if you were for or against Communism. Most of his authority, Rosenblatt believed, stemmed from an unwillingness or inability to understand the power the question generated. Rosenblatt was persuaded that the only effective way to challenge McCarthy was to inform and arouse the Establishment, both on and off Capitol Hill. The clearing house was a channel to provide information to senators, newsmen, businessmen, church leaders, and others about the menace McCarthy and his "ism" posed to themselves and to the nation in the guise of super-patriotism.[14]

On June 18 McCarthy announced the appointment of J. B. Matthews as executive director of the subcommittee. Francis Flanagan now became chief counsel of the full Senate Government Operations Committee, Cohn retained his position with the subcommittee, and assistant counsel Bobby Kennedy was given additional duties as an aide to Matthews. (Kennedy resigned on July 29 to enter private law practice. His letter of resignation to McCarthy was warm and appreciative.) The Matthews appointment interested Clearing House leaders intensely, and Lucille Lang began to prepare a dossier on the controversial ultraconservative.[15]

Joseph Brown Matthews, 59, had been a conservative Methodist minister and missionary in the 1920's and early 30's. In 1935 he abruptly renounced his past and became a Marxist and atheist. He joined the Socialist Party, wrote two radical books, and was soon active in 28 different left-wing front organizations. Three years later, at the age of 41, he made another complete about-face and became a right-wing anti-Communist. He was soon hired by the Dies Committee at a comfortable salary and fathered HUAC's extensive file system. In recent years he had worked for the Hearst Corporation as a highly paid anti-Communist consultant and was known to be close to many leaders of the second Red Scare.

Matthews had been of assistance to McCarthy since early 1950, when Joe was in desperate need of material to buttress his Lincoln Day speeches. Soon the senator presented him with a handsome desk set inscribed, "To J.

B. Matthews, a star-spangled American, from one of his pupils and admirers." Shortly after he hired Matthews three years later, Joe told reporters, "I had been trying to get him for a long time. I regard him as the best informed man in the United States on Communism."[16]

A few days before Matthews joined the subcommittee staff an article of his appeared in the July issue of the right-wing magazine *American Mercury*. Entitled "Reds and Our Churches," the piece began, "The largest single group supporting the Communist apparatus in the United States today is composed of Protestant clergymen." Clearing House leaders discovered the article almost two weeks later and decided to make good use of it. Rosenblatt and his friends now took the dossier and the article directly to Senators McClellan, Symington, and Jackson, pointing out that Matthews had long been critical of the Protestant clergy, first as a Marxist and then as a reactionary. The three subcommittee Democrats, who had not been consulted about the appointment in the first place, were irate. On July 2 they confronted McCarthy in his office and demanded that Matthews be fired. Joe refused, and both sides quickly prepared press releases. The Democrats accused Matthews of launching "a shocking and unwarranted attack against the American clergy." Joe denied that the article attacked the Protestant clergy (7,000 were Red-tainted, according to Matthews) and declared that he had no intention of investigating clergymen.[17]

The fracas hit the front pages, and the Clearing House called it to the attention of numerous religious leaders. Officials of the National Council of Churches and several major denominations denounced Matthews in the press and pulpit. Through Michigan clergymen, the Episcopal bishop of Detroit in particular, the Clearing House was able to pressure Senator Charles Potter into siding with the subcommittee Democrats, thus giving the dissidents a majority.[18]

During a heated subcommittee session on July 7 the Democrats, joined by Potter, called for Matthews' resignation. Joe refused to entertain the issue, contending that Matthews was a "nonprofessional" staff member whose employment was entirely at his discretion. The argument was patently false, not only because Matthews was clearly a "professional" but because under the Legislative Reorganization Act of 1946 even clerical staff was subject to approval by the majority. Perhaps not wishing to be identified with their fellow Republican on this occasion, Everett Dirksen did not attend the meeting and Karl Mundt left shortly after it began.[19]

The next day, after conferring with other leading Southern Democrats, John McClellan publicly challenged McCarthy's decision and said that if necessary he would take the case to the parent Committee on Government

Operations and then to the full Senate. Joe found himself at odds with the Senate Establishment on the Matthews matter; he was in the wrong and would undoubtedly suffer considerable humiliation as a consequence. Realizing this, he quickly made plans to retreat.[20]

Two Administration officials were a step ahead of the senator, however. Deputy Attorney General William Rogers and presidential speech writer Emmett John Hughes assumed that McCarthy would soon abandon Matthews, and they devised a plan to seal off that avenue of escape. Rogers, a onetime friend of Joe's, thought that the senator was becoming a political liability and should be curbed. The Matthews case, in his opinion, was the perfect opportunity to strike. As he told Hughes, "With all the Protestants up in arms, even a buddy of McCarthy's like Karl Mundt on his committee can hear the Lutherans screaming back in the Midwest." Rogers assured Hughes that his sentiments were shared fully by Vice-President Nixon.

Rogers and Hughes planned to encourage an open telegram of protest to the President from the National Conference of Christians and Jews. Eisenhower was to reply with a strong public censure of Matthews and McCarthy. The success of this scheme required haste; both the telegram and the reply would have to precede McCarthy's dismissal of Matthews, which was expected at any time. Two friendly Washington journalists sped to New York to confer with National Conference officials while Hughes obtained the assent of Sherman Adams and drafted the President's reply.

On the next day, July 9, Hughes discovered, after a morning of frantic telephone calls, that the National Conference telegram was resting on the desk of White House Special Counsel Bernard M. Shanley, who was not a party to the scheme. Meanwhile, rumors were swirling through Washington that McCarthy was about to dismiss Matthews and invite public approval of his own fair-mindedness. Rogers telephoned Hughes pleading, "For God's sake, we have to get that message out fast or McCarthy will beat us to the draw." Adams swiftly approved Hughes's speech draft and personally took it to the President. A few minutes later he reappeared with Eisenhower's endorsement of a slightly modified statement. The modifications meant that the stencil for the mimeographed press release would have to be redone. While this task was underway, Rogers telephoned from Nixon's office saying that Mundt and McCarthy had been conferring and were no doubt then on their way there with Matthews' resignation. Hughes urged Rogers to stall for ten minutes until the White House press release could make the news-ticker. Joe walked into the Vice-President's office just as Rogers put down the telephone. Rogers and Nixon immediately engaged him in conversation about a Senate speech he had made earlier that day. Joe rambled on for a time and then headed for the door. "Gotta rush now," he said. "I want to be sure I get the news of dumping Matthews to Fulton Lewis in time for him to break it on his broadcast." By now the President's message had already reached the press.[21]

The story of the exchange between the religious leaders and the President had the intended effect, making large front-page headlines throughout the nation. The National Conference telegram branded Matthews' charges "unjustified and deplorable," and continued, "destroying trust in the leaders of Protestantism, Catholicism or Judaism by wholesale condemnation is to weaken the greatest American bulwark against atheistic materialism and Communism." Eisenhower declared, "Generalized and irresponsible attacks that sweepingly condemn the whole of any group of citizens are alien to America." In short, the veteran anti-Communist expert was guilty of helping the Reds! Matthews promptly resigned, confirming an earlier statement by McCarthy that he had not read the *American Mercury* article when Matthews was hired. Joe accepted the resignation "very reluctantly" and endorsed Matthews' request for a hearing before the subcommittee.[22]

Senators Potter and Mundt (who had apparently been Lutheran-listening) joined the Democrats at a subcommittee meeting on July 10 in voting to deny Matthews the opportunity to defend his charges against the clergy. By a straight party vote of 4-3, however, McCarthy won sole hiring and firing authority over the subcommittee staff. Led by an angry John McClellan, the three Democrats resigned in protest and stalked from the room. Joe pretended to be unruffled by this unprecedented action, saying that it looked to him like "the old Democratic policy of either rule or ruin" and vowing that the work of the subcommittee would continue. "If they don't want to take part in uncovering the graft and corruption of the old Truman-Acheson administration, they are, of course, entitled" to resign.[23]

William S. White soon observed that the walkout was a direct attack on McCarthy's prestige in the Senate. "Officially, publicly, and studiedly to boycott one's fellow senator is about as grave a step as can be imagined. To lose face in the club that is the Senate is, sometimes, actually to lose all."[24]

When the subcommittee was scheduled to meet again on July 13, McCarthy was the only member to show up. At the recess of the closed-door session, Joe told reporters that he had uncovered evidence of "an alleged $150,000 shakedown against a friendly foreign government" by employees "in the old Acheson State Department." He declined to give any details, and the matter was soon forgotten.[25]

On the day the Democrats bolted, Harry Flood Byrd, the powerful Democratic senator from Virginia, issued a rare press release demanding that J. B. Matthews "give names and facts to sustain his charge or stand convicted as a cheap demagogue, willing to blacken the character of his fellow Americans for his own notoriety and personal gain." This was followed shortly by endorsements of the walkout by Democratic Senators Burnet R. Maybank of South Carolina and Robert Kerr of Oklahoma. In an obvious swipe at McCarthy, Maybank said there was no "place in our government for domineering, one-man rule regardless of political or religious affiliation." It was clear by now that Joe was in trouble not only with the White House and members of his subcommittee but also with the Southern bloc, the most influential group in the Senate.[26]

McCarthy suffered yet another setback during the first two weeks in July. His almost instinctive reaction to the initial confrontation with subcommittee Democrats over Matthews had been to create a diversion. On July 4 he leaked news of a forthcoming subcommittee report on the State Department filing system. Five days later, as the pressures to fire Matthews became irresistible, Joe gave a Senate speech in which he sharply criticized C.I.A. Director Allen W. Dulles, the Secretary of State's younger brother, for prohibiting the appearance of C.I.A. official William P. Bundy before the subcommittee. Joe announced that he would subpoena Bundy, Dean Acheson's son-in-law, in order to question him about a $400 contribution allegedly made to Alger Hiss's defense fund.[27]

McCarthy and his staff were planning eventually to conduct a full-scale investigation of the Central Intelligence Agency, the first undertaken by a congressional body. Don Surine had been at work for many months collecting what he later described as "tons" of documents obtained without permission from the C.I.A., Army Intelligence, and elsewhere, and lining up a large number of witnesses, "including generals." (One of those who leaked information and documents to the subcommittee staff, according to Surine, was former C.I.A. Director Walter Bedell Smith, Under Secretary of State in the Eisenhower Administration.) Surine was firmly convinced that K.G.B. agents had infiltrated the agency. McCarthy was of a like mind, and he told Roy Cohn that the proposed investigation interested him more than any other. Preliminary plans called for joint hearings with Styles Bridges' Senate Appropriations Committee.[28]

According to columnist Joseph Alsop, Eisenhower flatly refused to permit Bundy to submit to a McCarthy subpoena. Joe had been warned earlier that the President would not tolerate tampering with the C.I.A. After McCarthy's Senate speech, the National Security Council hurriedly met and voted to endorse the President's position on Bundy. Vice-President Nixon, the second ranking member of the council, informed Joe of the N.S.C. decision that same day. Over the weekend Nixon quietly contacted Potter and Dirksen and persuaded them to support the President and the council. With the Democrats off the subcommittee and Mundt, strongly pro-McCarthy but always anxious to avoid a clash with the Administration, teetering on the fence, McCarthy was a minority of one. At a private luncheon attended by the Vice-President and subcommittee Republicans, Nixon presented the political facts of life to McCarthy and persuaded him to retreat. A face-saving statement was issued by McCarthy and Director Dulles when the subcommittee next met, but the fact remained— and quickly became known—that Joe had been stopped in his tracks. Alsop crowed, "Sen. Joseph R. McCarthy has just suffered his first total, unmitigated, unqualified defeat by the White House."[29]

A storm of controversy surrounding McCarthy seemed to be gathering momentum almost daily during the muggy weeks of July. On the 13th Mike Monroney, with encouragement from the Clearing House, made a blistering Senate speech condemning the whole of Joe's anti-Communist career. The Oklahoma Democrat scornfully compared McCarthy and his staff to the FBI ("As the greatest crime detection agency in the world, I do not think that J. Edgar Hoover and his well-trained men have wasted the $470 million that the Congress has given them since 1947"), referred to the European travels of Cohn and Schine as the "keystone-cop" chase, and warned of grave national dangers implicit in a McCarthy probe of the C.I.A.[30]

During a television broadcast a few days later, Joe called Monroney's blast at Cohn and Schine "the most flagrant, the most shameful example of anti-Semitism." This drew the wrath of Herbert Lehman, who told the Senate that the remark was "pure and arrant demagogery, raising an ugly symbol in defense of indefensible conduct." Joe was so angry at Lehman that he countered by reading a 1948 letter from the New York senator to Alger Hiss, expressing support and friendship. (He read it into the record a second time later in the day.) The letter, he sneered, "will perhaps give a better picture of the great authority on how to fight Communism who now sets himself up to attack members of my committee staff." During a bitter exchange with Monroney, Joe asked, "Can the senator give me the name of a single Communist he has exposed during his long period in public life?"[31]

On July 17 retiring overseas information chief Dr. Robert L. Johnson, who had earlier appeared friendly to McCarthy, sent an open letter to the senator condemning a charge by subcommittee research director Karl Baarslag that overseas libraries "just don't go in for anti-Soviet literature." Senator Potter sighed wearily, "I've never seen anything like this committee. It seems we can't go fifteen minutes without running into some new problem." Joe's heated reply challenged Johnson's patriotism and threatened to leave the International Information Administration with "not one cent" to spend.[32]

On July 24 Arthur Eisenhower, the President's brother, called McCarthy "the most dangerous menace to America" and a "rabble-rouser." "When I think of McCarthy," he told a Las Vegas reporter, "I automatically think of Hitler." "He is a throwback to the Spanish inquisition." The Kansas City banker also charged the senator with having damaged United States prestige abroad and having hurt the Republican Party. Joe could only shrug in reply, "I don't hold Ike responsible for what his relatives say." The President himself declined to comment on his brother's remarks after learning that McCarthy had called upon him to do so. "I don't want to give him the satisfaction," he said. [33]

That same day McCarthy made front-page headlines by clashing with Under Secretary of State Walter Bedell Smith (perhaps as a screen to conceal their clandestine friendship) and by getting into a rousing fray with Sen. William Fulbright during a televised public hearing of the Senate Appropriations Committee. At one point Joe became so angry with Fulbright that he grabbed the gavel from acting chairman Homer Ferguson and began pounding it, demanding an answer to a question. Senators Ellender and McClellan were appalled by McCarthy's conduct. Karl Mundt tried unsuccessfully to restrain his colleague by reading aloud from a statute. Fulbright, in exasperation, said that he would answer questions from every member of the committee, "except the senator from Wisconsin, who is obviously bent on destroying my testimony."[34]

A week earlier Mike Monroney had introduced a resolution that would empower the Senate to cut off a line of investigation by one of its committees whenever it desired. On July 26 Monroney admitted that this was a slap at McCarthy and was an effort to prevent him from becoming a "one-man Senate." "The 83rd Congress," he said in the course of a television program, had produced a record of "molehills of legislation and mountains of McCarthy." Acting Senate Republican leader Knowland opposed the move, and it received little further attention. Joe accused Monroney of "taking over the job of whitewash and cover-up of Communism and corruption."[35]

When the Legislative-Judiciary Appropriation Bill was called up for action at month's end, Monroney was ready to propose an amendment that would have barred the use of investigative funds to finance any probe into any religious institution in the United States or into the C.I.A. Monroney abandoned the amendment upon learning that it lacked widespread support, but he had again made the point that McCarthy had enemies in the Senate who would not remain silent.[36]

John McClellan soon told reporters that he intended to try to curb McCarthy's power over his subcommittee during the next session of Congress. He had not taken such action earlier, he explained, because he had hoped, in vain, that Republicans would find a way to repress the junior senator from Wisconsin. Subcommittee members would have to return for operating funds the following year, McClellan said. "The resolution to give money can be amended, and the conditions stated under which they will get it."[37]

On August 4 Margaret Chase Smith thwarted an effort by McCarthy to obtain approval of a resolution permitting the subcommittee to issue independent reports during the congressional recess. Pointing to the absence of Democrats on the subcommittee, she proposed a successful amendment to the resolution requiring that recess reports be approved by a majority of the parent Government Operations Committee.[38]

Amid the proposals made by Mike Monroney, the story was leaked, undoubtedly by Nixon, that the subcommittee would soon be shifting its emphasis from Communism to charges of corruption under the Truman administration. The Vice-President was said to have encouraged such action because McClellan, Symington, and Jackson had no intention of returning to the subcommittee and all other Democrats were shunning appointment to the body. Without official bipartisanship, the G.O.P. body would appear to be attacking the G.O.P. administration if it continued on its present course. Joe was said to be enthusiastic about the new approach. He "will try to make Democrats wince as they prepare for next year's Congressional elections," wrote Jack Bell of the Associated Press.[39]

But Nixon and other G.O.P. leaders soon learned that this was simply more wishful thinking. Joe could not be restrained. On August 3 he charged the Administration with having made a "tremendous mistake" in choosing to continue aid to Allies that traded with Iron Curtain countries. In a Milwaukee speech three days later he sharply criticized the Administration for failure to fulfill a campaign promise to call to account "those responsible for our tremendous defeat in Korea." (The armistice ending the Korean War had been agreed upon in June. South Korean strongman Syngman Rhee and some right-wing allies in the United States, seeking a united Korea, were displeased by the terms of the agreement.)

On August 10 Joe told reporters he had evidence indicating that at least one member of the Communist party had access to secrets of the military establishment, the Atomic Energy Commission, and the C.I.A. He announced public hearings on subversion in government printing plants the next day. By the end of the month, sitting as a one-man subcommittee, he was holding hearings on Red infiltration of the Army. In early September he announced plans to call Army Secretary Robert T. Stevens before the subcommittee for interrogation.[40]

While many Republicans fumed, Joe's adversaries were encouraged by the summer's developments. The President's distaste for McCarthy, for one thing, was now public knowledge. After the Dartmouth speech, the message to the American Library Association, the telegram to the National Conference of Christians and Jews, and the reported resistance to a C.I.A. investigation, there was hope that Eisenhower would take an even more active approach toward the fractious Senator. Some observers saw the President's hand in a State Department decision of August 6 issuing a passport to William P. Bundy. Joe had strongly objected to Bundy's leaving the country for a vacation on the ground that since the C.I.A. official knew that the subcommittee wanted to question him he was technically under subpoena. This argument was flatly rejected in a letter from Under Secretary of State Donald B. Lourie, distributed to the press. *The New York Times* headline read, "State Department Rebuffs McCarthy."[41]

The J. B. Matthews affair, moreover, clearly damaged Joe. John Howe thought it "a serious blow to McCarthy." Maurice Rosenblatt wrote of Joe's "loss of momentum and prestige" and "the demonstration of his vulnerability." The major church magazines, including two Roman Catholic publications, voiced their objections to Matthews' charges and McCarthy's sympathetic commentary. Many senators, especially those from the South, were deeply disturbed by the attack on clergymen. The subsequent walk-out of the subcommittee Democrats was a serious matter, and powerful figures within the Senate Establishment were angered by Joe's "one-man rule." Jack Bell observed, "The Southerners have been around a long time; they have elephantine memories and where they consider their honor is impugned they are the most effective fighters in Congress." That statement was to prove prophetic.[42]

McCarthy's retreat on the proposed C.I.A. probe also emboldened his enemies. William Evjue cheered, "For the first time, McCarthyism is on the defensive." Maurice Rosenblatt, assessing the C.I.A. matter and the forced resignation of Matthews, wrote, "In the Senate cloakrooms the news that the bully can be beaten was received with increasing gleefulness." The attacks by Lehman, Monroney, McClellan, and Smith no doubt bore evidence of this exhilaration.[43]

Privately, Mike Monroney expressed dismay at McCarthy's conduct. He could not understand why Joe would have defended J. B. Matthews and so alienated the subcommittee Democrats that they resigned. Smart, cynical demagogues did not operate this way: Perhaps, he confided to a friend, McCarthy was "off balance." William Fulbright considered Joe "wild" at the time of their clash.[44]

Some of Joe's friends were equally puzzled and concerned. William F. Buckley later said that he thought the senator irresponsible at this time, and speculated that he was "drugged by the velocity of events." He wondered too if a biological breakdown of some sort was the source of the problem. When McCarthy began his struggle with the Army, Ed Nellor pled with him to reconsider; the Army was too powerful, Nellor argued. "You can't beat these people." Joe refused to listen, and Nellor sadly resigned. Ray Kiermas repeatedly begged his old friend to slow down, to weigh evidence more carefully. Robert E. Lee gave similar advice. But to no avail. Joe simply would not entertain pleas for caution. His anti-Communist zeal consumed him. His craving for public attention was insatiable. He was losing the ability to laugh at himself, a feature of his complex personality that had long charmed friends and acquaintances.[45]

Part of the explanation surely involves what Buckley referred to as the velocity of events. Armed with a zealous subcommittee staff, a large budget, and the power to subpoena, Joe was sometimes entangled in several probes and skirmishes at once. Leaks and tips continued to pour in upon him, and he seemed eager to exploit all of them. Moreover, he continued to accept scores of invitations for speeches. The increasingly frantic pace of his daily life, fed by an ever-growing sense of mission and self-importance, did not permit even brief pauses for the most elementary reflection.

Then too, Joe's drinking had become extremely heavy by this time. While he continued to appear in excellent physical condition, his alcoholism was slowly increasing its hold over him. Henry Jackson, arriving early one day for a morning executive session of the subcommittee, caught a glimpse of the chairman in the bathroom chug-a-lugging straight whiskey. Joe was more moody than before, more easily irritated, less able to restrain his temper.[46]

In early July he had even alienated people in his home town. When Dr. Nathan M. Pusey, the popular president of Lawrence College, was selected as the next president of Harvard University, Joe wrote a venomous letter to a Boston columnist saying, "Harvard's loss is Wisconsin's gain." He roasted the educator as "a man who has considerable intellectual possibilities but who has neither learned nor forgotten anything since he was a freshman in college." Joe labeled Pusey "a rabid anti-anti-Communist" and charged, "He appears to hide a combination of bigotry and intolerance behind a cloak of phony, hypocritical liberalism." Citizens of the Appleton area were stunned and shocked by this outburst, apparently the result of Pusey's co-sponsorship of the campaign polemic *The McCarthy Record*. The chairman of the Lawrence Board of Trustees concluded that "the senator has gone overboard," and one veteran G.O.P. official said that he felt "very badly" about the attack and hoped that McCarthy had been misquoted.[47]

Still, few observers predicted that McCarthy was in any immediate political danger, on the national or state level. The G.O.P. hierarchy maintained its formal support. The White House continued to hope for conciliation. William S. White reported, "The whole Republican attitude, in general, is one of ambivalence: disapproval, on balance, of Senator McCarthy but a lack of readiness to attempt any demonstration against him or to become publicly alienated from him." Politicians of both parties knew that Joe continued to stir fierce loyalties throughout the country. Floods of pro-McCarthy mail arrived regularly on Capitol Hill. The powerful right-wing media remained firmly behind the senator. Many congressmen (with little supporting evidence) were convinced that Joe commanded the allegiance of all the Roman Catholics in their districts.[48]

G.O.P. leaders on the whole continued to view McCarthy as a political asset. They thought, for example, that he would be of considerable assistance in the 1954 Congressional campaigns. As long as Republicans persisted in this belief, they would tolerate and even encourage Joe's activities. Democrats, with a few exceptions, and despite some grumbling among Southerners over procedural questions and personal affronts, were content at this point to remain quiescent. Their reluctance was in large part an unwillingness to appear soft on the Reds. [49]

20

DECLARATIONS
OF WAR

The McCarthy subcommittee—minus its Democrats—conducted several investigations in the late summer and fall of 1953, maintaining the constant attention of the press and remaining a regular fixture on daytime television in Washington and wherever it traveled. One minor probe of this period, often ignored by McCarthy critics and historians, was one of the most unusual of Joe's career.

Probably from sources within the FBI, McCarthy learned that the Government Printing Office continued to employ a highly suspicious bookbinder named Edward Rothschild. In the late 1930's and early 1940's Rothschild had been charged with being a Communist, with stealing classified data, and of trying to organize a Communist cell in the G.P.O. An FBI undercover agent had also informed her superiors that Mrs. Rothschild was a Communist party official. As early as 1943 the bureau was transmitting information to the agency about the Communist activities of the Rothschilds. At hearings before the Loyalty Board of the Government Printing Office in 1948, the FBI had given the board a list of 40 informants who could testify about the couple. Not one was called. Rothschild, under oath, denied party membership, Communist associations, and espionage. He was cleared and returned to the position he had held since 1930. The agency decided however, to restrict him from handling secret or confidential materials.

509

510

FBI officials boiled over Rothschild's retention. In September 1951, on request, they supplied additional information on the Rothschilds, without effect. The bureau's anger was compounded in mid-1953 when, under the new Administration regulations, Rothschild was given another clean security bill by the agency. One or more of the officials in the FBI clearly turned to McCarthy for redress. (Joe claimed that the case stemmed from a lead given in testimony during the overseas information program investigation.)

In closed-door hearings before the subcommittee in mid-August, the bookbinder testified that he had continued access to secret and confidential documents "up until this moment." Joe repeatedly leaked the proceedings of the sessions to reporters, claiming that Rothschild not only could get his hands on secret materials involving the C.I.A., the Atomic Energy Commission, and the Armed Forces, but also had access to top secret data concerning both the atomic and hydrogen bombs.

In open hearings before television cameras, Joe paraded several key witnesses against Rothschild, including a fellow employee who had gone to the Dies Committee in 1939 to complain about Rothschild's Communist activities. Rothschild himself pleaded the Fifth Amendment throughout his appearance, as did his wife and several others named as Communist associates of the couple. The G.P.O. immediately suspended the bookbinder without pay, after Joe called for such action, and Rothschild was later removed from government employment altogether. The hearings also resulted in the dismissal of the entire G.P.O. Loyalty Board panel. The agency head, desperately eager to please McCarthy, announced that the G.P.O. would return temporarily to a wartime security status. He soon declared that any agency employee taking the Fifth Amendment would thenceforth be fired.

Everett Dirksen said that he would propose legislation barring government employment to all persons invoking the Fifth Amendment before investigating committees. "Government employment is not a right, it is a privilege," the senator declared. The principle was swiftly adopted by the Secretary of the Army, also feeling heat from the McCarthy subcommittee, and then by the President for all employees in Executive departments.

(Joe said in June that anyone who invoked constitutional rights in refusing to tell a congressional committee about party membership "obviously is a Communist." In early September he declared that he would permit witnesses to plead the Fifth Amendment only if they stated that a *truthful* answer might tend to incriminate them. Such wording increased the suspicion that the complying witness was a Red. To choose alternative language before McCarthy virtually guaranteed a threat to be cited for contempt of Congress.)[1]

The case against Rothschild was by no means unassailable: the charges were old, the bookbinder's current access to secret information remained unclear, and the Fifth Amendment was not the conclusive statement of guilt many people thought it was. Nevertheless, the bulk of the evidence, especially from the public hearings, strongly suggests that the subcommittee could correctly claim to have discovered a genuine security risk. That does not justify, of course, the unproven assertion by McCarthyites that Rothschild was both a Communist and a spy in 1953. Nor does it excuse Joe's exaggerations about atomic and hydrogen bomb secrets; in fact, such information was unavailable to G.P.O. employees.

Joe and his allies would boast of this probe whenever challenged to cite their achievements. Roy Cohn said in November, "Our committee forced out of government Edward Rothschild, a Communist with access to secrets in the Government Printing Office, who invoked the Fifth Amendment." Fifteen years later he wrote, "This investigation, particularly the exposure of Rothschild, demonstrated the need for congressional committees like ours." If that was an overstatement, it should not erase the likelihood that the subcommittee had at least one positive contribution to its credit.

The G.P.O. investigation was distinctive in another way. Knowing that he had a good case, and eager to display his fairness in the aftermath of the Democrats' resignations, McCarthy was extremely calm and judicious during the public hearings. He was especially willing to extend every courtesy to Rothschild's two attorneys. At one point he permitted fifteen questions submitted by the lawyers to be asked of the FBI undercover agent; Senator Dirksen disallowed only one, pertaining to the witness's income. One of the attorneys, Charles E. Ford, declared, "I think the committee session at this day and this place is most admirable and most American." It was a rare moment in the subcommittee's history.[2]

In mid-September the subcommittee began what was ostensibly an investigation of Communist infiltration of the United Nations. The focus of the probe was one Julius Reiss, a onetime Army instructor and W.P.A. employee who, since 1950, had been a clerk employed by the Polish delegation to the United Nations. Reiss, also known as Joel Remes, had been a well-known Communist party leader for almost two decades. When called as a witness, he took the Fifth Amendment repeatedly, as McCarthy and his staff knew he would. Television viewers no doubt had the impression that the senator had nabbed another subversive. Joe commented sternly, "I might say that, Mr. Reiss, if you were in Communist Russia today and refused to answer whether you were an American spy, you would not be entitled to any Fifth Amendment." When the witness answered one question directly that he had evaded in executive session by taking the Fifth

Amendment (he denied ever hearing espionage advocated at a Communist party meeting), Joe lost his temper, shouting at one point, "I am getting very sick of you men engaged in the Communist conspiracy who come before this committee and abuse the privilege granted under the Fifth Amendment. It is a very important privilege. You are not going to use it to cover up your conspiracy, if I can help it."

Actually, the several hearings devoted to Reiss were a ruse by which to attack two leftist New York attorneys who had hired Reiss as a researcher during their defense of eleven Communist Party leaders charged with violating the Smith Act. The American Bar Association had recommended that Communist lawyers be disbarred, and Joe hoped to drive the pair from the profession. He invited an A.B.A. representative to be on hand for the public hearings. One of the attorneys, when called to the stand, took the Fifth Amendment frequently, thus qualifying in right-wing lingo as a "Fifth-Amendment Communist." The other, in executive session, chose to filibuster on the question of his alleged Communist activities and was recommended for a contempt citation. Joe angrily ordered the latter attorney removed from the hearing room by a policeman during a televised hearing.[3]

Joe took time out from the hearings to marry Jean Kerr on September 29, 1953, at St. Matthew's Cathedral in Washington. Their romance over the past several years had been stormy. Both strong-willed, the two quarreled often, broke up, and then patched things together again. The final rift was smoothed over just before Jean's mother announced the engagement. "I was fired three times," Jean later admitted. The major cause of the squabbling was Joe's constant attentions to other women. Jean once used her friendship with J. Edgar Hoover to have the FBI agent husband of a particularly attractive office secretary transferred to Alaska in order to remove her from Joe's sight. She told reporters that before their engagement she had laid down conditions for their marriage. She firmly declined to disclose them, however.

A few of McCarthy's close friends resented what they saw as Jean's aggressive pursuit of her employer. Ray Kiermas said later, "He wasn't the marrying kind." Willard Edwards thought that Joe, nearly 45, consented to marriage only to quash stories that he was homosexual.

At 29, Jean abandoned her Presbyterian past and converted to Roman Catholicism. Robert E. Lee made the arrangements through the clergy at St. Matthew's. On the wedding day, a cablegram arrived from Rome giving Pope Pius's "paternal and apostolic" blessing to the couple.

Close to 900 people gathered in the Cathedral for the ceremony, some 200 of whom were from Wisconsin. About 3,500 others milled around the outside of the cathedral for a look at the dignitaries as they arrived. Vice-President and Mrs. Nixon attended, as did presidential aides Sherman Adams, Wilton Persons, and Jack Martin. (The President sent his regrets, along with a letter of congratulation.) Numerous senators and congressmen were present, including newly married John F. Kennedy. Also on hand were C.I.A. Director Dulles (whose brother unaccountably failed to show up), former heavyweight boxing champion Jack Dempsey, Alice Roosevelt Longworth, Roy Cohn, Ed Nellor, Ray Kiermas, Tom Korb, and Urban Van Susteren. Mrs. Robert E. Lee was matron of honor, Mrs. Garvin E. Tankersley was a bridesmaid, and Joe's brother Bill served as best man.

At the conclusion of the mass, Mr. and Mrs. McCarthy turned slowly, smiled, and walked back down the middle aisle toward a waiting limousine, showers of rice, and a cheering crowd. Joe, beaming, waved at Nixon.[4]

Wealthy Texas businessman Ross Biggers told reporters in Houston that he and some twenty others had purchased a new Cadillac for the McCarthys as a wedding present. Delivery would be delayed, he explained, because Jean had selected a particularly plush Coupe de Ville model. Biggers said that when he asked the senator if he had ever owned a Cadillac, Joe replied, "Heck no, I've never even driven one." (When the car was delivered, the yarn was told that some 2,000 donors had purchased it, contributing sums from twenty-five cents to $100. "All those letters," Biggers said later, "convinced me that Joe is the most beloved man in America and, in a few quarters, the most hated. But thank God the ones that are backing him are loyal and those that are against him would destroy our beloved country.")[5]

The newlyweds flew to Spanish Cay in the British West Indies. Their wedding trip was brief, however, for within a week Roy Cohn reached Joe by shortwave radio and asked to meet with him immediately. At West Palm Beach, Florida, on October 8, Cohn told his employer of important new evidence of Communist infiltration into the Armed Forces. Joe and Jean packed their bags immediately, the senator announcing that he would open hearings in Washington on Monday morning.[6]

Joe was intensely interested at this time in investigations by the subcommittee staff of Communist infiltration of the Army. The first news of these probes surfaced on September 1 following the first of four executive sessions on the issue. Briefing reporters, as usual, about what had gone on behind the closed doors, Joe claimed that three Army civilian employees—

two clerks from the Quartermaster Corps in New York and a Signal Corps security guard in the same area—had ties with Communist activities. (The guard, for example, had signed a nominating petition for a Red gubernatorial candidate in 1946.) The next day, Joe summoned three high-ranking Army officers before the subcommittee and demanded the names of those who had cleared the suspects. Whoever was responsible for certifying the loyalty of "Miss Q," as Joe dramatically referred to one of the clerks, was, he said, "incompetent beyond words, or in sympathy with Communism." When the request was denied on the ground of President Truman's 1948 order, and when "Miss Q" was not immediately suspended, Joe flew into a rage. The stage was set for a bitter struggle between McCarthy and the Army that was to take many months to resolve and lead to the senator's political destruction.[7]

Joe publicly condemned Col. Robert A. Howard, Jr., commanding officer of the Quartermaster Inspection Service Command, for failing to respond as others had to his charges; by retaining "Miss Q," he said, Colonel Howard had "done a tremendous disservice to the Army by discrediting it so badly and thereby to his country." He was equally irate about the Army's adherence to the Truman order. The subcommittee, he said, was "having more difficulty with the Army than any other department." He told reporters that he had asked Army Secretary Robert T. Stevens, on vacation during the uproar, to appear at a closed hearing to explain the Pentagon's conduct.[8]

At an open hearing on September 8 Joe berated and humiliated Maj. Gen. Miles Reber, the General Staff Corps officer who had advised the Army to abide by the Truman directive. "Do not give me that, General," Joe bellowed at one point. "I want an answer to the question." He called the Army's action "the most unusual, the most unbelievable, the most unexplainable situation that I have ever heard of as long as I have been in Washington." He threatened to go all the way to Eisenhower to reverse the policy. "I cannot conceive that the President, who is elected upon a clean-up program, promises which he made from coast to coast, to clean out Communists and all types of crookedness and perversion, would whitewash those who are responsible." (Reber was soon transferred to Germany, in a move the Army called "routine.") At another hearing on September 11 Joe blamed "political carryovers from the old Administration" in the Pentagon for withholding the names of those he sought to expose and punish.[9]

McCarthy quickly increased the tempo of the battle by charging in the press that the Army had distributed "clearcut Communist propaganda" to 37 of its commands in 1952. He displayed photographic copies of 70 pages of a document entitled "Psychological and Cultural Traits of Soviet Siberia" and told reporters, "If you read this and believed it, you would move to Russia." Two days later the Army countered with the announcement that Joe had violated the law by disclosing "restricted" information. (This classification was the lowest of the designations used by the Army to safeguard information.) An Army spokesman also contended that a reading of the entire document, only 100 copies of which were ever reproduced, would refute the senator's allegation. Several sentences from the conclusion (which Joe had omitted) were released to the press, convincingly illustrating the document's pro-American, anti-Soviet slant.[10]

Boiling with rage at the Army's defiance, McCarthy summoned Gen. Richard C. Partridge, chief of Army Intelligence, to an executive session on September 21. With Army Secretary Stevens observing from the audience, Joe tore into Partridge for permitting the publication of the "Siberia" document and for approving of it when questioned.

> The Chairman. You come here and say it is a good, honest attempt. I wonder how much you know about the book. Do you know that this book quotes verbatim from Joe Stalin, without attributing it to him, as a stamp of approval of the United States Army? Are you aware of that?
> General Partridge. I don't know that it quotes from Joe Stalin or not.
> The Chairman. Don't you think before you testify you should take time to conduct some research to find out whether it quotes Joe Stalin and other notorious Communists? Don't you think you are incompetent to testify before you know that?
> General Partridge. No, sir.
> The Chairman. I don't want someone here who knows nothing about this document, just giving us conversation.

The next witness was Samuel McKee, civilian consultant to the Assistant Chief of Staff, Army Intelligence, and chairman of a committee that had reviewed the "Siberia" document in 1952 and passed it along. (A dissident member of that committee was probably the source of the tip to McCarthy.) McCarthy and Cohn took turns exposing and ridiculing his limited knowledge of Communist history and literature. Even though McKee was willing to express doubt about parts of the controversial document, Joe was unsparing in his criticism, calling the witness "completely and hopelessly incompetent" to hold his job.

At the close of the hearing, Robert Stevens stood up to make a brief statement. In public and in private, the Army Secretary had pledged his total support for the subcommittee. Shaken by the humiliation of Partridge and McKee, he could only say feebly in their defense, "I think they have tried to get before you the facts, right or wrong, to the best of their ability." This merely triggered another tirade against General Partridge. "We need someone who has some conception of the danger of Communism," Joe cried.[11]

Joe also called attention to a book entitled *U.S.S.R., A Concise Handbook,* edited by Dr. Ernest J. Simmons, a Columbia University professor of Russian literature. Joe labeled Simmons a Communist, and he and Cohn contended that many contributors to the book, including the historian Sir Bernard Pares, were Reds and espionage agents. Joe also claimed that the Army had used the volume "to indoctrinate our troops," at least through 1952. A public hearing of September 28 was devoted to the Simmons book and the "Siberia" document. Louis Budenz was one of three ex-Communists called upon to attest to the subversive nature of both works. Surveying the entire situation, Budenz claimed to see "the work of a concealed Communist" somewhere within the military. Joe also took another blast at General Partridge, who observed the proceedings quietly from the audience. (A short time later, Partridge was replaced as head of Army Intelligence and sent to Europe.)[12]

The investigation that had sent Roy Cohn scurrying to West Palm Beach to interrupt the McCarthys' honeymoon involved charges of Communist infiltration of the Army Signal Corps Center at Fort Monmouth, a 2,000-acre installation in northern New Jersey. Fort Monmouth was the Signal Corps' principal research, development, and training facility, employing 7,488 civilians, as well as troops. Among its laboratories was the Army's main radar research center, the Evans Signal Laboratory, at Belnar, ten miles from the fort.

Security at the Signal Corps Center came into question in mid-1952 when an East German scientist who escaped to the West reported having seen "many microfilmed copies of documents" from Fort Monmouth. The Signal Corps conducted an investigation, as did the FBI. The Air Force determined that the scientist was an unreliable witness, and the case was dropped. HUAC investigators poked around the facility in 1952 as well, checking out a charge that 57 secret documents had disappeared from the Signal Corps Intelligence Agency. That probe was also abandoned.

The McCarthy Subcommittee was secretly alerted to the possibility of subversives at Fort Monmouth by Maj. Gen. Kirke B. Lawton, Monmouth commander since December, 1951. Lawton was so security-conscious that he personally led one of several teams that periodically ransacked desks after hours to spot loose handling of classified material. FBI personnel probably also assisted McCarthy. In a November 1953 radio debate, Roy Cohn answered a question about Fort Monmouth by saying, "It is because what the FBI found was ignored that we have to have our investigation today." Throughout the public hearings on the issue McCarthy and Cohn would refer to the bureau's frustrations at being unable to convince the Army of Red infiltration at the Fort. The subcommittee would also reveal its possession of wiretap information.[13]

The subcommittee began closed-door hearings on August 31. News of the investigation became public shortly after the Army announced on October 6 that "several employees" at the Signal Corps laboratories at Fort Monmouth had been suspended for security reasons. The *Chicago Tribune* declared that two top American scientists and three others engaged in secret radar development had been suspended, adding that thirty others were under investigation. "Several figures" involved in the case of Julius and Ethel Rosenberg, the recently executed atomic bomb spies, were also reported linked to the inquiry.[14]

The names of three suspended employees leaked out the next day. One, Aaron H. Coleman, a top official at the Evans Signal Laboratory, said that he was being persecuted for having graduated in the same class at the City College of New York with Morton Sobell, a convicted member of the Rosenberg conspiracy. "I had no social relations with him after that. But in my capacity as a government project engineer I met him several times at the Reeves Instrument Corporation plant in New York." Coleman vowed to fight the suspension "because I am completely innocent."[15]

Joe, recently returned from his wedding trip, assured reporters that his subcommittee had unearthed a trail of "extremely dangerous espionage" that could "envelop the whole Signal Corps." The espionage was recent, he said, and dealt "with our entire defense against atomic attack."[16]

McCarthy and his staff conducted five days of closed-door hearings in mid-October. (Senators Dirksen and Potter sent representatives.) At the end of each session Joe again provided reporters with his interpretation of the day's events. (The testimony of only a single witness from the executive sessions would be published in full.) He painted a chilling picture of subversion and espionage and implied that he had uncovered a spy-ring masterminded by Julius Rosenberg, who had worked for the Army Signal Corps from 1940 until early 1945. *The New York Times* headlines typified the response of the press: "Army Radar Data Reported Missing," "Rosenberg Called Radar Spy Leader: McCarthy Says Ring He Set Up 'May Still Be in Operation' at Monmouth Laboratories," "Radar Witness Breaks Down: Will Tell All About Spy Ring," "Espionage in Signal Corps for Ten Years Is Charged." While Joe and Jean were away for a week on a speech-making jaunt to Arizona and Wisconsin, the hearings continued, and Cohn and Schine fed stories to eager reporters: "Monmouth Figure Linked to Hiss Ring," "Ex-U.N. Aide Linked to Spy Ring by Gold." When Joe returned, more large headlines appeared: "Ex-Spy Ring Figure in Arms Plant Job."

Joe and his staff took obvious pleasure in announcing the rising number of civilian employees at Fort Monmouth suspended by the Army: by October 15 there were ten, by the 23rd the figure was fifteen, a day later twenty, by the 27th the number had reached 27, and it would soon rise to 33. Several times Joe expressed his delight at the cooperation of Army Secretary Stevens and General Lawton. He told an enthusiastic crowd of 800 in Leonardo, New Jersey, that the situation at Fort Monmouth had been "incredibly bad" and that Lawton was determined to turn things around. "He's doing a great job."[17]

McCarthy, Stevens, Lawton, and Republican Senator H. Alexander Smith of New Jersey traveled together to Fort Monmouth on October 20. They conducted a two-hour inspection of the 100-acre Evans Signal Laboratory, after which Joe praised the secretary and the general and lauded President Eisenhower for his willingness to fire all employees in Federal departments who took the Fifth Amendment. "This is a very important step in making sure that all government employees are the true, loyal, fine type of people that the vast majority of them are." Senator Smith expressed his complete support of the subcommittee. Its investigation, he told reporters, "may have worldwide repercussions."[18]

The Army remained officially silent during the initial barrage of headlines. When Joe began discussing the charges of the East German scientist, however, and requested of Secretary Stevens that the 30-year-old refugee be brought to the United States to testify, the Army publicly reaffirmed a statement made in 1952 that it had found no missing documents and no evidence of espionage. Microfilm copies of Signal Corps data in Russian hands, a spokesman explained, were probably those turned over during the war under lend-lease agreements. (Actually, the Russians were not only given documents but had official representatives in Fort Monmouth handling classified materials. They were also supplied with classified communications equipment under lend-lease.) Unaffected by this explanation, Joe announced that he was sending a newly appointed investigator, former FBI agent James N. Juliana, to Germany to interview the scientist. When

Juliana returned, Joe described the scientist's charges to reporters at length and discounted the Army's statement about lend-lease. "McCarthy Charges Soviet Got Secrets," *The New York Times* headline read.[19]

A few days later Army officials were given further reason for concern when Cohn and Schine told reporters that McCarthy had authorized the subcommittee to call as witnesses members of the top screening board of the Department of the Army in Washington. The subcommittee had learned, they said, that the board had reinstated "many civilian employees suspected of Communist activities." Reporters were also told that a major general, now in Army Intelligence in Washington, would be questioned about his refusal in 1946 to suspend a civilian employee at Fort Monmouth found in unlawful possession of more than 40 classified Signal Corps documents. On October 30 Cohn went a step further, announcing that the subcommittee staff had compiled a list of all officials on regional and national security boards who passed upon security suspensions ordered by local commanders. Some of these officials, he said, would be questioned in public hearings.[20]

Secretary of Defense Charles E. Wilson had told reporters in mid-October that the Army was conducting its own investigation into security at Fort Monmouth. "It looks like it might be worse than just a security leak," he declared. On November 13 Secretary Stevens shocked and angered McCarthy by announcing that the Army probe had concluded that there were no suspected spies among the 33 civilians recently suspended and that no "current case" of subversion had been uncovered. He added that he did not think there had been any espionage in the Signal Corps during World War II. Joe ordered Cohn to prepare immediately for public hearings, telling reporters that the proceedings "will be of great interest to the American people."[21]

Three days later, Carl Greenblum, a 37-year-old electrical engineer from Wanamassa, New Jersey, admitted publicly to being the "mystery witness" who, according to McCarthy on October 16, had broken down and begun to cry after "some rather vigorous cross-examination by Roy Cohn." Joe said at the time that the witness had been lying, and that the confrontation with Cohn persuaded him to tell everything he knew about an espionage ring. After the incident before the subcommittee, word had somehow gotten out that Greenblum was the witness in question, and the feeling grew in his neighborhood that he was un-American. A hammer and sickle were painted on his house, a note placed on his front door read "Get out of town, you Nazis," and his three-year-old son was harassed. Greenblum then went to a local newspaper to tell his side of the story.

Greenblum said that he had broken into tears on the stand because his mother had died two days earlier and he was emotionally unprepared for Cohn's rapid barrage of questions. He vigorously denied having lied to the subcommittee. He acknowledged having had a "nodding acquaintance" with Morton Sobell and Julius Rosenberg, who had been a college classmate. But he had not liked Rosenberg, he said, and had had no social association with him. "I never had any sympathy for Communism," Greenblum said. "I had a revulsion toward it. There is an equation between Communism and totalitarianism and it has no place among free people." Reached by reporters, Joe preferred not to comment.[22]

The subcommittee held ten public hearings from late November through the end of the year, and five more in February and March, 1954. In all but one of the 1953 sessions McCarthy was the only senator present. The other Republican members later claimed to have been busy elsewhere. Forty witnesses testified, 34 of whom were suspected by McCarthy and his staff of being, or having been, Reds and spies. Twenty-five of the 34 took the Fifth Amendment when asked about Communist affiliations, and another refused to answer on the ground of the First Amendment. The steady parade of reluctant and belligerent witnesses produced headlines for months. Joe cleverly saved the most questionable and controversial witnesses for the several televised sessions.

In fact, however, the hearings confirmed the Army's judgment of the allegations by failing to display even slightly convincing evidence of espionage in the Army Signal Corps—at any time, with or without Julius Rosenberg. Not a single indictment of any individual would result from the investigation. The subcommittee showed that about a half dozen Communists had worked at Fort Monmouth from 1941-47 and that a tiny Communist cell had existed during and after the war at the Federal Telecommunications Laboratories of Nutley, New Jersey, a Signal Corps subcontractor. But no link could be made between the Communists, whose existence had long been known (several had been fired under the Truman administration; a union they dominated in Nutley had been expelled by the C.I.O.), and spying. A large percentage of those who took the Fifth Amendment about their Communist party affiliations specifically denied committing or even discussing espionage. The ex-Communists who cooperated fully with the subcommittee made the same firm denial.[23]

The best evidence the subcommittee could produce was presented on the first day of the public hearings before the television cameras. Roy Cohn introduced a deposition he had taken from convicted conspirator David Greenglass at Lewisburg prison. Greenglass repeated a story he had told at the Rosenberg trial involving Julius Rosenberg's wartime theft of a "proximity fuse" from the Signal Corps. He also enlarged his earlier account of Rosenberg's spying activities and said of other espionage efforts, "As far as I know these operations never stopped and could very possibly be continuing to this very day." The convict seemed suspiciously eager to please Cohn, with whom he had had prior dealings. In 1956 Robert Morris would bring Greenglass before the Senate Internal Security Subcommittee, where he would expand his story further.[24]

McCarthy was most effective when confronting Aaron H. Coleman, the only current employee at Fort Monmouth to be summoned before an open hearing. Testimony by the suspended chief of the Systems Section at the Evans Signal Laboratory revealed that he had been reprimanded and suspended for ten days in 1946 for "careless" handling of classified documents, and that over the years he had been friendly with several identified Communists. Joe's interrogation was skillful and shrewd; Coleman was sometimes evasive and crafty. But when the testimony had concluded, the most damaging thing Joe had established was that Coleman, at nineteen, had attended a single Young Communist League meeting with his college classmate Julius Rosenberg. The more than forty papers and personal notes found in Coleman's home after the war, intended for his private study, were of little importance; the reprimand was for failure to keep the documents in a safe with a three-combination lock. An appeal of the reprimand in late 1946 had prompted Army officials to observe that "the motives which led to your having had classified documents in your possession were highly praiseworthy." This was all a far cry from the spine-tingling revelations Joe had promised before the public hearings began. On October 23 he had told reporters that "an ex-Marine officer [Coleman] may have been the direct link between the laboratories and the Rosenberg spy ring."[25]

Throughout the public hearings Joe said that he wanted not only to expose Communists but to punish them. They were all spies, directly under the authority of the Soviet Union and dedicated to the destruction of the United States. He considered it his duty as a loyal American to see that they were jailed and fired from private and public employment. This passionately expressed attitude often led to a ruthlessness and rancor that astonished and frightened witnesses.

Ex-Communists, for example, unwilling to inform on past associates, were forced immediately to take the Fifth Amendment; a direct answer to any question about Communism meant waiving the right to use the Fifth Amendment in that entire area of investigation. From that point on they became "Fifth-Amendment Communists," and Joe would refer to them freely as Reds, traitors, and spies. Knowing they would continue to take the Fifth Amendment, on the advice of their attorneys, he would ask such questions as "Were you a spy yesterday?" From the predictable response, he would loudly conclude that he had uncovered current espionage.

Joe said repeatedly that the Fifth Amendment was a shield for the guilty. "Do you feel that you have a constitutional right to commit espionage?" he asked one witness. He ordered a policeman to remove a witness who pled the Fifth Amendment and attempted to make a few comments. "I want no speech from any man who refuses to tell whether he is destroying this nation." He bellowed at another witness, "Let me ask you this question: Julius Rosenberg was convicted of espionage and he has been executed. From your answers here, apparently you were engaged and still are engaged in the same type of espionage. Do you feel that you should be walking the streets of this country free, or that you should have the same fate as the Rosenbergs?" If at some point such a witness chose to answer a question in any way related to the Communist issue, Joe would claim that he had thereby automatically waived the right to plead the Fifth Amendment. If the witness persisted, Joe would threaten him with contempt of Congress. It was dangerous, for example, for an ex-Communist to deny that he had ever been a spy.[26]

Several witnesses had little or no connection with the investigation. They were Communists and ex-Communists Joe was trying to have disbarred or fired. One Brooklyn vice-principal, who had attended officer candidate school at Fort Monmouth for three months during the war, was summoned because his wife was reportedly a Red. (She had never worked at Fort Monmouth.) McCarthy and Cohn proceeded to grill him on the content of his high school social studies courses. Joe derisively referred to the witness at one point as "professor."[27]

Current employees of the Federal Telecommunications Laboratories were brought before the subcommittee because of a new company policy, supervised by an ex-FBI agent, calling for the immediate dismissal of anyone taking the Fifth Amendment. Joe tried to persuade other companies to take the same action. He urged the firing of one witness from his job with a company that sold eggs.[28]

Sometimes witnesses were asked about the occupations of brothers, sisters, and other relatives. Joe was searching for more suspects who could be revealed, condemned, and punished.[29]

The senator made it clear throughout the proceedings that he and his staff were working closely with the FBI. This added authority and prestige to the investigation and produced fear among many witnesses. One ex-

Communist agreed to cooperate with the subcommittee after FBI agents appeared at his front door shortly after he was subpoenaed. Another ex-Communist who broke down under the pressure urged others to confess to the FBI, slathered praise upon McCarthy for his fairness, and condemned leftists in the media for attacks upon the subcommittee. Joe appealed to one Federal Telecommunications employee to save her job by telling all she knew to the FBI. Agents could be produced within twenty minutes, he said, to take her testimony.[30]

The best that could be said of the Fort Monmouth investigation was that it may have tightened some rather loose postwar security procedures, both at the fort and at the Federal Telecommunications Laboratories. Several witnesses spoke of the sloppy handling of classified documents, and in a few cases Communists appear to have been taken too lightly by some security officials.[31]

But these debatable contributions do not begin to atone for the damage in ruined reputations and lost salaries and jobs suffered needlessly by sub-committee witnesses, both in closed and open hearings. Moreover, the suffering inflicted upon those suspended by the Army during the subcom-mittee probe should also be attributed to McCarthy. In a panic to prove themselves sufficiently attentive to the President's new security standards, Army officials persecuted almost fifty civilian employees. Charges in-cluded: attending a lecture by liberal *New York Post* columnist Max Lerner, having a brother who was a witness at the perjury trial of Alger Hiss, joining the Young Pioneers of America in 1933—at the age of twelve, having relatives who belonged to the still legal American Labor Party in New York, and for living with an allegedly subversive father—who swore he was never a member of the Communist party. Of over 120 charges against nineteen employees later analyzed by the Scientists' Committee on Loyalty and Security, only six involved Communist membership or affilia-tions; five of the six were denied under oath, and the sixth was the admission of attending Communist meetings at age twelve. Suspended employees were suspended without pay; the government bore none of the defendants' legal expenses; and attorneys for the employees were not furnished the names, addresses, or even descriptions of accusers. Eventu-ally, most of the accused won the right to return to their jobs, but the victory sometimes took years of litigation.[32]

Two newspapers in the Fort Monmouth area were among the first to condemn both the Army and subcommittee investigators. The *Asbury Park Press,* in a November 28 editorial, labeled most Army charges "ridiculously thin accusations" and warned that McCarthy's tactics could "easily become a threat to American principles of liberty and justice." The *Long Branch Daily Record* soon criticized what it called McCarthy's "reckless charges; his masterful dissemination of half-truths, insinuations, and innuendos; his assumption of the roles of prosecutor, judge, and jury, and now his threatened intimidation of the Army's loyalty review board; his callous disregard of the reputations of American citizens who have never been convicted of anything, much less accused; his snide 'ad-lib' comments; his abrogation of time-honored civil liberties." The major anti-McCarthy organs in the media quickly joined the attack. Jewish groups were particularly vocal, observing that virtually every subcommittee witness at the open hearings and almost all of the employees suspended by the Army were Jews.[33]

Morale at Fort Monmouth was said to be extremely low in the wake of the investigations. The post newspaper quoted a veteran engineer who referred to "the depression we now have." A committee of scientists bemoaned the "atmosphere of suspicion and distrust." One major basic research project was reportedly stalled by the confusion. General Lawton conceded that the Signal Corps might one day have to depend more upon outside research and development, but he told reporters that morale was "wonderful."[34]

The only military figure to speak out publicly against the Fort Monmouth hearings was retired Brigadier General Telford Taylor, former chief Allied prosecutor at the Nuremberg war crimes trial and currently a New York attorney. In a speech to a group of West Point cadets, Taylor denounced McCarthy as a "dangerous adventurer" making an "unscrupulous grab for publicity," and he labeled the senator's charges "groundless and shameful." He was also critical of Secretary Stevens, noting that the German Officers' Corps had been destroyed because it took up "false notions of playing politics with demagogues."[35]

Joe retaliated by showing reporters what he said was a photograph of the general's confidential civil service form, bearing a "flag" and carrying the notation "unresolved question of loyalty." "You will note," he said, "that the 'flagging' was not on security grounds, but on loyalty grounds." Joe called for the revocation of Taylor's reserve commission, demanded to know who let him address West Point cadets, and announced that his staff had been asked "to subpoena Mr. Telford Taylor, sometimes known as General Taylor." Taylor replied that a "flag" merely indicated that the file contained derogatory information, the sort that appears when anyone takes a firm position on public issues. He also expressed a willingness to appear before the subcommittee if summoned. When the chairman of the Civil Service Commission was asked about McCarthy's possession of the confidential document on Taylor, he said merely, "I've noticed in the past that some of his references have not been too accurate."[36]

Joe also tried to involve Taylor and diplomat John J. McCloy in a reported plot to place 125 German Communists in the office of the United States High Commissioner in Germany. The evidence for the charge, which Joe admitted he had not verified, came from a man who had been deposed earlier in the week by the State Department as a judge in Germany. The matter was not pursued once it made headlines. Moreover, Joe did not call Taylor before the subcommittee. He was content to smear him at the outset of a public hearing on Fort Monmouth.[37]

While McCarthy held executive hearings on Fort Monmouth, he announced plans to search for Communists within the General Electric Company plant in Schenectady, New York. General Electric, which had 131 plants across the country with 230,000 employees, handled government work for the Signal Corps and other military services, and Joe claimed that the new probe was linked to the hunt for spies in the Signal Corps laboratories.[38]

Closed hearings got underway on November 12 in Albany, with Joe again providing reporters with his own accounts of the proceedings. A brief open hearing occurred a week later, featuring testimony by William H. Teto, a 53-year-old upholstery-supply dealer. Teto announced that he had been an undercover agent for the FBI since 1941, counterspying on Communist cells in the General Electric Company. Joe dramatically declared that Teto would be given complete police protection, and he and Cohn proceeded to heap accolades upon J. Edgar Hoover. After Teto cited an estimate of the number of Communists at G.E., Joe demanded that all "Fifth-Amendment Communists" at the company be fired. On December 9 company officials reluctantly agreed to suspend all employees who took the Fifth Amendment and fire all admitted Communists immediately. There was considerable doubt about the legality (not to mention morality) of suspending and dismissing unionized workers on these grounds, but during the Red Scare such reservations were often ignored. Joe commended G.E. for its "fine" new policy.[39]

The subcommittee held five public hearings in early 1954, another that summer, two more in early December, and a final session on January 3, 1955. Three more FBI undercover agents testified, along with three ex-Communists who had earlier confessed to the FBI. Several dozen witnesses appeared, and many took the Fifth Amendment. In 1954 Joe broadened the probe to include the Allis-Chalmers, Bethlehem Steel, and Westinghouse corporations. Appropriate pressure was placed on these companies, as well, to dismiss all those who balked at the subcommittee's questions. Late that year the subcommittee recommended to the Secretary of Defense that the federal government withdraw or cancel all defense contracts with companies that continued to employ Communists and "Fifth-Amendment Communists."[40]

For all of the headlines and television time these hearings received, they achieved virtually nothing constructive or necessary. Not a single act of espionage or subversion could be attributed to the small number of employees who allegedly were or had been Communists. Even their proximity to classified information was often questionable. The occupations of witnesses included: production clerk, turret-lathe operator, grinder of castings, coil winder, drill-press operator, and research assistant at Harvard. One 64-year-old man, who had first been employed at G.E. in 1922, worked on street lights. The most damaging case against any of them came from an FBI undercover agent who said gravely, "A member of the Communist party can act as a listening post to some extent, in that he feels the pulse of the people in his shop."[41]

Roy Cohn later boasted that 32 people were fired as the result of the investigation. Of course, that was the major purpose of the probe. No crime had been committed; the names and activities of all Communists within the corporations under scrutiny were fully known by the FBI before the public hearings were held. McCarthy and his equally zealous staff members were again trying to punish those who, they believed, were plotting the annihilation of the United States. Displays of Joe's passion and fury were frequent—in closed as well as public hearings. He bitterly reviled those who took the Fifth Amendment, saying at one point, "I wish there were some way to make these conspirators testify, because the Fifth Amendment was for the purpose of protecting the individual, not for the purpose of protecting a conspiracy against this nation." He told hostile witnesses bluntly that he wanted them fired. He ordered several removed from the hearing room by force. When the 64-year-old G.E. witness expressed his unwillingness to be a political informer, Joe fired back, "We don't care what your politics are. We are interested in espionage, sabotage, and Communism, which has been named by the Supreme Court as a conspiracy against this country and not as a political party." A moment later, trying to persuade the witness to be cooperative, he said gently, "You don't seem to be a typical Communist; you do not seem to be an evil man."[42]

However much White House officials growled in private about McCarthy, the Administration revealed a consistent desire to continue to

use the Reds-in-government issue against Democrats. The initial spokesman for the attack was Attorney General Herbert Brownell, a shrewd party
professional who was generally thought to be the best political strategist in
the G.O.P. In a widely publicized interview with the editors of *U.S. News
and World Report,* released on August 31, 1953, Brownell claimed that
members of the still legal Communist party were "a greater menace now
than at any time," and he pointed especially to their presence in labor
unions. He praised the FBI ("I don't know of any more devoted group of
public officials"), congratulated congressional investigating committees,
and asserted that the Administration had restored confidence in the
Department of Justice.[43]

The White House announced in late October that 1,456 employees had
been forced off the federal government's payroll in the first four months of
the Eisenhower administration. Wholly without evidence, Joe claimed on a
"Meet the Press" television program that 90 percent of the dismissals had
been for "a combination of Communist activities and perversion." He told
an audience in Monroe, Wisconsin, "Believe me when I say 1,400 is only
scratching the surface."[44]

A few months later the Attorney General declared that the Administration had fired some 2,200 "security risks" since assuming power. Brownell
and other White House officials thereafter refused repeatedly to explain
how many actual spies were among the number. Many observers were
convinced that the statistic was released with the 1954 elections in mind.[45]

Brownell provoked a national uproar on November 6, 1953, by telling an
audience of Chicago business executives that former President Truman was
guilty of being deliberately and flagrantly soft on Communism. In 1946
Truman had named Assistant Secretary of the Treasury Harry Dexter
White the executive director of the International Monetary Fund. Brownell
charged that this action was taken despite FBI warnings sent to the White
House in December 1945 and February 1946 that White was a Communist
spy. Before making the accusation, the Attorney General discussed his
speech with Sherman Adams and James Hagerty, the President's press
secretary. According to Adams, Brownell thought that the charge "would
take away some of the glamour of the McCarthy stage play."[44]

Congressman Velde quickly announced that HUAC would subpoena
Truman, former Secretary of States James Byrnes, and former Attorney
General (now Supreme Court Justice) Tom Clark to testify on the White
case. (All three declined to appear.) Not to be outdone, Senator Jenner
declared that his subcommittee would soon hold hearings. Joe told reporters that he had already heard a similar case in closed session a month

earlier. Sen. Homer Ferguson, chairman of the Senate Republican Policy Committee, demanded an investigation of all "secret" government records "to determine just how much more evidence of Communist infiltration there is in Washington." Democratic National Chairman Stephen A. Mitchell indignantly observed that the Brownell charge was made soon after G.O.P. defeats in New Jersey and three days before a special congressional election in California.[47]

Many ultraconservatives, including McCarthy, had long been interested in the White case. It was also one of those matters that apparently continued to pique at least some FBI personnel. Congressman John McCormack of Massachusetts charged that Brownell had received his information directly from the bureau.[48]

Harry Dexter White had been a distinguished and powerful figure within the Roosevelt Administrations. After his transfer by Truman to the International Monetary Fund he remained in government until April 1947, when he resigned to enter private business. The President wrote him a warm letter praising his many years of public service. Secretly, White had been named by Whittaker Chambers and Elizabeth Bentley as part of an espionage ring in Washington that flourished in the late 1930s and early 1940s. When the allegation became public in 1948, White voluntarily appeared before HUAC and denied all ties to Communism and espionage. He died of a heart attack three days after protesting his innocence. A document later produced by Whittaker Chambers appeared to substantiate the charge against him.[49]

J. Edgar Hoover told the Jenner subcommittee, not long after the Brownell speech, that the bureau had sent seven warnings of espionage to the White House, from November 8, 1945, to July 24, 1946, containing White's name.

Truman contended in a nationally televised broadcast in mid-November 1953 that he had retained White in government service in order to keep from exposing a broader espionage investigation by the FBI. Whatever the exact facts of the matter, there should have been no question about Truman's patriotism and high-mindedness. Adlai Stevenson commented after Brownell's speech, "It is infamous that the man who has done more than anyone else to organize and fortify the free world against Communism should be subjected to such malicious political attack." President Eisenhower, who had been informed of the Attorney General's address only in general terms before its delivery (he had not heard of White), told a news conference he considered it inconceivable that Truman would have knowingly damaged the United States.[50]

Truman's television speech was filled with invective against Republicans, who were guilty, he said, of "shameful demagoguery." He charged the Administration with having embraced McCarthyism, and he defined the term in language that crackled with anger:

> It is the corruption of truth, the abandonment of our historical devotion to fair play. It is the abandonment of the "due process" of law. It is the use of the big lie and the unfounded accusation against any citizen in the name of Americanism or security. It is the rise to power of the demagogue who lives on untruth; it is the spread of fear and the destruction of faith in every level of our society.

Truman assured his viewers that the threat was beyond partisanship. "This horrible cancer is eating at the vitals of America and it can destroy the great edifice of freedom."[51]

McCarthy, in a towering rage, demanded equal time of the Federal Communications Commission. F.C.C. officials quickly complied. The reply was scheduled for a half hour on November 24 and was to be aired over all of the major television and radio networks.[52]

Joe's wrath was directed not only against Truman but increasingly against Eisenhower as well. The President had quietly dispatched White House aide I. Jack Martin, a former Taft adviser, to McCarthy bearing an offer: if Joe would conduct only executive hearings on the Army, minutes of the sessions would be delivered to Eisenhower personally and appropriate action would be taken. Joe resented this naive effort to stifle his headline-making, and he flatly rejected the proposal. Then, at his weekly news conference on November 11, the President had supported Truman's integrity and warned against what he called reckless, un-American methods of fighting Communism. On November 23 Eisenhower declared in a nationally broadcast address before the Anti-Defamation League of B'nai B'rith that it was a basic right of every man "to meet his accuser face to face." "In this country," he said, "if someone dislikes you or accuses you, he must come up in front. He cannot hide behind the shadows, he cannot assassinate you or your character from behind without suffering the penalties an outraged citizenry will inflict." Some observers interpreted this as a veiled slap at McCarthy and the entire security mania (for which Ike was in part responsible) that had gripped Washington. Since the implementation of Administration security regulations in late May, the only opportunity a suspended government employee had to meet his accuser was at a hearing in the appeal stage. Few cases ever got that far, which McCarthyites found encouraging. Scott McLeod revealed that 484 State Department employees ʰad been fired since January 20, and there had not been a single hearing under the new security regulations.⁵³

Joe was especially incensed by Eisenhower's recent statement that he hoped the internal subversion problem would have been dealt with so effectively that it would no longer be an issue in the 1954 elections. McCarthyites were determined to make Reds-in-government the principal theme of the campaigns, and Joe was preparing to take the crusade into contests all across the land.⁵⁴

In his nationally broadcast speech, Joe lashed out passionately against Truman, condemning him for deceit and appeasement and charging that his administration had been "crawling with Communists." Joe discussed at length the conflicting statements about Harry Dexter White and quoted J. Edgar Hoover to refute the former President's principal explanation for his conduct in 1946. He claimed that Truman had personally intervened to have a Communist agent reinstated to office in 1944. He was particularly emotional about Truman's use of the term "McCarthyism," saying, "The definition was identical, word for word, comma for comma, with the definition adopted by the Communist *Daily Worker,* which originated the term." He retaliated with a diatribe against what he called "Trumanism": "the placing of your political party above the interest of the country, regardless of how much the country is damaged thereby."

One expected such bombast from McCarthy against Democrats. But then Joe unexpectedly turned on the Eisenhower administration. He began by sharply criticizing the President's remark about the forthcoming campaigns. "The raw, harsh, unpleasant fact is that Communism is an issue and it will be an issue in 1954. . . . Practically every issue we face today, from high taxes to the shameful mess in Korea, is inextricably interwoven with the Communist issue." He proceeded to condemn the Administration for retaining China Hand John Paton Davies on the government payroll, for failing to take stronger action on behalf of American prisoners in Korea ("Are we going to continue to send perfumed notes, following the style of the Truman-Acheson regime?"), and for refusing to cut off aid to American allies that traded with Red China. "Once a nation has allowed itself to be reduced to a state of whining, whimpering appeasement," he cried, "the cost of retaining national honor may be high. But we must regain our national honor regardless of what it costs."⁵⁵

Columnist James Reston reported top White House staff members "hopping mad" about the speech, one aide calling it "a declaration of war against the President." Secretary of State Dulles was the first official to comment publicly. On December 1 he defended the Administration's policy to extend aid to nations trading in nonstrategic goods and commodities with Communist China and rejected what he called "blustering, domineering, or arrogant methods." (At stake was a very small quantity of trade, somewhere between $300 million and $375 million for 1953. The Republic of Columbia, South America, Harold Stassen pointed out, usually imported more annually.) Dulles said that McCarthy's attack hit at the very "heart of United States foreign policy." At a news conference the next day, the President stated that he was in "full accord" with Dulles and added firmly, "I repeat my previously expressed conviction that fear of Communists actively undermining our government will not be an issue in the 1954 elections."[56]

Joe called a news conference the following day and read a mildly conciliatory statement denying that he was challenging the President's leadership. Suddenly he departed from his text and urged Americans who agreed with him about the "blood trade with our mortal enemy" to write and wire the President. "Now I think President Eisenhower is an honorable man," he said, still ad-libbing. "I think he will follow the will of the American people if that will is made known to him." The news conference was televised and shown coast to coast that evening. Almost immediately telegrams began to pour in upon the White House; within twenty-four hours officials said that more than 4,300 had arrived, running more than two to one in favor of McCarthy. Joe quickly challenged the Administration's count, and contended that the actual response had been twice as large. He said he would soon seek an explanation of the "discrepancy" from Major General Persons, the President's congressional liaison chief. (By December 9, press secretary Hagerty stopped the tabulation, acknowledging receipt of about 25,000 telegrams and an equal number of letters. The President's viewpoint, he said, was "slightly ahead" in telegrams, while a majority of letters backed McCarthy. Columnist Arthur Krock commented, "Only a few thousandths of 1 percent of the American people acted on McCarthy's suggestion. And even this tiny trickle to the White House was closely divided.")[57]

On N.B.C.'s "American Forum of the Air" Joe expressed his belief in Secretary Dulles's sincerity but repeated his stand that the Administration's policy concerning trade with Red China was "a carry-over from the Truman-Acheson regime" and should be changed. On "Meet the Press," another televised program, he said, "The President would be a miracle man if he batted 100 percent. So, when he makes a mistake, I tell him about it."[58]

On December 18 Joe traveled to Chicago to address the same luncheon group that heard Attorney General Brownell attack Truman. Some 2,500 people turned out at the Executives Club of Chicago, the largest crowd in the organization's 43-year history. Joe reiterated his declaration that Reds-in-government would be "the issue" in the 1954 congressional elections, and he urged his listeners to "demand" of every candidate that he back his position on trade with Red China. The President, he said, was "doing a tremendously good job" in the White House. But if he were in the Senate, Joe said, "he would have the guts, brains and sense of duty to speak out as I am doing."[59]

H. Alexander Smith, chairman of the Senate Foreign Relations sub-committee on the Far East, was one of many Republican leaders becoming increasingly disturbed by the warfare between McCarthy and the Administration. Over the C.B.S. radio program "Capitol Cloakroom," the New Jersey senator called upon Joe to "get on the team and get on it soon."[60]

Eisenhower quickly made a move to unify his party by inviting McCarthy, Congressman Velde, Attorney General Brownell, and several others to the White House to discuss a legislative program that would include more effective action against subversives. Brownell thrilled the ultraconservatives by proposing legislation that would legalize evidence obtained by wiretapping and give the government the power to force a witness to testify, despite the Fifth Amendment. Velde called the discussion "very congenial" and said there was evidence at the White House of "cooperation of the highest type." Joe said, "I was not displeased at anything I heard." A half hour later he telephoned reporters and bubbled, "This is the first time I've had the opportunity to watch the President in action over a period of time. I was tremendously impressed with his handling of the conference and his detailed knowledge of every subject or piece of proposed legislation that was discussed."[61]

Richard Nixon then made another of his several attempts to mollify McCarthy. On December 30 Joe flew to Key Biscayne, Florida, where the Vice-President and Deputy Attorney General William Rogers were spending a few days in the sun. Nixon strongly advised his old friend to give the Administration a chance to clean the Reds out of Washington, stressing the good will of people like Army Secretary Stevens and emphasizing the fact that Republicans had to pull together. He also suggested that it would be wise for the Permanent Subcommittee on Investigations to probe something other than Communism. Joe accepted the advice (he always did), called a news conference, and announced that his subcommittee would broaden its inquiries to include tax cases settled on a low compromise basis during the Truman Administration. When either Nixon or Rogers leaked the story during the following week that the subcommittee would virtually bow out of the Red-hunting field, Joe bristled and flatly denied that he had even discussed such a matter with anyone, "from President Eisenhower on down." When Democrat Allen J. Ellender vowed to slash the subcommittee's budget for the coming year to reduce "wasteful" overlapping investigations, Joe dared him to try: "It will demonstrate that the Democrats are still the party that wants to cover up and whitewash treason, Communism and espionage."[62]

A variety of plans were soon said to be underway in the Senate, including one devised by Carl Hayden, a power in that body, to restrict the subcommittee's activities and cut its appropriations. Joe defiantly announced that he would seek sufficient funds to double his eleven-man investigative staff. Worried about his own subcommittee's budget, William Jenner then huddled with McCarthy and urged him to reconsider. "I think it was a mistake for him to concentrate so much in the field of subversion last year," Jenner told reporters, "and I don't think he'll do it this year." Joe gave in to the mounting pressure. He announced a major investigation of government operations in Alaska (saying soberly that he did not intend to hold public hearings there during the winter) and agreed to request $200,000 for the subcommittee, the same amount it had received the previous year. He also expressed a willingness to "lean over backward" to persuade the Democrats to return to the subcommittee. No doubt as a reward for these concessions, G.O.P. Senators placed him on the Rules Committee—a new assignment that increased his power in the Senate and gave him a voice and a vote in the struggles over committee appropriations.[63]

To further exhibit his concern for topics other than Communism, and to answer a published charge by his friend John Wyngaard that he was weak on the subject of farmer parity (then in the news in Washington), Joe asked Frank Waldrop of the *Washington Times-Herald* to write a speech for him on agriculture. As a lark, Waldrop dashed off a satire on standard agricultural oratory in a couple of hours and submitted it. Joe soon went before the same closed-door caucus of Republican senators that put him on the Rules Committee and read the speech practically verbatim, completely failing to see the humor Waldrop had intended. When word leaked out that Joe had called for price supports as high as 110 percent of parity, Washingtonians sniggered for weeks. To Waldrop, a veteran Capitol-watcher, this was proof that Joe was an amateur, an innocent, a vulnerable man out of his depth in a world of well-informed, shrewd, and ruthless power-brokers. Years later he scoffed at those who thought McCarthy a cynical politician;

the "parity" incident, he said, was "the irrevocable answer to Richard Rovere."[64]

In January 1954, after intensive peace-making efforts by Senators Knowland and Mundt, and a threat by Carl Hayden to cut off all subcommittee funds for lack of a "majority vote" on the body, Joe reluctantly agreed to the demands of subcommittee Democrats. He yielded exclusive authority to hire and fire staff members and agreed that minority senators could select their own counsel (they chose Bobby Kennedy) and a clerk. He also agreed that when the Democrats unanimously opposed public hearings on any issue, the question would be taken to the full Committee on Government Operations for decision by majority vote. McClellan, Jackson, and Symington backed the subcommittee's appropriation request and returned to their duties—six months and sixteen days after their dramatic walk-out. Jackson fussed a bit about one of the more extravagant claims of achievement made in the newly published subcommittee annual report, but the document was not formally challenged by the Democrats.[65]

The three senators were among many thousands of Americans who were shocked by the news in mid-January that McCarthy's national popularity had soared 16 percent since August. The Gallup poll reported that 50 percent of Americans interviewed held a favorable opinion of the senator. Republicans favored him by a whopping margin of 62 percent to 19 percent (with another 19 percent having no opinion), while Democrats were almost evenly divided, 39 percent to 38 percent (with 23 percent having no opinion). All major categories of occupational groups showed strong support: the "favorable" rating given by business and professional people was only a single point below the 50 percent given by manual workers. Of the major areas in the country, the East awarded McCarthy the highest approval, 55 percent, and the other regions were not far behind: 48 percent in the Midwest, 47 percent in the South, and 46 percent in the West.[66]

A painstaking analysis of McCarthy's many poll ratings by political scientist Michael Paul Rogin later concluded that perhaps the most significant characteristic of the senator's supporters was their party affiliation. Republicans, especially on the right-wing, were strongly pro-McCarthy. It is also true that Americans of both parties admired Joe simply because they identified him with anti-Communism. In the media the senator appeared to be the most outspoken, dedicated and active Red hunter in the country; his popularity reached its zenith during the much-publicized Fort Monmouth investigation. The Gallup polls consistently revealed the public's powerful aversion to Communism. In 1953, 81 percent of those polled thought that the Soviet Union sought world rule. Sixty-six percent did not believe that even ex-Communists should be allowed to teach in colleges and universities. Sixty-seven percent would not allow a pro-Communist to give a speech in their city. J. Edgar Hoover's popularity, 78 percent favorable (2 percent unfavorable), was higher than the President's. In early 1954, 74 percent thought there were still Communists in the federal government. McCarthy seemed to be hard at work tracking them down. Hadn't the FBI director himself vouched for his sincerity and integrity?[67]

There was another side to the January poll, however, that many headline writers overlooked. While the poll revealed a five to three ratio in favor of McCarthy, it also showed that those who had an opinion of the senator disapproved of his methods by a margin of 47 percent to 38 percent, with 15 percent declining to make a judgment. Manual workers gave the strongest backing to McCarthy's methods, but the margin was slim: 43 percent approval to 40 percent disapproval. The most frequently mentioned objections were "he goes too far," "he is too rough," and "uses methods like the Gestapo."[68]

Joe's power on election day was also called into question by the poll. Asked if they would be more or less likely to vote for a local G.O.P. candidate who had McCarthy's support, 45 percent said that the endorsement would not make a difference, while 26 percent replied "less likely." The favorable response of a mere 21 percent appeared to shatter the senator's claims to have a potent sway with voters.

When asked about the effect McCarthy was having on United States relations with our allies, 41 percent said "hurting" while 24 percent replied "helping." Pitted against Eisenhower for the G.O.P. presidential nomination in 1956, the President received 79 percent support to Joe's 9 percent.[69]

Newspapers carried several stories during the first month of 1954 pointing to increasing hostility toward McCarthy in some quarters. In Boston the intellectual community was outraged by McCarthy's treatment of Harvard physics professor Wendell H. Furry and Leon H. Kamin, a research assistant in Harvard's Department of Social Relations. In the course of the General Electric investigation, the two were brought into a televised public hearing and threatened, bullied, and slandered. Both men were ex-Communists, and both refused to take the Fifth Amendment. Their "crime" consisted of their unwillingness to provide McCarthy with the names of former Communist party associates. "Each time he refuses," the senator said angrily of Furry, "he will be cited for contempt. This will be another way, perhaps, of getting rid of Mr. Pusey's Fifth-Amendment

Communists." At one point Joe shouted, "To me it is inconceivable that a university which has had the reputation of being a great university would keep this type of creature on teaching our children."[70]

In New York *The Times* carried a letter signed by five distinguished former diplomats attacking the methods of Scott McLeod and assessing the "sinister results" of McCarthyism on the State Department. The signers, Norman Armour, Robert Woods Bliss, Joseph G. Grew, William Phillips, and G. Howland Shaw, asked if "we are not laying the foundations of a Foreign Service competent to serve a totalitarian government rather than the Government of the United States as we have heretofore known it." Without mentioning McCarthy by name, they warned, "Fear is playing an important part in American life at the present time."[71]

Press reports also indicated growing difficulties between McCarthy and the Army. Army officials were clearly disturbed by the senator's demand to question up to twenty former members of the Army's Loyalty and Security Appeals Board, which had passed on cases at Fort Monmouth. When the Army refused to produce the witnesses voluntarily, citing the Truman Executive Order that required secrecy on loyalty board appeals procedures, Joe threatened to subpoena the people in question. Private meetings between Army counsel John G. Adams and several G.O.P. congressional leaders and Administration officials, plus a personal visit by Adams to McCarthy, produced a delay in Joe's plans. But no one could be certain when the issue might suddenly resurface. Sherman Adams advised the Army counsel to prepare for a possible counterattack. It would involve the further adventures of Roy Cohn and G. David Schine.[72]

Schine had been drafted into the Army in early November and had reported to Fort Dix, New Jersey, for eight weeks of basic training. In late December Drew Pearson reported that Cohn had been calling Fort Dix's commander, Gen. Cornelius Ryan, two or three times a week to ask how Schine "was getting along," saying, "the senator wants to know." This resulted, the columnist said, in favored treatment of the subcommittee aide, such as being relieved of K.P. and guard duties. Pearson claimed that Ryan had asked Robert Stevens for advice, and that the Army Secretary replied, "This is one you've got to handle yourself."

The *Baltimore Sun* then quoted friends of Ryan who said that the general had complained of getting as many as four telephone calls in one day from Cohn. In late January the *New York Post* published an article on Schine based on interviews at Fort Dix. Schine's fellow recruits complained to reporters that the private lived the life of a visiting dignitary. He chatted with the company commander, regularly got weekends off, and was given an assortment of special privileges, such as freedom from K.P. and barracks cleaning duties. He often sat with the driver while a truck took inductees to and from rifle-range exercises. A recruit complained, "And one rainy day, after marching four miles to the rifle range, we got soaked taking target practice while Schine stayed in a heated communications shack and talked to some of the officers." The G.I.s also described Schine's luxurious special equipment. Said one:

> He had special mitten shaped gloves, with one finger, the trigger finger, separated from the rest. He had special boots, with straps and buckles on the side. He claimed the Army didn't have any that fitted him. He had a fur-lined hood, which he wore. He had an air mattress and a heavy down sleeping bag—and he never had to sweat out a full-time bivouac period at that.

Joe denied having personally taken any action on behalf of Schine, and he quoted General Ryan as saying that Schine was receiving "absolutely no special consideration." Sherman Adams was reliably informed that Cohn had in fact been applying considerable pressure on Ryan and that Schine had received favors. In his secret meeting with John G. Adams and others on January 21 concerning McCarthy's threat to subpoena the former members of the Loyalty and Security Appeals Board, the presidential assistant advised the Army counsel to prepare a detailed "chronology" of Cohn's actions. He thought it might prove to be a powerful weapon in the future should McCarthy escalate the controversy with the Army. On January 29 Army officials at Fort Dix announced a formal investigation of the charges surrounding Schine.[73]

The next day McCarthy held an executive hearing featuring testimony by Maj. Irving Peress, a dark, slightly balding, 36-year-old Army dentist stationed at Camp Kilmer, New Jersey. Peress had entered active duty as a captain on January 1, 1953. A short time later he submitted a form to the Army on which he wrote "federal constitutional privilege" concerning membership in any of the organizations declared subversive by the Attorney General. Following his basic training, Peress was sent to Fort Lewis, Washington, to await transportation to Yokahama, Japan. At his request, he received an emergency leave to return home to New York City because of the psychiatric problems of his wife and six-year-old daughter. He was then reassigned to Camp Kilmer, thirty miles from his home. Army Intelligence and the FBI were soon investigating the dentist as a possible security risk, and in August Peress took the Fifth Amendment again on an Army questionnaire. In early September he requested a promotion from captain to major. The promotion became effective on November 2.

During his appearance before McCarthy, Peress repeatedly pled the Fifth Amendment when asked about the Communist Party. Joe angrily implied that fellow Reds within the Army had helped the dentist's military career from the start, and he promised public hearings on the matter in mid-February. When he briefed reporters following the session, Joe listed the questions Peress had refused to answer, leaving the impression that he had discovered a subversive who was actively recruiting a Communist cell right under the Army's nose.[74]

Actually, the subcommittee had first learned about Peress in early December on a tip from Brig. Gen. Ralph W. Zwicker, the commanding officer at Camp Kilmer. (This would remain a well-guarded secret.) Zwicker had objected to Peress's promotion and had recommended that the dentist be relieved from duty immediately as a security risk. When Peress became a major, the general was outraged. After a conversation with General Lawton, a McCarthy sympathizer, Zwicker quietly approached the senator, supplying his staff with information on the case.[75]

In mid-January 1954 the Army finally got around to ordering Peress discharged, giving him the customary 90 days within which to select a termination date. He chose March 31. Thus Peress was on his way back to civilian life when McCarthy suddenly decided to haul him before the subcommittee and alert the press. It seemed obvious to Army and Administration officials that Joe intended to exploit the Peress case in his battle to force the Army to produce members of the Loyalty and Security Appeals Board. A Peress investigation could also be used to top stories and headlines about David Schine.

On February 1, two days after his appearance before McCarthy, Peress met with General Zwicker and asked for his immediate release from the Army. That same day McCarthy sent a letter by messenger to Secretary Stevens announcing a full probe of the case and recommending court-martial proceedings against Peress. With Stevens in the Far East, the letter was handled by John G. Adams.[76]

Joe's request for a $214,000 fund for his subcommittee came before the Senate on February 2. The debate, before packed galleries, lasted nearly three hours. The chief opponent of the appropriation was Allen J. Ellender of Louisiana, who tried annually to economize on the work of all investigating committees. Ellender's main argument was that the subcommittee was duplicating the work of others by probing Communists and subversion. Joe stormed and raged against the Southern Democrat, refusing to limit the future jurisdiction of the subcommittee and raising the possibility of new investigations into the *Amerasia* case ("one of the foulest cover-ups" in history) and the Voice of America. He claimed to have uncovered evidence of "very, very current espionage" at Fort Monmouth and declared that future hearings on the matter "will prove the most productive we ever held from the standpoint of decimating the ranks of the Communist party." (A report on the initial hearings had been placed on the desk of each senator a few days earlier.) Joe angrily demanded that the Army produce the former members of the Loyalty and Security Appeals Board, and he renewed his threat to subpoena them: "We intend to have those twenty persons, who cleared the Communists and sent them back to handle secret material, appear before the committee, so as to ascertain who hired them, who promoted them to those jobs, and why they cleared Communists." He also called upon the Army to court-martial Irving Peress, "who is a major in the United States Army as of this moment," and punish the officers who had failed to "expose" him or had played any part of his promotion. "This is the only way," he shouted, "to notify every Army officer that twenty years of treason are past and that this really is a new day."

When the heated clash ended, Joe demanded a roll-call vote on his request for funds. The implication was clear: he wanted to know exactly, in an election year, who was soft on the Reds. The vote was 85-1 in favor of the full appropriation. J. William Fulbright was the lone dissenter. Rarely, if ever, had the full Senate been brought to such shame by fear.[77]

Later that day, the Army announced Peress's honorable discharge. Joe was enraged by the unexpected action. "When they want to move fast," he said bitterly to Cohn, "they can shuffle those papers faster than you can see them." He publicly accused the Army of "highly improper" conduct and vowed to pursue the case further. Secretary Stevens, arriving in Washington from his Far East trip, promised a personal investigation of the honorable discharge. The Army and McCarthy were headed toward the most collossal collision of the decade.[78]

With his subcommittee fully funded for the coming year, McCarthy took off across the country for an eight-day round of Lincoln Day speeches. All expenses for the nine-city tour were picked up by the Republican National Committee, whose chairman, Leonard Hall, gave the senator his unequivocal endorsement. Joe's first appearance was in Charleston, West Virginia, the capital of the state in which he had found fame four years earlier. Before a crowd of 2,800 on a cold, wet night, he launched into flights of right-wing rhetoric so extreme that even veteran journalists must have flinched as they took notes. "The hard fact is," he said at one point, "that those who wear the label 'Democrat' wear with it the stain of a historic betrayal; wear it with the corrosion of unprecedented corruption; wear it with the blood of dying men who crawled up the hills of Korea while the politicians in the Democrat Party wrote invitations to the Communists to join them at the United Nations." The label "Democrat," he cried, was "stitched with the idiocy of a Truman; rotted by the deceit of an Acheson; corrupted by the red slime of a White."

With Jean at his side, Joe continued the slashing attacks in such places as Mt. Clemens, Michigan, and Aberdeen, South Dakota, as well as in Los Angeles and Dallas. Before a crowd of 1,000 at Eagles Hall in Madison he charged that John McCloy, former High Commissioner of Germany and currently head of the Chase National Bank of New York, had once issued an order for the destruction of all Army Intelligence files on Communists. McCloy denounced the story as "absolutely, utterly, and completely untrue," adding, "I've been a Republican longer than he has." A short time later Joe admitted "I was in error" about McCloy. But it was his only concession.

Reporters noticed that McCarthy rarely mentioned the President and seemed to ignore the Administration's accomplishments. During each speech he carried on his campaign to stop all aid to allies trading with Red China. "The question to be determined in this fall's election," he said, "is whether we are going to use American dollars indirectly to finance the blood trade." At a San Francisco news conference he told reporters he intended to press for a court-martial for "each and every" Army officer involved in the honorable discharge of Irving Peress, "a Fifth-Amendment Communist."

In Dallas, where he drew more than a thousand people to a $100-a-plate dinner, Joe gave his final address of the tour, so hoarse that he could barely speak. At a news conference he denied a report that Texas millionaires were backing him for the G.O.P. nomination in 1956 and gave his full support to the President. "The job he has been doing is not perfect. But it is so infinitely better than the job that has been done in the past twenty years of treason that there is no comparison." He twice refused to comment on the announcement that Gov. Allan Shivers would ask the Texas legislature to make membership in the Communist party a capital offense.[79]

After a brief vacation in the mountains of Mexico with right-wing movie actor Ward Bond and Texas millionaire Clint Murchison, Joe and Jean flew to New York to prepare for the scheduled public hearing on Peress. On the evening of February 17 a reckless driver rammed the taxicab in which Jean was riding. Joe stayed up with her all night and sent her to the hospital in the morning. When the televised hearing was called to order at the federal courthouse in Foley Square, Joe was suffering from a splitting headache.[80]

It was another "one-man" hearing, although Senators Dirksen and Potter had sent representatives. Army counsel Adams and General Zwicker were among the spectators. The first witness was Miss Ruth Eagle, a New York policewoman who had once belonged to the Communist party for two-and-one-half years as an undercover agent. She was called to document McCarthy's assertion that Peress was a Communist. Her testimony fell far short of that goal. When asked directly if Peress had been a member of the Communist party, the witness replied, "He appeared at our club meetings, and I believed that he was at that time." Cohn neglected to cite the dates of Miss Eagle's brief undercover activity, but at one point he said that her reports "go back to 1944."[81]

A few minutes after Irving Peress began to answer questions, Joe lost his temper completely and began to rail against the Army for granting the honorable discharge. He demanded the appearance that afternoon of the officer who signed the document, and gave the Army twenty-four hours to produce the names of all military personnel involved. "I think here you have the key to the deliberate Communist infiltration of our armed forces, the most dangerous thing. And the men responsible for the honorable discharge of a Communist are just as guilty as the man who belongs to the conspiracy himself." When Adams tried to answer a question at the end of a long McCarthy diatribe, Joe snapped, "John, I will not take any double-talk, any evasion on this."

Joe was savage toward Peress. The dentist refused to answer questions relating to Communism, so toward the conclusion of the hearing Joe hammered away at him to reveal the names, addresses, and occupations of relatives, in the hope that they might be persecuted by employers and neighbors. The witness was referred to repeatedly as a Communist conspirator.

Peress managed to land a few verbal blows of his own during the encounter, and at one point he quoted from Book seven of the Psalms: "His mischief shall return upon his own head and his violence shall come down upon his own pate." That line would later be recalled in connection with McCarthy's entire career.[82]

When the hearing recessed, John Adams released a letter of February 16 from Robert Stevens to McCarthy. In it the Army Secretary promised that hereafter commissions would not be awarded when loyalty data were refused and that honorable discharges would not be given to those failing to answer questions on the subject "when properly asked." He admitted that

the Army's system for discovering undesirables had broken down in the
Peress case and acknowledged that the dentist should not have been
promoted while under investigation. He contended, however, that the
Army did not possess sufficient evidence in the case to warrant a court-
martial. Stevens ordered the Inspector General of the Army to investigate
the entire matter.

Newspapers also carried some of McCarthy's comments on the letter,
made after the hearing. Joe termed Stevens' assertion that the Army lacked
enough facts to court-martial Peress a "completely incorrect statement."
He took issue with a phrase referring to political beliefs, calling it "Communist jargon." He suggested that Stevens must have been misinformed or
had merely signed a letter written by others, perhaps "holdover press
agents from the previous Administration." (Later studies would show that
a common bureaucratic logjam had prevented the Army from discharging
the dentist sooner. No credible evidence would ever be produced linking
Peress, a member of the left-wing American Labor Party, with subversion
or alleged subversives in the Army.)[83]

After leaving reporters, Joe skipped lunch to travel to Flower-Fifth
Avenue Hospital for a visit with Jean. There he received the gloomy news
that her ankle was fractured and would be in a cast for weeks. He returned
to the court house for a late afternoon hearing hungry, depressed, and
continuing to suffer from his headache. The scheduled witness at the
executive hearing was General Zwicker.[84]

That morning Zwicker had informed McCarthy privately that John
Adams had forbidden him to speak freely about the Peress case on the
ground of the Truman Executive order. Joe shrugged and appeared to take
this development in stride. Toward the end of the televised hearing,
however, the senator revealed a changed attitude when Zwicker balked at a
question. He warned, "I may say, General, you will be in difficulty if you
refuse to tell us what sensitive work a Communist was being considered for.
There is no Executive order for the purpose of protecting Communists. I
want to tell you right now, you will be asked that question this afternoon.
You will be ordered to make available that information." Still, Zwicker was
unprepared for what awaited him. He said a few days later, "Then I took the
stand and—boom! I never anticipated anything like it. It certainly was an
experience to me."[85]

Ralph Zwicker was a native of Stoughton, Wisconsin. He had grown up
in Madison and spent a year at the University of Wisconsin before entering
West Point. In World War II he served with the infantry in Normandy,
northern France. the Ardennes, the Rhineland, and Central Europe. His

decorations included the Silver Star, the Legion of Merit with Oak Leaf Cluster, the Bronze Star with two Oak Leaf Clusters and Arrowhead, the British Distinguished Service Order, and the French Legion of Honor and Croix de Guerre with Palm. After the war General Eisenhower publicly commended him. He graduated from the National War College and moved quickly up the ranks. He was assigned to Camp Kilmer in July 1953, four months after his promotion to brigadier general. A tall, trim, handsome man of 50, Zwicker seemed virtually a model of the professional soldier as he stepped before Senator McCarthy to take the oath.[86]

Zwicker was stiff, unfriendly, and unresponsive to questions, and Joe became angry with him almost immediately. The general denied having knowledge that Peress was a Communist, claimed that there was nothing he could have done to prevent the dentist's promotion, took refuge in the Executive order when asked about the honorable discharge, and even discredited the work of the subcommittee, by observing that it had unearthed no new evidence. McCarthy undoubtedly assumed that the general, a former ally, had been shaken badly by the discussion with John Adams concerning his testimony and was now more eager to protect his career than punish those responsible for Peress. Joe soon became abusive. "Don't be coy with me, General. . . . Don't you give me double-talk." "General," he bellowed at one point, "let's try and be truthful. I am going to keep you here as long as you keep hedging and hemming."

> General Zwicker. I am not hedging.
> The Chairman. Or hawing.
> General Zwicker. I am not hawing, and I don't like to have anyone impugn my honesty, which you just about did.
> The Chairman. Either your honesty or your intelligence; I can't help impugning one or the other . . .

Joe devised a hypothetical situation he considered identical to the Peress case and asked Zwicker if the general involved should not be removed from the military. When Zwicker tried to sidestep the question, Joe flew into a rage:

> The Chairman. You are ordered to answer it, General. You are an employee of the people.
> General Zwicker. Yes, sir.
> The Chairman. You have a rather important job. I want to know how you feel about getting rid of Communists.
> General Zwicker. I am all for it.

The Chairman. All right. You will answer that question, unless you take the Fifth Amendment. I do not care how long we stay here, you are going to answer it.

General Zwicker. Do you mean how I feel toward Communists?

The Chairman. I mean exactly what I asked you, General; nothing else. And anyone with the brains of a five-year-old child can understand that question. The reporter will read it to you as often as you need to hear it so that you can answer it, and then you will answer it.

General Zwicker. Start it over, please.

(The question was reread by the reporter.)

General Zwicker. I do not think he should be removed from the military.

The Chairman. Then, General, you should be removed from any command. Any man who had been given the honor of being promoted to general and who says, 'I will protect another general who protected Communists,' is not fit to wear that uniform, General. I think it is a tremendous disgrace to the Army to have this sort of thing given to the public. I intend to give it to them. I have a duty to do that. I intend to repeat to the press exactly what you said. So you know that. You will be back here, General.

McCarthy ordered Zwicker to reappear the following Tuesday for a public grilling.

The Chairman. In the meantime, in accordance with the order which you claim forbids you the right to discuss this case, you will contact the proper authority who can give you permission to tell the committee the truth about the case before you appear Tuesday, and request permission to be allowed to tell us the truth about the—

General Zwicker. Sir, that is not my prerogative, either.

The Chairman. You are ordered to do it.

General Zwicker. I am sorry, sir, I will not do that.

The hearing continued with the questioning of an Intelligence officer at Camp Kilmer. Very shortly, Joe attacked John Adams for "coaching" the witness and demanded that the Army counsel himself be sworn in as a witness. Adams refused, saying that he was Secretary Stevens's personal representative. Beside himself with anger, Joe ordered Adams, Zwicker, and the officers on the general's staff in attendance to leave the hearing room immediately. When they had filed out, he gaveled the session to a close.[87]

In a speech that evening at a dinner of the Traffic Club of New York, Joe said, "There was a disgraceful performance today, but I intend to find out who was responsible for covering up a Fifth-Amendment Communist who was an officer in the Army." He announced that General Zwicker would be recalled before an open hearing and said that he had asked the Army to produce its Adjutant General, Maj. Gen. William E. Bergin, as a witness. "It is up to Secretary Stevens to correct this situation quickly," he said. "He should take a new look at the top of the team to see whether this type of coddling of Communists will continue."

Joe also said that he was turning over the record of the Peress case to the Justice Department in the hope of obtaining criminal prosecution of the dentist for swearing falsely in his Army papers. He intended as well to have Peress cited for contempt for improperly invoking the Fifth Amendment seven times. The senator held, for example, that the witness's refusal to answer questions about relatives was not protected by the Constitution.[88]

The public was thoroughly confused by this time. The facts of the Peress case were far from clear. Was the dentist a Communist spy? If not, why did he persist in taking the Fifth Amendment? Was the Army hierarchy riddled with Reds? If not, what else could explain Peress's promotion and honorable discharge? If McCarthy did not have solid evidence in the matter, why was he so self-confident and outspoken? A senator would surely not make such grave charges lightly. Especially with a fellow Republican in the White House. It seemed clear to everyone that something was terribly wrong in Washington.

Moreover, newspapers were reporting hearings by a House Appropriations subcommittee into the Administration's claim to have fired 2,200 "security risks." Fewer than 5 percent of the cases, it was discovered, even involved suspected disloyalty. People had been dismissed for absurd reasons, including having relatives behind the Iron Curtain. Some cases were not dismissals at all but resignations or transfers. Not a single Communist had been found in any of the departments in Washington. Scott McLeod, a witness before the subcommittee, admitted that after a year in the State Department he had forced only eleven people from the payroll for "loyalty reasons," and seven of those cases had been initiated under the Truman administration. Columnists Joseph and Stewart Alsop observed, "Thus McLeod's personal score now stands at: Communists smoked out, 0; suspected dangerous thinkers abolished, 4." The public had every reason to be startled and puzzled.[89]

The confusion was compounded abroad, where many observers were convinced that America was in the grip of a witch-hunting hysteria. One newspaper in Copenhagen published a cartoon showing Truman being accused by McCarthy: "The committee has learned that the witness, Harry S. Truman, on July 21, 1945, had breakfast in Potsdam with a leading Communist named Joseph Stalin." The Peress and Zwicker affairs were to be followed closely by reporters and governments all over the world.[90]

General Zwicker returned to Camp Kilmer, incensed at McCarthy';s insults. He publicly disputed a report by the senator of a statement he had made in his testimony, calling it "slanted" and "absolutely not . . . truthful." He also wrote out a report on the encounter with McCarthy and sent it to the Pentagon. Chief of Staff Matthew B. Ridgeway immediately became indignant over the "affront" to one of his officers and consulted with Army Secretary Stevens. Other Army officials contacted the White House and Capitol Hill, complaining bitterly about McCarthy's conduct. The Army defied Joe's twenty-four-hour ultimatum to provide the names of all Army personnel connected with the promotion and discharge of Peress.

On Saturday morning, February 20, Stevens issued an order forbidding Army officers to appear before the subcommittee. He telephoned McCarthy in Albany to tell him of his order, and a stormy row ensued. According to "reliable sources," Joe asked Stevens if he would accept a subpoena to testify. When Stevens said he would take the matter under advisement, Joe snapped, "Well, then, consider yourself under subpoena," and he hung up. Army officials announced that evening that Stevens would appear before the senator the following Tuesday.

Stevens took Zwicker's report on the closed hearing of February 18 to Capitol Hill and gave a memorandum on it to subcommittee members. According to the memorandum, Joe had said to Zwicker: "You are a disgrace to the uniform. You're shielding Communist conspirators. You are going to be put on public display next Tuesday. You're not fit to be an officer. You're ignorant." The wording was inaccurate, but the substance of the quotation correctly conveyed McCarthy's attitude. Senators Jackson and McClellan said they would press immediately for the release of the hearing transcript.[91]

Joe, rushing between subcommittee hearings and almost nightly speaking engagements, taunted Stevens repeatedly, referring to him as "a fine, innocent, unknowing Secretary of the Army who refuses to clean house," a "good, loyal American" who was under the influence of "the wrong elements," and an "awful dupe." When Joe condemned the Secretary's order placing the subcommittee off limits as "unfair to loyal officers," Stevens fired back with a strongly worded statement defending his action. "I cannot permit the loyal officers of our armed services to be subjected to such unwarranted treatment. The prestige and morale of our armed forces are too important to the security of the nation to have them weakened by unfair attacks on our officer corps." He said that he himself would be "glad" to appear before the subcommittee because "since assuming office I have made it clear that I intend to take every necessary action to rid the Army of subversives." Joe, in Philadelphia to receive a "good citizenship" award from a chapter of the Sons of the American Revolution, said that the issue raised by Stevens "is whether the Army is supreme over the Congress . . . and can enjoy special dictatorial immunity in covering up its own wrongdoings."[92]

On Monday, February 22, in response to demands by both Republicans and Democrats, the unedited transcript of General Zwicker's testimony was made public. *The New York Times* published the entire document. Editorial outrage appeared immediately throughout the country. The *Times* described McCarthy as "arrogant, narrow-minded and reckless." The *Chicago Tribune,* abandoning its hard-line pro-McCarthy position, suggested that the senator learn to distinguish the role of investigator from the role of avenging angel; "We do not believe Senator McCarthy's behavior toward General Zwicker was justified and we expect it has injured his cause of driving the disloyal from the government service." Columnist David Lawrence, a longtime McCarthy apologist, sighed, "That was a bad mistake on the senator's part." Conservative columnist H. V. Kaltenborn dropped his support of McCarthy entirely: "He has become completely egotistic, arrogant, arbitrary, narrow-minded, reckless, and irresponsible. Power has corrupted him."[93]

Senator Potter, who had consistently backed McCarthy during hearings, was stunned when he read the transcript. He later termed Joe's conduct "a distorted, twisted, circus performance." Potter immediately fired Robert L. Jones, the staff man he had sent to the hearing, for making an "unauthorized" pro-McCarthy statement to reporters after the session. (Jones promptly announced his candidacy for the Senate seat held by Margaret Chase Smith. He had had McCarthy's support in the race even before his dismissal, including Joe's pledge to raise funds from his friends in Texas. Jones told the press he had quit Potter's staff and said in a formal statement: "It is obvious that very powerful sources were determined that I should not oppose Mrs. Smith in the Maine Republican primaries. I am thoroughly convinced that this is the handiwork of devious left-wing elements who are fearful of a bitter political showdown in Maine between the forces of Americanism and international liberalism.")[94]

General Zwicker, contacted by reporters at his home, said that he supported what McCarthy was trying to do "100 percent," adding, "but there's a way to do it." He explained that his reluctance to discuss the Peress case with the senator involved his duty to obey the Truman Executive order. "I'm an officer of the Army," he said. "There are certain things I'm not permitted to do. To begin with, I don't know who in the Department of the Army issued the order directing that Peress be given an honorable discharge. I'm not supposed to know."[95]

Stevens's appearance before the subcommittee was postponed two days at Senator Dirksen's request while he and other G.O.P. leaders worked frantically behind the scenes to avoid an embarrassing confrontation. Joe attempted to smother headlines produced by the Zwicker testimony by announcing a new case of a "known Communist" in the Army. He called for a public hearing the next day and invited the television networks to broadcast the session. He seemed curiously lighthearted all the while he talked with reporters; one newsman wrote, "Nearly every word of his statement was punctuated with chuckles . . ."[96]

Joe was no doubt relishing the thought of the humiliation he was about to inflict upon the Army. His new case concerned Mrs. Annie Lee Moss, a civilian employee of the Army Signal Corps. The tip had unquestionably come from FBI personnel, who also alerted HUAC. In 1951 J. Edgar Hoover had offered the Army and the Civil Service Commission an under-cover agent to testify to Mrs. Moss's Communist party activities. The agent was not summoned, and Mrs. Moss continued to be employed by the Signal Corps. Joe now had access to the agent and also, according to Don Surine, possessed a photostat of Mrs. Moss's Communist party membership card. Surine would later boast, "It was an open-and-shut damn deal."[97]

With the exception of Senator Symington, who was in Europe, all of the members of the subcommittee, plus the new minority counsel, Bobby Kennedy, were on hand for the public hearing of February 23. The witness was Mrs. Mary Stalcup Markward, who had been an undercover agent for the FBI from 1943 through October, 1949. She testified that she knew Mrs. Moss had been a Communist from party lists of card-carrying, dues-paying members. Senator McClellan raised the possibility that the Annie Lee Moss named by the witness might not be the same person currently employed by the Army. Rushing to upstage the subcommittee, HUAC had summoned Mrs. Moss to a closed-door hearing the day before, and con-gressmen had come away doubting that Mrs. Moss had been a Red. She did not take refuge in the Fifth Amendment at any time and had flatly denied any affiliation with the Communist party. Mrs. Markward admitted that she probably could not identify Mrs. Moss; she was not sure she had ever met her. But the current Mrs. Moss's employment record and address, she said, matched the data available to her in the 1940s.

Joe solemnly assured everyone that he, his staff, and the FBI had checked this case thoroughly and that there was no mistake: the Annie Lee Moss who was a Pentagon cafeteria worker in 1945 was the same woman who today was in the Army's code room in the Signal Corps "handling the incoding [sic] and decoding of confidential and top-secret messages. . . ." Mrs. Markward noted that Mrs. Moss's name had been dropped from the party rolls in 1945. Joe expressed complete confidence that she was still a Red. "There is nothing in the record to show that she ever broke with the party." Joe also took a well-aimed blast at Stevens:

> May I say at this time that I sincerely hope that all the facts in this case are brought to the attention of the Secretary of the Army. I think he has been grossly misinformed, misadvised. I do not think that Bob Stevens wants to protect Communists in the Army any more than any member of this committee does. I hope he gets all of the details of this case.[98]

After the hearing, the Army declared that Mrs. Moss had no access to codes, to the cryptographic rooms, or to "uncoded top-secret," secret, or confidential messages. She was simply a communications relay machine operator, "who feeds into or receives from automatic machines unintelligible code messages both classified and unclassified." Officials also said that an Army investigation of Mrs. Moss as a possible security risk was underway and had been started "prior to any action by the McCarthy subcommittee." Mrs. Moss, ill and at home, told reporters that she had "no knowledge of Communism whatsoever" and "never was a member of the Communist party or anything else." The United Press quoted her as saying that she had "never been in a code room in my life."[99]

The next morning, Roy Cohn opened the hearing by announcing that two top Communist leaders had been subpoenaed the evening before and had decided to confess all they knew to the FBI. Their testimony, Cohn said proudly, had confirmed the charge by Mrs. Markward concerning Annie Lee Moss. Joe expressed hope that the FBI would turn the witnesses over to the subcommittee later for public questioning. "I may say that the bureau has never been unreasonable in the past, and I am sure they will not be in this case." (The witnesses were never heard of again. Senator Dirksen told a reporter it was his "impression" that the man and wife described by Cohn were actually FBI undercover agents inadvertently subpoenaed as bonafide Communist party members.)[100]

Annie Lee Moss was then summoned to take the oath. Mrs. Moss, a black woman in her late forties, wore a fur-collared coat and a dark beret pulled down over the tops of her ears. She came into the hearing room slowly, leaning on the arm of her attorney. She appeared ill and was trembling as she went to the witness stand. She removed her glasses occasionally and wiped her eyes. After some considerable bickering with the attorney, Joe agreed to permit the witness to testify later when her health improved. He bluntly referred to her several times as a Communist and implied that her lawyer was too. When Senator Jackson objected to the accusation against the attorney, Joe angrily attacked him for his long absence from the subcommittee. "If you had been sitting with us over the past four months, watching members of the Communist conspiracy violating their oaths as lawyers and misinforming and misadvising clients, then you would not make the statement." Joe declared of Mrs. Moss, "I am not interested in this woman as a person at all." The issue was all-important: "Who in the military, knowing that this lady was a Communist, promoted her from a waitress to a code clerk? The information we have is that she has no special ability as a decoding clerk. We know that she has been handling classified material despite the statement issued last night by the military."

Two other witnesses appeared during the hearing. One, a woman described as having recruited Annie Lee Moss into the Communist party, took the Fifth Amendment on all questions. The second, Mrs. Charlotte Oram, also appealed to the Constitution when asked about party membership but said that until a day earlier she had neither seen nor heard of Annie Lee Moss. This directly contradicted testimony by Mrs. Markward, who claimed that Mrs. Oram had had access to the party records containing the suspect's name. When Mrs. Markward was asked if she recognized Mrs. Moss on the witness stand, she said that she could not be positive but that information in the party records indicated that the subcommittee had subpoenaed the right person. She specifically recalled that the Communist Annie Lee Moss, about ten years earlier, had been 38, a Negro, a worker in the Pentagon cafeteria, and had lived at an address very close, if not identical, to the address of the woman on the witness stand. Roy Cohn flatly ruled out any possibility of mistaken identity.[101]

After the hearing, the subcommittee Republicans walked to room P-54, a small office tucked away in a corridor near the rotunda. For the last two days Karl Mundt had been trying to get them together with Army Secretary Stevens to work out a peaceful settlement of their dispute. For the sake of

G.O.P. unity, all parties agreed to a luncheon the day before Stevens was to face McCarthy. Reporters were tipped off about the meeting, and when the door opened two hours later fifty newsmen and cameramen were on hand. Photographers swarmed into the room, taking shots of the senators and the luncheon plates splattered with remains of fried chicken. Joe was all smiles. Secretary Stevens sat stony-faced and silent on a green leather sofa. After a time, at the request of photographers, he agreed to smile and shake hands with McCarthy.

Mundt strode before a microphone and read a "memorandum of understanding" between the Army and the subcommittee. It sounded like a complete surrender by Stevens. The Army Secretary agreed to permit officers to appear before the subcommittee, agreed to furnish all the names of military personnel involved in the promotion and honorable discharge of Irving Peress, and agreed to make these men available to the subcommittee if it chose to question them. On the other hand, General Zwicker's reappearance before the senators was temporarily postponed, and the showdown meeting scheduled for the following day was canceled.

Thoroughly delighted with himself, Mundt spoke freely to reporters. Stevens could say little in response to the often hostile questions that greeted him. When one newsman asked if the memorandum was a "retreat," he replied simply, "I do not consider I am a person that capitulates or retreats."

Journalists speculated that the decision to come to terms with McCarthy had originated with the President. This was denied by Mundt and press secretary Hagerty. Eisenhower had returned to Washington earlier that day from a Palm Springs, California, golfing vacation and had first learned of the agreement, Hagerty said, from a news ticker in the White House.[102]

Robert Stevens was a friendly, well-meaning business executive. He had graduated from Yale, served in both world wars, and had been decorated with the Legion of Merit and the Distinguished Service Medal. He was heading the family textile firm in New Jersey when summoned to Washington two months earlier. Nothing in his experience had prepared him for the political machinations in which he was now embroiled. One quipster later observed that when Stevens walked into room P-54 to confront the likes of Mundt, Dirksen, and McCarthy, he was "like a goldfish in a tank of barracuda."[103]

A day earlier the Army Secretary had consulted privately with Nixon, Senator Knowland, Dirksen, John Adams, Deputy Attorney General William P. Rogers, and two White House aides about his upcoming appearance before the subcommittee. He was told frankly that he would get the worst of it if he had to face McCarthy. The Army looked weak on the Peress case. Moreover, Stevens' order concerning officers and the subcommittee would not hold up; the only official in the Executive branch immune from a subpoena was the President. There was a consensus that compromise was imperative, and Dirksen was dispatched to talk with Joe. Stevens's willingness to meet with the subcommittee Republicans the next day and to agree to their demands was a reflection of what he had heard from the Vice-President and the others. His agreeableness during what came to be called the "Chicken Luncheon" was grounded on a sincere desire to do what was best for his party and the Army. The memorandum, he hoped, had achieved at least a stalemate with the senator from Wisconsin.[104]

Stevens was also encouraged by the fact that the subcommittee senators had promised at the luncheon to extend fair treatment to the Army officers called upon to testify. After leaving the battery of reporters and cameramen, he returned to his office and told Army Chief of Staff Ridgeway, Assistant Secretary of Defense Fred A. Seaton, and others that he had defended the integrity of the officer corps by winning acceptance of a subcommittee policy in which officers would be treated in the future like gentlemen. When Pentagon officials read a copy of the memorandum a short time later and realized that it lacked any reference to the sensitive issue of subcommittee conduct, they knew that the Army Secretary was in trouble.

Within a few hours Stevens tasted the ashes. The initial press reaction to the memorandum, on the whole, was bitterly critical. The *New York Herald Tribune* declared, "Under severe party pressure, the Secretary of the Army surrendered to a senator who had humiliated and bullied an Army general." The *New York Post* wrote, "Secretary Stevens, after a two-hour brain-washing session with Joe McCarthy, unconditionally surrendered to the Piltdown politicians." The *Chicago Sun-Times* editorialized, "Secretary Stevens' unconditional surrender to Senator McCarthy is shocking and dismaying." The *Milwaukee Journal* stated, "If it was no retreat, it was total collapse." The *Detroit Free Press* compared February 24, 1954 to July 21, 1861: "That was the date of the first Battle of Bull Run." The *Washington Post* published a cartoon of Stevens handing McCarthy his sword, and the senator saying, "Okay, Bud, when I want you again I'll send for you."

According to *The New York Times,* the mood at the Pentagon was "bitter and gloomy." One senior staff member reportedly said, "Private Schine is the only man in the Army today with any morale." Army brass were privately referring to the secretary as "Retreating Robert." Adlai Stevenson told a reporter, "The abuse and humiliation to which General Zwicker has been exposed has now been officially condoned."

Stevens, reading the bad news on the ticker, became increasingly worried and despondent. The worst blow fell when a reporter quoted McCarthy saying shortly after the luncheon that the Army Secretary could not have given in "more abjectly if he had got down on his knees." (Joe later denied making the statement.)

Reporters began flocking outside Stevens's office, amid rumors that the secretary would resign. Stevens avoided newsmen and photographers for the rest of the day. That evening he telephoned several senators, sobbing and threatening to quit because he had "lost standing" at the Pentagon. He also called press secretary Hagerty and other White House staff members seeking guidance on how to respond to the crisis.

Nixon, Rogers, Sherman Adams, Hagerty, and several others quietly assembled in the White House and drafted a statement they hoped would be signed by all of the subcommittee Republicans. It was designed principally to mollify Stevens, who was reportedly "steaming mad." At Nixon's suggestion, the President summoned Everett Dirksen to the White House. The two men went over the document, and Eisenhower asked Dirksen to present it to his colleagues and obtain their signatures. "I'd like to see if you can do this," he said. The Illinois senator was also asked to consult with all members of the subcommittee to get Roy Cohn fired, to end one-man hearings, and to strip McCarthy of the power to issue subpoenas on his own.

The President, Hagerty noted in his diary, was "very mad and getting fed up—it's his army and he doesn't like McCarthy's tactics at all." He told his press secretary firmly, "This guy McCarthy is going to get into trouble over this. I'm not going to take this lying down." Eisenhower had tolerated McCarthy long enough. The effort to humiliate the Army exhausted his patience. The President would still refuse to attack the senator openly; his disdain for McCarthy was too great, and he feared a reaction in Congress that might be to the senator's advantage and further divide the G.O.P. He would, however, pay careful attention to Joe's every move and take several quiet steps to thwart his political power. "My friends tell me it won't be long in this Army stuff before McCarthy starts using my name instead of Stevens," Eisenhower told Hagerty. "He's ambitious. He wants to be President. He's the last guy in the world who'll ever get there, if I have anything to say."

Dirksen and his three Republican colleagues met for hours in a cloakroom not far from the Senate chamber. All were willing to say that Stevens had not capitulated and that all witnesses, in and out of uniform, would be treated with respect. But Joe firmly refused to accept wording that implied any past abuse of witnesses; to do otherwise would be a public admission of personal misconduct. The quartet finally agreed to sign a modified version of the Nixon draft, and at 4:00 P.M. the Vice-President carried the statement back to the White House and presented it to a group assembled in the East Wing.

The group group included Stevens, Acting Secretary of Defense Roger M. Kyes, Sherman Adams, William Rogers, Fred Seaton, White House counsel Bernard M. Shanley, and three White House aides. The conference lasted an hour and a half. When it broke up, Stevens was flatly unwilling to accept the statement submitted by the subcommittee Republicans, and hope for a quiet settlement of the situation seemed shattered. Nixon, Stevens, Adams, and Kyes then joined the President in his study for some further strategy-making.

Shortly before 6:00 P.M. Dirksen and McCarthy appeared before reporters. Informed about the meeting in the East Wing, they announced that there would be no statement released by the subcommittee Republicans. "There was a question," Dirksen said, "whether or not a certain word or phrase might be interpreted as critical of past conduct." As a peace-making gesture, he said also that he did not interpret the memorandum as a capitulation by Army Secretary Stevens. When Joe was asked if he agreed, he grinned broadly and said, "I agree on that. It was just a case of reaching an agreement." Surreptitiously, he gently kicked a correspondent in the shins as he made the statement.

By 6:00 P.M. the conferees in the President's study had agreed that Stevens would issue a statement in his own defense. The statement, revised by Nixon and strengthened by Eisenhower, had originally been intended for use by Stevens before the subcommittee. The Army Secretary was also given permission to make his presentation from the White House with the public understanding that it had the President's complete backing.

Fifteen minutes later reporters were admitted to Hagerty's office, where Stevens began reading his statement in a steady voice. The Secretary stated that the memorandum had been misinterpreted and that he had never "receded . . . from any of the principles upon which I stand." He continued, "I shall never accede to the abuse of Army personnel under any circumstances, including committee hearings. I shall never accede to them being browbeaten or humiliated. I do not intend them to be deprived of counsel when the matter under consideration is one of essential interest to me as Secretary, as was the case with General Zwicker." Stevens added, "From assurances which I have received from members of the subcommittee, I am confident that they will not permit such conditions to develop in the future."

When Stevens had finished, press secretary Hagerty told reporters, "On behalf of the President, he has seen the statement. He approves and endorses it 100 percent." A reporter then asked Stevens if he would continue as Army Secretary. When Stevens paused momentarily, Hagerty answered the question for him, "Of course."

Stevens returned to the Pentagon and was applauded by his staff. Smiling broadly, he said, "We've certainly got a Commander-in-Chief. He stepped right up and hit a home run."

Joe was in his office, surrounded by reporters, when a newsman took down the Stevens text by telephone and read it to the senator. His first reaction was an obscene phrase. Joe then charged that the Secretary had made a "completely false statement" by claiming assurances that future witnesses would not be "browbeaten or humiliated." He said that he made it clear to Stevens that if witnesses "are not frank and truthful—whether military personnel or not—they will be examined vigorously to get the truth about Communist activities." He added angrily, "I very carefully explained to the Secretary a number of times that he was Secretary of the Army and not running the committee." Joe was perturbed as well about the assertion that General Zwicker had been denied counsel. "He knows that Zwicker did not demand counsel."[105]

After the press conference, Joe took Urban Van Susteran (in Washington seeking a judgeship) and a *Time* magazine reporter home with him to the house he and Jean had moved into a month earlier. It was an eight-room, three-bath house on Third Street N.E., a short stroll from the Capitol. Jean's mother, Mrs. Elizabeth F. Kerr, had purchased it; the McCarthys rented half, and she lived in the other half. A dining room was stacked high with some 200 boxes—unopened wedding presents from the previous September. The kitchen contained a load of groceries that Jean had ordered by long-distance from her hospital bed. The telephone rang constantly. (Joe had a publicly listed number.) Twenty or thirty people trooped in and out during the evening, sampling bourbon, wandering into the kitchen, cornering the senator for an earnest conversation. Several times Joe sank into a chair muttering, "I'm getting old." The reporter later observed, "He is 44. His digestion is bad, and he has sinus trouble. But he is not slowing down, and he is decidedly not mellowing."[106]

The President's defense of his beleaguered Army Secretary appeared to trigger a rebellion in Washington against McCarthy's excesses. The day after Stevens read his defiant statement from the White House, G.O.P. leaders hastily summoned a session of the Senate Republican Policy Committee and set in motion a study aimed at curbing one-man inquiries by any senator. As the study was described to newsmen, it was clear that the Republicans were aiming at McCarthy. That same day, Senators McClellan and Jackson insisted successfully that Joe cancel a closed-door hearing he had scheduled in New York for February 27. The Democrats argued that they had not received adequate advance notice and would be unable to attend. The fact that Joe had summoned undisclosed "military personnel" for questioning no doubt intensified their objection. Senator Potter expressed the belief that in the future the other six members of the subcommittee would have a greater participation in the affairs of that body.[107]

Joe appeared uncustomarily conciliatory throughout the day. When asked for his reaction to the President's support of Stevens, he replied, "Eisenhower said he was against browbeating witnesses—I am too." He was obliged to add, however, that he would continue to expose Communists, "even if it embarrasses my own party."[108]

The influential political commentator Walter Lippmann then published a much-discussed column calling McCarthy "a candidate for supreme boss—for the dictatorship—of the Republican Party."

> This is the totalitarianism of the man: his cold, calculated, sustained and ruthless effort to make himself feared. That is why he has been staging a series of demonstrations, each designed to show that he respects nobody, no office, and no institution in the land, and that everyone at whom he growls will run away.

Lippmann believed that McCarthy's attacks on the Army were part of an effort to intimidate the Commander-in-Chief. He called for resistance to the senator, urging Republicans to realize the threat McCarthy posed to the G.O.P. and to the country.[109]

Columnists Joseph and Stewart Alsop also thought that Joe's long-range target was Eisenhower. "If the President permits just one more appeasement of Senator McCarthy, he can say goodbye to his own authority in his administration, in his party and in the Congress." *Time* magazine, in a cover-story on McCarthy, declared, "Politically, Joe is expendable, and the time to spend him appears to have come." The widely read magazine called for bold action by Eisenhower. "No one but the President can get McCarthy out of his dominant position in the headlines—a position from which he gives the false impression of dominating the government." Other voices in the press were equally adamant.[110]

On March 1 the Administration stripped Scott McLeod of his authority over State Department personnel. McLeod had been under fire for making five highly partisan Lincoln Day speeches and for causing turmoil among department employees. One Foreign Service veteran had recently resigned, complaining that McLeod had created a department "permeated by fear and intimidation." This action, announced on the authority of John Foster Dulles, was widely interpreted as a blow against McCarthy. Joe told reporters he would demand a full explanation from the Secretary of State.[111]

On March 2 Republican National Committee Chairman Leonard Hall met with reporters at the White House following a session with the President on McCarthy. While Hall tried to evade a number of questions, he had clearly lost the enthusiasm that had prompted him to call Joe a "great asset" to the G.O.P. just three weeks earlier. The Zwicker confrontation was foremost on his mind. "I don't think any one would say generals in our Army are not fighting Communism," he exclaimed. Hall also admitted that the McCarthy uproar could be hurting G.O.P. chances for victory in the fall elections.[112]

Hall's comments, made a day before the President's weekly news conference, stirred much excitement. Rumors were already all over Washington that Ike was boiling at McCarthy and would express himself in no uncertain terms when he met with reporters. Press secretary Hagerty would neither confirm nor deny the rumors. All of this was enough to prompt Joe to expect the worst. He announced a press conference immediately after the President had spoken and invited television cameras to be present. He then drafted an angry statement intended as a reply.[113]

The presidential news conference of March 3 was attended by a record-breaking 256 reporters. Eisenhower opened the proceeding by reading a prepared statement. It began with the admission that the Department of the Army had made "serious errors" in the Peress case. This was not news, for Stevens had said this a month earlier, and a chronology of the case released by the Army on February 26 had pointed to several bureaucratic snarls as Army officials processed the dentist's papers, investigated his loyalty reservations, and dispatched his personal file back and forth across the country. (Peress was promoted automatically, the Army explained, along with 7,000 other doctors and dentists, under an amendment of the Doctor's Draft Law. He was granted an honorable discharge because officials knew of no "overt act" on which to base charges. The Army had learned from an earlier case that it could not give a dishonorable discharge to a man for taking the Fifth Amendment on a loyalty form.) Eisenhower added that steps were being taken to insure that such mistakes would be avoided in the future. "I am confident," he said, "that Secretary Stevens will be successful in this effort."

Eisenhower's only references to McCarthy were cautious and indirect; the senator's name was not mentioned. He said that the Administration had not suggested that any subordinate "violate his convictions or principles or submit to any kind of personal humiliation when testifying before congressional committees or elsewhere." He backed the study of committee procedures underway in the Senate. He also made a vague reference to "disregard of the standards of fair play recognized by the American people." Beyond that, the President chose not to go. A battery of questions from reporters elicited little else on the subject. Many newsmen, hungry for headlines, were bitterly disappointed. At one point Joseph Alsop whispered to Willard Edwards, "Why, the yellow son of a bitch!"[114]

Edwards, a McCarthy confidant, realized that Joe's prepared reply was far too incendiary. He ran to the street, flagged a cab, and sped for the Senate Office Building. While Edwards was en route, Joe's secretary, Mary Driscoll, took down the President's statement in shorthand over the telephone. Three wire service reporters burst into the office a few minutes later and showed Joe the Associated Press lead. The quickly prepared story inaccurately described the statement as a strong anti-McCarthy attack. Joe hastily read Mary Driscoll's typewritten reproduction and saw the discrepancy between the news account and the actual statement. He made a few minor adjustments in his own prepared remarks and decided to strike one particularly volatile sentence: "Far too much wind has been blowing from high places in defense of this Fifth-Amendment Communist Army officer." But he still failed to appreciate how much stronger his statement was than the President's. By the time Willard Edwards reached the office, Joe was reading his reply to the reporters. Edwards interrupted, pleading with the senator to withdraw or modify his remarks. But Joe refused to listen. Edwards later wrote sadly, "It was all downhill for him from that day."[115]

Joe began by being condescending as well as self-righteous. He claimed that "this silly tempest in a teapot" had occurred only because "we dared to bring to light the cold, unpleasant facts about a Fifth-Amendment Communist officer who was promoted, given special immunity from duty outside the United States, and finally given an honorable discharge with the full knowledge of all concerned that he was a member of the Communist party." In a direct attack at Zwicker, he said, "If a stupid, arrogant, or witless man in a position of power appears before our committee and is found aiding the Communist party, he will be exposed. The fact that he might be a general places him in no special class so far as I am concerned."

Joe then turned to Eisenhower:

> I hope that the President realizes the reason for the gleeful
> shouting of every un-American element over what they con-
> sider a fight between those who honestly oppose Com-
> munism.
>
> I think that their joy will be shortlived. When the shouting
> and the tumult dies, the American people and the President
> will realize that this unprecedented mudslinging against the
> committee by extreme left-wing elements of the press and
> radio was caused because another Fifth-Amendment Com-
> munist in government was finally dug out of the dark recesses
> and exposed to public view.

Reporters also quoted the deleted sentence, crossed out of the statement in pencil.[116]

McCarthy's violent reaction to the President's moderately critical statement produced shock waves felt all over the country. Joe soon received telephone calls from several leading Republicans, including one Cabinet member, condemning him for extremism and announcing the cessation of any further relations. *The New York Times* wrote of "a struggle that might have lasting effects on the unity of the Republican party." A Democratic senator asked facetiously if "this open declaration of war requires approval by the Senate."[117]

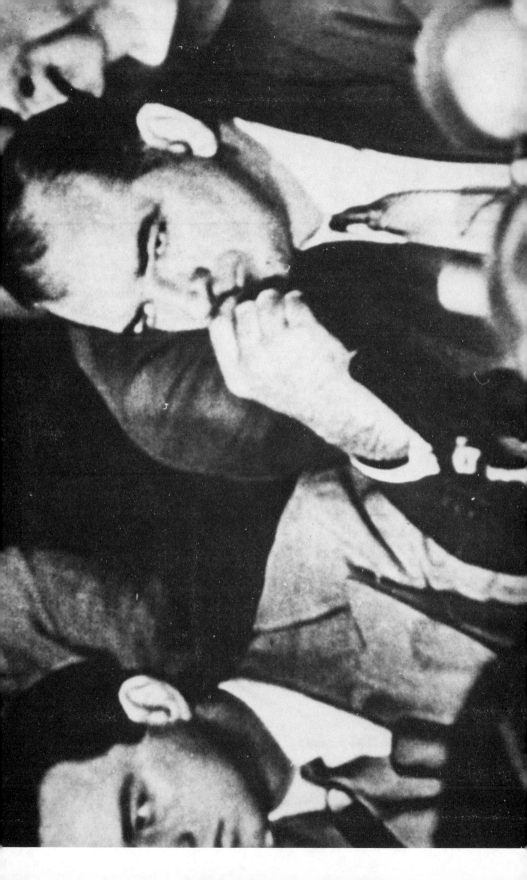

McCarthy and Roy Cohn during the 1954 Army-McCarthy hearings. (*Photos from the film* Point of Order *by Emile de Antonio)*

McCarthy and rural constituents, 1956. State Senator Gerald Lorge is seated directly across from McCarthy. *(Photo courtesy Gerald Lorge)*

McCarthy and his wife, Jean, shortly after the adoption of their daughter, Tierney, in early 1957. *(Photo courtesy Ray Kiermas)*

A NATIONAL
OBSESSION

Eisenhower was the target of harsh criticism for his failure to condemn McCarthy at the press conference. James Reston commented, "President Eisenhower turned the other cheek today, and Sen. Joseph R. McCarthy, always an obliging fellow, struck him about as hard as the position of the President will allow." The *Washington Post* thought that Joe's reply may have inadvertently done the President a favor: "His challenge gives Mr. Eisenhower another chance to substitute leadership for the weaseling of yesterday. For, left alone, the effect of Mr. Eisenhower's proclamation, no matter how well intentioned, could only be to compound the disgraceful surrender by Secretary Stevens." John F. Kane, special assistant to Army Secretary Stevens, resigned his post, protesting that his chief had not received the "fighting support" he deserved in the controversy with McCarthy. Herblock published a cartoon depicting a leering McCarthy clutching a bloody butcher's cleaver. Before him stood Eisenhower, drawing a feather from a scabbard. "Have a care, sir," said the President.[1]

Many observers attributed Eisenhower's approach toward McCarthy to politics. This was a favorite argument of Democrats: Ike would do nothing that might imperil G.O.P. success in the fall elections. On March 6, in a nationally broadcast speech delivered in Miami, Adlai Stevenson charged that "a group of political plungers had persuaded the President that McCarthyism is the best Republican formula for political success." He called the Republican Party "half McCarthy and half Eisenhower," and said that it had embarked on a campaign of "slander, dissension, and deception" in order to win the 1954 congressional elections."

Vacationing in Miami at the time, Joe announced that he would ask the networks for thirty minutes of equal time to reply. When Leonard Hall read this in the newspapers, he wired the networks himself, requesting equal time in the name of the Republican National Committee. "This is not a matter for personal rebuttal by any individual," he said in a formal statement. "We will designate our spokesman, who will speak for the party." Joe told reporters that Hall was "completely justified" in asking for time, and said that he would request an additional half hour. He threatened to file an appeal with the Federal Communications Commission if his demand was refused. It was widely known that his friend Robert E. Lee was on the F.C.C.

When Joe stepped off a plane in New York from Miami he learned that the networks had accepted Hall's request and rejected his. Infuriated, he vowed that the networks "will grant me time or learn what the law is. I guarantee that." Late that same day Hall announced that Vice-President Nixon would be delivering the Administration's reply to Stevenson.

Hall's move against McCarthy marked the first time a Republican leader had said openly that he favored someone else over the senator to represent the party and the Administration. It seemed certain from the start that Hall had presidential support. *The New York Times* reported, "The decision reflected increasing White House irritation with the methods employed by Senator McCarthy." Reporters soon learned that the President had lectured Republican congressional leaders in his office for 45 minutes, angrily insisting that McCarthy no longer be permitted to present himself as spokesman for the G.O.P. Eisenhower personally selected Nixon to make the network address. *Time* magazine commented, "It was a studied repudiation of Senator McCarthy."[2]

On the evening of March 8 the President made another revealing move. At the White House Correspondents Association dinner, he encouraged the president of the association to ask Robert Stevens to stand up and take a bow. This was unusual in that few people were ever introduced at the annual dinners. When the Army Secretary stood, Eisenhower quickly joined the reporters in vigorous clapping.[3]

The next day Republican Senator Ralph Flanders, the 73-year-old "quiet man" from Vermont, delivered a blistering attack against McCarthy from the Senate floor. McCarthy, he said, was "doing his best to shatter" the Republican party, "by intention or through ignorance." He belonged to a "one-man party" and "its name is 'McCarthyism,' a title which he has proudly accepted." Flanders surveyed international trouble spots and warned that the world "seems to be mobilizing for the great battle of Armageddon. Now is a crisis in the agelong warfare between God and the Devil for the souls of men." And what was McCarthy's role in this cataclysmic struggle? he asked. "He dons his war paint. He goes into his war dance. He emits his war whoops. He goes forth to battle and proudly returns with the scalp of a pink Army dentist."[4]

Republican senator John Sherman Cooper warmly congratulated his colleague, telling reporters that Flanders had shown "sanity and a sense of proportion" in appealing for "moderation." Democrat Herbert Lehman also had praise for the speech. Joe commented, "I am too busy to answer Republican heroes."[5]

The next day, in the Capitol basement, Joe threw an arm around Flanders and said, "Ralph, I looked up your record. You voted less for the Republicans than any man in the Senate." In fact, statistics showed that in 89 roll call votes in 1953, Flanders had agreed with the majority of his party 55 percent of the time while Joe scored 49 percent. McCarthy told a news conference later in the day that Flanders was "one of the finest old gentlemen I've ever met," and asserted that "he voted against Republican programs about as much as any Republican in the Senate." On the Senate floor Joe put his arms around the Vermonter from the rear, pretending to choke him.[6]

At his March 10 press conference, Eisenhower said that Flanders was doing a "service" by criticizing divisive elements within the Republican Party. *The New York Times* stated that the President's "unusual step" in commenting favorably on Flanders' speech "is a significant and encouraging piece of news." A few months later, Flanders revealed that the President had written him a personal "letter of appreciation" concerning the speech.[7]

The anger Eisenhower and Flanders were now displaying was part of a rising stream of hostility toward McCarthy that would quickly burst forth as a torrent. Increasingly, Americans were realizing that Joe was not just an Irish, two-fisted, anti-Communist. He was a rather frightening right-wing extremist who was capable of attacking anyone who stood in his path. Journalists, clergymen, professors, engineers, librarians, senators, generals, Cabinet members, the President—no one was safe.

Even McCarthy's staff members and personal friends were privately troubled by Joe's increasing abandonment of restraint and good sense. When he continued to demand equal time to answer Stevenson after the networks had agreed to present Nixon, Tom Korb wrote, "You have gone completely haywire," and warned, "you pushed your luck too far." But Joe did not listen. All personal criticism, he thought, was based either on ignorance or Communism. His zeal, no doubt intensified by his increasingly heavy drinking, had blinded him. He could neither see nor sense the shift of public opinion against him.[8]

On the evening of March 9 the distinguished newscaster Edward R. Murrow devoted the entirety of his popular "See It Now" show on C.B.S. television to an attack against McCarthy. The thirty-minute program, viewed in prime time in 36 cities, consisted largely of tapes and films of the senator. At the outset of the "report" (which Murrow would not admit was an attack) Joe was offered equal time to reply "if he believes we have done violence to his words or pictures." The editing portrayed Joe at his worst: belching, picking his nose, contradicting himself, giggling at his own vulgar humor ("Alger—I mean Adlai"), and harshly berating witnesses. Murrow asked his viewers, "Upon what meat does Senator McCarthy feed?" He answered solemnly, "Two of the staples of his diet are the investigations (protected by immunity) and the half truth. . . . It is necessary to investigate before legislating, but the line between investigation and persecution is a very fine one, and the junior senator has stepped over it repeatedly." McCarthy's actions, he said, "have caused alarm and dismay amongst our allies abroad and given considerable comfort to our enemies, and whose fault is that? Not really his; he didn't create the situation of fear, he merely exploited it, and rather successfully. Cassius was right: 'The fault, dear Brutus, is not in our stars, but in ourselves.'" The sharp contrast between McCarthy's low-grade loutishness and the broadcaster's sophistication, learning, and sincerity made a profound impression on viewers all across the country. Up until this time no one on network television had directly confronted McCarthy with his sins. No one had dared.

Murrow was a centrist liberal with strong views on civil liberties. When the eleven leaders of the American Communist party were convicted of conspiring to advocate the forcible overthrow of the government, he had warned, "We can't legislate loyalty," and reminded his audience that the party continued to be a legal political entity in the United States. He had made numerous references to McCarthy on his radio programs, and on the eve of the new year 1952 had sent the senator an "oral postcard" reading, "Look before you leap; the pool may be empty." In October 1953, "See It Now" had told the story of Lt. Milo Radulovich, a young Air Force Reserve officer who was classified a security risk because of the "questionable" activities of his father and sister. (The Air Force subsequently reconsidered its action.) In November it had presented "An Argument in Indianapolis," which showed the American Legion of that city trying to prevent a local chapter of the American Civil Liberties Union from hiring a hall. (A Roman Catholic church finally gave refuge to the chapter.) That same month Murrow had made a strong comment on Attorney General Brownell's charge against Harry Dexter White, and the "See It Now" cameras began filming the Jenner subcommittee's hearings on the case.

This activity did not escape the attention of McCarthyites. Outside the Senate caucus room one day, Don Surine sidled up to Morrow reporter Joe Wershba and threatened to expose the broadcaster as part of a "Moscow conspiracy." His evidence was a photostat of a 1935 article from Hearst's *Pittsburgh Sun-Telegraph* listing Murrow, along with twenty-five outstanding American educators, as part of an advisory committee for a summer school at Moscow University. The student exchange had been arranged by the Institute of International Education, where Murrow was employed for three years before joining C.B.S. in 1935. Surine's message was unmistakable: if Murrow would be quiet about the likes of what the McCarthy investigator called "this Radwich [Radulovich] junk," his record of "Communist affiliations" would not be exposed. News of the threat convinced Murrow that his television cameras should be turned directly upon McCarthy. The project, given the blessings of C.B.S. board chairman William S. Paley, was in preparation for two months before its presentation several hours after Ralph Flanders had spoken out on the Senate floor.

Public response to the program was described as the heaviest in C.B.S. history. Within 48 hours the network had received 12,924 calls commending the telecast and 1,367 opposing it. At the same time 3,267 complimentary telegrams arrived along with only 203 negative responses. Numerous commentators were ecstatic. John Crosby of the *New York Herald Tribune* wrote, "Right there television came of age." Jack Gould of *The New York Times* called the program "crusading journalism of high responsibility and genuine courage." Democratic Congressman Melvin Price of Illinois, a newspaperman, told the House, "It is indeed a rare thing when a T.V. network will stick its neck out by initiating or permitting to go over its facilities a hard-hitting, honest, unvarnished report on a highly charged, completely controversial issue."

The Far Right, of course, was furious. Murrow received a quantity of hate mail, some of it addressed to "Red" Murrow. One writer later suggested a suitable inscription for a new, Murrow-style Statue of Liberty: "Send me your Commies, pinkos, and crackpots, and I will put them on television." A Hearst newsman referred to the broadcaster as "Egghead R. Murrow." A C.B.S. colleague, Don Hollenbeck, who had openly endorsed the program on McCarthy, committed suicide after being attacked repeatedly by a Hearst newspaper as one of Murrow's "pinkos."

Joe sent a telegram to the Aluminum Company of America, sponsor of "See It Now," condemning its support of Murrow and indirectly threatening an investigation of some kind. (The company held firm but dropped its sponsorship a year later.) He accepted Murrow's invitation to reply, and the program was scheduled for April 6. Joe asked George Sokolsky to draft the speech.[9]

On March 10, during a hearing on Fort Monmouth, Joe angered Stuart Symington by attacking an absent Henry Jackson. Jackson had said on a television program that the subcommittee had not discovered any "new Communists." Joe shouted, "I do not like to have senators going out and misrepresenting the facts. If they sat and listened to the testimony they would know the number of current Communists, the danger of these men to the government." He constantly interrupted Symington as the Missouri senator tried to defend his fellow Democrat.[10]

After the hearing, Defense Secretary Charles E. Wilson sent a limousine for the senator to bring him to the Pentagon for lunch. (Joe hopped into the front seat beside the chauffeur.) Wilson had made headlines a few days earlier by characterizing as "just damn tommyrot" McCarthy's charge that the Army had coddled Communists during the Eisenhower administration. Wilson told reporters after the luncheon that Joe had been asked for advice on legislative proposals to deal with the issue of Communists called into the service by the draft. (Joe had suggested earlier that they be placed in special, disagreeable, labor camps.) In fact, Joe had been confronted with a 34-page Army report describing numerous and frequently scandalous efforts by Roy Cohn, over a seven-month period, to win favors for Pvt. G. David Schine. Wilson's price for withholding the report from the public was Cohn's immediate dismissal. Joe flatly refused.

The report was the document Sherman Adams had secretly advised the Army to prepare in the event that it sought to counterattack. (James Hagerty confided to his diary, "It's a pip.") The President and his counselors were convinced that the time was at hand. On the basis of the Army report, they had concluded that Cohn was responsible for McCarthy's attacks on the Army; they traced the young attorney's animosity to his quarrels with the Army over Schine. Cohn's dismissal, they believed, would help divert McCarthy's attentions elsewhere and protect the Army and the Administration from further humiliations and confrontations.

The night before the luncheon, Wilson had sent a copy of the report to Charles Potter, an old friend from Michigan, urging him to do what he could to persuade McCarthy to fire Cohn. Several senators, including Potter himself, and the chairman of the House Committee on Armed Services had separately requested full reports on Cohn's rumored interventions on behalf of Schine. Potter read the document and was shocked. He took it to Dirksen and Mundt, who both agreed with him that Cohn should be dismissed on the spot. That left McCarthy.

Potter cornered Joe in his office shortly after the luncheon with Wilson and insisted that Cohn must go. Joe angrily refused. While he hadn't read the report, he defended Cohn's innocence and claimed (correctly) that the Army was trying to blackmail him. He also threatened to have his friends Walter Winchell and George Sokolsky work Potter over in the press if he persisted with his demand. When Joe's temper subsided, he explained that he was not personally concerned about Schine. "Hell, Charlie," he said, "I don't care if they ship Schine to Siberia. But Roy worries about him." That was the stumbling block in the way of a compromise with the Army: Joe's concrete allegiance to Cohn. "If I got rid of Roy," he said, "it would be the greatest victory the Communists have scored up to now." He concluded the meeting by promising to discuss the matter further with subcommittee Republicans, and he offered Potter a drink.

Newsmen had known for months that Democrats on the subcommittee were unhappy with Cohn because the three senators had demanded the right to hire a "minority counsel" before returning to their duties. In early March they learned that subcommittee Republicans had reprimanded Cohn in January for pressuring Army officials about Schine and had ordered him to stop. They also discovered that the Republican National Committee had been quietly campaigning for Cohn's dismissal. Picking up rumors about the Potter-McCarthy meeting, reporters were waiting when the two senators emerged from Joe's office. They were eager to learn about Cohn's future. Joe denied that Potter had requested Cohn's resignation. He said, however, that he would resist any effort to remove the young attorney from the subcommittee staff. Cohn was "nearly indispensable."

Potter telephoned Secretary Wilson that evening with the news of McCarthy's intransigeance. Wilson was enraged, complaining not only about the fate of his offer but also about the Zwicker episode and the abuse that had been heaped upon Army personnel on behalf of Schine. "The man has gone too far," he said. Copies of the Army report were dispatched to each member of the subcommittee and several members of the Armed Services Committee. Twenty-four hours later the Administration would leak verbatim copies to the press. The war with McCarthy was underway.[11]

On Thursday morning, March 11, Annie Lee Moss appeared before the subcommittee in a public hearing. All of the senators were on hand, with the exception of Charles Potter, and a large crowd turned out to see the witness. Newspapers had made much of her first appearance before the subcommittee, and the *Washington Daily News* had taken up her case. She had been suspended from her job at the Pentagon two weeks earlier and was currently unemployed.

Now that Mrs. Moss was well enough to testify, it became apparent almost immediately that she was not the sort of person likely to be a Communist spy. She seemed inarticulate, very poorly educated, completely sincere, and wholly baffled by the charges leveled against her. In a soft voice, she denied any affiliation with Communists or the Communist party, said she had never been in a code room, and added that she knew nothing about coded messages.

As the testimony continued, sympathy for Mrs. Moss grew among the senators of both parties. She had been born in South Carolina, she said, and had not finished high school. When asked, "Did you ever hear of Karl Marx?" she replied, "Who's that?" She did not know the word "espionage." Her job in the Pentagon had been that of clerk-typist with an annual salary of only $3,300. She said she had never heard of Mrs. Markward, the FBI undercover agent. She also contended that there were three people named Annie Lee Moss living in Washington. Suddenly it dawned on everyone: McCarthy and Cohn had summoned and persecuted the wrong Annie Lee Moss!

(In fact, a careful reading of the hearings rules out mistaken identify. Mrs. Markward's description of the mid-1940s Communist of the same name fit the witness exactly. Either Mrs. Markward or Mrs. Moss was lying.) Cohn insisted that secret evidence existed, which he could not produce, proving that the witness was indeed the onetime Red. At that, Senators McClellan and Symington tore into Cohn, the former bitterly decrying the practice of "convicting people by rumor and hearsay and innuendo." The audience repeatedly applauded the attacks by Democrats. There were cheers when Symington said to the witness, "I may be sticking my neck out, but I believe you're telling the truth." Karl Mundt, chairing the hearing, made no effort to check the crowd's response or interfere with the denunciations of Cohn. (Joe had left the hearing room to confer with Fulton Lewis, Jr., about a network radio broadcast.) Stuart Symington brought the televised hearing to an emotional climax by telling the witness, a widow faced with going on welfare, that if the Army refused to reemploy her, he would personally see to it that she had a job. She was soon reinstated temporarily and later restored completely to duty.[12]

The Moss hearing was an unmitigated disaster for McCarthy and Cohn. It contributed to the alienation of subcommittee Democrats, blackened Cohn's reputation as an investigator, and helped shatter Joe's nationwide popularity. Walter Lippmann thought it was a major ingredient in "the breaking of a spell" cast by McCarthy over public opinion. Edward R. Murrow soon put excerpts of the hearing on "See It Now" and concluded the program by showing the President speaking about due process of law and of the American right "to meet your accuser face to face." A second wave of letters to C.B.S. followed, running nine to one in Murrow's favor. Some correspondents wrote of the "shocking" procedures employed against Mrs. Moss. Others said they were "sickened" by the persecution of a middle-aged black woman who could barely read English, let alone code.[13]

That evening McCarthy and Fulton Lewis, Jr., held a fifteen-minute question and answer session in a Washington studio billed as a reply to Adlai Stevenson. Joe took pokes at Stevenson and Flanders but aimed his hardest blows at Murrow, whom he called one of the "extreme Left-wing, bleeding heart elements of television and radio." He brandished the photocopy of the 1935 *Pittsburgh Sun-Telegraph* clipping and read the headline: "American Advisors to Communist Propaganda School." He tied Murrow to the Institute for International Education without describing what it was and without mentioning the prominent educators listed in the article. "This may explain why Edward R. Murrow, week after week, feels he must smear Senator McCarthy," Joe said. "Maybe he is worried about the exposure of some of his friends—I don't know." Murrow soon explained that the summer school project, which was perfectly legal, had been canceled by the Soviet Union before it began. Major newspapers carried the complete list of I.I.E. Advisory Council members, including John Dewey and Robert M. Hutchins.[14]

The next morning, March 12, newspapers contained stories on the Annie Lee Moss hearing, the Fulton Lewis broadcast, and the Army report. The report, described by the United Press as "sensational" and a "dynamite-laden document.... landing like a bombshell," received the most attention. *The New York Times* published the entire report and said in a huge front-page headline: ARMY CHARGES MCCARTHY AND COHN THREATENED IT IN TRYING TO OBTAIN PREFERRED TREATMENT FOR SCHINE. Cohn later wrote, "The shooting had begun."[15]

The chronology of the report began in mid-July 1953, with McCarthy summoning Maj. Gen. Miles Reber to his office. Joe requested a direct commission for G. David Schine, saying that speed was desirable since the young consultant might soon be drafted. During the meeting, Roy Cohn entered the office and emphasized the urgency of the situation. By the end of the month, however, three Pentagon officials had determined that Schine was unqualified for a direct commission, and the applicant was so notified. Throughout the period that Army officials scrutinized Schine's credentials, there were inquiries from the subcommittee staff about the status of the application.

On August 1 Cohn requested the Army's Office of the Chief of Legislative Liaison to explore the possibility of obtaining a reserve commission for Schine in either the Air Force or the Navy. Army officials complied, reporting negative results a few weeks later. Cohn then telephoned Army Secretary Stevens and obtained an appointment. Cohn attended the meeting in early October accompanied by Francis ("Frank") Carr, the 37-year-old, moon-faced ex-FBI man who served as executive director of the subcommittee. The two men chatted with Stevens for a time about plans for the Fort Monmouth investigation. Cohn then asked about an assignment in the New York City area for Schine when he was inducted. Stevens rejected the suggestion, asserting his belief that Schine should be treated as any other private in the Army. In mid-October, after a further request from Cohn, the Army Secretary softened his position somewhat and suggested that Schine might be granted fifteen days of temporary duty in New York between his induction and basic training for the completion of subcommittee business.

A few days later Joe, Jean, and John G. Adams found themselves together in New York, where subcommittee hearings were underway. Joe said frankly to the Army's general counsel that Schine was of no value to the subcommittee, that he was only interested in publicly, and that things had reached the point where the young man had become a pest. He added that he hoped nothing would obstruct the normal processes of the draft in this case. Joe gave Adams permission to relay his sentiments to Stevens. A short time later, Joe told Adams that while he continued to think Schine a nuisance he did not want Cohn to know of his views.

Cohn then began contacting Adams almost every day, in person and by telephone, about an assignment for Schine in the New York City area. After being rebuffed a number of times, Cohn threatened to expose the Army at its worst and show the country how poorly it was being run. He continued to ask about Schine's assignment while Adams attended executive sessions of the subcommittee.

On November 3 Schine was inducted into the Army and was placed on fifteen days temporary duty in New York to complete subcommittee duties. The next day Joe contacted Adams and requested that the temporary assignment be canceled. He was concerned that newsmen and others might raise questions about Schine's continued presence in the city. Cohn soon suggested that since it was the middle of the week, the temporary duty might be continued for a few more days. Adams complied with Cohn's wishes.

At the invitation of Army Secretary Stevens, McCarthy, Cohn, Carr, and Adams attended a luncheon at the Pentagon on November 6. The principal subject of conversation was the Fort Monmouth investigation, but before long Cohn asked when the Army would be able to arrange a New York City assignment for Schine. Joe now changed his tune and said that he too was interested in having Schine in New York. He suggested that the private be given the assignment of studying the pro-Communist leanings of West Point textbooks and that he report directly to Stevens. Cohn also requested that Schine be made available to the subcommittee while undergoing basic training at Fort Dix. Stevens said that Schine would be permitted to leave the post on weekends after his basic training if it was necessary for him to complete pending subcommittee work. He added that if a matter of urgency occurred, the private could also leave in the evenings after training. These concessions by Stevens were not routine, the Army report noted. Normally, soldiers in their first month of basic training were required to remain on the post.

On November 10 Schine was transported to Fort Dix to be processed in preparation for basic training. The next day Cohn and Carr called on General Ryan, the fort commander, asking to see Schine at the reception station. The request was granted. Schine was given a weekend pass the following day in response to a telephone call from some member of the subcommittee staff.

On November 17 Stevens and Adams lunched with McCarthy in New York. Afterward, Stevens, who was returning to Washington, gave Joe and members of his staff a ride in his plane to Maguire Air Force base, which adjoined Fort Dix. Private Schine was issued a pass that evening to see Joe and the others. Two days later, at the request of subcommittee staff man Thomas La Venia, Schine received a four-day pass.

The private's basic training began on November 23. Schine soon obtained a pair of two-day passes and began leaving the post almost every evening, returning late at night. General Ryan complained to Secretary Stevens about these privileges on December 6. Stevens thereupon authorized Ryan to prohibit Schine's weeknight excursions but asked that the private be kept available to the subcommittee on weekends. Ryan issued the appropriate order.

Three days later, at a hearing on Fort Monmouth, Cohn again spoke to Adams about Schine, abruptly turning his back on the Army counsel and terminating their conversation when Adams appeared insufficiently compliant. When Adams complained privately to McCarthy about Cohn's conduct, Joe agreed to write a letter to Stevens stating that the subcommittee had no further interest in Schine and that he hoped the young man would be treated the same as other soldiers. (The letter was written on December 22 and received by Stevens.) Joe also said that he would ask his staff to observe the same rule. When Adams returned to the Pentagon, Cohn telephoned to say that he would teach Adams what it meant to go over his head.

The next day, December 10, Joe invited Stevens, Adams, and Carr to lunch in Washington. Carr explained to the others that Cohn was too upset to attend and had departed for New York. Joe proceeded to pressure Stevens and Adams to obtain a New York area assignment for Schine at the conclusion of his first eight weeks at Fort Dix.

On December 11 Schine was informed that General Ryan had expanded his duties at the fort to include Saturday mornings. During the afternoon, Cohn telephoned Adams several times from New York, using "extremely vituperative language" and claiming that the Army had "double-crossed" him four times: when Schine was denied a commission, when he was not assigned immediately to New York, when his weeknight availability was canceled, and when he was required to remain on duty on Saturday mornings. The next day, Schine received a weekend pass.

On December 17 McCarthy spoke with Adams at the entrance to the U.S. Court House in New York. He said that he had learned of the extent to which his staff had been leaning on the Army, and he advised Adams that he wished nothing further to be done on the subcommittee's behalf with reference to Schine. After the hearings, when Adams, McCarthy, Cohn, and Carr were together, Adams suggested discussing the Schine matter, hoping to force Joe to reveal his views in front of his staff members. Cohn became "vituperative in his language," repeating his many complaints against the Army. Joe remained silent. As the party rode uptown in Cohn's car, Cohn continued his statement. Twice during the ride, and as Adams was getting out of the car, Joe requested Adams to ask Stevens to find a way to assign Private Schine to New York. He again suggested a study of West Point textbooks.

Adams soon checked with the Adjutant General of the Army to learn about Schine's qualification testing. He learned that the private had been found physically disqualified for service in the infantry because of a defect in his back. He was also told that Schine had been recommended to be an assistant criminal investigator and would probably be transferred to the Provost Marshall General School at Camp Gordon, Georgia, following his basic training. The course in the criminal investigator's school lasted eight weeks. Adams discussed his findings with Stevens, assuring the secretary that the proposed assignment would follow the normal course of action resulting from qualification testing.

On December 31 Adams telephoned Cohn to inform him of this development. Cohn asked repeatedly if Schine would be assigned to New York after his eight-week stint in Georgia. Adams said that he did not know. Private Schine, meanwhile, was receiving weekend and holiday passes.

On January 9, 1954, Adams was in Amherst, Massachusetts, filling a college speaking engagement. Frank Carr called to say that Cohn had been trying to reach him from New York. Cohn had learned that Schine was scheduled for K.P. duty on the following day, a Sunday, and he wanted Adams to intervene with General Ryan. Adams refused. He again declined when he received a call from Cohn.

About two days later, Cohn telephoned Adams to inquire about details surrounding Schine's duty at Camp Gordon. He wanted to know, among other things, whom to contact for the purpose of relieving Schine of duty when necessary. Adams then called Maj. Gen. William H. Maglin, the Provost Marshall General, to learn what was in store for Schine. He discovered that some of his initial information had been incorrect; for Schine to qualify as a criminal investigator, he would have to spend nearly five months at Camp Gordon. When Adams advised Cohn of this by telephone, Cohn exploded, saying that he would not stand for any more Army double-crosses. He ended the conversation by hanging up.

A day or so later, Adams called on Cohn and Carr in Cohn's subcommittee office to talk further about Schine. Cohn was shocked to learn that the chances were good that his friend would face overseas duty after his tour at Camp Gordon. He threatened to "wreck the Army" and cause Stevens to be "through as Secretary of the Army." Later that day, Adams told General Howard, the newly appointed commanding general at Camp Gordon, to ignore all pressures on behalf of the controversial private. He wanted Schine to receive exactly the same treatment as his peers.

Adams then contacted Stevens to apprise him of events. Since Stevens was about to leave for the Far East, to be gone a month, he contacted McCarthy directly. The two men met for two hours at the Carroll Arms hotel in Washington. On four or five occasions during the conversation Joe asked about the possibility of assigning Schine to New York after his tour at Camp Gordon. Stevens did not make a commitment.

In a conversation with Frank Carr on January 18, Adams asked if McCarthy had informed staff members of his two-hour session with Stevens. Carr said that he had heard nothing about it. Adams also informed him in detail about the length of time Schine would be required to spend at Camp Gordon. Carr immediately telephoned Cohn, on vacation in Florida, to tell him what he had heard. Cohn called Adams to confirm the story. He ended the conversation again by hanging up on Adams.

The next morning, Carr informed Adams that Cohn had cut short his vacation and returned to New York. He also stated that the subcommittee desired to interrogate a number of members of the Army's Loyalty-Security Appeals Board at 2:00 P.M. that day. When Adams reminded Carr of earlier understandings not to summon board members, there was no reply. That afternoon Adams himself appeared before McCarthy, Cohn, and Carr. Joe went on the record only once during the 45-minute session, saying that he wished to question Appeals Board members about various allegations concerning fraud, corruption, and personal misconduct.

On Friday evening, January 22, at the senator's invitation, Adams joined Joe and Jean at their Washington apartment for a lengthy chat. On many occasions during the evening Joe discussed a possible New York assignment for Schine, and he tried three times to obtain a commitment from his guest. Joe pointed out that the Army was walking into a long-range fight with Cohn, and that even if Cohn were no longer on the subcommittee he would continue his campaign against Army officials. Joe suggested that Cohn's friends in the press would begin producing articles charging the Army with favoritism in numerous other cases. Adams replied that he knew of no such favoritism, and he repeated his desire to see Schine treated like any other private. He was puzzled by McCarthy's references to the "original agreement" concerning Schine.

In early February Carr told Adams by telephone that the senator was angry over the rapid release of Irving Peress from the Army and was no longer willing to discuss matters with either Adams or Stevens. On February 16 Carr called Adams again to announce the summoning of General Zwicker and the acting G-2 officer of the First Army before the subcommittee. Cautiously, Carr made it clear that if the Army would do all that had been requested of it, its problems would be at an end. "Mr. Carr stated," the report concluded, "that if the Army would be reasonable, probably the committee would be reasonable."[16]

The Army report, obviously bearing the full authority of the Administration, was the most devastating attack ever launched against Joe McCarthy. The story of the senator's tolerance and wavering support of Cohn's bullying and blackmail threatened to destroy his popularity and political power. Even a slight acquaintance with the report produced disgust at the irrational and wholly irresponsible use of congressional authority on behalf of one Army draftee. Senator Potter issued a statement calling for an immediate executive session of the subcommittee to determine the facts of the case. "Assuming the information is accurate," he said, "Mr. Cohn should be removed immediately." In a joint statement, Senators McClellan, Symington, and Jackson also called for a meeting of the subcommittee. *The New York Times* stated editorially, "We should have preferred to see the present crackdown on Mr. McCarthy based on moral indignation over his whole philosophy—if one can call it that—instead of the specific outrages he has committed in recent weeks against the Army. But in any case the senator and his friends have now been truly hoist with their own petard."[17]

Joe was prepared to defend himself. Once he had rejected the appeals by Defense Secretary Wilson and Senator Potter he assumed correctly that it was only a matter of time before the report would find its way to reporters. On the evening of March 11 he had huddled with Cohn, Carr, and others to devise some sort of response. The plan that emerged was incredibly daring—as reckless and as fraudulent as Joe's improvisations on the Lee list in 1950. McCarthy and his associates decided to write eleven interoffice memoranda, back-date them, and claim that they came from the senator's files. In fact, anyone who knew McCarthy at all knew that he would never have written—or read—the sort of detailed memos that the group came up with. Some of them were comically awkward and crude, and were obviously designed to reply to the Army report. But Joe was determined to counterattack, a tactic that had always worked for him in the past.[18]

McCarthy and Cohn held a news conference at noon on March 12, several hours after the morning newspapers had carried the story of the Army report. With Cohn seated on his left, Joe praised his young assistant and said that he would fight to the last ditch to save his job. "There is only one man the Communists hate more than Roy Cohn," he declared. "That's J. Edgar Hoover." Joe denied any personal effort to obtain preferential treatment for Schine and said that the true purpose of the report was to "blackmail" him into calling off his investigations of the Army. He admitted, however, suggesting to Stevens that Schine receive an assignment in the New York area to study pro-Communist material in West Point textbooks and Army indoctrination courses. It remained a good idea, he said, to get a team of six or seven Army men with Schine's credentials to make such a study.

Cohn professed complete innocence. "I do say the statements to the effect that improper pressure was exerted by us are a lie. I do say I didn't say I would wreck the Army. I never threatened any one or did any other such absurd thing." He told reporters that he had no intention of resigning from the subcommittee.

Copies of the eleven memos were then distributed. They buttressed Joe's "blackmail" assertion completely, cleared Carr and Cohn of all charges contained in the Army report, and described Stevens and Adams as the foulest of villains. The documents were allegedly written over a more than five-month period beginning on October 2, 1953.

The authors wasted little time on subtlety. A memo dated December 9, 1953, had Carr writing to McCarthy: "I couldn't get you on the telephone. What I want to tell you is that I am getting fed up with the way the Army is trying to use Schine as a hostage to pressure us to stop our hearings on the Army." John Adams "refers to Schine as our hostage or the hostage whenever his name comes up." In another memo Carr described conversations with Adams about Schine, contrasting the attorney's perfidy with his own purity: "On a number of these occasions I have stated that it was my opinion that Schine should get an assignment for which he was qualified and in which he could actually be useful to the Army in an investigatory position. I have never, however, suggested that his assignment should be other than one which he is entitled to by all Army standards of fair play."

An unsigned memo dated November 6, 1953, portrayed Stevens telling McCarthy, Cohn, Carr, and Adams, at a Pentagon luncheon, that if the subcommittee revealed everything it knew about the Army Signal Corps, he would have to resign. Stevens then suggested that the subcommittee turn its attention away from the Army and toward the Navy, Air Force, and Defense Department. Adams chimed in to say that he and Stevens could provide "plenty of dirt" for the investigators.

One memo was dated January 14, 1954, the day the Army report said Cohn had promised to "wreck the Army" if Schine were sent overseas. It alleged that Adams told Cohn "this was the last chance" for Cohn to arrange a New York law partnership for him, with a guaranteed annual income of $25,000.

To substantiate the authenticity of all of this, a document dated March 11 told of McCarthy being informed of the Army report and ordering a search of the office files. Frank Carr was to look "for memoranda dictated concerning Schine."[19]

Pentagon officials were stunned by the counterattack; they had not anticipated Joe's incredible audacity. Secretary Stevens, in what one observer called "a high state of anguish," rushed through corridors, dodging reporters, on his way to consult with Adams and public relations advisers. Full replies were ready at dusk. Stevens called the allegation that he had urged the subcommittee to probe other Armed Services "utterly untrue" and "fantastic." Adams said that the entire "blackmail" charge was "fantastic and false," and he stood by the Army report.[20]

The other subcommittee Republicans were furious over McCarthy's sudden move. They had agreed with the chairman to hold a private meeting to discuss the Army report and question Roy Cohn under oath. Just before noon on the 12th, Joe abruptly canceled the meeting, in a telephone call to Potter, saying that he had to travel to Wisconsin that evening for a speech. A few minutes later, without consulting any of his G.O.P. colleagues, he and Cohn held their joint news conference and leveled the "blackmail" charges against the Army. Potter later wrote, "I have never seen Everett Dirksen angrier than he was that afternoon." The Illinois senator told a reporter that all of the subcommittee Republicans, and not just the chairman, had to take responsibility for staff members. "I do mean to meet it," he snapped. "There will be no fooling about it. The matter has gone far enough." Karl Mundt announced that he would soon make a formal motion to invite an impartial Senate committee to investigate the charges traded between the Army and McCarthy. He hoped that the subcommittee itself would not be forced to conduct the inquiry. "I don't want to have it conducted by a committee [on] which the staff is involved and the chairman is involved."[21]

On Friday evening, March 12, Joe flew to Wisconsin for a weekend speaking trip. (Speeches were scheduled in Chicago, Milwaukee, and Oklahoma City during the following week.) He left behind him an irate subcommittee, an enraged Army officialdom, and a near hysterical press. In Appleton, Joe announced that he had a "secret witness" who would support one of his charges against the Army.[22]

While Washington remained in an uproar over the Army-McCarthy battle, Richard Nixon went on network television and radio to make the Administration's formal reply to Adlai Stevenson. Before an audience estimated at 10 million, the stern-faced Vice-President rattled off some routine rhetoric about corruption and subversion in the previous administration ("We don't agree with Mr. Truman in kissing off that danger by calling it a 'red herring'"), and boasted that Republicans had separated from the government no fewer than: 422 subversives, 198 sexual perverts, 611 people convicted for felonies or misdemeanors, and 1,424 others with records indicating "untrustworthiness, drunkenness, mental instability, or possible exposure to blackmail." He asked at one point, "Isn't it wonderful, finally, to have a Secretary of State who isn't taken in by the Communists, who stands up to them?"

Nixon was less predictable when he turned to the subject of Senator McCarthy. The President, the Administration, and the "responsible leadership" of the Republican party, he said, insisted that procedures for dealing with Communism "must be fair and they must be proper." Some Red-hunters thought that Communists should be shot like rats, he observed. "Well, I'll agree; they're a bunch of rats, but just remember this. When you go out to shoot rats, you have to shoot straight, because when you shoot wildly it not only means that the rats may get away more easily, you make it easier on the rat, but you might hit someone else who's trying to shoot rats, too." Without mentioning McCarthy by name, Nixon criticized certain G.O.P. rat-shooters who had not practiced fairness. "Men who have in the past done effective work exposing Communists in this country have, by reckless talk and questionable methods, made themselves the issue, rather than the cause they believe in so deeply." In doing this, "they have allowed those whose primary objective is to defeat the Eisenhower administration, to divert attention from its great program to those individuals who followed those methods." Nixon added that the President, by contrast, "does not engage in personal vituperation and vulgar name-calling and promiscuous letter writing in asserting his leadership, and I say, Thank God that he doesn't. . . . I have never seen him mean; I have never seen him impulsive . . ."[23]

There could no longer be the slightest doubt about which side the White House was taking in the Army-McCarthy controversy. The Nixon attack gave McCarthy public notice that the Administration considered him a liability. This only made Joe angrier. When asked to comment on the Vice-President's speech, he said he thought the American people were "sick and tired" of the "constant yack-yacking" that he was not being gentle with Communists. Increasingly, as Urban Van Susteren later recalled, Joe referred in private to "that prick Nixon."[24]

On March 14 Roy Cohn appeared on the nationally televised program "Meet the Press." (He had been invited to appear a week later but when contacted demanded, "I want to go on *this* Sunday night." The Cabinet member who had been booked was told to wait.) He denied Army accusations against him and repeated his charge that Army officials had sought to use Private Schine as a "bargaining point" to stop the subcommittee investigation. He also developed his allegation that an offer was made to give him "dirt" on the Navy and Air Force. At a meeting he attended with Adams and Carr, he said, the Army counsel had offered to map Air Force bases where there were problems. Cohn said he thought it was "extremely disgraceful that sometime later a specific proposal was made to us that we go after an Air Force base wherein Mr. Adams told us there were a number of sex deviates . . . that would make excellent hearings for us."

In the course of the telecast, Cohn acknowledged that the subcommittee staff was being asked to sign a loyalty pledge to him. He denied, however, saying to two women who declined to sign that it "would be the worse for those that refused." All he knew about the pledge, he said, was that a staff member had told him it was being circulated.

Cohn's appearance on television, without the advance permission of the subcommittee, destroyed whatever sentiment might have existed among the senators to retain him on the staff. With the exception of McCarthy, all of the subcommittee members were now, in Cohn's words, "openly hostile."[25]

The subcommittee members met in executive session for two hours and forty-five minutes on March 16. It was a stormy meeting; Joe reportedly removed his coat and fought in his shirt sleeves to defend his interests. At a news conference afterward, the senators announced the unanimous approval of five resolutions. The subcommittee itself would conduct a full, public inquiry into the Army-McCarthy charges, which would be completed before the body took up any other work. Karl Mundt, the second ranking Republican, was to serve as temporary chairman during the investigation. A new counsel and staff would be employed (although Cohn and Carr were not suspended), to be approved by a majority vote of the senators. The subcommittee planned to meet in a week to receive a "progress report" on the search for the new employees. Two of the resolutions had been offered by McCarthy: the move to make the hearings public, and the suggestion to employ new counsel and staff members by majority vote.

Joe was smiling and affable; he shook hands several times with Senator McClellan before photographers. He told reporters that he willingly stepped down as chairman because he had complete confidence in Cohn. "I have frankly prejudged the case," he said. "I had to because these charges were brought to me months ago." He also said that he expected to testify under oath and participate as an active member of the subcommittee. He was unsure about whether he would vote on the subcommittee's final conclusions.

McCarthy appeared supremely self-confident. He no doubt thought he would simply take over the proceedings, as had been his practice since the Malmedy investigation, and have his way. If trouble arose, he could always depend upon Mundt to protect one of his own. (Roy Cohn thought, "But maybe things wouldn't be too bad. Senator Mundt, the chairman, was a wise, fair-minded man.") Mundt told reporters that he accepted the temporary chairmanship with great reluctance, and admitted that he had tried unsuccessfully to persuade his colleagues to give the investigatory task to another committee.

Still, there were several indications that McCarthy was in more trouble than he may have realized. The subcommittee files were put under lock and key, where Cohn, Carr and other members of the current staff would not have access to them. One of the resolutions specifically revoked Joe's power to order new hearings on other topics during the Army-McCarthy investigation, a clear acknowledgement of the chairman's penchant for diversionary tactics. Reporters also noticed that portion of another resolution which denied any subcommittee member "veto power" over the new staff. Referring to the new counsel, Henry Jackson said, "We are seeking a man with the diligence of a district attorney and the fair-mindedness of an eminent judge." Such a person was not likely to be sympathetic to McCarthy and his eleven memos.

Moreover, Senator McClellan, the senior Democrat, was assuming increasing leadership on the subcommittee. He sponsored three of the five resolutions and was to share the responsibility with Mundt for finding new staff members. It was widely known that McClellan had long been angry with McCarthy over his disregard of Senate rules and traditions. He also made little secret of his shock at the charges made against Annie Lee Moss and the Army and of his dislike and distrust of Roy Cohn. McClellan was a deeply conservative man with a stern sense of justice. His secure position within the Senate Establishment added considerable weight to his pronouncements. In short, he was not a man who could be attacked effectively by the Far Right; he was someone McCarthy had every reason to fear. The Arkansas senator told reporters that he hoped the forthcoming inquiry would reveal the "truth" to the public "as promptly and as expeditiously as possible."[26]

Joe also, of course, had good reason to worry about the President as the investigation approached. Eisenhower, whose popularity with the American people remained extremely high, had the power to severely damage if not destroy his public credibility. McCarthy critics continued to cry for an unequivocal statement by the President condemning the senator and all that he stood for. It was hoped that the clash with the Army would produce the long-awaited declaration; there had been definite signs in recent days of a growing boldness within the Administration.

Excitement could be sensed among newsmen as the President's weekly news conference got underway on March 17. Reporters scribbled frantically when Eisenhower said that he believed Robert Stevens had told the truth. But then he hedged, saying that Stevens could have made mistakes or have been misinformed on certain matters. The President spoke of fears of what unwise investigators might be doing as they tried to combat internal subversion, bribery, or deceit. He also said that he was taking the Army-McCarthy dispute seriously. But, to the deep disappointment of McCarthy's critics, he refused to attack the senator directly. Denis Brogan, a British observer of Americana, wrote, "Plenty of officials and plenty of Army officers are at the moment convinced that it is worse to have the senator than the President for an enemy. They will continue to think so and act on this until it becomes plain that the President is boss and means to be boss."[27]

That same day, Joe and Don Surine flew to Chicago and the first of the week's four scheduled speeches. Aboard the plane, Joe gave an interview to two reporters that revealed his fierce determination to counterattack and his complete unwillingness to soften his language or moderate his extremism. He blamed his row with the Army on "Pentagon politicians" appointed by the "Truman-Acheson regime" who were trying to block his search for Communists in government. "The voice was the voice of Stevens, but the hand was the hand of some holdover Pentagon politicians." He attacked the Senate Republican Policy Committee for recently suggesting rule changes that would ban one-man subcommittee hearings and provide basic protection for witnesses. "The rules," he said, "were good enough when we were investigating corruption and crooks. Why are the Communists in some special class?" He also asserted that the subcommittee's decision to drop all other inquiries during the Army-McCarthy investigation was in itself "a rather major, if temporary victory" for those "who fear exposure of Communists." In short, anyone who opposed him, regardless of party or position, was a Communist, a pro-Communist, or a dupe doing the work of the Communists. You were either for or against McCarthy—and opposition was a subversive activity.[28]

In Chicago the Democratic machine treated the senator like a visiting president from the moment his plane landed. He was introduced at a St. Patrick's Day dinner as a man who "today is driving the snakes out of America." As he began his speech, broadcast nationally by the Mutual network, there were cries of "Give 'em hell, Joe," and "Pour it on—you're in your own ball park." The capacity audience of 1,200 in the main ballroom at the Palmer House interrupted repeatedly with applause. The cheering was especially loud when Joe expressed his determination to continue the battle against subversion at all cost. He did not give "a tinker's damn" about attacks on his anti-Communist methods, he said, no matter "how high or how low" the critics in either political party were. He repeated the phrase "how high or how low," leaving the clear impression that he included the President in his denunciation. He added that he had not started the controversy with the Administration "but I think maybe I will have to finish it."[29]

The next day, before a wildly enthusiastic audience of 450 Chicago automobile dealers, Joe said that he would never be "a rubber stamp" for the President. He attacked Edward R. Murrow, John J. McCloy, the American Civil Liberties Union, and trade with Red China. He said of his conflict with Stevens and Adams that he was simply doing his job of "rooting out and exposing" Reds in the Army "when all hell broke loose." As he had the day before, Joe asked his audience to write to members of the subcommittee who favored a bar on one-man hearings and urge them to reconsider. He was thinking particularly of Everett Dirksen of Illinois, who had supported the rule change and, it was revealed, had proposed that Cohn be suspended for the duration of the Army-McCarthy probe.[30]

In Milwaukee, though suffering from exhaustion, laryngitis, and a wilting fever, Joe thrilled his audience of 500 at a Young Republican rally with attacks on "Ad-lie" Stevenson, Dean Acheson, and the Democratic Party. He listed "twenty counts" of treason against Democrats, and after each count asked, "As attorney for the defense, how plead you to this count, 'Ad-lie,' guilty or not guilty?" The audience soon began roaring "guilty!" at each pause in the "indictment." Joe made it clear as well that he was unsatisfied with the loyalty of all Republicans. He again promised to continue to "expose Communists . . . no matter how high or low are the Democrats or the Republicans who scream their maledictions at me." He drew thunderous applause by contrasting the late Robert Taft with current G.O.P. leaders. "During these days when the abuse and imprecations reach a new crescendo," he said, "I very greatly miss the moral support which I so long received from the tower of integrity and strength in the Republican party who no longer is with us—Senator Robert A. Taft—no chameleon was he."[31]

The following night, in Oklahoma City, Joe praised Eisenhower so faintly that some journalists turned the compliment into an attack. The President, he said, "is doing the best job he can, but I don't think he is a superman." If Ike were currently running for office, he continued, he would be "compelled" to campaign for him. Joe saved his strongest language for the mass media. In Milwaukee, to the delight of his audience, he had tossed documents from the speaker's stand to reporters, challenging them to check his quotations as he read them. Now he threatened to issue a report on the aim of the Communists "to infiltrate and control every media of information." The study, a "personal" project, would also reveal, he said, how "some politicians are in mortal fear of and therefore to some extent guided by" the media. If Americans wanted the true story of his dispute with high Army officials, Joe declared, they should write directly to his Washington office for information. "The more requests we get, the better I'll like it."[32]

Joe's vehemence about the media had broad ramifications. Increasingly, newspapers and magazines were turning against him editorially. Eugene Pulliam's *Arizona Republic,* for example, long a defender of the Far Right, commented, "The political obituary of . . . McCarthy . . . is being written in the news stories that greet—and disgust—Americans almost every morning these days. . . . Here is a man who had a great opportunity for service to his nation and who is spoiling it miserably." *Time* magazine ran a highly unflattering photograph of Cohn and Schine on its cover and was harshly critical of McCarthy. A survey of regional correspondents of *The New York Times* revealed growing hostility toward the senator in newspapers in every region of the country. The principal reason seemed to be his clash with the White House. The pro-Eisenhower *Houston Post* said, "The American people are against Communism and are with him [McCarthy] in the objective of rooting out Communism. But surely they will support the Administration's effort to prevent him from wrecking its plans for the country's good."[33]

Joe also perceived an increasing unfriendliness among reporters and was disturbed by slanted headlines and stories produced by representatives of the prestigious Associated Press and *The New York Times.* Journalists appeared to be deliberately trying to intensify the ill will between himself and the President. *The New York Times,* for example, reported the airline interview on the way to Chicago under the headline "McCarthy Criticizes Eisenhower for Backing New Inquiry Rules." In fact, Joe had done no such thing and had spent part of the interview telling reporters that the Communist party was trying to encourage fights between himself and the Administration. The Associated Press filed a story on the Chicago speech making McCarthy seem so anti-Eisenhower that Joe sent a telegram to the White House decrying the inaccuracy of the dispatch. The next day in

Milwaukee he upbraided A.P. correspondent John Chadwick for twisting his language. He then sought to punish the reporter by inviting a rival from the United Press to join him in a back room from which other newsmen had been barred.[34]

Journalists were also beginning to make much of Joe's sudden drop in the public opinion polls. The Gallup survey completed on March 2 showed a loss since January of four percentage points in the "favorable" category. Three weeks later the figure had fallen another eight points and stood at 38 percent. Forty-six percent of the public, according to Gallup, had an "unfavorable" view of the senator. When the San Francisco News asked its readers if they admired McCarthy, 644 said no and 161 yes. In Connecticut, citizens were invited to choose between Eisenhower and McCarthy as leader of the G.O.P. The President received 350 of the 351 votes cast.[35]

Newspapers, television and radio stations, and the newsreels were paying attention at the same time to a drive in Wisconsin to recall McCarthy. The effort was led by 50-year-old Leroy Gore, editor of the weekly Sauk-Prairie Star in tiny Sauk City, about 30 miles from Madison. Gore had been a Republican for 30 years and had supported McCarthy in 1952. He told reporters that his disillusionment with the senator stemmed from the Zwicker testimony, McCarthy's neglect of the dairy industry, and the general feeling he had that Joe had become a "menace" to the G.O.P. and the nation. By late March, Gore had distributed 15,000 petitions and was hoping to receive the necessary 403,804 notarized signatures within a 60-day period to call an election. The United Press reported that of the first 600 letters Gore received, only six had opposed his plan. The Milwaukee Journal soon said that Gore's mail from within Wisconsin was running 100 to one against McCarthy.

A state recall of a United States senator was of doubtful constitutionality. It was also thought unlikely, given the 1952 election returns, that enough signatures could be obtained, and in that event a reaction could occur favoring McCarthy. The Wisconsin Federation of Labor and the Wisconsin state C.I.O. soon announced that they would not support Gore's campaign. Democratic party leaders were equally unenthusiastic. Republicans threatened court action. But Gore promised to press on. "I'm just doing what I think is right," he said. He and friends soon established a state-wide organization called the "Joe Must Go" club that continued to collect signatures and considerable publicity.[36]

For years, of course, Joe had bristled at critics and questioned their patriotism. Now, as the attacks against him grew stronger and his popularity began to plummet, Joe increasingly expanded the ranks of what he saw as the Communist-inspired conspiracy at work to destroy him. The inclusion of the nation's major media outlets was part of a pattern. Even right-wing Republicans who had deserted him, such as Nixon, were perceived as doing the bidding of the Reds. "The enemy's ranks are closing," he shouted in Milwaukee. "They are going all out to rally support—from their stalwarts, from the bleeding hearts, from the well-meaning liberals, and from the chameleon politicians of both parties. They strive to hamstring our investigations." This belief was surely in large part why Joe continued to travel and make speeches at such a breakneck pace. He was appealing directly to the "real Americans" over the heads of the country's leading politicians and opinion-makers. The rank-and-file Republicans alone, it seemed, were ready to defend his fight against treason.[37]

While returning to Washington, Joe proposed that he and all other witnesses in the upcoming hearings submit to lie-detector tests. "The truth in this case is the important thing," he told reporters. Joe was bluffing again: he knew from similar suggestions made during the Hiss trial and the Bohlen nomination that there was little or no sympathy on Capitol Hill for such tests. The proposal made headlines, but it did nothing to stem the tide of anti-McCarthy sentiment in Washington and elsewhere that seemed to be gathering momentum almost daily.[38]

On Sunday, March 21, the Episcopal deans of the cathedrals of New York and Washington, D.C., preached fiery sermons in each other's pulpits, attacking the senator and his allies. Dr. James A. Pike called McCarthyism a "new tyranny," while the Very Rev. Francis B. Sayre, Jr., referred to it as "only another of the devil's disguises." Dean Sayre, related to former President Woodrow Wilson and widely known for his success in raising funds for the National Cathedral, lashed out at Joe directly. "For the sake of ten guilty ones he will damn an army. For the sake of twenty he is willing to wreck a whole administration. For the sake of thirty or forty or fifty, he will divide a nation right down to its democratic roots. . . . Little reckons he the diabolical consequences of his demoralizing tyranny."[39]

The next day, Senator Knowland, the G.O.P. floor leader, Senator Ferguson, chairman of the G.O.P. Policy Committee, and Leonard Hall, the Republican National Committee chairman, publicly agreed with a suggestion by Stuart Symington that McCarthy should drop his membership on the subcommittee for the duration of the forthcoming investigation and participate only as a witness. All three G.O.P. leaders were reportedly backed by the White House.[40]

Privately, the Republicans were afraid that Joe was coming apart mentally and physically. Hall confided to Nixon that the senator was "beginning to blow up" and was in no condition even to attend a hearing let alone participate in one. When Hall had called on Joe several days earlier, he had come to the door with a gun in his hand. Apparently he now carried one at all times, fearing for his life. Karl Mundt also shared his deep concern with Nixon after talking with Joe on the telephone until 2:00 A.M. Joe believed that his political future was in peril, Mundt said, and would agree to nothing that might impede his self-defense. Jean was almost in tears over the situation.[41]

At the root of the problem was one of the worst-kept secrets in Washington: Joe's heavy drinking. By the spring of 1954 the senator's alcoholic disease was becoming severe. It was affecting his judgment and feeding his fears. Films of his speeches at the time show him flabby and flushed, occasionally uncertain in his speech. An interview with the Associated Press in early April revealed his heavy dependence upon Roy Cohn for information. His temper flared easily; he was often highly emotional. Republican leaders had nightmares about what McCarthy might do to witnesses at the forthcoming hearings.[42]

Joe told reporters that he had "given no thought" to leaving the subcommittee and insisted on the uncurbed privilege of cross-examining those who testified against him. His only concession to critics was the surrender of his vote on subcommittee findings. He alleged that he and Mundt had agreed to that "days ago."[43]

On March 22 the president of the American Bar Association, William J. Jameson of Billings, Montana, declined an invitation to serve as special counsel for the investigation. (A.B.A. officials were reportedly afraid that Jameson's involvement in the dispute between McCarthy and the Army would cause "controversies" within the organization.) This was thought to be a blow to McCarthy and Mundt, who had supported Jameson. Joe referred to the upcoming inquiry later in the day as "this attempt to smear Cohn."[44]

The next day Joe called a subcommittee meeting for March 24 on Communist infiltration of defense plants. The Cohn affair had been "blown up," he argued, and was hindering the group's more serious work. His colleagues, however, would have none of this, and Joe was forced to cancel the session. The following day McCarthy reiterated his desire to resume the search for Reds. There were 130 suspects in defense plants alone, he said. (The day before he had mentioned 91.) He also appeared to be trying to minimize his own role in the coming probe. "Besides," he said, "this isn't my case—this is a case involving my chief counsel and the Army legal counsel." Senator McClellan, seeking to put sharp limits on Joe's role in the hearings, assured reporters that McCarthy was indeed "a party to the quarrel being investigated."[45]

An overflow crowd of 212 reporters attended the President's March 24 news conference, responding to the announcement that Eisenhower was willing to comment on the McCarthy dispute. When asked if he thought that the senator should participate in the coming investigation, the President said, "I am perfectly ready to put myself on record flatly, as I have before, that in America if a man is a party to a dispute, directly or indirectly, he does not sit in judgment on his own case." He would be no more specific than that, and refused to comment on McCarthy's insistence on the right of cross-examination. Still, it was obvious that the President was supporting the view of the Wisconsin senator's role in the hearings espoused by Republican leaders and a majority of the subcommittee members. Joe dismissed Eisenhower's statement with the observation that he had already given up his right to vote on subcommittee findings. He was unwilling to yield further.[46]

The media were preparing to give an unprecedented quantity of coverage to the struggle between the Army and McCarthy. The N.B.C. and A.B.C. networks announced plans to televise all hearings in the controversy. Scores of reporters and photographers were ready to pour into Washington. Walter Lippmann thought that McCarthy had become "a national obsession," and complained that more important matters such as Indo-China, Korea, and bills before Congress were barely being discussed. The influential columnist made no secret of his own views on the senator: "He has played no part in the great measures which the country has taken to resist the expansion of the Communist orbit—and here at home he has netted no spies but only a few minnows at the cost of terrible injustice or enormous injury to the good name of America, and the filling of our air with poison and stink."[47]

While the search for a special subcommittee counsel continued, Karl Mundt tried to minimize the significance of the impending hearings. The controversy involved no serious crimes such as treason or curruption, he said. "Involved here at best are misunderstandings and mistakes by one or more individuals connected with the Army or the Senate committee or both which have interfered with the orderly work of a growing number of officials both in the Army and in Congress." Mundt also took the position that McCarthy did not appear to be one of the "principal disputants" in the case. This statement confirmed the doubts of many about the objectivity of the subcommittee's acting chairman. Eisenhower confided to his press secretary, "You can't trust that fellow."[48]

On April 1 Mundt announced that the special subcommittee counsel would be Samuel P. Sears, a 58-year-old Boston attorney who had been president of the Massachusetts Bar Association and a member of the American Bar Association's board of delegates. Reporters quickly discovered that Sears had been a vigorous McCarthy supporter in 1952 and had once asserted that those taking the Fifth Amendment before congressional committees were "building an iron curtain to help conceal the efforts of Red Russia to destroy the United States." The Americans for Democratic Action cried "whitewash," and other McCarthy critics were equally perturbed. Within the next few days it was learned that Sears had a lengthy record of ultraconservative statements and actions. A few weeks earlier, in fact, Jean McCarthy had recommended him to represent her husband's position in a Boston debate. Facing dismissal, Sears resigned on April 6. Red-faced subcommittee Democrats assured reporters that the attorney, in his interview, had declared complete inpartiality toward McCarthy.

Mundt issued a statement revealing that the subcommittee had earlier sought the services of Judge Harold R. Medina of New York and that the idea had been quashed informally by members of the United States Supreme Court. He also explained that ten other distinguished attorneys had been considered and that Sears was the second to whom the post was formally offered. The senator assured the public, "We have continuously sought what help we could receive from the FBI in doing a name-check on potential choices and from all available sources in providing us with references and recommendations."[49]

The next day the subcommittee voted unanimously to employ Ray H. Jenkins of Knoxville, Tennessee, as special counsel. Jenkins, 57, was a wealthy, highly successful criminal lawyer, known for his courtroom theatrics. He was six-feet-two-inches tall, stocky, and had a massive head topped with a crew cut; he reminded some of a boxer dog when he set his jaw. A Taft Republican, he had been recommended to the subcommittee by Everett Dirksen. Jenkins told reporters, "I have no record, publicly or otherwise, with regard to Senator McCarthy or what has come to be called McCarthyism. I have no prejudice, and no bias."[50]

A few days earlier the Army had appointed Joseph Nye Welch to be its special counsel in the case. The 63-year-old attorney had been born on an Iowa farm, compiled excellent academic records at Grinnell College and Harvard Law School, and was enjoying a prosperous career with the prestigious Boston firm of Hale and Dorr. Short, paunchy, balding, Welch disguised a first-rate mind with a folksy charm and studied simplicity. Roy Cohn later described him as "a courtly gentleman with an old-fashioned grace of manner; a deft, sly wit, and an unerring sense for the jugular."

When asked about his position on McCarthy and McCarthyism, Welch responded, "I am a registered Republican and a trial lawyer. I'm just for facts."

Welch said at his appointment that two junior law associates from his firm, James D. St. Clair and Frederick G. Fisher, Jr., would join him in the case. All three were to serve without compensation. Two weeks later it was announced that Welch had dropped Fisher from the investigation immediately after learning that the young man had once belonged to the National Lawyers Guild, a target of HUAC attacks. "I didn't want a diversionary affair," Welch told reporters.[51]

The Army's unanticipated selection of a special counsel was another sign of its determination to defeat McCarthy and Cohn in the upcoming battle for public opinion. The appointment persuaded Joe, observing from the sidelines, to remain firm in his demand to cross-examine witnesses. Welch could not be permitted to go into the matter of the eleven memos, among other things, in the absence of fierce opposition.[52]

On April 6 Joe replied on television to the attacks of Edward R. Murrow. (The reply was actually a film made by Fox Movietone News. Joe sent the $6,336 bill to ALCOA, Murrow's sponsor, but the company would not pay it. C.B.S. ultimately covered the cost.) He repeated and slightly expanded his allegation about the 1934 summer school proposal and called the broadcaster "the leader and the cleverest of the jackal pack which is always found at the throat of anyone who dares to expose Communists and traitors." He made headlines, however, with a new charge: American research on the hydrogen bomb had been deliberately stalled for eighteen months, amid reports that Russia was "feverishly" pushing a similar project. (The United States had first exploded a hydrogen bomb in August 1952, and the Soviet Union had matched the achievement the following year.) "If there were no Communists in our government," he asked, "why did we delay?" He warned, "Our nation may well die because of that eighteen-month deliberate delay."

Many newspapers carried a full rebuttal by Murrow, and C.B.S. officials reported that the immediate response from the public was "overwhelmingly in favor of Murrow." Democratic Congressman Melvin Price of Illinois, a member of the Joint Congressional Committee on Atomic Energy, called the H-bomb charge "absolutely ridiculous," adding of McCarthy, "He showed complete ignorance." The President, at his weekly news conference the next day, said emphatically that he knew nothing about a delay in hydrogen bomb development. He said also that he had always regarded Edward R. Murrow as a friend.

(It was soon revealed that Joe was referring to charges surrounding famed physicist J. Robert Oppenheimer, who had been secretly suspended by the President in December from his position as consultant to the Atomic Energy Commission and denied access to secret materials. The charges concerned Oppenheimer's past associations with Communists and his opposition to the development of the hydrogen bomb. McCarthy, no doubt with the aid of FBI sources, had been quietly building a case against the scientist for some time. Subcommittee Republicans had sought to probe the matter as early as March 1953 but were dissuaded by White House officials. Joe heartily approved of Oppenheimer's suspension but played no further role in the sensational affair. Subcommittee members flatly ruled out any discussion of the case.)[53]

Hostility toward McCarthy appeared to be spreading rapidly as the hearings, scheduled for April 22, drew nearer. Bishop Bernard J. Sheil, the Roman Catholic auxiliary bishop of Chicago, made headlines on April 9 by strongly condemning the senator. In a speech before 2,500 cheering delegates to the C.I.O. United Auto Workers' Education Conference, the prelate described McCarthy as a "man on horseback" who threatened American freedoms. "Anticommunism is a serious business," he said, and not "a game to be played so publicity-mad politicos can build fame for themselves." The bishop emphasized that he was expressing his personal opinion and not that of the Church. He noted, however, that the Church stood firmly opposed to "lies, calumny, the absence of charity, and calculated deceit." This was devastating to McCarthy's image, for it was widely assumed that Roman Catholics were solidly behind the senator. Aides to the bishop soon reported that the response to his speech was nine to one in the bishop's favor. The radio station that carried the speech said its reaction was running twenty to one in favor of the bishop.[54]

There were also attacks by corporate executive Paul G. Hoffman, a personal friend of the President, and Philip M. Klutznik, president of B'nai B'rith. William Benton took out a full-page ad in *The New York Times* to ridicule McCarthy for dropping his $2,000,000 libel and slander suit and to solicit signatures for an anti-McCarthy campaign. (More than 10,000 people responded during the first week, contributing more than $16,000.) In Cleveland Kenneth D. Jackson, dean of the New York School of Social Work at Columbia University, warned of "a tragic and maybe irreparable breakdown of our service man's morale" unless McCarthy ended his struggle with the Army. Retired Maj. Gen. Arthur R. Wilson, who commanded Army troops in North Africa and Europe during World War II, sent a check for $100 to the commanding general at Fort Dix to be given to the first noncommissioned officer who punched Private Schine in the nose. In

Madison the "Joe Must Go" club reported obtaining nearly half the number of signatures required to hold a special recall election.[55]

While Joe nursed his extremely sore throat in Arizona, the subcommittee drew up procedural ground rules for the Army-McCarthy hearings. Passed unanimously, the rules altered customary procedures in order to insure maximum fairness and prohibit the sort of "one-man" tyranny that had become synonymous with McCarthy. Both sides in the controversy were to file written charges and submit their evidence in advance of the hearings. This material was to be made mutually available and given to the press. Each side was also to prepare a list of witnesses it wished to question publicly, including a synopsis of the testimony each witness was expected to give. Still unresolved was the question of McCarthy's membership on the subcommittee. At a news conference, subcommittee senators made it clear that they did not want Joe to be sitting with them at the bench questioning witnesses who sat below. They thought that all parties should be on a completely equal footing in the hearings, and that McCarthy should sit at the same level with Stevens, sharing the same rights of cross-examination. Joe continued to resist that proposal.[56]

On April 14 the Army gave the subcommittee its formal charges against McCarthy and his key aides. The document was supposed to remain confidential until the senator filed his counter-charges. Instead, it was leaked to reporters that evening, and Stuart Symington made it public the next day. There were 29 charges in all, and they followed the lines of the March 11 Army chronology describing the efforts to win favors for Schine. McCarthy was now tied to the events more closely than before, obviously to thwart his attempt to take himself out of the center of the controversy. Cohn, moreover, was now charged with hinting that the Fort Monmouth probe would be called off or soft-pedaled if Schine were well treated.[57]

Don Whitehead of the Associated Press reported Pentagon officials bitter and angry toward McCarthy over a broad range of issues, including the attacks on Zwicker and Stevens. They admitted that the Cohn-Schine affair was of secondary importance. Officials were viewing the forthcoming hearings, Whitehead wrote, as a chance to defend the integrity and prestige of the Army. One officer declared, "You don't compromise when your honor is involved." The reporter added, "A good many people, including some of McCarthy's colleagues in the Senate, think the inquiry could be the crossroads of the McCarthy career."[58]

Joe threatened to boycott the investigation until the subcommittee took steps to plug the news leak. At a press conference, Karl Mundt dismissed the leak as relatively unimportant and again suggested publicly that

McCarthy remove himself from the subcommittee during the investigation. If he continued to refuse, Mundt warned, the issue would be brought to the floor of the Senate for a final decision. Cohn later asserted, "the majority of the special committee appeared set upon a public lynching."[59]

Following a three-hour, closed-door session with four members of the subcommittee (including all of the Republicans), Joe agreed to step down temporarily and to file his detailed response to the Army's charges. In return, he and his associates, as well as Army officials and their counsel, were given the same right to cross-examine as subcommittee members. Joe was also permitted to select a Republican replacement from the parent Government Operations Committee. He chose ultraconservative Henry C. Dworshak of Idaho.[60]

On April 20 the controversy erupted anew with the filing by McCarthy, Cohn, and Carr of a 46-point, 5,000 word "bill of particulars." The statement denied the use of "improper means" to get favors for Schine and said that the Army report, "when placed in proper perspective," would be found "to have given greater aid and comfort to Communists and security risks than any other single obstacle [to investigating committees] ever designed."

The document's most sensational charge involved Assistant Secretary of Defense H. Struve Hensel, who had signed the Army's chronology and, Joe learned, had supervised its preparation. Hensel was alleged to have made cash profits from a ship supply company while serving as a procurement officer during World War II. (During the 1952 campaigns, Joe had made a similar charge against Stuart Symington, claiming that he had enjoyed "war profits" of more than $1,000,000 as head of the Emerson Electric Company.) To conceal this misconduct from the subcommittee, the statement charged, Hensel interested himself in the attempt to "discredit" McCarthy and his associates.

Stevens and Adams were attacked repeatedly. Adams was alleged to have said to subcommittee members in January that unless McCarthy was prevailed upon to drop his probe of the Army, he would circulate an "embarrassing report" about Cohn. He was also reported to have offered on numerous occasions to "break" General Lawton, commanding general at Fort Monmouth, in return for a promise of silence from McCarthy and the subcommittee staff.

Moreover, the document contended, Adams and Cohn had once been "close personal and social friends," in touch with each other as often as "dozens of times a week." Ordinary conversation between the two, "some jocular, some animated," had become in the Army report "violent, abusive and threatening" talk. The statement pointed to five instances when social relations between the two continued after Cohn was supposed to have made serious threats. "After Mr. Cohn is alleged to have set about 'wrecking' the Army, and causing the 'dismissal' of Mr. Adams' boss, Mr. Adams continued to invite Mr. Cohn to lunch, and to discuss a law partnership with him."

Hovering over all of the 46 points was the suspicion of subversion. "The pattern followed by Secretary Stevens and Mr. Adams is clear," the statement declared. "As long as only individual Communists were the object of the subcommittee's investigation, they made continuing offers of cooperation with the investigation. But as soon as the probe turned to the infinitely more important question of who was responsible for protecting Communist infiltration, and protecting Communists who had infiltrated, every conceivable obstacle was placed in the path of the subcommittee's search for truth." Even Joseph Welch was tainted: a law partner had belonged "in recent years" to an organization branded by HUAC as the "legal bulwark" of the Communist party and referred to by the Attorney General as the "legal mouthpiece" of the Communists. This, of course, was a reference to Fred Fisher, who was discharged, the document falsely contended, "only when his Communist-front connection became publicly known." The statement closed with the demand that Army officials make available to the subcommittee those "still serving under them who are responsible for the rise in the Army of a Communist conspirator against this country." The "conspirator" was Irving Peress.[61]

Hensel hotly denied the statement's charge against him, telling a national television audience, "Senator McCarthy is a liar but not a very clever liar." He explained that there was "absolutely nothing illegal" about his wartime business enterprise, which sold food exclusively to private businesses, and he dared McCarthy to repeat his allegation without congressional immunity. (Joe refused, saying it might delay the hearings.) Defense Secretary Charles Wilson emphatically supported Hensel and said that the Army-McCarthy dispute reminded him of the political maxim "if your opponent accuses you of being a liar, you don't deny it. You call him a horsethief." Reporters noted that Hensel had been confirmed by the Senate as Assistant Secretary of Defense on February 19 without objection.[62]

Newsmen could find no member of the subcommittee who recalled Adams making a threatening statement about Cohn. The three Democrats and Charles Potter flatly denied hearing the Army counsel say any such thing. Dirksen and Mundt declined comment.[63]

On the evening before the hearings were to begin, Joe was in Houston, the guest of his oil millionaire friend Hugh Roy Cullen. Addressing a crowd of 5,000 at the base of the San Jacinto Battlefield monument, in ceremonies staged by the Sons of the Republic of Texas, he warned of a plan to change subcommittee rules in order to hamstring the investigation of Reds. He cited the example of a proposal to require the presence of a certain number of senators at subcommittee hearings. Such a requirement, he said, had caused the invalidation by the United States Supreme Court of the perjury conviction of a Communist named Christoffel.

Questioned by reporters, Senator McClellan said, "I don't know what he's talking about," noting that there were no pending efforts to change sub-committee rules. The Associated Press pointed out that Milwaukee labor leader Harold Christoffel, after a second trial, was convicted of perjury and was currently in prison.[64]

That same evening the Gallup Poll reported that nearly eight out of ten adults surveyed said they had read or heard about the Army-McCarthy dispute. Forty-six percent of them believed Stevens; twenty-three percent sided with Joe.[65]

22

POINT OF ORDER

There was immense excitement throughout the country about the Army-McCarthy hearings. Most of the anticipation was generated, of course, by the media, which trumpeted the hearings as among the significant events of the decade. At first glance this appeared excessive, given the fact that much of the controversy focused upon the privileges of an Army private. But it was widely understood that the hearings were not actually about G. David Schine. The basic issue was Joe McCarthy. For years the senator had been condemning a wide assortment of individuals and institutions, and he appeared to be threatening the stability and integrity of one of the most popular administrations in American history. Now it was the attacker who was on trial. Millions would have the opportunity to look him squarely in the eye and judge for themselves what sort of man he was. Roy Cohn wrote later, "There was really but one name that was important, that of Joseph Raymond McCarthy. And one issue, McCarthy versus his enemies."[1]

Subcommittee members expected the hearings to last two weeks or more. Daily sessions were scheduled from 10:30 A.M. to 12:30 P.M., and from 2:30 P.M. to 4:30 P.M. The senators, three representatives of the Army, McCarthy, Cohn, and Carr were to be seated behind a 26-foot long mahogany table at one end of the ornate caucus room on the third floor of the Senate Office Building. Each day, the Army representatives and the

McCarthy group were to shift positions, equalizing their opportunities to be photographed by the three stationary television cameras covering the sessions.[2]

The special rules adopted for the hearings permitted Ray Jenkins, the subcommittee counsel, to question witnesses first, without time limit. He was to lead witnesses through a direct examination, enabling them to present their side of the case, and then he would switch to cross-examination, emphasizing the opposition's point of view. Chairman Mundt then had ten minutes to question the witness. Following that, each senator was given the same amount of time, alternating from Democratic to Republican sides of the table and from senior members down the line. At the conclusion of these questions, each side in the dispute, McCarthy and Welch or those associated with them, had ten minutes. The procedure would then be repeated, if necessary, until the interrogation of the witness was completed. Point three of the rules stipulated: "All examinations in each case shall proceed without interruption except for objections as to materiality and relevancy."[3]

On the opening day, April 22, the caucus room was jammed to capacity with more than 400 spectators and over 100 reporters. The audience was the largest ever to view a congressional hearing. Joseph Welch later recalled, "The first sight of the hearing room was a shock to a lawyer used to the traditionally ordered interiors of courtrooms. It was utter confusion. Photographers leaped up and down to get pictures. Messengers crawled beneath chairs. The cameras turned to follow the action. Spectators came and went. People sat, stood and moved in every square inch of space and the whole crowded room was bathed in the bright lights of television." Welch took one look through the doorway and recoiled in horror. A capitol patrolman on the scene was amused by the attorney's reaction. "Don't worry," he said, "in three days there won't be twenty people here."[4]

Senator Mundt opened the proceeding with a brief speech stressing the subcommittee's impartiality and commitment to "a maximum degree of dignity, fairness, and thoroughness." Senator McClellan, as the senior Democrat, echoed this sentiment, adding that the charges in the case were so "diametrically in conflict" that he saw no hope of reconciling them. The subcommittee's responsibility, he said, was to develop the facts and weigh the accusations. "It will be an arduous and a difficult task, one that is not pleasant to contemplate, but it is a job that must be done."

The hearing was only seventeen minutes old when Joe broke in and raised a "point of order"—a procedural subterfuge he would employ hundreds of times throughout the hearings to interject commentary. He objected to the charges raised by Adams and Stevens being labeled "Filed by the Department of the Army." "I maintain it is a disgrace and reflection upon every one of the million outstanding men in the Army to let a few civilians who are trying to hold up an investigation of Communists, label themselves as the Department of the Army." Joe was rude, emotional, and angry. He was establishing a pattern of interruption and harassment that would be repeated continuously throughout the hearings.

Roy Cohn later rated McCarthy's performance "miserable." "With his easily erupting temper, his menacing monotone, his unsmiling mien, and his perpetual five-o'clock shadow, he did seem the perfect stock villain. Central casting could not have come up with a better one." At first, people were shocked by the senator's often repellent behavior. In time, as they became rather accustomed to it day after day, Joe began to seem somehow humorous and pathetic. All over the country comedians, mimics, and smart alecks could be heard droning in the senator's flat voice, "Point of order, Mr. Chairman." The line almost always got a laugh. When the attacks turned to ridicule, Joe's political power was destroyed.[5]

The Army introduced three witnesses on the first day of the hearings. Maj. Gen. Miles Reber, a 35-year veteran and a winner of the Distinguished Service Medal, had flown from Germany to testify about the efforts of McCarthy and Cohn to obtain a speedy commission for G. David Schine. Reber did not feel that the senator was guilty of improper conduct, but he was critical of Cohn's persistent attempts to pressure him. Joe countered with an attack on the general's brother, Sam Reber, former acting United States High Commissioner for Germany. Joe claimed that the diplomat had resigned from the State Department in July 1953 "when charges that he was a bad security risk were made against him as a result of the investigations of this committee," and he alleged that this had influenced the general in his dealings with Cohn. The witness, pounding his hand in his fist, declared flatly, "I do not know and have never heard that my brother retired as a result of any action of this committee." Senator Jackson was appalled by Joe's tactic. Senator McClellan asked for a ruling on the issue, "because we may be trying members of everybody's family involved before we get through."

That afternoon, testimony by Secretary Stevens was interrupted to give Under Secretary of State Walter Bedell Smith an opportunity to appear. Smith, a secret ally of McCarthy's (Scott McLeod accompanied him to the hearing), described Cohn's contacts with him concerning a commission for Schine and said that in his judgment the young attorney's requests were neither extraordinary nor improper. Subcommittee members asked few questions. Joe thanked the retired Army general and said of him, "I think he has very many more important things to do than to discuss a private in the Army who had been promoted consistently until he is a private."

Secretary Stevens, in a lengthy statement, reviewed the Army chronology, attacked McCarthy's countercharges, and labeled the Schine case "an example of the wrongful seeking of privilege, of the perversion of power." He added several bits of new evidence to his account of events, including a threat allegedly made by Cohn when he was refused entrance to a special laboratory at Fort Monmouth. A colonel told Stevens that Cohn said "in substance": "This means war. Don't they think I am cleared for classified information? I have access to FBI files when I want them. . . . They did this on purpose to embarrass me. We will really investigate the Army now."[6]

On the second day of the hearings it was revealed that the Army possessed 50 to 100 transcripts of telephone conversations bearing on the case. For several years the appointment secretary to the Secretary of the Army had been secretly required to monitor virtually all telephone calls handled by his superior, making verbatim stenographic records for the files. A transcript of November 7, cited by Stevens, showed Joe deprecating Cohn's efforts on behalf of Schine. "Now, in that conversation," Stevens said, "Senator McCarthy says that one of the few things that he has trouble with Mr. Cohn about was David Schine. He said that 'Roy thinks that Dave ought to be a general and operate from a penthouse on the Waldorf Astoria,' or words to that effect. Senator McCarthy then said that he thought a few weekends off for David Schine might be arranged, or words to that effect. Perhaps for the purpose of taking care of Dave's girl friends."

Joe was enraged to learn of the Army's cache of evidence, calling the practice of monitoring telephone calls "one of the most indecent and dishonest things I ever heard of." The crowd in the jampacked hearing room laughed as he protested. A lengthy and heated argument filled much of the day concerning the admissibility of the transcripts as evidence. On a motion by Senator McClellan, and with the approval of all parties, the subcommittee voted unanimously to subpoena all relevant transcripts and introduce them into evidence in their chronological order. A number of legal questions remained involving the admission of the transcripts, and Mundt soon told reporters, "About half of the lawyers in town are working on this now. . . . We are just trying to make doggone sure we are on solid ground."[7]

In Milwaukee over the weekend, Joe called the hearings a "waste of time" and a "red-minnow burlesque." He said that Stevens was "inexperienced," and he hoped that someday the Secretary would wake up to "what is happening to him." Joe again complained about the existence of the transcribed telephone conversations. Bluffing, he said that he might have "possibly one or two" such transcripts in his own files.[8]

The next day, H. Struve Hensel filed his formal reply to McCarthy with the subcommittee, accusing the senator of "malicious lies" and offering to match his financial records against McCarthy's before the subcommittee or any other body. On his return to Washington, Joe issued a blistering attack against the Assistant Secretary of Defense. "He inadvertently tipped the hand of those who have been masterminding the smear attack upon my staff and disclosed the true purpose to be what I have stated it was since its inception—namely, an attempt to roadblock all investigations of graft, corruption, and communism, and divert the committee down the side road of investigating itself."[9]

Secretary Stevens took the stand on April 26 for the third of what would turn out to be thirteen consecutive days of testimony. Ray Jenkins examined him rigorously, probing for flaws in his account of events and demanding explanations for inconsistencies and omissions. The counsel was frequently harsh and sarcastic. Stevens faltered at times under the withering barrage of questions, and he occasionally became evasive and vague. He answered one question with "I don't think that I did, probably." When asked if he had wanted the subcommittee's probe at Fort Monmouth stopped, he replied, "Yes, sir," changed this to "No, sir," and then admitted seeking the "suspension" of the investigation (which he later denied).

The Army Secretary's testimony was filled with examples of extreme obsequiousness toward McCarthy, Cohn, and Schine. He conceded that McCarthy's investigation had accelerated the suspension of alleged security risks at Fort Monmouth. Moreover, he was unable to recall anything specific that Frank Carr had said or done that implicated him with the charges raised against McCarthy and Cohn. Mundt, Dirksen, and McCarthy made much of this failure.[10]

Joseph Welch was too clever to permit the continuation of such pillory without resistance. He had already revealed a capacity for showmanship by parading a bevy of top Army brass into the hearing room and positioning them so that television viewers would understand that he represented the Army rather than simply three "Pentagon politicians." During one hearing, Army Chief of Staff Matthew Ridgeway made a dramatic entrance and sat down right behind Secretary Stevens. Continuously irritated by this ploy, Joe would snap at one point, "I do think that we should know just how many generals and colonels are ordered over here by the civilians in the Pentagon; why they are here and not doing their work in the Army."

600 THE LIFE AND TIMES OF JOE McCARTHY

On April 27th, Welch seized upon the minor matter of a photograph introduced by Jenkins and magnified it into a major issue of the hearings. The resultant uproar lasted several days and produced hundreds of anti-McCarthy headlines across the country.[11]

The photograph in question had been taken on November 17, 1953. Earlier that day, Stevens had flown to New York and invited McCarthy, Cohn, and Carr to lunch. The discussion focused upon the Fort Monmouth probe and Joe's unhappiness about comments made by the Army Secretary at a press conference. After the meeting, Stevens flew his three guests in his private plane to McGuire Air Force Base, which adjoined Fort Dix. The senator and Cohn had mentioned at lunch a desire to see Schine, and Stevens, as usual, was bending over backward to be cooperative. Eight photographs were taken at Fort Dix, including one of Stevens, Schine, base commander Col. Kenneth Bradley, and Frank Carr. Schine requested a copy of the photograph showing him next to the Army Secretary, and when it arrived he placed it on a wall in his New York office. Without Schine's knowledge, the photograph had been altered by an Air Force sergeant to include only Schine, Stevens, and Bradley.

As Cohn prepared for the hearings, he remembered seeing the photograph in Schine's office and mentioned it to Jenkins. Cohn thought it would buttress his allegation that Stevens had asked to have his picture taken with Schine at a time when the Secretary was supposedly angry with the private over improper pressure tactics. (Stevens denied the charge and the truth of the matter was never settled.) Jenkins asked to see the photograph, and Schine brought it to Washington. Staff member James Juliana had two types of copies produced for presentation at the hearings: an exact duplication of the photograph that hung on Schine's wall and another showing only Stevens and Schine. Juliana later took full responsibility for editing Colonel Bradley out of one set of copies: "It was done because I had instructions to furnish Mr. Jenkins with a picture of Secretary Stevens and Mr. Schine." Jenkins, unaware that any alterations had been made, received a copy from Juliana containing only Stevens and Schine. He used it to allege that Stevens had asked to have his picture taken *alone* with Schine.

Welch opened the hearing on April 27 with the startling charge that Jenkins had presented as evidence "a doctored or altered photograph . . . as if it were honest." He contended that Stevens was "photographed in a group," argued that the Secretary was looking at Colonel Bradley rather than Schine (Stevens's eyeglass frames made it impossible to tell), and described Stevens's slight smile as "grim."

Called as a witness, Cohn expressed surprise that the photograph was incomplete but argued that it did not matter. He had not attempted to prove, he said, that Stevens had wanted to be photographed alone with Schine. The very existence of the photograph, he claimed, with or without Colonel Bradley, revealed Stevens's friendliness toward Schine.

Wrangling and quarreling over the facts in the case of the "doctored" photograph consumed many hours, strained senators' tempers, and undoubtedly bored tens of thousands of television viewers. Jenkins frustrated witnesses with lengthy and frequently needless and repetitious questions. Welch, eloquently hinting at a dark plot by McCarthyites, seemed never to get to the point. Most of the McCarthy aides called upon to testify, such as George Anastos, were only minor participants in the case. Reporters, meanwhile, wrote lengthy stories about the "fake," "cropped," and "shamefully altered" photograph. The fact that the original Air Force photograph, used by Welch, had been altered even before it reached Schine drew virtually no attention in the media.

Actually, there was little or no reason to condemn McCarthy staff members in the matter. Cohn had undoubtedly been unaware of Juliana's personal decision to alter the photograph. Juliana's alteration did not effect Cohn's assertions about Stevens and Schine. It seems certain that Jenkins, not Cohn, decided to use the picture to illustrate Stevens's alleged desire to be photographed alone with Schine. On the stand, Juliana, Schine, and others involved in handling the photograph were frank and believable.

Throughout the clamor, Joe did his best to get the facts of the case into the record quickly and return to the central issues of the hearings. He was finally successful on the afternoon of April 30 when Stevens returned to the witness stand and resumed his often bumbling performance. By this time, however, Welch, with the assistance of the media, had succeeded in casting a cloud of suspicion on the senator and his aides that would never fully dissipate. As Joe had learned years earlier, sensational allegations made larger headlines than complex, factual explanations.[12]

Welch's task was made easier by McCarthy's increasingly petulant behavior. By the conclusion of the seventh day of hearings, on April 30, Joe had clashed, at times bitterly, with almost every member of the subcommittee and Jenkins, as well as the Army counsel and Stevens. He had referred to the hearings as "this circus" and "this red-lined burlesque." During several of his outbursts, Joe seemed to lose his temper completely. Audience response in the hearing room seemed to be solidly anti-McCarthy.

In a row over the "doctored picture," he first directed his fire at Chairman Mundt, who was attempting to stem one of his many interruptions in the guise of a point of order.

Senator McCarthy. May I finish my point of order?

Senator Mundt. Counsel [Jenkins] advises the Chair that the senator is engaging in a statement or cross-examination rather than a point of order.

Senator McCarthy. I am getting rather sick of being interrupted in the middle of a sentence.

Senator Symington. I would like to say if this is not a point of order it is out of order. The counsel says it is not a point of order and it is not a point or order, if the counsel says it is not a point of order.

Senator McCarthy. Oh, be quiet.

Senator Symington. I haven't the slightest intention of being quiet. Counsel is running this committee, and you are not running it.

Senator McCarthy. Mr. Chairman, do I have the floor?

Senator Mundt. The Chair has the floor, and nobody is endeavoring to determine whether or not Senator McCarthy is speaking to a point of order.

Will you state your point of order and then speak to it?

Senator McCarthy. Mr. Chairman, may I suggest that when I start to say something, I not be interrupted in the middle of a sentence, and that Mr. Symington and no one else have the right to interrupt unless he addresses the Chair, and unless the Chair recognizes him. I am getting awfully sick of sitting down here at the end of the table and having whoever wants to interrupt in the middle of a sentence.

A few minutes later, he growled:

> Call it a point of order or call it what you may, when counsel for Mr. Stevens, and Mr. Hensel, and Mr. Adams makes a statement and he is allowed to do it without interruption, and if that statement is false, do I have a right to correct it, or do we find halfway through my statement that Mr. Welch should not have made his statement and therefore I cannot point out that he was lying?[13]

During a tedious interrogation of Schine by Jenkins concerning the altered photograph, Joe cried:

> I want to make the very strong point of order that this is the most improper exhibition I have ever seen. You have a lawyer here who brags about being one of the greatest crimi-

nal lawyers in the country, badgering this private and he has told him ten times now that he doesn't know whether or not George Anastos was there, but to the best of his recollection Anastos was not there.

He can't gain anything further by badgering this Army private. I think it is indecent, and I think the Chair should condemn it.[14]

Joe would become enraged when one of his staff members came under fire on the stand. Another such situation occurred on April 30 as Welch cleverly worked over James Juliana.

Mr. Welch. You did know what hung on Schine's wall when that was handed to you, sir.

Mr. Juliana. I did not know what hung on Schine's wall.

Mr. Welch. Did you think this came from a pixie? Where did you think this picture that I hold in my hand came from?

Mr. Juliana. I had no idea.

Senator Mundt. Senator McCarthy says he couldn't hear the question. It will be reread.

(Whereupon the question referred to was read by the reporter as above recorded.)

Senator McCarthy. Will counsel for my benefit define—I think he might be an expert on that—what a pixie is?

Mr. Welch. Yes. I should say, Mr. Senator, that a pixie is a close relative of a fairy.

Shall I proceed, sir? Have I enlightened you?

Senator McCarthy. As I said, I think you may be an authority on what a pixie is.[15]

Joe said nastily to Stevens at one point, "That is a simple question, Bob, and you should be able to answer it." He quickly compounded the insult with, "Let's be a little more honest here." He later charged the Secretary with "flagrant dishonesty."[16]

"May I have the Chair's attention," he bawled at Mundt during an exchange on rules. Later that day he again demanded Mundt's attention. "You can't listen to both at once. I know you have two ears, but you can't listen to both people at once." Two days later he suggested to the chairman that he "ask counsel for Mr. Stevens and Mr. Jenkins not to ask questions merely for the purpose of clearing their voices, but only ask them if they are looking for information."[17]

Not even timid Senator Dworshak was exempt from Joe's wrath. On

April 29 Joe objected to his line of questioning when it appeared critical of Schine. The Idaho Republican slammed a document on the table and fell silent. The next day, Joe said publicly that he regretted having selected Dworshak to serve on the subcommittee, and he threatened to reclaim his place on the body.[18]

Millions of spectators judged the hearings primarily on the impressions they received of the major participants. They had no other choice given the complex nature of the charges exchanged by the Army and McCarthy and given the format of the hearings, which frequently prevented prolonged attention to a single line of thought. Joe's sarcasm and malice contrasted sharply with Stevens's sincerity. (The Alsops called the Secretary "one of the Administration's leading innocents-at-large.") Cohn's brusque mannerisms and rapid-fire innuendos could not begin to compete in public popularity with Welch's folksy charm and wit.

A spot check made by the Gallup organization in eight major cities after the first several days of the hearings revealed that of the 66 percent following the controversy, 41 percent favored Stevens while only 17 percent favored McCarthy. A Gallup poll published in early May showed that 43 percent of those questioned would be less likely to vote for a candidate endorsed by McCarthy—a jump of 17 percent in five months. Newspapers also noted the defeat of former Republican Congressman J. Parnell Thomas in the April 20 New Jersey primary. Thomas had pledged "1000-percent" support for McCarthy, "his objectives, and his methods." A *Fortune* magazine study revealed faltering support of McCarthy among Texas businessmen because of the clash with Stevens and the Army. Clint Murchison said that Joe had begun to "bungle." Dallas editor E. M. Dealey deplored the "brutality" of the senator's methods.[19]

Many Republican leaders were anxious for the hearings to end, deploring the public spectacle of intraparty warfare. The President, angry and flushed, told a news conference he hoped the affair would conclude very quickly. Vice-President Nixon was quoted as saying that the hearings were getting to the "ridiculous stage." Senator Flanders told a constituent that the hearings were "a tragedy for the G.O.P. and a great field day for the Democratic Party." He added, "The responsibility for this thing lies squarely on the heads of the Republicans who have been obsessed with the value of McCarthy to the party. We are reaping what they have sown."[20]

Others were equally embarrassed by the proceedings. The bar association of St. Louis sent a telegram to the White House urging suspension of the hearings until adoption of a code of procedure, "for the sake of preserving the dignity of governmental processes in the United States."[21]

Joe's enemies were of a different mind, convinced that the senator was destroying himself daily before an audience of 20 million people. Senator Fulbright said that McCarthy was "using the same techniques of disruption and interruption the Communist leaders used in their conspiracy trial before Federal Judge Medina in New York." The Arkansas Democrat observed, "The hearing is a painful thing and it sickens me, but it is essential to wake up the American people to the truth about the man."[22]

After the eighth day of hearings, on May 3, the subcommittee, at Everett Dirksen's request, met privately with the major participants in the case to explore ways to conclude the hearings rapidly. Republicans proposed that McCarthy take the stand immediately and that no further witnesses be called. Welch and the subcommittee Democrats balked at the suggestion. Welch was intent on nailing McCarthy's coffin tightly. The Democrats, of course, had partisan considerations. Senator Symington said at the hearing the next morning, "There have been statements that these hearings are disheartening to the people. There have been statements that the American people are disgusted with these hearings. Well, many times something that is disgusting or disheartening nevertheless has to be done so that we have good in the long run."[23]

On the evening of May 3 Charles Potter secretly paid a visit to the White House at the invitation of the President. Eisenhower asked a number of questions about the hearings and passionately denounced McCarthy as "psychopathic" and "lawless." He urged an immediate end to the hearings and asked Potter to keep in touch with him. Two days later Eisenhower told a news conference that the hearings had damaged the nation's self-respect and injured its international prestige. He gave his unqualified support to Secretary Stevens.[24]

Jenkins and all of the senators except McCarthy had exhausted their supply of questions for the Army Secretary during the morning session on April 29. Thereafter, hour after hour, session after session, Joe and Roy Cohn kept hammering away at Stevens.

> Senator McCarthy. When did you first hear of the report? I am not asking you to pass on whether it is true or not. When did you first hear of the report or the allegation that Mr. Adams had made the statement that if we issued subpoenas for those who had cleared men with communistic backgrounds, that if we did that, there would be issued a report, a charge, call it what you may—
> Secretary Stevens. I never heard any such statement.

Senator McCarthy. Let me finish—emanating from your department, alleging misconduct on Mr. Cohn's part?

Secretary Stevens. I never heard any such statement.

Senator McCarthy. You never did?

Secretary Stevens. No, sir.

Senator McCarthy. Did you ever come to me and complain about any alleged misconduct on Mr. Cohn's part?

Secretary Stevens. Did I ever come to you?

Senator McCarthy. Yes.

Secretary Stevens. And complain about Mr. Cohn?

Senator McCarthy. Yes.

Secretary Stevens. I think you were well aware of what our attitude was with respect to the pressure Mr. Cohn was putting on us.

Senator McCarthy. Mr. Stevens, you can answer my question; will you? Did you ever complain to me of any misconduct or any pressure on the part of Mr. Cohn?

Secretary Stevens. Mr. Adams did, repeatedly.

Senator McCarthy. You are telling on what Mr. Adams did?

Secretary Stevens. That is right.

Senator McCarthy. I am asking you. Did you, Robert T. Stevens, ever complain to me about any misconduct on the part of my chief counsel?

Secretary Stevens. I complained to you about some things when you kept trying to get Schine assigned to New York, for example, Senator.

Senator McCarthy. I think you should answer this question, Mr. Secretary. There has been considerable complaint that you have been kept on the witness stand too long. You will be kept on—

Mr. Jenkins. May I suggest, Mr. Secretary, that the answer to the question is very simple and we certainly will get along much more expeditiously if you will answer his questions. That is, did you personally ever complain to Senator McCarthy about Mr. Cohn and Mr. Cohn's alleged efforts to get preferential treatment for Schine?

Secretary Stevens. I did not personally do that.

Mr. Jenkins. That is an answer, Senator.

Secretary Stevens. And for the reason that most of the pressure was coming on to Mr. Adams from Mr. Cohn, and Adams was therefore the one that complained.

Mr. Jenkins. All right.

Senator Mundt. Senator McCarthy?

Senator McCarthy. Did you not repeatedly praise Mr. Cohn to me?

Secretary Stevens. No, sir; I don't recall that.

Senator McCarthy. Don't you recall ever praising Mr. Cohn?

Secretary Stevens. I do not.

Senator McCarthy. You never said any good about him?

Secretary Stevens. I wouldn't say I never said anything good about him, but I don't recall going out of my way to praise him.

Senator McCarthy. Didn't you repeatedly praise Mr. Cohn to me?

Secretary Stevens. I do not recall ever having done that.

Senator McCarthy. Now, Mr. Stevens, as you know, Mr. Cohn has a background of having taken a large part in the prosecution of the Rosenberg case, the Rosenbergs who were executed, and the William Remington, the case of the second-string Communists, and, as you know very well, he was the attorney who presented the case before the grand jury which exposed 39 Communists in the U.N.—

Mr. Jenkins. Mr. Chairman, may I suggest that the Senator may ask those questions instead of making statements of fact.

Senator McCarthy. I will say, are you aware of those facts?

Secretary Stevens. Yes; I know about some of those facts.

Senator McCarthy. When you were talking to me on various occasions did we not discuss Mr. Cohn's background and did you not tell me that you felt that I was extremely lucky to have been able to persuade Mr. Cohn to come with the committee?

Secretary Stevens. Senator McCarthy, I am also interested in the military records of young people.

Mr. Jenkins. Mr. Secretary, may I suggest that you answer his question, please?

I dislike interrupting and I hope you know that. But when you do answer his questions directly he goes to another question and we are to that extent nearer the end of this investigation.

Senator Mundt. The Chair will add that, if you can do that, then you can make a statement of explanation afterward.

Secretary Stevens. Can I have the question?

Senator Mundt. Yes.

(The reporter read from his notes as requested.)

> Secretary Stevens. I have no recollection of any such statement.

On May 3 Joe brought up the Peress case, and the next day he sought to debate the Fort Monmouth charges. Efforts by Jenkins and others to restrict the questions to the topics at hand were brushed aside. Joe warned of individuals in the Army "much more dangerous than the Communists themselves," and he stormed and ranted at the hapless witness for helping to plot the destruction of his investigations. The *Washington Post* commented, "The Secretary's patience and obvious honesty in the face of questions which were sometimes insulting and frequently tricky have certainly won him the sympathy and respect of the American public."[25]

On the afternoon of May 4 Welch produced a letter from Army files that deflated a lengthy effort by McCarthy and Cohn to show that Stevens had been uncooperative during the Fort Monmouth investigation. To cover his chagrin, Joe impetuously whipped out a document from his briefcase that appeared to be a copy of a letter from J. Edgar Hoover to an Army general, dated January 26, 1951. Fifteen minutes earlier he had quietly asked Carr, "Shall I hit them with this one?" Carr had advised against it. Now Joe could no longer resist the temptation. He claimed that the document was one of a series of letters sent by the FBI Director to Army officials alerting them to security problems at the Signal Corps laboratories. Someone, he said, "was derelict when these repeated warnings from the FBI were ignored." Joe was bluffing; he did not know where the document had come from, and he did not understand what it actually was. He was to pay a high price for this hasty gamble.[26]

Senator Jackson and Welch immediately clamored for information about the document; it was labeled "Personal and Confidential, via liaison" and had typed at the bottom "Sincerely yours, J. Edgar Hoover, Director." The Army counsel denied any knowledge of it and spoke of "this purported copy." Joe, who claimed that his document was a copy of a letter that could be found in Army files, declared "I want to make it clear that I have gotten neither this letter nor anything else from the FBI." That evening, a search in the Pentagon produced no such letter. A subcommittee staff member, Robert Collier, was sent to Hoover with McCarthy's document. (Subcommittee members continually stumbled over each other to express their unbridled admiration for the director. Symington had earlier described the bureau as "one of the greatest organizations this country has ever or ever did have.")

The next morning, during an extremely stormy session, Collier revealed that the FBI had in its files a fifteen-page memorandum sent by Hoover to the same general on the same date. McCarthy's two-and-one-quarter page document contained information relating to the same subject, and in some instances it contained the exact language found in the memorandum, but it was not a copy of anything in the bureau files. Joe fought back with the claim that his letter was an exact copy of the memorandum with security information omitted. This was flatly contradicted by Collier on the basis of his consultation with Hoover. Welch crowed, "Mr. Collier, as I understand your testimony this document that I hold in my hand is a carbon copy of precisely nothing, is that right?" Collier was compelled to agree. Joe angrily counterattacked; "I think there should be certain rules, even on your part, Mr. Welch, certain rules of honesty in cross-examination." Cohn joined in to point out that the document dealt with suspected Fort Monmouth employee Aaron Coleman. He also claimed that the senator had spoken "with complete honesty" when introducing the letter. But the damage had been done, and newspapers ran blazing headlines declaring that Hoover had challenged the accuracy of McCarthy's evidence. The director, Richard Nixon revealed years later, was secretly telling the President at this time that McCarthy was impeding the investigation of Communists. Joe was now being almost completely written off by the forces that had created him. [27]

That afternoon, following a telephone conversation with Hoover, Collier testified in more detail about the differences between the McCarthy letter and the FBI memorandum. Joe's letter, he revealed, consisted of seven paragraphs taken verbatim from the memorandum. But evaluative comments ("Derogatory" or "No Derogatory") on individuals listed in both documents replaced bureau security information, and a parenthetical explanation had been added to account for the deletion of the material. McCarthy's document also contained a salutation, a closing, and other minor alterations. Thus it was clear that Welch was correct in claiming that the document Joe introduced into the hearings was not in fact a letter or a copy of a letter from J. Edgar Hoover.

Compounding the gravity of the situation, Hoover noted through Collier, was the fact that the FBI memorandum was highly classified. Joe had wanted to read all or part of his document into the record. At the director's suggestion, Mundt contacted the Attorney General for an opinion and refused to permit Joe to read a word of his "letter" aloud.

Hoover also emphasized, Collier said, that the designation "Espionage-R" found on both the memorandum and the McCarthy document was a routine notation and implied nothing. This bluntly contradicted Joe's claim that it proved those named in the documents were under investigation for Russian espionage.

Jenkins then called McCarthy to the stand. Joe said he had received his controversial document personally from a young officer in Army Intelligence in the spring of 1953: "I recall he stated very clearly the reason why he was giving me this information was because he was deeply disturbed because even though there were repeated reports from the FBI to the effect that there was Communist infiltration, indications of espionage in the top secret laboratories, the radar laboratories, that nothing was being done, he felt that his duty to his country was above any duty to any Truman directive to the effect that he could not disclose that information." In fact, Joe did not know where the letter had come from; it had apparently been received recently in the mail from an anonymous donor. McCarthy admitted being unaware of the fifteen-page FBI memorandum when he introduced his document as evidence and that he thought he possessed an exact copy of a letter from the Army files. While not revealing the specific contents of both documents, he noted that they contained 34 names and involved people "connected with the Sobel-Rosenberg spy ring."

When Welch took over the questioning, he dramatically contended that Joe's refusal to name his source of information violated the oath he had taken as a witness.

> Mr. Welch. The oath included a promise, a solemn promise by you to tell the truth, comma, the whole truth, comma, and nothing but the truth. Is that correct, sir?
>
> Senator McCarthy. Mr. Welch, you are not the first individual that tried to get me to betray the confidence and give out the names of my informants. You will be no more successful than those who have tried in the past, period.
>
> Mr. Welch. I am only asking you, sir, did you realize when you took that oath that you were making a solemn promise to tell the whole truth to this committee?
>
> Senator McCarthy. I understand the oath, Mr. Welch.
>
> Mr. Welch. And when you took it, did you have some mental reservation, some Fifth- or Sixth-Amendment notion that you could measure what you would tell?
>
> Senator McCarthy. I don't take the Fifth or Sixth Amendment.
>
> Mr. Welch. Have you some private reservations when you take the oath that you will tell the whole truth that lets you be the judge of what you will testify to?

Senator McCarthy. The answer is there is no reservation about telling the whole truth.

Mr. Welch. Thank you, sir.

Then tell us who delivered the document to you.

Senator McCarthy. The answer is no. You will not get that information.

Mr. Welch. You wish, then, to put your own interpretation on your oath and tell us less than the whole truth?

Senator McCarthy. Mr. Welch. I think I made it very clear to you that neither you nor anyone else will ever get me to violate the confidence of loyal people in this government who give me information about Communist infiltration. I repeat, you will not get their names, you will not get any information which will allow you to identify them so that you or anyone else can get their jobs.

When the Army counsel became interested in the details of the alleged donation of the document by the unnamed Army Intelligence officer, Joe became extremely evasive, sounding, Roy Cohn wrote later, "like the many dozens of witnesses he himself had criticized for being unresponsive at subcommittee hearings."

Mr. Welch. How soon after you got it did you show it to anyone?

Senator McCarthy. I don't remember.

Mr. Welch. To whom did you first show it?

Senator McCarthy. I don't recall.

Mr. Welch. Can you think of the name of anyone to whom you showed it?

Senator McCarthy. I assume that it passed on to my staff, most likely.

Mr. Welch. Name the ones on your staff who had it.

Senator McCarthy. I wouldn't know.

Mr. Welch. You wouldn't know?

Senator McCarthy. No.

Mr. Welch. Well, would it include Mr. Cohn?

Senator McCarthy. It might.

Mr. Welch. It would, wouldn't it?

Senator McCarthy. I say it might.

Mr. Welch. Would it include Mr. Carr?

Senator McCarthy. It might.

Although Joe was not legally required to disclose his source of information, as Jenkins and Mundt quickly pointed out, Welch had produced great theater and again contributed significantly to the destruction of McCarthy's public image.

When Welch's turn next came around, he attempted to stress the differences between Joe's document and the FBI memorandum, but Joe seemed undaunted by the damaging revelations that had dominated the hearing. "I consider it of tremendous importance, now that the authenticity has been established, that this is a verbatim copy, a verbatim copy, from the fifteen-page report, to show the committee and the people of this country the extent to which the FBI has done their usual outstanding job, tried to get action by sending through the reports, and the usual discouraging results, no action, nothing until a congressional committee took over."[28]

Subcommittee Democrats were determined to make the most of what journalists would soon call the "Case of the Purloined FBI Document." The next day, McClellan asked that hearing transcripts be forwarded to the Attorney General, and Symington, referring to "this obviously fraudulent letter," requested that every effort be made to identify McCarthy's informant. Joe exploded at Symington and Jackson, claiming they were part of the effort to obstruct the search for Reds. He soon claimed in a speech at Wausau that all three Democrats were "deliberately trying to prolong these hearings" and sneered, "Now one can see what the party of twenty years of treason stands for."[29]

Joe was becoming equally furious with the Administration. On May 6 Attorney General Brownell ruled that neither the FBI memorandum nor McCarthy's document should be made public. He said that the latter "constitutes an unauthorized use of information which is classified as Confidential." He also noted, "Mr. Hoover has examined the document and has advised me that he never wrote any such letter." Joe demanded that Brownell be called before the subcommittee in executive session for questioning about the decision, and he blasted the continued use of the Truman "blackout orders." He later told reporters that he would not be bound by Brownell's ruling unless J. Edgar Hoover also objected to the publication of the material. "I feel I have no duty, even remotely, to keep secret any information about Communists in the government and those who protect and cover them up, regardless of where I get the information." Contacted by reporters, Hoover had no comment.[30]

Joe's daily schedule during the hearings would have ruined the health of anyone else. He and Jean met nearly every morning at their home with Cohn, Carr, and Juliana for a breakfast strategy session. At 9:00 A.M., surrounded by bodyguards provided by the police department, they walked over to the Senate Office Building for the morning hearing. Lunch was often eaten at the nearby Carroll Arms hotel. By then Joe had invariably soaked his suit with perspiration and would bolt down food and drinks in his shirt sleeves. When the afternoon hearing recessed about 4:30, Joe and his aides would huddle in the senator's office for up to three hours. Dinner would follow, either at the McCarthy home or at the Colony restaurant, and then it was back to the office for more work. Jean, Cohn, and the others would usually go home about eleven. But Joe stayed on, shuffling through documents and transcripts. Sometimes he was accompanied by his long-time friend Mark Catlin of Appleton.

Catlin, a lobbyist in Washington, thought that Joe was actually enjoying the combat and the publicity surrounding the hearings. He would often talk about whom he would "get" the following day. He would also rattle on at length about the Communists in government, leaving his friend convinced of his complete sincerity. Catlin was shocked to see the extent of Joe's alcohol problem: he drank straight vodka all night. He seemed to doze off for periods of five or six minutes, but would awake abruptly and resume his work—and drinking. That was apparently the only sleep he got. Catlin would stumble home about 6:00 A.M., leaving the senator in his office. He could not understand how Joe was able to face the cameras only a few hours later.[31]

By the close of the twelfth day of hearings, May 7, Secretary Stevens was still on the witness stand, and very little light had been shed on the actual issues of the case despite the wide-ranging, repetitious, and frequently obnoxious interrogations by McCarthy and Cohn. Administration and Republican party leaders were becoming exceedingly anxious to call a halt to the proceedings. Cohn later wrote, "the hearings had already become a nuisance, a colossal bore, possibly the most monumental absurdity in our history." Acting as a White House intermediary, Wisconsin Republican leader Tom Coleman secretly approached a friend of Cohn's with a proposal: if Cohn would resign so would John Adams, and both would announce their joint action as a personal sacrifice to end the hearings, save taxpayers' money, and serve the nation. Joe, eager to halt what he some-times referred to as "this question of Schine's shoes" and anxious to resume his investigations, reluctantly agreed. Cohn began drafting his letter of resignation. But the Army would not go along with the plan. Everett Dirksen was furious, and asked the Administration to apply pressure on the Pentagon. When the White House refused, Dirksen resumed his own effort to stop the hearings.[32]

For two days the Illinois senator wrestled with details of a motion that would terminate Stevens' testimony, place McCarthy on the stand, and then shift the remainder of the hearings behind closed doors. Welch, Stevens, and the subcommittee Democrats opposed the proposal, while Joe and the Republicans favored it. During the debate, on the afternoon of May 11, Joe completely lost control of himself in a rage over some slight showmanship by Welch. For several minutes he passionately raged and thundered at the Army counsel, accusing him, among other things, of having "welched" on an earlier agreement.

> Mr. Chairman, may I say that I think it is a complete waste of time, from now on, to try to do anything except to go right straight through this, hear all the witnesses, unless the motion of the senator from Illinois is accepted. I think it is a waste of time to do any attempted dealing with Mr. Welch. The purpose of Mr. Stevens and Mr. Adams is now clear. They succeeded in calling the investigation of Communists off by making their smear attack upon my staff and upon me . . .
>
> Mr. Chairman, I urge that after this motion is acted upon that we have no more dealings, no more conversations, about how we can close the hearings. Let's hear all the witnesses, hear all of them in public, and I will ask that Mr. Welch be called. And, also, Mr. Chairman, I would like to make this request, and you perhaps may not be able to do this today, but, Mr. Chairman, in view of the fact that this committee is acting only in the hearings about four hours a day, in view of the fact that we have an investigation that we have been working on for six or eight months which the statute of limitations on criminal prosecutions is about to run out on, in view of the fact that as of this very moment, at 4:10, on May 11, 1954, there are roughly 100 and some 30 Communists in defense plants, I am going to ask the chair to call a meeting of the committee, and I will ask the permission then that we revoke the rule we originally made. We originally passed a rule that there be no hearings while this was in progress. I am sure that all of us who voted on that, and I voted for it, felt that we could dispose of these hearings in a matter of a week. Now, we realize that with the filibustering, procrastination, it may take months.
>
> Mr. Chairman, I think it is urgent that I have the permission of the committee. I am not asking for it here, but I would like to have an executive session, and receive the permission of the committee to hold hearings every evening, every Saturday, not on the military, but on Communists in defense

plants which have nothing to do with the military. I ask the Chair to call that executive session at his earliest convenience so that even while this circus is going on we may be able to defeat the purpose of Mr. Welch, Mr. Adams, and Mr. Stevens, and proceed to dig out Communists even during this circus. I think that is of the utmost importance, period.

Jenkins and Mundt were helpless for a time as they tried to restore order. The motion failed on a party-line vote, with Mundt reluctantly joining the Democrats to preserve the fairness of the chairmanship. A motion by McClellan to set time limits on interrogations also failed. The hearings were to proceed as originally planned (although soon expanded by 90 minutes each day). The senior Democrat sighed, "We are performing a public duty, a public trust. I may say, one of the most unpleasant and one of the most disagreeable ones I have ever had to perform in the course of my public service."[33]

With Stevens ill, John Adams took the stand on May 12. The 42-year-old native of South Dakota had been appointed the Army Secretary's principal legal adviser on October 1, 1953. A lifelong Republican, Adams had served in various capacities within the federal government after the war and was widely respected in Washington as a highly capable attorney. Unlike Stevens, he proved to be an articulate and informed witness.[34]

Jenkins spent two days in direct and cross examination. (Joe derisively read a newspaper during some of the testimony.) The careful and convincing account that emerged of Cohn's many efforts on behalf of Schine no doubt did serious damage to McCarthy's case. His vivid description of Cohn's conduct during a luncheon in New York, for example, drew gasps and laughter from the hearing room audience:

> Mr. Cohn became extremely agitated, became extremely abusive. He cursed me and then Senator McCarthy. The abuse went in waves. He would be very abusive and then it would kind of abate and things would be friendly for a few moments. Everybody would eat a little more, and then it would start again. It just kept on.

Adams said that Cohn's language was often obscene as well as abusive. "The thing that Cohn was angry about, the thing that he was so violent about, was the fact that, one, the Army was not agreeing to an assignment for Schine and, two, that Senator McCarthy was not supporting his staff in its effort to get Schine assigned to New York."

Joe's reaction to his aide's tirade was curious, Adams thought.

> This violence continued. It was a remarkable thing. At first
> Senator McCarthy seemed to be trying to conciliate. He
> seemed to be trying to conciliate Cohn and not to state
> anything contrary to what he had stated to me in the morn-
> ing. But then he more or less lapsed into silence.

After the luncheon, Adams said, Cohn drove him to Grand Central
Station to catch a train. En route, Cohn's violence flared up again, and he
stopped in the middle of four lanes of traffic and ordered Adams to "Get
there however you can." The Army counselor climbed out of the car and
darted through the traffic until he managed to flag a cab.

Adams also told of telephone conversations with Cohn's close friend
George Sokolsky. The Hearst columnist offered to stop the Army investi-
gation if Schine were allowed to enter a criminal investigators' course at
Camp Gordon almost seven weeks ahead of schedule. Carr had assured
Adams that Sokolsky had "a great deal of influence with the senator."

Adams responded effectively to a number of charges against himself and
the Army, in particular the allegation that Schine was used as a "hostage."
The witness was less credible, however, when he contended that neither he
nor Stevens had attempted to appease McCarthy and Cohn or had tried to
stop the Fort Monmouth investigation. His testimony was full of contradic-
tory evidence and statements on both counts. Especially revealing was
Adams's admission that he had deliberately leaked information about
Cohn's war with the Army to anti-McCarthy reporters and others a month
before the chronology was released.[35]

Senator Dirksen, still smarting over the Army's refusal to end the
hearings, took the offensive against Adams when Jenkins concluded his
questioning. At his own request, he was sworn in on the morning of May 15
and testified that in late January Adams had come to him privately with a
request to halt the subpoenaing of Army Loyalty Board members. The
Army counselor had also revealed his complaints about Cohn. Mundt then
followed Dirksen to the stand and told a similar story. Both were implying
blackmail. Potter reported being approached at the same time by a mutual
friend of Adams.

When Joe asked Dirksen bluntly if Adams had threatened to reveal
Cohn's misconduct if the subpoenas were not killed, the senator replied
cautiously, "I am not sure I came to any conclusion on that point at the time,
but I will say this: that this was the first time that a question of stopping the
subpoenas was coupled with the Cohn-Schine story as it came to me, and it
was the first I knew of it." If the two obviously pro-McCarthy Republicans

were not entirely persuasive, they at least provided further evidence of the Army's quiet counterattack against McCarthy and his aides early in the year.[36]

The secret involvement of the White House in the affair was inadvertently mentioned by Adams on his first day of testimony. In recounting events leading to the preparation of the chronology, he told of attending the January 21 meeting with Sherman Adams, Herbert Brownell, U.N. Ambassador Henry Cabot Lodge, and White House administrative assistant Gerald Morgan. He also revealed that Sherman Adams had suggested the chronology. When Senator Symington questioned the witness on the meeting two days later, he learned that Adams had been instructed not to discuss it. Subcommittee Democrats were as disturbed as McCarthy by this news and demanded to know the source of the order. Joe gasped, "I can't believe the White House would intervene in the case of a private." On May 17 the White House released a letter from the President to the Secretary of Defense prohibiting testimony on the meeting on the ground of the separation of powers.[37]

Joe raged about "an iron curtain" that someone had placed between the subcommittee and the truth about the charges against him and his aides. "I frankly thought all along Mr. Adams and Mr. Hensel were the people who had instigated this. Now there is no way of knowing who did." He did not blame the President; "I don't think his judgment is that bad, Mr. Chairman." Rather, some unknown person was behind this move.

> Now we are getting down to the meat of the case, Mr. Chairman, and that is, who was responsible for the issuance of the smear that has held this committee up for weeks and weeks and weeks, and has allowed Communists to continue in our defense plants, Mr. Chairman, handling top-secret material, as I said before, with a razor poised over the jugular vein of this nation? Who is responsible for keeping all these Army officers down here and all the senators tied up while the world is going up in flames?

Joe was particularly bitter about the presence of the Attorney General at the mysterious meeting, for Brownell had just renewed his stern warning against publishing any part of Joe's "Hoover letter," and he would be responsible for weighing conflicts in hearing testimony and filing perjury charges.

On Dirksen's motion, the subcommittee voted along party lines to recess for a week while the issue was explored further. Democrats feared that the move was another effort to curtail the proceedings, but Chairman Mundt assured everyone, "I think we all want these hearings to continue, and we want to get out all the facts."[38]

Joe should have realized immediately that it was the President who was directly responsible for the White House order. His sympathies toward Stevens and the Army in the dispute were certain, and it was naive to think that Sherman Adams, Brownell, and the others were acting with complete independence.

At his May 13 news conference, the President denounced the alleged disclosure of the "Hoover letter" to McCarthy as reprehensible and not in the best interests of the Army or of the United States. He also insisted that the Armed Forces could take care of themselves in the search for security risks. (Joe had no comment on the remarks.)[39]

Three days later the President invited Stevens to accompany him on a trip to North Carolina. Ike posed for numerous photographs with his Army Secretary and made his personal support unmistakable. Stevens soon told reporters, "The President has given me all the backing that I could have asked."[40]

On May 19 Eisenhower told a news conference that he would not rescind his order concerning the January 21 meeting, and he expressed astonishment that it had been used as a reason to suspend the hearings. One of the major purposes of the order, he said, was to keep the proceedings from being diverted to a side issue. The President called for the resumption of the hearings and declared that they should not end without providing the public with all of the facts in the case. This reflected his endorsement of the Army's determination to slug it out with McCarthy to the bitter end. Whenever the hearings resumed, Welch had told the subcommittee and millions of viewers, "the Army will be ready."[41]

Stevens called a news conference shortly after the President's to announce that the Army had made its charges against McCarthy, Cohn, and Carr on its own authority rather than that of higher officials. This was obviously a move designed to extricate the Administration from blame should the hearings be ended. It also undercut the charge that the full truth could not be obtained by future hearings.[42]

Joe continued to tell reporters he thought the President had not been "fully advised." He hinted at a boycott of further hearings, saying, "I just don't want to go ahead with a stacked deck." He called the presidential order a "gag" and complained, "It is ridiculous beyond comprehension to have the President and the Secretary of the Army say they want all the facts on the table in these hearings and then have them support this order."[43]

McCarthy raised Administration hackles further by delivering a Senate speech condemning as "criminal folly" the continuation of aid to Allies who shipped goods to Red China. Mutual Security Director Harold Stassen told reporters after a meeting with the President, "We need less headline hunters and more Eisenhower backers for the good of America."[44]

The subcommittee agreed on May 20 to resume the hearings the following Monday. Joe said he would be on hand but hedged when asked if he would testify publicly under oath. "I'm making no promise." He surprised reporters that same day by accusing the Administration—and by inference the President—of invoking the "Fifth Amendment" by refusing to permit testimony about the January 21 meeting. The Administration "must have something to hide," he said.[45]

In a speech at Fort Atkinson, Wisconsin, on May 22nd Joe gave the President a week to straighten himself out on the issues of his dispute with the Army or accept the responsibility for forcing the G.O.P. to "commit suicide before the television cameras."[46]

McCarthy's increasingly heated battle with the Administration occurred at a time when his public popularity continued to slide. A Gallup poll published in late May showed him with a 49 percent "unfavorable" rating. He was losing supporters in the press. Several G.O.P. leaders, including Sen. Homer Ferguson of Michigan, chairman of the Republican Policy Committee, stated publicly that Joe was unwelcome in their fall campaigns. A study by statistician Louis H. Bean, published in *Look* magazine under the title "The Myth of McCarthy's Strength" and given much press attention, showed that McCarthy had actually hurt G.O.P. candidates in 1952 and might do worse damage in 1954.[47]

As anyone could see, a direct confrontation with Eisenhower at this time would only further decrease McCarthy's popularity and political effectiveness. The warfare might also harm Republican candidates nationally a few months later. The situation cried out for compromise, as insiders like Karl Mundt quietly continued to plead. The slightest conciliatory gesture on McCarthy's part could perhaps be sufficient to heal the intraparty conflict. But Joe would have none of it. He and his friends had been attacked, and their search for Communists blocked. Someone was going to be sorry. Even if he lived in the White House.

When the hearings resumed on May 24, Stevens and Adams testified about the Army Secretary's assertion that the chronology was produced solely at the instigation of the Pentagon. Both witnesses tried mightily to minimize the influence of the secret meeting of January 21, but their testimony contained numerous equivocations and contradictions and probably resulted in persuading virtually everyone of the direct participation of top Presidential aides in the case.

After the hearing, McCarthy revealed to reporters that Vice-President Nixon had secretly asked Potter in March to request a copy of the Army chronology so that it might first reach subcommittee Republicans. Joe now understood the extent to which he had been attacked from the White House as well as from the Pentagon. He would soon suggest that the proceedings be labeled "smearings" instead of hearings. (Nixon soon told a Republican gathering in New York that the Administration was "smashing the Communist conspiracy to bits" without compromising the principles of American fair play. Referring to the Army-McCarthy hearings, he said scornfully, "I prefer professionals to amateurs on television.")[48]

Welch next introduced several Army officers from Fort Dix to testify about Schine's conduct while in basic training and about the pressure from Cohn and others to obtain special favors for the private. The Army displayed two charts on an easel, one revealing Schine's absences and telephone messages received by the commanding general and the other showing the privileges afforded an average trainee. Joe stormed and raged about the charts, calling them "dishonest" and "phony" and referring to Welch as a "clever little lawyer." His argument centered on the fact that the chart on Schine featured more black ink than its counterpart; black being commonly thought to be more negative than white, the chart was therefore obviously designed to deceive television viewers. Karl Mundt, increasingly willing to abandon his small claim to impartiality, heartily agreed. During the squabble, Joe and aide James Juliana strode to the chart on the average trainee and began blacking it in. In fact, as an Army witness soon made clear, the charts were both accurate and informative. Moreover, there was no evidence of deliberate deception by anyone in the Pentagon.[49]

The officers, including commanding General Ryan, documented many earlier reports of favoritism toward Schine (although Ryan denied that favoritism had been shown). The private had received sixteen passes during his eight weeks of training (the average was three or four). He had been permitted to make 250 long-distance telephone calls. He had gone "absent without leave" during a holiday without penalty, and the incident was not entered on his service record. Ryan pointed out that he was personally following orders given by Secretary Stevens—who had allegedly held Schine "hostage." He also described the constant pressure from McCarthy's office. The general and his aides received 29 telephone calls from Cohn and others, as well as several visits.

Schine's personal conduct was also discussed during the testimony. The private had offered a favor to his company commander an hour after they were introduced. He had bragged about intending to remake the American military Establishment along modern lines. When found sitting in the cab of a truck during a rainstorm while his fellow trainees were taking target practice, he said he was studying logistics. Schine was reprimanded on several occasions for breaches of discipline.[50]

McCarthy and Cohn protested vigorously against the introduction of much of this testimony, and when it continued Joe angrily stormed from the hearing room. "He is now recounting events in the private life of David Schine. I am not going to sit here and listen to it. May I say, Mr. Chairman, we have much more important work to do. We should be investigating Communists." Twenty minutes later he returned, angrily calling the full Committee on Government Operations into session at 5:30 P.M. that day to discuss other business. It was a petty method of revenge against his weary colleagues, but he had completely lost his temper. Joe then began attacking the *New York Post,* which had first carried stories on Schine at Fort Dix. He called the liberal, anti-McCarthy newspaper a "Communist sheet" and falsely claimed that James Wechsler, its editor, "has been one of the top officials of the Communist party." When Stuart Symington came to Wechsler's defense and pointed out that the subcommittee itself had once employed an ex-Communist, Joe sneered, "I may say to the senator from Missouri I am deeply disturbed when I find, after he came back to this committee apparently for the purpose of helping us dig out Communists, that the only time I hear him raise his voice at this table is when we appear to be hurting those who defended Communism." During much of the rest of the day he was virtually uncontrollable.[51]

On the afternoon of May 26, the twenty-first day of the hearings, the Army rested its case. Senator Dworshak, in response to a private meeting of the majority members of the subcommittee, immediately moved to dismiss the charges against Assistant Secretary of Defense Hensel and Frank Carr. The Republicans took the position that the evidence against both men was virtually nonexistent, and they contended (to save face for McCarthy) that the presidential order had blocked the discovery of further information on Hensel's activities. What they actually sought, of course, was a swift end to the public hearings. They also desired to remove Hensel and Carr as witnesses.[52]

Joe had virtually admitted to the entire subcommittee, during an executive session of May 17, that he had no evidence against Hensel. He told Hensel privately that he would be willing to drop his charges if he could find a way to do it that would not present him to the public as a "damn fool." (The Pentagon official demanded an open apology, and Joe refused.) When Hensel asked why he had been attacked in the first place, Joe replied that he was following a maxim taught him by an Indian named "Charlie," with whom he had once worked on a farm: When approached in an unfriendly manner, you kick your attacker below the belt as fast as possible until he is rendered helpless. Hensel revealed all of this after the conclusion of the hearings. On the witness stand, before millions of television viewers, he might have damaged McCarthy's credibility irreparably.[53]

The subcommittee Republicans were almost as eager to keep Frank Carr off the stand. For one thing, he had signed six of the back-dated "memoranda" presented as evidence against the Army. Senator Potter, among others, was deeply suspicious of the documents. Welch could be counted on to wage a spirited cross-examination of the McCarthy aide, and Carr's ability to respond convincingly was questionable.[54]

Welch and the subcommittee Democrats were furious over the G.O.P. maneuver. Hensel, they pointed out, had not been given the opportunity to defend himself against the charges raised by McCarthy, Cohn, and Carr. Carr's complicity in the actions of Cohn and McCarthy, they argued correctly, had been amply demonstrated. Moreover, there was further evidence against him to be presented. (The monitored telephone conversations, for example, were being studied prior to their planned release.) Welch addressed Dirksen, "Let me say this, Senator: If at the close of the case Mr. Carr is found free of all fault by you, you will see me advancing toward him smilingly. I have, sir, a genius for losing cases. I wish, however, not to lose them until the evidence is in."

Dworshak's motion passed by a straight party vote. A motion by McClellan to call Carr to the stand immediately was defeated in the identical fashion. Symington cried "whitewash" and promised to bring the Hensel case to the Senate floor and to the Armed Services Committee. All pretences of bipartisanship were now abandoned.[55]

The New York Times called the decision to release Hensel and Carr "a grave blunder" and declared: "The Republican members of the committee may not have been trying to cover up for Mr. McCarthy and Mr. Carr in relieving Mr. Hensel and Mr. Carr from the witness stand. But that is certainly the impression they have given." Columnist William S. White soon reported that the tactic "has brought a public reaction frightening to the Republicans." The hearings, he observed, "have drawn the Democrats together, in some areas of the controversy, as they had not been drawn in years."[56]

The subcommittee Democrats entered the hearing room the next day spoiling for a fight. Roy Cohn testified for less than thirty minutes before all three got into a nasty quarrel with McCarthy over his failure to share subcommittee documents with them. The case of the "purloined FBI document" then came up again, and Symington stated, "One of my oldest friends in the newspaper business the other day said that Edgar Hoover told him that if he released the document, that he would be jailed. . . . I have never said that anybody committed anything wrong in receiving it. But I do say that, regardless of his personal opinion, no man who takes an oath of office not to divulge secrets has the right to decide to do it." Joe's temper soared during the exchange, and he flew into the Democrats, recklessly challenging their integrity and patriotism. He showed equal disrespect for the Eisenhower administration. He complimented those in government who had provided him with materials in defiance of "any presidential directive," and he said, "If any administration wants to indict me for receiving and giving the American people information about Communism, they can just go right ahead and do the indicting." A few minutes later he angrily declared:

> As far as I am concerned, I would like to notify those two million federal employees that I feel it is their duty to give us any information which they have about graft, corruption, Communism, treason, and that there is no loyalty to a superior officer which can tower above and beyond their loyalty to their country. I may say that I hope the day comes when this administration notifies all federal employees that any information which they have about wrongdoing should be given to any congressional committee which is empowered to take it, period.[57]

Eisenhower was infuriated by the remarks. According to his press secretary, on May 28 he paced back and forth behind his desk at the White House fuming about "the complete arrogance of McCarthy."

> This amounts to nothing but a wholesale subversion of public services. McCarthy is making exactly the same plea of loyalty that Hitler made to the German people. Both tried to set up personal loyalty within the government while both were using the pretense of fighting Communism. McCarthy is trying deliberately to subvert the people we have in government, people who are sworn to obey the law, the Constitu-

tion, and their superior officers. I think this is the most disloyal act we have ever had by anyone in government of the United States.[58]

The White House issued a statement at the direction of Attorney General Brownell, and personally approved by the President, declaring that the Executive branch's responsibility "cannot be usurped by any individual who may seek to set himself above the laws of our land . . ." A short time later, in a speech approved by the White House, Brownell termed McCarthy's appeal for information an "open invitation to violate the laws." Senate Majority Leader Knowland and powerful Republican Sen. H. Alexander Smith also spoke out. Smith said he was deeply shocked by what he called "defiance of the Executive in this crisis," and he called Joe's statement "beyond belief." "We cannot tolerate one-man government either in the Executive or in our legislative bodies," he said. Knowland warned that Joe was treading on "highly dangerous and doubtful grounds."[59]

Subcommittee Democrats were to make much of McCarthy's appeal for confidential information, returning to it repeatedly during the remainder of the hearings to spotlight Joe's extremism and to embarrass the Administration, which by implication was allegedly unable to handle loyalty-security matters effectively on its own. The Democrats were also delighted on May 28 when Joe referred to "the past twenty or twenty-one years" of treason in government. The remark, made during an almost hysterical exchange with Senator Symington, extended his standard charge against the Democrats to encompass more than a year of the Eisenhower administration. Joe began an interview after the hearing with, "I hope to remain in the Senate and see many Presidents come and go . . ."[60]

On June 1 Ralph Flanders delivered an impassioned denunciation of McCarthy on the Senate floor. Joe was referred to as "Dennis the Menace," compared to Hitler, accused of anti-Semitism, anti-Protestantism, anti-Republicanism, and homosexuality, and condemned for allegedly helping the Reds.

> What we are now seeing is another example of economy of effort and expansion of success in the conquest of this country for Communism. The preliminary campaign is successfully under way. One of the characteristic elements of Communist and fascist tyranny is at hand, as citizens are set to spy upon each other. Established and responsible government is besmirched. Religion is set against religion, race against race. Churches and parties are split asunder. All is division and confusion.

> Were the junior senator from Wisconsin in the pay of the
> Communists, he could not have done a better job for them.

This ranked among the most extreme and irresponsible indictments of
McCarthy ever made, and it should have drawn the condemnation of
reasonable men within both parties. Instead, the speech was received in
silence, save for a chuckle or two from Democrats. It was left to Joe to reply,
and he did so in kind. During the hearing that afternoon, he angrily
pondered aloud whether Flanders' remarks had resulted from "senility or
viciousness."[61]

The subcommittee formally began to investigate the McCarthy side of
the struggle on May 27 with the appearance of Roy Cohn on the stand.
Cohn was questioned for nine days and proved to be an articulate, shrewd,
and frequently unconvincing witness. At one point he declared soberly,
"There was never any request by us for any kind of preferential treatment
for Schine." At other times he was circumspect, such as when questioned
about the eleven memoranda he and his friends had revealed in March:

> As far as I know, sir, they are memoranda from Senator
> McCarthy's file concerning various of these matters in our
> relations with Mr. Adams and Mr. Stevens . . .
> I would say that the November 6 one was probably dictated
> by me . . .
> I notice I mention my name last, which means I probably
> dictated it . . .
> As I recall it, I believe that was dictated after we had come
> back to this building from the meeting in Mr. Schine's office,
> and I believe Senator McCarthy, as he had done before on
> another occasion as I remember it, in a different investiga-
> tion, told me to dictate to Mary Driscoll a synopsis of what
> had gone on at the meeting.[62]

Ray Jenkins opened his cross-examination of Cohn with a question that
had crossed the minds of everyone who had followed the case: What drove
Cohn to seek Schine's frequent company during the weeks the inductee was
undergoing basic training? (Jenkins even rather indelicately probed the
possibility of homosexual ties, the unproved hypothesis that many anti-
McCarthyites took for granted.) When Cohn declared that Schine's knowledge of Subcommittee business was vast and indispensable, Jenkins asked
him to produce documents that would reveal Schine's labors during his
many absences from Fort Dix. Delay after delay followed, until it was finally
revealed that Cohn could only come up with a single six-page document.

Mr. Welch. Who wrote that?

Mr. Cohn. I believe Dave Schine did.

Mr. Welch. At what time?

Mr. Cohn. I don't know, sir.

Mr. Welch. Prior to his induction?

Mr. Cohn. I don't know. It might very well have been.

Mr. Welch. You wouldn't say it was afterward?

Mr. Cohn. No; I can't say that, sir.

Mr. Welch. So the first document I pick up is one that he might very well have done before his induction?

Mr. Cohn. Yes, sir.

To compound Cohn's embarrassment, Welch produced several receipts from restaurants and nightclubs, revealing that the two young men had not always been at work during Schine's leaves from military duty.[63]

Cohn did his best to field questions by Jenkins, Welch, Potter, McClellan, and Jackson on the eleven memoranda. But his answers did little to shake the skepticism that each revealed. Welch declared at one point, "I do not wish to conceal from anyone in this room that I have grave suspicions about the authenticity of these memoranda . . ." Welch's interrogation on the issue was especially incisive. During a session on June 9 he succeeded in getting Cohn to contend that he had ascended three flights of stairs to dictate a memorandum to McCarthy's secretary, Mary Driscoll, despite the presence of several staff stenographers in the office where an alleged conversation had taken place between himself and John Adams. When Mrs. Driscoll was called to the stand, Welch brilliantly dismantled her attempt to defend Cohn's assertion that she had typed all of the documents as they were dictated at different times over the months. At one point she said she had "no independent recollection" of any of the memoranda and had destroyed her shorthand notebooks. The audience burst into laughter twice as Welch led the veteran McCarthy staff member, obviously weak with fear, through a wholly unbelievable explanation of how she had allegedly filed the memoranda.[64]

During Cohn's testimony the transcribed telephone calls between Secretary Stevens and subcommittee senators were read into the record. Joe had been delaying their introduction for weeks, no doubt hoping to conceal the record of his personal lack of interest in Private Schine. Eschewing Joe's advice, Cohn now chose to place his own transcriptions and those of Carr and Schine into the record as well. Joe reluctantly followed suit with his own.

The monitored conversations turned out to be less important than anticipated. Cohn's merely provided further evidence of his arrogance and Secretary Stevens's obeisance. McCarthy's documented his anti-Communist zeal, his detached attitude toward Schine ("He is a good boy, but there is nothing indispensable about him"), and his curious awe of Cohn. Transcribed conversations by Dirksen, Potter, McClellan, Schine, and Carr (with Adams) were of even less significance.[65]

The transcribed conversations of Senator Symington were of a slightly more controversial quality, however, and they threw McCarthy and his aides into a rage that lasted for the remainder of the hearings and beyond. In chats with a distressed Secretary of the Army in February, Symington had revealed sympathy with Stevens and the Army and a distinct distaste for McCarthy ("This fellow might be sick, you know. . . . If you are going to play with McCarthy, you have got to forget about any of these Marquis of Queensberry rules"). The Missouri senator had also recommended that Stevens consult with his attorney, Clark Clifford, a highly knowledgeable Washington insider who had served as a top aide to President Truman. Stevens, Symington, and Clifford thereafter had a twenty-minute conversation about whether the Army Secretary should appear before McCarthy, sitting as a one-man subcommittee. The two Democrats advised against it, but Stevens elected not to accept the advice the following day.[66]

Joe, who had been feuding bitterly with Symington throughout the hearings, interpreted the presence of Clifford to signal a conspiracy of pro-Communist Fair Dealers to thwart the subcommittee's search for subversives. His thoughts now turned away from the Eisenhower administration; from this point on he fixed the blame for the hearings squarely upon Clifford, Symington, and other unnamed Democrats, who had allegedly "pulled the strings" for Stevens and Adams. Joe stormed and fumed for days, demanding that Symington disqualify himself and that both Symington and Clifford take the oath and testify at the hearings. Symington, the most emotional and openly partisan subcommittee Democrat, frequently responded in kind, and session after session exploded with angry, abusive, and often uncontrollable exchanges between the two senators. Joe twice referred to his colleague as "sanctimonious Stu," claimed he was running for President, labeled him "an alleged man," and called him "unfit" to serve on the subcommittee. Symington said that McCarthy wanted "just plain anarchy" in the United States; he itemized charges by the Hennings Committee and dared Joe to answer them; and at one point he shouted, "You better go to a psychiatrist." After one melee, Welch said wearily, "I am almost numb at what I have heard, it is so far removed from what we are trying to try here." The warfare even continued during an executive session.[67]

Symington undoubtedly won considerable public sympathy from the exchanges. On the whole, he seemed more reasonable and moderate than McCarthy, and he was far less vituperative. His explanation of the slight assistance given to Stevens earlier in the year was entirely believable and bore none of the sinister and subversive overtones McCarthy claimed to see. Both Symington and Clifford expressed a willingness to testify under oath. Joe's retreat from an earlier pledge to answer any and all questions about his own past, however, resulted in Symington's failure to take the stand. Subcommittee Republicans, eager to conclude the hearings, and no doubt leery of Joe's charges, blocked testimony by Clifford.[68]

Symington was convinced that McCarthy's repeated references to his transcribed conversations with Stevens were merely diversionary tactics, employed when things were going badly on the witness stand. Late in the hearings he cracked, "End run of diversion Number 1,620." He was surely correct, for Joe continually—often predictably—interrupted questioning whenever Welch and others appeared to be scoring too many points. While Mary Driscoll was floundering, for example, he brought up the Flanders speech and then suggested that all of the major figures in the case take lie-detector tests. When Senator Jackson seemed to be damaging Cohn on the sensitive issue of subcommittee files, Joe broke in with the charge of Communist infiltration of the C.I.A. When Welch put Cohn through a humiliating interrogation about the alleged number of subversives loose in defense plants, Joe called a meeting of the subcommittee to resume anti-Communist probes part-time. (Democrats boycotted the meeting, and nothing came of the ploy.)[69]

McCarthy's most famous attempt to divert the pattern of questioning occurred on the afternoon of June 9, with Roy Cohn still on the stand. During the morning session Welch had been causing Cohn considerable frustration with trenchant queries concerning one of the eleven memoranda. After the luncheon break, the Army attorney resumed his interrogation with a brilliant examination of the work habits of Cohn and Schine while the latter was on leave from the Army. When Cohn began to stumble, Joe excused himself, saying that he had to visit his office temporarily. When he returned several minutes later, he launched into a diatribe against Fred Fisher, Welch's young law associate who had been dropped from the case before the hearings began.

The tactic horrified Cohn, who squirmed in his seat and rolled his eyes skyward; his lips seemed to form the words "No! No!" Two days earlier he had made a private agreement with Welch: if the Army attorney would not bring up Cohn's military history (he had flunked the physical test for admission to West Point), the Fisher question would not be raised. McCarthy had agreed to the bargain. Now, however, in his desperation and anger, Joe impetuously decided to strike at Welch with everything he had. Cohn quickly scribbled a note to the senator. "This is the subject which I have committed to Welch we would not go into. Please respect our agreement as an agreement, because this is not going to do any good." Joe read the message and dismissed it. "I know Mr. Cohn would rather not have me go into this," he acknowledged a short time later. But by then he had fully committed himself to the attack.[70]

Slowly and malevolently, Joe droned:

> ... in view of Mr. Welch's request that the information be given once we know of anyone who might be performing any work for the Communist party, I think we should tell him that he has in his law firm a young man named Fisher whom he recommended, incidentally, to do work on this committee, who has been for a number of years a member of an organization which was named, oh, years and years ago, as the legal bulwark of the Communist party, an organization which always swings to the defense of anyone who dares to expose Communists. I certainly assume that Mr. Welch did not know of this young man at the time he recommended him as the assistant counsel for this committee, but he has such terror and such a great desire to know where anyone is located who may be serving the Communist cause, Mr. Welch, that I thought we should just call to your attention the fact that your Mr. Fisher, who is still in your law firm today, whom you asked to have down here looking over the secret and classified material, is a member of an organization, not named by me but named by various committees, named by the Attorney General, as I recall, and I think I quote this verbatim, as "the legal bulwark of the Communist party."

The substance of the charge, of course, was fraudulent, for Welch had been fully aware of Fisher's past and had publicly announced that because of it he was not asking the attorney to participate in the case.

Joe continued, a slight grin revealing the pleasure he took in heeding Indian Charlie's advice about striking below the belt.

> I am not asking you at this time to explain why you tried to foist him on this committee. Whether you knew he was a

member of that Communist organization or not, I don't know. I assume you did not, Mr. Welch, because I get the impression that, while you are quite an actor, you play for a laugh, I don't think you have any conception of the danger of the Communist party.

Chairman Mundt pointed out, when McCarthy had finished, that Welch had never recommended Fisher as a subcommittee counsel. Joe sputtered a few more sentences before Welch struck back.

"Until this moment, Senator," he began, "I think I never really gauged your cruelty or your recklessness."

Fred Fisher is a young man who went to the Harvard Law School and came into my firm and is starting what looks to be a brilliant career with us.

When I decided to work for this committee I asked Jim St. Clair, who sits on my right, to be my first assistant. I said to Jim, "Pick somebody in the firm who works under you that you would like." He chose Fred Fisher and they came down on an afternoon plane. That night, when he had taken a little stab at trying to see what the case was about, Fred Fisher and Jim St. Clair and I went to dinner together. I then said to these two young men, "Boys, I don't know anything about you except I have always liked you, but if there is anything funny in the life of either one of you that would hurt anybody in this case you speak up quick."

Fred Fisher said, "Mr. Welch, when I was in law school and for a period of months after, I belonged to the Lawyers Guild," as you have suggested, Senator. He went on to say, "I am secretary of the Young Republicans League in Newton with the son of Massachusetts' governor, and I have the respect and admiration of my community and I am sure I have the respect and admiration of the 25 lawyers or so in Hale & Dorr."

I said, "Fred, I just don't think I am going to ask you to work on the case. If I do, one of these days that will come out and go over national television and it will just hurt like the dickens."

So, Senator, I asked him to go back to Boston.

Little did I dream you could be so reckless and so cruel as to do an injury to that lad. It is true he is still with Hale & Dorr. It is true that he will continue to be with Hale & Dorr. It is, I regret to say, equally true that I fear he shall always bear a scar needlessly inflicted by you. If it were in my power to forgive you for your reckless cruelty, I will do so. I like to think I am a gentleman, but your forgiveness will have to come from someone other than me.

Stung by the powerful rhetoric, Joe tried to resume his attack upon Fisher. Welch interrupted:

> Mr. Welch. Senator, may we not drop this? We know he belonged to the Lawyers Guild, and Mr. Cohn nods his head at me. I did you, I think, no personal injury, Mr. Cohn.
> Mr. Cohn. No, sir.
> Mr. Welch. I meant to do you no personal injury, and if I did, I beg your pardon.
> Let us not assassinate this lad further, Senator. You have done enough. Have you no sense of decency, sir, at long last? Have you left no sense of decency?

When Joe again attempted to smear Fisher, Welch said sternly, "Mr. McCarthy, I will not discuss this with you further. You have sat within six feet of me and could have asked me about Fred Fisher. You have brought it out. If there is a God in heaven, it will do neither you nor your cause any good. I will not discuss it further. I will not ask Mr. Cohn any more questions. You, Mr. Chairman, may, if you will, call the next witness.[71]

The hearing room burst into applause. Mundt made no move to intervene. Joe, flushed and stunned, sat in silence.

Many of those close to McCarthy realized immediately how badly he had been hurt. Ray Kiermas, sitting in the audience, said later, "I was sick to my stomach." Ed Nellor, seated nearby, later recalled, "I got physically ill." Urban Van Susteren, who watched the confrontation on television, said years later, "It made me sick." Joe felt the pain of his humiliation keenly. Cohn wrote later, "The blow was terribly damaging to Senator McCarthy."[72]

The media had a field day with the incident. Newspapers ran photographs of Welch in tears and later showed him engulfed in congratulatory letters and telegrams. Headlines such as HAVE YOU NO SENSE OF DECENCY? were common. Filmed accounts of the clash were featured for weeks on television and in newsreels. (The encounter would be the climax of the highly partisan documentary film "Point of Order," compiled from television kinescopes of the hearings and viewed in theaters for years.)

Joe's conduct was censured by virtually all but the most hardline ultraconservatives. The right-wing *Wisconsin State Journal* said, "It was worse than reckless. It was worse than cruel. It was reprehensible." Columnist Doris Fleeson observed, "No one who saw that flower of evil will ever forget it." A satirical, anti-McCarthy phonograph record entitled "Point of Order" quickly proved to be a best-seller.[73]

Joe took the stand on the late afternoon of June 9. Ray Jenkins, whose McCarthyite sympathies had long been evident, led him through a gentle examination that permitted him, with the aid of a large map (obviously designed for television viewers), to deliver a lengthy and impassioned oration on internal subversion. Throughout his more than four days as a witness, Joe returned to the theme again and again, revealing a degree of earnest fanaticism that none of the attorneys or subcommittee members publicly questioned. (Indeed, no one during the hearings challenged any of the Red-Scare assumptions Joe freely repeated. Each of the senators expressed his deepest hatred of all Communists, his belief in the presence of Red spies within the federal government, and his highest respect for J. Edgar Hoover. Not one of them criticized the activities of Red-hunting congressional committees. None of them questioned the validity of the Fort Monmouth investigation. Welch called Irving Peress "a no-good Communist" and told McCarthy at one point, "You do good work. I admire the work you do, when it succeeds.")[74]

At times, on the witness stand, Joe was not as mentally agile as he had been earlier in the hearings. His thoughts became disconnected and his sentences rambled; he was often dependent upon Cohn for details. His difficulties surely stemmed in part from the fact that he was frequently required to lie. Joe said of Schine, "I think he is the most modest young man I have seen," and he claimed that the private's presence on the subcommittee staff was vital during his weeks at Fort Dix. "May I say, Mr. Jenkins, that I was surprised when I found there were only 65 phone calls to Dave Schine down at Fort Dix. . . . Those calls were to get information from the young man who more than anyone else was responsible for the exposure of Communism, Communist books, and the proposed waste of $18 million in the information program." He said of Cohn, "I think he is just a normal young man. He is very brilliant. I don't think that he has a hotter temper than anyone else." When confronted with his transcribed telephone calls ("I think for Roy's sake if you can let him come back for weekends or something so his girls won't get too lonesome—maybe if they shave his hair off, he won't want to come back"), Joe hedged and squirmed and was thoroughly unconvincing. He was even less persuasive when attempting to describe his alleged dictation of one of the eleven memoranda.[75]

After McCarthy's first full day on the stand, the subcommittee met in executive session to discuss the future of the hearings. By straight party votes, the Republicans succeeded in calling the sessions to a halt following the testimony of McCarthy and Carr (whom Joe had decided should appear). The Democrats were furious. Jackson could not believe that the hearings would end without an interrogation of Schine. (Jenkins and Welch sided with the Republicans on the issue.) Symington and McClellan were outraged that Clark Clifford was not to be summoned. In large part, of course, their blusterings had partisan overtones; the longer the hearings continued the more damage was done to the G.O.P. Symington even wanted to subpoena Don Surine, to expose his controversial departure from the FBI in 1950. After Cohn said that McCarthy would strongly oppose such a move, Symington's motion failed for lack of a second. (Surine had told Walter Winchell that Symington, in his youth, had been convicted of a felony. *Confidential* magazine, a highly popular scandal sheet, published the story, and the Missouri senator sought revenge against the investigator as well as his employer.)[76]

On the morning of June 11, while Jenkins proceeded through an extraordinarily uncritical cross-examination of McCarthy, Ralph Flanders entered the hearing room, strolled up to McCarthy, and handed him a message: "This is to inform you that I plan to make another speech concerning your activities in the Senate this afternoon as soon after the morning hour as I can get the floor. If you so desire, I would be glad to have you present." Joe flew into a rage and soon told reporters, "I think they should get a man with a net and take him to a good quiet place."

On the Senate floor, Flanders offered a resolution demanding that McCarthy be removed from the chairmanship of the Permanent Subcommittee on Investigations and its parent body if the senator did not within a reasonable time "purge himself of contempt" and answer six questions raised by the Hennings Committee in 1952. "It is no defense to call the charges a smear," Flanders said in his speech. "A smear is a most annoying thing and one which is perhaps—I would not speak definitely—not unknown to the junior senator from Wisconsin. But there is this about a smear: It can be removed by a dry-cleaning process which involves a vigorous application of the truth."[77]

Flanders had consulted no one before delivering his Senate address, and he had first thought of confronting McCarthy while walking to the Capitol that morning. He was severely criticized by Republican colleagues, who quickly dispatched his resolution to William Jenner's Rules Committee. Senate Democrats, on the whole, were also unsympathetic. "Anyhow," said one, "this is a Republican family fight. Joe's their problem; let them battle it out." Threats and hate mail poured in upon Flanders from across the country. But the 73-year-old Vermonter remained steadfast, and in a Senate speech of June 15 made it clear that he would not let the Rules Committee bury the matter. He also suggested that the public give "some thought to the question of whether a Fifth-Amendment Communist can, under any circumstances, in any conceivable way, by any conceivable person, find its parallel in a Fifth-Amendment senator." He wrote to Gen. Robert E. Wood in Chicago, "I cannot conceive of wanting to live, or wanting my children or grandchildren to live, in an America fashioned in the image of the junior senator from Wisconson."[78]

Late in the afternoon of June 11, Joe was presented with even more disturbing news. During the afternoon session Cohn had become highly irritated at Henry Jackson for ridiculing a silly document on psychological warfare written by Schine before he became a subcommittee consultant. (Eisenhower soon congratulated Jackson privately.) After the hearing, Cohn and minority counsel Bobby Kennedy almost came to blows over Cohn's threat to "get" the junior senator from Washington for having allegedly written something that was pro-Communist. It was reportedly a 1945 letter recommending an individual for federal employment who later became involved in a Senate Internal Security subcommittee probe. Bobby told reporters about the confrontation, and the story made front-page headlines. Jackson said that Cohn had made other threats against senators during the hearings. The incident buttressed John Adams's recollections of Cohn, damaged McCarthy's entire case against the Army, and made Cohn's ultimate departure from the subcommittee a certainty.[79]

On June 14 Frank Carr took the stand. The hefty ex-FBI man was the least credible witness to appear at the hearings, and his two days of testimony undoubtedly contributed greatly to the growing public cynicism about his side of the controversy. Carr was especially vulnerable in connection with the eleven memoranda, and McClellan, Jackson, and Welch questioned him intensely about the documents. When the witness was not forced into embarrassing assertions and explanations, he relied upon evasive language to protect himself. "I think that I could state definitely that it wasn't. My best recollection is that it wasn't. I am almost positive that it wasn't."[80]

Predictably, Joe interrupted the flow of questioning often with counter-charges, irrelevancies, and nasty asides. Late in the afternoon of June 14 he and Symington engaged in a quarrel that became so shrill and intense that Joe refused to quiet down even after Mundt had gaveled the hearing to a close.

You can run away if you like, Stu. You can run away if you
like. You have been here trying to smear the staff of this
committee, the young men who have been working to
uncover Communists. You jump up and run away without
answering the question. I have asked you a simple question.
Do you have any evidence of any kind to indicate that there is
any subversive amongst these young men? If not, if not, you
are leaving here this afternoon, leaving a smear upon the
name of each and every one of them. You shouldn't do that,
Mr. Symington. That is just dishonest. That is the same thing
that the Communist party has been doing too long.

The senators and the hundreds of people in the audience engaged each
other in conversation and filed out of the hearing room as Joe continued,
beside himself with rage. No one paid attention to the tirade. Not long
afterward, Symington would tell McCarthy triumphantly, "The American
people have had a look at you for six weeks. You are not fooling anyone . . .[81]

The proceedings concluded on June 17, a day filled with political
speeches by the senators, a final battle between Symington and McCarthy,
and a vow by Joe to summon former members of the Army Loyalty Board in
the near future and begin probes of the C.I.A. and Peress. As a final tribute
to the unwavering partisanship shown by both sides throughout the
hearings, Dirksen asked McCarthy to describe his service record during the
war. Joe went on at length, including the fictitious aspects he had injected
into his military history years earlier.[82]

The hearings had lasted 36 days. (The record was still held by the Pearl
Harbor investigations of 1945-46, which ran seventy days.) Thirty-two
witnesses had appeared; the transcript contained more than two million
words. Television time on the air totaled 187 hours. (Both the American
Broadcasting Company and the Dumont Television Network covered all of
the hearings "live." By a rough estimate, the entire coverage cost the five
television and radio networks nearly 10 million dollars' worth of broadcast
revenue.) In addition to the millions of people who had followed the
hearings over the media, some 115,000 had attended in person as part of
each day's crowd.[83]

Both sides claimed victory. Senator Potter, the only Republican on the
subcommittee even slightly capable of weighing the case objectively, was
correct in declaring in a press statement on the final day that the testimony
"was saturated with statements which were not truthful and which might
constitute perjury in a legal sense." Not one of the major witnesses in the

hearings had been entirely believable. Potter and the subcommittee Democrats called for the dismissal of all principals in the case, and McClellan implied that the Democrats' demand included Stevens and Adams as well as Cohn and Carr.[84]

If the testimony by Stevens and Adams had at times seemed to tarnish the Army's reputation, news of the extent to which they and other top military officials had sought to appease Cohn and McCarthy, in both the Schine affair and the Fort Monmouth case, was clearly harmful. Still, the Army emerged from the hearings in a far more positive light than its adversaries. Its belief that Cohn's zealous anxieties over Schine were at the root of its difficulties with McCarthy was undoubtedly correct. Its contention that Cohn, McCarthy, and Carr had attempted to obtain favors for Schine appeared virtually certain.

The major assertions by McCarthy, Cohn, and Carr were credible only to the diehards on the Far Right by the time the hearings ended. Few could believe that Schine had been held as a hostage, that the private's expertise had been necessary for the steady continuation of subcommittee business, that Army and Administration officials had attempted to coddle Reds and thwart the search for subversives, or that Struve Hensel, Stuart Symington, or Clark Clifford had masterminded a plot against the subcommittee. Only the most gullible could accept the eleven memoranda at face value.

Television, of course, was no doubt more responsible than the testimony itself for the widespread disfavor engulfing McCarthy. Joe's mannerisms and tactics had shocked and disgusted Americans. The clashes with Welch, homespun and witty, and Symington, handsome in his indignation, had been especially ruinous. Joe could not understand this simple truth because, as Cohn later observed, he was unable to view himself as others did. On the last day of the hearings he said, "Mr. Welch, you have seen me here for a long time. I don't think I have glared at anyone." He also expressed the firm conviction that the public would take his side of the controversy. "The American people are not going to be fooled. We have a pretty intelligent jury."[85]

After the hearings had concluded, Eisenhower privately congratulated Welch and his associate James St. Clair. Welch observed that if the hearings had accomplished nothing else, the Army had been able to keep McCarthy on television long enough for the public to get a good look at him. The President agreed.[86]

On the first day of September the subcommittee released a majority and a minority report and two supplementary statements (by Dirksen and Potter). All seven senators were in agreement on several issues: that

McCarthy was to blame for permitting Cohn to proceed with his efforts on behalf of Schine, that Cohn had exceeded the authority of his office, that Stevens was guilty of appeasement toward Cohn and McCarthy, that the Army Secretary and Adams had attempted to influence the Fort Monmouth investigation to some degree, and that neither Stevens nor Adams was "soft" on Communism. Beyond that, the reports tended to reflect the well-established views of both partisan groups, with the Republicans virtually absolving McCarthy of improper conduct, and the Democrats sharply condemning him for actions taken before and during the hearings.[87]

By this time, however, the Army-McCarthy hearings were of little interest. Cohn had left the subcommittee, Ralph Flanders had proposed McCarthy's censure, and a select committee of the Senate was already at work investigating a number of the most serious charges ever raised against the Wisconsin senator. Joe himself was heartbroken and increasingly alcoholic.

A MATTER OF
MORALITY AND
CONDUCT

For a time, Joe did not realize how severely the Army-McCarthy hearings had damaged his public image. Jean (who understood perfectly) continued to be encouraging, as did many friends and supporters. Right-wing newspapers made much of the narrow failure of the "Joe Must Go" campaign to force a special recall election in Wisconsin. The Republican state convention, chaired by Melvin Laird of Marshfield, greeted the senator enthusiastically and passed a resolution commending him for his "crusade against subversives." Joe assumed that he remained a potent political force and that the business of the subcommittee would promptly resume.[1]

It should have been obvious, however, that on the national level at least, McCarthy's effectiveness as a politician and anti-Communist crusader had been shattered by the televised hearings. Democratic Senator Monroney said that Joe's support of a Republican congressional candidate in the fall elections would be "the kiss of death," and many politicians of both parties agreed.[2]

The Gallup poll published after the hearings rated McCarthy's popularity at 34 percent, with 45 percent expressing disapproval. Four times as many college-trained people were strongly unfavorable as were strongly favorable. Least enthusiasm for the senator was found among business and professional people, 41 percent of whom expressed extreme disapproval as compared to 14 percent who said they approved highly.[3]

The press contained many indications of the poll's accuracy. In Sioux Falls, South Dakota, on June 13, Joe attracted an audience of American Legionnaires estimated to be only slightly more than one-half of the anticipated size. In Maine, Sen. Margaret Chase Smith defeated her McCarthy-backed opponent, Robert L. Jones, by a landslide five-to-one margin in a G.O.P. primary. In California, McCarthyite State Senator Jack Tenney was defeated by a politically moderate young housewife. In Connecticut, Republican senatorial candidate Clifford Case called McCarthy "a deeply divisive force" in the United States and said that if elected he would vote to strip the Wisconsinite of his subcommittee chairmanship and membership.[4]

In Washington there was a flurry of anti-McCarthy activity. Senator Lehman moved to deprive Joe of his committee chairmanships, and he told colleagues in a Senate speech that McCarthy had "grossly abused" his authority and "created public disrespect for Congress." The Senate Republican Policy Committee unanimously proposed a code of conduct in congressional investigations that would "assure the rights of witnesses" and protect people from "smears" by curbing "one-man" committee rule. Spokesmen for several national organizations, including the National Council of Churches, appeared before the Senate Rules subcommittee to demand changes in investigative procedures. Republican Senator Homer Ferguson urged resistance to efforts by the G.O.P. Senate leadership to delay action on reforms until after the elections.[5]

Joe returned to Washington from a nineteen-day vacation with Jean "south of the border" and quickly called a subcommittee meeting for July 15. Assuming he would resume his normal pattern of activities, he bullied and taunted Symington and Jackson throughout the closed-door session. With Cohn at his side, he resisted an effort led by Potter to force a "housecleaning" of the staff by refusing to recognize a proxy sent by McClellan. Afterward he told reporters confidently that he would soon hold one-man hearings in Boston to probe Communist infiltration of defense plants.

The next day, however, William Knowland forced Joe to abandon plans to hold hearings outside Washington during the closing weeks of Congress. The Senate Majority Leader was eager to quell the resurgence of partisan warfare on the subcommittee, especially now that Potter (known to have talked with the President on the matter) had sided with the Democrats. Ralph Flanders intensified the situation at the same time by announcing that he would call on the Senate a few days later to censure McCarthy.[6]

The move to censure reflected a new strategy by Flanders. His earlier resolution had never been given much of a chance at passage and had recently been opposed by the Senate Republican Policy Committee. Its defeat would have been tantamount to a vote of confidence for McCarthy. Few observers had high hopes for the censure resolution either. Republicans were leery of doing anything that might remotely hurt their chances at the polls; a single seat might determine which party controlled the Senate in 1955, and McCarthy was still popular, particularly in the New England states. Democratic Party leaders wished to stay aloof, saying that Joe was part of "the Republican mess in Washington." The White House also wanted to stay out of the struggle, claiming that this was the "Senate's baby." But Flanders was determined to press on, hoping that a vote of censure would be a cause to deny Joe his chairmanships after the elections. "We have come at the end of this century to a parting of the ways," he wrote in a speech to the Senate released on July 18. "On the one hand we move in the path and under the influence of the great Lincoln. If we turn the other way we choose the leadership of the junior senator from Wisconsin. In the words of Joshua, who led the children of Israel into the Promised Land, 'Choose you this day whom you will serve.'"[7]

Privately, Flanders had reason to be hopeful about the attack against McCarthy, for he was no longer battling alone. Since mid-June he had enjoyed the enthusiastic support of the Clearing House, the small but highly influential anti-McCarthy organization that had grown out of the National Committee for an Effective Congress in 1953. The liberal Republican businessman Paul G. Hoffman had raised $12,000 to mount a quiet campaign against the senator. Several activists, both paid and voluntary, were now joining Hoffman, lobbyist Maurice Rosenblatt, and others in contacting, persuading, and pressuring senators to back the Flanders resolution. Senators Fulbright, Hennings, Sparkman, Monroney, and Lehman worked among their fellow Democrats, while Flanders and John Sherman Cooper led the effort among Republicans. A letter to Lyndon B. Johnson asked the Senate Democratic leadership to take a public position on the resolution. A public telegram to each senator from twenty-three prominent Americans, including Paul Hoffman, labor leader Walter Reuther, Dean Erwin Griswold of the Harvard Law School, motion-picture mogul Samuel Goldwyn, and theologian Reinhold Niebuhr, urged bipartisan support for the resolution of censure.

By the evening of July 18, Clearing House leaders thought they had twenty-four "sure" and eighteen "very probable" votes. Twenty Senators were firmly against the resolution, while the rest were as yet unaccounted for. At a private meeting between Flanders and McClellan, arranged by Fulbright, the powerful Arkansas senator expressed a vital interest in the resolution. This was extremely significant, for McClellan was the key to many uncommitted Democratic votes, especially within the party's Southern hierarchy. In order to give McClellan time to wind up his primary campaign in Arkansas and return to Washington, Flanders delayed consideration of the vote on the resolution until July 30.[8]

Realizing that his dismissal from the subcommittee was imminent, Roy Cohn resigned on July 20. McCarthy swiftly transferred Don Surine to his personal staff to avoid the investigator's removal by his subcommittee colleagues. Staff member Thomas La Venia, a former Secret Service agent, was soon forced off the payroll. (The Defense Department had denied security clearances to Surine and La Venia due to incidents in their past.) Flanders remarked, "So far so good." He added, however, "This of course does not reach the heart of the problem represented by the junior senator from Wisconsin."[9]

Joe was especially bitter about the departure of his chief counsel, calling it a victory for Communists and fellow travelers. He also expressed the belief that Cohn was appreciated by the millions who had watched him during the hearings. "I know that they will resent as deeply as do I the treatment to which he has been subjected."[10]

A week later, Joe attended a banquet in New York's Hotel Astor honoring Cohn. He was applauded and cheered for nearly three minutes when introduced. The speech-making went on for hours, but no one reached the hearts of the audience more deeply than Rabbi Benjamin Schultz, who said, "The plain people know that the loss of Cohn is like the loss of a dozen battleships." "He is only beginning," Schultz exclaimed, and could be elected to almost any office in the United States at the moment. "America is for Cohn; the people are for Cohn; he stands for McCarthyism. God bless it." McCarthy, Westbrook Pegler, George Sokolsky, William F. Buckley, Fulton Lewis, Jr., John T. Flynn, Alfred Kohlberg, and the some 2,500 others in attendance applauded enthusiastically.[11]

On July 27 Joe appeared before the Senate Rules Committee to denounce proposals that would abolish one-man investigating committees. He vigorously defended his own record, contending that he used an "almost ideal set of rules," and asserting "on no occasion that I can recall have we concealed from a witness either the identity of an accuser or the nature of the accusation." In the course of his testimony, he blasted Annie Lee Moss and General Zwicker, and for the first time called Dorothy Kenyon a Communist. He declined to reveal the names of Mrs. Kenyon's accusers.[12]

Senate debate on the Flanders resolution began on July 30 before packed galleries. Flanders' opening speech contained three particulars: McCarthy's failure to respond to the Hennings Committee, the dispatch of Cohn and Schine to Europe (which raised "serious doubts as to the seriousness, responsibility, and intelligence" of the United States government, and which had "compromised" the honor of the nation and the Senate), and the senator's "habitual contempt for people," such as General Zwicker and Dorothy Kenyon. On the last point, Flanders said, "Unrebuked, it casts a blot on the reputation of the Senate itself. It also makes plain the impossibility of controlling exhibitions of innate character by any change in the rules. The senator can break rules faster than we can make them."

Flanders also took Joe to task for usurping the fields of two Senate subcommittees and for being an ineffective anti-Communist. The "one major feather in the war bonnet" of Senator McCarthy, he said, was Owen Lattimore, once accused of being a "top Soviet agent." As everyone knew, a federal court had recently dismissed major counts in Lattimore's indictment for perjury. "The senator's work has resulted in some desirable dismissals," Flanders said. "So far as I am aware he has never claimed credit for a single successful prosecution."

Leaders of both parties had taken the position that the Flanders resolution could not be a party issue. (Many Democrats were afraid of drawing the G.O.P. closer to McCarthy.) Nevertheless, it was soon obvious that numerous Republicans were determined to defeat the punitive action. Majority Leader Knowland quickly announced that he would vote against it. Senators Cordon and Malone sought to kill or delay it. Herman Welker denied that McCarthy had contempt for people, noting Joe's fondness for his own wife and children. Everett Dirksen delivered an hour-long oration accusing Communists and such liberal groups as the National Committee for an Effective Congress and Americans for Democratic Action of "jumping into bed" with Flanders.[13]

The following day, responding to criticism that the resolution was too general, Senator Fulbright offered six accusations of alleged misconduct. The bill of particulars included the Lustron charge, defiance of the Hennings Committee, the appeal to government employees for secret information, and the attacks on Zwicker, Mrs. Moss, and George C. Marshall. "His abuses have recalled to the minds of millions the most abhorrent tyrannies which our whole system of ordered liberty and balanced power was intended to abolish," Fulbright said. Sen. Wayne Morse soon suggested that McCarthy be censured on seven specific grounds. Flanders then introduced 33 particulars (drafted by the Clearing House), and the charges totaled 46, a number of which overlapped.

Republicans again registered disapproval of the resolution during the second day of debate, although Flanders picked up vocal support from G.O.P. moderates James H. Duff and John Sherman Cooper. Liberal Democrat Herbert Lehman spoke eloquently against McCarthy. But most senators, notably the Southern Democrats, remained quiet, and newspapers predicted the probable failure of the resolution.[14]

When Senator McClellan returned to Washington following a successful primary battle, he called for the creation of a special committee to study the charges against McCarthy, with instructions to report to the Senate before adjournment. H. Alexander Smith had suggested such a committee earlier, but the New Jersey Republican had sought to delay a report until after the elections. McClellan's proposal carried great weight with Minority Leader Lyndon Johnson, who had quietly been pondering such action against McCarthy for months. It appealed to many who preferred not to be asked to take a position on McCarthy during an election year. McCarthyites went along as well, hoping that a committee would scuttle the entire issue. The motion that passed on August 2, following a bitter debate that ended at 10:05 P.M., called for a select committee of three Democrats and three Republicans, appointed by the Vice-President on the recommendation of the respective party leaders. The vote was 75 to 12, with Flanders, Fulbright, Hennings, Lehman, and a number of others favoring outright censure in opposition.[15]

Joe was openly defiant throughout the debate. He told a "Catholic day" crowd of 15,000 at Johnstown, Pennsylvania, "I say to you now, there are no tactics too rough to weed out the underground influence which threatens the very heart of the American republic." On the Senate floor he relished the thought of having the right to cross-examine his critics: "I assure the American people that the senators who have made the charges will either indict themselves for perjury, or they will prove what consummate liars they are, by showing the difference between their statements on the floor of the Senate and their testimony in the hearing." That same day Joe made public a recent letter from former Secretary of War Harry H. Woodring alleging that George Marshall "would sell out his own grandmother for personal advantage." (At his news conference two days later, President Eisenhower delivered a dramatic two-minute encomium of the wartime Chief of Staff.)[16]

Privately, Joe was in torment. The Senate speeches comparing him to Hitler and implying that he was a crook and a homosexual galled and hurt him. He seemed unable to believe that the most powerful men in the Senate would seriously consider his censure. The public opinion polls and the condemnation by almost every major newspaper and magazine— including the Scripps-Howard chain—unquestionably increased his bitterness, as did the hostility of Hoover, Nixon, and others formerly close to him. Joe was becoming irritable, moody, secretive, and rigid. He drank almost constantly. Brent Bozell, a young attorney who arrived at McCarthy's office in August to provide legal counsel, soon confided to William F. Buckley that Joe's physical deterioration was such that he might die at any time.[17]

Lyndon Johnson was firmly convinced that McCarthy was a disruptive force in the Senate and believed that the time had come for his censure. Historically, the Senate had been extremely tolerant of its members, acknowledging and respecting their selection by the voters of their states. Many notorious mavericks had, at times, flaunted Senate rules and ignored their duties without penalty. But Joe had attacked a large number of Senators personally over the years, a serious violation of Senate traditions. Some of his recent targets, moreover, had been conservatives, which deeply disturbed the Senate Establishment. Audiences estimated at up to 20,000,000 had witnessed the verbal assaults. McCarthy had also impeded the flow of Senate business, and this earned him the wrath of many colleagues concerned with legislative achievements.

Responsibility for selecting members of the special committee fell upon Johnson and Knowland. The California Republican was no match for the Texan in intelligence or will, and, according to Johnson aide George Reedy, the result was that Johnson virtually hand-picked the committee. The Minority Leader saw to it that each member was conservative (to avoid the charge of being "soft"), honest, tough, and either quietly anti-McCarthy or sufficiently objective to be capable of censuring the Wisconsin senator. Publicly, Johnson called them "men who are symbols for patriotism, integrity, and judicial temperament." All six came from the South and West, where McCarthy had never enjoyed major support. Only one was up for reelection, and he faced token opposition.[18]

The ranking Democrat was Edwin C. Johnson of Colorado, who had been in the Senate since 1937 and had recently announced his retirement to run for governor of his state. Johnson, 70, was one of the most powerful men on Capitol Hill and a mentor and senior adviser of Lyndon Johnson. Although it was not widely known, he detested McCarthy for having ruined the reputation of a friend. In March the *Denver Post* had quoted him as saying, "In my opinion, there is not a man among the Democratic leaders of Congress who does not loathe Joe McCarthy." He told a closed-door meeting of the Democratic Policy Committee on July 29 that his mind was made up on McCarthy and that he was going to vote for the Flanders resolution. When appointed to the special committee, he told Lyndon Johnson privately, "I'll kill him."[19]

The other two Democrats were John C. Stennis of Mississippi and Samuel J. Ervin, Jr., of North Carolina, both Senate insiders. Stennis, 53, had been a lawyer and judge in his home state before going to Washington in 1947. Quiet, reserved, moderate, and known for fearless integrity, he was among the most respected men in the Senate. Ervin, 58, had enjoyed a lengthy career as an attorney and judge before being appointed to his seat the previous June. He was bright, witty, and learned, and was liked and admired by his colleagues.

Arthur Vivian Watkins of Utah was the senior Republican and chairman of the committee. Watkins, 67, was a graduate of Columbia University Law School and a former county attorney and judge. He had entered the Senate in November, 1946 and was currently a loyal Administration moderate. His service on the Senate Internal Security subcommittee was thought to protect him from attacks upon his patriotism. Watkins was a thin, gray, mild-mannered man who wore rimless glasses. A leader in the Mormon Church, he was respected for his scrupulous ethics, cold objectivity, and personal courage.

Frank Carlson of Kansas was a middle-of-the-road Republican known to be close to the President. A 61-year-old farmer-stockman of modest education and intellect, he had served six terms in the House and two terms as governor before his election to the Senate in 1950. Francis Case of South Dakota, 57, was a small, intense man. The son of a retired Methodist minister, he was one of capitol hill's rare teetotalers. He had come to Washington in 1937, following a career as a rancher and small-town newspaperman, and had served seven terms in the House before being elected to the Senate in 1951. He was known for his careful attention to legislative detail and was called the "amendingest senator" in service. Case was the only member of the Watkins Committee to be outside the inner club of the Senate.[20]

The selections won widespread approval. When Senator Knowland learned of the Democratic choices, he said, "I would be perfectly willing to go before them on trial of my life." Thomas Hennings said privately, "Lyndon, I don't see how you could possibly have done better." Nixon told reporters, "This is an outstanding committee." *The New York Times* declared, "The men selected command respect and support on both sides of the Senate chamber." McCarthy soon said that he was "completely satisfied" but could not resist telling an Illinois American Legion convention that "nice little boys in the Senate" had attacked "someone for doing the skunk-hunting job which they didn't have the guts to do themselves."[21]

Some observers were certain that McCarthy would trample the committee and emerge unscathed. Senator Fulbright was reported to have said,

"Joe can buffalo any committee on earth." Stewart Alsop, comparing McCarthy and Watkins, said that a "man-eating tiger" was about to face an "elderly mouse." A popular line in Washington at the time went: "The lion has been thrown into a den of lambs."[22]

As the Watkins Committee made preparations for hearings, Joe's fortunes continued to decline. An appearance at a Chicago White Sox game in Comiskey Park drew more boos than cheers from the crowd. A Gallup poll reported that the senator's "unfavorable" vote was up six points since June, to a record 51 percent. (Thirty-six percent were "favorable," while 13 percent had no opinion.) A series of well-documented articles in the *Christian Science Monitor* concluded that in fourteen months of public hearings, the McCarthy subcommittee had failed: (1) to find a single Communist spy whose guilt stood proved in court, (2) to secure a single indictment against anyone it charged with treason, (3) to uncover a single proved Communist working on a secret defense job. Reviewers were also praising a hard-hitting book entitled *McCarthy and the Communists,* by James Rorty and Moshe Decter, which condemned the senator's entire political career in detail.[23]

Still, McCarthy retained the support of a well-financed and zealous minority throughout the country, which saw the effort to censure the senator as a Red plot. William S. White estimated the number of hard-core McCarthyites in the Senate at fifteen and quoted one as saying of Joe's enemies, "They are powerful, but they will never pull this thing off." Moreover, the second Red Scare was far from over, a fact that could aid McCarthy. On August 24, Senate liberals, quivering with fear that political opponents would brand them "soft," spearheaded passage of the Communist Control Act, a statute calling the Communist party of the United States "the agency of a hostile foreign power" and declaring that it "should be outlawed." One observer wrote to Americans for Democratic Action, which had given its support, "A more blind, reactionary and un-American vote was never registered in the U.S. Senate."[24]

The Senate appropriated $30,000 for the Watkins Committee and agreed to pay McCarthy's legal expenses. The committee was granted broad powers, including the right to subpoena witnesses, request information from any source, and to otherwise establish its own procedures. Committee members were instructed "to act and make a report" before the Senate's adjournment.

The committee decided to conduct public hearings but elected to bar radio and television coverage and the taking of still pictures while the sessions were in progress. It adopted the procedural rules that applied on the floor of the Senate. The committee also barred hearsay evidence and agreed to accept evidence that was directly related to the charges against McCarthy—which excluded the issues weighed by the Gillette-Hennings Committee as well as the entire question of Communist subversion.

Joe's attorney, Edward Bennett Williams, was permitted to cross-examine witnesses, to object to procedures and specific questions, and to present evidence on McCarthy's behalf. He was also informed that either he or McCarthy could question a witness or raise an objection, but that once one of them spoke on a subject the other would be barred from participating. This was designed, of course, to prevent the shouting matches that had marred the Army-McCarthy hearings. (Watkins said later that what he had seen on television was "beyond belief.") Joe reluctantly agreed to Williams's demand that he remain silent during the hearings except when testifying.[25]

On August 24 the committee announced five categories of charges it would probe in public hearings: (1) McCarthy's treatment of the Gillette-Hennings Committee, (2) the invitation to government employees to give him classified information, (3) his possession and exploitation of the alleged J. Edgar Hoover letter, (4) his "abuses" against Senators Hendrickson and others, (5) his attack on General Zwicker. Watkins called these five "the most important" of the 46 specifications filed but did not preclude consideration of other allegations during the course of the hearings.[26]

Joe and Jean enjoyed a vacation in California prior to the hearings. A poolside photograph showed the senator aged and slightly bloated. On returning to Washington, Joe told a reporter that the inquiry was "a great waste of time" and said that he would call no defense witnesses. Some of the allegations would be acknowledged, he added. "For instance, the fact I said Senator Flanders was senile is unquestioned. It will be freely admitted. He can prove he's not if he can and wants to."[27]

The hearings opened on August 31 before a standing-room-only crowd in the Senate Caucus Room, site of the Army-McCarthy proceedings. The committee members were seated at random around the table rather than by party, emphasizing the bipartisan nature of the undertaking. Watkins began by reading the resolution guiding the investigation, describing procedural matters, and stressing the committee's belief that the hearings were not to be adversary in character. "We realize the United States Senate, in a sense, is on trial, and we hope our conduct will be such as to maintain the American sense of fair play and the high traditions and dignity of the United States Senate under the authority given it by the Constitution."[28]

Watkins and his colleagues were prepared for an immediate attack by McCarthy. The day before, in an executive session, he had angrily displayed the *Denver Post* clipping containing Edwin Johnson's hostile remark and wanted to know the committee's response. Prior to the hearing he had distributed his opening statement to reporters, a brief speech that challenged the patriotism and honesty of his critics.

Even before Joe was called to the stand, Watkins declared of the statement, "I want to say that we recognize that most of it is not material and relevant to the issues in this hearing as we understand them." When the matter of Senator Johnson's bias was raised, Watkins dismissed it as immaterial to the investigation. (Johnson claimed he did not say that he personally loathed McCarthy.) When Joe disregarded his attorney's instructions and attempted to take the offensive, Watkins responded sternly.

> Senator McCarthy. Mr. Chairman . . .
> The Chairman. Just a moment, Senator. You have filed no challenge; and, in the first place, I believe it is improper for you to do so, because we have not any jurisdiction.
> Senator McCarthy. Mr. Chairman, I should be entitled to know whether or not . . .
> The Chairman. The senator is out of order.
> Senator McCarthy. Can't I get Mr. Johnson to tell me . . .
> The Chairman. The senator is out of order.
> Senator McCarthy. . . . whether it is true or false?
> The Chairman. The senator is out of order. You can go to the senator and question and find out. That is not for this committee to consider. We are not going to be interrupted by these diversions and sidelines. We are going straight down the line.
> The committee will be in recess.

The chairman banged his gavel and continued to pound as McCarthy tried to speak. The crowd began to file out of the room. Joe reportedly said later, "This is the most unheard-of thing I ever heard of." James Reston observed, "Sen. Joseph R. McCarthy is in a tougher spot before the Watkins Committee now than at any other time since he became a world figure."[29]

There were nine public hearings, the last ending on September 13. The case against McCarthy took four days to present and consisted in large part of placing into the record many of the senator's insulting remarks and letters. Members of the committee were visibly distressed at times by the often violent language. Fulbright was "half-bright." Flanders was "senile." Hendrickson was the only human who ever lived so long "without brains or guts." Gillette was accused of "dishonesty." The committee counsel read aloud the entire confrontation between McCarthy and General Zwicker.

Joe was absent much of the time that his often torrid rhetoric reverberated through the hearing room. He remained quiet when present. A word in his own defense would have brought the crack of Watkins' gavel and further embarrassment. Reston thought Joe was like "an alley fighter in the Supreme Court" and mused, "He is fenced in for the first time and he is being hurt, for regardless of what the Senate does about his case, each day's hearing is a form of censure of its own."[30]

Outside the hearing room, much to his attorney's distress, Joe attacked Watkins for a slip of the tongue made during an interview and blasted Johnson for the *Denver Post* comment. He said that the absence of radio and television in the hearings made possible "completely false reporting." Other press conferences and filmed statements were to follow. Edward Bennett Williams later wrote, "Day by day our relationship with the committee worsened."[31]

Williams employed a number of approaches on his client's behalf. He moved to dismiss the charge alleging abuse of the Gillette-Hennings Committee on the ground that a senator could not be censured for conduct committed during a previous session of Congress. Having researched that issue, Watkins snapped, "We do not agree with you." Attempts to show that the committee had lacked legal authority and that its procedures had violated basic legal protections were also brushed aside as "wholly immaterial." McCarthy's conduct toward the committee members was the only issue in question, Watkins declared. On the stand, Joe noted, "There is no secret about how I felt about them." He claimed (falsely) that he had not received an invitation from the committee in late November 1952 to appear before it. He also claimed (falsely) to have notified the committee that he would only appear under subpoena.[32]

Williams argued that in calling upon government employees to supply him with information, McCarthy was merely echoing similar appeals from others, including the Internal Security subcommittee, on which Watkins sat. The chairman was hostile to this line of defense and blocked the presentation of much of Williams's argument. "We could go on for months here," he said. Joe testified that he had asked only for evidence of wrongdoing and not for classified information. His appeal, he asserted, invited employees to conform to the Criminal Code and to their oaths of office. Joe revealed not the slightest repentance for his actions. His earlier comments, he said, "certainly expressed my feelings then; they express my feelings now."[33]

Joe had no regrets about the "Hoover letter" either. It was his responsibility to investigate and expose wrongdoing and treason, he argued. "After talking to the officer, and discovering that there was wrongdoing, as evidenced by this document, I felt that I had the absolute duty to use the information contained in the document. I did that. I would do it again." Cohn testified, amidst a flurry of weasel words, that he had advised McCarthy that the document was unclassified.[34]

The blasts against Flanders and Hendrickson were also justified, Joe contended. "After the obscenities he had voiced about me," he said of the Vermont senator, "the ridiculous statements he had made, I was convinced he was senile." Hendrickson, Joe said, had signed the Hennings report without reading it.[35]

On the Zwicker charge, Williams took the position that the general had provoked McCarthy into attacking him. A witness was produced who said he had heard the general mutter "You s.o.b." at the senator from his seat in the audience even prior to his testimony. Zwicker was questioned, as were two McCarthy staff members who had received information from him. Joe, on the stand, called Zwicker "one of the most arrogant, one of the most evasive witnesses, that I have ever had before my committee, one of the most irritating." He had no second thoughts about his remarks to Zwicker. "I said he was not fit to wear the uniform of a general, and I think he was not. I think any man who says that it is right to give honorable discharges to known Communists is not fit to wear the uniform of a general. I said it then. I will say it now. I will say it again. I feel that as strongly as I feel anything." He promised to summon Zwicker before his subcommittee in the future and resume the questioning about Peress.[36]

Joe's defiance greatly influenced members of the committee. Watkins wrote later, "Each of us believed, I am sure, that if McCarthy (faced by the evidence and unswerving purpose of the Senate) would choose to purge himself from his contempt of the Senate his act would be accepted." The committee members may also have paid heed to a number of cogent letters from William Benton and Ralph Flanders. Benton called attention to facts surrounding Joe's refusal to appear before the Gillette-Hennings Committee. Flanders pointed to several highly controversial items in McCarthy's record as a senator and emphasized the necessity of censuring him. Flanders wrote, "We are faced with conduct by a senator which I believe is unparalleled and unprecedented in the history of the United States Senate. If we fail to meet this challenge we leave the Senate debased and in the future unprotected from the vilest sort of demagogy and unprincipled attacks upon members of the Senate."[37]

The Senate had chosen to recess rather than adjourn in order to be called back to consider the proposed censure. Under pressure from a number of senators running for reelection, however, the Majority and Minority Leaders agreed to postpone the censure debate until after the returns were in. Many McCarthy critics were distressed by the decision. Others, on the other hand, thought it enhanced the possibility of a successful move against the Wisconsin senator. Committee member Frank Carlson commented, "I don't think the atmosphere before election would be good for considering the kind of report we are issuing."[38]

On September 27 the Watkins Committee released a 68-page report which *Time* magazine, in a cover story, labeled "a ringing reassertion of the U.S. Senate's dignity." Unanimously and unequivocally, the committee members recommended that McCarthy be censured on two counts: his treatment of Senator Hendrickson and the Gillette-Hennings Committee, and his denunciation of General Zwicker. The well-documented and closely reasoned report called Joe's statement about Hendrickson "vulgar and insulting" and termed his conduct toward the committee "contemptuous, contumacious, and denunciatory, without reason or justification, and . . . obstructive to legislative processes." The six senators called Joe's berating of Zwicker "inexcusable" and "reprehensible." Citing a judicial decision discussing the orderly processes of legislative inquiries, they wrote: "The select committee is of the opinion that the very fact that 'the exercise of good taste and good judgment' must be entrusted to those who conduct such investigations placed upon them the responsibility of upholding the honor of the Senate. If they do not maintain high standards of fair and respectful treatment the dishonor is shared by the entire Senate."[39]

The committee came close to recommending censure on the ground of McCarthy's appeal to government employees.

> The select committee feels compelled to conclude that the conduct of Senator McCarthy in inviting federal employees to supply him with information, without expressly excluding therefrom classified documents, tends to create a disruption of the orderly and constitutional functioning of the executive and legislative branches of the government, which tends to bring both into disrepute. Such conduct cannot be condoned and is deemed improper.

The senators decided, however, to grant Joe the benefit of a few doubts and uncertainties that clung to the issue.[40]

The charge concerning the "Hoover letter" was dismissed because of "mitigating circumstances"—the stress and strain Joe was under during the Army-McCarthy hearings. Nevertheless, the committee stated that the accused had "committed grave error" and "manifested a high degree of irresponsibility" by offering to make public the contents of the document without consulting the Attorney General or subcommittee members.[41]

The report called Joe's remarks about Flanders "highly improper." It concluded, however, that they were induced by the Vermont senator's provocative conduct in the Senate caucus room and by his speeches on the Senate floor, and did not constitute a basis for censure.[42]

The bluntness and firmness of the bipartisan report caught Washington by surprise. Senate committees had investigated McCarthy four times in the past without producing anything remotely similar. McCarthyites such as Dirksen, McCarran, and Welker immediately expressed their determined opposition to the recommendations, while Lehman and Green and their allies pledged their support. Senate Leaders and the President remained cautiously silent.[43]

General Zwicker said that he was pleased with the report as it applied to him, and one veteran Pentagon observer predicted that the document would boost Army morale appreciably. A survey of newspaper opinion across the country showed widespread satisfaction with the Watkins Committee. The *Louisville Courier Journal* declared, "These six inoffensive and austere men have by their unanimity and moderation both destroyed the McCarthy myth and elevated the prestige of a senate which has suffered severe blows. They have done well and the nation owes them thanks." George Reedy confided to Lyndon Johnson, "There is a general feeling that the conclusion is foregone and that censure is a virtual certainty. At this point most of the press boys have even lost interest in the question of whether the censure will take place before or after the election."[44]

Republican chieftains had spread the word that McCarthy was unwelcome in the fall election campaigns. Even in Wisconsin, G.O.P. candidates thought their chances better without the assistance of their junior senator. Joe canceled a few speeches he had scheduled earlier and spent several weeks checking in and out of Bethesda Naval Hospital for treatment of his recurrent sinus problems. He was increasingly somber and despondent. The Watkins Committee report had hurt him deeply. At a news conference on October 13 he said he was "supporting all of the Republican candidates with one exception." This was a reference to New Jersey's Clifford Case, who had been openly hostile. Joe was also responding to the charge by ex-Communist Bella V. Dodd that Adelaide Case, the senatorial candidate's sister, had been active in Communist front groups in the 1940s. It soon turned out that Miss Dodd had condemned the wrong Adelaide Case. The other Adelaide was a New York college professor who had died in 1948.[45]

Even without McCarthy, Republicans all across the country employed Red Scare tactics against opponents. One radio advertisement featured a voice with a Russian accent saying, "Defeat the Republican congressional candidates in 1954! That is an order from Moscow! Return America to a New Deal-type administration." Vice-President Nixon, who campaigned in 95 cities in 30 states, labeled Democratic candidates "left-wingers," warned that the Democratic Party had tolerated internal subversion, and used the "numbers game" to show that the Eisenhower administration had fired legions of security risks. Adlai Stevenson called Nixon's journey an "ill-will tour" and described his campaigning as "McCarthyism in a white collar."[46]

For all of that, Democrats regained control of the House and Senate on November 2, prompting strategists and commentators to reevaluate the efficacy of right-wing campaign tactics. McCarthyite candidates were defeated in Illinois, Wyoming, Montana, Oregon, Michigan, and elsewhere. Joe's friend Charles Kersten lost his congressional seat to liberal Henry Reuss following a bitter campaign. McCarthy, on the other hand, blamed G.O.P. losses on the failure of candidates to speak forcefully about Communist infiltration of government. "Republicans have got to learn before next year that they can't duck the real issues and can't talk about sweet nothings."[47]

The debate on McCarthy's censure was scheduled to begin on November 8. The gravity of the undertaking was lost on no one. In its 165-year history, the Senate had only considered two motions of censure, and both were adopted. The first, in 1902, was a dual motion involving two South Carolina Democrats who had engaged in a fistfight on the Senate floor. The second, in 1929, was aimed at Republican Hiram Bingham for bringing the assistant to the president of the Connecticut Manufacturers Association into an executive session of the Senate Finance Committee as his aide. The resolution introduced by Flanders for the Senate's third confrontation with the question of censure read: "Resolved, that the conduct of the senator from Wisconsin, Mr. McCarthy, is unbecoming a member of the United States Senate, is contrary to senatorial traditions and tends to bring the Senate into disrepute, and such conduct is hereby condemned."

A Gallup poll published on November 5 showed that 49 percent of those interviewed disagreed with McCarthy's claim that the Watkins Committee had denied him a fair hearing. (Only 24 percent agreed, and they tended to be the less educated.) Three days later Gallup reported that of the 55 percent of the nation's voters who had followed the Watkins deliberations, 56 percent believed that McCarthy should be censured for his treatment of the Gillette-Hennings Committee (32 percent disagreed), and 47 percent thought he should be censured on the Zwicker charge (33 percent disagreed). Many on the Far Right were prepared to write Joe off. The *Los Angeles Mirror* declared that the Watkins Committee report "marks the end of Joe McCarthy as a major political force."[48]

Tens of thousands of others throughout the country, however, were eager to fight back against what they considered to be a pro-Communist assault upon the purest of patriots. The Hearst press, the *Chicago Tribune,* David Lawrence's *U.S. News and World Report,* the *Brooklyn Tablet,* and other organs of the Far Right led the way, condemning the Watkins Committee for bias, ignorance, and un-American activity. Hate mail poured in upon senators. Watkins received thousands of postcards, letters, and telegrams daily, many reading simply "Who Promoted Peress?" (The Army released a solid explanation on November 3, which attracted little attention from the media. Exhaustive investigations, the report stated, had "conclusively established that there was no collusion, conspiracy, or preferential treatment. . . . The evidence shows clearly that it was the system which was at fault.") Fulbright was called a "louse," "skunk," "coward," "dirty Red," and "jackass," among other things. Flanders told a correspondent that he had received 20,000 letters about McCarthy.[49]

At an annual Catholic War Veterans meeting in New York on November 8, Msgr. Edward R. Martin, a personal representative of Cardinal Spellman, declared, "I personally know that $5,000,000 has been pooled to kick McCarthy out of the Senate—only a small portion of what is pouring into Washington." The Catholic War Veterans of Brooklyn and Queens announced a nationwide campaign to collect signatures for a "Save McCarthy" petition. By early November the organization had gathered 250,000 signatures from 40 states. The C.W.V. and the *Brooklyn Tablet* were soon planning to join forces with a national organization called "Ten Million Americans Mobilized for Justice," which was attempting to obtain ten million signatures opposing McCarthy's censure.[50]

Before Joe stepped out on the Senate floor on November 8 he accepted two awards at a ceremony in Vice-President Nixon's Senate office. The American Coalition, a right-wing organization founded in 1928, presented him with a patriotic service medal. The coalition's president warned, "If you are destroyed then it follows, as night follows day, that your distinguished anti-Communist colleagues in the Congress and in the government will be savagely assaulted, and they too eliminated." Joe was also given a set of twenty-two bound volumes containing the 250,000 signatures collected by the New York veterans. He vowed to continue his work "even if the

Senate censures me—and I think they will—for fighting the dirtiest fighters in the world, Communists. I will go on until either the Communists lose or we die."[51]

Joe had no illusions about escaping censure. The Senate had never before held a special session for the sole purpose of disciplining one of its members, and he admitted freely that his opponents could muster the necessary majority vote. In public he tried to appear nonchalant, self-confident, and in great shape for a battle. "I can go fifteen rounds," he told reporters. He might lose the brawl, but a lot of people would be bloodied in the process. Beyond the range of the media, however, Joe was in more agony than friends had ever seen him. He was increasingly withdrawn and downcast. His drinking continued to accelerate. He began to enter his office through the private entrance and would sit alone for an hour or two before being discovered by staff members. The pain of the rejection he was about to suffer at the hands of his colleagues was acute.[52]

Of course, Joe might have extricated himself from this personally and politically damaging situation earlier, and several opportunities to do so were yet to appear. A cynical man would have wasted no time. But Joe was unprepared to give an inch in what he saw as his personal war to protect the flag. In his view, any punishment, no matter how severe, was preferable to compromise and appeasement. He would never yield to those doing the work of the Reds.

The Senate galleries were crowded on November 8 for the opening day of the unprecedented session. More than two-thirds of the senators were on hand, including nearly all of the Republicans. On every senator's desk had been placed a twenty-page pamphlet reproducing anti-McCarthy articles from the *Daily Worker*. The pink cover sheet read in large letters "THROW THE BUM OUT," and below were the words "Official Communist Party Line on Senator McCarthy." The message was far from subtle: to be against McCarthy was to be in favor of Marx and Lenin. Joe and Jean soon posed for a photograph with a copy of the *Daily Worker* urging the Senator's censure.[53]

On November 9 McCarthy released the text of a highly emotional speech scheduled for delivery on the Senate floor the following day. Unmistakably a product of Joe's own pen, the speech linked the quest for "my destruction" directly to Communists and their dupes. "From the moment I entered the fight against subversion back in 1950 at Wheeling, West Virginia, the Communists have said that the destruction of me and what I stand for is their number-one objective in this country." Joe pictured himself as the embodiment of "hard" anti-Communism. "Let me say, incidentally, that it is not easy for a man to assert that he is the symbol of resistance to Communist subversion—that the nation's fate is in some respects tied to his own fate." He likened himself to Martin Dies, "who in my opinion will go down in history as a heroic voice crying in the wilderness," a man "damned and humiliated and driven from public life." (Dies, one of Capitol Hill's most notorious Red-hunters, had announced his political retirement in 1944, following several years of criticism by President Roosevelt and congressional Democrats. In 1953 Joe had conferred privately with Dies and was warned "to expect abuse, ridicule, and every known device of 'character assassination' and mental torture.") As Roosevelt and Acheson had done the work of the Communist party by ruining Dies, Joe wrote, the Watkins Committee was likewise "the victim of a Communist campaign," the "involuntary agent" of the party.

> I would have the American people recognize, and contem-
> plate in dread, the fact that the Communist party—a rela-
> tively small group of deadly conspirators—has now extended
> its tentacles to that most respected of American bodies, the
> United States Senate; that it has made a committee of the
> Senate its unwitting handmaiden.

Joe acknowledged the likelihood of his censure but warned, "As you vote 'aye' on this resolution I urge you to weigh carefully the question: who has really won by this vote of censure?" He promised to continue "to serve the cause to which I have dedicated my life" no matter what happened.

> The Communists have now managed to have me investi-
> gated five times. If they fail to silence me this time—and
> make no mistake about it, they will fail—I will be investi-
> gated a sixth time and a seventh. But in a sense a new
> investigation of me is good news. It means that the Commu-
> nists have been hurt again.[54]

The censure debate began on November 10 with Watkins delivering a thoughtful and objective outline of the charges and the committee's recommendations. McCarthy was soon flying into the committee chairman, who appeared frail and said he was ill, with repeated challenges and questions. In a subtly effective address, Francis Case suggested that Joe's prepared speech, published in full in *The New York Times,* helped prove the contention that he had been contemptuous of a Senate committee. Joe did not deliver the speech, pleading lack of time, but inserted it into the

Congressional Record about forty minutes before adjournment. Many senators were quietly infuriated by the attacks upon Watkins and his colleagues. Lyndon Johnson was to say later that McCarthy's remarks "would be more fittingly inscribed on the wall of a men's room."[55]

Democrats stayed out of the struggle from the start. Johnson feared that Republicans would rally to McCarthy if they sensed that the debate was becoming partisan. Johnson was not a passive spectator, however. During the first session he blocked an effort by Knowland that would have enabled McCarthy backers to water down the censure resolution by introducing amendments. He also attempted to keep a firm hand on the liberals who were eager to enter the fray. "Lyndon Johnson and others are literally demanding that we refrain from rocking the boat," said Julius Edelstein, an assistant to Senator Lehman.[56]

Hundreds of McCarthy supporters descended upon Capitol Hill the following morning. Many carried small American flags and wore badges declaring "I Like McCarthy" and "I Like His Methods." A group from New York brought placards with such messages as "Senator McCarthy Is the Man Who Fulfilled the Ike Campaign Promises" and "Why Did Alger Hiss Want Trial in Vermont? Do You Know Senator Flanders?" The demonstrators buttonholed their senators, sat in the galleries, and gathered outside McCarthy's office. Senator Saltonstall told reporters that 60 people from Massachusetts had called on him, bringing signatures of 4,000 other McCarthy partisans. Shortly after 3:00 P.M. senators heard a tremendous roar of cheers from outside the chambers. Seconds later, Joe entered, wearing a broad grin.[57]

During the censure debate, Herman Welker vigorously defended McCarthy, calling him "one of the greatest living champions of human liberty, and one of the greatest living foes of Communist slavery." Francis Case raised eyebrows by suggesting that the senator might purge himself of the charges against him with a few apologies. But Joe was defiant throughout, deeply irritating a number of colleagues by objecting to the insertion into the *Congressional Record* of a radio broadcast praising the recently dismissed diplomat John Paton Davies. He also told a reporter, "As far as the [Gillette-Hennings] subcommittee is concerned, there is nothing I have done that I would have done differently."[58]

That evening a crowd of 3,000 gathered at Constitutional Hall to demonstrate their support of McCarthy. The affair had been arranged by Rabbi Benjamin Schultz, director of the American Jewish League Against Communism and a close friend of Roy Cohn. McCarthy was on hand, as were Senators Goldwater, Welker, and Mundt. Joe gave a fervent, tear-filled speech that deeply moved his audience. "Joe! Joe! Joe!" they screamed.[59]

There were increasing rumors of compromise within Republican circles during the third day of debate. Welker, Goldwater, and John Bricker stoutly defended McCarthy's record. Goldwater contended that censure would amount to a "global victory for Communism." John Stennis, on the other hand, decried what he called McCarthy's pattern of throwing "slush and slime" at all senators who criticized him. "I have no personal resentment toward the junior senator from Wisconsin for having made such statements," he said. "I feel sorry for him for having done so." Stennis strongly urged censure as a means of protecting the dignity of the Senate.[60]

Over the weekend, Joe and Jean traveled to Milwaukee with Barry Goldwater to attend a testimonial dinner at the Pfister Hotel. More than 1,500 people cheered and applauded throughout the evening and serenaded the senator with a special song. "Nobody's for McCarthy but the people, and we all love our Joe." Earlier that day Joe had told reporters, "I have no plans for doing any apologizing." Asked what effect the censure resolution, if passed, would have on his political fortunes, he replied, "None at all. I think I would not be up for censure except for the fact that I am exposing Communists."[61]

On the Sunday evening television program "Meet the Press" Senator Ervin, who had remained silent during the first three days of debate, spoke out sharply against McCarthy. He was particularly critical of the "unwitting handmaiden" speech in the *Congressional Record*. If the junior senator from Wisconsin did not believe the charges contained in the speech, Ervin said, there was "pretty solid" ground for expulsion from the Senate on the ground of "moral incapacity." If he did believe them, Ervin continued, then the senator had "mental delusions" and suffered from "mental incapacity." McCarthy was "giving the committee hell," Ervin charged, because he could not defend himself against its findings.[62]

At ten the next morning, November 15, Senator Watkins appeared before the McCarthy subcommittee in response to an earlier demand by McCarthy. Joe told reporters that he desired to learn if the Utah senator knew the identity of the "secret master" in the Defense Department who was allegedly responsible for protecting Peress. This was an act of pure spite and defiance by Joe and was a slap in the face for those Republicans, such as Dirksen and Knowland, who were working frantically behind the scenes to hammer out some sort of compromise.

In a small hearing room crowded with spectators and television and movie cameras, Joe badgered and attempted to humiliate his colleague. On several occasions he declared that Watkins had so little to say that he was wasting the subcommittee's time. When Watkins tried to interject a few words at one point, Joe said sarcastically, "Just a minute. Please, Senator. I will give you a gavel." At another point he accused Watkins of being "derelict" in his duty, adding "and that is putting it very, very mildly." The Utah senator was shocked by McCarthy's vitriolic, almost irrational behavior. He later wrote of "an unprecedented hearing, as far as I can ascertain, in the history of the Senate and especially in censure hearings."[63]

The regular proceedings later that day opened with a wild speech by William Jenner, who suggested that the censure resolution be tabled. The strategy of censure, he cried, "was initiated by the Communist conspiracy." Senator Case soon shocked everyone by announcing in a letter to Watkins that due to "new evidence" he would not vote to censure McCarthy on the Zwicker charge. This was considered to be the latest move by those Republicans seeking to soften the censure resolution. Its only apparent effect on the other members of the Watkins Committee was to steel their resolve. Senator Ervin took the floor, repeated the remarks he had made on television the day before, and called for McCarthy's expulsion.[64]

That same day Joe received a patriotic award from the New Jersey Department of the Army and Navy Union. He told his admirers during the ceremony, "I think I should warn you—they're going to vote censure. Not on the basis of facts, but on the basis of politics."[65]

On November 16, the fifth day of the debate, Senator Watkins gave a moving and emotional speech that lasted an hour and a half. Amid rumors that the Zwicker charge would be dropped because of Case's defection, Watkins strongly criticized McCarthy for recently referring to him in Milwaukee as stupid and cowardly. He also decried the *Congressional Record* speech and took Joe to task for calling the Senate session "a lynch bee" nine days earlier. Watkins believed McCarthy's conduct unprecedented and challenged the Senate to take action against him in order to defend its integrity. "How can the Senate hold up its head among other free deliberative bodies of the world unless it does something about this matter?" he asked. He invited his colleagues to add a section to the censure resolution calling attention to McCarthy's behavior during the current debate. "If no one moves such an amendment—and I shall give senators plenty of opportunity to do so—the man from Utah who has been called a coward will do it." Wallace Bennett, Watkins' Republican colleague from Utah, quickly announced that he would do the honors.[66]

Joe entered Bethesda Naval Hospital the next day for treatment of traumatic bursitis. While shaking hands with well-wishers in Milwaukee during the weekend, he had bumped his right elbow against the glass edge of a table top and sustained a bruise that soon developed painful complications. On November 18 the Senate agreed to adjourn until the 29th, when

McCarthy could return. (To make sure Joe was not stalling, the official Capitol physician consulted with doctors at the Naval Hospital and reported to the Majority Leader.) Lyndon Johnson called for prompt action at that time. "We shall have to redouble our efforts when we come back on November 29, unless we want to say to the people of this country—yes, Mr. President, to the people of the world—that the greatest deliberative body ever known is unable to come to a conclusion involving a matter of morality and conduct."[67]

Several friends, including Dirksen, Goldwater, Edward Bennett Williams, and Robert E. Lee, quietly visited McCarthy in the hospital during the next ten days, pleading with him to apologize to two members of the Senate who believed themselves insulted. Dirksen personally prepared three different drafts of a letter. Joe would concede nothing. "I will never let them think I would ever crawl," he told Dirksen. He threw a pen across the room at Goldwater and Williams, and started swearing and pounding on a table. To Lee he said simply, "Fuck 'em." [68]

The Southern bloc, weary and embarrassed by the entire proceeding, had apparently been prepared to vote against censure if McCarthy revealed sufficient repentance. Clearing House leaders were deeply worried about rumors of a compromise resolution that would merely slap McCarthy's wrists. Pro-McCarthy mail had continued to pour in upon senators, and reporters picked up talk of wavering by moderates. (Alexander Wiley left for Brazil, saying that even if he remained in Washington he would not take sides.) "Ten Million Americans Mobilizing for Justice," had opened a New York office and was widely distributing copies of a lengthy petition to be forwarded to the Senate. A portion of the petition read:

> 4. We point out that the Communists and their un-American cohorts, by vicious propaganda, and through willing stooges and blind but innocent dupes, already have victimized certain members of the United States Senate. The insidious influence of these enemies of our way of life was mainly responsible for the creation of the Watkins Committee, and for its incredible findings and conclusions. Now, these same subversive elements are again engaged in an all-out campaign of smear, slander, pressure, and political intimidation in a final attempt to destroy Senator Joseph R. McCarthy and the fundamental principles he symbolizes, and to nullify the great good that he has accomplished.

(Petitions said to bear 1,000,816 signatures reached Capitol Hill on

December 1. They were delivered by guards who stood over them with drawn pistols for the benefit of photographers.)[69]

However, McCarthy's defiance had sealed his fate. Censure was certain, and Joe and his partisans knew it. Joe said repeatedly that he hoped the vote would take place soon, so that he could resume his hunt for subversives.

On November 29, at McCarthy's suggestion, the Senate agreed to limit debate and begin voting two days later. Senator Bennett filed his resolution concerning McCarthy's conduct toward the Watkins Committee, and Edwin Johnson gave a lengthy speech supporting censure. Joe, his right arm bandaged from elbow to wrist and suspended in a sling, again made it clear that he would not apologize to anyone. Indeed, he proposed that resolutions to censure other senators be in order, but dropped the idea after Senator McClellan strongly objected.[70]

That evening a crowd of 13,000 (disappointing by previous estimates) roared its support of McCarthy at a rally in New York's Madison Square Garden sponsored by the Ten Million Americans Mobilizing for Justice. Jean and her mother appeared on Joe's behalf, and Roy Cohn was among the speakers. "If the Senate votes to censure," Cohn said, "it will be committing the blackest act in our whole history." The crowd cheered every reference to McCarthy, and expressed similar enthusiasm at the names of Douglas MacArthur, the late Pat McCarran, Westbrook Pegler, Senators Bricker and Knowland, and Cohn. Ralph Flanders was its major villain, and his rivals included Presidents Roosevelt and Truman, George Marshall, Dean Acheson, and *The New York Times*. At one point a woman photographer for *Life* magazine irritated members of the audience by taking pictures and was led from the arena by a detective amid cries of "Throw her out" and "Hang the Communist."[71]

On the evening of December 2, following three days of often heated speeches, parliamentary maneuvers, and the defeat of compromise resolutions offered by Dirksen, Mundt, and Bridges, the Senate voted 67 to 22 to "condemn" McCarthy for contempt and abuse of both the Gillette-Hennings Committee and the Watkins Committee. The Zwicker charge was dropped without a vote for a complex of reasons including the fear that censure of McCarthy for his conduct as a committee chairman would set a precedent limiting the powers of future chairmen in examining witnesses. (Lyndon Johnson warned Watkins privately that at least fifteen Democrats would not vote for it.) All of the 44 Democrats present voted for censure, while the Republicans were evenly divided—twenty-two on each side of the issue. Independent Wayne Morse of Oregon went with the majority. Joe voted "present."[72]

McCarthy's G.O.P. supporters, whose ranks included Majority Leader Knowland, were almost solidly from the Far Right. When the final resolution was passed, mocking laughter was heard among them. Styles Bridges rose to ask the Vice-President if the word "censure" appeared in the resolution in its final form. At this, Jenner, Welker, and Malone began laughing loudly. When Nixon observed that "censure" was not in the text of the resolution, Bridges said, "Then it is not a censure resolution." Nixon accordingly amended the title of the resolution to delete the word "censure," changing it to "Resolution relating to the senator from Wisconsin, Mr. McCarthy." Senator Fulbright patiently explained that the last such resolution, adopted in 1929, had also used the word "condemn." He proceeded, moreover, to quote from his dictionary, concluding, "Actually, 'condemn,' as I read it, is a more severe term than 'censure,' if there is any difference at all." Watkins and Stennis agreed. A few minutes later, William Jenner, near hysteria after hours of sparring and speech making, said of the entire investigation of McCarthy, "Let's do it over again. Let's do a retake."[73]

Later, outside the chamber, Joe was asked if he thought he had been censured. "Well, it wasn't exactly a vote of confidence," he replied. "I'm happy to have this circus ended," he continued, "so I can get back to the real work of digging out Communism, crime, and corruption. That job will start officially Monday morning, after ten months of inaction." He claimed to have "no personal feeling against anyone who voted on this matter." Miles McMillin assured readers of the *Madison Capital Times,* "It was obvious that he didn't care whether he was censured or not."[74]

DIES IRAE

Theoretically, McCarthy might have shrugged off the censure and gone about his business. He stood condemned for insulting and defying a Senate committee that had become seriously involved in partisan politics and had propagated charges that were often flagrantly inaccurate. He also stood condemned for attacking a committee that contained senators who had not been entirely objective toward the censure question and who had used harsh and inflammatory language themselves. These were not matters weighty enough to halt the advance of a "man on horseback," as Joe had often been portrayed. Moreover, censure carried no penalty. McCarthy's critics had said repeatedly in the hearings that they were not attacking his role as an anti-Communist investigator. (Indeed, several applauded his efforts.) And Joe was only 46, potentially able to enjoy a lengthy career in the Senate. On the surface of things, he could have resumed his search for Reds and headlines and scoffed at those who had wasted his time and thereby endangered the security of the nation.[1]

Instead, the censure destroyed McCarthy's spirit, accelerated his physical deterioration, and hastened his death. In part this was due to the realization that he was no longer a political figure of national significance. The grief resulting from the loss of many friends and supporters was also important. Joe was hurt deeply when colleagues began to turn their backs on him, leave the Senate floor when he rose to speak, and make excuses to be elsewhere when he joined them at lunch. Then too, the physical and mental exhaustion produced by months of public hearings and constant attack played a role. Roy Cohn later contended that the fight went out of McCarthy "because he had taken more punishment than a normal man could be expected to absorb." Joe's advanced alcoholism, of course, must be taken into account as well.[2]

After the hearings, Barry Goldwater confided to Arthur Watkins that McCarthy's drinking had caused his associates and staff members considerable distress during the debates. Joe had rebuffed efforts to contain his verbal excesses. Friendly colleagues took to hiding and discarding some of his prepared remarks in order to prevent further damage to their case. Everett Dirksen confided to Watkins, "I'd go crazy if I had another like him to defend."[3]

Joe soon began to be absent from numerous Senate proceedings. Friends would find him at home, a glass in his hand, talking bitterly about the past. Despair and self pity—new to McCarthy until recently—deepened with each passing month. He often arose late in the morning, watched television soap operas during the day, and stared for hours into the fire in his living room. He frequently refused telephone calls, even from intimates. "Always the censure was on his mind," Cohn wrote later. Joe took to whispering at Watkins as he passed his Senate seat, "How is the little coward from Utah?" He would later insert a bitter newsletter to constituents into the *Congressional Record* that referred to the Gillette-Hennings Committee as a "kangaroo court" and blasted Watkins for having committed the "greatest example of cowardice that the Senate has witnessed in its long history . . ." Joe assured his readers, "I had and have the utmost contempt for the Gillette Committee and also for the Watkins Committee, as well as the senators who tried to establish the rule that no senator could be criticized for his activities."[4]

Joe formally severed his relations with the Eisenhower administration a few days after the censure vote. On December 4 the President, who had remained aloof from the censure proceedings, invited Senator Watkins to the White House for a 45-minute chat. He then authorized his press secretary, James Hagerty, to tell reporters he had congratulated the Utah senator for a "very splendid job." Joe replied with a prepared statement in which he apologized for having campaigned for Eisenhower in 1952 and accused the President of a "shrinking show of weakness" toward the Communists. Hagerty's almost predictable response was to point to a presidential statement of June 4 giving the number of Reds the Administration had prosecuted. The press secretary assured newsmen that the Attorney General was at work bringing the figures up to date.[5]

Senator Knowland would not support McCarthy's blast at the President. Republican National Committee chairman Leonard Hall said that Joe had made "a great mistake." The Wisconsin Republican State Committee issued a statement commending Eisenhower for "working carefully, diligently, and aggressively" to remove subversives from government. The nation's press was virtually unanimous in denouncing McCarthy's attack. The *Chicago Sun-Times* wondered if the senator had "taken temporary leave of his senses." Denver's *Rocky Mountain News* declared, "He has simply blown his stack."[6]

In a private flight of fancy, Joe asked Don Surine to conduct a poll among G.O.P. leaders to determine his chances against Eisenhower for the presidential nomination in 1956. He did not have personal aspirations, he explained to William F. Buckley, but planned to swing all of his delegate support to William Knowland "and then we'd have a real anti-Communist President in the White House for a change." The poll revealed that about 3 percent of the Republican notables would openly back McCarthy. Joe was mortified by the findings, and his bitterness often came to the surface. He later called Dr. Milton Eisenhower, the President's brother, the "unofficial President" and "one of the most left-wingers you can find in the Republican party." He began one attack on the President's advisers by saying, "If Eisenhower were alive . . ."[7]

In early 1955 it became known that McCarthy was no longer welcome at the White House. Joe was the only committee chairman who failed to receive an invitation to one of two dinners held for Senate leaders. The First Lady's secretary told reporters that the omission was intentional and resulted from "a decision by the President and Mrs. Eisenhower." Joe soon told an audience in Kenosha that he would not blindly follow the Administration even if offered a White House invitation for his wife. Later he said, "The only feeling I have is one of amusement." In fact, Joe felt the President's snubs acutely. William Jenner later recalled, "They hurt. I could see them hurt." Many McCarthy followers were deeply angered by what they saw as the Chief Executive's haughtiness and pettiness. Westbrook Pegler no doubt captured this mood when he wrote, "Now I want to say that I would not accept an invitation to anything from Eisenhower because I consider him my social, moral, and ethical inferior."[8]

For the remainder of his career on Capitol Hill, Joe was often merely an obstructionist. He was one of three Republican senators the President said publicly could not be counted on to assist the Administration's legislative programs. He was the only senator to oppose the confirmation of liberal businessman James D. Zellerbach as ambassador to Italy. His was the only vote against confirmation of William J. Brennan, Jr., to the United States

Supreme Court. He was one of two senators to oppose the promotion of General Zwicker. He and Senator Malone cast the sole votes against the Austrian independence treaty.

In June 1955 McCarthy attacked the President for agreeing to engage in Big Four talks at Geneva. He then sought to embarrass Eisenhower by introducing a resolution to force participants to discuss Russia's satellite states. The Senate Foreign Relations Committee defeated the proposal 14-0. At Lyndon Johnson's insistence, the resolution was brought to the floor. Following a debate in which Joe challenged the patriotism of William Knowland, William Fulbright, and the President, it was crushed 77 to four. Fulbright viewed the stunning margin as "a further confirmation of the vote to condemn Senator McCarthy last December." In July a national magazine ran an article entitled "Whatever Happened to Joe McCarthy?" Henry Jackson answered the question by saying, "McCarthyism is no longer an issue. I don't even think about it."[9]

At approximately the same time, the press started to give Joe the "silent treatment." No doubt feeling guilty about their vital role in McCarthy's career, reporters now began to boycott news conferences and ignore press releases, while editors either refused to publish material on the senator or buried stories on back pages. *New York Times* reporter and columnist William S. White told a colleague he was going to write a lengthy piece on one of McCarthy's speeches and was sure he could get it published. The heavily edited article eventually appeared on page 52.[10]

Joe was deeply hurt by this unspoken policy of the journalists. Willard Edwards of the *Chicago Tribune* thought that more than anything else it led to his death. Joe had thrived on publicity for years; media coverage had been a significant part of his everyday life. Now, it seemed, no one was any longer interested in anything he had to say. *Time* magazine alluded to him as a "virtual stranger on Capitol Hill." One wit, thinking of the "Joe Must Go" slogan, said "Joe has gone." Senator Potter later recalled, "I think he was the loneliest man I ever saw."[11]

Joe's infrequent trips to Wisconsin revealed a serious erosion of his local popularity and political power. A "McCarthy Day" celebration at Boscobel in June 1955 drew 1,500 people, only a fraction of the 50,000 who were anticipated. Only a single reporter was on hand, and he represented the *Madison Capital Times,* which referred to the event as the "Boscobel blooper." Leroy Gore commented gleefully, "As a funeral director's son, I never saw so many pallbearers at one funeral in my life."[12]

In November, Postmaster General Summerfield forced the Senator to withdraw his nomination of a friend as temporary acting postmaster in

Appleton. A vote favoring natural gas producers, a short time later, earned the wrath of Wisconsin's Republican attorney general Vernon Thompson and prompted the *Milwaukee Journal* to dub McCarthy "the third senator from Texas." In early 1956, Roy L. Matson, editor of the once staunchly pro-McCarthy *Wisconsin State Journal,* told a group in Madison, "Time and the public's good sense have taken care of McCarthy. He's a dead pigeon."[13]

Joe played virtually no role in the state or national elections of 1956. In March his friend John Wyngaard reported, "He is rarely mentioned in political conversations today." Joe later sent letters to all G.O.P. candidates in Wisconsin offering assistance. Only a single aspirant accepted. Joe spoke on his behalf at a dinner held in October at a small tavern-restaurant in West Allis. The Republican gubernatorial candidate, scheduled to appear, sent his regrets at the last minute. Joe also endorsed Alexander Wiley's reelection and called for a Republican Congress so that McCarthyism might again flourish in the nation's capital. A reporter described his appearance:

> He spoke very slowly, pausing to laugh often and look at his wife Jean, who sat beside him. While others spoke, McCarthy usually stared at the floor. He seemed to be quite tense. He frequently interrupted speakers with unusually loud, slow handclaps, which the audience would take up.[14]

By the summer of 1956, Joe's alcoholism had become so severe that he began to be hospitalized periodically for detoxification. Jean told reporters in early September that he was in Bethesda Naval Hospital for treatment of a knee injury suffered on Guadalcanal while helping to repair a plane. Joe said later that "steel chips" had been removed. (McCarthy did have a fatty tumor removed from a leg a bit later, forcing him to wear a leg brace for a week, but he was not hospitalized for the treatment.) Privately, Jean pled with friends to help her save Joe's life.[15]

Later that month, Joe and Jean flew to Appleton for a visit. One evening, after a full day of drinking, Joe began to experience delirium tremens in front of his wife and friends, crying out that snakes were leaping at him. Jean, in great anguish, soon confided to Urban Van Susteren that Joe's alcohol consumption had damaged his liver. Van Susteren telephoned the senator's physician in Washington and learned that the liver condition was such that Joe would die in a short time unless he abstained from liquor completely. When Van Susteren confronted Joe about the matter the next morning, Joe flew into a rage. "Kiss my ass," he shouted. After a time, Van

Susteren angrily shoved a bottle of whiskey in front of his old friend and told him to drink it and end things without further disgracing himself and his family.[16]

At a reception in Shawano a few days later, Joe's physical appearance shocked and saddened many longtime friends. He seemed tired and sick, and he failed to recognize numerous people. Fred Sturm of Manawa thought he looked 80 years old. During a visit with Steve Swedish in Milwaukee, Joe broke down completely, telling his old friend of the pain he had suffered from the censure and his plunge from fame. "No matter where I go," he sobbed, "they look on me with contempt. I can't take it anymore."[17]

Jean bravely tried everything she could think of to raise his spirits. She had his Marine medals and anti-Communist awards framed and mounted on black velvet and displayed in a corner of the house where Joe would see them frequently. She read laudatory articles to him and assured him repeatedly that his star would rise again. She badgered him into announcing his intention to run for reelection in 1958—at a time when he talked privately about retiring to Arizona. She would not admit to anyone but a few intimates that Joe was in mortal peril. "Joe's in marvelous shape," Jean told reporters in Milwaukee, "except for his knee injury—lost 32 pounds since the beginning of Lent and feels wonderful." (For the rest of her life—twenty-three years—she would staunchly deny that Joe ever had a drinking problem.)[18]

For months the McCarthys had been trying to adopt a child. This was undoubtedly another effort by Jean to bring sunlight into Joe's ever-darkening world. With the personal assistance of Cardinal Spellman, they were able to bring home a five-week-old girl from the New York Foundling Home in January 1957. A friendly executive loaned them an entire railroad car for the happy journey. The infant was named Tierney Elizabeth, after each of her new grandmothers. Joe doted on the child and at times seemed something of his former self. The exhilaration was temporary, however, and Joe soon found himself again in the grip of the despair that was leading him toward death.[19]

In March, the McCarthys, accompanied by Jean's mother, traveled to Phoenix, Arizona, allegedly on Senate business. A family photograph showed Joe's face grotesquely bloated, his body gaunt.[20]

The senator soon traveled alone to Milwaukee to appear on a television quiz program. He arrived at the airport without an overcoat—to face ten-degree weather. He seemed listless and detached, and at dinner he merely toyed with his food. At one point in the evening he looked wearily at the ceiling and said to his host, businessman Raymond Dittmore, "Raymond, I've lived a million years." Later that night he made it clear to Dittmore that he was ready to die.[21]

The next day Dittmore drove him to Racine, where he was to give a speech on behalf of Lowell McNeill, a friend and avid partisan. McNeill went to the senator's hotel room at 4:00 P.M. to extend his greetings. Joe answered the door wearing nothing but jockey shorts. Throughout the 45-minute conversation that followed, he drank from a bottle of cheap brandy. At dinner he ate nothing. Afterward, he returned to the brandy.[22]

McCarthy returned to Wisconsin in April. Steve Swedish encountered him in Milwaukee in a hallway at the Pfister Hotel. He appeared ill and seemed to stagger slightly. He soon told of being persecuted constantly by Communists over the telephone. "They're murdering me," he cried.[23]

Mark Catlin of Appleton saw Joe at about the same time in Milwaukee. Joe's skin had a yellowish hue, the obvious sign of jaundice and liver damage. "He looked horrible," Catlin said later.[24]

The chief librarian of the *Milwaukee Journal* was shocked to observe McCarthy at a meeting of the Wauwatosa school board. A friend had brought the senator to the meeting unannounced to give a speech. Joe stumbled in a cloak room, became hopelessly entangled in coats, and had to be rescued. He was so drunk and sick he could barely speak. The librarian described the incident to *Journal* editors, who immediately assigned reporter Ed Bayley the task of writing McCarthy's obituary.[25]

Back in Washington, Joe ambled into the office of the Secretary of the Senate where two colleagues were having a drink. He filled a drinking glass to the brim with liquor and downed the contents in several uninterrupted gulps. He told his astonished observers that he had been to Bethesda Naval Hospital several times to "dry out" and that on the last occasion his doctor had said he would die if he had one more drop. He then proceeded to refill the glass and drink it dry.[26]

Joe was admitted to Bethesda Naval Hospital on April 28. Jean told reporters that his knee had been acting up again. The following day she said he had suffered a virus attack about ten days earlier and had a bad cold. In fact, Joe was hospitalized for a severe liver ailment. At 5:02 P.M. on Thursday, May 2, 1957, having received the last rites from a priest, he passed away. Jean was at his side.[27]

Hospital officials listed the cause of death as "acute hepatic failure," and the death certificate read "hepatitis, acute, cause unknown." The doctors acknowledged that McCarthy had suffered from the illness for several weeks and declared that the inflammation of the liver was a "noninfectious type"—meaning that it was not caused by a viral infection. They would not elaborate further. *Time* magazine reported unequivocably that Joe died of cirrhosis of the liver.[28]

McCarthyites soon began blaming infectious hepatitis for his death and took to denying that Joe drank excessively. Roy Cohn said in 1977, "I can categorically state he was not an alcoholic at any time." Some partisans even charged that the senator had been murdered, a tale that remains in currency on the extreme Right to this day. New Hampshire ultraconservative William Loeb wrote in the *Manchester Union Leader*:

> MCCARTHY WAS MURDERED BY THE COMMU-
> NISTS BECAUSE HE WAS EXPOSING THEM. WHEN
> HE BEGAN TO AROUSE THE UNITED STATES TO
> THE EXTENT OF THE COMMUNIST CONSPIRACY IN
> OUR GOVERNMENT, IN OUR SCHOOLS, IN OUR
> NEWSPAPERS, AND IN ALL BRANCHES OF AMERI-
> CAN LIFE, THE COMMUNIST PARTY REALIZED
> THAT IF IT WAS TO SURVIVE AND SUCCEED IN ITS
> CONSPIRACY TO SEIZE CONTROL OF THE UNITED
> STATES IT HAD TO DESTROY MCCARTHY BEFORE
> HE DESTROYED THE PARTY.[29]

Press reaction to the news of McCarthy's death was largely predictable. The most prestigious newspapers discussed the passing of a ruthless demagogue who had threatened American civil liberties, savaged government employees, and damaged the nation's image abroad. The *Chicago Tribune* said, "The senator was no Communist; hence he was no hero to the 'liberals.'" Newspapers in Western Europe were overwhelmingly critical of McCarthy. All major French papers referred to him as "the witch-hunter." In Austria, papers announced the death with such headlines as "Snooper Senator McCarthy Dies." "Inquisition" was used by London's conservative *Daily Telegraph*. "Senator McCarthy died yesterday in Washington," the British Labor Party's *News Chronicle* observed. "America was the cleaner by his fall and is cleaner by his death."[30]

All flags on government buildings, including the White House, were lowered to half-mast. Senators of all persuasions did their best to mourn a departed colleague. Karl Mundt said, "His passing takes out of the American political area a courageous fighter against Communism and a stalwart advocate of our traditional American concepts." John McClellan declared, "I found him to be a man of strong convictions and on occasions when I may have disagreed with him I am happy to say there were never any personalities involved. He will be missed from the Senate and the American scene."

Stuart Symington could only bring himself to say, "I am deeply distressed." (Symington would never again discuss McCarthy.)[31]

The President and Mrs. Eisenhower extended "profound sympathy" to Jean. Harry Truman said, "Too bad. I'm very sorry to hear the news of the senator's death." Dean Acheson told reporters he had "no comment at all." He quoted a Latin phrase which he translated as: "Say nothing about the dead unless it is good."[32]

The Republican dominated Wisconsin state senate, with four Democrats dissenting, adopted a resolution expressing sorrow at McCarthy's death and declaring: "History will record him as one of the most aggressive and courageous fighters against Communism . . . and a man who strove to awaken the public to dangers and the immediacy of the threat of Communists in our government." Miles McMillin commented a few days later, "The incident indicates the difficulties that arise when a public figure, particularly a highly controversial one, dies. There seems to be a strong belief among many that respect for death means that the past is changed, or at least forgotten."[33]

Thousands of people paid their respect to McCarthy at the Washington funeral home. A large silver crucifix stood behind the open casket, and candles gleamed at both ends of the bier. Joe was dressed in a dark blue suit; a rosary rested in his left hand. The Senate had sent a huge design of white carnations and lilies, one of scores of floral tributes that continued to arrive every hour.[34]

A formal service was held at St. Matthew's Cathedral on the morning of May 6. The Vice-President and Mrs. Nixon, Roy Cohn, William Knowland, and White House assistant I. Jack Martin, representing the President, were part of a crowd of 2,000. Among those participating in the requiem mass were 72 priests, monsignors, and bishops.[35]

At Jean's request, a funeral service followed in the Senate chamber—the first such ceremony since 1940. Jean sat quietly weeping in a chair just outside the open doors as one senator after another rose to extol her late husband. Barry Goldwater inserted prepared remarks into the *Congressional Record* that reflected much of the oratory: "Do not mourn Joe McCarthy. Be thankful that he lived, at the right time, and according to the talents vested in him by his Maker. Be grateful, too, that when it came his time to die, he passed on with the full assurance that, because he lived, America is a brighter, safer more vigilant land today."[36]

Following the Senate ceremony, the body was flown to Wisconsin, accompanied by Jean and the senator's entire office staff. The next day, some 30,000 Wisconsinites filed through St. Mary's Church in Appleton to view the open casket containing the pallid remains of the one-time local farm boy. Joe was laid to rest beside his parents, in St. Mary's cemetery, at a beautiful spot overlooking the Fox River. There, to this day, a small band of McCarthyites meets annually on May 2 to praise the senator's career. At other times during the years, the marble gravestone and the urns that border it have been defaced and vandalized by those holding a different interpretation of his history.[37]

Joe McCarthy was mourned by a great many. Jean received tens of thousands of messages of sympathy and condolence, many containing mass cards. "I can remember opening three letters in fifteen minutes one day which announced 15,000 masses," Mary Driscoll said later. Thousands of people responded to a radio appeal by Fulton Lewis, Jr., for funds to assist Tierney. (Through the efforts of Cardinal Spellman, Jean was able to keep her adopted daughter, despite a New York Foundling Home rule to the contrary.) Two decades later people glowed as they shared their memories of Joe's kindness, generosity, humor, intelligence, and industriousness. They often complained, however, that the qualities they most admired in McCarthy rarely, if ever, appeared in accounts of his life.[38]

Few journalists, and even fewer historians, have ever expressed sympathy for McCarthy since his death. Not a single college textbook from a major publisher is even neutral toward him. Books on his life and times bear such titles as *The Politics of Fear, The Great Fear, The Nightmare Decade, Days of Shame, Fear, the Accuser,* and *Decade of Fear.* Perhaps no other figure in American history has been portrayed so consistently as the essence of evil. He is our King John. Some writers have assigned him at least partial responsibility for America's inflexible China policy, the Vietnam War, Goldwater's capture of the G.O.P. in 1964, even Watergate. With Ronald Reagan's election in 1980, allusions to McCarthy and his "ism" were plentiful.

Of course, there is a great deal to be said against McCarthy. He was guilty of frequent lying and slander. Untold hundreds of Americans suffered directly from his zeal to find and punish subversives. (The cliché is true: he did not discover a single Communist.) He disrupted two Administrations and impeded serious congressional activity. He lent his support to a rigid foreign policy that would haunt the nation for generations. He backed efforts to curtail academic freedom and censure unpopular ideas. Evidence strongly suggests that he lowered morale throughout the federal government and damaged America's international prestige. These are extremely serious matters, wholly worthy of the historian's attention.

Still, Joe had many personal qualities that biographers and others have chosen to ignore. He was not the amoral, cynical, thieving, homosexual monster his critics described. Richard Rovere quoted an unidentified woman as saying, "He was a stinker. He was never 'sincere'—Christ, what a laugh. He never thought of *believing* in what he was doing." A serious biographer, as concerned with evidence as with polemics, could not have taken such a claim seriously.[39]

Nor was Joe the grave threat to the Constitution and to the nation he has seemed by some to be. He had no ideology or program of any significance. His ambition was limited. He did not terrify the American people or hold them in his spell, as some of his enemies claimed. (One public opinion poll sponsored by the Fund for the Republic concluded that in the summer of 1954, "The number of people who said that they were worried either about the threat of Communists in the United States or about civil liberties was, even by the most generous interpretation of occasionally ambiguous responses, *less than 1 percent!*") McCarthy could have been stopped cold at any time by, say, J. Edgar Hoover, Richard Nixon, or Dwight Eisenhower—men with authority, who knew when he was bluffing and lying. Ultimately, of course, he, more than anyone else, was responsible for his own destruction. Would-be dictators are made of far sterner stuff.[40]

Moreover, there was more to McCarthyism than McCarthy. Joe encountered the second Red Scare somewhat late. It burned intensely for some three years after his censure. Others surely share as much, if not more, blame for the ugliness that plagued the years 1948 to 1957—such as those who constantly encouraged McCarthy and filled his head with the fantasies of right-wing extremism.[41]

From any standpoint, it seems clear that McCarthy's life was profoundly tragic. His native intelligence and his formidable energy were largely squandered. He brought far more pain into the world than any man should. He was above all a reckless adventurer, an improviser, a bluffer. He once told a close friend, "Just remember, Gerry, he who does not live dangerously does not live at all."[42]

CHAPTER NOTES

PROLOGUE AND CHAPTER 1

1. *Milwaukee Journal*, November 14, 1954; *Chicago Tribune*, November 15, 1954; *Oshkosh Daily Northwestern*, November 15, 1954; Swedish interview. The song, never again performed, was written by Mrs. J. B. Matthews.
2. Swedish interview. For a similar incident during the month, see Roy Cohn, *McCarthy* (New York, 1968), p. 262. See also Korb interview, November 8, 1975.
3. See Weston A. Goodspeed, Melvin E. Bothwell, and Kenneth C. Goodspeed, *History of Outagamie County, Wisconsin* (Chicago, 1911), pp. 79, 82, 87, 96, 137-38, 142, 146, 707-8, 1090, 1222-23; Heenan (August 10, 1976), McCarthy interviews.
4. Heenan interviews, January 16, August 10, 1976; James Heenan Papers; Van Susteren (July 14, 1977), McCarthy, Feuerstein interviews.
5. Heenan (January 16, 1976), Van Susteren (November 25, 1975, February 21, 1976), interviews. For a photograph of Tim and Bid in front of their cabin in 1901, see the files of the *Appleton Post-Crescent*.

6. Heenan interview, January 16, 1976; *New York Times*, May 3, 1957. Vital statistics on the McCarthy children are as follows:
    1. Mary Ellen (Mrs. Fred A. Hoffman), b. April 3, 1902, d. January 11, 1951
    2. Margaret Olive (Mrs. Roman J. Kornely), b. March 16, 1904
    3. Stephen Timothy, b. April 9, 1905

4. William Patrick, b. March 16, 1907
5. Joseph Raymond, b. November 14, 1908, d. May 2, 1957
6. Howard Francis, b. April 30, 1910, d. June 4, 1960
7. Anna Mae (Mrs. Howard J. Long), b. November 26, 1912

7. *Births, Outagamie County,* XIII, 1081; *History of Outagamie County, Wisconsin,* pp. 1222-23; St. Mary's Church records; Mrs. Olive Kornely to the author, June 8, 1977; McCarthy interview.

8. See Werner, Mullarkey, Keller, Tegge, Kiermas, Kornely, Mrs. Olen Anderson, Korb (September 6, 1975) interviews; *Janesville Gazette,* February 12, 1951; *Milwaukee Sentinel,* May 7, 1957. Years later, Joe wrote of his "very religious mother" who had given him "a deep and abiding respect for the priesthood." Copy, Joe McCarthy to Robert Hartnett, January 6, 1953, Patrick McCarran Papers.

9. McCarthy, Van Susteren (November 25, 1975, February 21, 1976) interviews; "The Senate," *Time,* 69 (May 13, 1957), 28; Robert Fleming memorandum of April 24, 1951, box 3, Robert Fleming Papers.

10. *Green Bay Press-Gazette,* May 6, 1957.

11. Heenan interview, January 16, 1976; Heenan Papers; *Milwaukee Journal,* May 3, 1957.

12. Jack Anderson and Ronald W. May, *McCarthy: The Man, the Senator, the "Ism,"* (Boston, 1952), pp. 8-11.

13. Harold C. Livesay, *Andrew Carnegie and the Rise of Big Business* (New York, 1975), p. 27. See Thomas C. Reeves, "The Search for Joe McCarthy," *The Wisconsin Magazine of History,* 60 (Spring, 1977) 185-96.

14. Van Susteren (January 15, 1976), Heenan (January 16, 1976), McCarthy interviews.

15. Van Susteren interview, February 21, 1976.

16. McCarthy, Castonia, Walter Jolin, Yungwirth, and Heenan (August 10, 1976) interviews; Jack Alexander, "The Senate's Remarkable Upstart," *Saturday Evening Post,* 220 (August 9, 1947), 16; *Appleton Post-Crescent,* April 11, 1954.

17. See ibid.; McCarthy, Van Susteren (July 14, 1977) interviews.

18. McCarthy interview.

19. *Wisconsin State Journal,* July 16, 1946; Bob Schwartz memorandum, October 4, 1951, box 3, Fleming Papers; Sumnicht and Crabb interviews; Alexander, "The Senate's Remarkable Upstart," p. 16; Mrs. Wilma Witt to the author, February 20, 1976; *Oshkosh Daily Northwestern,* November 30, 1953; *Boston Sunday Globe,* August 18, 1946.

20. McCarthy interview.

21. Bob Schwartz memorandum, October 4, 1951, box 3, Fleming Papers; Alexander, "The Senate's Remarkable Upstart," pp. 16-17; *Wisconsin State Jour-*

nal, July 16, 1946; Mrs. G. Alton Een to the author, September 13, 1976; Testin interview; Testin scrapbooks.

22. Testin and Brown interviews.
23. After the operation, undergone at about eleven, Joe was left permanently with an annoying but not painful "pins and needles" sensation (paresthesia) on the left side of his face. Delaney interview; Dr. Adrian J. Delaney to the author, August 25, 1977.
24. Testin interview; Bob Schwartz memorandum, October 4, 1951, box 3, Fleming Papers; Korb interview, November 8, 1975. The *Time* editors chose not to print Tim's fatherly plea, electing instead to allege falsely that Joe ate meat on Fridays. "Congress," *Time,* LVIII (October 22, 1951), 21-24.
25. Testin interview.
26. Ibid.; *Wisconsin State Journal,* July 16, 1946. Cf. *Manawa Advocate,* May 9, 1957.
27. *Wisconsin State Journal,* July 16, 1946.
28. Ibid.
29. Bob Schwartz memorandum, October 4, 1951, box 3, Fleming Papers.
30. Testin scrapbooks and interview; Alexander, "The Senate's Remarkable Upstart," p. 17.
31. *Milwaukee Journal,* March 16, 1930.
32. See Hershberger, Brown, Testin, Mullarkey, McCarthy interviews; *Wisconsin State Journal,* July 16, 1946; *Oshkosh Daily Northwestern,* November 30, 1953.
33. Ibid.; Hershberger interview; New London and Hortonville *Press-Star,* February 9, 1977; copy, Hershberger to McCarthy, September 17, 1930, Heenan Papers.
34. Hershberger interview and papers.

CHAPTER 2

1. Testin, Lubeley interviews; Anderson and May notes, National Committee for an Effective Congress Papers (hereafter cited as NCEC). See a pro-McCarthy letter to the editor from Kuhn in *Milwaukee Journal,* August 13, 1951.
2. Mullarkey interview.
3. See College of Engineering catalogue, 1931-32, pp. 8, 54, Marquette University Archives; Lamers, Sturm, Hart interviews.
4. *Milwaukee Journal,* July 25, 1946.
5. Hanratty, Korb, Lamers, Wiechers, Lubeley, Hellman interviews; Helen Cromwell, *Dirty Helen: An Autobiography* (Los Angeles, 1966), pp. 242-45;

Anderson and May notes, NCEC; *Wisconsin State Journal,* July 16, 1946. The Cromwell autobiography should be read skeptically.

6. *Marquette Tribune,* October 16, 1930.
7. Hanratty interview. See the Olszyk interview.
8. Korb interview, September 6, 1975.
9. See *Marquette Tribune,* March 26, May 7, September 24, 1931; March 10, 17, April 28, May 5, 1932. A photograph of Joe in the ring is in *The Hilltop, 1931,* XVII, 257, Marquette University Archives, reproduced in *Milwaukee Journal,* May 3, 1957. See also *The Hilltop, 1933,* XIX, 143.
10. *Milwaukee Journal,* August 14, 1946; Saddy interview. Steve McCarthy thinks that Joe had two professional fights. McCarthy interview.
11. See *Marquette Tribune,* October 20, 1932; March 16, May 25, 1933; *Wisconsin News,* February 7, 1933.
12. Alexander, "The Senate's Remarkable Upstart," p. 17; Hanratty, Korb (September 6, 1975) interviews.
13. Marquette law school yearbooks, 1934, 1935, Marquette University Archives.
14. Schoenecker, Dammann, Hanratty, Flynn, Mullarkey, Korb (September 6, 1975) interviews; John C. Quinn to the author, July 18, 1975; Charles Curran to the author, June 26, 1975. For photographs of the fraternity members, see *The Hilltop, 1934,* XX, 245; XXI, 255, Marquette University Archives.
15. Dammann, Stoltz, Lamers, Bergen interviews. See *The Hilltop, 1933,* XIX, 207; XX, 195, Marquette University Archives.
16. Flynn interview.
17. Charles Curran to the author, June 26, September 15, 1975; Anderson and May, *McCarthy,* p. 27. Curran was active in both of McCarthy's successful Senate races.
18. Ibid.; Lamers interview, Charles Curran to the author, June 26, 1975. Joe's principal duty as president was to serve as chairman of a law banquet, given annually by the freshman class in honor of the graduating seniors. *Marquette Tribune,* April 27, May 11, 1933.
19. Charles Curran to the author, June 26, 1975; Flynn, Stoltz, Hanratty, Mullarkey, Korb (September 6, 1975) interviews.
20. *Madison Capital Times,* April 9, 1939; Hanratty interview.

CHAPTER 3

1. Hart (September 19, 1975), Parnell interviews.
2. Rummel interview by Glenn Silber; Alexander, "The Senate's Remarkable Upstart," p. 17; *Waupaca County Post,* January 9, 12, 1936.

3. Hart interview, October 6, 1975.

4. Hart (September 19, October 6, 1975), Parnell, Van Susteren (November 25, 1975), Kiermas, Mullarkey, Korb (November 8, 1975) interviews.

5. See Werner, Mrs. Agnes Buckley, Kiermas, Voy, Ed Nellor, Van Susteren (November 25, 1975, July 14, 1977) interviews.

6. Mullarkey, Mrs. Olen Anderson, Werner interviews.

7. See Jean Matheson to Ronald May, August 27, 1951, NCEC Papers; *Madison Capital Times,* May 2, 1952.

8. Hart interview.

9. *Wisconsin State Journal,* July 16, 1946; Voy, Parnell interviews; Mrs. Allen Voy to the author, October 23, 1976.

10. See *Waupaca County Post,* February 13, 20, 1936. See how this later became distorted by anti-McCarthyites: *Madison Capital Times,* March 13, 1954.

11. Meyer, Cattau interviews.

12. Alexander, "The Senate's Remarkable Upstart," p. 52; Mrs. Allen Voy to the author, October 23, 1976.

13. *Shawano County Journal,* February 13, 1936; Walter Jolin, Parnell, Cattau, Van Susteren (November 25, 1975) interviews.

14. *Madison Capital Times,* July 25, 1947.

15. Walter Jolin interview.

16. William T. Flarity Recollections, p. 8.

17. Meyer interview. The editorials were anonymous and cannot be distinguished from others run by the newspaper.

18. See *Shawano County Journal,* July 23, August 6, 13, October 15, 1936; *Shawano Evening Leader,* August 4, 1936; *Wisconsin State Journal,* July 17, 1946; *Madison Capital Times,* May 24, 31, 1954; Voy interview.

19. Ibid.

20. See Michael O'Brien, "Young Joe McCarthy, 1908-1944," *The Wisconsin Magazine of History,* 63 (Spring, 1980), 199-201.

21. Mrs. Allen Voy to the author, November 3, 1976.

22. *Shawano County Journal,* April 8, June 17, July 1, 1937.

23. Meyer interview.

24. Voy interview.

25. Werner interview.

26. Hart, Mullarkey, Swedish, Walter Jolin, Meyer, Van Susteren (November 25, 1975), Mrs. Olen Anderson interviews; Mary Louise Kenote to the author, September 25, 1975; Mrs. Wilma Witt to the author, February 20, 1976. For a photograph of Mary Louise Juneau and McCarthy, see *Milwaukee Journal,* October 8, 1939.

27. William T. Flarity Recollections, p. 5.

28. Voy interview.
29. William T. Flarity Recollections, p. 5; Mrs. Olen Anderson interview.
30. William T. Flarity Recollections, pp. 9-10; Alexander, "The Senate's Remarkable Upstart," pp. 15, 52; Hanratty interview.
31. Shawano *Evening Leader,* April 12, 1938.
32. See Robert Fleming's 1951 interview with Werner, box 3, Fleming Papers; Voy, Mrs. Olen Anderson interviews. See Werner's public comments in *Green Bay Press-Gazette,* October 2, 1946.
33. William T. Flarity Recollections, pp. 13-14; Mrs. Olen Anderson interview.
34. Voy, Mrs. Olen Anderson interviews.
35. Mrs. Olen Anderson interview. Mrs. Anderson, the former Dottie Druckrey, became deeply attached to Joe, and a few years later he attempted unsuccessfully to rekindle the relationship. She retains numerous mementos from her months with McCarthy, including ten paychecks, stenographic notes, and campaign postcards.
36. Van Susteren interview, January 15, 1976.
37. Mrs. Olen Anderson, Lorge interviews; Alexander, "The Senate's Remarkable Upstart," p. 52.
38. *Shawano County Journal,* December 28, 1938.
39. Keller interview; *Appleton Post-Crescent,* February 22, 1939. Cf. Werner's entry in the 1938 edition of Martindale-Hubbell (p. 1093) and in the April 1939 supplement (p. 15).
40. Cattau, Parnell interviews.
41. Appleton *Post-Crescent,* April 1, 1939.
42. Van Susteren interview, November 25, 1975.
43. Keller interview.
44. Van Straten interview.
45. Mullarkey, Mrs. Olen Anderson, Werner, Keller interviews. See McCarthy to Werner, September 21, 1938, and samples of the campaign postcards in Mr. Werner's possession.
46. *Appleton Post-Crescent,* April 4, 1939.
47. *Madison Capital Times,* April 9, 1939; *Wisconsin State Journal,* July 17, 1946.
48. William T. Flarity Recollections, pp. 13-15; Mrs. Olen Anderson, Werner, Walter Jolin, Korb (September 6, 1975) interviews; *Madison Capital Times,* May 2, 1952.
49. William T. Flarity Recollections, p. 12.
50. Anderson and May, *McCarthy,* p. 43; Fleming interview, September 17, 1951, box 3, Fleming Papers; Larry Jolin interview.

CHAPTER 4

1. Mrs. Olen Anderson interview.
2. *Appleton Post-Crescent,* July 3, 1939.
3. Van Susteren interview, November 25, 1975.
4. *Milwaukee Journal,* January 4, 1940; *Appleton Post-Crescent,* January 5, 1940.
5. Van Susteren, Keller, Stoltz interviews.
6. Werner, Keller, Mullarkey, Catlin interviews.
7. Anderson and May, *McCarthy,* p. 44; Alexander, "The Senate's Remarkable Upstart," pp. 52-53; Werner, Parnell, Mullarkey, Van Susteren (February 21, 1976) interviews.
8. Parnell, Van Susteren (November 25, 1975; February 5, 1977) interviews; *Wisconsin State Journal,* July 17, 1946. See editorial *Milwaukee Journal,* October 28, 1940; *Antigo Daily Journal,* February 1, 1940.
9. Anderson and May, *McCarthy,* p. 46.
10. Van Susteren interview, July 14, 1977.
11. Alexander, "The Senate's Remarkable Upstart," p. 52.
12. Anderson and May, *McCarthy,* pp. 45-46; Van Susteren interview, January 15, 1976.
13. Mullarkey interview.
14. Keller, Pusey, Van Susteren (November 25, 1975) interviews. See Dean Acheson, *Present at the Creation, My Years in the State Department* (New York, 1969), p. 370.
15. Van Susteren (November 25, 1975; February 21, 1976; August 9, 1976), Parnell interviews.
16. Van Susteren interview, November 25, 1975.
17. Ibid.
18. Van Susteren interviews, January 15, 1976, February 5, 1977; Michael O'Brien, "Senator Joseph McCarthy and Wisconsin: 1946-1957," unpublished doctoral dissertation, University of Wisconsin, 1971, p. 11.
19. See Brown, Mullarkey interviews.
20. Mrs. Wilma Witt to the author, February 20, 1976.
21. Johnson interview.
22. Flynn interview.
23. Anderson and May, *McCarthy,* p. 45.
24. Parnell interview.
25. Mrs. Wilma Witt to the author, February 20, 1976; Mrs. Agnes Buckley, Van Susteren (February 20, 1976) interviews.
26. Flynn interview.

27. Knowles interview.

28. Primary documents in the case are found in series 9/2/1, box 5, General Legal Files, Papers of the Wisconsin Department of Agriculture, Wisconsin State Archives, State Historical Society of Wisconsin. See esp. Edgar W. Zobal to Verlyn F. Sears, July 11, 1941, and copy, Gilbert Lappley to William Kirsch, October 15, 1941. Cf. Anderson and May, *McCarthy,* p. 50, which charges a "cover-up." See also 238 Wis. 258; *Appleton Post-Crescent,* July 9, 1941; Van Susteren (February 21, 1976), Parnell, Catlin, Kersten interviews. Cf. O'Brien, "Young Joe McCarthy, 1908-1944," pp. 212-17.

29. *Milwaukee Journal,* July 12, 1949.

30. Bob Schwartz memorandum, October 4, 1951, box 3, Fleming Papers.

31. Van Susteren interview, November 25, 1975.

32. *Appleton Post-Crescent,* June 4, (editorial), 6, 1942; *Green Bay Post-Gazette,* June 6, 1942.

33. *Milwaukee Journal,* November 14, 1951, June 8, 1952. Joe would first admit he had not entered the Marine Corps as a private while under investigation in 1954 for censure by the Senate. See U.S. Senate, Select Committee to Study Censure Charges, *Hearings On S. Res. 301,* 83d Cong., 2d sess. (hereafter referred to as *Watkins Committee Hearings*), p. 329.

34. Van Susteren interview, November 25, 1975.

35. Hanratty interview.

36. *Milwaukee Journal,* August 12, 1942.

CHAPTER 5

1. *Wisconsin State Journal,* July 18, 1946.

2. Day interview. See Patrick J. Maney, *"Young Bob" La Follette: A Biography of Robert M. La Follette, Jr., 1895-1953* (Columbia, Mo., 1978), p. 289.

3. Smedley interview.

4. *Milwaukee Journal,* June 8, 1952.

5. Ibid.; George B. Barnes to the author, July 13, 28, 1977.

6. Ibid.

7. Ibid.; Smedley, Todd, Wander, Munn interviews.

8. *Milwaukee Journal,* July 9, 1943; *Appleton Post-Crescent,* November 15, 1943.

9. *Milwaukee Sentinel,* July 21, 1944.

10. Glenn Todd to the author, October 15, 1977; G. M. Neufeld (of the Reference Section, Headquarters United States Marine Corps) to the author, October 6, 1977; copy, A. H. Manhard, Jr. (for the Commandant of the Marine Corps) to

Congressman Les Aspin, February 13, April 5, 1978. Robert Fleming of the *Milwaukee Journal* mistakenly attributed the letter of recommendation to Maj. Everett E. Munn, and this has become part of the standard account. *Milwaukee Journal,* June 8, 1952. This error was soon discovered by the Marine Corps. See John B. Farriter to Everett B. Munn, February 13, 1953, in Munn's possession.

11. Fleming, Van Susteren (February 21, 1976) interviews; Bob Schwartz memorandum, October 4, 1951, box 3, Fleming Papers; deposition, March 29, 1952, "Joseph R. McCarthy vs. The Post-Standard Company . . .," p. 8, in the possession of Syracuse attorney Tracy Ferguson.

12. Alexander, "The Senate's Remarkable Upstart," p. 16; Munn interview; press release, November 1, 1943, Headquarters United States Marine Corps.

13. *Milwaukee Journal,* June 8, 1952.

14. Deposition, March 29, 1952, "Joseph R. McCarthy vs. The Post-Standard Company . . . ," p. 8.

15. See "A Brief History of Marine Fighter/Attack Squadron 235 . . . ," Headquarters United States Marine Corps, 1969, p. 1; Robert Sherrod, *History of Marine Corps Aviation in World War II* (Washington, D.C., 1952), p. 465.

16. Press release, September 17, 1943, Headquarters United States Marine Corps.

17. *Eau Claire Leader,* January 31, 1947; Munn interview; Glenn Silber interview with Penn Kimball, a copy of which is in the author's possession.

18. Wander interview.

19. Ibid.

20. *Wisconsin State Journal,* July 18, 1946; Todd interview; Glenn Todd to the author, April 4, 1977.

21. Smedley, Montfort (May 24, 1977), Wander interviews; Alexander, "The Senate's Remarkable Upstart," p. 52; *Milwaukee Journal,* June 8, 1952; *Wisconsin State Journal,* July 18, 1946.

22. *Milwaukee Journal,* April 25, 1944; *Wisconsin State Journal,* July 18, 1946; *Madison Capital Times,* December 30, 1952; *Milwaukee Journal,* December 31, 1952.

23. Ibid.; G. M. Neufeld to the author, September 19, 1977; Todd, Munn interviews; Glenn Todd to the author, April 4, 19, 1977, April 27, 1978.

24. Wander interview.

25. Todd, Wander, Munn, Montfort (May 24, 1977), Smedley interviews; copy, A. H. Manhard to Les Aspin, February 13, 1978. In 1951 Joe wrote to Montfort, "As you recall, I did make a few trips in the back seat and shot hell out of the coconut trees." Joe McCarthy to W. H. Montfort, July 18, 1951, in Dr. Montfort's possession.

26. *Milwaukee Journal,* December 31, 1952. Cf. Constantine Brown in *Washington Evening Star,* December 31, 1952.

27. Van Susteren interview, February 5, 1977; *Madison Capital Times,* September 29, 1946.
28. Van Susteren interview, February 5, 1977; U.S. Senate, Subcommittee on Privileges and Elections, *Investigations of Senators Joseph R. McCarthy and William Benton, Report,* 82d Cong., 1st sess., 1952, hereafter cited as the *Hennings Committee Report; Madison Capital Times,* July 21, 25, 28, 1947.
29. *Milwaukee Journal,* June 8, 1952.
30. *Appleton Post-Crescent,* November 15, 1943. See also *Milwaukee Sentinel,* January 25, March 3, 1944; *Shawano Leader,* April 6, 1944; *Green Bay Press Gazette,* April 12, 1944.
31. *Milwaukee Journal,* June 8, 1952; Anderson and May, *McCarthy,* p. 60.
32. Ibid., p. 61; Montfort (May 24, 1977), Thompson interviews.
33. Walter Melchior to Alexander Wiley, March 13, 1944, Alexander Wiley Papers; *Milwaukee Journal,* April 25, 1944.
34. Ibid., July 13, 1944.
35. Korb (September 6, 1975), Pusey interviews.
36. *Hennings Committee Report,* pp. 27, 43; Korb interview, September 6, 1975.
37. *Madison Capital Times,* February 15, 1947; *Milwaukee Journal,* July 6, 1950; *Hennings Committee Report,* pp. 28-29.
38. *Milwaukee Journal,* April 25, 1944; Herman F. Heckert to Alexander Wiley, May 23, 1944, Wiley Papers; Kersten interview.
39. Anderson and May, *McCarthy,* p. 69; copy, Alexander Wiley to Ronald K. Wilde, May 31, 1944, Harold A. Meyer to Alexander Wiley, August 27, 1944, Wiley Papers; Hagene interview; *Milwaukee Journal,* August 13, 1944.
40. Van Susteren (February 5, 1977), Korb (June 3, 1976) interviews.
41. *Appleton Post-Crescent,* April 1, 1939, January 29, 1944; Fred Felix Wettengel to Alexander Wiley, June 7, 1944, copy, Fred Felix Wettengel to Fred R. Zimmerman, June 7, 10, 1944, Wiley Papers; Eli Waldron, "Joe McCarthy's Home Town," *The Reporter,* VI (May 13, 1952), 19-24. See Keller, Dohr, Brooker, Crabb interviews.
42. *Milwaukee Journal,* June 8, 1944.
43. Ibid., September 29, 1946.
44. Copy, Alexander Wiley to B. Snella, April 24, 1944, copy, Alexander Wiley to M. F. Cudahy, September 9, 1944, copy, Alexander Wiley to S. C. Van Gordon, March 24, 1944, Oscar Schmiege to Alexander Wiley, August 9, 1944, Arthur A. Tiller to Alexander Wiley, September 6, 1944, Walter Melchior to Alexander Wiley, March 13, 1944, Wiley Papers.
45. "Gen. George Catlett Marshall" folder, box 3, Fleming Papers; Glenn Todd to the author, September 16, 1977; *Chicago Tribune,* July 21, 1944.
46. *Milwaukee Sentinel,* July 21, 1944.

47. *Milwaukee Journal,* August 4, 14, 1944.

48. Anderson and May, *McCarthy,* p. 70; Harold A. Meyer to Alexander Wiley, August 27, 1944, Wiley Papers. For a photograph of Colby and McCarthy, see *Appleton Post-Crescent,* July 22, 1944.

49. See Anderson and May, *McCarthy,* pp. 68-69. See McCarthy's "Guest Editorial" in the *Wisconsin State Journal,* August 13, 1944.

50. Seymour Gmeiner to Alexander Wiley, August 18, 1944, Walter K. Miller to Alexander Wiley, May 8, 1944, copy, Fred Felix Wettengel to Fred R. Zimmerman, June 10, 1944, Wiley Papers.

51. *The Wisconsin Blue Book, 1946* (Madison, 1946), p. 595.

52. Copy, Alexander Wiley to Leathem D. Smith, August 18, 1944, Wiley Papers; Philipp interview.

53. Harold A. Meyer to Alexander Wiley, August 27, 1944, Wiley Papers.

54. Elmer R. Honkamp to Alexander Wiley, September 15, 1944, ibid.

55. Michael F. Cudahy to Alexander Wiley, August 25, September 7, 1944, Alexander Wiley to Joe McCarthy, September 18, October 5, 1944, Joe McCarthy to Alexander Wiley, September 11, 28, 1944, Wiley Papers.

56. *Milwaukee Journal,* November 14, 1951. He was relieved of active duty on February 20, 1945, and his resignation "under honorable conditions" was accepted on March 29.

57. Ibid.; *Milwaukee Sentinel,* January 29, 1945; *Appleton Post-Crescent,* January 31, 1945.

58. Joe McCarthy to William M. Lamers, May 12, 1945, Marquette University Archives; Van Susteren televised interview, 1975, Glenn Silber, Madison, Wisconsin.

59. Glenn Todd to the author, April 4, 1977; *Wisconsin State Journal,* July 18, 1946.

CHAPTER 6

1. John Wyngaard in the *La Crosse Tribune,* July 21, 1951. See the biographical sketch in the Thomas Emmet Coleman Papers, the obituary in the *Milwaukee Journal,* February 5, 1964, and the Eddy (May 24, 1976), Philipp, Tegge, Van Susteren (August 9, 1976), Knowles, Catlin, Bayley (July 8, 1977), and Larry Jolin interviews.

2. Eddy interview, May 24, 1976.

3. Ibid. See John Wyngaard in the *St. Paul Pioneer Press,* December 9, 1945. On Coleman and La Follette, see *Milwaukee Journal,* August 18, 1946.

4. Hennings Committee Report.

5. Tegge interview.
6. Miles McMillin in *Madison Capital Times,* September 29, 1946.
7. Ibid.
8. *Appleton Post-Crescent,* May 8, 1945.
9. See Eddy (May 24, 1976), Tegge, McNeil interviews.
10. Eddy interview, July 12, 1977.
11. *Milwaukee Journal,* December 2, 1945. See John Wyngaard in *Superior Evening Telegram,* October 20, 1945.
12. See copy, William T. Evjue to William Dufty, October 6, 1947, box 6, William T. Evjue Papers; Herbert Jacobs Recollections.
13. *Madison Capital Times,* December 9, 26, 1945.
14. Ibid., December 14, 1945, January 5, 1946.
15. Bayley interview, July 8, 1977; Wyngaard interview; Laird interview. In 1952 Coleman told the National Press Club in Washington, "Joe McCarthy is not embarrassing to me. I've known him as long as anybody. I don't know whether his table manners or his looks are just right, but the people of Wisconsin are not embarrassed by him." *Milwaukee Journal,* October 30, 1952.
16. Eddy (May 24, 1976), Tegge interviews; Anderson and May, *McCarthy,* pp. 78-79. See the Wyngaard column in *Appleton Post-Crescent,* May 13, 1946.
17. *Madison Capital Times,* December 9, 1945.
18. *Milwaukee Journal,* February 19, 1946.
19. *Madison Capital Times,* November 16, 1945.
20. See Roger T. Johnson, *Robert M. La Follette, Jr. and the Decline of the Progressive Party in Wisconsin* (Madison, 1964), pp. 102-22.
21. *Wisconsin State Journal,* March 18, 1946.
22. Ibid.
23. *Madison Capital Times,* April 27, 1946; *Eau Claire Leader,* April 28, 1946.
24. Eddy interview, May 24, 1976; *Milwaukee Journal,* April 29, 1946.
25. Van Susteren interview, January 15, 1976.
26. Alexander, "The Senate's Remarkable Upstart," pp. 53, 57.
27. Eddy interview, May 24, 1976; O'Brien, "Senator Joseph McCarthy and Wisconsin," p. 19; Van Susteren interview, January 15, 1976.
28. Alexander, "The Senate's Remarkable Upstart," p. 57; O'Brien, "Senator Joseph McCarthy and Wisconsin," pp. 19-20; Van Susteren interview, January 15, 1976.
29. Eddy interview, May 24, 1976; John Wyngaard in *Appleton Post-Crescent,* May 13, 1946.
30. Ibid., May 6, 1946; Anderson and May, *McCarthy,* pp. 81-82.
31. *Madison Capital Times,* May 6, 14, 1946; *Milwaukee Journal,* May 16, 1946.

32. *Appleton Post-Crescent,* July 9, 1946.

33. *Madison Capital Times,* June 29, July 1, 1946.

34. See O'Brien, "Senator Joseph McCarthy and Wisconsin," p. 22.

35. Tegge interview; *Milwaukee Journal,* October 23, 1946.

36. Kiermas interview.

37. Hagerty interview.

38. Townsend interview, June 26, 1975.

39. See Townsend, Swedish, Fleming, Kiermas, Bayley (July 7, 1977) interviews; *Milwaukee Journal,* March 20, 1954.

40. Ibid., July 26, 1946. Joe opposed a postwar veterans' bonus. *Rhinelander News,* June 20, 1946.

41. *Superior Telegram,* July 10, 1946; Alexander, "The Senate's Remarkable Upstart," p. 57; Anderson and May, *McCarthy,* p. 87. Arriving late for an appearance before the Manitowoc Joes' Club, McCarthy said simply, "It's late. Anyway this isn't an occasion for speechmaking. It's an occasion for celebration. Let's eat." *Manitowoc Herald-Times,* March 21, 1946.

42. Flanagan interview. Interestingly, McCarthy was highly sensitive to physical pain, his own and that of others. In the late 1940s he became violently nauseated at the sight of a hospitalized son of a friend. Delaney interview.

43. Van Susteren interview, January 15, 1976; Secretary of State of Wisconsin, *Political Contributions of the 1946 Primary Elections,* folders 2062, 4480.

44. *Wisconsin State Journal,* July 23, 1946.

45. Ibid., July 25, 28, 1946. Joe had first dared La Follette to debate in late March. See *Racine Journal-Times,* April 1, 1946.

46. *Madison Capital Times,* August 1, 1946. Another G.O.P. candidate, Perry J. Stearns, charged that La Follette voted with the "Communist New Deal" on domestic issues and with fascist elements "such as the America Firsters" on international affairs. *Milwaukee Journal,* August 5, 1946. Earlier in the campaign, McCarthy had declared that he saw little value in condemning Russia or the "Russian attitude." Those loudest in their protests, he said, were "inviting another war." *Rhinelander News,* June 20, 1946.

47. *Milwaukee Journal,* August 6, 1946.

48. Telegram, Joseph R. McCarthy to Robert M. La Follette, Jr., August 8, 1946, box 535, Robert M. La Follette, Jr., Papers.

49. *Milwaukee Journal,* August 9, 1946.

50. "La Follette's Defeat," *Life,* XXI (August 26, 1946), 26-27.

51. Johnson, *Robert M. La Follette, Jr.,* pp. 111, 154; copy, Robert M. La Follette, Jr., to John E. Dickinson, May 16, 1946, box 533, Robert M. La Follette, Jr., Papers.

52. Johnson, *Robert M. La Follette, Jr.,* pp. 151-54. See Maney, *"Young Bob" La*

Follette, pp. 287-304. See also Laird interview and *New York Times,* February 25, 1953; Morris Rubin interview, May 29, 1967, Cornell University.

53. Quoted in a McCarthy advertisement, *Milwaukee Journal,* August 4, 1946.

54. See Johnson, *Robert M. La Follette, Jr.,* pp. 136-37; *Milwaukee Journal,* August 11, 1946.

55. Johnson, *Robert M. La Follette, Jr.,* pp. 137-57; David M. Oshinsky, *Senator Joseph McCarthy and the American Labor Movement* (Columbia, Missouri, 1976), pp. 23-43.

56 See *Political Contributions of the 1946 Primary Elections,* folders 1897, 4364; campaign flyers in John K. Kyle Papers, box 5; Bayley interview, July 8, 1977.

57. Johnson, *Robert M. La Follette, Jr.,* pp. 155-56.

58. *Milwaukee Journal,* August 9, 1946.

59. Oshinsky, *Senator Joseph McCarthy,* pp. 39-41; *Eau Claire Leader,* July 4, 1946; *Milwaukee Journal,* August 5, 6, 12, 1946.

60. O'Brien, "Senator Joseph McCarthy and Wisconsin," pp. 40-41; *New York Times,* August 13, 1946.

61. Eddy interview; memoranda in Eddy Papers; *Milwaukee Journal,* August 16, 1946. Miles McMillin soon called the effort "Operation Kindergarten." *Madison Capital Times,* August 25, 1946.

62. *The Wisconsin Blue Book,* 1948, p. 604; *Milwaukee Journal,* August 14, 1946. In Milwaukee County McCarthy won 48,596 to 38,437; in Racine, 5,569 to 4,370; in Kenosha, 3,576 to 3,410. He carried 33 of 71 counties.

63. Estes Kefauver to Robert M. La Follette, Jr., August 19, 1946; Edwin C. Johnson to Robert M. La Follette, Jr., September 15, 1946, box 534, La Follette Papers.

64. See Johnson, *Robert M. La Follette, Jr.,* p. 157. Coleman thought that the issue of La Follette's wartime radio profits was decisive in the election. See copy, Thomas E. Coleman to Carroll Reece, August 30, 1946, Cyrus Philipp Papers.

65. *Madison Capital Times,* August 13, 1946; Marquis Childs in *Appleton Post-Crescent,* August 19, 1946.

66. See editorial, *Madison Capital Times,* April 26, 1950; Anderson and May, *McCarthy,* p. 104; Lately Thomas, *When Even Angels Wept, The Senator Joseph McCarthy Affair—A Story Without a Hero* (New York, 1973), p. 44. Cf. *The Progressive* (April 1954), XVIII, 65. In 1951 Joe bitterly denounced the "Communists have the same right . . ." quotation. U.S. Senate, Subcommittee of the Committee on Foreign Relations, *Nomination of Philip C. Jessup, Hearings,* 82d Cong., 1st sess., 1951, p. 84 (hereafter cited as *Jessup Hearings*). In 1954 he denied having accepted or encouraged Red support in 1946. "If you'll check, you'll find that they took more bitter pot-shots at me. There was no Communist support that I know of." Saul Pett article in *New York Times,* April 12, 1954.

67. Kiermas interview.
68. See Oshinsky, *Senator Joseph McCarthy,* pp. 43-45. Some Polish-Americans voted Republican in 1946 because they were upset over the Yalta agreements. The president of the Wisconsin Young Democrats, a Polish-American, switched to the G.O.P. in April. Athan G. Theoharis, *The Yalta Myths, An Issue in U.S. Politics, 1945-1955* (Columbia, Missouri, 1970), pp. 52-53. See also John H. Fenton, *Midwest Politics* (New York, 1966), p. 48.
69. Oshinsky, *Senator Joseph McCarthy,* pp. 28-33.
70. *The Wisconsin Blue Book, 1948* (Madison, 1948), pp. 599, 604.
71. *Madison Capital Times,* August 16, 1946; *Milwaukee Journal,* November 6, 1946.
72. *Madison Capital Times,* October 8, 1946. The budget is in the Philipp Papers.
73. In O'Brien, "Senator Joseph McCarthy and Wisconsin," p. 46.
74. *Milwaukee Journal,* September 4, 10, 28, 1946.
75. Ibid., October 11, 1946; Anderson and May, *McCarthy,* pp. 118-20. See telegram, Fred Felix Wettengel to Marvin B. Rosenberry, October 25, 1946; copy, Marvin B. Rosenberry to H. F. Grapen, October 2, 1946, Marvin B. Rosenberry Papers.
76. *Madison Capital Times,* September 26, October 11, 1946; *Milwaukee Journal,* September 27, 29, 1946; *Kenosha Labor,* October 3, 1946; *Green Bay Press-Gazette,* October 17, 1946; Van Susteren (February 21, 1976), Kersten (May 17, 1971), Stoltz, Werner interviews. The most exaggerated account of the "quickie" divorces is in Anderson and May, *McCarthy,* pp. 73-77. The initial charges were devised by a Democratic attorney in Appleton and given to Miles McMillin of the *Capital Times.* O'Brien, "Senator Joseph McCarthy and Wisconsin," p. 49.
77. *Milwaukee Journal,* September 28, October 2, 10, 1946; Racine *Labor,* October 11, 1946; Anderson and May, *McCarthy,* pp. 111-113; Van Susteren interview, February 14, 1977; *Madison Capital Times,* October 17, 1946. On Murphy, see copy, Joe McCarthy to Alexander Wiley, September 28, 1944, Wiley Papers; *Chicago Tribune,* December 27, 1947. Col. McCormick said later, under oath, that he had no recollection of McCarthy's visit. McCormick deposition, pp. 60-68, box 4, Roberts Papers.
78. *Madison Capital Times,* October 21, 1946.
79. Ibid., October 22, 29, 1946.
80. Quoted in John Lewis Gaddis, *The United States and the Origins of the Cold War 1941-1947* (New York, 1972), pp. 58-59.
81. Oshinsky, *Senator Joseph McCarthy,* pp. 52-53; Paul Bullock, "'Rabbits and Radicals,' Richard Nixon's 1946 Campaign Against Jerry Voorhis," *Southern California Quarterly,* LV (Fall, 1973), 319-59; *Milwaukee Journal,* October 2, 11, November 6, 1946; *Madison Capital Times,* October 17, 1946.

82. See Peter H. Irons, "American Business and the Origins of McCarthyism: The Cold War Crusade of the United States Chamber of Commerce," in Robert Griffith and Athan Theoharis (eds.), *The Specter, Original Essays on the Cold War and the Origins of McCarthyism* (New York, 1974), pp. 77-82.

83. Donald F. Crosby, "The Politics of Religion: American Catholics and the Anti-Communist Impulse," in ibid., pp. 20-38.

84. Committee on Un-American Activities, 79th Cong., 2d sess., *Investigation of Un-American Activities and Propaganda* (Washington, D.C., 1947), pp. 2-3.

85. See Joe McCarthy to Kenneth S. Wherry, October 11, 1946, Kenneth S. Wherry Papers.

86. *Milwaukee Journal,* October 17, 1946.

87. See Oshinsky, *Senator Joseph McCarthy,* pp. 54-55.

88. *Madison Capital Times,* October 22, 1946.

89. *Milwaukee Journal,* October 23, 1946.

90. For a paraphrase of the definition, see *Madison Capital Times,* October 23, 1946.

91. Ibid.

92. Ibid., October 25, 1946.

93. *Eau Claire Leader,* October 16, 1946.

94. *Janesville Daily Gazette,* October 30, 1946.

95. *Appleton Post-Crescent,* November 2, 1946; *Green Bay Press-Gazette,* November 2, 1946. Both newspapers were run by close friends and advisers of McCarthy. See the Wyngaard interview.

96. O'Brien, "Senator Joseph McCarthy and Wisconsin," p. 53.

97. Ibid., p. 54; *Madison Capital Times,* October 25, 1946.

98. *Milwaukee Journal,* October 2, 1946; *Chippewa Herald-Telegram,* October 11, 1946.

99. *Eau Claire Leader,* October 16, 1946.

100. *Milwaukee Journal,* October 23, 1946.

101. *Madison Capital Times,* October 31, 1946.

102. *Milwaukee Journal,* November 10, 1946.

103. *The Wisconsin Blue Book, 1948,* pp. 670, 672, 675. See Louis H. Bean, *Influences in the 1954 Mid-Term Elections* (Washington, 1954), pp. 10-13.

104. *Milwaukee Journal,* November 6, 10, 1946; McCarthy, Townsend (June 26, 1975) interviews.

CHAPTER 7

1. Donald R. Matthews, *U.S. Senators and Their World* (Chapel Hill, 1960), pp. 64-65; Eddy (May 24, 1976), Hart interviews.

2. Robert Griffith, *The Politics of Fear, Joseph R. McCarthy and the Senate* (Lexington, 1970), p. 14; Parnell, Mullarkey interviews. A very few McCarthy friends accept the "inferiority" thesis, most notably Tom Korb.

3. Lorge interview; *Milwaukee Sentinel,* December 3, 1946; *Wisconsin State Journal,* December 3, 1946; Alexander, "The Senate's Remarkable Upstart," p. 57; "Senate Newcomer," *Newsweek,* 39 (December 16, 1946), 2-3; editorial, *Marinette Eagle-Star,* December 4, 1946.

4. Alexander, "The Senate's Remarkable Upstart," p. 57; *Eau Claire Leader,* January 31, 1947.

5. *Appleton Post-Crescent,* January 2, 1947.

6. Townsend interview.

7. Alexander, "The Senate's Remarkable Upstart," p. 57.

8. Van Straten, Kiermas interviews.

9. Kiermas interview; Miles McMillin in the *Madison Capital Times,* April 11, 1948; Alexander, "The Senate's Remarkable Upstart," p. 16.

10. Kiermas interview; *Appleton Post-Crescent,* August 15, 1947.

11. Kiermas, Reedy interviews; Eleanor Harris, "The Private Life of Senator McCarthy," *The American Weekly,* August 16, 1953, p. 7. Mr. and Mrs. Kiermas vouched for the accuracy of the Harris article in their interview with the author.

12. Kiermas, Korb (September 6, 1975), Henderson, Bayley (July 8, 1977) interviews; Harris, "The Private Life of Senator McCarthy," p. 5.

13. Alexander, "The Senate's Remarkable Upstart," p. 16; *Appleton Post-Crescent,* August 15, 1947.

14. Kiermas, Wyngaard interviews; *Madison Capital Times,* September 3, 1949; John Wyngaard to the author, May 31, 1977; "Congress," *Time,* LVIII (October 22, 1951), 22.

15. Kiermas, Van Susteren (January 15, 1976) interviews.

16. Kiermas, Van Susteren (November 25, 1975) interviews.

17. Van Susteren interview, July 14, 1977.

18. Harris, "The Private Life of Senator McCarthy," p. 5.

19. Anderson interview; Jack Anderson, *Confessions of a Muckraker: The Inside Story of Life in Washington During the Truman, Eisenhower, Kennedy and Johnson Years* (New York, 1979), pp. 176-79.

20. Alexander, "The Senate's Remarkable Upstart," pp. 16, 58; Korb interview, September 6, 1975. In 1953, with McCarthy at the height of his political power, a native of Russia would claim that the senator spoke Russian without an accent, "not even a brogue." *New York Times,* June 23, 1953. See also Ibid., January 8, 1954.

21. See Eric F. Goldman, *The Crucial Decade—And After: America, 1945-1960*

(New York, 1960), p. 55; Alonzo L. Hamby, *Beyond the New Deal: Harry S. Truman and American Liberalism* (New York, 1973), p. 137.

22. *New York Times,* January 15, 1947; *Appleton Post-Crescent,* January 23, 1947.

23. George H. Gallup, *The Gallup Poll: Public Opinion, 1935-1971,* 3 vols. (New York, 1972), I, 606.

24. *Appleton Post-Crescent,* January 24, 1947; Oshinsky, *Senator Joseph McCarthy,* p. 65.

25. *New York Times,* February 2, 3, 1947.

26. Ibid., May 27, 1947.

27. See Oshinsky, *Senator Joseph McCarthy,* pp. 82-86.

28. U.S. Senate, Committee on Banking and Currency, *Rent Control, Hearings,* 80th Cong., 1st sess., 1947, pp. 79-80, 173-74; *Appleton Post-Crescent,* February 3, 1947; *Madison Capital Times,* March 13, June 2, 1947.

29. *New York Times,* February 7, 13, 1947. See also ibid., September 16, 19, 1949.

30. *Congressional Record,* 80th Cong., 1st sess., March 10, 1947, p. 1811.

31. Ibid., March 12, 1947, p. 1935; U.S. Senate, Subcommittee of the Committee on Banking and Currency, *Sugar Controls, Hearings,* 80th Cong., 1st sess., 1947, pp. 124, 129, 151, 210-20, 225-29, 232-36, et passim.

32. See "G.O.P. Rebels' Key Position," *U.S. News and World Report,* 22 (May 16, 1947), 20-21; *Congressional Record,* 80th Cong., 1st sess., March 26, 1947, pp. 2598-2611, March 27, 1947, pp. 2697-2732; *New York Times,* March 27, 28, 1947; "Pen in Hand," *U.S. News and World Report,* 22 (April 14, 1947), 28.

33. Earl B. Wilson, *Sugar and Its Wartime Controls, 1941-1947* (New York, [1948], I, 4-5, 144, 152-53; IV, 1313; *New York Times,* May 14, June 5, 1947; "Sugar So Plentiful Some May Go Abroad," *Business Week,* September 13, 1947, p. 44.

34. Anderson and May, *McCarthy,* pp. 128-33; *Madison Capital Times,* May 28, 1952; *Hennings Committee Report,* pp. 38-39.

35. Richard Rovere, *Senator Joe McCarthy* (New York, 1959), pp. 105-6.

36. *Washington Post,* May 14, 1952; *New York Times,* June 5, 1947.

37. Townsend (January 5, 1978), Van Susteren (January 5, 1978), interviews; "Pepsi-Cola's Walter Mack," *Fortune,* 36 (November, 1947), 176, 178, 181-82, 184, 187-88, 190; *Madison Capital Times,* September 3, 1949; *New York Times,* September 4, 7, 1949; U.S. Senate, Subcommittee of the Committee on Expenditures in the Executive Departments, *Influence in Government Procurement, Hearings,* 81st Cong., 1st sess., 1949, pp. 289-337, 475-84, 497-540, 561-63, 570-73, 578-83, 590-96.

38. *Washington Post,* May 14, 1952; "Twelve Full Ounces, That's a Lot," *Fortune,* 35 (January, 1947), 143; *Madison Capital Times,* June 13, 1952; U.S. Senate,

Subcommittee of the Committee on Banking and Currency, *Sugar Controls, Hearings,* 80th Cong., 1st sess., 1947, pp. 139-41, 145-72, 200-229.

39. *New York Times,* December 10, 13, 1947.

40. "Anti-Communist Momentum," *U.S. News and World Report,* 22 *(March 28, 1947), 34, 36.*

41. Quoted in Hamby, *Beyond the New Deal,* p. 163.

42. In Henry Steele Commager, *Freedom and Order, A Commentary on the American Political Scene* (New York, 1966), pp. 73-74.

43. *Congressional Record,* 80th Cong., 1st sess., July 15, 1947, pp. 8492-93.

44. See David E. Lilienthal, *The Journals of David E. Lilienthal: Volume II, The Atomic Energy Years, 1945-1950* (New York, 1964), pp. 128-66; *Milwaukee Journal,* March 12, 1947; *Congressional Record,* 80th Cong., 1st sess., March 25, 1947, p. 2530, April 3, 1947, pp. 3085-3116, April 9, 1947, p. 3241. McCarthy paired with Sen. Warren Magnuson, a Lilienthal supporter, on an earlier vote to recommit and on confirmation.

45. *Town Meeting, Bulletin of America's Town Meeting of the Air,* 12 (April 3, 1947), 3-23; *New York Herald Tribune,* April 4, 1947.

46. *Madison Capital Times,* April 6, 1947.

47. *Congressional Record,* 80th Cong., 1st sess., April 22, 1947, p. 3793.

48. Ibid., May 9, 1947, pp. 4879-4884.

49. *Madison Capital Times,* July 5, 1947.

50. Ibid., February 10, 13, 14, 18 (editorial), 1947; editorial, *Appleton Post-Crescent,* February 18, 1947. See the editorial in the *Wisconsin State Journal,* February 15, 1947.

51. Van Susteren interview, February 5, 1977; *Madison Capital Times,* June 3, 4, July 28, 31, August 6 (editorial), 1947.

52. Ibid., June 4, 1947.

CHAPTER 8

1. Richard O. Davies, *Housing Reform During the Truman Administration* (Columbia, Missouri, 1966), p. 41.

2. Ibid., pp. 33-38.

3. Ibid., pp. 47-49.

4. *New York Times,* April 24, 1947.

5. Ibid., August 28, September 3, 1947.

6. Ibid., August 20, 1947; Davies, *Housing Reform During the Truman Administration,* p. 68.

7. *Congressional Record,* 80th Cong., 1st sess., July 11, 1947, p. 8657, July 25, pp. 10185-87; *New York Times,* July 12, 25, 1947.

8. Ibid., August 20, 1947; *Madison Capital Times,* August 20, 1947. See copy, Joe McCarthy to Charles Tobey, [August, 1947], box 116, Charles Tobey Papers.

9. *Congressional Record,* 80th Cong., 1st sess., July 19, 1947, pp. 9356-57, 9377-88; *New York Times,* July 20, 1947.

10. Ibid., September 3, 1947.

11. See U.S. Senate, Joint Committee on Housing, *Study and Investigation of Housing, Hearings,* 80th Cong., 1st sess., 1948, p. 345, hereafter cited as *Housing Hearings.* On the McCarthy bill, see *Congressional Record,* 80th Cong., 1st sess., June 23, 1947, p. 7553, July 25, pp. 10138-39.

12. *New York Times,* September 3, 1947.

13. Ibid., August 28, September 5, 1947.

14. See Joe McCarthy to Ralph A. Gamble, February 10, 1948, J. Howard McGrath Papers. In all but one of the hearings outside Washington, McCarthy served as chairman, sometimes presiding alone. Gamble, active on other fronts, also permitted Joe to function as chairman during two of the Washington hearings, due to his expertise.

15. *Housing Hearings,* pp. 153, 1778-79, 862.

16. Ibid., pp. 2397, 1777.

17. Ibid., pp. 2101-3, 2465-66, 861, 1779; *New York Times,* October 15, 1947.

18. *Housing Hearings,* pp. 140-41, 2039; U.S. House of Representatives, Sub committee of the Joint Committee on Housing, *High Cost of Housing, Report,* 80th Cong., 2d sess., 1948, pp. 9-10; Davies, *Housing Reform During the Truman Administration,* pp. 43-58. The contention that McCarthy was interested in prefabricated housing in order to wangle favors for the Harnischfager Corporation of Milwaukee is undocumented and unpersuasive. See Anderson and May, *McCarthy,* p. 141; Oshinsky, *Senator Joseph McCarthy,* p. 73; *Housing Hearings,* p. 2450; Korb interviews, September 6 and November 8, 1975.

19. See *Housing Hearings,* pp. 267-69, 765-68, 855-57, 871-73, 882-92.

20. See ibid., pp. 5029-41, 5133-54, 5203-4, 5907-8; *New York Times,* January 16, 29, 1948.

21. *Madison Capital Times,* February 2, 1948.

22. *New York Times,* September 3, 1948.

23. See *Housing Hearings,* pp. 151, 173-78, 283-95, 329-30, 382-95, 912, 1739, 2433-34, 2442-44, 2461.

24. See ibid., pp. 165-73, 194-98, 314, 4710-11, 5101-26, 5271-5300; Oshinsky, *Senator Joseph McCarthy,* pp. 76-77.

25. *Housing Hearings,* pp. 254-55, 5748-50.

26. Joe McCarthy to Ralph A. Gamble, February 10, 1948, McGrath Papers; *Madison Capital Times,* February 12, 1948.

27. *Public Papers of the Presidents of the United States, Harry S. Truman, January 1 to December 31, 1948* (Washington, 1964), pp. 156-63; *Madison Capital Times,* February 27, March 1, 1948; *New York Times,* February 28, March 2, 1948; Wendt interview.

28. *New York Times,* March 16, 1948; *Congressional Record,* 80th Cong., 2d sess., March 15, 1948, pp. 2796-97, 2800-2801, 2815-27; April 15, 1948, pp. 4414, 4496, 4514; U.S. House of Representatives, Joint Committee on Housing, *Final Majority Report,* 80th Cong., 2d sess., March 15, 1948. On March 22, Joe had his remarks and his housing report published separately in a Senate report. U.S. Senate, Joint Committee on Housing, *Housing Study and Investigation, Individual Views,* Report no. 1019, 80th Cong., 2d sess., March 22, 1948.

29. *Congressional Record,* 80th Cong., 2d sess., April 14, 1948, pp. 4411-25; April 15, 1948, pp. 4478-4522; April 20, 1948, pp. 4594-4618; April 21, 1948, pp. 4670-83; April 22, 1948, pp. 4728-38.

30. Ibid., June 19, 1948, pp. 9086-92; Davies, *Housing Reform During the Truman Administration,* p. 83.

31. Ibid., pp. 79-80.

32. *Eau Claire Leader,* January 31, 1947; *Madison Capital Times,* May 25, 1947, March 16, 1948; *Milwaukee Journal,* June 5, 1947; Alexander, "The Senate's Remarkable Upstart," p. 58; *New York Times,* November 14, 1947.

33. Miles McMillin in the *Madison Capital Times,* April 11, 1948; Olsyzk, Korb (September 6, 1975) interviews.

34. Copy, Joe McCarthy to "Dear Folks," March 31, 1948, box 3, Fleming Papers.

35. *Madison Capital Times,* April 25, 1948; Laird interview.

36. *New York Times,* May 21, 26, 1948; Irwin Ross, *The Loneliest Campaign, The Truman Victory of 1948* (New York, 1968), pp. 43-57.

37. See McCarthy's comment on the plank in *Congressional Record,* 80th Cong., 2d sess., August 5, 1948, p. 9863. See also Donald Bruce Johnson and Kirk H. Porters, *National Party Platforms, 1840-1972* (Urbana, 1973), p. 452.

38. Ibid., p. 432.

39. Harry S. Truman, "Message to the Special Session of the Eightieth Congress," July 27, 1948, Harry S. Truman Papers, OF 63; Harry S. Truman, *Years of Trial and Hope* (New York, 1956), pp. 241-42.

40. *New York Times,* July 28, 29, 1948.

41. Copy, Joe McCarthy to Robert A. Taft, August 2, 1948, McGrath Papers; *New York Times,* August 3, 1948.

42. *Congressional Record,* 80th Cong., 2d sess., August 5, 1948, pp. 9855-72.

43. Ibid., August 6, 1948, pp. 9915-35; Ralph E. Flanders, *Senator from Vermont* (Boston 1961), pp. 220-21; *New York Times,* August 7, 1948.

44. Quoted in Davies, *Housing Reform During the Truman Administration,* pp. 36, 62.

45. *New York Times,* August 11, 1948; Davies, *Housing Reform During the Truman Administration,* pp. 95-100.

46. *Congressional Record,* 81st Cong., 1st sess., April 14, 1949, p. 4611; Davies, *Housing Reform During the Truman Administration,* p. x.

47. O'Brien, "Senator Joseph McCarthy and Wisconsin," pp. 62-63; *Madison Capital Times,* August 22, November 14, 1948. For further McCarthy efforts to stimulate housing, see *New York Times,* August 23, September 25, 1948.

48. See *Congressional Record,* 81st Cong., 1st sess., April 14, 1949, pp. 4581-86, 4603-20; April 18, 1949, pp. 4716-18; April 19, 1949, pp. 4728-40, 4752-69; April 20, 1949, pp. 4791-4821; April 21, 1949, pp. 4836-4903; *New York Times,* April 22, 1949. For McCarthy's attempt to curb a special rent-control extension for the District of Columbia, see ibid., March 30, April 11, 1949. He told the Senate, "Although it may not seem important, it is perhaps the one measure of this session which most clearly puts the finger on us to show whether we are legislating for the best interests of the nation or for our own convenience and pleasure."

49. See Davies, *Housing Reform During the Truman Administration,* pp. 108-12.

50. *Milwaukee Journal,* March 1, 1949.

51. *Madison Capital Times,* June 16, 1950.

52. See Anderson and May, *McCarthy,* pp. 152-57; Hennings Committee Report, pp. 15-19; *Congressional Record,* 81st Cong., 2d sess., June 19, 1950, pp. A4527-34; U.S. Senate, Subcommittee of the Committee on Banking and Currency, *Proposed Disposition of Lustron Plant, Hearings,* 82d Cong., 1st sess., February 13, 1951; U.S. Senate, Subcommittee of the Committee on Banking and Currency, *Study of Reconstruction Finance Corporation, Hearings,* 82d Cong., 1st sess., part 2, February 21, 22, 23, 26, 27, and March 1, 1951; U.S. Senate, Subcommittee on Privileges and Elections of the Committee on Rules and Administration, *Investigation of Senator Joseph R. McCarthy, Hearings,* 82d Cong., 2d sess., September 28, 1951, May 12, 13, 14, 15, and 16, 1952. A slightly garbled defense is in Joe McCarthy, *McCarthyism, The Fight for America* (New York, 1952), pp. 93-94. Much more revealing is the 1952 deposition "Joseph R. McCarthy vs. The Post-Standard Company, Samuel I. Newhouse, and Robert L. Vorhees," pp. 167-200. After Lustron's bankruptcy, Joe negotiated selling the rights to his article to the Harnischfager Corporation of Milwaukee. The company offered $5,000, but the deal was never closed.

See Thomas Korb to Joe McCarthy, June 16, 1950, Joe McCarthy to Thomas Korb, June 21, 1950, Korb Papers; *Washington Star,* May 18, 1952. For the outside incomes of senators in 1976, see *Milwaukee Journal,* July 10, 1977.

CHAPTER 9

1. Hugh Butler to Joseph R. McCarthy, January 8, 1949, box 207, Hugh A. Butler Papers.
2. *New York Post,* September 4, 1951; Joe McCarthy to Robert A. Taft, January 7, 1949, box 502, Robert Taft Papers.
3. *New York Times,* March 14, 1948; Joe McCarthy to Joseph R. Jones, December 6, 1948, in the possession of historian Allen Yarnell.
4. Minetti (March 1, 14, 1977), Korb (September 6, 1975) interviews; *Milwaukee Journal,* May 4, 1949; deposition of Joseph R. McCarthy, September 26, 1951, pp. 73-82, box 3, William A. Roberts Papers. Urban Van Susteren also urged McCarthy to forget the Malmedy issue for fear that it would damage him politically, especially with the members of the American Legion, who were clamoring for the execution of Nazi war criminals. Joe "brushed me aside with the remark that I was wasting his time and not to irritate him any more with such conversation because he had made up his mind. . . . I knew full well that he was saying that his sense of justice would never let him rest if he didn't do as he did." Urban P. Van Susteren to the author, July 24, 1978.
5. See Frederick J. Libby, *To End War, The Story of The National Council for Prevention of War* (Nyack, New York, 1969).
6. Finucane interview, March 15, 1977; U.S. Senate, Committee on Armed Services, *Malmedy Massacre Investigation, Hearings,* 81st Cong., 1st sess., pp. 952, 960. (This document will hereafter be referred to as *Malmedy Hearings.*)
7. *New York Times,* January 7, 1949. The Supreme Court denied the petition by a 4-4 vote on jurisdictional grounds.
8. "War Crimes," *Time,* LIII (January 17, 1949), 19.
9. *Congressional Record,* 81st Cong., 1st sess., January 27, 1949, p. 599; ibid., February 8, 1949, pp. 956-59; Finucane interview, July 22, 1978.
10. Edward L. Van Roden, "American Atrocities in Germany," *The Progressive,* XIII (February, 1949), 21-22.
11. *New York Times,* March 2, 1949.
12. Ibid., March 5, 1949.
13. Ibid.
14. *Malmedy Hearings,* pp. 1602-15; also see pp. 5-6.

15. Pusey interview; O'Brien, "Senator Joseph McCarthy and Wisconsin," pp. 62, 72, 358.

16. *Malmedy Hearings*, pp. 98, 636-37, 837.

17. *Congressional Record*, 81st Cong., 1st sess., January 27, 1949, pp. 598-99; *Malmedy Hearings*, pp. 280, 531.

18. Ibid., 280, 637; *New York Times*, April 16, 1949.

19. *Malmedy Hearings*, p. 803.

20. *Congressional Record*, 81st Cong., 1st sess., October 19, 1949, p. 14975.

21. See *Malmedy Hearings*, pp. 1280, 1284, 1420.

22. Hunt too had serious doubts initially about the accuracy of the German charges. See ibid., pp. 109-10, 147-48, 168-69.

23. See ibid., pp. 209, 349, 373, 981, 1568; Minetti (March 14, 1977), Korb (September 6, 1975), Finucane (March 15, 1977) interviews.

24. See *Malmedy Hearings*, pp. 8, 11, 12, 15, 19, 98, 180, 188, 223-24, 636. Joe also charged that "Jap diaries" had revealed "mock trials" of captured Marines in the Pacific. He noted that American justice in that region after the war had been unexceptionable. See ibid., pp. 8, 26, 88.

25. Ibid., pp. 33-69.

26. Ibid., pp. 72-101.

27. Ibid., pp. 102-12. Joe was eager to stress the patriotism of his position and cited personal support by American Jews and combat veterans. See ibid., pp. 171, 185.

28. See ibid., pp. 154-90, 543-54, 897-907.

29. Ibid., pp. 190-221; see also pp. 1145-68.

30. See ibid., pp. 225-63, 301-19, 949-1028, 1073-1125.

31. See ibid., pp. 98, 112, 265-69.

32. Ibid., pp. 173-74. In 1952 McCarthy said of Baldwin, "I have a high regard for Ray. I like Ray. I like him a lot, and I think he is a good friend of mine yet." *Hartford Courant*, October 29, 1952.

33. *Malmedy Hearings*, pp. 270-300, 473-543.

34. There were several major inaccuracies in the petition. Everett later explained that he was not given access to the trial records while writing his petition and was working from memory! See ibid., pp. 380-84, 386-96, 1569.

35. Ibid., pp. 403-71, and see pp. 571-608.

36. Ibid., pp. 457-59.

37. Ibid., pp. 609-39, 658-803, 837-40; Korb interview, September 6, 1975; *Madison Capital Times*, May 20, 1949. As a judge, McCarthy had ordered lie-detector tests given on several occasions. E.g., *Milwaukee Sentinel*, January 8, 1946.

38. *Malmedy Hearings*, pp. 844-59, 862-81, 883-96, 939-49.

39. Ibid., pp. 927-39, 946, 1042, 1419-20.

40. See *Congressional Record,* 81st Cong., 1st sess., July 26, 1949, pp. 10160-75; *Green Bay Press-Gazette,* July 27, 28, 29, 30, 1949. Joe tried unsuccessfully to have the newspaper articles published in the *Reader's Digest.* See Joe McCarthy to John T. Flynn, July 11, 1949, John T. Flynn Papers.

41. In box 4, Fleming Papers.

42. *Malmedy Hearings,* pp. 1240-1336.

43. Ibid., pp. 1369-1432.

44. Ibid., pp. 1513-23, 1550, 1594-98.

45. Ibid., pp. 1523-28, 1545-52, 1616-28.

46. Ibid., pp. 1555-70.

47. *Congressional Record,* 81st Cong., 1st sess., October 14, 1949, pp. 14511-34. See U.S. Senate, Committee on Armed Services, *Malmedy Massacre Investigation, Report,* 81st Cong., 1st sess., 1949.

48. See *Malmedy Hearings,* pp. 403-40, 427, 441-71, 1050, 1061, 1165-66, 1279, 1369-1432, 1556-58. Of course, as McCarthy pointed out, the chief prosecuting attorney, Colonel Ellis, also lacked relevant experience. Low salaries and the unavailability of qualified personnel after the war figured prominently in the problem. See ibid., pp. 912-13, 1417.

49. See ibid., pp. 135, 188, 363, 546-48, 850, 906, 1156, 1319, 1321, 1327-28, 1332-35. When Polish guards arrived at Schwabisch Hall they mistreated prisoners slightly until reprimanded by American officials. Ibid., pp. 577, 647, 807.

50. Ibid., pp. 58, 1201, 1280-83; *Green Bay Press Gazette,* July 28, 1949.

51. See *Malmedy Hearings,* pp. 72-101, 1145-68, 1197-1205; William L. Shirer, *The Rise and Fall of the Third Reich* (New York, 1959), pp. 1422-23.

52. *Madison Capital Times,* February 16, 1951; Rovere, *Senator Joe McCarthy,* p. 112. Rovere, as usual, took the story from the 1952 campaign polemic by Jack Anderson and Ronald May. Their chapter on Malmedy is wildly inaccurate. Compare, for example, their excerpts from the hearings on pages 162-63 with the hearings themselves, pages 1459-60. On his own, Rovere suggested that Aschenauer was introduced personally to McCarthy "probably through pro-Nazis among Wisconsin German-Americans"!

53. See *Malmedy Hearings,* pp. 204, 981, 1027, 1432-51, 1453-65, 1528, 1567; Finucane interview, March 15, 1977. Those most interested in defending the prisoners' charges were from the Far Right politically. E.g., Freda Utley, *The High Cost of Vengeance* (Chicago, 1949), pp. 185-95.

54. Copy, Miles McMillin to Abe Fortas, April 3, 1950, William T. Evjue Papers; Anderson and May, *McCarthy,* p. 164; *The Daily Compass,* March 21, 1950; *New York Times,* July 19, 1954. See also the Korb interview of September 6,

1975. During World War II the Harnischfager Corporation was one of ten companies ordered by the President's Committee on Fair Employment Practices to stop discriminating against workers because of race or religion. *New York Herald Tribune,* April 13, 1942. For Walter Harnischfager's views on Germany, see the *Milwaukee Journal,* October 27, 1944, June 14, 1947, October 14, 1948.

CHAPTER 10

1. See *Appleton Post-Crescent,* May 11, 1957; *Milwaukee Journal,* May 3, 1957.

2. On the hospitalization, see *New York Times,* July 22, 1949; *Milwaukee Journal,* May 3, 1957.

3. See O'Brien, "Senator Joseph McCarthy and Wisconsin," pp. 66-67, 74; Robert Fleming memoranda of his Washington trip of January 1-6, 1951, in box 3, Fleming Papers; Tyler Abell (ed.), *Drew Pearson Diaries, 1949-1959* (New York, 1974), p. 74. Boardman privately expressed an opinion on the case, however, and conducted research on it for the board. See W. Wade Boardman to Edward J. Dempsey et al., July 9, 1949, and W. Wade Boardman to State Board of Bar Commissioners, October 18, 1948, Edward J. Dempsey Papers. Dempsey was president of the State Board of Bar Commissioners.

4. Copy, Miles McMillin to Arthur McLeod, July 7, 1948, ibid; *Madison Capital Times,* July 8, 1949.

5. Joe McCarthy to Arthur W. McLeod, July 27, 1948, R. T. Reinholdt to Edward J. Dempsey, August 2, 1948, Arthur W. McLeod to Joseph R. McCarthy, August 9, 1948, Harlan B. Rogers to R. T. Reinholdt, August 25, 1948, Dempsey Papers; *Madison Capital Times,* September 9, 1948.

6. *Madison Capital Times,* September 19, 1948, December 15, 1948; copy, Edward J. Dempsey to Harlan B. Rogers, September 14, 1948, Dempsey Papers.

7. *Madison Capital Times,* December 15, 1948.

8. Ibid., January 11, 1949; W. T. Doar to R. T. Reinholdt et al., n.d., Dempsey Papers.

9. H. B. Rogers to members of the board, August 12, 1948, ibid; *Madison Capital Times,* June 19, 1949.

10. *Milwaukee Journal,* July 12, 1949; *Madison Capital Times,* July 13, 1949.

11. Ibid., July 13, 14, 15, 21, 1949; editorial, *Green Bay Press-Gazette,* July 18, 1949. Only ten Wisconsin newspapers carried stories of the decision. Three of the five newspapers that defended the senator failed to mention his censure. The *Appleton Post-Crescent* edited Wyngaard's column to include only favorable commentary. See O'Brien, "Joseph McCarthy and Wisconsin," pp. 71-72.

12. *Green Bay Press-Gazette,* July 13, 1949; *Madison Capital Times,* July 14, 1949.

Privately, Boardman wrote to the board's counsel, "I feel very proud to be a member of the board that filed the complaint and not at all unhappy with the result." W. Wade Boardman to Harlan B. Rogers, July 13, 1949.

13. See *Green Bay Press-Gazette,* November 14, 1949; *Milwaukee Journal,* April 20, 1955. McCarthy deliberately overpaid his federal taxes slightly so that the refund would embarrass his critics. Kiermas interview.

14. The statement was published in full in the *Green Bay Press-Gazette,* November 14, 1949, and in the *Appleton Post-Crescent.*

15. On Parker, see Aldric Revell in *Madison Capital Times,* November 15, 1949; Bayley interview, July 8, 1977; Miles McMillin quoted in O'Brien, "Senator Joseph McCarthy and Wisconsin," p. 91; Jacobs Recollections; and the obituary in *Milwaukee Journal,* May 19, 1978.

16. See *Madison Capital Times,* November 9, 10, 11, 1949; telegram, Joe McCarthy to William T. Evjue, November 10, 1949, Evjue Papers. Parker had actually signed the affidavit in early 1948, but a few weeks later he was named city editor, left the union, and thus did not file the document with the N.L.R.B. See *Madison Capital Times,* January 31, 1949, August 6, 1951; copy, William T. Evjue to Joseph Short, August 3, 1951, Evjue Papers.

17. *Madison Capital Times,* November 11, 1949. Cf. the distorted and undated account in Anderson and May, *McCarthy,* pp. 272-73.

18. Copy, Joe McCarthy to John Nestigen, December 3, 1949, Korb Papers; *Racine Journal Times,* December 6, 1949.

19. See *Chicago Tribune,* April 27, 28, 1950; *Washington Star,* August 5, 1951; *Madison Capital Times,* August 6, 1951.

20. O'Brien, "Joseph McCarthy and Wisconsin," pp. 92-93.

21. Ibid., p. 365; Madison *Capital Times,* November 10, 11, 1949. See Jean Kerr to T. W. Korb, November 14, 1949, Korb Papers.

22. McCarthy, *McCarthyism, The Fight for America,* p. 2.

23. "Senator McCarthy Answers Some Important Questions," *Cosmopolitan,* May, 1952, pp. 39-40.

24. Surine interview, April 7, 1977; *Congressional Record,* 81st Cong., 1st sess., September 15, 1949, pp. 12877-80, 12926-31. McCarthy raised the subject in one political speech. See *Kenosha Evening News,* November 16, 1949.

25. Cohn, *McCarthy,* pp. 8-10. Roy Cohn, *McCarthy: The Answer to "Tail Gunner Joe,"* (New York, 1977) is a thinly disguised reprint of the earlier volume. See also Cohn interview.

26. *Milwaukee Sentinel,* November 11, 1949; *Green Bay Press-Gazette,* November 12, 1949; *Kenosha Evening News,* November 16, 1949; *Philadelphia Evening Bulletin,* December 4, 1949; *Milwaukee Journal,* December 7, 1949; *Congressional Record,* 81st Cong., 2d sess., January 5, 1950, p. 86; *Madison Capital Times,*

December 12, 1949; *Milwaukee Sentinel,* January 22, 1950; *Congressional Record,* 81st Cong., 2d sess., January 25, 1950, p. 895, February 8, 1950, p. 1635. Joe attempted unsuccessfully to have his own subcommittee investigate the spy charge, made by arch-conservative columnist Victor Riesel. In December he offered to volunteer the services of his subcommittee to look into charges of wartime spying by the Soviet Union. This allegation involved atomic materials and secrets and came from ultraconservative Fulton Lewis, Jr. See *New York Times,* December 4, 1949.

27. Nellor, Minetti (March 14, 1977) interviews.

28. *Congressional Record,* 81st Cong., 1st sess., October 19, 1949, pp. A6625-27, A6631-32; see the list of office employees in box 5, Fleming Papers; Kiermas, Nellor interviews; Karl H. Cerny to the author, October 3, 1978; Drew Pearson in *Madison Capital Times,* April 19, 1950.

29. See *New York Times,* May 5, June 14, 20, September 1, 3, 4, 7, 13, October 13, 1949. See also General Vaughan's amusing recollections in Ovid Demaris, *The Director, An Oral Biography of J. Edgar Hoover* (New York, 1975), pp. 111-12.

30. Quoted in Goldman, *The Crucial Decade—And After: America, 1945-1960,* p. 137.

31. Catlin interview. Cf. Jim Bishop, *A Bishop's Confession* (Boston, 1981), pp. 233-34.

32. The leading exception is Michael O'Brien. See his "McCarthy and McCarthyism: The Cedric Parker Case, November 1949," in Griffith and Theoharis (eds.), *Original Essays on the Cold War and the Origins of McCarthyism,* pp. 226-38.

33. Anderson and May, *McCarthy,* pp. 172-73. On the pension plan, see copy, Elmer Thomas to Joe McCarthy, February 6, 1950, Elmer Thomas Papers; copy, Paul H. Douglas to Joe McCarthy, February 21, 1950, Paul H. Douglas Papers.

34. See Donald F. Crosby, *God, Church, and Flag: Senator Joseph R. McCarthy and the Catholic Church, 1950-1957* (Chapel Hill, 1978), pp. 50-52; Edmund A. Walsh to Marquis Childs, April 25, 1951, Marquis Childs Papers. On Walsh, see *New York Times,* November 1, 1956.

35. See Woods, Fleming interviews. See also Pearson's column in *Madison Capital Times,* March 14, 1950, and the special report on the subject in ibid., September 29, 1951. In mid-January, 1950 Joe again brandished a photostatic copy of a document in a tussle with Navy Secretary Francis P. Matthews over an appointment. See *Congressional Record,* 82d Cong., 2d sess., January 18, 1950, p. 512.

36. Lorge, Kiermas, Korb (November 8, 1975), Minetti (June 24, 1975), Laird interviews; Glenn Silber interview with Penn Kimball; Cohn, *McCarthy,* pp. 66-67; David E. Koskoff, *Joseph P. Kennedy, A Life and Times* (Englewood

Cliffs, New Jersey, 1974), pp. 363-65; Victor Lasky, *J.F.K., The Man and The Myth* (New York, 1977), p. 137; Gail Cameron, *Rose, A Biography of Rose Fitzgerald Kennedy* (New York, 1971), pp. 105-06. Cf. Joan and Clay Blair, Jr., *The Search for J.F.K.* (New York, 1976), pp. 307-08.

37. Eddy (July 29, 1976), Kiermas, Korb (November 8, 1975, August 2, 1976), Van Susteren (November 25, 1975), Waldrop, Nellor (June 6, 1979) interviews.

38. *Washington Star,* September 18, 1953; *La Crosse Tribune,* September 27, 1953; *Appleton Post-Crescent,* October 12, 1953; Richard Wilson, "The Ring Around McCarthy," *Look,* 17 (December 1, 1953), 30-32; Nellor (June 6, 1979), Kiermas, Korb (September 6, November 8, 1975), Reedy, Cocke, Edwards (November 17, 1976), William F. Buckley, Jr., Minetti (March 14, 1977, January 10, April 12, 1978) interviews.

CHAPTER 11

1. Earl Latham, *The Communist Controversy in Washington, From the New Deal to McCarthy* (Cambridge, Mass., 1966), pp. 3-4.

2. Ibid., pp. 71, 149-50, 359-62.

3. Martin Grodzins, *The Loyal and the Disloyal, Social Boundaries of Patriotism and Treason* (Chicago, 1956), p. 232.

4. See Robert K. Murray, *Red Scare: A Study in National Hysteria, 1919-1920* (Minneapolis, 1955); Stanley Coben, *A. Mitchell Palmer* (New York, 1963); William Preston, Jr., *Aliens and Dissenters: Federal Suppression of Radicals, 1903-1933* (New York, 1966).

5. Alan Barth, *The Loyalty of Free Men* (New York, 1951), p. 10.

6. See August Raymond Ogden, *The Dies Committee, A Study of The Special House Committee for the Investigation of Un-American Activities 1938-1944* (Washington, D.C., 1945); Walter Goodman, *The Committee: The extraordinary career of the House Committee on Un-American Activities* (New York, 1968); Robert Stripling, *The Red Plot Against America* (Drexel Hill, Pennsylvania, 1949), p. 23. Ogden (p. 296) concludes: "It stands in the history of the House of Representatives as an example of what an investigating committee should not be."

7. See Michal R. Belknap, *Cold War Political Justice: The Smith Act, the Communist Party, and American Civil Liberties* (Westport, Connecticut, 1977).

8. Gallup, *The Gallup Poll,* I, 640, II, 873; "The Quarter's Polls," *Public Opinion Quarterly,* 12 (Summer, 1948), 350-51.

9. See David Caute, *The Great Fear: The Anti-Communist Purge Under Truman*

and Eisenhower (New York, 1978), pp. 70-81; Chamber of Commerce of the U.S.A., *A Program for Community Anti-Communist Action* (Washington, D.C., 1948).

10. Dean Acheson, *A Democrat Looks at His Party* (New York, 1955), p. 127. For the interesting hypothesis that the politics of anti-Communism started on the federal level and spread to the states, see Robert Griffith, "American Politics and the Origins of 'McCarthyism,'" in Griffith and Theoharis (eds.), *The Specter,* pp. 15-16.

11. There were four investigations of subversive activities in the 79th Congress (1945-47), twenty-two during the 80th (1947-49), and twenty-four during the 81st (1949-51). See ibid., p. 13.

12. Goodman, *The Committee,* pp. 167-89.

13. Robert K. Carr, *The House Committee on Un-American Activities* (Ithaca, New York, 1952), p. 216.

14. Goodman, *The Committee,* pp. 272-96.

15. The bill died in the Senate, with Administration opposition. See ibid., pp. 228-30.

16. Ibid., pp. 231-39.

17. Of those named initially, only Remington was still employed by the government. See Herbert L. Packer, *Ex-Communist Witnesses, Four Studies in Fact Finding* (Stanford, California, 1962), pp. 52-120; Latham, *The Communist Controversy in Washington,* passim; Elizabeth Bentley, *Out of Bondage* (New York, 1951).

18. Cabell Phillips, *The 1940s: Decade of Triumph and Trouble* (New York, 1975), pp. 368-69.

19. Latham, *The Communist Controversy in Washington,* p. 417.

20. The best contemporary account is Alistair Cooke, *A Generation on Trial, U.S.A. vs. Alger Hiss* (New York, 1950). The most scholarly treatment is Allen Weinstein, *Perjury: The Hiss-Chambers Case* (New York, 1978). See Whittaker Chambers, *Witness* (New York, 1952), and Alger Hiss, *In the Court of Public Opinion* (New York, 1957). On the FBI's leaks to Nixon and the ultraconservative media, see Athan Theoharis, *Spying on Americans, Political Surveillance from Hoover to the Huston Plan* (Philadelphia, 1978), p. 164.

21. Goldman, *The Crucial Decade,* p. 113.

22. Quoted in Goodman, *The Committee,* p. 273.

23. See U.S. House of Representatives, Committee on Un-American Activities, *100 Things You Should Know About Communism . . . ,* 82d Cong., 1st sess., May 14, 1951.

24. Cited in Carey McWilliams, *Witch Hunt: The Revival of Heresy* (Boston, 1950), p. 192.
25. *New York Times,* June 17, 1949.
26. Quoted in E. J. Kahn, Jr., *The China Hands: America's Foreign Service Officers and What Befell Them* (New York, 1975), p. 207.
27. U.S. House of Representatives, Committee On Un-American Activities, *Annual Report . . . ,* 81st Cong., 2d sess., March 15, 1950, p. 23.
28. George F. Kennan, *American Diplomacy, 1900-1950* (Chicago, 1951), p. 49.
29. W. A. Swanberg, *Luce and His Empire* (New York, 1972), pp. 2-7, 183-4, 214.
30. See Latham, *The Communist Controversy in Washington,* pp. 219-68; Theodore H. White, *In Search of History, A Personal Adventure* (New York, 1978), pp. 70-161; Kahn, *The China Hands,* passim; Herbert Feis, *The China Tangle: The American Effort in China from Pearl Harbor to the Marshall Mission* (Princeton, 1953), passim; Joseph W. Esherick (ed.), *Lost Chance in China, The World II Despatches of John S. Service* (New York, 1974), passim.
31. See Ross Y. Koen, *The China Lobby in American Politics* (New York, 1974), passim; Swanberg, *Luce and His Empire,* pp. 250-53, 265-73, 282-83; John N. Thomas, *The Institute of Pacific Relations: Asian Scholars and American Politics* (Seattle, 1974), pp. 48-49.
32. See the China Lobby articles by Max Ascoli, Charles Werbenbaker, and Philip Horton in *The Reporter,* VI (April 15 and 29, 1952); Drew Pearson in Madison *Capital Times,* September 15, 1951, April 25, 1953.
33. See Kahn, *The China Hands,* pp. 49-50, 174, 188-92; Koen, *The China Lobby in American Politics,* pp. 50-55, 59-60, 76-77; Thomas, *The Institute of Pacific Relations,* pp. 36-44. Cf. Joseph C. Keeley, *The China Lobby Man* (New Rochelle, New York, 1969) and Irene Corbally Kuhn, "He Lobbies Against Communism," *American Legion Magazine,* (July, 1952), pp. 14-15, 58-60. Kohlberg's interesting history warrants further study. In 1940 he offered himself to the Royal Canadian Air Force as a kamikaze pilot after deciding that Japan was planning the conquest of China. He repeated the offer a year later to an assistant secretary of the United States Navy. Thomas, *The Institute of Pacific Relations,* p. 38. In the fall of 1949 he produced commotion by accusing the New York Public Library of having Communists and pro-Communists in positions of authority. *Milwaukee Journal,* April 11, 1950.
34. Quoted in Griffith, *The Politics of Fear,* pp. 47-48.
35. See Richard M. Fried, *Men Against McCarthy* (New York, 1976), pp. 14-15.
36. *Chicago Tribune,* February 4, 1950.
37. Ibid., February 7, 8, 1950.
38. Nellor (May 7, 1977), Edwards (November 17, 1976) interviews; Mrs. Garvin

Tankersley to the author, January 10, 1979; deposition of Joseph R. McCarthy, September 26, 1951, pp. 317, 322-30, box 3, Roberts Papers. Waters joined the McCarthy staff on January 25 and resigned on March 7, 1950. See box 5, Fleming Papers.

39. See Griffith, *The Politics of Fear,* pp. 48-49; Fried, *Men Against McCarthy,* p. 44. Two copies of the Wheeling speech are in U.S. Senate, Subcommittee of the Committee on Foreign Relations, *State Department Employee Loyalty Investigation, Hearings,* 81st Cong., 2d sess., 1950, pp. 1758-67. (Hereafter cited as *Tydings Committee Hearings.*)

40. E.g., "List of U.S. Aides Accused of Red Connections," *Chicago Sunday Tribune,* February 5, 1950. See also Willard Edwards's articles in the *Chicago Tribune,* February 6, 8, 1950. Edwards claimed on February 5 that there were 2,200 disloyal federal officials and employees, and that more than 500 occupied "key posts where they have access to confidential information." This was obviously discounted in Washington as typical right-wing blather, and no one deigned to reply. Of course, it was another matter for a senator to make similar claims.

41. See Francis J. Love to the author, May 23, 1975.

42. *Wheeling Intelligencer,* February 10, 1950.

43. See "Report of Preliminary Investigation of Senator William Benton's Charges against Joseph R. McCarthy Relating to Senate Resolution 187," an unpublished report by the staff of the Senate Subcommittee on Privileges and Elections, box 78, Robert C. Hendrickson Papers; William F. Buckley, Jr., and L. Brent Bozell, *McCarthy and His Enemies, The Record and its Meaning* (Chicago, 1954), pp. 41-51.

44. Two days after the speech, Gieske wrote an editorial stating that McCarthy had "shocked his audience when he charged there are over fifty persons of known Communistic affiliation still sheltered in the U.S. Department of State." By that time, however, McCarthy was claiming that he had 57 names, and Gieske may have read that number back into the Wheeling speech. Editorial, *Wheeling Intelligencer,* February 11, 1950. Cf. Buckley and Bozell, *McCarthy and His Enemies,* p. 49, for a clever twist of this evidence. See also John Howe to William Benton, March 30, April 6, 1954, and William Benton to John Howe, April 5, 1954, box 4, William Benton Papers.

45. See *Congressional Record,* 81st Cong., 2d sess., February 20, 1950, pp. 1953, 1958; "The McCarthy Issue . . . Pro and Con," *U.S. News and World Report,* 31 (September 7, 1951), 37.

46. McCarthy, *McCarthyism, The Fight for America,* p. 9. Cf. "Senator McCarthy answers some important questions," *Cosmopolitan,* May, 1952, p. 40.

47. Bem Price story in *Washington Star,* April 5, 1954.

48. Edwin R. Bayley, *Joe McCarthy and the Press.* (Madison, 1981), pp. 18-19.

49. Francis J. Love to the author, May 23, 1975.
50. *Denver Post,* February 11, 1950. See Griffith, *The Politics of Fear,* p. 53, fn 2.
51. Lee, Edwards (November 17, 1976), Nellor (May 7, 1977) interviews. May 7, 1977, The Lee list is in the *Tydings Committee Hearings,* pp. 1771-1813. Alfred Friendly, "The Noble Crusade of Senator McCarthy," *Harper's,* 20 (August, 1950), 34-42, is a useful analysis. In fact, four different committees of the Republican-controlled 80th Congress investigated the same files and information on which McCarthy based his charges and chose not to submit a report or charge a single State Department employee with disloyalty. U.S. Senate, Committee on Foreign Relations, *State Department Employee Loyalty Investigation, Report,* 81st Cong., 2d sess., 1950, p. 9. (Hereafter cited as *Tydings Committee Report.*)
52. *Denver Post,* February 11, 1950. Joe asserted that the President's Loyalty Board had listed 289 Department employees as "bad risks" and that 205 of them were still on the payroll.
53. Clinton P. Anderson, *Outsider in the Senate, Senator Clinton Anderson's Memoirs* (New York, 1970), p. 103. "Card-carrying Communist" was a common expression at the time, however inaccurate. See the Associated Press story "540,000 Reds in U.S., Hoover Tells Senators," *Chicago Tribune,* February 8, 1950.
54. He added, "Certainly this label is not deserved by hundreds of thousands of loyal American Democrats throughout the nation and by the sizable number of able and loyal Democrats in both the Senate and the House." *New York Times,* February 12, 1950.
55. Bayley, *Joe McCarthy and the Press,* pp. 21, 26-27, 29; *Nevada* State Journal, February 12, 1950.
56. Bayley, *Joe McCarthy and the Press,* pp. 26-28; *Reno Gazette,* February 13, 1950.
57. Ibid.; *Milwaukee Journal,* February 13, 1950.
58. Bayley, *Joe McCarthy and the Press,* pp. 29-30.
59. *New York Times,* February 14, 1950.
60. Bayley, *Joe McCarthy and the Press,* p. 30.
61. Ibid.; p. 32; editorial, *Washington Post,* February 14, 1950.
62. Bayley, *Joe McCarthy and the Press,* p. 33; *Los Angeles Times,* February 15, 1950.
63. *Huronite and Daily Plainsman,* February 16, 21, 1950.
64. *Milwaukee Journal,* February 15, 1950.
65. Bayley, *Joe McCarthy and the Press,* pp. 35-36; Fleming, Reddin interviews. See John Hoving, "My Friend McCarthy," *The Reporter,* 2 (April 25, 1950), pp. 28-31.
66. *Chicago Tribune,* February 19, 1950.

CHAPTER 12

1. Bayley, *Joe McCarthy and the Press,* p. 36. See Douglass Cater, "The Captive Press," *The Reporter,* 2 (June 6, 1950), pp. 17-20.
2. Kelly interview. Frank Kelly was assistant to the Majority Leader from January 1949 until April 1952 and sat next to Lucas on the evening of February 20.
3. Cf. Richard Rovere's assertion that McCarthy had no speech. *Senator Joe McCarthy,* pp. 125-27.
4. See *Milwaukee Journal,* February 21, 1950; *New York Times,* February 28, 1950; Anderson, *Confessions of a Muckraker,* pp. 190-91. Joe proceeded to link Lloyd with Hiss. Fellow A.D.A. liberal Hubert Humphrey staunchly defended him. *Congressional Record,* 81st Cong., 2d sess., February 28, 1950, pp. 2456, 2494-95.
5. Buckley and Bozell, *McCarthy and His Enemies,* p. 60. McCarthy's Senate speech is in *Congressional Record,* 81st Cong., 2d sess., February 20, 1950, pp. 1952-81. For the correlation between McCarthy's cases and those in the Lee list, see *Tydings Committee Hearings,* pp. 1815-17. McCarthy always denied, even privately, that his 81 cases of February 20 had come from the Lee list. Lee interview.
6. *New York Times,* February 22, 1950.
7. *Congressional Record,* 81st Cong., 2d sess., February 21, 1950, pp. 2062-68; February 22, 1950, pp. 2129-50; *New York Times,* February 23, 1950.
8. Ibid., February 24, 1950.
9. Ibid., February 25, 1950; *Madison Capital Times,* February 28, 1950. Lucas had expressed a similar thought at the conclusion of McCarthy's speech of February 20. When Frank Kelly asked if he would make a formal reply, Lucas said, "I'm not going to get into a pissing contest with a skunk." Kelly interview.
10. *New York Times,* February 26, 1950.
11. Demaris, *The Director,* p. 167. See William C. Sullivan, *The Bureau: My Thirty Years in Hoover's FBI* (New York, 1979), pp. 45-46, 267. At his Los Angeles press conference, Joe declared, "I want to know why the Federal Bureau of Investigation has been barred from projects like Los Alamos—the atomic installation. I want to know why the State Department has the power of veto over what the FBI does." *Los Angeles Times,* February 15, 1950.
12. Nichols interview. See Theoharis, *Spying on Americans,* pp. 133-34, 163-65, 200. On Nichols and Hoover, see Demaris, *The Director,* pp. 65-69, 90,

99-104; Nellor interview, June 6, 1979. For more on Sokolsky, see Warren I. Cohen, *The Chinese Connection: Roger S. Greene, Thomas W. Lamont, George E. Sokolsky and American-East Asian Relations* (New York, 1978), pp. 71-87, 260-72, 282-88.

13. See Nichols, Surine (July 30, 1977, June 20, 1980), Korb (September 6, November 8, 1975), Nellor (June 6, 1979), Delaney interviews; *Madison Capital Times,* August 15, 1952. Surine tried unsuccessfully to resign before Hoover fired him. McCarthy would always contend that Surine resigned and was not dismissed. See copies of the relevant documents in box 3 of the Roberts Papers, especially copy, J. Edgar Hoover to A. S. Monroney, April 3, 1951. On Surine's later relationship with the bureau, see memorandum, SAC Baltimore to J. Edgar Hoover, March 24, 1950; memorandum, Scheidt to J. Edgar Hoover, April 30, 1950; memorandum, J. Edgar Hoover to Clyde Tolson and D. M. Ladd, May 1, 1950; memorandum, D. M. Ladd to J. Edgar Hoover, May 19, 1950; memoranda, Guy Hottel to J. Edgar Hoover, May 24, June 23, September 19, 20, 1950; memorandum, Baltimore office to J. Edgar Hoover, October 13, 1950; memorandum, A. H. Belmont to D. M. Ladd, July 24, 1951; memorandum, W. A. Branigan to A. H. Belmont, July 14, 1953; memorandum, J. Edgar Hoover to New York office, October 27, 1953, all in the Owen Lattimore Collection.

14. Earl Mazo, *Richard Nixon: A Political and Personal Portrait* (New York, 1959), pp. 140-41; Nellor (May 7, 1977), Anderson interview; Anderson, *Confessions of a Muckraker,* p. 185; Anderson and May, *McCarthy,* p. 191; Richard Nixon, *RN: The Memoirs of Richard Nixon* (New York, 1979), I, 168-69.

15. Anderson interview; Anderson, *Confessions of a Muckraker,* pp. 181-85, 208.

16. Nellor interview, May 7, 1977. Nellor had played an important role in the early stages of the Hiss case. See *New York Sun,* August 12, 1948. Later in 1950 Nellor went to work for columnist and broadcaster Fulton Lewis, Jr., while continuing to write for McCarthy. Nellor was instructed to serve as the link between the journalist and the senator. Lewis paid Nellor's salary; the speech writer's services cost Joe nothing. See Nellor interview, June 6, 1979.

17. Kersten interview, May 15, 1971; *Madison Capital Times,* April 12, 19, 1950. See Nixon, *RN,* I, 52, 69.

18. See box 13, folder 3, Thomas E. Coleman Papers.

19. Copy, Walter Harnischfager to Joe McCarthy, March 14, 24, 1950; copy, Tom Korb to Joe McCarthy, March 29, April 14, June 15, 1950, Korb Papers. Korb warned McCarthy, however, against accepting information from right-wing extremist Joe Kamp and Alfred Kohlberg. Harnischfager noted, "I trust that you will be able to keep the investigation on a high plane."

20. Lee interview; *Tydings Committee Hearings,* p. 1111. See the frank comments by Bridges in *Milwaukee Journal,* April 15, 1950.

21. Nellor interview, January 11, 1979; *Milwaukee Journal,* April 11, 1950; *Madison Capital Times,* October 11, 1952; *Minneapolis Morning Tribune,* April 15, 19, 1950. Judd said that he argued vainly for two hours with McCarthy not to make certain charges.

22. *Tydings Committee Hearings,* pp. 537, 581, 661-65, 1480-82, 1099; Kiermas, Waldrop, Nellor (January 11, June 6, 1979), Minetti (April 12, 1978) interviews. In mid-January, 1950 Fulton Lewis, Jr., ran into McCarthy and Whittaker Chambers in Nixon's office. Fulton Lewis, Jr., deposition, box 4, Roberts Papers.

23. Lee, Nellor (May 7, 1977, January 11, 1979), Surine (April 7, 1977), Waldrop, Edwards (November 17, 1976) interviews.

24. Ibid.

25. Nellor interview, May 7, 1977, January 11, 1979.

26. See *Tydings Committee Hearings,* pp. 1-32.

27. See *Congressional Record,* 81st Cong., 2d sess., January 24, 1950, p. 816; January 25, 1950, p. 905; January 26, 1950, p. 1006.

28. *Madison Capital Times,* March 8, 1950. The State Department created an ad hoc group, under the leadership of Adrian S. Fisher, the department's legal adviser, to research and reply to McCarthy's charges. In the spring of 1950, President Truman named Herb Maletz and unofficial adviser Max Lowenthal to help shape White House rebuttals to Joe's attacks. Fried, *Men Against McCarthy,* pp. 55, 59; Francis H. Thompson, *The Frustration of Politics: Truman, Congress, and the Loyalty Issue, 1945-1953* (Rutherford, New Jersey, 1979), p. 121. See the unsigned Lowenthal memorandum "The McCarthy Business," May 5, 1950, Internal Security file, Spingarn Papers.

29. *Washington Times-Herald,* March 9, 1950.

30. Telegram, Joe McCarthy to Tom Coleman, March 8, 1950, box 13, Coleman Papers.

31. *Tydings Committee Hearings,* pp. 33-72; *Madison Capital Times,* March 9, 1950.

32. *New York Times,* March 9, 1950; *Madison Capital Times,* March 11, 1950.

33. Ibid., March 10, 1950.

34. Copy, Emerson P. Schmidt to Joe McCarthy, March 7, 1950, box 13, Coleman Papers.

35. *Tydings Committee Hearings,* pp. 73-84. When Joe finally located the title of Hanson's book, after considerable fumbling ("I might say, Mr. Chairman, that this is my own filing system—"), he called it "Human Endeavor."

36. Ibid., pp. 85-87, 91.

37. It is uncertain exactly when Joe initially learned of Lattimore. See Owen Lattimore, *Ordeal by Slander* (Boston, 1950), pp. 4-5.

38. Acheson, *Present at the Creation*, p. 364.

39. *Tydings Committee Hearings*, pp. 92-108, 1876.

40. Ibid., pp. 109-75, 292.

41. See ibid., pp. 255-56. See Buckley and Bozell, *McCarthy and His Enemies*, pp. 145-46 concerning Joe's no doubt impromptu assertion that a Truman cabinet member had recommended Duran to the U.N.

42. *Tydings Committee Report*, pp. 30, 200-205. See "Congress," *Time*, LVIII (October 22, 1951), 24.

43. *Tydings Committee Report*, p. 94.

44. Ibid., p. 74.

45. *Tydings Committee Hearings*, pp. 171-75.

46. Ibid., pp. 176-214, 258; *Washington Post*, March 15, 1950.

47. *Madison Capital Times*, March 15, 17, 1950; *Washington Post*, March 15, 1950; *Washington Evening Star*, March 14, 1950.

48. *Madison Capital Times*, March 14, 1950; *The Daily Compass*, March 21, 1950.

49. See Fleming interview.

50. *Milwaukee Journal*, March 17, 1950; *Madison Capital Times*, March 18, 1950.

51. *Tydings Committee Hearings*, pp. 215-75.

52. *New York Times*, March 23, 1950.

53. *Madison Capital Times*, March 21, 1950.

54. *Tydings Committee Hearings*, pp. 277-92. Concerned about the sources of McCarthy's charges against Lattimore, FBI agents discovered that Don Surine possessed material taken from bureau investigative reports. Agents in Baltimore, where Surine had worked, were ordered not to have further dealings with the former agent. Surine assured FBI officials that he had not benefitted from a bureau leak. Memorandum, J.P. Mohr to J. Edgar Hoover, March 23, 1950; memorandum, SAC Baltimore to J. Edgar Hoover, March 24, 1950, Lattimore Collection. According to Lou Nichols, the bureau considered Lattimore "part and parcel" of the Communist party. The "top spy" charges, Nichols said later with a grin, were simply products of McCarthy's ego. Nichols interview. See Anderson, *Confessions of a Muckraker*, p. 199, and Abell (ed.), *Drew Pearson Diaries, 1949-1959*, p. 119.
p. 119.

55. *New York Times*, March 24, 1950; Kersten interview, May 15, 1971; Keeley, *The China Lobby Man*, pp. 1-3, 98-99; Buckley interview.

56. See *New York Times*, March 24, 25, 28, 29, 1950; *Congressional Record*, 81st Cong., 2d sess., March 27, 1950, pp. 4098-4107. There are several versions of

Taft's statement. See William S. White, *The Taft Story* (New York, 1954), p. 54; *Milwaukee Journal,* March 25, 1950; James T. Patterson, *Mr. Republican: A Biography of Robert A. Taft* (Boston, 1972), pp. 444-49. Taft often denied making any such comment. E.g., *Madison Capital Times,* June 6, 1950. *The New York Times* account of March 23, which was at least one source of the quotation, did not quote Taft directly.

57. *New York Times,* March 23, 1950; *Madison Capital Times,* March 23, 1950.

58. *New York Times,* March 24, 25, 27, 1950; *Tydings Committee Hearings,* p. 484.

59. *Madison Capital Times,* March 24, 1950.

60. *New York Times,* March 27, 1950; Anderson and May, *McCarthy,* p. 213; Anderson, *Confessions of a Muckraker,* p. 196; *Madison Capital Times,* March 27, 1950. Cf. McCarthy, *McCarthyism, The Fight for America,* p. 20.

61. *New York Times,* March 27, 1950. See Brien McMahon's defense of the Administration in ibid., March 26, 1950.

62. *Tydings Committee Hearings,* pp. 293-313; *Madison Capital Times,* March 27, 1950.

63. *Tydings Committee Hearings,* pp. 315-39.

64. *New York Times,* March 28, 1950.

65. Ibid., March 26, 28, 1950.

66. *Madison Capital Times,* March 27, 1950; *Tydings Committee Hearings,* pp. 295, 343-44.

67. Ibid., pp. 341-71.

68. *Washington Post,* March 29, 1950; Herbert Block, *The Herblock Book* (Boston, 1952), pp. 144-45; *Washington Star,* May 18, 1952; Buckley and Bozell, *McCarthy and His Enemies,* p. 62; editorial, *Milwaukee Sentinel,* February 3, 1954; Nellor interview, June 6, 1979. Joe sometimes blamed the Communist party for the term. "The McCarthy Issue," *U.S. News and World Report,* 31 (September 7, 1951), 31; *New York Times,* November 25, 1953.

69. Nellor (January 11, 1979), Kersten (May 15, 1971) interviews.

70. Ibid.

71. Nellor interview, January 11, 1979; *Milwaukee Journal,* April 1, 1950.

72. Ibid.; telegram, Joe McCarthy to Tom Coleman, March 30, 1950, Coleman Papers.

73. *Congressional Record,* 81st Cong., 2d sess., March 30, 1950, pp. 4375-93; *New York Times,* March 31, 1950; *Madison Capital Times,* March 30, 31, 1950; *Milwaukee Journal,* April 1, 1950.

74. *Madison Capital Times,* March 31, 1950. McCarthy turned over more than fifty documents on Lattimore to the FBI after the speech. Much of the material had arrived in the mail and was of little or no value; some of it had

come from anonymous informants. The bureau carefully checked each point in the March 30 speech and interviewed J. B. Matthews to make sure that the senator had given agents everything important he had on the matter. Memorandum, Clyde Tolson to J. Edgar Hoover, March 30, 1950; memorandum, Guy Hottel to J. Edgar Hoover, March 31, 1950; J. Edgar Hoover to SAC New York, April 20, 1950; memorandum, D. M. Ladd to J. Edgar Hoover, May 10, 1950; memorandum, J. Edgar Hoover to James M. McInerney, April 28, May 11, 1950; memorandum, C. E. Hennrich to A. H. Belmont, May 15, 1950, all in the Lattimore Collection. For a summary and analysis of the materials Joe submitted to the bureau, see memorandum, C. E. Hennrich to A. H. Belmont, June 27, 1950, ibid.

75. *New York Times,* March 31, 1950. The State Department had just named former G.O.P. Senator John Sherman Cooper a consultant to Acheson and was wooing Vandenberg in the hope of reinvigorating bipartisanship. Ibid., March 29, 30, 1950.
76. *Madison Capital Times,* April 1, 1950.
77. *Milwaukee Journal,* April 2, 1950.
78. *New York Times,* March 31, 1950.
79. *Madison Capital Times,* April 1, 3, 1950.
80. Ibid., March 29, April 3, 4, 1950. After his March 30 speech, Joe turned over to the FBI information he and his staff had collected on Lattimore. A few days later Tydings and McCarthy exchanged heated letters about the committee's desire to obtain the documents. Joe defied the committee, pleading his desire to protect his sources, and ignored a deadline set by Tydings. The committee later obtained access through the Justice Department to certain items it requested. Ibid., March 31, April 5, 1950; *Tydings Committee Hearings,* pp. 1895-96
81. Ibid., pp. 373-416.
82. *Madison Capital Times,* April 1, 1950; Lattimore, *Ordeal by Slander,* pp. 1-59.
83. *Madison Capital Times,* April 3, 1950.
84. Ibid., April 6, 1950.
85. Lattimore, *Ordeal by Slander,* pp. 59-60.
86. On Kohlberg, see *Madison Capital Times,* April 8, 1950; *Milwaukee Journal,* April 11, 1950. Kohlberg told an audience in Larchmont, New York, "It took a man with the guts and dumbness of Senator McCarthy to start this investigation. Men in the Senate who know more than McCarthy remain silent because they know they will be smeared."
87. The document had come from Kohlberg and had been used as early as 1948 in an article in *China Monthly.* See *Milwaukee Journal,* April 15, 1950; Lattimore, *Ordeal by Slander,* p. 97.

88. See ibid., p. 94; *Madison Capital Times,* April 8, 1950; *Tydings Committee Hearings,* pp. 417-86. Sen. Styles Bridges told a Milwaukee audience, "I don't know if Owen Lattimore is a Communist or not. But when it takes 14 typewritten pages to summarize the FBI report on him—I say that man is no man to represent my country." *Milwaukee Journal,* April 15, 1950.

89. *Madison Capital Times,* April 6, 7, 1950.

90. *Milwaukee Journal,* April 9, 1950; *Madison Capital Times,* April 29, 1950.

91. Ibid., April 10, 11, 1950; Millard Tydings, "Memorandum for the President," April 12, 1950, OF 419-K, Truman Papers.

92. *Madison Capital Times,* April 13, 26, 27, 1950. In return, Joe harshly denounced Evjue and Cedric Parker. *Chicago Tribune,* April 27, 28, 1950. See copy, William T. Evjue to Esther Van Wagoner Tufty, August 22, 1950, box 138, Evjue Papers. Evjue was feeding anti-McCarthy information to Abe Fortas and newspapers across the country. See copy, William T. Evjue to Abe Fortas, April 3, 1950, ibid.; *Madison Capital Times,* April 4, 6, 10, 1950; *Baltimore Sun,* April 12, 1950; *Tydings Committee Hearings,* p. 802.

93. See ibid., pp. 487-88, 520-21; Packer, *Ex-Communist Witnesses,* pp. 121-24. See also Anderson, *Confessions of a Muckraker,* pp. 201-02.

94. *Tydings Committee Hearings,* pp. 487-558; *Madison Capital Times,* April 20, 1950. Kersten alerted the FBI to Budenz's knowledge of Lattimore as soon as he learned of it. Agents grilled Budenz so intensely that when Kersten later visited him, he and his wife were in tears from the pressure. Kersten interview, May 15, 1971. Jean Kerr tried unsuccessfully to bolster Budenz's credibility with J. Edgar Hoover. Memorandum, J. Edgar Hoover to Clyde Tolson and D. M. Ladd, May 1, 1950, Lattimore Collection. The bureau's Lou Nichols later judged Budenz a basically sound witness but acknowledged that he went too far and was too often after headlines. Nichols interview.

95. *Tydings Committee Hearings,* pp. 558-70.

96. A copy of the speech is in the Korb Papers. See *Madison Capital Times,* April 21, 1950.

97. Ibid., April 24, 1950; *Milwaukee Journal,* April 30, 1950.

98. Ibid.; *Madison Capital Times,* May 1, 1950.

99. See "Report of Preliminary Investigation of Senator William Benton's Charges against Joseph McCarthy Relating to Senate Resolution 187," pp. 13-14.

100. *Madison Capital Times,* April 25, 1950; Lattimore, *Ordeal by Slander,* pp. 132-35.

101. *Tydings Committee Hearings,* pp. 571-630.

102. *Madison Capital Times,* April 26, 28, 1950. In 1953, with Republicans in power, Hanson was fired by Harold Stassen.

103. *Tydings Committee Hearings,* pp. 631-60.
104. Ibid., pp. 660-67, 1479-82; *Madison Capital Times,* April 18, 26, May 1, 1950; copy, "Confidential, Preliminary Report," box 5, Roberts Papers. Huber had gone to the FBI before contacting Kerley. Kerley then introduced Huber to McCarthy and Robert Morris at J. B. Matthews's New York penthouse on April 14. Kerley, Huber, McCarthy, and Matthews met again ten days later. The following morning, Joe traveled to Washington with the perspective witness. Huber actually knew virtually nothing about Lattimore; he told FBI agents that it would not be necessary for him to spend more than five minutes on a witness stand. Bureau reports make it clear that Huber was at least emotionally unstable. See memoranda, Scheidt to J. Edgar Hoover, May 3, 4, 1950; memoranda, J. Edgar Hoover to the Attorney General, May 3, 11, 1950, in the Lattimore Collection.
105. *Tydings Committee Hearings,* pp. 669-707. Browder also cleared Kenyon, Hanson, Vincent, and Service of having direct or indirect associations with the Communist Party.
106. Ibid., pp. 709-35.
107. *Congressional Record,* 81st Cong., 2d sess., May 3, 1950, p. 6259; *Madison Capital Times,* April 27, 1950.
108. *Tydings Committee Hearings,* pp. 737-96.
109. Ibid., pp. 799-921. See Lattimore, *Ordeal by Slander,* pp. 189-90.
110. *Madison Capital Times,* May 1, 1950.
111. *New York Times,* May 19, 1950.
112. *Minneapolis Tribune,* April 30, 1950; "The Quarter's Polls," *Public Opinion Quarterly,* 14 (Fall, 1950), 596.
113. *Milwaukee Journal,* May 4, 1950.
114. *Madison Capital Times,* May 4, 1950; New York Times, May 5, 1950.
115. A copy of the speech is in the Korb Papers. In an attached letter, Jean Kerr wrote, "The whole office worked on it until 4 this morning." See *Chicago Tribune,* May 7, 1950.

CHAPTER 13

1. Delaney, Richard Gaillard, Mrs. Richard Gaillard, Kiermas, Surine (April 7, 1977), Nellor (May 7, 1977) interviews. See Nixon, *RN,* I, 183.
2. See Kersten (May 15, 1971), Surine (April 7, 1977) interviews.
3. Bayley, *Joe McCarthy and the Press,* pp. 67-68. About this same time McCarthy complained that Associated Press writer Marvin Arrowsmith was hostile

toward him and was inserting his prejudice into his widely read dispatches. A case could be made to sustain the charge. Charles A. Hazen of the *Shreveport, Louisiana Times* soon made a formal complaint against the A.P.'s Washington Bureau, charging "left-wing bias" in stories about McCarthy. Hazen's 66-page statement was considered and dismissed by a committee of the A.P. Managing Editors Association. "The AP has yet to detect one instance of willful bias in its news report." See *New York Post,* September 20, 1951; Robert Fleming memorandum, August 8, 1951, box 3, Fleming Papers.

4. Anderson interview; Anderson, *Confessions of a Muckraker,* p. 194.

5. *Janesville Gazette,* May 8, 1950. For a chronological list of McCarthy's appearances at this time, see box 4 of the Fleming Papers.

6. See *Hennings Committee Report,* pp. 19-26; deposition, "Joseph R. McCarthy vs. The Post-Standard Company . . . ," pp. 33-34, 74-76, 149-51; Surine deposition, box 4, Roberts Papers. It is uncertain if the funds raised by Tom Coleman went into the special account. See Joe McCarthy to Tom Coleman, June 28, 1950, Coleman Papers.

7. Lee, Surine (April 7, June 8, 1977), Nellor (June 6, 1979), Van Susteren (February 5, 1977) interviews. The alleged would-be assassin was brought before the McCarthy subcommittee in June, 1953 and took the Fifth Amendment repeatedly. U.S. Senate, Permanent Subcommittee on Investigations, *Communist Party Activities, Western Pennsylvania, Hearing,* 83d Cong., 1st sess., June 18, 1953, passim. As early as May 1950 Surine was complaining to FBI agents that his telephone was tapped and his mail tampered with. He suspected the State Department. Memorandum, Guy Hottel to J. Edgar Hoover, May 24, 1950, Lattimore Collection.

8. Anderson, *Outsider in the Senate,* pp. 101-105.

9. See *Tydings Committee Hearings,* pp. 1239-40. FBI officials searched diligently and unsuccessfully for the source of the "100-percent" quotation. Memorandum, D.M. Ladd to J. Edgar Hoover, March 31, 1950, Lattimore Collection.

10. *Madison Capital Times,* May 4, 1950.

11. *Tydings Committee Hearings,* pp. 923-67, 2501. Bielaski's O.S.S. superior, who received the documents taken from the *Amerasia* office, testified that he had no knowledge of an "A-bomb" document. Ibid., pp. 1194-95. Bielaski had played a major role in keeping the *Amerasia* case alive. He admitted providing materials for Republican Congressman George A. Dondero of Michigan, a persistent critic of the case's handling. Bielaski's sister was ultraconservative Mrs. Ruth Shipley, director of the State Department's Passport Office in the early 1950s. See Caute, *The Great Fear,* p. 246.

12. *Tydings Committee Hearings,* pp. 967-99, 1165-70, 1183-84. Corroborative

testimony was presented on May 26 by attorney Robert M. Hitchcock, who had worked with McInerney on the case. He noted that many of the documents in question had actually been declassified while still marked "classified." See ibid., pp. 1101-51.

13. Ibid., pp. 1053-74.
14. "Significantly, on the last day Larsen testified he stated, in the presence of a member of the subcommittee staff, that Levine telephoned him on the night before his appearance before us as a witness suggesting that he, Larsen, 'go easy on the *Plain Talk* article.' At the same time, Levine suggested that he would effect a lucrative arrangement on Larsen's behalf for the writing of some syndicated articles on the Far East." *Tydings Committee Report,* p. 148. Levine and his associate Ralph de Toledano filed strong protests against Larsen's testimony and the committee's interpretation of it. Ralph de Toledano to Millard Tydings, July 16, 1950, box 1108, and Don Levine to Theodore F. Green, August 12, 1950, box 1105, Green Papers. Cf. Larsen's "draft" and the article published in *Plain Talk, Tydings Committee Hearings,* pp. 1739-53, 2492-2501.
15. Ibid., pp. 1075-1164.
16. *Janesville Gazette,* May 8, 1950; *Madison Capital Times,* May 15, 22, 26, 31, 1950.
17. Copy, memorandum, William Benton to John Howe, February 21, 1955, box 4, Benton Papers; *Congressional Record,* 81st Cong., 2d sess., May 9, 1950, p. 6696, May 11, 1950, pp. 6969-75; *Madison Capital Times,* May 18, 26, 27, 1950.
18. Ibid., May 16, 27, 1950.
19. Ibid., May 16, 1950.
20. *New York Times,* June 2, 1950; Margaret Chase Smith, *Declaration of Conscience* (New York, 1972), pp. 3-21, 112; Kiermas interview. Right-wing newspapers played down the importance of the declaration. The *Wisconsin State Journal* observed in bold face type that the statement "Doesn't Mention McCarthy." Of course, Senate rules did not permit mention of Joe's name in the attack. See Evjue's editorial "Spotting Propanganda" in the *Madison Capital Times,* June 3, 1950.
21. Ibid., June 6, 1950. Liberal Republican Governors Earl Warren of California and James Duff of Pennsylvania also declared against McCarthy. Thomas Dewey, outgoing Governor of New York, was noncommital. Ibid., June 19, 1950.
22. *New York Times,* June 2, 1950.
23. *Madison Capital Times,* June 6, 1950.
24. Ibid., June 7, 1950; *New York Times,* June 18, 1950.
25. See Stewart Alsop, "The Artful Dodger," in *Madison Capital Times,* June 14,

1950. Of course, McCarthy may have obtained the rest of the more than 100-page report from which his excerpt was taken. He would never reveal the names of those he had in mind, however.

26. A copy of the speech is in the Korb Papers. See *Milwaukee Journal,* June 9, 1950; *Madison Capital Times,* June 9, 1950.

27. *New York Times,* June 18, 1950.

28. *Tydings Committee Hearings,* pp. 1229-56. Robert Morris asked Peurifoy if he knew that John Service had passed secret documents to "Mr. Gatley," a Soviet secret agent. Peurifoy did not, and the identity of this person was never revealed. Morris probably meant Mark Gayn. See ibid., p. 1246; Buckley and Bozell, *McCarthy and His Enemies,* p. 151.

29. *Madison Capital Times,* June 21, 1950. On committee leaks, see *Tydings Committee Hearings,* pp. 1196-1203, 1211, 1241, 1247.

30. Ibid., pp. 1257-1349; *Tydings Committee Report,* pp. 75-76, 91-92. When Philip Jaffe appeared before the committee he pled the Fifth Amendment concerning everything but his name and address. *Tydings Committee Hearings,* pp. 1213-27. He was cited for contempt of Congress. In an executive session, Chief Counsel Morgan said that he had "no doubt" about Jaffe being a Communist and an espionage agent, and Tydings said that he was inclined to agree. Ibid., pp. 1459-60. Cf. *Tydings Committee Report,* p. 103. See Kahn, *The China Hands,* pp. 161-62; Philip J. Jaffe, *The Amerasia Case, From 1945 to the Present* (New York, 1979), pp. 1, 18-38.

31. *Madison Capital Times,* June 22, 1950. For examples of Service's more awkward testimony about his past, see *Tydings Committee Hearings,* pp. 1327-34, 1372-73, 1439-42, 1445-52.

32. Ibid., pp. 1391-1422. Cf. *Tydings Committee Report,* pp. 89-90.

33. *Ashland Daily Press,* August 1, 1950. Service was reinstated to duty on August 13, 1945, after the grand jury had voted against indictment. Acheson took the oath of office as Under Secretary of State on August 27. In September Service was sent to Tokyo to work in General MacArthur's occupation headquarters.

34. *The Gallup Poll,* II, 911-12; *Minneapolis Tribune,* July 16, 1950. The Minnesotans polled voted 46.5 percent to 40 percent, however, to support the proposition that McCarthy had not proved there were a number of Communists or Communist sympathizers in the State Department.

35. *Tydings Committee Report,* p. 167; *Christian Science Monitor,* July 19, 1950.

36. See *Tydings Committee Report,* pp. 168-89; memorandum, January 1-6, 1951, box 3, Fleming Papers; "Memorandum of Pros and Cons on the proposal to establish a Commission on Internal Security and Individual Rights," June 26, 1950, "Memorandum for the Files," June 23, 1950, box 31, Spingarn Papers. In May, Tydings had urged the appointment of a commission to study McCarthy's

81 cases. The White House floated the idea and dropped it after Republicans objected. See Spingarn memorandum, May 22, 1950, ibid.; *Madison Capital Times,* June 5, 7, 1950. The Tydings Committee's evaluation of the 81 names was reconfirmed by the State Department during the Eisenhower Administration. See ibid., January 17, 1955.

37. See Demaris, *The Director,* pp. 118-19; *Tydings Committee Report,* pp. 166-67; *Congressional Record,* 81st Cong., 2d sess., July 20, 1950, p. 10712. The report's author, Edward P. Morgan, was also an ex-FBI agent. Morgan later told Robert Fleming that before he was named chief counsel, Don Surine had come to him asking for "just one case, because we're in the middle of this thing now without a single case." Shortly after Morgan's appointment, McCarthy called to say, "Ed, if I could have named the counsel myself, I'd have chosen you." Later, McCarthy's tune changed, and he spread stories around Washington that cost Morgan's law firm clients. He also sent agents to harrass clients. Memorandum, January 1-6, 1951, box 3, Fleming Papers; Morgan, Nellor (June 6, 1979) interviews.

38. Ibid.; U.S. Senate, Committee on Foreign Relations, *State Department Employee Loyalty Investigation, Individual Views,* 81st Cong., 2d sess., July 20, 1950. Thirty-five pages of the transcript of the committee's final session, held on June 28, were somehow omitted from the published hearings. Lodge angrily reported this to the Senate, alleging deliberate fraud. Brien McMahon contended that the omission was a mistake. In any case, the pages were subsequently published by the committee and contained nothing more important than a belated and irrelevant charge by Robert Morris against Theodore Geiger, assistant to Marshall Plan administrator Paul Hoffman. "He is doing work that is quasi-State Department in character," Morris said. "I have gone and gotten some witnesses together who will testify that he was a member of the same Communist party unit as they were ..." Weary, and disgusted with Morris, Tydings snapped, "Turn it over to the FBI or do something with it." McCarthy and his allies would henceforth charge an attempted cover-up and refer to "Part 3" of the Tydings Committee report. In 1978 McCarthy's widow, in an interview with the author, was still contending that Democrats had tried to suppress the 35 pages. The senator himself did not pursue the Geiger case. See Buckley and Bozell, *McCarthy and His Enemies,* pp. 169-71; U.S. Senate, Committee on Rules and Administration, *Maryland Senatorial Election of 1950, Hearings,* 82d Cong., 1st sess., 1951, pp. 506-7, 1105, 1122 (hereafter cited as *Maryland Hearings*); Minetti interview, April 10, 1978.

39. *New York Times,* July 18, 1950.

40. *Madison Capital Times,* July 18, 1950. Joe, however, urged Republicans not to block the report's filing. "It will perform a valuable function in that a reading

of it by any fair-minded person will indicate the extent to which the subcommittee has gone to protect Communists in Government, and to vilify those
who attempt to expose such Communists." *New York Times,* July 18, 1950.

41. *Madison Capital Times,* July 18, 24, 1950.

42. *Christian Science Monitor,* July 21, 1950.

43. See Smith, *Declaration of Conscience,* p. 27; Reedy interview.

44. See memorandum, January 1-6, 1951, box 3, Fleming Papers.

45. See Buckley and Bozell, *McCarthy and His Enemies,* p. 49; *Madison Capital
    Times,* July 21, 1950. On August 4, self-assured, Joe charged Tydings with
    fraud and urged the Senate and the press to force the Maryland senator to play
    the recording. *Congressional Record,* 81st Cong., 2d sess., August 4, 1950, pp.
    11794-95. Tydings did not reply. More than a year later, McCarthy foe William
    Benton played the record at a public Senate hearing, and it was correctly
    identified. *Madison Capital Times,* September 28, 1951. Tydings stated in 1952
    that he had never claimed to possess a recording of McCarthy at Wheeling.
    This was technically correct. Ibid., September 4, 1952.

46. *Congressional Record,* 81st Cong., 2d sess., July 20, 1950, pp. 10686-89,
    10691-10717; *New York Times,* July 21, 1950. Later, Tydings publicly offered
    a $25,000 reward to anyone, including McCarthy, who could prove that there
    were either 205 or 57 card-carrying Communists in the State Department in
    early 1950. Millard E. Tydings, "McCarthyism: How It All Began," *The Re-
    porter,* 7 (August 19, 1952), 15.

47. *Congressional Record,* 81st Cong., 2d sess., July 21, 1950, pp. 10773-92,
    10798-10803; *New York Times,* July 22, 1950. Jenner was referring to
    Davies's best-selling *Mission to Moscow,* published in 1942. McCarthy enjoyed
    incensing Jenner, whose reputation for intellectual prowess was very modest.
    "I got old Bill wound up today," he would say with a laugh. Nellor interview,
    June 6, 1979.

48. Joseph and Stewart Alsop, "Why Has Washington Gone Crazy?" *Saturday
    Evening Post,* 223 (July 29, 1950), 20. This piece, sharply critical of McCarthy,
    prompted Joe to assert that it followed the Communist party line "almost 100
    percent." *Madison Capital Times,* August 9, 1950.

49. McCarthy. *McCarthyism, The Fight for America,* p. 74.

50. See *Congressional Record,* 81st Cong., 2d sess., July 25, 1950, pp. 10912-58;
    McCarthy, *McCarthyism, The Fight for America,* pp. 12-13, 17, 29; Buckley
    and Bozell, *McCarthy and His Enemies,* pp. 202-205, 274.

51. The State Department released the instructions issued in 1946 concerning the
    files. *New York Times,* July 13, 1950. Cf. the affidavit reproduced in Mc-
    Carthy, *McCarthyism, The Fight for America,* pp. 71-72. See *Tydings
    Committee Report,* pp. 171-72.

52. See Buckley and Bozell, *McCarthy and His Enemies,* pp. 351-59; McCarthy, *McCarthyism, The Fight for America,* p. 74; *New York Times,* July 13, 1950; *Tydings Committee Hearings,* pp. 1251-52.

53. McCarthy, *McCarthyism, The Fight for America,* p. 74. Several right-wingers, no doubt with Hoover's assistance, correctly observed that the director never said that the materials in the relevant State Department files were complete in their entirety. The director could only account for the bureau's own material. In light of McCarthy's contentions about the files, however, the point is irrelevant. See *Maryland Hearings,* pp. 1067-75.

54. *Madison Capital Times,* July 31, 1950. On May 1, 1950 the Wisconsin American Legion staged a nationally publicized "day under Communism" in the tiny city of Mosinee. It featured a mock coup, a "takeover" of the local newspaper, propaganda leaflets, the "arrest" of the mayor, and the "liquidation" of the police chief. Two ex-Communists were on hand to add authenticity. See Howard R. Kleuter and James J. Lorence, *Woodlot and Ballot Box, Marathon County in the Twentieth Century* (Wausau, Wisconsin, 1977), pp. 364-66.

CHAPTER 14

1. Nellor interview, June 6, 1979; Anderson and May, *McCarthy,* pp. 8-9; *Madison Capital Times,* August 2, 1950, September 29, 1951.

2. Ibid., October 19, 24, 25, November 1, 1950.

3. See ibid., June 30, July 7, 10, August 24, 29, 30, 1950; *Milwaukee Journal,* July 6, August 31, 1950, July 2, 1952. Kersten failed to file state income tax returns for 1943, 1944, and 1945. McKinnon, his law partner and brother-in-law, did not file federal or state returns from 1936 to 1945. Both men paid up and continued to practice law. See ibid., January 28, 1947; *Madison Capital Times,* October 24, 1947; W. Wade Boardman to Edward J. Dempsey, et al., July 9, 1948, Dempsey Papers. Howard McCarthy paid an additional $203.05 plus $18.05 interest for the years 1946-47. Tim's estate was assessed $68.08 plus $40.42 in interest in 1946. *Milwaukee Journal,* July 6, 1950.

4. Ibid., January 22, 1951; *Madison Capital Times,* March 8, 1951. In 1950 McCarthy paid $1,175.78 in state income taxes on a total income of $22,025. *Milwaukee Journal,* June 8, 1951.

5. Surine (April 7, May 12, 1977), Kersten (May 15, 1971), Cocke, Nellor (May 7, 1977) interviews; *Duluth News-Tribune,* February 18, 1951; deposition, "Joseph R. McCarthy vs. The Post-Standard Company . . . ," pp. 76-79, 157.

6. Nellor (May 7, 1977, January 11, June 6, 1979), Surine (May 13, 1977), Cocke, Nichols interviews; deposition of Donald A. Surine, box 4, Roberts Papers.

McCarthy's office files were always in near total disarray, in part because of the staggering quantity of materials arriving each day, but also because of Joe's carelessness and frequent absence from his office. Nellor (May 7, 1977, June 6, 1979), William F. Buckley, Jr., Edwards (November 17, 1976) interviews. Joe once confessed, "I wouldn't know where to start in the files." Deposition, "Joseph R. McCarthy vs. The Post-Standard Company . . . ," p. 131.

7. Robert Fleming memorandum of August 8, 1951, box 3, Fleming Papers; copy, "Confidential Report Dated February 25, 1951," box 5, Roberts Papers; Edwards (November 17, 1976), Kiermas, Fleming, Nellor (June 6, 1979) interviews; *Hennings Committee Report,* pp. 20-26.

8. Nellor (May 7, 1977, June 6, 1979), Lee, Kiermas, Van Susteren (November 25, 1975), Richard Gaillard, Korb (November 8, 1975) interviews; Charles J. V. Murphy, "Texas Business and McCarthy," *Fortune,* 49 (May, 1954), 100-1, 208, 211-12, 214, 216; *Madison Capital Times,* September 25, 1950. After the 1952 elections, Jean Kerr, Victor Johnston, and Robert E. Lee were employed briefly by Texas billionaire H. L. Hunt to help prepare "Facts Forum," a right-wing network radio program. Hunt's penury, Jean said later, probably prevented him from making any significant financial contributions to McCarthy. Jean despised the Texan and resigned without taking a cent in salary. See Henry Hurt III, *Texas Rich, The Hunt Dynasty from the Early Oil Days through the Silver Crash* (New York, 1981), pp. 157-58; Minetti interview, April 12, 1978.

9. For a fairly complete list, see box 4, Fleming Papers. See also *Portland Oregonian,* August 20, 1951; *Milwaukee Journal,* August 31, October 26, 1950; deposition, "Joseph R. McCarthy vs. The Post-Standard Company . . . , p. 58. Much was made of an analysis published by the *Congressional Quarterly* in April 1951 revealing that McCarthy had the second worst attendance record in the Senate on 20 key votes. Twelve of the 20, however, were taken while Joe was in the hospital recovering from a sinus operation. *Milwaukee Journal,* April 17, 1951; *Madison Capital Times,* May 14, 1951.

10. *Milwaukee Journal,* March 2, 1951; *Madison Capital Times,* July 24, 1952; Van Susteren (January 15, 1976, February 5, 1977), Kiermas, Nellor (May 7, 1977), Surine (April 7, 1977), Delaney, Richard Gaillard, Brown interviews. On speaking fees, see *Milwaukee Journal,* June 8, 1951. Cf. Robert Fleming memorandum of September 17, 1951, box 3, Fleming Papers.

11. Fleming, Bayley (July 7, 1977), Henderson interviews; *Madison Capital Times,* September 17, 1951.

12. Osman interview. Interestingly, Joe left meetings hurriedly, often pretending to be summoned by a long-distance telephone call. He would sometimes fight his way out of a crowd.

13. Copy, "Speech of Senator Joe McCarthy," April 23, 1951, Racine Public Library; *Janesville Gazette,* April 9, 1951.
14. *Manawa Advocate,* June 21, 1951.
15. Henderson, Fleming interviews; *Madison Capital Times,* September 17, 1951.
16. *Wausau Daily Record-Herald,* October 6, 1950.
17. See box 3, Philipp Papers. The booklet also contained the documents and photograph described in McCarthy's Wausau speech (fn 16).
18. Henderson, Kiermas, Nellor (May 7, 1977) interviews; deposition, "Joseph R. McCarthy vs. The Post-Standard Company . . . ," pp. 72-73.
19. Copy, "Speech of Senator Joe McCarthy," April 23, 1951, Racine Public Library. See the full text of a typical McCarthy speech of this period in *Kenosha Evening News,* October 20, 1950.
20. See editorial, *Madison Capital Times,* November 29, 1950.
21. See O'Brien, "Senator Joseph McCarthy and Wisconsin," pp. 293-310; *Twin Rivers [Wisconsin] Reporter,* November 3, 1950.
22. See the editorial in *Madison Capital Times,* December 4, 1950; McCarthy form letter of August 3, 1950, box 77, Evjue Papers; *Eau Claire Leader,* September 5, 1951; *Madison Capital Times,* March 17, 1952; editorial, *Chicago Sun-Times,* June 30, 1952.
23. Bayley (July 7, 1977), Fleming, Henderson interviews; *Madison Capital Times,* September 17, 1951.
24. See box 1108, Green Papers.
25. *New York Times,* July 3, 6, 7, 14, 15, 16, September 9, 1950.
26. Ibid., July 3, 1950. For an excellent analysis of the origins of American involvement in the war, see John W. Spanier, *The Truman-MacArthur Controversy and the Korean War* (New York, 1965), pp. 15-64. See also Glenn D. Paige, *The Korean Descision: June 24-30, 1950* (New York, 1968).
27. *New York Times,* July 7, 1950; copy, Joe McCarthy to the President, July 12, 1950, Korb Papers.
28. *Milwaukee Journal,* October 6, 1950; *Wausau Daily Record-Herald,* October 6, 1950; *Manawa Advocate,* June 21, 1951.
29. See Harper, *The Politics of Loyalty,* pp. 144-62; William R. Tanner and Robert Griffith, "Legislative Politics and 'McCarthyism': The Internal Security Act of 1950," in Griffith and Theoharis (eds.), *The Specter,* pp. 174-89; Milton R. Konvitz, *Expanding Liberties, Freedom's Gains in Postwar America* (New York, 1966), pp. 134-67; Paul H. Douglas, *In the Fullness of Time, The Memoirs of Paul H. Douglas* (New York, 1971), pp. 306-9; Hubert Humphrey to Estes Kefauver, September 19, 1950, Legislation, 81st Congress, Kefauver Papers; *Congressional Record,* 81st Cong., 2d sess., September 8, 1950, p. 14439, September 12, 1950, p. 14628, September 20, 1950, p. 15261, Sep-

tember 23, 1950, p. 15726. When the Administration asked J. Edgar Hoover to help defeat the McCarran bill, the director chose to remain silent. See memorandum, Stephen Spingarn to J. Edgar Hoover, August 22, 1950, Internal Security folder, Spingarn Papers.

30. *Milwaukee Journal,* October 31, 1950.

31. Mazo, *Richard Nixon,* pp. 73-83; Fried, *Men Against McCarthy,* p. 110. Cf. Bullock, "'Rabbits and Radicals,' Richard Nixon's 1946 Campaign Against Jerry Voorhis," p. 349.

32. For a good survey of the contests, see Fried, *Men Against McCarthy,* pp. 95-121.

33. See "Address in Kiel Auditorium, St. Louis," November 4, 1950, *Truman Papers, 1950,* pp. 697-703.

34. *Congressional Record,* 81st Cong., 2d sess., September 23, 1950, p. A6901.

35. *Milwaukee Journal,* October 22, 1950; Nellor to the author, July 19, 1979. For a supreme example of Nellor's skill with words, see "Rep. Broyhill Rebuts Attack by Muskie," *Washington Star,* September 18, 1970.

36. *Milwaukee Journal,* October 31, 1950.

37. Ibid., August 31, October 6, November 10, 1950; *Madison Capital Times,* September 30, November 1, 1950.

38. Kiermas, Nellor (June 6, 1979) interviews.

39. Nellor interview, June 6, 1979; *Maryland Hearings,* pp. 182-90, 425, 536-37, 1103-4.

40. See ibid., pp. 277, 285, 291-92; U.S. Congress, Senate, 82d Cong., 1st sess., Committee on Rules and Administration, *Maryland Senatorial Election of 1950,* 1951, p. 44 (hereafter cited as *Maryland Report*).

41. See *Maryland Hearings,* pp. 220, 288-98, 307, 1105.

42. See ibid., pp. 33, 232-33, 253, 257, 310-11, 327, 379, 431-32, 499-504, 1103-5, 1112-13, 1177; Murphy, "Texas Business and McCarthy," p. 211; copy, "Address by Senator Joseph R. McCarthy before the Republican Club of the District of Columbia," October 30, 1950, Tydings Papers.

43. *Maryland Hearings,* pp. 33-36, 220-21, 257, 325, 471-78, 500, 653-54, 844-45, 1103-28; Kiermas interview; *Maryland Report,* p. 32.

44. *Maryland Hearings,* pp. 246-49, 328, 369-87, 399-404, 425-37, 439-49, 1108-14.

45. Ibid., pp. 222-23, 230-31, 471-82, 485-88, 541-79, 650-55, 844-45, 1116; Nellor interview, June 6, 1979.

46. *Maryland Hearings,* pp. 20-27, 256, 579-93, Nellor interview, June 6, 1979. In response to strenuous objections by Tydings, the network permitted the senator to use one Lewis program for rebuttal. A 3- to 4-minute "technical error" marred the first broadcast, and Tydings was given a second opportunity.

47. *Baltimore American,* November 5, 1950; *Maryland Hearings,* pp. 15-16, 505-15.
48. Ibid., pp. 302-6.
49. A copy of the tabloid is in box 4, Fleming Papers. Tydings included in his denials the charge that he had sponsored a Lattimore speech. He and his wife had once loaned their names to a fund-raising campaign for Bryn Mawr College, he explained, without knowing that Lattimore was a participant. See *Maryland Hearings,* pp. 1060, 1063.
50. Ibid., pp. 371, 382, 386-98.
51. Ibid., pp. 13, 343-45, 353, 357, 363, 533.
52. Ibid., pp. 1107-08, 1121-25.
53. *Milwaukee Journal,* February 9, 1951; *Madison Capital Times,* May 14, 1951; deposition, "Joseph R. McCarthy vs. The Post-Standard Company . . . ," pp. 40-43; "The McCarthy Issue . . . Pro and Con," *U.S. News and World Report,* 31 (September, 1951), 31. See also *Maryland Report,* pp. 24-25, 45-46. When up for reelection in 1956, Senator Butler said, "I freely admit that this picture was in bad taste and a mistake of judgment." *Milwaukee Journal,* October 16, 1956.
54. *Maryland Hearings,* p. 19; Kiermas interview.
55. On November 6 Jean Kerr had Ewell Moore give Fedder $115 to pay those who completed some 11,000 postcards. Moore was accompanied to Baltimore by McCarthy staff members George Greeley and Mary Driscoll. Munday paid Fedder in full on December 26, in return asking for Butler's letter of guaranty. The total cost of Fedder's services was $18,099.59.
56. This account of Fedder's "ride" is based on an analysis of testimony appearing throughout the *Maryland Hearings* and interviews with Kiermas and Nellor (June 6, 1979). Surine declined to discuss the incident in an interview.
57. *Washington Post,* November 10, 1950.
58. See Fried, *Men Against McCarthy,* pp. 109-21; William Howard Moore, *The Kefauver Committee and the Politics of Crime, 1950-1952* (Columbia, Missouri, 1974), pp. 149-58; Robert Fleming in *Milwaukee Journal,* November 10, 1950; Miles McMillin in *Madison Capital Times,* November 11, 1950; Donald J. Kemper, *Decade of Fear, Senator Hennings and Civil Liberties* (Columbia, Missouri, 1965), pp. 28-29; Daniel James, "Did the GOP Win?" *New Leader,* XXXIII (November 20, 1950), 2-3; Gus Tyler, "The Mid-Term Paradox," *New Republic,* CXXIII (November 27, 1950), 14-15.
59. See the interview with Millard Tydings in *U.S. News and World Report,* 29 (November 17, 1950), 33; *Maryland Hearings,* pp. 238, 243, 449-57, 460-64, 736, 770, 822-42; Fried, *Men Against McCarthy,* pp. 137-39. Roman Catholics, about 20 percent of Maryland's population, played no exceptional role in

Tydings' defeat, despite fears by liberals that McCarthy had heavily influenced their votes. See Donald F. Crosby, *God, Church, and Flag: Senator Joseph R. McCarthy and the Catholic Church, 1950-1957* (Chapel Hill, 1978), pp. 70-74; Harry W. Kirwin, *The Inevitable Success: Herbert R. O'Conor* (Westminster, Maryland, 1962), pp. 508-11.

60. See Fried, *Men Against McCarthy,* p. 121.
61. See ibid., pp. 96-101, 111, 118-19; *New York Times,* January 7, 1951.
62. *Madison Capital Times,* June 4, August 7, 1951; Joe McCarthy to Tom Korb, January 8, 1951, Korb Papers.
63. Nellor (May 7, 1977, June 6, 1979), Mrs. Regina Nellor interviews; Ed Nellor to the author, May 26, 1977.

CHAPTER 15

1. See Fried, *Men Against McCarthy,* pp. 156-58; Presidential News Conference of December 19, 1950, *Truman Papers, 1950,* p. 751; Acheson, *Present at the Creation,* p. 631; Koskoff, *Joseph P. Kennedy,* pp. 353-57, 367; The Gallup Poll, II, 953-54, 961. These polls consistently reveal the public's painful ignorance of political affairs. In late 1950 and during 1951, 34 percent could not identify Acheson, 45 percent were unfamiliar with the term "Cold War," 54 percent did not know what the Voice of America was, 51 percent could not identify Robert Taft, 27 percent were unable to identify the United Nations, only 3 percent knew the approximate population of South Korea, only 35 percent could identify N.A.T.O., and 51 percent said that they could not define the electoral college. See ibid., pp. 953-54, 963, 991, 996, 1004, 1009, 1015, 1028.
2. *Washington Post,* November 30, 1950; *Chicago Tribune,* December 7, 1950.
3. McCarthy deposition, box 3, Roberts Papers, pp. 407-10, 414-19; Pearson deposition, ibid., pp. 18-47, 51-108, 130-39, 144; Westbrook Pegler deposition, box 4, ibid., pp. 71-73, 102-11, 149-52; Kiermas, Reedy, Nellor (May 7, 1977), Van Susteren (November 25, 1975, March 16, 1981), Woods interviews; memoranda, Warren Woods to the files, May 17, November 2, 1951, box 6, Roberts Papers; *Madison Capital Times,* December 14, 1950; Anderson, *Confessions of a Muckracker,* p. 214; copy, Tom Korb to Joe McCarthy, December 14, 1950. Abell (ed.), *Drew Pearson Diaries,* pp. 123-24, 128, is not to be trusted on this score. See Woods interview.
4. See *Congressional Record,* 81st Cong., 2d sess., December 15, 1950, pp. 16634-41; *Madison Capital Times,* December 16, 1950; Evjue in ibid., February 28, 1951. Surine possessed a transcript of an FBI wiretap involving Karr.

Copy, "Confidential, Preliminary Report," March 7, 1951, box 5, Roberts Papers. This report and others like it in the Roberts Papers were written by a Pearson spy in McCarthy's office.

5. *Madison Capital Times,* December 16, 1950.
6. Nellor interview, June 6, 1979; editorial, *Washington Post,* December 24, 1950. By 1954 Lewis appeared on some 500 radio stations and fifty television stations, and his audience was estimated at 16,000,000 people. Booton Herndon, *Praised and Damned, The Story of Fulton Lewis, Jr.* (New York, 1954), p. 1.
7. *Madison Capital Times,* January 6, 1951.
8. Woods interview; see copy, memorandum, Warren Woods to W. A. Roberts, May 14, 1953, box 6, Roberts Papers; copy, memorandum, Edward G. Villalon to W. A. Roberts, January 30, 1956, box 3, ibid. Research for the suit, including the taking of several important depositions, yielded much information that was distributed by Pearson and published by anti-McCarthy newspapers. The influential Anderson and May campaign polemic of 1952 was an offshoot. Pearson personnel worked closely with the *Madison Capital Times* and *Milwaukee Journal.* See copy, Warren Woods to Robert Fleming, August 13, 1951, box 3, ibid.; memorandum, Warren Woods to Drew Pearson, August 24, 1951, box 6, ibid.; memorandum, Warren Woods to Jack Anderson, August 24, 1951, ibid.; copy, memorandum, Joe McCarthy to Wisconsin Radio Stations, September 7, 1951, box 3, ibid.; Robert Fleming to Warren Woods, September 22, 1951, ibid.
9. *Madison Capital Times,* January 27, February 13, 1951; Smith, *Declaration of Conscience,* pp. 21-24.
10. *Madison Capital Times,* February 2, 1951. Wherry's biographer assures us, "He detested demagogues such as McCarthy . . ." Marvin E. Stromer, *The Making of a Political Leader, Kenneth S. Wherry and the United States Senate* (Lincoln, Nebraska, 1969), p. 19.
11. The relationship between Surine and McCarran was so close that at one point the investigator stored "hot" C.I.A. documents in the basement of the senator's Washington home. See "The McCarthy Issue . . . Pro and Con," *U.S. News and World Report,* pp. 29, 39; Surine (April 7, May 13, 1977, February 11, 1979), Nellor (May 7, 1977) interviews; copy, "Confidential, Preliminary Report, undated, pp. 3, 9-10, "Confidential Report Dated February 25, 1951," p. 6, box 5, Roberts Papers. Cf. Eva Adams to the author, May 19, 1977.
12. *New York Times,* February 10, 17, 1951.
13. "Further Preliminary Report," February 7, 1951, "Further Confidential Report," February 17, 1951, box 5, Roberts Papers; I.P.R. press releases of February 16, 21, 23, 27, 1951, box 2, Evjue Papers; *New York Times,* February

10, 11, 17, 1950; *Madison Capital Times,* February 14, 1951; Anderson and May, *McCarthy,* pp. 343-46; Kiermas interview. Drew Pearson's spy, in the document of February 7 cited above, noted that FBI agents "took statements of Matthews and Surine to see if any Federal laws had been violated." Surine would later contend that he risked his life for the I.P.R. files. See Surine interviews of March 29, May 13, September 29, 1977; U.S. Senate, Subcommittee of the Committee on Foreign Relations, *Nomination of Philip C. Jessup to be United States Representative to the Sixth General Assembly of the United Nations, Hearings,* 82d Cong., 1st sess., 1951, p. 87 (hereafter cited as *Jessup Hearings*).

14. Quoted in Crosby, *God, Church, and Flag,* p. 32. Cf. Cohn, *McCarthy,* p. 269.

15. See Harper, *The Politics of Loyalty,* pp. 135-40, 164-85; Fried, *Men Against McCarthy,* pp. 161-69; Athan Theoharis, "The Escalation of the Loyalty Program," in Barton Bernstein (ed.), *Politics and Policies of the Truman Administration* (Chicago, 1972), pp. 256-59.

16. See *New York Post,* July 22, 1951; Kahn, *The China Hands,* pp. 227-31, 237-46.

17. *Madison Capital Times,* July 16, 26, August 10, 1951; *New York Times,* August 10, (editorial) 11, 1951; *Congressional Record,* 81st Cong., 2d sess., August 9, 1951, pp. 9703-13.

18. *Madison Capital Times,* December 14, 1951.

19. U.S. Senate, Committee on Armed Services, *Nomination of Anna M. Rosenberg to be Assistant Secretary of Defense, Hearings,* 81st Cong., 2d sess., 1950; Alfred J. Friendly, "Case History of a Smear," *The Progressive,* 15 (May, 1951), 5-9; Nellor interview, June 6, 1979; Anderson and May, *McCarthy,* pp. 309-14; Arnold Forster and Benjamin R. Epstein, *The Troublemakers* (New York, 1952), pp. 25-61; *New York Times,* December 6, 1950; *Madison Capital Times,* December 31, 1951. See also Fulton Lewis, Jr., deposition, box 4, "Confidential, Preliminary Report," box 5, Roberts Papers. Ed Nellor, who tried to protect Surine during his testimony before the Armed Services Committee, thought years later that the entire Rosenberg incident may have been a plot against McCarthy by his enemies! Nellor interview, June 6, 1979. See also Ed Nellor to the author, October 8, 1979.

20. Editorial, *Madison Capital Times,* January 3, 1951; *Milwaukee Journal,* January 12, 1951.

21. Smith, *Declaration of Conscience,* pp. 24-26.

22. *Maryland Hearings,* pp. 1-5.

23. Ibid., pp. 7-28, 181-213. Senator Taft's campaign manager later admitted handling $250,000 in unreported cash.

24. Ibid., pp. 541-79. Kiermas, Surine, and Ewell Moore had discussed matters a short time earlier with the sympathetic Assistant Counsel Ralph E. Becker at Becker's home. Ibid., pp. 575-78.

25. Deposition, Joseph R. McCarthy vs. The Post-Standard Company . . . ," pp. 40-46, 49-72. McCarthy also conferred with Ewell Moore before he testified and appears to have sent Moore to veteran Washington attorney Robert L'Heureux for advice. *Maryland Hearings,* pp. 621-24, 799-811.

26. *Maryland Report,* pp. 34-35, 72-73.

27. Kemper, *Decade of Fear,* p. 38; *New York Times,* July 6, 1951.

28. The report did make two indirect references to the senators, however, in its requests for action by the Rules Committee. See *Maryland Report,* p. 8.

29. *Milwaukee Journal,* August 3, 1951.

30. Robert S. Allen in *Madison Capital Times,* August 14, 1951. The full Rules Committee, at Joe's request, modified the Maryland election report by eliminating a reference to Jean Kerr's endorsement of the composite photograph. *New York Times,* August 9, 1951.

31. *Washington Star,* February 12, 1951; *New York Times,* February 13, 14, 1951; editorial, *Madison Capital Times,* February 14, 1951.

32. *Washington Daily News,* October 15, 1951; *Madison Capital Times,* October 16, 1951. Davis was also found guilty of giving information about Leftists to the United States Consulate General in Geneva and to the American embassy in Paris.

33. Ibid., October 17, 1951.

34. Joe McCarthy to Tom Coleman, June 28, 1950, box 13, Coleman Papers.

35. *Maryland Hearings,* pp. 678-79; Nellor interview, June 6, 1979.

36. See deposition, "Joseph R. McCarthy vs. The Post-Standard Company . . . ," pp. 79-98, 130-65; Gary May, *China Scapegoat: The Diplomatic Ordeal of John Carter Vincent* (New York, 1979), p. 184; "Report of Preliminary Investigation of Senator William Benton's Charges against Joseph A. McCarthy Relating to Senate Resolution 187," box 78, Hendrickson Papers. Don Surine's deposition is in the County Clerk's Office, Syracuse, New York. The Davis affidavit cited by McCarthy in his deposition, pp. 84-87, was taken by a highly sympathetic investigator and must be judged accordingly. On Davis and Evjue, see memorandum, Esther Tufty to William Evjue, November 15, 1951, box 138, Evjue Papers.

37. Deposition, "Joseph R. McCarthy vs. The Post-Standard Company . . . ," p. 211; Tracy H. Ferguson to the author, June 6, 1978; "Clarifying Editorial Ends McCarthy Suit," *Editor and Publisher* 86 (March 21, 1953), 36. The editorial apology also exonerated McCarthy of the standard charges involving the

Lustron booklet and of his direct involvement in the composite photograph ploy used in the Maryland campaign.

38. *Milwaukee Journal*, April 8, 1951; *Janesville Gazette*, April 9, 1951. McCarthy also charged in Fort Atkinson that a "close relative" of a *Milwaukee Journal* editor had raised money for the Alger Hiss defense fund and had made eleven telephone calls to the newspaper's editorial writers on the day Louis Budenz testified before the Tydings Committee. He also claimed that two members of the *Journal*'s editorial staff had contributed to the fund, and "you can see why they go down the party line." The entire allegation, as the *Journal* soon proved, was a bluff and a smear. The "close relative" was Louis S. Weiss, deceased brother-in-law of a *Journal* executive. See Robert Fleming memoranda of April 7, 23, 24, 1951; Richard H. Field to Robert Fleming, April 20, 1951, box 3, Fleming Papers; editorial, Milwaukee *Journal*, April 17, 1951. At the 1952 G.O.P. State Convention, Joe made the same charge, slightly altering the facts. Ibid., June 14, 1952.

39. Van Susteren interview, January 15, 1976; *Milwaukee Journal*, April 12, 1951.

40. Ibid.

41. Ibid., April 13, 14, 1951.

42. Spanier, *The Truman-MacArthur Controversy and the Korean War*, pp. 212-213; "Action on M-Day," *Time*, 57 (April 23, 1951), 26.

43. *The Gallup Poll*, II, 981, 989; copy, "Speech of Senator Joe McCarthy," April 23, 1951, Racine, Wisconsin Public Library.

44. *Congressional Record*, 82d Cong., 1st sess., June 14, 1951, pp. 6556-6603.

45. *Madison Capital Times*, June 15, 16, August 9, September 28, 1951; Joe McCarthy, *America's Retreat from Victory, The Story of George Catlett Marshall* (New York, 1951), pp. 174-80.

46. *Milwaukee Journal*, April 21, 1950; editorial, *Madison Capital Times*, December 8, 1950; McCarthy, *America's Retreat from Victory*, p. 4.

47. *Marinette Eagle-Star*, July 2, 1951; McCarthy, *America's Retreat from Victory*, pp. 6-7; McCarthy deposition, box 3, Roberts Papers, pp. 89-91. The publication was quietly subsidized by Joe's friends, including officials of the Harnischfager Corporation and the Republican Party of Wisconsin. See Jean Kerr to Tom Korb, August 24, 1951; copy, Tom Korb to Jean Kerr, August 28, 1951, Korb Papers; copy, Wayne J. Hood to Henry E. Ringling, August 29, 1951, box 4, Hood Papers. The book was republished by McCarthy in 1952 under the title *The Story of General George Marshall*.

48. Cater, "Is McCarthy Slipping?," p. 26; Rovere, *Senator Joe McCarthy*, pp. 175-77.

49. Minetti (March 14, 1977), Surine (April 7, 1977), Buckley interviews; *New York Times*, May 5, 1962; John Chamberlain, "Forrest Davis, RIP," *National*

Review, 12 (May 22, 1962), 357, 386; Beth A. Hoffman to the author, March 30, 1978; editorial, *Madison Capital Times,* January 11, 1952. McCarthy sent thousands of copies of the Senate speech and the book throughout Wisconsin under his senatorial franking privilege. In a form letter to high school teachers, Joe wrote, "I tried to keep this history as objective as possible." Editorial, ibid., February 26, 1952.

50. Buckley interview; Chamberlain, "Forrest Davis, RIP," p. 357. Surine later contended that McCarthy supervised the touch-up of the manuscript from start to finish and was thoroughly familiar with the finished product when he delivered it to the Senate. Surine interview, April 7, 1977. See p. 141 of *America's Retreat from Victory* for an example of an insertion of McCarthyana.

51. *Madison Capital Times,* June 15, 1951.

52. *New York Herald Tribune,* June 15, 1951.

53. *Milwaukee Journal,* August 7, 1951; *Congressional Record,* 82d Cong., 1st sess., August 6, 1951, pp. 9498-9501.

54. "Democrats Fume at McCarthy, But He Has Them Terrorized," *Newsweek,* 38 (April 20, 1951), 19; Anderson and May, *McCarthy,* p. 316; copy, William Benton to Harold Fey, August 29, 1951, box 4, Benton Papers.

CHAPTER 16

1. See Sidney Hyman, *The Lives of William Benton* (Chicago, 1969), pp. 194, 406, 442.

2. Ibid., pp. 449, 461-62.

3. Ibid., pp. 455-56; "The McCarthy Issue," *U.S. News and World Report,* 31 (September 7, 1951), 32, 34; *Hennings Committee Report,* pp. 1-2; *Milwaukee Journal,* August 7, 1951.

4. *New York Times,* August 9, 1951; Cater, "Is McCarthy Slipping?" p. 26.

5. Ibid.; *Madison Capital Times,* August 10, 1951; *Newsweek,* 38 (August 20, 1951), p. 19; William S. White in *New York Times,* September 9, 1951; John Howe to William Benton [August, 1951], Box 4, Benton Papers.

6. Editorial, *Madison Capital Times,* July 30, August 2, 1951. The White House requested a copy of the story from Evjue. Joseph Short, Truman's secretary, wrote: "That July fourth petition project of yours made one of the most interesting stories I have read in a long time. I believe we can make good use of it in our effort to point out what McCarthyism is doing to the country. You certainly have done a great job in Wisconsin along the same line." See Joseph

Short to William Evjue, July 27, 1951, and copy, William Evjue to Joseph Short, August 3, 1951, box 137, Evjue Papers. For Hunter's reflections on his petition and McCarthy, see *Madison Capital Times,* April 16, 1979.

7. Ibid., August 15, 1951; *New York Times,* September 9, 1951.
8. *Madison Capital Times,* August 31, 1951. Tobin had spoken out against McCarthy earlier. See Crosby, *God, Church, and Flag,* pp. 75-76.
9. *Congressional Record,* 82d Cong., 1st sess., August 20, 1951, pp. 10319-37; *Maryland Report,* pp. 41-74.
10. "The McCarthy Issue ... Pro and Con," *U.S. News and World Report,* pp. 29, 31, 41. This article also contains an interview with Benton, who reflects the fear and willingness to persecute "suspects" that some liberals as well as conservatives equated with patriotism at the time.
11. Joe McCarthy to Guy Gillette, September 17, 1951, in *Hennings Committee Report,* p. 60; *Madison Capital Times,* September 18, 19, 1951; Kemper, *Decade of Fear,* p. 43; *Congressional Record,* 82d Cong., 1st sess., September 21, 1951, p. 11857.
12. *Madison Capital Times,* September 19, 1951; Kemper, *Decade of Fear,* p. 43.
13. *Madison Capital Times,* September 20, 21, 1951.
14. Ibid., September 22, 1951; *Congressional Record,* 82d Cong., 1st sess., September 21, 1951, pp. 11857-58.
15. *New York Times,* September 23, 1951.
16. *Madison Capital Times,* September 26, 1951; *Milwaukee Journal,* September 27, 1951.
17. The series appeared from September 4 through 23, 1951 and was distributed nationally by the C.I.O.
18. Anderson interview; Anderson, *Confessions of a Muckraker,* pp. 207-8; *Washington Star,* September 27, 1951.
19. See Warren Woods to Robert Fleming, August 13, September 4, October 29, 1951, box 4, Fleming Papers; Woods interview.
20. See Fleming memoranda of August 8, October 2, 1951, box 3, Fleming Papers; Millard Tydings to Robert Fleming, April 10, 1951, and undated Fleming memorandum, box 4, ibid.
21. See the Bob Schwartz materials in box 3, ibid.; "Congress," *Time,* LVII (October 22, 1951), 21-24. A month earlier, Luce's *Life* magazine had urged backers of Robert Taft to repudiate all ties with McCarthy. "Somebody must forego the pleasure of further groin-and-eyeball fighting." Cf. Swanberg, *Luce and His Empire,* pp. 297-302. Luce quietly permitted Robert Fleming to study *Time*'s files on McCarthy, which assisted the reporter in discrediting Joe's "war wound" claims. Fleming interview.
22. *Eau Claire Leader,* September 5, 1951; *Madison Capital Times,* September 20, November 10, 27, 1951, June 18, 25, 1952.

23. Ibid., September 26, 1951.
24. Guy Gillette to Joseph R. McCarthy, September 25, 1951, in *Hennings Committee Report*, p. 61; *Madison Capital Times*, September 28, 1951.
25. Ibid.; Anderson, *Confessions of a Muckraker*, p. 250; Hyman, *The Lives of William Benton*, p. 462.
26. William Benton to Guy Gillette, October 5, 1951, in *Hennings Committee Report*, p. 105; *Madison Capital Times*, October 26, November 12, 1951. Joe called Tydings a "clever little faker" and assured him, "The fight against Communists will go on, Millard, regardless of how much you yap at my heels." He also claimed that Tydings had failed to ask the State Department for the names of the 205 cited in James Byrnes's letter! Ibid.
27. *Washington Daily News*, October 23, 1951; William S. White in *New York Times*, October 28, 1951.
28. *Jessup Hearings*, pp. 162-63.
29. Ibid., pp. 164-69. Cf. ibid., p. 497.
30. Ibid., pp. 78, 989-1022; U.S. Senate, Subcommittee to Investigate the Administration of the Internal Security Act and Other Internal Security Laws, *Institute of Pacific Relations, Hearings*, 82d Cong., 1st sess., 1951, pp. 513-701, 1077-1110. McCarran kept a close watch on the Sparkman hearings, providing the Alabama senator with questions and evidence. *Jessup Hearings*, p. 599. He attended a portion of the October 2 hearings featuring McCarthy.
31. *Madison Capital Times*, September 20, 1951.
32. *Jessup Hearings*, pp. 1-39.
33. Ibid., pp. 41-60, 601-22, 685-872; *Madison Capital Times*, September 26, October 3, 13, 1951. Stassen declared his candidacy for the presidential nomination in December, some liberals dubbing him "the white-collar McCarthy." He hinted opposition to McCarthy in mid-February, 1952, and by early April, following Robert A. Taft's primary victory in Wisconsin, he publicly denounced Joe's "wild-swinging recklessness." The two men feuded bitterly for the remainder of McCarthy's career. Ibid., (editorial) December 29, 1951, February 15, 20, April 8, 1952, March 30, 1953, May 22, June 4, 1954, April 11, 1955. In 1956 Stassen sought to drop Richard Nixon from the ticket for being too right-wing. Twenty-four years later he was still seeking the presidential nomination.
34. *Jessup Hearings*, pp. 41-153. The political climate was such that no one during the hearings challenged the relevance of a citation by HUAC or a state un-American activities committee. Joe considered such a citation "proof" of a charge and beyond dispute. See ibid., p. 74.
35. Ibid., p. 211; *Madison Capital Times*, October 3, 1951.
36. Ibid.; *Jessup Hearings*, p. 106. Shortly, Joe publicly released excerpts from

minutes of a Loyalty Review Board meeting, revealing criticism of the State Department's handling of the loyalty program. He would not reveal his source. A board examiner, Miriam M. Dehaas, was later suspended for leaking the information. *New York Times,* January 6, 1952; *Madison Capital Times,* September 5, 1952.

37. *New York Times,* October 19, 1951; Jackson interview, April 10, 1968.

38. *New York Times,* October 20, 21, 23, 1951; *Madison Capital Times,* October 24, 1951. See the McCarthy advertisement in *Milwaukee Journal,* October 31, 1951. See also McCarthy, *McCarthyism, The Fight for America,* p. 13.

39. Guy Gillette to Joseph R. McCarthy, October 1, 1951; Joe McCarthy to Guy Gillette, October 4, 1951, in *Hennings Committee Report,* pp. 61-62.

40. *Madison Capital Times,* October 26, November 2, 1951.

41. Ibid., November 14, 24, 1951.

42. Ibid., December 7, 10, 1951; Joe McCarthy to Guy Gillette, December 6, 7, 1951, in *Hennings Committee Report,* pp. 62-63. See also Guy Gillette to Joseph R. McCarthy, December 11, 1951; Joe McCarthy to Guy Gillette, December 19, 1951; Guy Gillette to Joseph R. McCarthy, December 21, 1951, in ibid., pp. 64-65.

43. Guy Gillette to Joseph R. McCarthy, December 6, 1951, in ibid., p. 63; *Madison Capital Times,* December 8, 1951.

44. *Hennings Committee Report,* pp. 14, 106-7.

45. Ibid.; *Madison Capital Times,* December 28, 1951, January 5, 1952; copy, memorandum, John P. Moore to Guy Gillette, January 11, 1952, box 18, Hendrickson Papers. Buckley reportedly had a record of mental instability. See Anderson, *Confessions of a Muckraker,* p. 261; Frances Low, "McCarthy Under Fire," *The Progressive,* 16 (May, 1952), 18-19.

46. "Report of Preliminary Investigation of Senator William Benton's Charges Against Joseph R. McCarthy Relating to Senate Resolution 187," passim; *Madison Capital Times,* February 27, 1952.

47. The subcommittee later raised the possibility that McCarthy may have leaked the report himself. The story first appeared in the *Providence Journal-Bulletin,* a Republican newspaper. See ibid., February 20, 1952; *Hennings Committee Report,* p. 13; Anderson and May, *McCarthy,* p. 323.

48. *Madison Capital Times,* January 16, 17, 19, 24, 28, 1952; Robert C. Hendrickson to Daniel J. P. Hendrickson, January 25, 1952, box 21, Hendrickson Papers; copies, memoranda, William Benton to John Howe, December 20, 1954, January 6, February 21, 1955, box 4, Benton Papers; Anderson and May, *McCarthy,* p. 322; *Congressional Record,* 82d Cong., 2d sess., March 18, 1952, pp. 2446-47; Smith, *Declaration of Conscience,* pp. 31-36. Joe privately upbraided Mrs. Smith at this time for recommending to a Wisconsin priest a well-documented analysis of McCarthy's charges and evidence entitled

"McCarthy versus the State Department" by Duke University sociologist Hornell Hart. Joe had tried unsuccessfully to coerce Duke officials into preventing publication of the 36-page study. It was released in mimeographed form on December 17, 1951. Ibid., p. 36; *Madison Capital Times*, January 25, 1952. See Hornell Hart, "McCarthyism Versus Democracy," *New Republic*, 126 (February 25, 1952), 10-13.

49. Copy, memorandum, William Benton to John Howe, February 21, 1951, box 4, Benton Papers; William S. White in *New York Times*, January 27, 1952; editorial, *Madison Capital Times*, February 20, 1952.

50. *Beloit News*, January 28, 1952; editorial, *Madison Capital Times*, February 17, 1952.

51. Ibid., February 25, 1952.

52. Ibid., January 31, February 8, 1952; Harper, *The Politics of Loyalty*, pp. 221-22. Nash was a native of Wisconsin Rapids, Wisconsin. His sister had recently co-sponsored an advertisement in the *Wisconsin Rapids Daily Tribune* condemning McCarthyism. See *Madison Capital Times*, January 31, February 1, 4, 5, 8, August 29, 1952.

53. *Wheeling News-Register*, February 10, 1952. Joe soon charged on the Senate floor that Mrs. Keyserling was a former Communist and that she belonged to "an unlimited number of Communist fronts." Leon Keyserling branded the story "entirely false and nonsensical." *Madison Capital Times*, April 22, 1952. McCarthy's charges against the Keyserlings had already been investigated by various official agencies. See editorial, *Boston Herald*, April 24, 1952.

54. *Madison Capital Times*, February 13, 1952.

55. Ibid., February 12, 1952. McCarthy reportedly grilled Snow and Deputy Undersecretary of State Carl Humelsine repeatedly and mercilessly in secret sessions of the McCarran Committee. See Robert S. Allen in ibid., April 22, 1952.

56. Guy Gillette to Carl Hayden, March 6, 1952, in *Hennings Committee Report*, pp. 2-5; *Madison Capital Times*, February 21, March 8, 1952.

57. See Richard L. Strout in *Christian Science Monitor*, March 30, 1952.

58. Copy, Joe McCarthy to William Benton, March 18, 1952, copy, William Benton to Joseph R. McCarthy, March 18, 1952, box 5, Benton Papers; copy, Joe McCarthy to William Benton, May 7, 1952, box 4, ibid.; *Washington Post*, March 19, 1952; *Madison Capital Times*, March 26, 27, 28, 29, 1952.

59. Van Susteren interview, November 25, 1975. McCarthy dropped the suit in March, 1954, three days before a scheduled pre-trial conference. Van Arkel interview; *New York Times*, March 6, 1954.

60. Joe McCarthy to Carl Hayden, March 21, 1952, in *Hennings Committee Report*, pp. 67-68.

61. Ibid., pp. 5, 69-79; *Madison Capital Times*, April 11, 1952; *Congressional*

Record, 82d Cong., 2d sess., April 10, 1952, pp. 3833-3934; *Milwaukee Journal,* April 13, 1952. Darrell St. Claire had been one of Assistant Secretary of State William Benton's congressional liaison officers shortly after the war. He was at this time in touch with Benton aide John Howe, providing information and advice. See copy, confidential memorandum, John Howe to Senator Benton, April 14, 1952, box 4, Benton Papers; Hyman; *The Lives of William Benton,* p. 351. Senators Gillette, Smith, Monroney, Hendrickson, and Hayden denied, however, that St. Clair had played any role in the subcommittee's investigation.

62. Kelly, Reedy interviews.

63. When William F. Buckley first became acquainted with McCarthy he marveled at the Senator's lack of sophistication and his lack of interest in ideological matters. "He drove me crazy for his lack of intellectual precision," Buckley later recalled. Over lunch one day in 1952 Buckley asked Joe to articulate the argument against torturing the truth out of one of Russia's top American spies. "Bill," Joe replied indignantly, "don't tell anyone you ever asked me that question." He simply refused to deal with it. Buckley interview.

64. Kiermas interview.

65. Van Susteren (February 20, August 10, 1976, February 5, 1977), Osman, Henderson, Bayley (July 7, 1977) interviews; Harvey Matusow, *False Witness* (New York, 1955), pp. 144, 148.

66. Van Susteren (August 9, 1976), Brown, Gaillard, McNeil, Brooker, Lee, Korb (September 6, 1975) interviews; *Madison Capital Times,* July 24, August 11, 1952; *Eau Claire Leader,* October 16, 1952.

67. *Madison Capital Times,* August 11, September 4, 1952; *Appleton Post-Crescent,* November 5, 1952.

68. *Madison Capital Times,* April 19, May 7, 1952; Guy Gillette to Joseph R. McCarthy, May 7, 10, 1952, Joe McCarthy to Guy Gillette, May 8, 11, 1952, in *Hennings Committee Report,* pp. 79-84.

69. *Washington Star,* May 18, 1952; Brooker interview.

70. *Madison Capital Times,* May 17, June 2, 21, 30, 1952.

71. Ibid., June 2, 12, 1952; *New York Times,* July 3, 1952. See the Gillette-McCarthy correspondence in *Hennings Committee Report,* pp. 86-93. A short time earlier, newspapers reported that Lattimore was about to pay a visit behind the Iron Curtain. Fearing the professor's flight, the State Department issued an order preventing such a trip. The story turned out to be a hoax, and the State Department apologized profusely. *New York Times,* July 3, 1952.

72. Ibid., July 4, 1952; *Madison Capital Times,* July 4, 1952. Subcommittee Associate Counsel Wellford H. Ware, a Republican lawyer hired at Senator

Hendrickson's request, may have leaked Benton's tax records to McCarthy. See Luther H. Evans to William Benton, August 8,1952; copy, Gerald Van Arkel to William Benton, August 11, 1952; memoranda, John Howe to William Benton, August 12, 22, 1952, box 4, Benton Papers.

73. *Washington Post,* July 6, 1952; *Congressional Record,* 82d Cong., 2d sess., July 5, 1952, pp. 9537-39, 9542-44.

74. Marquis Childs and Drew Pearson in *Madison Capital Times,* September 6, 1952; Hyman, *The Lives of William Benton,* p. 464.

75. See *Hennings Committee Report,* pp. 8, 14-15, 93-94; copy, telegram, Herman Welker to Carl Hayden, September 8, 1952, box 4, Benton Papers; *Madison Capital Times,* September 9, 1952.

76. Guy M. Gillette to Carl Hayden, September 10, 1952, in *Hennings Committee Report,* p. 95.

77. Memorandum, John Howe to William Benton, August 22, 1952, box 4, Benton Papers.

78. Hyman, *The Lives of William Benton,* pp. 464-65, 482; *Hennings Committee Report,* p. 8. The legality of Hayden's subcommittee membership was cleared with the Senate parliamentarian. See unsigned memorandum [Grace Johnson], "Composition of Subcommittee on Privileges and Elections," box 120, Hayden Papers; *Watkins Committee Hearings,* pp. 359-62, 364-68, 535-40.

79. See Kemper, *Decade of Fear,* p. 57; U.S. Senate, Special Committee on Investigation of Cover on Mail of Senators, *Report No. 2510,* 83d Cong., 2d sess., 1954. There was no examination of the contents of the mail and apparently no delay in delivery.

80. Robert Hendrickson to William Benton, November 14, 1952, box 4, Benton Papers.

81. Anderson, *Confessions of a Muckraker,* pp. 257-58.

82. Paul J. Cotter to Joseph R. McCarthy, November 7, 1952, Ray Kiermas to Paul J. Cotter, November 10, 1952, in *Hennings Committee Report,* pp. 96-97; Van Susteren interview, February 20, 1976.

83. Copy, Mary K. Gardner to Guy Gillette, September 14, 1954, copy, William Benton to Robert C. Hendrickson, September 15, 1954, box 5, Benton Papers; *Hennings Committee Report,* pp. 9-10.

84. Hyman, *The Lives of William Benton,* p. 482; Anderson, *Confessions of a Muckraker,* pp. 257-58.

85. Thomas C. Hennings, Jr., to Joseph R. McCarthy, November 21, 1952, in *Hennings Committee Report,* pp. 98-99; telegram, Thomas C. Hennings, Jr., to Joseph R. McCarthy, November 21, 1952, in U.S. Senate, Select Committee to Study Censure Charges, *Report on Resolution to Censure,* 83d Cong., 2d

sess., p. 15 (hereafter cited as *Watkins Committee Report*). A more strongly worded version of the Hennings telegram, never sent, was published in the *Hennings Committee Report*, p. 99, no doubt to strengthen the subcommittee's case against McCarthy.

86. Joe McCarthy to Thomas C. Hennings, Jr., November 28, December 1, 1952, in ibid., pp. 101-04. See also ibid., p. 9.

87. Anderson, *Confessions of a Muckraker*, pp. 258-59; Hyman, *The Lives of William Benton*, p. 483; *New York Times*, December 25, 1952; copy, memorandum, William Benton to John Howe, September 17, 1954, box 5, Benton Papers; *Hennings Committee Report*, pp. 45-51. Benton always staunchly defended his conduct in the Cosgriff affair, and no legal steps were taken against him. McCarthy initially learned of the banker's gift from hearings held in March, 1951 by the Senate subcommittee of the RFC of the Senate Banking and Currency Committee.

88. Copy, memorandum, William Benton to John Howe, September 17, 1954, box 5, Benton Papers; *Watkins Committee Hearings*, p. 306.

89. Anderson, *Confessions of a Muckraker*, pp. 259-60; *Watkins Committee Hearings*, pp. 362-64.

90. Copy, memorandum, John Howe to William Benton, October 12, 1954, box 5, Benton Papers.

91. *Madison Capital Times*, January 3, 1953; *Milwaukee Journal*, January 3, 1953; editorial, *New York Post*, January 5, 1953; copy, memorandum, William Benton to John Howe, August 31, 1954, box 5, Benton Papers.

92. Memorandum, William Benton to John Howe, November 23, 1954, box 4, ibid.; *Hennings Committee Report*, pp. 1-15, 45.

93. Ibid., pp. 15-19.

94. Ibid., pp. 19-27; Drew Pearson in *Los Angeles Times*, February 5, 1955; Matusow, *False Witness*, pp. 177-83; Van Susteren interview, January 15, February 20, 1976. Van Straten denied to reporters that McCarthy had played any part in the soybean transaction. "This is a private matter, and nothing that concerns the Senate." *Milwaukee Journal*, January 3, 1953. He told the author that Joe loaned him the $10,000. Van Straten interview. Joe had undoubtedly received a tip on the soybean shares. He had an active account at the time with Daniel F. Rice and Company of Chicago, whose specialty was the grain futures market. "Mortgage the house and buy rye," McCarthy once advised Van Susteren excitedly by telephone. Van Susteren interview, February 15, July 14, 1977.

95. *Hennings Committee Report*, pp. 27-38.

96. Ibid., pp. 39-43; Kiermas interview. McCarthy and Kiermas exchanged funds informally and frequently in response to gambling and investment needs.

Kiermas thought later that at least $50,000 was handled between the two over the years. For McCarthy on Kiermas and the Hennings Report, see *New York Times,* January 30, 1953.

97. The report merely agreed with Benton that he had "badly handled" the Cosgriff donation. *Hennings Committee Report,* pp. 45-52.

98. *Milwaukee Sentinel,* January 3, 1953; editorial, *New York Post,* January 5, 1953; *Madison Capital Times,* January 5, 9, 19, 20, March 25, 1953; *New York Times,* March 26, 1953; Brock, *Americans for Democratic Action,* p. 146; H. H. Wilson, "The Senate Sellout," *The Nation,* 176 (January 24, 1953), 64; Willard Shelton, "The Shame of the Senate," *The Progressive,* 17 (February, 1953), 7-10; Griffith, *The Politics of Fear,* p. 187; "McCarthy: A Documented Record," *The Progressive,* 18 (April, 1954), passim. Cf. editorial, *Madison Capital Times,* January 22, 1953; "Report on McCarthy," *Commonweal,* 57 (January 23, 1953), 393. The 2,500 copy supply of the Hennings Report was quickly exhausted, giving rise to the false rumor among liberals that Senator Jenner had pidgeonholed the document. Kemper, *Decade of Fear,* p. 62.

99. *Madison Capital Times,* January 15, 1953; editorial, *New York Post,* January 5, 1953; O'Brien, "Senator Joseph McCarthy and Wisconsin," p. 210.

100. *Milwaukee Journal,* January 3, 1953; *Milwaukee Sentinel,* January 3, 1953.

101. Copy, memorandum, John Howe to William Benton, October 12, 1954, box 5, Benton Papers; Marquis Childs in *Washington Post,* January 6, 1953; Thomas Hennings to Ralph Torreyson, February 7, 1953, box 84, Hennings Papers. Chavez was seated "without prejudice" anyway, as was Republican William Langer.

102. *Milwaukee Journal,* January 3, 1953; *New York Times,* January 3, 4, 1953.

103. Anderson, *Confessions of a Muckraker,* p. 260.

104. Copy, memorandum, John Howe to William Benton, October 12, 1954, box 4, Benton Papers; *Milwaukee Journal,* September 6, October 17, 1953; *Washington Post,* October 17, 1953.

CHAPTER 17

1. See Jean Kerr to Tom Korb, October 27, 1951; copy, Tom Korb to Jean Kerr, October 29, 1951, Korb Papers; Jean Kerr to Wayne Hood, November 30, December 3, 1951, box 6, Hood Papers. Excerpts of the book appeared in the May 1952 issue of *Cosmopolitan,* a Hearst publication. Walter Harnischfager quietly channeled $400 through the Jolles Foundation of New York to have 800 copies distributed to educational institutions and libraries. Copy, Walter

Harnischfager to Joe McCarthy, June 4, 1952; Walter Harnischfager to the Jolles Foundation, June 16, 1952, Korb Papers.

2. Copy, Tom Korb to Otis Gomillion, October 18, 1951; copy, Tom Korb to Richard S. Falk, November 28, 1951, ibid; *Madison Capital Times,* December 10, 1951.

3. Ibid., December 12, 1951; *Milwaukee Journal,* December 12, 1951; Korb (September 6, 1975), Townsend (June 25, 1975) interviews.

4. Editorials, *Madison Capital Times,* August 13, 21, 1952; Mary Tom Savage to Tom Korb, February 13, 1952, Korb Papers; *Milwaukee Journal,* August 29, 1952; copy, Margaret Hampton to McCarthy Club members, August 9, 1952, Korb Papers. The club reported spending $57,000.64 by the September 9 primary. *Madison Capital Times,* September 22, 1952.

5. *Milwaukee Journal,* October 24, 1951, January 30, 1952; O'Brien, "Senator Joseph McCarthy and Wisconsin," pp. 162-69; Matusow, *False Witness,* p. 141. Columnist Joseph Alsop later reported the rumor that Joe had threatened to make Kohler's divorce a campaign issue, prompting the Governor to abandon his Senatorial ambitions. *Chicago Sun-Times,* October 14, 1952. Kohler denied the story. Kohler interview, Columbia University.

6. "Hope in Wisconsin," *The Progressive,* 16 (March, 1952), 3-4; Reuss, Doyle interviews; O'Brien, "Senator Joseph McCarthy and Wisconsin," pp. 158-61, 169-75; editorial, *Chicago Sun-Times,* June 30, 1952.

7. *Milwaukee Journal,* June 3, 1951; Aldric Revell in *Madison Capital Times,* August 23, 1951.

8. Wendy, Bayley (July 7, 1977) interviews; Rubin (June 29, 1967) interview, Cornell University.

9. Wisconsin Citizens' Committee on McCarthy's Record, *The McCarthy Record* ([Madison], 1952). The book was serialized in the *Milwaukee Journal* and *Sheboygan Press.* See *Madison Capital Times,* June 30, September 3, 1952.

10. Ibid., May 3, 1952; Aldric Revell in ibid., August 23, 1951; John B. Oakes, "Report on McCarthy and McCarthyism," *New York Times Magazine,* November 2, 1952, p. 12.

11. Copy, Wayne Hood to Anne Hale Wilson, November 1, 1951; Harold Hornburg to Wayne Hood, February 29, 1952, box 2, Hood Papers; copy, Cyrus Philipp to Walter S. Hallanan, August 28, 1952, box 3, Philipp Papers; copy, Margaret Hampton to McCarthy Club members, August 9, 1952, Korb Papers.

12. *The Wisconsin Blue Book, 1954* ([Madison, 1954]), pp. 626-27; *New York Times,* January 22, 1952; Taft form letter, February 16, 1952, box 81, Evjue Papers; Townsend (June 26, 1975), Korb (September 6, 1975), Sumnicht, Tegge interviews; *Madison Capital Times,* July 9, 1952.

13. *New York Times,* June 6, 27, 1952; *Madison Capital Times,* September 17, 1951.

14. Ibid., June 13, 1952; *Milwaukee Journal,* June 14, 1952. See the statement by Zimmerman in "Why McCarthy Should Be Repudiated," *The Nation,* 175 (August 30, 1952), pp. 168-69.

15. *Milwaukee Journal,* July 9, 1952; *Madison Capital Times,* July 9, 1952.

16. See Herbert S. Parmet, *Eisenhower and the American Crusades* (New York, 1972), pp. 92-94.

17. *Milwaukee Journal,* July 9, 1952; *Official Report of the Proceedings of the Twenty-fifth Republican National Convention . . .* (Washington, D.C., [1952]), p. 68.

18. Ibid., pp. 141-42.

19. *Madison Capital Times,* July 10, 1952.

20. *Official Report of the Proceedings of the Twenty-fifth Republican National Convention . . . ,* pp. 142-47; *Madison Capital Times,* July 10, 1952.

21. Tegge interview.

22. Editorials, *Milwaukee Sentinel,* July 10, 1952, *New York Times,* July 10, 1952; *Madison Capital Times,* July 10, 1952.

23. *Official Report of the Proceedings of the Twenty-fifth Republican National Convention . . . ,* pp. 309-15.

24. Parmet, *Eisenhower and the American Crusades,* pp. 101, 122-24; Kersten interview, October 8, 1971; *New York Times,* August 14, 26, 1952.

25. "Republicans," *Time,* LX (September 22, 1952), 24.

26. *Madison Capital Times,* July 12, 1952.

27. Ibid., July 23, 1952; *New York Times,* July 27, 1952.

28. *Madison Capital Times,* August 27, 1952.

29. Ibid., August 11, 1952.

30. Ibid., (editorial), July 9, August 7, 18, 27, 29, 30, 1952; *Milwaukee Journal,* August 28, 1952; Olsyzk interview; *Ashland Daily Press,* August 19, 1952; Matusow, *False Witness,* pp. 135-46.

31. *Madison Capital Times,* September 3, 4, 1952. A *Congressional Quarterly* study showed that McCarthy sided with the majority of Democrats and Republicans 82 percent of the time in 1952. The average senator went along with the bipartisan majority 78.5 percent of the time. Liberal Paul Douglas scored 50 percent, while John M. Butler and Lyndon Johnson had 95 percent records. In 1951 McCarthy's percentage was 83, while Senator Wiley's was 84. Ibid., September 2, 1952.

32. *Chicago Tribune,* August 19, 1952; *Madison Capital Times,* September 4, 5, 1952; *Lakewood Herald-American,* September 4, 1952; O'Brien, "Senator Joseph McCarthy and Wisconsin," pp. 171-75; Wendt interview; Joseph Alsop in *Chicago Sun-Times,* September 7, 1952.

33. Doyle interview; *Madison Capital Times,* September 2, 1952.

34. Ibid.
35. Ibid., September 4, 5, 1952; *Ashland Daily Press,* September 4, 1952; *Major Campaign Speeches of Adlai E. Stevenson, 1952* (New York, 1953), pp. 271-72.
36. *Madison Capital Times,* September 5, 1952.
37. A copy of the tabloid is in the Evjue Papers.
38. Matusow, *False Witness,* p. 146.
39. *The Wisconsin Blue Book, 1954,* p. 656; "The Campaign," *Time,* LX (September 22, 1952), 23; copy, Tom Korb to Edmund E. Lincoln, September 25, 1952, Korb Papers.
40. Schmitt quoted in Graham Hovey, "How McCarthy Sold Wisconsin," *New Republic,* 127 (September 22, 1952), 10; "The Campaign," *Time,* LX (September 22, 1952), 24; editorial, *New York Journal American,* September 10, 1952; editorial, *New York Times,* September 14, 1952; "McCarthyism: Is It a Trend?" *U.S. News and World Report,* 33 (September 19, 1952), 21.
41. Doyle interview; O'Brien, "Senator Joseph McCarthy and Wisconsin," pp. 183-88; *Appleton Post-Crescent,* October 22, 1952; *Beloit Daily News,* November 1, 1952.
42. O'Brien, "Senator Joseph McCarthy and Wisconsin," pp. 182, 184-85; Hovey, "How McCarthy Sold Wisconsin," p. 11; editorial, *Madison Capital Times,* September 15, 1952; editorial, *Milwaukee Journal,* September 10, 1952.
43. *Beloit Daily News,* September 29, 1952; *Eau Claire Leader,* October 16, 1952.
44. *New York Times,* April 27, 1952; John Wyngaard in *Green Bay Press-Gazette,* October 3, 1952.
45. The Alsops in *Chicago Sun-Times,* August 5, 1952; Dwight D. Eisenhower, *The White House Years: Mandate for Change, 1953-1956* (Garden City, New York, 1963), p. 317; Emmet John Hughes, *The Ordeal of Power, A Political Memoir of the Eisenhower Years* (New York, 1962), p. 38; *Milwaukee Journal,* August 20, 1952; Kersten interview; William S. White in *New York Times,* August 22, 1952.
46. *Madison Capital Times,* August 22, 1952.
47. Ibid., August 23, 1952.
48. Eisenhower, *The White House Years,* p. 317; Hughes, *The Ordeal of Power,* p. 39.
49. Robert Cutler, *No Time for Rest* (Boston, 1965), p. 287; Hughes, *The Ordeal of Power,* p. 38; *New York Times,* September 11, 1952.
50. Cutler, *No Time for Rest,* pp. 287-88; *Madison Capital Times,* October 3, 4, 1952; *New York Times,* October 3, 4, 1952; Parmet, *Eisenhower and the American Crusades,* pp. 131-32; Eisenhower, *The White House Years,* pp. 318-19; Sherman Adams, *Firsthand Report, The Story of the Eisenhower*

Administration (New York, 1961), pp. 30-33; Dohr, Larry Jolin interviews; Joseph Alsop in *Chicago Sun-Times,* October 14, 1952; Walter Kohler interview, Columbia University. McCarthy made a private visit to Eisenhower's Milwaukee quarters that evening. Cutler, *No Time for Rest,* p. 288. Joe was physically shaken because of a minor automobile accident he had been involved in the day before. *Madison Capital Times,* October 3, 1952.

51. Ibid., October 9, 1952.

52. Editorial, ibid., October 11, 1952; *New York Post,* October 6, 1952.

53. Hughes, *The Ordeal of Power,* pp. 19-20.

54. *Montana Standard,* October 13, 15, 1952; *Milwaukee Journal,* October 13, 1952; *Las Vegas Sun,* October 13, 14, 15, 1952; *Arizona Republic,* October 19, 1952; *Seattle Daily Times,* October 23, 24, 1952; Matusow, *False Witness,* pp. 160-61, 166-71; Fried, *Men Against McCarthy,* pp. 240-41. See *Congressional Record,* 83d Cong., 1st sess., March 25, 1953, p. 2291. Right after Joe's slip of the tongue in Las Vegas, Greenspun falsely claimed in print that the senator was a homosexual. He obtained his "evidence" from Drew Pearson attorney Warren Woods, who was highly skeptical of it. Joe retaliated in 1954 by having the government file charges against the editor for publishing a column "tending to incite murder or assassination." A jury found Greenspun innocent. See the article by Lawrence Martin in *Denver Post,* February 7, 1954, and Greenspun's privately published *A Few Columns on Joe McCarthy* (Las Vegas, 1977). See also Woods interview.

55. *New York Times,* October 1, 1952; *Hartford Courant,* October 1, 29, 1952; *St. Louis Post-Dispatch,* October 9, November 1, 1952; *Detroit Free Press,* October 10, 1952; *Indianapolis Star,* October 20, 1952; *Wheeling Intelligencer,* October 22, 1952; *Montana Standard,* October 31, 1952; Fried, *Men Against McCarthy,* pp. 241, 244. Joe appeared in Tyler, Texas, on October 17 for an American Legion anti-Communist rally described by sponsors as "nonpartisan." Fulton Lewis, Jr., introduced him as "a man hated by everybody but Americans." *St. Louis Post-Dispatch,* October 18, 1952. Joe apparently did not campaign in Utah or New Mexico, as his office later reported to statistician Louis Bean.

56. Kiermas, Surine (July 18, 1980) interviews; Cohn, *McCarthy,* pp. 67-68; Crosby, *God, Church, and Flag,* pp. 109-11; Whalen, *The Founding Father,* pp. 411-20; Lasky, *J.F.K., The Man and the Myth,* pp. 184-92, 298; Arthur Krock, *Memoirs, Sixty Years on the Firing Line* (New York, 1968), p. 319; Hyman, *The Lives of William Benton,* p. 480. Cf. Herbert S. Parmet, *Jack: The Struggles of John F. Kennedy* (New York, 1980), pp. 249-50; Walter Trohan, *Political Animals, Memoirs of a Sentimental Cynic* (Garden City, N.Y., 1975), p. 249. See Westbrook Pegler in *Arizona Republic,* October 17, 1952. Accord-

ing to John Fox, owner of the *Boston Post,* McCarthy refused to respond when Fox sought the senator's endorsement of Lodge. Whalen, *The Founding Father,* p. 420. The senior Kennedy denied all reports of personal campaign assistance to his son.

57. Kersten interview, May 15, 1971; Blair, *The Search for J.F.K.,* pp. 551-55; Koskoff, *Joseph P. Kennedy, A Life and Times,* p. 410; Crosby, *God, Church and Flag,* p. 109; Lasky, *J.F.K., The Man and the Myth,* pp. 191, 297. In 1950, Joe Kennedy had quietly sent a $1,000 campaign contribution to Richard Nixon through his son John. John made it clear that he personally preferred Nixon to Helen Gahagan Douglas. Nixon, *RN,* I, 91-92.

58. McNeill interview.

59. The Alsops in *Chicago Sun-Times,* October 25, 1952; McCarthy Broadcast Dinner form letter, October 9, 1952, Korb Papers.

60. Surine interviews, May 27, 1977, August 1, 1980.

61. *New York Herald Tribune,* October 28, 1952. Two weeks earlier, William Jenner had declared, "Stevenson's campaign manager is Wilson Wyatt, former chairman of the ruthless and reckless gang of Marxist lobbyists who call themselves 'ADA.' Stevenson's speeches are largely written by Professor Arthur Schlesinger, Jr., one of the top ADA commissars . . ." Brock, *Americans for Democratic Action,* p. 140.

62. *Madison Capital Times,* November 3, 1952; Willard H. Pedrick, "Senator McCarthy and the Law of Libel: A Study of Two Campaign Speeches," *Northwestern University Law Review,* 48 (May-June, 1953), 135-62.

63. *Milwaukee Journal,* October 31, 1952; *Appleton Post-Crescent,* November 4, 1952.

64. *Madison Capital Times,* November 3, (editorial) 4, December 4, 1952, February 6, 1956; Murphy, "Texas Business and McCarthy," p. 211; copy, Henry Harnischfager to David Frame, January 23, 1953, Korb Papers; Gaillard, Van Susteren (November 25, 1975, August 9, 1976, July 14, 1977, March 1, 1980), McNeill, Korb (November 8, 1975), Kiermas, Surine (July 25, 1980) interviews. Right-wing extremist John T. Flynn made a confidential contribution that earned McCarthy's personal thanks. Joe McCarthy to John T. Flynn, November 28, 1952, Flynn Papers.

65. O'Brien, "Senator Joseph McCarthy and Wisconsin," p. 190; Oshinsky, *Senator Joseph McCarthy and the American Labor Movement,* pp. 145-56; Doyle interview; *Madison Capital Times,* November 10, 1952. McCarthy reported that he personally collected $24,087 and spent $18,869. Fairchild claimed to have received only $1,819 personally, spending $1,343 on his campaign. Governor Kohler reported receiving nothing and spending a mere $1,194! Ibid.

66. Oshinsky, *Senator Joseph McCarthy and the American Labor Movement,* pp. 140-44.

67. Anderson and May, *McCarthy,* p. 377; Anderson interview; Anderson, *Confessions of a Muckraker,* pp. 254-55. Joe was extremely bitter about the former book. He refused to get on the same elevator with Anderson one day, saying that he didn't want the journalist to "stink it up." Anderson interview.

68. *Milwaukee Journal,* November 3, 4, 1952; *Appleton Post-Crescent,* November 4, 1952.

69. Crosby, *God, Church, and Flag,* pp. 113-14; Fried, *Men Against McCarthy,* p. 245.

70. Ibid.

71. Ibid., p. 244.

72. Ibid., pp. 243-44.

73. Ibid., p. 243; Matusow, *False Witness,* pp. 166-69.

74. Campaign materials from the Henry M. Jackson Papers; Brock, *Americans for Democratic Action,* p. 145; Fried, *Men Against McCarthy,* pp. 242-43.

75. Copy, William Benton to Millard Tydings, April 5, 1954, box 4, Benton Papers.

76. Parmet, *Eisenhower and the American Crusades,* pp. 109, 133; Fried, *Men Against McCarthy,* p. 233; Goldman, The Crucial Decade—And After, p. 226; *Milwaukee Journal,* October 24, 1952. "Today," Nixon wrote in 1978, "I regret the intensity of those attacks." Nixon, *RN,* I, 136.

77. *Major Campaign Speeches of Adlai E. Stevenson, 1952,* p. 282.

78. See Fried, *Men Against McCarthy,* p. 231; Parmet, *Eisenhower and The American Crusades,* pp. 127, 132, 141-43; Hughes, *The Ordeal of Power,* pp. 31-33. A G.O.P. senatorial "truth squad," staffed by McCarthyite senators, followed Truman throughout the campaign, condemning his administration for its approach to the internal Communist conspiracy. E.g., *New York Times,* October 7, 1952.

79. See Fried, *Men Against McCarthy,* pp. 237-38, 242-44, 246-47.

80. *Major Campaign Speeches of Adlai E. Stevenson, 1952,* pp. 21, 32, 127, 129-31, 194, 273-75, 298.

81. *Appleton Post-Crescent,* November 5, 1952.

82. Korb interview, September 6, 1975.

83. See O'Brien, "Senator Joseph McCarthy and Wisconsin," pp. 190, 200-3; Crosby, *God, Church and Flag,* pp. 95-98; Oshinsky, *Senator Joseph McCarthy and the American Labor Movement,* pp. 147-55; Nelson Polsby, "Towards an Explanation of McCarthyism," *Political Studies,* 8 (October, 1960), 258-63; editorial, *Chicago Sun-Times,* June 30, 1952; editorial, *Madison Capital Times,* September 15, 1952; Michael Paul Rogin, *The Intellectuals and McCarthy: the Radical Specter* (Cambridge, Mass., 1967), p. 99; Louis H. Bean, *Influences in*

the 1954 Mid-Term Elections (New York, 1954), p. 11. Rogin, *The Intellectuals and McCarthy,* pp. 59-100, 215-60 are especially valuable.

84. *Appleton Post-Crescent,* November 5, 1952; *Arizona Republic,* November 8, 1952.

85. Bean, *Influences in the 1954 Mid-Term Elections,* pp. 1-2, 18-22; Fried, *Men Against McCarthy,* p. 249.

86. Crosby, *God, Church, and Flag,* pp. 102-03; Hyman, *The Lives of William Benton,* pp. 480-81; Bean, *Influences in the 1954 Mid-Term Elections,* pp. 23-24; copy, undated memorandum, William Benton to Maurice Rosenblatt, attached to copy, John Howe to Henry Kaiser, July 14, 1953, box 4, Benton Papers. McCarthy did not make special overtures to Roman Catholics. The Wisconsin campaign was without discernible religious overtones. See Crosby, *God, Church, and Flag,* pp. 91-95.

87. Louis Harris, *Is There a Republican Majority?* (New York, 1956), pp. 32, 203-04, 223; Angus Campbell, et al., *The Voter Decides* (Evanston, Illinois, 1954), p. 52; Angus Campbell et al., *The American Voter* (New York, 1960), pp. 50-51; *The Gallup Poll,* II, 1135; Rogin, *The Intellectuals and McCarthy,* p. 247. Asked by Gallup pollsters in late 1952 why they voted for Eisenhower, 42 percent cited corruption in government, 24 percent noted Korea, and 9 percent mentioned Communism in government. *The Gallup Poll,* II, 1115. See also p. 1118.

88. Arthur Krock in *New York Times,* November 5, 1952; William S. White in ibid., January 18, 1953. Krock, a personal friend of Joseph P. Kennedy and his family, noted that in the defeat of Henry Cabot Lodge, "Mr. McCarthy unquestionably felt no pain." Ibid., November 6, 1952.

89. *Madison Capital Times,* December 16, 1952; Lewis quoted in May, *China Scapegoat,* p. 262. On Hoover and Vincent, see ibid., pp. 206-08, 234-35, 286-87. The behavior of ultraconservative Hiram Bingham, Review Board chairman, was highly irregular during this probe. His vote against Vincent, which was decisive, might well have been politically inspired. Earlier, McCarthy had asserted publicly that he could not conceive of "any good American" leaving Jessup, Davies, and Carter in the State Department. See ibid., pp. 240-41, 244-59; *Madison Capital Times,* November 21, 1952.

90. Ibid., December 29, 1952.

CHAPTER 18

1. *Major Campaign Speeches of Adlai E. Stevenson, 1952,* p. 309.

2. *New York Times,* November 21, 1952; Griffith, *The Politics of Fear,* p. 208. The other five were: Majority Leader Taft; conservative Eugene D. Millikin of

Colorado, G.O.P. Conference head and chairman of the Finance Committee; William F. Knowland, chairman of the Policy Committee; Styles Bridges, chairman of the Appropriations Committee; and freshman Frank Carlson of Kansas, a close friend of Eisenhower. *New York Times,* January 4, 1953.

3. See William S. White in ibid., January 18, 1953.

4. Johnson in William S. White, *The Professional: Lyndon B. Johnson* (Boston, 1964), pp. 49-50; copy, J. W. Fulbright to William Benton, March 4, 1953, box 4, Benton Papers; Reedy interview.

5. Mazo, *Richard Nixon,* p. 145.

6. *Madison Capital Times,* November 20, 21, 1952.

7. May, *China Scapegoat,* pp. 264-70. Dulles's leniency toward Vincent enraged McCarthyites. Joe said, "Under no circumstances should anyone like Vincent, having been rejected by the Loyalty Board, be entitled to any pension." Ibid., pp. 273-77. Dulles turned to Walter Judd, Vincent's longtime adversary, for advice on filling the post of Assistant Secretary of State for the Far East. Ibid., p. 269. On Davies, see *New York Times,* November 6, 1954.

8. Ibid., January 23, 1953.

9. Actually, Lourie was a political novice who had learned of McLeod from a Chicago neighbor. After an agreeable luncheon meeting in Washington with McLeod, Lourie offered him the post. The business executive was soon to regret his hasty move. Hughes, *The Ordeal of Power,* pp. 74-75.

10. *Wisconsin State Journal,* November 9, 1952; *Washington Times Herald,* January 4, 1953; *Madison Capital Times,* November 29, December 29, (Robert S. Allen) 31, 1952.

11. Cohn, *McCarthy,* pp. 47-48, 66; Robert F. Kennedy, *The Enemy Within* (New York, 1960), pp. 176, 307.

12. Whalen, *The Founding Father,* p. 445; Koskoff, *Joseph P. Kennedy,* pp. 439-41; Krock, *Memoirs,* pp. 318-22; Arthur M. Schlesinger, Jr., *Robert Kennedy and His Times* (New York, 1978), pp. 91, 101-2, 107, 113-14.

13. *New York Times,* January 3, 1953; Cohn, *McCarthy,* p. 48.

14. *New York Times,* January 3, 1953; "The Self-Inflated Target," *Time,* LXIII (March 22, 1954), 23, 26; Cocke, Kiermas, Minetti (March 14, 1977), Swedish, Van Susteren (December 26, 1975), Korb (September 6, 1975) interviews.

15. "The Self-Inflated Target," p. 23; Demaris, *The Director,* pp. 159-60, 164-66; Cohn, *McCarthy,* pp. 47-48. Cohn soon became closely associated with Hoover and his assistant Lou Nichols. Nichols interview.

16. Sokolsky in *New York Journal American,* July 24, 1959; Cohn, *McCarthy,* pp. 45-48, 111, 141.

17. *New York Times,* January 25, 1954; Catlin, Van Susteren (December 26, 1975), Edwards (November 17, 1976), Townsend (June 26, 1975) interviews.

Cohn was highly sensitive to the fact that many American liberals, radicals, and Communists were Jewish. He soon joined Sokolsky, Alfred Kohlberg, Eugene Lyons, and others in creating the American Jewish League against Communism. Cohn, *McCarthy,* pp. 249-50.

18. Richard Rovere, "The Adventures of Cohn and Schine," *The Reporter,* 9 (July 21, 1953), 9-11; Rovere, *Senator Joe McCarthy,* pp. 193-95; "Self-Inflated Target," *Time,* LXIII (March 22, 1945), 26.
19. *New York Times,* January 6, 8, February 5, 1953; *Madison Capital Times,* January 26, 1953.
20. Ibid., January 31, 1953.
21. Ibid.; Joe McCarthy to Dwight D. Eisenhower, January 21, 1953, George M. Humphrey to Dwight D. Eisenhower, February 3, 1953, OF 148-B, Eisenhower Papers; memorandum, Charles Willis to Bernard M. Shanley, April 22, 1953, OF 103-P, ibid. The request for Internal Revenue materials was routinely granted. The Hennings Committee, of course, had been given the same privilege while investigating McCarthy.
22. *New York Times,* January 27, 29, February 4, 5, 7, 1953; William Shannon in *Madison Capital Times,* February 4, 1953; Joe McCarthy to Dwight D. Eisenhower, February 3, 1953, Joe McCarthy to Sherman Adams, February 4, 1953, GF9-D-1, Eisenhower Papers; Cohn, *McCarthy,* pp. 52-53; Eisenhower, *The White House Years, Mandate for Change,* p. 320; *Congressional Record,* 83d Cong., 1st sess., February 6, 1953, pp. 926-34. See also Joe McCarthy to John T. Flynn, November 28, 1952, January 7, 1953, Flynn Papers.
23. *New York Times,* February 6, 1953; Charles E. Bohlen, *Witness to History, 1929-1969* (New York, 1973), pp. 309-13; Adams, *Firsthand Report,* p. 94.
24. Ibid., pp. 91-93; Athan G. Theoharis, *The Yalta Myths, An Issue in U.S. Politics, 1945-1955* (Columbia, Missouri, 1970), pp. 158-65.
25. Bohlen, *Witness to History,* pp. 314-20.
26. Ibid., p. 321.
27. Ibid., pp. 321-22; Parmet, *Eisenhower and the American Crusades,* p. 240; John Robinson Beal, *John Foster Dulles, 1888-1959* (New York, 1959), pp. 141-42; *Madison Capital Times,* March 21, 24, 1953. McLeod sought to fire Bohlen's brother-in-law, Charles W. Thayer, Consul General in Munich, over a morals episode involving a Russian woman some years earlier. Thayer was summoned to appear before the McCarthy subcommittee but was permitted to escape the ordeal through resignation. Bohlen, *Witness to History,* p. 323; *Madison Capital Times,* March 26, 1953.
28. Bohlen, *Witness to History,* p. 322.
29. Ibid., pp. 322-23; Hughes, *The Ordeal of Power,* pp. 82-83; *Madison Capital Times,* March 17, 1953.

30. Bohlen, *Witness to History,* p. 324.
31. Ibid., pp. 324-27; *Madison Capital Times,* March 19, 1953.
32. Ibid., March 19, 20, 21, 1953; *Congressional Record,* 83d Cong., 1st sess., March 20, 1953, pp. 2155-57. According to Emmet John Hughes, a White House staff member was assigned to McLeod to see that he was kept "secure" from any public place where he might be served a subpoena. Hughes, *The Ordeal of Power,* p. 75.
33. Adams, *Firsthand Report,* pp. 94-95; Bohlen, *Witness to History,* p. 336; *Congressional Record,* 83d Cong., 1st sess., March 23, 1953, pp. 2192, 2194; Hughes, *The Ordeal of Power,* p. 83; Mazo, *Richard Nixon,* p. 145.
34. *Madison Capital Times,* March 23, 1953.
35. Ibid., March 24, 1953; *Congressional Record,* 83d Cong., 1st sess., March 23, 1953, pp. 2187-2208; Bohlen, *Witness to History,* pp. 328-29.
36. Ibid., pp. 330-33; *Congressional Record,* 83d Cong., 1st sess., March 25, 1953, pp. 2277-2300.
37. *Madison Capital Times,* March 26, 1953.
38. Childs in *Kansas City Times,* March 27, 1953; copy, Dwight D. Eisenhower to Harry Bullis, OF 99-R, Eisenhower Papers; Hughes, *The Ordeal of Power,* p. 81.
39. *Congressional Record,* 83d Cong., 1st sess., March 27, 1953, pp. 2374-92. Of nine absentees, six Democrats and two Republicans favored confirmation. Curiously, William Jenner, away on Senate business, made no announcement.
40. Taft in William S. White, *The Taft Story* (New York, 1954), p. 239. Asked if the Bohlen struggle meant a rupture in relations with McCarthy, Taft told reporters, "no, no, no, no." *New York Times,* March 28, 1953.
41. Childs in *Kansas City Times,* March 27, 1953; Utley in *Chicago Sun-Times,* March 25, 1953.
42. See *Madison Capital Times,* March 27, 1953. For an able summary of the Bohlen case, see the booklet by James N. Rosenau, *The Nomination of "Chip" Bohlen* (New York, 1958).
43. William S. White, *Citadel, The Story of the U.S. Senate* (New York, 1956), pp. 257-58.
44. *New York Times,* October 4, 1952, February 3, 1953.
45. See Ralph Lord Roy, *Communism and the Churches* (New York, 1960), pp. 232-48, 254-60.
46. *New York Times,* February 5, 7, 15, 17, 22, 1953; U.S. Senate, Permanent Subcommittee on Investigations, *State Department-File Survey, Hearings,* 83d Cong., 1st sess., 1953.
47. *New York Times,* February 13, 1953. The Foreign Relations Committee had a subcommittee already studying the Voice. Formerly chaired by Senator Ful-

bright, it would now be headed by Bourke Hickenlooper and conduct hearings simultaneously with the McCarthy Subcommittee. By April, six congressional inquiries into the Voice were in progress.

48. Ibid.; Martin Merson, *The Private Diary of a Public Servant* (New York, 1955), pp. 33-35, 38.

49. See ibid., pp. 22-23.

50. Ibid., pp. 22, 38-39, 56-57, 92-93, 119; Philip Horton, "Voices Within the Voice," *The Reporter*, 9 (July 21, 1953), 25-29.

51. Merson, *The Private Diary of a Public Servant*, pp. 31-32, 50-55; *New York Times*, February 14, 15, 17, March 1, 11, 1953; U.S. Senate, Permanent Subcommittee on Investigations, *State Department Information Program-Voice of America, Hearings*, 83d Cong., 1st sess., 1953 (hereafter referred to as *Voice Hearings*), pp. 19, 696. McCarthyites sought a high position in I.I.A. for McKesson, undoubtedly to strengthen their control over the agency. See Merson, *The Private Diary of a Public Servant*, pp. 56-57, 71, 95, 97. See also U.S. Senate, Permanent Subcommittee on Investigations, *Waste and Mismanagement in Voice of America Engineering Projects, Report*, 83d Cong., 2d sess., 1954. The subcommittee's finding (p. 10): "Poor planning, reckless disregard for taxpayers' money, incompetence, stupidity, or worse was the rule and not the exception . . ."

52. *New York Times*, February 18, 19, April 12, 1953; *Madison Capital Times*, February 24, 1953; Merson, *The Private Diary of a Public Servant*, pp. 1-7, 9.

53. Ibid., p. 12; *New York Times*, February 19, 1953; *Voice Hearings*, pp. 98-114.

54. *New York Times*, February 20, June 11, 16, 22, 23, 28, July 31, 1953; Merson, *The Private Diary of a Public Servant*, pp. 14-16; Martin Merson interview, John Foster Dulles Oral History, Princeton University. Out of over 100,000 titles by 85,000 authors, I.I.S. centers reported possessing only 39 titles by eight authors who were known Communists. Merson, *The Private Diary of a Public Servant*, p. 44. The subcommittee's final report claimed, "Over 30,000 books by Communists and those who have aided the Communist cause were in use . . ." U.S. Senate, Permanent Subcommittee on Investigations, *State Department Information Program-Information Centers, Report*, 83d Cong., 2d sess., 1954, p. 12.

55. Merson, *The Private Diary of a Public Servant*, pp. 16-19; *New York Times*, February 25, 1953.

56. Ibid., February 26, March 19, 1953; Merson, *The Private Diary of a Public Servant*, pp. 42-45.

57. *New York Times*, February 21, 1953.

58. Ibid., February 22, 28, April 15, 1953; Merson, *The Private Diary of a Public Servant*, pp. 24-26.

59. *New York Times,* February 28, 1953; *Madison Capital Times,* February 26, 1953.
60. *New York Times,* February 27, 1953. Matthews was heard in executive session. Ibid., March 1, 1953.
61. Ibid., March 3, 1953; *Voice Hearings,* pp. 298-305, 320-21, 324, 487.
62. *New York Times,* March 3, May 20, 1953; *Voice Hearings,* pp. 310-12.
63. *New York Times,* March 1, 5, 6, April 15, 1953; Merson, *The Private Diary of a Public Servant,* pp. 47-48, 62-67; *Voice Hearings,* pp. 331-87, 495-520. See James A. Wechsler, *The Age of Suspicion* (New York, 1953), pp. 4-5, 21-32.
64. *New York Times,* March 7, 1953; *Voice Hearings,* pp. 522-40.
65. Wechsler, *The Age of Suspicion,* p. 264.
66. *New York Times,* March 14, 1953; *Voice Hearings,* pp. 702-18.
67. *Madison Capital Times,* April 25, 30, May 8, 1953; Wechsler, *The Age of Suspicion,* pp. 266-316; U.S. Senate, Permanent Subcommittee on Investigations, *State Department Information Program-Information Centers, Hearings,* 83d Cong., 1st sess., 1953 (hereafter referred to as *Information Centers Hearings*), pp. 253-81, 289-324.
68. *New York Times,* March 7, 8, June 4, 1953.
69. Ibid., March 25, 1953; *Information Centers Hearings,* pp. 1-39.
70. *New York Times,* March 9, 16, 1953.
71. Ibid., March 10, 18, 30, 31, April 2, 14, 15, 16, 17, 18, May 21, 23, 24, 1953; *Madison Capital Times,* March 30, 31, April 2, 3, 9, May 26, 1953; Marquis Childs in *Kansas City Times,* June 2, 1953; U.S. Senate, Permanent Subcommittee on Investigations, *Control of Trade with the Soviet Bloc, Hearings,* 83d Cong., 1st sess., 1953; Beal, *John Foster Dulles,* pp. 148-49; Schlesinger, *Robert Kennedy and His Times,* pp. 108-12; Cohn, *McCarthy,* pp. 68-70; Mazo, *Richard Nixon,* pp. 145-46. Cf. Eleanor Lansing Dulles, "Footnote to History: A Day in the Life of Senator Joe McCarthy," *World Affairs,* 148 (Fall, 1980), 156-162.
72. Mazo, *Richard Nixon,* p. 146. Persons may well have been a secret source of White House information for McCarthy. See Surine (August 30, October 30, 1980), Korb (September 6, 1975) interviews; Hagerty Diary, February 28, March 24, May 12, 1954.
73. *New York Times,* April 18, 1951; *Washington Post,* April 26, 1953. Joe later claimed falsely that Cohn and Schine did not hold "formal" press conferences during the trip. See *Information Centers, Hearings,* pp. 197-98.
74. Horton, "Voices Within the Voice," pp. 28-29; *Information Centers Hearings,* pp. 187, 194.
75. Ibid., pp. 129-38, 159-65, 213; Cohn, *McCarthy,* p. 81.
76. In a deposition of a year earlier, McCarthy admitted that he had never heard of

Commonweal. Deposition, "Joseph R. McCarthy vs. The Post-Standard Company . . . ," pp. 217-18.

77. See *New York Times,* April 6, 8, 12, 15, 18, 19, 20, 21, 22, 1953; Drew Pearson in *Madison Capital Times,* April 22, 1953; Rovere, "The Adventures of Cohn and Schine," p. 9; Cohn, *McCarthy,* p. 82.

78. *Voice Hearings,* pp. 214-18; *Information Centers Hearings,* pp. 171-201, 221-42; Theodore Kaghan, "The McCarthyization of Theodore Kaghan," *The Reporter,* 9 (July 21, 1953), 17-25; *New York Times,* April 8, May 12, June 11, 16, 1953. Well-known radio commentator Raymond Swing resigned as the Voice of America's principal political analyst to protest Kaghan's forced departure. He condemned the State Department's "spineless failure . . . to stand by its own staff." Ibid., May 20, 1953.

79. *Madison Capital Times,* April 29, 1953; *New York Times,* May 13, 15, 16, 1953; *Congressional Record,* 83d Cong., 1st sess., May 14, 1953, pp. 4909-14.

80. *New York Times,* April 23, May 14, 19, 20, 24, 28, June 2, 10, 11, 1953; *Madison Capital Times,* June 10, 1953. See U.S. Senate, Permanent Subcommittee on Investigations, *State Department—Student-Teacher Exchange Program, Hearings,* 83d Cong., 1st sess., 1953.

81. Merson, *The Private Diary of a Public Servant,* pp. 120-71; *New York Times,* July 1, 2, 7, 10, 21, 22, 1953. For the subcommittee's reports on the I.I.A. investigations, see U.S. Senate, Permanent Subcommittee on Investigations, *Voice of America, Report,* 83d Cong., 2d sess., 1954; U.S. Senate, Permanent Subcommittee on Investigations, *State Department Information Program-Information Centers, Report,* 83d Cong., 2d sess., 1954; *New York Times,* January 11, 18, 1954. For a more detailed account of the I.I.A. probe, see Latham, *The Communist Controversy in Washington,* pp. 323-49.

CHAPTER 19

1. William S. White, "Joe McCarthy, The Man With the Power," *Look,* 17 (June 16, 1953), 32.

2. "A Vigorous Individual," *Time,* LXII (September 7, 1953), 21-22. Spellman declared, "He is against Communism and he has done and is doing something about it. He is making America aware of the dangers of Communism." *Madison Capital Times,* August 6, 1953.

3. *New York Times,* April 28, 1953.

4. *Wisconsin State Journal,* April 23, 1953; editorial, *The Christian Century,* LXX (May 6, 1953), 531; James Burnham in *Davenport [Iowa] Daily Times,* May 15, 1953; *Madison Capital Times,* June 13, 1953.

5. White, "Joe McCarthy, The Man with the Power," p. 30.
6. *New York Times,* June 15, 17, 1953.
7. Ibid., June 18, 1953.
8. Ibid., June 27, 28, 1953; *Madison Capital Times,* July 5, 1953.
9. *New York Times,* April 30, June 12, 1953; *Washington Daily News,* July 20, 1953; Kiermas interview.
10. *Madison Capital Times,* June 29, 30, 1953.
11. *Washington Daily News,* May 25, 1953; *Christian Science Monitor,* May 27, 1953; *Madison Capital Times,* July 21, 1953; G. Bromley Oxnam to William Benton, March 11, 1954, box 5, Benton Papers. A leading Japanese daily called McCarthy a "modern emperor of Tsin" and asked, "Where is freedom of speech in America? This despot can become another Hitler. Eisenhower can do nothing with him. He is like a satan." *Kansas City Times,* June 27, 1953.
12. *Washington Daily News,* May 25, 1953; *Milwaukee Journal,* May 30, 1953.
13. See Griffith, *The Politics of Fear,* pp. 228-29.
14. Ibid., pp., 225-27; Rosenblatt, Van Arkel interviews.
15. *New York Times,* June 19, 1953; Cohn, *McCarthy,* pp. 68-69.
16. *Washington Star,* July 9, 1953. Friends of McCarthy later remembered Matthews as a true believer with a serious drinking problem. See Buckley, Kiermas, Edwards (November 17, 1976), Waldrop, Nichols, Nellor (June 6, 1979), Lee interviews.
17. Copy, memorandum, John Howe to William Benton, July 10, 1953, box 4; George E. Agree to William Benton, July 23, 1953, box 5, both in the Benton Papers; *New York Times,* July 3, 1953.
18. Copy, memorandum, John Howe to William Benton, July 10, 1953, box 4, Benton Papers; *New York Times,* July 4, 5, 6, 1953.
19. Ibid., July 8, 1953.
20. Ibid., July 9, 1953. Clearing House leaders had already developed strategy for use in the full committee and on the Senate floor. Copy, memorandum, John Howe to William Benton, July 10, 1953, box 4, Benton Papers.
21. Hughes, *The Ordeal of Power,* pp. 83-85.
22. *New York Times,* July 10, 1953. See Cohn, *McCarthy,* pp. 60-61 for a possible explanation of the inflammatory sentence in Matthews' article. Cf. Kiermas interview.
23. *Madison Capital Times,* July 10, 11, 1953. HUAC agreed to hear Matthews' testimony. Testifying before HUAC in 1947, J. Edgar Hoover had expressed "a real apprehension so long as Communists are able to secure ministers of the Gospel to promote their evil work and espouse a cause that is alien to the religion of Christ and Judaism." *New York Times,* July 31, 1953. Still, Hoover was disturbed by the Matthews flap, probably because Matthews was too

specific, claiming to know the names of 7,000 pro-Red clergymen. Nichols interview.

24. *New York Times,* July 12, 1953.
25. *Madison Capital Times,* July 13, 1953. The State Department later dismissed the allegation as without substance. *New York Times,* January 21, 1954.
26. White in ibid., July 12, 1953; *Madison Capital Times,* July 13, 1953. For a perceptive summary of the Matthews affair by Maurice Rosenblatt, see the copy of *Congressional Report,* July 22, 1953, box 4, Benton Papers.
27. *New York Times,* July 5, 10, 1953; *Congressional Record,* 83d Cong., 1st sess., July 9, 1953, pp. 8277-78.
28. Surine interviews of May 13, 27, 1977, and May 19, July 18, 1980; Cohn, *McCarthy,* p. 64.
29. Alsop in *Madison Capital Times,* July 17, 1953; Arthur Krock in *New York Times,* July 26, 1953; Cohn, *McCarthy,* pp. 63-64. See *New York Times,* July 15, August 11, 1953. In early 1955 McCarthy submitted information on the C.I.A. to Gen. Mark W. Clark, chairman of a Hoover Commission task force to study the agency. Six months later, the task force declared there was no "valid ground" for McCarthy's charge that the C.I.A. was seriously infiltrated by Communists. Ibid., January 15, June 29, 1955. See Victor Marchetti and John D. Marks, *The CIA and the Cult of Intelligence* (New York, rev. ed., 1980), pp. 185-94. Surine remained convinced, years later, that the Army-McCarthy hearings were deliberately designed by the Administration to protect the agency from investigation. Surine interviews of May 27, 1977, and May 19, 1980.
30. *Congressional Record,* 83d Cong., 1st sess., July 13, 1953, pp. 8619-21.
31. Lehman, in reply, wanted to know why McCarthy had allegedly accepted Red support in the election of 1946. Joe retaliated by claiming that Lehman had appointed three Communists to UNRRA during the period he served as Director-General. See ibid., July 20, 1953, p. 9179, July 21, 1953, pp. 9346-48, 9352-54; *Washington Daily News,* July 20, 1953.
32. *Madison Capital Times,* July 17, 21, 1953.
33. Ibid., July 24, 1953; *New York Times,* July 25, 1953.
34. Ibid. The hearing was transferred to larger quarters and televised on orders from McCarthy, ostensibly with the approval of ailing Styles Bridges. Other committee members were not consulted in advance.
35. *Madison Capital Times,* July 27, 1953.
36. *New York Times,* July 30, 1953.
37. Ibid., August 3, 1953.
38. *Madison Capital Times,* August 4, 1953.
39. Ibid., July 27, 1953.

40. Ibid., August 4, 6, September 5, 1953; *New York Times,* August 11, 12, 1953.
41. The C.I.A. pointed out that Bundy had been cleared repeatedly on security grounds. Director Dulles denied McCarthy's request to see the agency's recorded version of the reasons Bundy had contributed to the Hiss defense fund. Ibid., August 7, 1953.
42. Copy, memorandum, John Howe to William Benton, July 10, 1953, box 4, Benton Papers; Rosenblatt in *Congressional Report,* July 22, 1953, ibid.; editorial, *Madison Capital Times,* August 18, 1953; Bell in ibid., July 27, 1953.
43. Editorial, ibid.; *Congressional Report,* July 22, 1953, box 4, Benton Papers.
44. Copy, memorandum, Thomas Wheeler to William Benton and John Howe, July 31, 1953, ibid.; Fulbright interview.
45. Buckley, Nellor (May 7, 1977), Kiermas, Lee interviews.
46. Jackson interview; William W. Prochnau and Richard W. Larsen, *A Certain Democrat: Senator Henry M. Jackson, A Political Biography* (New York, 1972), p. 139.
47. *Milwaukee Journal,* July 1, 3, 1953; Pusey, Keller, Van Susteren (February 21, 1976), Dohr, Sumnicht interviews; "McCarthy and a Besieged Army," *Life,* 36 (March 8, 1954), 29. According to Ray Kiermas, Joe had also received a letter describing how Pusey ridiculed him at parties. Kiermas interview. Joe would wage a vendetta against Pusey and Harvard for years, in part because the university president refused to dismiss faculty members for taking the Fifth Amendment before congressional committees. In late 1953 Joe said that a bill was being prepared that would deny tax-exemption for all educational institutions employing "Fifth-Amendment Communists." *New York Times,* November 6, December 19, 1953.
48. White in ibid., July 26, 1953. A Gallup poll of June, 1953 showed that only 12 percent of Catholics expressed high approval of McCarthy while 15 percent expressed intense disapproval. See Agnes E. Meyer in *Milwaukee Journal,* November 2, 1953. Pollster Louis Bean concluded in mid-1954, "There is no denying that he still rates more favorably among Catholics than among Protestants and Jews, but that does not mean that his influence can sway the vote of a Catholic community." *Washington Post,* May 18, 1954. McCarthy enjoyed support from the widely read *Our Sunday Visitor,* and the *Brooklyn Tablet* and *Baltimore Catholic.* But the intellectual Catholic weeklies *America* and *Commonweal* strongly opposed him. While New York's Francis Cardinal Spellman openly favored Joe, and influential Bishop Fulton J. Sheen often privately consulted with him, the senator would never receive any official Church endorsement. See William R. Bechtel, "The Protestant Church Under Fire," *New Republic,* 128 (July 27, 1953), pp. 10-12; Crosby, *God, Church, and Flag,* pp. 228-51; Nellor interview, June 6, 1969.

49. William S. White predicted incorrectly that the death of Robert A. Taft on July 31 would split the G.O.P., as it removed "the one real bridge" between the somewhat liberal Eastern faction and the more conservative and McCarthyite Midwestern wing. Joe commented, "The greatest man I have ever known died today." *New York Times,* August 1, 1953.

CHAPTER 20

1. *New York Times,* June 22, 1953; U.S. Senate, Permanent Subcommittee On Investigations, *Communist Infiltration Among Army Civilian Workers, Hearings,* 83d Cong., 1st sess., September 8, 1953, p. 6, September 28, 1953, p. 31.

2. U.S. Senate, Permanent Subcommittee on Investigations, *Security-Government Printing Office, Hearings,* 83d Cong., 1st sess., 1953, passim; U.S. Senate, Permanent Subcommittee on Investigations, *Annual Report,* 83d Cong., 2d sess., 1954, pp. 15-18 (hereafter referred to as *Subcommittee Annual Report, 1954*); *New York Times,* August 11, 12, 13, 14, 15, 18, 19, 20, 21, 22, 23, 30, September 1, 1953; *The American Forum of the Air,* XVI (November 22, 1953), pp. 7-8; Cohn, *McCarthy,* pp. 53-54. Security in the G.P.O. was clearly lax at times. The subcommittee investigation found a gambling ring in operation among employees that had been discovered and reported in early 1948.

3. U.S. Senate, Permanent Subcommittee on Investigations, *Security-United Nations, Hearings,* 83d Cong., 1st sess., 1953, passim; *Subcommittee Annual Report, 1954,* pp. 38-40. In mid-October the subcommittee held two public hearings on the 1944 transfer of occupation currency plates from the United States to the Soviet government. The issue had already been examined by a joint committee of the Senate in 1947, and the (no doubt exaggerated) claim had been made that the wartime action had cost Americans some $255,000,000. The probe generated few headlines and was abandoned. See U.S. Senate, Permanent Subcommittee on Investigations, *Transfer of Occupation Currency Plates-Espionage Phase, Hearings,* 83d Cong., 1st sess., 1953, passim, esp. pp. 8-13. See also *New York Times,* October 20, 21, 22, 1953; Cohn, *McCarthy,* pp. 56-58; *Subcommittee Annual Report, 1954,* pp. 35-38; Packer, *Ex-Communist Witnesses,* pp. 60, 62, 115-16; Nichols interview.

4. Edwards (November 17, 1976, June 5, 1979), Kiermas, Reedy, Woods, Lee, Nellor (June 6, 1979) interviews; *Appleton Post-Crescent,* September 29, 1953; *Kansas City Star,* September 29, 1953; *Milwaukee Sentinel,* September 5, 1956; Cohn, *McCarthy,* pp. 93-94.

5. *Kansas City Star,* September 29, 1953; *Milwaukee Journal,* October 22, 1953; Murphy, "Texas Business and McCarthy," pp. 101, 208. When Joe wrecked the car in Wisconsin by hitting a deer, the Texas businessmen promptly, and quietly, bought him a replacement. Nellor interview, June 6, 1979.
6. *New York Times,* October 10, 1953; *Appleton Post-Crescent,* October 12, 1953.
7. *New York Times,* September 1, 2, 3, 1953.
8. Ibid., September 4, 5, 1953. "Miss Q," Doris Walters Powell, was later suspended from government service. The *Subcommittee Annual Report, 1954,* p. 5, claimed that she invoked the Fifth Amendment during her appearance before the subcommittee. This is extremely doubtful, as Joe made no mention of such an action in his press briefing. The testimony was never published, and Mrs. Powell was not asked to appear in a public hearing. The date of Mrs. Powell's confrontation with the subcommittee is incorrectly cited in the *Annual Report,* perhaps an attempt to confuse the accused with another witness, Mrs. Marvel J. Cooke, who took the Fifth Amendment on that day when questioned about Mrs. Powell. See the comments by Mrs. Powell's attorney in *New York Times,* September 9, 1953.
9. U.S. Senate, Permanent Subcommittee on Investigations, *Communist Infiltration Among Army Civilian Workers, Hearings,* 83d Cong., 1st sess., 1953, pp. 9-23, 52; *Madison Capital Times,* September 11, 1953.
10. Ibid., September 10, 11, 1953.
11. U.S. Senate, Permanent Subcommittee on Investigations, *Communist Infiltration in the Army, Hearings,* 83d Cong., 1st sess., 1953, pp. 85-105.
12. Ibid., September 28, 1953, passim; *New York Times,* September 29, 1953.
13. Minetti (March 14, 1977), Cohn interviews; *New York Times,* January 11, 1954; *The American Forum of the Air,* XVI (November 22, 1953), p. 6; U.S. Senate, Permanent Subcommittee on Investigations, *Army Signal Corps-Subversion and Espionage, Hearings,* 83d Cong., 1st and 2d sess., 1954, pp. 40-42, 61-62, 73-74 (hereafter referred to as *Fort Monmouth Hearings*). Asked if the subcommittee had wiretap evidence, Joe said, "We have done no wiretapping." *New York Times,* December 18, 1953.
14. *Washington Post,* October 7, 1953.
15. *New York Times,* October 8, 1953.
16. Ibid., October 13, 1953.
17. *Newark Star-Ledger,* October 22, 1953.
18. *Boston Post,* October 21, 1953; *New York Times,* October 21, 1953.
19. Ibid., October 18, 21, 22, 1953.
20. Ibid., October 27, 28, 31, 1953; *New York Herald Tribune,* October 28, 1953.
21. *New York Times,* October 14, November 15, 1953.
22. Ibid., October 17, November 17, 1953. See Cohn's remarks in *The American*

Forum of the Air, XVI (November 22, 1953), p. 10. Greenblum was later suspended. *New York Times,* February 12, 1954.

23. See *Fort Monmouth Hearings,* pp. 25-33, 43-50, 133-43, 202-07, 237-52, 264-67, 275-81, 285-91, 382, 407-09, 413-34, 462-70.

24. See ibid., pp. 18-25; Walter and Miriam Schneir, *Invitation to an Inquest* (New York, 1973), pp. 127, 157, 277-79, 293-96, 344-49.

25. *Fort Monmouth Hearings,* pp. 77-113; *New York Times,* January 12, 1954; Cohn, *McCarthy,* pp. 166-67. Joe declared that he would seek indictments against Coleman for espionage and perjury. The next day he told reporters, "It is not our function to develop cases of espionage." *New York Times,* December 10, 11, 1953. Coleman was later reinstated.

26. *Fort Monmouth Hearings,* pp. 35-50, 118, 130-31, 141, 151-53, 161, 202-07, 242-43, 249, 251, 268-71, 281, 287, 302-04, 358.

27. Ibid., pp. 113-43, 167-72, 192-202, 207-23.

28. Ibid., pp. 252, 274, 277, 307. For months the Jenner subcommittee had been calling Fifth Amendment teachers into open hearings in order to get them fired. See Alan Barth, *Government by Investigation* (New York, 1955), pp. 169-76.

29. *Fort Monmouth Hearings,* pp. 338, 343, 425-26.

30. Ibid., pp. 256-57, 275-81, 375-82, 411-13, 426-41. An FBI spokesman insisted that the subcommittee had received none of the bureau's confidential file information, officially or unofficially. *New York Times,* December 12, 1953.

31. *Fort Monmouth Hearings,* pp. 99-100, 107, 275-81, 380, 385, 418.

32. *New York Times,* January 11, 13, 1954; Scientists' Committee on Loyalty and Security, "Fort Monmouth One Year Later," *Bulletin of the Atomic Scientists,* 11 (April, 1955), 148-50. The subcommittee may also have been responsible for the suspension of twelve employees at the Griffiss Air Force Base radar research center in Rome, New York. Joe told reporters, "It all has to do with Communist activities, and when you are dealing with Communist activities, you are involving espionage." *New York Times,* December 15, 16, 1953.

33. Ibid., January 11, 13, 1954. Many of the Jews had attended the City College of New York during the Depression.

34. *New York Times,* January 11, 1954; *Milwaukee Journal,* November 15, 1953. When Lawton was given a "disability" discharge not long afterward, McCarthyites were convinced that the Army was retaliating for his cooperation with the subcommittee. Cohn, *McCarthy,* p. 95; Minetti (March 14, 1977, April 12, 1978), Surine (June 20, 1980) interviews.

35. *New York Times,* November 28, 1953.

36. Ibid., December 6, 10, 13, 1953. Taylor, a member of the National Committee for an Effective Congress, had told a Bronxville, New York, audience in

February that congressional inquiries had become a "vicious weapon of the extreme right against their political opponents." See his excellent study, *Grand Inquest: The Story of Congressional Investigations* (New York, 1955).

37. *New York Times,* December 11, 12, 1953.

38. *New York Herald Tribune,* November 9, 1953.

39. *New York Times,* November 13, 14, 17, 19, 20, December 10, 1953; U.S. Senate, Permanent Subcommittee on Investigations, *Subversion and Espionage in Defense Establishments and Industry, Hearings,* 83d and 84th Cong., 1st and 2d sess., 1953-55, pp. 1-10, 131 (hereafter cited as *G.E. Hearings*).

40. See ibid., pp. 199-200.

41. Ibid., p. 126. Cf. Joe's statement on p. 135.

42. Cohn, *McCarthy,* p. 55; *G.E. Hearings,* pp. 63-64, 84. At least initially, McCarthy also sought to use the investigation to damage the United Electrical, Radio and Machine Workers of America, the recognized bargaining agent at G.E. that had been expelled by the C.I.O. in 1949 as Communist-dominated. *New York Times,* November 13, 25, December 10, 1953. The union was not a prominent part of the hearings, but several witnesses were members, and William Teto attacked it in a public session. *G.E. Hearings,* pp. 141-42.

43. "Communists in the U.S. a Greater Menace Now," *U.S. News and World Report,* 35 (September 4, 1953), pp. 40-44, 49-50.

44. *New York Times,* December 17, 1953; *Madison Capital Times,* November 3, 1953.

45. See ibid., January 22, 1954; *New York Times,* January 25, 27, 1954.

46. Ibid., November 7, 1953; Adams, *Firsthand Report,* p. 140.

47. *New York Times,* November 8, 11, 1953. The Republican candidate won in California.

48. *Madison Capital Times,* November 17, 1953. See James Reston in *New York Times,* November 17, 1953, and Herbert Lehman in ibid., December 12, 1953.

49. See Latham, *The Communist Controversy in Washington,* pp. 175-79, 369-72.

50. See Cabell Phillips, *The Truman Presidency, The History of a Triumphant Succession* (New York, 1966), pp. 358-60; *Madison Capital Times,* November 12, 16, 17, 1953; *New York Times,* November 8, 17, 1953; *Washington Star,* November 12, 1953.

51. *New York Times,* November 17, 1953.

52. Ibid., November 21, 1953. In October, the Administration announced the interim appointment of McCarthy's close friend Robert E. Lee to the Federal Communications Commission. Everett Dirksen and Styles Bridges were Lee's principal sponsors. The Clearing House and Mike Monroney fought the

nomination, but it passed the Senate in early 1954 by a better than two-to-one margin. Griffith, *The Politics of Fear,* pp. 235-37; Lee interview.

53. Cohn, *McCarthy,* pp. 111-12; *Washington Star,* November 12, 1953; *New York Times,* November 24, 1953; James Reston in ibid., November 25, 1953. Cohn also contended that Ike sent his brother, Dr. Milton Eisenhower, to George Sokolsky to explore an accommodation with McCarthy. Dr. Eisenhower has denied the story. See Parmet, *Eisenhower and the American Crusades,* p. 338.

54. Ibid., November 19, 1953.

55. Ibid., November 25, 1953. A reference to "the Augean stables," use of "Stygian blackness," and a quotation in Latin from Cato betray the pen of another author of the speech.

56. Ibid., November 26, December 2, 3, 1953; *Madison Capital Times,* December 8, 1953. Senators Jenner and Welker agreed with McCarthy about the forthcoming elections, as did Leonard Hall, chairman of the Republican National Committee. For the hostile British reaction to McCarthy's position on trade with Red China, see *New York Times,* December 14, 1953.

57. *Madison Capital Times,* December 4, 5, 1953; *New York Times,* December 6, 7, 13, 1953. Joe's appeal for telegrams and letters no doubt stemmed from the favorable response to his November 24 speech. He had reported to Tom Korb, "We have received over 1,000 wires and over 10,000 letters. Of these, approximately 100 were unfriendly." Joe McCarthy to Tom Korb, December 3, 1953, Korb Papers.

58. *New York Times,* December 7, 1953; *New York Post,* December 14, 1953.

59. *New York Times,* December 19, 1953; *Madison Capital Times,* December 19, 1953.

60. Ibid.

61. *New York Times,* December 20, 1953.

62. *Madison Capital Times,* January 5, 1954; *Washington Post,* January 6, 1954; Mazo, *Richard Nixon,* pp. 147-48.

63. *New York Times,* January 9, 12, 13, 1954.

64. Editorial, *Madison Capital Times,* December 30, 1953, January 14, 1954; William S. White in *New York Times,* January 13, 1954, Waldrop interview.

65. *New York Times,* January 15, 18, 23, (James Reston) 24, 27 (W. H. Lawrence) 31, 1954. Jackson's objection concerned the alleged savings of $18,000,000 after the Voice of America probe. The annual report claimed that the staff had interviewed some 1,200 people in the course of undertaking 157 distinct investigations and 445 preliminary inquiries! *Subcommittee Annual Report, 1954,* p. 3.

66. *The Gallup Poll,* II, 1201-02; *Washington Post,* January 15, 1954. In April, 1953, Joe's Gallup rating was 19 percent favorable, 22 percent unfavorable,

and (incredibly) 59 percent no opinion. The "favorable" figure rose to 35 percent in June, and was 34 percent in August.

67. *The Gallup Poll,* II, 1136, 1163, 1191, 1197, 1213; Rogin, *The Intellectuals and McCarthy,* pp. 232-60.

68. *The Gallup Poll,* II, 1202-03; *Washington Post,* January 16, 1954.

69. *The Gallup Poll,* II, 1203-04; *Washington Post,* January 16, 1954.

70. *G.E. Hearings,* pp. 22-46; "Investigations," *Time,* LXIII (January 24, 1954), 20. Furry and Kamin were both cited for contempt of Congress by the Senate. *New York Times,* August 12, 1954.

71. Ibid., January 17, 1954. Dulles respectfully rejected the evaluation. "I find no evidence of any cringing on the part of the Foreign Service personnel," he told reporters. Ibid., January 20, 1954.

72. See ibid., January 23, 1954.

73. Ibid., November 5, 1953, January 30, 1954; *Madison Capital Times,* December 12, 22, 24, 1954, February 4, 1954; Adams, *Firsthand Report,* pp. 143-45.

74. *New York Times,* January 31, 1954; U.S. Senate, Permanent Subcommittee on Investigations, *Communist Infiltration in the Army, Hearings,* 83d Cong., 2d sess., 1954, pp. 107-18.

75. See Minetti (March 14, 1977, April 12, 1978), Korb (September 6, 1975), Surine (July 18, 1980) interviews; Cohn, *McCarthy,* pp. 96-99; *Watkins Committee Hearings,* pp. 438, 455, 465-66, 482-83, 500-501, 505-07, 515-19; Arthur V. Watkins, *Enough Rope* (Englewood Cliffs, New Jersey, 1969), pp. 22, 64-68; Edwin Johnson in *Congressional Record,* 83d Cong., 2d sess., November 29, 1954, p. 16158.

76. See Cohn, *McCarthy,* pp. 101-02.

77. *Congressional Record,* 83d Cong., 2d sess., February 2, 1954, pp. 1086-1103; *New York Times,* February 3, 1954.

78. See Cohn, *McCarthy,* pp. 101-02; *Washington Post,* February 4, 1954; *New York Times,* February 4, 1954.

79. *Madison Capital Times,* February 5, 8, 11, 12, 1954; *New York Post,* February 8, 1954; "A Word for Joe," *Time,* LXIII (February 15, 1954), 18.

80. See *Watkins Committee Hearings,* p. 186; Edwards interview, November 17, 1976; McCarthy mss. in Edwards Papers.

81. U.S. Senate, Permanent Subcommittee on Investigations, *Communist Infiltration in the Army, Hearings,* 83d Cong., 2d sess., 1954, pp. 119-23. Cf. *New York Times,* February 19, 1954.

82. U.S. Senate, Permanent Subcommittee on Investigations, *Communist Infiltration in the Army, Hearings,* 83d Cong., 2d sess., 1954, pp. 123-43. See Charles Potter, *Days of Shame* (New York, 1965), p. 87. Peress soon reported that "fascist hoodlums" had thrown rocks through the windows of his home,

adding that he had received 30 unsigned hate letters. "This is the terror that stems from McCarthyism," he said. *New York Times,* March 1, 1954.

83. Ibid., February 19, 1954. The Administration soon put the Armed Forces under the security risk standards applied to civilian federal employees. The new directive, among other things, provided that those invoking the Fifth Amendment or refusing to answer questions about alleged subversive affiliations or associations would not be drafted or accepted as volunteers. Secretary of Defense Wilson told reporters, "As I stated previously, one single Communist in the Armed Forces is one too many." The Doctor Draft Act was also altered, with Wilson's assistance, to prevent another Peress case. See ibid., April 9, 1954; E. Bruce Geelhoed, *Charles E. Wilson and Controversy at the Pentagon, 1953 to 1957* (Detroit 1979), pp. 92-94.

84. Edwards interview, November 17, 1976; McCarthy mss. in Edwards Papers; *Watkins Committee Hearings,* p. 190; *New York Times,* February 21, 1954.

85. U.S. Senate, Permanent Subcommittee on Investigations, *Communist Infiltration in the Army, Hearings,* 83d Cong., 2d sess., 1954, p. 137; Minetti (March 14, 1977, April 12, 1978), Korb (September 6, 1975), Edwards (November 17, 1976) interviews; *New York Times,* February 23, 1954. Cf. Cohn, *McCarthy,* pp. 103-04.

86. *Madison Capital Times,* February 23, 1954.

87. U.S. Senate, Permanent Subcommittee on Investigations, *Communist Infiltration in the Army, Hearings,* 83d Cong., 2d sess., 1954, pp. 145-57; *New York Times,* February 19, 23, 1954.

88. Ibid., February 19, 1954.

89. See the Alsops in *Madison Capital Times,* February 15, 1954, and the editorial of February 20, 1954, ibid.

90. Ibid.; Drew Middleton in *New York Times,* February 18, 1954.

91. Ibid., February 21, 1954; *Madison Capital Times,* February 20, 22, 1954.

92. *New York Times,* February 21, 1954; *Madison Capital Times,* February 22, 1954.

93. Editorial, *New York Times,* February 23, 1954; editorial, *Chicago Tribune,* February 25, 1954; Lawrence in *Madison Capital Times,* March 4, 1954; Kaltenborn in ibid., March 1, 1954.

94. *New York Times,* February 23, 1954; Potter, *Days of Shame,* pp. 85, 152-60.

95. *New York Times,* February 23, 1954.

96. Ibid.

97. Surine interview, June 8, 1977. Joe specifically denied having had access to FBI reports in the case. He and Mundt were openly critical of the Army's failure to heed Hoover's warning in 1951. *Fort Monmouth Hearings,* pp. 324, 326-27, 329.

98. Ibid., pp. 310-29; *New York Times,* February 24, 1954.

99. Ibid.

100. See ibid., February 25, 1954.

101. *Fort Monmouth Hearings,* pp. 332-52.

102. *New York Times,* February 25, 1954. See James C. Hagerty Diary, February 23, 1954, James C. Hagerty Papers; copy, Karl E. Mundt to Fred Christopherson, March 1, 1954, FF2, Karl E. Mundt Papers.

103. In "Investigations," *Time,* LXIII (March 8, 1954), 24.

104. See ibid., pp. 23-24.

105. Hagerty Diary, February 24, 1954; *New York Times,* February 26, 28, 1954; "Investigations," *Time,* March 8, 1954, pp. 23-25.

106. *Washington Star,* January 23, 1954; Foster Shannon to Ralph Flanders, September 24, 1957, Flanders Papers; "Investigations," *Time,* March 8, 1954, p. 21.

107. *New York Times,* February 27, 1954.

108. Ibid.

109. *Washington Post,* March 1, 1954.

110. *Madison Capital Times,* March 3, 1954; "The Presidency," *Time,* LXIII (March 8, 1954), 20.

111. *New York Times,* March 2, 3, 1954. McLeod remained in charge of department security matters.

112. *Madison Capital Times,* March 2, 1954; *New York Times,* March 3, 1954.

113. Ibid.; McCarthy mss., Edwards Papers.

114. *New York Times,* March 4, 1954; McCarthy mss., Edwards Papers. Eisenhower rejected much harsher anti-McCarthy language contained in an earlier draft of his statement. See the draft in OF 99-P, Eisenhower Papers. See also Hagerty Diary, March 1, 2, 3, 1954. On the Peress case in general, see the analysis in A-76-26, box 4, Fred Seaton Papers.

115. McCarthy mss., Edwards Papers. For the Army chronology, see *New York Times,* February 27, 1954.

116. Ibid., March 4, 1954. A short time later, Joe read the statement before television cameras, "stopping every sentence or so in order to give the cameras time to get a new angle." See James Reston in ibid.

117. McCarthy mss., Edwards Papers; *New York Times,* March 4, 1954.

CHAPTER 21

1. *New York Times* March 4, 6, 1954; *Washington Post,* March 4, 1954.

2. *New York Times,* March 9, 1954; "Investigations," *Time,* LXIII (March 22,

1954), 21-22; Mazo, *Richard Nixon,* p. 149; Hagerty Diary, March 8, 9, 1954. Joe's anger over the rejection of his demand for equal time was such that at a press conference on March 9 he turned his back on N.B.C. and C.B.S. cameras, saying he would do nothing for either network. Robert E. Lee, Joe's friend on the F.C.C., declared that he thought the decision by the networks "very fair." Despite additional blustering, Joe did not appeal the decision. *New York Times,* March 10, 1954.

3. Ibid., March 9, 1954.
4. *Congressional Record,* 83d Cong., 2d sess., March 9, 1954, p. 2886. See copy, Ralph Flanders to Robert E. Wood, March 22, 1954, box 2, Flanders Papers.
5. *New York Times,* March 10, 1954.
6. Ibid., March 11, 1954.
7. Ibid., March 11, August 4, 1954. Said Eisenhower, "I was very much interested in reading the comments you made in the Senate today. I think America needs to hear from more Republican voices like yours." Copy, Dwight D. Eisenhower to Ralph Flanders, March 9, 1954, OF 99-R, Eisenhower Papers.
8. Copy, Tom Korb to Joe McCarthy, March 10, 1954, Korb Papers. Joe replied two weeks later, failing even to mention his old friend's criticism. Joe McCarthy to Tom Korb, March 24, 1954, ibid.
9. *New York Times,* March 11, 1954; Alexander Kendrick, *Prime Time, The Life of Edward R. Murrow* (New York, 1969), pp. 47-50, 53-54, 58, 61, 66, 74-75, 81, 362-63, 471; Fred W. Friendly, *Due to Circumstances Beyond Our Control* (New York, 1967), pp. 29-46, 62-66; "Radio-TV Take the State in New McCarthy Tempest," *Broadcasting-Television,* 46 (March 15, 1954), 31-33.
10. *Fort Monmouth Hearings,* pp. 420-21.
11. *New York Times,* March 5, 11, 12, 1954; Potter, *Days of Shame,* pp. 24-32, 62-64; Cohn, *McCarthy,* pp. 113-15, 120-21, 124-26; Hagerty Diary, March 9, 10, 11, 12, 1954.
12. *Fort Monmouth Hearings,* pp. 443-62; *New York Times,* March 12, 27, 1954; "Committee vs. Chairman," *Time,* LXIII (March 22, 1954), 27. Available evidence does not reveal conclusively which of the two women was committing perjury. Mrs. Markward's inability to recognize Mrs. Moss on the stand leaves one uneasy. So does the testimony of Charlotte Oram, a local Communist who said she had never heard of Mrs. Moss. The near illiteracy displayed by Mrs. Moss prompts one to wonder how she was able to function as a typist, pass a civil service examination, and apply for a real estate license. Moreover, her explanation for receiving the *Daily Worker* and her description of rooming with a known Communist are not entirely convincing.

Cohn, in recent years, has pointed to a favorable evaluation of Mrs. Markward's overall credibility by the Subversive Activities Control Board. He also notes an SACB finding of 1958 that Communist party records reveal membership by an Annie Lee Moss of 72 R Street, S.W., Washington, D.C. Mrs. Moss did make a single reference in her testimony to that address. Mrs. Markward, however, who said she based her charges on party records, did not mention it. In 1954, Cohn, Mrs. Markward, and Frank Carr repeatedly linked Mrs. Moss with a Second Street residence during the war. Moreover, in 1959 the S.A.C.B. was less than enthusiastic about Mrs. Markward's overall reliability. "Upon a reassessment of her credibility, however, we conclude that Markward's testimony should be assayed with caution." See Cohn, *McCarthy,* p. 123; Roy Cohn to the author, February 19, 1981; *Fort Monmouth Hearings,* pp. 339-40; *Reports of the Subversive Activities Control Board* (Washington, D.C., 1966), I, 93-4, 98-9; "Here's an 'Informer' the Reds Should Not Have Tangled With," *Saturday Evening Post,* 231 (December 27, 1958), 10. There was another Mrs. Annie Lee Moss listed in the 1954 District of Columbia telephone book (p. 787). Cf. the letter from M. Stanton Evans in *National Review,* 6 (February 14, 1959), 514.

13. Lippmann in *Washington Post,* March 25, 1954; Kendrick, *Prime Time,* pp. 73-74; Friendly, *Due to Circumstances Beyond Our Control,* pp. 47-51; Marya Mannes, "The People vs. McCarthy," *The Reporter,* 10 (April 27, 1954), p. 26.
14. *New York Times,* March 12, 1954.
15. Cohn, *McCarthy,* p. 126.
16. *New York Times,* March 12, 1954. Carr was hired in July, 1953 to replace J. B. Matthews. In the bureau's New York City office, he had been in charge of the investigation that led to the indictment and conviction of the eleven Communist party leaders. See *Madison Capital Times,* July 16, 1953.
17. *New York Times,* March 13, 1954.
18. The story of the March 11 scheme came from a McCarthy confidant who, on this point, preferred to remain anonymous. Cf. Cohn, *McCarthy,* p. 126.
19. *New York Times,* March 13, 1954.
20. "The Self-Inflated Target," *Time,* LXIII (March 22, 1954), p. 27; *New York Times,* March 13, 1954.
21. Ibid.; Potter, *Days of Shame,* pp. 112-13; *Madison Capital Times,* March 13, 1954.
22. *New York Times,* March 15, 1954.
23. Ibid., March 14, 1954; Mazo, *Richard Nixon,* pp. 149-50; Nixon, *RN,* I, 177-80. Nixon's reference to "promiscuous letter writing" pointed to the flood of hate mail being received by those publicly critical of McCarthy. See Potter, *Days of Shame,* pp. 121-27.
24. *Madison Capital Times,* March 15, 1954; Van Susteren interview, November 25, 1975.
25. *New York Times,* March 15, 1954; Cohn, *McCarthy,* pp. 125-29.
26. *New York Times,* March 17, 1954; Cohn, *McCarthy,* pp. 131-32.

27. *New York Times,* March 18, 1954; Brogan in *Washington Daily News,* March 19, 1954.
28. *New York Times,* March 18, 1954.
29. Ibid.
30. Ibid., March 19, 1954.
31. Ibid., March 20, 1954; *Milwaukee Journal,* March 20, 1954.
32. *New York Times,* March 21, 1954.
33. "Investigations," *Time,* March 22, 1954, p. 22; *New York Times,* March 21, 1954. The same issue of the *Times* surveyed a number of scalding anti-McCarthy editorials from newspapers in Paris, Bonn, and London.
34. Ibid., March 18, 20, 1954; *Milwaukee Journal,* March 20, 1954. On March 17 the *Washington Post* purchased the *Times-Herald,* the only pro-McCarthy newspaper in the nation's capital. Joe thought this a serious blow, and he was no doubt correct. See Bayley, *Joe McCarthy and the Press,* pp. 151-52.
35. *The Gallup Poll,* II, 1220, 1225; *New York Times,* March 21, 1954.
36. *Milwaukee Journal,* March 20, 24, 1954; *New York Times,* March 22, 24, 1954.
37. *Milwaukee Journal,* March 20, 1954; *New York Times,* March 21, 1954. Joe accepted no fees for the week's speeches. See ibid., March 17, 1954.
38. Ibid., March 22, 1954.
39. *Milwaukee Journal,* March 22, 1954. Army counsel John Adams had come to Dean Sayre, frightened and intimidated by the McCarthy-Cohn affair, seeking spiritual assistance. During the Army-McCarthy hearings, Adams would telephone the clergyman each morning, and they would pray together for strength. Sayre interview.
40. *Madison Capital Times,* March 22, 1954; *New York Times,* March 23, 1954.
41. Nixon, *RN,* I, 180-81.
42. *Washington Star,* April 8, 1954. Cohn declared in the joint interview, "We have never gotten an FBI file, and we have never gotten a tip from the FBI."
43. *New York Times,* March 23, 1954.
44. Ibid.
45. *Madison Capital Times,* March 24, 1954; *New York Times,* March 25, 1954; Hagerty Diary, March 23, 24, 1954.
46. *New York Times,* March 25, 1954.
47. *Washington Post,* March 25, 1954.
48. *New York Times,* March 28, 1954; Hagerty Diary, March 23, 1954.
49. Ibid., April 8, 11, 1954.
50. Ibid., April 8, 11, 1954.
51. Ibid., April 3, 15, 16, 1954; Cohn, *McCarthy,* p. 132; *Madison Capital Times,* April 15, 1954. Fisher had also been engaged in organizing a guild chapter with assistance from a Communist organizer. Three Administration officials,

including James Hagerty, participated in the decision to drop the young attorney from the case. Hagerty Diary, April 2, 1954.

52. See the remarks of Karl Mundt on "Meet the Press" in *New York Times,* April 5, 1954.

53. *Madison Capital Times,* April 7, 14, 1954; *New York Times,* May 9, 19, 1954; Friendly, *Due to Circumstances Beyond Our Control,* pp. 54-61; John Major, *The Oppenheimer Hearing* (New York, 1971), pp. 9-16, 269. Atomic Energy Commission Chairman David Lilienthal soon said that the decision to develop an H-bomb, made on January 31, 1950, had been delayed at most just over four months by top level discussions about the advisability of creating such a weapon. McCarthyite Senator Bourke B. Hickenlooper charged a short time later that the bomb had been delayed "several years." *New York Times,* April 8, 17, 1954. See Hagerty Diary, April 7, 1954.

54. *Madison Capital Times,* April 9, 1954; *New York Times,* April 10, 1954; *Washington Post,* April 13, 1954. See Crosby, *God, Church, and Flag,* pp. 163-69; John Cogley, *A Canterbury Tale: Experiences and Reflections, 1916-1976* (New York, 1976), pp. 46-47.

55. *Washington Star,* April 9, 1954; *New York Times,* April 7, 9 (editorial) 12, 16, 1954. See copy, George R. Donahue et al. to Karl Mundt, June 4, 1954, box 5, Benton Papers.

56. *New York Times,* April 13, 14, 1954.

57. *Madison Capital Times,* April 15, 1954.

58. Ibid.

59. *New York Times,* April 16, 17, 1954; Cohn, *McCarthy,* p. 136.

60. *New York Times,* April 20, 21, 1954.

61. Ibid. The reference to Welch and Fisher went unnoticed by reporters at the time. On the Symington charge, see *St. Louis Post-Dispatch,* November 1, 1952.

62. *New York Times,* April 21, 1954; *Washington Star,* April 21, 1954; *Madison Capital Times,* April 21, 1954.

63. *New York Times,* April 21, 1954.

64. Ibid., April 22, 1954.

65. *Madison Capital Times,* April 21, 1954. Democrats backed Stevens by almost four to one, while Republicans were virtually evenly divided.

CHAPTER 22

1. Cohn, *McCarthy,* p. 138; editorial, *New York Times,* April 22, 1954.

2. Ibid. At the first hearing 120 reporters were on hand, along with three

television crews, 12 fixed and three roving newsreel cameramen, and 36 still cameramen. Bayley, *Joe McCarthy and the Press,* p. 204.

3. *Washington Star,* April 21, 1954.

4. *New York Times,* April 23, 1954; Joseph N. Welch, "The Lawyer's Afterthoughts," *Life,* 37 (July 26, 1954), 100.

5. Cohn, *McCarthy,* p. 208.

6. U.S. Senate, Special Subcommittee on Investigations, *Special Senate Investigations on Charges and Countercharges Involving: Secretary of the Army Robert T. Stevens, John G. Adams, H. Struve Hensel, and Senator Joe McCarthy, Roy M. Cohn, and Francis P. Carr, Hearings,* 83d Cong., 2d sess., 1954 (hereafter referred to as *Army-McCarthy Hearings*), pp. 27-99; *New York Times,* April 23, 1954. See the colonel's testimony on Cohn's Fort Monmouth outburst in *Army-McCarthy Hearings,* pp. 1432-45.

7. Ibid., pp. 101-75; *New York Times,* April 24, 25, 1954.

8. Ibid.

9. Ibid., April 26, 1954.

10. *Army-McCarthy Hearings,* pp. 177-254.

11. See ibid., pp. 188, 338, 398-402; Cohn, *McCarthy,* p. 142.

12. *Army-McCarthy Hearings,* pp. 182, 202-04, 255-58, 268-303, 325, 389-91, 451-556; Cohn, *McCarthy,* pp. 152-54. Cf. Potter, *Days of Shame,* pp. 183-84, 252-56.

13. *Army-McCarthy Hearings,* pp. 257-59.

14. Ibid., p. 486. Joe apologized to Jenkins for this remark. Ibid., p. 492.

15. Ibid., p. 543.

16. Ibid., pp. 328, 372.

17. Ibid., pp. 359, 372, 510.

18. Ibid., pp. 472, 550; *New York Times,* April 30, 1954.

19. *Madison Capital Times,* May 1, 3, 1954; Murphy, "Texas Business and McCarthy," pp. 100-01, 211.

20. *New York Times,* April 30, May 1, 1954; copy [Ralph Flanders] to Eva B. Briggs, May 10, 1954, box 2, Flanders Papers. See copy, Dwight D. Eisenhower to Harry A. Bullis, May 6, 1954, OF 99-R-1, Eisenhower Papers.

21. *Madison Capital Times,* May 1, 1954.

22. *Washington Star,* April 30, 1954.

23. *Army-McCarthy Hearings,* pp. 574-77, 651-66.

24. See Potter, *Days of Shame,* pp. 13-23, 182-90; *New York Times,* May 6, 1954.

25. *Army-McCarthy Hearings,* pp. 591-602, 635-39, 641-42, 667-97; editorial, *Washington Post,* May 5, 1954.

26. Edwards interview, November 11, 1976; Cohn, *McCarthy,* pp. 165-70. See Carr's testimony in *Army-McCarthy Hearings,* pp. 2718-19, 2721-24.

27. Ibid., pp. 531, 703-13, 718, 720-44; Nixon, *RN,* I, 183.

28. Edwards interview, November 11, 1976; *Madison Capital Times,* May 20, 1954; *Army-McCarthy Hearings,* pp. 748-74; Cohn, *McCarthy,* pp. 173-74. See *Watkins Committee Hearings,* p. 393. Following an investigation, Army officials denied that an officer had delivered the document to McCarthy. *New York Times,* August 12, 1954.

29. *Army-McCarthy Hearings,* pp. 782-84; *New York Times,* May 9, 1954. It was later revealed that Americans for Democratic Action chairman Joseph L. Rauh, top officials of the *Washington Post,* and other prominent liberals had been hoodwinked during much of 1954 by one Paul Hughes, who falsely represented himself as a member of McCarthy's staff. Hughes was paid almost $11,000 for fake information that the liberals thought came straight from the senator's files. McCarthyites were to make much of this clandestine effort to obtain purloined documents. See William F. Buckley, Jr., *Up from Liberalism* (n.p., 1965), pp. 70-84; Cohn, *McCarthy,* pp. 177-80; Surine interviews of April 7, May 13, 1977.

30. *Army-McCarthy Hearings,* pp. 819-21, 830-33; *Madison Capital Times,* May 7, 1954. Joe opened the afternoon hearing of May 10 with a tribute to Hoover on his 30th anniversary as FBI Director.

31. Cohn, *McCarthy,* pp. 139-40; "Investigations," *Time,* LXIII (May 3, 1954), 19; Catlin interview.

32. Cohn, *McCarthy,* pp. 156-57. The same proposal had been made to James Hagerty on March 25 by Senators Welker and Hickenlooper, following a luncheon with McCarthy and Mundt. Hagerty Diary, March 25, 1954.

33. *Army-McCarthy Hearings,* pp. 934-39, 969-1006, 1008, 1184.

34. See the biography of Adams in *New York Times,* March 13, 1954.

35. *Army-McCarthy Hearings,* pp. 1009-1147; *New York Times,* May 13, 1954.

36. *Army-McCarthy Hearings,* pp. 1177-97. Cf. Cohn, *McCarthy,* pp. 160-62.

37. *Army-McCarthy Hearings,* pp. 1059, 1169-74, 1213, 1249. See Hagerty Diary, May 14, 17, 1954.

38. *Army-McCarthy Hearings,* pp. 1262-65, 1278-86. See the fervid editorial in the *New York Times,* May 19, 1954.

39. Ibid., May 13, 1954.

40. *Madison Capital Times,* May 19, 1954; *New York Times,* May 22, 1954; Hagerty Diary, May 18, 1954.

41. *Madison Capital Times,* May 19, 1954; *Army-McCarthy Hearings,* p. 1283. See Hagerty Diary, May 11, 12, 14, 1954.

42. *Madison Capital Times,* May 19, 1954.

43. Ibid., May 19, 20, 1954.

44. Ibid., May 22, 1954. See Hagerty Diary, May 20, 1954.

45. *Madison Capital Times,* May 20, 1954; *New York Times,* May 21, 1954. See Hagerty Diary, May 21, 1954.

46. *Madison Capital Times,* May 24, 1954.
47. Ibid., (editorial) May 19, 24, 1954; *New York Times,* May 17, 23, 1954; *Washington Post,* May 18, 1954; Louis Bean, "The Myth of McCarthy's Strength," *Look,* 18 (June 1, 1954), 108. Bean's full study, which appeared in the spring under the title *Influences in the 1954 Mid-Term Elections,* was sponsored and distributed by the anti-McCarthy Clearing House. Each member of Congress received a complimentary copy. See *New York Times,* February 4, 1954; copy, memorandum, John Howe to William Benton, July 16, 1953, box 4, Benton Papers; Van Arkel interview.
48. *Army-McCarthy Hearings,* pp. 1295-1379, 1540; *Madison Capital Times,* May 24, 1954; *Washington Post,* May 28, 1954. Nixon said later that he had not watched any of the hearings and had advised his friends to follow the same course. Mazo, *Richard Nixon,* p. 150.
49. *Army-McCarthy Hearings,* pp. 1388-1431, 1495-73.
50. Ibid., pp. 1381-83, 1391, 1393-96, 1409, 1477-82, 1493-94. Despite his many absences from Fort Dix, Schine received a rating of "superior" in training. His rating for character was a low "fair." Ibid., pp. 1390, 1392, 1489.
51. Ibid., pp. 1491, 1496-97, 1502-12, 1515; *Madison Capital Times,* May 26, 1954.
52. *Army-McCarthy Hearings,* pp. 1522-32.
53. *New York Times,* June 21, 1954.
54. Potter, *Days of Shame,* p. 271.
55. *Army-McCarthy Hearings,* pp. 1526-51. Dirksen apparently tricked Potter into voting with the majority by telling him that the President favored such a move. In fact, Eisenhower had made no such recommendation and was upset by the subcommittee decision. Hagerty Diary, May 26, 27, 28, 1954.
56. *New York Times,* May 27, 30, 1954.
57. *Army-McCarthy Hearings,* pp. 1568-75.
58. Hagerty Diary, May 28, 1954.
59. *New York Times,* May 29, 30, 1954; *Madison Capital Times,* May 31, June 18, 1954. Democratic Senator A. S. "Mike" Monroney, coauthor of the Congressional Reorganization Act of 1946, denied McCarthy's claim that the act justified his appeal to government employees. *New York Times,* June 6, 1954.
60. *Army-McCarthy Hearings,* p. 1722; *New York Times,* May 29, 1954.
61. *Congressional Record,* 83d Cong., 2d sess., June 1, 1954, pp. 7389-90; *New York Times,* June 2, 1954; *Army-McCarthy Hearings,* p. 1827. Joe unsuccessfully demanded that Flanders be subpoenaed by the subcommittee. See ibid., pp. 1883, 1919-20, 1942-43.
62. Ibid., pp. 1801, 1803, 1874.
63. Cohn said that Schine had contributed substantially to several published subcommittee reports, but he was unable to document the claim. See ibid., pp. 1665-73, 1680, 2406-24, 2803-06.

64. Ibid., pp. 1816-52, 1839-40, 1845, 2379-80, 2389-90.
65. Ibid., pp. 1972-73, 2088-2225. McCarthyites leaked a transcription they hoped would damage Stevens to the *Chicago Tribune* a day before all of the monitored conversations were made public. *New York Times,* June 7, 1954.
66. *Army-McCarthy Hearings,* pp. 2118-26, 2970-71.
67. Ibid., pp. 2226-41, 2281-85, 2325, 2339-41, 2350-54, 2359-62, 2704-07, 2909-10.
68. See ibid., pp. 2327-43.
69. Ibid., pp. 1827-28, 1850-51, 1899-1904, 1945-48, 2907; *New York Times,* June 4, 1954. The renewed threat to investigate the C.I.A. angered the President, who leaked a story of his determination to prevent such a probe and conferred with congressional leaders on the matter. Ibid., June 7, 1954; Hagerty Diary, June 8, 1954.
70. *Army-McCarthy Hearings,* pp. 2045-56, 2254; Cohn, *McCarthy,* pp. 200-203; Edward Bennett Williams, *One Man's Freedom* (New York, 1962), p. 61.
71. *Army-McCarthy Hearings,* pp. 2426-30. Welch may have rehearsed his attack on McCarthy, anticipating the Fisher incident. See Griffith, *The Politics of Fear,* fn 46, pp. 259-60. On numerous occasions during the hearings the veteran attorney was highly ineffective. See *Army-McCarthy Hearings,* pp. 2045-49, 2081-86, 2268-72, 2606-09. Frederick G. Fisher bore his "scar" well, becoming a highly successful attorney. See *Milwaukee Journal,* October 24, 1976.
72. Kiermas, Nellor (June 6, 1979); Van Susteren (November 25, 1975) interviews; Cohn, *McCarthy,* p. 204.
73. *Madison Capital Times,* June 11, 1954; *Washington Star,* June 10, 1954; *Christian Science Monitor,* June 17, 1954.
74. *Army-McCarthy Hearings,* pp. 2269, 2431-44, 2879. Cohn went so far as to proclaim that he and his associates "worship" the FBI director. Ibid., p. 1792.
75. Ibid., pp. 2455, 2467, 2480, 2503, 2507-08, 2510, 2550-54, 2557.
76. Ibid., pp. 2517-44; Surine interview, June 8, 1977.
77. *Army-McCarthy Hearings,* pp. 2559-60; *Madison Capital Times,* June 11, 1954; *Congressional Record,* 83d Cong., 2d sess., June 11, 1954, pp. 8032-33.
78. Flanders interview, Columbia University; *New York Times,* June 15, 16, 1954; *Congressional Record,* 83d Cong., 2d sess., June 15, 1954, pp. 8240-42; copy, Ralph Flanders to Robert E. Wood, August 14, 1954, box 11, Flanders Papers.
79. *Army-McCarthy Hearings,* pp. 2613-17, 2621-23; *New York Times,* June 12, 1954; Cohn, *McCarthy,* pp. 70-72; Schlesinger, *Robert Kennedy,* p. 121; Prochnau and Larsen, *A Certain Democrat,* pp. 146-47; Jackson interview. *The New York Times* story noted that Kennedy had "remained on very friendly terms with Senator McCarthy himself."
80. *Army-McCarthy Hearings,* p. 2759. See especially the encounter with Welch, pp. 2278-90, 2794-2801.

81. Ibid., pp. 2704-07, 2911. On June 15 Joe reserved seats behind the witness chair for friends, who applauded, cheered and waved when he entered the hearing room. Ibid., pp. 2709-10; *Madison Capital Times,* June 15, 1954.

82. See *Army-McCarthy Hearings,* pp. 2887-89, 2956, 2973-74.

83. *New York Times,* June 18, 1954.

84. Ibid.; *Madison Capital Times,* June 18, 1954.

85. *Army-McCarthy Hearings,* pp. 2903, 2939.

86. Hagerty Diary, June 18, 1954.

87. See U.S. Senate, Special Subcommittee on Investigations, *Charges and Countercharges Involving: Secretary of the Army Robert T. Stevens, John G. Adams, H. Struve Hensel and Senator Joe McCarthy, Roy M. Cohn, and Francis P. Carr, Report,* 83d Cong., 2d sess., 1954, pp. 79-102. Bobby Kennedy wrote the solid but somewhat cautious Democratic minority report. *New York Times,* July 31, 1954; Schlesinger, *Robert Kennedy,* p. 122. Neither report challenged the authenticity of the eleven memoranda introduced by McCarthy, Cohn, and Carr. See Ray Jenkins's pro-McCarthy recollections in "The Army vs. McCarthy," *Newsweek,* 73 (May 5, 1969), 16-17.

CHAPTER 23

1. Nellor (May 7, 1977), Henderson interviews; *Madison Capital Times,* June 7, 12, 13, 1954. The recall drive collected nearly 400,000 signatures, of which about 335,000 were valid and notarized. Two historians of the subject concluded, "More people had signed this protest than had ever signed any notarized petition in the nation's history, and they had dealt a massive blow to the myth of McCarthy's invincibility." See David P. and Esther S. Thelen, "Joe Must Go: The Movement to Recall Senator Joseph R. McCarthy," *Wisconsin Magazine of History,* LXIX (Spring, 1966), 185-209. McCarthyites harassed and frightened Leroy Gore and his family during the campaign. See *Madison Capital Times,* April 19, May 11, 1954, and Leroy Gore, *Joe Must Go* (New York, 1954), pp. 25, 92-99, 136, 148-72.

2. *Washington Star,* June 14, 1954.

3. *Madison Capital Times,* June 23, 1954. Cf. G. D. Wiebe, "The Army-McCarthy Hearings and the Public Conscience," *Public Opinion Quarterly,* XXI (Winter, 1958-59), 492-93.

4. *New York Times,* June 14, July 7, 1954; editorial, *Madison Capital Times,* June 22, 1954; Thomas Stokes in *Washington Star,* June 23, 1954.

5. *New York Times,* June 18, July 2, 7, 14, 1954.

6. Ibid., July 16, 17, 1954; *Washington Star,* July 16, 1954.

7. *New York Times,* July 17, 18, 19, 1954.

8. See Griffith, *The Politics of Fear,* pp. 276-85; Fried, *Men Against McCarthy,*

pp. 293-96; Maurice Rosenblatt to Lyndon B. Johnson, July 27, 1954, Senate Papers, box 374, Lyndon B. Johnson Papers; Rosenblatt, Van Arkel interviews.

9. *Madison Capital Times,* July 20, 1954. On the two security clearances, see *Army-McCarthy Hearings,* pp. 2703-06, 2819; Surine interview, June 8, 1977; *New York Times,* June 18, 19, 24, 1954.

10. Ibid., July 21, 1954.

11. See Murray Kempton in *New York Post,* July 29, 1954; Frank Gibney, "After the Ball," *Commonweal,* LX (September 3, 1954), 531-35.

12. *Washington Star,* July 27, 1954; *New York Times,* July 28, 1954.

13. *Congressional Record,* 83d Cong., 2d sess., July 30, 1954, pp. 12729-42; *New York Times,* July 31, 1954.

14. *Congressional Record,* 83d Cong., 2d sess., July 31, 1954, pp. 12893-12927; *New York Times,* August 1, 1954.

15. *Congressional Record,* 83d Cong., 2d sess., August 2, 1954, pp. 129422-89; *Washington Star,* August 2, 1954; *New York Times,* August 3, 1954. See the transcripts of monitored telephone calls between McClellan and Johnson, and minutes of the Democratic Policy Committee for July 29, August 2, 5, 1954 in Senate Papers, boxes 364, 374, Johnson Papers.

16. *Washington Star,* August 2, 1954; *New York Times,* August 3, 5, 1954.

17. Nellor (May 7, 1977), Edwards (November 17, 1976), Buckley interviews. See Cohn, *McCarthy,* p. 221. Many accepted Joe's public facade of complete self-confidence. E.g., Watkins, *Enough Rope,* p. 34.

18. Reedy interview; *Madison Capital Times,* August 5, 1954. See William S. White, *Citadel: The Story of the U.S. Senate* (New York, 1956), pp. 128, 132; Rowland Evans and Robert Novak, *Lyndon B. Johnson, The Exercise of Power* (New York, 1966), pp. 81-85; Merle Miller, *Lyndon, An Oral Biography* (New York, 1980), pp. 166, 170-72.

19. *New York Times,* August 6, 1954; *Denver Post,* March 12, 1954; minutes, Democratic Policy Committee, July 29, 1954, Senate Papers, box 374, Johnson Papers; Reedy interview. Cf. Sam J. Ervin, Jr. to the author, February 6, 1981.

20. See *New York Times,* August 6, 1954; White, *Citadel,* pp. 129-31. Powerful Senators Eugene Millikin of Colorado and Walter George of Georgia had declined an invitation to serve on the committee. Seeking Catholic representation on the body, Johnson had approached Mike Mansfield, John Kennedy, and John Pastore. They too declined. Minutes, Democratic Policy Committee, August 5, 1954, Senate Papers, box 364, Johnson Papers.

21. Ibid.; *Madison Capital Times,* August 5, 1954; editorial, *New York Times,* August 7, 1954; *Milwaukee Journal,* August 8, 21, 1954.

22. Watkins, *Enough Rope,* pp. 31, 35.

23. *Milwaukee Journal,* August 8, 1954; *Madison Capital Times,* August 23, 1954;

Christian Science Monitor, August 24, 25, 26, 27, 1954; James Rorty and Moshe Decter, *McCarthy and the Communists* (Boston, 1954), see esp. pp. 86-103.

24. White in *New York Times,* August 15, 1954; Brock, *Americans for Democratic Action,* p. 157. See Mary Sperling McAuliffe, *Crisis on the Left; Cold War Politics and American Liberals, 1947-1954* (Amherst, Mass., 1978), pp. 132-44.

25. See Watkins, *Enough Rope,* pp. 33-34, 36; Williams, *One Man's Freedom,* pp. 60, 62-64. Williams declined to accept compensation from committee funds.

26. Ibid., August 25, 1954. The groupings included a total of thirteen charges selected from the 46.

27. *Madison Capital Times,* August 30, 1954.

28. *Watkins Committee Hearings,* pp. 1-14.

29. Ibid., pp. 14-38; Watkins, *Enough Rope,* pp. 36-37, 41-42; Reston in *New York Times,* September 2, 1954.

30. Ibid.

31. Ibid., September 3, 1954; Williams, *One Man's Freedom,* p. 63.

32. *Watkins Committee Hearings,* pp. 17-20, 53-58, 298-305, 359-73, 384-87.

33. Ibid., pp. 262-78, 404, 410-13, 417-21.

34. Ibid., pp. 314-15, 388-90, 409-10, 413-16, 429, 443-47.

35. Ibid., pp. 306-11, 388, 425-28.

36. Ibid., pp. 175-204, 333, 345, 453-510, 514-20. Joe spent four days on the witness stand.

37. See Watkins, *Enough Rope,* pp. 79-80; the Alsops in *Washington Post,* September 29, 1954; copy, telegram, William Benton to Arthur Watkins, September 13, 1954; copy, William Benton to Arthur Watkins, September 15, 1954; copy, memorandum, John Howe to William Benton, September 17, 1954, box 5, Benton Papers. See also Ralph Flanders to Arthur Watkins, September 6, 10, 11 (five letters), 16, 1954, Arthur Watkins Papers. Flanders was receiving assistance in preparing these briefs by a Clearing House volunteer working in his office. Copy, memorandum, John Howe to William Benton, September 7. 1954, box 5, Benton Papers.

38. See *New York Times,* September 25, 1954; James Reston in ibid., September 26, 1954; copy, J. W. Fulbright to William Benton, September 18, 1954, box 5, Benton Papers.

39. "The Censure of Joe McCarthy," *Time,* LXIV (October 4, 1954), 21; *Watkins Committee Report,* pp. 30-1, 60-1.

40. Ibid., pp. 38-39.

41. Ibid., pp. 44-45.

42. Ibid., p. 46.

43. *New York Times,* September 28, 1954.

44. Ibid., September 28, 29, 1954; George Reedy to Lyndon Johnson, September 27, 1954, Senate Papers, box 117, Johnson Papers.

45. *New York Times,* September 19, 1954; John Wyngaard in *Madison Capital Times,* September 27, 1954; *Newark Star-Ledger,* October 14, 19, 1954.

46. See Matthews, *U.S. Senators and Their World,* p. 71; Mazo, *Richard Nixon,* pp. 152-56; Nixon, *RN,* I, 195-201. Nixon vigorously supported Clifford Case, who won a narrow victory. A year later, the Administration was claiming that 3,614 federal employees had been dismissed for security reasons. *New York Times,* September 27, 1955.

47. Editorial, *Milwaukee Journal,* November 7, 1954; *New York Times,* November 5, 1954. Joe entered the Illinois race against Paul Douglas by sending a public telegram to the senator accusing him of cowardice and hypocrisy for dodging the question of how he would vote on the McCarthy censure resolution. *Chicago Tribune,* November 2, 1954.

48. *Washington Post,* November 6, 1954; *Madison Capital Times,* November 1, 18, 1954.

49. Watkins, *Enough Rope,* pp. 115-16, 287-91; copy, Ralph Flanders to Clifford O. Simpson, October 22, 1954, box 11, Flanders Papers.

50. See Crosby, *God, Church, and Flag,* pp. 200-02; Watkins, *Enough Rope,* p. 117. A spokesman for the Archdiocese of New York said that the monsignor was designated by Cardinal Spellman to represent him at such functions but had "the sole responsibility of conveying the greetings and blessings of the cardinal—and nothing else." *New York Times,* November 10, 1954.

51. *Madison Capital Times,* November 8, 1954; *New York Times,* November 9, 1954.

52. See Cocke interview.

53. *New York Times,* November 9, 1954.

54. Ibid., November 10, 1954; Martin Dies, *Martin Dies' Story* (New York, 1963), pp. 176-77.

55. *Congressional Record,* 83d Cong., 2d sess., November 10, 1954, pp. 15921-54; *New York Times,* November 11, December 2, 1954.

56. Ibid., November 11, 1954; copy, Julius Edelstein to Arthur M. Schlesinger, Jr., November 11, 1954, box 5, Benton Papers.

57. *Madison Capital Times,* November 11, 1954; *New York Times,* November 12, 1954.

58. *Congressional Record,* 83d Cong., 2d sess., November 11, 1954, pp. 15959-80; *New York Times,* November 12, 1954. On Davies, see ibid., November 6, 1954.

59. See ibid., November 12, 1954; Watkins, *Enough Rope,* pp. 117-18.

60. *Congressional Record,* 83d Cong., 2d sess., November 12, 1954, pp. 15986-16009; *New York Times,* November 13, 1954.

61. *Madison Capital Times,* November 13, 1954.

62. *New York Times,* November 15, 1954.

63. Watkins, *Enough Rope,* pp. 84-106; *Madison Capital Times,* November 15, 1954; *New York Times,* November 16, 1954. Watkins placed the entire transcript of the encounter in the *Congressional Record,* and *The New York Times* published excerpts.

64. *Congressional Record,* 83d Cong., 2d sess., November 15, 1954, pp. 16011-41; *New York Times,* November 16, 1954; Watkins, *Enough Rope,* pp. 139-41.

65. *New York Times,* November 16, 1954.

66. *Congressional Record,* 83d Cong., 2d sess., November 16, 1954, pp. 16052-61; *New York Times,* November 5, 8, 17, 1954; Watkins, *Enough Rope,* pp. 144-46.

67. *Congressional Record,* 83d Cong., 2d sess., November 18, 1954, pp. 16132-3; Sumnicht interview; *New York Times,* November 18, 19, 1954. Senator Mundt told a confidant, "Joe has been obviously under a strain, and his thinking has been about as straight as a corkscrew the past two weeks. The meetings around the country have sort of gone to his head, and even his best friends are having difficulty getting him to sit down and work out some strategy which would deter or nullify the censure resolution." Copy, Karl E. Mundt to W. E. O'Brien, November 22, 1954, FF7, Mundt Papers.

68. *Memorial Services . . . Joseph Raymond McCarthy, Late a Senator from Wisconsin* (Washington, D.C., 1957), pp. 81, 90, 96-97; Lee, Henderson interviews; Williams, *One Man's Freedom,* pp. 67-68; Barry Goldwater, *With No Apologies* (New York, 1979), p. 61.

69. Ibid.; copy, memorandum, John Howe to William Benton, November 24, 1954, box 4, Benton Papers; *Milwaukee Journal,* November 18, 1954; *Chicago Tribune,* November 18, 1954. On pressures from the Right, see also Flanders interview, Columbia University, and the pro-McCarthy materials in the scrapbooks of the George Moseley Papers. Clint W. Murchison stoutly defended McCarthy in a personal letter to Lyndon Johnson. "At the present time I believe I can handle him," the Texas millionaire wrote, "even to the point, if necessary, of getting him to bolt the Republican Party at some future date." Clint W. Murchison to Lyndon B. Johnson, November 24, 1954, Senate Papers, box 117, Johnson Papers. See also memorandum, George Reedy to Lyndon B. Johnson, November 29, 1954, ibid., urging the Minority Leader to resist compromise.

70. *Congressional Record,* 83d Cong., 2d sess., November 29, 1954, pp. 16149-80; *New York Times,* November 30, 1954.

71. *New York Times,* November 30, 1954; *Madison Capital Times,* November 30, 1954.

72. *Congressional Record,* 83d Cong., 2d sess., December 2, 1954; p. 16392; *New York Times,* December 3, 1954; Watkins, *Enough Rope,* p. 149. John F. Kennedy did not vote on the fate of his old friend, later claiming he was too ill at the time. This explanation has not convinced many serious students of the subject. See Crosby, *God, Church, and Flag,* pp. 205-15.

73. *New York Times,* December 3, 4, 1954; *Madison Capital Times,* December 3, 1954. Cf. *Congressional Record,* 83d Cong., 2d sess., December 2, 1954, pp. 16392-95. Nixon later denied changing the title of the resolution. Mazo, *Richard Nixon,* pp. 150-51.

74. *New York Times,* December 3, 1954; *Madison Capital Times,* December 3, 6, 1954.

CHAPTER 24

1. The assumptions underpinning the second Red Scare went virtually unchallenged in the hearings. Sen. Edwin Johnson introduced an amendment to the censure resolution placing the Senate on record as being opposed to Communism and determined that its committees would continue to expose it diligently. Senator McClellan promised to pursue the Peress matter further. (In July, 1955 the Government Operations Committee, in a report signed by McCarthy, excluded subversion as a factor in the case. See *New York Times,* July 15, 1955.)

2. See Watkins, *Enough Rope,* p. 183; *Memorial Services . . . Joseph Raymond McCarthy, Late a Senator from Wisconsin,* pp. 201-02; Cohn, *McCarthy,* p. 243; Hagerty, Minetti (March 14, 1977, April 12, 1978), Van Susteren (November 25, 1975), Knowles, Cocke interviews.

3. Watkins, *Enough Rope,* pp. 181-82.

4. Cohn, *McCarthy,* pp. 254, 256; Watkins, *Enough Rope,* pp. 182, 184; Flanders, *Senator from Vermont,* p. 268.

5. *New York Times,* December 5, 1954; Hagerty Diary, December 3, 4, 6, 1954; *Madison Capital Times,* December 7, 1954. The President refused to reply to McCarthy at his weekly news conference.

6. Ibid., December 8, 1954; John Wyngaard in *Wausau Record-Herald,* December 18, 1954; *New York Times.* December 9, 1954.

7. Cohn, *McCarthy,* pp. 253-54; *Milwaukee Journal,* May 3, 1957.

8. *Madison Capital Times,* January 20, February 28, 1955; *Arizona Republic,* March 13, 1957; *Memorial Services . . . Joseph Raymond McCarthy, Late a Senator from Wisconsin,* p. 205; Pegler in *Appleton Post-Crescent,* March 11, 1957.

9. *New York Times,* June 17, 22, 23, 1955; *Congressional Record,* 84th Cong., 1st sess., June 16, 1955, pp. 8422-30, June 20, 1955, pp. 8721-25, June 22, 1955, pp. 8933-60; Cohn, *McCarthy,* p. 255; "Whatever Happened to Joe McCarthy?" *Picture Week,* I (July 16, 1955), 4-9.

10. See Edwards (November 17, 1976), Bayley (July 7, 1977) interviews; Drew Pearson in *Wisconsin CIO News,* May 10, 1957.

11. Edwards interview, November 17, 1976; Cohn, *McCarthy,* p. 255; John W. Caughey, *In Clear and Present Danger* (Chicago, 1958), p. 175; Potter, *Days of Shame,* p. 296. Joe's loneliness was such that occasionally he would drop by the Karl Mundt home and wash dishes. See the unpublished manuscript by Mundt, FF9, Mundt Library.

12. *Madison Capital Times,* June 6, 13, 1955; "Post Mortem," *The Progressive,* 19 (July, 1955), 4.

13. Sumnicht interview; *Appleton Post-Crescent,* December 1, 1955; *St. Paul Pioneer Press,* February 19, 1956; *Madison Capital Times,* March 1, 1956. Joe told Warren Knowles, seeking support for an appointment as a federal judge, that his endorsement would only hurt him. Knowles interview.

14. Wyngaard in *Waukesha Daily Freeman,* March 24, 1956; *Milwaukee Journal,* October 26, 1956, May 3, 1957.

15. *Milwaukee Sentinel,* September 5, 1956, May 3, 1957; *Appleton Post-Crescent,* September 22, 1956; David Balliet, "I'll Miss Joe McCarthy," *Chicago Sunday Tribune Magazine,* June 30, 1957, pp. 19-20.

16. Van Susteren interviews, February 5, July 14, 1977.

17. Sturm, Meyer, Voy, Mr. and Mrs. Olen Anderson, Cattau, Swedish interviews.

18. *Milwaukee Sentinel,* September 5, 1956; *Appleton Post-Crescent,* November 17, 1956; Hanratty interview; "The Passing of McCarthy," *Time,* LXIX (May 13, 1957), 29.

19. See Balliet, "I'll Miss Joe McCarthy," p. 34; Lee, Edwards (November 17, 1976) interviews; Cohn, *McCarthy,* p. 261.

20. *Arizona Republic,* March 13, 1954.

21. Dittmore interview. See Reedy, Purtell, Fleming interviews.

22. McNeill interview.

23. Swedish interview.

24. Catlin interview.

25. Bayley interview, July 7, 1977.

26. Confidential source.

27. *Milwaukee Journal,* May 3, 1957.

28. Ibid.; "The Passing of McCarthy," *Time,* p. 28. The fatality rate of hepatitis was only about 5 to 10 percent. Moreover, Joe did not respond to the normal treatments for the ailment. *New York Times,* May 3, 1957. For undocumented and highly questionable allegations that Joe was violent while in the hospital,

see Drew Pearson in *Wisconsin CIO News,* May 10, 1957, and Cook, *The Nightmare Decade,* pp. 539-40. Copies of the death certificate are on file at the county register of deeds office in Appleton. McCarthy's hospital records are unavailable to scholars. Q. E. Crews, Jr., to the author, September 28, 1977.

29. See *Chicago Tribune,* April 13, 1977; Korb (September 6, 1975), Purtell interviews; *Appleton Post-Crescent,* May 7, 1957; Cohn, *McCarthy,* pp. 260-62; Loeb editorial in box 13, Flanders Papers; Medford Evans, *The Assassination of Joe McCarthy* (Boston, 1970). There is no truth to the 1978 allegation that McCarthy was a morphine addict before his death. See Maxine Cheshire, "Drugs and Washington, D.C.," *Ladies Home Journal,* XCV (December, 1978), 180, 182; Bergen interviews; Harry J. Anslinger and Will Oursler, *The Murderers: The Story of the Narcotic Gangs* (New York, 1961), p. 181.

30. Editorial, *Chicago Tribune,* May 4, 1957; *Milwaukee Journal,* May 3, 1957; Buckley, *Up from Liberalism,* pp. 29-30.

31. *New York Times,* May 3, 1957; Amelia Graves [secretary to Senator Symington] to the author, November 8, 1976.

32. *New York Times,* May 3, 1957.

33. *Milwaukee Journal,* May 3, 1957; McMillin in *Wisconsin CIO News,* May 10, 1957. One of the dissenting Democrats was Henry Maier, later the longtime mayor of Milwaukee. Gaylord Nelson of Madison, later a Democratic U.S. senator (1963-81), left the chamber to avoid voting.

34. *Milwaukee Journal,* May 4, 1957; *Memorial Services . . . Joseph Raymond McCarthy, Late a Senator from Wisconsin,* p. 231.

35. Ibid.

36. Ibid., pp. 39, 232; *Appleton Post-Crescent,* August 16, 1957.

37. See ibid., May 6, 7, 8, 1957. See also ibid., February 21, May 20, 1968; *Milwaukee Journal,* May 7, 1962. Jean, who married Washington attorney G. Joseph Minetti in 1961, would never participate in the graveside services honoring McCarthy. (A similar service is held annually at St. Patrick's Cathedral in New York.) She was scornful of the John Birch Society, whose members, she said, played a major role in the ceremonies. See *Appleton Post-Crescent,* May 7, 1972; Minetti interview, March 1, 1977. Her favorite eulogy of McCarthy was by William S. Schlamm, which first appeared in the *National Review* and was inserted into the *Congressional Record* by Senator Hruska. See *Memorial Services . . . Joseph Raymond McCarthy, Late a Senator from Wisconsin,* pp. 195-99; Minetti interviews, March 14, September 27, 1977.

38. *Appleton Post-Crescent,* October 28, 1957; Lee interview; *Milwaukee Journal,* May 4, 1957. See Mrs. Ruth McCormick Tankersley's recollections in *Chicago Tribune,* May 4, 1957. The McCarthy estate totaled $179,942. It consisted of $86,558.90 in insurance, $83,680.98 in personal property (including 6,300

shares of oil stock), $5,584.25 interest in jointly held property, and $4,118.71 jointly held interest in the senator's Washington home. *Appleton Post-Crescent*, May 1, 1959.

39. Rovere, *Senator Joe McCarthy*, p. 248.
40. See Samuel A. Stouffer, *Communism, Conformity, and Civil Liberties* (New York, 1955), pp. 59 et passim.
41. On civil liberties after the McCarthy censure, see Thomas C. Reeves, *Freedom and the Foundation, The Fund for the Republic in the Era of McCarthyism* (New York, 1969), pp. 96-293.
42. Lorge interview.

SELECTIVE
BIBLIOGRAPHY

Interviews and Conversations
with the Author

Jack Anderson
Mr. and Mrs. Olen A. Anderson
Karl Baldwin
Edwin R. Bayley
Thomas J. Bergen
Dave Brooker
Gordon Brown
Dr. and Mrs. Robert B. Brown
Agnes (Mrs. William) Buckley
 [of Racine, Wis.]
William F. Buckley, Jr.
Don Castonia
Louis Cattau
Mark S. Catlin, Jr.
Madelaine (Mrs. Earle) Cocke
Roy Cohn
Howard Crabb
Albert W. Dammann
Leo Day
Margaret (Mrs. Herbert J.)
 De Bruin

Dr. Adrian J. Delaney
Raymond Dittmore
Mr. and Mrs. Raymond P. Dohr
James E. Doyle
Loyal Eddy
Willard Edwards
Charles B. Elston
Ray L. Feuerstein
James Finucane
Patrick Flanagan
Robert Fleming
Gerald T. Flynn
J. William Fulbright
Dr. and Mrs. Richard A. Gaillard
Paul Gratke
Margaret (Mrs. Edgar) Hagene
Katheryn (Mrs. Walter) Hagerty
Fr. Raphael Hamilton
Charles Hanratty
Edward J. Hart
Richard Harvey, Jr.

783

Mr. and Mrs. James S. Heenan, Sr.
Margaret (Mrs. Hugo) Hellman
Dion Henderson
Mr. and Mrs. Leo Hershberger
Henry M. Jackson
Mr. and Mrs. Russell Johnson
Mr. and Mrs. Larry Jolin
Walter Jolin
Mr. and Mrs. Gustavus Keller
Frank Kelly
Charles Kersten
Mr. and Mrs. Ray Kiermas
Warren Knowles
Thomas Korb
Olive (Mrs. Roman) Kornely
Melvin R. Laird
William M. Lamers
Robert E. Lee
Gerald D. Lorge
George H. Lubeley
Mrs. Richard McCarthy
Stephen McCarthy
Lowell McNeill
Fr. Linus J. Merz
Ruth (Mrs. Harold A.) Meyer
Merle Miller
Jean (Mrs. Joseph G.) Minetti
W. H. Montfort
Edward P. Morgan
Clifford Mullarkey
Everett E. Munn
Mr. and Mrs. Ed Nellor
Gaylord Nelson
Lou Nichols
Mr. and Mrs. Edmund G. Olsyzk
Richard O'Melia
Loren H. Osman
Andrew Parnell

Cyrus Philipp
William Proxmire
Dr. Robert F. Purtell
Nathan Pusey
George Reedy
John Reddin
Henry Reuss
Herbert Romerstein
Maurice Rosenblatt
Fred Saddy
Fr. Francis B. Sayre, Jr.
Harold V. Schoenecker
Loraine E. Schuffler
Ken Smedley
Robert Stoltz
Fred Sturm
Francis H. Sumnicht
Donald A. Surine
Steve Swedish
Mr. and Mrs. Lloyd Tegge
Honor Testin [now Mrs. Gordon Brown]
John F. Thompson
Glenn Todd
Harold Townsend
Gerhard P. Van Arkel
Henry J. Van Straten
Urban P. Van Susteren
Mr. and Mrs. Allen Voy
Frank Waldrop
Mr. and Mrs. Jerome Wander
Frances Wendt
Francis A. Werner
Virginia (Mrs. Theodore) Wiechers
Warren Woods
John Wyngaard
Mr. and Mrs. Herman Yungwirth

The 90-minute television program "Joe McCarthy: an American Ism," first shown nationally over the Public Broadcasting System in 1979, was based upon the author's interviews.

LETTERS TO THE AUTHOR

Eva Adams
Dr. George B. Barnes
Fr. John F. Cronin
Charles P. Curran
Francis T. Davis
Beulah (Mrs. G. Alton) Een
Sam J. Ervin, Jr.
Tracy H. Ferguson
Frederick H. Gloe
Hank Greenspun
Mary Helen Juneau
Mary Louise Kenote
Francis J. Love
John C. Quinn
Bazy (Mrs. Garvin) Tankersley
Wilma (Mrs. M. J.) Witt

In addition, a number of interviewees supplemented their recollections with correspondence.

INTERVIEWS BY OTHERS

Herbert Brownell, Dwight D. Eisenhower Library
Dwight D. Eisenhower, Dulles Oral History Project, Princeton
    University
Ralph Flanders, Columbia Oral History Collection
Penn Kimball, televised by Glenn Silber, Madison, Wisconsin
Walter Kohler, Columbia Oral History Collection
Miles McMillin, Cornell Oral History Project
Morris H. Rubin, Cornell Oral History Project
W. H. Rummel, televised by Glenn Silber, Madison, Wisconsin
G. David Schine, Columbia Oral History Collection
Urban P. Van Susteren, televised by Glenn Silber, Madison, Wisconsin
Arthur Watkins, Columbia Oral History Collection

MANUSCRIPTS

Americans for Democratic Action MSS, State Historical Society of Wisconsin

William E. Benton MSS, State Historical Society of Wisconsin

Hugh A. Butler MSS, Nebraska State Historical Society

Marquis Childs Papers, State Historical Society of Wisconsin

Thomas E. Coleman MSS, State Historical Society of Wisconsin

Edward J. Dempsey MSS, State Historical Society of Wisconsin

Paul Douglas MSS, Chicago Historical Society

John Foster Dulles MSS, Princeton University and Dwight D. Eisenhower Library

Loyal Eddy Papers, in Mr. Eddy's possession

Willard Edwards MSS, in Mr. Edwards's possession

Dwight D. Eisenhower Papers, Dwight D. Eisenhower Library

William T. Evjue MSS, State Historical Society of Wisconsin

Ralph Flanders MSS, State Historical Society of Wisconsin

William T. Flarity MSS, in Robert Griffith's possession

Robert Fleming MSS, State Historical Society of Wisconsin

John T. Flynn MSS, University of Oregon

Theodore F. Green MSS, Library of Congress

James C. Hagerty MSS, Dwight D. Eisenhower Library

Carl Hayden MSS, Arizona State University

James Heenan, Sr. Papers, in Mr. Heenan's possession

Robert C. Hendrickson MSS, Syracuse University

Wayne Hood MSS, State Historical Society of Wisconsin

Henry M. Jackson Papers, in Senator Jackson's possession

Herbert Jacobs MSS, State Historical Society of Wisconsin

"Joe Must Go" Campaign Papers, State Historical Society of Wisconsin

Lyndon B. Johnson Papers, Lyndon B. Johnson Library

Estes Kefauver MSS, University of Tennessee

Ray Kiermas Papers, in the author's possession

Thomas W. Korb MSS, in Mr. Korb's possession

John K. Kyle MSS, State Historical Society of Wisconsin

Robert M. La Follette, Jr. MSS, Library of Congress

Owen Lattimore F.B.I. Files, copies in the possession of Prof. Robert P. Newman of the University of Pittsburgh

Patrick McCarran MSS, Division of Archives, Office of the Nevada Secretary of State

Joseph R. McCarthy Scrapbooks, State Historical Society of Wisconsin

J. Howard McGrath Papers, Harry S. Truman Library
George Van Horn Molseley Papers, Library of Congress
Karl Mundt MSS, Dakota State College
National Committee for an Effective Congress MSS, in the possession of
    Maurice Rosenblatt, Washington, D.C.
Cyrus Philipp MSS, State Historical Society of Wisconsin
William A. Roberts MSS, State Historical Society of Wisconsin
Marvin B. Rosenberry MSS, State Historical Society of Wisconsin
Richard Rovere MSS, State Historical Society of Wisconsin
Fred Seaton MSS, Dwight D. Eisenhower Library
Stephen J. Spingarn Papers, Harry S. Truman Library
Robert A. Taft MSS, Library of Congress
Honor Testin Scrapbooks, in Mrs. Gordon Brown's possession
Elmer Thomas MSS, University of Oklahoma
Charles Tobey MSS, Dartmouth College
Harry S. Truman Papers, Harry S. Truman Library
Millard E. Tydings MSS, University of Maryland
U.S. Marine Corps Papers, History and Museums Division, Department
    of the Navy
Arthur Watkins MSS, Brigham Young University
Kenneth S. Wherry MSS, Nebraska State Historical Society
Alexander Wiley MSS, State Historical Society of Wisconsin

A large quantity of Joe McCarthy materials is on deposit at Marquette University. The papers have remained closed due to resistance first from Jean McCarthy and more recently by Joseph Minetti, Jean's second husband. Insiders have assured the author that the material is virtually worthless. One calls it "McCarthy's third-class mail." Joe's widow possessed a much smaller and possibly more important collection. Efforts by the author to learn more about it, before and after Mrs. Minetti's death, were unsuccessful. For more on the McCarthy Papers, see Reeves, "The Search for Joe McCarthy," pp. 185-96. The author's McCarthy collection, including almost all of the research materials used in writing this book, are at the State Historical Society of Wisconsin.

GOVERNMENT DOCUMENTS

U.S. Congress. *Congressional Record,* vols. 93-102, 1947-1956.
U.S. House of Representatives: Committee on Un-American Activities.
    Annual Report, 81st Cong., 2d sess., 1950.

_____. Committee on Un-American Activities. *Investigation of Un-American Activities and Propaganda,* 79th Cong., 2d sess., 1947.

_____. Committee on Un-American Activities. *100 Things You Should Know About Communism in the U.S.A.,* 82d Cong., 1st sess., 1951.

_____. Subcommittee of the Joint Committee on Housing. *High Cost of Housing, Report,* 80th Cong., 2d sess., 1948.

_____. Joint Committee on Housing. *Final Majority Report,* 80th Cong., 2d sess., 1948.

U.S. Senate: Committee on Armed Services. *Malmedy Massacre Investigation. Hearings . . . ,* 81st Cong., 1st sess., 1949.

_____. Committee on Armed Services. *Malmedy Massacre Investigation. Report,* 81st Cong., 1st sess., 1949.

_____. Committee on Armed Services. *Nomination of Anna M. Rosenberg to Be Assistant Secretary of Defense. Hearings . . . ,* 81st Cong., 2d sess., 1950.

_____. Subcommittee of the Committee on Banking and Currency. *Proposed Disposition of Lustron Plant. Hearings . . . ,* 82d Cong., 1st sess., 1951.

_____. Subcommittee of the Committee on Banking and Currency. *Study of Reconstruction Finance Corporation. Hearings . . . ,* 82d Cong., 1st sess., 1951.

_____. Subcommittee of the Committee on Banking and Currency. *Sugar Controls. Hearings . . . ,* 80th Cong., 1st sess., 1947.

_____. Committee on Banking and Currency. *Defense Housing Act. Hearings . . . ,* 82d Cong., 1st sess., 1951.

_____. Committee on Banking and Currency. *Rent Control. Hearings . . . ,* 80th Cong., 1st sess., 1947.

_____. Subcommittee of the Committee on Expenditures in the Executive Departments. *Influence In Government Procurement. Hearings . . . ,* 81st Cong., 1st sess., 1949.

_____. Subcommittee of the Committee on Foreign Relations. *Nomination of Philip C. Jessup to be United States Representative to the Sixth General Assembly of the United Nations. Hearings. . . .* 82d Cong., 1st sess., 1951.

_____. Subcommittee of the Committee on Foreign Relations. *State Department Employee Loyalty Investigation. Hearings . . . ,* 81st Cong., 2d sess., 1950.

_____. Committee on Foreign Relations. *State Department Employee Loyalty Investigation, Individual Views.* 81st Cong., 2d sess., 1950.

_____. Committee on Foreign Relations. *State Department Employee Loyalty Investigation. Report . . . ,* 81st Cong., 2d sess., 1950.

————. Committee on Government Operations. Permanent Subcommittee on Investigations. *Annual Report . . .* , 83d Cong., 2d sess., 1954.

————. Committee on Government Operations. Permanent Subcommittee on Investigations. *Army Signal Corps-Subversion and Espionage. Hearings . . .* , 83d Cong., 1st and 2d sess., 1954.

————. Committee on Government Operations. Permanent Subcommittee on Investigations. *Communist Infiltration Among Army Civilian Workers. Hearings . . .* , 83d Cong., 1st sess., 1953.

————. Committee on Government Operations. Permanent Subcommittee on Investigations. *Communist Infiltration in the Army. Hearings . . .* , 83d Cong., 1st and 2d sess., 1953-1954.

————. Committee on Government Operations. Permanent Subcommittee on Investigations. *Communist Party Activities, Western Pennsylvania. Hearings . . .* , 83d Cong., 1st sess., 1953.

————. Committee on Government Operations. Permanent Subcommittee on Investigations. *Control of Trade with the Soviet Bloc. Hearings . . .* , 83d Cong., 1st sess., 1953.

————. Committee on Government Operations. Permanent Subcommittee on Investigations. *Security—Government Printing Office. Hearings . . .* , 83d Cong., 1st sess., 1953.

————. Committee on Government Operations. Permanent Subcommittee on Investigations. *Security—United Nations. Hearings . . .* , 83d Cong., 1st sess., 1953.

————. Committee on Government Operations. Permanent Subcommittee on Investigations. *State Department Files Survey. Hearings . . .* , 83d Cong., 1st sess., 1953.

————. Committee on Government Operations. Permanent Subcommittee on Investigations. *State Department Information Program—Information Centers. Hearings . . .* , 83d Cong., 1st sess., 1953.

————. Committee on Government Operations. Permanent Subcommittee on Investigations. *State Department Information Program—Information Centers. Report . . .* , 83d Cong., 2d sess., 1954.

————. Committee on Government Operations. Permanent Subcommittee on Investigations. *State Department Information Program—Voice of America. Hearings . . .* , 83d Cong., 1st sess., 1953.

————. Committee on Government Operations. Permanent Subcommittee on Investigations. *State Department—Student-*

Teacher Exchange Program. Hearings . . . , 83d Cong., 1st sess., 1953.

——. Committee on Government Operations. Permanent Subcommittee on Investigations. *Subversion and Espionage in Defense Establishments and Industry. Hearings . . . ,* 83d Cong., 1st and 2d sess., 1954.

——. Committee on Government Operations. Permanent Subcommittee on Investigations. *Transfer of Occupation Currency Plates—Espionage Phase. Hearings . . . ,* 83d Cong., 1st sess., 1953.

——. Committee on Government Operations. Permanent Subcommittee on Investigations. *Voice of America. Report . . . ,* 83d Cong., 2d sess., 1954.

——. Committee on Government Operations. Permanent Subcommittee on Investigations. *Waste and Mismanagement in Voice of America Engineering Projects. Report . . . ,* 83d Cong., 2d sess., 1954.

——. Committee on Government Operations. Special Subcommittee on Investigations. *Charges and Countercharges Involving Secretary of the Army Robert T. Stevens, John G. Adams, H. Struve Hensel, and Senator Joe McCarthy, Roy M. Cohn, and Francis P. Carr. Hearings . . . ,* 83d Cong., 2d sess., 1954.

——. Committee on Government Operations. Special Subcommittee on Investigations. *Special Senate Investigation on Charges and Countercharges Involving: Secretary of the Army Robert T. Stevens, John G. Adams, H. Struve Hensel, and Senator Joe McCarthy, Roy M. Cohn, and Francis P. Carr. Senate Report 2507,* 83d Cong., 2d sess., 1954.

——. Committee on the Judiciary. Subcommittee to Investigate the Administration of the Internal Security Act and Other Internal Security Laws. *Institute of Pacific Relations. Hearings . . . ,* 82d Cong., 1st and 2d sess., 1951-52.

——. Committee on Rules and Administration. Subcommittee on Privileges and Elections. *Investigation of Joseph R. McCarthy. Hearings . . . ,* 82d Cong., 2d sess., 1952.

——. Committee on Rules and Administration. Subcommittee on Privileges and Elections. *Investigation of Senators Joseph R. McCarthy and William Benton. Report,* 82d Cong., 2d sess., 1952.

——. Committee on Rules and Administration. Subcommittee on Privileges and Elections. *Maryland Senatorial Election of 1950. Hearings . . . ,* 82d Cong., 1st sess., 1951.

———. Committee on Rules and Administration. *Maryland Senatorial Election of 1950. Report . . . ,* 82d Cong., 1st sess., 1951.

———. Joint Committee on Housing. *Housing Study and Investigation, Individual Views. Report,* 80th Cong., 2d sess., 1948.

———. Joint Committee on Housing. *Study and Investigation of Housing. Hearings . . . ,* 80th Cong., 1st sess., 1948.

———. *Report of the Select Committee to Study Censure Charges,* 83d Cong., 2d sess., 1954.

———. Select Committee to Study Censure Charges. *Hearings . . . ,* 83d Cong., 2d sess., 1954.

———. Special Committee on Investigation of Cover on Mail of Senators. *Report . . . ,* 83d Cong., 2d sess., 1954.

U.S. Senate and House: *Memorial Services Held in the Senate and House of Representatives of the United States, Together with Remarks Presented in Eulogy of Joseph Raymond McCarthy.* 85th Cong., 1st sess., 1957.

BOOKS, ARTICLES, AND DISSERTATIONS

Acheson, Dean. *Present at the Creation: My Years in the State Department.* New York: Norton, 1969.

Adams, Sherman. *Firsthand Report, The Story of the Eisenhower Administration.* New York: Harper and Row, 1961.

Alexander, Jack. "The Senate's Remarkable Upstart," *Saturday Evening Post,* 220 (August 9, 1947), 15-17, 52-53, 57-58.

Alsop, Joseph and Stewart. "Why Has Washington Gone Crazy," *Saturday Evening Post,* 223 (July 29, 1950), 20+.

Anderson, Clinton P. *Outsider in the Senate, Senator Clinton Anderson's Memoirs.* New York: World, 1970.

Anderson, Jack. *Confessions of a Muckraker: The Inside Story of Life in Washington During the Truman, Eisenhower, Kennedy and Johnson Years.* New York: Random House, 1979.

Anderson, Jack and Ronald W. May. *McCarthy: The Man, the Senator, the "Ism."* Boston: Beacon Press, 1952.

Barth, Alan. Government by Investigation. New York: Viking Press, 1955.

———. *The Loyalty of Free Men.* New York: Viking Press, 1951.

Bayley, Edwin R. *Joe McCarthy and the Press.* Madison: University of Wisconsin Press, 1981.

Beal, John Robinson. *John Foster Dulles: 1888-1959.* New York: Harper, 1959.

Bean, Louis H. *Influences in the 1954 Mid-Term Elections.* Washington, D.C.: Public Affairs Institute, 1954.

Bell, Daniel (ed.). *The Radical Right.* New York: Doubleday Anchor, 1964.

Bernstein, Barton J. (ed.). *Politics and Policies of the Truman Administration.* Chicago: Quadrangle, 1972.

Bishop, Jim. *A Bishop's Confession.* Boston: Little, Brown, 1981.

Blair, Joan and Clay, Jr. *The Search for J.F.K.* New York: Berkeley Medallion, 1976.

Block, Herbert. *The Herblock Book.* Boston: Beacon Press, 1952.

Bohlen, Charles E. *Witness to History, 1929-1969.* New York: Norton, 1973.

Bontecou, Eleanor. *The Federal Loyalty-Security Program.* Ithaca: Cornell University Press, 1953.

Brock, Clifton. *Americans for Democratic Action: Its Role in National Politics.* Washington, D.C.: Public Affairs Press, 1962.

Buckley, William F., Jr. and L. Brent Bozell. *McCarthy and His Enemies, The Record and its Meaning.* Chicago: Regnery, 1954.

Bullock, Paul. " 'Rabbits and Radicals,' Richard Nixon's 1946 Campaign Against Jerry Voorhis," *Southern California Quarterly,* LV (Fall, 1973), 319-59.

Campbell, Angus, Philip E. Converse, Warren E. Miller, and Donald E. Stokes. *The American Voter.* New York: Wiley, 1960.

Campbell, Angus, Gerald Gurin, and Warren E. Miller. *The Voter Decides.* Evanston, Illinois: Row Peterson, 1954.

Carr, Robert K. *The House Committee on Un-American Activities.* Ithaca, New York: Cornell University Press, 1952.

Cater, Douglass. "The Captive Press," *The Reporter,* 2 (June 6, 1950), 17-20.

Caute, David. *The Great Fear: The Anti-Communist Purge Under Truman and Eisenhower.* New York: Simon and Schuster, 1978.

Chamberlain, John. "Forrest Davis, RIP," *National Review,* 12 (May 22, 1962), 357, 386.

Cohn, Roy. *McCarthy.* New York: New American Library, 1968.

Commager, Henry Steele. *Freedom and Order, A Commentary on the American Political Scene.* New York: George Braziller, 1966.

"Congress," *Time,* LVIII (October 22, 1951), 21-4.

Cook, Fred J. *The Nightmare Decade, The Life and Times of Senator Joe McCarthy.* New York: Random House, 1971.

Crosby, Donald F. *God, Church, and Flag: Senator Joseph R. McCarthy and the Catholic Church, 1950-1957.* Chapel Hill: University of North Carolina Press, 1978.

Cutler, Robert. *No Time For Rest.* Boston: Little, Brown, 1966.

Davies, Richard O. *Housing Reform During the Truman Administration.* Columbia, Missouri: University of Missouri Press, 1966.

Demaris, Ovid. *The Director, An Oral Biography of J. Edgar Hoover.* New York: Harper's Magazine Press, 1975.

Donner, Frank J. *The Un-Americans.* New York: Ballantine, 1961.

Dorsen, Norman and John G. Simon. "McCarthy and the Army: A Fight on the Wrong Front," *Columbia University Forum,* 7 (Fall, 1964), 21-8.

Douglas, Paul H. *In the Fullness of Time, The Memoirs of Paul H. Douglas.* New York: Harcourt, Brace, Jovanovich, 1971.

Dulles, Eleanor Lansing. "Footnote to History: A Day in the Life of Senator Joe McCarthy," *World Affairs,* 143 (Fall, 1980), 156-62.

Eisenhower, Dwight D. *The White House Years: Mandate for Change, 1953-1956.* Garden City, N.Y.: Doubleday, 1963.

Evans, Rowland and Robert D. Novak. *Lyndon B. Johnson: The Exercise of Power.* New York: New American Library, 1968.

Fenton, John H. *Midwest Politics.* New York: Holt, Rinehart and Winston, 1966.

Flanders, Ralph. *Senator from Vermont.* Boston: Little, Brown, 1961.

Flynn, John T. *The Lattimore Story.* New York: Devin-Adair, 1953.

Forster, Arnold and Benjamin R. Epstein. *The Troublemakers.* Garden City, N.Y.: Doubleday, 1952.

Freeland, Richard M. *The Truman Doctrine and the Origins of McCarthyism: Foreign Policy, Domestic Politics, and Internal Security, 1946-1948.* New York: Knopf, 1972.

Fried, Richard M. *Men Against McCarthy.* New York: Columbia University Press, 1976.

Friendly, Alfred J. "Case History of a Smear," *The Progressive,* 15 (May, 1951), 5-9.

————. "The Noble Crusade of Senator McCarthy," *Harpers,* 20 (August, 1950), 34-42.

Friendly, Fred W. *Due to Circumstances Beyond Our Control.* New York: Random House, 1967.

Gaddis, John Lewis. *The United States and the Origins of the Cold War, 1941-1947.* New York: Columbia University Press, 1972.

Gallup, George H. *The Gallup Poll, 1935-1971.* 3 vols. New York: Random House, 1972.

Goldman, Eric F. *The Crucial Decade—And After: America, 1945-1960.* New York: Vintage Books, 1960.

Goldwater, Barry. *With No Apologies.* New York: Morrow, 1979.

Goodman, Walter. *The Committee: The extraordinary career of the House Committee on Un-American Activities.* New York: Farrar, Straus and Giroux, 1968.

Gore, Leroy. *Joe Must Go.* New York: Julian Messner, 1954.

Greenspun, Hank. *A Few Columns on Joe McCarthy.* Las Vegas: Hank Greenspun, 1977.

Griffith, Robert. *The Politics of Fear: Joseph R. McCarthy and the Senate.* Lexington, Kentucky: University Press of Kentucky, 1970.

Griffith, Robert and Athan Theoharis (eds.). *The Specter, Original Essays on the Cold War and the Origins of McCarthyism.* New York: New Viewpoints, 1974.

Grodzins, Morton. *The Loyal and the Disloyal: Social Boundaries of Patriotism and Treason.* Chicago: University of Chicago Press, 1956.

Hamby, Alonzo L. *Beyond the New Deal: Harry S. Truman and American Liberalism.* New York: Columbia University Press, 1973.

Harris, Eleanor. "The Private Life of Senator McCarthy," *The American Weekly,* August 16, 1953, pp. 4-5, 7; August 23, 1953, pp. 7, 9, 12.

Harper, Alan D. *The Politics of Loyalty: The White House and the Communist Issue, 1946-1952.* Westport, Conn.: Greenwood, 1969.

Harris, Louis. *Is There a Republican Majority?* New York: Harper and Row, 1956.

Hart, Hornell. "McCarthyism Versus Democracy," *New Republic,* 126 (February 25, 1952), 10-13.

Herndon, Booton. *Praised and Damned, The Story of Fulton Lewis, Jr.* New York: Duell, Sloan and Pearce, 1954.

Hoving, John. "My Friend McCarthy," *The Reporter,* 2 (April 25, 1950), 28-31.

Hughes, Emmet John. *The Ordeal of Power, A Political Memoir of the Eisenhower Years.* New York: Atheneum, 1963.

Hyman, Sidney. *The Lives of William Benton.* Chicago: University of Chicago Press, 1969.

Johnson, Roger T. *Robert M. La Follette, Jr. and the Decline of the Progressive Party in Wisconsin.* Madison: State Historical Society of Wisconsin, 1964.

Kaghan, Theodore. "The McCarthyization of Theodore Kaghan," *The Reporter,* 9 (July 21, 1953), 17-25.

Kahn, E. J., Jr. *The China Hands: America's Foreign Service Officers and What Befell Them.* New York: Viking Press, 1975.

Keeley, Joseph. *The China Lobby Man: The Story of Alfred Kohlberg.* New Rochelle, N.Y.; Arlington House, 1969.

Kemper, Donald J. *Decade of Fear, Senator Hennings and Civil Liberties.* Columbia, Missouri: University of Missouri Press, 1965.

Kendrick, Alexander. *Prime Time, The Life of Edward R. Murrow.* New York: Avon, 1969.

Kendrick, Frank J. "McCarthy and the Senate." Ph.D. dissertation, University of Chicago, 1962.

Koen, Ross Y. *The China Lobby in American Politics.* New York: Harper and Row, 1974.

Koskoff, David E. *Joseph P. Kennedy, A Life and Times.* Englewood Cliffs, New Jersey: Prentice-Hall, 1974.

Krock, Arthur. *Memoirs: Sixty Years on the Firing Line.* New York: Popular Library, 1968.

Latham, Earl. *The Communist Controversy in Washington, From the New Deal to McCarthy.* Cambridge, Mass.: Harvard University Press, 1966.

Lattimore, Owen. *Ordeal by Slander.* Boston: Little, Brown, 1950.

Lilienthal, David E. *The Journals of David E. Lilienthal. Vol. II: The Atomic Energy Years, 1945-1950.* New York: Harper and Row, 1964.

McAuliffe, Mary Sperling. *Crisis on the Left: Cold War Politics and American Liberals, 1947-1954.* Amherst, Massachusetts: University of Massachusetts Press, 1978.

"McCarthy: A Documented Record," *The Progressive,* 18 (April, 1954), 1-92.

McCarthy, Joe. *America's Retreat from Victory, The Story of George Catlett Marshall.* New York: Devin-Adair, 1951.

————. *McCarthyism, The Fight for America.* New York: Devin-Adair, 1952.

"McCarthy Issue . . . Pro and Con, The," *U.S. News and World Report,* 31 (September 7, 1951), 24-41.

"McCarthyism: Is it a Trend?" *U.S. News and World Report,* 33 (September 19, 1952), 21-22.

McWilliams, Carey. *Witch Hunt: The Revival of Heresy*. Boston: Little, Brown, 1950.

Maney, Patrick J. *'Young Bob' La Follette: A Biography of Robert M. La Follette, Jr., 1895-1953*. Columbia, Missouri: University of Missouri Press, 1978.

Marchetti, Victor and John D. Marks. *The CIA and the Cult of Intelligence*. New York: Dell, rev. ed., 1980.

Matthews, Donald R. *U.S. Senators and Their World*. Chapel Hill: University of North Carolina Press, 1960.

Matusow, Harvey. *False Witness*. New York: Cameron and Kahn, 1955.

May, Gary. *China Scapegoat: The Diplomatic Ordeal of John Carter Vincent*. New York: New Republic Books, 1979.

Mazo, Earl. *Richard Nixon, A Political and Personal Portrait*. New York: Harper and Bros., 1959.

Merson, Martin. *The Private Diary of a Public Servant*. New York: Macmillan, 1955.

Meyer, Karl E. "The Politics of Loyalty: From La Follette to McCarthy in Wisconsin, 1918-1952." Ph.D. dissertation, Princeton University, 1956.

Miller, Merle. *Lyndon, An Oral Biography*. New York: G. P. Putnam, 1980.

Murphy, Charles J. V. "Texas Business and McCarthy," *Fortune*, 49 (May, 1954), 100-1, 208, 211-12, 214, 216.

Nixon, Richard. *RN: The Memoirs of Richard Nixon*. Vol. 1., New York: Warner Books, 1979.

O'Brien, Michael. *McCarthy and McCarthyism in Wisconsin*. Columbia, Missouri: University of Missouri Press, 1980.

————. "Young Joe McCarthy, 1908-1944," *The Wisconsin Magazine of History*, 63 (Spring, 1980), 179-232.

O'Brien, Michael. "Young Joe McCarthy, 1908-1944," *The Wisconsin Magazine of History*, 63 (Spring, 1980), 179-232.

Ogden, August Raymond. *The Dies Committee: A Study of the Special House Committee for Investigation of Un-American Activities, 1938-1944*. Washington, D.C.: Catholic University Press, 1945.

Oshinsky, David M. *Senator Joseph McCarthy and the American Labor Movement*. Columbia, Missouri: University of Missouri Press, 1976.

Packer, Herbert L. *Ex-Communist Witnesses, Four Studies in Fact Finding*. Stanford: Stanford University Press, 1962.

Parmet, Herbert S. *Eisenhower and the American Crusades*. New York: Macmillan, 1972.

————. *Jack: The Struggles of John F. Kennedy.* New York: Dial, 1980.

Patterson, James T. *Mr. Republican: A Biography of Robert A. Taft.* Boston: Houghton Mifflin, 1972.

Pedrick, Willard H. "Senator McCarthy and the Law of Libel: A Study of Two Campaign Speeches," *Northwestern University Law Review,* 48 (May-June, 1953), 135-62.

Phillips, Cabell. *The Truman Presidency, The History of a Triumphant Succession.* New York: Macmillan, 1966.

Polsby, Nelson. "Towards an Explanation of McCarthyism," *Political Studies,* 8 (October, 1960), 250-71.

Potter, Charles. *Days of Shame.* New York: Coward-McCann, 1965.

Prochnau, William W. and Richard W. Larsen. *A Certain Democrat: Senator Henry M. Jackson, A Political Biography.* New York: Prentice-Hall, 1972.

Reeves, Thomas C. *Freedom and the Foundation, The Fund for the Republic in the Era of McCarthyism.* New York: Knopf, 1969.

————. (ed.). *McCarthyism.* Hinsdale, Illinois: Dryden, 1973.

————. "McCarthyism: Interpretations Since Hofstadter," *The Wisconsin Magazine of History,* 60 (Autumn 1976), 42-54.

————. "Tail Gunner Joe: Joseph R. McCarthy and the Marine Corps," *The Wisconsin Magazine of History,* 62 (Summer 1979), 300-11.

————. "The Search for Joe McCarthy," *The Wisconsin Magazine of History,* 60 (Spring 1977), 185-96.

Rogin, Michael Paul. *The Intellectuals and McCarthy, the Radical Specter.* Cambridge, Mass.: The M.I.T. Press, 1967.

Rorty, James and Moshe Decter. *McCarthy and the Communists.* Beacon Press, 1954.

Rovere, Richard H. *Senator Joe McCarthy.* New York: Harcourt, Brace, 1959.

Roy, Ralph Lord. *Communism and the Churches.* New York: Harcourt, Brace, 1960.

Schlesinger, Arthur M., Jr., *Robert Kennedy and His Times.* New York: Ballantine, 1978.

Schneir, Walter and Miriam. *Invitation to an Inquest.* New York: Penguin, 1973.

Scientists' Committee on Loyalty and Security. "Fort Monmouth One Year Later," *Bulletin of the Atomic Scientists,* 11 (April, 1955), 148-50.

"Self-Inflated Target, The," *Time,* LXIII (March 22, 1954), 23-7.

"Senate Newcomer," *Newsweek,* 39 (December 16, 1946), 2-3.

"Senator McCarthy Answers Some Important Questions," *Cosmopolitan,* May 1952, pp. 39-41, 143-54.

Smith, Margaret Chase. *Declaration of Conscience.* Edited by William C. Lewis, Jr. Garden City, N.Y.: Doubleday, 1972.

Stouffer, Samuel A. *Communism, Conformity, and Civil Liberties.* New York: Doubleday, 1955.

Straight, Michael. *Trial by Television.* Boston: Beacon Press, 1954.

Sullivan, William C. *The Bureau: My Thirty Years in Hoover's FBI.* New York: Norton, 1979.

Swanberg. W. A. *Luce and his Empire.* New York: Scribners, 1972.

Thelen, David P. and Esther S. "Joe Must Go: The Movement to Recall Senator Joseph R. McCarthy," *The Wisconsin Magazine of History,* XLIX (Spring 1966), 185-209.

Theoharis, Athan G. *Seeds of Repression: Harry S. Truman and the Origins of McCarthyism.* Chicago: Quadrangle, 1971.

_____. *Spying on Americans: Political Surveillance from Hoover to the Huston Plan.* Philadelphia: Temple University Press, 1978.

_____. *The Yalta Myths: An Issue in U.S. Politics, 1945-1955.* Columbia, Missouri: University of Missouri Press, 1970.

Thomas, John N. *The Institute of Pacific Relations: Asian Scholars and American Politics.* Seattle: University of Washington Press, 1974.

Thomas, Lately. *When Even Angels Wept: The Senator Joseph McCarthy Affair—A Story Without a Hero.* New York: Morrow, 1973.

Thompson, Francis H. *The Frustration of Politics: Truman, Congress, and the Loyalty Issue, 1945-1953.* Rutherford, New Jersey: Fairleigh Dickinson University Press, 1979.

Trohan, Walter. *Political Animals, Memoirs of a Sentimental Cynic.* Garden City, N.Y.: Doubleday, 1975.

Tydings, Millard E. "McCarthyism: How It All Began," *The Reporter,* 7 (August 19, 1952), 11-15.

Van Roden, Edward L. "American Atrocities in Germany," *The Progressive,* XIII (February 1949), 21-22.

"Vigorous Individual, A," *Time,* LXII (September 7, 1953), 21-22.

Waldron, Eli. "Joe McCarthy's Home Town," *The Reporter,* VI (May 13, 1952), 19-24.

Watkins, Arthur. *Enough Rope.* Englewood Cliffs, New Jersey: Prentice-Hall, 1969.

Wechsler, James A. *The Age of Suspicion.* New York: Random House, 1953.

Welch, Joseph N. "The Lawyer's Afterthoughts," *Life,* 37 (July 26, 1954), 97-98, 100, 102, 104-06, 108.

Whalen, Richard. *The Founding Father: The Story of Joseph P. Kennedy.* New York: New American Library, 1964.

White, Theodore H. *In Search of History, A Personal Adventure.* New York: Harper and Row, 1978.

White, William S. *The Professional: Lyndon B. Johnson.* Boston: Houghton Mifflin, 1964.

———. *Citadel: The Story of the U.S. Senate.* New York: Harper, 1956.

———. "Joe McCarthy, The Man with the Power," *Look,* 17 (June 16, 1953), 29-33.

———. *The Taft Story.* New York: Harper and Row, 1954.

Wiebe, G. D. "The Army-McCarthy Hearings and the Public Conscience," *Public Opinion Quarterly,* XXI (Winter 1958-59), 490-502.

Williams, Edward Bennett. *One Man's Freedom.* New York: Atheneum, 1962.

Wilson, Richard. "The Ring Around McCarthy," *Look,* 17 (December 1, 1953), 29-33.

Wisconsin Citizens' Committee on McCarthy's Record. *The McCarthy Record.* Madison: The Wisconsin Citizens' Committee on McCarthy's Record, 1952.

INDEX

Acheson, Dean, 209, 215, 219, 253, 255, 269, 270, 278, 299, 312-13, 324, 328-29, 347-48, 378, 401, 673

Adams, John G., 536-37, 538, 541-44, 551, 570-74, 576-77, 592-93, 597, 606, 614, 615-17, 619-20, 626, 636, 637

Adams, Sherman, 438-40, 471, 500, 513, 527, 536-37, 553, 566, 617

Aiken, George, 238, 297

Alfonsi, Paul, 196

Alsop, Joseph, 312, 316, 436, 440, 496, 502-3, 545, 556, 558, 604

Alsop, Steward, 312, 316, 374, 436, 496, 545, 556, 604, 647

Amerasia case, 123-24, 224, 290-96, 300-3, 305, 307, 356, 539

American Action, Inc., 98-99, 102

American Civil Liberties Union, 215

American Federation of Labor, 89, 142, 205, 448

American Legion, 192-93, 207, 209, 379-80, 429

Americans for Democratic Action, 124, 241, 404, 414, 445, 447, 588, 643

Anastos, George, 601, 603

Anderson, Clinton P., 120, 228, 269, 290

Anderson, Jack, ix, 114, 121, 156, 158, 184, 188, 202, 241, 247, 264, 288, 316, 383-84, 408, 409, 415, 448-49, 497

Andrews, Bert, 480

Andrews, T. Coleman, 415

Armour, Norman, 473, 536

Army investigations, 506, 513-25, 536-59, 561-63, 566-637

Arundel, Russell M., 121-23, 403

Aschenauer, Rudolf, 183-84

Aschenbrenner, Ed, 22-23

Atlee, Clement, 491

Auden, W. H., 480

Avery, Sewall, 247-48

Baarslag, Karl, 489, 503

Baldwin, Raymond E., 167-70, 172-74, 176-84, 377

801

Ball, Joseph H., 107, 116, 264
Barkley, Alben W., 309, 415
Barnes, George B., 47
Barrett, Frank, 441, 455
Barth, Alan, 207, 480
Baruch, Bernard, 361
Bauer, Robert A., 483
Bayley, Edwin R., 420, 671
Beall, J. Glenn, 450
Bean, Louis H., 455, 619
Bell, Jack, 505, 506
Benet, Stephen Vincent, 480
Bennett, Wallace, 334, 344-45, 660, 662
Bentley, Alvin, 337, 412, 442
Bentley, Mrs. Alvin, 412
Bentley, Elizabeth, 211, 306, 325, 388,
     528
Benton, William B., 158, 264-65, 296,
     330, 344, 351, 361, 366, 372, 392,
     397; anti-McCarthy moves of, 374-
     86, 388, 396, 406-10, 413, 443, 497,
     590; at 1952 Democratic National
     Convention, 428-29; description of,
     377; and election of 1952, 407, 442,
     451, 455; lawsuit against McCarthy,
     398-99; McCarthy resolution against,
     400, 404-5; and Watkins Committee,
     651
Berndt, Margaret T., 338
Bielaski, Frank, 291-93, 300
Biemiller, Andrew J., 100
Biggers, Ross, 513
Bingham, Hiram, 355-56, 391, 654
Birkhead, Kenneth, 384, 385, 497
Blau, Fred, 102
Bliss, Robert Woods, 536
Block, Herbert (Herblock), 266-67, 316,
     334, 372, 413, 440, 561
Boardman, W. Wade, 188, 190
Bobrowicz, Edmund, 94, 103
Boggs, Hale, 135
Bogolepov, Igor, 473
Bohlen, Charles E., 468-76
Bond, Ward, 430, 540

Bowles, Chester, 377
Bozell, L. Brent, 242, 645
Braden, Spruille, 256
Bradley, Kenneth, 600-1
Bradley, Omar, 136
Brennan, William J., Jr., 667-68
Brewster, Owen, 241, 345, 388, 418
Bricker, John W., 100, 151, 450, 474, 659
Bridges, Styles, viii, 123, 180, 220, 222,
     248, 251, 265, 269, 288, 387, 399,
     423-24, 462, 468, 469-70, 472-74,
     502, 662, 663
Brogan, Dennis, 581
Browder, Earl, 192, 196, 249, 281, 305,
     339-40, 485
Brownell, Herbert, 442, 494, 527-28, 532,
     565, 612, 617, 624
Brunauer, Esther Caukin, 254-55, 264-66,
     305, 356
Brunauer, Stephen, 255, 264-66, 325, 356
Buckley, Daniel G., 394-95, 465
Buckley, William F., Jr., 242, 373-74, 451,
     467, 507, 642, 645, 667
Budenz, Louis, 248, 267-68, 275-77, 279-
     83, 305, 307, 327, 384, 388, 516
Bundy, William P., 502, 506
Burnham, James, 494
Burns, James MacGregor, 442
Buseby, Fred, 254
Butler, Hugh, 100, 161
Butler, John Marshall, 335-39, 341, 343,
     345, 362, 364, 418, 460, 475
Byers, Robert, Jr., 158, 403
Byers, Robert, Sr., 158
Byrd, Harry F., 180, 501-2
Byrnes, James F., 224, 226, 278, 361, 527
Byrnes, John W., 100, 438
Byrnes, Mildred, 16

Cain, Harry P., 60, 135, 144, 151, 361,
     418, 423, 441, 450, 455
Callahan, William, 225-26
Campbell, Alex, 333-34
Campbell, William, 65

Canaan, Jack, 54

Canall, Margaret Ellen, 2

Capehart, Homer, 117, 134, 201, 223, 241, 311, 333, 344, 380, 418, 475

Carlson, Frank, 646, 652

Carr, Francis, 570-77, 579-80, 592, 595, 599-600, 611, 612, 616, 618, 621-22, 626-27, 633, 634, 636

Carr, Robert K., 210

Carter, Edward C., 352-53

Case, Adelaide, 653

Case, Clifford, 640, 653

Case, Francis, 646, 657, 658, 660

Cater, Douglass, 373, 378

Catlin, Mark, Jr., 40-41, 53, 75, 202, 613, 671

Cattau, Louis, 22-23, 28

Chadwick, John, 584

Chaffee, Zechariah, Jr., 404

Chamberlain, John, 374

Chambers, Joseph M., 168

Chambers, Whittaker, 206, 211-14, 249, 446, 480, 528

Chapple, John, 326

Chavez, Dennis, 269, 296, 415

Chennault, Claire, 217, 220

Cherkasky, Ben, 40

Cherne, Leo, 127

Childs, Marquis, 260, 343, 473, 475

"China Hands," 217-18, 220

China Lobby, 215, 219-21, 282, 372, 413

Christoffel, Harold R., 267, 594

Churchill, Winston, 328

Clark, Tom, 527

Clay, Lucius D., 164, 166, 183-84

"Clearing House," the, 497-99, 503, 641, 643, 661

Clifford, Clark, 627-28, 633, 636

Clubb, O. Edmund, 356

Cohen, Meyer, 431

Cohn, Roy, 198-99, 442, 446, 476, 513, 586, 595, 640, 672, 673; description of, 463-65; and Army investigations, 513, 515, 517-22, 536-37, 541, 566-

67, 569-80, 583, 588, 591-93; in Army-McCarthy hearings, 597-601, 604-18, 620-37; and General Electric investigation, 525-26; and Government Printing Office probe, 511; and McCarthy censure, 651, 662; and Moss, Annie Lee, 549-50, 568-69; resignation of, from McCarthy Subcommittee, 642; and Voice of America investigation, 484, 488-91, 503

Colby, James, 56, 58

Coleman, Aaron H., 517, 521, 609

Coleman, Thomas E., 112, 146-47, 268, 340, 367; during Army-McCarthy hearings, 613; and campaign of 1946, 68-76, 79, 81, 83, 89-90, 93-95; and campaign of 1952, 417, 422; description of, 64-66; on McCarthyism, 283; after Wheeling speech, 247-48, 252, 254

Collier, Robert, 608-9

Commager, Henry Steele, 126

Communist China, 215-21

Communist Control Act of 1954, 647

Communist Party in America, 205-11

Compton, Wilson M., 477-79

Conant, James B., 467-68, 490

Condon, Edward U., 210

Congress of Industrial Organizations (C.I.O.), 88-89, 94, 99-100, 102-4, 117-18, 142, 193, 206, 448

Connally, Tom, 242-43, 269, 272-74, 276, 308

Cooper, John Sherman, 563, 641, 644

Coplon, Judith, 214, 306

Cordon, Guy, 643

Cornelison, Frank, 75

Corry, Patricia, 113

Cosgriff, Walter, 400, 409

Cotter, Paul J., 406-8

Counihan, Maybelle, 24, 46

Cousins, Norman, 316

Crabb, Howard, 5

Crosby, John, 565
Crouch, Paul, 446-47
Crowley, Leo T., 84
Cullen, H. R., 319, 419, 594
Cummings, William Garfield, 446-47
Curran, Charles, 17
Currie, Lauchlin, 211

Davies, The Rev. A. Powell, 497
Davies, John Paton, 217-18, 356, 461, 530
Davies, Joseph E., 311, 480
Davis, Charles, 365-70, 386, 395
Davis, Forrest, 373-74
Day, Leo, 45
Dealey, E. M., 604
Dean, Vera Micheles, 480
Dear, John, 235
Decter, Moshe, 647
De Mille, Cecil B., 430
Dempsey, Jack, 513
Dennett, Raymond, 390
Dennis, Eugene, 191
Denton, R. Harold, 154
Desmond, Frank, 225-26
De Sola, Ralph, 358-62
De Voto, Bernard, 445
Dewey, John, 480, 569
Dewey, Thomas E., 100, 146-47, 150, 328
Dickens, Randolph, Jr., 368-69
Dickstein, Samuel, 207
Dies Committee, 207-8, 357
Dies, Martin, 207, 657
Dilworth, Richardson, 333
Dirksen, Everett, 319, 395-96, 398, 418,
    499, 511; and Army investigations,
    548, 549-50, 551, 552, 553-54, 567,
    577, 582, 588, 593, 599, 636; in
    Army-McCarthy hearings, 605, 613-
    14, 616-17, 622, 627, 635; and
    Bohlen case, 471, 473-74; in
    campaign of 1950, 332, 335, 343,
    345; and Fifth Amendment, 510;
    and McCarthy's censure, 643, 653,
    661, 662, 666

Di Salle, Michael V., 452
Dittmore, Raymond, 670-71
Dodd, Bella V., 280-81, 305, 653
Dohr, Raymond P., 438-39
Dondero, George A., 294-95
Dostal, Edward V., 80
Douglas, Helen Gahagan, 332, 334
Douglas, Paul, 330-31, 378, 382
Doyle, James, 419, 431
Driscoll, Mary, 558, 626, 628, 674
Druckrey, Dottie, 26-27, 33
Duff, James, 333, 343-44, 393, 644
Dulles, Allen W., 502-3, 513
Dulles, Foster Rhea, 480
Dulles, John Foster, 262, 427-28, 453,
    461, 469-72, 479, 480-81, 487, 491,
    513, 531, 557
Duran, Gustavo, 224, 256, 258, 305, 325,
    380, 384-85
Durfee, James R., 67
Dwinell, John S., 182
Dworshak, Henry C., 241, 460, 474, 592,
    603-4, 621-22

Eagle, Ruth, 541
Eastland, James, 347, 351
Eberlein, Michael G., 21-26, 96
Ecton, Zales, 441, 450, 455
Eddy, Loyal, 65-66, 68-69, 74-75, 78, 92,
    109
Edelstein, Julius, 658
Edwards, Willard, 223, 249, 319, 512,
    558, 668
Einstein, Albert, 222
Eisenhower, Arthur, 504
Eisenhower, Dwight D., 504, 644, 673;
    and Army investigations, 529, 551,
    553-59, 561-63, 578, 580-81, 587,
    604-5, 617-18, 623-24, 634, 636; and
    Bohlen, Charles E., 468-75; and
    campaigns of 1952, 422-23, 427,
    436-40, 451-53; and campaigns of
    1954, 530-31, 561-62; and Central
    Intelligence Agency, 502-3, 506; and

Conant, James, 467; and Greek shipowners dispute, 487; and Jessup, Philip, 261; loyalty program of, 461-62, 494, 510, 529-30; and Matthews, J. B., 500-1; and McCarthy censure, 653, 666; on Murrow, Edward R., 589; and Oppenheimer, J. Robert, 589-90; on Rosenberg, Anna, 361; State of the Union address of, 476; and White, Harry Dexter, 528

Eisenhower, Milton, 264, 427, 667
Eklund, Laurence, 107-8
Elections, of 1946, 115; of 1950, 270, 331-46; of 1952, 449-56; of 1954, 654
Ellender, Allen J., 133, 143, 145, 150, 466, 533, 538
Ellis, Burton F., 169-70, 177
Epstein, Benjamin, 361
Ervin, Samuel J., Jr., 646, 659-60
Everett, Willis M., Jr., 164, 169, 175-76, 180-82, 184
Evjue, William T., 68-69, 76-77, 91, 99, 106, 120-21, 130-31, 140, 143, 151, 188-96, 199, 276, 289, 296-97, 316-17, 362, 365, 369, 379, 386, 395, 396, 410, 420, 430-31, 435, 454, 506

Fairchild, Thomas R., 335, 419-20, 431, 434-35, 447-49, 453-54
Fairfield, William S., 235
Falk, Harold, Sr., 80
Fanton, Dwight, 166-68, 173-75
Farrand, John E., 365, 367-70, 395
Fast, Howard, 479-80
Fedder, William, 340-43, 345, 363-64, 369, 380
Federal Bureau of Investigation (FBI), 101, 127, 206, 212, 246, 291-95, 298-303, 306, 312-14, 318, 324, 352, 510, 517, 522-23, 528, 548, 590
Ferber, Edna, 480
Ferguson, Homer, 77, 242, 276, 295, 351, 355, 466, 468, 470, 504, 528, 585, 619, 640

Ferguson, J. Donald, 321
Ferguson, Joseph T., 333
Field, Frederick Vanderbilt, 276, 281, 305, 322
Field, Marshall, 431-97
Fine, John, 333
Finucane, James, 172-73, 183-84
Fish, Hamilton, 207
Fisher, Frederick G., Jr., 589, 593, 628-31
Flanagan, Francis, 168, 462, 480-81, 486, 498
Flanagan, Patrick, 83
Flanders, Ralph, 262; on Army-McCarthy hearings, 604; and Bohlen nomination, 472; and housing investigation, 135, 138, 139, 143-44, 149, 151; McCarthy, efforts against, 184-85, 414, 562-63, 624-25, 633-34, 637, 640-43, 648, 651, 653, 655; and sugar rationing, 118-20; and Tydings Committee, 311
Flarity, William, 24-25
Fleeson, Doris, 632
Fleming, Robert, 232, 344, 370-71, 384, 418
Fletcher, Charles K., 135
Floberg, John F., 52
Foley, Raymond M., 150, 153
"Flying Badgers," 90-94
Flynn, Gerald T., 16
Flynn, John T., 220-21, 467, 642
Ford, Charles E., 511
Forrestal, James, 197, 349, 432
Forster, Arnold, 361
Fortas, Abe, 272, 296
Freedman, Benjamin H., 357-61
Freedom House, 497
Fried, Louis, 343
Friedrich, Carl J., 165
Fuchs, Klaus, 201, 222
Fulbright, J. William, 115, 388-91, 408, 414, 460, 491, 504, 507, 539, 605, 641-43, 644, 646-47, 655, 663, 668

Fund for the Republic, 675
Furry, Wendell H., 535

Gamble, Ralph, 135-37
Gayn, Mark, 290, 301
George, Walter, 469
Gibson, Hugh, 473
Gieske, Herman E., 226
Gillette, Guy, 343, 362-63, 378, 381, 385,
    388, 391-96, 398, 401, 404-6, 469
Ginsberg, Isidore, 139-40, 193
Goldman, Eric, 110, 214
Goldwater, Barry, xiv, 441, 455, 474, 658-
    659, 661, 666, 673, 674
Goldwyn, Samuel, 641
Golos, Jacob, 211
Gomillion, Otis, 80-81, 107, 319, 417
Goodland, Walter E., 65, 71, 75-76, 89-
    90, 94-95, 100, 107
Goodman, Walter, 209, 210
Goodwin, William J., 248
Gore, Leroy, viii, 584, 639, 668
Gould, Jack, 565
Graham, Frank, 330, 345-46
Greek shipowners dispute, 485-88, 505,
    530-31, 540, 619
Green, John Raeburn, 381-82, 395
Green, Theodore F., 244, 252, 259, 264,
    270, 278, 306, 327, 653
Greenblum, Carl, 519-20
Greenglass, David, 520-21
Greenspun, Hank, 441
Grew, Joseph G., 302-3, 324, 473, 536
Griffith, Robert, 110
Griswold, Erwin, 641

Hagene, Margaret F., 56
Hagerty, James, 527, 531, 551, 553-55,
    557, 566, 666
Hagerty, Mr. and Mrs. Walter, 80
Hall, Leonard, 539, 557, 562, 585-86, 667
Hallanan, Walter S., 424
Hammett, Dashiell, 480, 491
Hand, Learned, 461

Hanratty, Charles, 12-14, 18, 25, 43
Hanson, Haldore, 254, 265-66, 279-80,
    305
Harbaugh, J. I., Jr., 165
Harnischfager, Walter, 65, 80, 184, 248
Harriman, W. Averell, 429
Harris, Reed, 483
Harsh, Joseph C., 308, 375
Hart, Ed, 20-21, 24, 109
Harvey, Paul, 327
Hatch Act of 1939, 208
Hayden, Carl, 378, 383, 396, 398-400,
    404-11, 414-15, 533-34
Hearst newspapers, 101, 207, 248, 291,
    347, 427, 655
Hearst, William Randolph, 427, 434
Heenan, James, 5
Heil, Joseph, 65
Heil, Julius P., 74
Hellman, Hugo, 12
Hellman, Lillian, 480
Henderson, Dion, 321, 402
Hendrickson, Robert C., 298, 362-63,
    365, 380-81, 385, 396, 405-11, 414,
    648, 651, 652
Hennings Committee Report, 411-15
Hennings, Thomas, Jr., 159, 344, 362,
    364, 381-83, 385, 386, 405-11, 414-
    15, 641, 644, 646
Hensel, H. Struve, 592-93, 599, 621-22,
    636
Hermann, A. G., 423
Hershberger, Leo D., 7-10, 418
Hershey, Lewis B., 328
Hickenlooper, Bourke, 201, 244, 247, 249,
    252, 258-59, 261, 263, 265, 270, 274-
    75, 278, 280, 300, 304, 306, 308, 309,
    387, 474, 491
Hill, Perry, 196
Hiss, Alger, 211-14, 221, 432-33, 453
Hitchcock, Robert M., 296
Hlavaty, Julius H., 483-84
Hoan, Daniel, 95
Hobbs, Samuel F., 290, 292

Hoey, Clyde, 460
Hoffman, Paul G., 423, 436, 497, 590, 641
Holder, Cale J., 428
Holland, William, 353
Hollenbeck, Don, 565-66
Honkamp, Elmer, 59
Hood, Wayne, 417, 422
Hoover, Herbert, 347, 355, 424, 478
Hoover, J. Edgar, 101, 112, 124, 265, 299-300, 363, 449, 512; and *Amerasia* case, 291, 303, 324; and Army-McCarthy hearings, 608-9, 612; and Bohlen, Charles, 472; and Cohn, Roy, 464; and Fuchs case, 222; and Lattimore, Owen, 263, 274-75; and Lilienthal, David, 126-27; and loyalty files, 263, 265; McCarthy, friendship with, 203-4, 245, 288, 493-94, 535; and Moss, Annie Lee, 548; and Surine, Don, 246; and Tydings, Millard, 306, 307-8, 312-14; and White, Harry Dexter, 528
House Committee on Un-American Activities (HUAC), 101, 124, 191, 195-96, 208-15, 220, 221, 253, 254, 256, 330, 353, 466, 476, 527, 548
Housing Act of 1948, 149-50
Housing Act of 1949, 150-52
Hoving, John, 232
Howard, Robert A., Jr., 514
Howe, John, 379, 385, 497, 506
Howlett, Pat, 34-36, 39
Huber, John, 280-81
Hughes, Emmet John, 437, 440, 452, 474, 496, 500
Hull, Cordell, 278
Humphrey, George M., 415
Humphrey, Hubert, 269, 330-31, 378, 448, 460
Hunt, H. L., 319, 337
Hunt, Lester C., 168-69, 173, 177, 179
Hunter, John Patrick, 379
Hunter, Ken, 248-49, 295

Hurley, Patrick, Jr., 217-19, 221, 323, 424
Hutchins, Robert M., 361, 377, 480, 569

Immell, Ralph M., 76, 89-90, 94-95
Institute of Pacific Relations, 254-55, 276, 281, 352-54, 388, 445
Isaacs, Harold R., 356
Ives, Irving, 262, 298, 311, 408

Jackson, Henry M., 507; and Army-McCarthy hearings, 580, 597, 612, 626, 628, 633, 634, 640; and elections of 1952, 441, 450, 452; and McCarthy Subcommittee, 460, 484, 499, 501, 505, 534, 546, 550, 556, 566, 575; on McCarthyism, 392, 668
Jackson, Kenneth D., 590
Jaffe, Philip, 254, 276, 290, 293, 294, 300-3, 324-25
Jameson, William J., 586
Jenkins, Ray H., 588, 596, 599, 600-1, 602, 603, 606-8, 610, 615-16, 625, 632, 633
Jenner, William, 145, 281, 309, 311-12, 351, 365, 371, 372, 398, 418, 436-37, 442, 450, 455, 466, 476, 494, 527, 528, 533, 565, 660, 663
Jessup, Philip C., 251-52, 261, 268, 269, 305, 325, 387-92, 395
"Joe Must Go" campaign (see Gore, Leroy)
Johnson, Edwin C., 93, 474, 645, 648-50, 662
Johnson, Louis, 328
Johnson, Lyndon, viii, 180, 308, 359, 460, 644, 645, 658, 661, 662, 668
Johnson, Robert L., 479, 491, 503-4
Johnston, Victor, 68, 91-92, 110, 112, 146
Jolin, Gerald, 55-56
Jolin, Mr. and Mrs. Walter, 22
Jones, Robert L., 547, 640
Jonkel, Jon M., 336-341, 345, 363
Judd, Walter, 220, 248
Juliana, James N., 518-19, 600-1, 603,

612, 620
Juneau, Mary Louise, 24

Kaghan, Theodore, 490
Kai-shek, Chiang, 215-21, 256
Kaltenborn, H. V., 547
Kamin, Leon H., 535
Kamp, Joseph P., 220
Kane, John F., 561
Kaplan, Raymond, 485
Karney, Rex, 58
Karr, David, 349-50
Karsten, Frank M., 283
Kearney, The Rev. James F., 256
Kefauver, Estes, 93, 168, 170, 179, 330-
    31, 344, 429
Keller, Gus, 28-29
Kem, James, 428, 442, 455
Kennan, George F., 215, 300
Kennedy, Eunice, 203
Kennedy, John F., 203, 267, 442-44, 460,
    467, 513
Kennedy, Joseph P., 203, 347, 442-43,
    447, 462-63
Kennedy, Patricia, 203
Kennedy, Robert, 203, 463, 464, 486, 488,
    498, 534, 548, 634
Kenney, Mary Jane, 224
Kenny, Delbert J., 75-76, 89
Kenyon, Dorothy, 250-53, 258-60, 305,
    542-43
Kerley, Larry E., 248, 280-81
Kerr, Mrs. Elizabeth F., 247, 267, 555,
    662, 670
Kerr, Jean Fraser (McCarthy), 199, 249,
    316, 323, 540, 555, 640, 648, 656,
    659, 662; and adopted daughter, 670,
    674; and Army investigation, 570,
    574, 588, 612-13, 639; and campaign
    of 1952, 417, 433; description of,
    204, 288; and Gillette subcommittee,
    395, 407; and Lattimore speech, 262,
    267; and Lustron booklet, 153-56;
    and Marshall speech, 374; in

Maryland campaign, 336-41, 363-65,
    380; and McCarthy's illness and
    death, 586, 669-74; wedding of, 512-
    13
Kerr, Robert, 290, 502
Kersten, Charles, 129, 288, 289, 317, 443;
    and campaign of 1944, 56; and
    campaign of 1946, 70, 100; and
    campaign of 1950, 343; and
    campaign of 1954, 654; and
    Eisenhower, 428, 436; and
    Lattimore, Owen, 262, 267, 277, 279;
    McCarthy staff, joins, 247; and
    Yalta, 468
Keyserling, Leon, 397
Kidd, Earl, 75
Kidney, John A., 50
Kiermas, Delores, 112-14
Kiermas, Ray, 203, 335, 349, 407, 507,
    513, 631; and campaign of 1946, 79,
    93; description of, 78-79; and Lodge,
    Henry Cabot, 442-43; McCarthy,
    financial dealings with, 318, 319,
    413; on McCarthy, 114, 287, 512;
    McCarthy staff, joins, 112; and
    Maryland campaign, 338, 340-43,
    363; on Smith, Margaret Chase, 297
Kilgore, Harley M., 283, 330-31, 442, 450
Kimball, Dan A., 52
Kimball, P. T., 53
Klein, Julius, 371
Klutznik, Philip M., 590
Knight, Frances, 478
Knowland, William, 180, 220, 248, 273,
    276, 472-73, 504, 534, 551, 585, 624,
    640, 643, 645-46, 658, 663, 667, 668,
    673
Kohlberg, Alfred, 250, 282, 642; and
    Amerasia case, 291; and America's
    Retreat from Victory, 374; and
    China Lobby, 215, 220; description
    of, 220-21; and Hanson, Haldore,
    254; and Jessup, Philip C., 388; and
    Larsen, Emmanuel, 295, 302; and

Lattimore, Owen J., 255, 256, 262, 273, 277, 279; McCarthy, gives information to, 248, 262, 273, 288; McCarthy, gives money to, 337; and Vincent, John Carter, 461

Kohler, Walter, 65

Kohler, Walter, Jr., 74, 147, 333, 335, 343, 419, 428, 429, 437-39, 444, 454

Korb, Thomas, 80, 248, 346, 349, 513, 563-64; and campaign of 1944, 54; and campaign of 1952, 417, 418, 422, 434, 453; on McCarthy, 171, 453; and Malmedy investigation, 162, 178, 184, 185; at Marquette, 13, 14

Kordas, Mr. and Mrs. Leopold, 97

Korean War, 308, 327-29, 345, 348, 452, 505

Kornely, Roman, 55-56

Kornely, Mrs. Roman (Olive McCarthy), 2, 6, 20, 56

Kraus, Charles H., 200, 202

Kretzmann, Edwin, M. J., 482-83

Krock, Arthur, 456, 486, 531

Kyes, Roger M., 554

Ladd, D. Milton, 293, 302

La Follette, Philip, 63-65, 146

La Follette, Robert M., 63

La Follette, Robert M., Jr., 38, 63-65, 69-72, 75-94, 199

Laird, Melvin, 147, 639

Lamers, William, 16-17

Lane, Arthur Bliss, 430

Lane, W. Preston, 336, 344-45

Lang, Lucille, 497, 498

Langer, William, 129, 164-65, 312, 331, 442

Langlie, Arthur, 451-52

Lappley, Gilbert, 40-41

Larsen, Emmanuel, 257, 290, 292-95, 299, 300, 301, 305

Latham, Earl, 206, 213

Lattimore, Owen J., 217, 255, 262-64,

267-69, 272-74, 276-83, 291, 295, 302, 305, 307, 321-22, 404, 464, 643

La Venia, Thomas, 571, 642

Lawrence, David, 547, 655

Lawton, Kirke B., 516-18, 524, 538, 592

Lee, Robert E., 248, 289, 507, 661; on Federal Communications Commission, 562; and Kerr, Jean, 512; and "Lee list," 227-28, 250; in Maryland campaign, 337, 363

Lee, Mrs. Robert E., 337, 513

Leer, Eugen, 184

Lehman, Herbert H., 239, 269, 330, 345, 378, 387, 496, 503, 563, 640, 641, 644, 653

Levine, Don, 295

Lewis, Fulton, Jr., 314, 327, 338, 349-50, 357, 359-61, 363-64, 395, 406, 430, 457, 568-69, 642, 674

Libby, Frederick J., 163, 167, 173, 184

Lilienthal, David E., 126-27, 201

Lippmann, Walter, 556, 569, 587

Litow, Max, 70, 97

Lloyd, David, 241, 247

Lloyd, Harold, 430

Lodge, Henry Cabot, 111, 241; and Army investigations, 617; description of, 244; and campaign of 1952, 442-44; and Gillette subcommittee, 395-96; and Korean War, 328; on Tydings Committee, 244, 247, 249, 251, 270, 274, 292, 304, 306-7, 308, 311, 312

Loeb, James, 124

Loeb, William, 220-21, 672

Long, Russell, 348

Longworth, Alice Roosevelt, 513

Lourie, Donald B., 462, 477, 478, 480, 506

Love, Francis J., 225-27

Lubeley, George H., 11

Lucas, Scott, 120, 162, 168, 236-37, 241-43, 273, 283, 284, 332, 334-35, 343-44

Luce, Clare Boothe, 100, 221

Luce, Henry R., 100, 216, 220, 384-85

Lucey, Patrick, 435
Lustron Corporation, 139, 152-58, 278,
    386, 395, 403, 404, 411, 413
Lyons, Roger, 482
Lynd, Robert S., 405

McCardle, Carl, 478
McCarey, Leo, 430
McCarran, Pat, 220, 330, 347, 351, 355,
    365, 470-71, 474, 495, 653
McCarran Act, 329-31, 345
McCarran Committee, 351-54, 356, 388,
    390, 397, 404, 464
McCarthy, Anna Mae, 4-5
McCarthy, Bridget, 2-5, 20
McCarthy, Howard, 20, 55-56, 66, 317
McCarthy, Joseph R., ancestry of, 1-2;
    and alcohol, xv, 15, 39, 45, 78, 320,
    401-2, 507, 564, 586, 637, 656, 666,
    669-72; anti-Communism,
    introduction to, 80, 84-85, 99, 101-5,
    129, 191-204; and anti-Semitism, 5,
    184, 367-362, 465, 503; and Army
    investigations, 506, 513-25, 536-59,
    561-63, 566-637; in Army-McCarthy
    hearings, 595-639; and Bohlen,
    Charles E., 468-476; and campaign
    of 1936, 22-23; and campaign of
    1939, 25-31; and campaign of 1944,
    38-39; 52-59, 74, 99, 130-31, 289,
    407, 413, 415; and campaign of
    1945, 60; and campaign of 1946, 60,
    66-108, 188-90; and campaign of
    1948, 145-48; and campaign of 1950,
    334-35; and campaign of 1952, 417-
    49, 453-57; and campaign of 1954,
    530-32, 540, 619; and campaign of
    1956, 669; censure of, by Senate, xiv-
    xv, 640-663, 665; and Central
    Intelligence Agency, 257, 280, 318,
    502-3, 505-6, 628, 635; as college
    student, 11-18; and Conant, James,
    467-68; and Davis, Charles, 365-70;
    death of, 671-72; as Democrat, 18,

22-23, 57, 59, 70, 75; and disabled
    veterans, 136-37, 144-45; and
    divorce cases, 96-98, 102, 105;
    education of, 3-18; estate of, 781-82;
    and Fifth Amendment, 510-12, 518,
    521-22, 526, 535-36; and "five
    percenter" investigation, 200; and
    fur industry, 118, 197-98; and
    General Electric investigation, 525-
    26, 535; and Gillette-Hennings
    subcommittee, 375, 378-87, 392-416;
    and Government Printing Office
    probe, 509-11; and Greek
    shipowners dispute, 485-88, 505,
    530-31, 540, 619; as grocery
    manager, 5-8, 11; as high school
    student, 7-10; and homosexuality, 4,
    112, 257, 383, 512, 624, 644, 675;
    and housing investigations, 106, 118,
    133-59, 192-93; and Jessup, Philip,
    387-92; as judge, 34-42, 56-58, 60,
    76-77, 95-98, 104, 188-90; and labor,
    73-73, 88-91, 94, 103-4, 106, 116-18,
    129, 448, 454; as lawyer, 18-31; and
    McCarran Committee, 351-54, 404;
    and *Madison Capital Times,* 1949
    attack on, 191-97; and Malmedy
    case, 162-85; in Marine Corps,
    43-61, 128; Marshall, George,
    speech on, 371-74; in Maryland
    campaign, 335-45, 363-65, 380-81,
    386, 395; and Matthews, J. B., affair,
    498-502, 506; parents of, 2-5;
    Pearson, Drew, assault on, 348-49;
    platform techniques of, 194, 197,
    320-27; and polls, 283, 303-4, 456,
    534, 584, 594, 604, 619, 639-40, 647,
    654-55, 675; speech of February 20,
    1950, 235-42, 284, 386, 395; and
    sugar rationing, 118-23, 403; tax
    problems of, 55, 130-31, 190-91,
    193, 317; and Texans, 319, 337, 447,
    513, 540, 547, 594, 604, 669; as True
    Believer, 202, 287-90, 320, 401; and

Tydings Committee, 249-314; and
United Nations probe, 511-12; and
Voice of America investigation, 477-
85, 491, 495, 503-4; voting record of,
117-18; wedding of, 512-13;
Wheeling speech of, 222-27, 278-79,
386, 394, 395; youth of, 1-5
McCarthy, Mary Ellen, 2
McCarthy, Olive (see Kornely, Mrs.
Roman)
McCarthy Record, The, 420-21, 430
McCarthy, Stephen Patrick, 1-2
McCarthy, Stephen Timothy, 2, 5, 107
*McCarthy: The Man, the Senator, the
"Ism,"* ix, 448-49
McCarthy, Tierney Elizabeth, 670, 674
McCarthy, Timothy, 2-5, 20, 55-56, 317
McCarthy, William Patrick, 2, 413, 513
"McCarthyism," 266-67
McCarthyism, The Fight For America,
197, 226, 417, 419, 429
McClellan, John L., 504, 505, 556, 640;
and Army-McCarthy hearings, 575,
579, 580, 586-87, 594, 596, 597, 598,
612, 622, 626, 627, 633, 634, 636; on
Cohn and Schine, travels of, 488;
description of, 580; and McCarthy,
censure of, 642, 644, 662; on
McCarthy, death of, 672; McCarthy
Subcommittee, joins, 460; McCarthy
Subcommittee, resigns from, 499-
501; McCarthy Subcommittee,
returns to, 534; and Moss, Annie
Lee, 548, 568; and Zwicker, Ralph
W., 546
McCloy, John J., 525, 540
McCormack Act of 1938, 208
McCormack, John, 207, 528
McCormick newspapers, 207, 248
McCormick, Robert R., 98
McFarland, Ernest W., 379, 400, 441, 455
McGovern, William, 418
McGranery, James, 432, 464
McGrath, J. Howard, 263, 265, 270, 274-

75, 393
McGuire, Martin R. P., 479
McInerney, James M., 292-93, 294, 302-3
McKee, Samuel, 515-16
McKeller, Kenneth, 347
McKesson, Lewis J., 478
McKinnon, Arlo J., 57, 70, 317
McLeod, R. W. Scott, 248, 462, 469-472,
478, 530, 536, 545, 556-557, 597
McMahon, Brien, 238-39, 241-42, 244,
252-53, 262, 269, 279, 293, 295, 296,
306, 311, 334, 344, 382
McMillen, Rolla C., 135, 138
McMillin, Miles, 67, 69, 74, 99, 184, 188,
195, 316, 327, 397, 418, 420, 425,
427, 433, 448, 663, 673
McMurray, Howard J., 87-88, 94-96, 98-
99, 102-6, 188
McNeill, Lowell, 444, 671
MacArthur, Douglas, 146-47, 318, 329,
370-71, 378, 423-24
Mackey, D. John, 336
Mack, Walter, 121-22
MacKay, John A., 497
MacLeish, Archibald, 445
Magnuson, Warren, 129, 334, 344
Mahoney, George, 336
Malmedy case, 162-85, 360, 377, 386, 395,
421
Malone, George W., 222, 312, 441, 455,
474, 643, 663, 668
Mandel, Benjamin, 352
Mandell, William Marx, 485
Mansfield, Mike, 219, 441, 450
Maragon, John, 121-22
Markward, Mary Stalcup, 548-50, 568
Marshall, George C., 123, 127, 219, 261,
278, 322, 357, 371-74, 386, 436-49,
643, 644
Martin, Msgr. Edward R., 655
Martin, I. Jack, 513, 529, 673
Martin, Joseph W., Jr., 100, 370-71, 372
Maryland campaign of 1950, 335-45, 362-
65, 380-81

Matson, Roy L., 669
Matthews, J. B., and Budenz, Louis, 277, 279; description of, 498-499; on Dies Committee, 208; and Huber, John, 281; and Institute of Pacific Relations papers, 352-53; McCarthy, gave information to, 248, 256, 288, 348; on McCarthy Subcommittee, 498-501; Protestant clergy, attack upon, 499-502; and Rosenberg, Anna, 357-61
Matthews, Troup, 482
Matusow, Harvey, 402, 412, 430, 434, 441, 445, 446-47, 450
May, Andrew J., 84
May, Ronald W., ix, 202, 383, 385, 448-49, 497
Maybank, Burnet, 155, 161-62, 502
Mayer, Louis B., 430
Medina, Harold, 201
Menjou, Adolphe, 430
Merson, Martin, 479, 481, 483
Meyer, Harold A., 22, 59
Meyer, Ruth, 23
Milland, Ray, 430
Miller, Ruth McCormick (Mrs. Garvin Tankersley), 336-39, 341, 513
Miller, Steve, 417, 465
Millikin, Eugene, 334, 344
Mitchell, Harry B., 270
Mitchell, Hugh, 451
Mitchell, Kate, 290, 301
Mitchell, Stephen A., 528
Monaghan, Hugh M., III, 336
Monroney, A. S., 362-63, 369, 394, 396, 398, 405-6, 411, 503-5, 506-7, 639, 641
Montfort, W. H., 51-52
Moody, Blair, 396, 442, 455
Moore, Ewell, Jr., 341-43
Moore, John, 404
Morgan, Dennis, 430
Morgan, Edward P., 244-45, 277, 278-79, 282, 299, 306, 309, 310, 449
Morgan, Gerald, 617

Morris, Robert, 245, 277, 279, 281, 292, 336, 352-53, 367, 462, 465
Morse, Wayne, 69, 107, 298, 313, 414, 643, 662
Morton, Alfred H., 480-81
Moss, Annie Lee, 548-50, 567-69, 642, 643
Mullarkey, Clifford, 11, 14, 36, 110
Mundt, Karl, 273, 276, 319, 329-30, 346, 504, 534, 658; and Army investigations, 550-51, 567, 577; and Army-McCarthy hearings, 579-80, 587, 588, 591-93, 596, 598, 599, 601, 607, 609, 612, 615, 616, 618, 619, 620, 630, 634; and Bohlen, Charles E., 474-475; and campaign of 1952, 436; and Central Intelligence Agency, 503; and Greek shipowners dispute, 486; and Hiss case, 214, 221, 241; and Institute of Pacific Relations papers, 352-53; and Jessup, Philip, 251, 387; on McCarthy, 586, 672; and McCarthy, censure of, 662; McCarthy Subcommittee, joins, 460; and Matthews, J. B., controversy, 499-501; and Moss, Annie Lee, hearing, 568; and Voice of America investigation, 483, 485, 491
Mundt-Nixon bill, 210, 329-30
Munn, Everett E., 49-50, 52
Mundy, Cornelius P., 339, 343
Murchison, Clint W., 319, 337, 447, 540, 604
Murphy, George, 430
Murphy, James Maxwell, 98
Murray, James E., 358
Murray, Robert, 83
Murrow, Edward R., 398, 564-66, 569, 589
Myers, Francis, 344
Myers, Paul A., 225

Nash, Phileo, 397
Nathan, Robert, 431

National Committee for an Effective Congress, 448, 497, 641, 643 (see Clearing House)

National Council for Prevention of War, 163-65, 167, 169, 172, 183-84

Nationalist Chinese, 215-21

Neely, Matthew, 283-84

Nellor, Ed, 199, 230, 288, 319, 335, 346, 513; and Army-McCarthy hearings, 631; and Lattimore speech, 267-68; and "Lee list," 227, 250; and McCarthy informants, 318; McCarthy, observations on, 249, 287; McCarthy staff, joins, 247; McCarthy, urges to be cautious, 323, 507; and Maryland campaign, 338; and Pearson, Drew, attack on, 349-50; and Rosenberg, Anna, attack on, 359-60; and Wheeling speech, 223

Nelson, Gaylord, 335, 395, 418, 419

Neuhausler, Johann, 183

Nichols, Louis B., 245-46, 293

Nicholson, Donald, 271

Niebuhr, Reinhold, 641

Nilles, George, 342-43

Nimitz citation, 47-49, 57, 433

Nimitz Commission, 355-56

Nixon, Richard M., 270, 319, 350-51, 393, 513; and campaign of 1946, 100; and campaign of 1950, 332, 343, 346; and campaign of 1952, 423, 424, 436, 451; and campaign of 1954, 654; and Herblock, 316; and Hiss case, 212, 221, 222; and HUAC, 124, 210, 214; and Jessup, Philip C., 387; McCarthy, aid to, 246-47, 248, 288, 423; and MacArthur dismissal, 371; and Mundt-Nixon bill, 210, 329-30; and Sulgrave incident, 348-49; as Vice-President, 460, 464, 471, 486-88, 500, 505, 532-33, 551-54, 562, 577-78, 604, 620, 646, 663, 673

O'Brien, Pat, 430

O'Conor, Herbert, 336, 351

O'Donnell, John, 372

O'Konsky, Alvin, 100

Olds, Leland, 199-201

O'Mahoney, Joseph, 441, 455

Oppenheimer, J. Robert, 589-90

Oram, Charlotte, 550

Osterloth, Mrs. Frank, 6-7

Oxnam, Bishop G. Bromley, 476, 497

Paley, William S., 565

Palmer, A. Mitchell, 206-7

Panuch, J. Anthony, 250

Pares, Bernard, 516

Parker, Cedric, 191-96, 199, 379

Parnell, Andrew, 20, 28, 35, 40-42, 110

Partridge, Richard D., 515-16

Patman, Wright, 135, 138, 140

Pearson, Drew, 114, 289, 384, 386; and Benton, William, 385; and Colony Club story, 202, 260; and Independence Day, 1951, stunt, 379; and Gillette-Hennings subcommittee, 395, 405, 408-9, 413; and Lattimore, Owen J., 264, 275; and "Lee list" speech, 243; and Lloyd, David, 247; and Lustron charge, 278; McCarthy, attacks on, 197, 348-50, 380, 385, 441; McCarthy, friendship with, 188, 247; and Maryland campaign, 343; and Matusow, Harvey, 412; and Rosenberg, Anna, 360; and Schine, G. David, 536; spy of, 318

Pedrick, Willard H., 445-46

Pegler, Westbrook, 348, 430, 442, 642

Peiper, Joachim, 163, 179

Pepper, Claude, 345-46

Peress, Irving, 537-46, 548, 552, 557, 558, 574, 593, 608

Perl, William R., 176-77, 182

Persons, Wilton B., 439, 444-45, 460, 471, 488, 513, 531

Philipp, Cyrus, 65, 422

Phillips, Cabell, 212

Phillips, William, 536
Pickard, Sam, 65
Pierce, Robert, 75
Pike, The Rev. James A., 585
Pilat, Oliver, 383-85
Polland, Milton R., 121-22
Poorbaugh, Jack, 405-6
Popular Front, 206
Posniak, Edward G., 313
Potter, Charles, 414, 442, 455, 460, 501,
    503-4, 547, 556, 567, 575, 577, 593,
    605, 616, 620, 626, 627, 635-36, 640,
    668
Powell, Dick, 430
Price, Melvin, 565, 589
Progressivism in Wisconsin, 63-65, 71,
    106
Proxmire, William, 158, 335, 431
Puerifoy, John E., 229, 231, 260, 275, 283,
    299-300, 314
Purtell, William A., 455
Pusey, Nathan M., 507-8, 535

Quaker Dairy case, 39-42, 99, 105, 296,
    386

Radulovich, Milo, 564-65
Rains, Albert, 135
Rankin, John, 209, 358-59
Rauh, Joseph, 431
Raymond, John M., 165, 171
Reagan, Ronald, 674
Reber, Miles, 514, 569, 597
Reece, B. Carroll, 100
Reedy, George, 349, 406, 645, 653
Rees, Edward J., 142
Reid, Mrs. Ogden, 419
Reidl, John, 43, 54, 58, 166
Reiss, Julius, 511-12
Remington, William, 211, 311, 325, 463
Reston, James, 91, 283, 332, 486, 530,
    561, 649, 650
Reuss, Henry S., 419-20, 428, 431, 434-
    35, 654

Reuther, Walter, 641
Revell, Aldric, 421
Revercomb, Chapman, 135, 442, 450, 455
Rhee, Syngman, 328
Richardson, Seth, 263, 271-72, 355
Ridgeway, Matthew B., 546, 552, 599
Ringler, Paul, 232
Ringling, Henry, 437
Roberts, Mr. and Mrs. Chester G., 97
Roberts, Glenn D., 86
Roberts, William A., 202
Rogers, Harlan P., 189
Rogers, William P., 157, 442, 460, 488,
    500, 532-33, 551, 554
Rogin, Michael Paul, 454, 456, 534
Roosevelt, Eleanor, 253, 264, 480, 497
Roosevelt, Franklin D., Jr., 371
Rorty, James, 647
Rosenberg, Anna M., 357-62
Rosenberg, Ethel, 463-64, 465
Rosenberg, Julius, 307-8, 463-64, 465,
    517-18, 520-22
Rosenberry, Marvin B., 41-42, 96, 99, 296
Rosenblatt, Maurice, 497-99, 506, 641
Rosenfeld, A. H., 180
Roth, Andrew, 290, 293, 294, 300-1
Rothschild, Edward, 509-11
Rovere, Richard, ix, 110, 121, 183, 373,
    534, 675
Royal, Walter Moore, 153
Royall, Kenneth C., 123, 163-66, 169
Rubin, Morris H., 420
Rummel, W. H., 19
Rushmore, Howard, 465
Russell, Richard, 180, 236, 359, 377
Ryan, Cornelius, 536-37, 571-73, 620
Ryan, James T., 80

Sabath, Adolph J., 126, 224
Saddy, Fred, 13
Saltonstall, Leverett, 180, 262, 269, 658
Sartre, John Paul, 480
Sayre, The Rev. Francis B., 585
Schiff, Dorothy, 431

Schine, G. David, and Army
investigations, 518-19, 536-37, 569-
79, 583, 591, 597-601, 606, 615-16,
620-21, 625-28, 632, 633, 634, 636,
637; description of, 465-66; and
Voice of America investigation, 488-
91, 503
Schlamm, William S., viii
Schlesinger, Arthur, Jr., 445-46, 480
Schmidt, Emerson P., 247, 254
Schmitt, Len, 420, 430-31, 434
Schoepple, Andrew, 418, 474
Schricher, Henry, 450
Schuh, Matt, 66, 403
Schultz, Rabbi Benjamin, 642, 658
Schuman, Frederick L., 257, 258, 305
Scott, Randolph, 430
Scripps-Howard newspapers, 101, 248,
291, 296, 475, 644
Sears, Samuel P. 588
Seaton, Fred A., 552, 554
Service, John Stewart, 217-19, 231, 257,
260, 261, 268-69, 274, 290-91, 293,
300-3, 305, 307, 323-25, 356
Shanley, Bernard M., 554
Shannon, William V., 383, 385
Shapley, Harlow, 230, 237, 256, 258, 305
Shaw, G. Howland, 536
Shearon, Marjorie, 358, 361
Sheen, Bishop Fulton J., 101, 276
Sheil, Bishop Bernard J., 590
Shelton, Willard, 414
Shivers, Allan, 540
Shoenecker, Harold V., 15
Shumacker, Ralph, 168
Silvermaster, Nathan Gregory, 211
Simmons, Ernest J., 516
Simmons, Roscoe, 337-38, 363-64
Simpson, Gordon, 163-64, 171-72, 179
Smedley, Ken, 46, 51-52
Smith Act, 201, 208, 209, 211
Smith, Frank, 338
Smith, Gerald L. K., 88, 358-60
Smith, H. Alexander, 262, 298, 388, 392,

491, 518, 532, 624, 644
Smith, Margaret Chase, 415; and
"Declaration of Conscience," 297-98,
350-51, 380-81; and Gillette
subcommittee, 381, 383, 396, 399;
on Government Operations
Committee, 460, 505; and Hennings
speech, 382; McCarthy, personal
relationship with, 297; McCarthy,
votes for, 308; and Maryland
campaign investigation, 362-63, 365,
380-81; and Senate race of 1954,
547, 640
Smith, Tony, 249, 267
Smith, Walter Bedell, 469, 481, 502, 504,
597-98
Smith, Willis, 351
Snow, Conrad E., 271, 393, 397-98
Sobell, Morton, 517, 520
Sokolsky, George, 246, 248, 281, 288, 353,
355, 360, 464, 566, 567, 616, 642
Sparkman, John J., 135, 138, 389-92, 452,
472, 641
Spellman, Francis Cardinal, 101, 493,
655, 670, 674
Spingarn, Stephen, 306
Stachel, Jack, 276
Stassen, Harold E., 107, 112, 145-47, 390,
422, 486-87, 531, 619
St. Clair, James D., 589, 630, 636
St. Claire, Darrell, 400, 406
Stearns, J. Perry, 75, 95
Steinman, Louise Tinsley, 348
Stennis, John C., 646, 659, 663
Stevens, Robert T., 538, 541; in Army-
McCarthy hearings, 591, 592-93,
597-615, 618, 619-20, 626-27, 636,
637; at "Chicken Luncheon," 550-52,
561; description of, 551; and
Eisenhower, 553-57, 562, 581; and
Fifth Amendment, 510; at Fort
Monmouth, 518; and McCarthy,
eleven memos of, 576-77; and
McCarthy Subcommittee, 506, 514,

515-16, 541-42, 546, 549, 550-55;
and Schine, G. David, issue of,
570-74
Stevenson, Adlai E., 372, 429, 432-33,
435-36, 440, 443, 444-46, 451-53,
459, 552, 561-62, 654
Stilwell, Joseph W., 216-17
Stimson, Henry L., 262, 265, 269
Stoffel, Margaret, 2
Stoltz, Robert, 16
Stone, I. F., 184, 260
Stotler, Thomas, 352-53
Straight, Michael, 256
Strandlund, Carl G., 154-56
Strong, Herbert, 165
Strout, Richard, 304
Sturm, Fred, 670
Sullivan, William C., 245
Sulzberger, Arthur Hays, 440
Summerfield, Arthur E., 247-48, 668
Sumnicht, Francis, 5
Sundstrom, Frank, 135, 155
Surine, Donald A., 197, 350, 407, 581;
and Central Intelligence Agency,
502; and Davis, Charles, 367, 369;
departure from FBI of, 246, 386,
393, 395, 633; description of, 246,
288, 341; Hoover, J. Edgar,
relationship to, 246; and Institute of
Pacific Relations papers, 352-54;
and Larsen, Emmanuel, 295; and
Lattimore, Owen J., 262, 267; and
Lodge, Henry Cabot, 443; and
loyalty files, 314; and McCarthy
informants, 318; McCarthy,
observations on, 249, 287, 462; on
McCarthy personal staff, 246, 252,
289, 642; and McCarthy presidential
poll, 667; on McCarthy
Subcommittee, 465, 642; and
Marshall, George, 373, 374; in
Maryland campaign, 338, 340-343,
363-364; on Moss, Annie Lee, 548;
and Murrow, Edward R., 565; and

Rosenberg, Anna, case, 359-60; and
Stevenson, Adlai, 444-45;
Symington, Stuart, charge against,
633; wiretaps on, 230, 290
Sutton, Pat, 371
Swanke, Tony, 23, 30-31
Swedish, Steve, xiii-xv, 670, 671
Sweeney, Thomas B., 225
Symington, Stuart, 640; and Army
investigations, 575, 585, 591; in
Army-McCarthy hearings, 602, 605,
608, 612, 617, 621, 622, 624, 627-28,
633, 634-35, 636; and campaign of
1952, 442, 452, 592; and Greek
shipowners dispute, 488; Jackson,
Henry, defends, 566; on McCarthy,
death of, 673; McCarthy
Subcommittee, bolts, 501, 505;
McCarthy Subcommittee, joins, 460,
534; and Matthews, J. B., 499, 501;
Moss, Annie Lee, defends, 568; and
Rosenberg, Anna, 361; and
Wechsler, James, 484

Taber, John, 248, 250, 477-78
Taft-Hartley bill, 117, 129
Taft-Ellender-Wagner bill, 134, 137-38,
140-41, 143-44, 148
Taft, Robert A., 107, 111, 112, 373; and
Bohlen, Charles E., 470-72, 475; in
campaign of 1946, 100; and
campaign of 1950, 332-33, 343, 344;
and campaign of 1952, 386, 422,
423, 427-28; and Coleman, Tom,
247; and Conant, James B., 467-68;
description of, 115; and housing
legislation, 133-36, 144-45, 148-49,
151; and Jessup, Philip C., 392; on
Kennedy, Joseph P., 347; on Korean
War, 328-29; La Follette, Robert M.,
Jr., endorsement of, 69, 88; and
Lattimore, Owen J., 269-70; and
Lilienthal, David E., 126-27;
McCarthy, committee assignments

of, 162; McCarthy, defense of, 269-70, 380, 422; McCarthy, encouragement of, 263; McCarthy, tribute by, 582; and Marshall, George C., 386; and Taft-Hartley bill, 117, 129; on Truman, impeachment of, 371; on Truman State Department, 220, 270, 328, 422; on Tydings Committee Report, 308; on Voice of America, 485; voting record of, 117-18

Tankersley, Garvin, 339-40

Tankersley, Mrs. Garvin (see Miller, Ruth McCormick)

Taylor, Glen H., 135

Taylor, Telford, 524-25

Tegge, Lloyd, 77-78, 422, 425, 427

Ten Million Americans Mobilizing for Justice, 661-62

Tenney, Jack, 640

Terry, Dr. Luther, 181

Testin, Honor, 6-8

Teto, William H., 525

Theis, Bill, 288

Thomas, Elbert D., 344

Thomas, J. Parnell, 210, 213, 604

Thomas, Norman, 102

Thompson, Dorothy, 260

Thompson, John F., 54

Thompson, Vernon, 669

Thorpe, Elliott R., 277

Thye, Edward, 298

Tierney, Dennis, 2

Tobey, Charles W., 115, 119-20, 135-36, 138, 143-45, 149, 151, 179, 269, 273, 298, 408, 471

Tobin, Maurice J., 380

Todd, Glenn A., 48, 50-52, 60

Townsend, Harold, 79-80, 93, 95, 107, 111, 122, 417, 422

Truman, Harry S., 76, 86, 111, 115, 215, 262, 347, 377, 381, 673; and *Amerasia* case, 293; anti-Communist policies of, 123; and Benton, William, charges of, 396-97; in campaign of 1946, 100; and campaign of 1948, 145, 147-48; and campaign of 1950, 334; and campaign of 1952, 431, 452; and China, 218-19; on "Declaration of Conscience," 298; and Hiss case, 212; and housing, 133, 143, 145, 150-52; and HUAC, 210-211; and hydrogen bomb, 201, 222, 328; and Jessup, Philip, 388, 392; and Korean War, 328-329; and Lattimore, Owen J., 269; and loyalty files, 210, 263, 270-71, 284; loyalty programs of, 124-25, 209, 355-56; and McCarran Act, 330-31; and McCarthy, charges of, 232, 243, 269, 275-76, 379-80, 397, 427; on McCarthy, death of, 673, and MacArthur, Douglas, 370; and White, Harry Dexter, 528-29

Tse-tung, Mao, 215-16, 218

Tufty, Esther Van Wagoner, 316

Tydings Committee, 239, 243-47, 249-85, 290-95, 299-314, 321-23; report of, 304-6

Tydings, Millard E., 296, 403; on "Declaration of Conscience," 298; description of, 243-44; Fleming, Robert, aid to, 384; on McCarthy, labor proposal of, 129; and Malmedy investigation, 167, 180, 386; Maryland campaign of, 334-46, 362-64, 380; and Tydings Committee investigation, 243-44, 249-54, 258, 260-64, 268, 271, 273-75, 278, 284, 291, 293, 300, 306, 308-14, 322

Tyler, S. R., 366

United States Chamber of Commerce, 101, 209, 247

Utley, Clifton, 475

Utley, Freda, 220-24, 268, 281-82, 305, 489

Van Arkel, Gerhard P., 497

Vandenberg, Arthur H., 162, 220, 269, 329

Van Doren, Mark, 166

Van Roden, Edward L., 163-65, 168, 172-73, 175, 179

Van Straten, Henry J., 29, 78-79, 112, 412-13

Van Susteren, Urban P., 25, 28, 34, 37-39, 42-43, 48, 60, 74, 83, 92, 97, 99, 102-3, 114, 131, 196, 320, 349, 399, 401, 412, 447, 513, 555, 578, 631, 669-70

Vaughan, Harry, 200, 297

Velde, Harold, 466, 476, 494, 527, 532

Vincent, John Carter, 217-18, 221, 305, 365-66, 368, 456-57, 461

Vogeler, Mr. and Mrs. Robert, 425

Voice of America investigation, 268, 477-85, 488-91, 503-4

Voy, Mae, 21, 23-24

Wadleigh, H. Julian, 224, 230, 237

Wagner, Robert F., 133, 135, 150

Waldrop, Frank, 248, 349, 533-34

Wallace, Henry A., 71, 104, 123-24, 192, 217, 256, 328

Walsh, The Rev. Edmund A., 202-3

Walter, Arnold, 12

Walter, Jack, 12

Wander, Jerome, 50, 52

Warren, Earl, 393, 422

Waters, George, 223, 250

Watkins, Arthur V., 349, 351, 646-51, 655, 657-60, 663, 666

Watkins Committee, 645-662, 666

Watson, L. R., 74

Wayne, John, 326, 430

Wechsler, James, 445, 484, 621

Wedemeyer, Albert C., 217

Weinstein, Allen, 213

Welch, Joseph Nye, 588-89, 593, 596, 599-605, 608-12, 614, 615, 618, 620, 622, 626, 627-31, 632, 633, 634, 636

Welker, Herman, 345-46, 395-96, 398,

404, 405-6, 418, 474, 643, 653, 658-59, 663

Wendt, Francis, 143

Werner, Edgar V., 25-31, 34-35, 95

Werner, Francis, 24, 29

West, Jack, 367-68

Wettengel, Fred Felix, 56-58, 75, 95-96

Wherry, Kenneth B., 119-20, 220, 241, 243, 248, 269, 271, 276, 280, 282-84, 295, 309, 310, 312, 351, 362, 365, 395

Whitaker, James K., 225

White, Harry Dexter, 211, 527-28, 530, 565

White, Lincoln, 296

White, Theodore H., 216, 480

White, Walter, 480

White, William S., 270, 380, 382, 456, 476, 481, 493, 495, 501, 508, 622, 647, 668

Whitehead, Don, 591

Whiting, A. N., 30

Whitney, Courtney, 318

Wiedman, Clark, 158

Wiley, Alexander, 38, 98, 111, 129, 276, 415, 430, 669; and Attlee, Clement, McCarthy attack on, 491; and Bohlen, Charles E., 469, 471-73; and campaign of 1944, 53, 54, 57, 59; and campaign of 1950, 333, 335, 343; and campaign of 1952, 428; and Eisenhower loyalty program, 462; and fur industry, 118; and Lilienthal, David E., 127; and McCarthy, censure of, 661; and McCarthy, defense of, 270, 333; and Mundt-Nixon bill, 330; and Voice of America investigation, 477

Williams, Edward Bennett, 373, 384, 648, 650-51, 661

Willoughby, Charles A., 318, 426

Wilson, Arthur R., 590-91

Wilson, Charles E., 519, 566-67, 593

Wilson, H. H., 414

Winchell, Walter, 209, 327, 464, 567, 633
Withers, Garrett, 238-39
Witsell, Edward F., 325
Wolcott, Jesse P., 134-35, 143-45, 148-51
Woltman, Frederick, 310
Wood, John S., 210
Wood, Robert E., 444, 634
Woodring, Harry H., 644
Woods, Warren, 350, 384, 497
Wyatt, Wilson, 139, 445
Wyngaard, John, 111, 113, 190, 533

Yost, Norman L., 226-27
Young, Merl, 156

Zeidler, Carl, 38-39, 42, 53
Zellerbach, James D., 667
Zimmerman, Fred R., 56-57, 107, 146,
    418, 423, 428, 453-54
Zwicker, Ralph W., viii, 538, 541, 542-48,
    551, 555, 557, 558, 574, 591, 642-43,
    648, 651, 652, 653, 662, 668